CLASS 10

CBSE QUESTION & CONCEPT BANK

CHAPTER-WISE & TOPIC-WISE

SCIENCE

EDITION : Fourth

Published By: Physicswallah Limited

Physics Wallah Publication

ISBN : 978-93-7818-447-5

MRP : 675/-

Mobile App: Physics Wallah (Available on Play Store)

Website: www.pw.live

Youtube Channel: Physics Wallah - Alakh Pandey
Alakh Pandey - Class 10
Physics Wallah Foundation
NCERT Wallah

Email: publication@pw.live

SKU Code: BKP2603019478

ABOUT THE AUTHOR

Meet **Samridhi Sharma**, popularly known to her students as "**Pookie Ma'am** 🎀". With a warm smile, energetic teaching style, and laser-sharp clarity, she transforms even the trickiest science concepts into simple and fun lessons.

With **8+ years of** dedicated online teaching experience **in PW** and reputed schools, she's mentored **lakhs of students**, guiding many to **top-ranks** in the **Central Board of Secondary Education (CBSE)** exams — including securing **Rank 1** and **Rank 2**. She teaches students aiming for the school and board exams up to Class 12 and also mentors **Olympiad** and **NTSE** aspirants.

She believes in both theory and hands-on learning. To give equal importance to practical understanding, she launched **Experimental Kits** for Classes 9 and 10.

Her track record speaks volumes, and her pookie gang knows: when she says you can do it, she means it.

A post graduate of the University of Delhi with a **Master's in Botany**, she has also cleared top-tier national exams—**UGC-NET** (Environmental Sciences), **GATE** (Life Sciences) and **CTET**—showcasing her academic strength and commitment.

Her teaching isn't just about covering the syllabus—it's about helping you own it: clear your doubts, apply your knowledge, and approach exam day with calm and confidence.

With Pookie Ma'am as your guide and Question & Concept Bank Book in your hands—you're set to smash Board Exams.

PREFACE

In this era of cutthroat competition among Class 10th aspirants for great marks in Board Exams, only a few are prepared enough to achieve it. During the preparation, a student needs the most relevant study material to cover all topics, practice efficiently, and excel in Board exams and other 10th level competitive exams.

While there is an abundance of study materials available in the market, what we felt was missing was a self-driven and well-planned study material. We have addressed this issue by introducing the CBSE Class 10th Question & Concept Bank.

CBSE Class 10th Question & Concept Bank is a book that covers all the important concepts and theories, along with a rich amount of practice questions. This book is designed to provide you with the perfect guidance you need. The study material is consistent with the syllabus offered in NCERT Books and has been curated by the **Physics Wallah Editorial Team** under the careful observation of Physics Wallah Faculties.

Their invaluable contributions have enriched the very essence of our books.

This book consists of the following features:

The content is made in such a way that you can invest your time to make a strong fundamental that will get compounded and will pay you the interest in every upcoming year of your competitive exam's preparation and board exam preparation.

This will help you stay ahead of your competitors.

Our content will help you secure excellent marks in CBSE Class 10th Board Exam.

Following are the different sections that we have provided to develop your skills:

In Theory:

- Concept Maps
- NCERT Definitions
- Important Facts
- Classification
- Difference Between
- Real Life Application Based Questions
- Myth Busters
- Mnemonics
- Memes

In Questions (Competency Based):

- Multiple Choice Questions
- Assertion and Reason
- Subjective Questions (with VSA, SA, LA and Case-Based Questions as per Latest Board Exam Pattern)
- NCERT and NCERT Exemplar Questions
- Mistake 101: What not to do!
- Nailing the Right Answer
- Key Takeaways
- Hand Drawn Diagrams
- Answer Keys & Explanations with Marking Scheme as per Latest CBSE Board Pattern
- Topper's Explanations

Includes Questions & Explanations from:

Sample Question Paper issued by CBSE – **(CBSE SQP)**

Additional Practice Questions issued by CBSE – **(CBSE APQ)**

Competency Focused Practice Questions issued by CBSE – **(CFPQ)**

Previous Year Questions in CBSE Board Exams

A step to make our book even better for our students:

Provide your valuable feedback
or
Report the Error

View Errata
(Error Correction from our end)

SYLLABUS ISSUED BY CBSE

SCIENCE
Code No. (086)
CLASS-X

Time: 03 Hours **(80 marks)**

Unit No.	Unit Name	Marks
I	Chemical Substances-Nature and Behaviour	25
II	World of Living	25
III	Natural Phenomena	12
IV	Effects of Current	13
V	Natural Resources	05
	Total	**80**
	Internal assessment	**20**
	Grand Total	**100**

Theme: Materials

Unit I: Chemical Substances - Nature and Behaviour

Chemical Reactions and Equations

Chemical reactions, Chemical equation, Balanced chemical equation, types of chemical reactions: combination, decomposition, displacement, double displacement, precipitation, endothermic exothermic reactions, oxidation and reduction.

Acids, Bases and Salts

Acids and Bases – their definitions in terms of furnishing of H^+ and OH^- ions, identification using indicators, chemical properties, examples and uses, neutralization, concept of pH scale (Definition relating to logarithm not required), importance of pH in everyday life; preparation and uses of Sodium Hydroxide, Bleaching powder, Baking soda, Washing soda and Plaster of Paris.

Metals and Non-metals

Properties of metals and non-metals; Reactivity series; Formation and properties of ionic compounds; Basic metallurgical processes; Corrosion and its prevention.

Carbon and its Compounds

Covalent bonds – formation and properties of covalent compounds. Versatile nature of carbon, Hydrocarbons – saturated and unsaturated, Homologous series. Nomenclature of alkanes, alkenes, alkyne and carbon compounds containing functional groups (halogens, alcohol, ketones, aldehydes). Chemical properties of carbon compounds (combustion, oxidation, addition and substitution reaction). Ethanol and Ethanoic acid (only properties and uses), soaps and detergents.

Theme: The World of the Living

Unit II: World of Living

Life processes

'Living Being'. Basic concept of nutrition, respiration, transport and excretion in plants and animals.

Control and co-ordination in animals and plants

Tropic movements in plants; Introduction of plant hormones; Control and co-ordination in animals: Nervous system; Voluntary, involuntary and reflex action; Chemical co-ordination: animal hormones.

Reproduction

Reproduction in animals and plants (asexual and sexual) reproductive health - need and methods of family planning. Safe sex vs HIV/AIDS. Child bearing and women's health.

Heredity and Evolution

Heredity; Mendel's contribution- Laws for inheritance of traits: Sex determination: brief introduction.

Theme: Natural Phenomena

Unit III: Natural Phenomena

Reflection of light by curved surfaces; Images formed by spherical mirrors, centre of curvature, principal axis, principal focus, focal length, mirror formula (Derivation not required),magnification.

Refraction; Laws of refraction, refractive index.

Refraction of light by spherical lens; Image formed by spherical lenses; Lens formula(Derivation not required); Magnification. Power of a lens.

Functioning of a lens in human eye, defects of vision and their corrections, applications of spherical mirrors and lenses.

Refraction of light through a prism, dispersion of light, scattering of light, applications in dailylife (excluding colour of the sun at sunrise and sunset).

Theme: How Things Work

Unit IV: Effects of Current

Electric current, potential difference and electric current. Ohm's law; Resistance, Resistivity, Factors on which the resistance of a conductor depends. Series combination of resistors, parallel combination of resistors and its applications in daily life. Heating effect of electric current and its applications in daily life. Electric power, Interrelation between P, V, I and R. Magnetic effects of current : Magnetic field, field lines, field due to a current carrying conductor, field due to current carrying coil or solenoid; Force on current carrying conductor, Fleming's Left Hand Rule, Direct current. Alternating current: frequency of AC. Advantage of AC over DC. Domestic electric circuits.

Theme: Natural Resources

Unit V: Natural Resources

Our environment

Eco-system, Environmental problems, Ozone depletion, waste production and their solutions. Biodegradable and non-biodegradable substances.

Note for the Teachers:

The NCERT text books present information in boxes across the book. These help students to get conceptual clarity. However, the information in these boxes would not be assessed in the year-end examination.

CHAPTER-WISE WEIGHTAGE AND TREND ANALYSIS

SCIENCE										
CHAPTERS	**2022**		**2023**		**2024**		**2025**		**2026**	
	DL	**ODL**	**DL**	**ODL**	**DL**	**ODL**	**DL**	**ODL**	**DL**	**ODL**
Chemical Reactions and Equations	–	–	8	6	7	7	6	6	5	4
Acids, Bases and Salts	–	–	8	10	4	5	6	6	5	7
Metals and Non-metals	–	–	4	6	8	7	6	7	8	8
Carbon and its Compounds	5	5	7	6	6	6	6	6	7	6
Periodic Classification of Elements (*Rationalised*)	5	5	–	–	–	–	–	–	–	–
Life Processes	–	–	10	10	5	8	8	6	5	6
Control and Coordination	–	–	3	1	6	6	7	7	6	9
How do Organisms Reproduce?	6	7	6	5	6	10	7	7	16	11
Heredity and Evolution (*Some portion is Rationalised*)	7	6	6	6	6	1	4	5	5	6
Light – Reflection and Refraction	–	–	12	9	7	10	7	6	7	6
The Human Eye and the Colourful World (*Some portion is Rationalised*)	–	–	2	5	5	2	5	6	5	8
Electricity (*Some portion is Rationalised*)	6	6	11	8	7	8	6	7	12	7
Magnetic Effects of Electric Current (*Some portion is Rationalised*)	6	6	5	5	6	5	7	6	6	11
Sources of Energy (*Rationalised*)	–	–	–	–	–	–	–	–	–	–
Our Environment	5	5	5	5	4	5	5	5	5	5
Sustainable Management of Natural Resources (*Rationalised*)	–	–	–	–	–	–	–	–	–	–

**The marks allotment mentioned above is chapter-wise and includes internal choice questions as well. Therefore, the total might not match the Maximum Marks of the respective Previous Year Paper. Here, DL is Delhi, ODL is Outside Delhi.*

Question Typology

YEAR	Objective Questions		Subjective Questions			
	MCQs	A/R	VSA	SA	LA	Case-Based type
2026	16	4	6	7	3	3
2025	16	4	6	7	3	3
2024	16	4	6	7	3	3
2023	16	4	6	7	3	3
2022 (Term II)	-	-	7	6	0	2
2022 (Term I)	43	5		-	-	12

Evolving Trends in CBSE Exam Patterns

2022

Term I

- Rationalized syllabus adopted from this year onwards.
- 50/60 questions were needed to attempt.
- All sections were featured solely in objective format.
- Introduction of a dedicated section for 4-mark Case-based questions.

Term II

- Total number of questions reduced.
- All sections were featured solely in subjective format.
- The number of questions in subpart format increased from this year onwards.

2023

- The number of sections in the paper increased to 5 sections (A, B, C and D).
- The total number of questions has increased.
- Since 2020 objective questions have increased by 60%.
- Since 2020 Assertion/ *Reason questions* have increased by 50%.
- Competancy based questions increased in number.
- Activity based questions were introduced.

2024

- No changes in exam pattern

2025

- 50% of the marks were allocated to competency-based questions, while the rest of the exam pattern remained unchanged.

2026

- Number of sections reduced to 3 (A, B, C) and divided into Biology, Chemistry, and Physics.
- Total number of questions remains same i.e., 39.
- No change in number of each typology (MCQ, A/R, VSA, SA, LA, CBQ)
- Number of internal choices is same as before.

HOW TO USE THIS BOOK

This book is structured to support your learning journey of preparing for your board exams through a variety of engaging and informative elements. Here's how to make the most of it:

CBSE Solved Paper of 2026 with Handwritten Style Answers: *Get yourself updated with the latest Board Question Papers. With handwritten answers, learn the practical application of concepts and effective answering techniques to achieve higher scores.*

CBSE Solved Paper

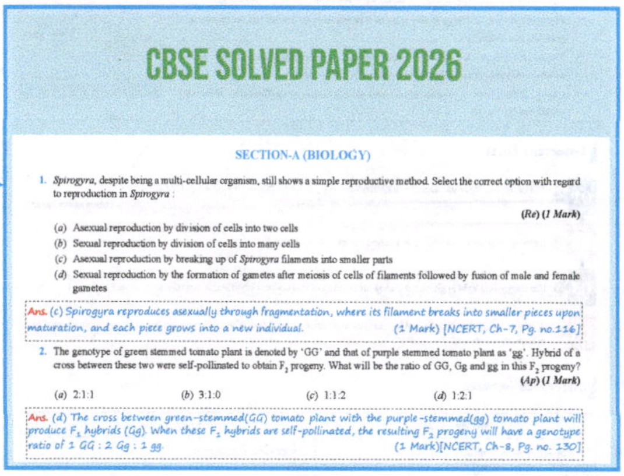
CBSE SOLVED PAPER 2026

SECTION-A (BIOLOGY)

1. *Spirogyra*, despite being a multi-cellular organism, still shows a simple reproductive method. Select the correct option with regard to reproduction in *Spirogyra* :

(Re) (1 Mark)

(*a*) Asexual reproduction by division of cells into two cells
(*b*) Sexual reproduction by division of cells into many cells
(*c*) Asexual reproduction by breaking up of *Spirogyra* filaments into smaller parts
(*d*) Sexual reproduction by the formation of gametes after meiosis of cells of filaments followed by fusion of male and female gametes

Ans. (c) Spirogyra reproduces asexually through fragmentation, where its filament breaks into smaller pieces upon maturation, and each piece grows into a new individual. (1 Mark) [NCERT, Ch-7, Pg. no.116]

2. The genotype of green stemmed tomato plant is denoted by 'GG' and that of purple stemmed tomato plant as 'gg'. Hybrid of a cross between these two were self-pollinated to obtain F_2 progeny. What will be the ratio of GG, Gg and gg in this F_2 progeny?

(Ap) (1 Mark)

(*a*) 2:1:1 (*b*) 3:1:0 (*c*) 1:1:2 (*d*) 1:2:1

Ans. (d) The cross between green-stemmed(GG) tomato plant with the purple-stemmed(gg) tomato plant will produce F_1 hybrids (Gg). When these F_1 hybrids are self-pollinated, the resulting F_2 progeny will have a genotype ratio of 1 GG : 2 Gg : 1 gg. (1 Mark)[NCERT, Ch-8, Pg. no. 130]

At the start of every chapter, you'll find a thoughtfully chosen image and a quote that captures the main idea and motivation of the topic. This approach aims to get your interest and give you a glimpse of the theme ahead.

Before diving into the details, we outline the syllabus and analyze the weightage given to each topic over the past five years. This helps you prioritize your study focus based on the significance of each section.

Preview

SYLLABUS & WEIGHTAGE

LIST OF CONCEPT NAMES	YEARS				
	2020	2022 TERM-1	2023	2024	2025
Types of Changes and Characteristics of Chemical Reactions (Physical and Chemical Changes)	1 Q (1 M)	—	—	—	—
Chemical Equations and their Balancing	1 Q (3 M) 1 Q (5 M)	2 Q*	1 Q (1 M)	1 Q (2 M)	1 Q (1 M)
Types of Chemical Reactions (Combination, decomposition, displacement, double displacement, precipitation, endothermic exothermic reactions, oxidation and reduction)	1 Q (3 M)	6 Q*	3 Q (1 M) 1 Q (3 M)	1 Q (1 M) 1 Q (2 M) 1 Q (3 M)	1 Q (2 M) 1 Q (3 M)
Effect of Oxidation Reactions (Corrosion and Rancidity)	—		—	—	—

*For the year 2021, the exam was not conducted.
*All questions were of MCQ type and carried equal marks.

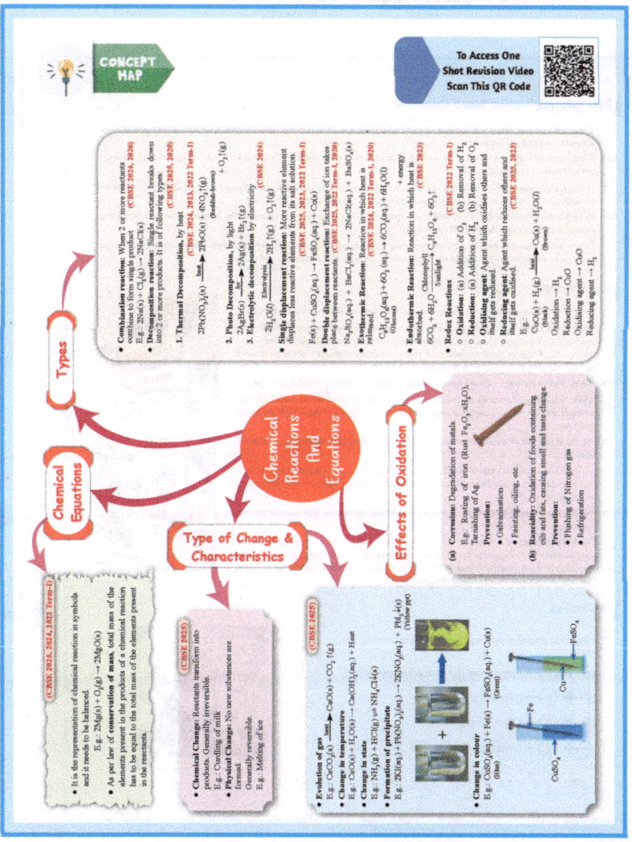

Concept Map

The concept map appears to be a comprehensive study aid that outlines key concepts in a structured format. Use it to understand the chapter's structure and as a quick reference to recall important highlights.

A QR Code to access One Shot Revision Video of the chapter.

TYPES OF CHANGES AND CHARACTERISTICS OF CHEMICAL REACTIONS 1

NCERT Definitions (Commonly asked in 1 mark)

- **Reactants:** Substances that **undergo** chemical changes in a reaction.
- **Products:** New substances **formed** as a result of a chemical reaction.
- **Physical State:** The state in which a substance exists (solid, liquid, gas, aqueous).
- **Physical Change:** A change in which **no new substances** are formed and the change is generally **reversible**
- **Chemical Change:** A process in which substances (reactants) transform into **new substances** (products) and the change is generally **irreversible**.
- **Chemical Reaction:** A process where substances (reactants) transform into different substances (products).

Important Facts

01 The protective layer on magnesium ribbon which is cleaned by rubbing it with a sand paper. *~Magnesium oxide*

02 Burning a candle wax involves both chemical and physical changes.

03 Dazzling white light is given out during the burning of magnesium ribbon and is harmful to the eyes.

04 A chemical reaction is indicated by changes like colour change, temperature change, evolution of gas, state change, or precipitate formation.

Difference Between

Physical Change	Chemical Change
No new substance is formed.	New substances are formed.
Usually reversible.	Usually irreversible.
Involves changes in physical properties like shape, size, state.	Involves changes in chemical properties and composition.
No energy change is involved.	Energy is absorbed or evolved.
Example: Melting of ice, Tearing of paper.	Example: Burning of paper.

NCERT Definitions: *It simplifies complex topics into brief, easy-to-understand explanations.*

Important Facts: *Quick, bullet point facts that are crucial for exams.*

Classification

Functions of an Eye		
S. No.	**Function**	**Description**
1.	Adjustment to Light	Iris and pupil regulate light entry
2.	Refraction of Light	Lens bends light rays to form a sharp image
3.	Visual Processing	Retina converts light into electrical signals for the brain

Vision Defects and Corrections of an Eye			
S. No.	**Defect**	**Causes**	**Correction**
1.	Myopia (Nearsightedness)	Elongated eyeball or increased lens power	Concave lenses
2.	Hypermetropia(Farsightedness)	Compressed eyeball or decreased lens power	Convex lenses
3.	Presbyopia	Age-related hardening of the lens	Bifocal lenses
4.	Cataract	Lens clouding typically due to aging	Surgical removal and lens replacement
5.	Astigmatism	Irregular curvature of cornea or lens	Cylindrical lenses

Difference Between

Pupil v/s Iris	
Pupil	**Iris**
The opening that allows light into the eye	Muscular ring around the pupil that gives eye color
Size adjusts to light intensity	Controls the size of the pupil
Does not have color	Pigmented to provide eye color
Directly involved in light entry	Indirectly involved by adjusting pupil size
Remains black in appearance	Can have various colors

Myopia v/s Hypermetropia	
Myopia (Nearsightedness)	**Hypermetropia (Farsightedness)**
Caused by an elongated eyeball	Caused by a compressed eyeball
Distant objects are blurred	Close objects are blurred
Corrected with concave lenses	Corrected with convex lenses
Far point is closer than normal	Near point is farther than normal
Light focuses before the retina	Light focuses behind the retina

Classification: *It organizes complex information into clear categories, making it easier for students to grasp differences, recognize patterns, and predict properties or behaviors in their learning.*

Difference Between: *Side-by-side comparisons to help distinguish similar concepts.*

Real Life Application Based Questions

1. **Have you ever wondered why cutting an apple and leaving it out causes it to turn brown? Explain what type of change i occurring and why it happens?**

Ans. When you cut an apple, it turns brown. Browning of apple takes place due to oxidation and this is a chemical change. Hence, w cannot restore it to original colour.

2. **While cooking pasta, Priya observed two processes: boiling water to cook pasta and frying onions until they turned brow Identify which process is a physical change and which is a chemical change?**

Ans. Boiling water to cook pasta is a physical change because boiling water involves **changing the state of water** from liquid to g (steam) without altering its chemical composition.

Frying onions causes them to turn brown, indicating the chemical change because a **chemical reaction** occurs and the process i irreversible and results in the formation of new substances with different flavours and colours.

Myth Buster

- **Myth: All physical changes are reversible, and all chemical changes are irreversible.**

  Fact: While many physical changes are reversible (like melting and freezing of water), some are not (like breaking a glass, cutting of an apple). Similarly, not all chemical changes are irreversible. For example, the **synthesis of water** is a chemical change that can be reversed through electrolysis to yield hydrogen and oxygen gases.

- **Myth: Physical changes always involve states of matter transitions (solid, liquid, gas).**

  Fact: While state transitions are common examples of physical changes, not all physical changes involve them. Dissolving sugar in water is a physical change without a state transition.

- **Myth: If you mix two substances and they react, they must have undergone a chemical change.**

  Fact: While mixing two substances can lead to a chemical reaction, it is not always the case. For example, mixing alcohol and water alters neither's chemical composition, illustrating a physical change.

- **Myth: The burning of a candle is just a physical change because you can see the wax melting.**

  Fact: The burning of a candle is actually a chemical reaction. When a candle burns, the wax combines with oxygen in the air to form new substances like carbon dioxide and water vapour, indicating a chemical change. The melting of wax is a physical change, but the actual burning (combustion) is a chemical change.

Mnemonics

- **DROP**-To remember characteristics of chemical change

  - D → Dramatic change in chemical composition
  - R → Release of gas
  - O → Observed energy change
  - P → Production of new substance

Real-Life Application Based Questions: *Exercises that connect theory with practical scenarios. It will enhance your understanding and relevance of concepts.*

Myth Buster: *Clear up common misconceptions to ensure your understanding is accurate.*

Mnemonics: *Memory aids to help you retain and recall information.*

COMPETENCY BASED SOLVED EXAMPLES

Multiple Choice Questions (1 M)

1. Which of the following metals exist in their native state in nature? (*Un*)
   (*i*) Ca (*ii*) Pt (*iii*) Al (*iv*) Ag
   (*a*) (*i*) and (*ii*) (*b*) (*ii*) and (*iii*)
   (*c*) (*ii*) and (*iv*) (*d*) (*iii*) and (*iv*)
2. Aluminium is used in **thermit** welding because (*Un*)
   (*a*) Aluminium is a metal that has lightweight
   (*b*) Aluminium is a strong oxidising agent
   (*c*) Aluminium has more affinity for oxygen
   (*d*) Aluminium is considered a reactive metal
3. During purification of a metal by electrolysis, what happens at the negative electrode? (*Re*) (CBSE APQ, 2023)
   (*a*) Metal ions lose electrons to become neutral atoms.
   (*b*) Neutral metal atoms gain electrons to become ions.
   (*c*) Neutral metal atoms lose electrons to become ions.
   (*d*) Metal ions gain electrons to become neutral metal atoms
4. Which of the following metals are obtained by electrolysis of their chlorides in the molten state? (*Ap*) (NCERT Exemplar)
   (*i*) Na (*ii*) Ca (*iii*) Fe (*iv*) Cu
   (*a*) (*i*) and (*iv*) (*b*) (*iii*) and (*iv*)
   (*c*) (*i*) and (*iii*) (*d*) (*i*) and (*ii*)
5. In the electrolytic refining of copper, the electrolyte used is (*Un*)
   (*a*) CuO (*b*) $Cu(OH)_2$
   (*c*) Acidified $CuSO_4$(aq) (*d*) $CuSO_4$(s)

Assertion and Reason (1 M)

Direction: The following questions consist of two statements – Assertion (A) and Reason (R). Answer these questions by selecting the appropriate option given below:

(*a*) Both A and R are true, and R is the correct explanation of A.
(*b*) Both A and R are true, but R is not the correct explanation of A.
(*c*) A is true, but R is false
(*d*) A is false, but R is true.

1. **Assertion (A):** One of the steps involved in copper extraction is $Cu_2S + 2Cu_2O \longrightarrow 6Cu + SO_2$
   Reason (R): Cu_2S is the reducing agent in this reaction, while Cu_2O is the oxidising agent. (*Un*)
2. **Assertion (A):** Highly reactive metals are extracted by electrolytic reduction.
   Reason (R): Metals are deposited at the cathode in electrolytic reduction. (*Un*)
3. **Assertion (A):** Zinc oxide can be reduced to zinc metal on heating with carbon.
   Reason (R): Carbon is less reactive than zinc. (*Un*) (CBSE APQ, 2023)

Subjective Questions

Very Short Answer Type Questions (2 M)

1. **Priya is studying the occurrence of metals in nature. She has samples of five metals: gold, aluminium, lead, iron, and silver. These metals occur in different forms in nature. Some occur in native state, and some in the combined state with other elements.** (*Un*)
   (A) Identify the metal(s) that are most likely to be found in their native state and those found in a combined state in the Earth's crust, which are positioned at the bottom of the reactivity series.
   (B) What is the name of the process in which sulphide ores are heated strongly in the presence of excess air to convert them into oxides?

Ans. (A)
- Gold and silver are often found in a native state and lies at the bottom of the reactivity series due to its low reactivity. (*½ M*)
- Silver can be found in the combined state as their sulphide or oxide ores or in the free state. It lies at the bottom of the reactivity series due to their low reactivity. (*½ M*)

(B) The process of converting sulphide ores into oxides by heating strongly in the presence of excess air is called roasting. (*1 M*)

Hints & Explanations

Multiple Choice Questions

1. (*c*) Pt and Ag are present in the bottom of the reactivity series and are the least reactive. Therefore, can exist in their native state in nature.
2. (*c*) Aluminium is used in thermit welding because aluminium has more affinity for oxygen. It can be understood from the following reaction:
   $Fe_2O_3(s) + 2Al(s) \rightarrow Al_2O_3(s) + 2Fe(l) + Heat$
3. (*d*) At negative electrode, *metal ions gain electrons to become neutral metal atoms in electrolysis.*
4. (*d*) Highly reactive metals like Na, Mg, Ca which are placed in the higher part of the reactivity series cannot be obtained by heating with carbon.
   Therefore, they are obtained by electrolysis of their chlorides in the molten state.

Solved Examples

For each topic, solved examples are provided including tagging of Competencies, PYQs, CBSE SQPs, etc., that exemplify how to approach and solve questions. This section is designed to reinforce your learning and improve problem solving skills.

MISCELLANEOUS EXERCISE

Multiple Choice Questions (1 M)

1. Which of the following is non-metal but is lustrous? (*Un*) (NCERT Exemplar)
   (*a*) Iodine (*b*) Mercury
   (*c*) Carbon (*d*) Bromine
2. Electrical wires have a coating of insulating material. The material, generally used is (*Un*) (NCERT Exemplar)
   (*a*) Sulphur (*b*) Graphite
   (*c*) PVC (*d*) All can be used
3. Krunal connected a copper plate and an iron plate to the positive and negative terminals of a battery respectively along with a switch. He immersed the plates into a beaker containing acidified copper sulphate solution.
   Which of the following is likely to happen when the current is started? (*Ap*) (CFPQ)
   (*a*) Iron will be deposited on the copper plate.
   (*b*) Copper will continue to be deposited on the iron plate.
   (*c*) No reaction will occur at the iron plate or at the copper plate.
   (*d*) The copper already deposited on the iron plate will go back into the solution.
4. In the list given below, a metal to the right is more reactive than a metal that is to its left.

Copper	Tin	Nickel	Cobalt	Iron	Zinc

The table below gives the colour of the metal sulpahte salt solutions.

ANSWER KEYS

Multiple Choice Questions

1. (*a*) 2. (*c*) 3. (*b*) 4. (*c*) 5. (*b*) 6. (*a*) 7. (*d*) 8. (*c*) 9. (*d*) 10. (*d*)
11. (*b*) 12. (*d*) 13. (*b*) 14. (*a*) 15. (*d*) 16. (*a*) 17. (*c*) 18. (*d*) 19. (*b*) 20. (*b*)
21. (*c*) 22. (*c*) 23. (*c*) 24. (*c*) 25. (*b*)

Assertion and Reason

1. (*d*) 2. (*d*) 3. (*a*) 4. (*a*) 5. (*c*) 6. (*c*) 7. (*b*) 8. (*c*)

Case Based Questions

Case Based-II

(*i*) (*d*) (*ii*) (*a*) (*iii*) (*c*) (*iv*) (*b*)

HINTS & EXPLANATIONS

Multiple Choice Questions

1. (*a*) Iodine is the only non-metal which is lustrous, that is, has a shiny appearance.
2. (*c*) An insulating material that is used in coating of electrical wire is PVC (Polyvinyl chloride).
3. (*b*) When the current is started, the iron plate (cathode, negative terminal) attracts Cu^{2+} ions from the solution, which are reduced to form metallic copper. Thus, copper continues to deposit on the iron plate.

11. (*b*) Iron is more reactive than copper. Therefore, iron displaces copper from copper sulphate solution, resulting in the formation of iron sulphate and deposition of copper on the iron nail, giving it the colour of reddish brown. This displacement reaction can be represented as:
    $Fe(s) + CuSO_4(aq) \rightarrow FeSO_4(aq) + Cu(s)$
12. (*d*) Gold(Au) will get dissolved in conc. HCl and conc. HNO_3, 3 : 1 mixture (aqua regia).

At the end of each chapter, you'll find additional exercises intended to test your grasp of the material. These are great for revision and to prepare for exams.

Answer Key and Explanations including Topper's Explanations, Mistake 101, Nailing the right answer and Key takeaway to know how to write the ideal answer.

Answer Key

MOCK TEST PAPER-1

Time allowed : 3 hours **Maximum Marks : 80**

NOTE:

(*i*) *Q.P. Code given on the right hand side of the question paper should be written on the title page of the answer-book by the candidate.*
(*ii*) *Please check that this question paper contains **39** questions.*
(*iii*) ***Please write down the Serial Number of the question in the answer-book at the given place before attempting it.***
(*iv*) *15 minute time has been allotted to read this question paper. The students will read the question paper only and will not write any answer on the answer-book during this period.*

GENERAL INSTRUCTIONS:

Read the following instructions carefully and follow them:

(*i*) *This question paper contain **39** questions. **All** questions are **compulsory**.*
(*ii*) *The question paper is divided into three sections - **A**, **B** and **C**.*
Section A : Biology (30 marks)
Section B : Chemistry (25 marks)
Section C : Physics (25 marks)
(*iii*) *The question paper has MCQs, VSAs, SAs, LAs and CBQs. Marks are given against each question.*
(*iv*) *There are case based questions (CBQs) with three sub-questions and are of 4 marks each.*
(*v*) ***Divide your answer sheet into three sections as per the question paper -***
Section A (Biology), Section B (Chemistry) and Section C (Physics).
It is compulsory to answer each question in its respective section. Do not mix answers of one section into the other section.
(*vi*) *Instructions are given with each section and question, wherever necessary.*
(*vii*) *Kindly note that a separate question paper has been provided for visually impaired candidates.*
(*viii*) *There is no overall choice in the question paper. However, an internal choice has been provided in few questions. Only one of the choices in such questions must be attempted.*

SECTION - A

1. Identify *A* in the given flowchart representing the reflex arc. 1

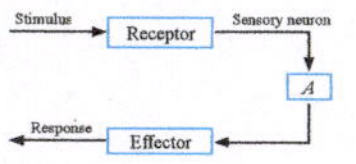

(*a*) Spinal cord (*b*) Brain (*c*) Spinal nerve (*d*) PNS

Mock Test

Mock Test Papers: Test your preparedness with our Mock Test Papers designed to mirror the format and difficulty of real exams. Use the detailed explanations to identify areas of strength and opportunities for improvement.

CONTENTS

Upcoming CBSE SQPs/ APQs can be accessed through this QR

Questions have been categorized according to the Bloom's Taxonomy (as per CBSE Board). The following abbreviations have been used in the book:

(*Un*) - Understanding (*Re*) - Remembering (*Ap*) - Applying
(*An*) - Analysing (*Cr*) - Creating (*Ev*) - Evaluating

CBSE SOLVED PAPER 2026

Time allowed : 3 hours	Maximum Marks : 80

GENERAL INSTRUCTIONS:

Read the following instructions carefully and follow them:

*(i) This question paper contain **39** questions. **All** questions are **compulsory**.*

*(ii) The question paper is divided into **three** sections - **A**, **B** and **C**.*

Section A : Biology (30 marks)

Section B : Chemistry (25 marks)

Section C : Physics (25 marks)

(iii) The question paper has MCQs, VSAs, SAs, LAs and CBQs. Marks are given against each question.

*(iv) There are case based questions (CBQs) with three sub-questions and are of **4** marks each.*

(v) Divide your answer sheet into three sections as per the question paper - Section A (Biology), Section B (Chemistry) and Section C (Physics).

It is compulsory to answer each question in its respective section. Do not mix answers of one section into the other section.

(vi) Instructions are given with each section and question, wherever necessary.

(vii) Kindly note that a separate question paper has been provided for visually impaired candidates.

(viii) There is no overall choice in the question paper. However, an internal choice has been provided in few questions. Only one of the choices in such questions must be attempted.

SECTION-A (BIOLOGY)

1. *Spirogyra*, despite being a multi-cellular organism, still shows a simple reproductive method. Select the correct option with regard to reproduction in *Spirogyra*: ***(Re)*** ***(1 Mark)***

(*a*) Asexual reproduction by division of cells into two cells

(*b*) Sexual reproduction by division of cells into many cells

(*c*) Asexual reproduction by breaking up of *Spirogyra* filaments into smaller parts

(*d*) Sexual reproduction by the formation of gametes after meiosis of cells of filaments followed by fusion of male and female gametes

Ans. (c) Spirogyra reproduces asexually through fragmentation, where its filament breaks into smaller pieces upon maturation, and each piece grows into a new individual. (1 Mark) [NCERT, Ch-7, Pg. no.116]

2. The genotype of green stemmed tomato plant is denoted by 'GG' and that of purple stemmed tomato plant as 'gg'. Hybrid of a cross between these two were self-pollinated to obtain F_2 progeny. What will be the ratio of GG, Gg and gg in this F_2 progeny? ***(Ap)*** ***(1 Mark)***

(*a*) 2:1:1 (*b*) 3:1:0 (*c*) 1:1:2 (*d*) 1:2:1

Ans. (d) The cross between green-stemmed(GG) tomato plant with the purple-stemmed(gg) tomato plant will produce F_1 hybrids (Gg). When these F_1 hybrids are self-pollinated, the resulting F_2 progeny will have a genotype ratio of 1 GG : 2 Gg : 1 gg. (1 Mark)[NCERT, Ch-8, Pg. no. 130]

3. Identify the type of tropic movement that is responsible for the movement of the pollen tube towards an ovule from the following options. **(Re) (1 Mark)**

(*a*) Hydrotropism (*b*) Geotropism (*c*) Chemotropism (*d*) Phototropism

Ans. (c) The pollen tube moves towards the ovule because it responds to chemicals released by the ovule. This type of movement is called chemotropism. (1 Mark)[NCERT, Ch-6, Pg. no.107]

4. If the stomatal pore is open, it indicates which situation from the following? **(Un) (1 Mark)**

(*a*) The guard cells have shrunk.
(*b*) The water comes out of the guard cells.
(*c*) Large amount of water is lost through stomata.
(*d*) The guard cells have swelled due to inflow of water.

Ans. (d) When the stomatal pore is open, it means the guard cells are full of water, causing them to swell and open the pore for gas exchange. (1 Mark)[NCERT, Ch-5, Pg. no. 83]

5. Which of the following limits the number of trophic levels in a food chain ? **(Un) (1 Mark)**

(*a*) Availability of water
(*b*) Deficient food supply
(*c*) Decrease in energy at higher levels
(*d*) Pollution in air

Ans. (c) The number of trophic levels in a food chain is limited because energy is lost at each level, making it harder to sustain many levels. Only about 10% of the energy is passed on. (1 Mark)[NCERT, Ch-13, Pg. no. 210]

6. The following events occur during the process of photosynthesis. Choose the option that indicates the correct events. **(Re) (1 Mark)**

(i) Oxidation of carbon dioxide to carbohydrates
(ii) Conversion of light energy into chemical energy
(iii) Absorption of light energy by chlorophyll
(iv) Conversion of hydrogen and oxygen into water

Options:

(*a*) (i) and (ii) (*b*) (ii) and (iii) (*c*) (iii) and (iv) (*d*) (i) and (iv)

Ans. (b) The events occur during the process of photosynthesis are: (i) Absorption of light energy by chlorophyll. (ii) Conversion of light energy to chemical energy and splitting of water molecules into hydrogen and oxygen. (iii) Reduction of carbon dioxide to carbohydrates. (1 Mark)[NCERT, Ch-5, Pg. no. 82]

7.

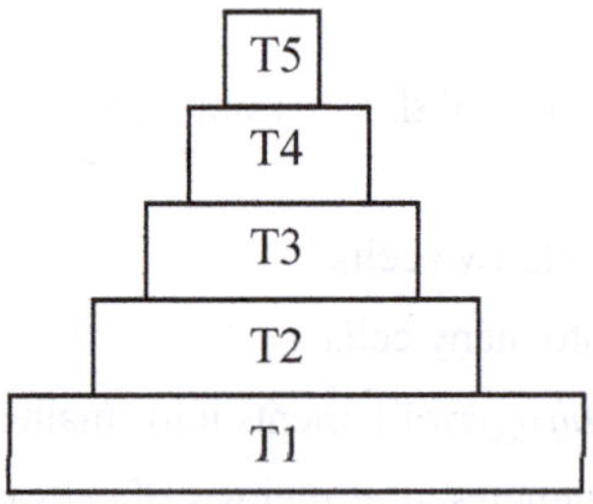

In the given figure, identify the trophic level having maximum concentration of harmful chemicals. **(Ap) (1 Mark)**

(*a*) T1 (*b*) T5 (*c*) T4 (*d*) T3

Ans. (b) As harmful chemicals are not degradable, they accumulate progressively at each trophic level. This process is termed as biological magnification, and as a result, the highest concentration of these chemicals is found at the top trophic level (T5). (1 Mark)[NCERT, Ch-13, Pg. no. 212]

For Questions number 8 and 9, two statements are given - one labelled as Assertion (A) and the other labelled as Reason (R). Select the correct answer to these questions from the codes (*a*), (*b*), (*c*) and (*d*) as given below.

(*a*) Both Assertion (A) and Reason (R) are true and Reason (R) is the correct explanation of Assertion (A).
(*b*) Both Assertion (A) and Reason (R) are true, but Reason (R) is **not** the correct explanation of Assertion (A).
(*c*) Assertion (A) is true, but Reason (R) is false.
(*d*) Assertion (A) is false, but Reason (R) is true.

8. **Assertion (A):** There are generally a greater number of individuals at the lower trophic levels of an ecosystem.

Reason (R): The greatest number is of the producers. *(Un) (1 Mark)*

Ans. (b) As energy decreases at each successive trophic level due to energy loss (mainly through heat and metabolism), fewer individuals can be supported at higher trophic levels. This is why there are generally more individuals at lower trophic levels, with the greatest number being producers.
(1 Mark)[NCERT, Ch-13, Pg. no. 210]

9. **Assertion (A):** Blood plasma transports carbon dioxide in dissolved form, while oxygen is transported by respiratory pigments.

Reason (R): Carbon dioxide is more soluble in water than in oxygen. *(Un) (1 Mark)*

Ans. (a) Blood plasma transports carbon dioxide dissolved in water, while oxygen is transported by respiratory pigments like hemoglobin. This is because carbon dioxide is more soluble in water than oxygen.
(1 Mark)[NCERT, Ch-5, Pg. no. 90]

10. (*a*) "The timing and the amount of hormone secreted by a gland are regulated in the human body." Justify this statement with the help of an example. *(Un) (2 Marks)*

OR

(*b*) Electrical impulse is an excellent means to transmit information in the animal body, but there are some limitations to the use of electrical impulses. State any two limitations. *(Un) (2 Marks)*

Ans. (a) The timing and amount of hormone secretion are regulated by feedback mechanisms in the human body. For example, cells of the pancreas detect high blood sugar and secretes insulin to lower it. As sugar levels decrease, insulin secretion is reduced. This ensures hormones are secreted in the right amounts and at the right time. (2 Marks) [NCERT, Ch-6, Pg. no. 111]

OR

(b) Two limitations of electrical impulses are:

- Electrical impulses can only reach cells connected by nervous tissue, not every cell in the animal body. (1 Mark)
- After transmitting an electrical impulse, cells need time to reset before generating and transmitting a new impulse, so they cannot constantly transmit electrical impulses. (1 Mark) [NCERT, Ch-6, Pg. no. 108]

11. Do all variations in a species have equal chances of surviving in the environment in which they find themselves? Explain. *(Un) (2 Marks)*

Ans.
- No, all variations in a species do not have equal chances of surviving in the environment. (1 Mark)
- Variations that provide an advantage for survival are more likely to be passed on, while others may not survive due to environmental pressures. For example, bacteria that can resist heat have a better chance of surviving in hot conditions. (1 Mark)

[NCERT, Ch-8, Pg. no. 128, 129]

12. Suggest two ways of dealing with waste generated at home. *(Ap) (2 Marks)*

Ans. Two ways of dealing with waste generated at home:

- Segregating waste into biodegradable and non-biodegradable categories for separate disposal. This helps in reducing the overall environmental impact. (1 Mark)
- Biodegradable waste can be buried as they can be broken down by biological processes, such as by bacteria or other microorganisms. They decompose naturally and do not persist in the environment for long. (1 Mark)

[NCERT, Ch-13, Pg. no. 214,215]

13. Observe the following diagrams : **(*An*) (*3 Marks*)**

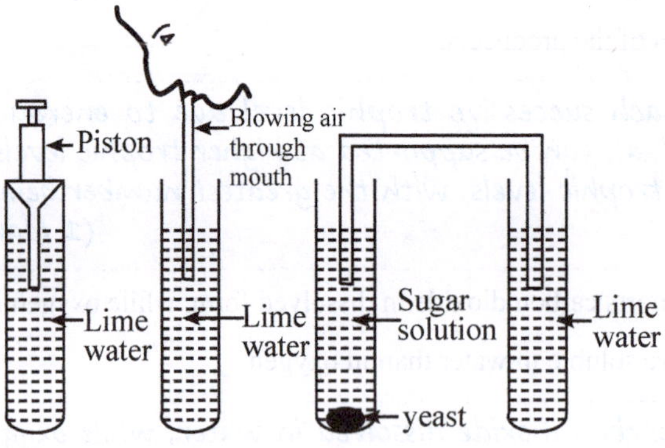

(*a*) What change will be observed in Cases ' P ', ' Q ' and ' R ' ? Give reasons.

(*b*) In which case :

(*i*) is aerobic respiration taking place? (*ii*) is fermentation taking place?

Ans. (a) • Case P: The lime water takes a longer time to turn milky because atmospheric air contains very little carbon dioxide. (½ Mark)

• Case Q: Exhaled air contains more carbon dioxide, which reacts with lime water to form insoluble calcium carbonate, turning it milky. (½ Mark)

• Case R: The lime water turns milky because yeast respires anaerobically and ferments sugar, releasing carbon dioxide that reacts with lime water to form calcium carbonate. (½ Mark)

(b) (i) Aerobic Respiration is occurring in Case Q, where oxygen is used to break down glucose. (¾ Mark)

(ii) Fermentation is occurring in Case R, where anaerobic respiration (fermentation) takes place in yeast, producing CO_2 and ethanol. (¾ Mark)

[NCERT, Ch-5, Pg. no. 87, 88]

14. (*a*) Giving two examples, justify the statement that the sex of the offspring in all animals is not always genetically determined.

(*b*) Differentiate between the sex chromosomes of male and female human beings. **(*Un*) (*3 Marks*)**

Ans. (a) The sex of offspring is not always genetically determined as:

• In few reptiles, the temperature at which fertilized eggs are kept determines whether the animals developing in the eggs will be male or female. (1 Mark)

• In other animals, such as snails, individuals can change sex, indicating that sex is not genetically determined. (1 Mark)

(b)

Aspect	Females sex chromosome	Males sex chromosome
Chromosomes	XX; Have a perfect pair of X chromosomes	XY;Have a mismatched pair, one X and one Y
Size of Chromosomes	Both X chromosomes are of the same size	X chromosome is normal-sized and the Y chromosome is shorter

(1 Mark)

[NCERT, Ch-8, Pg. no. 132]

15. Attempt either (*a*) or (*b*) :

(*a*) (*i*) Name an organ that helps in the formation of male germ cells in humans and also mention the condition that favours the formation of male germ cells.

(*ii*) In male reproductive system, write the pathway followed to deliver male germ cells to the site of fertilisation.

(*iii*) Mention the main physical feature of the male germ cell that helps it move towards the female germ cell.

(*Re*) (*2 + 2 + 1 = 5 Marks*)

OR

(*b*) Radha has three children. She does not want to have more children. Radha visits a nearby hospital, to know the methods to prevent pregnancy.

(*i*) Mention the name of any two ways other than the surgical methods, following which Radha can avoid unwanted pregnancies.

(*ii*) Name the surgical methods to prevent pregnancy.

(*iii*) Give one example each of sexually transmitted diseases caused by bacteria and virus.

(*Re, An*) (*2 + 2 + 1 = 5 Marks*)

Ans. (a)

(i) • Testes help in the formation of male germ cells (sperms). (1 Mark)

• Favorable Condition for sperm formation is temperature lower than the normal body temperature, which is why the testes are located outside the abdominal cavity in the scrotum. (1 Mark)

(ii) The pathway followed by male germ cells (sperms) to reach the site of fertilization is as follows:

Sperm is produced in the testes

↓

Travels through the vas deferens

↓ (mixes with secretions from the seminal vesicles and prostate gland)

Sperm moves through the urethra

↓

Released during sexual intercourse through penis

↓

Enter vaginal passage

↓

Reaches to the uterus after travelling through cervix

↓

Moves upward and reaches oviduct(site of fertilisation)

(2 Marks)

(iii) The long tail of the sperm helps it move towards the female germ cell (egg) during fertilisation.

(1 Mark)

[NCERT, Ch-7, Pg. no. 123]

OR

(b) (i) Two ways Radha can avoid unwanted pregnancies:

1. Contraceptive Pills: These pills alter the hormonal balance in the body to prevent ovulation. (1 Mark)
2. Condoms: They act as a mechanical barrier to prevent sperm from reaching the egg. (1 Mark)

(ii) Surgical methods to prevent pregnancy are:

- Tubectomy (in female) and (1 Mark)
- Vasectomy (in male) (1 Mark)

(iii) Examples of sexually transmitted diseases caused by:

- Bacteria: Gonorrhoea (½ Mark)
- Virus: HIV/AIDS (½ Mark)

[NCERT, Ch-7, Pg. no. 125]

16. Read the following passage and answer the questions that follow :

A middle–aged person is facing some cognitive changes in himself. His early symptoms included mild forgetfulness. For example, forgetting where he left his mobile or failing to find words to complete his sentences. He was facing problems in driving a car, climbing up and down the stairs, inserting a plug into an outlet. He slowly developed a sad mood and anxiety. ***(Re, Un)***

(*a*) What are voluntary actions ? ***(1 Mark)***

(*b*) Which part of the brain is responsible for precision of voluntary actions? ***(1 Mark)***

(*c*) (*i*) Explain the role of the medulla? ***(2 Marks)***

OR

(*c*) (*ii*) How do the animal muscles move ? ***(2 Marks)***

Ans. (a) Voluntary actions are the movements or activities that are consciously controlled by the brain, such as walking, speaking, or picking up objects. (1 Mark)

(b) The cerebellum is responsible for the precision and coordination of voluntary actions. (1 Mark)

(c) (i)

- The medulla in the hind-brain controls involuntary actions, i.e. those actions that occur automatically without conscious control. (1 Mark)
- Example: Blood pressure, salivation, and vomiting. (Any two) (1 Mark)

OR

(c) (ii) Animal muscles move when nerve impulses reach them. The muscle fibers change shape, specifically shortening, due to special proteins in muscle cells. These proteins rearrange in response to the electrical impulses, causing the muscle to contract. (2 Marks)

[NCERT, Ch-6, Pg. no. 103-105]

SECTION-B (CHEMISTRY)

17. Tamarind is a natural source of which acid ? ***(Re) (1 Mark)***

(*a*) Acetic acid (*b*) Tartaric acid (*c*) Oxalic acid (*d*) Citric acid

Ans. (b) Tamarind is a natural source of tartaric acid, responsible for its sour taste. (1 Mark)

[NCERT, Ch- 2 , Pg. no. 28]

18. Rain water is called' acid rain' when its : ***(Re) (1 Mark)***

(*a*) pH falls below 7.2. (*b*) pH falls below 14. (*c*) pH is above 7. (*d*) pH falls below 5.6.

Ans. (d) When the pH falls below 5.6, it is called acid rain. (1 Mark) [NCERT, Ch- 2 , Pg. no. 26]

19. Which of the following are combination reactions ? **(Un) (1 Mark)**

(i) $2KClO_3 \longrightarrow 2KCl + 3O_2$

(ii) $MgO + H_2O \longrightarrow Mg(OH)_2$

(iii) $4Al + 3O_2 \longrightarrow 2Al_2 O_3$

(iv) $Zn + FeSO_4 \longrightarrow ZnSO_4 + Fe$

(*a*) (i) and (iii)
(*b*) (iii) and (iv)
(*c*) (ii) and (iv)
(*d*) (ii) and (iii)

Ans. (d) A combination reaction is when two or more substances combine to form one single product.

(ii) $MgO + H_2O \rightarrow Mg(OH)_2$

(iii) $4Al + 3O_2 \rightarrow 2Al_2O_3$ (1 Mark)

[NCERT, Ch- 1 , Pg. no.6-7]

20. A metal carbonate reacts with a solution X which forms a salt, water and a gas Y . What are X and Y ? **(Ap) (1 Mark)**

(*a*) X -Sodium hydroxide, Y - Carbon dioxide
(*b*) X -Sodium hydroxide, Y - Hydrogen
(*c*) X -Hydrochloric acid, Y - Carbon dioxide
(*d*) X - Hydrochloric acid, Y - Hydrogen

Ans. (c) General reaction:

Metal carbonate + Acid $\longrightarrow$ Salt + Water + CO_2

$Na_2CO_3 + 2HCl \longrightarrow 2NaCl + H_2O + CO_2$

X = Hydrochloric acid (1 Mark)

Y = Carbon dioxide gas

[NCERT, Ch- 2 , Pg. no. 20-21]

21. When Mg metal is treated with hot water, it starts floating on the surface of the water. The reason for its different behaviour is: **(Un) (1 Mark)**

(*a*) Mg is a lighter element than water.
(*b*) Mg reacts with water to produce H_2 gas which helps in floating.
(*c*) Mg reacts with water to produce N_2 gas which helps in floating.
(*d*) Mg reacts with water to form CO_2 gas which helps in floating.

Ans. (b) Magnesium reacts with hot water to form magnesium hydroxide and hydrogen. It also starts floating due to the bubbles of hydrogen gas sticking to its surface

$Mg + 2H_2O \longrightarrow Mg(OH)_2 + H_2\uparrow$ (1 Mark)

[NCERT, Ch- 3 , Pg. no. 43]

22. A student notices that her silver jewellery turned dull and had a grey-black coating over it after wearing for a few months. What results in the change in colour of the silver metal ? **(Un) (1 Mark)**

(*a*) The polish over the jewellery was removed after wearing for a few months.
(*b*) The jewellery comes in contact with air, moisture and acids and corrodes.
(*c*) Dust particles over the jewellery change its colour.
(*d*) Its colour changes due to rusting.

Ans. (b) Silver jewellery turns grey-black because it reacts with air (especially sulphur compounds), moisture and acidic substances, forming a layer of silver sulphide (Ag_2S) on the surface. (1 Mark)

[NCERT, Ch- 1 , Pg. no. 13]

23. When ferrous sulphate crystals are heated in a test tube, we observe that: **(Ap) (1 Mark)**

(*a*) A colourless gas with no smell is evolved.

(*b*) A brown gas is evolved.

(*c*) The green colour of the salt fades and a gas with the smell of burning sulphur is evolved.

(*d*) The green colour of the salt fades and no gas is evolved.

Ans. (c) On heating ferrous sulphate crystals, the green colour fades and a gas with burning sulphur smell (SO_2) is released.

$$\underset{\text{(Ferrous sulphate)}}{2FeSO_4(s)} \xrightarrow{\text{Heat}} \underset{\text{(Ferric oxide)}}{Fe_2O_3(s)} + SO_2(g) + SO_3(g)$$

(1 Mark)

[NCERT, Ch- 1 , Pg. no. 8]

For Question number 24, two statements are given - one labelled as Assertion (A) and the other labelled as Reason (R). Select the correct answer to this question from the codes (*a*), (*b*), (*c*) and (*d*) as given below.

(*a*) Both Assertion (A) and Reason (R) are true and Reason (R) is the correct explanation of Assertion (A).

(*b*) Both Assertion (A) and Reason (R) are true, but Reason (R) is not the correct explanation of Assertion (A).

(*c*) Assertion (A) is true, but Reason (R) is false.

(*d*) Assertion (A) is false, but Reason (R) is true.

24. Assertion (A): Carbon shows the property of catenation.

Reason (R): C–C bond is weak due to its small size.

(Re) (1 Mark)

Ans. (c) Carbon forms bonds with other carbon atoms to make long chains; this property is called catenation.

Carbon forms very strong bonds because of its small atomic size, making its compounds highly stable. (1 Mark)

[NCERT, Ch- 4 , Pg. no.62]

25. Answer the following :

(*a*) Why should chemical equations be balanced ?

(*b*) Name the oxidising and reducing agent in the following equation : **(Un) (2 Marks)**

$4Na + O_2 \longrightarrow 2Na_2O$

Ans. (a) According to the law of conservation of mass, atoms are neither created nor destroyed in a reaction, that is, the total mass of the elements present in the products of a chemical reaction has to be equal to the total mass of the elements present in the reactants.. Therefore, chemical equations must be balanced. (1 Mark)

(b) $4Na + O_2 \rightarrow 2Na_2O$

- Sodium gains oxygen, so it is oxidised → hence sodium is the reducing agent
- Oxygen is reduced (accepts electrons) → hence oxygen is the oxidising agent (1 Mark)

[NCERT, Ch- 1 , Pg. no. 3,12-13]

26. Answer the following :

(*a*) Why can the oxides of highly reactive metals not be reduced by carbon ?

(*b*) Why do ionic compounds have high melting and boiling points ?

(*c*) Why is a solder, an alloy of lead and tin, used for welding electrical wires together? **(Un) (3 Marks)**

Ans. (a) Highly reactive metals cannot be reduced by carbon because they have a stronger affinity for oxygen, forming very stable oxides. Therefore, their oxides are extracted by electrolytic reduction instead of carbon reduction. (1 Mark)

(b) Ionic compounds have high melting and boiling points because a large amount of energy is required to break the strong inter-ionic forces of attraction between oppositely charged ions. (1 Mark)

(c) Solder is used for joining electrical wires because it has a low melting point and melts easily to form a firm joint. (1 Mark)

[NCERT, Ch- 3 , Pg. no. 48-49, 52]

27. Attempt either (*a*) or (*b*):

(*a*) (*i*) Write one example each of one metal that is so soft that it can be cut with a knife, and one non-metal that is a good conductor of electricity.

(*ii*) Using the electronic configuration, explain how Mg atom combines with oxygen to form magnesium oxide by transfer of electrons. [Atomic number : Mg = 12, O = 8]

(*Un*) (*3 Marks*)

OR

(*b*) Give reasons:

(*i*) Metal sulphides and carbonates should be converted to their metal oxides in the process of extraction of metals.

(*ii*) Aluminium oxide is considered as an amphoteric oxide.

(*iii*) Metals like Na, K, Ca and Mg are never found in their free state in nature. **(*Un*) (*3 Marks*)**

Ans. (a) (i)

- Metal that can be cut with a knife: Sodium (very soft metal) (½ Mark)
- Non-metal that conducts electricity: Graphite (form of carbon) (½ Mark)

(ii) Magnesium (Mg) has electronic configuration 2,8,2. Oxygen (O) has electronic configuration 2,6 (1 Mark)

Magnesium loses 2 electrons to form Mg^{2+} ion

Oxygen gains 2 electrons to form O^{2-} ion

Formation of MgO:

$$\underset{[2,\,8,\,2]}{Mg} \longrightarrow \underset{[2,\,8]}{Mg^{2+}} + 2e^-$$

$$O + 2e^- \longrightarrow O^{2-}$$
[2, 6] [2, 8]

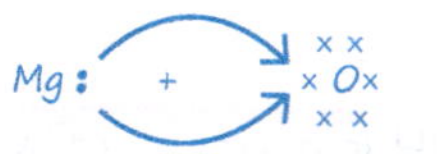

$\longrightarrow [Mg^{2+}]\,[O^{2-}]$

$$Mg^{2+} + O^{2-} \longrightarrow MgO$$ (1 Mark)

[NCERT, Ch- 3 , Pg. no.40, 47-48]

OR

(b) (i) Metal sulphides and carbonates are first converted into metal oxides because metals are more easily extracted from their oxides. Sulphides are converted by roasting and carbonates by calcination. (1 Mark)

(ii) Aluminium oxide is amphoteric because it reacts with both acids and bases to form salt and water. (1 Mark)

$$Al_2O_3 + 6HCl \rightarrow 2AlCl_3 + 3H_2O$$

$$Al_2O_3 + 2NaOH \rightarrow 2NaAlO_2 + H_2O$$

(Sodium aluminate)

(iii) Metals like Na, K, Ca and Mg are highly reactive, so they readily combine with air, water and other substances and hence are not found in free state in nature. (1 Mark)

[NCERT, Ch- 3 , Pg. no. 41, 50-51]

28. Read the following passage and answer the questions that follow : In the given diagram, when electricity is passed through an aqueous solution of a common salt, a substance 'Z' is produced, along with the evolution of gases 'X' and 'Y'. When a burning matchstick is brought near the gas 'Y', it burns with a pop sound, whereas 'X' is used for disinfecting drinking water. When 'X' is passed through slaked lime, an insoluble substance 'A' is produced. ***(Ap)***

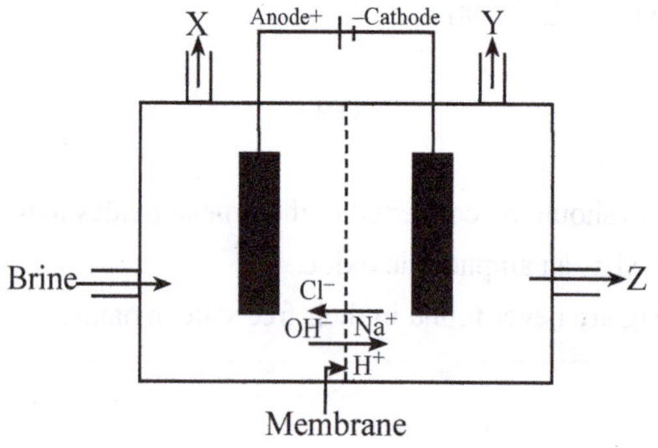

(*a*) Write the names of the gases 'X' and 'Y'. ***(1 Mark)***

(*b*) Write the balanced chemical equation for the formation of substance 'Z'. ***(1 Mark)***

(*c*) (i) What happens : ***(2 Marks)***

(I) If a drop of red litmus solution is added to the aqueous solution of substance 'Z'?

(II) If CO_2 gas is passed through ammoniacal solution of aqueous NaCl ?

OR

(*c*) (ii) Identify the substance 'A' and write the balanced chemical equation of the reaction which takes place in its preparation. ***(2 Marks)***

Ans. (a) Gas X → Chlorine (Cl_2) is used for disinfecting water (½ Mark)

Gas Y → Hydrogen (H_2) (burns with pop sound) (½ Mark)

(b) Substance Z = Sodium hydroxide (NaOH)

$$2NaCl(aq) + 2H_2O(l) \rightarrow 2NaOH(aq) + Cl_2(g) + H_2(g)$$ (1 Mark)

(c) (i)

(I) On adding red litmus to solution Z (NaOH), It turns red litmus to blue because NaOH is basic (1 Mark)

(II) On passing CO_2 through ammoniacal NaCl solution, white precipitate of sodium bicarbonate is formed

$$NaCl + NH_3 + H_2O + CO_2 \rightarrow NaHCO_3 \downarrow + NH_4Cl$$

[NCERT, Ch- 3 , Pg. no. 26, 30-31]

(1 Mark)

OR

(c) (ii) Substance A = Bleaching powder $Ca(ClO)_2$ (1 Mark)

Bleaching powder is produced by the action of chlorine on dry slaked lime $[Ca(OH)_2]$.

$2Ca(OH)_2 + 2Cl_2 \rightarrow Ca(ClO)_2 + CaCl_2 + 2H_2O$

(1 Mark) [NCERT, Ch- 3 , Pg. no. 30-31]

29. Attempt either (*a*) or (*b*): **(Ap) (5 Marks)**

(*a*) A carbon compound 'P' of molecular formula C_2H_6O is found to be neutral when tested with red and blue litmus. A gas that burns with a pop sound is produced when sodium metal reacts with compound 'P'.

(*i*) Identify the compound 'P'.

(*ii*) The carbon compound 'P' is heated with conc. H_2SO_4 at 443 K to produce compound 'Q'.

(I) Write the chemical equation for the reaction.

(II) What is the role of conc. H_2SO_4 in this reaction?

(*iii*) What is likely to be observed on heating compound 'P' with ethanoic acid with an acid as a catalyst? Write the chemical equation for the reaction.

OR

(*b*) (*i*) Write the structural formula of benzene.

(*ii*) State the reason why carbon can neither form C^{4+} cation nor C^{4-} anion.

(*iii*) What type of bond is formed between carbon and hydrogen ?

(*iv*) How is ethanol converted to ethanoic acid ?

(*v*) Complete the following chemical equation:

$CH_3COOC_2H_5 + NaOH \longrightarrow$ **(Un) (5 Marks)**

Ans. (a) Molecular formula = C_2H_6O

- It is neutral to litmus (so not an acid or base)
- With sodium metal it releases a gas with pop sound → this gas is hydrogen

Alcohols show this reaction with sodium.

Therefore:

(i) Compound P is Ethanol (C_2H_5OH) (½ Mark)

Reaction with sodium:

$2C_2H_5OH + 2Na \rightarrow 2C_2H_5O^-Na^+ + H_2\uparrow$ (½ Mark)

(ii) (I) Concentrated sulphuric acid removes water (H_2O) from ethanol. So ethanol changes into ethene (an alkene).

$$\underset{\text{(Ethanol)}}{C_2H_5OH} \xrightarrow{\text{Conc. } H_2SO_4,\ 443K} \underset{\text{(Ethene)}}{C_2H_4} + H_2O$$

(1 Mark)

(II) Role of conc. H_2SO_4:

It acts as a dehydrating agent (removes water). (1 Mark)

(iii) Heating ethanol with ethanoic acid in presence of an acid, this is called esterification.

An ester with a sweet smell is formed. (1 Mark)

Reaction:

$$C_2H_5OH + CH_3COOH \xrightarrow{Conc.\ H_2SO_4} CH_3COOC_2H_5 + H_2O$$ (1 Mark)

Ethyl ethanoate
(pleasant fruity smell)

[NCERT, Ch-4 , Pg. no.72-73]

OR

(b) (i) Benzene is a six-carbon ring with alternating double bonds: (1 Mark)

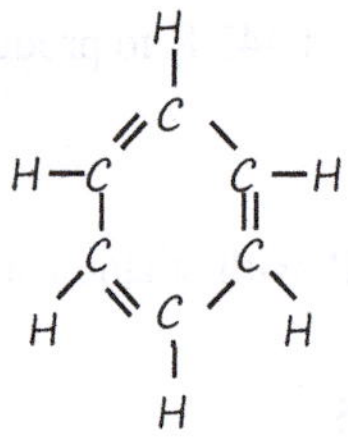

Benzene – C_6H_6

(ii) Carbon cannot form C^{4+} or C^{4-} ions because losing four electrons requires a very large amount of energy, and gaining four electrons would be difficult for the nucleus to hold. Therefore, carbon attains stability by sharing electrons and forming covalent bonds. (1 Mark)

(iii) The bond that occurs between Carbon (C) and Hydrogen (H) is a covalent bond. (1 Mark)

(iv)

$$CH_3-CH_2OH \xrightarrow{Acidified\ K_2Cr_2O_7\ +\ Heat} CH_3\ COOH$$

(1 Mark)

(v) $CH_3COOC_2H_5 + NaOH \rightarrow CH_3COONa + C_2H_5OH$ (1 Mark)

[NCERT, Ch- 4 , Pg. no. 59, 65,71,74]

SECTION-C (PHYSICS)

30. A thin beam of white light falls on a face of a glass prism and a spectrum is obtained on a screen. Which of the following options is the correct sequence of colours from top to bottom on the screen? ***(Un) (1 Mark)***

(*a*) Red, Green, Yellow, Violet, Blue
(*b*) Red, Yellow, Green, Blue, Violet
(*c*) Violet, Blue, Green, Yellow, Red
(*d*) Violet, Red, Green, Yellow, Blue

Ans. (b) When white light passes through a glass prism, dispersion occurs.

- Red deviates the least.
- Violet deviates the most.

On the screen, the colour that deviates least appears at the top, and the most deviated appears at the bottom.

(1 Mark) [NCERT, Ch 10, Pg. no. 167]

31. From the following options choose the one which gives negative magnification greater than one : ***(Un) (1 Mark)***

(*a*) Concave mirror; Nature of image - real
(*b*) Concave mirror; Nature of image - virtual
(*c*) Convex mirror; Nature of image - real
(*d*) Convex mirror; Nature of image - virtual

Ans. (a)

- Negative magnification → image is real and inverted.
- Magnification greater than 1 → image is enlarged.

Only a concave mirror can form a real, enlarged image (when the object is between F and C).

(1 Mark) [NCERT, Ch 9, Pg. no. 143]

For Question number 32, two statements are given - one labelled as Assertion (A) and the other labelled as Reason (R). Select the correct answer to this question from the codes (*a*), (*b*), (*c*) and (*d*) as given below.

(*a*) Both Assertion (A) and Reason (R) are true and Reason (R) is the correct explanation of Assertion (A).

(*b*) Both Assertion (A) and Reason (R) are true, but Reason (R) is not the correct explanation of Assertion (A).

(*c*) Assertion (A) is true, but Reason (R) is false.

(*d*) Assertion (A) is false, but Reason (R) is true.

32. **Assertion (A):** Direction of force exerted on a current-carrying conductor placed in a magnetic field remains same if the directions of both magnetic field and current flowing through the conductor are reversed.

Reason (R): The direction of force exerted on a current-carrying conductor placed in an external magnetic field can be determined by using magnetic compass. ***(An)* (*1 Mark*)**

Ans. (c) The assertion is true because according to Fleming's Left-Hand Rule, force direction depends on both current and magnetic field.

If both are reversed, their effects cancel each other, so the force direction remains unchanged.

The reason is false because a magnetic compass shows the direction of the magnetic field, not the direction of force.

(1 Mark) [NCERT, Ch 12 , Pg. no. 202]

33.

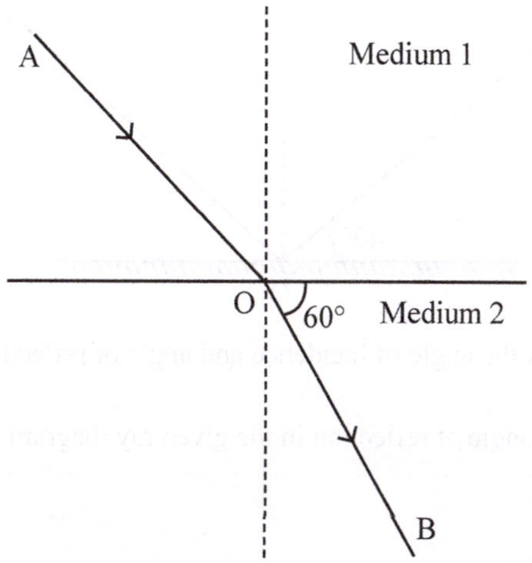

Use the above given ray diagram to calculate the angle of incidence. Given that the refractive index of Medium 2 with respect to the Medium 1 is $\sqrt{3}$. ***(Ap)* (*2 Marks*)**

Ans. Given:

Refractive index $_1\mu_2 = \sqrt{3}$

Angle shown (60°) is with the surface.

So, angle of refraction

$r = 90° - 60° = 30°$ (1 Mark)

Using Snell's Law:

$$_1\mu_2 = \frac{\sin i}{\sin r} \Rightarrow \sqrt{3} = \frac{\sin i}{\sin 30^\circ} \Rightarrow \sqrt{3} = \frac{\sin i}{\frac{1}{2}}$$

$$\sin i = \frac{\sqrt{3}}{2} \Rightarrow i = 60^\circ$$ (1 Mark)

[NCERT, Ch 9 , Pg. no.148]

34. Attempt either (*a*) or (*b*):

(*a*) How does the focal length of eye lens change as the distance of the object from the eyes is altered? Explain.

OR

(*b*) Why is the concave lens used as a corrective lens for a myopic eye ? **(*Un*) (*2 Marks*)**

Ans. (a) When the object is far away, the ciliary muscles relax, the lens becomes thin, and the focal length increases. (1 Mark)

When the object is near, the ciliary muscles contract, the lens becomes thick, and the focal length decreases. This adjustment is called accommodation. (1 Mark)

[NCERT, Ch 10 , Pg. no.162]

OR

(b) In myopia (short-sightedness), distant objects form an image in front of the retina.

A concave lens diverges the incoming light rays so that the image forms on the retina, enabling clear vision of distant objects. (2 Marks) [NCERT, Ch 10, Pg. no. 163]

35.

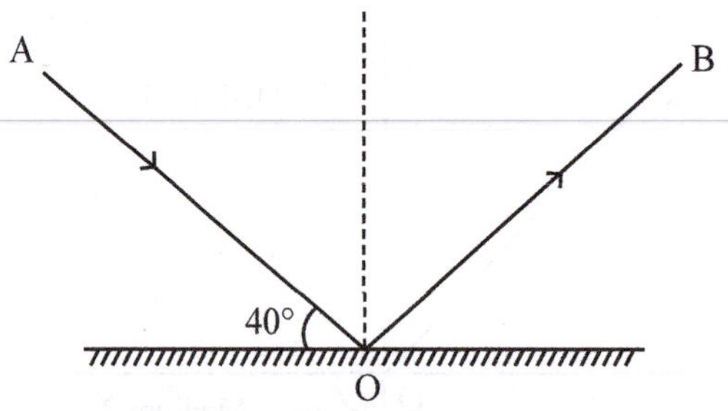

(*a*) State the laws which help to find out the angle of incidence and angle of reflection in the ray diagram given above. **(*2 Marks*)**

(*b*) Find out the angle of incidence and angle of reflection in the given ray diagram. **(*Re, Ap*) (*1 Mark*)**

Ans. (a) Laws of Reflection

1. The incident ray, reflected ray and the normal at the point of incidence lie in the same plane.

2. The angle of incidence (i) is equal to the angle of reflection (r). (2 Marks)

(b) Given angle with the mirror surface = 40°

Angle of incidence is measured from the normal, so:

$i = 90^\circ - 40^\circ = 50^\circ$

By law of reflection

$r = i = 50^\circ$ (1 Mark)

36. The values of current I flowing in a given resistor for the corresponding values of potential difference V applied across the ends of resistor are given below in the table :

I (Amperes)	0.4	0.8	1.2	1.6	2.0
V (Volts)	1.2	2.4	3.6	4.8	6.0

Plot a graph between V and I and calculate the resistance of that resistor. ***(Ap, Cr) (3 Marks)***

Ans. Graph between V and I

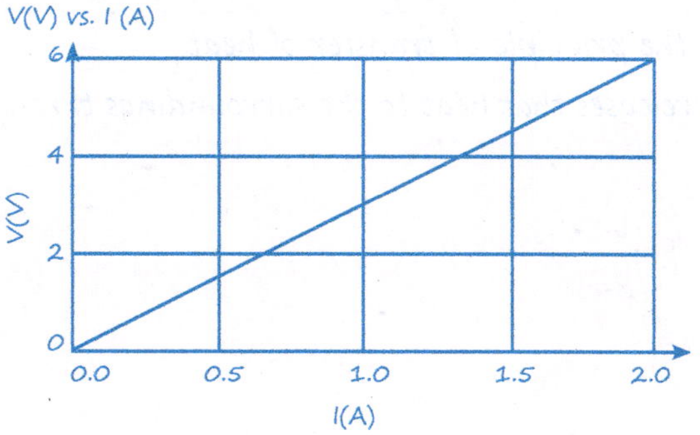

[NCERT, Ch 11 , Pg. no. 176]

(2 Marks)

Resistance: $R = \frac{V}{I}$

Taking any pair: $R = \frac{1.2}{0.4} = 3\Omega$

(Checking another $\frac{6.0}{2.0} = 3\Omega$) (1 Mark)

37. What is scattering of light ? How is scattering of light different from reflection of light? Explain. ***(An) (3 Marks)***

Ans. Scattering of light is the phenomenon in which light is deviated in different directions when it strikes small particles (like dust, air molecules, etc.) in a medium.

Example: Blue colour of the sky. (1 Mark)

Scattering of Light	Reflection of Light
Light is deviated in different directions when it strikes small particles.	Light bounces back from a surface into the same medium.
Occurs due to dust, smoke, air molecules, etc.	Occurs from a smooth surface like a mirror.
Does not follow fixed angle laws.	Follows the laws of reflection (i = r).
Example: Blue colour of the sky.	Example: Image formed in a mirror.

(2 Marks)

[NCERT, Ch 10 , Pg. no. 169]

38. Read the following passage and answer the questions that follow :

Swati, a class 10 student, observes that when she passes close to the refrigerator in her kitchen, she feels the heat, although the things kept inside the refrigerator are cool.

(*a*) Describe the cause of heating in the above-mentioned case. **(*1 Mark*)**

(*b*) A current *I* flows through a resistor of resistance *R* when the potential difference across it is *V*. Applying Ohm's law, write the formula for amount of heat produced by the resistor in time *t*. **(*1 Mark*)**

(*c*) (i) Write any two practical applications of heating effect of electric current.

OR

(*c*) (ii) Define the commercial unit of electric energy and express it in Joules (J). **(*Re, Un, Ap*) (*2 Marks*)**

Ans. (a) The refrigerator works on the principle of transfer of heat.

It removes heat from inside and releases that heat to the surroundings through the condenser coils at the back, so we feel warmth near it. *(1 Mark)*

(b) Using Ohm's Law V = IR

Heat produced in time t:

$H = Pt = VIt$

Substituting V = IR:

$H = I^2Rt$ *(1 Mark)*

(c) (i) Two practical applications of heating effect

1. Electric iron

2. Electric heater *(2 Marks)*

OR

(c) (ii) Commercial unit of electric energy

The commercial unit of electric energy is kilowatt-hour (kWh). *(2 Marks)*

[NCERT, Ch 11 , Pg. no. 188]

39. (*a*) (i) State the rules to determine the following:

(I) Direction of magnetic field produced around a current-carrying straight conductor.

(II) Direction of force experienced by a current-carrying straight conductor placed in a magnetic field which is perpendicular to it.

(ii) (I) Draw the magnetic field lines due to a current-carrying solenoid.

(II)

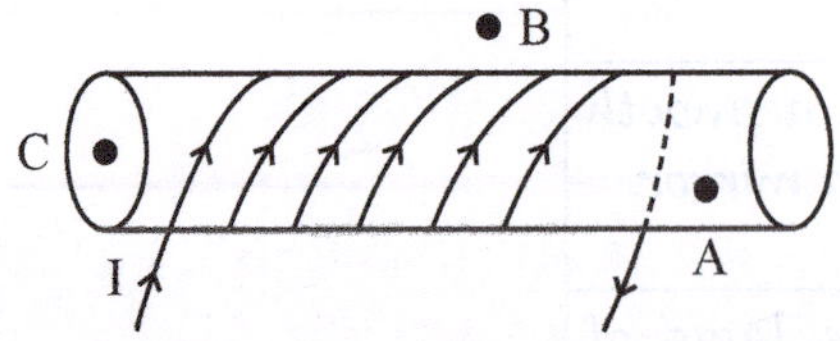

Three points A,B and C are marked in the above given diagram of the current-carrying solenoid. Out of the three points A,B and C, at which point is the magnetic field strength maximum and at which point is it minimum ? **(*Re, An, Cr*) (*5 Marks*)**

OR

(*b*) (i) (I) In the given circuit diagram, a battery *B*, a key *K*, a resistance *R* and a thick copper wire XY are connected in series and a compass is placed near the wire. What is the purpose of this arrangement?

(II) What conclusion do you draw from it?

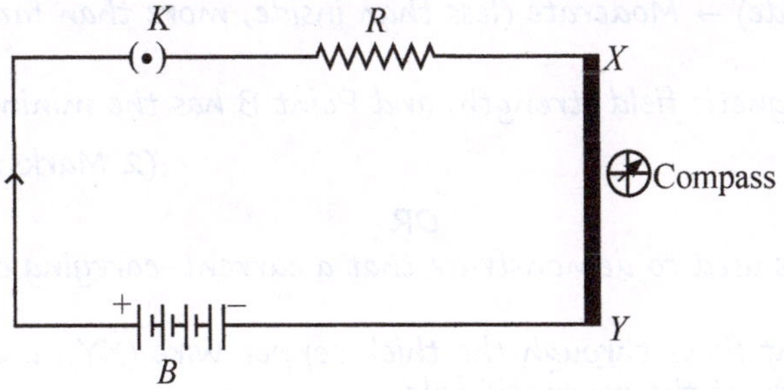

(ii) Give reasons :

(I) There is either a convergence or a divergence of magnetic field lines near the ends of a current-carrying straight solenoid.

(II) The current-carrying solenoid, when suspended freely, aligns along a particular direction.

(III) The burnt-out fuse should be replaced by another fuse of identical rating. **(*Un*) (*5 Marks*)**

Ans. (a) (i) (I) Direction of magnetic field around a current-carrying straight Conductor is given by

Right Hand Thumb Rule:

If the conductor is held in the right hand such that the thumb points in the direction of current, then the curled fingers show the direction of magnetic field lines around the conductor.

(1 Mark) [NCERT, Ch12 , Pg. no. 200]

(II) Direction of force on a current-carrying conductor in a magnetic field is given by

Fleming's Left Hand Rule:

Stretch the thumb, forefinger and middle finger of the left hand mutually perpendicular.

- Forefinger → Direction of magnetic field
- Middle finger → Direction of current
- Thumb → Direction of force (motion)

(1 Mark) [NCERT, Ch12 , Pg. no. 200, 203]

(ii) (I) Magnetic field lines due to a current-carrying solenoid

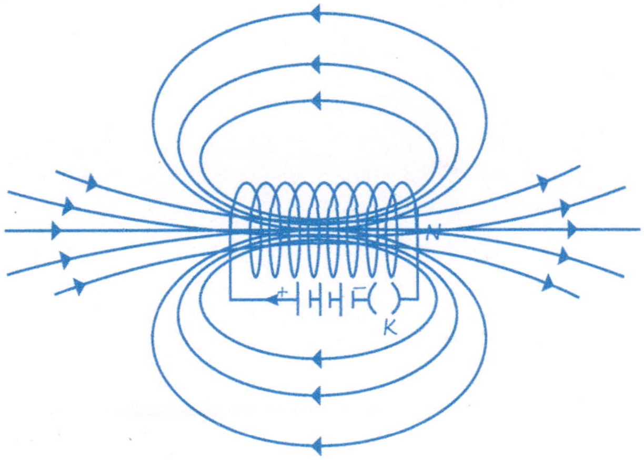

(1 Mark)

(iii) From the diagram:

Point A → Inside the solenoid → **Maximum magnetic field**

Point B → Outside the solenoid (away from ends) → **Minimum magnetic field**

Point C → Near the end (outside) → Moderate (less than inside, more than far outside)

Point A has the maximum magnetic field strength, and Point B has the minimum magnetic field strength.

(2 Marks) [NCERT, Ch12 , Pg. no. 201]

OR

Ans. (b) (i) (I) This arrangement is used to demonstrate that a current-carrying conductor produces a magnetic field around it.

When the key is closed, current flows through the thick copper wire (XY), and the compass needle deflects, showing the presence and direction of the magnetic field.

(1 Mark)

(II) When current flows through the wire XY, the compass needle deflects.

This shows that a current-carrying conductor produces a magnetic field around it.

If the direction of current is reversed, the compass deflects in the opposite direction, proving that the direction of magnetic field depends on the direction of current.

(1 Mark)

(ii)

(I) Near the ends of a solenoid, magnetic field lines either converge or diverge because:

A current-carrying solenoid behaves like a bar magnet.

Magnetic field lines emerge from the north pole (diverge) and enter the south pole (converge), so convergence and divergence occur near the ends. (1 Mark)

(II) A freely suspended current-carrying solenoid aligns in a particular direction because:

A current-carrying solenoid acts like a bar magnet.

Hence, it aligns itself along the North–South direction under the influence of Earth's magnetic field.(1 Mark)

(III) A burnt-out fuse should be replaced by one of identical rating because:

The fuse is designed to melt at a specific current value.

If a higher rating fuse is used, it may not melt during overload, causing damage or fire hazard. (1 Mark)

[NCERT, Ch12 , Pg. no. 201]

CBSE SOLVED PAPER 2025

Time allowed : 3 hours **Maximum Marks : 80**

GENERAL INSTRUCTIONS:

Read the following instructions very carefully and strictly follow them:

*(i) This question paper comprises **39** questions. **All** questions are compulsory.*

*(ii) This question paper is divided into **five** sections - **A, B, C, D** and **E**.*

*(iii) **Section A** - Questions No. **1** to **20** are Multiple Choice Questions. Each question carries **1** mark.*

*(iv) **Section B** - Questions No. **21** to **26** are Very Short Answer type questions. Each question carries **2** marks. Answer to these questions should be in the range of **30** to **50** words.*

*(v) **Section C** - Questions No. **27** to **33** are Short Answer type questions. Each question carries **3** marks. Answer to these questions should be in the range of **50** to **80** words.*

*(vi) **Section D** - Questions No. **34** to **36** are Long Answer type questions. Each question carries **5** marks. Answer to these questions should be in the range of **80** to **120** words.*

*(vii) **Section E** - Questions No. **37** to **39** are of **3** source-based/case-based units of assessment carrying **4** marks each with sub-parts.*

(viii) There is no overall choice. However, an internal choice has been provided in some sections. Only one of the alternatives has to be attempted in such questions.

SECTION-A

Select and write the most appropriate option out of the four options given for each of the questions no. 1 to 20. There is no negative marking for incorrect response.

1. Given below are the structures of some hydrocarbons. Select the two structures which are related to each other from the given options: ***(An) (1 Mark)***

(i) 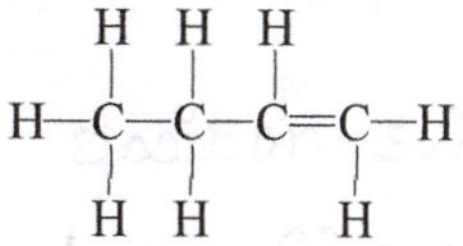
(ii) 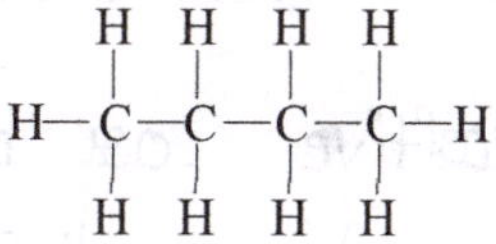
(iii) 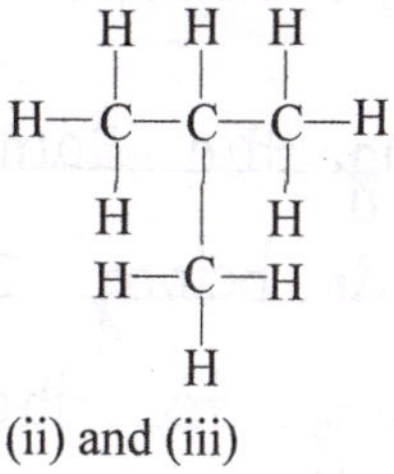
(iv) 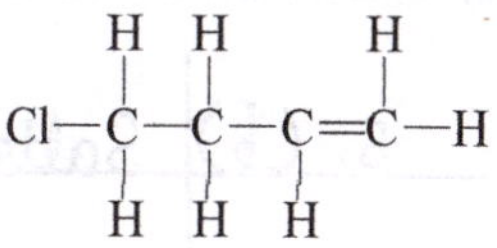

(*a*) (i) and (iv) (*b*) (ii) and (iv) (*c*) (ii) and (iii) (*d*) (i) and (iii)

1. (c) (ii) and (iii) are isomers since they have the same molecular formula of C_4H_{10}. Hence, they both are related to each other.

2. Choose the ***incorrect*** statement about the common reaction used in hydrogenation of vegetable oils. ***(Un) (1 Mark)***

(*a*) It is an addition reaction.

(*b*) It takes place in the presence of nickel or palladium catalyst.

(*c*) The product contains only single bonds between carbon atoms.

(*d*) It is an addition reaction which occurs in the presence of an acid catalyst.

2. (d) Hydrogenation of vegetable oils is an addition reaction that occurs using a nickel catalyst or palladium catalyst to give saturated hydrocarbons.

3. Consider the following chemical equation: ***(Ev) (1 Mark)***

$p\,Al + q\,H_2O \rightarrow r\,Al_2O_3 + s\,H_2$

To balance this chemical equation, the values of 'p','q',r' and 's' must be respectively:

(*a*) 3,2,2,1 (*b*) 2,3,3,1 (*c*) 2,3,1,3 (*d*) 3,1,2,2

3. (c) The complete balanced equation is:

$2Al + 3H_2O \longrightarrow Al_2O_3 + 3H_2$

Hence, p = 2, q = 3, r = 1, s = 3

4. Study the following cases: ***(1 Mark)***

(i) $CuSO_4 + Mg \rightarrow$ (ii) $FeSO_4 + Pb \rightarrow$ (iii) $CaSO_4 + Al \rightarrow$ (iv) $ZnSO_4 + Ca \rightarrow$

The case/cases in which new product (s) will form is/are: ***(Un)***

(*a*) Only (i) (*b*) Only (iii) (*c*) (i) and (iv) (*d*) (i), (ii) and (iv)

4. (c) According to reactivity series, only reaction (i) and (iv) will take place.

$CuSO_4 + Mg \longrightarrow MgSO_4 + Cu$

$ZnSO_4 + Ca \longrightarrow CaSO_4 + Zn$

5. Which of the given option represents a family of salts? ***(1 Mark)(Re)***

(*a*) $NaCl, Na_2SO_4, CaSO_4$ (*b*) $K_2SO_4, Na_2SO_4, CaSO_4$ (*c*) $NaNO_3, CaCO_3, Na_2CO_3$ (*d*) $MgSO_4, CuSO_4, MgCl_2$

5. (b) Salts having the same positive or negative radicals are said to belong to a family. K_2SO_4, Na_2SO_4, and $CaSO_4$ belong to the family of sulphate salts.

6. Match Column-I with Column-II and select the correct option from the choices provided. ***(Re) (1 Mark)***

	Column-I		Column-II
A.	Site of fertilisation of egg with the sperm	(i)	Vagina
B.	Site of implantation of embryo	(ii)	Uterus
C.	Site of entry of sperm into the female reproductive tract	(iii)	Oviduct
D.	Site through which the waste materials generated by the developing embryo are removed	(iv)	Placenta
		(v)	Cervix

(a) A -(ii), B -(i), C -(v), D -(iv) (b) A -(iii), B -(i), C -(v), D -(iv)
(c) A -(iv), B -(ii), C -(iii), D -(i) (d) A -(iii), B -(ii), C -(i), D -(iv)

6. (d) fertilisation of egg and sperm occurs in the oviduct, embryo implants in the uterus, sperm enters through the vagina, and the placenta removes waste from the developing embryo's blood, ensuring proper nutrient and waste exchange.

7. The part of the hind-brain controlling involuntary actions such as salivation and vomiting in humans is: **(Re) (1 Mark)**
(a) Cerebellum (b) Cerebrum (c) Pons (d) Medulla

7. (d) The medulla in the hindbrain controls involuntary actions like salvation and vomiting, regulating essential reflexes for body function.

8. Select a pair of bisexual flowers from the following : **(Re) (1 Mark)**
(a) Papaya and mustard (b) *Hibiscus* and mustard (c) *Hibiscus* and papaya (d) *Hibiscus* and watermelon

8. (b) Hibiscus and Mustard are bisexual flowers, Containing both Stamen (male) and carpels (female), enabling Self and cross-pollination.

9. The plant hormone present in greater concentration in the areas of rapidly dividing cells is: **(Re) (1 Mark)**
(a) Auxin (b) Cytokinins (c) Gibberellins (d) Abscisic acid

9. (b) Cytokinins promote cell division and are found in high concentrations in actively growing regions like fruits and seeds.

10. Temporary finger-like extensions on the cell surface to take in food is formed in: **(Re) (1 Mark)**
(a) *Paramoecium* (b) *Amoeba* (c) *Leishmania* (d) *Rhizopus*

10. (b) Amoeba forms pseudopodia, a temporary finger-like extensions, to engulf food through phago-cytosis, aiding movement and nutrition intake.

11 A wire of length '*l*' in gradually stretched so that its length increases to 3*l*. If its original resistance is R, then its new resistance will be: **(Ev) (1 Mark)**

(*a*) 3R (*b*) 6R (*c*) 9R (*d*) 27R

11. (c) The resistance R of a wire is given by $R = \rho \frac{l}{A}$
When the wire is stretched to 3 times its original length (3l), the volume of the wire remains the same, so

$$l \times A = (3l) \times A' = A' = \frac{A}{3}$$

Thus, the new resistance R' becomes

$$R' = \rho \frac{3l}{A/3} = \rho \frac{3l \times 3}{A} = 9\rho \frac{l}{A} = 9R$$

12. Which one of the following statements is ***not*** true about a bar magnet ? **(Re) (1 Mark)**

(*a*) It sets itself in north-south direction when suspended freely.

(*b*) It has attractive power for iron filings.

(*c*) It produces magnetic field lines.

(*d*) The direction of magnetic field lines inside a bar magnet is from its north pole to its south pole.

12. (d)
- Outside the magnet, magnetic field lines run from the north pole to the south pole.
- Inside the magnet, they run from the south pole to the north pole to form closed loops.

13. Absolute refractive index of water and glass is $\frac{4}{3}$ and $\frac{3}{2}$ respectively. If the speed of light in glass is 2×10^8m/s, the speed of light in water is: **(Ev) (1 Mark)**

(*a*) $\frac{9}{4} m/s$ (*b*) $\frac{7}{3}$ m/s (*c*) $\frac{16}{9}$ m/s (*d*) $\frac{9}{8}$ m/s

13. (a) The absolute refractive index n of a medium is given by

$$n = \frac{c}{v}$$

for glass :

$$n_g = \frac{c}{v_g}$$

Substituting values :

$$\frac{3}{2} = \frac{c}{2 \times 10^8}$$

Solving for c :

$$c = \frac{3}{2} \times 2 \times 10^8 = 3 \times 10^8 \text{ m/s}$$

for water

Using the same formula :

$$n_w = \frac{c}{v_w}$$

Substituting values :

$$\frac{4}{3} = \frac{3 \times 10^8}{v_w}$$

Solving for v_w :

$$v_w = \frac{3 \times 10^8}{4/3} = 3 \times 10^8 \times \frac{3}{4} = \frac{9}{4} \times 10^8 \text{ m/s}$$

14. When a beam of white light passes through a region of very fine dust particles, the colour of light that scatters the most in that region is : **(Re) (1 Mark)**

(*a*) red (*b*) orange (*c*) blue (*d*) yellow

14(c) When a beam of white light passes through fine dust particles, the color that scatters the most is blue.

This phenomenon is called Rayleigh scattering, where shorter wavelength of light scatter more ~~rat~~ readily, and blue light has the shortest wavelength in the visible spectrum.

15. The strength of the magnetic field produced inside a current carrying long straight solenoid does not depend upon: **(Un) (1 Mark)**

(a) Area of cross-section of the tube of the solenoid

(b) Number of turns per unit length in the solenoid

(c) Direction of current flowing through the coil of the solenoid

(d) Material of the core of the solenoid

15. (c) While the direction of the current determines the polarity of the magnetic field (north or south pole), it does not affect the strength of the field inside the solenoid.

16. Other than the abiotic components, which of the given biotic components are ***not*** required to make an aquarium with small herbivorous fishes a self-sustaining system? **(Un) (1 Mark)**

(i) Aquatic plants and aquatic animals

(ii) Terrestrial plants and terrestrial animals

(iii) Decomposers as bacteria and fungi

(iv) Consumers as clown fishes and sea urchins

(a) (i) and (iv) (b) (ii) and (iii) (c) (i) and (iii) (d) (ii) and (iv)

16. (d) A self-sustaining aquarium with herbivorous fish needs aquatic plants for oxygen and food and decomposers for nutrient cycling. Terrestrial organism and specific consumers like clownfish and sea urchins are unnecessary.

For Questions number 17 to 20, two statements are given - one labelled as Assertion (A) and the other labelled as Reason (R). Select the correct answer to these questions from the codes (a), (b), (c) and (d) as given below.

(a) Both Assertion (A) and Reason (R) are true and Reason (R) is the correct explanation of Assertion (A).

(b) Both Assertion (A) and Reason (R) are true, but Reason (R) is ***not*** the correct explanation of Assertion (A).

(c) Assertion (A) is true, but Reason (R) is false.

(d) Assertion (A) is false, but Reason (R) is true.

17. **Assertion (A):** In our actions of writing or talking, our nervous system communicates with the muscles.

Reason (R): Cranial nerves and spinal nerves form the peripheral nervous system. **(Re) (1 Mark)**

17. (b) The nervous system controls voluntary actions by sending signals to muscles, while Reason (R) mentions the PNS components, it does not explain how the CNS communicates with the body through the PNS.

18. Assertion (A): Use of jute bags for shopping reduces pollution.

Reason (R): Jute is biodegradable and its bag may be reused as and when needed.

(Un) (1 Mark)

18. (a) Using jute bags reduces pollution because jute is biodegradable and reusable, unlike plastic bags that contribute to environmental pollution. Jute bags decompose naturally and can be used multiple times, making them an eco-friendly alternative to plastic.

19. Assertion (A): Hydrogen gas is not evolved when a metal reacts with nitric acid.

Reason (R): Nitric acid is a strong reducing agent and reduces the hydrogen produced in the reaction to water.

(An) (1 Mark)

19. (c) Hydrogen gas is not evolved when a metal reacts with nitric acid. It is because HNO_3 is a strong oxidising agent. It oxidises the H_2 produced to water and itself gets reduced to any of the nitrogen oxides (N_2O, NO, NO_2).

20. Assertion (A): Magnetic field lines around a bar magnet never intersect each other.

Reason (R): Magnetic field produced by a bar magnet is a quantity that has both magnitude and direction.

(Un) (1 Mark)

20. (b) Both A and R are true but R is not the correct explanation for A.

The assertion is correct because magnetic field lines, by their very nature, indicate the direction of the magenetic field at every point, and if they were to intersect, it would imply the existence of two different directions at the same point, which is impossible. Although the reason is true (magnetic fields are vector quantities with both magnitude and direction), it does not explain why the field lines never intersect. The non-intersecting property is due to the uniqueness of the magnetic field vector at any given point rather than simply because it is a vector quantity.

SECTION-B

Questions no. 21 to 26 are Very Short Answer Type questions.

21. (*a*) List the possible sources of energy required in decomposition reactions. Illustrate any one with a suitable example. ***(Re) (2 Marks)***

21. (a) Decomposition reactions require an external source of energy to break down compound into simpler substances. The common sources of energy include:

(1) Heat (Thermal decomposition)

(2) Light (Photodecomposition)

(3) Electricity (Electrolytic decomposition)

Example: Decomposition of silver chloride into silver and chlorine by light.

$$2AgCl(s) \xrightarrow{\text{Sunlight}} 2Ag(s) + Cl_2(g)$$

OR

(*b*) What is observed when hydrated ferrous sulphate crystals are heated in a dry boiling tube? Give balanced chemical equation (s) of the reactions(s) that occur (s). ***(Un) (2 Marks)***

21. (b) ferrous sulphate crystals ($FeSO_4 \cdot 7H_2O$) lose water when heated and the colour of the crystals changes. It then decomposes to ferric oxide (Fe_2O_3), sulphur dioxide (SO_2) and sulphur trioxide (SO_3)

The balanced chemical equation is :

$$2FeSO_4(s) \xrightarrow{Heat} Fe_2O_3(s) + SO_2(g) + SO_3(g)$$

(Ferrous sulphate) (ferric oxide)

22. Giving reason, state the advantage of using baking powder over baking soda for the preparation of bread or cakes.

(Un) (2 Marks)

22. Baking powder is a mixture of baking soda (Sodium hydrogencarbonate) and a mild edible acid such as tartaric acid. When baking powder is heated or mixed in water, the following reaction takes place :

$$NaHCO_3 + H^+ \longrightarrow CO_2 + H_2O + \text{Sodium salt of acid}$$

(from any acid)

Carbon dioxide produced during the reaction can cause bread or cake to rise making them soft and spongy. Thus baking powder is used over baking soda in bakery.

23. State the main function of arteries. Why do they have thick and elastic walls?

(Re, Un) (2 Marks)

23.
- Main function of arteries : Arteries carry oxygenated blood from the heart to different parts of the body.
- Arteries carry blood under high pressure from the heart. To sustain this force, they have thick, elastic walls that prevent rupture and maintain continuous blood flow.

24. (A) Explain how the proteins control the 'characteristics' in an organism with the help of an example of 'short height' trait in pea plant.

24.(A) Proteins control traits by regulating hormone production.

Example: In pea plants if a gene controls height by producing an enzyme that regulates growth hormone. A functional enzyme results in more hormone, making the plant tall, while a less efficient enzyme produces less hormone, leading to short plants.

(B) Name the information source of making proteins in a cell. **(Un, Re) (2 Marks)**

(B) The DNA in a cell provides the genetic information required for protein synthesis.

25. (A) A student has difficulty in reading his textbooks but can read the blackboard clearly while sitting in the last row. Name the defect of vision the student is suffering from. List two reasons due to which this defect arises. Write the nature of the lenses required to correct this defect. **(An) (2 Marks)**

25.(A) The student is suffering from hypermetropia (far-sightedness), where the near point of clear vision is abnormally far from the eye. This defect arises primarily due to:

1. An eyeball that is shorter than normal, causing the image of near objects to be focused behind the retina.

2. Insufficient refractive power of the cornea or lens, which fails to adequately converge light rays from close objects onto the retina.

To correct this deffect, convex (converging) lenses are used. These lenses increase the overall refractive power of the eye, thereby shifting the image forward onto the retina for clear near vision.

OR

(B) Draw a ray diagram to show the path of a ray of light falling obliquely on one of the refracting faces of a triangular glass prism and mark the angle of deviation on it. ***(Cr) (2 Marks)***

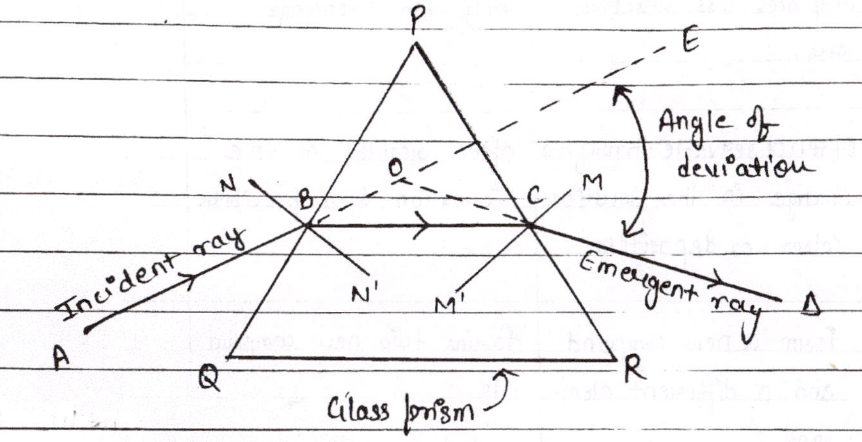

26. A voltage source sends a current of 2 A to a resistor of $40\,\Omega$ connected across it for 5 minutes. Calculate the electrical energy supplied by the source. ***(Ev) (2 Marks)***

26. First we determine the voltage across the resistor using Ohm's law:

$V = I \times R = 2A \times 40\Omega = 80V$

The power supplied by the source is:

$P = V \times I = 80V \times 2A = 160\,W.$

Since the time is given in minutes, convert 5 minutes to seconds:

$t = 5\,min \times 60s/min = 300s$

Thus, the electrical energy supplied is:

$E = P \times t = 160W \times 300s = 48,000\,J.$

SECTION-C

Questions no. 27 to 33 are Short Answer Type questions.

27. How is a double displacement reaction different from a displacement reaction? Explain giving example in the form of balanced chemical equations. ***(Re) (3 Marks)***

27. Displacement reaction and double displacement reaction:

Displacement Reaction	Double Displacement Reaction
Involves a single element being replaced in a compound	Involves exchanges of different atoms or groups of atoms (ions)
More reactive element displaces less reactive one.	No element displacement, only ion exchange.
Often observable through a change in the solution colour or deposition.	often results in the formation of a precipitate
form a new compound and a different element.	forms two new compounds
Example: Iron nail in Copper sulphate solution $Fe + CuSO_4 \rightarrow FeSO_4 + Cu$	Example: Reaction of sodium sulphate with barium chloride. $Na_2SO_4(aq) + BaCl_2(aq) \rightarrow BaSO_4(s) + 2NaCl(aq)$

28. (*a*) Common salt is an important raw material for various chemicals of daily use. State in brief the method of preparation of (i) Sodium hydroxide, and (ii) Sodium hydrogen carbonate from common salt. Write balanced chemical equations of the reactions that occur. ***(Ap) (3 Marks)***

28.(a) (i) When electricity is passed through an aqueous solution of sodium chloride (called brine), it decompose to form sodium hydroxide. The process is called the chlor-alkali process.

The balanced chemical equation that is involved is:

$2NaCl(aq) + 2H_2O(l) \longrightarrow 2NaOH(aq) + Cl_2(g) + H_2(g)$

(ii) Sodium hydrogencarbonate ($NaHCO_3$) is produced using sodium chloride as shown below;

$NaCl + H_2O + CO_2 + NH_3 \longrightarrow NH_4Cl + NaHCO_3$

(Ammonium chloride) (sodium hydrogencarbonate)

OR

(*b*) Design an experimental set-up to demonstrate that "Alcohol and glucose contain hydrogen but are not categorised as acids". Also give the reason to justify this fact. **(*An*) (*3 Marks*)**

28. (b) The experimental setup is shown below:

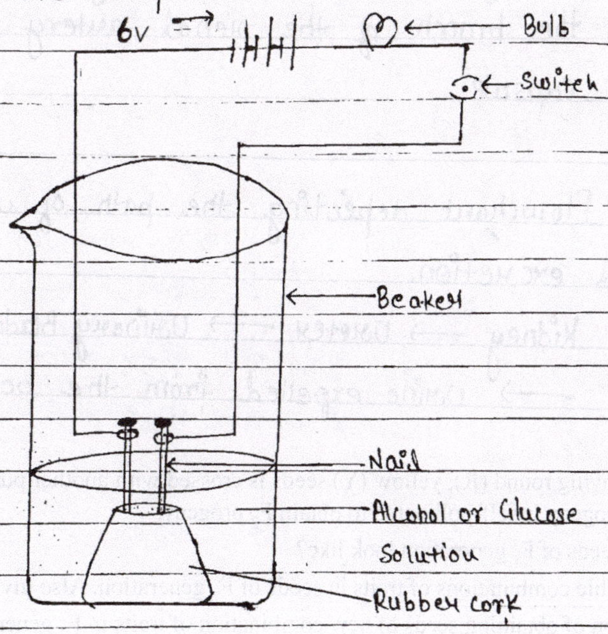

In this experiment, the bulb not glowing in the presence of glucose and alcohol solutions suggest that these substances do not conduct electricity. This is because they do not dissociate into ions in solution.

Even though both glucose and alcohol contain hydrogen atoms, they do not release free ions (such as H^+ or OH^-) in water, which are required for electrical conductivity. Thus, these solutions cannot be classified as acids.

29. (A) Enlist any two nitrogenous waste products removed from the blood of human kidney.

(B) Name the capillary cluster formed by the branch of renal artery in the Bowman's capsule.

(C) Depict in the form of a flow chart the path of the urine formed in each kidney until it is finally passed out through the urethra. **(*Re, Cr*) (*3 Marks*)**

29. (A) Two nitrogenous waste products removed by the kidney.

- Urea
- Uric acid

(B) The glomerulus is the capillary cluster formed by the branch of the renal artery in Bowman's Capsule.

(C) Flowchart depicting the path of urine formation and excretion.

Kidney ⟶ Ureter ⟶ Urinary Bladder ⟶ Urethra ⟶ Urine expelled from the body.

30. A pure pea plant having round (R), yellow (Y) seeds is crossed with another pure pea plant having wrinkled (r), green (y) seeds. Subsequently F_1 progeny is self-pollinated to obtain F_2 progeny. ***(An) (3 Marks)***

(A) What do the seeds of F_1 generation look like?

(B) Give the possible combinations of traits in seeds of F_2 generation. Also give their ratio.

(C) State the reason of obtaining seeds of new combination of traits in F_2 generation.

30. (P generation) RRYY (Round, Yellow) × rryy (Wrinkled, Green)

(Gamete) RY ry

(F_1 generation) RrYy (Round, Yellow)

↓ selfing

(F_2 generation)

	RY	Ry	rY	ry
RY	RRYY (Round, Yellow)	RRYy (Round, Yellow)	RrYY (Round, Yellow)	RrYy (Round, Yellow)
Ry	RRYy (Round, Yellow)	RRyy (Round, Green)	RrYy (Round, Yellow)	Rryy (Round, Green)
rY	RrYY (Round, yellow)	RrYy (Round, Yellow)	rrYY (wrinkled, Yellow)	rrYy (wrinkled, Yellow)
ry	RrYy (Round, Yellow)	Rryy (Round, Green)	rrYy (wrinkled, Yellow)	rryy (wrinkled, Green)

(A) The F_1 generation seeds will all be round and yellow because round (R) and Yellow (Y) are dominant traits over wrinkled (r) and green(y).

(B)

Possible combination of traits in F_2 generation	Genotypic Combination	Ratio
Round, Yellow	RRYY, RRYy, RrYY, RrYy	9/16
Round, Green	RRyy, Rryy	3/16
Wrinkled, Yellow	rrYY, rrYy	3/16
Wrinkled, Green	rryy	1/16

(C) New combinations arise due to the independent assortment of genes during gamete formation. The alleles for seed shape (R, r) and Seed color (Y, y) segregate independently, leading to new trait combinations.

31. A person has to keep reading material much beyond 25 cm (say at 50 cm) from the eye for comfortable reading. Name the defect of vision he is suffering from. List two causes responsible for arising of this defect. Draw labelled diagram showing correction of this defect using eye-glasses. Are these glasses convergent or divergent of light? ***(Cr) (3 Marks)***

31. The defect of vision that the person is suffering from is called 'Hyperopia' or 'Farsightedness'. This condition occurs when the eye is too short or the cornea has too little curvature, causing light to focus behind the retina instead of directly on it. As a result, the person can see distant objects clearly but struggles to see nearby objects.

Two causes of hyperopia are:

- Shortened eyeball – The eyeball becomes to small in length, which reduces the distance between the retina and the eye lens.

- Elongated eye lens – The focal length of the eye lens becomes too long, which reduces the eye len's ablity to converge.

To correct hyperopia convex lenses (converging lenses) are used in eyeglasses. These lenses help to bend the light rays inward so that they focus direct-ly on the retina, allowing for clear vision at close distances.

Hypermetropic eye:

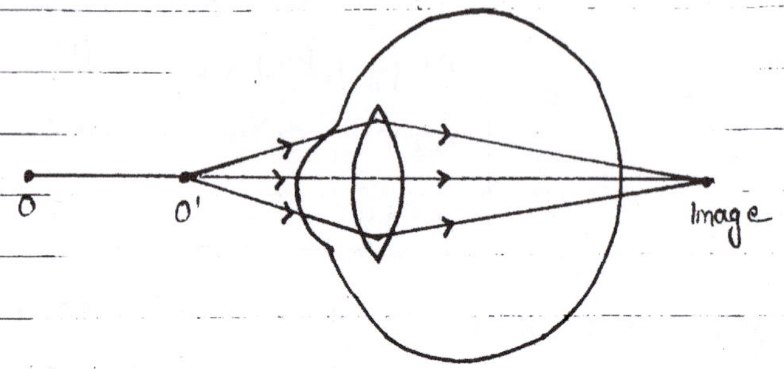

Correction using convex lens

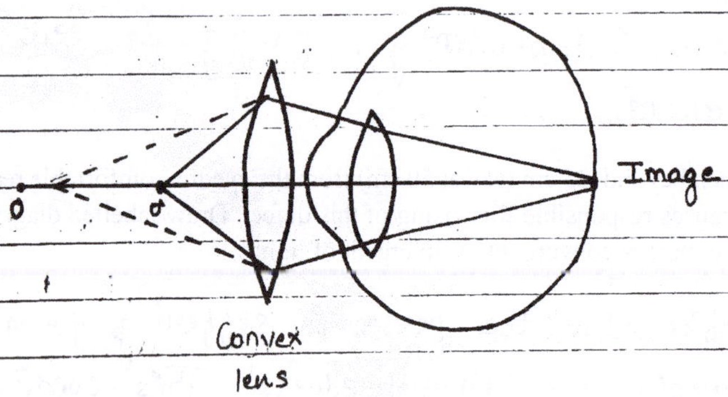

32. (A) Draw a labelled diagram to show the pattern of magnetic field lines on a horizontal white board due to a straight current carrying conductor passing perpendicular through its centre. If the direction of current in the conductor is vertically downwards, mark the **direction of (i) current, and (ii) magnetic field lines.**

32. (a)

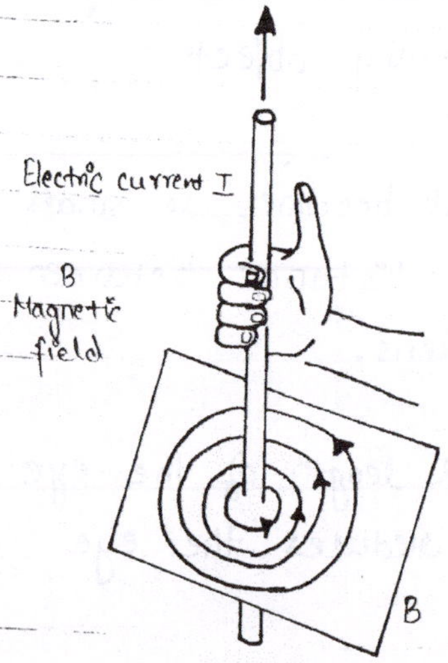

(B) State the right hand thumb rule and check whether the directions marked on the diagram are in accordance with this rule.

(Cr, Re) (3 Marks)

(b) Right hand thumb rule:
Statement: Point the thumb of the right hand in the direction of the current (here, into the board). Then, the curl of the fingers gives the direction of the magnetic field lines.
Verification: With the thumb pointing downward (into the board), the fingers naturally curl in a clockwise direction when seen from above. This confirms that the magenetic field lines in the diagram are correctly drawn as clockwise, in accordance with the right hand thumb rule.

33. (A) "In a food chain energy flow is unidirectional." Give two reasons for the given statement.

33.(A) Energy flow in a food chain is unidirectional because:

- One-way transfer of energy: Energy captured by autotrophs doesn't return to the sun, and energy passed to herbivores doesn't revert to autotrophs.
- Energy loss at each step: Due to the 10% law, most energy is lost as heat, limiting its transfer to the next level.

(B) If 10,000 J energy is available at the producer level, how much energy will be available to the secondary consumers? Give reason to justify your answer.

(Un, Ap) (3 Marks)

(B) Energy at producer level = 10,000 J
using the 10% Law which states that only 10% of energy is passed from one trophic level to the next, while 90% is lost as heat.

- Primary consumers receive:
  10% of 10,000 J = 1,000 J
- Secondary consumers receive:
  10% of 1,000 J = 100 J

Thus, 100 J of energy will be available to the secondary consumers.

SECTION-D

Questions no. 34 to 36 are Long Answer Type questions.

34. (A) (*i*) "In refraction of light through a rectangular glass slab, the emergent ray is always parallel to the direction of the incident ray". Why? Explain with the help of a ray diagram. What happens when a ray of light falls normally on one of the faces of a rectangular glass prism? Draw diagram.

34.(A) Refraction through a rectangular glass slab:
When a ray enters a glass slab at an angle, it refracts toward the normal because the speed of light decreases in glass. On reaching the second surface, the ray goes from glass to air and refracts away from the normal. The geometry of the slab is such that the second refraction cancels the angular deviation produced at the first surface. Thus, the emergent ray is parallel to the incident ray, even though it is laterally shifted.

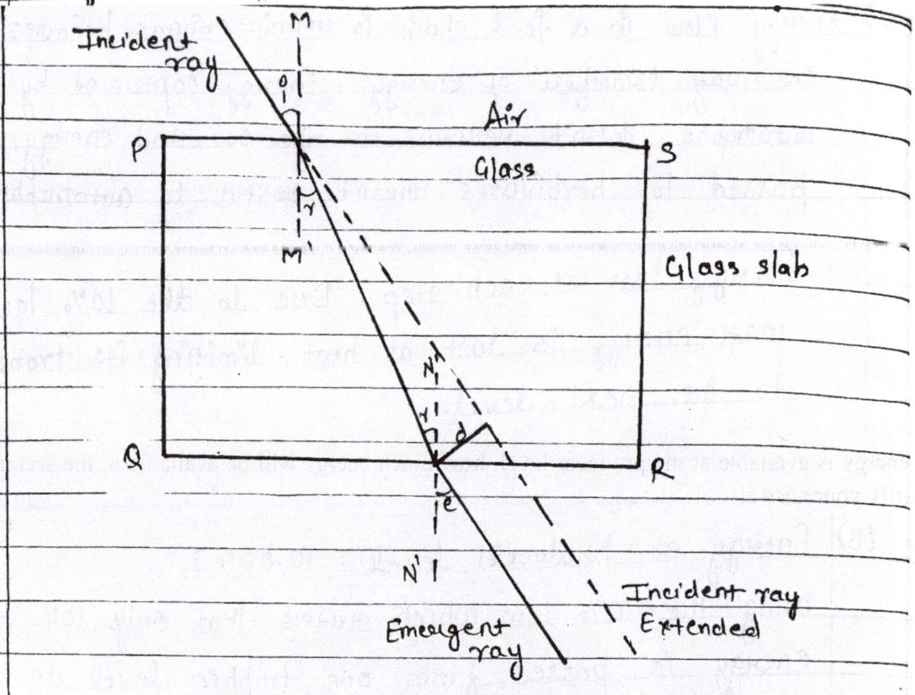

Normal incidence on a rectangular glass prism:
When the ray falls perpendicularly (normal incidence) on one face, the angle of incidence is 0°. According to Snell's law, no refraction occur because sin 0° = 0; hence, the ray travels straight through without bending. There may be a lateral shift, but the direction remains unchanged.

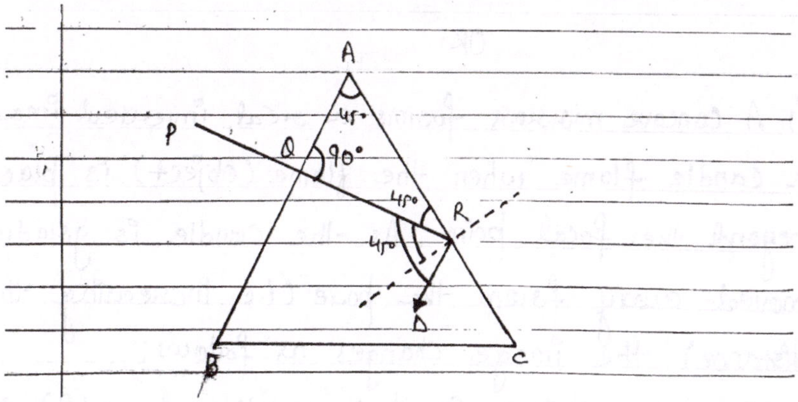

(*ii*) An object is placed at a distance of 30 cm from the optical centre of a concave lens of focal length 20 cm. Use Lens formula to determine the position of the image formed in this case. **(*Cr, Ev*) (*5 Marks*)**

(ii) Using the lens formula

$$\frac{1}{f} = \frac{1}{v} + \frac{1}{u}$$

Here, for a concave lens, the focal length f is negative and by sign convention, the object distance u is also taken as negative. Thus,

$f = -20 cm$

$u = -30 cm$

Substitute into the lens formula:

$$\frac{1}{-20} = \frac{1}{v} + \frac{1}{-30} = \frac{1}{-20} = \frac{1}{v} - \frac{1}{30}$$

Rearrange to solve for $\frac{1}{v}$:

$$\frac{1}{v} = -\frac{1}{20} + \frac{1}{30}$$

$$\frac{1}{v} = -\frac{3}{60} + \frac{2}{60} = -\frac{1}{60}$$

Thus, $v = -60 cm$

The negative sign indicates that the image is virtual and formed on the same side of the lens as the object.

OR

(B) (*i*) A student wishes to study the image formation by a concave mirror using candle flame as object. State the type of the image formed by the mirror and mention the change in the image formed, if any, that he observes when the candle flame is gradually moved away from the pole of the mirror. Draw a ray diagram to show the image formation when the object distance is nearly equal to the radius of curvature of the mirror.

OR

(B) (i) A concave mirror forms a real, inverted image of a candle flame when the flame (object) is placed beyond the focal point. As the candle is gradually moved away from the pole (i.e. increasing the object distance), the image changes as follows:

- When the object is between the focus (F) and the centre of curvature (C), the image is real, is inverted, and magnified and appears beyond C.

- When the object is exactly at C (i.e. when the object distance ≃ radius of curvature), the image is real, inverted, of the same size as the object and is formed at C.
- For further increases in object distance (object beyond C), the image remains real and inverted but becomes diminished and moves closer to F.

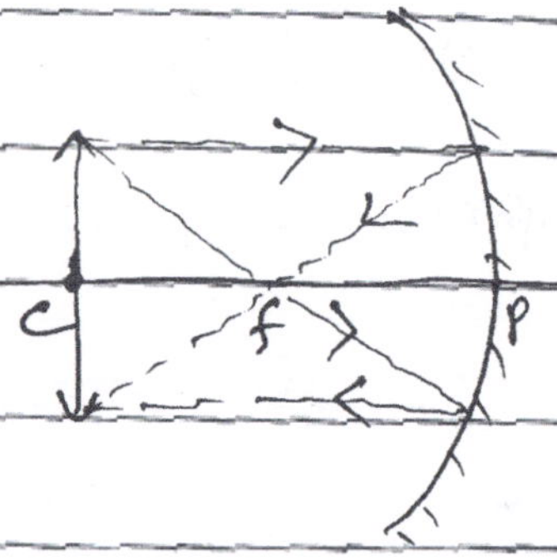

(*ii*) A convex mirror used for rear-view on an automobile has a focal length of 3.0 m. If a bus is located at 6.0 m from this mirror, use mirror formula to find the position of the image of the bus as seen in the mirror. **(*Cr, Ev*) (*5 Marks*)**

(ii) Using the mirror formula

$$\frac{1}{f} = \frac{1}{v} + \frac{1}{u}$$

Where

$u = -6m$

$f = 3m$

putting in mirror formula

$$\frac{1}{3} = \frac{1}{v} + \frac{1}{-6}$$

$$\frac{1}{3} + \frac{1}{6} = \frac{1}{v}$$

$$\frac{6+3}{18} = \frac{1}{v}$$

$$\frac{9}{18} = \frac{1}{v}$$

$$v = 2m$$

35. (*a*) (*i*) Consider the following metals:

K, Ca, Al, Cu, Ag, Fe

Select from the above metals, a metal which

I. does not react with oxygen even at high temperature.

II. reacts with oxygen at ordinary temperature and forms a protective oxide layer which prevents the metal from further oxidation.

III. catches fire when kept in the open.

IV. does not burn in oxygen but the hot metal is coated with a black coloured oxide layer.

(*ii*) What are amphoteric oxides? With the help of balanced chemical equations show that aluminium oxide is an amphoteric oxide.

(*iii*) What are alkalis? Give one example. ***(Un) (5 Marks)***

35.(a) (i)

I: Silver (Ag) does not react with oxygen even at high temperature.

II: Al reacts with oxygen at ordinary temperature and forms a protective oxide layer which prevents the metal from further oxidation.

III: Potassium catches fire when kept in open

IV: Copper does not burn, but the hot metal is coated with a black coloured layer of copper(II) oxide.

(ii) Metal oxides which react with both acids as well as bases to produce salts and water are known as amphoteric oxides.

Aluminium oxide reacts with acids and bases in the following manner:

$Al_2O_3 + 6HCl \longrightarrow 2AlCl_3 + 3H_2O$

$Al_2O_3 + 2NaOH \longrightarrow 2NaAlO_2 + H_2O$

(Sodium aluminate)

(iii) An alkali is a base that dissolves in water. Most metal oxides are insoluble in water but some of these dissolve in water to form alkalis.

Example: Sodium oxide dissolve in water to produce sodium hydroxide which is an alkali

$Na_2O(s) + H_2O(l) \longrightarrow 2NaOH(aq)$

OR

(*b*) (*i*) With the help of balanced chemical equations state the process of extracting (I) mercury from its ore called cinnabar. and (II) copper from its sulphide ore.

(*ii*) Silver and copper articles slowly lose their shiny surfaces when exposed to air. Name the compounds formed on (I) silver articles, and (II) copper articles in the form of coating. ***(Un) (5 Marks)***

(b) (i) (I) Cinnabar (HgS) is an ore of mercury. When it is heated in air, it is first converted into mercuric oxide (HgO). Mercuric oxide is then reduced to mercury on further heating.

$2HgS(s) + 3O_2(g) \xrightarrow{Heat} 2HgO(s) + 2SO_2(g)$

$2HgO(s) \xrightarrow{Heat} 2Hg(l) + O_2(g)$

(II) Copper which is found as Cu_2S in nature can be obtained from its ore by just heating in air.

$2Cu_2S + 3O_2(g) \xrightarrow{Heat} 2Cu_2O(s) + 2SO_2(g)$

$2Cu_2O + Cu_2S \xrightarrow{Heat} 6Cu(s) + SO_2(g)$

(ii) (I) Silver sulphide, Ag_2S

(II) Basic copper carbonate, $CuCO_3 , Cu(OH)_2$

36. (A) (*i*) Identify the parts 'X' and 'Y' in the figure given below:

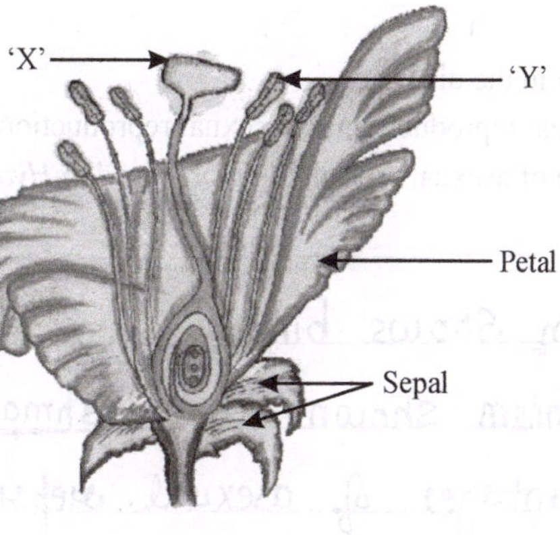

(*ii*) Name the yellowish coloured structures produced by the part labelled as 'Y'.

(*iii*) Write the name of the process by which these are transferred to the part labelled as 'X'.

(*iv*) Explain the process of seed formation in a flowering plant. **(Re, Un) (5 Marks)**

36.(A) (i) X – Stigma
Y – Anther

(ii) The anther (Y) produces pollen grains, which are yellow-colored and contain male gametes for fertilization.

(iii) The process by which pollen grains are transferred to the stigma is called pollination.

(iv) Process of seed formation in a flowering plant:

- Pollination – Transfer of pollen grains from the anther to the stigma.
- Fertilization – Pollen reaches the ovule in the ovary where the male gamete fuses with the female gamete to form a zygote.
- Embryo formation – The zygote divides repeatedly to form an embryo inside the ovule.
- Seed and fruit formation – The ovule develops in a seed, while the ovary ripens into a fruit, which protects the seed.

OR

(B) (*i*) Name the type of asexual mode of reproduction shown in the given figure.

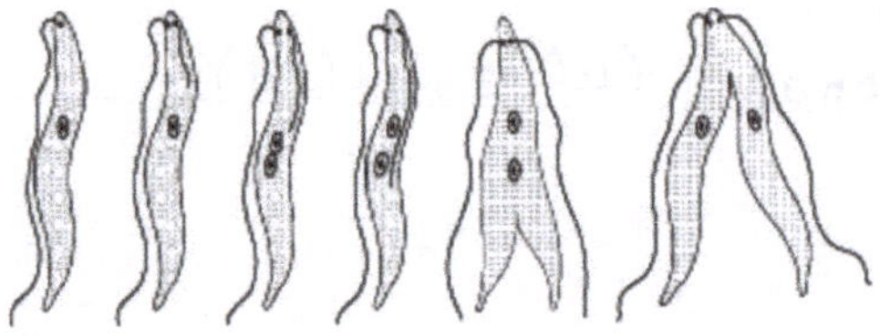

(a) (b) (c) (d) (e) (f)

(*ii*) Identify the unicellular organism in the diagram.

(*iii*) List any two advantages of asexual reproduction over sexual reproduction.

(*iv*) Name and explain any one mode of asexual reproduction observed in *Hydra*. **(*Re, Un*) (*5 Marks*)**

(B) (i) The diagram shows binary fission.
(ii) The organism shown is Leishmania
(iii) Two advantages of asexual reproduction over sexual reproduction
(1) Faster reproduction - Asexual reproduction is rapid, allowing quick population growth without requiring a mate.
(2) Genetic stability - offspring are genetically identical to the parent, ensuring stability of traits in favorable conditions.
(iv) Hydra reproduces asexually by budding. A small outgrowth forms due to repeated cell division, gradually enlarges, and develops tentacles. Once fully matured, it detaches from the parent and becomes an independent organism allowing rapid reproduction.

SECTION-E

The following questions are Source-based/Case-based questions. Read the case carefully and answer the questions that follow.

37. 'A' and 'B' are two salts used for washing purposes. Salt 'A' is used for bathing also. Four test tubes I, II, III and IV as mentioned below are taken. **(*An*)**

I. Rain water + solution of salt 'A'

II. Rain water + solution of salt. 'B'

III. Tubewell water + solution of salt 'A'

IV. Tubewell water + solution of salt 'B'

The test tubes are shaken one by one almost identically for the same time and the lengths of foam formed in each test tube is noted.

(*i*) In which one of the four test tubes is the foam formed the minimum? **(*1 Mark*)**

(*ii*) Differentiate between salt A and salt B. **(*1 Mark*)** (*iii*) (A) What are esters? What happens when an ester reacts with an alkali (say sodium hydroxide)? Give chemical equation for the reaction. **(2 Marks)**

37. (i) The foam formation is the minimum in test tube III (Tubewell water + solution of salt 'A')
This is because salt A is used for bathing purposes and is likely to be a soap purposes and tubewell water contains salts of magnesium and calcium, which cause water hardness and prevent foam formation.

(ii)

Salt A	Salt B
Used for both bathing and washing purposes.	Used only for washing purposes
Likely to be a soap (sodium or potassium salt of fatty acid	Likely to be a detergent (synthetic cleaning agent that works in hard water)
Does not form foam in hard (tubewell) water due to the presence of calcium and magnesium salts.	Forms foams easily in both rainwater and tubewell water.

(iii) (A) Esters are sweet-smelling substances formed by reaction of an acid and an alcohol.
On treating with sodium hydroxide, which is an alkali, the ester is converted back to alcohol and sodium salt of carboxylic acid.
The chemical equation for the reaction of ester with an alkali is:

$$CH_3COOC_2H_5 \xrightarrow{NaOH} C_2H_5OH + CH_3COONa$$

Or

(*iii*)(B) What is the cause of hardness of water? Sometimes it is observed that while bathing foam is formed with difficulty and an insoluble substance is formed. Name this substance and write the cause of its formation. ***(2 Marks)***

(iii) (B) Hardness of water is due to the presence of calcium and magnesium salts.
While bathing foam is formed with difficulty due to the formation of the insoluble substance called scum which remains after washing with water.
This is caused by the reaction of soap with the calcium and magnesium salts, which cause the hardness of water.

38. A person while climbing up a rocky hill comes into a panic state and fear. His body starts reacting in a "flight-or-fight" condition to adjust to the dangerous and stressful situation. ***(An)***

Based on the above facts, answer the questions that follow.

(*i*) (A) Name the hormone secreted in the blood of the person in this situation. ***(2 Marks)***

Or

(*i*) (B)Name the source gland of the hormone secreted in this condition. ***(2 Marks)***

(*ii*) State any two responses in the body of the person as a result of the secretion of this hormone. ***(1 Mark)***

(*iii*) How does the action of the chemical signal in terms of hormones differ from the electrical impulses *via* nerve cells? ***(1 Mark)***

38 (i) (A) The hormone secreted in this situation is Adrenaline.
It is released in response to stress or fear, triggering the fight-or-flight response.

Or

(i) (B) The hormone Adrenaline is secreated by a pair of gland called Adrenal Glands.
These glands are located above the kidneys.

(ii) Two responses in the body due to adrenaline secretion
• The heart beats faster, supplying more oxygen to muscles for immediate action.

• The diaphragm and rib muscles contract, allowing faster oxygen intake, supporting the body's fight or flight response.

(iii) Hormonal action is slow, traveling through blood to affect multiple organs, while nerve impulses are fast, transmitting electrical signals for immediate responses.

39. As shown in the diagram, an electric circuit consisting of an ammeter, a voltmeter, 4 cells of 1.5 V each, a plug key with a gap XY was set up. Voltmeter and ammeter readings were recorded in the observation table for four arrangements as given below: ***(An)***

Arrangement No. 1- only resistor R_1 in gap XY

Arrangement No. 2- only resistor R_2 in gap XY

Arrangement No. 3- Resistors R_1 and R_2 in series in gap XY

Arrangement No. 4- Resistors R_1 and R_2 in parallel in gap XY

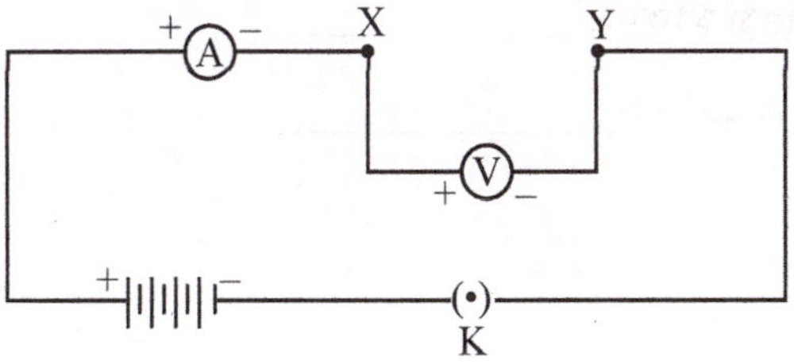

Based on the observations, four V-I graphs A, B, C and D as shown in figure were drawn. Study these graphs.

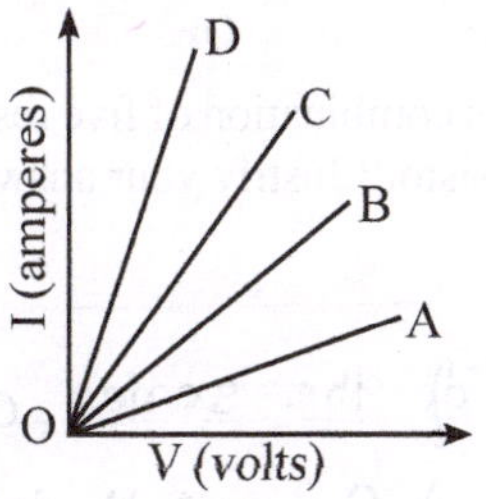

(*i*) Which one of the graphs represents the series combination of R_1 and R_2? ***(1 Mark)***

(*ii*) Which one of these graphs represents the parallel combination of R_1 and R_2? ***(1 Mark)***

(*iii*)(A) Show an arrangement of three resistors, each of resistance 10 Ω, so that the combination has a resistance of 15 Ω. Give justification for your answer. ***(2 Marks)***

39 (i) In a series circuit, the total resistance increases, resulting in a lower current for the same voltage.

The V-I graph with the least slope (smallest current) corresponds to the highest resistance.
Hence, graph A represents the series combination of R_1 and R_2

(ii) In a parallel circuit, the total resistance decreases, leading to a higher current for the same voltage.
The V-I graph with the steepest slope (highest current) corresponds to the lowest resistance.
Hence, graph D represents the parallel combination of R_1 and R_2

(iii) (A) We can combine two resistors in parallel and then add the third in series:
Parallel combination of two 10 Ω resistors:

$$R_p = \frac{10 \times 10}{10 + 10} = 5\Omega$$

Adding a third 10 Ω resistor in series

$$R_{eq} = 5 + 10 = 15\Omega$$

Or

(*iii*)(B) A battery of 6 V is connected with a series combination of five resistors of 0.1 Ω, 0.2 Ω, 0.3 Ω, 0.4 Ω and 0.5 Ω. How much current would flow through the 0.3 Ω resistor? Justify your answer. ***(2 Marks)***

(iii) (B) Total resistance of the series circuit:

$$R_{total} = 0.1 + 0.2 + 0.3 + 0.4 + 0.5$$
$$= 1.5\Omega$$

Total current using Ohm's law:

$$I = \frac{V}{R} = \frac{6\,V}{1.5\,\Omega} = 4A$$

Since it is a series circuit, the same 4A current flow through all resistors, including the 0.3 Ω resistor.

1 CHEMICAL REACTIONS AND EQUATIONS

"Chemical reactions are like miniature universes, full of secrets and wonders, constantly reminding us of the magic hidden in the atoms."

~Marie Curie

SYLLABUS & WEIGHTAGE

LIST OF CONCEPT NAMES	YEARS				
	2020	2022 TERM-I	2023	2024	2025
Types of Changes and Characteristics of Chemical Reactions (Physical and Chemical Changes)	1 Q (1 M)	—	—	—	—
Chemical Equations and their Balancing	1 Q (3 M) 1 Q (5 M)	2 Q*	1 Q (1 M)	1 Q (2 M)	1 Q (1 M)
Types of Chemical Reactions (Combination, decomposition, displacement, double displacement, precipitation, endothermic & exothermic reactions, oxidation and reduction)	1 Q (3 M)	6 Q*	3 Q (1 M) 1 Q (3 M)	1 Q (1 M) 1 Q (2 M) 1 Q (3 M)	1 Q (2 M) 1 Q (3 M)
Effect of Oxidation Reactions (Corrosion and Rancidity)	—	—	—	—	—

** All questions were of MCQ type and carried equal marks.*

For the year 2021, the exam was not conducted.

CONCEPT MAP

To Access One Shot Revision Video Scan This QR Code

Chemical Reactions And Equations

Chemical Equations

Represented as

CBSE 2025, 2024, 2022 Term-I

- It is the representation of chemical reaction in symbols and it needs to be balanced.
  E.g.: $2Mg(s) + O_2(g) \rightarrow 2MgO(s)$
- As per law of **conservation of mass**, total mass of the elements present in the products of a chemical reaction has to be equal to the total mass of the elements present in the reactants.

Type of Change & Characteristics

CBSE 2025

- **Chemical Change:** Reactants transform into products. Generally irreversible.
  E.g.: Curdling of milk
- **Physical Change:** No new substances are formed
  Generally reversible.
  E.g.: Melting of ice

- **Evolution of gas**
  E.g.: $CaCO_3(s) \xrightarrow{heat} CaO(s) + CO_2\uparrow(g)$
- **Change in temperature**
  E.g.: $CaO(s) + H_2O(s) \rightarrow Ca(OH)_2(aq.) + Heat$
- **Change in state**
  E.g.: $NH_3(g) + HCl(g) \rightleftharpoons NH_4Cl\downarrow(s)$
- **Formation of precipitate** CBSE 2025
  E.g.: $2KI(aq.) + Pb(NO_3)_2(aq.) \rightarrow 2KNO_3(aq.) + PbI_2\downarrow(s)$ (Yellow ppt)

- **Change in colour**
  E.g.: $CuSO_4(aq.) + Fe(s) \rightarrow FeSO_4(aq.) + Cu(s)$
  (Blue) (Green)

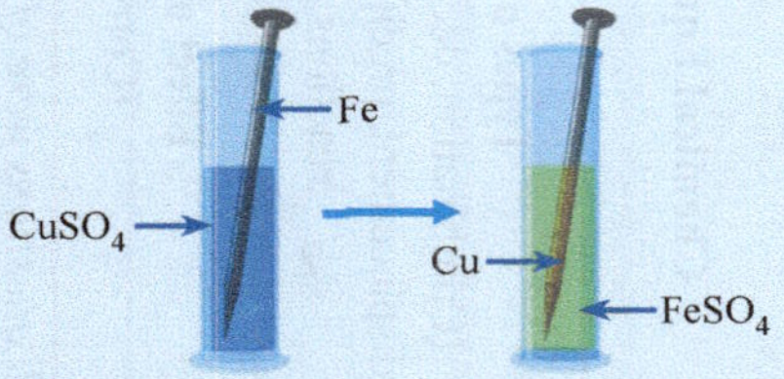

Effects of Oxidation

(a) **Corrosion:** Degradation of metals.
E.g.: Rusting of iron (Rust $Fe_2O_3 \cdot xH_2O$), Tarnishing of Ag.
Prevention:
- Galvanisation
- Painting, oiling, etc.

(b) **Rancidity:** Oxidation of foods containing oils and fats, causing smell and taste change.
Prevention:
- Flushing of Nitrogen gas
- Refrigeration

Types

- **Combination reaction:** When 2 or more reactants combine to form single product CBSE 2024, 2020
  E.g.: $2Na(s) + Cl_2(g) \rightarrow 2NaCl(s)$
- **Decomposition reaction:** Single reactant breaks down into 2 or more products. It is of following types: CBSE 2025, 2020
  1. **Thermal Decomposition,** by heat CBSE 2024, 2023, 2022 Term-I
     $2Pb(NO_3)_2(s) \xrightarrow{heat} 2PbO(s) + 4NO_2\uparrow(g) + O_2\uparrow(g)$ (Reddish-brown)
  2. **Photo Decomposition,** by light
     $2AgBr(s) \xrightarrow{hv} 2Ag(s) + Br_2\uparrow(g)$
  3. **Electrolytic decomposition** by electricity CBSE 2024
     $2H_2O(l) \xrightarrow{Electrolysis} 2H_2\uparrow(g) + O_2\uparrow(g)$
- **Single displacement reaction:** More reactive element displaces less reactive elements from its salt solution. CBSE 2025, 2023, 2022 Term-I
  $Fe(s) + CuSO_4(aq.) \rightarrow FeSO_4(aq.) + Cu(s)$
- **Double displacement reaction:** Exchange of ion takes place between reactants. CBSE 2025, 2022 Term-I, 2020
  $Na_2SO_4(aq.) + BaCl_2(aq.) \rightarrow 2NaCl(aq.) + BaSO_4(s)$
- **Exothermic Reaction:** Reaction in which heat is released. CBSE 2024, 2022 Term-I, 2020
  $C_6H_{12}O_6(aq.) + 6O_2(aq.) \rightarrow 6CO_2(aq.) + 6H_2O(l) + energy$ (Glucose)
- **Endothermic Reaction:** Reaction in which heat is absorbed. CBSE 2023
  $6CO_2 + 6H_2O \xrightarrow[Sunlight]{Chlorophyll} C_6H_{12}O_6 + 6O_2\uparrow$
- **Redox Reactions** CBSE 2022 Term-I
  - **Oxidation:** (a) Addition of O_2 (b) Removal of H_2
  - **Reduction:** (a) Addition of H_2 (b) Removal of O_2
  - **Oxidising agent**: Agent which oxidises others and itself gets reduced.
  - **Reducing agent**: Agent which reduces others and itself gets oxidised. CBSE 2025, 2023

  E.g.:
  $CuO(s) + H_2(g) \xrightarrow{heat} Cu(s) + H_2O(l)$
  (Black) (Brown)
  Oxidation → H_2
  Reduction → CuO
  Oxidising agent → CuO
  Reducing agent → H_2

TYPES OF CHANGES AND CHARACTERISTICS OF CHEMICAL REACTIONS

1

NCERT Definitions (Commonly asked in 1 mark)

- **Reactants:** Substances that **undergo** chemical changes in a reaction.
- **Products:** New substances **formed** as a result of a chemical reaction.
- **Physical State:** The state in which a substance exists (solid, liquid, gas, aqueous).
- **Physical Change:** A change in which **no new substances** are formed and the change is generally **reversible**
- **Chemical Change:** A process in which substances (reactants) transform into **new substances** (products) and the change is generally **irreversible.**
- **Chemical Reaction:** A process where substances (reactants) transform into different substances (products).

Important Facts

01 The protective layer on magnesium ribbon which is cleaned by rubbing it with a sand paper.
~Magnesium oxide

02 Burning a candle wax involves both chemical and physical changes.

03 Dazzling white light is given out during the burning of magnesium ribbon and is harmful to the eyes.

04 A chemical reaction is indicated by changes like colour change, temperature change, evolution of gas, state change, or precipitate formation.

Difference Between

Physical Change	Chemical Change
No new substance is formed.	New substances are formed.
Usually reversible.	Usually irreversible.
Involves changes in physical properties like shape, size, state.	Involves changes in chemical properties and composition.
No energy change is involved.	Energy is absorbed or evolved.
Example: Melting of ice, Tearing of paper.	Example: Burning of paper.

Real Life Application Based Questions

1. **Have you ever wondered why cutting an apple and leaving it out causes it to turn brown? Explain what type of change is occurring and why it happens?**

Ans. When you cut an apple, it turns brown. Browning of apple takes place due to oxidation and this is a chemical change. Hence, we cannot restore it to original colour.

2. **While cooking pasta, Priya observed two processes: boiling water to cook pasta and frying onions until they turned brown. Identify which process is a physical change and which is a chemical change?**

Ans. Boiling water to cook pasta is a physical change because boiling water involves **changing the state of water** from liquid to gas (steam) without altering its chemical composition.

Frying onions causes them to turn brown, indicating the chemical change because a **chemical reaction** occurs and the process is irreversible and results in the formation of new substances with different flavours and colours.

Myth Buster

❒ **Myth: All physical changes are reversible, and all chemical changes are irreversible.**

Fact: While many physical changes are reversible (like melting and freezing of water), some are not (like breaking a glass, cutting of an apple). Similarly, not all chemical changes are irreversible. For example, the **synthesis of water** is a chemical change that can be reversed through electrolysis to yield hydrogen and oxygen gases.

❒ **Myth: Physical changes always involve states of matter transitions (solid, liquid, gas).**

Fact: While state transitions are common examples of physical changes, not all physical changes involve them. Dissolving sugar in water is a physical change without a state transition.

❒ **Myth: If you mix two substances and they react, they must have undergone a chemical change.**

Fact: While mixing two substances can lead to a chemical reaction, it is not always the case. For example, mixing alcohol and water alters neither's chemical composition, illustrating a physical change.

❒ **Myth: The burning of a candle is just a physical change because you can see the wax melting.**

Fact: The burning of a candle is actually a chemical reaction. When a candle burns, the wax combines with oxygen in the air to form new substances like carbon dioxide and water vapour, indicating a chemical change. The melting of wax is a physical change, but the actual burning (combustion) is a chemical change.

❒ **Myth: All chemical reactions are dangerous and involve explosions or the release of toxic gases.**

Fact: Many chemical reactions are safe and occur regularly in everyday life, such as the browning of fruit or the digestion of food.

❒ **Myth: In a chemical reaction, the mass of the products is greater than the mass of the reactants due to the energy release.**

Fact: According to the law of conservation of mass, the total mass of the reactants is always equal to the total mass of the products in a chemical reaction. Energy does not contribute to mass in a measurable way in chemical reactions.

Mnemonics

❒ **DROP**-To remember characteristics of chemical change

- D → Dramatic change in chemical composition
- R → Release of gas
- O → Observed energy change
- P → Production of new substance

COMPETENCY BASED SOLVED EXAMPLES

Multiple Choice Questions (1 M)

1. Which of the following is not a physical change? *(Ap)*

(*a*) Boiling of water to give water vapour

(*b*) Melting of ice to give waters

(*c*) Dissolution of salt in water

(*d*) Combustion of Liquefied Petroleum Gas (LPG)

2. Which of the following is a NECESSARY condition for ALL chemical reactions? **(*Un*) (CFPQ)**

(*a*) The reactants should be in the same state.

(*b*) Energy should be supplied to the reactants.

(*c*) The reactants should be at the same temperature.

(*d*) There should be physical contact between the reactants.

3. In which of the following, the identity of initial substance remains unchanged? **(*Ap*) (CBSE 2020)**

(*a*) Curdling of milk

(*b*) Formation of crystals by process of crystallisation

(*c*) Fermentation of grapes

(*d*) Digestion of food

4. Which one of the following processes involve chemical reactions? **(*Un*) (NCERT Exemplar)**

(*a*) Storing of oxygen gas under pressure in a gas cylinder

(*b*) Liquefaction of air

(*c*) Keeping petrol in a china dish in the open

(*d*) Heating copper wire in presence of air at high temperature

Assertion and Reason (1 M)

Direction: **The following questions consist of two statements – Assertion (A) and Reason (R). Answer these questions by selecting the appropriate option given below:**

(*a*) Both A and R are true, and R is the correct explanation of A.

(*b*) Both A and R are true, but R is not the correct explanation of A.

(*c*) A is true, but R is false.

(*d*) A is false, but R is true.

1. **Assertion (A):** Tearing of paper is a physical change, although it cannot be reversed.
   Reason (R): Chemical change is a reaction involving the changes in chemical properties or composition, resulting in the formation of a new substance. *(Un)*

2. **Assertion (A):** Mixing salt and water is a physical change
   Reason (R): Mixing salt and water does not result in the formation of new substances. The salt dissolves in water, forming a homogeneous solution, but the chemical composition of both salt and water remains unchanged. *(An)*

3. **Assertion (A):** Pungent smelling gas is produced when sulphur burns in air.
   Reason (R): Sulphur trioxide is formed on reaction of sulphur with oxygen. *(Un)*

Subjective Questions

Very Short Answer Type Questions (2 M)

1. Explain why the following examples are considered as chemical changes. *(Un)*

(*a*) Respiration (*b*) Cooking of food

Ans. (*a*) Respiration is an example of chemical change because carbohydrates from the food we eat undergoes oxidation and produces water, carbon-dioxide and energy, that is, formation of new products takes place. *(1 M)*

(*b*) Cooking of food is an example of chemical change because food once prepared cannot revert back into the form from which it is prepared. *(1 M)*

> **Mistakes 101 : What not to do!**
>
> Student may fail to explain the irreversible nature of the change in cooking food and may lack clarity on the concept of new products being formed in chemical changes.

2. Grapes hanging on the plant do not ferment but after being plucked from the plant can be fermented. Under what conditions do these grapes ferment? Is it a chemical or a physical change? **(*Ap*) (NCERT Exemplar)**

Ans. Grapes ferment after being plucked when yeast is present and conditions are anaerobic, that is, absence of oxygen. *(1 M)*

In this process of fermentation, sugars are converted to alcohol and carbon dioxide and since new products are formed, therefore, it is a chemical change. *(1 M)*

3. "Dil. HCl is added to Zn granules." How will you prove that chemical change has taken place here? Support your response with two arguments. **(*Ap*) (CBSE SQP, 2023)**

Ans. Chemical change has taken place because of the following characteristics shown during the reaction:

- Bubbles of gas/ Evolution of gas
- Change in colour (Zn-silvery grey to black)
- Change in temperature *(2 M)*

Short Answer Type Questions (3 M)

1. (*a*) Why should a magnesium ribbon be cleaned before burning in air? **(NCERT Intext)**

(*b*) Give two characteristics of the chemical reaction which occurs on adding potassium iodide solution to lead nitrate solution. **(*Re*)**

Ans. (*a*) Magnesium ribbon should be cleaned with sand paper before burning in air because the ribbon develops a coating of magnesium oxide due to its reaction with oxygen. This oxide layer impedes the ribbon's ability to react efficiently. By cleaning, typically with sandpaper, this layer is removed. *(1 M)*

(*b*) On adding potassium iodide to lead nitrate solution, the following two characteristics are observed:

- Yellow ppt of lead iodide will form *(1 M)*
- Colour changes from colourless to yellow. *(1 M)*

Nailing the Right Answer

For a full credit answer, students are advised to mention the colour change that occurs during the reaction.

Mistakes 101 : What not to do!

Students may mistakenly mention only one characteristic instead of providing two characteristics as asked.

2. (*a*) Define physical change. State its two characteristics.

(*b*) Give two examples of physical changes.

Ans. (*a*) A change in which no new substance is formed and the change can be reversible or irreversible. *(1 M)*

It's two characteristics are:

1. Change in state *(½ M)*
2. Change in size *(½ M)*

(*b*) The two examples of physical changes are:

1. Melting a sugar cube *(½ M)*
2. Mixing sand and water *(½ M)*

Long Answer Type Questions (5 M)

1. (*a*) Differentiate between physical and chemical change. (*Ap*)

(*b*) Which among the following are physical or chemical changes ?

***(i)* Evaporation of petrol**

***(ii)* Burning of Liquefied Petroleum Gas (LPG)**

***(iii)* Heating of an iron rod to red hot.**

***(iv)* Sublimation of solid ammonium chloride**

Ans. (*a*)

Physical Change	Chemical Change
No new substance is formed. *(½ M)*	Formation of new substances takes place. *(½ M)*
It affects the physical properties such as colour, shape, size, etc. *(½ M)*	It affects the chemical as well as physical properties. *(½ M)*
Original substance can be recovered *(½ M)*	It is generally not possible to recover the original substance. *(½ M)*

(*b*) (*i*) It is a physical change as no new chemical substance is formed. *(½ M)*

(*ii*) It is a chemical change because LPG on burning forms CO_2 and H_2O. *(½ M)*

(*iii*) It is a physical change because in heating it only gets changes into red hot and there is no any chemical change. *(½ M)*

(*iv*) It is a physical change because solid NH_4Cl changes into NH_4Cl vapour and no new chemical substance is formed. *(½ M)*

2. State what is a chemical reaction. A chemical reaction is often accompanied by external indications or characteristics which include - (*a*) Colour change (*b*) Effervescence or gas evolved (*c*) Evolution or absorption of heat (*d*) Formation of a precipitate. With reference to each of the above, write the indication seen during-

(*i*) Addition of dilute acid to active metal

(*ii*) Addition of dilute hydrochloric acid to silver nitrate

(*iii*) Addition of water to quicklime

(*iv*) Thermal decomposition of mercury oxide. (*Ap*)

Ans. A chemical reaction is chemical change where substances will react with each other and results in the formation of a new substance. *(1 M)*

(*i*) When dilute acid is added to an active metal, the test tube becomes hot, which means heat is produced. Evolution of hydrogen gas also takes place. *(1 M)*

(*ii*) Addition of dilute HCl to silver nitrate will result in the formation of white ppt of AgCl. *(1 M)*

(*iii*) On adding water to quicklime, the solution boils and the release of heat is accompanied by a hissing sound.*(1M)*

(*iv*) In thermal decomposition of mercury oxide, the colour of mercury changes from red to silver. *(1 M)*

Hints & Explanations

Multiple Choice Questions

1. (*d*) Combustion of LPG is a chemical change and not a physical change.
2. (*d*) For a chemical reaction, it is necessary that there is physical contact between the reactants.
3. (*b*) The composition of the starting substance does not change during the crystallisation process since it just crystallised.
4. (*d*) In first three options given here, there is no involvement of chemical reaction. When copper is heated in presence of air at high temperature, copper undergoes oxidation reaction to give out copper oxide.

Assertion and Reason

1. (*b*) Tearing of paper is a physical change because no new substance having different composition is formed.
2. (*a*) Mixing of salt and water does not result in the formation of new substances. In this, chemical composition of salt and water will not change.
3. (*c*) SO_2 is formed on the reaction of sulphur with oxygen and it is of pungent smell.

2 CHEMICAL EQUATIONS AND THEIR BALANCING

NCERT Definitions (Commonly asked in 1 mark)

- **Chemical Equation:** A **symbolic representation** of a chemical reaction in the form of symbols and formulae.
- **Word-Equation:** A representation of a chemical reaction using the **names of the reactants and products, with an arrow between them.**
- **Skeletal Chemical Equation:** An unbalanced chemical equation **showing only the formulas** of the reactants and products.
- **Balanced Chemical Equation:** A chemical equation where the number of atoms for each element is the same on both sides of the equation, adhering to the law of conservation of mass.

Important Facts

01 The total mass of reactants equals the total mass of products in a chemical reaction.
~ **Law of Conservation of Mass**

02 To balance equations, **coefficients** are placed in front of compounds, not subscripts within formulas.

03 The gaseous, liquid, aqueous and solid states of reactants and products are represented by the notations (g), (l), (aq.) and (s), respectively.

Difference Between

Balanced Equation vs Skeletal Equations

Characteristics	Balanced Equations	Skeletal Equations
Law of conservation of mass	Follow law of conservation of mass	Doesn't follow law of conservation of mass
Balancing	**Equal** number of atoms for each element on both sides	**Unequal** number of atoms, balancing is required.
Mass	Mass is **conserved**	Mass is **not conserved** until balanced
Example Reactions	$2H_2(g) + O_2(g) \rightarrow 2H_2O\ (l)$	$Fe + O_2 \rightarrow Fe_3O_4$

Myth Buster

- **Myth: Equal numbers of molecules of reactants and products indicate a balanced equation.**

  Fact: A balanced chemical equation has an equal number of each type of atom on both sides of the equation, not necessarily an equal number of molecules. Balancing is about the conservation of atoms, not the count of molecules.

- **Myth: The physical states of reactants and products are not essential in a chemical equation.**

  Fact: Including the physical states (solid, liquid, gas, aqueous) in a chemical equation provides crucial information about the conditions of the reaction.

- **Myth: The amount of a substance in a chemical equation is represented by its subscript numbers.***

  Fact: The subscript in a chemical formula represents the number of atoms of each element in a molecule, not the quantity of the substance. The coefficients in front of chemical formulas indicate the number of molecules or moles of a substance involved in the reaction.

- **Myth: The arrow in a chemical equation can be read as "yields" or "produces," indicating that the reaction always goes to completion.***

  Fact: The arrow in a chemical equation indicates the direction of the reaction. While it is often read as "yields," this does not mean that all reactants are completely converted into products.

** Concepts beyond the board exam syllabus, offering deeper insight and critical thinking on NCERT topics.*

COMPETENCY BASED SOLVED EXAMPLES

Multiple Choice Questions (1 M)

1. In which of the following chemical equations, the abbreviations represent the correct states of the reactants and products involved at reaction temperature?

(*Un*) (NCERT Exemplar)

(*a*) $2H_2(l) + O_2(l) \rightarrow 2H_2O(g)$

(*b*) $2H_2(g) + O_2(l) \rightarrow 2H_2O(l)$

(*c*) $2H_2(g) + O_2(g) \rightarrow 2H_2O(l)$

(*d*) $2H_2(g) + O_2(g) \rightarrow 2H_2O(g)$

2. In her chemistry class, Emma is studying the thermal decomposition of lead nitrate. She comes across the balanced chemical equation for the reaction:

$2\,Pb(NO_3)_2 \rightarrow 2PbO + 4\,NO_2 + O_2$

Emma wonders what the coefficients of PbO and NO_2 in the equation (2 and 4, respectively) tell her about the substances produced. Can you help Sarah determine which of the following options is correct? (*Un*)

(*a*) the ratio of the number of moles produced of the two substances

(*b*) the ratio of the number of atoms in the two substances

(*c*) the ratio of the mass produced of the two substances

(*d*) the ratio of the densities of the two substances

3. Consider the following unbalanced equation: (*Ap*)

$aAl + bH_2SO_4 \rightarrow cAl_2(SO_4)_3 + dH_2$

The correct set of coefficients to balance the equation is:

(*a*) 2, 3, 1, 3 (*b*) 4, 6, 2, 3

(*c*) 3, 1, 2, 3 (*d*) 2, 6, 1, 3

4. It is important to balance the chemical equations to satisfy the law of conservation of mass. Which of the following statements of the law is incorrect?

(*Re*) (CBSE 2022 Term-1)

(*a*) The total mass of the elements present in the reactants is equal to the total mass of the elements present in the products.

(*b*) The number of atoms of each element remains the same, before and after a chemical reaction.

(*c*) The chemical composition of the reactants is the same before and after the reaction.

(*d*) Mass can neither be created nor can it be destroyed in a chemical reaction.

5. When ammonia (NH_3) reacts with oxygen (O_2) to produce nitrogen monoxide (NO) and water (H_2O), the balanced chemical equation is: (*An*)

(*a*) $4NH_3 + \frac{3}{2}O_2 \rightarrow 4NO + 6H_2O$

(*b*) $2NH_3 + \frac{5}{2}O_2 \rightarrow 2NO + 3H_2O$

(*c*) $NH_3 + O_2 \rightarrow NO + H_2O$

(*d*) $3NH_3 + 4O_2 \rightarrow 3NO + 6H_2O$

Assertion and Reason (1 M)

Direction: **The following questions consist of two statements – Assertion (A) and Reason (R). Answer these questions by selecting the appropriate option given below:**

(*a*) Both A and R are true, and R is the correct explanation of A.

(*b*) Both A and R are true, but R is not the correct explanation of A.

(*c*) A is true, but R is false.

(*d*) A is false, but R is true.

1. **Assertion (A):** The balancing of chemical equations is based on law of conservation of mass.

   Reason (R): Total mass of reactants is equal to total mass of products. ***(Re)***

2. **Assertion (A):** The following chemical equation, $2C_2H_6 + 7O_2 \rightarrow 4CO_2 + 6H_2O$ is a balanced chemical equation.

   Reason (R): In a balanced chemical equation, the total number of atoms of each element may or may not equal on both side of the equation. ***(Un)***

Subjective Questions

Very Short Answer Type Questions (2 M)

1. **(*a*) What is the basis of balancing chemical equation?** ***(Un)***

   (*b*) Write a balanced chemical equation for the reaction between sodium chloride and silver nitrate indicating the physical state of the reactants and the products. ***(Ap)***

Ans. (*a*) A chemical reaction is balanced on the basis of law of conservation of mass which states that mass can neither be created nor destroyed. *(1 M)*

(*b*) $AgNO_3(aq.) + NaCl(aq.) \longrightarrow AgCl\downarrow(s) + NaNO_3(aq.)$ *(1 M)*

2. **Write a balanced chemical equation with state symbols for the following reactions.** ***(Ap)*** **(NCERT Intext)**

   (*i*) Solutions of barium chloride and sodium sulphate in water react to give insoluble barium sulphate and the solution of sodium chloride.

   (*ii*) Sodium hydroxide solution (in water) reacts with hydrochloric acid solution (in water) to produce sodium chloride solution and water.

Ans. The balanced chemical equations with state symbols are:

(*i*) $BaCl_2(aq.) + Na_2SO_4(aq.) \rightarrow BaSO_4\downarrow(s) + 2NaCl(aq.)$ *(1 M)*

(*ii*) $NaOH(aq.) + HCl(aq.) \rightarrow NaCl(aq.) + H_2O(l)$ *(1 M)*

Short Answer Type Questions (3 M)

1. **Write balanced chemical equations for the following reactions.**

   (*i*) Silver bromide on exposure to sunlight decomposes into silver and bromine,

   (*ii*) Sodium metal reacts with water to form sodium hydroxide and hydrogen gas.

   (*iii*) Photosynthesis in Plants ***(Un)***

Ans. (*i*) $2AgBr(s) \xrightarrow{\text{Sunlight}} 2Ag(s) + Br_2(g)$ *(1 M)*

(*ii*) $2Na(s) + 2H_2O(l) \longrightarrow 2NaOH(aq.) + H_2(g)$ *(1 M)*

(*iii*) $6CO_2(aq.) + 6H_2O(l) \xrightarrow[\text{Chlorophyll}]{\text{Sunlight}} C_6H_{12}O_6(aq.) + 6O_2(aq.)$ *(1 M)*

2. **Complete and balance the following equations:**

   (*a*) $NaOH + \_\_ \longrightarrow Na_2SO_4 + H_2O$

   (*b*) $Ca(OH)_2 + \_\_ \longrightarrow CaCO_3 + H_2O$

   (*c*) $FeSO_4 + \text{heat} \longrightarrow Fe_2O_3 + \_\_ + \_\_$ ***(Un)***

Ans. (*a*) $2NaOH + H_2SO_4 \longrightarrow Na_2SO_4 + 2H_2O$ *(1 M)*

(*b*) $Ca(OH)_2 + CO_2 \longrightarrow CaCO_3 + H_2O$ *(1 M)*

(*c*) $2FeSO_4 + \text{heat} \longrightarrow Fe_2O_3 + SO_2(g) + SO_3(g)$ *(1 M)*

> **Nailing the Right Answer**
>
> While balancing the equation, it is advisable to first balance the compound which contains the highest number of atoms, either on product or reactant side. Also, select the element in that compound which has the maximum number of atoms.

3. **Complete the missing components/variables given as x and y in the following reactions**

   (*a*) $Pb(NO_3)_2(aq.) + 2KI(aq.) \longrightarrow PbI_2(x) + 2KNO_3(y)$

   (*b*) $Cu(s) + 2AgNO_3(aq.) \longrightarrow Cu(NO_3)_2(aq.) + x(s)$

   (*c*) $Zn(s) + H_2SO_4(aq.) \longrightarrow ZnSO_4(x) + H_2(y)$ ***(Ap)***

Ans. (*a*) $Pb(NO_3)_2(aq.) + 2KI(aq.) \rightarrow PbI_2(s) + 2KNO_3(aq.)$

Hence, x is (s) and y is (aq.). *(1 M)*

(*b*) $Cu(s) + 2AgNO_3(aq.) \rightarrow Cu(NO_3)_2(aq.) + 2Ag(s)$

Hence, x is 2Ag. *(1 M)*

(*c*) $Zn(s) + H_2SO_4(aq.) \rightarrow ZnSO_4(aq.) + H_2(g)$

Hence, x is (aq.) and y is (g). *(1 M)*

Long Answer Type Questions (5 M)

1. **(*a*) What is a balanced chemical equation? Why should chemical equations be balanced?** ***(Un)*** **(NCERT)**

   (*b*) Write the balanced chemical equation for the following reaction:

   (*i*) Phosphorus burns in presence of chlorine to form phosphorus pentachloride.

   (*ii*) Burning of natural gas.

   (*iii*) The process of respiration. ***(Ap)***

Ans. (*a*) Balanced chemical equation can be defined as equation which has an equal number of atoms of different elements in the reactants and products. *(1 M)*

An equation should be balanced so that it follows law of conservation of mass, according to which, mass can neither be created and nor be destroyed in a chemical reaction. *(1 M)*

(*b*) (*i*) $P_4(s) + 10Cl_2(g) \longrightarrow 4PCl_5(s)$ *(1 M)*

(*ii*) $CH_4(g) + 2O_2(g) \longrightarrow CO_2(g) + 2H_2O(g)$ + heat energy *(1 M)*

(*iii*) $C_6H_{12}O_6(aq.) + 6O_2(aq.) \longrightarrow 6CO_2(aq.) + 6H_2O(l)$ + energy *(1 M)*

Mistakes 101 : What not to do!

Failing to balance the chemical equation properly is a common error. Make sure the number of atoms of each element on both sides of the equation is the same.

2. (*i*) Translate the following statements into chemical equations and then balance them.

(*a*) Hydrogen gas combines with nitrogen to form ammonia.

(*b*) Hydrogen sulphide gas burns in air to give water and sulphur dioxide.

(*c*) Barium chloride reacts with aluminium sulphate to give aluminium chloride and a precipitate of barium sulphate.

(*d*) Potassium metal reacts with water to give potassium hydroxide and hydrogen gas.

(*Ap*) (NCERT)

(*ii*) Write the balanced equation for the following word reaction. **(*Un*)**

Hydrogen + Chlorine → Hydrogen chloride

Ans. (*i*) (*a*) $3H_2(g) + N_2(g) \rightarrow 2NH_3\uparrow(g)$ *(1 M)*

(*b*) $2H_2S(g) + 3O_2(g) \rightarrow 2SO_2\uparrow(g) + 2H_2O(l)$ *(1 M)*

(*c*) $3BaCl_2(aq.) + Al_2(SO_4)_3(aq.) \rightarrow 2AlCl_3(aq.) + 3BaSO_4\downarrow(s)$ *(1 M)*

(*d*) $2K(s) + 2H_2O(l) \rightarrow 2KOH(aq.) + H_2\uparrow(g)$ *(1 M)*

(*ii*) $H_2(g) + Cl_2(g) \rightarrow 2HCl(g)$ *(1 M)*

Hints & Explanations

Multiple Choice Questions

1. (*c*) During the formation of water (in liquid form), both H_2 and O_2 are in gaseous state.
2. (*a*) In a chemical equation, the coefficients (the numbers in front of the chemical formulas) represent the mole ratio of the substances involved in the reaction.
3. (*a*) The balanced equation is: $2Al + 3H_2SO_4 \rightarrow Al_2(SO_4)_3 + 3H_2\uparrow$

   Thus, the correct set of coefficients are: 2,3,1,3.
4. (*c*) Statement (*c*) is incorrect because chemical composition of the reactants and products is not same before and after a chemical reaction. This is because new compounds are formed as products.
5. (*b*) The balanced chemical equation is:

$$2NH_3 + \frac{5}{2}O_2 \rightarrow 2NO + 3H_2O$$

Assertion and Reason

1. (*a*) The balanced chemical equation is based on the law of conservation of mass as total mass of reactants is equal to that of products.
2. (*c*) Reason is false as in a balanced equation, the total number of atoms must be equal on both sides of the reaction.

3 TYPES OF CHEMICAL REACTIONS

NCERT Definitions (Commonly asked in 1 mark)

- **Combination Reaction:** A chemical reaction in which two or more reactants **combine** to form a single product.

  Burning of coal

  $C(s) + O_2(g) \rightarrow CO_2(g)$

- **Decomposition Reaction:** A reaction where a single reactant **breaks down** into two or more simpler products.

  $2FeSO_4(s) \xrightarrow{Heat} Fe_2O_3(s) + SO_2(g) + SO_3(g)$

  (Ferrous sulphate) (Ferric oxide)

- **Displacement Reaction:** In this reaction, a more reactive element **displaces** the less reactive element from its salt solution.

  $Fe(s) + CuSO_4(aq.) \longrightarrow FeSO_4(aq.) + Cu(s)$

  (Copper sulphate) (Iron sulphate)

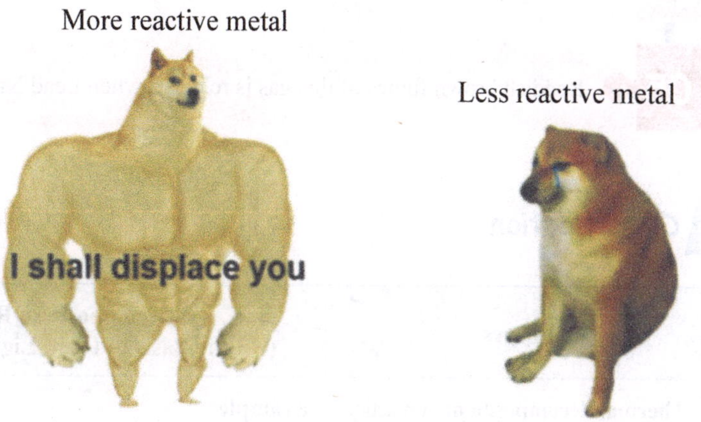

- **Double Displacement Reaction:** A reaction where **exchange of ions** between reactants take place to form new products.

  $Na_2SO_4(aq.) + BaCl_2(aq.) \rightarrow BaSO_4(s) + 2NaCl(aq.)$

  (Sodium sulphate) (Barium chloride) (Barium sulphate) (Sodium chloride)

- **Precipitation Reaction:** A reaction that results in the **formation of an insoluble product** (precipitate) from soluble reactants.

  $Na_2SO_4(aq.) + BaCl_2(aq.) \rightarrow BaSO_4(s) + 2NaCl(aq.)$

  (Sodium sulphate) (Barium chloride) (Barium sulphate) (Sodium chloride)

  (white precipitate)

- **Exothermic Reaction:** Reactions in which **heat is released** along with the formation of products

  $C_6H_{12}O_6(aq.) + 6O_2(aq.) \rightarrow 6CO_2(aq.) + 6H_2O(l) + energy$

  (Glucose)

- **Endothermic Reaction:** Reactions in which **heat is absorbed** along with the formation of products

  $6CO_2 + 6H_2O \xrightarrow[Sunlight]{Chlorophyll} C_6H_{12}O_6 + 6O_2\uparrow$

- **Redox Reaction:** A chemical reaction in which one reactant gets oxidised while the other gets reduced during a reaction. Such reactions are called **oxidation-reduction reactions** or redox reactions.

  Oxidation

  $CuO + H_2 \xrightarrow{Heat} Cu + H_2O$

  Reduction

- **Oxidation:** A process involving the **loss of electrons** or **addition of oxygen** or **removal of hydrogen.**

  $2Cu + O_2 \xrightarrow{Heat} 2CuO$

- **Reduction:** A process involving the **gain of electrons** or **removal of oxygen** or **addition of hydrogen.**

  $H_2 + Br_2 \rightarrow 2HBr$

- **Oxidising Agent (Oxidant):** Substance which itself undergoes reduction but **causes oxidation.**
- **Reducing Agent (Reductant):** Substance which itself undergoes oxidation but **causes reduction.**

Important Facts

01 A solution used for white washing. **~ Slaked lime**

02 The compound formed which gives a shiny finish upon white washing when calcium hydroxide reacts with CO_2 in air. **~ Calcium carbonate**

03 Decomposition of vegetable matter into compost releases energy. **~ Exothermic reaction.**

04 It is quick lime and it is used in the manufacturing of cement. **~ Calcium oxide**

05 Reddish brown fumes of this gas is released when Lead Nitrate is heated. **~ NO_2**

Classification

Types	Decomposition Reactions (On the Basis of Heat, Light and Electricity)	Diagram Depicting Reactions
Thermal decomposition: A reaction where a single reactant breaks down into two or more simpler products due to **heating**.	**Examples** $2Pb(NO_3)_2(s) \xrightarrow{Heat} 2PbO(s) + 4NO_2(g) + O_2(g)$ (Lead nitrate) (Lead oxide) (Nitrogen dioxide) (Oxygen)	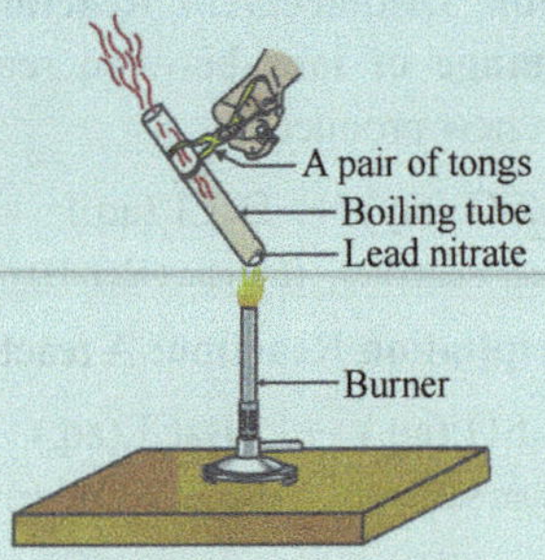
Photochemical decomposition: A reaction where a single reactant breaks down into two or more simpler products due to **light**.	$2AgCl(s) \xrightarrow{Sunlight} 2Ag(s) + Cl_2(g)$	
Electrolytic decomposition: A reaction where a single reactant breaks down into two or more simpler products due to **electricity**.	$2H_2O(l) \rightarrow 2H_2(g) + O_2(g)$	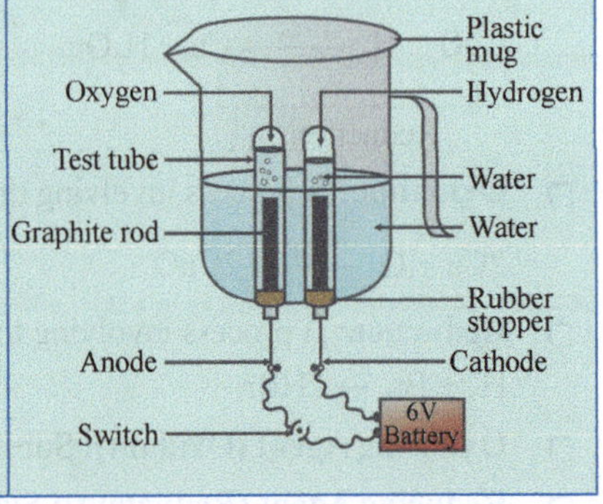

Difference Between

Displacement Reaction vs Double Displacement Reaction	
Displacement Reaction	**Double Displacement Reaction**
Involves a single element being replaced in a compound.	Involves exchange of different atoms or groups of atoms (ions).
More reactive element displaces less reactive one.	No element displacement, only ion exchange.
Often observable through a change in the solution colour or deposition.	Often results in the formation of a precipitate.
Forms a new compound and a different element.	Forms two new compounds.
Example: Iron nail in copper sulphate solution.	**Example:** Reaction of sodium sulphate with barium chloride.

Combination Reaction vs Decomposition Reaction	
Combination Reaction	**Decomposition Reaction**
Two or more substances combine to form a single product.	A single substance breaks down into two or more simpler products.
Usually exothermic (releases heat).	Usually endothermic (absorbs heat).
Simpler reactants form a more complex product.	A complex reactant breaks down into simpler products.
Does not require energy for initiation.	Requires energy like heat, light, or electricity for initiation.
Example: Formation of water from hydrogen and oxygen.	**Example:** Decomposition of calcium carbonate to calcium oxide and carbon dioxide.

Exothermic Reaction vs Endothermic Reaction	
Exothermic Reaction	**Endothermic Reaction**
Releases energy, usually in the form of heat.	Absorbs energy from the surroundings.
Temperature of the surroundings increases.	Temperature of the surroundings decreases.
Example: Combustion of fuels.	**Example:** Photosynthesis in plants.

Oxidation vs Reduction	
Oxidation	**Reduction**
Gain of oxygen	Loss of oxygen
Loss of hydrogen.	Gain of hydrogen
Example: Rusting of iron (iron oxidizes to iron oxide).	**Example:** Copper oxide reduced to copper when heated with hydrogen.

Real Life Application Based Questions

1. Describe a redox reaction that is essential for life and energy production.

Ans. In **photosynthesis**, carbon dioxide and water combine in the presence of sunlight to produce glucose and oxygen, providing essential energy and oxygen for life on Earth and is also a redox reaction.

2. How does decomposition play a role in black and white photography?

Ans. In photography, silver bromide decomposes to silver and bromine under light, enabling image formation on photographic film.

3. How does a displacement reaction facilitate the extraction of metals?

Ans. In metallurgy, displacement reactions help extract metals from their ores, such as using carbon to displace iron from iron oxide.

4. What is the role of redox reactions in galvanic cells?*

Ans. Redox reactions in galvanic cells involve the transfer of electrons from a reducing agent to an oxidizing agent, generating an electric current used to power electronic devices.

** Concepts beyond the board exam syllabus, offering deeper insight and critical thinking on NCERT topics.*

Myth Buster

- **Myth: Atoms change into different types of atoms during a chemical reaction.**

  Fact: Atoms do not change their identity during chemical reactions. Chemical reactions involve the rearrangement of atoms to form new substances, but the types of atoms remain the same.

- **Myth: In displacement reactions, any metal can displace any other metal from its compound.**

  Fact: Displacement reactions depend on the reactivity series of metals. A more reactive metal can displace a less reactive metal from its compound, not the other way around.

- **Myth: Oxidation reactions always involve oxygen.***

  Fact: Oxidation refers to the loss of electrons in a substance or the increase in oxidation state. While it often involves gaining oxygen, it can also occur through the loss of hydrogen or electrons.

- **Myth: Chemical reactions can create or destroy atoms.**

  Fact: Chemical reactions rearrange atoms in different ways, but they do not create or destroy them. The number and type of atoms remain constant before and after the reaction, adhering to the law of conservation of mass.

COMPETENCY BASED SOLVED EXAMPLES

Multiple Choice Questions (1 M)

1. $Fe_2O_3 + 2Al \longrightarrow Al_2O_3 + 2Fe$ **(*Un*) (NCERT Exemplar)**

The above reaction is an example of a

(*a*) combination reaction.
(*b*) double displacement reaction
(*c*) decomposition reaction
(*d*) displacement reaction

2. Some types of chemical reactions are listed below.

- decomposition -combination
- displacement -double displacement

Which two of the following chemical reactions are of the SAME type? (*An*) (CBSE APQ, 2023)

(*P*) $AgNO_3 + NaCl \rightarrow AgCl + NaNO_3$
(*Q*) $Mg + 2HCl \rightarrow MgCl_2 + H_2$
(*R*) $CH_4 + 2O_2 \rightarrow CO_2 + 2H_2O$
(*S*) $2KOH + H_2SO_4 \rightarrow K_2SO_4 + H_2O$

(*a*) *P* and *Q* (*b*) *Q* and *R*
(*c*) *R* and *S* (*d*) *P* and *S*

3. Three beakers labelled as A, B and C each containing 25 mL of water were taken. A small amount of NaOH, anhydrous $CuSO_4$ and NaCl were added to the beakers A,B and C respectively. It was observed that there was an increase in the temperature of the solutions contained in beakers A and B, whereas in case of beaker C, the temperature of the solution falls. Which one of the following statement(s) is(are) correct? (*An*) (NCERT Exemplar)

(*i*) In beakers A and B, exothermic process has occurred.
(*ii*) In beakers A and B, endothermic process has occurred.
(*iii*) In beaker C exothermic process has occurred.
(*iv*) In beaker C endothermic process has occurred.

(*a*) (*i*) only (*b*) (*ii*) only
(*c*) (*i*) and (*iv*) (*d*) (*ii*) and (*iii*)

4. The emission of brown fumes in the given experimental set-up is due to (*Re*) (CBSE 2023)

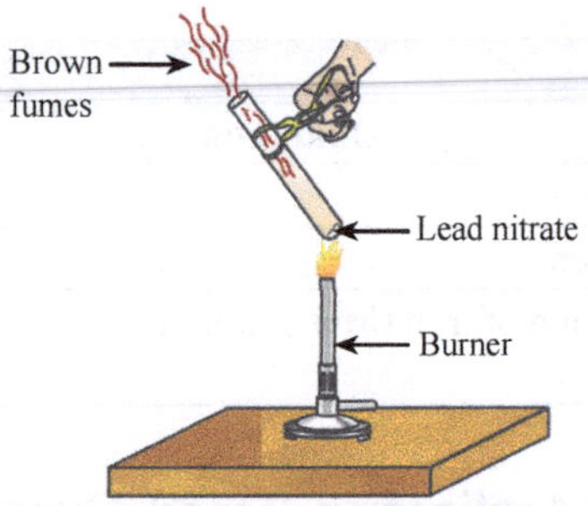

(*a*) thermal decomposition of lead nitrate which produces brown fumes of nitrogen dioxide.
(*b*) thermal decomposition of lead nitrate which produces brown fumes of lead oxide.
(*c*) oxidation of lead nitrate forming lead oxide and nitrogen dioxide.
(*d*) oxidation of lead nitrate forming lead oxide and oxygen.

(*Un*)

5. When 50g of lead powder is added to 300 ml of blue copper sulphate solution, after a few hours, the solution becomes colourless. This is an example of (*An*) (CBSE SQP, 2024)

(*a*) Combination reaction
(*b*) Decomposition reaction
(*c*) Displacement reaction
(*d*) Double displacement reaction

* *Concepts beyond the board exam syllabus, offering deeper insight and critical thinking on NCERT topics.*

Assertion and Reason (1 M)

Direction: The following questions consist of two statements – Assertion (A) and Reason (R). Answer these questions by selecting the appropriate option given below:

(*a*) Both A and R are true, and R is the correct explanation of A.

(*b*) Both A and R are true, but R is not the correct explanation of A.

(*c*) A is true, but R is false.

(*d*) A is false, but R is true.

1. **Assertion (A):** In the given reaction,

$Zn(s) + CuSO_4(aq.) \longrightarrow ZnSO_4(aq.) + Cu(s)$

Zn acts as a reductant but itself gets reduced.

Reason (R): In a redox reaction, oxidant gets reduced by accepting electrons and reductant gets oxidized by losing electrons. ***(Ap)***

2. **Assertion (A):** The colour of aqueous solution of copper sulphate turns colourless when a piece of lead is added to it.

Reason (R): Lead is more reactive than copper, and hence displaces copper from its salt solution. ***(Ap)* (CBSE 2023)**

Subjective Questions

Very Short Answer Type Questions (2 M)

1. **While cooking in an aluminium vessel, Sudeshna burned some food till all that was left was a completely charred and black residue. She just left the blackened vessel heating on the stove. After an hour she found that the vessel was completely clean, with no trace of any blackness.**

(*a*) Write a chemical equation to explain what happened to the charred, black residue that made it disappear.

(*b*) Name the type of reaction referred to in (*a*).

***(An)* (CFPQ)**

Ans. (*a*) The blackened residue left in the aluminium vessel is likely carbon (charred food). When exposed to heat in the presence of oxygen, carbon reacts with oxygen to form carbon dioxide, which is a gas and escapes from the vessel. *(½ M)*

The reaction can be written as:

$C(s) + O_2(g) \longrightarrow CO_2(g)$ *(½ M)*

(*b*) The type of reaction is combustion or oxidation or combination, as carbon reacts with oxygen to produce carbon dioxide. *(1 M)*

2. **A solution of a substance 'X' is used for white washing.**

(*i*) Name the substance 'X' and write its formula.

(*ii*) Write the reaction of the substance 'X' named in (*i*) above with water ***(Un)* (NCERT Intext)**

Ans. (*i*) Substance 'X': Lime (Calcium Oxide) *(½ M)*

Formula: CaO *(½ M)*

(*ii*) Reaction with Water: When Calcium Oxide (CaO) reacts with water (H_2O), it forms Calcium Hydroxide ($Ca(OH)_2$), which is also known as slaked lime. The chemical reaction is as follows: *(1 M)*

$$\underset{\text{(Quick lime)}}{CaO(s)} + H_2O(l) \longrightarrow \underset{\text{(Slaked Lime)}}{Ca(OH)_2(aq.)}$$

3. **Answer the following questions:**

(*a*) Write the balanced chemical equation of any one reaction that cannot be classified as combination, decomposition, simple displacement or double displacement. (CFPQ)

(*b*) Examine the following reaction:

$Fe(s) + 2HCl(aq) \rightarrow FeH_2(aq) + Cl_2(g)$

What changes are needed in the equation above to correctly represent the reaction between iron (Fe) and hydrochloric acid (HCl)? ***(An)***

Ans. (*a*) The chemical equation is:

$6\,CO_2 + 6\,H_2O \rightarrow C_6H_{12}O_6 + 6O_2$ *(1 M)*

(*b*) The correct reaction is:

$Fe(s) + 2HCl(aq) \rightarrow FeCl_2(aq) + H_2(g)$

Changes Needed:

- FeH_2 (aq) should be changed to $FeCl_2$ (aq) *(½ M)*
- Cl_2 (g) should be changed to H_2 (g) *(½ M)*

4. **What is observed when a solution of sodium sulphate is added to a solution of barium chloride taken in a test tube? Write equation for the chemical reaction involved and name the type of reaction in this case.**

***(Un)* (CBSE 2018)**

Ans. When the solution of sodium sulphate is added to the solution of barium chloride, then the white insoluble precipitate of barium sulphate is formed. *(½ M)*

The following reaction takes place:

$BaCl_2(aq.) + Na_2SO_4(aq.) \rightarrow 2NaCl\,(aq.) + BaSO_4(s)\downarrow$ *(1 M)*

The above reaction is an example of double displacement reaction as the two reactant compounds exchange their ions to form two different compounds. *(½ M)*

> **Nailing the Right Answer**
>
> To ensure full credit, mention about the precipitation in double displacement reaction. Clearly write balanced chemical equation to adhere to the law of conservation of mass. Use proper chemical symbols and states for all reactants and products.

Short Answer Type Questions (3 M)

1. **Decomposition reactions require energy either in the form of heat or light or electricity for breaking down the reactants. Write one equation each for decomposition reactions where energy is supplied in the form of heat, light and electricity.** ***(Re)* (CBSE 2018)**

Ans. 1. Decomposition by heating:

$$CaCO_3(s) \xrightarrow{\text{Heat}} CaO\ (s) + CO_2\ (g) \uparrow$$

Here, calcium carbonate on heating gives quick lime (CaO) and carbon dioxide. *(1 M)*

2. Decomposition by light

$$2AgCl(s) \xrightarrow{\text{Sunlight}} 2Ag(s) + Cl_2(g)$$ *(1 M)*

3. Decomposition by electricity

$$2H_2O(l) \xrightarrow{\text{Electricity}} 2H_2(g) + O_2(g)$$

Breaking down of water into hydrogen and oxygen on passing electricity is known as electrolysis of water. *(1 M)*

2. The reactants of two reactions are given below.

(1) $Ca + 2H_2O \rightarrow$

(2) $CaO + H_2O \rightarrow$

(*a*) Write the chemical formula of the common product formed in the two reactions.

(*b*) Identify the type of reaction that will occur in (1) and (2) **(*An*) (CFPQ)**

Ans. (*a*) The common product formed in both reactions is calcium hydroxide. *(½ M)*

The chemical formula of calcium hydroxide is $Ca(OH)_2$. *(½ M)*

(*b*) Type of Reactions:

1. $Ca + 2\ H_2O \rightarrow Ca(OH)_2 + H_2$

Type of Reaction: Single displacement reaction (Calcium displaces hydrogen from water to form calcium hydroxide and hydrogen gas). *(1 M)*

2. $CaO + H_2O \rightarrow Ca(OH)_2$

Type of Reaction: Combination reaction (Calcium oxide reacts with water to form calcium hydroxide). *(1 M)*

3. The diagram below shows the set-up in which electrolysis of water takes place.

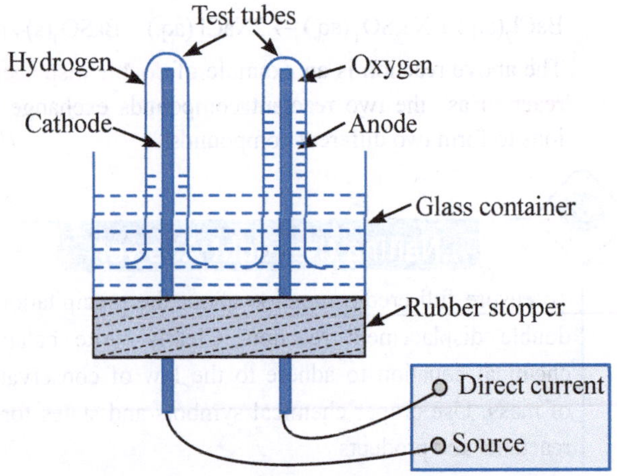

1. What type of reaction takes place?

2. Explain why this is an example of an endothermic reaction?

3. The test tube containing hydrogen is removed carefully from the apparatus. A lit match stick is brought near the mouth of this test tube. The gas burns with an explosive "pop" sound. Write a balanced chemical equation for this reaction and indicate whether energy is absorbed or released. **(*An*) (CFPQ)**

Ans. 1. Decomposition / Electrolytic decomposition *(½ M)*

2. This is an example of an endothermic reaction because energy in the form of electrical energy is absorbed. *(1 M)*

3. Balanced equation: *(1½ M)*

$$2H_2\ O + \text{energy} \rightarrow 2H_2 + O_2$$

The energy will get absorbed in this reaction.

4. (*a*) State any two observations when an electric current is passed through acidulated water, in a container having each electrode covered by test tubes filled with water.

(*b*) Write the ratio of the mass of the gas collected at the cathode to the mass of the gas collected at the anode. **(*An*) (CBSE 2024)**

Ans. (*a*) The following are the two observations that are observed:

1. At the cathode, hydrogen gas is released, which can be observed as bubbles rising in the test tube covering the cathode. *(1 M)*

2. At the anode , oxygen gas is released, observable as fewer bubbles in the test tube covering the anode compared to the cathode because oxygen is produced in a lesser volume. *(1 M)*

(*b*) The ratio of the mass of the gas collected at the cathode (hydrogen) to the mass of the gas collected at the anode (oxygen) can be derived from the electrolysis process and the chemical equation: $2H_2O \rightarrow 2H_2 + O_2$ *(½ M)*

From this, it's evident that twice the volume of hydrogen gas is produced compared to oxygen gas. *(½ M)*

Long Answer Type Questions (5 M)

1. Which among the following changes are exothermic or endothermic in nature? **(*Ev*) (NCERT Exemplar)**

(*a*) Decomposition of ferrous sulphate

(*b*) Dilution of sulphuric acid

(*c*) Dissolution of sodium hydroxide in water

(*d*) Dissolution of ammonium chloride in water

(*e*) Formation of ammonia gas

Ans. **Exothermic reactions:** Those reactions which involves release of heat.

Among the given reactions, the exothermic reactions are:

(*b*) Dilution of sulphuric acid *(1 M)*

(*c*) Dissolution of sodium hydroxide in water *(1 M)*

(*e*) Formation of ammonia gas *(1 M)*

Endothermic reaction: Those reactions which involves absorption of heat.

Among the given reactions, the endothermic reactions are:-

(*a*) Decomposition of ferrous sulphate *(1 M)*

(*d*) Dissolution of ammonium chloride in water *(1 M)*

2. **Identify the oxidising agent (oxidant) in the following reaction:** *(Ap)*

(*a*) $Pb_3O_4 + 8HCl \rightarrow 3PbCl_2 + Cl_2 + 4H_2O$

(*b*) $2Mg + O_2 \rightarrow 2MgO$

(*c*) $Cr_2O_7^{2-} + 3SO_3^{2-} + 8H^+ \rightarrow 2Cr^{3+} + 3SO_4^{2-} + 4H_2O(l)$

(*d*) $V_2O_5 + 5Ca \rightarrow 2V + 5CaO$

(*e*) $3Fe + 4H_2O \rightarrow Fe_3O_4 + 4H_2$

Ans. (*a*) Pb_3O_4 is losing oxygen and hence getting reduced. Therefore, Pb_3O_4 acts as an oxidizing agent. *(1 M)*

(*b*) Magnesium gains oxygen and gets oxidized. Hence, Magnesium is reducing agent and O_2 will be oxidising agent. *(1 M)*

(*c*) $Cr_2O_7^{2-}$ is losing oxygen and hence getting reduced. Therefore, $Cr_2O_7^{2-}$ acts as an oxidizing agent. *(1 M)*

(*d*) V_2O_5 is losing oxygen and hence getting reduced. Therefore, V_2O_5 acts as an oxidizing agent. *(1 M)*

(*e*) H_2O is losing oxygen and hence getting reduced. Therefore, H_2O acts as an oxidizing agent. *(1 M)*

Mistakes 101 : What not to do!

Students should not confuse between oxidizing and reducing agents. Students should remember that the oxidizing agent is reduced and substance that is oxidized is the reducing agent.

Hints & Explanations

Multiple Choice Questions

1. (*d*) displacement reaction.
In this reaction, aluminium (Al) displaces iron (Fe) from iron oxide (Fe_2O_3), forming aluminium oxide (Al_2O_3) and elemental iron (Fe). This is a classic example of a displacement reaction.

2. (*d*) P and S, both corresponds to double displacement reaction while 'Q' is single displacement reaction and 'R' is combustion reaction

3. (*c*) Exothermic processes will increase the temperature whereas endothermic processes will decrease the temperature.

4. (*a*) This is a thermal decomposition reaction. When lead nitrate undergoes thermal decomposition, brown fumes of nitrogen dioxide are produced.

5. (*c*) Displacement reaction

Assertion and Reason

1. (*d*) In the given reaction, Zn acts a reductant and gets oxidised.

2. (*a*) Lead is more reactive than copper, hence, it will displace the copper from its salt solution which results in the formation of lead sulphate which is colourless.

EFFECT OF OXIDATION REACTIONS

4

NCERT Definitions (Commonly asked in 1 mark)

- **Corrosion:** The process by which metals are **chemically attacked** by air, moisture, or other substances in their environment.
- **Rancidity:** The process of **oxidation of food** (containing fats and oils) when exposed to air, light, or moisture, leading to unpleasant smell and taste.
- **Antioxidants:** The substances which **prevent oxidation** and are generally added to food items containing fats and oils to prevent rancidity.

Important Facts

01 Rust is **reddish-brown** in colour.

02 The chemical formula for rust is typically represented as $Fe_2O_3.nH_2O$*

Difference Between

Rusting v/s Tarnishing	
Rusting	**Tarnishing**
Rusting refers to the corrosion of **iron or steel**.	Tarnishing refers to corrosion of metals **other than iron**.
The process involves the oxidation of iron in the presence of water and oxygen, leading to the formation of **iron oxide** (rust).	For example, silver tarnish is a result of silver reacting with hydrogen sulfide (H_2S) in the air, forming **a black layer of silver sulphide** (Ag_2S) on the surface.
Rusting leads to significant material loss and structural weakness, making it a major concern, especially in industries and infrastructure involving iron and its alloys.	Tarnishing does not usually lead to significant material loss but can affect the appearance and surface properties of the metal.

Real Life Application Based Questions

1. The Statue of Liberty has turned green. Why ?*

Ans. The Statue of Liberty turned green due to the oxidation of its copper coating, forming a patina that protects the underlying metal from further corrosion.

2. How do manufacturers prevent rancidity in packaged food items like chips?

Ans. Manufacturers use inert gases like nitrogen to flush chips bags, limiting oxygen exposure and preventing the oxidation of fats, thereby inhibiting rancidity and extending shelf life.

3. Why are antioxidants important in our diet, and how do they relate to the concept of rancidity?*

Ans. Antioxidants in our diet prevent cell damage by neutralizing harmful molecules called free radicals. They help in avoiding rancidity in foods by slowing down the oxidation of fats, keeping food fresh and safe.

** Concepts beyond the board exam syllabus, offering deeper insight and critical thinking on NCERT topics.*

4. **Give reason, why cosmetics have recommendation "Store these products in cool, dark places" ?**

Ans. Many cosmetics, including creams, lotions, and lip balms, contain oils and fats that can go rancid. When these products are exposed to air, light, or heat, the oils can get oxidized, leading to a change in smell, colour, and texture, and potentially causing skin irritation or allergic reactions. To prevent this, cosmetic manufacturers often add antioxidants and use airtight packaging. This is why it is recommended to store cosmetics products in cool and dark places.

Myth Buster

- **Myth: All metals corrode at the same rate and under the same conditions.**
  Fact: Different metals have different rates of corrosion and react differently to environmental conditions. For example, iron rusts when exposed to water and oxygen, while silver tarnishes in the presence of sulphur compounds in the air.
- **Myth: Food manufacturers use nitrogen in chips bags merely to fill the space and prevent crushing.**
  Fact: While nitrogen does help prevent chips from being crushed, its primary function in chips bags is to displace oxygen. This prevents oxidation of the chips, maintaining their freshness and preventing rancidity.
- **Myth: Both rusting and corrosion terms are same and can be used interchangeably.**
  Fact: Corrosion is the process where materials, like metals, wear away due to reactions with their surroundings such as air, moisture, acids, etc. Rusting is a type of corrosion that only happens to iron and steel, forming red or orange rust. Hence, corrosion includes rusting. So, while all rusting is corrosion, not all corrosion is rusting. Hence, both these terms are different and should not be used interchangeably.
- **Myth: Silver tarnishing and iron rusting are completely different processes and do not share any commonalities.**
  Fact: Both silver tarnishing and iron rusting are forms of corrosion, a broader term that describes the degradation of metals due to chemical reactions with their environment. While the specific chemicals involved differ (oxygen and moisture for iron, sulphur compounds for silver), both processes are fundamentally oxidation reactions.

COMPETENCY BASED SOLVED EXAMPLES

Multiple Choice Questions (1 M)

1. **Silver jewellery becomes black on prolonged exposure to air, it is due to the formation of** *(Un)*
   (a) Ag_2S and Ag_3N (b) Ag_2S
   (c) Ag_3N (d) $Ag_2O + Ag_2S$
2. **Which of the following metals is the most resistant to corrosion?** *(Un)*
   (a) Iron (b) Gold
   (c) Copper (d) Aluminium
3. **Fatty foods become rancid due to** *(Re)*
   (a) Oxidation (b) Corrosion
   (c) Hydrogenation (d) Reduction

Assertion and Reason (1 M)

Direction: The following questions consist of two statements – Assertion (A) and Reason (R). Answer these questions by selecting the appropriate option given below:

(a) Both A and R are true, and R is the correct explanation of A.
(b) Both A and R are true, but R is not the correct explanation of A.
(c) A is true, but R is false.
(d) A is false, but R is true.

1. **Assertion (A):** Corrosion of iron is called rusting.
   Reason (R): Corrosion of iron occurs in presence of air and water. *(Re)*
2. **Assertion (A):** Iron articles are painted so as to prevent them from rusting.
   Reason (R): When the surface of iron is coated with paint, its surface does not come in contact with oxygen and moisture therefore, rusting does not take place. *(Un)*
3. **Assertion (A):** Formation of rust on iron is a chemical change.
   Reason (R): Rust is formed when iron reacts with oxygen and water in the presence of air. The resulting iron oxide is chemically different from the original iron, making it a chemical change. *(Un)*

Subjective Questions

Very Short Answer Type Questions (2 M)

1. **Uzma peeled and cut some potatoes and left them in an open bowl. After a few minutes, she observed that the cut potato pieces had turned brown.**
   Radhika also peeled and cut some potatoes. She kept the cut potato pieces immersed in a bowl of water. The potato pieces in water did NOT turn brown.
   Explain the difference in the reaction of the cut potato pieces in the two cases. *(An)* **(CFPQ)**

Ans. • The browning of the potato pieces kept in the open bowl is likely to be due to an oxidation reaction between the potato and air. *(1 M)*

• The oxidation is prevented by keeping the potato under water as it is not in contact with air. *(1 M)*

2. (a) Define antioxidants ***(Re)***

(b) Give one method to prevent rusting.

Ans. (*a*) Antioxidants are substances which prevents oxidation. These are added to foods containing fats and oils to prevent it from being rancid. *(1 M)*

(*b*) Rusting can be prevented by greasing or oiling the iron article. *(1 M)*

Short Answer Type Questions (3 M)

1. (a) Why do we galvanize iron particles? ***(Un)***

(b) Give one example where corrosion is an advantage rather than a disadvantage.

Ans. (*a*) To prevent rusting, iron particles are galvanized. It is the process of coating iron with a protective layer of zinc. *(1 M)*

Here, layer of zinc works as a protective layer. It acts as a barrier to against various corrosive elements. *(½ M)*

(*b*) The example where corrosion is an advantage is the case of aluminium which when exposed to moist air gets covered with a thin impervious layer of aluminium oxide (Al_2O_3). The protective oxide layer prevents the metal from further oxidation. *(1½ M)*

2. (a) Define rancidity.

(b) Oil and fat containing food items are flushed with nitrogen. Why? ***(Re)*** **(NCERT)**

Ans. (*a*) Rancidity is defined as the bad smell and taste of food which takes place due to oxidation of fats or oils. *(1 M)*

(*b*) Oil and fat containing food items are flushed with nitrogen to increase their shelf life and maintain quality. This process, involves replacing the oxygen in the packaging with nitrogen. *(1 M)*

Oxygen can cause oxidative rancidity in oil and fat-rich foods.

Nitrogen is an inert gas and by flushing out oxygen and filling the packaging with nitrogen, this process slows down the oxidation of fats and oils, thus preserving the freshness, taste, and texture of the food. *(1 M)*

Long Answer Type Questions (5 M)

1. (a) What happens when food materials containing fats and oils are left for a long time? List two observable changes and suggest two ways by which this phenomenon can be prevented. ***(Ap)***

(b) A shiny brown coloured element 'X' on heating in air becomes black in colour. Name the element 'X' and the black coloured compound formed. ***(Ap)*** **(NCERT)**

Ans. (*a*) When food materials containing fats and oils are left for a long time, they become rancid. Food gets spoiled in such a way that it becomes unfit to eat. *(1 M)*

Two observable changes are:

(*i*) Change in taste *(½ M)*

(*ii*) Change in smell *(½ M)*

Two methods of prevention:

(*i*) Adding antioxidants which prevent rancidity *(½ M)*

(*ii*) Refrigerating food helps to slow down rancidity *(½ M)*

(*b*) A shiny brown element 'X' which on heating in air becomes black in colour is basically Copper element and black coloured compound formed is Copper oxide. *(1 M)*

The reaction that takes place is:

$$\underset{\text{copper}}{2Cu(s)} + \underset{\text{oxygen}}{O_2(g)} \longrightarrow \underset{\text{copper oxide}}{2CuO(s)} \quad (1\ M)$$

Nailing the Right Answer

Students should clearly list the observable changes like taste and smell. Explain Prevention Methods: Describe how adding antioxidants, using nitrogen gas, and refrigeration can prevent rancidity. Provide specific and concise information without unnecessary details.

Hints & Explanations

Multiple Choice Questions

1. (*b*) Silver reacts with H_2S in air to form silver sulphide
$2Ag + H_2S \longrightarrow Ag_2S + H_2$

2. (*b*) Gold is a noble metal and does not react with oxygen or moisture in the air, hence it is the most resistant to corrosion.

3. (*a*) Rancidity is oxidation of oils & fats.

Assertion and Reason

1. (*b*) The correct reason for given assertion is that corrosion occurs due to oxidation of iron.

2. (*a*) Both assertion and reason are correct and reason is the correct explanation of assertion.

3. (*a*) The resultant iron oxide differs from the original iron in terms of chemical composition and properties and hence, indicates a chemical change.

MISCELLANEOUS EXERCISE

Multiple Choice Questions (1 M)

1. Select from the following a process in which a combination reaction is involved: **(*Un*) (CBSE 2024)**
   (*a*) Black and White photography
   (*b*) Burning of coal
   (*c*) Burning of methane
   (*d*) Digestion of food

2. Olivia is studying single displacement reactions in her chemistry class. She comes across the following reaction:
   $AB + C \rightarrow AC + B$
   Olivia is curious about the ion type of A in the product and the stability comparison between AB and AC. After considering the possible outcomes, she wonders which of the following is true about the reactants and products. Help Olivia select the correct option: **(*Un*)**

Type of ion of A in product	Stability of AB as compared to AC
A. cation	less stable
B. anion	less stable
C. cation	more stable
D. anion	more stable

   (*a*) A (*b*) B
   (*c*) C (*d*) D

3. Which of the following among the given options will be required to identify the gas evolved when dilute HCl acid reacts with Zn metal? **(*An*)**
   (*a*) Red litmus paper (*b*) pH paper
   (*c*) Lime water (*d*) A burning splinter

4. $MnO_2 + 4HCl \rightarrow MnCl_2 + 2H_2O + Cl_2$
   The reaction given above is a redox reaction because in this case: **(*Un*) (CBSE 2024)**
   (*a*) MnO_2 is oxidised and HCl is reduced.
   (*b*) HCl is oxidised.
   (*c*) MnO_2 is reduced.
   (*d*) MnO_2 is reduced and HCl is oxidised.

5. Gautam has to courier a sample of silver bromide powder to a laboratory for analysis.
   Which of the following containers can he use to pack the sample? **(*Ev*) (CFPQ)**
   (P) Transparent glass bottle
   (Q) Opaque plastic bottle
   (R) Black paper packet
   (*a*) Only P (*b*) Only P or Q
   (*c*) Only Q or R (*d*) Any of P, Q or R

6. A chemical equation is said to be balanced if **(*Re*)**
   (*a*) Compounds are same on both sides
   (*b*) Molecules are same on both sides
   (*c*) Number of atoms are same on both sides
   (*d*) Number of electrons are same on both sides

7. $MnO_2 + xHCl \rightarrow MnCl_2 + yH_2O + zCl_2$
   In order to balance the above chemical equation, the values of *x*, *y* and *z* respectively are: **(*Ap*) (CBSE 2023)**
   (*a*) 6, 2, 2 (*b*) 4, 1, 2
   (*c*) 4, 2, 1 (*d*) 2, 2, 1

8. In balanced chemical equation **(*Ap*)**
   $aKMnO_4 + bH_2SO_4 \longrightarrow cK_2SO_4 + dMnSO_4 + eH_2O + f[O]$
   Which of the following alternatives are correct?
   (*a*) $a = 2, b = 3, c = 1, d = 2, e = 3, f = 5$
   (*b*) $a = 1, b = 2, c = 1, d = 3, e = 2, f = 3$
   (*c*) $a = 2, b = 3, c = 2, d = 3, e = 2, f = 5$
   (*d*) $a = 3, b = 1, c = 3, d = 3, e = 1, f = 3$

9. 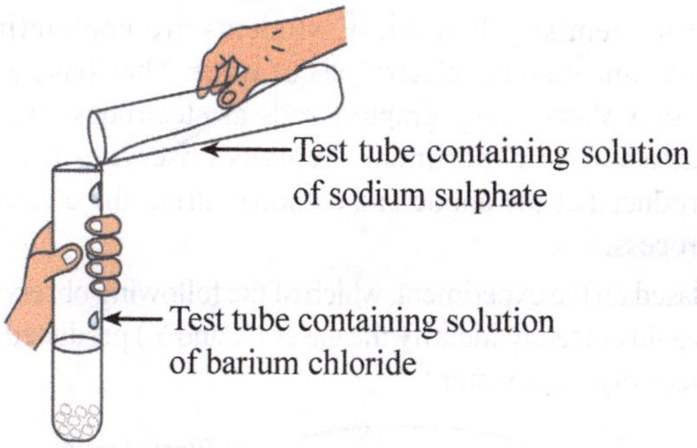

   Identify the product which represents the solid state in the above reaction. **(*Un*) (CBSE SQP, 2023)**
   (*a*) Barium chloride (*b*) Barium sulphate
   (*c*) Sodium chloride (*d*) Sodium sulphate

10. 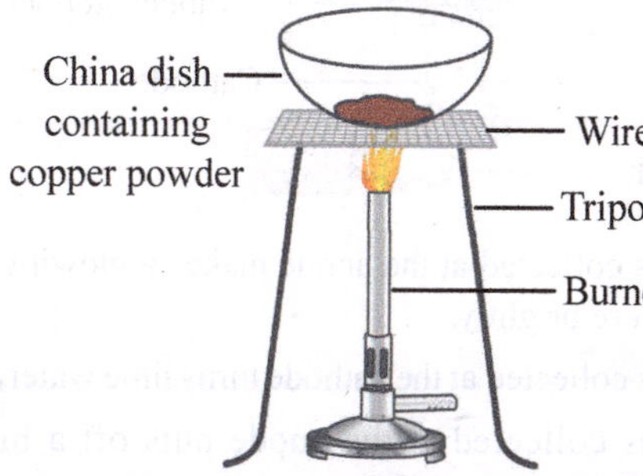

   Which of the following observations is correct for the above given experimental diagram? **(*Un*) (CBSE APQ, 2023)** (*a*) Red-coloured copper is reduced to black-coloured copper(I) oxide

(*b*) Red-coloured copper is oxidized to red-coloured copper(I) oxide

(*c*) Red-coloured copper is reduced to black-coloured copper (II) oxide

(*d*) Red-coloured copper is oxidized to black coloured copper(II) oxide

11. Ammonium nitrate (NH_4NO_3) is a commonly used fertilizer. When ammonium nitrate decomposes, it produces nitrogen gas (N_2), water vapour (H_2O), and oxygen gas (O_2). Write a balanced chemical equation for this decomposition reaction. **(*Ap*)**

(*a*) $2NH_4NO_3 \rightarrow 2N_2 + 4H_2O + O_2$

(*b*) $NH_4NO_3 \rightarrow N_2 + 2H_2O$

(*c*) $NH_4NO_3 \rightarrow N_2 + 4H_2O + 2O_2$

(*d*) $NH_4NO_3 \rightarrow N_2 + H_2O + O_2$

12. Which of the following pair of reactants can undergo a displacement reaction under appropriate conditions? **(*Ap*)**

(*a*) $MgSO_4 + Fe$ (*b*) $ZnSO_4 + Fe$

(*c*) $MgSO_4 + Pb$ (*d*) $CuSO_4 + Fe$

13. The gas that gives a black precipitate with aqueous $Pb(NO_3)_2$ solution and a white precipitate with aqueous $ZnCl_2$ solution is **(*Re*)**

(*a*) CO_2 (*b*) NO_2

(*c*) NH_3 (*d*) H_2S

14. In a chemistry laboratory, students are conducting an experiment on the electrolysis of water. They have a setup with a plastic mug, graphite rods as electrodes, and a 6V battery. The experiment involves observing the gases produced at the anode and cathode during the electrolysis process.

Based on the experiment, which of the following observations would correctly identify the gases (X and Y) produced in the electrolysis of water? **(*An*)**

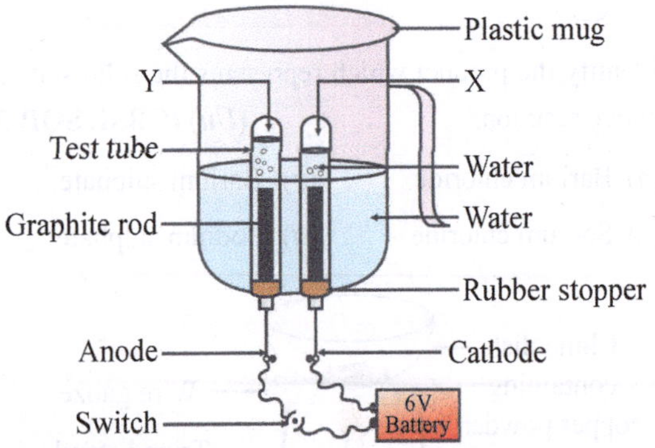

(A) The gas collected at the anode makes a glowing splint burn more brightly.

(B) The gas collected at the cathode turns lime water milky.

(C) The gas collected at the anode puts off a burning matchstick.

(D) The gas collected at the cathode produces a pop sound when exposed to a burning matchstick.

Select the correct option:

(*a*) Only (A) (*b*) Both (A) and (D)

(*c*) Only (C) (*d*) Both (B) and (C)

15. Select from the following a decomposition reaction in which source of energy for decomposition is light: **(*Re*) (CBSE 2024)**

(*a*) $2FeSO_4 \rightarrow Fe_2O_3 + SO_2 + SO_3$

(*b*) $2H_2O \rightarrow 2H_2 + O_2$

(*c*) $2AgBr \rightarrow 2Ag + Br_2$

(*d*) $CaCO_3 \rightarrow CaO + CO_2$

16. Calcium oxide reacts vigorously with water to produce calcium hydroxide. **(*Un*)**

$CaO(s) + H_2O(l) \longrightarrow Ca(OH)_2(aq.)$

This reaction can be classified as:

(A) Combination reaction

(B) Exothermic reaction

(C) Endothermic reaction

(D) Decomposition reaction

Which of the following is the correct option?

(*a*) (A) and (C) (*b*) (C) and (D)

(*c*) (A), (C) and (D) (*d*) (A) and (B)

17. Which of the following displacement reactions will occur if the indicated reactants are mixed? **(*Un*)**

A. $3Mg(s) + 2AlCl_3(aq.) \longrightarrow 3MgCl_2(aq.) + 2Al(s)$

B. $Zn(s) + MgCl_2(aq.) \longrightarrow ZnCl_2(aq.) + Mg(s)$

C. $Cu(s) + Pb(NO_3)_2(aq.) \longrightarrow Cu(NO_3)_2(aq.) + Pb(s)$

D. $Ni(s) + 2AgNO_3(aq.) \longrightarrow Ni\ (NO_3)_2(aq.) + 2Ag(s)$

(*a*) A, B (*b*) C, D

(*c*) B, C (*d*) A, D

18. Which of the following statements about the reaction given below are correct? **(*Un*) (CBSE 2022, Term I)**

$$MnO_2 + 4HCl \rightarrow MnCl_2 + 2H_2O + Cl_2$$

(*i*) HCl is oxidized to Cl_2

(*ii*) MnO_2 is reduced to $MnCl_2$

(*iii*) $MnCl_2$ acts as an oxidizing agent

(*iv*) HCl acts as an oxidizing agent

(*a*) (*ii*), (*iii*) and (*iv*) (*b*) (*i*), (*ii*) and (*iii*)

(*c*) (*i*) and (*ii*) only (*d*) (*iii*) and (*iv*) only

19. When hydrogen sulphide gas is passed through a blue solution of copper sulphate, a black ppt. of copper sulphide is obtained and the sulphuric acid that is formed remains in the solution. The reaction is an example of **(*Un*) (CBSE 2020)**

(*a*) A combination reaction

(*b*) A displacement reaction

(*c*) A decomposition reaction

(*d*) A double displacement reaction

20. A chemistry teacher is conducting a demonstration for their students to illustrate the decomposition of hydrogen peroxide (H_2O_2), a common household disinfectant and bleaching agent. The teacher wants to show how hydrogen peroxide decomposes to produce water and oxygen gas. Write a balanced chemical equation for this decomposition reaction. ***(Un)***

(*a*) $2H_2O_2 \rightarrow 2H_2O + O_2$ (*b*) $H_2O_2 \rightarrow H_2O + O_2$

(*c*) $H_2O_2 \rightarrow H_2O + 2O_2$ (*d*) $2H_2O_2 \rightarrow H_2O + O_2$

21. In an experiment with 100 mL 0.1 M solution of Copper Chloride, by mistake 5 gm of a mixture containing equal weights of Tin, Silver, Lead and Calcium, was added. Finally after some time the solution gets completely decolourised. Which of the following statements is correct regarding this experiment? ***(An)***

(*a*) Silver reacts with copper chloride to give silver chloride

(*b*) Calcium reacts with copper chloride to give calcium chloride

(*c*) All the metals react with copper chloride

(*d*) Only lead reacts with copper chloride forming white precipitate of lead chloride.

22. Rekha dropped a metal piece A in the solution of another metal B. After some time, a new colourless compound C is formed. A, B, C respectively can be ***(An)***

(*a*) Cu, $ZnSO_4$, $CuSO_4$ (*b*) Mg, NaCl, $MgCl_2$

(*c*) Mg, $CuSO_4$, $MgSO_4$ (*d*) Fe, $ZnSO_4$, $FeSO_4$

23. The reaction between iron(III) chloride ($FeCl_3$) and sodium hydroxide (NaOH) results in the formation of iron(III) hydroxide ($Fe(OH)_3$) and sodium chloride (NaCl). Identify the type of reaction, and what is the colour of $Fe(OH)_3$ precipitate? ***(Un)***

(*a*) Double displacement reaction, yellowish brown

(*b*) Combination reaction, white

(*c*) Displacement reaction, green

(*d*) Decomposition reaction, brown

24. Shweta went for a journey by train in June 2018. Her train was to depart at 7 am. Her mother packed 'Bread Pakodas' for her lunch. However, Shweta did not eat them till evening. In the evening, when she opened her lunch box, she felt an unpleasant smell. The taste of Pakodas was also sour. This happened due to ________ ***(Re)***

(*a*) Thermal Decomposition (*b*) Calcination

(*c*) Isomerism (*d*) Rancidity

25. Reo is studying different types of exothermic reactions in the laboratory. In one experiment, he observes that both water and carbon dioxide are produced in the gaseous state. In another experiment, he notes that water is produced in the liquid state and carbon dioxide is formed in the aqueous state.

Which of the following reactions corresponds to each scenario described above?

(A) In which both water and CO_2 are produced in the gaseous state.

(B) In which water is produced in the liquid state and CO_2 is in the aqueous state. ***(An)***

Options:

(*a*) Reaction 1 (A): The combustion of methane with oxygen.

Reaction 2 (B): The reaction between glucose and oxygen.

(*b*) Reaction 1 (A): The combustion of propane with oxygen.

Reaction 2 (B): The reaction of carbon monoxide with water.

(*c*) Reaction 1 (A): The reaction between sodium bicarbonate and acetic acid.

Reaction 2 (B): The combustion of methane with oxygen.

(*d*) Reaction 1 (A): The reaction of calcium carbonate with water.

Reaction 2 (B): The reaction between sodium carbonate and acetic acid.

26. "A group of students conducted an experiment to observe the effect of different environments on the rate of iron corrosion. They placed identical iron nails in three different setups: one exposed to salty water, another exposed to dry air, and the last one buried in moist soil."

Based on the scenario, which setup is most likely to show the highest rate of corrosion in iron nails? ***(An)***

(*a*) Salty water

(*b*) Dry air

(*c*) Moist soil

(*d*) All setups show equal rates of corrosion

Assertion and Reason (1 M)

Direction: The following questions consist of two statements – Assertion (A) and Reason (R). Answer these questions by selecting the appropriate option given below:

(*a*) Both A and R are true, and R is the correct explanation of A.

(*b*) Both A and R are true, but R is not the correct explanation of A.

(*c*) A is true, but R is false.

(*d*) A is false, but R is true.

1. Assertion (A): When 1g of ammonium chloride (NH_4Cl) is added to a test tube containing 2g of barium hydroxide ($Ba(OH)_2$), the bottom of the test tube becomes cold.

Reason (R): The reaction between ammonium chloride and barium hydroxide is an endothermic and decomposition reaction. ***(An)***

2. Assertion (A): Burning of a candle is considered a physical as well as chemical change.

Reason (R): Melting of wax is a physical change, the melted wax turns into vapours and then burns which is a chemical change. ***(Un)***

3. **Assertion (A):** All the chemical equations must be balanced.

Reason (R): Atoms are either created or destroyed in chemical reaction. ***(Re)***

4. **Assertion (A):** Copper can easily displace silver on reacting with aqueous solution of silver nitrate.

Reason (R): Silver is more reactive than copper. ***(Ap)***

5. **Assertion (A):** Reaction of Quicklime with water is an exothermic reaction.

Reason (R): Quicklime reacts vigorously with water releasing a large amount of heat. ***(Un)* (CBSE 2023)**

6. **Assertion (A):** Photosynthesis is considered as an example of an endothermic reaction.

Reason (R): In the process of photosynthesis, energy gets released. ***(Un)***

7. **Assertion (A):** When CO_2 gas is passed through lime water, a white precipitate is formed initially.

Reason (R): White precipitate formed is of $CaCO_3$ which is formed during the reaction. ***(Re)***

8. **Assertion (A):** Paint is applied on the iron articles.

Reason (R): To enhance electrical conductivity of iron articles. ***(Un)***

9. **Assertion (A):** Gold and silver do not corrode in moist air.

Reason (R): It is because they have low reactivity. ***(Ap)***

10. **Assertion (A):** Nitrogen is flushed in potato chips packets to prevent rancidity.

Reason (R): Nitrogen prevents contact of chips to air and thus prevents oxidation. ***(Un)***

Subjective Questions

Very Short Answer Type Questions (2 M)

1. On opening a bottle of soda, Nishchal observed that there was a lot of effervescence and some of the soda water bubbled out of the bottle.

(*a*) Write the equation for the chemical reaction taking place.

(*b*) Identify the type of reaction. ***(Ap)* (CFPQ)**

2. During a laboratory experiment, you are given solutions of lead nitrate ($Pb(NO_3)_2$) and potassium iodide (KI). When these solutions are mixed, a yellow precipitate forms. ***(Ap)***

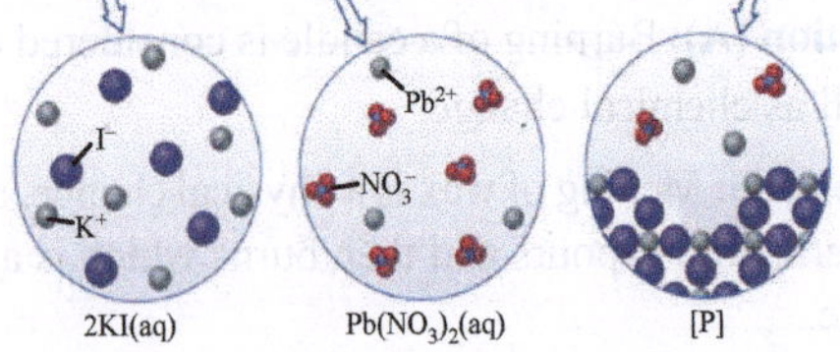

(*a*) Identify the compound that gives yellow precipitate, P.

(*b*) Briefly explain the reaction.

3. Identify the substances that are oxidised and the substances that are reduced in the following reactions. ***(Un)* (NCERT Intext)**

(*i*) $4Na(s) + O_2(g) \rightarrow 2Na_2O(s)$

(*ii*) $CuO(s) + H_2(g) \rightarrow Cu(s) + H_2O(l)$

4. What is meant by a balanced chemical equation? Why is it necessary for the equation to be balanced? ***(Re)* (CBSE 2024)**

5. A student took a small amount of copper oxide in a conical flask and added dilute hydrochloric acid to it with constant stirring. He observed a change in colour of the solution. ***(Un)* (CBSE 2023)**

(*i*) Write the name of the compound formed and its colour.

(*ii*) Write a balanced chemical equation for the reaction involved.

6. Write the balanced equation of the reactions given below. ***(Ap)***

(*a*) Iron metal reacts with a solution of tin (II) chloride.

(*b*) Iron reacts with hydrochloric acid.

7. Answer the following questions: ***(An)***

(*a*) Dilip was comparing combination reactions with decomposition reactions.

Which class of chemical substances may be the product of a decomposition reaction but NOT a product of a combination reaction? **(CFPQ)**

(*b*) Provide an example of a reaction in which both displacement and redox processes occur.

8. Eight identical, iron blocks are placed on the ground in the two arrangements X and Y as shown below. The block arrangement are kept moist by sprinkling water every few hours.

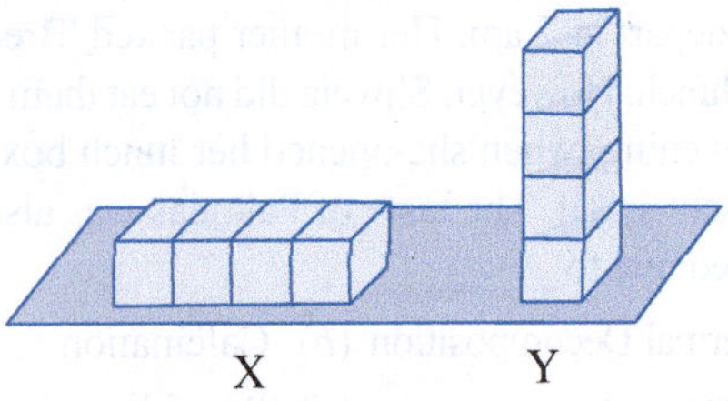

Which of the arrangements is likely to gather more rust after ten days? Justify your answer. ***(An)* (CFPQ)**

Short Answer Type Questions (3 M)

1. Write one chemical equation each for the chemical reaction in which the following have taken place: ***(Un)* (CBSE 2024)**

(*i*) Change in colour

(*ii*) Change in temperature

(*iii*) Formation of precipitate

Mention colour change/temperature change (rise/fall)/ compound precipitated along with equation.

2. (*i*) While electrolysing water before passing the current some drops of an acid are added. Why? Name the gases liberated at cathode and anode. Write the relationship between the volume of gas collected at anode and the volume of gas collected at cathode.
   (*ii*) What is observed when silver chloride is exposed to sunlight? Give the type of reaction involved.
   (*Re*) (CBSE 2023)

3. 2g of silver chloride is taken in a China dish and the China dish is placed in sunlight for some time. What will be your observation in this case? Write the chemical reaction involved in the form of a balanced chemical equation. Identify the type of chemical reaction. **(*Ap*) (CBSE 2019)**

4. Complete and balance the following chemical equations: **(*Ap*) (CBSE 2020)**
   (*i*) $NaOH(aq.) + Zn_{(s)} \rightarrow$
   (*ii*) $CaCO_3(s) + H_2O(l) + CO_2(g) \rightarrow$
   (*iii*) $HCl(aq.) + H_2O(l) \rightarrow$

5. On adding a drop of barium chloride solution to an aqueous solution of sodium sulphite, white precipitate is obtained.
   (*a*) Write a balanced chemical equation of the reaction involved
   (*b*) What other name can be given to this precipitation reaction?
   (*c*) On adding dilute hydrochloric acid to the reaction mixture, white precipitate disappears. Why?
   (*Un*) (NCERT Exemplar)

6.

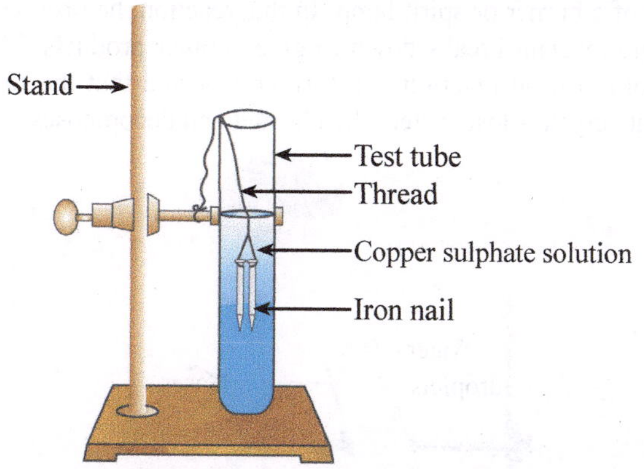

Study the experimental set-up shown in the diagram and write chemical equation for the chemical reaction involved. Name and define the type of reaction. List two other metals which can be used in place of iron to show the same type of reaction with copper sulphate solution. **(*Ap*) (CBSE 2024)**

7. Tina finds a paper covered with a white substance in a chemistry lab. She keeps the paper near the window of the lab and comes back to pick it up after five hours to take it home, She noticed that the white substance had turned grey,
   (*a*) What could be the most likely substance on the paper that Tina found?
   (*b*) The substance changed from white to grey, Write the chemical equation for this reaction.
   (*c*) State ONE application of this property of the substance seen in daily life. **(*An*) (CFPQ)**

8. (*a*) Identify the reducing agent in the following reactions:
   (*i*) $4NH_3 + 5O_2 \rightarrow 4NO + 6H_2O$
   (*ii*) $H_2O + F_2 \rightarrow HF + HOF$
   (*iii*) $Fe_2O_3 + 3CO \rightarrow 2Fe + 3CO_2$
   (*iv*) $2H_2 + O_2 \rightarrow 2H_2O$
   (*b*) Define a redox reaction in terms of gain or loss of oxygen. **(*Un*) (CBSE 2023)**

Long Answer Type Questions (5 M)

1. (*a*) In her chemistry class, Lily is studying redox reactions. She comes across the following equation representing the reaction between zinc oxide and hydrochloric acid:
   $ZnO + 2HCl \longrightarrow ZnCl_2 + H_2O$
   She wonders about the nature of this reaction. Lily asks herself the following questions:
   (*i*) Is this a double displacement reaction? Can you explain why or why not?
   (*ii*) Is this a redox reaction? Justify your answer.
   (*iii*) Can you name another type of reaction that this is an example of.
   (*b*) Why is the electrolysis of water considered an endothermic reaction? **(*An*)**

2. Balance the following chemical equations and identify the type of chemical reaction. **(*Ap*) (NCERT Exemplar)**
   (*a*) $Mg(s) + Cl_2(g) \longrightarrow MgCl_2(s)$
   (*b*) $HgO(s) \xrightarrow{Heat} Hg(l) + O_2(g)$
   (*c*) $Na(s) + S(s) \xrightarrow{Fuse} Na_2S(s)$
   (*d*) $TiCl_4(l) + Mg(s) \longrightarrow Ti(s) + MgCl_2(s)$
   (*e*) $CaO(s) + SiO_2(s) \longrightarrow CaSiO_3(s)$

3. (*a*) Identify the substance oxidized, substance reduced, oxidizing agent, reducing agent in the following reaction – $3MnO_2 + 4Al \longrightarrow 3Mn + 2Al_2O_3$ **(*Un*)**
   (*b*) What is the colour of ferrous sulphate crystals? How does the colour change after heating? Explain with the help of a chemical equation. Also, name the products formed on strongly heating ferrous sulphate crystals. **(*Re*)**

4. (*a*) A brown substance "X" on heating in the air forms a substance "Y". When hydrogen gas is passed over heated "Y". It again changes back into "X".
   (*i*) Name the substances X and Y.
   (*ii*) Name the chemical processes occurring during both changes.
   (*iii*) Write chemical equations. **(*Un*)**
   (*b*) What do you mean by a precipitation reaction? Explain by giving examples. **(*Un*) (NCERT)**

5. (*a*) What is the difference between displacement and double displacement reactions? Write equations for these reactions. **(*Re*) (NCERT)**
   (*b*) Why are decomposition reactions called the opposite of combination reactions? Write equations for these reactions. **(*Re*) (NCERT)**

Case Based Questions

Case Based-I: Alok was conducting an experiment to study the reaction between calcium carbonate and hydrochloric acid. He mixed a small piece of calcium carbonate with hydrochloric acid in a test tube. He observed that the mixture produced a fizzing sound and a gas evolved. ***(Un)***

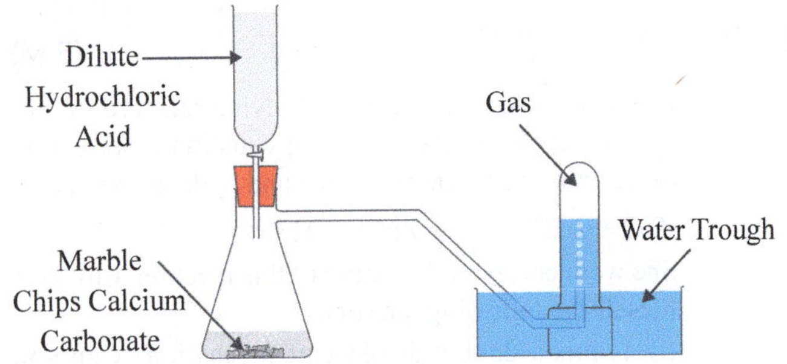

(*i*) What is the name of the gas evolved during the reaction? *(1 M)*

(*ii*) How did Alok identify the gas evolved during the reaction? *(1 M)*

(*iii*) What is the name of the product formed during the reaction? *(1 M)*

(*iv*) What is the importance of balancing chemical equations? *(1 M)*

Case Based-II: A student conducted an experiment by mixing hydrochloric acid and sodium hydroxide solution in a beaker. The student noticed that the temperature of the solution increased and the mixture turned into a neutral solution. Based on the observations, the student concluded that a chemical reaction had taken place. ***(Un)***

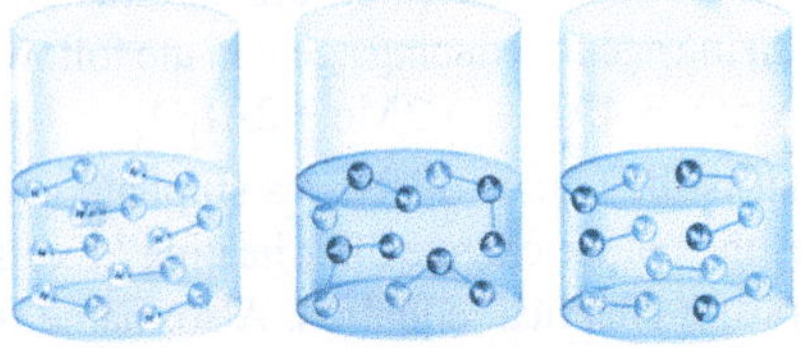

(*i*) What is the balanced chemical equation for the reaction between hydrochloric acid and sodium hydroxide? *(1 M)*

(*ii*) Why does the temperature of the solution increase during the reaction between hydrochloric acid and sodium hydroxide? *(1 M)*

(*iii*) (*a*) What is the chemical name for the compound formed during the reaction between hydrochloric acid and sodium hydroxide? *(1 M)*

(*b*) What type of reaction is occurring between hydrochloric acid and sodium hydroxide? *(1 M)*

Case Based-III: Displacement reactions involve the replacement of one element by another element in a compound. Typically, a more reactive element will displace a less reactive one from its compound. These reactions, specifically when one element replaces another in a compound, are commonly referred to as single displacement reactions. However, they are often simply called displacement reactions. Also, the reactions in which there is an exchange of ions between the reactants are called double displacement reactions. ***(An)***

(*i*) (*a*) Identify substance 'A' in the following chemical reaction and provide a balanced chemical equation for the reaction:

Aluminium chloride ($AlCl_3$) is mixed with ammonium hydroxide (NH_4OH), resulting in the formation of 'A' along with ammonium chloride (NH_4Cl). *(1 M)*

(*b*) $Al + CuSO_4 \rightarrow$ *(1 M)*

(*ii*) Using the provided experimental setup where dry hydrogen is passed over a heated oxide of metal X, describe the observations and reactions that lead to the formation of a reddish-brown residue. Identify the metal X and explain the chemical processes involved.

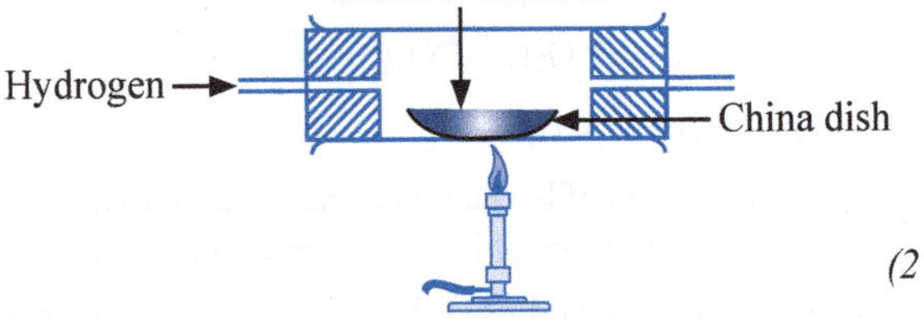

(2 M)

OR

Describe the chemical reaction that occurs when zinc reacts with dilute sulphuric acid. Include details about the gas evolved, its properties, and any observations during the reaction. *(2 M)*

Case Based-IV: Ravi took about 2 g ferrous sulphate crystals in a dry boiling tube. He then heat the boiling tube over the flame of a burner or spirit lamp. In this reaction, he observe that a single reactant breaks down to give simpler products. This is a decomposition reaction. He further reported that the ferrous sulphate crystals lose water when heated and decomposes. ***(Un)***

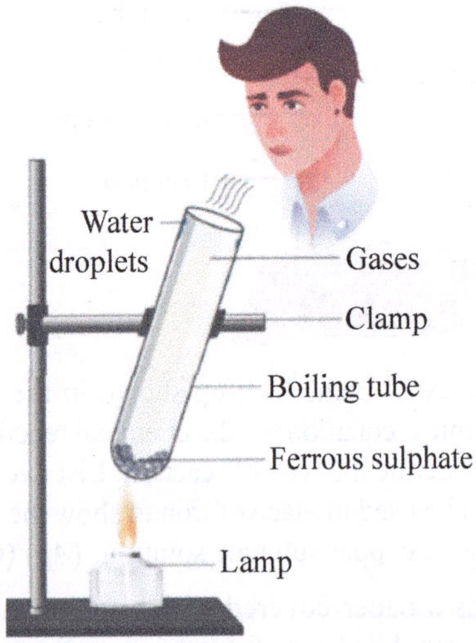

(*i*) What compound is formed when SO_2 is passed through water? *(1 M)*

(*ii*) What is the colour of ferric oxide? *(1 M)*

(*iii*) Write 4 observations of this experiment. *(2 M)*

OR

How many water molecules are present in ferrous sulphate crystals? Write its colour before and after on prolong heating. *(2 M)*

ANSWER KEYS

Multiple Choice Questions

1. (b)	2. (a)	3. (d)	4. (d)	5. (c)	6. (c)	7. (c)	8. (a)	9. (b)	10. (d)
11. (a)	12. (d)	13. (d)	14. (b)	15. (c)	16. (d)	17. (d)	18. (c)	19. (d)	20. (a)
21. (b)	22. (c)	23. (a)	24. (d)	25. (a)	26. (a)				

Assertion and Reason

1. (c)	2. (a)	3. (c)	4. (c)	5. (a)	6. (c)	7. (a)	8. (c)	9. (a)	10. (a)

HINTS & EXPLANATIONS

Multiple Choice Questions

1. (*b*) The chemical reaction involved in the burning of coal is $C(s) + O_2(g) \rightarrow CO_2(g)$

   Since, in the above reaction, C combines with O_2 to give single product CO_2, therefore, it is a combination reaction.

2. (*a*) A in AC is a cation (because it forms an ionic bond with the anion C). Since C displaces B, it implies that C is more reactive than B. For the reaction to proceed, AC must be more stable than AB, as the formation of AC is thermodynamically favorable (due to C's higher reactivity and ability to form a more stable bond with A). This implies AB is less stable compared to AC.

3. (*d*) When Zn metal reacts with dilute HCl acid, then hydrogen gas will be evolved and hence, by using a burning splinter, hydrogen gas can be identified. The reaction is:

   $Zn + 2HCl \rightarrow ZnCl_2 + H_2\uparrow$

4. (*d*) In the given reaction, MnO_2 is getting reduced as its oxidation state changes from +4 to +2 in $MnCl_2$. Similarly, HCl is getting oxidised as its oxidation state changes from −1 to 0 in Cl_2.

5. (*c*) Silver bromide (AgBr) is photosensitive and decomposes in light.
   - **P (transparent glass bottle)** allows light, so it is unsuitable.
   - **Q (opaque plastic bottle)** and **R (black paper packet)** block light, making them suitable.

6. (*c*) If an equal number of atoms are present on both sides of an equation, then it is said to be balanced.

7. (*c*) This is an oxidation-reduction reaction. A complete balanced equation is:

   $MnO_2 + 4HCl \rightarrow MnCl_2 + 2H_2O + Cl_2$

   $x = 4; y = 2; z = 1$

8. (*a*) The balanced chemical equation is:

   $2KMnO_4 + 3H_2SO_4 \rightarrow K_2SO_4 + 2MnSO_4 + 3H_2O + 5[O]$

9. (*b*) The reaction that occurs is:

   $Na_2SO_4 + BaCl_2 \rightarrow BaSO_4 + 2NaCl$

   Hence, $BaSO_4$ is present in solid state in the given reaction.

10. (*d*) From the figure, it is observed that red-coloured copper is oxidized to black coloured copper(II) oxide. The reaction that takes place is:

    $$\underset{\text{(Red)}}{2Cu} + O_2 \xrightarrow{\text{Heat}} \underset{\text{(Black)}}{2CuO}$$

11. (*a*) For a balanced chemical equation, atoms of each type should be equal on both sides of the reaction. So, the correct balanced equation will be represented as:

    $2NH_4NO_3 \rightarrow 2N_2 + 4H_2O + O_2$

12. (*d*) A more reactive metal will displace less reactive from its salt solution.

    $CuSO_4 + Fe \rightarrow FeSO_4 + Cu$

13. (*d*) $Pb(NO_3)_2 + H_2S \rightarrow \underset{\text{(Black precipitate)}}{PbS\downarrow} + 2HNO_3$

    $ZnCl_2 + H_2S \rightarrow \underset{\text{(White precipitate)}}{ZnS\downarrow} + 2HCl$

14. (*b*) In the electrolysis of water, the gas collected at the cathode is hydrogen, which produces a pop sound when exposed to a burning matchstick. The gas collected at the anode is oxygen, which makes a glowing splint burn more brightly.

15. (*c*) A decomposition reaction in which source of energy for decomposition is light is

    $2AgBr(s) \rightarrow 2Ag(s) + Br_2(g)$

16. (*d*) In a combination reaction, two or more reactants will combine to form a single product. In this reaction, heat will be evolved, so it is exothermic.

17. (*d*) According to reactivity series, a more reactive metal can displace less reactive metal from its salt solution. So, according to this, reactions given in options in (A) and (D) will take place.

18. (c) In the given reaction, MnO_2 loses oxygen and forms $MnCl_2$. Therefore, it is said that MnO_2 is reduced to $MnCl_2$. Whereas, HCl loses hydrogen and forms Cl_2. Therefore, it is said that HCl is oxidized to Cl_2.

19. (d) $CuSO_4 + H_2S \rightarrow CuS\downarrow + H_2SO_4$ is an example of double displacement type of reaction.

20. (a) The balanced equation for the decomposition of H_2O_2 is: $2H_2O_2 \rightarrow 2H_2O + O_2$

21. (b) All metals except silver are more reactive than copper. Thus, they can react with copper chloride and can decolourise it.

When calcium reacts with copper chloride, calcium chloride will be formed, which is white in colour.

22. (c) Mg is more reactive than copper, hence will displace copper from $CuSO_4$.

The reaction that occurs is:

$$\underset{(A)}{Mg} + \underset{(B)}{CuSO_4} \rightarrow \underset{(C)}{MgSO_4} + Cu$$

23. (a) The reaction between iron (III) chloride ($FeCl_3$) and sodium hydroxide (NaOH) is a double displacement reaction and it results in the formation of iron(III) hydroxide ($Fe(OH)_3$) which is a yellowish brown precipitate and sodium chloride (NaCl).

24. (d) Due to rancidity, smell and taste of food becomes bad.

25. (a) Reaction 1 (A): The combustion of methane with oxygen.

$$CH_4\,(g) + 2O_2\,(g) \rightarrow CO_2\,(g) + 2H_2O\,(g)$$

Reaction 2 (B): The reaction between glucose and oxygen.

$$\underset{\text{(Glucose)}}{C_6H_{12}O_6\,(aq)} + 6O_2\,(aq) \rightarrow 6CO_2\,(aq) + 6H_2O\,(l) + \text{energy}$$

26. (a) Salty water accelerates the process of corrosion due to the presence of electrolytes that facilitate the movement of electrons, speeding up the oxidation process in metals like iron.

Assertion and Reason

1. (c) When we mix barium hydroxide with ammonium chloride, the bottom of the test tube becomes cold due to the absorption of heat. So, it is an endothermic reaction. The reaction between ammonium chloride and barium hydroxide is not a decomposition reaction, because decomposition reaction involves the breaking down of a single compound into simpler substances.

2. (a) Burning of a candle is both a chemical and a physical change. The physical change occurs when the wax of candle melts and it loses its shape.

The chemical change is combustion of fuel in presence of oxygen to produce carbon dioxide.

3. (c) Atoms can neither be created nor be destroyed in a chemical reaction.

4. (c) Copper can displace silver from its salt solution because it is placed above in the reactivity series. Copper is more reactive than silver.

5. (a) Heat is released during an exothermic reaction along with the formation of products.

6. (c) Photosynthesis process is known as an endothermic reaction as energy in the form of sunlight is absorbed by the green plants.

7. (a) Lime water is calcium hydroxide. It reacts with CO_2 gas to form a white precipitate of calcium carbonate.

$$\underset{\text{(lime water)}}{Ca(OH)_2} + CO_2(g) \longrightarrow \underset{\text{(White ppt)}}{CaCO_3(s)} + H_2O(g)$$

8. (c) Iron articles are painted to prevent them from rusting.

9. (a) Gold and silver both have very low reactivity due to which they do not corrode in moist air.

10. (a) Nitrogen is flushed to avoid potato chips becoming rancid by preventing oxidation.

Subjective Questions

Very Short Answer Type Questions

1. (a) When the bottle is opened, the pressure is released, and carbonic acid (H_2CO_3) decomposes back into carbon dioxide and water. The chemical reaction involved in this process is

$$H_2CO_3(aq) \longrightarrow CO_2(g) + H_2O(l)$$

The bubbling and effervescence happen due to the release of CO_2 gas from the carbonic acid. *(1 M)*

(b) It is decomposition reaction. *(1 M)*

2. (a) The compound that forms the yellow precipitate is lead iodide (PbI_2). *(½ M)*

(b) When lead nitrate reacts with potassium iodide, a double displacement reaction occurs.

The reaction can be represented by the following balanced chemical equation:

$Pb(NO_3)_2 + 2KI \rightarrow PbI_2 + 2KNO_3$ *(½ M)*

In this reaction, lead nitrate ($Pb(NO_3)_2$) and potassium iodide (KI) exchange ions, resulting in the formation of lead iodide (PbI_2), which is an insoluble yellow precipitate, and potassium nitrate (KNO_3), which remains in solution. *(1 M)*

3. (i) $4Na(s) + O_2\,(g) \rightarrow 2Na_2O(s)$

Oxidised: Na is oxidised as it undergoes addition of oxygen. *(½ M)*

Reduced: Oxygen (O_2) is reduced. *(½ M)*

(ii) $CuO(s) + H_2(g) \rightarrow Cu(s) + H_2O(l)$

Oxidised: Hydrogen (H_2) is oxidised as the addition of oxygen takes place. *(½ M)*

Reduced: Copper oxide (CuO) is reduced as the removal of oxygen takes place. *(½ M)*

4. A balanced chemical equation is the one which has the equal number of atoms of each element on both the sides of the equation. *(1 M)*

It is necessary for a equation to be balanced so that it follows the law of conservation of mass i.e., the mass should remain conserved, before and after a chemical reaction. *(1 M)*

5. (*i*) When CuO (Copper oxide) is mixed with dilute HCl (Hydrochloric acid), it will give a bluish-green colour salt of cupric chloride ($CuCl_2$) and water. *(1 M)*

(*ii*) The reaction between CuO and dil. HCl is shown as: *(1 M)*

$$\underset{\text{(Copper oxide)}}{CuO(s)} + \underset{\text{(Hydrochloric acid)}}{2HCl(aq.)} \rightarrow \underset{\text{(Cupric chloride)}}{CuCl_2(aq.)} + H_2O(l)$$

6. (*a*) $Fe + SnCl_2 \rightarrow Sn + FeCl_2$ *(1 M)*

(*b*) $Fe + 2HCl \rightarrow FeCl_2 + H_2$ *(1 M)*

7. (*a*) Elements like H_2, O_2, and N_2 can be products of decomposition reactions, but they are not the products of combination reactions, where compounds are formed instead. *(1 M)*

(*b*) A good example of a reaction where both displacement and redox processes occur is:

$Zn(s) + CuSO_4(aq) \rightarrow ZnSO_4(aq) + Cu(s)$ *(1 M)*

8. Arrangement Y is likely to gather more rust because: *(1 M)*

(*i*) Rusting is a surface phenomenon. *(½ M)*

(*ii*) Arrangement Y has a larger surface area exposed to air *(½ M)*

Short Answer Type Questions

1. (*i*) In the below reaction, the colour changes from colourless ($Pb(NO_3)_2$) to yellow (PbI_2).

$Pb(NO_3)_2(aq) + 2KI(aq) \rightarrow PbI_2(s) + 2KNO_3(aq)$ *(1 M)*

(*ii*) The action of dilute sulphuric acid on zinc releases heat, thus, results in temperature rise.

$Zn(s) + H_2SO_4(aq) \rightarrow ZnSO_4(aq) + H_2(g)$ *(1 M)*

(*iii*) The reaction of Barium chloride with sodium sulphate produces Barium sulphate as the precipitate. The reaction occurs as:

$BaCl_2(aq) + Na_2SO_4(aq) \rightarrow BaSO_4(s)\downarrow + 2NaCl(aq)$ *(1 M)*

2. (*i*) To make water more conductive before electrolysis, acid is added to the solution. This makes it simple for the current to move through the solution. *(½ M)*

At the cathode, hydrogen gas is released, whereas at the anode, oxygen gas is released. *(½ M)*

The cathode gas collection volume is twice as large as the anode gas collection volume.

$2H_2O(l) \rightarrow 2H_2(g) + O_2(g)$ *(1 M)*

Nailing the Right Answer

Students should clearly explain the purpose of adding drops of acid and identify gases correctly. They should correctly write which gas is released at cathode and which one at anode. Describe the relationship between the volume of gas collected at the anode and cathode using balanced chemical equation.

(*ii*) Silver metal and chlorine gas are produced during the decomposition of silver chloride when it is exposed to light. The reaction is known as photolytic reaction. *(1 M)*

The reaction that takes place is:

$2AgCl \xrightarrow{\text{Sunlight}} 2Ag + Cl_2$

3. When 2g of silver chloride is taken in a china dish and is placed in sunlight for some time, the solution turns grey. *(1 M)*

This is a decomposition reaction. *(1 M)*

The balanced chemical reaction that occurs is:

$2AgCl \xrightarrow{\text{Sunlight}} 2Ag + Cl_2$ *(1 M)*

4. The complete balanced equations are:

(*i*) $2NaOH + Zn \rightarrow Na_2ZnO_2 + H_2$ *(1 M)*

(*ii*) $CaCO_3 + CO_2 + H_2O \rightarrow Ca(HCO_3)_2$ *(1 M)*

(*iii*) $HCl + H_2O \rightarrow H_3O^+ + Cl^-$ *(1 M)*

5. (*a*) The reaction between barium chloride ($BaCl_2$) and sodium sulphite (Na_2SO_3) can be represented as:

$BaCl_2(aq.) + Na_2SO_3(aq.) \rightarrow BaSO_3(s) + 2NaCl(aq.)$ *(1 M)*

(*b*) This precipitation reaction can also be called as double displacement reaction. *(1 M)*

(*c*) The reaction can be represented as:

$BaSO_3(s) + 2HCl(aq.) \rightarrow BaCl_2(aq.) + SO_2(g) + H_2O(l)$ *(½ M)*

The formation of soluble barium chloride and the release of SO_2 gas cause the white precipitate to disappear. *(½ M)*

6. The chemical equation involved for the chemical reaction is

$Fe(s) + CuSO_4(aq.) \rightarrow FeSO_4(aq.) + Cu(s)$ *(1 M)*

The above reaction is a type of displacement reaction. *(½ M)*

This is a type of chemical reaction in which a more reactive element displaces the less reactive element from it's salt solution. *(½ M)*

The other two metals that can be used in place of Fe are the metals that are more reactive from copper. It can be seen from the reactivity series. Hence, magnesium and aluminium can be taken. *(1 M)*

Topper's Explanation

(1) $Fe(s) + CuSO_4(aq) \longrightarrow FeSO_4(aq) + Cu(s)$

(2) Displacement reaction. In this reaction, a more reactive element displaces a less reactive element from its compound (solution)

(3) Zinc (Zn) & Aluminium (Al).

7. (*a*) The most likely substance on the paper that Tina found could be silver chloride (AgCl) or silver bromide (AgBr) *(1 M)*

(*b*) $2AgCl \rightarrow 2Ag + Cl_2$ *(1 M)*

OR

$2AgBr \rightarrow 2Ag + Br_2$

(*c*) Used in black and white photography *(1 M)*

8. (*a*) A substance which gets oxidized is known as reducing agent.

(*i*) NH_3 - Reducing agent as it is getting oxidized to NO. *(½ M)*

(*ii*) H_2O - Reducing agent as it is getting oxidized to HOF. *(½ M)*

(*iii*) CO - reducing agent as it is getting oxidized to CO_2. *(½ M)*

(*iv*) H_2 - reducing agent as it is getting oxidized to H_2O. *(½ M)*

(*b*) In a redox reaction, reduction and oxidation takes place simultaneously.

Oxidation - It is defined as the gain of oxygen. *(½ M)*

Reduction - It is defined as the loss of oxygen. *(½ M)*

Long Answer Type Questions

1. (*a*) (*i*) Yes, it is. *(½ M)*

There is an exchange of ions between the reactants:

- Zinc oxide (ZnO) reacts with hydrochloric acid (HCl), resulting in the formation of zinc chloride ($ZnCl_2$) and water (H_2O). This ion exchange characterises a double displacement reaction. *(1 M)*

(*ii*) No, this is not a redox reaction. *(½ M)*

Since none of the reactants have gained or lost an electron. *(1 M)*

(*iii*) This reaction is an example of a neutralisation reaction as an acid (HCl) and a base (ZnO) are reacting together to form a salt($ZnCl_2$) and water (H_2O). *(1 M)*

(*b*) The electrolysis of water is considered endothermic because it requires the input of electrical energy to break the water molecules into hydrogen and oxygen gases. *(1 M)*

2. (*a*) $Mg(s)+Cl_2(g) \rightarrow MgCl_2(s)$ *(½ M)*

This type of reaction is called a combination reaction or a synthesis reaction. *(½ M)*

(*b*) $2HgO(s) \xrightarrow{\text{Heat}} 2Hg(l) + O_2(g)$ *(½ M)*

This is a thermal decomposition reaction. *(½ M)*

(*c*) $2Na(s) + S(s) \xrightarrow{\text{Fuse}} Na_2S(s)$ *(½ M)*

This is a combination reaction. *(½ M)*

(*d*) $TiCl_4(l) + 2Mg(s) \longrightarrow Ti(s) + 2MgCl_2(s)$ *(½ M)*

This is a displacement reaction. *(½ M)*

(*e*) $CaO(s) + SiO_2(s) \longrightarrow CaSiO_3(s)$ *(½ M)*

This is a combination reaction. *(½ M)*

3. (*a*) MnO_2 is getting reduced to Mn as oxygen is getting removed from it. *(½ M)*

Al is getting oxidised to Al_2O_3 as oxygen is getting added to it. *(½ M)*

Also,Oxidizing agent- MnO_2 *(½ M)*

Reducing agent-Al *(½ M)*

(*b*) • The colour of ferrous sulphate crystals is green. *(½ M)*

• On heating, $FeSO_4.7H_2O$ gets decomposed to form ferrous sulphate which is white in colour. Then on further heating, it decomposes to give reddish brown solid substance Fe_2O_3. *(½ M)*

When ferrous sulphate crystals are heated strongly, the products obtained are: Fe_2O_3, SO_2 and SO_3. This is a decomposition reaction. *(1 M)*

The chemical reaction that takes place is:

$$\underset{\text{Anhydrous ferrous Sulphate (white)}}{2FeSO_4(s)} \xrightarrow{\text{heat}} \underset{\text{Ferric oxide (brown)}}{Fe_2O_3(s)} + SO_2\uparrow(g) + SO_3\uparrow(g)$$ *(1 M)*

4. (*a*) (*i*) *X*- Copper *(½ M)*

Y- Copper (II) oxide. *(½ M)*

(*ii*) In the first reaction, oxidation will take place, while the second one is a redox reaction. *(1 M)*

(*iii*) $\underset{\text{Copper 'X'}}{2Cu(s)} + \underset{\text{Oxygen}}{O_2(g)} \xrightarrow{\text{Heat}} \underset{\text{Copper (II) oxide 'Y'}}{2CuO(s)}$ *(½ M)*

$\underset{\text{Copper (II) oxide 'Y'}}{CuO(s)} + \underset{\text{Hydrogen}}{H_2(g)} \xrightarrow{\text{Heat}} \underset{\text{Copper 'X'}}{Cu(s)} + \underset{\text{Water}}{H_2O(l)}$ *(½ M)*

(*b*) A reaction in which an insoluble solid, known as the precipitate, is formed is called a precipitation reaction. *(1 M)*

For example:

$Na_2CO_3(aq.) + CaCl_2(aq.) \rightarrow CaCO_3(s)\downarrow + 2NaCl(aq.)$ *(1 M)*

5. (*a*)

Displacement Reactions	Double Displacement Reactions
A more reactive metals displaces a less reactive metal from its salt solution.	Two reactants in the solution mutually exchange their ions.
The general reaction is represented as: $A + B-C \rightarrow A-C + B$	The general reaction is represented as: $AB + CD \rightarrow AC + BD$
Example: Reaction between iron and copper sulphate. In this reaction, more reactive Fe displaces less reactive Cu from its $CuSO_4$ solution.	Example: Reaction between silver nitrate and sodium chloride. In this reaction, $AgNO_3$ and NaCl exchange Cl^- and NO_3^- ions mutually between them.
The balanced chemical equation is as follows: $Fe(s) + CuSO_4(aq.) \rightarrow Cu(s) + FeSO_4(aq.)$	The balanced chemical equation is as follows: $AgNO_3(aq.) + NaCl(aq.) \rightarrow AgCl(s) + NaNO_3(aq.)$

(3 M)

(*b*) In combination reaction, two or more simpler substances combine together to form a single product. In decomposition reaction, a single compound splits to give rise to two or more simple substances. Hence they are opposite to each other. *(1 M)*

Example of decomposition reaction:

$$\underset{\text{Copper carbonate}}{CuCO_3(s)} \xrightarrow{\text{Heat}} \underset{\text{Copper oxide}}{CuO(s)} + \underset{\text{Carbon dioxide}}{CO_2(g)} \quad (½ M)$$

Example of combination reaction.

$C(s) + O_2(g) \rightarrow CO_2(g)$ *(½ M)*

Case Based Questions

Case Based-I

(*i*) According to the given information, gas evolved is CO_2. *(1 M)*

(*ii*) He identified the gas by passing it through lime water. Lime water turns milky on passing CO_2 gas through it. *(1 M)*

(*iii*) The name of the product formed during the reaction is calcium chloride ($CaCl_2$). *(1 M)*

(*iv*) It helps to conserve the mass of reactants and products. *(1 M)*

Case Based-II

(*i*) The balanced equation is:

$HCl + NaOH \rightarrow NaCl + H_2O$ *(1 M)*

(*ii*) In the reaction between HCl and NaOH, heat is evolved which means the reaction will be exothermic and hence, temperature will increase. *(1 M)*

(*iii*) (*a*) The reaction between HCl and NaOH is:

$HCl + NaOH \rightarrow NaCl + H_2O$ *(½ M)*

The compound formed is sodium chloride (NaCl). *(½ M)*

(*b*) The reaction between an acid and a base is known as an acid-base reaction or neutralization reaction. *(1 M)*

Case Based-III

(*i*) (*a*) In the given chemical reaction, substance 'A' is aluminium hydroxide ($Al(OH)_3$). The balanced chemical equation for the reaction is as follows:

$$AlCl_3(aq.) + 3NH_4OH(aq.) \rightarrow \underset{(A)}{Al(OH)_3(s)} + 3NH_4Cl(aq.)$$

(1 M)

(*b*) In this displacement reaction, aluminium (Al) displaces copper from copper sulphate ($CuSO_4$), resulting in the formation of aluminium sulphate ($Al_2(SO_4)$ and copper metal (Cu). The balanced chemical equation is:

$2Al + 3CuSO_4 \rightarrow Al_2(SO_4)_3 + 3Cu$ *(1 M)*

(*ii*) The reddish-brown residue is likely to be copper (Cu). When hydrogen reduces copper oxide (CuO), it forms copper metal (Cu). Copper has a characteristic reddish-brown colour. The chemical process involved is a reduction reaction, where hydrogen acts as a reducing agent, leading to the formation of the metal in its elemental form. *(1 M)*

The reaction occurs as:

$$\underset{\text{Copper oxide}}{CuO} + \underset{\text{Hydrogen}}{H_2} \xrightarrow{\text{Heat}} \underset{\text{Copper (Reddish-brown)}}{Cu\downarrow} + \underset{\text{Water vapour}}{H_2O} \quad (1 M)$$

Mistakes 101 : What not to do!

Not correctly identifying the metal X or providing an incomplete explanation of the chemical processes involved in the formation of the reddish-brown residue.

OR

When zinc (Zn) reacts with dilute sulphuric acid (H_2SO_4), a chemical reaction takes place. The reaction can be represented as:

$Zn + H_2SO_4 \rightarrow ZnSO_4 + H_2\uparrow$ *(1 M)*

During this reaction, zinc sulphate ($ZnSO_4$) is formed, and hydrogen gas (H_2) is evolved. Hydrogen gas is colourless, odourless, and burns with a pop sound when ignited. As the reaction progresses, you would observe the formation of bubbles (due to the evolution of hydrogen gas) and the solution turning cloudy as zinc sulphate is produced. *(1 M)*

Key Takeaways

This question teaches students single displacement reactions and their characteristics. Observations like bubbling and solution cloudiness indicate a chemical reaction.

Case Based-IV

(*i*) SO_2 on reaction with water forms sulphurous acid. *(½ M)*

$$\underset{\text{sulphur dioxide}}{SO_2(g)} + \underset{\text{water}}{H_2O(l)} \rightarrow \underset{\text{Sulphurous acid}}{H_2SO_3(l)} \quad (½ M)$$

(*ii*) Generally, the colour of ferric oxide is brown. *(1 M)*

(*iii*) (*a*) Water vapour will be evolved. *(½ M)*

(*b*) Change in colour will take place. *(½ M)*

(*c*) Pungent and suffocating odour of SO_2 gas will be produced. *(½ M)*

(*d*) Reddish brown coloured solid i.e.; Fe_2O_3 is obtained. *(½ M)*

OR

- The chemical formula of ferrous sulphate crystals is $FeSO_4.7H_2O$. Hence, it contains 7 water molecules. *(1 M)*
- Before heating it is green in colour and on heating, it loses water molecules to become anhydrous (white) and then on further heating, it decomposes to give reddish brown solid substance Fe_2O_3. *(½ M)*
- The chemical reaction involved is:

$$\underset{\substack{\text{(Ferrous sulphate)}\\\text{(Green)}}}{2FeSO_4(s)} \xrightarrow{\text{Heat}} \underset{\substack{\text{(Ferric oxide)}\\\text{(Reddish brown)}}}{Fe_2O_3(s)} + SO_2(g) + SO_3(g) \quad (½ M)$$

2 ACIDS, BASES AND SALTS

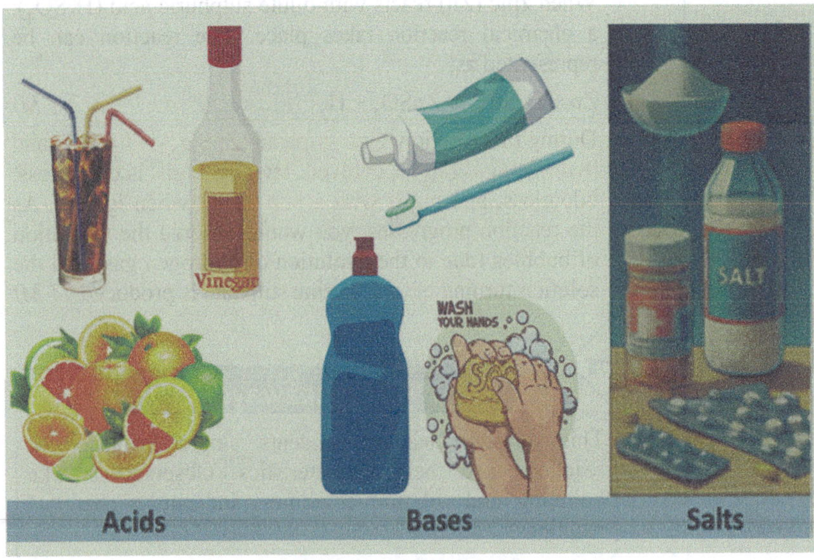

Acids, bases, and salts play a crucial role in our daily lives, influencing everything from health to food products. The tanginess of citrus fruits, fizz in soft drinks and the sharp taste of vinegar enhance the flavours in our food. Bases are key ingredients in soap, detergents and toothpaste while common salts season our meals and antacids helps relieve indigestion.

SYLLABUS & WEIGHTAGE

LIST OF CONCEPT NAMES	YEARS				
	2020	2022 TERM-1	2023	2024	2025
Acids, Bases & Indicators (Definitions in terms of furnishing of H^+ and OH^- ions, General properties, Examples and uses, neutralization)	—	3 Q*	1 Q (2 M)	1 Q (1 M)	1 Q (3 M)
pH and Importance of pH (Concept of pH scale , importance of pH in everyday life)	—	2 Q*	1 Q (1 M)	2 Q (1 M each)	—
Salts (Preparation and uses of Sodium Hydroxide, Bleaching powder, Baking soda, Washing soda and Plaster of Paris)	1 Q (5 M)	3 Q*	1 Q (1 M) 1 Q (2 M) 1 Q (3 M)	1 Q (1 M)	1 Q (1 M) 1 Q (2 M) 1 Q (3 M)

**All questions were of MCQ type and carried equal marks.*

For the year 2021, the exam was not conducted.

CONCEPT MAP

To Access One Shot Revision Video Scan This QR Code

Acids, bases and Salts

pH SCALE (CBSE 2024, 2022 Term-I)

- pH = –log[H^+]
- The values on the pH scale range from 0 to 14.
- For acidic solutions, pH < 7
- For neutral solutions, pH = 7
- For basic solutions, pH > 7

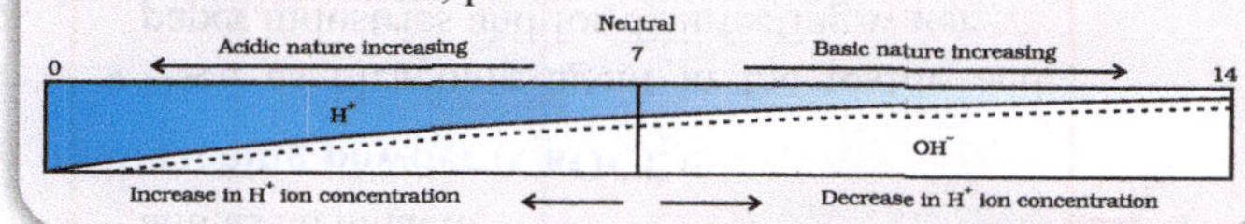

Bases

Classification

Strong Bases	Weak Bases
Produce more OH– ions in aqueous solutions	Produce less OH^- ions in aqueous solutions
E.g. → NaOH	E.g. → NH_4OH

Properties

Physical Properties (CBSE 2022 Term-I)
- Bitter in taste
- Aqueous solution conducts electricity
- Soapy in touch
- Bases that are soluble in water : Alkali

Note: All alkalis are bases but all bases are not alkali.

Chemical Properties
- Base + Metal → Salt + H_2↑ (CBSE 2020)
- Base + Non-metal oxide → Salt + H_2O

Indicators

Type

Synthetic Indicators
- Methyl orange (Natural colour → orange)
  Acid → Red colour,
  Base → Yellow colour
  (CBSE 2022 Term-I, 2020)
- Phenolphthalein (Natural colour → colourless)
  Acid → Colourless,
  Base → Pink colour

Type

Natural Indicators
- Turmeric

Turmeric

Acid → Yellow colour,
Base → Red colour
- Red Cabbage

Red Cabbage

Acid → Red colour,
Base → Green colour
- Litmus paper (CBSE 2022 Term-I)

Acid → Turns blue litmus red
Base → Turns red litmus blue

Type

Olfactory indicators
(based on odour/smell)

Onion

Vanilla extract

Clove oil

Acids

Classification

Strong Acids	Weak Acids
Produce more H^+ ions in aqueous solutions	Produce less H^+ ions in aqueous solutions
E.g. → HCl, HNO_3, H_2SO_4	E.g. → Citric acid

Sources (CBSE 2022 Term-I)

Natural source	Acid	Natural source	Acid
Vinegar	Acetic acid	Sour milk (Curd)	Lactic acid
Orange	Citric acid	Lemon	Citric acid
Tamarind	Tartaric acid	Ant sting	Methanoic acid
Tomato	Oxalic acid	Nettle sting	Methanoic acid

Properties

Physical Properties
- Sour in taste
- Aqueous solution conducts electricity
- Corrosive in nature

Chemical Properties
- Metal + Acid →
  Metal salt + H_2↑ (burns with a pop sound)
- Metal Carbonate + Acid →
  Metal salt + CO_2↑ + H_2O
  (turns lime water milky)
  (CBSE 2023, 2022 Term-I)
- Metal Hydrogen Carbonate + Acid →
  Metal Salt + CO_2↑ + H_2O
- Neutralisation: Acid + Base → Salt + Water
- Metal oxide + Acid → Salt + H_2O

Salts

Acids, bases and Salts → Salts

Types of salts CBSE 2025, 2024, 2022 Term-I

Basic	Acidic	Neutral
• Salts of strong base + weak acid • pH > 7 • E.g; Na_2CO_3, K_3PO_4 etc.	• Salts of strong acid + weak base • pH < 7 • E.g; NH_4Cl, $(NH_4)_2SO_4$ etc.	• Salts of strong acid + strong base • pH = 7 • E.g; NaCl, $NaNO_3$ etc.

Uses:

Common Salt (NaCl):

- Important raw material for formation of many compounds.

Caustic Soda (NaOH):

- Used in the manufacturing of soaps and detergents.

Washing Soda ($Na_2CO_3 \cdot 10H_2O$): CBSE 2020

- Remove permanent hardness of water.

Baking soda ($NaHCO_3$): CBSE 2022 Term-I

- Used in the manufacturing of baking powder and as an antacid.

Bleaching powder ($CaOCl_2$):

- Used as bleaching agent in the textile and paper industries and for disinfecting water.

Plaster of Paris (POP):

- Used as plasters for setting broken and fractured bones; for making moulds.

Examples

- **Common Salt (NaCl)** CBSE 2025

  $NaOH\,(aq) + HCl\,(aq) \rightarrow NaCl\,(aq) + H_2O\,(l)$

- **Caustic Soda (NaOH)** CBSE 2025, 2020

  Chlor-Alkali Process:

  $\underset{\text{(Brine)}}{2NaCl\,(aq)} + 2H_2O(l) \xrightarrow{\text{Electrolysis}} 2NaOH\,(aq) + \underset{\text{At anode}}{Cl_2\uparrow} + \underset{\text{At cathode}}{H_2\uparrow}$

- **Washing Soda ($Na_2CO_3 \cdot 10H_2O$)** CBSE 2025, 2023, 2020

  $Na_2CO_3 + 10H_2O \rightarrow Na_2CO_3 \cdot 10H_2O$

- **Baking soda ($NaHCO_3$)** CBSE 2025, 2023

  $NaCl + NH_3 + H_2O + CO_2 \rightarrow NaHCO_3 + NH_4Cl$

  $2NaHCO_3 \xrightarrow{\text{heat}} Na_2CO_3 + CO_2\uparrow + H_2O$

- **Bleaching powder ($CaOCl_2$)** CBSE 2020

  $\underset{\text{(Slaked lime)}}{Ca(OH)_2} + Cl_2 \rightarrow CaOCl_2 + H_2O$

- **Blue vitriol ($CuSO_4 \cdot 5H_2O$)** CBSE 2023

  $\underset{\text{(Blue)}}{CuSO_4 \cdot 5H_2O} \xrightarrow{\text{heat}} \underset{\text{(White)}}{CuSO_4} + 5H_2O$

- **Plaster of Paris (POP)** CBSE 2023, 2022 Term-I

  $\underset{\text{(Gypsum)}}{CaSO_4 \cdot 2H_2O} \xrightarrow{\text{heat/100°C}} \underset{\text{(POP)}}{CaSO_4 \cdot \frac{1}{2}H_2O} + 1\frac{1}{2}H_2O$

1 ACIDS, BASES AND INDICATORS

NCERT Definitions (Commonly asked in 1 mark)

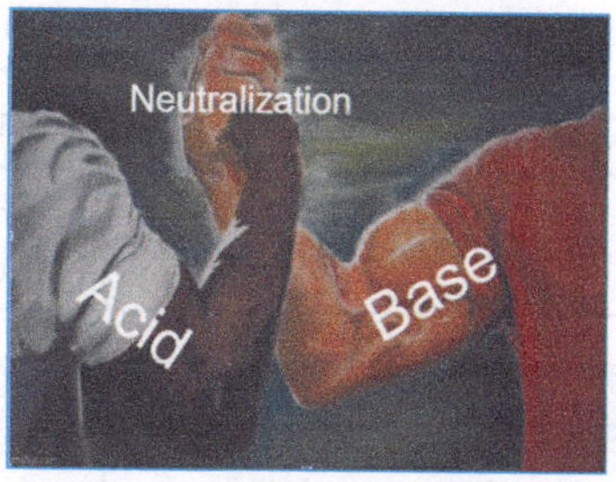

- **Acids:** The substances that dissociate in aqueous solution to give **H^+ ions**. For example, HCl, HNO_3.
- **Bases:** The substances that dissociate in aqueous solution to give **OH^- ions**. For example, NaOH, KOH.
- **Neutralization:** The reaction between an acid and a base to produce water and salt.

  Acid + Base → Salt + Water

  Example: $HCl + NaOH \rightarrow NaCl + H_2O$
- **Indicators:** The chemical compounds that change its colour in presence of an acid or a base. For example: Litmus, methyl orange, phenolphthalein.

Indicator	Colour in Acid	Colour in Base
Litmus (Blue/Red)	Blue turns red	Red turns blue
Phenolphthalein	Colourless	Pink
Methyl Orange	Red	Yellow

- **Olfactory indicators:** A substance that gives a **distinct odour** in acidic and basic medium. For example: Onion, vanilla extract, clove oil etc.

- **Dilution:** Mixing an acid or base with water results in decrease in the concentration of ions (H_3O^+/OH^-) per unit volume.

Important Facts

01 A plant belonging to the division *Thallophyta* is used to extract litmus solution (a purple dye). *~Litmus*

02 Gas which turns lime water milky but excess of it makes solution colourless. *~CO_2*

03 Metallic oxides are **basic** in nature and non-metallic oxides are **acidic** in nature.

04 Strong acids and bases conduct electricity due to the production of ions in solution, while substances like glucose and alcohol do not conduct electricity since they are non ionisable.

05 Dissolving an acid in water is an **exothermic reaction**, that is why, during dilution, the acid must always be added slowly to water with constant stirring.

Classification

Acids (On the Basis of their Strength)		
Characteristics	**Strong Acids**	**Weak Acids**
Ionisation	Completely dissociate in water	Partially dissociate in water
Concentration	Produces more $[H^+]$ ions	Produces less $[H^+]$ ions
Conductivity	High conductivity	Low conductivity
Reaction with Metals	Reacts more vigorously	Reacts less vigorously
Examples	Hydrochloric acid (HCl), Sulphuric acid (H_2SO_4), Nitric acid (HNO_3)	Acetic acid (CH_3COOH), Carbonic acid (H_2CO_3)

Bases (On the Basis of their Strength)		
Characteristics	**Strong Bases**	**Weak Bases**
Ionisation	Completely dissociate in water	Partially dissociate in water
Concentration	Produces more $[OH^-]$ ions	Produces less $[OH^-]$ ions
Conductivity	High conductivity	Low conductivity
Reaction with Metals	Reacts more vigorously	Reacts less vigorously
Examples	Sodium hydroxide (NaOH), Potassium hydroxide (KOH)	Ammonium hydroxide (NH_4OH), Zinc hydroxide $[Zn(OH)_2]$

Acids (On the Basis of Source)		
Type	**Characteristics**	**Examples**
Organic Acid	Contains carbon; found naturally; typically weaker	Acetic acid (CH_3COOH), Citric acid ($C_6H_8O_7$)
Inorganic Acid	Does not contain carbon; derived from one or more inorganic compounds; generally stronger	Hydrochloric acid (HCl), Sulphuric acid (H_2SO_4)

Indicators		
Type	**Characteristics**	**Examples**
Natural	Derived from plants; colour changes depend on pH	Litmus, turmeric, red cabbage juice
Synthetic	Man-made chemicals; specific colour changes at certain pH	Phenolphthalein, methyl orange
Olfactory	Change in smell is observed instead of colour change	Vanilla extract, onion juice

Difference Between **(Commonly asked in 2-3 marks)**

Acids vs Bases (On the Basis of Physical Properties)		
Characteristics	**Acids**	**Bases**
Taste	Sour in taste	Bitter in taste
Effect on litmus	Turns blue litmus red	Turns red litmus blue

In water	Give H^+ ions in aqueous solution	Give OH^- ions in aqueous solution
pH	pH < 7	pH > 7
Touch	Non Soapy	Soapy

Acids vs Bases (On the basis of Chemical Properties)		
Characteristics	**Acids**	**Bases**
Reaction with metal carbonates	Acid reacts with metal carbonates to give salt, carbon dioxide and water. $Na_2CO_3(s) + 2HCl\ (aq) \rightarrow 2NaCl\ (aq) + H_2O\ (l) + CO_2\ (g)$	No reaction
Reaction with metal hydrogen carbonate	Acid reacts with metal hydrogen carbonates to give salt, carbon dioxide and water. $NaHCO_3(s) + HCl\ (aq) \rightarrow NaCl\ (aq) + H_2O\ (l) + CO_2\ (g)$	No reaction
Reaction with oxides	Acids react with metal oxides to give salt and water. $CuO + H_2SO_4 \rightarrow CuSO_4 + H_2O$	Bases react with non-metal oxides to give salt and water. $Ca(OH)_2 + CO_2 \rightarrow CaCO_3 + H_2O$

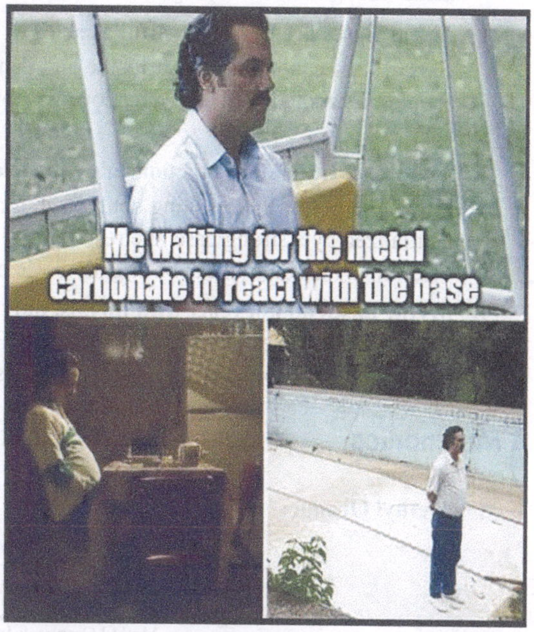

Alkali vs Base	
Alkali	**Base**
Bases that dissolve in water are alkalis.	Bases may or may not be water soluble.
All alkali are bases	All bases are not alkali.
Examples are NaOH, KOH, $Ca(OH)_2$.	Examples are CuO, $Mg(OH)_2$.

Real Life Application Based Questions

1. **What role does acids like citric acid, acetic acid, and ascorbic acid play in food and beverages?**

Ans. These acids serve multiple purposes in food and beverages. Citric acid, for example, adds a flavour and acts as a preservative in soft drinks, while acetic acid gives vinegar its distinctive sour taste. Ascorbic acid, also known as vitamin C, is essential for nutrition and also helps to preserve the freshness of food by acting as an antioxidant.

2. **Do you know significance of acids in pharmaceuticals, specifically mentioning acetylsalicylic acid?***

Ans. Acids are integral in pharmaceuticals for creating effective medications. **Acetylsalicylic acid**, commonly known as aspirin, is an excellent example. It is used as a pain reliever and an anti-inflammatory medication, helping to reduce fever.

3. **Why is sulphuric acid important in the functioning of lead-acid batteries?**

Ans. Sulphuric acid is used in lead-acid batteries to because it participates in the electrochemical reactions that generate electrical energy with lead, helps in voltage regulation through its concentration, and provides conductivity necessary for the flow of electricity.

4. **In what way do bases contribute to the effectiveness of household cleaning products?**

Ans. Bases such as sodium hydroxide or ammonia are effective in cleaning because they react with fatty acids present in grease and oils to produce soap and glycerol in a reaction known as saponification. This process transforms greasy residues into soap, which is washable with water, making the cleaning process much more effective.

** Concepts beyond the board exam syllabus, offering deeper insight and critical thinking on NCERT topics.*

Myth Buster

- **Myth: All acids are dangerous and can burn your skin.**

  Fact: Not all acids are highly corrosive. While strong acids like sulphuric acid or hydrochloric acid can cause burns, many weak acids like acetic acid (vinegar) or citric acid (found in citrus fruits) are relatively harmless and widely used in everyday life.

- **Myth: Bases are not as harmful as acids.**

  Fact: Bases can be just as corrosive and dangerous as acids. Strong bases like sodium hydroxide can cause severe burns and should be handled with care. The potential for harm depends on the strength and concentration of the base, not the fact that it is a base.

- **Myth: Neutralization reactions always yield a neutral solution with a pH of 7.**

  Fact: The pH of the resulting solution in a neutralization reaction depends on the acid and base involved. If a strong acid is neutralized by a strong base, the resulting solution will be neutral (pH 7). However, if a weak acid reacts with a strong base, or vice versa, the solution can be slightly basic or acidic respectively.

- **Myth: Bases do not react with metals, only acids do.**

  Fact: Certain bases can react with metals. For example, when sodium hydroxide (a base) reacts with zinc, hydrogen gas is released, similar to the reaction between acids and certain metals.

Mnemonics

- **Methyl Orange:**

"My Aunt's Rug Became Yellow"

My	Aunt's	Rug	Became	Yellow
↓	↓	↓	↓	↓
Methyl Orange →	In Acid →	Turns Red	In Base →	Turns Yellow

- **Phenolphthalein:**

"Paintings At College Bring Peace"

Paintings	At	College	Bring	Peace
↓	↓	↓	↓	↓
Phenolphthalein →	In Acid →	Turns Colourless	In Base →	Turns Pink

- **Litmus:**
  - B A R

    ↓ ↓ ↓

    Blue $\xrightarrow{\text{Acid}}$ Red
  - R B B

    ↓ ↓ ↓

    Red $\xrightarrow{\text{Base}}$ Blue

COMPETENCY BASED SOLVED EXAMPLES

Multiple Choice Questions (1 M)

1. Acid present in tomato is: ***(Re)***

(a) Methanoic acid (b) Acetic acid

(c) Lactic acid (d) Oxalic acid

2. Which of the following phenomena occur, when a small amount of acid is added to water? ***(An)***

(i) Ionisation **(ii) Neutralisation**

(iii) Dilution **(iv) Salt formation**

(a) (i) and (ii) (b) (i) and (iii)

(c) (ii) and (iii) (d) (ii) and (iv)

3. What happens when a solution of an acid is mixed with a solution of a base in a test tube? ***(An)***

(i) The temperature of the solution increases

(ii) The temperature of the solution decreases

(iii) The temperature of the solution remains the same

(iv) Salt formation takes place

(a) (i) only (b) (i) and (iii)

(c) (ii) and (iii) (d) (i) and (iv)

4. **In the experimental setup given below, it is observed that on passing the gas produced in the reaction in the solution 'X', the solution 'X' first turns milky and then colourless.** ***(An)* (CBSE, 2023)**

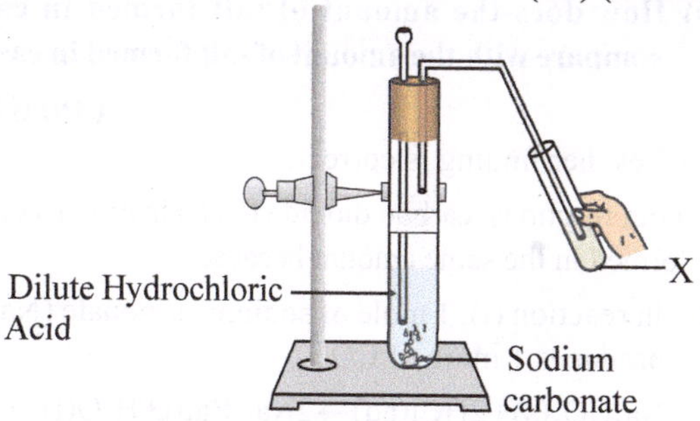

The option that justifies the above stated observation is that 'X' is aqueous calcium hydroxide and

(*a*) it turns milky due to carbon dioxide gas liberated in the reaction and after sometime it becomes colourless due to formation of calcium carbonate.

(*b*) it turns milky due to formation of calcium carbonate and on passing excess of carbon dioxide it becomes colourless due to formation of calcium hydrogen carbonate which is soluble in water.

(*c*) it turns milky due to passing of carbon dioxide through it. It turns colourless as on further passing carbon dioxide, sodium hydrogen carbonate is formed which is soluble in water.

(*d*) the carbon dioxide liberated during the reaction turns lime water milky due to formation of calcium hydrogen carbonate and after some time it turns colourless due to formation of calcium carbonate which is soluble in water.

5. **Which of the following is(are) true when HCl (g) is passed through water?** ***(Un)***

(*i*) It does not ionise in the solution as it is a covalent compound.

(*ii*) It ionises in the solution

(*iii*) It gives both hydrogen and hydroxyl ion in the solution

(*iv*) It forms hydronium ion in the solution due to the combination of hydrogen ion with water molecule

(*a*) (*i*) only (*b*) (*iii*) only

(*c*) (*ii*) and (*iv*) (*d*) (*iii*) and (*iv*)

6. **Select from the following the statement which is true for bases.** ***(Un)***

(*a*) Bases are bitter and turn blue litmus red.

(*b*) Bases have a pH less than 7.

(*c*) Bases are sour and change red litmus to blue.

(*d*) Bases turn pink when a drop of phenolphthalein is added to them.

7. **Which of the following oxide(s) is/are soluble in water to form alkalies?** ***(Un)***

(*i*) Na_2O **(*ii*) SO_2**

(*iii*) K_2O **(*iv*) NO_2**

(*a*) (*i*) and (*iii*) (*b*) (*i*) only

(*c*) (*ii*) and (*iv*) (*d*) (*iii*) only

8. **Sodium hydroxide is termed an alkali while Ferric hydroxide is not because:** ***(An)***

(*a*) Sodium hydroxide is a strong base, while Ferric hydroxide is a weak base.

(*b*) Sodium hydroxide is a base which is soluble in water while Ferric hydroxide is also a base but it is not soluble in water.

(*c*) Sodium hydroxide is a strong base while Ferric hydroxide is a strong acid.

(*d*) Sodium hydroxide and Ferric hydroxide both are strong bases but the solubility of Sodium hydroxide in water is comparatively higher than that of Ferric hydroxide.

Assertion and Reason (1 M)

Direction: The following questions consist of two statements – Assertion (A) and Reason (R). Answer these questions by selecting the appropriate option given below:

(*a*) Both A and R are true, and R is the correct explanation of A.

(*b*) Both A and R are true, but R is not the correct explanation of A.

(*c*) A is true, but R is false.

(*d*) A is false, but R is true.

1. **Assertion (A) :** It is advised that while diluting an acid one should add water to acid and not acid to water keeping the solution continuously stirred.

Reason (R) : The process of dissolving an acid into water is highly exothermic. ***(Un)***

2. **Assertion (A):** On adding sulphuric acid to water the resulting aqueous solution get corrosive.

Reason (R): Hydronium ions are responsible for corrosive action. ***(Un)***

3. **Assertion (A):** Phenolphthalein is an acid-base indicator.

Reason (R): Phenolphthalein gives different colours in acidic and basic medium. ***(Re)***

4. **Assertion (A):** A damp red litmus paper turns blue when exposed to a basic gas.

Reason (R): Basic gases increase the OH^- ion concentration on the moist surface of the litmus paper, causing it to turn blue. ***(Un)***

5. **Assertion (A):** Hydrochloric acid (HCl) is stronger than acetic acid (CH_3COOH).

Reason (R): HCl dissociates partially in water, releasing less H^+ ions compared to the complete dissociation of acetic acid. ***(Un)***

Subjective Questions

Very Short Answer Type Questions (2 M)

1. **Write the name of the acid present in the following substances:** ***(Re)***

(*i*) Tamarind **(*ii*) Orange**

Ans. (*i*) Tamarind – Tartaric acid *(1 M)*

(*ii*) Orange – Citric acid *(1 M)*

2. **Why does an aqueous solution of an acid conduct electricity?** **(*Un*) (NCERT Intext)**

Ans. An aqueous solution of an acid conducts electricity due to the presence of ions in the solution. *(1 M)*

When an acid dissolves in water, it dissociates into positively charged hydrogen ions (H^+) and the corresponding negatively charged ions. *(½ M)*

These ions facilitate the flow of electric charge through the solution. *(½ M)*

3. **Why should curd and sour substances not be kept in brass and copper vessels?** **(*Ap*) (NCERT Intext)**

Ans. Curd and sour substances should not be kept in brass and copper vessels because of the following reason:

1. **Chemical reaction:** These substances contain acids that can react with copper and brass to form copper compounds that are toxic if ingested, potentially leading to food poisoning. *(1 M)*
2. **Metal Corrosion:** The acidic reaction can also corrode the metal, damaging the vessel and contaminating the food with metal ions, which are unsafe for health. *(1 M)*

4. **A student adds a spoon full of powdered sodium hydrogen carbonate to a flask containing ethanoic acid. List two main observations, he must note in his note book, about the reaction that takes place. Also, write chemical equation for the reaction.** **(*An*)**

Ans. On adding sodium hydrogen carbonate to ethanoic acid,

I. Brisk effervescence will be formed. *(½ M)*

II. Evolution of colourless and odourless gas with evolution of heat. *(½ M)*

The involved chemical reaction is:

$$CH_3COOH + NaHCO_3 \rightarrow CH_3COONa + H_2O + CO_2\uparrow$$ *(1 M)*

5. **What will be the action of the following substances on litmus paper? Dry HCl gas, Carbonated soft drink, Curd, Soap solution.** **(*Ap*)**

Ans. Dry HCl gas - No effect *(½ M)*

Carbonated soft drink-Turns blue litmus paper to red colour *(½ M)*

Curd-Turns blue litmus paper to red colour *(½ M)*

Soap solution-Turns red litmus paper to blue colour *(½ M)*

Short Answer Type Questions **(3 M)**

1. **Sunita carried out the following reactions in the laboratory:**
   - **(*i*) Complete neutralisation of one mole of sodium carbonate with hydrochloric acid**
   - **(*ii*) Complete neutralisation of one mole of sodium bicarbonate with hydrochloric acid**

   She found that the amount of carbon dioxide formed in both the reactions was the same.
   - **(*a*) Is her finding correct? Justify your answer.**
   - **(*b*) How does the amount of salt formed in case (*i*) compare with the amount of salt formed in case (*ii*)?**

   (*An*) (CFPQ)

Ans. (*a*) Yes, her finding is correct. *(1 M)*

In both reactions, carbon dioxide (CO_2) is produced, and it is formed in the same amount because:

- In reaction (i), 1 mole of sodium carbonate (Na_2CO_3) produces 1 mole of CO_2.

  $$Na_2CO_3(s)+2HCl(aq)\rightarrow 2NaCl(aq)+H_2O(l)+CO_2(g)$$ *(½ M)*

- In reaction (ii), 1 mole of sodium bicarbonate ($NaHCO_3$) also produces 1 mole of CO_2.

  $$NaHCO_3(s)+HCl(aq)\rightarrow NaCl(aq)+H_2O(l)+CO_2(g)$$ *(½ M)*

(*b*) The amount of salt (NaCl) formed in case (*i*) is twice the amount formed in case (*ii*). Specifically, 2 moles of NaCl are formed in reaction (*i*) compared to 1 mole of NaCl formed in reaction (*ii*). *(1 M)*

2. **2 mL of sodium hydroxide solution is added to a few pieces of granulated zinc metal taken in a test tube. When the contents are warmed, a gas evolves which is bubbled through a soap solution before testing. Write the equation of the chemical reaction involved and the test to detect the gas. Name the gas which will be evolved when the same metal reacts with dilute solution of a strong acid.** **(*Ap*) (CBSE 2018)**

Ans. • When zinc is added to a sodium hydroxide solution, then sodium zincate (Na_2ZnO_2) and hydrogen gas are generated. The chemical reaction that occurs is:

$$2NaOH + Zn \rightarrow Na_2ZnO_2 + H_2\uparrow$$ *(1 M)*

When the candle flame is held close to the evolved gas, then it keeps burning with a pop sound showing the evolution of Hydrogen gas. *(½ M)*

Now, when the same metal Zn reacts with the dilute solution of a strong acid (H_2SO_4), then the following reaction occurs:

$$Zn + H_2SO_4 \rightarrow ZnSO_4 + H_2\uparrow$$ *(1 M)*

Thus, hydrogen gas is being evolved. *(½ M)*

Topper's Explanation:

$NaOH\ (aq.) + Zn\ (s) \xrightarrow{\Delta} Na_2ZnO_2 + H_2$
(sodium hydroxide solution) (sodium zincate) 1

Thus, in this reaction, hydrogen gas is evolved 1

As the gas is passed through soap solution, bubbles filled with hydrogen gas come out. Bring a candle near the bubbles evolved, 1 the bubble bursts & the gas inside it starts burning with a pop sound & extinguishes the candle. This tests the presence of H_2 gas in them

Even if the zinc metal reacts with a solution of strong acid, hydrogen gas is produced / evolved.
[Eg: $Zn + 2HCl \rightarrow ZnCl_2 + H_2$]

3. A solution P is taken in a flask and two drops of phenolphthalein indicator is added to it. The graph below shows how the pH of the mixture changes as a solution Q is added dropwise to the flask with stirring.

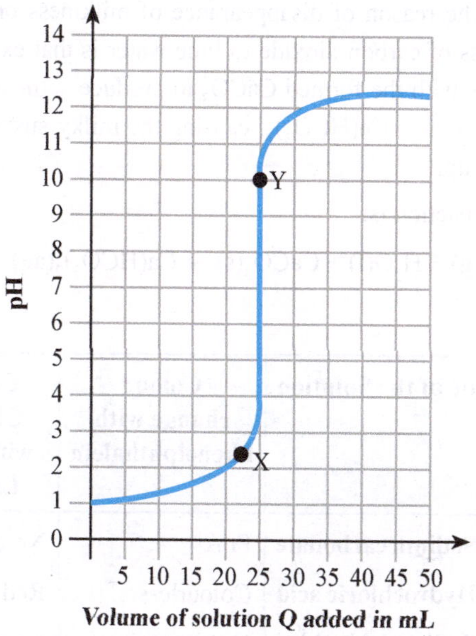

(a) Identify the nature of solutions P and Q.

(b) What will the colour of the solution in the flask be at points X and Y?

(c) Identify the type of reaction taking place in the flask.

(An) (CFPQ)

Ans. (a) Nature of solutions P and Q:

- Solution P: Acidic *(½ M)*
- Solution Q: Basic *(½ M)*

(b) Phenolphthalein is an indicator which remains colourless in acidic solution and becomes pink in basic solutions.

- At point X: The solution is acidic, hence, the solution will be colourless at point X. *(½ M)*
- At point Y: The solution is basic, hence, the solution will be pink at point Y. *(½ M)*

(c) The reaction taking place in the flask is a neutralisation reaction, where an acid (solution P) reacts with a base (solution Q) to form water and a salt. *(1 M)*

4. A student prepared solutions of (i) an acid and (ii) a base in two separate beakers. She forgot to label the solutions and litmus paper is not available in the laboratory. Since both the solutions are colourless, how will she distinguish between the two? (Ap) (NCERT Exemplar)

Ans. In the absence of litmus, other indicators such as phenolphthalein, methyl orange etc. might be used. Natural indicator such as turmeric can also be used to distinguish between acidic and basic solutions. *(1 M)*

Some common indicators with characteristic colour are given below:

Indicator	Acid solution	Basic solution	Neutral solution
Phenolphthalein	Colourless	Pink	Colourless
Turmeric	Yellow	Red	Yellow

(1×2 = 2)

Long Answer Type Questions (5 M)

1. (a) Compounds such as alcohols and glucose also contain hydrogen but are not categorised as acids. Describe an activity to prove it.

(b) Why does distilled water not conduct electricity, whereas rain water does? (Un) (NCERT)

Ans. (a) Two nails are inserted on the wooden or rubber cork and placed in a beaker as shown in figure below.

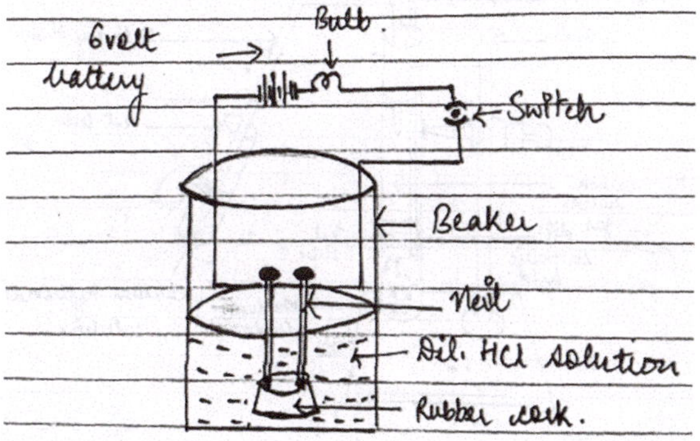

(1 M)

- Iron nail is connected to a bulb, then a 6 volt battery and a wire is connected to a switch. Some alcohol or glucose is poured to dip the nails in the glucose or alcohol solution.
- The switch is turned on and we will see the bulb is not glowing despite being connected to the switch.
- The beaker is emptied then and HCl solution is added. This time, the bulb glows.
- This proves that acid can conduct electricity but alcohol and glucose will not conduct electricity. *(2 M)*

(b) Distilled water does not contain any ionic compounds in it. *(½ M)*

While rainwater contain a lot of more compounds that has ions. *(½ M)*

Rainwater will dissolve acidic gas such as CO_2 from the air and CO_2 gas will form carbonic acid. This means that it has H^+ ions and carbonate ions. Thus, with the presence of acids, rainwater will conduct electricity. *(1 M)*

Key Takeaways

This teaches students that acid contains free ions and therefore it can conduct electricity. Covalent compounds don't have free ions therefore, they cannot conduct electricity.

2. **Describe an activity to demonstrate the reaction of acids with metal carbonates and metal hydrogen carbonates.** ***(Cr)***

Ans. Take two test tubes and label them as 'I' and 'II'.

Take about 0.5 g of a metal carbonate such as potassium carbonate in test tube I and 0.5 g of a metal hydrogen carbonate such as potassium hydrogen carbonate in test tube II.

Add about 3 mL of acid such as dilute sulphuric acid to both the test tubes.

A gas will be produced in both the test tubes. Pass the gas through lime water. *(2 M)*

The limewater will turn milky. This shows that the gas produced in the reaction is carbon dioxide.

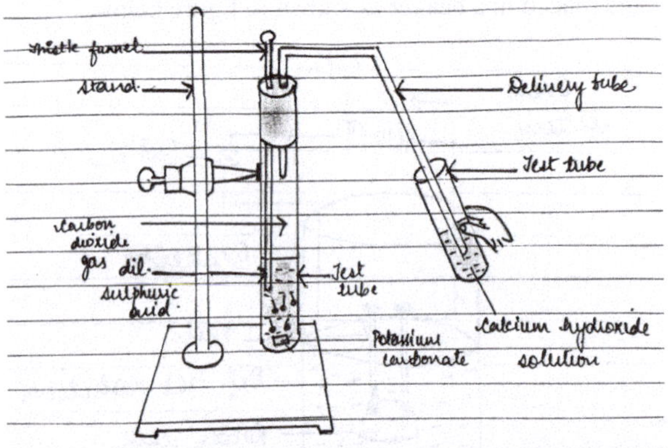

Passing carbon dioxide gas through calcium hydroxide solution

(1 M)

The chemical reactions involved in the process are as follows:

Test tube I:

$K_2CO_3 + H_2SO_4 \longrightarrow K_2SO_4 + CO_2\uparrow + H_2O$ *(½ M)*

Test tube II:

$2KHCO_3 + H_2SO_4 \longrightarrow K_2SO_4 + 2CO_2\uparrow + 2H_2O$ *(½ M)*

Reaction of limewater with carbon dioxide:

$Ca(OH)_2 + CO_2 \longrightarrow CaCO_3\downarrow + H_2O$ *(½ M)*

Lime water — White ppt.

On passing excess carbon dioxide the following reaction takes place:

$CaCO_3(s) + H_2O(l) + CO_2(g) \longrightarrow Ca(HCO_3)_2(aq)$

(Soluble in water)

(½ M)

3. *(i)* **Explain the reason of disappearance of milkiness on passing excess of carbon dioxide to lime water?**

(ii) **To the three solutions given below, a few drops of phenolphthalein and blue litmus were added separately. Mention the change in colour in each case.** ***(Ap)***

Name of the Solution	Colour Change with Phenolphthalein	Colour Change with Blue Litmus
(a) Sodium carbonate		
(b) Hydrochloric acid		
(c) Sodium chloride		

Ans. *(i)* The reason of disappearance of milkiness on passing excess of carbon dioxide to lime water is that excess CO_2 reacts with the formed $CaCO_3$ to produce soluble calcium bicarbonate, $Ca(HCO_3)_2$, causing the milky suspension to clear up. *(1 M)*

The reaction is:

$CO_2(g) + H_2O(l) + CaCO_3(s) \rightarrow Ca(HCO_3)_2(aq)$ *(1 M)*

(ii)

Name of the Solution	Colour change with Phenolphthalein	Colour Change with Blue Litmus
***(a)* Sodium carbonate**	Pink	No change
***(b)* Hydrochloric acid**	Colourless	Red
***(c)* Sodium chloride**	No change	No change

(1×3 = 3M)

Hints & Explanations

Multiple Choice Questions

1. *(d)* Acid present in tomato is Oxalic acid.
2. *(b)* When acid dissolves in water it ionizes to give H^+ ions. The process of dissolving an acid in water that results in decrease in concentration of H^+ ions per unit volume is known as dilution.
3. *(d)* When a solution of an acid is mixed with a solution of a base, *neutralisation reaction occurs which results in the* formation of salt and water with the evolution of heat.
4. *(b)* Calcium hydroxide turns milky due to the formation of calcium carbonate which on passing excess of CO_2 forms calcium hydrogen carbonate which makes the solution clear again.
5. *(c)* Though HCl gas is a covalent compound, but being a strong acid, it ionises in the aqueous solution to produce hydronium and chloride ions.

   $HCl(g) + H_2O(l) \rightarrow H_3O^+(aq) + Cl^-(aq)$
6. *(d)* Bases turn pink when a drop of phenolphthalein is added to them as, phenolphthalein is a weak acid and it gives pink colour when added to base.

7. (*a*) Generally, metal oxides are basic in nature and non-metallic oxides are acidic in nature. Some of the metal oxides form alkali when dissolved in water. In the given oxides, sodium and potassium oxides are metallic in nature and they form sodium and potassium hydroxides respectively.

$Na_2O(s) + H_2O(l) \rightarrow 2NaOH(aq)$

$K_2O(s) + H_2O(l) \rightarrow 2KOH(aq)$

Here, SO_2 and NO_2 due to acidic in nature will not form alkalies in water.

8. (*b*) The bases which dissolves in water are known as alkali. NaOH is a base which dissolve in water while $Fe(OH)_3$ is insoluble in water but it can act as base.

Assertion and Reason

1. (*d*) The assertion incorrectly advises adding water to acid, which is dangerous due to the highly exothermic reaction; the correct procedure is to add acid to water.

2. (*a*) Since, sulphuric acid is a strong acid, therefore it readily forms hydronium ions when dissolved in water which are responsible for its corrosive action.

3. (*a*) Phenolphthalein may be represented as Hph.

$$\underset{\text{(Colourless)}}{Hph} \rightleftharpoons \underset{\text{(Colourless)}}{H^+} + \underset{\text{(Pink)}}{Ph^-}$$

In acidic medium, excess of H^+ ions are present and therefore equilibrium is towards left and hence solution is colourless. While in basic medium, OH^- ions combine with H^+ ions to form unionized water molecules and therefore equilibrium shifts toward right and hence solution has pink colour. Therefore, phenolphthalein is an acid base indicator.

4. (*a*) Basic gases indeed cause an increase in the surface concentration of OH^- ions on litmus paper, which is responsible for the colour change to blue.

5. (*c*) The strength of an acid in water is determined by its ability to dissociate and release H^+ ions. HCl being a strong acid, dissociates completely.

2 pH AND IMPORTANCE OF pH

NCERT Definitions (Commonly asked in 1 mark)

- **Universal indicator:** A mixture of several indicators that exhibits different colours at various hydrogen ion concentrations, and is used to determine the pH value of a solution.
- **pH scale:** A scale ranging from **0 to 14** that measures the concentration of hydrogen ions in a solution, indicating its acidity or alkalinity.

  $pH = -\log[H^+]$

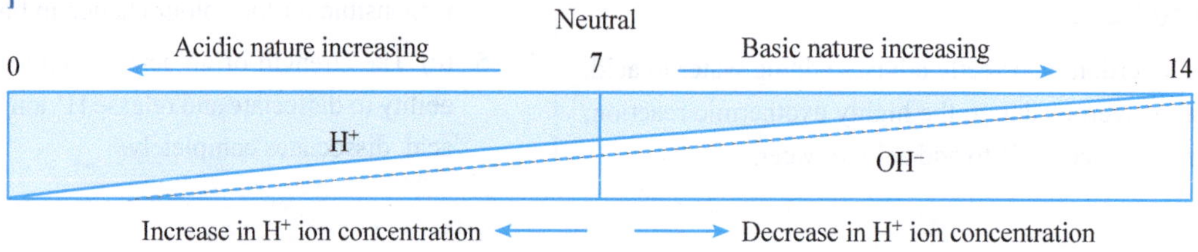

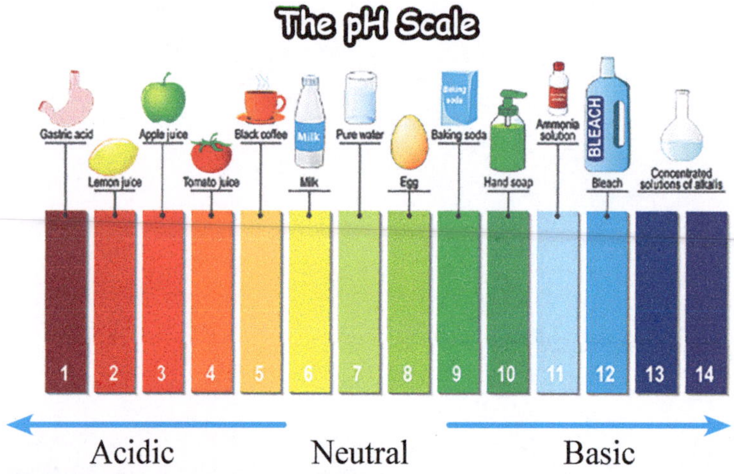

	pH ≈ 6.5
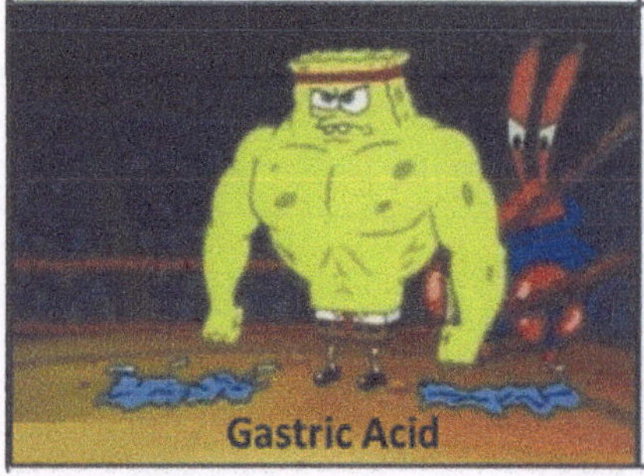	pH ≈ 2

❒ **Acid rain:** It is rain with pH less than 5.6, caused due to the absorption of pollutants like sulphur dioxide and nitrogen oxides from the atmosphere. It can cause harm to the environment by affecting plant life, aquatic animals, and infrastructure.

❒ **Antacids:** Bases that are used to **neutralize** excess stomach acid to relieve pain and irritation. Example: Milk of Magnesia

Important Facts

01 Human body functions optimally within a narrow pH range of 7.0 to 7.8.

02 Thick clouds of acid, suggesting a very acidic environment, is present in the atmosphere of Venus. ***~ Sulphuric Acid***

03 An **antacid** neutralize the excess of hydrochloric acid present in our stomach that causes acidity. ***~ Milk of Magnesia***

04 A basic substance is used to neutralise the honeybee sting or hair of nettle leaves sting, containing methanoic acid. ***~ Baking soda***

05 Hardest substance of the body made up of calcium hydroxyapatite. ***~ Tooth enamel***

Real Life Application Based Questions

1. **Why do farmers test soil pH before planting crops like blueberries or broccoli?***

Ans. Different crops require specific soil pH levels for **optimal growth and nutrient uptake**. Blueberries prefer acidic soil, while broccoli thrives in slightly alkaline conditions. Testing soil pH enables farmers to adjust it. They can use lime to raise pH or sulphur to lower it to ensure the best environment for their crops.

2. **How does monitoring the pH of a lake help protect its aquatic life?**

Ans. Aquatic organisms are sensitive to their environment's pH. Monitoring lake pH helps detect changes that might indicate pollution, such as acid rain effects, allowing for timely interventions to restore balance and protect the ecosystem, ensuring the survival and health of aquatic species.

3. **Rajesh always monitors pH during the production of fermented foods like yogurt. Do you know why?**

Ans. The pH level influences the taste, texture, and safety of fermented foods. In yogurt production, pH monitoring ensures the right acidity level is achieved for desirable flavour and texture, while also inhibiting harmful bacteria, ensuring the product is safe and consistent in quality.

Myth Buster

- **Myth: Life can exist in any pH condition as long as there is water and other essential elements.**

  Fact: Living organisms require specific pH ranges to survive. For example, human blood must maintain a pH range of 7.35 to 7.45. Extreme pH levels, whether too acidic or too alkaline, can be harmful or even lethal to living organisms. This is why acid rain, with a pH less than 5.6, can have detrimental effects on aquatic life and vegetation.

- **Myth: Using any base can neutralize excess stomach acid without any side effects.**

  Fact: While bases can neutralize stomach acid, not all bases are safe to ingest. Antacids like **magnesium hydroxide** are formulated to be effective and safe for treating excess stomach acid. In contrast, stronger bases could cause severe harm if ingested.

- **Myth: pH levels are only crucial for scientists and don't have much impact on daily life.**

  Fact: pH levels play a significant role in everyday life, affecting everything from agriculture and water quality to human health and hygiene. For example, soil pH can influence plant growth, while the pH of personal care products can affect skin and hair health.

- **Myth: Acidity and basicity both are inversely related to pH value.**

  Fact: It should be noted that i.e., lower the value of pH, higher will be the acidity but basicity is directly related to pH value i.e., higher the value of pH, higher will be the basicity.

** Concepts beyond the board exam syllabus, offering deeper insight and critical thinking on NCERT topics.*

COMPETENCY BASED SOLVED EXAMPLES

Multiple Choice Questions (1 M)

1. A student added a drop of universal indicator to 1.00 mL of given solution and found that a green colour is produced. The pH value of the solution will be ***(Un)***

(*a*) 7 – 9 (*b*) 0 – 3

(*c*) 10 – 12 (*d*) 4 – 6

2. Which of the following statements is correct about an aqueous solution of an acid and of a base?
***(Un)* (NCERT Exemplar)**

(*i*) Higher the pH, stronger the acid

(*ii*) Higher the pH, weaker the acid

(*iii*) Lower the pH, stronger the base

(*iv*) Lower the pH, weaker the base

(*a*) (*i*) and (*iii*) (*b*) (*ii*) and (*iii*)

(*c*) (*i*) and (*iv*) (*d*) (*ii*) and (*iv*)

3. The pH of three solutions X, Y, Z is 6, 4, 8 respectively. Which of the following is the correct option from the following? ***(Ap)***

(*a*) X > Y > Z decreasing acidic strength

(*b*) X < Y < Z increasing acidic strength

(*c*) Y > X > Z is decreasing acidic strength

(*d*) Z > Y > X decreasing acidic strength

4. You are having five solutions X, Y, Z, A and B with pH values as follows:

X = 1.8, Y = 7, Z = 8.5, A = 8 and B = 5

Which solution would be most likely to liberate hydrogen with magnesium powder? ***(Ap)***

(*a*) Solution X and Y (*b*) Solution X

(*c*) Solution Z (*d*) All of the above

5. The pH of the gastric juices released during digestion is ***(Re)* (NCERT Exemplar)**

(*a*) less than 7 (*b*) more than 7

(*c*) equal to 7 (*d*) equal to 0

6. The table below has information regarding pH and the nature (acidic/basic) of four different solutions. Which one of the options in the table is correct? ***(Ap)***

Option	Solution	Colour of pH paper	Approximate pH value	Nature of solution
(*a*)	Lemon juice	Orange	3	Basic
(*b*)	Milk of magnesia	Blue	10	Basic
(*c*)	Gastric juice	Red	6	Acidic
(*d*)	Pure water	Yellow	7	Neutral

7. Tooth decay begins at the pH of: ***(Un)* (CBSE 2024)**

(*a*) 5.1 (*b*) 5.8

(*c*) 6.5 (*d*) 8.0

8. Which of these graphs how the pH of milk changes as it forms curd? ***(Ap)* (CFPQ)**

(*a*)
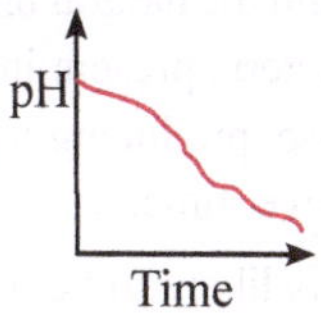

(*b*)
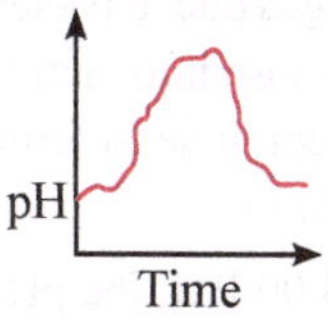

(*c*)
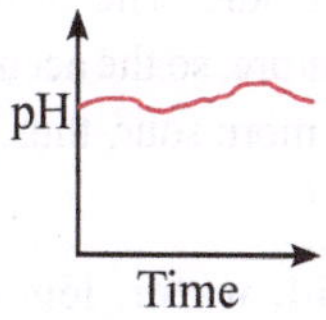

(*d*)
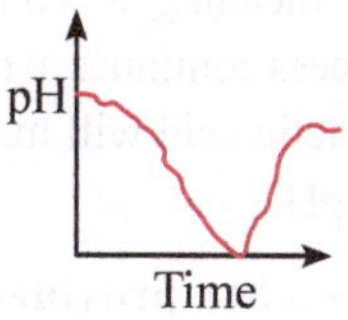

Assertion and Reason (1 M)

Direction: **The following questions consist of two statements – Assertion (A) and Reason (R). Answer these questions by selecting the appropriate option given below:**

(*a*) Both A and R are true, and R is the correct explanation of A.

(*b*) Both A and R are true, but R is not the correct explanation of A.

(*c*) A is true, but R is false.

(*d*) A is false, but R is true.

1. **Assertion (A):** Most of factories wastes are considered acidic in nature.

 Reason (R): Usually bases are added to all factory wastes before discharging into the water bodies. ***(Un)***

2. **Assertion (A):** Acetic acid is present in Ant's sting.

 Reason (R): The body part where ant bite is treated with moist baking soda. ***(Re)***

3. **Assertion (A):** Pure water is neither acidic nor basic.

 Reason (R): The pH of a solution is directly proportional to its $[H^+]$ concentration. ***(Un)***

4. **Assertion (A):** Universal indicator can show a wide range of colours each corresponding to a different pH value.

 Reason (R): Each colours represents a particular concentration of hydrogen ions in the solution. ***(Un)***

Subjective Questions

Very Short Answer Type Questions (2 M)

1. Farida checks the pH of a bottle of milk at 10:00 AM and finds it to be 6.0. She leaves the milk bottle on the table at room temperature (30 °C). She checks the pH of the milk again at 4:00 PM.

How is the pH of the milk at 4:00 PM likely to compare with the pH of milk at 10:00 AM? Justify your answer. *(Ap)* **(CFPQ)**

Ans. At 10:00 AM, the pH of the milk is 6.0, which is slightly acidic. As Farida leaves the milk bottle at room temperature (30°C) for several hours, the milk will undergo some changes due to bacterial activity and the natural breakdown of lactose into lactic acid. The bacteria present in the milk will continue to ferment the lactose, producing lactic acid, which lowers the pH of the milk over time. *(1 M)*

By 4:00 PM, the pH of the milk is likely to be lower than 6.0, meaning it would be more acidic. The fermentation process continues at room temperature, so the accumulation of lactic acid will make the milk more sour, thus lowering the pH. *(1 M)*

2. A teacher provided acetic acid, water, lemon juice, aqueous solution of sodium hydrogen carbonate and sodium hydroxide to students in the school laboratory to determine the pH values of these substances using pH papers. One of the students reported the pH values of the given substances as 3, 12, 4, 8 and 14 respectively. Which one of these values is not correct? Write its correct value stating the reason. *(Ap)*

Ans.

Given Substance	Given pH	
Acetic acid	3	Correct
Water	12	Incorrect
Lemon Juice	4	Correct
Aq. Sodium hydrogencarbonate	8	Correct
Aq. Sodium Hydroxide	14	Correct

The pH value of water is incorrect as for water the pH value is 7 not 12. *(2 M)*

3. Do basic solutions also have H^+ (aq) ions? If yes, then why are these basic? *(Un)* **(NCERT Intext)**

Ans. Yes, Basic solutions have H^+ ions. *(1 M)*

These are basic because hydroxide ions present are more in basic solution than H^+ ions. *(1 M)*

4. pH is measured using a pH meter, which comprises a detecting unit consisting of a pH sensitive glass electrode and an indicating unit which indicates the pH as shown below. *(An)* **(CFPQ)**

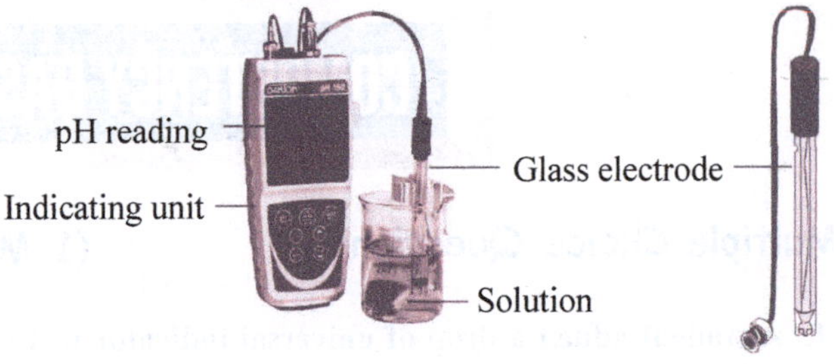

pH meter

To measure the pH of a solution, the glass electrode is dipped into the solution and the pH is displayed on the screen of the indicating unit. Before measuring the pH of another solution, the glass electrode is rinsed with distilled water and dried carefully with tissue paper.

How is the pH reading of the second solution likely to be affected if the glass electrode is not dried with tissue paper in the following cases?

(i) If the second solution being measured is acidic in nature

(ii) If the second solution being measured is basic in nature

Ans. (i) The pH meter will indicate a slightly higher pH reading than the actual pH of the solution if the second solution is acidic. *(1 M)*

(ii) The pH meter will indicate a slightly lower pH reading than the actual pH of the solution if the second solution is basic. *(1 M)*

Short Answer Type Questions (3 M)

1. A milkman adds a very small amount of baking soda to fresh milk.

(a) Why does he shift the pH of the fresh milk from 6 to slightly alkaline?

(b) Why does this milk take a long time to set as curd? *(Ap)* **(NCERT)**

Ans. (a) Milk man shifted the pH of the fresh milk from 6 to slightly alkaline to avoid milk from getting spoil and sour due to formation of lactic acid. *(1½ M)*

(b) This milk will take long time to set into curd because the lactic acid produced here will first neutralise the pH then the pH is reduced to turn milk into curd. *(1½ M)*

2. (i) What is the role of acid in our stomach?

(ii) Why does pain occur in the stomach during indigestion?

(iii) What can be done to relieve this pain? *(Ap)*

Ans. (i) Our stomach produces hydrochloric acid, which helps in the digestion of food. *(1 M)*

(ii) During indigestion, the stomach produces too much of this acid and this causes pain and irritation. *(1 M)*

(iii) Antacids are used to get rid of this pain. Antacids are mild bases that neutralize the excess acid present in the stomach. Magnesium hydroxide or milk of magnesia is often used to treat acidity in the stomach. *(1 M)*

3. **Farmers are using a large number of pesticides and fertilizers in their fields to increase crop production and to enhance their profits. But by doing so they are causing damage to the soil as well as to the environment.**

(*a*) Do you agree with this statement?

(*b*) Why should we avoid eating fruits and vegetables without washing them properly? ***(Un)***

Ans. (*a*) Plants need a specific pH range for their healthy growth. By the usage of large number of pesticides and fertilizers, pH of the soil changes which makes it more acidic or basic. Therefore, due to long term use of pesticides and fertilizers, the soil becomes infertile. This leads to soil erosion causing damage to the environment. Hence, the use of these pesticides and fertilizers should be restricted. *(2 M)*

(*b*) We need to wash vegetables and fruits properly before eating them because pesticides and chemical fertilizers are harmful for human consumption. *(1 M)*

Long Answer Type Questions (5 M)

1. **(*a*) You have four solutions A, B, C and D. The pH of solution A is 6, B is 9, C is 12 and D is 7.**

(*i*) Identify the most acidic and most basic solutions respectively.

(*ii*) Arrange the above four solutions in the increasing order of H^+ ion concentration.

(*iii*) State the change in colour of pH paper on dipping in solution C.

(*b*) Tooth enamel is one of the hardest substance in our body. Explain the changes in pH of mouth which indicates tooth decay. How does tooth paste help in preventing it? ***(An)***

Ans. (*a*) (*i*) Lower the pH, more will be the acidity and higher the pH, more will be the basicity. Therefore,

'A' is most acidic with pH = 6

'C' is most basic with pH = 12 *(1 M)*

(*ii*) Lesser the pH value, more will be the hydrogen ion concentration.

The increasing order of H^+ ion concentration: C < B < D <A. *(1 M)*

(*iii*) pH paper is an indicator which is used to determine the pH value of a solution. The pH paper changes their colour in the presence of an acid or a base. Highly acidic solutions give red colour and highly basic solutions give blue colour with pH papers.

pH paper will turn blue in colour in solution 'C; with pH = 12. *(1 M)*

(*b*) • Tooth enamel, made up of calcium hydroxyapatite (a crystalline form of calcium phosphate) is the hardest substance in the body. *(½ M)*

- It does not dissolve in water, but is corroded when the pH in the mouth is below 5.5. Tooth decay starts when the pH of the mouth is lower than 5.5. *(½ M)*
- Bacteria present in the mouth produce acids by degradation of sugar and food particles remaining in the mouth after eating. *(½ M)*
- Toothpastes are generally basic in nature and hence neutralise the acid present in mouth and hence prevents tooth decay. *(½ M)*

Hints & Explanations

Multiple Choice Questions

1. (*a*) The universal indicator, is a mixture of several indicators. It shows different colours at different concentrations of hydrogen ions in a solution. It shows green colour in the pH value range of 7-9.
2. (*d*) Stronger the acid, lesser is the pH and stronger the base, higher is the pH.
3. (*c*) pH is inversely proportional to the acidic strength. As acidic strength increases pH decreases thus the correct order is Y > X > Z.
4. (*b*) Solution X would liberate hydrogen with Mg because pH value is least for X solution i.e., 1.8. Therefore, it is the most acidic among all the given solutions.
5. (*a*) The pH of gastric juice is about 1.2 i.e., it is acidic in nature and hence pH value will be less than 7.
6. (*b*) Milk of magnesia is basic in nature having pH around 10.
7. (*a*) Tooth decay starts when the pH of the mouth is lower than 5.5. Hence, among all the given pH values, at pH 5.1, tooth decay starts.
8. (*a*) Graph A shows a consistent decrease in pH over time, which could represent the steady production of lactic acid.

Assertion and Reason

1. (*a*) As factory wastes are considered acidic in nature, their direct discharge into water bodies will lead to damage of aquatic life. Thus, before discharging of acidic waste it is neutralised with addition of bases.
2. (*d*) Formic or methanoic acid is present in Ant's sting. The body part where ant bite is treated with moist baking soda which neutralises the acids secreted by the ant bite.
3. (*c*) The pH of a solution is inversely proportional to its $[H^+]$ concentration.
4. (*a*) A universal indicator shows various colours corresponding to different pH levels, each indicating the solution's acidity or basicity. These colour changes directly reflect the concentration of hydrogen ions in the solution. The pH value associated with each colour provides an approximate measure of that hydrogen ion concentration.

3 SALTS

NCERT Definitions (Commonly asked in 1 mark)

- **Salts:** Salts are ionic compounds composed of positive ions (cations) and negative ions (anions) that are held together by ionic bonds. They are formed by the neutralization reaction between acids and bases. Example: Sodium chloride (NaCl)
- **Family of Salts:** Group of salts having the same positive or negative radicals. Examples: Na_2SO_4 and NaCl are sodium family salts; KCl and NaCl are chloride family salts etc.

- **Chlor-alkali process:** It is an industrial method for the electrolytic production of chlorine gas (Cl_2), sodium hydroxide (NaOH), and hydrogen gas (H_2) from the electrolysis of a sodium chloride (NaCl) solution(brine).

  $2NaCl(aq) + 2H_2O(l) \rightarrow 2NaOH(aq) + Cl_2(g)\uparrow + H_2(g)\uparrow$
- **Water of Crystallisation:** The **number of water molecules** associated with each formula unit of the salt is constant and forms a fixed ratio. This water is called water of crystallisation.

  Example: $CuSO_4 \cdot 5H_2O$, $CaSO_4 \cdot 2H_2O$ etc.

Important Facts

01 A chemical compound used for bleaching, produced by the action of chlorine on dry slaked lime. ~ *Bleaching Powder*

02 The chemical name of salt is sodium bicarbonate and it is used in cooking and as a mild non-corrosive base. ~ *Baking Soda*

03 The chemical name of salt is Sodium carbonate decahydrate and it is used as a cleaning agent and for water softening. ~ *Washing Soda*

04 The chemical name of salt is Calcium sulphate hemihydrate and it is used for casting moulds and for immobilizing broken bones. ~ *Plaster of Paris*

05 Salt used in making Plaster of Paris through dehydration. ~ *Gypsum*

Classification

Types of Salts (On the basis of their nature)			
Property	**Neutral Salt**	**Acidic Salt**	**Basic Salt**
Definition	Salt formed from the reaction of a **strong acid** and a **strong base**.	Salt derived from a **strong acid** and a **weak base**.	Salt resulting from a **strong base** and a **weak acid**.
Typical pH	Typically has a pH of 7.	Generally has a pH **less than** 7.	Usually has a pH **greater than** 7.
Example Reaction	Sodium chloride (NaCl): $HCl + NaOH \rightarrow NaCl + H_2O$	Ammonium sulphate $(NH_4)_2SO_4$: $H_2SO_4 + 2NH_4OH \rightarrow (NH_4)_2SO_4 + 2H_2O$	Sodium acetate (CH_3COONa) : $CH_3COOH + NaOH \rightarrow CH_3COONa + H_2O$

Real Life Application Based Questions

1. **How does sodium hydroxide contribute to the soap and detergent manufacturing process?**

Ans. Sodium hydroxide plays a critical role in soap and detergent manufacturing through a process called saponification. In this process, it reacts with oils and fats to create soap, a substance that can mix with both oil and water, allowing it to remove dirt and grease.

2. **Rohit used baking soda in fire extinguishers. Do you know what is the advantage of using it?**

Ans. Baking soda is used in some types of fire extinguishers as a non-toxic and non-corrosive agent to combat fires. It releases carbon dioxide when heated or combined with an acid, helping to smother the fire by cutting off the oxygen supply.

3. **What makes baking soda a valuable component in personal care products?**

Ans. Baking soda, or sodium bicarbonate, is commonly used in personal care products such as toothpaste, deodorant, and bath products due to its mild abrasive, neutralizing, and odour-absorbing properties. It helps in maintaining pH balance, neutralizing acidic odours, and gently scrubbing away surface stains, contributing to personal hygiene and care.

4. **What role does Plaster of Paris play in building construction?**

Ans. Plaster of Paris is widely used in building construction to create decorative mouldings and coatings for walls and ceilings. It's easy-to-mould property when mixed with water, followed by quick-setting into a hard form, makes it ideal for creating intricate designs and smooth finishes on interior surfaces.

Myth Buster

❒ **Myth: All salts are neutral compounds with a pH of 7.**

Fact: The pH of a salt solution depends on the **strength of the acid and base** from which the salt is derived. Salts from a strong acid and a strong base are neutral (pH = 7), but salts from a strong acid and a weak base are acidic (pH < 7), and those from a strong base and a weak acid are basic (pH > 7).

❒ **Myth: Salts do not contain water because they are dry crystalline substances.**

Fact: Many salts contain water of crystallization, which is integral to their crystal structure. For example, hydrated copper sulphate ($CuSO_4 \cdot 5H_2O$) appears blue due to this water. When heated, the water is removed, and the salt turns white, demonstrating that the 'dry' appearance of salts can be deceptive.

❒ **Myth: The primary use of sodium chloride is in food seasoning and preservation.**

Fact: While sodium chloride is widely used as a seasoning and preservative in the food industry, its application extend far beyond this. It is a critical raw material in the chemical industry, used in the production of numerous substances including sodium hydroxide, chlorine, hydrochloric acid, and many other chemicals.

Mnemonics

- **Half** way round the **Paris**, I drove in **2 gypsies**

$$CaSO_4 \cdot \frac{1}{2}H_2O + 1\frac{1}{2}H_2O \rightarrow CaSO_4 \cdot 2H_2O$$

(Plaster of Pairs) (Gypsum)

- **"Chlorine gas is given off at the anode, and hydrogen gas at the cathode".**

Chloe **a**te **h**ot dog with the **cat**

↓ ↓ ↓ ↓

Chlorine Anode Hydrogen Cathode

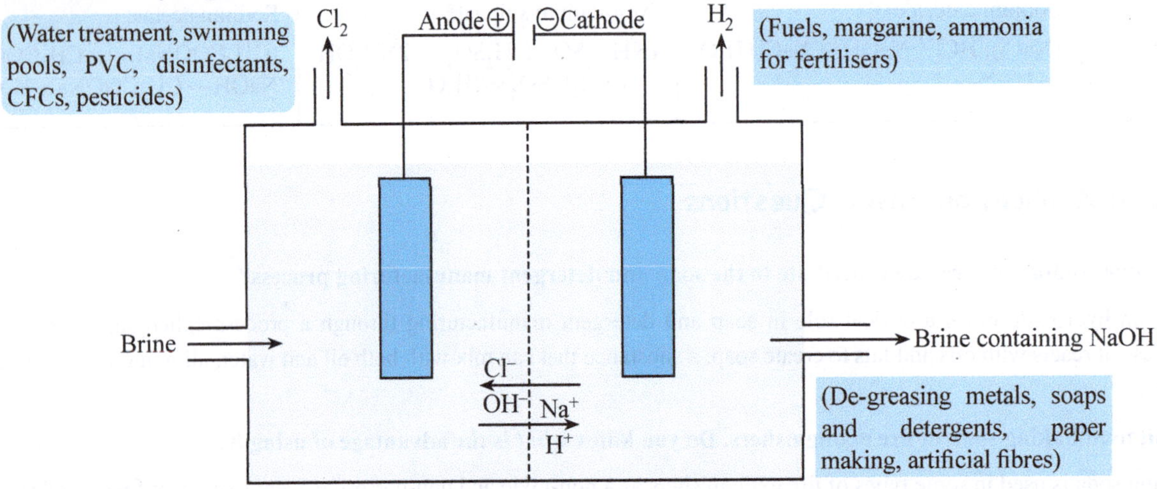

COMPETENCY BASED SOLVED EXAMPLES

Multiple Choice Questions (1 M)

1. Sodium carbonate is a basic salt because it is a salt of ***(Un)*** **(NCERT Exemplar)**

(*a*) strong acid and strong base
(*b*) weak acid and weak base
(*c*) strong acid and weak base
(*d*) weak acid and strong base

2. If 10 mL of H_2SO_4 is mixed with 10 mL of $Mg(OH)_2$ of the same concentration, the resultant solution will give the following colour with universal indicator: ***(Ap)*** **(CBSE 2020)**

(*a*) Red (*b*) Yellow
(*c*) Green (*d*) Blue

3. Which of the following salts do not have the water of crystallization? ***(Re)*** **(CBSE 2022-Term I)**

(*i*) Bleaching Powder (*ii*) Plaster of Paris
(*iii*) Washing soda (*iv*) Baking soda
(*a*) (*ii*) and (*iv*) (*b*) (*i*) and (*iii*)
(*c*) (*ii*) and (*iii*) (*d*) (*i*) and (*iv*)

4. Study the following table and choose the correct option: ***(Ap)*** **(CBSE 2022-Term I)**

	Salt	Parent Acid	Parent Base	Nature of Salt
(*a*)	Sodium Chloride	HCl	NaOH	Basic
(*b*)	Sodium Carbonate	H_2CO_3	NaOH	Neutral
(*c*)	Sodium Sulphate	H_2SO_3	NaOH	Acidic
(*d*)	Sodium Acetate	CH_3COOH	NaOH	Basic

5. The name of the salt used to remove permanent hardness of water is: ***(Re)*** **(CBSE 2023)**

(*a*) Sodium hydrogen carbonate ($NaHCO_3$)
(*b*) Sodium chloride (NaCl)
(*c*) Sodium carbonate decahydrate ($Na_2CO_3 \cdot 10H_2O$)
(*d*) Calcium sulphate hemihydrate ($CaSO_4 \cdot \frac{1}{2}H_2O$)

6. **Match the chemical substances given in Column-I with their appropriate application given in Column-II** (*Re*) **(NCERT Exemplar)**

Column-I	Column-II
A. Bleaching powder	(*i*) Preparation of glass
B. Baking soda	(*ii*) Production of H_2 and Cl_2
C. Washing soda	(*iii*) Decolourisation
D. Sodium chloride	(*iv*) Antacid

(*a*) A - (*ii*), B-(*i*), C-(*iv*), D-(*iii*)

(*b*) A - (*iii*), B-(*ii*), C-(*iv*), D-(*i*)

(*c*) A - (*iii*), B-(*iv*), C-(*i*), D-(*ii*)

(*d*) A - (*ii*), B-(*iv*), C-(*i*), D-(*iii*)

7. **Baking soda is a mixture of:** (*Re*) **(CBSE 2020)**

(*a*) Sodium carbonate and acetic acid

(*b*) Sodium carbonate and tartaric acid

(*c*) Sodium hydrogen carbonate and tartaric acid

(*d*) Sodium hydrogen carbonate and acetic acid

Assertion and Reason (1 M)

Direction: The following questions consist of two statements – Assertion (A) and Reason (R). Answer these questions by selecting the appropriate option given below:

(*a*) Both A and R are true, and R is the correct explanation of A.

(*b*) Both A and R are true, but R is not the correct explanation of A.

(*c*) A is true, but R is false

(*d*) A is false, but R is true.

1. **Assertion (A):** All salts form neutral solutions with pH = 7.

Reason (R): Salts are formed by the neutralisation of an acid with a base. (*Un*)

2. **Assertion (A):** Salts of a strong acid and weak base are basic in nature.

Reason (R): It has a pH value less than 7. (*Un*)

3. **Assertion (A):** Bleaching powder is represented as $Na_2CO_3.10H_2O$.

Reason (R): Bleaching powder is produced by the action of chlorine on dry slaked lime (*Re*)

4. **Assertion (A):** The chemical name of baking soda is sodium hydrogencarbonate.

Reason (R): Baking soda is an acidic salt. (*Re*)

Subjective Questions

Very Short Answer Type Questions (2 M)

1. **Why the salt solutions of strong acid and strong bases are neutral?** (*An*)

Ans. Salt solutions of strong acids and strong bases are neutral because they do not hydrolyse in water as both the acid and base neutralize each other and hence, solution become neutral in nature. (*2 M*)

2. **Sophia is a lab technician working in a high school chemistry lab. She was tasked with preparing different salts and observing their behaviour when subjected to heat. One day, Sophia decided to experiment with a salt (X) made from a strong acid (H_2SO_4) and a weak base ($Fe(OH)_2$). She carefully heated the salt and noticed a change in its colour.**

(*a*) What happens to the colour of the salt (X) when it is heated, and why?

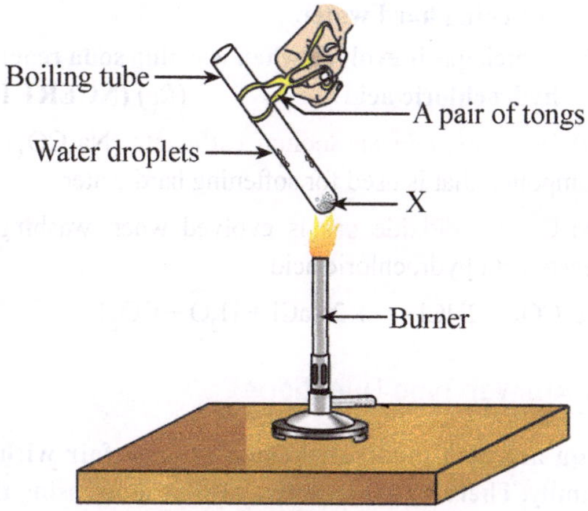

(*b*) How many water molecules are present in one formula unit of salt (X)? (*An*)

Ans. (*a*) The salt X is ferrous sulphate ($FeSO_4$). Ferrous sulphate, when hydrated ($FeSO_4.7H_2O$), is light green due to the presence of water of crystallisation. On heating, the water in the crystals is removed, resulting in the formation of anhydrous ferrous sulphate ($FeSO_4$), which changes the crystals' colour from light green to white. (*1 M*)

(*b*) One formula unit of hydrated ferrous sulphate ($FeSO_4.7H_2O$) contains seven water molecules. These water molecules are referred to as water of crystallisation. (*1 M*)

3. **What is the chemical name of brine and bleaching powder? How bleaching powder is formed?** (*Re*)

Ans. Chemical name of brine is aqueous sodium chloride solution which is represented as NaCl(aq.). (*½ M*)

Chemical name of Bleaching powder is calcium hypochlorite $Ca(OCl)_2$. (*½ M*)

Bleaching powder in obtained by the action of chlorine on dry slaked lime that is Calcium hydroxide. (*½ M*)

The complete reaction is given as.

$Ca(OH)_2 + Cl_2 \rightarrow CaOCl_2 + H_2O$ (*½ M*)

4. **(*a*) (*i*) A compound 'X' which is prepared from gypsum has the property of hardening when mixed with proper quantity of water.**

Identify 'X' and write its chemical formula. (*Re*) **(CBSE 2023)**

(*ii*) State the difference in chemical composition between baking soda and baking powder:

Ans. (*a*) (*i*) Since, compound X gets hardened when mixed with water, therefore, X is Plaster of Paris and its chemical formula is $CaSO_4.1/2H_2O$. (*1 M*)

(*ii*) Baking soda is sodium hydrogen carbonate ($NaHCO_3$) and it is added to make cooking faster. (*½ M*)

Baking powder consists of baking soda in addition to cream of tartar and cornstarch. (*½ M*)

5. Answer the following questions

(*a*) Name the sodium compound which is used for softening hard water.

(*b*) Which gas is evolved when washing soda reacts with hydrochloric acid? (*Re*) (NCERT Intext)

Ans. (*a*) Washing soda or Sodium carbonate (Na_2CO_3) is the compound that is used for softening hard water. (*1 M*)

(*b*) Carbon dioxide gas is evolved when washing soda reacts with hydrochloric acid. (*½ M*)

$Na_2CO_3 + 2HCl \longrightarrow 2NaCl + H_2O + CO_2\uparrow$ (*½ M*)

Short Answer Type Questions (3 M)

1. You are at a medical-themed science fair with your family. There's an interactive exhibit showcasing the use of a white powder in medicine. The presenter engages the audience: (*Ap*)

(*a*) What's the name and chemical formula of the white powder used by doctors to support fractured bones?"

(*b*) When we mix this powder with water, it undergoes a transformation into a hard solid. Can someone explain this process and write down the balanced chemical equation?"

(*c*) "Can anyone share another medical application where this white powder is used effectively?"

Ans. (*a*) The chemical name of the powder is calcium sulphate hemihydrate. (*½ M*)

Its formula is:

$CaSO_4.\frac{1}{2}H_2O$ (*½ M*)

(*b*) When this white powder is mixed with water, a solid hard mass gypsum is formed. (*½ M*)

$CaSO_4.\frac{1}{2}H_2O + \frac{3}{2}H_2O \rightarrow CaSO_4.2H_2O$ (*½ M*)

(*c*) It is used for making toys, materials for decoration and to make surfaces smooth. (*1 M*)

Mistakes 101 : What not to do!

Students may mistakenly state that the white powder used by doctors for supporting fractured bones is calcium carbonate ($CaCO_3$) instead of calcium sulphate ($CaSO_4.\frac{1}{2}H_2O$). They may confuse the compounds or fail to recognize the correct chemical formula.

2. Identify the acid and the base from which sodium chloride is obtained. Which type of salt is it? When is it called rock salt? How is rock salt formed? (*Un*) (CBSE 2019)

Ans.
- Sodium chloride is obtained from a strong acid i.e. hydrochloric acid (HCl) and a strong base i.e. sodium hydroxide (NaOH). (*½ M*)
- Sodium chloride (NaCl) is a neutral salt as pH of its aqueous solution is 7. (*½ M*)
- It is called rock salt when sodium chloride is found in mineral form. These deposits of salt are large crystals which are often brown due to impurities. (*1 M*)
- Beds of rock salt are formed when seas get evaporated over a long period of time, leaving behind salt deposits. (*1 M*)

3. List the important products of the Chlor-alkali process. Write one important use of each.

OR

How is washing soda prepared from sodium carbonate? Give its chemical equation. State the type of this salt. Name the type of hardness of water which can be removed by it? (*Re*) (CBSE, 2020)

Ans. The reaction involved in the Chlor-alkali process is:

$2NaCl(aq) + 2H_2O(l) \rightarrow 2NaOH(aq) + Cl_2(g) + H_2(g)$ (*½ M*)

The important products formed in this process are sodium hydroxide (NaOH), chlorine gas (Cl_2) and hydrogen gas (H_2). Chlorine gas is given off at the anode, and hydrogen gas at the cathode. Sodium hydroxide solution is formed near the cathode. (*1 M*)

Uses of the products:

(*i*) H_2: Used as fuels, for manufacturing ammonia for fertilizers. (*½ M*)

(*ii*) Cl_2: Used in the water treatment, for manufacturing PVC, in pesticides etc. (*½ M*)

(*iii*) NaOH: It is widely used in the preparation of soaps and detergents, in paper making or artificial fibres etc. (*½ M*)

OR

Washing soda is prepared by recrystallisation of sodium carbonate. (*½ M*)

The involved chemical reaction is

$Na_2CO_3 + 10H_2O \longrightarrow Na_2CO_3.10H_2O$ (*½ M*)

- Washing soda is a basic salt. Since it is made from strong base, NaOH and weak acid, H_2CO_3. (*1 M*)
- It is used for removing permanent hardness of water. (*1 M*)

4. Answer the following questions

(*a*) Why is it said that the dehydration of copper sulphate crystals is a reversible process?

(*b*) What will happen if a solution of sodium hydrogen carbonate is heated? Give the equation of the reaction involved. (*Ap*)

Ans. (*a*) The dehydration of copper sulphate crystals is a reversible process because blue coloured copper sulphate crystals become white on strongly heating due to loss of water of crystallisation. (½ M)

When water is added to the anhydrous salt, the blue colour reappears due to formation of hydrated copper sulphate. (1 M)

(*b*) Sodium hydrocarbonate on heating yields sodium carbonate and carbon dioxide gas. (½ M)

$$2NaHCO_3 \xrightarrow{\text{heat}} Na_2CO_3 + H_2O + CO_2\uparrow \quad (1\ M)$$

5. Answer the following questions:

(*a*) Write three uses of the compound of calcium that exists as a yellowish-white powder and is obtained by the action of chlorine on dry slaked lime.

(*b*) How is bleaching powder manufactured? Write the properties of Bleaching powder. (*Re*)

Ans. (*a*) The compound referred in the question is bleaching powder. Some of its uses are given below:

(*i*) It is used for bleaching purposes in textile industries, paper factories, and in the laundry. (½ M)

(*ii*) It is used as an oxidizing agent in chemical industries. (½ M)

(*iii*) It is used as a disinfectant in the process of water purification. (½ M)

(*b*) Bleaching powder is prepared by the action of chlorine gas (Cl_2) on dry slaked lime. (½ M)

$$\underset{\text{Slaked lime}}{Ca(OH)_2} + \underset{\text{Chlorine}}{Cl_2} \longrightarrow \underset{\text{Bleaching powder}}{CaOCl_2} + \underset{\text{Water}}{H_2O}$$

(½ M)

The properties of bleaching powder are: (½ M)

(*i*) It is a white-yellow coloured powder which gives the odour of chlorine.

(*ii*) It is soluble in water.

Long Answer Type Questions (5 M)

1. A few crystals of ferrous sulphate were taken in a dry boiling tube and heated. Tiny water droplets were observed in the tube after some time.

(*i*) From where did these water droplets appear? Explain.

(*ii*) What colour change will be observed during heating?

(*iii*) How many molecules of water are attached per molecule of $FeSO_4$ crystal? Write the molecular formula of crystalline forms of (I) Copper sulphate, and (II) Sodium carbonate.

(*iv*) State how is Plaster of Paris obtained from gypsum. Write two uses of Plaster of Paris. (*Un*) (CBSE 2024)

Ans. (*i*) When ferrous sulphate crystals are heated,the water droplets comes out of the crystals and appear as free water which can be seen in the test tube. (½ M)

$$FeSO_4.7H_2O + \text{Heat} \rightarrow FeSO_4 + 7H_2O \quad (½\ M)$$

(*ii*) During heating, green colour of $FeSO_4$ crystal will fade and the crystal will become white in colour. (1 M)

(*iii*) Seven molecules are attached to per molecule of $FeSO_4$ crystal. (½ M)

(I) $CuSO_4.5H_2O$ (½ M)

(II) $Na_2CO_3.10H_2O$ (½ M)

(*iv*) POP is obtained when gypsum at 373 K (100°C) is heated which when loses water molecules and becomes calcium sulphate hemihydrate ($CaSO_4$. ½ H_2O). This is called Plaster of Paris. (½ M)

$$CaSO_4.2H_2O \xrightarrow{100°C} CaSO_4 \cdot \frac{1}{2}H_2O + 1\frac{1}{2}H_2O$$

Uses of POP

1. It is used by doctors as plaster for supporting fractured bones in the right position. (½ M)

2. Used for making decoration items and toys. (½ M)

Topper's Explanation:

(i) crystals of ferrous sulphate has 1 water molecules of crystallisation. These are present as an essential part of crystal in fixed numbers per unit formula of the compound. On heating ferrous sulphate crystals, these molecules of water comes out of the crystals and becomes free water which can be seen in the test-tube.

$FeSO_4 \cdot 7H_2O \xrightarrow{\Delta} FeSO_4 + 7H_2O$.

(ii) Green colour of $FeSO_4$ crystal will fade and the crystal will become white in colour.

(iii) seven molecules.
(I) $CuSO_4 \cdot 5H_2O$
(II) $Na_2CO_3 \cdot 10H_2O$

(iv) When gypsum is heated at 100°C (373K), then it loses 1½ molecule of water of crystallisation to become plaster of paris with only ½ molecule of water of crystallisation.

$CaSO_4 \cdot 2H_2O \xrightarrow{100°C} CaSO_4 \cdot \frac{1}{2}H_2O + 1\frac{1}{2}H_2O$

uses of P.O.P:-
① for setting fractured bones in right position.
② for making decoration items & toys.

Hints & Explanations

Multiple Choice Questions

1. (*d*) Sodium carbonate is a basic salt because it is formed by combination of strong base (NaOH) and weak acid (carbonic acid).

$$2NaOH + H_2CO_3 \longrightarrow Na_2CO_3 + 2H_2O$$

2. (*c*) $$\underset{\text{(Acid)}}{H_2SO_4(aq)} + \underset{\text{(Base)}}{Mg(OH)_2(aq)} \longrightarrow \underset{\text{(Salt)}}{MgSO_4(aq)} + \underset{\text{(Water)}}{2H_2O}$$

$MgSO_4$ salt formed is slightly acidic nearly a neutral salt and hence universal indicator will give the green colour in this solution.

The colours that indicate the pH of a solution, after adding a universal indicator, are

pH range	Description	Colour
< 3	Strong acid	Red
3 – 5	Weak acid	Orange or Yellow
7	Neutral	Green
8 – 11	Weak alkali	Blue
> 11	Strong alkali	Indigo or Violet

3. (*d*) (*i*) Bleaching powder: Its chemical formula is $CaOCl_2$. It has zero water of crystallization.

(*ii*) Plaster of Paris: Its chemical formula is $CaSO_4.1/2H_2O$. It has half water of crystallization.

(*iii*) Washing soda: Its chemical formula is $Na_2CO_3.10H_2O$. It has ten water of crystallization.

(*iv*) Baking soda: Its chemical formula is $NaHCO_3$. It has zero water of crystallization.

Hence, bleaching powder and baking soda has zero water of crystallization.

4. (*d*) Option (*d*) is correct because sodium acetate is formed when acetic acid (weak acid) and sodium hydroxide (strong base) is reacted with each other. Since, sodium hydroxide is a strong base and acetic acid is a weak acid, therefore, the overall salt solution will be basic.

5. (*c*) Permanent hardness of water is removed by sodium carbonate decahydrate ($Na_2CO_3.10H_2O$).

6. (*c*) A-(*iii*), B-(*iv*), C-(*i*), D-(*ii*)

Bleaching powder - Decolourisation

Baking soda - Antacid

Washing soda - Preparation of glass

Sodium chloride - Production of H_2 and Cl_2

7. (*c*) Baking soda is mixture of sodium hydrogen carbonate and tartaric acid.

Assertion and Reason

1. (*d*) Only neutral salts form neutral solutions with pH = 7.

2. (*d*) Salts of a strong acid and weak base are acidic with pH value less than 7.

3. (*d*) Bleaching powder is represented as $CaOCl_2$.

4. (*c*) Baking soda is a mild non-corrosive basic salt.

MISCELLANEOUS EXERCISE

Multiple Choice Questions (1 M)

1. Hydrangea plants develop blue or pink flowers depending on the availability of aluminium from the soil. When the soil is acidic, aluminium is more available to the roots, resulting in blue flowers. When the soil is alkaline, the availability of aluminium decreases, resulting in pink flowers.

The graph below is of the pH of the soil at different sections of a field.

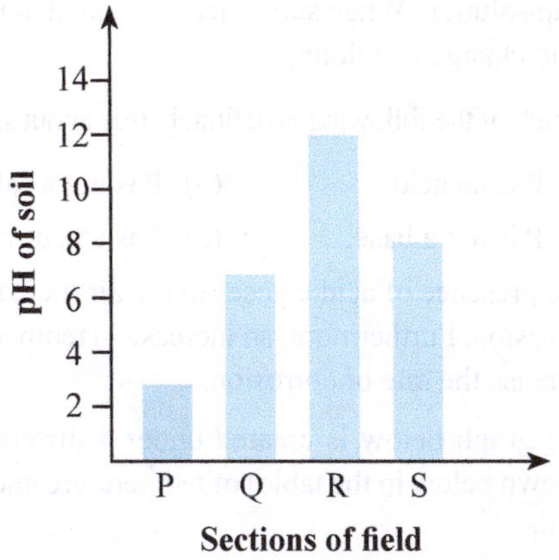

In which section of the field will the flowers on ALL the hydrangea plants definitely be blue in colour and in which section will the flowers on ALL the hydrangea plants definitely be pink in colour? **(*An*) (CFPQ)**

Option	Blue flowers	Pink flowers
W	Section P and Q	Section R and S
X	Section R and S	Section P and Q
Y	Section P, Q and S	Section R
Z	Section P	Section R

(*a*) W (*b*) X
(*c*) Y (*d*) Z

2. *Match List-I with List-II and select the correct answer by using the codes given below the list:* **(*Re*)**

	List-I (Name of Acid)		List-II (Source)
A.	Lactic acid	(*i*)	Tamarind
B.	Oxalic acid	(*ii*)	Curd
C.	Acetic acid	(*iii*)	Tomato
D.	Tartaric acid	(*iv*)	Vinegar

	A	B	C	D
(*a*)	(*i*)	(*iv*)	(*ii*)	(*iii*)
(*b*)	(*ii*)	(*i*)	(*iv*)	(*iii*)
(*c*)	(*ii*)	(*i*)	(*iii*)	(*iv*)
(*d*)	(*ii*)	(*iii*)	(*iv*)	(*i*)

3. Which of the following gives the correct increasing order of acidic strength? **(*Re*) (NCERT Exemplar)**

(*a*) Water < Acetic acid < Hydrochloric acid
(*b*) Water < Hydrochloric acid < Acetic acid
(*c*) Acetic acid < Water < Hydrochloric acid
(*d*) Hydrochloric acid < Water < Acetic acid

4. Solid Calcium oxide reacts vigorously with water to form Calcium hydroxide accompanied by the liberation of heat. From the information given above it may be concluded that this reaction **(*Un*) (CBSE 2024)**

(*a*) is endothermic and pH of the solution formed is more than 7.
(*b*) is exothermic and pH of the solution formed is 7.
(*c*) is endothermic and pH of the solution formed is 7.
(*d*) is exothermic and pH of the solution formed is more than 7.

5. Study the experimental set up shown in given figure and choose the correct option from the following: **(*An*) (CBSE 2022-Term-1)**

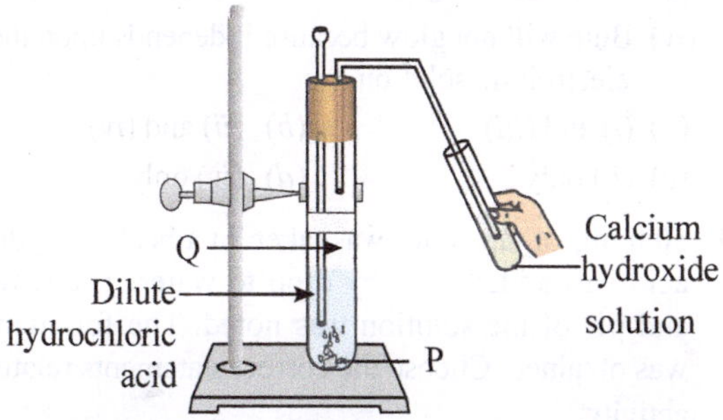

	P	Q	Change observed in calcium hydroxide solution
(*a*)	K_2CO_3	Cl_2 gas	No change
(*b*)	$KHCO_3$	CO_2 gas	No change
(*c*)	$KHCO_3$	H_2 gas	Turns milky
(*d*)	K_2CO_3	CO_2 gas	Turns milky

6. If a few drops of a concentrated acid accidentally spills over the hand of a student, what should be done? **(*Un*) (NCERT Exemplar)**

(*a*) Wash the hand with saline solution
(*b*) Wash the hand immediately with plenty of water and apply a paste of sodium hydrogen carbonate
(*c*) After washing with plenty of water, apply solution of sodium hydroxide on the hand
(*d*) Neutralise the acid with a strong alkali

7. 10 mL of a solution of NaOH is found to be completely neutralised by 8 mL of a given solution of HCl. If we take 20 mL of the same solution of NaOH, the amount HCl solution (the same solution as before) required to neutralise it will be **(*Ap*) (NCERT Intext)**

(*a*) 4 mL (*b*) 8 mL
(*c*) 12 mL (*d*) 16 mL

8. In an attempt to demonstrate electrical conductivity through an electrolyte, the following apparatus was set up. **(*Ap*) (NCERT Exemplar)**

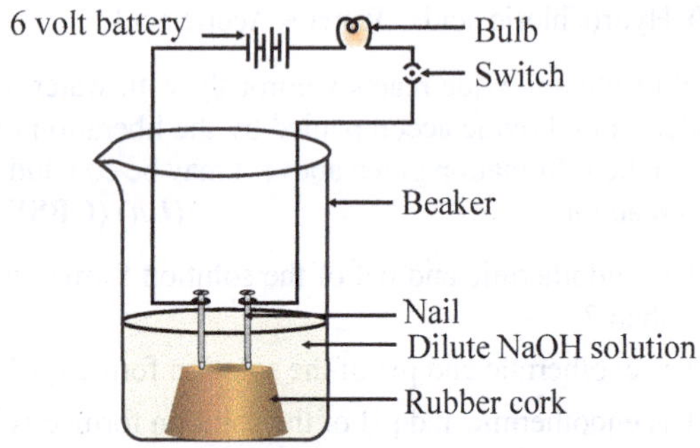

Which among the following statement(s) is/are correct?

(*i*) Bulb will not glow because electrolyte is not acidic.
(*ii*) Bulb will glow because NaOH is a strong base and furnishes ions for conduction.
(*iii*) Bulb will not glow because circuit is incomplete.
(*iv*) Bulb will not glow because it depends upon the type of electrolytic solution.

(*a*) (*i*) and (*iii*) (*b*) (*ii*) and (*iv*)
(*c*) (*ii*) only (*d*) (*iv*) only

9. 50.0 mL of tap water was taken in a beaker. Hydrochloric acid was added drop by drop to water. The temperature and pH of the solution was noted. The following graph was obtained. Choose the correct statements related to this activity. **(*An*)**

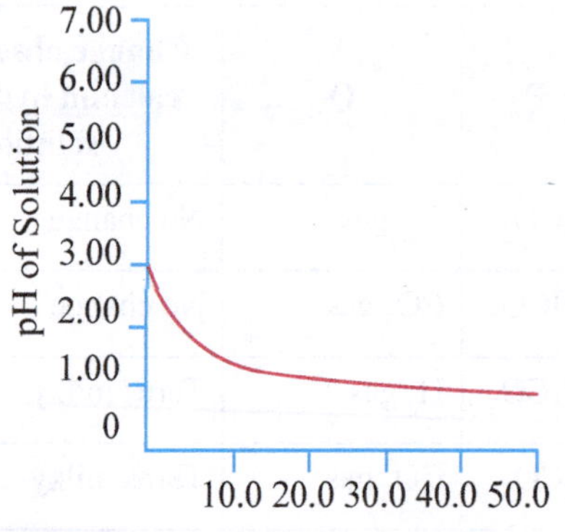

Volume of HCl added (mL)

(*i*) The process of dissolving an acid in water is highly endothermic.
(*ii*) The pH of the solution increases rapidly on addition of acid.
(*iii*) The pH of the solution decreases rapidly on addition of acid.
(*iv*) The pH of tap water was around 7.0.

(*a*) (*i*) and (*ii*) (*b*) (*i*) and (*iii*)
(*c*) (*iii*) and (*iv*) (*d*) (*ii*) and (*iv*)

10. 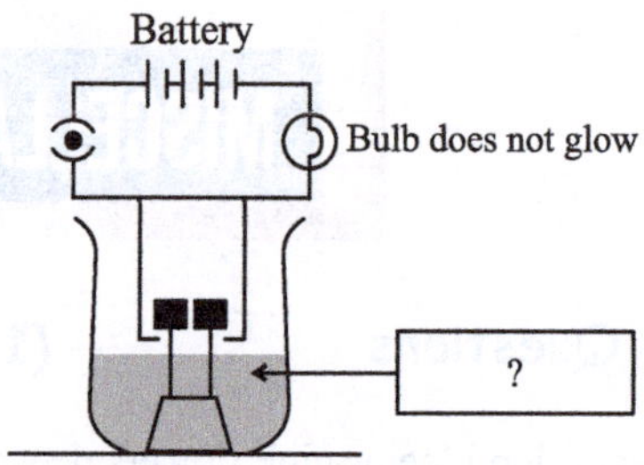

The solution in the given figure is likely to be **(*An*) (CBSE SQP, 2024)**

(*a*) HNO_3 (*b*) C_2H_5OH
(*c*) H_2SO_4 (*d*) CO_2 in water

11. The yellow colour of turmeric changes to red on addition of soap solution. When substance P is added to turmeric, there is no change in colour. **(*Ap*)**

Which of the following is definitely true about substance P?

(*a*) P is an acid. (*b*) P is not a salt.
(*c*) P is not a base. (*d*) P is a neutral substance.

12. The presence of acidic gases in the air increases the rate of corrosion. Furthermore, an increase in temperature can also increase the rate of corrosion.

The graph below is created under 4 different conditions (shown below in the table) of temperature and acidic nature of air.

Condition	Temperature (in °C)	pH value
1	20	6
2	30	6
3	30	7
4	20	7

Which of the graphs represents condition 2? **(*An*) (CFPQ)**

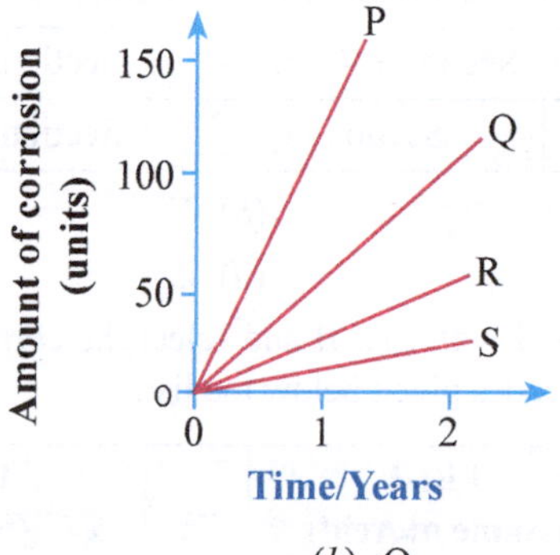

(*a*) P (*b*) Q
(*c*) R (*d*) S

13. Sulphur powder is heated on a spatula. A piece of both, moist blue and red litmus papers are brought one by one near the gas evolved during heating. The action of gas on the moist litmus papers will be: **(*Re*)**

(*a*) No change in colour in both the litmus papers.
(*b*) Blue litmus paper becomes red.
(*c*) Red litmus paper becomes blue.
(*d*) Blue litmus paper turns black.

14. Two salts 'X' and 'Y' are dissolved in water separately. When phenolphthalein is added to these two solutions, the solution 'X' turns pink and the solution 'Y' does not show any change in colour, therefore 'X' and 'Y' are **(Ap)**

	(X)	(Y)
(a)	Na_2CO_3	NH_4Cl
(b)	Na_2SO_4	$NaHCO_3$
(c)	NH_4Cl	Na_2SO_4
(d)	$NaNO_3$	Na_2SO_4

15. Sheetal has two test tubes, one containing dilute hydrochloric acid and the other dilute sulphuric acid but they are not labelled. Adding which of the following to the test tubes will help her to find out which test tube contains hydrochloric acid and which contains sulphuric acid? **(An) (CFPQ)**

(a) Blue litmus paper (b) Zinc metal strips

(c) Sodium carbonate (d) Barium carbonate

16. An unknown solution in a test tube was given to a student, when universal indicator solution is added to test tube, it turned out violet. The unknown solution is: **(Un)**

(a) Vinegar solution (b) Iodine solution

(c) Caustic Soda solution (d) Baking soda solution

17. Equal volumes of hydrochloric acid and sodium hydroxide solutions of same concentration are mixed and the pH of the resulting solution is checked with a pH paper. What would be the colour obtained? **(Ap)**

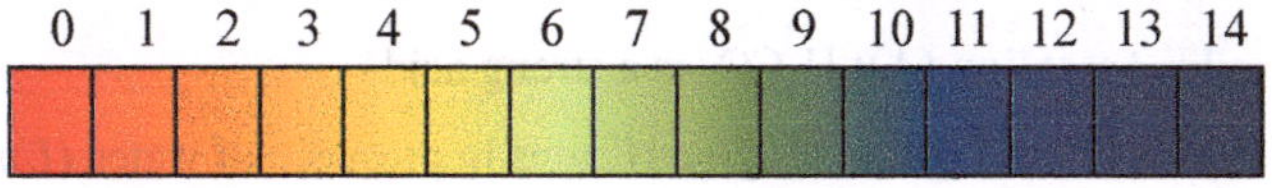

(a) Red (b) Yellow

(c) Yellowish green (d) Blue

18. Sonia has aqueous solutions of three salts, sodium acetate, sodium chloride and ammonium chloride in three test tubes. The test tubes are not labeled. On checking, she finds the pH of the solutions to be 4.6, 7.0 and 8.9.

Which of the following correctly matches the salts with their respective pH? **(An) (CBSE APQ, 2023)**

	pH 4.6	pH 7.0	pH 8.9
A	sodium acetate	sodium chloride	ammonium chloride
B	sodium chloride	ammonium chloride	sodium acetate
C	ammonium chloride	sodium acetate	sodium chloride
D	ammonium chloride	sodium chloride	sodium acetate

(a) A (b) B

(c) C (d) D

19. A man is using excess quantities of chemical fertilizers in fields for a number of years. The crop productivity gradually began to decrease inspite of using chemical fertilizers. Which of the following are correct statements? **(Un)**

1. The soil has become more acidic in nature
2. The soil has become more alkaline in nature
3. The productivity of crop is enhanced by adding slaked lime to the soil.
4. The productivity of crop is enhanced by adding some organic matter.
5. The productivity of crop can be enhanced by adding NaCl.

(a) 1 and 5 (b) 1 and 3

(c) 2 and 5 (d) 2 and 4

20. Payal has to arrange the following in DECREASING order of hydroxide ion concentration. Wine (pH 4.0), milk of magnesia (pH 10.5), blood (pH 7.4) **(An)**

Which of the following arrangements is correct?

(a) wine → milk of magnesia → blood

(b) blood → milk of magnesia → wine

(c) milk of magnesia → blood → wine

(d) wine → blood → milk of magnesia

21. You are provided with aqueous solutions of three salts- A, B and C, 2-3 drops of blue litmus solution, red litmus solution and phenolphthalein were added to each of these solution in separate experiments. The change in colours of different indicators were recorded in the following table. **(An)**

Sample	With blue Litmus Solution	With red Litmus Solution	With Phenolphthalein Solution
A	No change	No change	No change
B	Turns red	No change	No change
C	No change	Turns blue	Turns pink

On the basis of above observations, identify A, B and C from the following options:

(a) $A = NH_4Cl$, $B = NaCl$, $C = CH_3COONa$

(b) $A = NH_4Cl$, $B = CH_3COONa$, $C = NaCl$

(c) $A = NaCl$, $B = NH_4Cl$, $C = CH_3COONa$

(d) $A = CH_3COONa$, $B = NH_4Cl$, $C = NaCl$

22. When four dilute solutions of (I) HCl, (II) common salt, (III) caustic soda and (IV) milk of magnesia are tested with universal indicator, then which of the following is the correct observation? **(Ap)**

(a) I-Green, II-violet, III-Blue, IV-Red

(b) I-Green, II-Blue, III-Violet, IV-Red

(c) I-Red, II-Green, III-Violet, IV-Blue

(d) I-Red, II-Violet, III-Green, IV-Blue

23. Consider the following compounds:

$FeSO_4$; $CuSO_4$; $CaSO_4$; Na_2CO_3

The compound having maximum number of water of crystallisation in its crystalline form in one molecule is: **(*Un*) (CBSE 2024)**

(*a*) $FeSO_4$ (*b*) $CuSO_4$

(*c*) $CaSO_4$ (*d*) Na_2CO_3

24. A researcher is studying a compound 'X' which is a by-product in the production of bleaching powder and is neutral in nature.

$Ca(OH)_2 + Cl_2 \rightarrow CaOCl_2 + X$

'X' is also formed when an acid reacts with a specific substance.The researcher is interested in identifying the type of substance that, when reacted with an acid, produces compound 'X.'

Which of the following substances, when reacted with an acid, will produce compound 'X'? **(*An*)**

(A) Metal (B) Non-metal

(C) Base (D) Metallic oxide

(E) Non-metallic oxide

(F) Metal carbonate or metal hydrogen carbonate

(*a*) (A), (C), (D) and (E) (*b*) (B), (D) and (E)

(*c*) (C), (D) and (F) (*d*) (B), (D), (E) and (F)

25. 'Z' is a substance that is water soluble and its aqueous solution turns red litmus to blue and release H_2 gas on reaction with zinc metal. It is prepared by electrolysis of NaCl (aq). What is Z? **(*Ap*)**

(*a*) $NaNO_3$ (*b*) $NaClO_3$

(*c*) NaOH (*d*) NH_4OH

26. In one of the industrial processes used for manufacture of NaOH, a gas A is formed as by-product. The gas A reacts with lime water to give a compound B which is used as a bleaching agent in chemical industry. The compounds A and B could be **(*Ap*)**

(*a*) H_2 and $NaHCO_3$ respectively

(*b*) H_2 and Na_2CO_3 respectively

(*c*) Cl_2 and $CaOCl_2$ respectively

(*d*) Cl_2 and $NaHCO_3$ respectively

27. Adding which of the following to a colourless solution would give an indication that the solution could possibly be hydrochloric acid? **(*Ap*)**

(*a*) Copper metal strips (*b*) Silver metal strips

(*c*) Calcium carbonate (*d*) Sodium chloride

28. An acid (X) with sodium hydrogen carbonate is used in making the cakes fluffy and spongy. It is due to the release of (Y) gas in the reaction. Here, X and Y are **(*Un*)**

(*a*) (X) : Oxalic acid and (Y) : CO_2

(*b*) (X) : Tartaric acid and (Y) : O_2

(*c*) (X) : Citric acid and (Y) : H_2

(*d*) (X) : Tartaric acid and (Y) : CO_2

29. When sodium chloride (NaCl) is mixed with water and carbon-dioxide and ammonia, two products A and B are produced. On heating A, sodium carbonate is obtained as product. And when sodium carbonate reacts with sufficient water, product C is formed. What are A, B and C? **(*Ap*)**

(*a*) A = NaOH, B = H_2O and C is washing soda

(*b*) A = Na_2CO_3, B = NH_4Cl and C = Baking soda

(*c*) A = NH_4Cl, B = $NaHCO_3$ and C = Washing soda

(*d*) A = $NaHCO_3$, B = NH_4Cl and C = $Na_2CO_3.10H_2O$

30. The correct order of increasing pH values of the aqueous solutions of baking soda, rock salt, washing soda and slaked lime is **(*An*)**

(*a*) Baking soda < Rock salt < Washing soda < Slaked lime

(*b*) Rock salt < Baking soda < Washing soda < Slaked lime

(*c*) Slaked lime < Washing soda < Rock salt < Baking soda

(*d*) Washing soda < Baking soda < Rock salt < Slaked lime

Assertion and Reason (1 M)

Direction: The following questions consist of two statements – Assertion (A) and Reason (R). Answer these questions by selecting the appropriate option given below:

(*a*) Both A and R are true, and R is the correct explanation of A.

(*b*) Both A and R are true, but R is not the correct explanation of A.

(*c*) A is true, but R is false.

(*d*) A is false, but R is true.

1. **Assertion (A):** H_2CO_3 is a strong acid.
   Reason (R): Acids give H^+ ions in presence of water. **(*Un*)**

2. **Assertion (A):** Ammonia (NH_3) solution is an alkali.
   Reason (R): Ammonia solution turns blue litmus paper red. **(*Re*)**

3. **Assertion (A):** Carbonic acids (H_2CO_3) is found in almost all soft drinks.
   Reason (R): Carbonic acid is an organic acid. **(*Re*)**

4. **Assertion (A):** CH_3COOH is used as vinegar in cooking and food preservatives.
   Reason (R): Strong acids ionise almost completely in aqueous solution and hence produce a large amount of H^+ ions. **(*Un*)**

5. **Assertion (A):** In basic solutions, phenolphthalein gives pink colour.
   Reason (R): Phenolphthalein is a natural indicator. **(*Re*)**

6. **Assertion (A):** Higher the hydrogen ion concentration, lower is the pH value.
   Reason (R): For acidic solution, pH > 7. **(*Un*)**

7. **Assertion (A):** Pure water is neutral.
   Reason (R): The pH of a solution is directly proportional to the concentration of hydrogen ions present in it. **(*Re*)**

8. **Assertion (A):** Salts are the products of an acid-base reaction.
   Reason (R): Salt may be acidic or basic. **(*Un*)**

9. **Assertion (A):** Tooth decay starts when the pH of the mouth is lower than 5.5.
Reason (R): Tooth enamel is made up of calcium hydroxyapatite and is the softest substance in the body. ***(Re)***

10. **Assertion (A):** $CaOCl_2$ is the chemical formula of bleaching powder.
Reason (R): Calcium oxide reacts with chlorine to form bleaching powder. ***(Re)***

Subjective Questions

Very Short Answer Type Questions (2 M)

1. Name the acid present in
(*a*) Honeybee sting
(*b*) Hair of nettle leaves ***(Re)***

2. Ramesh has four conical flasks containing dilute nitric acid (HNO_3), dilute hydrochloric acid (HCl), dilute sulphuric acid (H_2SO_4) and dilute sodium hydroxide (NaOH) respectively. The beakers are not labelled, and he does not have any pH indicator.
By making mixtures of pairs of the substances, which solution will Ramesh be able to identify and what observation will help him to make this identification? ***(Un)***

3. Why do acids not show acidic behaviour in the absence of water? ***(Un)* (NCERT)**

4. Dry ammonia gas has no action on litmus paper, but a solution of ammonia in water turns red litmus paper blue. Why is it so? ***(An)***

5. Name the type of reaction where salt and water are obtained as products. Give an example of basic salt. ***(Un)***

6. While performing an experiment in his laboratory, Ajay by mistake dropped a little copper oxide into hydrochloric acid solution. He observed some changes in the solution. Account for his observation. ***(Ap)***

7. In which of the given cases will the bulb glow? ***(An)***

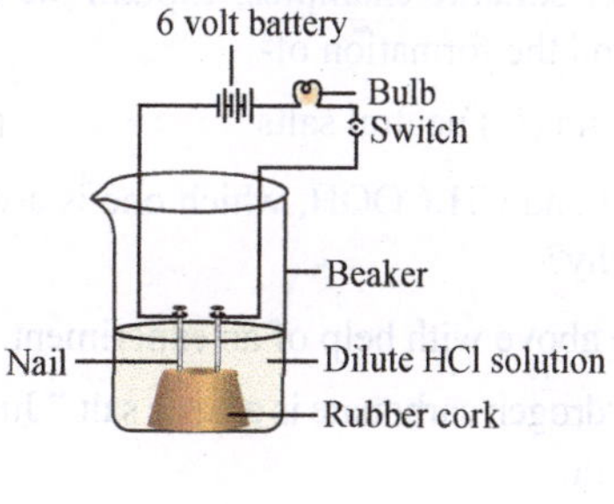

Case I

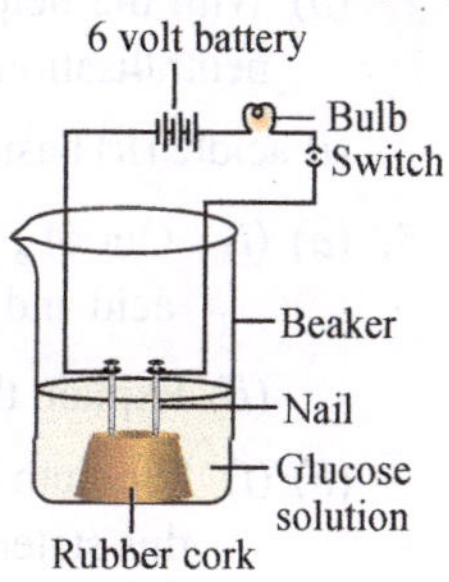

Case II

8. Answer the following questions
(*a*) If the pH of a vegetable soup is 6.5, how is the taste of the soup likely to be?
(*b*) What effect does an increase in concentration of H^+ (aq.) in a solution have on the pH of solution? ***(Re)***

9. Among KOH, NaCl, and H_2SO_4, which compound has the highest pH value? ***(Ap)***

10. A knife which is used to cut a fruit was immediately dipped into water containing drops of blue litmus solution. If the colour of the solution is changed to red, what inference can be drawn about the nature of the fruit and why? ***(Un)* (CBSE 2023)**

11. Write balanced chemical equation for the reaction that occurs when:
(*i*) blue coloured copper sulphate crystals are heated and
(*ii*) Sodium hydrogen carbonate is heated during cooking. ***(Re)* (CBSE 2023)**

12. The industrial process used for the manufacture of caustic soda involves electrolysis of an aqueous solution of compound 'X'. In this process, two gases 'Y' and 'Z' are liberated. 'Y' is liberated at cathode and 'Z', which is liberated at anode, on treatment with dry slaked lime forms a compound 'B'. Name X, Y, Z and B. ***(Un)* (CBSE 2023)**

13. Salts are formed by the neutralisation reaction between an acid and a base. Complete the following table by filling the missing data: ***(Un)* (CBSE APQ, 2023)**

S. No.	Name of the Salt	Formula	Parent Base	Parent Acid
1	Ammonium Chloride	NH_4Cl	....	....
2	Copper Sulphate	....	$Cu(OH)_2$	....

Short Answer Type Questions (3 M)

1. Blue litmus solution is added to two test tubes A and B containing dilute HCl and NaOH solution respectively. In which test tube a colour change will be observed? State the colour change and give its reason. ***(Un)* (CBSE 2019)**

2. You are given three test tubes. The three test tubes contain distilled water, acidic solution and the basic solution respectively. There is only red litmus paper available in order to identify what is there in each test tube. How will you find out what is in each of the test tubes? ***(Ap)* (NCERT Intext)**

3. What is observed when 2 mL of dilute hydrochloric acid is added to 1 g of sodium carbonate taken in a clean and dry test tube? Write chemical equation for the reaction involved. ***(Un)* (CBSE 2019)**

4. A substance 'X' is used as a building material and is insoluble in water. When it reacts with dil. HCl, it produces a gas which turns lime water milky.
(*a*) Write the chemical name and formula of 'X'.
(*b*) Write chemical equations for the chemical reactions involved in the above statements. ***(Un)* (CBSE 2023)**

5. 20 mL of water and 15 mL of sulphuric acid are to be mixed in a beaker. ***(Re)***
(*a*) State the method that should be followed with reason.
(*b*) What is this process known as?

6. 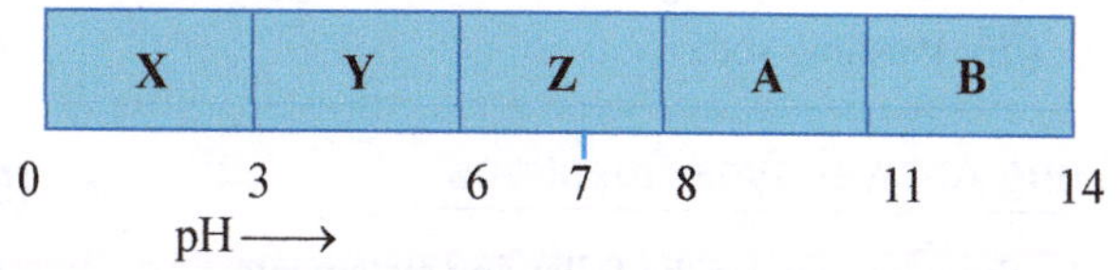

In which region will the given substances be present? ***(Ap)***
(*i*) Coffee
(*ii*) Blood
(*iii*) Milk of magnesia

7. Salt A is commonly used in bakery products which on heating gets converted into another salt B, which is used to remove the hardness of water, along with this, evolution of gas C takes place. The gas C, when passed through lime water, turns it milky. Identify A, B and C. ***(Ap)***

8. (*a*) The pH of a sample of tomato juice is 4.6. How is this juice likely to be in taste ? Give reason to justify your answer.

   (*b*) How do we differentiate between a strong acid and a weak base in terms of ion-formation in aqueous solutions?

   (*c*) The acid rain can make the survival of aquatic animals difficult. How? ***(An)* (CBSE 2024)**

9. (*a*) What is the colour of $FeSO_4.7H_2O$ crystals? Will there is any colour change upon heating the $FeSO_4.7H_2O$ crystal? Give balanced chemical equation for the changes.

   (*b*) What is the chemical formula of the compound used by doctors for plastering fractured bones? ***(Re)***

10. A sulphate salt of Group 2 element of the Periodic Table is a white, soft substance, which can be moulded into different shapes by making its dough. When this compound is left in open for some time, it becomes a solid mass and cannot be used for moulding purposes. Identify the sulphate salt and why does it show such a behaviour? Give the reaction involved. ***(Un)* (NCERT Exemplar)**

11. (*a*) In the given series of reactions, name the compounds X and Z.

    (*b*) Which type of reaction is X to Z?

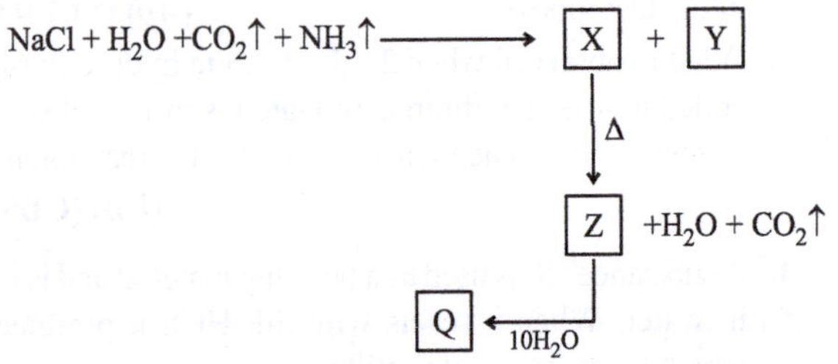

    (*c*) You are given 3 unknown solutions A, B, and C with pH values of 6, 8 and 9.5 respectively. In which solution will the maximum number of hydronium ions be present? Arrange the given samples in the increasing order of H^+ ion concentration. ***(An)* (CBSE SQP, 2024)**

12. How can the given substances be produced from common salt?

    (*i*) Sodium hydroxide

    (*ii*) Sodium hydrogen carbonate

    (*iii*) Washing soda ***(Un)***

Long Answer Type Questions **(5 M)**

1. State reasons for the following statements: ***(Ap)***

   (*a*) Tap water conducts electricity whereas distilled water does not.

   (*b*) Dry hydrogen chloride gas does not turn blue litmus red whereas dilute hydrochloric acid does.

   (*c*) During summer season, a milk man usually adds a very small amount of baking soda to fresh milk.

   (*d*) For a dilution of acid, acid is added into water and not water into acid.

   (*e*) Ammonia is a base but does not contain hydroxyl group.

2. (*a*) What will be the pH of solution obtained on adding potassium hydroxide to sulphuric acid? Explain why.

   (*b*) On adding an element 'X' to caustic soda (NaOH), a salt is produced along with a gas. This gas, formed in the process when bubbled with soap solution, burns with a pop sound when a burning matchstick is taken near it. Also, 'X' is used in the process of galvanization. What will 'X' produce with HCl?

   (*c*) Why does applying baking soda to a bee-stung area give relief? ***(An)***

3. (*a*) A metal compound 'A' reacts with dil. sulphuric acid to produce effervescence, The gas evolved extinguishes a burning candle. If one of the compound formed in the above reaction is calcium sulphate, then name the compound 'A' and the gas evolved? Also, write a balanced chemical equation for the reaction that occurred.

   (*b*) (*i*) How does antacid help to relieve indigestion in stomach? Name one antacid.

   (*ii*) A farmer treats the soil with $CaCO_3$. What is the nature of soil? Why does the farmer treat the soil with $CaCO_3$? ***(An)***

4. (*a*) Consider the following solutions: Distilled water, solution of glucose, rain water, solution of acetic acid.

   Among the given solutions, which solution(s) will

   (*i*) conduct electricity (*ii*) have no effect on litmus

   Explain giving reasons.

   (*b*) With the help of suitable examples, explain the term neutralisation and the formation of-

   (*i*) acidic (*ii*) basic and (*iii*) neutral salts ***(Un)***

5. (*a*) (*i*) Out of HCl and CH_3COOH, which one is a weak acid and why?

   (*ii*) Explain the above with help of an experiment.

   (*b*) (*i*) "Sodium hydrogen carbonate is a basic salt." Justify this statement.

   (*ii*) How is it converted into washing soda? ***(Un)***

6. A remarkable property of acids is that they can 'dissolve' metals. When metals are added to an acid, they disintegrate and disappear into the acid. ***(An)* (CFPQ)**

   (*a*) State one other common observation when metals 'dissolve' in acids. Explain the reason for this observation.

   (*b*) If the acid with the 'dissolved' metal is evaporated, can we get the metal back? Why or why not?

   (*c*) In this question, the word 'dissolve' is used within quotes. This is because it is not actually an example of dissolving. What is the MAIN difference between a metal 'dissolving' in an acid and sugar dissolving in water?

Case Based Questions

Case Based-I:

1. $A + H_2O \xrightarrow{\text{ELECTROLYSIS}} X + Y\uparrow + Z\uparrow$
   (X: CAUSTIC SODA; Y: ANODE; Z: CATHODE)

2. $A \xrightarrow{\text{ELECTROLYSIS}} M + Y\uparrow$
   (A: MOLTEN; M: CATHODE; Y: ANODE)

3. $M + CH_3COOH \longrightarrow P + Z\uparrow$

4. $CH_3COOH + Q \xrightarrow[H_2SO_4]{\text{Conc.}} R$

5. $R + X \longrightarrow P + Q$ **(*Ap*) (CBSE SQP, 2024)**

(*i*) Derive the names of A, Y, Z, M, P & R *(3 M)*

Attempt either subpart (ii) or (iii).

(*ii*) Improvise an activity to test Z. *(1 M)*

OR

Name the process in which compounds X, Y & Z are formed from (A). Justify your response. *(1 M)*

Case Based-II: Salts play a very important role in our daily life. Sodium chloride which is known as common salt is used almost in every kitchen. Baking soda is also a salt used in faster cooking as well as in baking industry. The family of salts is classified on the basis of cations and anions present in them. **(*Un*) (CBSE 2024)**

(*i*) Identify the acid and base from which Sodium chloride is formed. *(1 M)*

(*ii*) Find the cation and the anion present in Calcium sulphate. *(1 M)*

(*iii*) "Sodium chloride and washing soda both belong to the same family of salts." Justify this statement. *(2 M)*

OR

Define the term pH scale. Name the salt obtained by the reaction of Potassium hydroxide and Sulphuric acid and give the pH value of its aqueous solution. *(2 M)*

Case Based-III: A chemist named John is studying the reactions of a substance 'X' with various chemicals. 'X' is a commonly used compound in laboratories and industries, often utilized for cleaning metals and known for producing chloride ions in solution. Here are the observations:

1. When 'X' reacts with a metal 'Y', a gas 'A' is produced which burns with a pop sound.
2. When 'X' reacts with 'Z', a different gas 'B' is produced.
3. The gas 'B' reacts with water in the presence of sunlight to form a substance 'W' and another gas 'C' and water.
4. The substance 'W' contains hydrogen atoms but is not categorized as an acid.
5. The gas 'A' is known to be used in the reduction of a metal oxide 'V'.
6. When 'V' reacts with 'X', the resulting solution turns blue-green. **(*An*)**

Based on these observations, answer the following questions:

(*i*) Identify 'X' and 'W'. *2 M)*

(*ii*) Out of 'V' and 'B', which one is non-metallic oxide? Also, identify gas 'A'. *(2 M)*

OR

What is the effect of the blue litmus solution on the compound formed by the reaction of V and X? *(2 M)*

Case Based-IV: In the diagram given below when electricity is passed through an aqueous solution of a common salt, A substance 'Z' is produced along with the evolution of gases 'X' and 'Y'. When a burning matchstick is brought near the gas 'Y' it burns with a pop sound, whereas X is used for disinfecting drinking water. When gas 'X' is passed through a solution of slaked lime, an insoluble substance 'A' is produced. **(*Ap*) (CBSE APQ, 2023)**

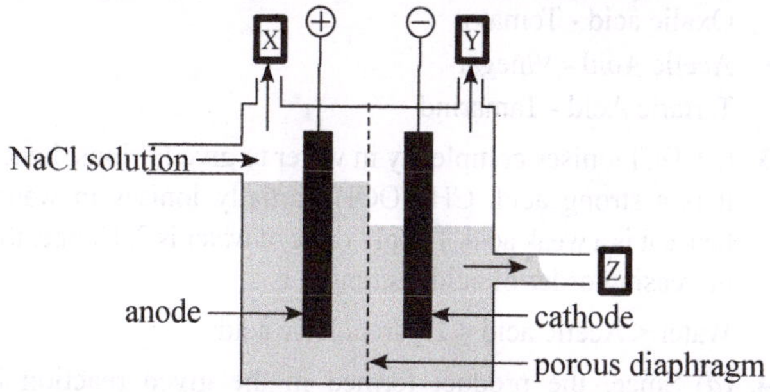

(*i*) Write the name of gases 'X' and 'Y'. *(1 M)*

(*ii*) Write the balanced chemical equation for the formation of substance 'A'. *(1 M)*

(*iii*) Write your observations: *(2 M)*

(*i*) If a drop of blue litmus solution is added to the aqueous solution of substance 'Z'

(*ii*) If methyl orange is added to substance 'Z'

OR

Write a balanced chemical reaction that takes place when 'X' and 'Y' react with each other. The product so produced will turn blue litmus red only when wet, why? *(2 M)*

ANSWER KEYS

Multiple Choice Questions

1. (*d*)	2. (*d*)	3. (*a*)	4. (*d*)	5. (*d*)	6. (*b*)	7. (*d*)	8. (*c*)	9. (*c*)	10. (*b*)
11. (*c*)	12. (*a*)	13. (*b*)	14. (*a*)	15. (*d*)	16. (*c*)	17. (*c*)	18. (*d*)	19. (*b*)	20. (*c*)
21. (*c*)	22. (*c*)	23. (*d*)	24. (*c*)	25. (*c*)	26. (*c*)	27. (*c*)	28. (*d*)	29. (*d*)	30. (*b*)

Assertion and Reason

1. (*d*)	2. (*c*)	3. (*c*)	4. (*b*)	5. (*c*)	6. (*c*)	7. (*c*)	8. (*b*)	9. (*c*)	10. (*c*)

HINTS & EXPLANATIONS

Multiple Choice Questions

1. (*d*) Blue flowers will definitely be in Section P (low pH, acidic soil). Pink flowers will definitely be in Section R (high pH, alkaline soil).
2. (*d*) Lactic Acid - Curd
   Oxalic acid - Tomato
   Acetic Acid - Vinegar
   Tartaric Acid - Tamarind
3. (*a*) HCl ionises completely in water to give H^+ ions, hence it is a strong acid. CH_3COOH partially ionises in water, hence it is a weak acid. The pH value of water is 7. Hence, the increasing order of acidic strength is :

   Water < Acetic acid < Hydrochloric acid
4. (*d*) Since, the product formed in the given reaction is calcium hydroxide, $Ca(OH)_2$, which is the base and the reaction is accompanied by the liberation of heat, therefore, the reaction is exothermic and the pH of the solution formed is more than 7.
5. (*d*) On observing the experimental setup given in the above figure, the best suitable option is given in (*d*).

   If P is potassium carbonate and when it is treated with dil HCl solution, it reacts vigorously producing carbon dioxide gas that is Q. The released CO_2 gas turns lime water ($Ca(OH)_2$) milky due to the formation of calcium carbonate. The complete observed reactions are given as,

   $$\underset{\text{Potassium carbonate}}{K_2CO_3(s)} + 2HCl(l) \rightarrow H_2O(l) + \underset{\text{Carbon dioxide}}{CO_2(g)}\uparrow + \underset{\text{Potassium chloride}}{2KCl(aq)}$$

   $$\underset{\substack{\text{Calcium hydroxide}\\\text{(Lime water)}}}{Ca(OH)_2(aq)} + \underset{\substack{\text{Carbon}\\\text{dioxide}}}{CO_2(g)} \rightarrow \underset{\substack{\text{Calcium carbonate}\\\text{(White ppt)}\\\text{(Makes limewater}\\\text{milky)}}}{CaCO_3(s)} + \underset{\text{Water}}{H_2O(l)}$$
6. (*b*) Sodium hydrogen carbonate is a mild non-corrosive base and can be used to neutralise the acid.
7. (*d*) 10 mL of NaOH requires 8 mL of HCl solution to neutralise

   20 mL of NaOH requires = $(8 \times 20/10)$ = 16mL of HCl
8. (*c*) NaOH is a strong electrolyte and it ionises in water to produce ions (Na^+ and OH^-), hence the solution will conduct electricity and the bulb will glow.
9. (*c*) The process of dissolving an acid in water is exothermic in nature.

   The pH of tap water is around 7.0 i.e., neutral and on addition of HCl to the beaker containing tap water, the pH of the solution decreases.
10. (*b*) C_2H_5OH
11. (*c*) When substance P is added to turmeric, there is no change in colour, this implies, that, P can be an acid or a neutral substance, but definitely not a base.
12. (*a*) Corrosion increases with:

    1. Lower pH (more acidic).
    2. Higher Temperature (30°C > 20°C).

    Since condition 2 involves higher temperature and acidic air (pH 6), it is expected to have a higher rate of corrosion compared to conditions with less acidic air or lower temperature.

    - Condition 2 corresponds to graph P, as it represents significant corrosion due to high temperature (30°C) and acidic air (pH 6).
13. (*b*) When the sulphur powder is heated on a spatula, the gas evolved is sulphur dioxide (SO_2). Since SO2 is an oxide of non-metal so, it will be acidic in nature and turns blue litmus paper to red.
14. (*a*) Phenolphthalein is an indicator that turns pink in basic solutions, and remains colourless in neutral and acidic solutions. Based on this information, Salt 'X' must be basic and Salt 'Y' can be either neutral or acidic.

    In the given choices,Na_2CO_3 (Sodium Carbonate) is basic, and NH_4Cl (Ammonium Chloride) is acidic.
15. (*d*) Barium carbonate reacts differently with dilute hydrochloric acid (HCl) and dilute sulphuric acid (H_2SO_4) because of the solubility of the resulting salts. The formation of a white precipitate when using barium carbonate indicates the presence of sulphuric acid, as barium sulphate is insoluble. In contrast, no precipitate forms with hydrochloric acid due to the solubility of barium chloride.

16. (*c*) The violet colour change indicates that an unknown solution is highly alkaline in nature.

17. (*c*) When equal volumes of strong acid and base are mixed, they neutralize each other to give a salt solution with a pH of 7. A pH paper strip dipped in this salt solution will turn yellowish-green.

The reaction takes place as follows:

$HCl + NaOH \longrightarrow NaCl + H_2O$

18. (*d*) Ammonium chloride has pH around 4.6.

Sodium chloride has pH around 7.0 and sodium acetate has pH around 8.9.

19. (*b*) Use of excessive chemical fertilizers will lead to soil acidification which means soil pH is lower. Thus, the pH of the acidic soil is increased by adding slaked lime as it is basic in nature.

20. (*c*) A higher pH value indicates a lower concentration of hydrogen ions (H^+) and a higher concentration of hydroxide ions (OH^-), making the solution more basic.

Thus, the correct arrangement is (c) milk of magnesia → blood → wine.

21. (*c*) A = NaCl (neutral in nature)

B = NH_4Cl (Acidic in nature)

C = CH_3COONa (Basic in nature)

22. (*c*) HCl is acidic in nature (pH < 7), common salt is neutral (pH = 7), caustic soda (NaOH) is highly basic in nature (pH > 7) and milk of magnesia also basic in nature (pH > 7) but less basic than caustic soda.

The colours that indicate the pH of a solution, after adding a universal indicator, are:

pH range	Description	Colour
< 3	Strong acid	Red
3 – 6	Weak acid	Orange or Yellow
7	Neutral	Green
8 – 11	Weak alkali	Blue
> 11	Strong alkali	Indigo or Violet

23. (*d*) Na_2CO_3 is the compound which has maximum number of water of crystallisation in its crystalline form and it exists as $Na_2CO_3 \cdot 10H_2O$.

Others exists as:

$FeSO_4 \cdot 7H_2O$, $CuSO_4 \cdot 5H_2O$, $CaSO_4 \cdot 2H_2O$.

24. (*c*) Since, compound X is neutral, so it is water which is also a byproduct in the production of bleaching powder. Water is formed when an acid reacts with a base, metallic oxide, or metal carbonate. Therefore, substances (C), (D), and (F) are the correct ones, as they react with acids to produce water, which has a pH of 7.0.

- Base + Acid → Salt + Water
- Metal oxide + Acid → Salt + Water
- Metal carbonate/Metal hydrogencarbonate + Acid → Salt + Carbon dioxide + Water

25. (*c*) On electrolysis of NaCl (aq), NaOH is produced.

$$2NaOH + Zn \longrightarrow \underset{\text{Sodium Zincate}}{Na_2ZnO_2} + H_2\uparrow$$

26. (*c*) The gas released during the manufacture of NaOH is chlorine, Cl_2(A).

$2NaCl(aq) + 2H_2O(l) \longrightarrow 2NaOH(aq) + Cl_2(g) + H_2(g)$

Cl_2 will be released at anode.

Cl_2(A) when reacts with lime water, a compound known as bleaching powder, $CaOCl_2$ (B) is obtained.

$Ca(OH)_2(aq) + Cl_2(g) \longrightarrow CaOCl_2(s) + H_2O(l)$

27. (*c*) $CaCO_3 + 2HCl \longrightarrow CaCl_2 + H_2O + CO_2$

28. (*d*) The acid (X) is tartaric acid which undergoes reaction with sodium hydrogen carbonate. It makes cakes fluffy and spongy. This happens due to the release of CO_2 gas (Y) in the reaction.

$$NaHCO_3(s) + \underset{\text{(from any acid)}}{H^+(aq)} \longrightarrow CO_2(g) + H_2O(l) + \text{sodium salt of acid}$$

29. (*d*) $NaCl + H_2O + NH_3 + CO_2 \longrightarrow NH_4Cl(B) + NaHCO_3(A)$;

$2NaHCO_3(A) + \text{heat} \longrightarrow Na_2CO_3 + H_2O + CO_2$;

$Na_2CO_3 + 10H_2O \longrightarrow Na_2CO_3.10H_2O$ (C = washing soda)

30. (*b*) Rock salt = NaCl,

Baking soda = $NaHCO_3$

Washing soda = $Na_2CO_3 . 10H_2O$

Slaked lime = $Ca(OH)_2$

Therefore, the increasing order of pH value is:

Rock Salt < Baking Soda < Washing Soda < Slaked lime.

Assertion and Reason

1. (*d*) H_2CO_3 (carbonic acid) is a weak acid.
2. (*c*) Ammonia solution, which is alkaline in nature turns the red litmus paper to blue.
3. (*c*) Soft drinks contain carbonic acids.

   Carbonic acid is a weak mineral acid.
4. (*b*) Vinegar having chemical formula CH_3COOH is used in cooking and food preservatives.

   Strong acids ionise almost completely in aqueous solution.
5. (*c*) Phenolphthalein remains colourless in acidic solution and becomes pink in colour in basic solutions. Phenolphthalein is a synthetic indicator.
6. (*c*) For acidic solution, pH < 7.
7. (*c*) Pure water is neutral i.e. it is neither acidic nor basic.

   As, pH = $-\log [H^+]$

   If the concentration of $[H^+]$ ions is larger then pH value will be less or vice versa. Hence, the pH of a solution is inversely proportional to the concentration of hydrogen ions present in it.
8. (*b*) Salts are formed as a result of neutralisation reaction. Salts may be acidic or basic in nature.
9. (*c*) Tooth decay starts when the pH of the mouth is lower than 5.5. Tooth enamel is made up of calcium hydroxyapatite (a crystalline form of calcium phosphate) and is the hardest substance in the body.
10. (*c*) Bleaching powder is produced by the action of chlorine on dry slaked lime [$Ca(OH)_2$].

Subjective Questions

Very Short Answer Type Questions

1. (*a*) Formic acid is present in honeybee sting. Bee-sting injects this acid in our skin which causes pain and irritation. *(1 M)*

(*b*) Formic acid is present in hair of nettle leaves too. Nettle is a herbaceous plant which grows in the wild. Its leaves have stinging hair, which cause painful stings when touched accidentally. *(1 M)*

2. Ramesh can identify the sodium hydroxide (NaOH) solution by mixing it with each of the acids (HNO_3, HCl, and H_2SO_4). When NaOH is mixed with an acid, it undergoes a neutralization reaction. *(1 M)*

The observation that will help him to make this identification is the increase in temperature, which will cause the flask to feel warm to the touch. Neutralization reactions between an acid and a base are exothermic and release heat. *(1 M)*

3.
- Acids do not show acidic behaviour in the absence of water because acids release hydrogen ions (H^+) when they dissolve in water. Without water, there's no medium for this ionization to occur. *(1 M)*
- It is due to hydrogen ions that they show acidic properties. *(1 M)*

4.
- Dry ammonia gas has no action on litmus paper, but a solution of ammonia in water turns red litmus paper blue because ammonia dissolves in water to form ammonium hydroxide (NH_4OH) which is base and it turns red litmus into blue. *(1 M)*
- Dry NH_3 gas will not change into OH^- ions and cannot turn red litmus to blue. *(1 M)*

5. When an acid reacts with a base, salt and water are produced. Such reactions are known as neutralisation reactions. *(1 M)*

Sodium acetate (CH_3COONa) is an example of basic salt as it is formed form strong base NaOH and weak acid CH_3COOH *(1 M)*

6. The metal oxides react with acids to produce salt and water. Hence, HCl reacts with copper oxide (CuO) to produce copper chloride which is green in colour. *(1 M)*

The reaction involved in this process is shown below:

$CuO(s) + 2HCl(dil.) \longrightarrow CuCl_2(aq) + H_2O(l)$ *(1 M)*

7. The bulb will glow in case I. Ionic solutions have the capability to conduct electricity. HCl when dissolved in water furnishes ions in its solution, hence the bulb will glow in case-I. *(1 M)*
Glucose is a covalent compound, therefore the aqueous solution of glucose does not dissociate to give ions and hence bulb will not glow in case-II. *(1 M)*

8. (*a*) The pH of a vegetable soup is 6.5, the taste of the vegetable soup likely to be slightly sour because it is weakly acidic. *(1 M)*

(*b*) If a solution has higher the concentration of H^+, then lower will be the pH value of the solution. *(1 M)*

9. The lower the concentration of hydrogen ions, the higher is the pH value. *(1 M)*
Among the given compounds, KOH is basic in nature. Thus, it has the lowest hydrogen ion concentration. Hence, KOH has the highest pH value. *(1 M)*

10. For acidic solutions, colour of litmus changes from blue to red. *(1 M)*
According to question, the colour of the knife changes to red when dipped in blue litmus solution, hence the nature of the fruit is acidic. *(1 M)*

11. (*i*) On heating crystals of copper sulphate (blue in colour), anhydrous copper sulphate is formed. The balanced reaction is:

$$\underset{\text{(Blue)}}{CuSO_4\cdot 5H_2O} \xrightarrow{\text{heat}} \underset{\text{(Colourless)}}{CuSO_4} + 5H_2O$$ *(1 M)*

(*ii*) Sodium hydrogen carbonate on heating forms sodium carbonate, water, and carbon dioxide gas.

$2NaHCO_3 \rightarrow Na_2CO_3 + H_2O + CO_2\uparrow$ *(1 M)*

12. Electrolysis of aqueous solution of NaCl (X) is used for the production of caustic soda (NaOH). It's reaction is:

$$\underset{(X)}{2NaCl(aq)} + 2H_2O(l) \rightarrow 2NaOH(aq) + \underset{(Z)}{Cl_2\uparrow(g)} + \underset{(Y)}{H_2\uparrow(g)}$$ *(1 M)*

Reaction of Z with dry slaked lime ($Ca(OH)_2$) is:

$$Ca(OH)_2 + \underset{(Z)}{Cl_2} \rightarrow \underset{(B)}{CaOCl_2} + H_2O$$ *(1 M)*

Mistakes 101 : What not to do!

Students might make an error in writing correctly what exactly is represented by B, X, Y and Z due to confusion. They should be very careful while mentioning which letter represents which compound/element.

13. 1. Parent Base: Ammonium hydroxide (NH_4OH) *(½ M)*
Parent Acid: Hydrochloric acid.(HCl) *(½ M)*
2. Formula: $CuSO_4$ *(½ M)*
Parent Acid: Sulphuric acid (H_2SO_4) *(½ M)*

Short Answer Type Questions

1.
- When blue litmus solution is added to two test tubes, A containing dilute HCl and B containing NaOH solution, a colour change will be observed in test tube A. Blue litmus paper turns red under acidic conditions and remains blue in basic solutions. *(1 M)*
- Test Tube A (dilute HCl): The blue litmus solution turns red because HCl is an acid *(1 M)*
- Test Tube B (NaOH solution): The blue litmus solution remains blue because NaOH is a base. *(1 M)*

2. The content in each of the test tubes can be identified by noticing the colour change on the red litmus paper.
- Acidic Solution: If the red litmus paper remains red after being dipped into the solution, this test tube likely contains the acidic solution. Acids do not change the colour of red litmus paper. *(1 M)*

- Basic Solution: If the red litmus paper turns blue, this indicates that the test tube contains a basic solution. Bases have the property of turning red litmus paper blue. *(1 M)*
- Distilled Water: If there's no change in the colour of the red litmus paper, indicating it remains red, this test tube could contain the distilled water. Distilled water is neutral and does not change the colour. *(1 M)*

3. • When 2 mL of dilute hydrochloric acid is added to 1 g of sodium carbonate taken in a clean and dry test tube, a brisk effervescence is observed during the reaction, which confirms that the released gas is carbon dioxide. *(½ M)*

- Acids react with metal carbonate to give salt, water and carbon dioxide as the product. *(½ M)*
- Sodium carbonate reacts with an acid, i.e., hydrochloric acid to give sodium chloride along with carbon dioxide and water. *(1 M)*

  The chemical reaction involved is:

  $$Na_2CO_3(s) + 2HCl(aq.) \rightarrow 2NaCl(aq.) + H_2O(l) + CO_2\uparrow(g)$$ *(1 M)*

4. (*a*) The chemical name of the substance 'X' is Calcium carbonate and its chemical formula is $CaCO_3$. *(1 M)*

(*b*) Reaction of 'X' with dilute HCl:

$$CaCO_3(s) + 2HCl(aq) \longrightarrow CaCl_2(aq) + H_2O(l) + CO_2(g)$$ *(1 M)*

Reaction of the produced gas (CO_2) with lime water ($Ca(OH)_2$):

$$CO_2(g) + Ca(OH)_2(aq) \longrightarrow CaCO_3(s) + H_2O(l)$$ *(1 M)*

Topper's Explanation

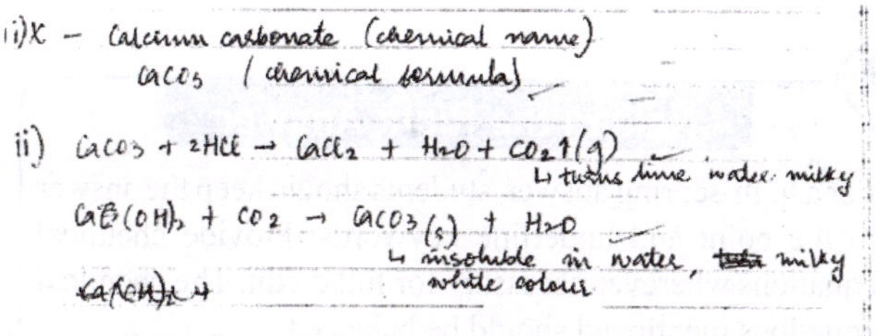

5. (*a*) The process of dissolving an acid in water is a highly exothermic one. The acid is to be added slowly in water with constant stirring to avoid the mixture to be splashed out. *(1 M)*

The reaction is highly exothermic in nature therefore, constant cooling should be done. *(½ M)*

(*b*) The process is known as dilution. Dilution is the process of adding a solvent (usually water) to reduce the concentration of the solute. *(1½ M)*

6. (*i*) Coffee is slightly acidic in nature. Thus, it will be present in region Y. *(1 M)*

(*ii*) Blood is very slightly alkaline in nature. Thus, it will be present in region Z. *(1 M)*

(*iii*) Milk of magnesia is basic in nature. However, it is not a very strong base. Thus, it will be present in region A. *(1 M)*

Key Takeaways

This question teaches students that different pH value indicates different hydrogen ion concentrations, hence different degree of acidity and alkalinity.

pH << 7 - strongly acidic (≈ 1-3)

pH < 7 - slightly acidic (≈ 4-6)

pH = 7 neutral

pH > 7 - slightly basic (≈ 8-10)

pH >> 7 - strongly basic (≈ 11-14)

7. • Baking soda is a salt which is used in bakery products. On heating, it produces sodium carbonate, and carbon dioxide.

$$2NaHCO_3 \longrightarrow Na_2CO_3 + H_2O + CO_2\uparrow$$ *(1 M)*

- Sodium carbonate is generally used to remove the hardness of the water. *(1 M)*
- CO_2 gas will turn the lime water milky due to the formation of $CaCO_3$ which is insoluble. *(1 M)*

  $$CO_2 + Ca(OH)_2 \longrightarrow CaCO_3 + H_2O$$

  Thus, A = Sodium bicarbonate, $NaHCO_3$

  B = Sodium carbonate, Na_2CO_3

  C = Carbon dioxide, CO_2

8. (*a*) As we know that, pH less than 7 corresponds to acidic behaviour and the pH more than 7 corresponds to basic behaviour. Since, the pH of a sample of tomato juice is 4.6, therefore, it is likely to be sour in taste. *(1 M)*

(*b*)

Strong Acid	Weak Base
1. A strong acid is the one that will furnish more [H^+] ions in the aqueous solution.	1. A weak base is the one that will furnish less [OH^-] ions in the aqueous solutions.
Example: Hydrochloric Acid	**Example:** Ammonium Hydroxide

(½ × 2 = 1 M)

(*c*) When the pH of rain water is less than 5.6, it is called acid rain. When such rain flows into the river, it lowers the pH of the river water. As a result, the survival of aquatic life in such river becomes difficult. *(1 M)*

9. (*a*) Pale green is the colour of $FeSO_4.7H_2O$ crystals. *(½ M)*

Yes, colour will change. It becomes dirty white on heating. *(½ M)*

$$\underset{\text{Pale green}}{FeSO_4 \cdot 7H_2O} \xrightarrow{\text{heat}} \underset{\text{Dirty white}}{FeSO_4} + 7H_2O$$ *(1 M)*

(*b*) Plaster of Paris is used for plastering fractured bones. *(½ M)*

It has the chemical formula $CaSO_4.\frac{1}{2}H_2O$. *(½ M)*

10. The sulphate salt should be calcium sulphate hemihydrate, which is white and soft substance and can be moulded into different shapes. *(½ M)*

- Calcium sulphate hemihydrate is commonly known as Plaster of Paris.
- Plaster of paris has half a molecule of water of crystallization. *(½ M)*

When plaster of paris is left open for some time, it absorbs moisture to form the compound, Gypsum which is hard to make moulds. *(1 M)*

$$\underset{\text{(Plaster of Pairs)}}{CaSO_4 \cdot \frac{1}{2}H_2O} + 1\frac{1}{2}H_2O \longrightarrow \underset{\text{(Gypsum)}}{CaSO_4 \cdot 2H_2O}$$ *(1 M)*

11. (*a*) $X = NaHCO_3$; $Z = Na_2CO_3$ *(½ + ½ M)*

(*b*) Decomposition reaction *(½ M)*

(*c*)
- Solution A will have the maximum number of hydronium ions. *(½ M)*
- Increasing order or H^+ ions $C < B < A$ *(1 M)*

12. (*i*) Preparation of sodium hydroxide from sodium chloride:

On passing electricity through an aqueous solution of sodium chloride, sodium hydroxide is formed along with chlorine gas and hydrogen gas. *(½ M)*

$$2NaCl(aq) + 2H_2O(l) \longrightarrow 2NaOH(aq) + Cl_2(g) + H_2(g)$$ *(½ M)*

(*ii*) Preparation of sodium hydrogen carbonate from sodium chloride:

On passing carbon dioxide and ammonia gas through salt solution, sodium hydrogen carbonate is formed. *(½ M)*

$$NaCl + H_2O + CO_2 + NH_3 \longrightarrow NH_4Cl + \underset{\text{(Sodium hydrogen carbonate)}}{NaHCO_3}$$ *(½ M)*

(*iii*) Preparation of washing soda from sodium chloride:

First sodium hydrogen carbonate is obtained from sodium chloride. Then, on heating sodium hydrogen carbonate, sodium carbonate is formed. Washing soda is then obtained by recrystallisation of sodium carbonate. *(½ M)*

$$2NaHCO_3 \xrightarrow{\text{heat}} Na_2CO_3 + H_2O + CO_2\uparrow$$

$$Na_2CO_3 + 10H_2O \longrightarrow Na_2CO_3.10H_2O$$ *(½ M)*

Long Answer Type Questions

1. (*a*) Tap water conducts electricity because it contains ions, distilled water does not contain any ions to conduct electricity, because of which it doesn't conduct electricity. *(1 M)*

(*b*)
- Due to absence of water, dry hydrogen chloride gas do not dissociate to give H^+ ions and hence, does not turn blue litmus red. *(½ M)*
- The dilute hydrochloric acid dissociates in the presence of water to give H^+ ions and hence, turns blue litmus to red. *(½ M)*

(*c*) During summer season, a milk man usually adds a very small amount of baking soda to fresh milk, because it will not allow milk to produce lactic acid that makes milk taste sour. *(1 M)*

(*d*) For a dilution of acid, acid is added into water and not water into acid because adding water to acid is highly exothermic in nature that will cause burn if splashed out. *(1 M)*

(*e*) Ammonia does not contain hydroxyl group but it is a base because ammonia dissolves in water to give NH_4OH and hence, furnishes OH^- ions. Thus, it is basic in nature. *(1 M)*

2. (*a*) pH of solution will be neutral. On addition of KOH to H_2SO_4, the effects of acid and base are nullified. It is known as acid-base neutralisation reaction. In this reaction, salt and water are produced. *(1 M)*

$$H_2SO_4 + 2KOH \longrightarrow K_2SO_4 + 2H_2O$$ *(1 M)*

(*b*) 'X' is a metal which reacts with alkali (NaOH) to produce salt and hydrogen gas. Zinc is one such metal. *(½ M)*

It is also used in the galvanisation process. Therefore, 'X' is zinc. *(½ M)*

$$\underset{\text{Metal}}{Zn} + 2NaOH \longrightarrow \underset{\text{Salt}}{Na_2ZnO_2} + H_2\uparrow$$ *(½ M)*

H_2 gas released burns with a pop sound.

On adding hydrochloric acid to metal, salt and hydrogen gas are produced again.

$$Zn + 2HCl \longrightarrow ZnCl_2 + H_2\uparrow$$ *(½ M)*

(*c*) A bee-sting injects formic acid on the skin, which causes burning, pain and irritation. *(½ M)*

Methanoic acid is a weak acid. If a mild base such as sodium hydrogen carbonate or baking soda is applied to the stung area, it neutralizes the acid and provides relief. *(½ M)*

Nailing the Right Answer

For a high-scoring answer, students should keep the answer to the point and underline keywords. Provide chemical equations wherever necessary for full credit. The chemical equations mentioned should be balanced.

3. (*a*) The compound 'A' is $CaCO_3$ and its name is calcium carbonate. *(1 M)*

The gas liberated is CO_2 as it extinguishes a burning candle. *(1 M)*

$$\underset{\text{(A)}}{CaCO_3} + H_2SO_4(\text{dil.}) \longrightarrow \underset{\text{Calcium sulphate}}{CaSO_4} + H_2O + CO_2\uparrow$$ *(1 M)*

(*b*) (*i*) Antacid neutralises excess of acid produced in the stomach. $NaHCO_3$ is an example of an antacid. *(1 M)*

(*ii*) The nature of soil is acidic. *(½ M)*

The farmer wants to make the soil neutral by adding $CaCO_3$ that has basic nature which is good for crops. *(½ M)*

4. (*a*) (*i*) Solutions of acetic acid (CH_3COOH) and rain water will conduct electricity. *(½ M)*

Both the solutions contain ions which can conduct electricity. Rain water is slightly acidic in nature as it contains carbonic acid. *(½ M)* (*ii*) Distilled water is neutral in nature. Glucose is a molecular compound and hence does not furnish any kind of ions on dissolving in water. (½ M)

Hence, the solution of glucose is also neutral in nature. Thus, these solutions have no effect on litmus. (½ M)

(*b*) In neutralisation type of chemical reaction, an acid and base react together to form salt and water with evolution of heat. (½ M)

(*i*) When neutralisation of a strong acid with a weak base takes place, it forms acidic salt. Example:

$$HCl + NH_4OH \longrightarrow \underset{\text{acidic salt}}{NH_4Cl} + H_2O \quad (½\ M)$$

(*ii*) When neutralisation of a weak acid with a strong base takes place, it forms basic salt. Example:

$$NaOH + CH_3COOH \longrightarrow \underset{\text{basic salt}}{CH_3COO^- Na^+} + H_2O \quad (1\ M)$$

(*iii*) When neutralisation of a strong acid with a strong base takes place, it forms neutral salt. Example:

$$NaOH + HCl \longrightarrow \underset{\text{neutral salt}}{NaCl} + H_2O \quad (1\ M)$$

5. (*a*) (*i*) CH_3COOH is weaker acid than HCl because HCl (hydrochloric acid) when comes in contact with water, liberates more H^+ ions into the solution as compared to the number of hydrogen ions liberated by the same amount of CH_3COOH (acetic acid) into the solution. Hence, CH_3COOH is a weak acid. (1 M)

(*ii*) **Experiment:** When two separate electrolytic cells are made, one with HCl(aq) as an electrolyte and the other cell with CH_3COOH(aq) as an electrolyte, in both the cells when a bulb is connected to check the voltage produced in the respective cells, we find that the bulb connected to the cell with HCl glows brighter as compared to the other cell. (½ M)

From this, it is proved that HCl (hydrochloric acid) is a stronger acid because when there are more ions in the solution there will be more conduction of electricity and hence the bulb would glow brighter. (½ M)

(*b*) (*i*) When a strong base such as NaOH reacts with a weak acid such as H_2CO_3, it results in a basic salt and water. (½ M)

$$NaOH + H_2CO_3 \longrightarrow \underset{\text{basic salt}}{NaHCO_3} + H_2O$$

Hence, we can justify that sodium hydrogen carbonate ($NaHCO_3$) is a basic salt. (½ M)

(*ii*) Washing soda can be prepared by heating of sodium hydrogen carbonate followed by recrystallisation.

(½ M)

$$2NaHCO_3 \xrightarrow{\Delta} Na_2CO_3 + H_2O + CO_2\uparrow$$

(1 M)

$$Na_2CO_3 + 10H_2O \xrightarrow{\text{Recrystallisation}} Na_2CO_3.10H_2O$$

(½ M)

6. (*a*) When metals dissolves in acid , it displaces hydrogen atoms from the acids as hydrogen gas and forms a compound called a salt.

Observation: Bubbling is seen (1 M)

Reason: Because hydrogen gas is produced. (1 M)

(*b*) No, we cannot get the metal back, if the acid with the dissolved metal is evaporated. (1 M)

This is because the metal is present as the part of the salt solution. (1 M)

(*c*) Metal dissolving in an acid is a chemical change, while the sugar dissolving in water is a physical change.

(1 M)

Case Based Questions

Case Based-I

(*i*) A - Sodium chloride, Y - Chlorine gas, Z - Hydrogen gas, M - Sodium metal, P - Sodium ethanoate & R - Ethyl ethanoate/ester (½ × 6 = 3 M)

Student to attempt either subpart (ii) or (iii).

(*ii*) Any activity similar to the given figure (1 M)

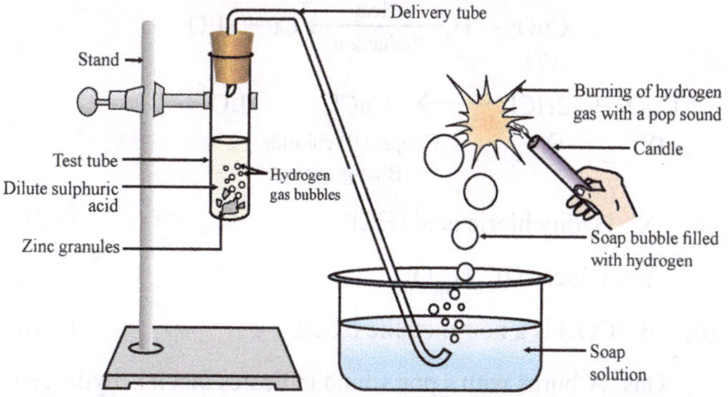

Fig.: Reaction of zinc granules with dilute sulphuric acid and testing hydrogen gas by burning

OR

Chlor alkali process

The process is called the chlor-alkali process because of the products formed chlor for chlorine and alkali for sodium hydroxide. (1 M)

Case Based-II

(*i*) Sodium chloride is NaCl and is formed by the reaction of acid, HCl and the base, NaOH. (½ × 2 = 1 M)

(*ii*) The cation and the anion present in calcium sulphate is Ca^{2+} and SO_4^{2-} respectively. (½ × 2 = 1 M)

(*iii*) Salts containing the same positive or negative radicals are known to belong to a family. (1 M)

Sodium chloride (NaCl) and washing soda ($Na_2CO_3{\cdot}10H_2O$) both belong to the family of sodium salts, since both contain the same positive radical i.e., sodium ions. (1 M)

OR

A pH scale is a scale used for measuring hydrogen ion concentration in a solution. *(½ M)*

The salt obtained by the reaction of potassium hydroxide and sulphuric acid is potassium sulphate.

$$KOH + H_2SO_4 \rightarrow \underset{\text{Potassium Sulphate}}{K_2SO_4} + H_2O$$ *(1 M)*

Since, this salt is formed by the reaction of strong base and strong acid, therefore, its pH would be 7(neutral). *(½ M)*

Case Based-III

The involved reactions are:

$$\underset{(X)}{2HCl} + \underset{\substack{(Y)\\ \text{(Any metal)}}}{Mg} \longrightarrow MgCl_2 + \underset{\substack{(A)\\ \text{(Burns with a}\\ \text{pop sound)}}}{H_2\uparrow}$$

$$\underset{(X)}{2HCl} + \underset{(Z)}{Na_2CO_3} \longrightarrow 2NaCl + H_2O + \underset{(B)}{CO_2\uparrow}$$

$$\underset{(B)}{6CO_2} + 12H_2O \xrightarrow[\text{Sunlight}]{\text{Chlorophyll}} \underset{\substack{\text{Glucose}\\ (W)}}{C_6H_{12}O_6} + \underset{(C)}{6O_2\uparrow} + 6H_2O$$

$$\underset{(V)}{CuO} + \underset{(A)}{H_2} \xrightarrow[\text{Reduction}]{\text{Heat}} Cu + H_2O$$

$$\underset{(V)}{CuO} + \underset{(X)}{2HCl} \longrightarrow \underset{\substack{\text{Copper (II) chloride}\\ \text{(Blue-green)}}}{CuCl_2} + H_2O$$

(*i*) 'X': Hydrochloric acid (HCl) *(1 M)*

'W': Glucose ($C_6H_{12}O_6$) *(1 M)*

(*ii*) 'B' (CO_2) is a non-metallic oxide. *(1 M)*

Gas 'A' burns with a pop sound indicates that it is hydrogen gas (H_2). *(1 M)*

OR

$$\underset{(V)}{CuO} + \underset{(X)}{2HCl} \longrightarrow \underset{\substack{\text{Copper (II) chloride}\\ \text{(Blue-green)}}}{CuCl_2} + H_2O$$ *(1 M)*

The compound formed, copper (II) chloride ($CuCl_2$), is acidic in nature. *(½ M)*

It will turn the blue litmus solution to red. *(½ M)*

Case Based-IV

(*i*) When electricity is passed through an aqueous solution of a common salt, it decomposes to form sodium hydroxide(Z). The chemical reaction that occurs is:

$$2NaCl(aq) + 2H_2O(l) \longrightarrow \underset{(Z)}{2NaOH(aq)} + \underset{(X)}{Cl_2(g)} + \underset{(Y)}{H_2(g)}$$

X = Cl_2 gas *(½ M)*

Y = H_2 gas *(½ M)*

H_2 gas burns with a pop sound when a burning matchstick is brought near it.

(*ii*) The balanced chemical equation for the formation of substance 'A' is:

$$Ca(OH)_2 + Cl_2 \longrightarrow \underset{(A)}{CaOCl_2} + H_2O$$ *(1 M)*

(*iii*) (*i*) Blue litmus does not cause any colour change, since Z is a base. *(1 M)*

(*ii*) When methyl orange is added to substance Z, that is NaOH, it changes its colour to yellow. *(1 M)*

OR

The balanced chemical reaction that takes place when 'X' and 'Y' react with each other is:

$$H_2(g) + Cl_2(g) \longrightarrow 2HCl(g)$$ *(1 M)*

The Hydrogen Chloride gas produced turns only wet blue Litmus red as HCl get dissociated in water to give out H^+ ion. *(1 M)*

❑❑❑

3 METALS AND NON-METALS

"The body of car or any other automobile is made of steel or aluminium to make it strong and durable. These cars run on fuels like petrol and diesel that are made from long compressed dead decaying organic material made of hydrogen and carbon that are non-metals. Thus, we can see how metals and non-metals together play a crucial role in shaping of the current world."

SYLLABUS & WEIGHTAGE

LIST OF CONCEPT NAMES	YEARS				
	2020	2022 TERM-I	2023	2024	2025
Properties of Metals & Non-metals and The Reactivity Series	—	7 Q*	2Q (1 M) 1Q (4 M)	1 Q (1 M)	2 Q (1 M each) 1 Q (5 M)
Formation and Properties of Ionic Compounds	—	1 Q*	—	—	—
Basic Metallurgical Processes	1 Q (5 M)	—	—	1 Q (3 M)	1 Q (3 M)
Corrosion and Its Prevention	—	—	—	1 Q (1 M)	1 Q (2 M)

** All questions were of MCQ type and carried equal marks.*

For the year 2021, the exam was not conducted.

Metals & Non-metals

METALS

Corrosion
- Rusting of Iron: $4Fe + 2x.H_2O + 3O_2 \rightarrow 2Fe_2O_3 \cdot xH_2O$ Rust (Brick red)
- Tarnishing of Copper: CBSE 2025
  $2Cu + H_2O + CO_2 + O_2 \rightarrow Cu(OH)_2 \cdot CuCO_3$ Basic copper carbonate (green)
- Tarnishing of Silver: $2Ag + H_2S \rightarrow Ag_2S + H_2$ Silver Sulphide (black) CBSE 2025

Prevention
- Applying oil or grease
- Applying paint.
- By Galvanisation.
- By Alloying

Alloys: A homogeneous mixture of two or more metals or a metal and a non-metal
1. Brass → Cu + Zn
2. Bronze → Cu + Sn CBSE 2024
3. Solder → Pb + Sn
4. Stainless Steel → Fe + Cr + Ni

Physical Properties CBSE 2023
- Solid (Exception- Hg)
- Malleable and ductile (Exception- Zn, Hg) CBSE 2025
- Sonorous (Exception- Na, K)
- Lustrous- shiny (Exception-Bi)
- High M.P. & B.P. (Exception-Ga)
- High density (Exception- Li, Na and K)
- Good conductors of heat and electricity
- Hard (Exception- Na, K)

Chemical Properties
- Metal + Oxygen → Metal Oxide CBSE 2023
  $4Na + O_2 \rightarrow 2Na_2O$
- Amphoteric oxides: Reacts with both acids and bases CBSE 2025, 2024, 2023
  $Al_2O_3 + 6HCl \text{ (Acid)} \rightarrow 2AlCl_3 + 3H_2O$
  $Al_2O_3 + 2NaOH \text{ (Base)} \rightarrow 2NaAlO_2 + H_2O$
- Metal oxide + Water → Metal Hydroxide CBSE 2023, 2022 Term-I
  $Na_2O(s) + H_2O(l) \rightarrow 2NaOH(aq)$
- Metal + Water → Metal Oxide + Hydrogen CBSE 2022 Term-I
  Metal Oxide + Water → Metal Hydroxide
  $2K + 2H_2O \rightarrow 2KOH + H_2\uparrow$
- Metal + Steam → Metal oxide + Hydrogen Gas CBSE 2022
  $2Al(s) + 3H_2O(g) \rightarrow Al_2O_3(s) + 3H_2(g)$
- Metal + Acid → Salt + Hydrogen Gas CBSE 2022 Term-I
  $2Na + 2HCl \rightarrow 2NaCl + H_2\uparrow$
- Metal + Hydrogen → Metal Hydride
  $2Na + H_2 \rightarrow 2NaH$
- Metal + Base → Metal Salt + Hydrogen Gas
  $Zn + 2NaOH \rightarrow Na_2ZnO_2 + H_2$

Extraction of metals CBSE 2025, 2024, 2020

Ore → Concentration of ore →
- Metals of high reactivity (Na, K, Al) → Electrolysis of molten ore → Pure metal
- Metals of medium reactivity (Zn, Fe, Pb) → Carbonate ores → Calcination / Sulphide ores → Roasting → Oxide of metal → Reduction to metal → Purification of metal
- Metals of low reactivity (Hg, Cu, Ag) → Sulphide ores → Roasting → Metal → Refining → Electrolytic Refining

Steps involved in the extraction of metals from ores

Reactivity Series CBSE 2025, 2022 Term-I

A metal with high reactivity can displace a metal with low reactivity from its salt solution.

K > Na > Ca > Mg > Al > Zn > Fe > Sn > Pb > H > Cu > Hg > Ag > Au > Pt

NON-METALS

Physical Properties
- Solid and gas (Exception-Br)
- Soft and brittle (Exception-Diamond)
- Non sonorous
- Low M.P. and B.P.
- Non malleable and non ductile
- Dull ((Exception- iodine and graphite)
- Poor conductor of heat and electricity (Exception- graphite)

Chemical properties
- Non metal + Oxygen → Non metallic Oxide
  $C(s) + O_2(g) \rightarrow CO_2(g)$ CBSE 2023
- Non metal + Water → No Reaction
- Non metal + Acid/Base → No Reaction

IONIC COMPOUNDS

Formation of Ionic compounds CBSE 2025, 2022 Term-I, 2020

Formed by the complete transfer of electrons from a metal to a non-metal. Ex. Formation of $MgCl_2$

$Mg \rightarrow Mg^{2+} + 2e^-$ (cation) ; $Cl + e^- \rightarrow Cl^-$ (anion)

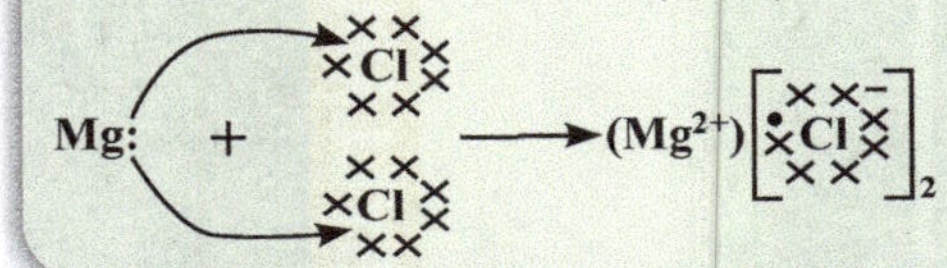

Physical properties of Ionic compounds CBSE 2020
- Crystalline Solid
- High M.P and B.P.
- Soluble in water & insoluble in solvents like kerosene.
- Good conductors of electricity in aqueous solution and molten state
- Do not conduct electricity in solid state.

1 PROPERTIES OF METALS & NON-METALS AND THE REACTIVITY SERIES

NCERT Definitions (Commonly asked in 1 mark)

- **Malleability:** The ability of metals to be deformed under pressure into **thin sheets**.
- **Ductility:** The property of metals to be drawn into **wires**.
- **Electrical Conductivity:** The ability of a substance(metals) to allow the **flow of electricity**.
- **Reactivity Series:** A series in which metals are arranged in order of their reactivity from **highest to lowest**.
- **Metallic Lustre:** The property of metal by which they exhibit **shining** surface.
- **Sonority:** The property of metal by which they produce **sound** on striking hard surfaces.
- **Amphoteric Oxides:** Oxides that show both **acidic** and **basic** properties.

Important Facts

01 The metal that remains liquid at room temperature and is often used in thermometers. *~ Mercury*

02 A substance which despite being a non-metal, can conduct electricity and is used in pencils. *~ Graphite*

03 A non metal, the hardest natural substance known with very high melting and boiling point. *~ Diamond*

04 The most ductile metal. *~ Gold*

05 Some bases soluble in water. *~ Alkalis*

06 Metals which are poor conductors of heat. *~Lead and Mercury*

07 Copper does not react with dilute HCl.

Difference Between

Metals vs. Non-metals(On the Basis of Physical Properties)		
Physical Properties	**Metals**	**Non-metals**
State (at room temperature)	Mostly solid (except mercury which is liquid)	Mostly solid or as gases (except bromine which is liquid.)
Hardness	Generally hard (except, Na and K)	Generally soft (except diamond)
Malleability	Malleable	Brittle (break into pieces when hammered)
Ductility	Ductile	Non-ductile
Conductivity	Good conductors of heat and electricity	Poor conductors (except graphite)
Appearance	Lustrous (shiny)	Non-lustrous (except iodine)
Sonorous	Produce sound	Do not produce sound
Density	High density	Low density

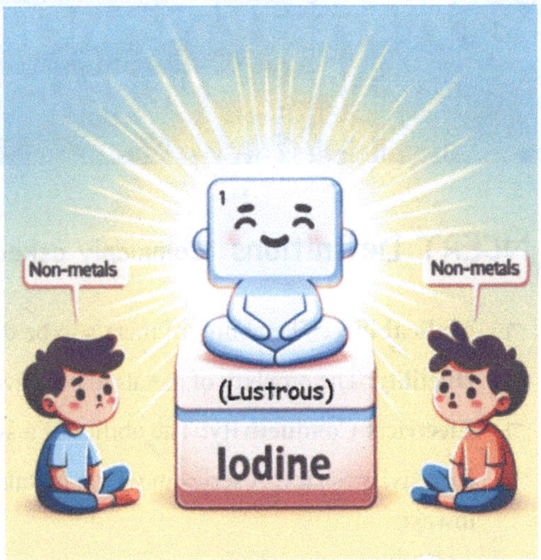

Metals vs. Non-metals (On the Basis of Chemical Properties)		
Chemical Properties	**Metals**	**Non-metals**
Nature of Oxide	Generally basic (Eg-Na_2O, K_2O), but also forms amphoteric oxides (Eg-Al_2O_3, ZnO)	Generally acidic (Eg- CO_2, SO_2, NO_2) but also forms neutral oxide. (Eg- N_2O, CO, NO)
Reaction with Water	**Reactivity:** Metals like Na,K react violently with cold water. Magnesium does not react with cold water. Some metals (like Fe, Al, Zn), do not react either with cold or hot water, but they react with steam. **Products formed:** Metal hydroxide or Metal oxide	Generally do not react with water.
Reaction with Acids	Reactive metals reacts with acids to give a salt and hydrogen gas.	Do not displace hydrogen from dilute acids.

Real Life Application Based Questions

1. **You notice that all the electrical wires used have a coating of polyvinylchloride (PVC) or rubber-like material. Why is it important to use such coated wires for electrical connections?**

Ans. The PVC or rubber-like coating on electric wires acts as an insulator (bad conductor of electricity) **to prevent electric shocks**. Also, these materials are resistant to heat and fire, reducing the risk of fires from short circuits.

2. **Gold is a very soft metal, yet it's widely used for making jewellery. How is this possible?**

Ans. Pure gold is indeed soft, which makes it unsuitable for making durable jewellery. Therefore, it's alloyed with other metals like copper or silver to make it harder and more resistant to wear and tear, which is why gold alloys are commonly used for jewellery.

3. **Why are aluminium foils commonly used for wrapping food?**

Ans. Aluminium foils are used for wrapping food because aluminium is **malleable**, meaning it can be made into thin sheets that can be easily bent or wrapped around objects. Also, the smooth, shiny surface of aluminium reflects the heat radiation emitted by food back towards it. In this way food **remains warm** for a longer duration of time. Aluminium also has **good corrosion resistance,** is **non-toxic,** and **doesn't impart any taste** to the food. Hence, aluminium foils are commonly used for wrapping food.

4. **While cooking, if a small piece of aluminium foil accidentally falls into the flame of a gas stove, it burns with a bright flame. However, a copper coin does not. Can you explain how it is based on the reactivity series?**

Ans. Aluminium is **more reactive** than copper and when it burns, it reacts with oxygen to form aluminium oxide, emitting a lot of heat and light. **Copper**, **being less reactive**, does not easily react with oxygen to burn in a gas flame.

Myth Buster

- **Myth: The physical state of a substance at room temperature is indicative of whether it is a metal or a non-metal.**
  Fact: While metals are commonly solid at room temperature (except mercury which is liquid), this is not a definitive way to classify elements as metals or non-metals since there are exceptions to this generalization.

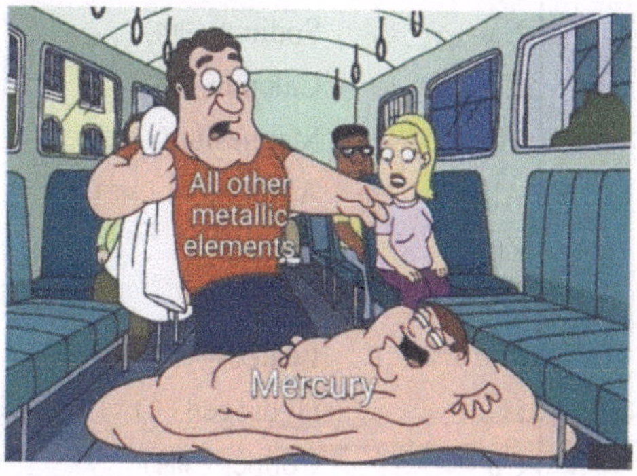

- **Myth: All metals react with water.**
  Fact: Metals exhibit varying reactivity with water. While some, like potassium and sodium, react vigorously, others, like aluminium, iron, and zinc, do not react with cold or hot water but will react with steam.
- **Myth: Metal oxides are always basic in nature.**
  Fact: While many metal oxides are basic, some, like aluminium oxide and zinc oxide, exhibit amphoteric properties, meaning they can act as both acids and bases.
- **Myth: All non-metals are poor conductors of heat and electricity.**
  Fact: Graphite, a form of carbon and a non-metal, is a good conductor of electricity, which makes it an exception to the general rule that non-metals are poor conductors.
- **Myth: The reactivity series is only useful for predicting reactions between metals and acids.**
  Fact: The reactivity series not only predicts the outcomes of reactions between metals and acids but also provides insight into other reactions, such as single displacement reactions, where a more reactive metal can displace a less reactive metal from its compound.
- **Myth: Metals cannot be cut easily due to their hardness.**
  Fact: Alkali metals such as sodium, and potassium are so soft that they can be cut with a knife, demonstrating that not all metals share the same level of hardness.
- **Myth: All metals have high melting points.**
  Fact: While many metals are hard and have high melting points, metals like gallium and caesium have very low melting points and can melt just from the warmth of a human hand.

Mnemonics

METALS- Properties

- M → Malleable
- E → Electrical Conductor
- T → Thermal Conductor
- A → Alloy Forming
- L → Lustrous
- S → Sonorous/Solid

- **Best conductors of heat:** Silver(Ag) and Copper (Cu).

"Happy Students Celebrated"

Happy → Heat
Students → Silver
Celebrated → Copper

- **Aqua regia:** Freshly prepared mixture of concentrated HCl and concentrated HNO_3 in the ratio of 3 : 1. It can dissolve gold, even though neither of these acids can do so alone.

"3 Hens made 1 Nest"

3 → 3 parts
Hens made → Hydrochloric acid
1 → 1 part
Nest → Nitric acid

To HCl and HNO_3 alone

To aqua regia

❒ To remember Reactivity series

REACTIVITY SERIES TRICK		
K	Potassium (काशी)	Most reactive
Na	Sodium (नाथ)	
Ca	Calcium (का)	
Mg	Magnesium (माली)	
Al	Aluminium (आलू)	
Zn	Zinc (जरा)	Reactivity decreases
Fe	Iron (फके)	
Pb	Lead (पकाता)	
H	Hydrogen (है)	
Cu	Copper (कौन)	
Hg	Mercury (है)	
Ag	Silver (आगे)	
Au	Gold (आओ)	Least reactive

COMPETENCY BASED SOLVED EXAMPLES

Multiple Choice Questions (1 M)

1. Metals are lustrous and shine especially when their freshly cut surfaces are exposed.
Salma cut pieces and compared the lustre of the freshly cut surfaces of the following metals.
aluminium, sodium, copper, iron
The freshly cut surface of which of these metals is likely to lose its lustre first on exposure to air? **(*Un*) (CBSE APQ,2023)**

(*a*) aluminium (*b*) sodium
(*c*) copper (*d*) iron

2. In a laboratory experiment, a student is given a sample of an unknown element and is asked to determine its identity. The student observes that the element has a high melting point, is a good conductor of electricity, and forms a basic oxide when reacted with oxygen.
Based on these observations, the student proposes two possible identities for the unknown element: it could be metal 'X' or metal 'Y. Which identity, if any, is more likely, and why? **(*An*)**

(*a*) Metal 'X' is more likely because it has a higher melting point than metal 'Y.'
(*b*) Metal 'Y' is more likely because it forms a basic oxide, which is a characteristic of metals.
(*c*) Both metal 'X' and metal 'Y' are equally likely, and the observations do not provide sufficient information to distinguish between them.
(*d*) Neither metal 'X' nor metal 'Y' is likely because the observations are inconsistent.

3. Aluminium is used for making cooking utensils. Which of the following properties of aluminium are responsible for the same? **(*Ap*) (NCERT Exemplar)**

(*i*) Good thermal conductivity
(*ii*) Good electrical conductivity
(*iii*) Ductility
(*iv*) High melting point

(*a*) (*i*) and (*ii*) (*b*) (*i*) and (*iii*)
(*c*) (*ii*) and (*iii*) (*d*) (*i*) and (*iv*)

4. The oxide which can react with HCl as well as KOH to give corresponding salt and water is **(*Re*) (CBSE 2024)**

(*a*) CuO (*b*) Al_2O_3
(*c*) Na_2O (*d*) K_2O

5. Which of the following oxide(s) would be obtained on the prolonged reaction of iron with steam? **(*Re*) (NCERT Exemplar)**

(*a*) FeO (*b*) Fe_2O_3
(*c*) Fe_3O_4 (*d*) Fe_2O_3 and Fe_3O_4

6. Study the diagram given below and identify the gas formed in the reaction. **(*Ap*)(CBSE 2022 Term-1)**

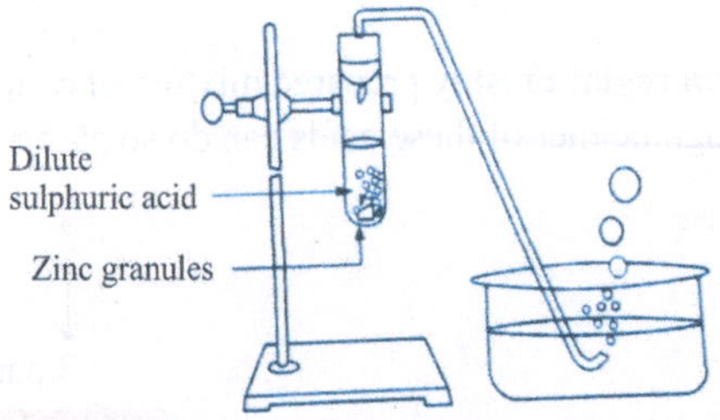

(*a*) Carbon dioxide which extinguishes the burning candle.
(*b*) Oxygen due to which the candle burns more brightly.
(*c*) Sulphur dioxide which produces a suffocating smell.
(*d*) Hydrogen which while burning produces a popping sound.

Assertion and Reason (1 M)

Direction: The following questions consist of two statements – Assertion (A) and Reason (R). Answer these questions by selecting the appropriate option given below:

(*a*) Both A and R are true, and R is the correct explanation of A.
(*b*) Both A and R are true, but R is not the correct explanation of A.
(*c*) A is true, but R is false
(*d*) A is false, but R is true.

1. **Assertion (A):** On adding dil. HCl to a test tube containing a substance 'X', a colourless gas is produced which gives a pop sound when a burning match stick is brought near it.
Reason (R): In this reaction metal 'X' is displaced by Hydrogen. ***(Un) (CBSE SQP, 2024)***
2. **Assertion (A):** Metals are sonorous.
Reason (R): They are generally brittle in the solid state, and they break into pieces when hit by a hammer. ***(Un)***
3. **Assertion (A):** Carbon reacts with oxygen to form carbon dioxide, which is an acidic oxide.
Reason (R): Non-metals form acidic oxides. ***(Re)***
4. **Assertion (A):** $Fe_2O_3 + 2Al \rightarrow Al_2O_3 + 2Fe$
The above chemical equation is an example of displacement reaction.
Reason (R): Aluminium being more reactive than iron, displaces Fe from its oxide. ***(Un)***

Subjective Questions

Very Short Answer Type Questions (2 M)

1. (*a*) **The densities of water and magnesium metal at different temperatures are given in the table below.**

Temperature	Density of magnesium metal	Density of water
25 °C (room temperature)	1.738	0.99
100 °C (boiling point of water)	-	0.958
650 °C (melting point of magnesium)	1.64	-

'Magnesium floats in boiling water because its density decreases on heating.'
Is the statement above true or false? If true, give a reason. If false, correct it. **(CFPQ)**

(*b*) **Name the oxide that dissolves in water to produce alkali.** ***(An)***

Ans. (*a*) The statement "Magnesium floats in boiling water because its density decreases on heating" is false. *(½ M)*
Magnesium floats because of the bubbles of hydrogen gas sticking to its surface as it reacts with hot water. *(½ M)*

(*b*) Sodium oxide dissolves in water to produce alkali. *(½ M)*

$Na_2O(s) + H_2O(l) \rightarrow 2NaOH(aq)$ *(½ M)*

2. **Why do we use copper and aluminium wire for the transmission of electric current?** ***(Ap)***

Ans. We use copper and aluminium wire for the transmission of electric current because of the following two reasons:
1. They are good conductors of electric current. *(1 M)*
2. They are ductile that, can be easily drawn into wires. *(1 M)*

3. **Give an example of a metal which** ***(Re)*** **(NCERT Intext)**
(*i*) is a liquid at room temperature.
(*ii*) can be easily cut with a knife.
(*iii*) is the best conductor of heat
(*iv*) is a poor conductor of heat

Ans. (*i*) Mercury *(½ M)*
(*ii*) Sodium *(½ M)*
(*iii*) Silver *(½ M)*
(*iv*) Lead *(½ M)*

4. **The blue-coloured solution of the sulphate salt of metal W is taken in a beaker. Metal powders X, Y and Z are added one after the other to the beaker. The colour changes occuring in the solution are shown below.**

$$\underset{\text{Blue solution}}{W\text{-}SO_4} \xrightarrow{\text{Metal X}} \underset{\text{solution}}{\text{Colourless}} \xrightarrow{\text{Metal Y}} \underset{\text{solution}}{\text{Pink}} \xrightarrow{\text{Metal Z}} \underset{\text{solution}}{\text{Green}}$$

State what colour change, if any, will occur if metal X is again added to the green solution in the beaker. Explain why. ***(An)*** **(CFPQ)**

Ans. No colour change will occur. *(1 M)*
Metal X is less reactive than metal Z, or metal X is lower than metal Z in the reactivity series. *(1 M)*

Short Answer Type Questions (3 M)

1. **(*i*) Write two properties of gold which make it the most suitable metal for ornaments.**
(*ii*) Name two metals which have low densities.
(*iii*) Name two metals which melt when you keep them on your palm. ***(Re)***

Ans. (*i*) The two properties of gold which make it the most suitable metal for ornaments are
1. Malleability (can be beaten into thin sheets) and ductility (can be drawn into thin wires). *(½ M)*
2. Noble element (Gold being a noble element does not react with air, water, acids etc. and hence does not get corroded). *(½ M)*

(*ii*) Sodium and Potassium have low densities. *(½ × 2 = 1 M)*
(*iii*) Gallium and Caesium are the two metals which melt when you keep them on your palm. *(½ × 2 = 1 M)*

2. **Imagine you are a forensic chemist called upon to investigate a series of incidents where a man posing as a goldsmith went door to door, offering to polish old gold ornaments. After treating the jewellery, the ornaments sparkled but lost significant weight, causing distress among the owners. Additionally, you are often consulted by engineers who need advice on materials for constructing hot water tanks.**
Based on this scenario, answer the following questions: ***(Ap)***
(A) Based on your knowledge of chemistry, identify the likely solution used by the man to clean the gold ornaments. Explain the chemical process that caused the gold ornaments to lose weight despite appearing polished.
(B) Explain why copper is preferred over steel (an alloy of iron) for making hot water tanks.

Ans. (A)

- **Likely Solution:** The man probably used aqua regia, a mixture of concentrated hydrochloric acid and concentrated nitric acid in the ratio of 3: 1, which is known to dissolve gold. *(1 M)*
- **Chemical Process:** Aqua regia dissolve the outer layer of the gold to form gold chloride. Due to this, inner layer become shiny. This will cause a loss of weight of ornaments. *(1 M)*

(B) Copper (Cu), rather than Steel (an alloy of Iron (Fe)), is used to make hot water tanks because copper does not react with water or steam, while Iron reacts with steam to corrode the tank. *(1 M)*

3. Samples of four metal A, B, C and D were taken and added to the following solution one by one. The results obtained have been tabulated as follows. ***(Ap)* (NCERT Intext)**

Metal	Iron (II) Sulphate	Copper(II) Sulphate	Zinc Sulphate	Silver Nitrate
A	No reaction	Displacement		
B	Displacement		No reaction	
C	No reaction	No reaction	No reaction	Displacement
D	No reaction	No reaction	No reaction	No reaction

Use the Table above to answer the following questions about metals A, B, C and D.

***(i)* Which is the most reactive metal?**

***(ii)* What would you observe if B is added to a solution of Copper(II) sulphate?**

***(iii)* Arrange the metals A, B, C and D in the order of decreasing reactivity.**

Ans. (*i*) Metal B is the most reactive as it gives displacement reaction with iron (II) sulphate. *(½ M)*

(*ii*) When metal B is added to copper (II) sulphate solution, a displacement reaction will take place because of which the blue colour of copper (II) sulphate solution will fade and a red-brown deposit of copper will be formed on metal B. *(1 M)*

(*iii*) Metal B displays the highest reactivity as it has the capability to displace iron from its salt solution.

Comparatively, Metal A exhibits lower reactivity as it displaces copper from its salt solution.

Metal C demonstrates even lower reactivity since it can only displace silver from its salt solution.

Lastly, Metal D is the least reactive among the mentioned metals as it cannot displace any other metal from its salt solution. *(1 M)*

Therefore, the sequence of decreasing reactivity for the metals is B > A > C > D *(½ M)*

Key Takeaways

This question teaches students that, the reactivity of metals can be compared by their ability to displace other metals from their salt solutions. A more reactive metal can displace a less reactive metal from its salt solution. The reactivity series can be determined by observing reactions between metals and metal salt solutions.

4. A solution of $CuSO_4$ was kept in an iron pot. After a few days, the iron pot was found to have a number of holes in it. Explain the reason in terms of reactivity. Write the equation of the reaction involved. ***(Ap)* (NCERT Exemplar)**

Ans.
- A solution of $CuSO_4$ was kept in an iron pot. After a few days, the iron pot was found to have a number of holes in it.
- This is because according to reactivity series, Fe is more reactive as compared to Cu.
- Reactivity series is a series in which elements are arranged in the decreasing order of their reactivity.
- Therefore, Fe displaces Cu from $CuSO_4$ and forms $FeSO_4$.
- Since Fe from iron pot is participating in the reaction, hence holes are formed in the vessel. *(2 M)*
- The reaction takes place as

  $Fe + CuSO_4 \rightarrow FeSO_4 + Cu$ *(1 M)*

5. Sakshi was comparing the reactivity of different metals for her science project. She added iron filings in four test tubes A, B, C, D containing aqueous solutions of $ZnSO_4$, $CuSO_4$, $FeSO_4$ and $Al_2(SO_4)_3$ respectively as shown in the figure – ***(Ap)* (CBSE APQ, 2023)**

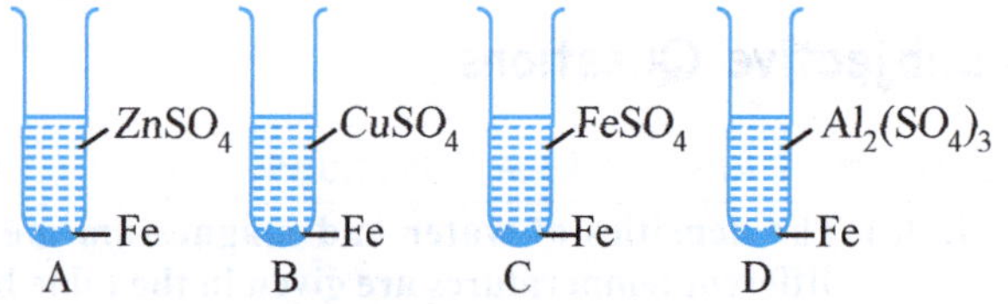

***(a)* In which of the test tubes she will observe the reaction to be most vigorous**

***(b)* What is the reason for her observation?**

(c) Write a well-balanced equation of the reaction in (*b*).

Ans. (*a*) In Test Tube-B, the reaction will be most vigorous. *(1 M)*

(*b*) Copper lies lower than Iron in the reactivity series so displacement reaction will take place and Fe will displace Cu from its $CuSO_4$ solution. *(1 M)*

(c) $Fe(s) + CuSO_4(aq.) \rightarrow FeSO_4(aq.) + Cu(s)$ *(1 M)*

Long Answer Type Questions (5 M)

1. Give reasons for the following:

***(i)* Generally, no hydrogen gas is evolved when metals react with dilute nitric acid.**

***(ii)* Sodium hydroxide solution cannot be kept in aluminium containers.**

***(iii)* Reaction of calcium with water is less violent.**

***(iv)* Sodium is kept immersed in kerosene.**

(v)* Aluminium reacts with dilute hydrochloric acid slowly in the beginning.** ***(Ap)

Ans. (*i*) When a metal reacts with nitric acid, no hydrogen gas is produced because HNO_3 is a powerful oxidising agent, it oxidises the generated H_2 to water, and itself gets reduced to any of the nitrogen oxides (N_2O, NO, NO_2). *(1 M)* (*ii*) NaOH cannot be stored in an aluminium vessels because Na being highly reactive, reacts with aluminium and corrodes the metal and produces highly flammable hydrogen gas. *(1 M)*

(*iii*) The reaction of calcium with water is less violent as the heat evolved is not sufficient for the hydrogen to catch fire. *(1 M)*

(*iv*) Sodium reacts so vigorously that it catch fire if kept in the open. Hence, to protect them and to prevent accidental fires, they are kept immersed in kerosene oil. *(1 M)*

(*v*) This is because aluminium is shielded by a layer of aluminium oxide, Al_2O_3. It will take some time for the hydrochloric acid to eat through this protective layer, but once it does, the reaction will proceed rapidly with hydrogen gas beginning to bubble out of the solution. *(1 M)*

2. (*a*) What would be observed when: (*Un*)

(*i*) Some zinc pieces are put in a copper sulphate solution.

(*ii*) Some silver pieces are put in a green-coloured ferrous sulphate solution.

(*b*) What is the reactivity series of metals? Arrange the following metals in the order of their increase in reactivity.

Gold, copper, iron and magnesium.

(*c*) What would you observe when zinc is added to a solution of iron(II) sulphate? Write the chemical reaction that takes place. (NCERT Intext)

Ans. (*a*) (*i*) When Zn pieces are put in $CuSO_4$ solution, then the blue solution of copper will become colourless, and reddish brown copper metal will be deposited. This is because Zn being more reactive displaces Cu from its salt solution.

$$\underset{}{Zn(s)} + \underset{\text{(Blue)}}{CuSO_4\,(aq)} \rightarrow \underset{\text{(colourless)}}{ZnSO_4\,(aq)} + \underset{\text{(reddish brown)}}{Cu\downarrow(s)}$$

(1 M)

(*ii*) $Ag(s) + FeSO_4\,(aq) \rightarrow$ No reaction

This reaction will not take place because 'Ag' is less reactive than iron. *(1 M)*

(*b*) The series of metals in which metals are arranged in decreasing order of their reactivity is known as the reactivity series of metals. *(1 M)*

The given metals can be arranged in increasing order as: *(1 M)*

Au < Cu < Fe < Mg

(*c*) When zinc is added to a solution of iron(II) sulphate, then the green colour of iron sulphate fades and the solution becomes colourless due to the formation of zinc sulphate. *(½ M)*

The chemical reaction that takes place is:

$$Zn(s) + FeSO_4(aq) \rightarrow ZnSO_4(aq) + Fe(s) \quad (½\ M)$$

Mistakes 101 : What not to do!

Based on the misunderstanding of the reactivity series, students might predict incorrect outcomes for displacement reactions.

Hints & Explanations

Multiple Choice Questions

1. (*b*) The freshly cut surface of sodium is likely to lose its lustre first on exposure to air, because sodium is most reactive among the given metals.
2. (*c*) Both metal 'X' and metal 'Y' are equally likely, and the observations do not provide sufficient information to distinguish between them.
3. (*d*) Al should have high melting point so that utensil doesn't melt on flame. Also, it should have good thermal conductivity so that heat can be transferred from the flame to the food inside the vessel.
4. (*b*) Al_2O_3 is an amphoteric oxide which can react with HCl (an acid) as well as KOH (a base) to give corresponding salt and water.
5. (*c*) The prolonged reaction of iron with steam produces Fe_3O_4, and the reaction takes place as
$$3Fe(s) + 4H_2O(g) \rightarrow Fe_3O_4\,(s) + 4H_2\uparrow(g)$$
6. (*d*) According to the given diagram, it is clear that zinc granules are present in a test tube, and dilute H_2SO_4 is poured on it. Zinc, which is more reactive than hydrogen, displaces it and form zinc sulphate. Hydrogen gas is also formed during this. H_2 gas is combustible in nature therefore, it burns with a popping sound when a burning match stick is brought near to this.

Assertion and Reason

1. (*c*) A is true but R is false
2. (*c*) Assertion is True, but the Reason is false.
   Metals are generally hard, thus, they do not break into pieces when hit by a hammer, rather, they convert into thin sheets.
3. (*a*) Generally, non-metals form acidic or neutral oxides. Carbon dioxide is an oxide of carbon(a non-metal). Hence, it's an acidic oxide.
4. (*a*) Al being more reactive than Fe can displace it from its oxide, Fe_2O_3. Therefore, the given reaction is a displacement reaction.

FORMATION AND PROPERTIES OF IONIC COMPOUNDS

2

NCERT Definitions (Commonly asked in 1 mark)

- **Electrostatic Forces:** The **forces of attraction** between positively and negatively charged ions in an ionic compound.
- **Ionic Compounds/Electrovalent Compounds:** Compounds composed of ions held together by electrostatic forces and formed by the transfer of electrons from a metal to a non-metal.
- **Ionic Bond:** A chemical bond formed between **two ions** with **opposite charges**. Ionic bonds form when one atom(metals) gives up one or more electrons to another atom(non metal).

Important Facts

01 An electrically charged atom or group of atoms. *~ Ion*

02 Ionic compounds consist of only ions and not molecules.

03 NaCl does not exist as molecule but as aggregate of oppositely charged ions.

04 Ionic bond is also called as electrovalent bond.

05 Reactivity of elements is explained on the element's tendency to attain completely filled valence shell.

Real Life Application Based Questions

1. **In a kitchen experiment, you decide to observe how table salt (sodium chloride) dissolves in water. Given that table salt is formed through an ionic bond, how does this ionic interaction influence salt's ability to dissolve in water during cooking?**

Ans. The ionic nature of table salt means that it consists of positively charged sodium ions and negatively charged chloride ions. Water molecules, which are polar, interact with these ions, dissolving them and thereby making salt an excellent seasoning and preservative in cooking due to its high solubility.

2. **Considering that ionic compounds conduct electricity when dissolved, how does this property benefit athletes through sports drinks?**

Ans. When ionic compounds like electrolytes dissolve in water, they release ions that are essential for nerve impulse transmission and muscle function. For athletes, consuming sports drinks with electrolytes helps maintain essential body functions, especially during prolonged physical activity.

Myth Buster

- **Myth: Ionic compounds always involve a metal and a non-metal.**

  Fact: Most ionic compounds consist of metals and non-metals, with metals losing electrons and non-metals gaining them. However, certain compounds, such as ammonium nitrate (NH_4NO_3), are ionic and contain only non-metal elements.

- **Myth: Ionic compounds always conduct electricity.**

  Fact: Ionic compounds do not conduct electricity in their solid state because their **ions are fixed** in place within the crystal lattice. However, when melted or dissolved in water, they can conduct electricity due to the free movement of ions.

- **Myth: All ionic compounds are soluble in water.**

  Fact: Solubility in water varies among ionic compounds. While many are soluble, such as sodium chloride, others like barium sulphate are insoluble due to the specific interactions between the ions and water molecules.

- **Myth: The formation of ionic compounds is always exothermic and never include any endothermic steps.***

  Fact: While the formation of an ionic lattice from ions is generally exothermic due to the **release of lattice energy**, the overall process of forming ionic compounds from elements includes endothermic steps like ionization, which requires energy.

* *Concepts beyond the board exam syllabus, offering deeper insight and critical thinking on NCERT topics.*

COMPETENCY BASED SOLVED EXAMPLES

Multiple Choice Questions (1 M)

1. The electronic configurations of three elements, A, B and C are A — 2, 8; B — 2, 8, 7 and C — 2, 8, 2. Which of the following statement is correct? ***(Ap)*** **(NCERT Exemplar)**

(*a*) A is a metal

(*b*) B is non-metal

(*c*) C is a non-metal

(*d*) B is a metal and C is a non-metal

2. An element 'M' has 50% of the electrons filled in the 3rd shell as in the 2nd shell. The atomic number of 'M' is: ***(Un)*** **(CBSE SQP, 2023)**

(*a*) 10 (*b*) 12

(*c*) 14 (*d*) 18

3. Which of the following are not ionic compounds? ***(Un)*** **(NCERT Exemplar)**

(*i*) KCl (*ii*) HCl

(*iii*) CCl_4 (*iv*) NaCl

(*a*) (*i*) and (*ii*) (*b*) (*ii*) and (*iii*)

(*c*) (*iii*) and (*iv*) (*d*) (*i*) and (*iii*)

4. Reaction between B and A forms compound D. B loses electrons, and A gains electrons. Which of the following properties is not shown by compound D? ***(An)***

(*a*) Has low melting point

(*b*) Has high melting point

(*c*) Occurs as solid

(*d*) Conducts electricity in the molten state

5. Which of the following structures correctly depicts the compound $CaCl_2$? ***(Un)*** **(CBSE 2022 Term 1)**

(*a*) 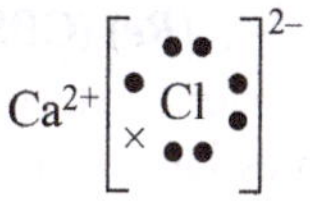

(*b*) 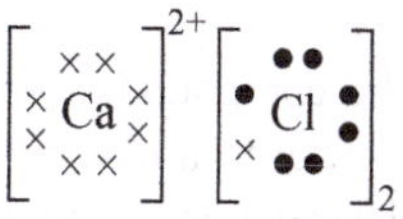

(*c*) 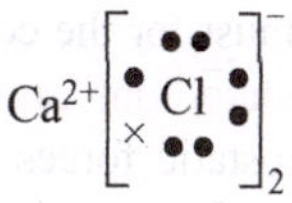

(*d*) 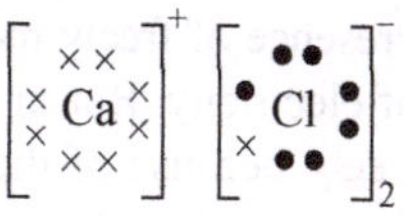

Assertion and Reason (1 M)

Direction: The following questions consist of two statements – Assertion (A) and Reason (R). Answer these questions by selecting the appropriate option given below:

(*a*) Both A and R are true, and R is the correct explanation of A.

(*b*) Both A and R are true, but R is not the correct explanation of A.

(*c*) A is true, but R is false

(*d*) A is false, but R is true.

1. **Assertion (A):** Potassium Chloride is an ionic compound.

   Reason (R): Metal (K) and non-metal (Cl) react by mutual transfer of electrons. ***(Un)***

2. **Assertion (A):** Ionic solids are good conductors of electricity.

   Reason (R): Ionic solids consists of anions and cations. ***(Un)***

Subjective Questions

Very Short Answer Type Questions (2 M)

1. Leena in a chemistry lab was conducting an experiment to investigate the properties of a newly discovered compound, XY. During her analysis, she discovered that atoms of X lost one electron each, while atoms of Y gained one electron each to form this compound.
Based on her observations, can you determine the nature of the bond that exists between atoms X and Y in compound XY? ***(Un)***

Ans. The atoms of X lose electrons while the atoms of Y gain electrons. Hence, there is transfer of electrons from atoms of X to atoms of Y. *(1 M)*
The bond formed by the transfer of electrons is known as ionic bond. The nature of bond in the compound XY is ionic. *(1 M)*

2. Why do ionic compounds conduct electricity in a molten state? ***(Re)***

Ans. Ionic compounds will conduct electricity in a molten state because they contain free ions that will move in a molten state. *(1 M)*
For a compound to conduct electricity, it must contain free ions. Presence of free ions are responsible for the conduction of electricity. *(1 M)*

Short Answer Type Questions (3 M)

1. What are ionic compounds? Why do ionic compounds not conduct electricity in the solid state? ***(Re)* (CBSE 2019)**

Ans. The compounds formed by the transfer of electrons from a metal to a non-metal are known as ionic compounds or electrovalent compounds. *(1 M)*
Presence of freely moving ions is must for the conduction of electricity. But in case of solid state, ions cannot move freely because of the strong electrostatic forces that hold them together. As a result, in their solid state, ionic solids do not conduct electricity. *(2 M)*

2. The electronic configuration of some elements is given in the table below. ***(Un)* (CBSE APQ, 2023)**

Elements	Electronic Configuration
P	2, 8, 8
Q	2, 8, 8, 1
R	2, 6
S	2, 5
T	2, 8, 2
U	2, 8, 7

(*a*) Identify any two pairs of elements that will react to form compounds by a transfer of electrons.
(*b*) Write the molecular formula of the compounds formed by the pairs of elements identified in (*a*).

Ans. (*a*) The two pairs of elements that will react to form compounds by a transfer of electrons are:
- *Q* and *R*
- *Q* and *U*
- *T* and *R*
- *T* and *U*

(Any two of the above) *(1 × 2 = 2 M)*

(*b*) The correct molecular formulas of the compounds formed in (*a*) are:
- Q_2R
- QU
- TR
- TU_2

(Any two of the above) *(½ × 2 = 1 M)*

Nailing the Right Answer

For a student to accurately answer the above question, he needs to know the tendency of elements to complete their octet. Elements with 1, 2 electrons in valence shell tend to lose electrons to elements with 6, 7 electrons in their valence shell, to ensure the octet of all elements in the compound is complete.

Long Answer Type Questions (5 M)

1. (*i*) In the formation of a compound between two atoms P and R, P loses two electrons and R gains one electron.
(*a*) What is the nature of the bond between P and R?
(*b*) Suggest the formula of the compound formed between P and R.
(*ii*) On a similar concept, explain the formation of the $MgCl_2$ molecule.
(*iii*) Why does common salt conduct electricity only in the molten state?
(*iv*) The melting point of NaCl is high. Why? ***(Un)***

Ans. (*i*) (*a*) Ionic bond is formed between P and R. *(½ M)*
(*b*) $(P^{2+})(R^-)_2$, i.e., PR_2 is the formula of the compound. *(½ M)*

(*ii*) $Mg \rightarrow Mg^{2+} + 2e^-$ *(½ M)*
$2Cl + 2e^- \rightarrow 2Cl^-$ *(½ M)*
$(Mg^{2+})(Cl^-)_2$ *(1 M)*

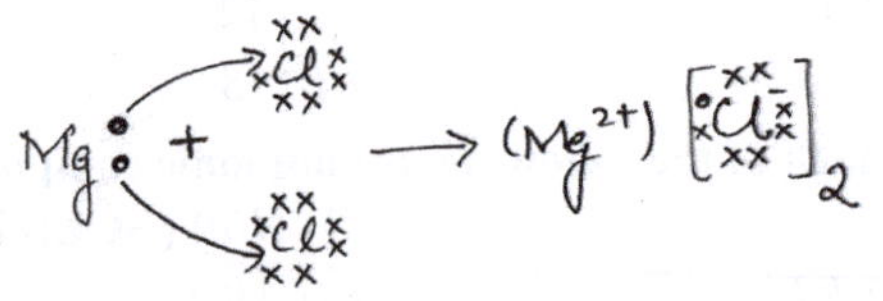

Formation of magnesium chloride

(*iii*) NaCl is the common salt and it is composed of Na^+ and Cl^- ions which are free to move in a molten state, but in solid state, they are not free to move.
Therefore, common salt conducts electricity only in the molten state *(1 M)*

(*iv*) NaCl is an ionic compound and possesses a strong force of attraction between Na^+ and Cl^-, thus, a large amount of energy is required to break the bond. Therefore, it possesses a high melting point. *(1 M)*

Key Takeaways

This question teaches students that ionic bonds are formed between atoms when one loses electrons and another gains electrons and they conduct electricity only during molten state. Their strong electrostatic forces leads to high melting point.

2. (*a*) Write electron dot structures of Ca (Atomic no. 20) and O (Atomic no. 8).

(*b*) Show the formation of calcium oxide by transfer of electrons.

(*c*) Name the ions present in this compound.

(*d*) List four important characteristics of this compound.

(CBSE 2020)

Ans. (*a*) Ca (atomic number 20) = 2, 8, 8, 2 *(½ M)*

It's electron dot structure is:

:Ca

O (atomic number 8) = 2, 6 *(½ M)*

It's electron dot structure is:

×× O ×× ××

(*b*) Ca + O ⟶ $(Ca^{2+})[:O:]^{2-}$ *(1 M)*

(*c*) The ions present in this compound are:

(*i*) Calcium ion (Ca^{2+}) *(½ M)*

(*ii*) Oxide ion (O^{2-}) *(½ M)*

(*d*) Calcium oxide is an ionic compound and its characteristics are:

- Soluble in water
- Conducts electricity in molten state
- High melting point and boiling point
- Solids and are somewhat hard *(½ × 4 = 2 M)*

Topper's Explanation

26 a) Calcium → ·Ca·

~~Oxygen → :O:~~

Oxygen → :Ö:

b) Ca ⟶ Ca^{2+} + $2e^-$
(2,8,8,2) (2,8,8)

O + $2e^-$ ⟶ O^{2-}

·Ca· + :O: ⟶ Ca^{2+} + $[O]^{2-}$

⟶ $Ca^{2+}O^{2-}$

⟶ CaO

c) The ions present are Ca^{2+} – calcium ion which is a cation

O^{2-} – oxide ion which is an anion

d) CaO is an ionic compound. Its properties are

- High melting and boiling point
- hard solid, brittle – breaks when pressure is applied
- soluble in water
- insoluble in organic solvents like petrol, kerosene
- conducts electricity is molten ~~and~~ aqueous states
- Does not conduct electricity in solid state.
- Imparts specific colour to the flame.

Hints & Explanations

Multiple Choice Questions

1. (*b*) According to the given electronic configuration, A is a noble gas, Neon (2, 8), B is Chlorine (2, 8, 7) and C is Magnesium (2, 8, 2).

Hence, B is a non-metal, and C is a metal.

2. (*c*) An element with Atomic number-14 has the following electronic configuration:

K L M N

2 8 4

Hence, this element satisfies the given condition.

3. (*b*) HCl and CCl_4 are not ionic compounds as they are not formed by the transfer of electrons but rather formed by sharing of electrons.

4. (*a*) The reaction between B and A results in the formation of ionic compound, D.

Since, it is an ionic compound, therefore, it has a high melting point, is solid and good conductor of electricity in the molten state.

5. (*c*) The outer shell of calcium contains 2 electrons whereas, chlorine contains 7 electrons. To get stable electronic configuration, calcium must donates its two outer shell electrons to both the chlorine atoms. In this way all the three atoms get stabilized. This can be shown by the following figure,

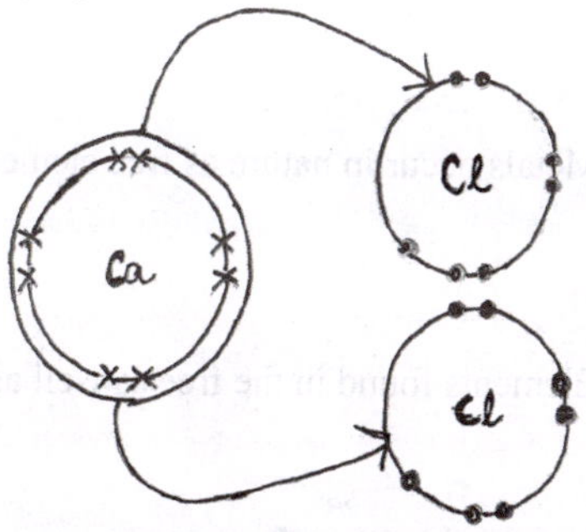

During this arrangement of electrons, calcium attains +2 charge and each chlorine get one-one negative charge. Hence, the arrangement given in option (*c*) is correct.

Assertion and Reason

1. (*a*) Potassium chloride is an ionic molecule in which potassium loses one electron, which is gained by chlorine, resulting in mutual electron transfer from metal to non-metal.

2. (*d*) • Ions are fixed in place in an ionic solid. They remain in their position within the crystal lattice. They don't move much inside the lattice, hence they can't conduct electricity because they don't have any charge carriers.

• Ionic solids are made up of ions that are both positive (cations) and negative (anions). The electrostatic force of attraction between these ions keeps them together.

3 BASIC METALLURGICAL PROCESSES

NCERT Definitions (Commonly asked in 1 mark)

- **Metallurgy:** The science and technology of extracting metals from their ores and then refining them for use.
- **Gangue:** The commercially **worthless** material that surrounds or is closely mixed with a wanted mineral in an ore deposit.
- **Thermit Reaction:** Reduction of iron (lll) oxide to iron by aluminium is called thermit reaction. This reaction is highly exothermic and is used to join railway tracks or cracked machine parts.
- **Refining of Metal:** The process of purifying impure metals to obtain their pure form.
- **Electrolytic Refining:** A technique that uses electrolysis to purify a metal, where impure metal is made the anode and the pure metal is deposited at the cathode.
- **Concentration of Ore:** The process of ***removing impurities*** and increasing the concentration of metal in an ore.

I am being "concentrated"

Important Facts

01 Metals occur in nature as free elements or in the form of their compounds.

02 Elements found in the free as well as in the combined state. *~ Copper and Silver*

03 Metals are found as their oxides because oxygen is abundant on Earth and reacts with many elements to form oxides.

04 The sulphide ore of mercury. *~ Cinnabar*

05 All the metals which are placed above copper in the reactivity series are found only in the form of their compounds.

06 All ores are minerals but all the minerals are not ores.

Classification

Classification of Metals on the Basis of Reactivity			
Reactivity Category	**Metals (Examples)**	**Occurrence in Nature**	**Extraction Method**
High Reactivity	Potassium (K), Sodium (Na), Calcium (Ca), Magnesium (Mg), Aluminium (Al)	Found in the combined state in nature. Not found in free state due to high reactivity.	**Electrolysis:** Electrolytic reduction of molten ores to extract metal.
Medium Reactivity	Zinc (Zn), Iron (Fe), Lead (Pb)	Mainly found as oxides, sulphides, or carbonates in the earth's crust.	**Reduction using Carbon:** Reduction of metal oxides with carbon or carbon monoxide in a blast furnace.
Low Reactivity	Copper (Cu), Silver (Ag), Gold (Au)	Often found in the free (native) state due to low reactivity. Copper and Silver are also found in combined state as their sulphide or oxide ores.	Physical separation and minor chemical processes for purification. For those in combined state, various chemical reduction processes are carried out, depending on the specific metal.

Difference Between

Ore Vs. Mineral		
Aspect	**Ore**	**Mineral**
Definition	A mineral from which the metal can be extracted conveniently and economically.	The elements or compounds, which occur naturally in the earth's crust
Percentage of metal	Ores contain a large percentage of metal.	Minerals contain a low percentage of metal.
Examples	Cinnabar and Bauxite are examples of ores from which mercury and aluminium are extracted, respectively.	Quartz and feldspar are examples of minerals that may not be used as ores.
Purpose	Extracted specifically for metal production.	Studied for various uses, including their economic value, and used as gems, building materials, etc.

Roasting Vs. Calcination		
Aspect	**Roasting**	**Calcination**
Definition	Roasting is a process of heating the ore in the presence of excess air or oxygen.	Calcination is a process of heating the ore in the absence or limited supply of air.
Objective	To convert sulphide ores into oxides	To convert carbonate ores into oxides.
Result	Results in the formation of oxides from sulphides.	Results in the decomposition of carbonates to oxides.
Examples	Roasting of zinc sulphide to zinc oxide. $2ZnS(s) + 3O_2(g) \xrightarrow{\text{Heat}} 2ZnO(s) + 2SO_2(g)$	Calcination of Zinc carbonate to zinc oxide $ZnCO_3(s) \xrightarrow{\text{Heat}} ZnO(s) + CO_2(g)$
Evolution of gas	Sulphur dioxide is released	Carbon dioxide is released.
Environment	Requires oxygen for the reaction.	Does not require oxygen

Real Life Application Based Questions

1. **How does the process of electrolytic refining ensure the safety of medical tools?**

Ans. Electrolytic refining purifies metals to such a degree that the tools made from them are safe for medical procedures. This high level of purity is necessary to prevent adverse reactions in patients and to ensure that medical instruments are free of any impurities that might harbour bacteria or cause infections.

2. **What is the significance of the thermit reaction in welding railway tracks and how does it contribute to the safety of rail transport?**

Ans. The thermit reaction is utilized to weld railway tracks due to its ability to produce intense heat without requiring external power sources. This exothermic reaction between aluminium powder and an iron oxide results in molten iron, which welds the tracks together, creating strong, seamless joints that ensure smooth and safe train operations.

Mnemonics

❑ **The process of roasting and calcination along with their conditions can be learned as follows:**

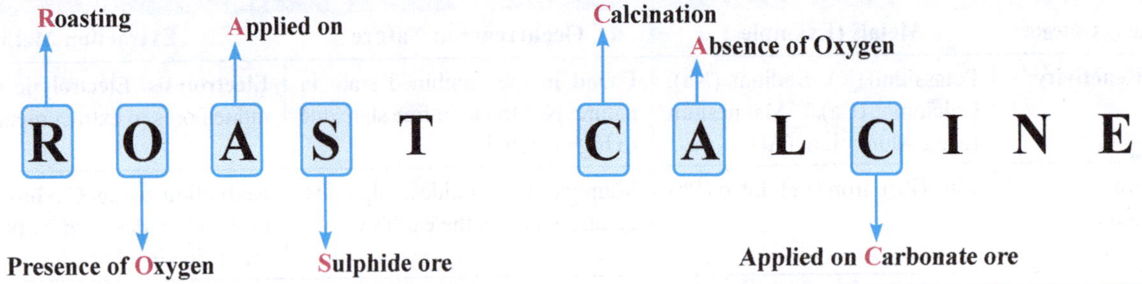

COMPETENCY BASED SOLVED EXAMPLES

Multiple Choice Questions (1 M)

1. **Which of the following metals exist in their native state in nature?** *(Un)*
   (*i*) Ca (*ii*) Pt (*iii*) Al (*iv*) Ag
   (*a*) (*i*) and (*ii*) (*b*) (*ii*) and (*iii*)
   (*c*) (*ii*) and (*iv*) (*d*) (*iii*) and (*iv*)
2. **Aluminium is used in thermit welding because** *(Un)*
   (*a*) Aluminium is a metal that has lightweight
   (*b*) Aluminium is a strong oxidising agent
   (*c*) Aluminium has more affinity for oxygen
   (*d*) Aluminium is considered a reactive metal
3. **During purification of a metal by electrolysis, what happens at the negative electrode?** **(*Re*) (CBSE APQ, 2023)**
   (*a*) Metal ions lose electrons to become neutral atoms.
   (*b*) Neutral metal atoms gain electrons to become ions.
   (*c*) Neutral metal atoms lose electrons to become ions.
   (*d*) Metal ions gain electrons to become neutral metal atoms
4. **Which of the following metals are obtained by electrolysis of their chlorides in the molten state?** **(*Ap*) (NCERT Exemplar)**
   (*i*) Na (*ii*) Ca (*iii*) Fe (*iv*) Cu
   (*a*) (*i*) and (*iv*) (*b*) (*iii*) and (*iv*)
   (*c*) (*i*) and (*iii*) (*d*) (*i*) and (*ii*)
5. **In the electrolytic refining of copper, the electrolyte used is** *(Un)*
   (*a*) CuO (*b*) $Cu(OH)_2$
   (*c*) Acidified $CuSO_4$(aq) (*d*) $CuSO_4$(s)

Assertion and Reason (1 M)

Direction: The following questions consist of two statements – Assertion (A) and Reason (R). Answer these questions by selecting the appropriate option given below:

(*a*) Both A and R are true, and R is the correct explanation of A.
(*b*) Both A and R are true, but R is not the correct explanation of A.
(*c*) A is true, but R is false
(*d*) A is false, but R is true.

1. **Assertion (A):** One of the steps involved in copper extraction is $Cu_2S + 2Cu_2O \longrightarrow 6Cu + SO_2$
   Reason (R): Cu_2S is the reducing agent in this reaction, while Cu_2O is the oxidising agent. *(Un)*
2. **Assertion (A):** Highly reactive metals are extracted by electrolytic reduction.
   Reason (R): Metals are deposited at the cathode in electrolytic reduction. *(Un)*
3. **Assertion (A):** Zinc oxide can be reduced to zinc metal on heating with carbon.
   Reason (R): Carbon is less reactive than zinc.
   (*Un*) (CBSE APQ, 2023)

Subjective Questions

Very Short Answer Type Questions (2 M)

1. **Priya is studying the occurrence of metals in nature. She has samples of five metals: gold, aluminium, lead, iron, and silver. These metals occur in different forms in nature. Some occur in native state, and some in the combined state with other elements.** *(Un)*
   (A) Identify the metal(s) that are most likely to be found in their native state and those found in a combined state in the Earth's crust, which are positioned at the bottom of the reactivity series.
   (B) What is the name of the process in which sulphide ores are heated strongly in the presence of excess air to convert them into oxides?

Ans. (A)
- Gold and silver are often found in a native state and lies at the bottom of the reactivity series due to its low reactivity. *(½ M)*
- Silver can be found in the combined state as their sulphide or oxide ores or in the free state. It lies at the bottom of the reactivity series due to their low reactivity. *(½ M)*

(B) The process of converting sulphide ores into oxides by heating strongly in the presence of excess air is called roasting. *(1 M)*

2. **What is a thermit reaction? Write a chemical equation for this reaction and mention its one use.** ***(Re)***

Ans. The reduction of iron oxide to iron by aluminium is called a thermit reaction. It is highly exothermic in nature. *(1 M)*

The reaction takes place as:

$Fe_2O_3(s) + 2Al(s) \rightarrow 2Fe(l) + Al_2O_3(s) + Heat$ *(½ M)*

Thermit reaction is used for the welding of railway tracks (joining metals) called as thermit welding. *(½ M)*

3. **What is anode mud? Name the common elements present in the anode mud in electrolytic refining of copper.** ***(Re)***

Ans. Anode mud is the insoluble impurity that settle down at the bottom of the anode during electrolytic refining. *(1 M)*

The common elements present in the anode mud in electrolytic refining of copper are antimony, selenium, tellurium, silver, gold and platinum. *(1 M)*

4. **A metallic element, M, has the following properties:** ***(An)*** **(CFPQ)**
   - floats on water
   - can be cut with a knife
   - occurs naturally as its chloride, of formula MCl
   - its oxide dissolves in water to form the hydroxide

   (*a*) State the method of manufacture of the metal M.

   (*b*) Name the major by product obtained in the process.

Ans. (*a*) The metal, M that best describes the above properties is either Na or K and these metals are present high up in the reactivity series, hence will be manufactured by the electrolysis of their molten chloride *(1 M)*

(*b*) The major by-product obtained in this process is Chlorine. *(1 M)*

Short Answer Type Questions **(3 M)**

1. **E is an element amongst copper, zinc, aluminium and iron. It shows following properties:** ***(An)***

   (*i*) One of its ores is rich in E_2O_3

   (*ii*) E_2O_3 is not attacked by water,

   (*iii*) It forms two chlorides ECl_2 and ECl_3.

   Name the element and justify your answer.

Ans. The formation of ECl_2 and ECl_3 of the E element shows that the element E has the variable valency of 2 and 3 respectively. Out of the elements that are given, only Fe exists in divalent and trivalent form.

(*i*) The ore rich in Fe_2O_3 is haematite. *(1 M)*

(*ii*) Haematite is not attacked by the water. *(1 M)*

(*iii*) The two chlorides are: Iron(II)chloride or $FeCl_2$ and Iron(III)chloride or $FeCl_3$. *(1 M)*

2. **How is the method of extraction of metals high up in the reactivity series different from that for metals in the middle? Why can the same process not be applied for them? Name the process used for the extraction of these metals.** ***(Un)*** **(CBSE 2019)**

Ans. The method of extraction of metals high up in the reactivity series is different from that for metals in the middle because:

- Metals high up in the reactivity series generally occur in the form of oxides which are quite stable. They cannot be obtained from their compounds by heating with carbon. For example, carbon cannot reduce the oxides of sodium, magnesium, calcium, aluminium, etc., to the respective metals. This is because these metals have high affinity for oxygen than carbon. Thus, these metals are obtained by the electrolysis of their molten chlorides, and this process is called electrolytic reduction. *(1 M)*
- Metals in the middle occur in the form of carbonates and sulphides, which are first converted into oxides by various methods and then into metals. *(1 M)*

The same process cannot be applied to them due to the differences in their reactivity. *(½ M)*

The process used for their extraction is calcination or roasting, followed by reduction. *(½ M)*

3. **During extraction of metals, electrolytic refining is used to obtain pure metals.**

   (*a*) Which material will be used as anode and cathode for refining of silver metal by this process?

   (*b*) Suggest a suitable electrolyte also.

   (*c*) In this electrolytic cell, where do we get pure silver after passing electric current?

   (Ap) **(NCERT Exemplar)**

Ans. (*a*) For the electrolytic refining of the silver metal, following are used as anode and cathode.

Anode: Impure Silver *(½ M)*

Cathode: Pure Silver *(½ M)*

(*b*) **Electrolyte:** Any salt solution of silver, such as $AgNO_3$, can be used as an electrolyte. *(1 M)*

(*c*) After passing the electric current, we get pure silver at the **cathode**. *(1 M)*

Mistakes 101 : What not to do!

In this question, students may mistakenly identify the anode material as pure silver instead of impure silver, which is essential for the electrolytic refining process to remove impurities. Students may get confused about which product is obtained at cathode due to misunderstanding of the flow of ions during the electrolytic refining process.

4. **An ore on treatment with dil. HCl gives off the smell of rotten eggs. Name the type of this ore. How can the metal be obtained from its concentrated ore?** **(CBSE 2019)**

Ans. (*a*) H_2S is the gas which smells like that of rotten eggs. Therefore the ore is a sulphide ore. *(½ M)*

This sulphide ore is concentrated by froth-flotation process.

The metal is obtained from the concentrated ore in the given two steps: *(½ M)*

(*i*) **Roasting:** Roasting involves heating the ore strongly in the presence of air. The metal sulphide gets converted into metal oxide along with evolution of sulphur dioxide (SO_2) gas.

$2ZnS(s) + 3O_2 \xrightarrow{Heat} 2ZnO(s) + 2SO_2(g)\uparrow$ *(1 M)*

(*ii*) **Reduction with carbon:** The metal oxide on heating with carbon, gets reduced to free metal.

$ZnO(s) + C(s) \rightarrow Zn(s) + CO(g)\uparrow$ *(1 M)*

Topper's Explanation

8. Smell of rotten eggs is usually produced by Sulphur.

∴ It must be a sulphide ore.

let us suppose that the ore is Zinc blende (ZnS).

Concentration of ore

First of all, the ore is concentrated by the method of froth floatation.

Conversion into metal oxide

Then it is ~~roasted~~ converted into its metal oxide via Roasting in supply of excess air.

For eg. $ZnS + O_2 \xrightarrow[\Delta]{\text{Roasting}} ZnO + SO_2\uparrow$

Zinc sulphide ore; (excess air); zinc Oxide; sulphur dioxide (pungent smell)

Conversion into metal

It is then converted into its metal form by using a reducing agent like Carbon, Aluminium etc.

for eg. $ZnO + C \xrightarrow{\text{reduction}} Zn + CO$

zinc oxide; (reducing agent) Carbon; zinc metal (contaminated); Carbon monoxide

It is further refined to get it in its pure form.

Long Answer Type Questions (5 M)

1. Two ores X and Y were taken. On heating these ores, it was observed that

(a) ore X gives CO_2 gas, and

(b) ore Y gives SO_2 gas.

Write steps to convert these ores into metals, giving chemical equations of the reactions that take place. **(An) (CBSE 2020)**

Ans. (a) Ore X is a carbonate ore. *(½ M)*

The steps involved in the extraction of this carbonate ore into metal are:

(i) **Calcination:** The carbonate ore is heated strongly in the limited supply of oxygen to produce metal oxide with the evolution of CO_2 gas.

$$XCO_3 \xrightarrow{\text{heat}} XO + CO_2\uparrow \quad (1\ M)$$

(ii) **Reduction:** The oxide ore is reduced with carbon, C.

$$XO + C \rightarrow X + CO\uparrow \quad (1\ M)$$

(b) Ore Y is a sulphide ore. *(½ M)*

The steps involved in the extraction of this sulphide ore into metal are:

(i) **Roasting:** The sulphide ore is heated strongly in the presence of oxygen to produce metal oxide with the evolution of SO_2 gas.

$$2XS + 3O_2 \xrightarrow{\text{heat}} 2XO + 2SO_2\uparrow \quad (1\ M)$$

(ii) **Reduction:** The oxide ore is reduced with carbon, C.

$$XO + C \rightarrow X + CO\uparrow \quad (1\ M)$$

Nailing the Right Answer

To ensure full credit, students should clearly identify the ore type (carbonate or sulphide).

Describe the calcination and reduction steps distinctly. Provide balanced chemical equations with proper symbols. Ensure to show the evolution of gases accurately and maintain the sequence of steps.

2. Carbon cannot reduce the oxides of sodium, magnesium and aluminum to their respective metals. Why? Where are these metals placed in the reactivity series? How are these metals obtained from their ores? Take an example to explain the process of extraction along with chemical equations. **(An) (CBSE 2020)**

Ans. Carbon cannot reduce the oxides of sodium, magnesium, and aluminium because their reactivity exceeds that of carbon and also they have more affinity for oxygen. *(1 M)*

In the reactivity series, these metals are placed at the top above carbon. *(1 M)*

Electrolytic reduction (Electrolysis) is a process used to recover metals with high reactivity, such as sodium, magnesium, and aluminium from their respective ores. *(1 M)*

For example, sodium is obtained by the electrolysis of its molten chloride. The metal is deposited at the cathode (the negatively charged electrode), whereas, chlorine is liberated at the anode (the positively charged electrode). *(1 M)*

The reactions are:

At cathode: $Na^+ + e^- \rightarrow Na$ *(½ M)*

At anode: $2Cl^- \rightarrow Cl_2 + 2e^-$ *(½ M)*

Hints & Explanations

Multiple Choice Questions

1. (c) Pt and Ag are present in the bottom of the reactivity series and are the least reactive. Therefore, can exist in their native state in nature.
2. (c) Aluminium is used in thermit welding because aluminium has more affinity for oxygen. It can be understood from the following reaction:

   $Fe_2O_3(s) + 2Al(s) \rightarrow Al_2O_3(s) + 2Fe(l) + \text{Heat}$
3. (d) At negative electrode, metal ions gain electrons to become neutral metal atoms in electrolysis.
4. (d) Highly reactive metals like Na, Mg, Ca which are placed in the higher part of the reactivity series cannot be obtained by heating with carbon.

   Therefore, they are obtained by electrolysis of their chlorides in the molten state.
5. (c) In the electrolytic refining, a solution of the metal salt is used as an electrolyte. Hence, an aqueous solution of acidified $CuSO_4$ is used as an electrolyte.

Assertion and Reason

1. (c) Cu(I) gets reduced while sulphur gets oxidised. Hence, Cu(I) acts as the oxidising agent while S in Cu_2S acts as reducing agent.
2. (b) Metals towards the top of the reactivity series are extremely reactive. They cannot be obtained by heating their compounds with carbon. This is due to the fact that these metals have a higher affinity for oxygen than carbon. These metals are thus produced using electrolytic reduction.

   Also, in this process, metals are deposited at the cathode.
3. (c) Carbon is more reactive than zinc.

4 CORROSION AND ITS PREVENTION

NCERT Definitions (Commonly asked in 1 mark)

- **Corrosion:** The gradual destruction or chemical alteration of a metal due to reaction with environmental agents like oxygen, water, acids, or salts.
- **Rusting:** A form of corrosion that specifically affects iron and steel, resulting in the formation of reddish-brown oxide on their surface.
- **Tarnishing:** A type of corrosion that occurs on the surface of metals such as silver or copper, as it undergoes a chemical reaction with sulphur or other non-metals, leading to a dull surface or discolouration.
- **Anodising:** Anodising is a process that involves coating a metal, usually aluminium, with a protective oxide layer by making it the anode in an electrolytic cell, which increases its resistance to corrosion.
- **Galvanisation:** The process of applying a protective zinc coating to steel or iron to prevent rusting.
- **Alloy:** A mixture of two or more elements, where at least one is a metal, designed to have enhanced properties compared to its component elements.

Important Facts

01 An alloy formed when one of the metals is mercury.

~Amalgam

02 An alloy that has a low melting point and is used for welding electrical wires together and is made of lead and tin (Pb and Sn).

~Solder

03 Pure gold, known for its softness, making it unsuitable for crafting durable jewellery.

~24 Carat Gold

04 By alloying iron with nickel and chromium, stainless steel is created, which is both hard and resistant to rust.

05 In India, 22 carat gold is used for making ornaments.

Difference Between

Rusting v/s Tarnishing

Factors	Rusting	Tarnishing
Metals Affected	Iron and steel	Silver and Copper
Chemical Product formed	Iron oxide ($Fe_2O_3.xH_2O$)	Silver sulphide (Ag_2S) and Copper carbonate ($Cu(OH)_2.CuCO_3$)
Environmental Conditions	Presence of moisture and oxygen	Exposure to sulphur compounds and moist carbon dioxide
Appearance	Reddish-brown flaky coating	Black coating on silver and green coating on copper
Structural Impact	Can lead to significant structural damage	Primarily affects appearance, less structural impact
Prevention	Protective coatings, galvanizing, corrosion-resistant alloys	Polishing, protective coatings, anti-tarnish agents

Real Life Application Based Questions

1. **Why do you often see older vehicles with rust, especially in coastal areas?**

Ans. Saltwater accelerates the rusting process due to the presence of salt, which speeds up the chemical reaction between iron and oxygen in the air or water, leading to quicker corrosion.

2. **How does wrapping underground pipes in plastic help prevent corrosion?**

Ans. Wrapping pipes with plastic provides a physical barrier against moisture and soil-borne corrosive substances, which can cause the pipes to corrode and leak.

3. **Why do silver jewellery and utensils need to be polished over time?**

Ans. Silver tarnishes due to corrosion when it reacts with hydrogen sulphide in the air, forming a black layer of silver sulphide. Polishing removes this layer, restoring the shine.

4. **Why are galvanized pipes often used in outdoor constructions?**

Ans. Galvanized pipes are coated with zinc, which protects the steel or iron beneath from corrosion.

Myth Buster

- **Myth: Corrosion is purely a surface phenomenon.**
  Fact: While corrosion often appears on the surface, it can penetrate deep into the material, compromising structural integrity from within.
- **Myth: Rust can be prevented entirely.**
  Fact: Rust can be minimized and controlled, but due to the ubiquitous presence of oxygen and moisture in most environments, it's challenging to prevent entirely without appropriate protective measures.
- **Myth: All corrosion is harmful and unwanted.**
  Fact: Some forms of corrosion can actually protect a material. For instance, the oxide layer on aluminium can prevent further corrosion.
- **Myth: Dry environments prevent corrosion.**
  Fact: While dry environments reduce the risk of some types of corrosion, they do not prevent it entirely. Corrosion can still occur due to other factors like exposure to chemicals or pollutants in the air, even in dry conditions. For example: oxidation of iron occurs at high temperatures without water.

Mnemonics

- **The different alloys and their composition can be learned as:**

1. **Brass:** An alloy of copper and zinc (Cu and Zn)

   "Brave Cows Zip"

   Brave → Brass, Cows → Copper, Zip → Zinc

2. **Bronze:** An alloy of copper and tin (Cu and Sn)

   "Bronze Coins Twinkle"

   Bronze → Bronze, Coins → Copper, Twinkle → Tin

3. **Solder:** An alloy of lead and tin (Pb and Sn)

   "Lost his Shoulder"

   LosT his Shoulder → Lead(Pb) Tin(Sn) Solder

4. **Stainless steel:** An alloy of nickel, iron and chromium (Ni + Fe + Cr)

   "New Ferrari Car"

   New → Ni, Ferrari → Fe, Car → Cr

COMPETENCY BASED SOLVED EXAMPLES

Multiple Choice Questions (1 M)

1. Galvanisation is a process of coating iron articles with a layer of zinc to prevent the iron from rusting. **(*Un*) (CBSE APQ, 2023)**

The iron is protected even if the zinc coating is scratched and iron is exposed.

Which of the following is true about how zinc prevents the rusting of iron?

(*P*) A galvanised iron article does not undergo oxidation.

(*Q*) The zinc coating prevents contact of iron with air.

(*R*) Zinc undergoes corrosion more easily than iron.

(*a*) only *P* (*b*) only *Q*

(*c*) only *P* and *Q* (*d*) only *Q* and *R*

2. Stainless steel is a very useful material for our life. In stainless steel, iron is mixed with **(*Re*) (NCERT Exemplar)**

(*a*) Ni and Cr (*b*) Cu and Cr

(*c*) Ni and Cu (*d*) Cu and Au

3. Chirag is conducting an experiment to investigate the conditions under which iron rusts, three test tubes are set up as shown in the image.

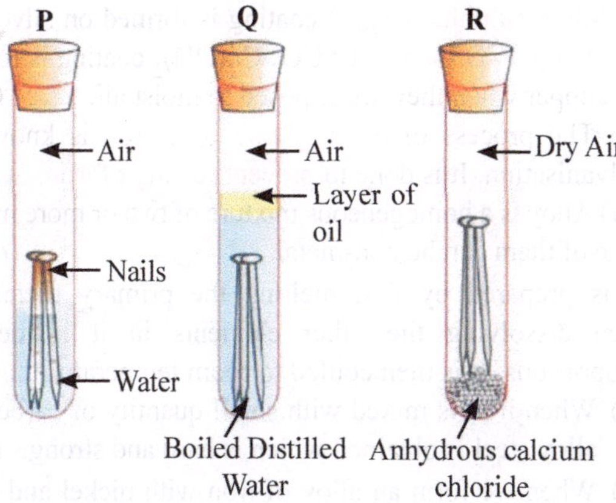

Each test tube contains iron nails under different conditions:

- **Tube P:** Contains air and water.
- **Tube Q:** Contains boiled distilled water (with no dissolved air) and a layer of oil on top.
- **Tube R:** Contains dry air and anhydrous calcium chloride (a drying agent).

Which test tube(s) will show rust formation on the iron nails after a few days? **(*Ap*)**

(*a*) Only Tube P (*b*) Only Tube Q

(*c*) Only Tube R (*d*) Both Tube P and Tube Q

4. Which of the following is an alloy of copper and tin? **(CBSE 2024)**

(*a*) Nichrome (*b*) Brass

(*c*) Constantan (*d*) Bronze

Assertion and Reason (1 M)

Direction: The following questions consist of two statements – Assertion (A) and Reason (R). Answer these questions by selecting the appropriate option given below:

(*a*) Both A and R are true, and R is the correct explanation of A.

(*b*) Both A and R are true, but R is not the correct explanation of A.

(*c*) A is true, but R is false

(*d*) A is false, but R is true.

1. Assertion (A): For the prevention of corrosion, the process of anodising is used.

Reason (R): Anodising is the process of coating iron with a layer of zinc. **(*Un*)**

2. Assertion (A): Solder is used for welding electrical wires together.

Reason (R): It has a low melting point. **(*Un*)**

3. Assertion (A): Rusting of iron is endothermic in nature.

Reason (R): As the reaction is slow, the release of heat is barely evident. **(*Un*) (CBSE SQP, 2023)**

Subjective Questions

Very Short Answer Type Questions (2 M)

1. Silver jewellery loses its shine when kept for some time. Give reason for same. Explain with the help of the chemical equation. **(*Un*)**

Ans. Silver will react with the sulphur present in the air, and it will become silver sulphide, Ag_2S, that is black in colour, so the shine is lost. *(1 M)*

The chemical reaction takes place as:

$2Ag + H_2S \rightarrow Ag_2S\downarrow + H_2\uparrow$ *(1 M)*

2. A green layer is slowly-slowly formed on a copper plate that is left exposed to air for a long time in a bathroom. What is the chemical formula of this green substance? Explain with the help of the chemical equation. **(*Re*)**

Ans. The copper plate acquire a green layer due to the formation of basic copper carbonate, and the chemical formula of this layer is $[CuCO_3 \cdot Cu(OH)_2]$. *(1 M)*

The chemical reaction takes place as:

$2Cu + H_2O + CO_2 + O_2 \rightarrow \underset{\text{Basic Copper Carbonate (green)}}{Cu(OH)_2 .CuCO_3}$ *(1 M)*

3. Read the following statements. **(*An*) (CFPQ)**

(P) Stainless steel does not rust.

(Q) Iron, nickel and chromium form an alloy.

Does statement (Q) present a valid explanation for statement (P)? Justify your answer.

Ans. Yes, statement (Q) explains statement (P). *(½ M)*

This is because stainless steel contains chromium, which forms a protective layer preventing rust. The alloy of iron, nickel, and chromium enhances corrosion resistance, making stainless steel durable against rusting. *(1½ M)*

4. Name an alloy that contains a non-metal as one of its constituents. Give its composition and two uses. ***(Re)***

Ans. Steel is an alloy in which non-metal carbon is one of the component. It is made up of iron and carbon (about 0.05%). *(1 M)*

Uses:

- Most of the tableware and utensils we use on a daily basis are made of stainless steel. *(½ M)*
- Most automobiles' bodies, doors, motors, suspensions, and interiors are made primarily of steel. *(½ M)*

5. Imagine you are an engineer at a manufacturing plant. You are tasked with selecting materials for a new product that requires high strength and resistance to corrosion. Your supervisor asks you to consider using an alloy, instead of pure metals for this application. Alloy is known to be a homogeneous mixture of two or more metals, or a metal and a non-metal, with improved properties compared to its constituent elements. ***(Un)***

(A) Identify two examples of alloys, and list their constituent elements.

(B) Why iron is not used in its pure state? What makes iron hard and strong?

Ans. (A) Two examples of alloys are:

Brass: Constituent elements are copper (Cu) and zinc (Zn). *(½ M)*

Bronze: Constituent elements are copper (Cu) and tin (Sn). *(½ M)*

(B) Iron is never used in its pure state because pure iron is very soft and stretches easily when hot. *(½ M)*

Iron when mixed with a small amount of carbon (about 0.05 %), makes it hard and strong. *(½ M)*

Short Answer Type Questions (3 M)

1. List three differentiating features between the processes of galvanisation and alloying. ***(Re)* (CBSE 2020)**

Ans.

Galvanization	Alloying
Galvanization is the process of *putting a protective zinc* coating on steel or iron to prevent rusting.	Alloying is the process of *mixing two or more metals* or a metal and a non-metal.
It is accomplished using electrolysis, which is analogous to anodising.	Alloying is done by first melting the primary metal and then adding the other elements in definite proportions, followed by cooling it down to room temperature.
The characteristics of the inner metal are not affected throughout the galvanisation process.	Alloying changes the qualities of metals, such as conductivity, strength, and so on.

(3 M)

2. Equal sized bars of aluminium and iron are exposed to the environment as shown below.

***(Ap)* (CBSE APQ,2023)**

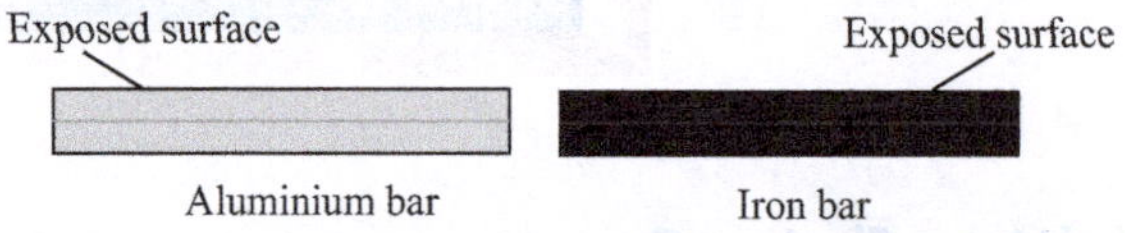

Which of them is likely to corrode till the level marked by the line FIRST? Justify your answer.

Ans. - The iron bar will corrode till the level marked by the line first. *(1 M)*

- Iron gets oxidised on exposure to air and moisture. The layer of rust formed on the surface allows air and moisture to pass through and reach the metal, causing corrosion to continue. *(1 M)*

- Aluminium gets oxidised on exposure to air. The layer of oxide formed on the surface forms a protective coating that prevents air from reaching the metal and thus prevents further corrosion. *(1 M)*

Long Answer Type Questions (5 M)

1. *(i)* Write the chemical name of the coating that will form on silver and copper articles when these are left exposed to moist air.

(ii) **Explain the term galvanisation. Why it is done?**

(iii) **Define an alloy. How are alloys prepared? How do *the properties* of iron change when:**

(a) **a small quantity of carbon,**

(b) **nickel and chromium are mixed with it?** ***(Un)***

Ans. (*i*) Silver sulphide (Ag_2S) coating is formed on silver and basic copper carbonate $CuCO_3 \cdot Cu(OH)_2$ coating is formed on copper when they are exposed to moist air. *(1 M)*

(*ii*) The process of coating zinc over iron is known as galvanisation. It is done to prevent rusting of iron. *(1 M)*

(*iii*) Alloy is a homogeneous mixture of two or more metals. One of them can be non-metal. *(½ M)*

It is prepared by first melting the primary metal and then dissolving the other elements in it in definite proportions. It is then cooled to room temperature. *(½ M)*

(*a*) When iron is mixed with small quantity of carbon, an alloy steel is obtained which is hard and strong. *(1 M)*

(*b*) When we form an alloy of iron with nickel and chromium, we get an alloy that is stainless steel which is hard and does not get rusted. *(1 M)*

2. Three pieces of a rust free iron rod are completely coated with the following: ***(Ap)* (CFPQ)**

(i) **Plastic**

(ii) **Oil paints**

(iii) **Zinc**

An identical scratch is made on each piece, thus exposing the iron. The pieces of iron are kept exposed to moist air for 10 days and then checked for rust formation.

(a) **State if rusting will be observed at the point of the scratch on the three iron pieces.**

(b) **Give reason for your answer in each case.**

(c) **Name the process of applying a protective zinc coating to steel or iron.**

Ans. (*a*) (*i*) Rust will be seen on the plastic coated iron pieces (½ *M*)

(*ii*) Rust will be seen on the painted iron piece. (½ *M*)

(*iii*) No rust will be seen on the zinc coated iron piece. (1 *M*)

(*b*) (*i*) The iron rod is in contact with air and moisture. (½ *M*)

(*ii*) The iron rod is in contact with air and moisture. (½ *M*)

(*iii*) Zinc is more reactive than iron and gets oxidised in preference to the iron object. (1 *M*)

(*c*) Galvanisation is the process of applying a protective zinc coating to steel or iron. (1 *M*)

Nailing the Right Answer

To ensure full credit students should clearly state the observation for each type of coating. Provide a concise reason for the rust formation based on the properties of the materials. Highlight the importance of understanding the reactivity series for predicting rust formation.

Hints & Explanations

Multiple Choice Questions

1. (*d*) only Q and R

2. (*a*) When iron is combined with nickel and chromium, stainless steel is formed.

3. (*a*) Rusting of iron requires both water and oxygen. In Tube P, both air (oxygen) and water are present, providing the necessary conditions for rusting to occur. Tube Q has water but no dissolved air, a layer of oil separates air from nails and boiled distilled water and Tube R has dry air with no moisture, so neither Tube Q nor Tube R will show rust formation.

4. (*d*) Bronze is an alloy of copper(Cu) and tin(Sn).

Assertion and Reason

1. (*c*) Anodising is the formation of a thick oxide layer of aluminium. When exposed to air, aluminium forms a thin oxide coating. This aluminium oxide coating protects it from further corrosion.

   Hence, A is True but R is false.

2. (*a*) Solder, a lead and tin (Pb and Sn) alloy, has a low melting point and as a result, it is used to join electrical wires.

3. (*d*) The process of rusting is an exothermic reaction. It's because the combination reaction between iron and damp air produces heat. However, the reaction is so slow, that the release of heat is barely evident.

   Hence, assertion is false and reason is true.

MISCELLANEOUS EXERCISE

Multiple Choice Questions (1 M)

1. Which of the following is non-metal but is lustrous? **(*Un*) (NCERT Exemplar)**

   (*a*) Iodine (*b*) Mercury
   (*c*) Carbon (*d*) Bromine

2. Electrical wires have a coating of insulating material. The material, generally used is **(*Un*) (NCERT Exemplar)**

   (*a*) Sulphur (*b*) Graphite
   (*c*) PVC (*d*) All can be used

3. Krunal connected a copper plate and an iron plate to the positive and negative terminals of a battery respectively along with a switch. He immersed the plates into a beaker containing acidified copper sulphate solution.

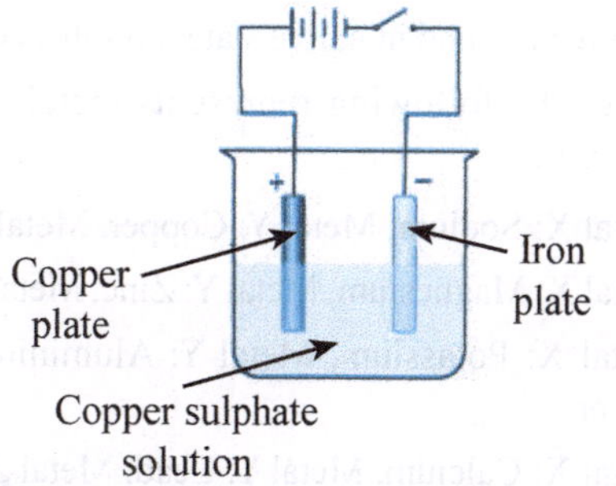

   Which of the following is likely to happen when the current is started? **(*Ap*) (CFPQ)**

   (*a*) Iron will be deposited on the copper plate.
   (*b*) Copper will continue to be deposited on the iron plate.
   (*c*) No reaction will occur at the iron plate or at the copper plate.
   (*d*) The copper already deposited on the iron plate will go back into the solution.

4. *In the list given below, a metal to the right is more reactive than a metal that is to its left.*

Copper	Tin	Nickel	Cobalt	Iron	Zinc

   The table below gives the colour of the metal sulpahte salt solutions.

Metal salt solution	Colour of aqueous metal salt solution
Copper sulphate	blue
Tin sulphate	yellow
Nickel sulphate	green
Cobalt sulphate	pink
Iron sulphate	green
Zinc sulphate	colourless

Adding nickel and iron metal to which of the following solutions will show that iron is more reactive than nickel? **(*An*) (CFPQ)**

(*a*) Copper sulphate (*b*) Tin sulphate
(*c*) Cobalt sulphate (*d*) Zinc sulphate

5. Metals are good conductors of electricity and their conductivity can be compared by connecting them to a circuit.
Salma took strips of different metals and compared their electrical conductivity. The metals she used were: zinc, silver, lead, and nickel.

Which of these metals is likely to show the highest electrical conductivity? **(*Un*)**

(*a*) Zinc (*b*) Silver
(*c*) Lead (*d*) Nickel

6. An element reacts with oxygen to give a compound with a high melting point. This compound is also soluble in water. The element is likely to be **(*Ap*) (NCERT)**

(*a*) Calcium (*b*) Carbon
(*c*) Silicon (*d*) Iron

7. The number of shells required to write the electronic configuration of Potassium (At. No. 19) **(*Un*) (CBSE 2024)**

(*a*) 1 (*b*) 2
(*c*) 3 (*d*) 4

8. The metal X does not react with cold water but floats on hot water with formation of colourless bubbles. Which of the following represents metal X. **(*Re*) (CBSE APQ, 2023)**

(*a*) Aluminium (*b*) Copper
(*c*) Magnesium (*d*) Lead

9. Two elements A and B on burning in air give corresponding oxides. Oxides of both A and B are soluble in water. The aqueous solution of oxide of A is alkaline and reacts with aqueous solution of oxide of B to give another compound. Identify A and B. **(*Un*)**

(*a*) A and B both are metals
(*b*) A and B are non-metals
(*c*) A is non-metal and B is metal
(*d*) A is metal and B is non-metal

10. Copper is used for making cooking utensils. Which of the following physical properties of copper is NOT responsible for the same? **(*Un*) (CBSE 2023)**

(*a*) Malleability (*b*) High melting point
(*c*) Thermal conductivity (*d*) High reactivity

11. Aashi is conducting a laboratory experiment, in which two test tubes are set up as shown in the image. **(*An*)**

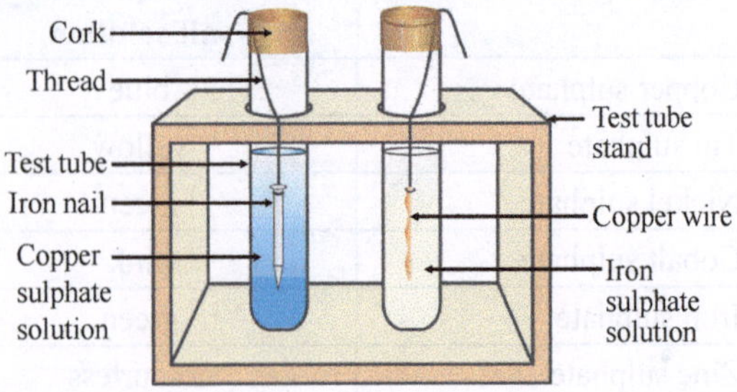

The first test tube contains an iron nail immersed in a copper sulphate solution, while the second test tube contains a copper wire immersed in an iron sulphate solution. Both test tubes are sealed with corks and suspended in a test tube stand. Which of the following observations is most likely to occur after a few hours?

(*a*) The copper wire in the iron sulphate solution will be coated with iron.
(*b*) The iron nail in the copper sulphate solution will be coated with copper.
(*c*) The copper sulphate solution will turn brown.
(*d*) The iron sulphate solution will turn blue.

12. 2 mL each of conc. HNO_3, HCl and a mixture conc. HCl and conc. HNO_3 in the ratio of 3 : 1 are taken in test tubes labelled as X, Y and Z. A small piece of metal is added in each test tube. No change has taken place in test-tubes X and Y, but the metal got dissolved in test tube Z, respectively. The metal is: **(*Un*)**

(*a*) Pb (*b*) Al
(*c*) Cu (*d*) Au

13. Identify the most and least reactive elements on the basis of the given sequence of reactions. **(*An*)**

$P + QA \rightarrow PA + Q$ ...(i)
$P + QB \rightarrow PB + Q$
$R + PA \rightarrow RA + P$ ...(ii)

(*a*) P and R (*b*) R and Q
(*c*) R and P (*d*) P and Q

14. On adding dilute sulphuric acid to a test tube containing a metal 'X', a colourless gas is produced when a burning match stick is brought near it. Which of the following correctly represents metal 'X'? **(*Un*) (CBSE SQP, 2023)**

(*a*) Sodium (*b*) Sulphur
(*c*) Copper (*d*) Silver

15. Which of the following pairs will give displacement reactions? **(*Un*) (NCERT)**

(*a*) NaCl solution and copper metal
(*b*) $MgCl_2$ solution and aluminium metal
(*c*) $FeSO_4$ solution and silver metal
(*d*) $AgNO_3$ solution and copper metal

16. Ria, a high school student, is working on her chemistry homework. She needs to identify three metals (X, Y, and Z) based on their extraction methods and reaction properties as described below.

- **Metal X:** Obtained by electrolysis of their molten chloride, its oxide is soluble in water.
- **Metal Y:** Extracted by heating alone and forms black oxide.
- **Metal Z:** Found in native state, dissolves in aqua regia.

Which of the following represents metals X, Y and Z respectively? **(*Ap*)**

(*a*) Metal X: Sodium, Metal Y: Copper, Metal Z: Gold
(*b*) Metal X: Magnesium, Metal Y: Zinc, Metal Z: Platinum
(*c*) Metal X: Potassium, Metal Y: Aluminium, Metal Z: Silver
(*d*) Metal X: Calcium, Metal Y: Lead, Metal Z: Copper

17. An element X (atomic number 12) reacts with another element Y (atomic number 17) to form a compound Z. Which of the following statements are true regarding this compound? **(*Re*)**

(*i*) Molecular formula of Z is XY_2.

(*ii*) It is soluble in water.

(*iii*) X and Y are joined by sharing of electrons.

(*iv*) It would conduct electricity in the molten state.

(*a*) (*ii*) and (*iii*) (*b*) (*i*) and (*iii*)

(*c*) (*i*), (*ii*) and (*iv*) (*d*) (*i*) and (*iv*)

18. Which among the following alloys contain mercury as one of its constituents? **(*Re*) (NCERT Exemplar)**

(*a*) Stainless steel (*b*) Alnico

(*c*) Solder (*d*) Zinc amalgam

19. Which of the following is an example of roasting? **(*Re*)**

(*a*) $ZnCO_3 \xrightarrow{\Delta} ZnO + CO_2$

(*b*) $2ZnS + 3O_2 \rightarrow 2ZnO + 2SO_2$

(*c*) $ZnO + C \rightarrow Zn + CO$

(*d*) $HCl + NaOH \rightarrow NaCl + H_2O$

20. An electrolytic cell consists of **(*Un*) (NCERT Exemplar)**

(*i*) positively charged cathode

(*ii*) negatively charged anode

(*iii*) positively charged anode

(*iv*) a negatively charged cathode

(*a*) (*i*) and (*ii*) (*b*) (*iii*) and (*iv*)

(*c*) (*i*) and (*iii*) (*d*) (*ii*) ad (*iv*)

21. Metals like sodium, potassium, calcium and magnesium are extracted by electrolysis of their chlorides in the molten state. These metals are not extracted by reduction of their oxides with carbon because **(*Un*)**

(*i*) reduction with carbon is very expensive

(*ii*) carbon readily makes alloys with these metals.

(*iii*) carbon has less affinity for oxygen than these metals

(*iv*) carbon is a weaker reducing agent than these metals.

(*a*) (*i*) and (*ii*) (*b*) (*ii*) and (*iii*)

(*c*) (*iii*) and (*iv*) (*d*) (*iv*) and (*i*)

22. Ravi has three metal samples: Aluminium, iron, and copper. He placed each metal in a separate test tube containing hydrochloric acid. After a few minutes, he recorded the following observations: **(*Ap*)**

Test Tube 1: Rapid formation of bubbles

Test Tube 2: Slow formation of bubbles

Test Tube 3: No observable reaction

Which of the following correctly matches the metals with their respective observations?

	Rapid formation of bubbles	Slow formation of bubbles	No observable reaction
A.	Aluminium	Copper	Iron
B.	Iron	Aluminium	Copper
C.	Aluminium	Iron	Copper
D.	Iron	Copper	Aluminium

(*a*) A (*b*) B

(*c*) C (*d*) D

23. Which one of the following figures correctly describes the process of electrolytic refining? **(*Re*) (NCERT Exemplar)**

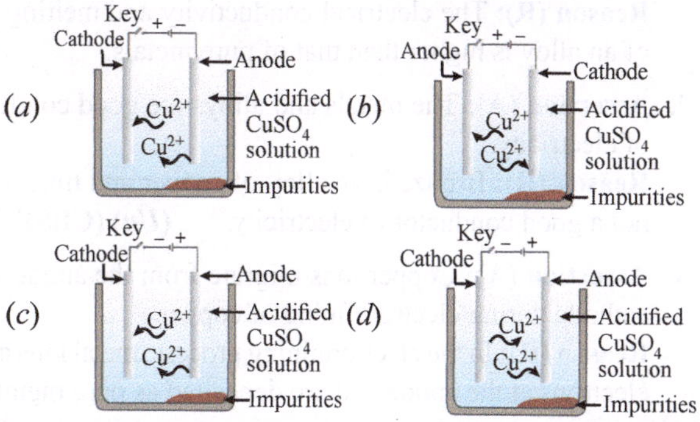

24. Arjun has two test tubes, one containing a small piece of sodium and the other containing a small piece of copper. He wants to identify which test tube contains sodium and which contains copper, but the test tubes are not labelled.
Adding which of the following solutions to the test tubes will help him visually identify the sodium and copper? **(*Ap*)**

(*a*) only water

(*b*) only dilute hydrochloric acid

(*c*) either water or dilute hydrochloric acid

(*d*) None of these

25. Which one of the following correctly represents Sodium oxide? **(*Un*) (CBSE SQP, 2023)**

(*a*) $Na^{+2}\ 2[\overset{\times\times}{\underset{\times\times}{{}_\times O_\times}}]^{-2}$ (*b*) $2Na^{+}\ [\overset{\times\times}{\underset{\times\times}{{}_\times O_\times}}]^{-2}$

(*c*) $2Na^{+}\ 2[\overset{\times\times}{\underset{\times\times}{{}_\times O_\times}}]^{-1}$ (*d*) $Na^{+1}\ [\overset{\times\times}{\underset{\times\times}{{}_\times O_\times}}]^{-2}$

Assertion and Reason **(1 M)**

Direction: The following questions consist of two statements – Assertion (A) and Reason (R). Answer these questions by selecting the appropriate option given below:

(*a*) Both A and R are true, and R is the correct explanation of A.

(*b*) Both A and R are true, but R is not the correct explanation of A.

(*c*) A is true, but R is false

(*d*) A is false, but R is true.

1. **Assertion (A):** Gold and silver are the least malleable metals.
Reason (R): The ability of the metals to be beaten into thin sheets is known as malleability. **(*Un*)**

2. **Assertion (A):** Magnesium chloride is a covalent compound.
Reason (R): Metals and non-metals react by mutual transfer of electrons. **(*Un*)**

3. **Assertion (A):** Aluminium oxide (Al_2O_3) is an amphoteric oxide.
Reason (R): Aluminium oxide reacts with acids as well as bases. **(*Re*)**

4. **Assertion (A):** The ores of many metals are oxides.
Reason (R): Oxygen is a very reactive element and abundant on the Earth. **(*Un*)**

5. **Assertion (A):** Chromium oxide is generally reduced to chromium by heating with Al powder.
Reason (R): The reduction of chromium oxide by aluminium is highly endothermic. **(*Re*)**

6. **Assertion (A):** An alloy is known as an amalgam if one of the metals is mercury.
Reason (R): The electrical conductivity and melting point of an alloy is higher than that of pure metals. ***(Un)***

7. **Assertion (A):** The metals and alloys are good conductors of electricity.
Reason (R): Bronze is an alloy of copper and tin, and it is not a good conductor of electricity. **(*Un*) (CBSE 2020)**

8. **Assertion (A):** Copper ions migrate from the anode to the cathode during electrorefining of copper.
Reason (R): In the electrorefining process, metal ions accept electrons at the anode and are deposited as pure metal.
(*Re*) (CBSE APQ, 2023)

Subjective Questions

Very Short Answer Type Questions (2 M)

1. You are given a hammer, a battery, a bulb, wires and a switch. **(*Ap*) (NCERT)**
(*a*) How could you use them to distinguish between samples of metals and non-metals?
(*b*) Assess the usefulness of these tests in distinguishing between metals and non-metals.

2. Identify the metal in the following. ***(Re)***
(*a*) Metal that does not react with oxygen even at high temperatures.
(*b*) The most ductile metal.

3. Answer the following questions: ***(Re)***
(*a*) (*i*) Generally, non-metals have low boiling point, but which non-metal has high boiling point?
(*ii*) Name one metal which has a low melting point.
(*b*) Give reasons why copper is used to make hot water tanks and not steel (an alloy of iron). **(NCERT)**

4. Answer the following questions:
(*a*) Listed here is the reactivity of certain metals.

Metal	Reaction with air	Reaction with water	Reaction with dilute acids
Gold	Does not oxidise or burn	No reaction	No reaction
Sodium	Burns vigorously to form an oxide	Violent reaction	Violent reaction
Zinc	Burns to form an oxide	Reacts on heating	Reacts to produce hydrogen
Platinum	No reaction	Does not dissolve or react	No reaction

From the list above, identify the metal(s) that are likely to be found in a pure state in the Earth's crust.
(*b*) A metal oxide on being heated with carbon does NOT produce carbon dioxide. Give a possible explanation for this behaviour of the metal oxide. **(*Ev*) (CFPQ)**

5. You are a scientist working in a chemical research laboratory. Your team is investigating the reactivity of different metals with water to develop safer storage and handling procedures. During an experiment, you observe the following:
• Metal Y does not react with cold water but reacts with steam, forming an oxide and releasing hydrogen gas.

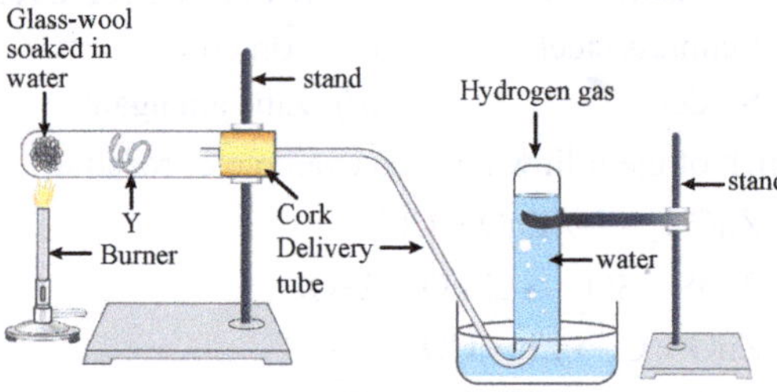

• Metal Z reacts violently with cold water, producing a hydroxide and hydrogen gas.

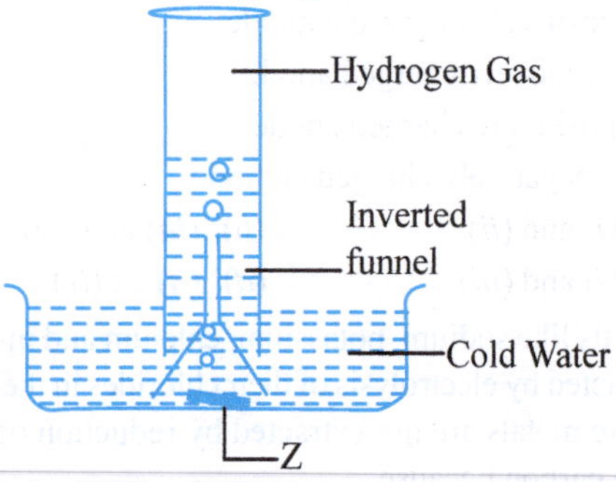

Identify metals Y and Z. ***(Un)***

6. (*a*) How do non-metals react with acid? Explain.
(*b*) Why is sodium kept immersed in kerosene oil? ***(Un)***
(NCERT Intext)

7. You are an engineer working for a railway maintenance company. Your team is responsible for repairing and joining railway tracks and cracked machine parts. During your work, you utilize a special metal, 'M', known for its unique properties and effectiveness in various industrial applications. The metal 'M' has the following properties. ***(Ap)***
• Do not react with cold or hot water but react with steam.
• Act as a reducing agent to reduce metal oxides to metals.
• Its reaction with metal oxide is used to join railway tracks or cracked machine parts.
• Its oxide acts as a protective layer and prevents atmospheric corrosion from penetrating below the oxide layer.
(*a*) Identify Metal 'M'.
(*b*) In the thermit reaction, which substance acts as the reducing agent? Write the chemical reaction involved.

8. (*a*) Write the balanced chemical equation for the reaction that is prevented by storing potassium metal under kerosene.
(*b*) Identify the type of chemical reaction that is prevented.
(*Un*) (CBSE APQ, 2023)

9. Name two metals which will displace hydrogen from dilute acids, and two metals which will not? **(Un) (NCERT)**

10. Give reasons: **(Ap) (CBSE 2019)**
 (a) Platinum, gold and silver are used to make jewellery.
 (b) Metals like sodium and potassium are stored under oil.

OR

Silver articles become black when kept in open for some time, whereas copper vessels lose their shiny brown surfaces and gain a green coat when kept in open. Name the substances present in air with which these metals react and write the name of the products formed.

11. You must have seen tarnished copper vessels being cleaned with lemon or tamarind juice. Explain why these sour substances are effective in cleaning the vessels. **(Un) (NCERT)**

12. Iron does not burn on heating but iron filings burn vigorously when sprinkled in the flame of the burner. Explain. **(Un)**

13. Why iron is not used in its pure state? What makes iron hard and strong? **(Un)**

14. Imagine you are a metallurgist working in a copper refining plant. During the electrolytic refining process of copper, you are explaining to a new trainee how the process works. During the electrolytic refining of copper, impure copper is used as the anode, and a thin sheet of pure copper is used as the cathode. An aqueous solution of copper(II) sulphate ($CuSO_4$) is used as the electrolyte. **(Un)**
 (a) During the electrolytic refining of copper, what happens to insoluble impurities, and where are they found after the process?
 (b) In the electrolytic refining of copper, if the impure copper anode starts to decrease in mass, what happens to the mass of the pure copper cathode, and why?

Short Answer Type Questions (3 M)

1. To compare the reactivity of magnesium and aluminium two friends carried out the following tests.
 • Shardul reacted the metals with hydrochloric acid.
 • Ashwin reacted the metals with boiling water.
 Whose test will differentiate between the two metals based on their reactivity? Explain why. **(An) (CFPQ)**

2. What are amphoteric oxides? Give an example. Write balanced chemical equations to justify your answer. **(Re) (CBSE 2019)**

3. 1.2 mL of sodium hydroxide solution is added to a few pieces of granulated zinc metal taken in a test tube. When the contents are warmed, a gas evolves which is bubbled through a soap solution before testing. Write the equation of the chemical reaction involved and the test to detect the gas. Name the gas which will be evolved when the same metal reacts with dilute solution of a strong acid. **(Un)**

4. Out of three metals P, Q and R, P is less reactive than Q and R is more reactive than P and Q both. Suggest an activity to arrange P, Q and R in order of their decreasing reactivity. **(Ap) (CBSE 2019)**

5. Give the formula of the stable binary compounds that would be formed by the combination of following pairs of elements. **(Un) (NCERT Exemplar)**
 (a) Mg and N_2 (b) Li and O_2
 (c) Al and Cl_2

6. A metal X is obtained from its chloride salt by exposure to sunlight. **(Un) (CBSE APQ, 2023)**
 (a) In which section of the reactivity series of metals-top, middle or bottom, is it likely to be placed? Justify your answer.
 (b) Identify the type of reaction the chloride salt of metal X undergoes on exposure to sunlight.

7. (a) Anirudh took two metal oxides; aluminium oxide and magnesium oxide as shown in the pictures given below. But he forgot to label them. How will you guide/ help Anirudh to identify the oxides and label them?

 (b) In an activity Aishu was given two substances; Copper Sulphide (Cu_2S) and Copper Oxide (Cu_2O) to obtain copper from these compounds. She was able to extract Copper successfully. Illustrate with the help of chemical equations how Aishu might have completed the activity. **(An) (CBSE SQP, 2024)**

8. The given reaction shows one of the processes to extract the metals like Iron and Manganese. **(Un) (CBSE SQP, 2023)**
 $MnO_2(s) + Al(s) \rightarrow Mn(l) + Al_2O_3(s) + Heat$
 (a) Give reason why the above reaction is known as a thermit reaction.
 (b) Identify the substance oxidised and reduced in the above reaction.
 (c) Give a reason why Aluminum is preferably used in thermit reactions.

9. Name the ore of mercury and state the form in which it is found in nature. Write the chemical equations along with the condition required for the reactions involved in the extraction of mercury from its ore. **(Un) (CBSE 2024, 2019)**

10. Metal 'A' is used in the thermit process as a reducing agent. When 'A' is heated with oxygen it gives an oxide 'B' which is amphoteric in nature. Identify A and B. Illustrate with the help of chemical equations, the reaction of B with HCl and NaOH respectively. **(Ap) (CBSE APQ, 2023)**

11. Draw a labeled diagram to show electrolytic refining of copper. State what happens when electric current is passed through the electrolyte taken in this case. **(Ap) (CBSE 2024)**

12. A teacher asks her students to identify a metal, M. She gives them the following clues to help them. **(*Ap*) (CFPQ)**
   (P) Its oxide reacts with both HCl and NaOH.
   (Q) It does not react with hot or cold water but reacts with steam.
   (R) It can be extracted by electrolysis of its ore.
   (*a*) Identify the metal.
   (*b*) Write the chemical equations for the reaction of the metal with HCl and NaOH respectively.
   (*c*) What would happen if the metal is reacted with iron oxide?

Long Answer Type Questions (5 M)

1. You are a junior scientist working in a metallurgy lab, and you've been assigned to investigate the properties and reactions of two mysterious metals, X and Y. Based on your experiments and observations, you have gathered the following information:
   - Metal X displaces Metal Y from its solution, indicating that X is more reactive than Y.
   - Metal X is a key component of Alloy A, which has a low melting point and is widely used in welding electrical wires together.
   - Metal Y, when heated in air, forms a black oxide. It is commonly found in nature in combined states such as sulphide and oxide ores.
   - Metal Y reacts with a moist acidic oxide to form a green substance.

   With this information, you need to answer the following questions: **(*Un*)**
   (*a*) Considering the properties and reactivity of Metal Y, is it typically extracted by the electrolysis of its molten chloride? Justify your answer based on standard metallurgical practices.
   (*b*) Both Metal X and Metal Y react with oxygen to form oxides. Do these metals react with water (at room temperature) to liberate hydrogen gas?
   (*c*) Identify Alloy A and list its constituents.
   (*d*) If Metal Y is refined electrolytically, at which electrode (anode or cathode) would you obtain the pure metal?
   (*e*) Metal Y reacts with a moist acidic oxide to form a green substance. Identify this green substance. Write the reaction involved.
2. (*i*) Write the electron-dot structures for sodium, oxygen and magnesium.
   (*ii*) Show the formation of Na_2O and MgO by the transfer of electrons. **(*Cr*) (NCERT Intext)**
   (*iii*) What are the ions present in these compounds?
3. Explain the following: **(*Un*) (NCERT Exemplar)**
   (*a*) Reactivity of Al decreases if it is dipped in HNO_3
   (*b*) Carbon cannot reduce the oxides of Na or Mg
   (*c*) NaCl is not a conductor of electricity in solid state whereas it does conduct electricity in aqueous solution as well as in molten state
   (*d*) Iron articles are galvanised.
   (*e*) Metals like Na. K, Ca and Mg are never found in their free state in nature.
4. (*a*) An ore on treatment with dilute HCl produces brisk effervescence. Name the type of ore with one example. What are the steps that will be required to obtain metal from the enriched ore? Also, write the chemical equations for the reactions involved in the process. **(CBSE 2019)**
   (*b*) Copper coin is immersed in silver nitrate aqueous solution, $AgNO_3$, for some time. What changes will take place in the coin and in the colour of the solution? Write a balanced chemical equation of the reaction involved. **(*Un*)**
5. (*a*) List in tabular form three chemical properties on the basis of which we can differentiate between a metal and a non-metal.
   (*b*) Give reasons for the following:
      (*i*) Most metals conduct electricity well.
      (*ii*) The reaction of iron (III) oxide [Fe_2O_3] with heated aluminium is used to join cracked machine parts.
   (*Un*) (CBSE 2019)
6. Write balanced chemical equations to explain what happens, when **(*Un*) (CBSE 2020)**
   (*i*) Mercuric oxide is heated.
   (*ii*) Mixture of cuprous oxide and cuprous sulphide is heated.
   (*iii*) Aluminum is reacted with manganese dioxide.
   (*iv*) Ferric oxide is reduced with aluminum.
   (*v*) Zinc carbonate undergoes calcination.

   OR

   (*i*) By the transfer of electrons, illustrate the formation of bond in magnesium chloride and identify the ions present in this compound.
   (*ii*) Ionic compounds are solids. Give reasons.
   (*iii*) With the help of a labeled diagram show the experimental set up of action of steam on a metal.

Case Based Questions

Case Based-I: Meet Alex and Mia, two budding scientists. They embarked on a mission to explore the reactivity of different metals. By observing Potassium's explosive reaction with water, Zinc's subtle fizzing with dilute acid, and the inert nature of Silver, they uncovered the unique behaviour of each metal. This journey sparked their curiosity about the reactivity series and its implications in various industrial processes and everyday life. **(*Un*)**
(*i*) Arrange the following metals in order of their reactivity, starting from the most reactive: Potassium, Zinc, Copper, Aluminum, Silver. *(1 M)*
(*ii*) If a metal A is higher in the reactivity series than a metal B, what can you infer about their tendencies to react with water? *(1 M)*
(*iii*) (*a*) A metal X reacts vigorously with water, while a metal Y reacts mildly with steam. Which metal is higher in the reactivity series and why? *(1 M)*
(*b*) Why are metals like gold and platinum often found in a pure state in nature and not as compounds? *(1 M)*

Case Based-II: A student, took four metals P, Q, R and S and carried out different experiments to study the properties of metals. Some of the observations were:
- All metals could not be cut with knife except metal R.
- Metal P combined with oxygen to form an oxide M_2O_3, which reacted with both acids and bases.

- Reaction with water.

  P – Did not react either with cold or hot water but reacted with steam.

  Q – Reacted with hot water and the metal started floating.

  R – Reacted violently with cold water.

  S – Did not react with water at all.

(*Ap*) (CBSE 2022 Term 1)

Based on the above observations answer the following:

(*i*) Out of the given metals, the metal Q is (*1 M*)

(*a*) Iron (*b*) Zinc

(*c*) Potassium (*d*) Magnesium

(*ii*) Metal which forms amphoteric oxides is (*1 M*)

(*a*) P (*b*) Q

(*c*) R (*d*) S

(*iii*) The increasing order of the reactivity of the four metals is (*1 M*)

(*a*) P < Q < R < S (*b*) S < R < Q < P

(*c*) S < P < Q < R (*d*) P < R < Q < S

(*iv*) Out of the given metals, the one which needs to be stored using Kerosene is (*1 M*)

(*a*) P (*b*) R

(*c*) S (*d*) Q

Case Based-III: Pure gold is very soft and therefore not suitable for making jewellery. To make it hard, gold is alloyed with other metals. The purity of gold is measured in carats according to the table below. Carat number is the number of parts of gold in 24 parts **(*Ap*)**

Carat Number	Number of Parts of Gold in 24 Parts	Number of Parts of other Metals in 24 Parts
24	24	0
22	22	2
18	18	6
14	14	10
12	12	12

(*i*) What is the percentage of gold in 18 carat gold? Name any two metals that are used to make 22 carat gold. (*2 M*)

(*ii*) Like gold, pure iron is also comparatively soft and also undergoes rusting. Name the substance that is mixed with iron.

(*a*) to make it hard. (*1 M*)

(*b*) to change it to stainless steel to prevent rusting. (*1 M*)

OR

(*ii*) (*a*) What type of mixture is an alloy? (*1 M*)

(*b*) How does the electrical conductivity of an alloy compare with that of the pure metal? (*1 M*)

Case Based-IV: Almost all metals combine with oxygen to form metal oxides. Metal oxides are generally basic as nature. But some metal oxides show both basic as well as acidic behaviour. Different metals show different reactivities towards oxygen. Some react vigorously while some do not react at all.

(*Un*) (CBSE 2023)

(*i*) What happens when copper is heated in air? (Give the equation of the reaction involved). (*1 M*)

(*ii*) Why are some metal oxides categorized as amphoteric? Give one example. (*1 M*)

(*iii*) Complete the following equations: (*2 M*)

(*a*) $Na_2O(s) + H_2O(l) \rightarrow$

(*b*) $Al_2O_3 + 2NaOH \rightarrow$

OR

On burning Sulphur in oxygen a colourless gas is produced. (*2 M*)

(*a*) Write chemical equation for the reaction.

(*b*) Name the gas formed.

(*c*) State the nature of the gas.

(*d*) What will be the action of this on a dry litmus paper?

Case Based-V: The metals produced by various reduction processes are not very pure. They contain impurities, which must be removed to obtain pure metals. The most widely used method for refining impure metals is electrolytic refining. **(*Un*)**

(*i*) What is the cathode and anode made of in the refining of copper by this process? (*1 M*)

(*ii*) Name the solution used in the above process and write its formula. (*1 M*)

(*iii*) How copper gets refined when electric current is passed in the electrolytic cell? (*2 M*)

OR

You have two beakers 'A' and 'B' containing copper sulphate solution. What would you observe after about 2 hours if you dip a strip of zinc in beaker 'A' and a strip of silver in beaker 'B'?

Give reason for your observations in each case. (*2 M*)

Case Based-VI: The melting points and boiling points of some ionic compounds are given below: **(*Un*) (CBSE 2023)**

Compound	Melting Point (K)	Boiling Point (K)
NaCl	1074	1686
LiCl	887	1600
$CaCl_2$	1045	1900
CaO	2850	3120
$MgCl_2$	981	1685

These compounds are termed ionic because they are formed by the transfer of electrons from a metal to a non-metal. The electron transfer in such compounds is controlled by the electronic configuration of the elements involved. Every element tends to attain a completely filled valence shell of its nearest noble gas or a stable octet.

(*i*) Show the electron transfer in the formation of magnesium chloride. (*1 M*)

(*ii*) List two properties of ionic compounds other than their high melting and boiling points. (*1 M*)

(*iii*) While forming an ionic compound, say sodium chloride, how does sodium atom attain its stable configuration? (*2 M*)

OR

Give reasons: (*2 M*)

(*a*) Why do ionic compounds in the solid state not conduct electricity?

(*b*) What happens at the cathode when electricity is passed through an aqueous solution of sodium chloride?

ANSWER KEYS

Multiple Choice Questions

1. (*a*)	**2.** (*c*)	**3.** (*b*)	**4.** (*c*)	**5.** (*b*)	**6.** (*a*)	**7.** (*d*)	**8.** (*c*)	**9.** (*d*)	**10.** (*d*)
11. (*b*)	**12.** (*d*)	**13.** (*b*)	**14.** (*a*)	**15.** (*d*)	**16.** (*a*)	**17.** (*c*)	**18.** (*d*)	**19.** (*b*)	**20.** (*b*)
21. (*c*)	**22.** (*c*)	**23.** (*c*)	**24.** (*c*)	**25.** (*b*)					

Assertion and Reason

1. (*d*)	**2.** (*d*)	**3.** (*a*)	**4.** (*a*)	**5.** (*c*)	**6.** (*c*)	**7.** (*b*)	**8.** (*c*)

Case Based Questions

Case Based-II

(*i*) (*d*) (*ii*) (*a*) (*iii*) (*c*) (*iv*) (*b*)

HINTS & EXPLANATIONS

Multiple Choice Questions

1. (*a*) Iodine is the only non-metal which is lustrous, that is, has a shiny appearance.

2. (*c*) An insulating material that is used in coating of electrical wire is PVC (Polyvinyl chloride).

3. (*b*) When the current is started, the iron plate (cathode, negative terminal) attracts Cu^{2+} ions from the solution, which are reduced to form metallic copper. Thus, copper continues to deposit on the iron plate.

4. (*c*) Iron is more reactive than nickel. When added to cobalt sulphate, iron displaces cobalt, forming iron sulphate and depositing cobalt. Nickel, being less reactive, cannot displace cobalt. This reaction confirms that iron is more reactive than nickel.

5. (*b*) Silver is known to have the highest electrical conductivity among all metals, making it the best conductor of electricity in this set.

6. (*a*) Calcium oxide has a high melting point and is soluble in water. Thus, the element is calcium.

7. (*d*) The electronic configuration of potassium (K) is

	K	L	M	N (shells)
K :	2	8	8	1

Hence, four shells are required.

8. (*c*) Magnesium does not react with cold water. It reacts with hot water to form magnesium hydroxide and hydrogen (colourless bubbles). It also starts floating due to the bubbles of hydrogen gas sticking to its surface.

9. (*d*) A is metal as the oxide of metal will dissolve in H_2O to give basic solution. The aqueous solution of oxide of element A reacts with aqueous solution of oxide of element B, Hence, solution of oxide of element B is acidic as reaction between two basic solution does not take place. Hence element B is non-metal as nonmetals oxides are acidic in nature.

10. (*d*) High reactivity is not responsible for copper being used for making cooking utensils.

11. (*b*) Iron is more reactive than copper. Therefore, iron displaces copper from copper sulphate solution, resulting in the formation of iron sulphate and deposition of copper on the iron nail, giving it the colour of reddish brown. This displacement reaction can be represented as:

$Fe(s) + CuSO_4(aq) \rightarrow FeSO_4(aq) + Cu(s)$

12. (*d*) Gold(Au) will get dissolved in conc. HCl and conc. HNO_3, 3 : 1 mixture (aqua regia).

13. (*b*) The most reactive element is R and Q is the least reactive element because R easily displaces P from its salt and P easily displaces Q from its salt, but Q cannot displace P as well as R.

14. (*a*) The element X is sodium. Na metal reacts with dilute H_2SO_4 to produce H_2 gas which burns with a pop sound when a burning match stick is brought near it.

The reaction that occurs is:

$H_2SO_4 + 2Na \rightarrow Na_2SO_4 + H_2$

15. (*d*) Copper is more reactive than silver and will readily displace it from its salt solution, $AgNO_3$.

The reaction that occurs is:

$Cu + 2AgNO_3 \rightarrow Cu(NO_3)_2 + 2Ag\downarrow$

16. (*a*)
- **Metal X: Sodium**
  - Sodium is obtained by electrolysis of molten sodium chloride.
  - Sodium oxide is soluble in water, forming sodium hydroxide.
- **Metal Y: Copper**
  - Copper can be obtained from its ore by just heating in air.
  - Copper oxide is black.
- **Metal Z: Gold**
  - Gold is found in the native state.
  - Gold dissolves in aqua regia.

17. (*c*) Atomic number of element 'X' is 12 so it is Mg and the atomic number of element 'Y' is 17 so, it is Cl.
Mg and Cl do not form bond by sharing of electrons. They form bond by the transfer of electrons from metal to non-metal. Hence,the molecular formula of compound Z is $MgCl_2$. and is an ionic compound. Therefore, it would conduct electricity in molten state and is soluble in water.
18. (*d*) Zinc Amalgam is Zn-Hg, hence it contains mercury as one of its constituents.
19. (*b*) The sulphide ores are converted into their oxides by heating strongly in the presence of excess air. This process is known as roasting.
20. (*b*) A positively charged anode and a negatively charged cathode make up an electrolytic cell.
21. (*c*) The oxides of some of the moderately reactive metals like zinc is extracted with carbon as a reducing agent. As a result, a free metal is obtained. High reactive metals like sodium, potassium, calcium and magnesium cannot be extracted with carbon as a reducing agent. As, these metals are stronger reducing agents than carbon and carbon has less affinity for oxygen than these metals. Therefore, carbon will not be able to remove oxygen from their oxides.
22. (*c*) Aluminium reacts rapidly with hydrochloric acid, producing hydrogen gas and causing rapid formation of bubbles. Iron reacts slowly with hydrochloric acid, producing hydrogen gas at a slower rate. Copper does not react with hydrochloric acid, resulting in no observable reaction.
23. (*c*) Represents correctly the process of electrolytic refining.
24. (*c*) When water is added to the test tubes, the sodium will react vigorously, producing hydrogen gas and heat, which can cause the evolved hydrogen gas to catch fire. Copper will not react with water.
When dilute hydrochloric acid is added to the test tubes, sodium will react vigorously, producing hydrogen gas and forming sodium chloride. Copper does not react with dilute hydrochloric acid.
25. (*b*) $2Na^+ [\overset{\times\times}{\underset{\times\times}{{}^\times_\times O {}^\times_\times}}]^{-2}$

Assertion and Reason

1. (*d*) Gold and silver are the most malleable metals, that is, they can be beaten into thin sheets easily by hammering them.
2. (*d*) Magnesium chloride is an ionic compound.
3. (*a*) Amphoteric oxides reacts with both acids and bases.
4. (*a*) Oxygen is reactive and abundant on the Earth, therefore, ores of many metals are oxides.
5. (*c*) The reduction of chromium oxide by aluminium is highly exothermic.
6. (*c*) The electrical conductivity and melting point of an alloy is lower than that of pure metals.
7. (*b*) Metals conduct electricity due to the presence of free electrons. Because alloys are metal mixtures, they have somewhat similar properties to metals. As a result, they, too, are good electrical conductors, but their conductivity is less than that of pure metals.
Bronze is a metal alloy made of copper and tin and does not conduct electricity.
8. (*c*) In the electrorefining process, metal ions accept electrons at the cathode and are deposited as pure metal. The reaction that takes place at cathode is

$$M^{n+} + ne^- \rightarrow \underset{\text{Pure metal}}{M\,(s)}$$

Subjective Questions

Very Short Answer Type Questions

1. (*a*) To distinguish between samples of metals and non-metals:
Conductivity Test: Connect the sample with the battery, wires, and switch to form a simple circuit. If the bulb lights up, the material is a metal (conducts electricity). If not, it's a non-metal. *(½ M)*
Hammer Test: Strike the sample with the hammer. If it can be flattened or shaped without breaking, it is likely a metal. Non-metals are typically brittle and get shattered. *(½ M)*
(*b*) **Usefulness of Tests:**
Conductivity Test: Effective, as metals are generally good conductors while non-metals are insulators. *(½ M)*
Hammer Test: Useful, but limited, as some metals can also be brittle, and non-metals can sometimes be malleable. *(½ M)*

Key Takeaways

This question teaches students about the basic properties of metals and non-metals. Metals being good conductors of electricity cause the bulb to light up. Metals are generally malleable and can be flattened or shaped when hammered, unlike most non-metals. This question helps students to critically evaluate and reflect upon nature of metals and non-metals.

2. (*a*) The two metals that does not react with oxygen even at high temperatures are:-
(1) Silver *(½ M)*
(2) Gold *(½ M)*
(*b*) Gold is the most ductile metal. *(1 M)*
3. (*a*) (*i*) Diamond is one of the non metal which has high boiling point. *(½ M)*
(*ii*) Ga is a metal which has low melting point. *(½ M)*
(*b*) Copper (Cu) does not react with cold water, hot water, or steam. However, iron (Fe) does react with steam. If the hot water tanks are made of steel (an alloy of iron), then iron would react vigorously with the steam formed from hot water. *(1 M)*
4. (*a*) Gold and platinum *(1 M)*
(*b*) The metal oxide does not produce carbon dioxide when heated with carbon because the metal in metal oxide is highly reactive and has a greater affinity for oxygen than carbon. *(1 M)*

5. Metal Y is likely to be either aluminium (Al), zinc (Zn), or iron (Fe), as these metals do not react with cold water but react with steam to form their respective oxides and hydrogen gas. *(1 M)*

Metal Z is likely to be either sodium (Na) or potassium (K) as these metals react violently with cold water to form their respective hydroxides and hydrogen gas. *(1 M)*

6. (*a*) Generally, non-metals do not prefer to react with acids because, when a substance reacts with acid, it provides electrons to the H^+ ions. But in the case of non-metals, they accept electrons by themselves. *(1 M)*

(*b*) Sodium is kept immersed in kerosene oil because

(1) Na is highly reactive *(½ M)*

(2) If kept open, can react with oxygen to catch fire and can cause damage. *(½ M)*

7. (*a*) Metal 'M' is Aluminium (Al). *(1 M)*

(*b*) In the thermit reaction, aluminium acts as the reducing agent, losing electrons to reduce iron(III) oxide to molten iron. *(½ M)*

$Fe_2O_3(s) + 2Al(s) \rightarrow 2Fe(l) + Al_2O_3(s) + \text{heat}$ *(½ M)*

8. (*a*) $4K + O_2 \rightarrow 2K_2O$ *(1 M)*

(*b*) Combination reaction OR oxidation reaction or redox reaction *(1 M)*

9. Iron and aluminium will displace hydrogen from dilute acid, since they are more reactive than that of hydrogen. *(1 M)*

Mercury and copper cannot displace hydrogen from dilute acid, since they are less reactive than that of hydrogen. *(1 M)*

10. (*a*) Platinum, gold and silver are used to make jewellery because these metals are very less reactive, thus they are not affected by air, moisture or most chemicals. These metals are lustrous, malleable and ductile in nature and has high corrosion resistance nature. *(1 M)*

(*b*) Sodium and potassium readily react with water to produce a lot of heat. So, hydrogen evolved in the reaction leads to fire. Therefore, in order to prevent contact with water, these metals are stored under oil like kerosene. *(1 M)*

OR

When silver is exposed to air, it combines with the sulphur in the air to generate a coating of silver sulphide. *(1 M)*

$$2Ag + H_2S \rightarrow \underset{\text{Silver sulphide}}{Ag_2S} + H_2$$

Copper vessels lose their shiny brown surface as copper reacts with moist CO_2 in the air, forming a green layer of copper carbonate and copper hydroxide. *(1 M)*

$$2Cu + H_2O + CO_2 + O_2 \rightarrow \underset{\text{Copper hydroxide}}{Cu(OH)_2} + \underset{\text{Copper carbonate}}{CuCO_3}$$

11. Lemon or tamarind juice contains citric acid, which reacts with tarnish (copper carbonate) on copper vessels. The acid neutralises basic copper carbonate and dissolves the layer, leaving the copper surface clean. This acidic action facilitates the removal of tarnish and restores the shiny appearance of the copper. *(2 M)*

12. Iron doesn't burn when heated because it has a strong molecular force of attraction (lesser surface area exposed to flame), which prevent it from reaching its ignition temperature. *(1 M)*

However, iron filings, being smaller particles, quickly attain the ignition temperature when sprinkled in flames due to their larger surface area, allowing them to burn vigorously. *(1 M)*

13. Iron is never used in its pure state because pure iron is very soft and stretches easily when hot. *(1 M)*

Iron when mixed with a small amount of carbon (about 0.05 %), makes it hard and strong. *(1 M)*

14. (*a*) Insoluble impurities do not dissolve in the electrolyte and settle at the bottom of the anode and are known as anode mud. *(1 M)*

(*b*) The mass of the pure copper cathode increases because copper ions from the anode dissolve into the electrolyte and are then deposited onto the cathode, forming pure copper. *(1 M)*

Short Answer Type Questions

1. Ashwin's test, where the metals are reacted with boiling water, will differentiate between magnesium and aluminium based on their reactivity. Magnesium readily reacts with boiling water to produce hydrogen gas, forming magnesium hydroxide ($Mg(OH)_2$).

In contrast, Aluminium does not react with boiling water, but reacts only with steam. *(1 M)*

$Mg + 2H_2O(l) \rightarrow Mg(OH)_2 + H_2$

$Al + H_2O(l) \rightarrow \text{no reaction}$ *(½ M)*

Hydrochloric acid might not differentiate the two metals effectively, as both react with hydrochloric acid, producing hydrogen gas and corresponding salts. *(1 M)*

$Mg + 2HCl \rightarrow MgCl_2 + H_2$

$2\,Al + 6HCl \rightarrow 2\,AlCl_3 + 3H_2$ *(½ M)*

2. Amphoteric oxides are those oxides which can react with both acids and bases. **Example:** Aluminium oxide(Al_2O_3), can react with both acids and bases. *(1 M)*

The balanced chemical equations are:

$Al_2O_3 + 6HCl \rightarrow 2AlCl_3 + 3H_2O$ *(1 M)*

$Al_2O_3 + 2NaOH \rightarrow 2NaAlO_2 + H_2O$ *(1 M)*

3. When zinc is added to a sodium hydroxide solution, sodium zincate (Na_2ZnO_2) and hydrogen gas are generated.

$2NaOH + Zn \rightarrow Na_2ZnO_2 + H_2\uparrow$ *(1 M)*

When the burning splint is held near the evolved gas, it continues to burn with a pop sound, indicating hydrogen gas evolution. *(1 M)*

$ZnSO_4$ is formed with the evolution of hydrogen gas, when the same metal, Zn, interacts with the strong acid H_2SO_4.

$Zn + H_2SO_4 \rightarrow ZnSO_4 + H_2\uparrow$ *(1 M)*

4. Step 1 → Take salt solution of metal P, Q and R.

Step 2 → According to question, R > Q > P, Since R is more reactive than Q and P, so displacement reaction take place.

(1) $\underset{(s)}{R} + \underset{(aq)}{\text{Salt of } Q} \rightarrow \underset{(aq)}{\text{Salt of } R} + \underset{(s)}{Q}$ *(½ M)*

$\underset{(s)}{R} + \text{Salt of } \underset{(aq)}{P} \rightarrow \text{Salt of } \underset{(aq)}{R} + \underset{(s)}{P}$ (½ M)

(2) $\underset{(s)}{Q} + \text{Salt of } \underset{(aq)}{R} \rightarrow \underset{(aq)}{\text{No reaction}}$ (½ M)

$\underset{(s)}{Q} + \text{Salt of } \underset{(aq)}{P} \rightarrow \text{Salt of } \underset{(aq)}{Q} + \underset{(s)}{P}$ (½ M)

(3) $\underset{(s)}{P} + \text{Salt of } \underset{(aq)}{R} \rightarrow \text{No reaction}$ (½ M)

$\underset{(s)}{P} + \text{Salt of } \underset{(aq)}{Q} \rightarrow \text{No reaction}$ (½ M)

5. (*a*) $3Mg(s) + N_2(g) \rightarrow Mg_3N_2(s)$ (*1 M*)
(Magnesium nitride)

(*b*) $4Li(s) + O_2(g) \rightarrow 2Li_2O(s)$ (*1 M*)
(Lithium oxide)

(*c*) $2Al(s) + 3Cl_2(g) \rightarrow 2AlCl_3(s)$ (*1 M*)
(Aluminium chloride)

6. (*a*) - Bottom section (*1 M*)

- Metals at the bottom of the reactivity series are the least reactive. They occur in their free state; their compounds are unstable and hence easily converted to metal. (*1 M*)

(*b*) Photolytic decomposition (*1 M*)

7. (*a*) Aqueous solution of magnesium oxide turns red litmus to blue. Aluminium oxide is amphoteric and insoluble in water. Thus, it does not change the colour of either blue or red litmus. (*3 M*)

OR

Magnesium oxide reacts with acid only whereas Aluminium oxide reacts with acids and bases, which means it is amphoteric in nature.

(*b*) $2Cu_2S + 3O_2(g) \xrightarrow{\text{Heat}} 2Cu_2O(s) + 2SO_2(g)$ (*1 M*)

$2Cu_2O + Cu_2S \xrightarrow{\text{Heat}} 6Cu(s) + SO_2(g)$ (*1 + 1 M*)

8. (*a*) The above reaction is known as a thermit reaction as the reaction is highly exothermic reaction.

OR

The metal (Mn/Fe) obtained will be in molten/liquid state. (*1 M*)

(*b*) Substance oxidised – Al(s) (*½ M*)

Substance reduced – $MnO_2(s)$ (*½ M*)

(c) Aluminium is preferably used in thermit reactions as it is placed above Fe and Mn in reactivity series of metals. (*1 M*)

9. Cinnabar is the ore of mercury and it is found as sulphide ore in the nature. (*1 M*)

When it is heated in air, it is first converted into mercuric oxide (HgO). Mercuric oxide is then reduced to mercury on further heating.

$2HgS(s) + 3O_2(g) \xrightarrow{\text{Heat}} 2HgO(s) + 2SO_2(g)$

$2HgO(s) \xrightarrow{\text{Heat}} 2Hg(l) + O_2(g)$ (*1 M*)

Hence, condition required are heating and presence of oxygen. (*1 M*)

Topper's Explanation

28. (1) Cinnabar. I Mercury is found in its sulphide ore in nature.

(2) $2HgS + 3O_2 \xrightarrow{\Delta} 2HgO + 2SO_2$

$2HgO \xrightarrow{\Delta} 2Hg + O_2$

The condition required is heat. In first reaction presence of oxygen is also needed to oxidise mercury.

10. Metal 'A' is Aluminium (Al) as it is used as reducing agent in thermit process. (*½ M*)

The reaction of A when heated with oxygen (O_2) is

$4Al + 3O_2 \rightarrow 2Al_2O_3$
(B)

Hence, B is Al_2O_3 (Aluminium oxide) and it is amphoteric in nature. (*½ M*)

The chemical equations illustrating amphoteric nature of B are:

$Al_2O_3 + 6HCl \rightarrow 2AlCl_3 + 3H_2O$ (*1 M*)

$Al_2O_3 + 2NaOH \rightarrow 2NaAlO_2 + H_2O$ (*1 M*)

11. The diagram for the electrolytic refining of copper is shown below:

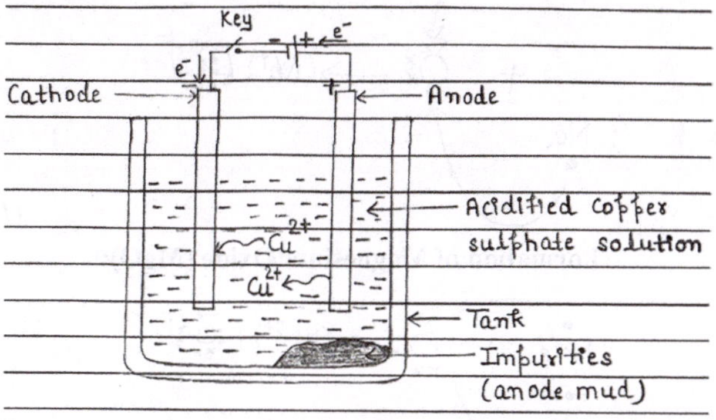

(*½ M*)

In this process, the anode is made up of impure copper and cathode is made up of thin strip of pure copper. (*½ M*)

On passing the current through the electrolyte, the pure metal from the anode dissolves into the electrolyte and an equivalent amount of pure metal from the electrolyte is deposited on the cathode. (*1 M*)

12. (*a*) The given information identifies the metal as Aluminium. (*½ M*)

(*b*) $Al_2O_3 + 2NaOH \rightarrow 2NaAlO_2 + H_2O$ (*1 M*)

$Al_2O_3 + 6HCl \rightarrow 2AlCl_3 + 3H_2O$ (*1 M*)

(*c*) It would displace iron to form aluminium oxide. (*½ M*)

Long Answer Type Questions

1. According to the given information, Metal X can be lead (Pb) or tin (Sn) and Metal Y is Copper (Cu).

(*a*) No, Metal Y is not extracted by the electrolysis of its molten chloride. Electrolysis is a common method used to extract metals that are placed at the top of the activity series. Y is copper metal that is placed low in the activity series. (*1 M*) (*b*) Metals X (Pb or Sn) and Y (Cu) react with oxygen to form oxides. However, neither metal X (lead or tin) nor metal Y (copper) react with water (at room temperature) to liberate hydrogen gas. *(1 M)*

(*c*) Alloy A is likely solder, commonly used for welding electrical wires together. Solder typically contains lead (Pb) and tin (Sn). *(1 M)*

(*d*) In the electrolytic refining of copper (Metal Y), the pure metal is obtained at the cathode. *(1 M)*

(*e*) Metal Cu (Copper) reacts with moist air and carbon dioxide (acidic oxides) to form a green substance known as basic copper carbonate. *(½ M)*

The reaction that occur is:

$$2Cu + H_2O + CO_2 + O_2 \longrightarrow Cu(OH)_2 + CuCO_3$$

(½ M)

2. (*i*) The electron-dot structures for Na, O, and Mg are as follows:

Na	O	Mg
2, 8, 1	2, 6	2, 8, 2

(1 M)

(*ii*) **Formation of Sodium Oxide (Na_2O):**

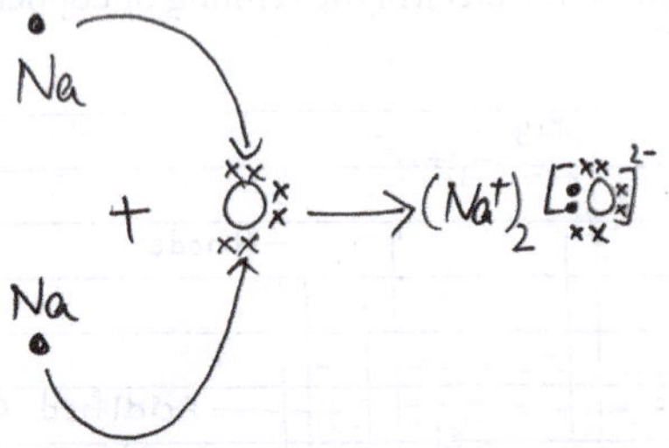

(1 M)

Formation of Magnesium Oxide (MgO):

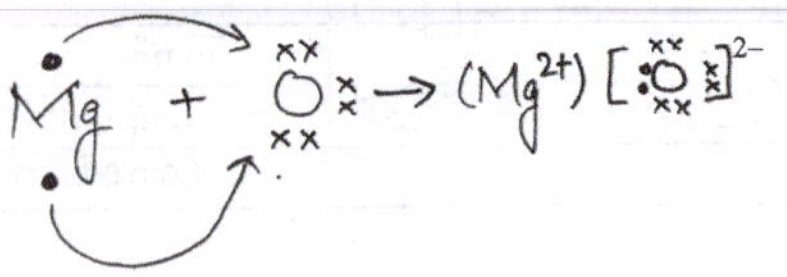

(1 M)

(*iii*) The ions present in these compounds are:

Sodium ion: Na^+ *(½ M)*

Oxide ion: O^{2-} *(½ M)*

Magnesium ion : Mg^{2+} *(½ M)*

Oxide ion: O^{2-} *(½ M)*

3. (*a*) Nitric acid, being a potent oxidizing agent, induces the deposition of an aluminium oxide layer when aluminium is immersed in it. Consequently, the reactivity of aluminium diminishes upon immersion in nitric acid. *(1 M)*

(*b*) Sodium and magnesium, being highly reactive metals, exhibit a stronger affinity to oxygen than to carbon. Consequently, carbon proves ineffective in reducing the oxides of sodium or magnesium. *(1 M)*

(*c*) NaCl is an example of an ionic compound. Its electrical conductivity is due to the mobility of Na^+ and Cl^- ions. In the solid state, the movement of these ions is not possible due to its rigid structure but in aqueous solution or molten state, the ions can move freely. Hence, NaCl do not conduct electricity in solid state, whereas it does conduct electricity in aqueous solution as well as in molten state. *(1 M)*

(*d*) Iron readily reacts with atmospheric oxygen and forms rust. Galvanization (coating with zinc) of iron articles is employed as a preventive measure against rusting. *(1 M)*

(*e*) Sodium (Na), potassium (K), calcium (Ca), and magnesium (Mg) are characterized by high reactivity, forming compounds readily with a variety of elements. Consequently, these metals are not naturally found in their free state due to their affinity for compound formation. *(1 M)*

4. (*a*) The type of ore is carbonate ore.

Brisk effervescence with acid is observed due to the evolution of carbon dioxide gas, during the reaction of an acid with carbonate ore. Example:

$$ZnCO_3(s) + 2HCl\ (aq) \rightarrow ZnCl_2(s) + H_2O\ (l) + CO_2\ (g)$$

(1 M)

The steps involved in the extraction of this carbonate ore into metal are:

(*i*) **Calcination:** The carbonate ore is heated strongly in the limited supply of oxygen to produce metal oxide with the evolution of CO_2 gas.

$$ZnCO_3(s) + HEAT \rightarrow ZnO(s) + CO_2(g)$$ *(1 M)*

(*ii*) **Reduction:** The oxide ore is then reduced with carbon to extract the metal.

$$ZnO(s) + C(s) \rightarrow Zn(s) + CO(g)$$ *(1 M)*

(*b*) Copper is considered more reactive than silver hence it will displace silver from silver nitrate ($AgNO_3$) solution and silver will be deposited on copper coin. The colour of solution will change to blue due to the formation of $Cu(NO_3)_2$. *(1 M)*

$$Cu(s) + 2AgNO_3\ (aq) \rightarrow Cu(NO_3)_2\ (aq) + 2Ag(s)$$

(1 M)

5. (*a*)

Property	Metals	Non-Metals
1. Nature of ions	Metals are electropositive elements and hence, lose one or more electrons to form positive ions,	Non-metals are electronegative elements, and hence gain one or more electrons to form negative ions.
2. Nature of oxides	Metals form basic oxides	Non-metals form either acidic or neutral oxides.
3. Reaction with water	Most of the metals displace hydrogen from water or steam	Non-metals generally do not react with water or steam

(3 M)

(*b*) (*i*) Metals are good conductors of electricity because they contain free electrons which can move easily through the metal lattice and conduct electric current. *(1 M)* (*ii*) In the thermit process, iron (III) oxide is heated with aluminium, which results in the evolution of high amount of heat which melts iron. This molten iron is used to fill cracked machine parts.

$Fe_2O_3(s) + 2Al(s) \rightarrow 2Fe(l) + Al_2O_3(s) + \text{Heat}$ *(1 M)*

6. (*i*) When mercuric oxide (HgO), a red solid, is heated to extremely high temperatures, it decomposes into mercury (Hg), a grey residue, and oxygen gas (O_2).

$2HgO \xrightarrow{\text{Heat}} 2Hg + O_2$ *(1 M)*

(*ii*) Copper metal is formed as a by product when a mixture of cuprous oxide and cuprous sulphide is heated, along with the generation of SO_2 gas.

$2Cu_2O + Cu_2S \xrightarrow{\text{Heat}} 6Cu + SO_2$ *(1 M)*

(*iii*) Aluminium oxide (Al_2O_3) and manganese (Mn) are formed as a byproduct when aluminium reacts with manganese dioxide.

$3MnO_2 + 4Al \longrightarrow 2Al_2O_3 + 3Mn + \text{heat}$ *(1 M)*

(*iv*) When ferric oxide is reduced with aluminium, a residue of aluminium oxide (Al_2O_3) and iron (Fe) is formed.

$Fe_2O_3 + 2Al \longrightarrow Al_2O_3 + 2Fe + \text{heat}$ *(1 M)*

(*v*) When zinc carbonate is calcined (heated in the absence of air), zinc oxide, ZnO is formed as a residue along with the evolution of CO_2 gas.

$ZnCO_3 \xrightarrow{\text{Heat}} ZnO + CO_2$ *(1 M)*

OR

(*i*) The formation of bonds in magnesium chloride is given below:

$Mg \longrightarrow Mg^{2+} + 2e^-$

2, 8, 2   2, 8

(Magnesium cation) *(½ M)*

$Cl + e^- \longrightarrow Cl^-$ *(½ M)*

2, 8, 7   2, 8, 8

(Chloride anion)

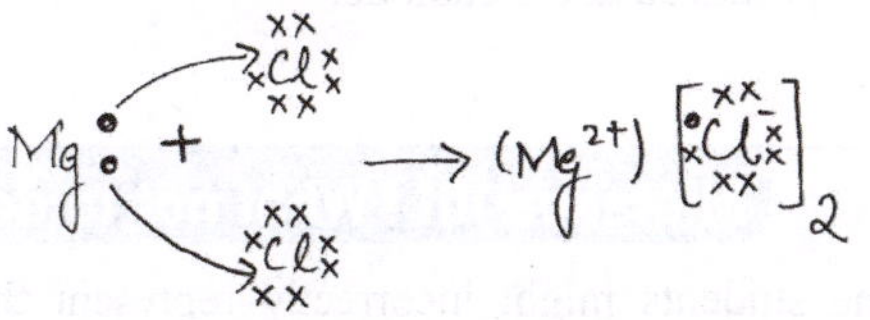

Formation of magnesium chloride

(1 M)

(*ii*) Ionic compounds are composed of oppositely charged ions bound together by a strong electrostatic attraction. As a result, they are hard solids. *(1 M)*

(*iii*) The well labelled diagram for the action of steam on metal is given below:

Action of steam on metal

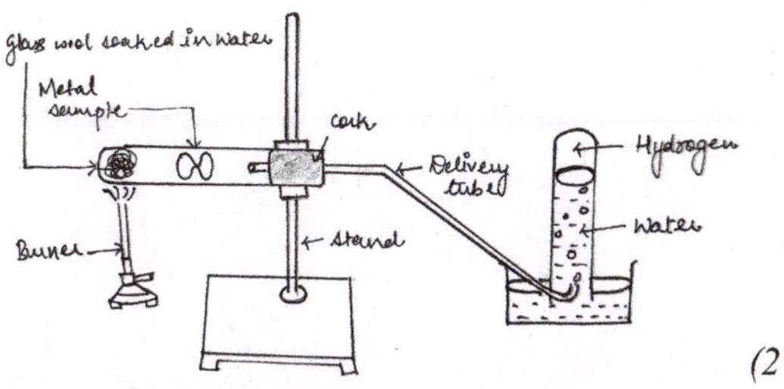

(2 M)

Case Based Questions

Case Based-I

(*i*) The metals can be arranged starting from the most reactive as:-

Potassium, Aluminium, Zinc, Copper, Silver. *(1 M)*

(*ii*) If metal A is higher in the reactivity series than metal B, metal A will have a stronger tendency to react with water and displace hydrogen gas, compared to metal B. *(1 M)*

(*iii*) (*a*) Metal X is higher in the reactivity series than metal Y. This is evident from X's vigorous reaction with water and Y's milder reaction with steam. *(1 M)*

(*b*) Metals like gold and platinum are found in a pure state because they are very unreactive due to their low positions in the reactivity series. They don't readily combine with other elements to form compounds. *(1 M)*

Case Based-II

(*i*) (*d*) Magnesium reacts with hot water to form magnesium hydroxide and hydrogen. It starts floating due to the bubbles of hydrogen gas sticking to the surface. *(1 M)*

(*ii*) (*a*) $2Al + 3H_2O \longrightarrow Al_2O_3 + 3H_2$ *(1 M)*

(*iii*) (*c*) The four metals are:

P : Al

Q : Mg

R : K/Na

S : Cu/Ag/Au

Thus, the correct order of reactivity is $S < P < Q < R$.

(1 M)

(*iv*) (*b*) 'R' is highly reactive, therefore, needs to be stored in kerosene. *(1 M)*

Case Based-III

(*i*) The percentage of gold in 18 carat gold is (18/24) × 100 = 75% *(1 M)*

The two metals that are used to make 22 carat gold are

1. Silver *(½ M)*
2. Copper *(½ M)*

(*ii*) (*a*) Carbon(0.05%) is mixed with iron to make it hard. *(1 M)*

(*b*) Metals like nickel and chromium are mixed with iron to change it to stainless steel to prevent rusting. *(1 M)*

OR

(*ii*) (*a*) An alloy is a homogeneous mixture of two or more metals, or a metal and a non-metal. *(1 M)*

(*b*) The electrical conductivity of an alloy is less than that of the pure metal. *(1 M)*

Case Based-IV

(*i*) When copper is heated in air, it combines with oxygen to form copper(II) oxide, a black oxide.

$2Cu + O_2 \rightarrow 2CuO$

(Copper)   Copper(II) oxide *(1 M)*

(*ii*) Some metal oxides, such as aluminum oxide and zinc oxide, show both acidic as well as basic behaviour. Such metal oxides that react with both acids, as well as bases to produce salts and water are known as amphoteric oxides. (½ M)

Aluminium oxide is one such oxide and reacts in the following manner with acids and bases –

$Al_2O_3 + 6HCl \rightarrow 2AlCl_3 + 3H_2O$

$Al_2O_3 + 2NaOH \rightarrow 2NaAlO_2 + H_2O$ (½ M)

(Sodium aluminate)

(*iii*) (*a*) $Na_2O(s) + H_2O(l) \rightarrow 2NaOH\ (aq)$ (1 M)

(*b*) $Al_2O_3 + 2NaOH \rightarrow 2NaAlO_2 + H_2O$ (1 M)

(Sodium aluminate)

OR

(*a*) SO_2 gas is formed on burning sulphur in oxygen. The chemical reaction is

$S + O_2 \longrightarrow SO_2$ (½ M)

(*b*) SO_2 (Sulphur dioxide) is formed. (½ M)

(*c*) SO_2 formed is acidic in nature. (½ M)

(*d*) SO_2 turns moist blue litmus paper red but it does not have any action on dry litmus paper due to the absence of H^+ ions in the dry state. (½ M)

Case Based-V

(*i*) In the electrolytic refining process, the impure metal is made the anode and a thin strip of pure metal is made the cathode. (1 M)

(*ii*) A solution of the metal salt is used as an electrolyte. In this case, the metal salt is acidified copper sulphate solution. (1 M)

(*iii*) When electric current is passed through the cell, copper from the impure anode dissolves into the electrolyte as copper ions. (1 M)

These ions then migrate towards the cathode, where they gain electrons and deposit as pure copper. (1 M)

OR

In beaker 'A', since, the strip of zinc is dipped, and zinc being more reactive than copper, therefore, will displace it from its salt solution,copper sulphate. The reaction that occurs is

$Zn + CuSO_4 \rightarrow ZnSO_4 + Cu$ (1 M)

In beaker 'B', since, the strip of silver is dipped, and silver being less reactive than copper, therefore, will not displace it from its salt solution and no reaction will occur. (1 M)

Case Based-VI

(*i*)

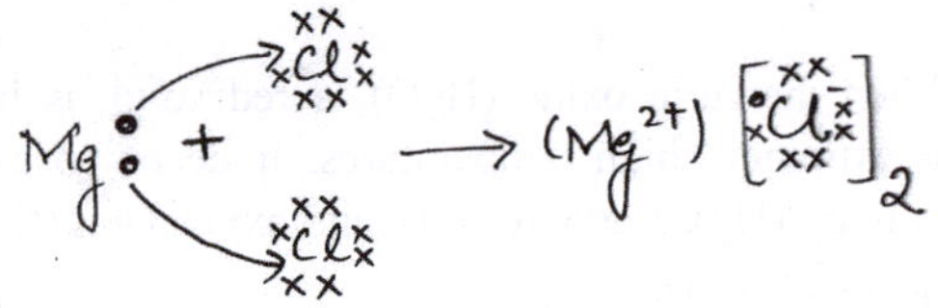

Formation of magnesium chloride (1 M)

(*ii*) • Ionic compounds conduct electricity in solution or in molten state. (½ M)

• Ionic compounds are generally soluble in water and insoluble in solvents like kerosene, petrol etc. (½ M)

(*iii*) By losing one electron, Na attains noble gas configuration and it forms ionic compound NaCl. Cl gains one electron given by Na to achieve noble gas configuration. (½ M)

$Na \rightarrow Na^+ + e^-$ (½ M)

$Cl + e^- \rightarrow Cl^-$ (½ M)

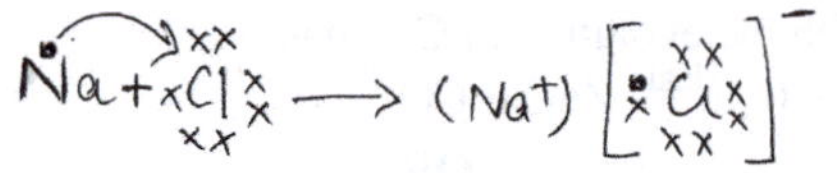 (½ M)

OR

(*a*) Ionic compounds in the solid state have rigid structure and movement of ions is not possible in rigid str ucture. Hence, ionic solids do not conduct electricity. (1 M)

(*b*) When electricity is passed through an aqueous solution of sodium chloride, it decomposes to form sodium hydroxide. Cl_2 gas is produced at the anode and H_2 gas is produced at the cathode. (1 M)

Mistakes 101 : What not to do!

Some students might incorrectly represent the electron transfer process in the formation of magnesium chloride, leading to loss of marks. Students might provide an *incomplete or inaccurate explanation of how sodium atom* attains its stable configuration.

4 CARBON AND ITS COMPOUNDS

Carbon is one of the most versatile element and forms the core of all the life. From the foods we eat, made from organic compounds, to the medicines that heal us; from the DNA that carries our genetic blueprint, to the industries and automobiles that power our civilizations with fossil fuels—carbon is the common thread. Lets discover carbon's unique ability to form countless compounds, providing the foundation for life on Earth and the countless innovations of human industry.

SYLLABUS & WEIGHTAGE

LIST OF CONCEPT NAMES	YEARS				
	2020	2022 TERM-II	2023	2024	2025
Occurrence, Versatile Nature and Bonding in Carbon	1 Q (1 M)	2 Q (3 M each)	—	1 Q (2 M)	—
Hydrocarbons and Compound Containing Functional Groups. (Saturated and unsaturated hydrocarbons, Carbon compounds containing functional groups like halogens, alcohol, ketones, aldehydes, alkanes and alkynes).	1 Q (1 M)	—	—	1 Q (1 M) 1 Q (2 M)	—
Homologous Series, Nomenclature and Isomerism	2 Q (1 M each)	1 Q (2 M)	1 Q (1 M)	1 Q (1 M) 1 Q (2 M)	1 Q (1 M)
Chemical Properties of Carbon Compounds (Combustion, oxidation, addition and substitution reaction)	—	—	1 Q (2 M)	—	1 Q (1 M)
Some Important Carbon Compounds: Ethanol and Ethanoic Acid.	1 Q (2 M)	—	1 Q (3 M)	1 Q (4 M)	1 Q (2 M)
Soaps and Detergents.	1 Q (1 M) 1 Q (2 M)	—	1 Q (5 M)	—	1 Q (2 M) 2 Q (1 M each)

For the year 2021, the exam was not conducted.

CONCEPT MAP

To Access One Shot Revision Video Scan This QR Code

Carbon and its Compounds

Bonding in Carbon – The Covalent Bond

Covalent bond: CBSE 2024, 2022 Term-II 2020

Sharing of electrons between atoms.

It can neither form C^{4-} anion nor C^{4+} cation.

It can only share its valence electrons.

Carbon's tetravalency forms diverse compounds.

Electron Dot Structure CBSE 2024, 2023, 2022 Term-II

Hydrogen: H–H Oxygen: O=O Nitrogen: N≡N

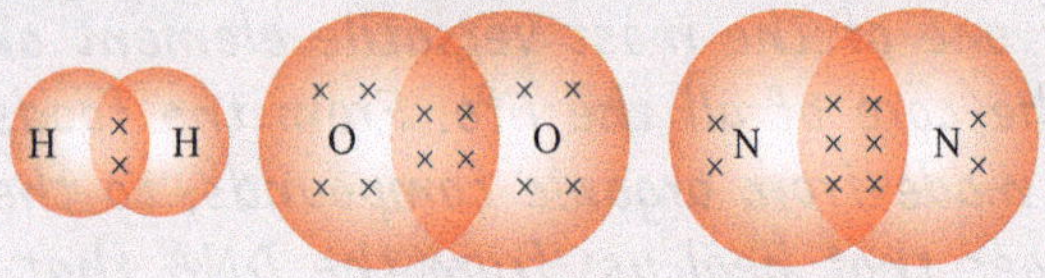

Allotropes of Carbon

CBSE 2022 Term-II

- **Diamond:** Tetrahedral, 3-D arrangement, hardest natural substance.
- **Graphite:** Hexagonal layers, smooth and slippery, conducts electricity.
- **Fullerene:** atoms arranged in the shape of a football

Diamond

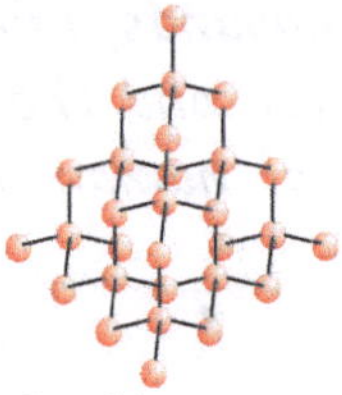

Fullerene

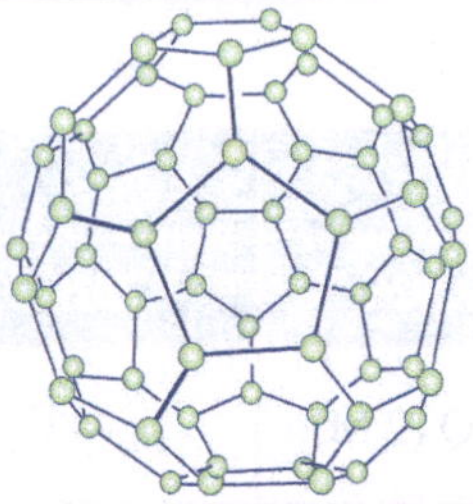

Graphite

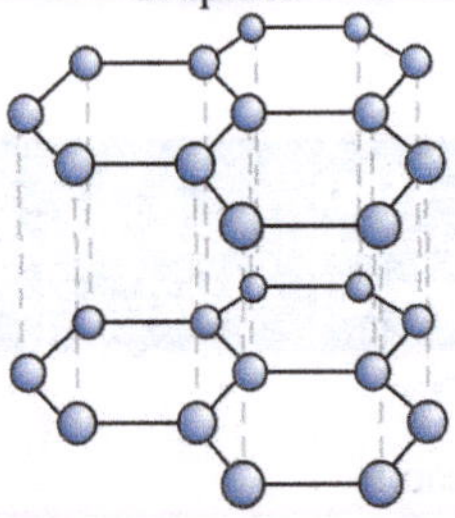

Versatile Nature of Carbon

SATURATED AND UNSATURATED CARBON COMPOUNDS

CBSE 2025, 2023, 2022 Term-II

- **Saturated (Alkanes): Single** carbon-carbon bonds.

  General formula: C_nH_{2n+2}.

  Example: Ethane (C_2H_6).

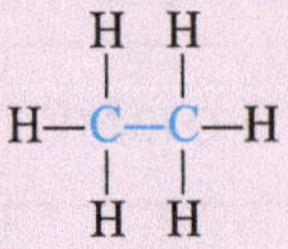

- **Unsaturated**

  (Alkenes): Double carbon-carbon bonds.

  General formula: C_nH_{2n}.

  Example: Ethene (C_2H_4).

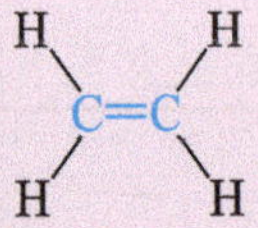

  (Alkynes)

  Triple carbon-carbon bonds.

  General formula: C_nH_{2n-2}.

  Example: Ethyne (C_2H_2).

  H–C≡C–H

NOMENCLATURE OF CARBON COMPOUNDS

CBSE 2024, 2022 Term-II, 2020

Prefix + Root word + Primary suffix + secondary suffix

Class of compounds	Prefix/Suffix	Example
1. Halo alkane	Prefix- **chloro, bromo,** etc.	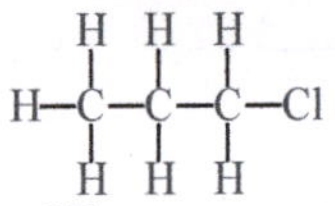 Chloropropane 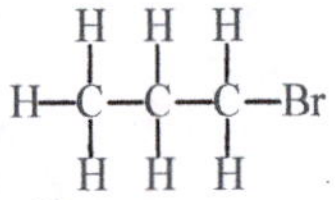 Bromopropane
2. Alcohol	Suffix - **ol**	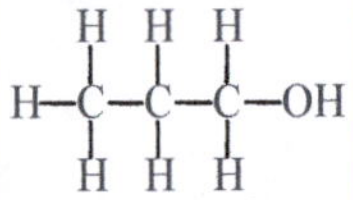 Propanol
3. Aldehyde	Suffix - **al**	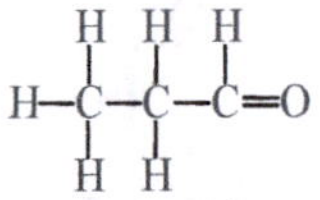 Propanal
4. Ketone	Suffix - **one**	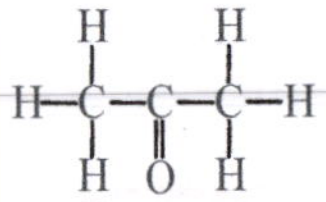 Propanone
5. Carboxylic acid	Suffix - **oic acid**	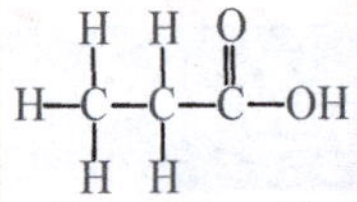 Propanoic acid
6. Alkenes	Suffix - **ene**	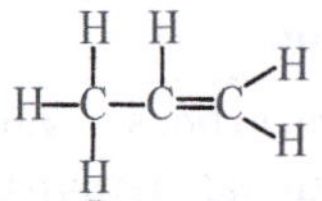 Propene
7. Alkynes	Suffix - **yne**	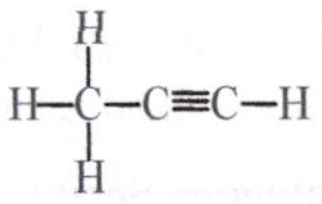 Propyne

Reasons

Catenation: Carbon atoms form **long chains.**

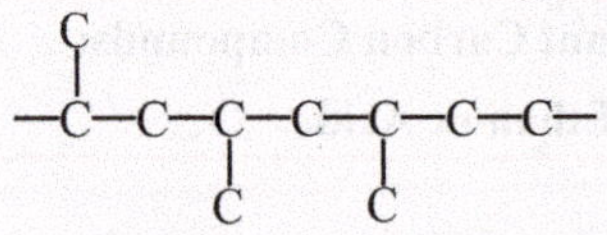

Tetravalency: Carbon has a **valency of four,** it is capable of bonding with four other atoms of carbon or atoms of some other mono-valent element.

Carbon and its Compounds

Chemical Properties

CBSE 2024, 2022 Term-II, 2020

HOMOLOGOUS SERIES

Series of compounds in which the same functional group substitutes for hydrogen in a carbon chain.

Characteristics

Differ by **$-CH_2$** and 14 u molecular mass.
Identical chemical properties.

- **Combustion:** The process of burning of carbon compounds in O_2.
  1. $C + O_2 \rightarrow CO_2$ + heat and light CBSE 2025, 2023
  2. $CH_4 + 2O_2 \rightarrow CO_2 + 2H_2O$ + heat and light
- **Oxidation:** Addition of oxygen.

$$CH_3-CH_2OH \xrightarrow[\text{or acidified } K_2Cr_2O_7+\text{Heat (Oxidizing Agent)}]{\text{Alkaline } KMnO_4+\text{Heat}} CH_3COOH + H_2O$$

CBSE 2025, 2024, 2020

- **Substitution:** In the presence of sunlight, Cl can replace the hydrogen of saturated hydrocarbon.

  $CH_4 + Cl_2 \rightarrow CH_3Cl + HCl$ (in the presence of sunlight)
- **Addition:** Unsaturated compound + Reagent → Saturated compound. Eg.: Hydrogenation of vegetable oil. CBSE 2025, 2023

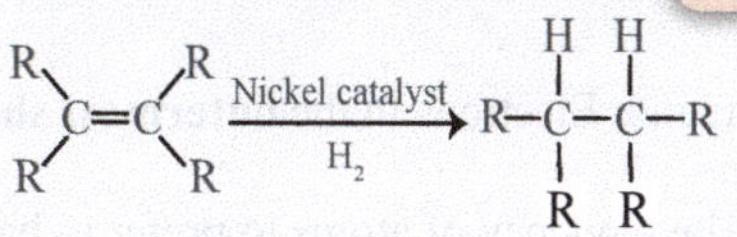

Some Important Carbon Compounds

- **Ethanol (C_2H_5OH):**

  Properties: Volatile, good solvent

  Uses: Medicines, anti-freeze, alcoholic beverages

  Reaction: $2Na + 2CH_3CH_2OH \rightarrow 2CH_3CH_2O^-Na^+ + H_2$ (Sodium ethoxide) CBSE 2024, 2023, 2020

  $C_2H_5OH + 3O_2 \rightarrow 2CO_2 + 3H_2O$ + heat + light

  $CH_3-CH_2OH \xrightarrow[H_2SO_4]{\text{Hot Conc.}} CH_2=CH_2 + H_2O$ CBSE 2025, 2024, 2023

  Denatured alcohol: Undrinkable alcohol with toxic substances like methanol. **Absolute Alcohol:** Pure ethanol.

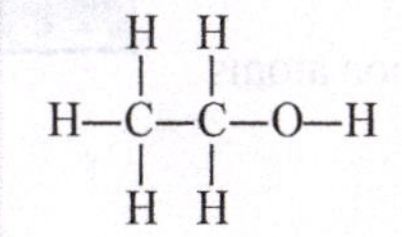

  Tincture of iodine: Solution of iodine in alcohol, used as an antiseptic.

- **Ethanoic Acid (CH_3COOH):**

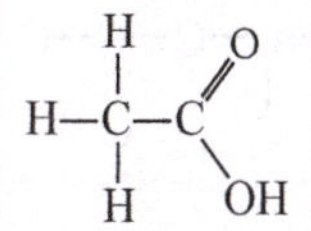

  Properties: Weak acid.

  Uses: Vinegar, food preservation, in making perfumes.

  Reaction:

  CH_3-COOH (Ethanoic acid) $+ CH_3-CH_2OH$ (Ethanol) $\underset{}{\overset{\text{Acid}}{\rightleftharpoons}} CH_3-\underset{\parallel\atop O}{C}-O-CH_2-CH_3 + H_2O$ (Ester) CBSE 2025, 2024, 2020

  Saponification: $CH_3COOC_2H_5 \xrightarrow{NaOH} C_2H_5OH + CH_3COONa$ CBSE 2025, 2020

  $NaOH + CH_3COOH \rightarrow CH_3COONa + H_2O$

  $2CH_3COOH + Na_2CO_3 \rightarrow 2CH_3COONa + H_2O + CO_2\uparrow$ CBSE 2025

  $CH_3COOH + NaHCO_3 \rightarrow CH_3COONa + H_2O + CO_2\uparrow$

Soaps and Detergents

SOAPS

CBSE 2023, 2020

- They are sodium or potassium salts of long-chain carboxylic acids.
- *Most filth is oily in nature, and oil does not dissolve in water.*
- The ionic end of soap interacts with water, whereas the carbon chain interacts with oil.
- Thus, the soap molecules form **micelles**, which have one end facing the oil droplet and the other ionic end facing the outside. Micelle, thus helps in pulling out the dirt in water.

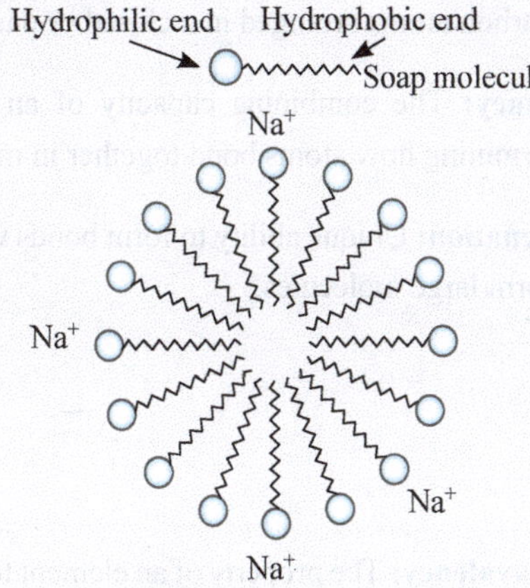

- Soap forms insoluble precipitate of calcium and magnesium salts in hard water called scum CBSE 2025

DETERGENTS

CBSE 2020

- Detergents are generally sodium salts of sulphonic acids or ammonium salts with chlorides or bromides ions, etc.
- They remain effective in hard water.
- Detergents are usually used to make shampoos and products for cleaning clothes.

OCCURRENCE, VERSATILE NATURE AND BONDING IN CARBON

1

NCERT Definitions (Commonly asked in 1 mark)

- **Covalent Bond:** A type of chemical bond where atoms **share pairs of electrons** to attain stable electronic configurations.

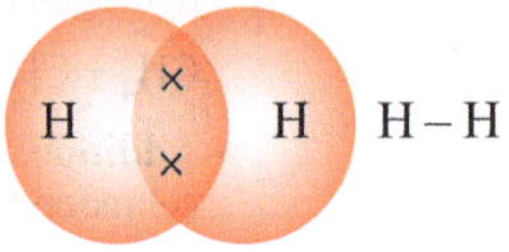

- **Valence Electrons:** Electrons in the **outermost shell** of an atom that are involved in bonding.

- **Octet Rule:** The tendency of atoms to prefer to have eight electrons in the valence shell, which gives them the same electronic configuration as a noble gas. This state of having **eight electrons** in the **outermost shell** is associated with stability in chemical compounds.

- **Electron Dot Structure:** A diagram showing the arrangement of valence electrons around atoms in a molecule.

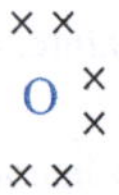

- **Allotropes:** They are different molecular or crystalline forms of the same element,exhibiting different physical properties.

- **Fullerenes:** A class of carbon allotropes characterised by molecules of carbon atoms arranged in a closed or partially closed mesh.

- **Valency:** The combining capacity of an element, important in determining how atoms bond together in molecules.

- **Catenation:** Unique ability to form bonds with other carbon atoms to form large molecules.

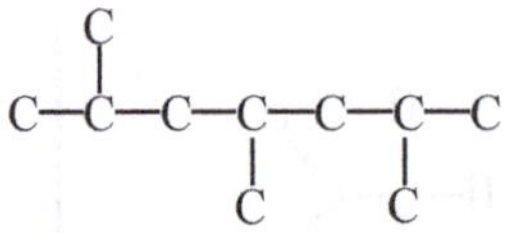

- **Tetravalency:** The property of an element to exhibit the valency of four. Example: Carbon, which contains four valence electrons.

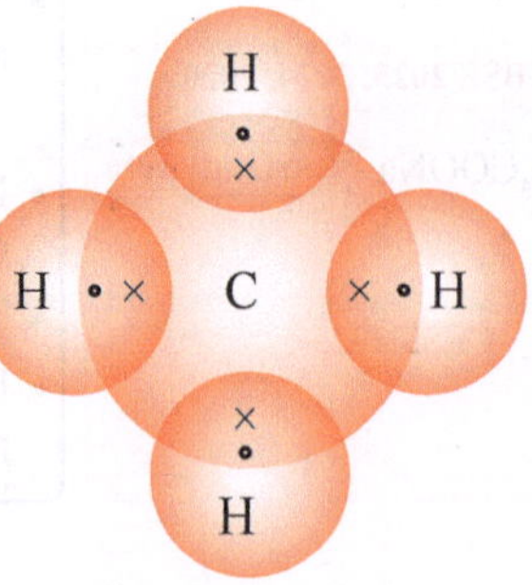

Important Facts

01 The Earth's crust has only 0.02% carbon in the form of minerals (like carbonates, hydrogencarbonates, coal and petroleum) and the atmosphere has 0.03% of carbon dioxide.

02 Widely used as a fuel and is a major component of bio-gas and Compressed Natural Gas (CNG). *~Methane*

03 Diamonds can be synthesised by subjecting pure carbon to very high pressure and temperature.

04 An element with valency 1. *~Hydrogen*

Classification

Allotrope of Carbon	Structure	Properties	Uses
Diamond	Tetrahedral structure, each carbon atom bonded to four others.	Hardest substance known, good conductor of heat, poor conductor of electricity, high refractive index.	Jewellery, cutting tools.
Graphite	Hexagonal arrays in layers, each carbon atom bonded to three others, one of these is a double bond.	Smooth and slippery, good conductor of electricity, not as hard as diamond.	Lubricants, pencils, batteries.
C-60 Buckminsterfullerene	Spherical structure, carbon atoms arranged in a football shape.	Resembles a geodesic dome, different reactivity compared to diamond and graphite.	Research, potential applications in materials science, medical science.

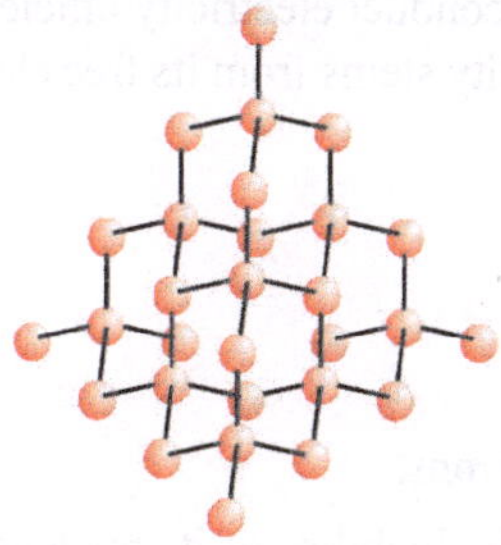

The structure of diamond

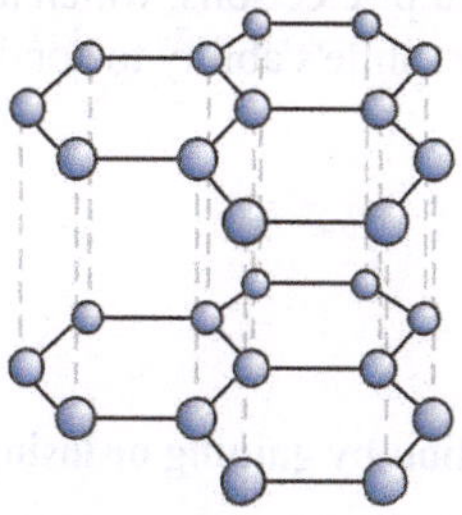
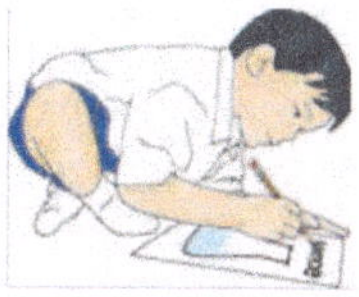

The structure of graphite

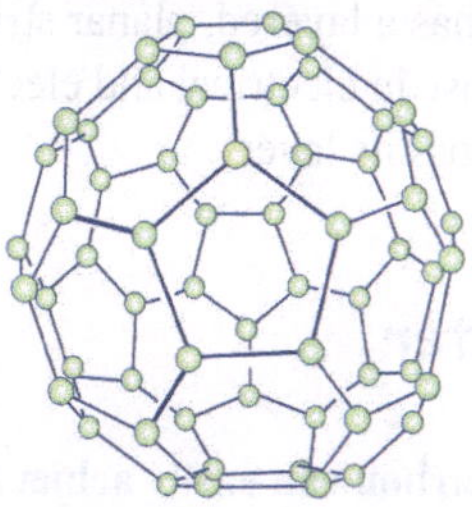

The structure of C-60 Buckminsterfullerence

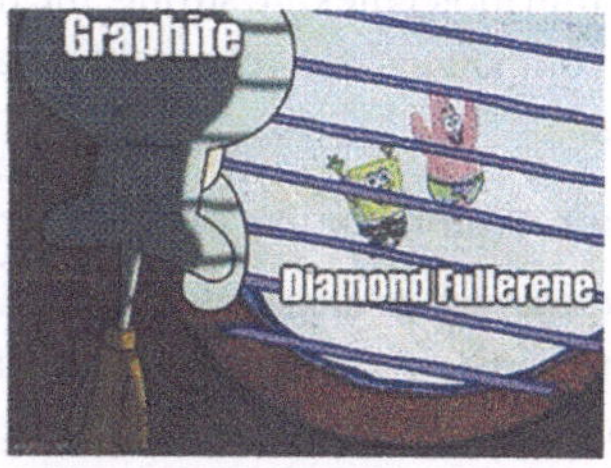

Difference Between

Characteristic	Ionic Compound	Covalent Compound
Bond Formation	Transfer of electrons from one atom to another, typically between metals and non-metals	Sharing of electron pairs between atoms, typically between non-metals
Melting and Boiling Points	High melting and boiling points	Low melting and boiling points.
Conductivity	Conduct electricity in solution or in the molten state due to free-moving ions.	Poor conductors of electricity as no ions are present.
State at room temperature	Usually solid	Can be gases, liquids, or solids.
Solubility	Often soluble	Variable
Examples	Salts, such as sodium chloride (NaCl)	Water (H_2O), Oxygen (O_2), Methane (CH_4), etc.

Real Life Application Based Questions

1. Graphite is used as a lubricant. Explain how the structure of graphite contributes to its effectiveness in this role.

Ans. Graphite has a layered, planar structure and since these layers can easily slide over each other, graphite serves as an excellent lubricant.

2. Diamonds are not only used in jewellery but also in cutting and drilling equipment. Why?

Ans. Diamonds are renowned for being the hardest natural substance on Earth. This extreme hardness makes them ideal for use in cutting and drilling tools as they can cut through almost any material. Additionally, diamonds have a high thermal conductivity, meaning they can dissipate heat quickly, which is beneficial in high-speed cutting processes, where temperature can affect performance.

3. Why are diamonds favoured for jewellery like engagement rings?

Ans. Diamond's brilliance and durability, due to strong covalent bonding, make them ideal for jewellery that lasts a lifetime.

4. Why is graphite used in electrical and electronic applications?

Ans. Graphite has a layered, planar structure with delocalised pi-electrons, which allows it to conduct electricity efficiently, making it ideal for use in electrical and electronic applications. Graphite's ability to conduct electricity stems from its free electrons moving easily across its layers.

Myth Buster

- **Myth: Carbon can easily achieve noble gas configuration by gaining or losing four electrons.**

  Fact: Carbon cannot easily gain or lose four electrons due to energy constraints and the inability of its nucleus to effectively manage the change in electron number. Instead, carbon achieves stability by sharing electrons, forming covalent bonds.

- **Myth: Covalent bonds are strong and result in substances with high melting and boiling points.**

  Fact: While covalent bonds within molecules are strong, the intermolecular forces in most carbon-based compounds are relatively weak, leading to low melting and boiling points.

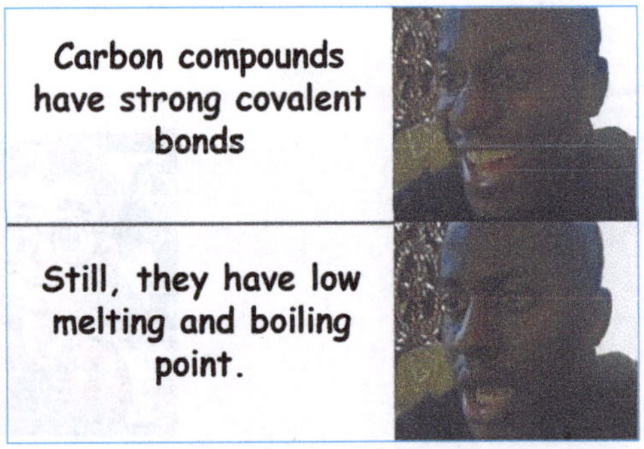

- **Myth: All forms of pure carbon exhibit similar physical properties.**

  Fact: Different allotropes of carbon, such as diamond, graphite, and fullerenes, have vastly different physical properties due to the different ways the carbon atoms are bonded together. For example, diamond is extremely hard, while graphite is soft and slippery, and fullerenes have unique shapes and properties.

Mnemonics

In **diamond**, each carbon atom is bonded to four other carbon atoms forming a rigid **three-dimensional** structure.

In **graphite**, each carbon atom is bonded to three other carbon atoms in the same plane giving a **hexagonal** array.

"Mary watched 3-D movie wearing a diamond necklace while his husband ate grapes"

Mary watched **3-D** movie wearing a **d**iamond necklace while his **h**usband ate **g**rapes

3-D → 3-Dimensional; d → Diamond; h → Hexagonal; g → Graphite

COMPETENCY BASED SOLVED EXAMPLES

Multiple Choice Questions (1 M)

1. Imagine you are a scientist working in a laboratory. You are asked to synthesise a certain allotrope of carbon. Your instructions are to subject pure carbon to very high pressure and temperature. This allotrope is known for its hardness and high melting point. Unlike another common allotrope of carbon, it is not smooth and slippery, and it does not conduct electricity. ***(Re)***

What allotrope of carbon are you synthesizing?

(*a*) Diamond (*b*) Graphite

(*c*) Fullerene (*d*) Coke

2. The electron dot structure of chlorine molecule is: ***(Ap)*** **(CBSE, 2023)**

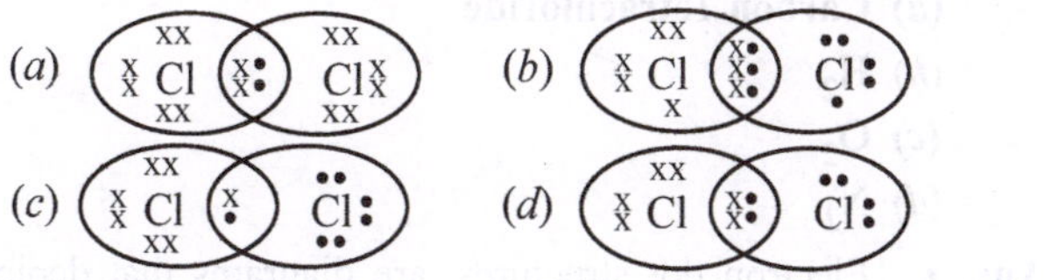

3. Carbon compounds:

(*i*) are good conductors of electricity.

(*ii*) are bad conductors of electricity.

(*iii*) have strong forces of attraction between their molecules.

(*iv*) have weak forces of attraction between their molecules.

The correct statements are: ***(Un)***

(CBSE 2024, NCERT Exemplar)

(*a*) (*i*) and (*ii*) (*b*) (*ii*) and (*iii*)

(*c*) (*ii*) and (*iv*) (*d*) (*i*) and (*iii*)

4. In her chemistry class, Sarah is reviewing the bonding in ethyne (C_2H_2) by looking at its electron dot structure. She notices the connection between the two carbon atoms and starts wondering about the number of electron pairs they share. Can you help Sarah figure out how many pairs of electrons are shared between the two carbon atoms in ethyne? ***(An)***

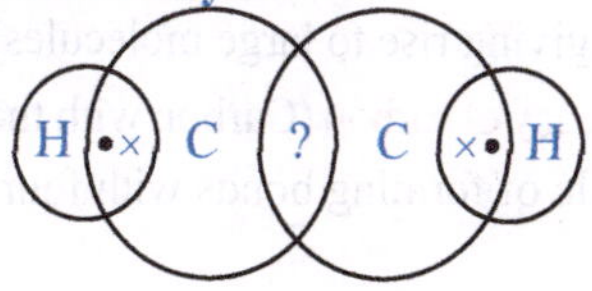

(*a*) 4 (*b*) 1

(*c*) 2 (*d*) 3

Assertion and Reason (1 M)

Direction: The following questions consist of two statements – Assertion (A) and Reason (R). Answer these questions by selecting the appropriate option given below:

(*a*) Both A and R are true, and R is the correct explanation of A.

(*b*) Both A and R are true, but R is not the correct explanation of A.

(*c*) A is true, but R is false.

(*d*) A is false, but R is true.

1. **Assertion (A):** Carbon has a strong tendency to either lose or gain electrons to attain noble gas configuration.

   Reason (R): Carbon has four electrons in its outermost shell and has the tendency to share electrons with carbon or other elements. ***(Un)*** **(CBSE 2020)**

2. **Assertion (A):** Graphite is slippery to touch.

   Reason (R): In graphite, the various layers of carbon atoms are held together by weak van der waal's forces of attraction. ***(Re)***

3. **Assertion (A):** Carbon forms a very strong bond with elements like oxygen, hydrogen, nitrogen etc.

   Reason (R): One reason for the formation of strong bonds is its bigger size. ***(Un)***

Subjective Questions

Very Short Answer Type Questions (2 M)

1. In electron dot structure, the valence shell electrons are represented by crosses or dots. (*Ap*) (NCERT Exemplar)

(*a*) The atomic number of chlorine is 17. Write its electronic configuration.

(*b*) Draw the electron dot structure of chlorine molecule.

Ans. (*a*) The electronic configuration of chlorine is -

KLM- 2,8,7 *(1 M)*

(*b*) The electron dot structure of chlorine molecule is-

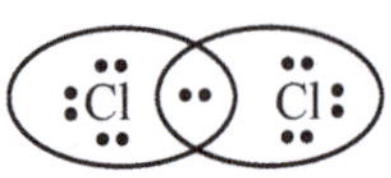

(1 M)

2. Which two characteristic features of carbon when put together give rise to large number of carbon compounds? (*Un*)

Ans. Carbon creates a huge number of compounds due to the following two properties:

(*i*) Catenation (ability to form bonds with other atoms of carbon, giving rise to large molecules). *(1 M)*

(*ii*) Tetravalency of carbon (Carbon with the valency of four, is capable of forming bonds with four other atoms) *(1 M)*

Short Answer Type Questions (3 M)

1. (*a*) What is buckminsterfullerene? How does it relate to diamond and graphite?

(*b*) Why is diamond utilised in the manufacture of cutting tools but graphite is not?

(*c*) Why is graphite utilised in the manufacture of dry cell electrodes yet diamond is not? (*Re*)

Ans. (*a*) Buckminsterfullerene is an allotrope of carbon-containing clusters of 60 carbon atoms linked together to create spherical molecules. It burns on heating to form carbon dioxide, and nothing is left behind. This shows that it is made up of carbon only, like diamond and graphite. *(1 M)*

(*b*) Diamond is used to make cutting tools, but graphite is not because diamond is a highly hard substance, while graphite is a soft substance. *(1 M)*

(*c*) Graphite is utilised to make dry cell electrodes, whereas diamond is not because graphite is an excellent conductor of electricity, and diamond is not. *(1 M)*

2. (*a*) Why are covalent compounds generally poor conductors of electricity?

(*b*) Catenation is the ability of an atom to form bonds with other atoms of the same element. Both carbon and silicon exhibit it. Compare the ability of catenation of the two elements. Give reasons. (*Un*)(NCERT Exemplar)

Ans. (*a*) Covalent compounds do not undergo dissociation in an aqueous solution. Also, these compounds do not contain any free ions. *(½ M)*

Due to absence of flow of electrons/ions, these are the poor conductors of electricity. *(½ M)*

(*b*) Both carbon and silicon show catenation. But compounds made with silicon are more reactive and less stable. In contrast, bonds formed by carbon are very strong, so organic compounds are more stable than silicon compounds. Thus, we can say that carbon shows better catenation than silicon. *(2 M)*

3. State the reasons, why carbon cannot

(*a*) Lose four electrons to form C^{4+} cation, and

(*b*) Gain four electrons to form C^{4-} anion.

How does carbon overcome this problem to form compounds? (*Un*) (CBSE 2022 Term-II)

Ans. (*a*) Carbon atom cannot lose their four electrons to form C^{4+} cations because it would require a large amount of energy to remove four extra electrons leaving behind a carbon cation with six protons in its nucleus holding on to just two electrons. *(1 M)*

(*b*) Carbon atom cannot gain four electrons to form C^{4-} anion because it would be difficult for the carbon nucleus to hold ten electrons with six protons, that is, with four extra electrons. *(1 M)*

To overcome this problem, carbon forms four covalent bonds by sharing its valence electrons with other carbon atoms or with atoms of other elements to complete its octet. *(1 M)*

Long Answer Type Questions (5 M)

1. What are electron dot structures? Give the electron dot structure of the following. (*Ap*)

(*a*) Carbon Tetrachloride

(*b*) H_2

(*c*) O_2

(*d*) N_2

Ans.
- Electron dot structures, are diagrams that depict the chemical bonds that exist between atoms in a molecule. They also show the total number of lone pairs in each of the atoms that may exist in the molecule. *(1 M)*
- **The electron dot structure are given below:**

(*a*)

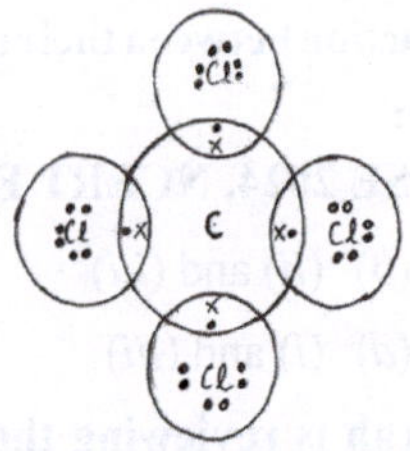

(1 M)

(*b*)

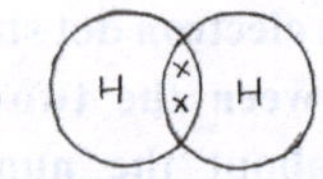

(1 M)

(c) 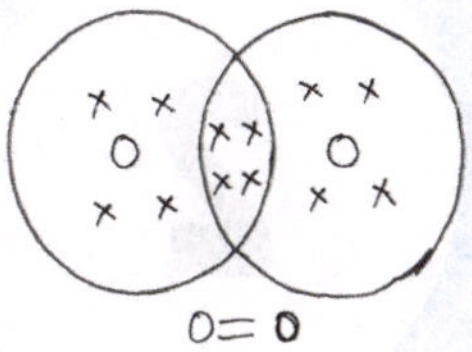

(1 M)

(d) 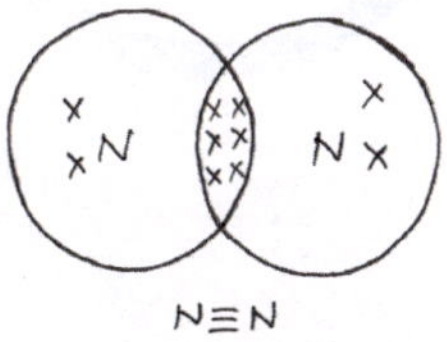

(1 M)

Nailing the Right Answer

Students should clearly and neatly draw the electron dot structures to fetch full marks. Students should remember to count the total valence electrons and make sure that electrons around the central atom are either 2 or 8. Double and triple bonds should be shown accurately and with precision.

Hints & Explanations

Multiple Choice Questions

1. (*a*) Diamonds are formed by subjecting pure carbon to very high pressure and temperature. They have a rigid three-dimensional structure where each carbon atom is bonded to four other carbon atoms, making them extremely hard and giving them a high melting point. Unlike graphite, which is smooth and slippery, diamonds are not conductive and are known for their exceptional hardness.
2. (*c*) This is the correct representation of electron dot structure of chlorine molecule.
3. (*c*) Carbon compounds are bad conductors of electricity as they do not have any free electrons for conduction. Also, they have weak forces of attraction between their molecules as the atoms are joined together through covalent bonds.
4. (*d*) In the given electron dot structure of ethyne, the two carbon atoms are triple-bonded to each other. A triple bond consists of three shared pairs of electrons. Therefore, the number of pairs of electrons shared between the two carbon atoms is 3.

Assertion and Reason

1. (*d*) Carbon has a valency of four because its outermost shell contains four electrons. To obtain the octet state, four more electrons are required. Carbon cannot lose or gain four electrons, since, it would require a large amount of energy to do so. Instead, it shares electrons with another carbon or with other elements to achieve the octet state.
2. (*a*) Graphite is smooth and slippery due to its layered structure, which allows it to slide over each other. Because of the weak van der waal's force of attraction, the bond is readily dissolved, and they slide over each other. This causes graphite to be slipperier.
3. (*c*) Carbon tends to form strong bonds due to its small size.

HYDROCARBONS AND COMPOUNDS CONTAINING FUNCTIONAL GROUP

2

NCERT Definitions (Commonly asked in 1 mark)

- **Hydrocarbons: Organic compounds** consisting solely of **hydrogen and carbon.**
- **Saturated Compounds:** Organic compounds with only **single bonds** between carbon atoms, **Example:** methane (CH_4) and ethane (C_2H_6).
- **Unsaturated Compounds:** Organic compounds that contain **double or triple carbon-carbon bonds. Example:** ethene (C_2H_4) and ethyne (C_2H_2).
- **Functional Groups:** Specific groups of atoms within molecules that are responsible for the characteristic chemical reactions of those molecules.

Hetero Atom	Class of Compounds	Formula of Functional Group
Cl/Br	Halo- (Chloro/bromo) alkane	—Cl, —Br (substitutes for hydrogen atom)
Oxygen	1. Alcohol	–OH
	2. Aldehyde	—C(=O)—H
	3. Ketone	—C(=O)—
	4. Carboxylic acid	—C(=O)—OH

Important Facts

01 This element forms compounds with hydrogen which have chains of upto seven or eight atoms, and this element compounds are very reactive. ***~Silicon***

02 The scientist who debunked the vital force theory by synthesizing urea, an organic compound, from ammonium cyanate. ***~Friedrich Wöhler***

03 The reactivity of organic compounds correlates with the type of carbon-carbon bonds present, with unsaturated compounds being more reactive than their saturated counterparts.

04 A saturated hydrocarbon where carbon atoms are arranged in a ring structure, represented as C_6H_{12}. ***~Cyclohexane***

05 An example of an unsaturated ring, C_6H_6, illustrating aromatic hydrocarbons. ***~Benzene***

Classification

Difference Between

Saturated Hydrocarbons v/s Unsaturated Hydrocarbons		
Property	**Saturated Hydrocarbons**	**Unsaturated Hydrocarbons**
Bond Type	Single bonds only	Double or triple bonds
Types	Alkanes	Alkenes, Alkynes
Hydrogen to Carbon Ratio	Maximum (General formula: C_nH_{2n+2})	Less than maximum (Alkenes: C_nH_{2n}, Alkynes: C_nH_{2n-2})
Reactivity	Less reactive	More reactive

Real Life Application Based Questions

1. **Ramesh is a scientist and is making gasoline using alkanes. Why are alkanes suitable for use in gasoline?**

Ans. Alkanes **burn cleanly**, producing a hot, blue flame and much energy, ideal for efficient gasoline.

2. **How do alkenes contribute to the production of rubber?***

Ans. Alkenes provide the **reactive double bonds** necessary for rubber's elasticity and strength.

3. **Name an organic compound which contains ketone as a functional group and is used in the nail polish removers?**

Ans. Acetone is commonly used in many nail polish removers due to its miscibility with water, and its rapid evaporation rate. Also, it effectively dissolves nail polish, facilitating its removal using a cotton swab or cloth.

4. **Why are mixtures of hydrocarbons like coal and natural gas used to generate electricity?**

Ans. Coal and natural gas are used to generate electricity because their hydrocarbon content combusts to release large amounts of energy, powering electricity generation.

Myth Buster

- **Myth: All hydrocarbons having the general formula, C_nH_{2n}, belongs to the alkene family.**
  Fact: Not all hydrocarbons with the general formula, C_nH_{2n}, belongs to the alkene family. For example, Cyclohexane with the molecular formula, C_6H_{12} though satisfies the general formula of alkenes, that is, C_nH_{2n} but in actual it is a cycloalkane.
- **Myth: All carbon compounds have same stability due to carbon's ability to form covalent bonds.**
  Fact: While it's true that carbon forms very strong covalent bonds due to its small size and tetravalency, not all carbon compounds exhibit the same level of stability. **Reactivity varies** greatly among different organic compounds, **depending on their functional groups and structure**. For example, some carbon compounds with multiple bonds or certain functional groups can be quite reactive.
- **Myth: Saturated hydrocarbons are always straight-chained.**
  Fact: Saturated hydrocarbons, or alkanes, can have a variety of structures, including **straight chains, branched chains, and rings**. The term 'saturated' refers to the single bonds between carbon atoms, not the shape of the carbon chain.

** Concepts beyond the board exam syllabus, offering deeper insight and critical thinking on NCERT topics.*

Mnemonics

- Unsaturated compounds have double or triple bonds.
  Saturated compounds have single bonds.
  "The uninvited guest couldn't decide between two or three slices of cake, so they satiated their hunger with just one"

  The **un**invited guest couldn't decide between **two** or **three** slices of cake, so they **sat**iated their hunger with just **one**.

  un → Unsaturated; two → Double; three → Triple; sat → Saturated; one → Single

- The mnemonics used to remember the first four members of the homologous series of alcohols.
  "My elephant packed big peanuts"

  My → Methanol; **e**lephant → Ethanol; **p**acked → Propanol; **b**ig → Butanol; **p**eanuts → Pentanol

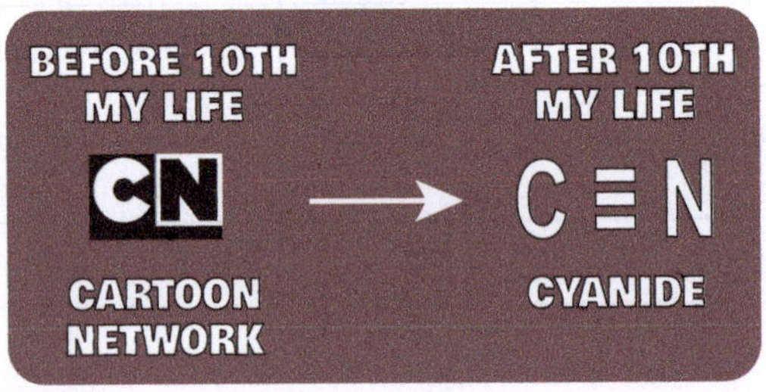

COMPETENCY BASED SOLVED EXAMPLES

Multiple Choice Questions (1 M)

1. Identify the unsaturated compounds from the following. *(Ap)* **(NCERT Exemplar)**

(*i*) Propane (*ii*) Propene
(*iii*) Propyne (*iv*) Chloropropane
(*a*) (*i*) and (*ii*) (*b*) (*ii*) and (*iv*)
(*c*) (*iii*) and (*iv*) (*d*) (*ii*) and (*iii*)

2. Which among the following contains a double bond? **(*Un*)**

(*a*) H_2 molecule (*b*) CO_2 molecule
(*c*) N_2 molecule (*d*) None of these

3. In which of the following compounds, — OH is the functional group? **(*Un*) (NCERT Exemplar)**

(*a*) Butanone (*b*) Butanol
(*c*) Butanoic acid (*d*) Butanal

4. Which of the chemicals below does not have a carbonyl group? **(*Un*)**

(*a*) Alcohol (*b*) Aldehyde
(*c*) Ketone (*d*) Carboxylic acid

Assertion and Reason (1 M)

Direction: The following questions consist of two statements – Assertion (A) and Reason (R). Answer these questions by selecting the appropriate option given below:

(*a*) Both A and R are true, and R is the correct explanation of A.
(*b*) Both A and R are true, but R is not the correct explanation of A.
(*c*) A is true, but R is false.
(*d*) A is false, but R is true.

1. Assertion (A): Methane is simplest saturated hydrocarbon which is a major component of natural gas.
Reason (R): Ethanol has formula CH_3OH. **(*Un*)**

2. Assertion (A): Benzene, a ring-structured compound, is classified as an saturated hydrocarbon.
Reason (R): Despite its stable ring structure, benzene contains alternating double bonds that classify it as unsaturated. **(*Re*)**

Subjective Questions

Very Short Answer Type Questions (2 M)

1. Write the molecular formula of ethene and draw its electron dot structure. *(Ap)* **(CBSE, 2019)**

Ans. The molecular formula of ethene is C_2H_4. *(1 M)*

Its electron dot structure is:

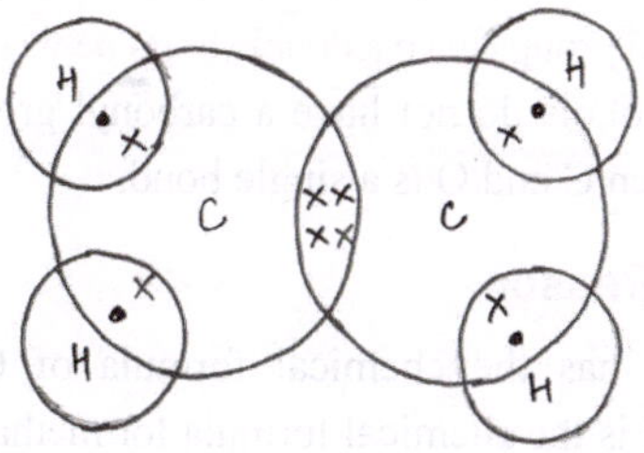

(1 M)

Nailing the Right Answer

Students should make a neat diagram and correctly placed crosses and dots. The circles should be drawn clearly and their arrangement should be absolutely accurate in order to ensure full credit. In the end they should recheck that the octet is complete.

2. Name the functional group present in each of the following organic compounds. *(Re)*

(a) C_2H_5Cl

(b) C_2H_5OH

Ans. The functional group present in the following organic compounds are -

(a) (–Cl) Halogen (Chloro) *(1 M)*

(b) (–OH) Alcohol *(1 M)*

Short Answer Type Questions (3 M)

1. Unsaturated hydrocarbons contain multiple bonds between the two C-atoms and show addition reactions. Give the test to distinguish ethane from ethene.

(Re) **(NCERT Exemplar)**

Ans Saturated hydrocarbons (containing single bond) generally burn with a clean flame. Unsaturated hydrocarbons (containing double or triple bond) burn with yellow flame and produce lot of soot. *(1 M)*

When Ethane and Ethene are exposed to flame, they can be differentiated. Ethane, as a saturated hydrocarbon, produces a clear flame, but ethene, as an unsaturated hydrocarbon, produces a yellow flame with a lot of black smoke. *(2 M)*

2. Categories the following compounds in Alkane, Alcohols, Alkene and Alkyne Category?

$C_{10}H_{22}$, C_6H_{12}, C_7H_{12}, C_4H_{10}, $C_7H_{15}OH$, *(Un)*

Ans The general formula for alkanes, alkenes, and alkynes is C_nH_{2n+2}, C_nH_{2n}, and C_nH_{2n-2}, respectively, where 'n' represents the number of carbon atoms. *(1 M)*

Among the given compounds, alkanes are $C_{10}H_{22}$, and C_4H_{10}, as they correspond to the general formula of alkanes.

C_6H_{12} is an alkene and C_7H_{12} is an alkyne. *(1 M)*

Alcohol consists of –OH as the functional group. Hence, $C_7H_{15}OH$ is an alcohol. *(1 M)*

Long Answer Type Questions (5 M)

1. (a) What are hydrocarbons? Give examples.

(b) Give the structural differences between saturated and unsaturated hydrocarbons with two examples each.

(c) What is a functional group? Give examples of four different functional groups. *(Un)* **(NCERT Exemplar)**

Ans. (a) Compounds of carbon and hydrogen are called hydrocarbons. Example, methane, ethane etc. *(1 M)*

(b) Saturated hydrocarbons contain carbon-carbon single bonds. Unsaturated hydrocarbons contain at least one carbon-carbon double or triple bond. *(1 M)*

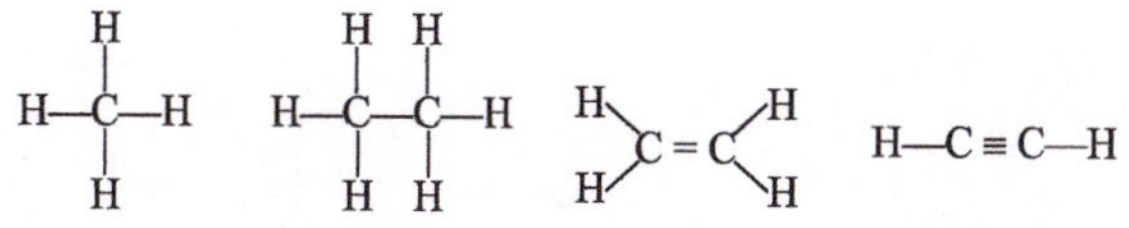

Methane Ethane — Saturated hydrocarbons

Ethene Ethyne — Unsaturated hydrocarbons

(1 M)

(c) Functional group - An atom/group of atoms joined in a specific manner which is responsible for the characteristic chemical properties of the organic compounds. *(1 M)*

Examples are the hydroxyl group (–OH), aldehyde group (–CHO), carboxylic group (–COOH) and ketone group (–CO). *(1 M)*

2. What do you understand by the term alkanes? There are four compounds X, Y, Z and W containing different functional groups. Compound X has an alcoholic functional group with three carbons. Similarly, compounds Y, Z and W contain ketonic, acidic and chloride functional groups with a total three carbon atoms. What should be the name of all the compounds X, Y, Z and W? *(An)*

Ans Saturated hydrocarbons are called alkanes, that is, compounds with only single bonds. *(1 M)*

Compound X contains an alcoholic functional group (–OH) with three carbon atoms, then the formula of the compound X must be $CH_3CH_2CH_2OH$. The name of the compound is Propanol. *(1 M)*

Similarly, compound Y contains ketonic functional group (–CO–) with total three carbon atoms, then the formula of the compound Y must be $H_3C–CO–CH_3$. The name of the compound is Propanone. *(1 M)*

Similarly, compound Z contains an acidic functional group (–COOH) with a total three carbon atoms, then the formula of the compound Z must be $CH_3CH_2–COOH$. The name of the compound is Propanoic acid. *(1 M)*

Similarly, compound W contains a chloride functional group (–Cl) with three carbon atoms, then the formula of the compound W must be $CH_3CH_2CH_2$-Cl. The name of the compound is Chloropropane. *(1 M)*

Hints & Explanations

Multiple Choice Questions

1. (*d*) Propene is an alkene, and propyne is an alkyne. Hence, both are unsaturated compounds.
2. (*b*) CO_2 molecule contains a double bond as it exists as $O=C=O$.
3. (*b*) Butanol has –OH as the functional group. Its chemical formula is $CH_3CH_2CH_2CH_2OH$.
4. (*a*) Carbonyl groups have a double bond between carbon and oxygen. Alcohols do not have a carbonyl group since the bond between C and O is a single bond.

Assertion and Reason

1. (*c*) Ethanol has the chemical formula of CH_3CH_2OH. CH_3OH is the chemical formula for methanol.
2. (*d*) Benzene's classification as unsaturated due to its double bonds, even within a ring structure, is correctly explained by the reason.

3 HOMOLOGOUS SERIES, NOMENCLATURE AND ISOMERISM

NCERT Definitions (Commonly asked in 1 mark)

- **Homologous Series:** **A series of compounds** in which the **same group/functional group** substitutes for hydrogen in a carbon chain. Compounds within a homologous series demonstrate a consistent difference in molecular mass of 14 u and the addition of **CH_2 units,** despite having similar chemical properties.
- **Nomenclature:** Nomenclature is the system of **naming chemical compounds** based on their structure and composition, making it easier to identify and study them.
- **Isomerism:** The property of the compounds by which they possess same molecular formula, but differ in their properties and structures.
- **Structural Isomers:** Compounds with identical molecular formula but different structures.

Important Tables

- For any compound, complete IUPAC name consists of: Prefix + Root word + Primary suffix + secondary suffix

Group	Prefix
$—CH_3$	Methyl
$—CH_2CH_3$ or $—C_2H_5$	Ethyl
$—CH_2CH_2CH_3$ or $—C_3H_7$	Propyl
—F	Fluoro
—Cl	Chloro
—Br	Bromo
—I	Iodo

Number of Carbon Atoms	Root Word
C_1	Meth-
C_2	Eth-
C_3	Prop-
C_4	But-
C_5	Pent-
C_6	Hex-
C_7	Hept-
C_8	Oct-
C_9	Non-
C_{10}	Dec-

Type of Bond	Primary Suffix
$C—C$	-ane
$C=C$	-ene
$C\equiv C$	-yne

Functional Group	Secondary Suffix
—OH	—ol
—CHO	—al
$—\overset{\overset{O}{\parallel}}{C}—$	—one
—COOH	—oic acid

Nomenclature of Organic Compounds		
Class of Compounds	**Prefix/Suffix**	**Example**
1. Halo alkane	Prefix-chloro, bromo, etc.	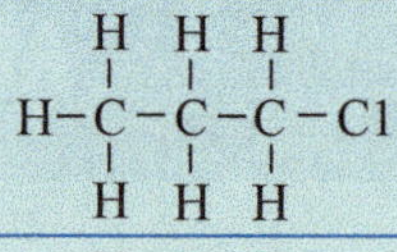 Chloropropane
2. Alcohol	Suffix-ol	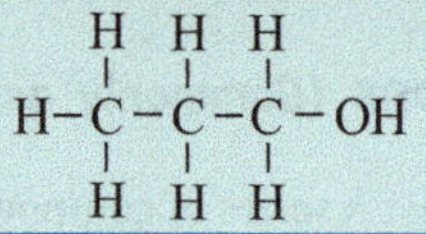 Propanol
3. Aldehyde	Suffix-al	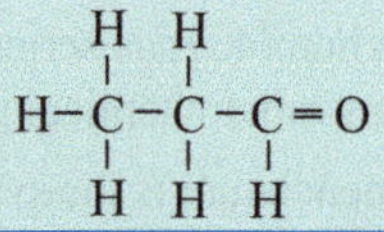 Propanal
4. Ketone	Suffix-one	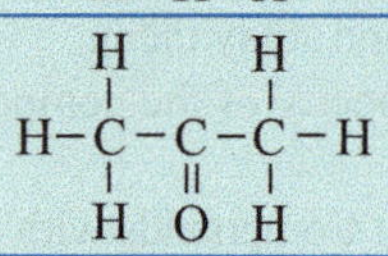 Propanone
5. Carboxylic acid	Suffix-oic acid	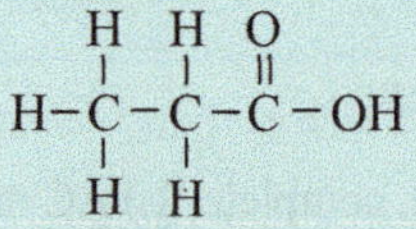 Propanoic acid
6. Alkenes	Suffix-ene	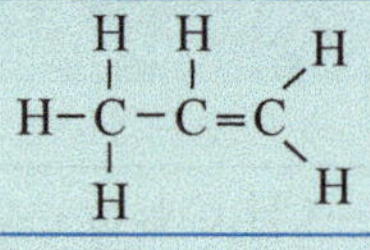 Propene
7. Alkynes	Suffix-yne	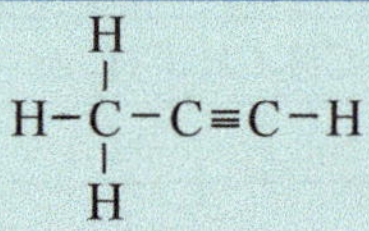 Propyne

Important Facts

01 The chemical properties, which are determined solely by the functional group, remain similar in a homologous series.

02 In a homologous series, the melting and boiling points increases with increasing molecular mass.

Real Life Application Based Questions

1. What is the significance of nomenclature in real world? Why IUPAC nomenclature came into existence in the first place?

Ans. Before IUPAC standardised the rules of nomenclature, there was confusion within the scientific community regarding naming of the chemical compounds. Hence,scientists framed a systematic method for naming organic compounds based on their structures which will be accepted universally. So that scientists, researchers and educators throughout the world could unambiguously communicate in a common language.

2. Why is it important to understand hydrocarbon nomenclature when considering different fuels for environmental science?

Ans. Knowing the hydrocarbon structure helps predict combustion properties, guiding the use of various hydrocarbons like methane, ethane, and propane for specific applications like heating and cooking.

3. Even though Methane and Butane belongs to a homologous series but they have different applications. Provide some applications for each.

Ans. Methane is a major constituent of natural gas and is used majorly in electricity generation. Propane and Butane are major constituents of liquefied petroleum gas (LPG) which is used as a fuel in heating appliances, and cooking equipment.

Myth Buster

- **Myth: The length of the carbon chain does not affect the chemical properties of compounds in a homologous series.**

  Fact: While the functional group largely determines the chemical properties in a homologous series, subtle differences can arise with changes in chain length or branching. These variations can affect reactivity and the mechanisms of chemical reactions, though the fundamental properties governed by the functional group remain similar.

- **Myth: Compounds with the same molecular formula have the same structure.**

  Fact: Compounds with the same molecular formula may have different structures, known as isomers. These structural variations can lead to different physical and chemical properties. For instance, butane and isobutane both have the formula C_4H_{10} but have different structures and, therefore, different properties.

- **Myth: All compounds in a homologous series have the same physical properties.**

  Fact: While compounds in a homologous series have similar chemical properties due to the presence of the same functional group, their physical properties such as melting point, boiling point, and solubility vary. These properties change progressively with increasing molecular mass within the series

Mnemonics

Number of Carbon Atoms	Root Word
C_1	Meth-
C_2	Eth
C_3	Prop-
C_4	But-
C_5	Pent-
C_6	Hex-
C_7	Hept-
C_8	Oct-
C_9	Non-
C_{10}	Dec-

"My Energetic Puppy Barks Proudly at Home; However, Older Napping Dogs Dream."

My	Energetic	Puppy	Barks	Proudly	Home;	However,	Older	Napping	Dogs
↓	↓	↓	↓	↓	↓	↓	↓	↓	↓
Meth	Eth	Prop	But	Pent	Hexane	Heptane	Octane	Nonane	Decane

COMPETENCY BASED SOLVED EXAMPLES

Multiple Choice Questions (1 M)

1. Consider the structures of the three cyclic carbon compounds A, B and C given below and select the correct option from the following: *(Ap)* **(CBSE, 2023)**

A. 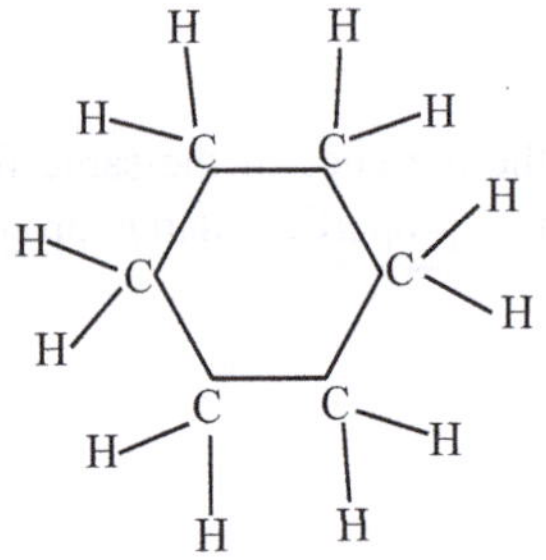

B. 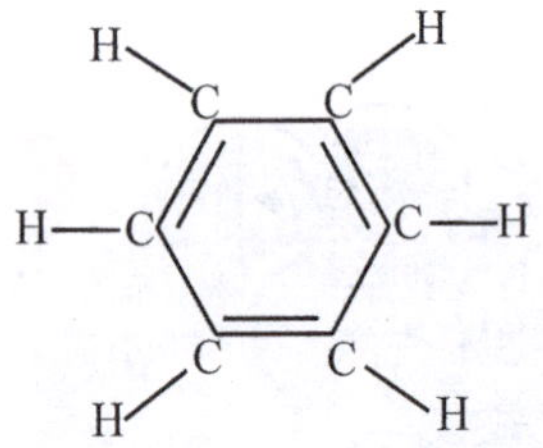

C. 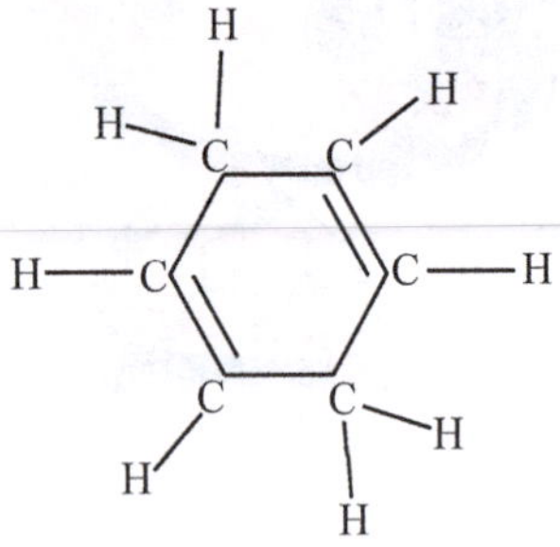

(*a*) *A* and *C* are isomers of hexane and *B* is benzene.

(*b*) *A* is an isomer of hexane, *B* is benzene and *C* is an isomer of hexene.

(*c*) *A* is a saturated cyclic hydrocarbon and *B* and *C* are unsaturated cyclic hydrocarbons.

(*d*) *A* is cyclohexane and *B* and *C* are the isomers of benzene.

2. Consider the following statements about homologous series of carbon compounds:

A. All succeeding members differ by $-CH_2$ unit.

B. Melting point and boiling point increases with increasing molecular mass.

C. The difference in molecular masses between two successive members is 16 u.

D. C_2H_2 and C_3H_4 are NOT the successive members of alkyne series.

The correct statements are- *(Un)* **(CBSE 2024)**

(*a*) (A) and (B) (*b*) (B) and (C)

(*c*) (A) and (C) (*d*) (C) and (D)

3. The correct structural formula of butanoic acid is *(Un)* **(NCERT Exemplar)**

(*a*) 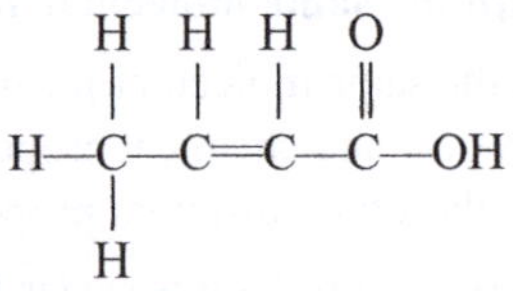

(*b*) 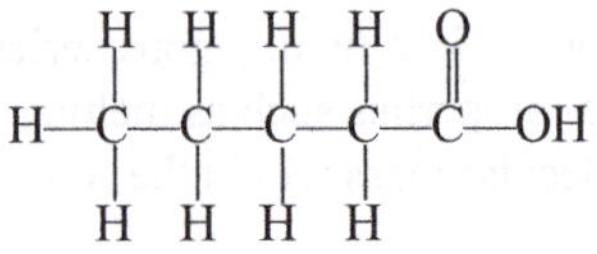

(*c*) 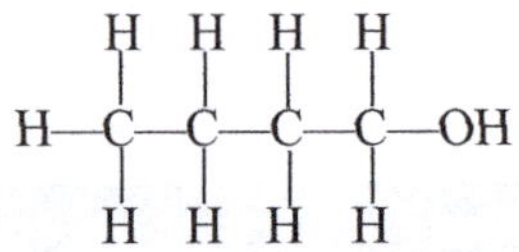

(*d*) 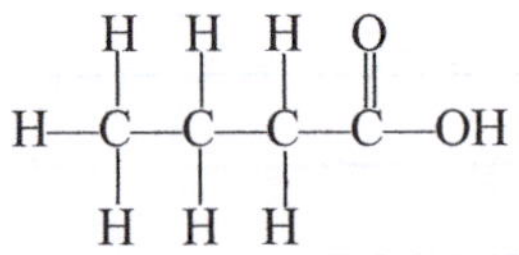

4. Which of the following are correct structural isomers of butane? *(Ap)* **(NCERT Exemplar)**

(*i*) 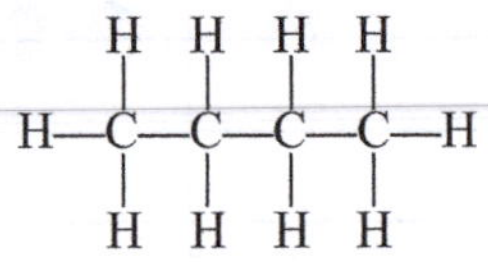

(*ii*) 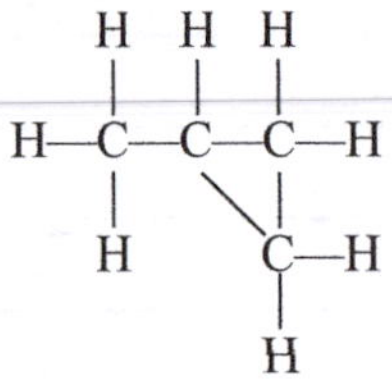

(*iii*) 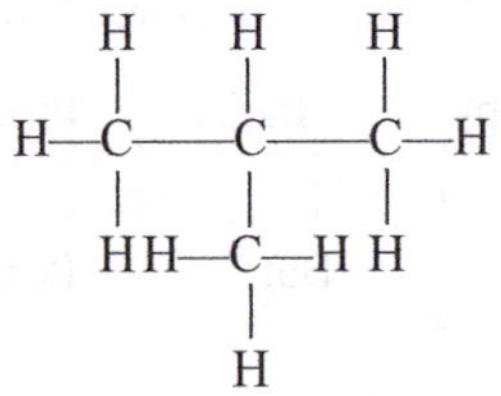

(*iv*) 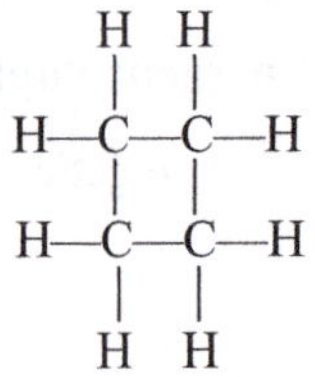

(*a*) (i) and (iii) (*b*) (ii) and (iv)

(*c*) (i) and (ii) (*d*) (iii) and (iv)

Assertion and Reason (1 M)

Direction: The following questions consist of two statements – Assertion (A) and Reason (R). Answer these questions by selecting the appropriate option given below:

(*a*) Both A and R are true, and R is the correct explanation of A.

(*b*) Both A and R are true, but R is not the correct explanation of A.

(*c*) A is true, but R is false

(*d*) A is false, but R is true.

1. **Assertion (A):** Following are the members of a homologous series : CH_3OH, CH_3CH_2OH, $CH_3CH_2CH_2OH$
Reason (R): A series of compounds with same functional group but differing by $-CH_2-$ unit is called a homologous series. **(*Un*) (CBSE 2020)**

2. **Assertion (A):** Isomers have the same molecular formula but different structural formulas.
Reason (R): Isomers arise due to the different possible arrangements of atoms within a molecule. **(*Re*)**

3. **Assertion (A):** Butane exhibits isomerism.
Reason (R): Butane is a saturated hydrocarbon. **(*Un*)**

Subjective Questions

Very Short Answer Type Questions (2 M)

1. **Consider the carbon compounds having following molecular formula: (*An*) (CBSE, 2022 Term II)**
(i) C_3H_6 *(ii)* C_3H_8
(iii) C_4H_6 *(iv)* C_6H_6
(v) C_6H_{12}
(*a*) State the number of double covalent bonds present in C_3H_6.
(*b*) Write the formula of first member of the homologous series to which the carbon compound C_4H_6 belongs.
(*c*) Which one of the above compounds forms ring structure of carbon atoms?
(*d*) Identify, which of the above compounds, is a member of alkane series.

Ans. (*a*) Number of double covalent bonds present in C_3H_6 is one. This is shown in the following figure,

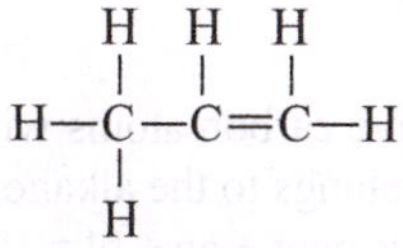

(½ M)

(*b*) C_4H_6 belongs to the C_nH_{2n-2} series. Therefore, the formula of the first member of homologous series to which the carbon compound C_4H_6 belongs is C_2H_2. (½ M)

(*c*) The compound C_6H_6 forms a ring structure and its name is benzene. (½ M)

(*d*) In the given compounds, C_3H_8 belongs to the alkane series, because the general formula of alkane series is C_nH_{2n+2}. (½ M)

2. **Organic compounds belonging to different homologous series can be isomers. For example, propanal and propanone are isomers.**
Can an alkane and an alcohol be isomers? Why or why not? (*Un*) (CFPQ)

Ans. (*a*) No, they cannot be isomers because isomers have same molecular formula but their structural arrangements are different. (*1 M*)

(*b*) Alkanes have only carbon and hydrogen atoms, while alcohols have oxygen atoms too, hence, their molecular formulas are different. (*1 M*)

Short Answer Type Questions (3 M)

1. **Write the structural formulae of all the isomers of hexane. (*An*) (NCERT Exemplar)**

Ans. Below are the structural formulae of all isomers of hexane (*3 M*)

(*a*) 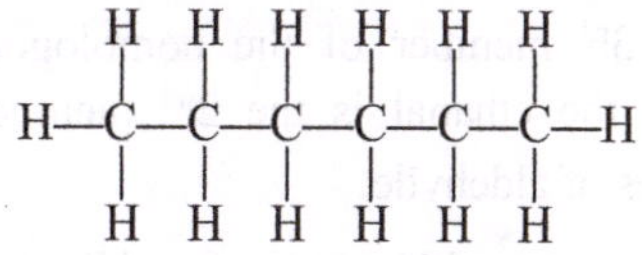

(*b*) 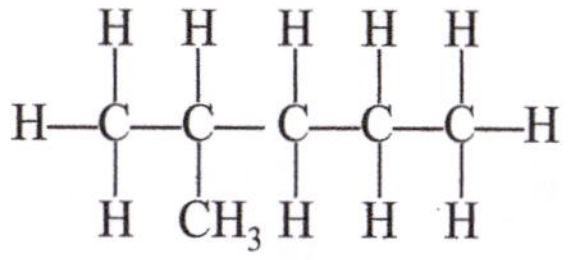

(*c*) 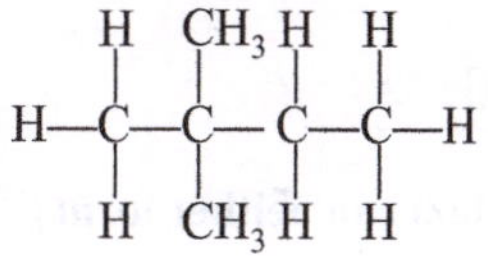

(*d*) 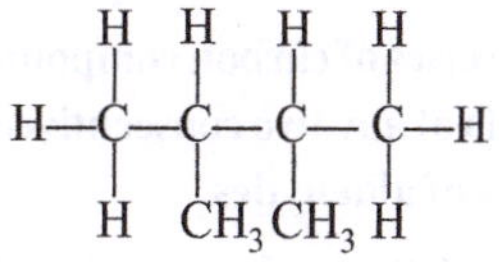

(*e*) 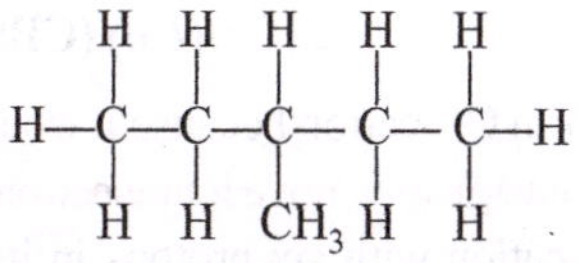

> **Mistakes 101 : What not to do!**
> Students commonly make these mistakes of not including all five isomers. They tend to forget one or more isomers in such type of questions. Make sure no isomer is repeated. Always remember to include the proper number of hydrogen atoms to maintain the correct molecular formula, which is C_6H_{14}.

2. **Consider the following organic compounds:**

(i) 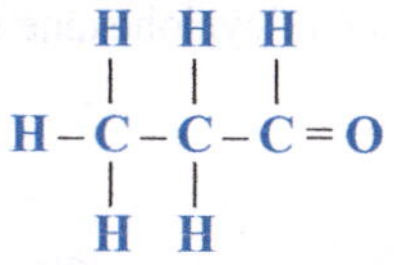 *(ii)* 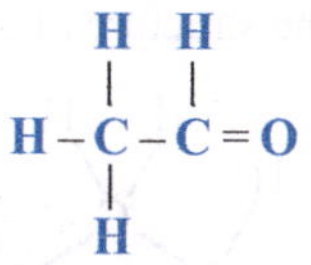

(*a*) Name the functional group present in their compounds.
(*b*) Write the general formula for the compounds of this functional group.

(c) State the relationship between these compounds and draw the structure of any other compound having similar functional group. ***(Un)*** **(CBSE 2022 Term-II)**

Ans. (*a*) Aldehydic functional group is present in both structures. *(½ M)*

(*b*) General formula of the compounds with aldehydic functional group: $C_nH_{2n}O$. *(½ M)*

(*c*) These both compounds are belongs to homologous series of aldehydes. These compounds differ by $-CH_2$ group where first structure is Propanal and the 2nd structure is ethanal. *(½ M)*

Propanal is the 3rd member of the homologous series of aldehyde and the ethanal is the 2nd member of the homologous series of aldehyde. *(½ M)*

4th member of this series will be butanal and its structure is: *(1 M)*

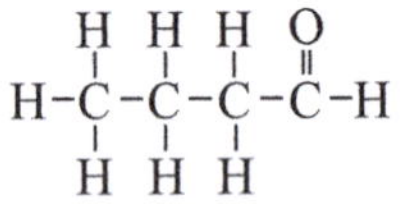

Long Answer Type Questions **(5 M)**

1. (*a*) Give reason why carbon can neither form C^{4+} cations nor C^{4-} anions but form covalent compounds.

(*b*) What is homologous series of carbon compound? Write the molecular formula of any two consecutive members of homologous series of aldehydes.

(*c*) Draw the structure of the molecule of cyclohexane (C_6H_{12}). ***(Un)*** **(CBSE 2024)**

Ans. (*a*) Carbon cannot form C^{4+} cation because it would require a large amount of energy to remove four electrons leaving behind a carbon cation with six protons in its nucleus holding on to just two electrons. *(1 M)*

Carbon cannot form C^{4-} anion because it would be difficult for the nucleus with six protons to hold on to ten electrons, that is, four extra electrons. *(1 M)*

(*b*) A homologous series is a series of compounds in which the same functional group substitutes for hydrogen in a carbon chain and successive members differs by the $-CH_2$ unit or by 14u molecular mass. *(1 M)*

Example: The molecular formula for the two consecutive members of a homologous series of aldehydes are HCHO, CH_3CHO. *(½ × 2 = 1 M)*

(*c*) The structure of the molecule of cyclohexane is

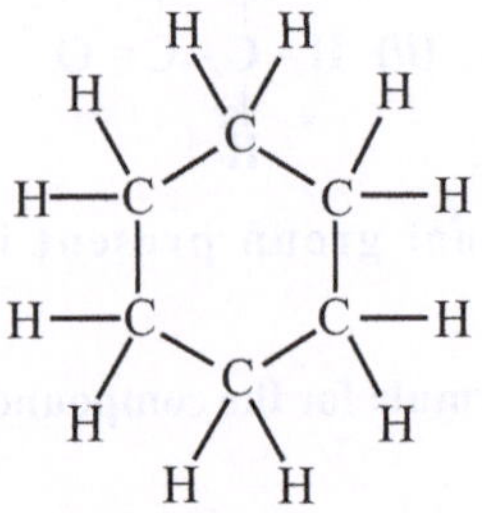

(1 M)

2. Write the name of the following compounds.
(Un) **(NCERT Exemplar)**

(*a*) 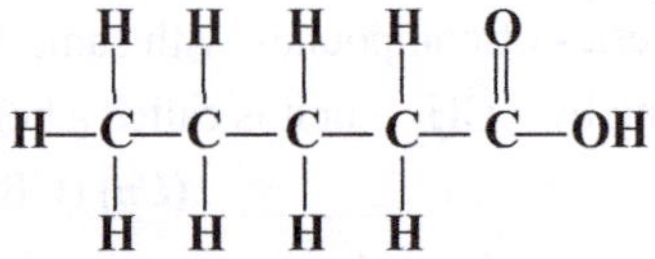

(*b*) 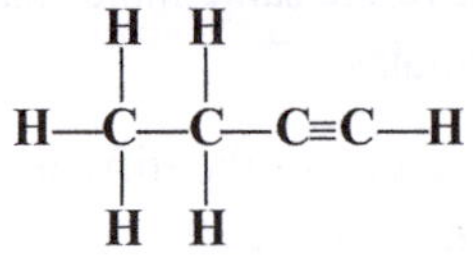

(*c*) 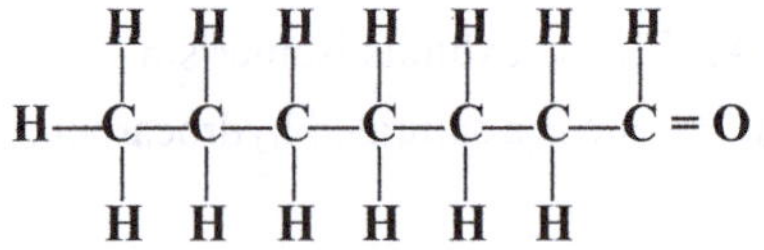

(*d*) 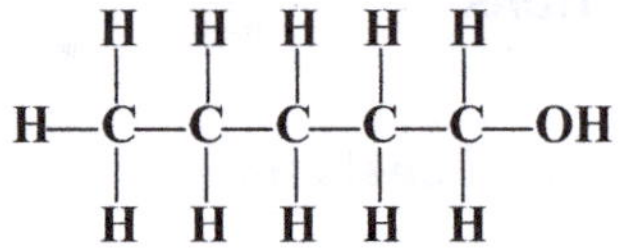

(*e*) 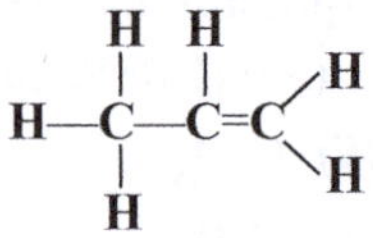

Ans. (*a*) Since, the parent chain consists of five carbon-atoms, hence, prefix 'pent' will be used. As there are only single bonds, thus, belongs to alkanes. Also, the functional group is –COOH (carboxylic acid), therefore, the suffix used is 'oic' acid.

Thus, the correct IUPAC name is Pentanoic acid. *(1 M)*

(*b*) Since, the chain consists of four carbon-atoms and belongs to an alkene, therefore, the correct IUPAC name is Butyne. *(1 M)*

(*c*) The given compound has seven carbon atoms in the main chain with the functional group –CHO and belongs to alkanes.

Thus, the correct IUPAC name is

Hept + an + al → Heptanal
(Hept ↓ Prefix; an ↓ alkane; al ↓ aldehyde) *(1 M)*

(*d*) The given compound has five carbon atoms with –OH as the functional group and it belongs to the alkane family. Thus, the correct IUPAC name is pent + an + ol = Pentanol. *(1 M)*

(*e*) The given compound has three carbon atoms, and it belongs to the alkene family. Thus, the correct IUPAC name is Propene. *(1 M)*

Nailing the Right Answer

To ace these kind of questions students should count the number of carbon atoms to determine the prefix. Identify the functional group to determine the suffix. Note the type of bonds between carbon atoms (single, double, triple) to figure out the family. Remember the IUPAC nomenclature rules, and prioritize the functional groups according to their precedence. Check for any branches or substituents, and name them as prefixes, placing them in ascending order by carbon number.

3. (*i*) **Draw the structure of the following compounds:**

(*a*) **Butanoic acid** (*b*) **Chloropentane**

(*ii*) **How are structure (*i*) and structure (*ii*) given below related to one another? Give reason to justify your answer.**

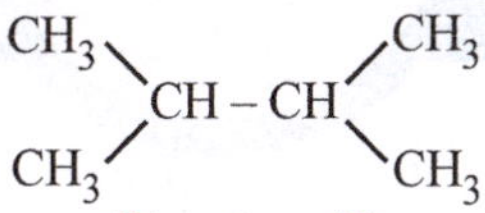

Structure (*i*)

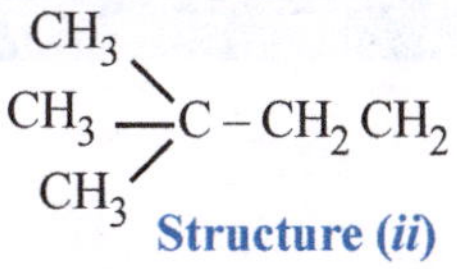

Structure (*ii*)

Draw one more possible structure for above case.

(*iii*) **Differentiate between saturated and unsaturated carbon compounds on the basis of their general formula.** **(*Un*) (CBSE 2023)**

Ans. (*i*) Structure of butanoic acid is shown as: (½ M)

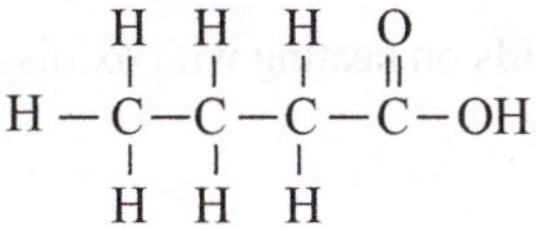

Structure of Chloropentane is shown as: (½ M)

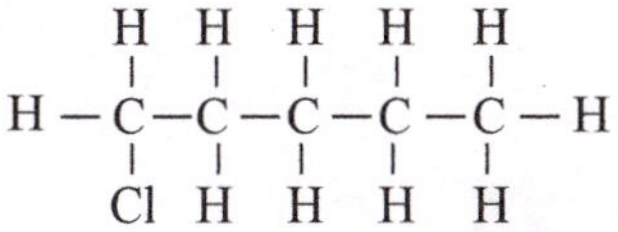

(*ii*)

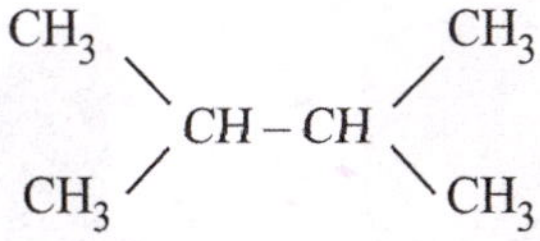

Structure (*i*)

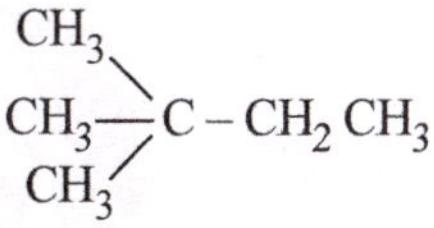

Structure (*ii*)

(1 M)

Structure (*i*) is 2,3-dimethylbutane and structure (*ii*) is 2,2-dimethylbutane

Both structures are isomers to each other due to same molecular formula (C_6H_{14}) but different in arrangement of atoms.

One more possible isomer of the compound is:

$H_3C — CH_2 — CH_2 — CH_2 — CH_2 — CH_3$ (1 M)

n-hexane

(*iii*)

Saturated Hydrocarbons	Unsaturated Hydrocarbons
Those compounds that have single carbon-carbon bond in their carbon chain or ring.	Those compounds that have at least one double or triple carbon-carbon bond in their carbon chain or ring.
If carbon atoms are connected by single bonds, then it is referred to as alkane.	If carbon atoms are connected by double bonds, then it is referred to as alkene.
General formula of the alkane is: C_nH_{2n+2}.	General formula of the alkene is: C_nH_{2n} If carbon atoms are connected by triple bonds, then it is referred to as alkyne. General formula of the alkyne is: C_nH_{2n-2}.

(2 M)

Hints & Explanations

Multiple Choice Questions

1. (*c*) Compound (*A*) is cyclohexane, a saturated cyclic hydrocarbon. Compound (*B*) and (*C*) are unsaturated hydrocarbons.
2. (*a*) In a homologous series, the difference in molecular masses between two successive members is 14u (not 16u). C_2H_2 and C_3H_4 are the successive members of the alkyne series as they differ by the $-CH_2$ unit and corresponds to the same general formula of alkynes series.
3. (*d*)

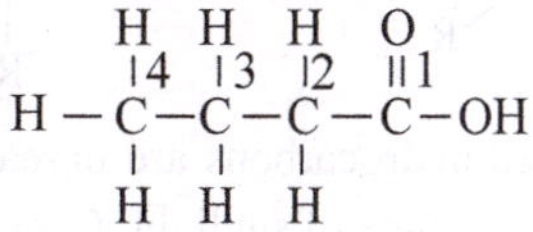

(Butanoic acid)

4. (*a*) The chemical formula of Butane is C_4H_{10}, here structure (*ii*) and (*iv*) have 8 hydrogen atoms, therefore, they are incorrect.

Assertion and Reason

1. (*a*) Since, the given compounds differ by $-CH_2$ unit, therefore, they belong to the homologous series.
2. (*a*) The assertion correctly explains the concept of isomerism, with the reason detailing the underlying cause
3. (*b*) For a molecule to exhibit isomerism, it must have more than 3 carbon atoms. Since in butane, there are 4 carbon atoms, therefore, will exhibit isomerism.

Since, butane has the presence of single bonds, therefore, it is a saturated hydrocarbon.

CHEMICAL PROPERTIES OF CARBON COMPOUNDS 4

NCERT Definitions (Commonly asked in 1 mark)

- **Combustion:** Carbon in all of its allotropic forms can **burn in oxygen** which results in the formation of CO_2 along with large amount of heat and energy.
  (*i*) $C + O_2 \rightarrow CO_2 + \text{heat} + \text{energy}$
  (*ii*) $CH_4 + O_2 \rightarrow CO_2 + H_2O + \text{heat} + \text{light}$
- **Oxidation:** Carbon in all carbon compounds like alcohols can be **oxidised to carboxylic acids** on heating with oxidising agents like $KMnO_4$.

$$CH_3 - CH_2OH \xrightarrow[\text{Or aciddified } K_2Cr_2O_7\text{+Heat}]{\text{Alkaline } KMnO_4 \text{ + Heat}} CH_3COOH$$

- **Addition:** Unsaturated hydrocarbons **add hydrogen** in the presence of catalysts like **Pd or Ni** to yield saturated hydrocarbons. This reaction is generally used in the **hydrogenation of vegetable oil** in the presence of a Ni catalyst.

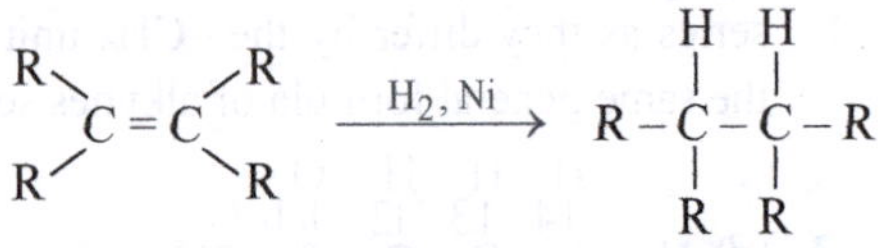

- **Substitution:** Saturated hydrocarbons are unreactive in the presence of most of the reagents. In the presence of sunlight, Cl can replace the hydrogen one by one. It is known as substitution reaction.

$$CH_4 + Cl_2 \rightarrow CH_3Cl + HCl$$

Saturated HC in the presence of sunlight

Saturated HC in the presence of other reagents

Important Facts

01 Carbon dioxide, heat, and light are products of combustion reactions involving carbon or its compounds.

02 In combustion, **saturated hydrocarbons** burn with a **clean flame**, whereas **unsaturated ones** produce a yellow, sooty flame.

03 The presence of **smoke** and **soot** in combustion indicates **incomplete burning**, usually due to limited air supply.

04 A flame only occurs when gaseous substances burn, which is why materials like coal or charcoal can emit heat without a flame.

05 Vegetable oils, often unsaturated, are preferred over animal fats due to health considerations related to saturated fatty acids.

Difference Between

Property	Combustion	Oxidation
Definition	A chemical reaction between a fuel and an oxidant releasing energy as heat and light.	A chemical reaction where a substance loses electrons and gain oxygen.
Process Type	Fast and exothermic.	Can be slow or fast, and exothermic or endothermic.
Temperature	High temperatures	Varies, can occur at low or high temperatures.
Products	Typically water and carbon dioxide (complete combustion).	Produces oxides; specific products depend on the substance and conditions.
Example	Burning of wood or coal.	Rusting of iron

Property	Addition	Substitution
Reaction Type	Combines two or more substances into a new compound.	Replaces an atom or group of atoms in a molecule .
Mechanism	Opens a double or triple bond to add new atoms.	Involves bond-breaking and bond-forming steps.
Types of Compounds	Unsaturated compounds (alkenes, alkynes)	Saturated compounds (alkanes) or aromatic compounds
Product Formation	Single product with all atoms from the reactants	Two products, one with the substitnent, one with the replaced atom
Example	Hydrogenation of ethene to ethane	Chlorination of methane to chloromethane

Real Life Application Based Questions

1. **Rashi noticed that the bottoms of her cooking pots were getting increasingly blackened, even though she cleans them regularly. What does this indicate about her gas stove?**

Ans. The blackening of the pots indicates **incomplete combustion** due to blocked air holes on the gas stove.

2. **Why is the oxidation of alcohols to carboxylic acids important in the chemical industry?**

Ans. This oxidation process is vital for synthesizing important chemicals like acetic acid, used in vinegar and as a precursor for various industrial products.

3. **How is the combustion of carbon compounds crucial in electricity generation?***

Ans. Combustion of carbon compounds in power plants produces heat that is used to create steam that drives turbines, generating electricity efficiently.

Myth Buster

- **Myth: All carbon compounds burn in oxygen to give only carbon dioxide and water along with energy.**

  Fact: While many carbon compounds combust to produce carbon dioxide and water, the actual products can vary based on the substance's structure and the combustion conditions. Incomplete combustion can produce carbon monoxide or soot (carbon), especially if the oxygen supply is limited.

- **Myth: The presence of a flame always indicates complete combustion.**

** Concepts beyond the board exam syllabus, offering deeper insight and critical thinking on NCERT topics.*

Fact: A flame indicates that combustion is occurring, but it does not guarantee complete combustion. Incomplete combustion can occur, producing soot and other incomplete oxidation products, even when a flame is present.

- **Myth: Oxidation reactions in carbon compounds are limited to combustion.**

  Fact: While combustion is a common oxidation reaction, carbon compounds can undergo various types of oxidation reactions. For instance, alcohols can be oxidized to carboxylic acids using oxidizing agents like potassium permanganate or potassium dichromate.

- **Myth: Fossil fuels are readily available and can be considered infinite resources.**

  Fact: Fossil fuels like coal and petroleum are finite resources formed over millions of years from the remains of ancient organisms. Their availability is limited, and their continued use is unsustainable in the long term, necessitating the shift toward renewable energy sources.

Mnemonics

PAN- In addition reaction, nickel and palladium is used as a catalyst.

- P → Palladium
- A → Addition Reaction
- N → Nickel

COMPETENCY BASED SOLVED EXAMPLES

Multiple Choice Questions (1 M)

1. $CH_3–CH_2–OH \xrightarrow{\text{Alkaline } KMnO_4 + \text{Heat}} CH_3–COOH$

In the above given reaction, alkaline $KMnO_4$ acts as **(*Un*) (NCERT Exemplar)**

(*a*) reducing agent (*b*) oxidising agent
(*c*) catalyst (*d*) dehydrating agent

2. During a chemistry experiment, Ethan is studying the combustion of various carbon compounds. He observes the following compounds undergoing complete combustion in oxygen:

(P) CH_3COOH **(Q) CH_3CH_2COOH**
(R) $CH_3CH{=}CH_2$ **(S) $CH_3CH_2CH_2OH$**

Ethan is curious to know which of these compounds will produce the same amount of carbon dioxide (CO_2) when the same number of molecules of each compound undergo complete combustion. Can you help Ethan identify which of the compounds will produce the same amount of CO_2? **(*An*)**

(*a*) Only P and Q (*b*) Only Q and S
(*c*) Only P, Q and R (*d*) Only Q, R and S

3. Chlorine reacts with saturated hydrocarbons at room temperature in the **(*Re*) (NCERT Exemplar)**

(*a*) absence of sunlight
(*b*) presence of sunlight
(*c*) presence of water
(*d*) presence of hydrochloric acid

Assertion and Reason (1 M)

Direction: The following questions consist of two statements – Assertion (A) and Reason (R). Answer these questions by selecting the appropriate option given below:

(*a*) Both A and R are true, and R is the correct explanation of A.
(*b*) Both A and R are true, but R is not the correct explanation of A.
(*c*) A is true, but R is false.
(*d*) A is false, but R is true.

1. Assertion (A) : Ethene undergoes addition reactions.
Reason (R): It is a saturated compound. **(*Un*)**

2. **Assertion (A):** Saturated hydrocarbons are generally less reactive than unsaturated ones.

Reason (R): The absence of double or triple bonds in saturated hydrocarbons makes them less likely to participate in addition reactions. *(Un)*

Subjective Questions

Very Short Answer Type Questions (2 M)

1. Why is the conversion of ethanol to ethanoic acid an oxidation reaction? Explain with the help of the chemical reaction. *(Ap)*

Ans. The conversion of ethanol to ethanoic acid is considered an oxidation reaction because it involves the gain of oxygen or the loss of hydrogen. *(1 M)*

$$CH_3-CH_2OH \xrightarrow[\text{Or acidified } K_2Cr_2O_7 + \text{Heat}]{\text{Alkaline } KMnO_4 + \text{Heat}} CH_3COOH$$ *(1 M)*

2. (a) A mixture of oxygen and ethyne is burnt for welding. Can you tell why a mixture of ethyne and air is not used? **(NCERT Intext)**

(b) Which of the following hydrocarbons undergo addition reactions:
C_2H_6, C_3H_8, C_3H_6, C_2H_2. *(Ap)* **(NCERT Exemplar)**

Ans. (a) Oxygen and ethyne is burnt for welding,but a mixture of ethyne and air is not used because burning of ethyne in air produces a sooty flame due to incomplete combustion, which is not hot enough to melt metals for welding. *(1M)*

(b) C_3H_6 (Propene) and C_2H_2 (Ethyne or Acetylene) are the hydrocarbons that undergo addition reactions. *(1 M)*

Key Takeaways

From this question students learn that unsaturated hydrocarbons undergo addition reactions and saturated hydrocarbons do not typically participate in addition reactions.

Short Answer Type Questions (3 M)

1. What happens when 5% alkaline potassium permanganate solution is added drop by drop to warm propyl alcohol (propanol) taken in a test tube ? Explain with the help of a chemical equation. *(Un)* **(CBSE 2019)**

Ans. When we add 5% alkaline potassium permanganate solution drop by drop to warm propyl alcohol, the purple colour of potassium permanganate begins to fade. *(1 M)*

During this reaction, the alcohols are converted into carboxylic acids as carbon compounds can be easily oxidised. Propanoic acid is the end product of this reaction. *(1 M)*

$$CH_3CH_2CH_2OH + 2[O] \xrightarrow[\text{or acidified } K_2Cr_2O_7]{\text{Alkaline } KMnO_4;\text{Heat}} CH_3CH_2COOH + H_2O$$ *(1 M)*

2. (a) Under what conditions an oxidation reaction can be called as combustion reaction? Illustrate your answer with example.

(b) Addition reactions and substitution reactions are types of organic reactions. Which type of reaction is shown by:

(i) ethane (ii) ethene *(Un)*

Ans. (a) When complete oxidation of fuel takes place with the release of a high amount of heat and light, it is called a combustion reaction. Hence, for an oxidation reaction to be called as combustion reaction, it must undergo complete oxidation. *(½ M)*

For examples:

- Burning of coal

$$C + O_2 \rightarrow 2CO_2 + \text{Heat} + \text{Light}$$ *(½ M)*

(b) (i) Ethane shows substitution reactions. In the presence of sunlight, when chlorine is added to it, chlorine can replace the hydrogen atoms one by one. The reaction takes place as

$$CH_3-CH_3 + Cl_2 \rightarrow CH_3CH_2Cl + HCl$$ *(1 M)*

(ii) Ethene shows the addition reactions. Ethene adds hydrogen in the presence of catalysts such as palladium or nickel to give saturated hydrocarbons. The reaction is shown below:

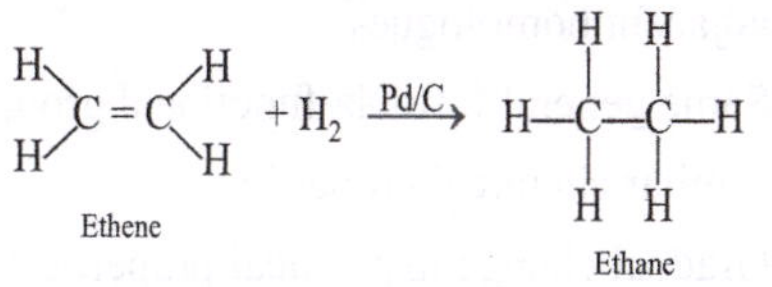

(1 M)

3. In his chemistry lab, Jack burns one mole of an alkane P in excess oxygen, which produces 6 moles of carbon dioxide and 7 moles of water. Jack is curious about the identity of this alkane and its behaviour during combustion.

(a) Based on the reaction, can you help Jack determine the chemical formula and the chemical name of the compound?

(b) Will this compound produce a clear or sooty flame upon burning? Justify your answer. *(An)*

Ans. (a) Chemical Formula and Name of Alkane 'P':

- Formula: C_6H_{14} *(1 M)*
- Name: Hexane *(1 M)*

(b) Hexane will burn with a clear (blue) flame because it is a saturated hydrocarbon. *(1 M)*

Long Answer Type Questions (5 M)

1. (a) "Keerthi thinks that Substitution reaction occurs in saturated Hydrocarbons, on the contrary Krishi thinks, it occurs in unsaturated Hydrocarbons." Justify with valid reasoning whose thinking is correct.

(*b*) **"Methane and Propane and their Isomers are used as fuels" Comment. Draw the electron dot structure of the immediate lower homologue of Propane. Give any two characteristics of homologues of a given homologous series.**

(*c*) **A mixture of oxygen and ethyne is burnt for welding. Can you predict why a mixture of ethyne and air is not used?** **(*An*) (CBSE SQP, 2024)**

Ans. (*a*) Keerthi's thinking is correct as substitution reactions occur in saturated hydrocarbons, hydrogen atoms are replaced with heteroatoms in saturated hydrocarbons. Whereas in unsaturated hydrocarbons an addition reaction occurs, simple molecules are added across double and/ or triple bonds. *(1 M)*

(*b*) Methane and propane undergo combustion reaction in presence of oxygen and produce large amount of energy. *(1 M)*

The lower homologue of propane is ethane has the following electron dot structure:

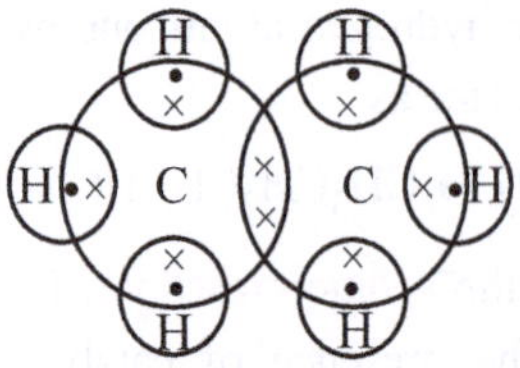

(1 M)

ANY TWO *CHARACTERISTICS*

- Difference in $-CH_2-$ / 14 u molecular mass of any two adjacent homologues.
- Same general formula/functional group
- Similar chemical properties
- Gradual change in physical properties *(1 M)*

(*c*) The mixture of ethyne and oxygen in sufficient amounts undergoes complete combustion to fire a clean blue flame. In presence of insufficient supply of oxygen or in presence of air, ethyne does not undergo complete combustion and produces sooty flame. *(1 M)*

2. (*a*) **Two carbon compounds X and Y have the the molecular formula C_4H_8 and C_5H_{12} respectively. Which one of these is most likely to show addition *reaction? Justify your answer. Also give the chemical* equation to explain the process of addition reaction in this case.**

(*b*) **Give reason for the following: Acetylene burns with a sooty flame.**

(*c*) **What happens when methane burns in oxygen?** **(*Ap*)**

Ans. (*a*) All unsaturated hydrocarbons (containing double or triple bonds) have tendency to get converted to saturated hydrocarbons (single bonds) by adding small molecules such as hydrogen (H_2), halogens (X_2), etc. Such reactions are called addition reactions. *(1 M)*

Compound X i.e., C_4H_8 belongs to alkene series (C_nH_{2n}) while compound Y i.e., C_5H_{12} belongs to alkane series (C_nH_{2n+2}). Thus, compound X will undergo addition reaction. *(1 M)*

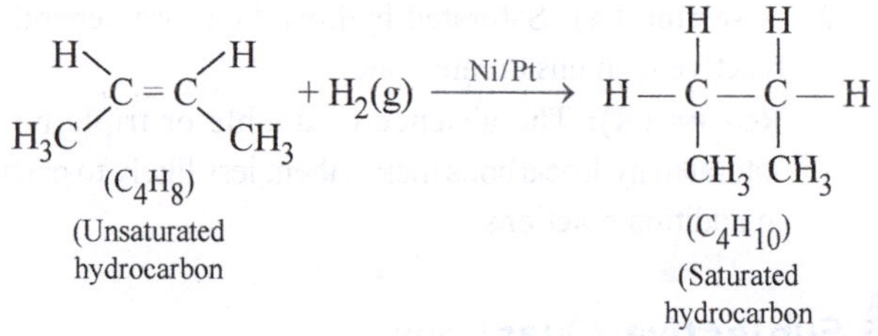

(1 M)

(*b*) Acetylene burns with a sooty flame. The formula of acetylene is HC ≡ CH. It is an unsaturated hydrocarbon where the carbon content is more than the hydrogen content. As a result, carbon is not completely burned, and the unburned carbon settles as soot. Hence, it burns with a sooty flame. *(1 M)*

(*c*) When methane is burned in O_2, CO_2 and H_2O are produced.

$CH_4(g) + 2O_2(g) \rightarrow CO_2(g)\uparrow + 2H_2O(l)$ *(1 M)*

Nailing the Right Answer

Carefully identify the type of hydrocarbon (alkane, alkene, alkyne) by looking at the molecular formula and the type of bonds. Know that unsaturated hydrocarbons (alkenes and alkynes) typically undergo addition reactions. Be *familiar with the combustion process, understanding that* complete and incomplete combustion. Balance chemical equations accurately, showing the conservation of mass.

Hints & Explanations

Multiple Choice Questions

1. (*b*) An oxidizing agent is one that causes oxidation of other substances. Since $KMnO_4$ causes the oxidation of CH_3CH_2OH to CH_3COOH, therefore, acts as an oxidising agent.

2. (*d*)

- P (acetic acid) produces $2CO_2$.
- *Q (propanoic acid), R (propene), and S (propanol) each* produce $3CO_2$.

So, Q, R and S produce the same amount of carbon dioxide.

3. (*b*) Chlorine reacts with saturated hydrocarbons at room temperature in the presence of sunlight. The reaction takes place as

$$\underset{\text{Methane}}{CH_4} + \underset{\text{Chlorine}}{Cl_2(g)} \xrightarrow{\text{sunlight}} \underset{\text{Chloromethane}}{CH_3Cl} + \underset{\text{Hydrochloric acid}}{HCl(l)}$$

Assertion and Reason

1. (*c*) Ethene is an unsaturated compound.

2. (*a*) The reactivity of hydrocarbons is tied to their saturation level, with unsaturated ones being more reactive due to the presence of double or triple bonds.

5 SOME IMPORTANT CARBON COMPOUNDS: ETHANOL AND ETHANOIC ACID

NCERT Definitions (Commonly asked in 1 mark)

- **Ethanol (Alcohol):** A liquid carbon compound, active in alcoholic beverages, used widely in medical applications due to its solvent properties, and is soluble in water.

- **Absolute Alcohol:** Absolute alcohol is **pure ethanol** without any water or impurities, typically used in industrial processes, laboratory settings, and as a solvent.
- **Denatured Alcohol:** Ethanol made unfit for drinking by adding poisonous substances like methanol to it. Dyes are also added to colour the alcohol blue so that it can be identified easily.

- **Glacial Acetic Acid:** Glacial acetic acid is a concentrated form of acetic acid where it is almost **100% pure**, known for solidifying at cooler temperatures and used in various chemical processes.
- **Esterification:** A reaction where an **acid** reacts with an **alcohol**, often in the presence of an acid catalyst, to form an **ester, a sweet-smelling substance** used in perfumes and flavours.

$$\underset{\text{(Ethanoic acid)}}{CH_3{-}COOH} + \underset{\text{(Ethanol)}}{CH_3{-}CH_2OH} \overset{\text{Acid}}{\rightleftharpoons} \underset{\text{(Ester)}}{CH_3{-}\overset{\overset{\Large O}{\|}}{C}{-}O{-}CH_2{-}CH_3} + H_2O$$

- **Saponification:** A process where an **ester** reacts with an **alkali** to form an **alcohol** and a **carboxylic acid salt**, a principle used in soap making.

$$CH_3COOC_2H_5 \xrightarrow{NaOH} C_2H_5OH + CH_3COONa$$

Important Facts

01 A by-product of sugar refining from sugarcane, fermentable into ethanol, used in alcohol-based fuel. ***~Molasses***

02 The conversion of ethanol to ethene by dehydration at high temperatures using concentrated sulphuric acid.

03 This alcohol affects the optic nerve, causing blindness. It gets oxidised to methanal which coagulates the protoplasm, in much the same way an egg is coagulated by cooking. ***~Methanol***

04 A salt is formed when ethanoic acid reacts with a base like sodium hydroxide or with carbonates and hydrogencarbonates. ***~Sodium Acetate***

05 A 5-8% solution of acetic acid in water. ***~Vinegar***

Important Reactions

Reaction of Ethanol			
Reaction Type	**Reactants**	**Products**	**Chemical Equation**
Reaction with Sodium	Ethanol + Sodium	Sodium Ethoxide + Hydrogen	$2Na + 2CH_3CH_2OH \rightarrow 2CH_3CH_2O^-Na^+ + H_2$
Dehydration	Ethanol + Concentrated Sulphuric Acid (Hot)	Ethene + Water	$CH_3CH_2OH \xrightarrow{\text{conc. } H_2SO_4} CH_2 = CH_2 + H_2O$

Reaction of Ethanoic Acid			
Reaction Type	**Reactants**	**Products**	**Chemical Equation**
Esterification Reaction	Ethanoic acid + Ethanol	Ester (Ethyl acetate) + Water	$CH_3COOH + CH_3CH_2OH \rightarrow CH_3COOCH_2CH_3 + H_2O$
Saponification	Ester + Sodium hydroxide	Ethanol + Sodium acetate	$CH_3COOC_2H_5 + NaOH \rightarrow C_2H_5OH + CH_3COONa$
Reaction with a Base	Ethanoic acid + Sodium hydroxide	Sodium acetate + Water	$CH_3COOH + NaOH \rightarrow CH_3COONa + H_2O$
Reaction with Carbonates	Ethanoic acid + Sodium carbonate	Sodium acetate + Water + Carbon dioxide	$2CH_3COOH + Na_2CO_3 \rightarrow 2CH_3COONa + H_2O + CO_2\uparrow$
Reaction with Hydrogen carbonates	Ethanoic acid + Sodium hydrogencarbonate	Sodium acetate + Water + Carbon dioxide	$CH_3COOH + NaHCO_3 \rightarrow CH_3COONa + H_2O + CO_2\uparrow$

Real Life Application Based Questions

1. Can you explain the importance of the esterification reaction in industrial applications?

Ans. The esterification reaction between ethanoic acid and ethanol produces esters, which are used in making perfumes and flavouring agents due to their sweet smell and non-toxic nature, enhancing product appeal and safety.

2. What role does ethanoic acid play in the food industry?

Ans. Ethanoic acid, commonly known as acetic acid, is used as a preservative in pickles, and other food items due to its acidic properties which inhibit microbial growth, thereby extending the shelf life of food products.

3. Explain how the reaction of ethanoic acid with sodium carbonate is applied in fire extinguishers.

Ans. Ethanoic acid reacts with **sodium carbonate** in fire extinguishers to release **carbon dioxide**, which smoothers flames by displacing oxygen, demonstrating an application in safety equipment.

Myth Buster

- **Myth: Consuming any alcohol in moderation, including ethanol, is completely safe and has no long-term health effects.**

  Fact: While moderate consumption of certain alcoholic beverages may have some reported health benefits, ethanol itself, especially in its pure form, is highly toxic. Even moderate consumption can lead to significant health issues over time, including liver disease, addiction, and increased risk of various cancers.

- **Myth: Ethanol and methanol can be used interchangeably in industrial applications due to their similar chemical structures.**

  Fact: Despite their structural similarities, ethanol and methanol have very different properties and toxicities. Methanol is far more toxic than ethanol and can cause severe or fatal outcomes if ingested, inhaled, or absorbed through the skin.

- **Myth: Ethanoic acid, being an organic compound, is weaker than all inorganic acids, and therefore is not hazardous.**

Fact: While ethanoic acid (acetic acid) is indeed a weaker acid compared to many inorganic acids like hydrochloric acid or sulphuric acid, it can still pose hazards, particularly in concentrated forms. Glacial acetic acid; for instance, can cause severe burns upon skin contact and can be damaging if ingested or inhaled.

- **Myth: Denatured alcohol can be purified by simple distillation or filtration to remove additives, making it safe to consume.***

Fact: Denatured alcohol contains additives that are toxic and often designed to be difficult to separate from the ethanol. Even if one were to attempt distillation or filtration, trace amounts of these toxic substances could remain, posing serious health risks if ingested. The purpose of denaturation is to deter the consumption of industrial or laboratory ethanol.

** Concepts beyond the board exam syllabus, offering deeper insight and critical thinking on NCERT topics.*

COMPETENCY BASED SOLVED EXAMPLES

Multiple Choice Questions (1 M)

1. Vinegar is a solution of ***(Un)*** **(NCERT Exemplar)**

(*a*) 50%-60% acetic acid in alcohol
(*b*) 5%-8% acetic acid in alcohol
(*c*) 5%-8% acetic acid in water
(*d*) 50%-60% acetic acid in water ***(Un)***

2. A compound Y on treatment with alkaline $KMnO_4$ followed by acidification gives a compound X. Compound X also reacts with compound Y in the presence of few drops of H_2SO_4 to form a sweet smelling compound Z. The compound X, Y and Z are, respectively. ***(Ap)***

(*a*) Ethanoic Acid, Sodium Ethanoate, Ethane
(*b*) Ethanoic Acid, Ethanol, Ethyl Ethanoate
(*c*) Ethanoic Acid, Ethanal, Ethene
(*d*) Ethanol, Ethanoic Acid, Sodium Ethanoate

3. In the given sequence of reaction,

$$P \xrightarrow[\text{potassium dichromate}]{\text{Acidified}} \text{Ethanoic acid} \xrightarrow{P} R$$

The final product R is? ***(Ap)***

(*a*) A carboxylic acid (*b*) An alcohol
(*c*) An aldehyde (*d*) An ester

4. A compound with which of the following functional groups is MOST LIKELY to cause the decomposition of baking soda to produce carbon dioxide?

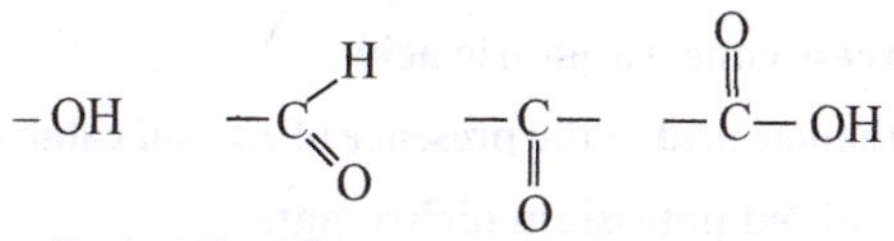

P Q R S

(An) **(CFPQ)**

(*a*) P (*b*) Q
(*c*) R (*d*) S

Assertion and Reason (1 M)

Direction: The following questions consist of two statements – Assertion (A) and Reason (R). Answer these questions by selecting the appropriate option given below:

(*a*) Both A and R are true, and R is the correct explanation of A.
(*b*) Both A and R are true, but R is not the correct explanation of A.
(*c*) A is true, but R is false.
(*d*) A is false, but R is true.

1. Assertion (A): Ethanoic acid reacts with ethyl alcohol in presence of conc. H_2SO_4 to form ethyl ethanoate.
Reason: (R): Esters are used in ice creams and cold drinks. ***(Re)***

2. Assertion (A): Esterification is a process in which a sweet smelling substance is produced.
Reason: (R): When esters react with sodium hydroxide an alcohol and sodium salt of carboxylic acid are obtained. ***(Re)*** **(CBSE 2020)**

3. Assertion (A): Ethanoic acid is also known as glacial acetic acid.
Reason (R): The melting point of pure ethanoic acid is 290 K and hence, it often freezes during winters in cold climates. ***(Re)*** **(CBSE 2020)**

4. Assertion (A): To prevent the misuse of industrial ethanol, it is denatured by adding substances like methanol.
Reason (R): Denaturing makes ethanol toxic to consume, thereby, deterring its use as a beverage. ***(Un)***

Subjective Questions

Very Short Answer Type Questions (2 M)

1. A carbon compound is a constituent of beer, whisky and some cough syrups. Identify the compound and write its formula. ***(Re)*** **(CBSE 2020)**

Ans. The compound is Ethanol. and it is commonly called alcohol and is the active ingredient of all alcoholic drinks. *(1 M)*

The chemical formula of Ethanol is C_2H_5OH. *(1 M)*

2. Combustion analysis of compound X revealed the ratio of its elements in a molecule to be carbon : hydrogen : oxygen :: 3 : 6 : 2. The compound undergoes esterification to yield an ester and water.

(*a*) Identify the compound X. Write its chemical formula.

(*b*) Write the balanced equation for the combustion of compound X. **(*An*) (CFPQ)**

Ans. (*a*) Propanoic acid *(½ M)*

C_2H_5COOH *(½ M)*

(*b*) $2C_2H_5COOH + 7O_2 \rightarrow 6CO_2 + 6H_2O + \text{energy}$ *(1 M)*

3. Heating an alcohol with concentrated sulphuric acid results in the dehydration of the alcohol to give the alkene as shown by the reaction of ethanol to give ethene.

$$CH_3CH_2\,OH \xrightarrow{\text{Hot conc. sulphuric acid}} CH_2{=}\,CH_2$$

Pramila heated 2-butanol (shown below) with concentrated sulphuric acid.

This also

$$CH_3CH_2\underset{\displaystyle OH}{\underset{|}{C}}HCH_3$$

Write the structural formulae of all the possible products of the reactions. **(*Ap*) (CFPQ)**

Ans. The structural formulae for the possible products are -

$CH_3CH{=}\,CHCH_3$ *(1 M)*

$CH_3CH_2\,CH{=}CH_2$ *(1 M)*

Short Answer Type Questions (3 M)

1. An organic compound X with formula C_2H_6O is an active ingredient in all alcoholic drinks. When a small piece of sodium is added to compound X, a new compound Y is formed. Identify X and write the balanced chemical equation to show the change. **(*An*)**

Ans. • Ethanol is commonly called alcohol and is the active ingredient of all alcoholic drinks. Hence, the given organic compound X with formula C_2H_6O is Ethanol i.e. C_2H_5OH. *(1 M)*

• Alcohols react with sodium leading to the evolution of hydrogen gas. The following reaction takes place when a small piece of sodium is added to compound X:

$$\underset{\text{(Ethanol)}}{2Na + 2CH_3CH_2OH} \rightarrow \underset{\text{(Sodium ethoxide)}}{\underset{(Y)}{2CH_3CH_2ONa}} + H_2\uparrow \quad (1M)$$

Here, the compound Y is sodium ethoxide. *(1 M)*

Key Takeaways

Student shall learn from this question that metals react with alcohols to produce hydrogen gas and a metal alkoxide. Balancing chemical equations is essential to accurately represent the conservation of mass in a reaction

2. Name the organic compound which is added to make ethanol unfit for drinking purposes. What is the name of the mixture formed? **(*Re*)**

Ans. • The organic compound which is added to make ethanol unfit for drinking purposes is methanol. It is a poisonous substance that prevents the misuse of ethanol produced for industrial use. *(1 M)*

Dyes are also added to colour the alcohol blue so that it can be identified easily. *(1 M)*

• The mixture so formed is known as methylated spirit or denatured alcohol. *(1 M)*

3. How would you distinguish experimentally between an alcohol and a carboxylic acid? **(*Un*)**

Ans. • An alcohol contains the functional group –OH and the carboxylic acid contains the functional group –COOH. *(1 M)*

• Carboxylic acids reacts with sodium carbonate (Na_2CO_3) to produce CO_2 gas which turns lime water milky. On the other hand, alcohols do not give this reaction. Therefore, this experiment can be used to distinguish an alcohol and a carboxylic acid. *(1 M)*

• Reaction of Carboxylic acid with Na_2CO_3 is as follows:

$2CH_3COOH + Na_2CO_3 \rightarrow 2CH_3COONa + H_2O + CO_2\uparrow$ *(1 M)*

Long Answer Type Questions (5 M)

1. (*a*) Name a commercially important carbon compound having functional group –OH and write its molecular formula.

(*b*) Write chemical equation to show its reaction with

(1) Sodium metal

(2) Excess conc. sulphuric acid

(3) Ethanoic acid in the presence of an acid catalyst

(4) Acidified potassium dichromate

Also write the name of the product formed in each case. **(*Un*) (CBSE 2024)**

Ans. (*a*) A commercially important carbon compound having the functional group –OH is Ethanol and its molecular formula is C_2H_5OH. *(½ × 2 = 1 M)* (*b*) (1) Reaction of ethanol with sodium metal:

$$2Na + 2CH_3CH_2OH \rightarrow \underset{\text{(Sodium ethoxide)}}{2CH_3CH_2O^-Na^+} + H_2$$

The product obtained in this reaction is sodium ethoxide. *(1 M)*

(2) Reaction of ethanol with excess conc. sulphuric acid:

$$CH_3-CH_2OH \xrightarrow[H_2SO_4]{\text{Hot Conc.}} CH_2 = CH_2 + H_2O$$

The product obtained in this reaction is ethene. *(1 M)*

(3) Reaction of ethanol with ethanoic acid:

$$\underset{\text{(Ethanoic acid)}}{CH_3-COOH} + \underset{\text{(Ethanol)}}{CH_3-CH_2OH} \overset{\text{Acid}}{\rightleftharpoons} \underset{\text{(Ester)}}{CH_3-\overset{O}{\overset{\|}{C}}-O-CH_2-CH_3} + H_2O$$

The product obtained in this reaction is ester. *(1 M)*

(4) Reaction of ethanol with acidified potassium dichromate:

$$CH_3-CH_2OH \xrightarrow{\text{Acidified } K_2Cr_2O_7 + \text{Heat}} CH_3COOH$$

The product obtained in this reaction is ethanoic acid. *(1 M)*

2. (*a*) In tabular form, distinguish between ethanol and ethanoic acid under the following headings:

(*i*) Physical state

(*ii*) Smell

(*iii*) Taste

(*iv*) $NaHCO_3$ test

(*v*) Ester test

(*b*) Write a chemical reaction to show the dehydration of ethanol. **(*Un*)**

Ans. (*a*)

Properties	Ethanol	Ethanoic Acid
Physical State	Colourless liquid	Colourless liquid
Smell	Pleasant smell	Vinegar like smell
Taste	Burning taste	Sour taste
$NaHCO_3$ test	No reaction	Produce brisk effervescence due to CO_2.
Ester test	Ethanol reacts with acetic acid in the presence of conc. H_2SO_4 to form fruity smell compound, ester.	Ethanoic acid reacts with ethyl alcohol in the presence of conc. H_2SO_4 to form fruity smell compound, ester.

(4 M)

(*b*)

$$\underset{\text{Ethanol}}{CH_3CH_2OH} \xrightarrow[443K]{\text{Conc.}H_2SO_4} \underset{\text{Ethene}}{CH_2 = CH_2} + H_2O$$

(1 M)

3. A carbon compound 'P' on heating with excess conc. H_2SO_4 forms another carbon compound 'Q' which on addition of hydrogen in the presence of nickel catalyst forms a saturated carbon compound 'R'. One molecule of 'R' on combustion forms two molecules of carbon dioxide and three molecules of water. Identify P, Q and R and write chemical equations for the reactions involved. **(*An*)**

Ans. Compound 'P' will be ethanol which forms ethene in the presence of Conc. H_2SO_4. *(1 M)*

$$\underset{\substack{\text{Ethanol}\\ \text{(P)}}}{C_2H_5OH} \xrightarrow[443\text{ K}]{\text{Conc. }H_2SO_4} \underset{\substack{\text{Ethene}\\ \text{(Q)}}}{CH_2=CH_2} + H_2O$$

(1 M)

'Q' is Ethene which in the presence of Ni forms Ethane (R).

(1 M)

$$\underset{\text{Ethene}}{CH_2=CH_2} \xrightarrow[H_2]{\text{Ni catalyst}} \underset{\text{Ethane}}{CH_3-CH_3}$$

(1 M)

Ethane (R) on combustion forms CO_2 and H_2O.

$$C_2H_6 + \frac{7}{2}O_2 \longrightarrow 2CO_2 + 3H_2O$$

(1 M)

Nailing the Right Answer

Know that unsaturated hydrocarbons (alkenes and alkynes) typically undergo addition reactions. Be familiar with the combustion process, must have understanding of both complete and incomplete combustion. Balance chemical equations accurately, showing the law of conservation of mass.

Topper's Explanation

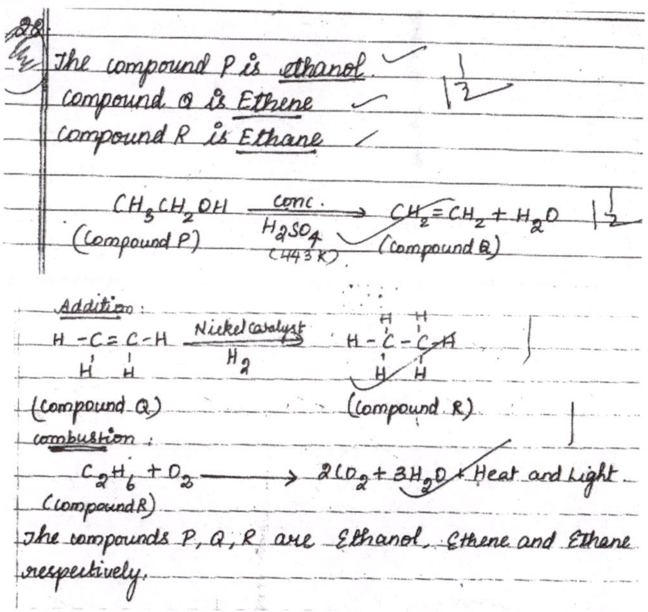
The compound P is ethanol.
compound Q is Ethene
compound R is Ethane

CH_3CH_2OH (Compound P) —conc. H_2SO_4 (443K)→ $CH_2=CH_2 + H_2O$ (Compound Q)

Addition:
H–C=C–H (Compound Q) —Nickel catalyst, H_2→ H–C–C–H (Compound R)

combustion:
$C_2H_6 + O_2$ (Compound R) ——→ $2CO_2 + 3H_2O$ + Heat and Light

The compounds P, Q, R are Ethanol, Ethene and Ethane respectively.

Hints & Explanations

Multiple Choice Questions

1. (*c*) 5-8% solution of acetic acid in water is called vinegar
2. (*b*) As a sweet-smelling compound Z is formed, hence this characteristic of compound Z shows that it is an ester which is formed by the reaction of an alcohol with a carboxylic acid in the presence of conc. H_2SO_4. Also, X is formed by the acidification of compound Y, therefore, Y should be alcohol, and X should be a carboxylic acid.

$$\underset{\text{Ethanol}}{\underset{(Y)}{C_2H_5OH}} \xrightarrow[\text{KMnO}_4]{\text{alkaline}} \underset{\text{Ethanoic acid}}{\underset{(X)}{CH_3COOH}}$$

$$\underset{(Y)}{C_2H_5OH} + \underset{(X)}{CH_3COOH} \xrightarrow[H_2SO_4]{\text{Conc.}} \underset{\text{(ester)}}{\underset{\text{Ethylethanoate}}{\underset{(Z)}{CH_3COOC_2H_5}}}$$

3. (*d*)

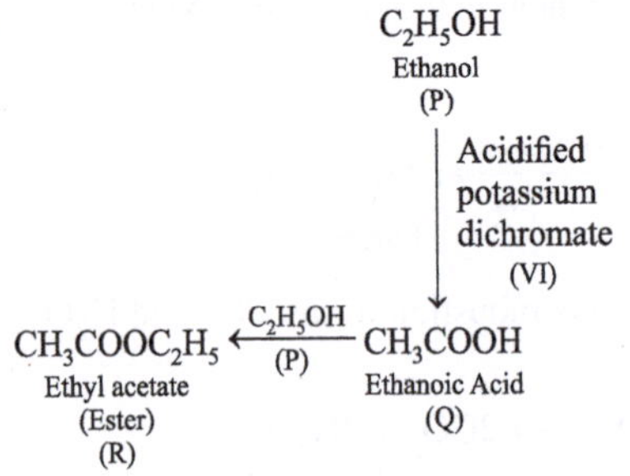

4. (*d*) Carboxylic acid groups decompose to give CO_2 gas.

Assertion and Reason

1. (*b*) Esters are sweet smelling and are used in ice creams and cold drinks.
2. (*b*) Esterification is the reaction of carboxylic acid with alcohol to produce the sweet-smelling chemical ester.

   When an ester interacts with sodium hydroxide, it produces an alcohol as well as the sodium salt of carboxylic acid. This is referred to as ester hydrolysis.
3. (*a*) Glacial acetic acid is pure ethanoic acid. This is due to the fact that acetic acid, when it reaches its melting point, generates a glacier and hence, glacial acetic acid.

   This melting point is significantly higher than that of ice. Because of this, it freezes and creates a glacier in the winter.
4. (*a*) The purpose of denaturing ethanol is to prevent its consumption, which is effectively achieved by adding toxic substances.

SOAPS AND DETERGENTS

6

NCERT Definitions (Commonly asked in 1 mark)

- **Micelles:** When the molecules of soap interact with dirt and water, the ionic-end or hydrophilic end protrudes outwards and dissolve in water while the carbon chain or hydrophobic end interacts with oil and protrudes inwards. The soap molecules, thus form structures called micelles.

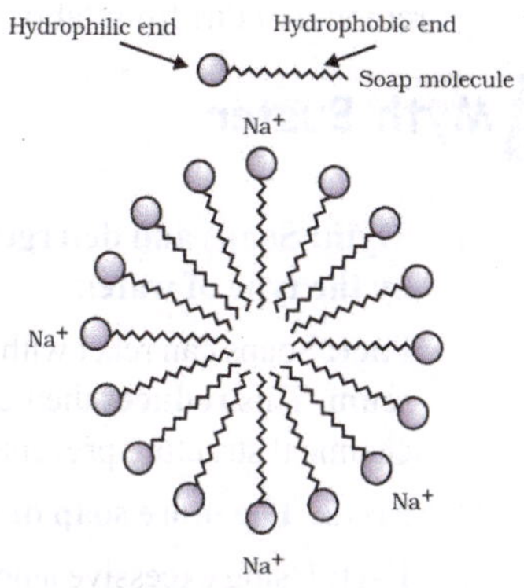

- **Hydrophilic:** Property of a molecule or a part of a molecule that is typically **attracted** or interacts with **water.**
- **Hydrophobic:** Property of a molecule or a part of a molecule that **repels water** and typically interacts with oils or fats.
- **Hard Water:** Water that contains **high concentrations of calcium, magnesium, or other mineral salts,** which can reduce the effectiveness of soap.
- **Soaps:** Soaps are **sodium or potassium salts of long-chain carboxylic acids.**
- **Detergents:** Detergents are **cleansing agents** made of **sodium salts of sulphonic acids or ammonium salts with chlorides or bromides ions,** etc.

Important Facts

01 Hard water contains hydrogencarbonates/ sulphates/chlorides of calcium or magnesium.

02 The insoluble substance that remains after washing with water, caused by the reaction of soap with the calcium and magnesium salts. ***~ Scum***

03 Works well in hard water unlike soaps because they do not form insoluble precipitates with the Ca^{2+} and Mg^{2+} ions present in hard water. ***~ Detergents***

04 The process of beating clothes or scrubbing to enhance the cleaning efficiency by spreading the detergent or soap throughout the material and dislodging dirt. ***~ Agitation***

Difference Between

Soaps Vs. Detergents

Feature	Soaps	Detergents
Composition	Sodium or potassium salts of long-chain carboxylic acids	Sodium salts of sulphonic acids or ammonium salts
Example*	Sodium stearate	Sodium lauryl sulphate
Effectiveness in Hard Water	Less effective due to formation of scum	More effective as they do not form scum
pH	Generally mild	Can be harsh (alkaline)
Usage	More commonly used for personal hygiene (bathing, hand washing) and washing clothes.	Broad usage including laundry, dishes, and industrial applications
Cleaning Efficiency	Less efficient in hard water due to precipitate formation	More efficient in hard water as they do not form insoluble precipitates.

** Concepts beyond the board exam syllabus, offering deeper insight and critical thinking on NCERT topics.*

Real Life Application Based Questions

1. **How does the process of forming micelles make soap effective in cleaning oily dirt from clothes?**

Ans. Soap molecules form micelles around oily dirt with hydrophobic tails trapping the oil and hydrophilic heads facing outwards. This emulsifies oil in water, allowing it to be rinsed away, effectively cleaning clothes.

2. **Why does hard water reduce the effectiveness of soap when washing clothes or bathing?**

Ans. Hard water contains calcium and magnesium, which react with soap to form insoluble scum. This reaction reduces the soap's ability to form micelles, necessitating more soap for effective cleaning.

3. **Explain the importance of agitation when washing clothes with soap.**

Ans. Agitation helps to disperse soap molecules throughout the water, allowing micelles to form more efficiently and improving the removal of dirt from fabrics during the wash cycle.

Myth Buster

- **Myth: Soaps and detergents work in the same way under all water conditions, and their cleaning efficiency is not affected by the type of water.**

  Fact: Soaps can react with minerals in hard water, such as calcium and magnesium, to form insoluble precipitates known as **soap scum.** This **reduces** their cleaning efficiency. In contrast, detergents are designed to be effective even in hard water because their chemical structure prevents them from forming such precipitates, maintaining their cleaning power regardless of water hardness.

- **Myth: The more soap or detergent you use, the cleaner your clothes or dishes will be.**

  Fact: Using excessive amounts of soap or detergent does not necessarily enhance cleaning and can actually be counterproductive. Overuse can lead to **residue buildup** on fabrics and surfaces and can contribute to environmental pollution.

- **Myth: All detergents are harsh and can damage fabrics and surfaces.**

  Fact: While some detergents can be harsh, especially on certain delicate fabrics, there are many formulations designed to be gentle, while still effective at cleaning. Detergent manufacturers often produce specialized products for different uses, including those suitable for delicate fabrics or sensitive skin.

- **Myth: Soap is always better for the environment than detergent.**

  Fact: While it's true that some soaps are made from natural ingredients and are biodegradable, not all soaps are environmentally friendly, especially if they use unsustainable palm oil or other environmentally harmful ingredients. Detergents, on the other hand, can contain synthetic chemicals that may not break down easily in the environment. However, there are eco-friendly detergents available that are designed to minimize environmental impact.

Mnemonics

- The ionic-end of soap is hydrophilic, while the carbon chain is hydrophobic.

  "In Philadelphia, Cats Photograph"

  In → Ionic; Philadelphia, → Hydrophilic; Cats → Carbon; Photograph → Phobic

COMPETENCY BASED SOLVED EXAMPLES

Multiple Choice Questions (1 M)

1. Which of the following is not correctly matched? **(*Re*) (NCERT Exemplar)**

(*a*) Hard soaps - sodium salts of fatty acids.

(*b*) Soft soaps - potassium salts of fatty acids.

(*c*) Hydrophilic - water insoluble

(*d*) None of these

2. In the soap micelles? **(*Re*) (NCERT Exemplar)**

(*a*) the ionic end of soap is on the surface of the cluster while the carbon chain is in the interior of the cluster.

(*b*) ionic end of soap is in the interior of the cluster and the carbon chain is out of the cluster

(*c*) both ionic end and carbon chain are in the interior of the cluster

(*d*) both ionic end and carbon chain are on the exterior of the cluster

3. Observe the following table carefully

Samples	Hard Water	Soap or Detergent Added	Observation (After Shaking 5 Minutes)
A	10 mL	Soap (5 drops)	White curd like Scum formed
B	15 mL	Detergent (5 drops)	White curd like Scum is formed
C	8 mL	Soap (5 drops)	Lot of lather is formed
D	12 mL	Detergent (5 drops)	Lot of lather is formed

Which among the given test tubes give correct result? **(*An*)**

(*a*) A & B (*b*) C & D

(*c*) A & D (*d*) B & D

4. Several factories were pouring their wastes in rivers A and B. Water samples were collected from these two rivers. It was observed that sample collected from river A was acidic while that of river B was basic. The factories located near A and B are **(*An*) (CBSE 2020)**

(*a*) Soaps and detergents factories near A and alcohol distillery near B.

(*b*) Soaps and detergents factories near B and alcohol distillery near A.

(*c*) Lead storage battery manufacturing factories near A and soaps and detergents factories near B.

(*d*) Lead storage battery manufacturing factories near B and soaps and detergents factories near A.

Assertion and Reason (1 M)

Direction: **The following questions consist of two statements – Assertion (A) and Reason (R). Answer these questions by selecting the appropriate option given below:**

(*a*) Both A and R are true, and R is the correct explanation of A.

(*b*) Both A and R are true, but R is not the correct explanation of A.

(*c*) A is true, but R is false

(*d*) A is false, but R is true.

1. **Assertion (A):** Detergents are more effective cleansing agents than soaps in hard water.

Reason (R): They do not form precipitates with Ca^{2+} and Mg^{2+} present in hard water. **(*Un*)**

Subjective Questions

Very Short Answer Type Questions (2 M)

1. Answer the following questions:

(*a*) Give reason, why washing clothes with soap in hard water is not effective?

(*b*) Will a micelle be formed, if soap is dissolved in organic solvent like ethanol? **(*Un*)**

Ans. (*a*) Soap reacts with Ca^{2+} and Mg^{2+} ions present in hard water to form insoluble precipitates called scum. Hence, washing clothes with hard water is not effective. *(1 M)*

(*b*) Since, the hydrocarbon chains of soap molecules are soluble in organic solvents like ethanol, hence, micelle will not be formed if soap is dissolved in ethanol. *(1 M)*

2. People use a variety of methods to wash clothes. Usually after adding the soap, they 'beat' the clothes on a stone, or beat it with a paddle, scrub with a brush or the mixture is agitated in a washing machine. Why is agitation necessary to get clean clothes?

(*Un*) (NCERT Intext)

Ans. Agitation in washing clothes is crucial because it helps to distribute the soap and water evenly through the fabric, which loosens dirt and stains. *(1 M)*

When the wetted clothes in soap solution are agitated (or beaten), the micelles containing dirt particles get removed from the surface of dirty clothes and go into the water and the dirty clothes gets cleaned. *(1 M)*

3. In three test tubes A, B and C, three different liquids namely distilled water, underground water and distilled water in which a pinch of calcium sulphate is dissolved, respectively are taken. Equal amount of soap solution is added to each test tube and the contents are shaken. In which test tube will the length of the foam (lather) be longest? Justify your answer. ***(An)*** **(CBSE 2019)**

Ans. • Test tube A contains distilled water, which is considered soft water with no free ions, and so the length of foam in test tube A will be the longest. *(½ M)*

• Test tube B includes underground water that contains ions such as Mg^{+2}, Ca^{+2} that react with soaps to generate salts of fatty acids known as scum, which is insoluble in water and hence has a shorter foam length than test tube A. *(½ M)*

• Test tube C includes distilled water with $CaSO_4$, which contains Ca^{+2} ions that react with soaps to generate fatty acid salts, i.e., scum, and hence the length of foam in test tube C is less than that in test tube A. *(½ M)*

As a result, the length of foam in test tube A will be the longest. *(½ M)*

Nailing the Right Answer

Identify the characteristics of the liquids in each test tube. Understand how the ions present in the liquids affect the formation of foam. Compare the reactions of the different liquids with the soap solution to determine the length of foam.

Short Answer Type Questions (3 M)

1. What are detergents chemically? Write any two merits and two demerits of using detergents for cleansing. Explain the reason, why detergents are suitable for washing, even in the case of water having calcium and magnesium ions? ***(Un)***

Ans. Detergents are generally sodium salts of sulphonic acids or ammonium salts with chlorides or bromides ions. *(½ M)*

Merits:

(*i*) Detergents can even work well in hard water. *(½ M)*

(*ii*) They are more effective than soaps. *(½ M)*

Demerits:

(*i*) They are more expensive than soaps. *(½ M)*

(*ii*) Some of them having branched hydrocarbons are non-biodegradable. *(½ M)*

Detergents are suitable for washing even in hard water having Mg^{2+} and Ca^{2+} ions because they do not form insoluble precipitates with the calcium and magnesium ions. *(½ M)*

Long Answer Type Questions (5 M)

1. Compound 'X' works well with hard water. It is used for making shampoos & products for cleaning clothes. Compound 'X' is not 100% biodegradable and causes water pollution. Compound 'Y' does not work well with hard water and it is 100% biodegradable and does not cause water pollution.

(*a*) Identify compound X,

(*b*) Identify Y.

Also, provide reasons for your answer. ***(Ap)***

Ans. (*a*) X is detergent because detergents function well with hard water, are not totally biodegradable, and pollute the water. *(½ M)*

Reason: Detergents include long-chain hydrocarbons, therefore they are not biodegradable, and contaminate the environment. *(1 M)*

The charged ends of detergents do not form insoluble precipitates with the calcium and magnesium ions in hard water, which is why they perform effectively in hard water. *(1 M)*

(*b*) Y is a soap because soaps do not work well with hard water and are 100 % biodegradable. (½ M)

Reason: Soaps form insoluble precipitates with the calcium and magnesium ions. These insoluble salts separate as the scum Therefore, they do not work well with hard water. *(1 M)*

Also, since they do not have much long hydrocarbons chain, therefore, they are 100% biodegradable and do not cause water pollution. *(1 M)*

2. (*i*) With the help of diagram, explain the formation of micelles, when soap is applied on oily dirt.

(*ii*) Take two test tubes X and Y with 10 mL of hard water in each. In test tube 'X', add few drops of soap solution and in test tube 'Y' add a few drops of detergent solution. Shake both the test tubes for the same period.

(1) In which test tube the formation of foam will be more? Why?

(2) In which test tube is a curdy solid formed? Why? ***(Un)***

Ans. (*i*) • Most dirt is oily in nature, and oil does not dissolve in water. *(½ M)*

• The molecules of soap are sodium or potassium salts of long-chain carboxylic acids. *(½ M)*

• The ionic end of soap interacts with water, while the carbon chain interacts with oil. The soap molecules, thus, form structures called micelles where one end of the molecules is towards the oil droplet while the ionic-end faces outside. This forms an emulsion in water. *(½ M)*

- The soap micelle thus helps in pulling out the dirt in water, and we can wash our clothes clean. *(½ M)*

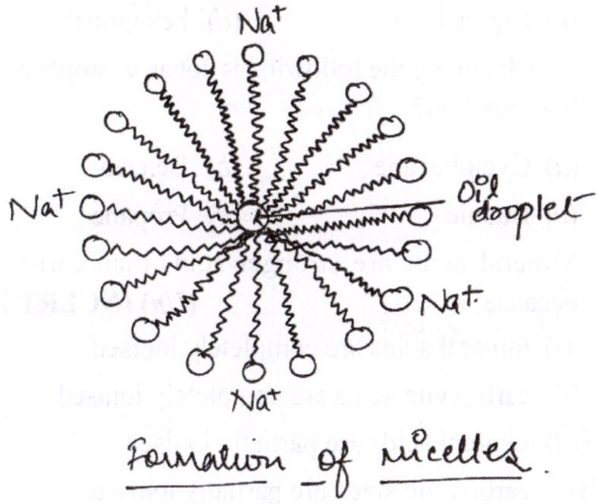

(1 M)

(*ii*) (1) In Test Tube Y, there will be more foam formation as it contains detergents. The charged ends of these compounds do not form insoluble precipitates with the calcium and magnesium ions in hard water. Thus, they remain effective in hard water. *(1 M)*

(2) In Test Tube X, a curdy solid is formed due to the presence of soap solution. This is caused by the reaction of soap with the calcium and magnesium salts present in hard water, which results in the formation of an insoluble substance (scum) which remains on clothes after washing with water. *(1 M)*

Hints & Explanations

Multiple Choice Questions

1. (*c*) Hydrophilic means water loving, and hydrophilic compounds are generally water soluble.

2. (*a*) In the soap micelles, the ionic end of soap is on the surface of the cluster while the carbon chain is in the interior of the cluster.

3. (*c*) Soaps do not form lather in hard water, it forms white scum. Detergent forms lather easily even with hard water.

4. (*c*) Acidic wastes are produced by lead factories.

However, the wastes produced by the soap and detergent industry are basic.

As a result, the factories near A might be lead storage battery companies, whereas those near B must be soap and detergent factories.

Assertion and Reason

1. (*a*) Detergents are typically sodium salts of sulphonic acids or ammonium salts containing chlorides or bromide ions. In hard water, the charged ends of these compounds do not form insoluble precipitates with the calcium and magnesium ions. As a result, they are more effective in hard water than soaps.

MISCELLANEOUS EXERCISE

Multiple Choice Questions (1 M)

1. You are conducting a lab session for a high school chemistry class. The students are learning about the structure and bonding of water molecules. They have been introduced to the concept of covalent bonds and the sharing of electrons between atoms. The students are tasked with depicting a water molecule, showing the nature of bonding between one oxygen atom and two hydrogen atoms. You ask the students to draw the electron dot structure of a water molecule. Which of the following diagrams correctly shows the electron dot structure of a water molecule? **(*An*)**

   (*a*) H·Ọ̈·H (*b*) H:Ọ̈·H
   (*c*) H:Ọ̈:H (*d*) H:O:H

2. The main reason for the huge number of carbon compounds are **(*Re*)**
   (*a*) catenation
   (*b*) tetravalency of carbon
   (*c*) tendency to form multiple bonds
   (*d*) all of these

3. Carbon dioxide molecule contains **(*Re*)**
   (*a*) single covalent bond (*b*) double covalent bond
   (*c*) triple covalent bond (*d*) ionic bond

4. 1 mole of ethene and 1 mole of ethyne are separately made to completely undergo addition reaction to form the respective saturated compound. **(*An*) (CFPQ)**

   Which of the following will be DIFFERENT for the two reactions?

   (P) the number of moles of the saturated compound formed
   (Q) the number of moles of the hydrogen consumed

   (*a*) only P (*b*) only Q
   (*c*) both P and Q (*d*) neither P nor Q

5. Imagine, you are conducting an experiment in your chemistry class to study the combustion characteristics of different carbon compounds. You burn ethanol, camphor, and naphthalene and observe the nature of the flame and the production of smoke. **(*Un*)**
   Which of the following is most likely to produce a yellow flame?
   (*a*) Only Camphor
   (*b*) Camphor and Naphthalene
   (*c*) Ethanol and Naphthalene
   (*d*) Only Naphthalene

6. Which one of the following statement is incorrect about graphite and diamond? **(*Re*)**
   (*a*) Graphite is smooth and slippery.
   (*b*) Graphite is a good conductor of electricity.
   (*c*) Diamond is good conductor
   (*d*) Physical properties of graphite and diamond are different.

7. Structure of diamond is **(*Re*)**
   (*a*) linear (*b*) tetrahedral
   (*c*) trigonal (*d*) hexagonal

8. Which among the following is not an example of a saturated hydrocarbon? **(*Un*)**
   (*a*) Cyclohexane (*b*) Benzene
   (*c*) Butane (*d*) Propane

9. Mineral acids are stronger acids than carboxylic acids because **(*Un*) (NCERT Exemplar)**
   (*i*) mineral acids are completely ionised
   (*ii*) carboxylic acids are completely ionised
   (*iii*) mineral acids are partially ionised
   (*iv*) carboxylic acids are partially ionised
   (*a*) (*i*) and (*iv*) (*b*) (*ii*) and (*iii*)
   (*c*) (*i*) and (*ii*) (*d*) (*iii*) and (*iv*)

10. You are working on a project in an organic chemistry laboratory, and you need to synthesise ethane starting from ethanol. You consider several possible reaction pathways to achieve this transformation.
    Which of the following reaction sequences will successfully convert ethanol to ethane? **(*Ap*)**
    (*a*) Oxidation followed by dehydration
    (*b*) Dehydration followed by addition of H_2
    (*c*) Oxidation followed by addition of H_2
    (*d*) Dehydration followed by oxidation

11. The structure of three hydrocarbons are given below.

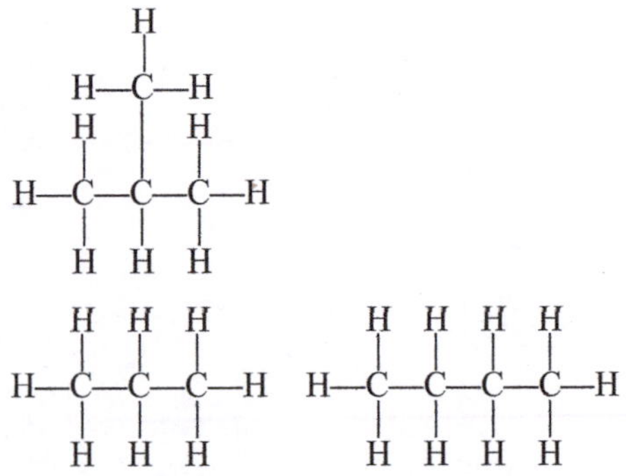

    Select the statement which is correct for all the above three compounds? **(*Ap*) (NCERT Exemplar)**
    (*a*) They are isomers of each other
    (*b*) They have the same general formula
    (*c*) They have the same physical properties
    (*d*) None of these

12. Ethane, with the molecular formula C_2H_6 has **(*Un*) (NCERT)**
    (*a*) 6 covalent bonds. (*b*) 7 covalent bonds.
    (*c*) 8 covalent bonds. (*d*) 9 covalent bonds.

13. The functional groups present in the following compound are **(Un)**

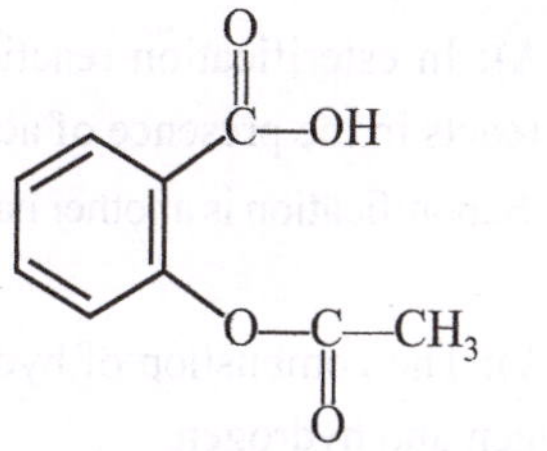

(*a*) Alcohol, ketone and ester
(*b*) Ester and carboxylic acid
(*c*) Carboxylic acid and ketone
(*d*) Ester and alcohol

14. Which of the following is incorrect? **(Un)**

(*a*) $CH_3—CH_2—C(=O)—CH_3$ Butanone

(*b*) $CH_3—CH_2—C(H)=O$ Propanal

(*c*) $CH_3—CH_2—C(=O)—OH$ Butanal

(*d*) $CH_3—CH_2—CH_2—CH_2—OH$ Butanol

15. Which of the following forms a homologous series? **(Ap)**

(*a*) Ethane, Ethylene, Acetylene
(*b*) Ethane, Propane, Butanone
(*c*) Methanol, Ethanol, Propanoic acid
(*d*) Butane, 2-Methyl Butane, 2, 3, dimethyl Butane

16. What happens when bromine water is added to ethene? **(Un)**

(*a*) $CH_2 = CH_2 + Br_2(aq) \rightarrow Br–CH_2–CH_2–Br$
(*b*) $CH_2 = CH_2 + Br_2(aq) \rightarrow CH_2=CH–Br$
(*c*) $CH_2 = CH_2 + Br_2(aq) \rightarrow H_3C—HC(Br)_2$
(*d*) None of these

17. The IUPAC name of the given compounds (X) and (Y) respectively are: **(Ap)**

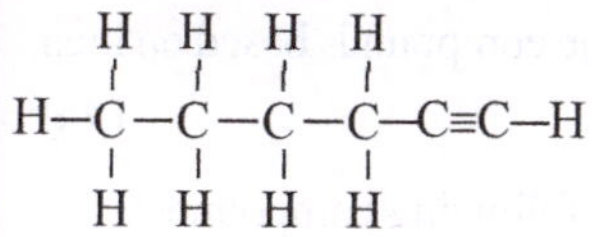

(X)

and

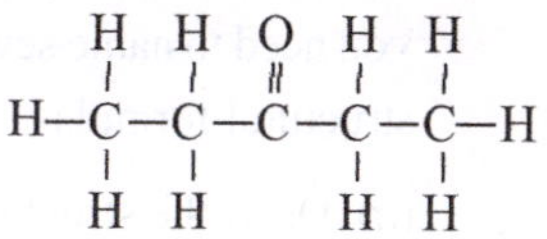

(Y)

(*a*) Pent-1-yne and Pentanal
(*b*) Hex-1-yne and Pentan-3-one
(*c*) Hex-1-ene and Pentan-3-one
(*d*) Hex-1-yne and Hexan-3-one

18. Write IUPAC name of: **(Ap)**

$CH_3—CH(CH_3)—CH_3$

(*a*) 2, 2-dimethyl propane (*b*) 2-methyl butane
(*c*) 2, 2 dimethyl ethane (*d*) 2-methyl propane

19. $HC \equiv CH \xrightarrow[+H_2]{Pd} \boxed{X}$

$\uparrow$ Hot conc H_2SO_4

C_2H_5OH

Which of the following correctly represents 'X' in the above chemical changes? **(Un) (CBSE APQ, 2023)**

(*a*) Ethane (*b*) Ethene
(*c*) Ethyne (*d*) Ethanoic acid

20. While cooking, if the bottom of the vessel is getting blackened on the outside, it means that **(An) (NCERT)**

(*a*) the food is not cooked completely,
(*b*) the fuel is not burning completely.
(*c*) the fuel is wet.
(*d*) the fuel is burning completely.

21. When a vegetative oil is treated with Hydrogen in the presence of Nickel catalyst it forms fat (Vegetable Ghee). This is an example of **(Un)**

(*a*) Displacement reaction
(*b*) Decomposition reaction
(*c*) Addition reaction
(*d*) Double displacement reaction

22. Which among the following is an example of substitution reaction? **(Ap)**

(*a*) $CH_2 = CH_2 + H_2 \xrightarrow{H_2/Pd} CH_3–CH_3$
(*b*) $CH_3CH_2OH + H_2 \xrightarrow{KMnO_4 (alkaline)} CH_3COOH$
(*c*) $CH_4 + Cl_2 \xrightarrow{hv} CH_3Cl + HCl$
(*d*) $C + O_2 \rightarrow CO_2$ + heat and light

23. Which among the following reactions is known as esterification reaction? **(Re)**

(*a*) $CH_3COOH + NaHCO_3 \rightarrow CH_3COONa + H_2O + CO_2$
(*b*) $CH_3COOH + NaOH \rightarrow CH_3COONa + H_2O$
(*c*) $C_2H_5OH + CH_3COOH \xrightarrow{H^+} CH_3COOC_2H_5 + H_2O$
(*d*) $CH_3COOC_2H_5 + NaOH \rightarrow CH_3COONa + C_2H_5OH$

24. Which of the following represents saponification reaction? **(Re) (NCERT Exemplar)**

(*a*) $CH_3COONa + NaOH \xrightarrow{CaO} CH_4 + Na_2CO_3$
(*b*) $CH_3COOH + C_2H_5OH \xrightarrow{H_2SO_4} CH_3COOC_2H_5 + H_2O$
(*c*) $2CH_3COOH + 2Na \rightarrow 2CH_3COONa + H_2$
(*d*) $CH_3COOC_2H_5 + NaOH \rightarrow CH_3COONa + C_2H_5OH$

25. The soap molecule has a **(Re) (NCERT Exemplar)**

(*a*) hydrophilic head and a hydrophobic tail
(*b*) hydrophobic head and a hydrophilic tail
(*c*) hydrophobic head and a hydrophobic tail
(*d*) hydrophilic head and a hydrophilic tail

26. In a chemistry lab, students are performing two activities to understand the properties of hard and soft water.

In Activity 1, they compare the lather forming capacity of soap in distilled water and hard water.

In Activity 2, they compare the lather forming capacity of soap and detergent in hard water. The goal is to observe which substance forms more lather and if any precipitates are formed.

Based on the results of the two activities, which conclusion can be drawn about the ability of soap and detergent to form lather in hard water? ***(Un)***

(*a*) Soap forms more lather in hard water than in soft water and does not form any precipitates.

(*b*) Detergent forms a curdy precipitate in hard water, while soap does not.

(*c*) Soap does not form lather in hard water and produces a white curdy precipitate, while detergent forms lather in hard water.

(*d*) Both soap and detergent form the same amount of lather in hard water and produce a curdy precipitate.

Assertion and Reason (1 M)

Direction: The following questions consist of two statements – Assertion (A) and Reason (R). Answer these questions by selecting the appropriate option given below:

(*a*) Both A and R are true, and R is the correct explanation of A.

(*b*) Both A and R are true, but R is not the correct explanation of A.

(*c*) A is true, but R is false

(*d*) A is false, but R is true.

1. **Assertion (A):** Graphite is chemically more reactive than diamond. ***(Re)***

   Reason (R): Diamond is very hard but graphite is soft.

2. **Assertion (A):** Propane (C_3H_8) is the third member of alkane. ***(Un)***

   Reason (R): It is obtained from general formula C_nH_{2n+2}.

3. **Assertion (A):** In a homologous series of alcohols the formula for the second member is C_2H_5OH and the third member is C_3H_7OH

   Reason (R): The difference between the molecular masses of the two consecutive members of a homologous series is 144. ***(Ap)* (CBSE 2020)**

4. **Assertion (A):** Esterification is a process in which a sweet smelling substance is produced.

   Reason (R): When esters react with sodium hydroxide an alcohol and sodium salt of carboxylic acid are obtained. ***(Re)* (CBSE 2020)**

5. **Assertion (A):** The IUPAC name of $H_3C–CH=CH—C≡C–H$ is pent-3-en-1-yne and not pent-2-en-4-yne.

   Reason (R): Lowest locant rule for multiple bonds is preferred. ***(Un)***

6. **Assertion (A):** Ethanol turns blue litmus red. ***(Un)***

   Reason (R): It reacts with sodium metal to evolve H_2 gas.

7. **Assertion (A):** In esterification reaction, carboxylic acid and alcohol reacts in the presence of acid to give ester.

   Reason (R): Saponification is another name for esterification reaction. ***(Re)***

8. **Assertion (A):** The combustion of hydrocarbons typically releases oxygen and hydrogen. ***(Un)***

   Reason (R): Combustion is a chemical reaction that occurs in the presence of oxygen, and produces energy in the form of heat and light.

9. **Assertion (A):** Animal fats are healthier than vegetable oils.

   Reason (R): Vegetable oils generally have long unsaturated carbon chains while animal fats have saturated carbon chains. ***(Re)***

10. **Assertion (A):** Soaps are generally biodegradable but do not work well with hard water.

    Reason (R): Some detergents are non-biodegradable but work well with hard water. ***(Re)***

Subjective Questions

Very Short Answer Type Questions (2 M)

1. What are covalent compounds? Why are they different from ionic compounds? ***(Un)* (CBSE 2016)**

2. (*a*) Why is carbon tetravalent?

   (*b*) What would be the electron dot structure of a molecule of sulphur which is made up of eight atoms of sulphur? ***(Ap)* (NCERT Intext)**

3. You are conducting an organic chemistry experiment in the laboratory where you are asked to work with various carbon compounds. The aim of your experiment is to draw the structures of specific organic compounds. Additionally, you need to name several organic compounds based on their structural formulas. ***(An)***

   (*a*) Draw the structures for the following compounds:

   (*i*) Bromopentane

   (*ii*) Butanone

   (*b*) Name the following compounds based on their structural formulas provided:

   (*i*) 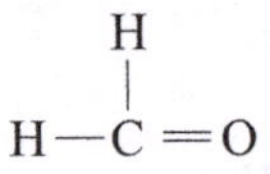

   (*ii*) 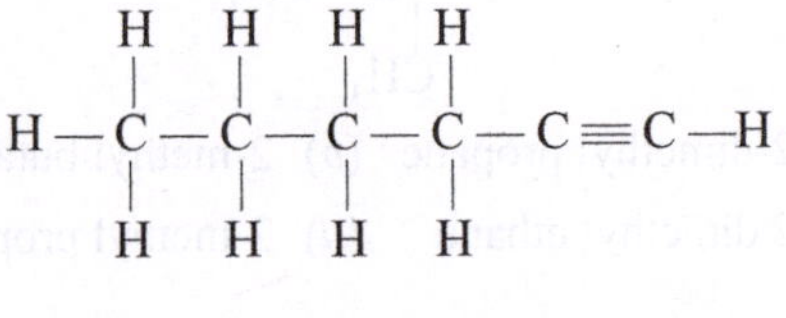

4. (*a*) What is meant by a saturated hydrocarbon? Give one example.

(*b*) An alkane has 11 carbon atoms arranged within ring structures as shown below.

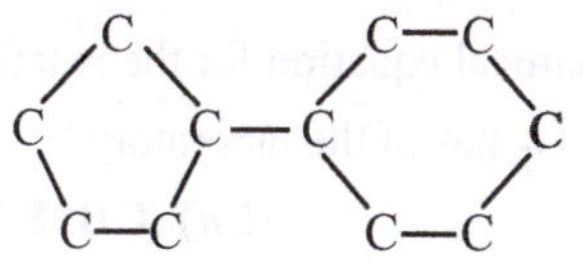

What is the molecular formula of the alkane? (*Ap*) (CFPQ)

5. You are conducting an experiment to observe the behaviour of soap and detergent when mixed with hard water and soft water. You have four equal-sized samples of soap and detergent solutions, which you expose to hard water and soft water in separate test tubes as shown in the images below. (*Ap*)

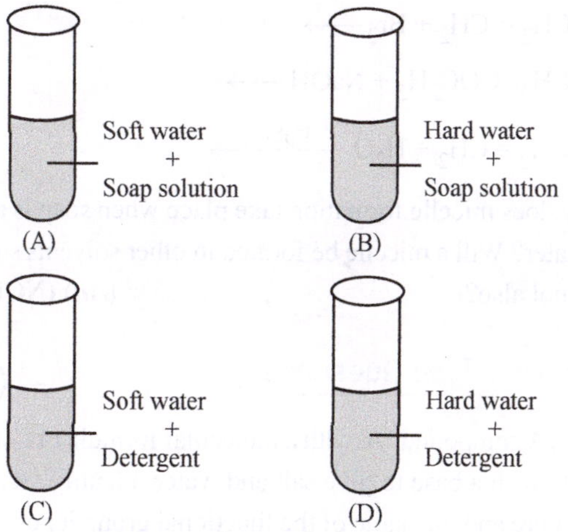

(*a*) In which test tube is a white curdy precipitate likely to form? Justify your answer.

(*b*) When greasy dirt or oil is mixed with soapy water, the soap molecules arrange themselves into tiny clusters. What are these clusters called?

6. The melting and boiling points of carbon compounds are generally low and they are largely non-conductors of electricity. State two conclusions based on these two properties. (*Un*) (CBSE 2024)

7. You are performing an experiment in the chemistry laboratory to observe the reaction between an alcohol and a carboxylic acid in the presence of acid catalyst. You place the reaction mixture in a test tube and heat it in a water bath using a burner, as shown in the setup below. During the reaction, you notice that the resulting product, "P" emits a fruity smell. (*Ap*)

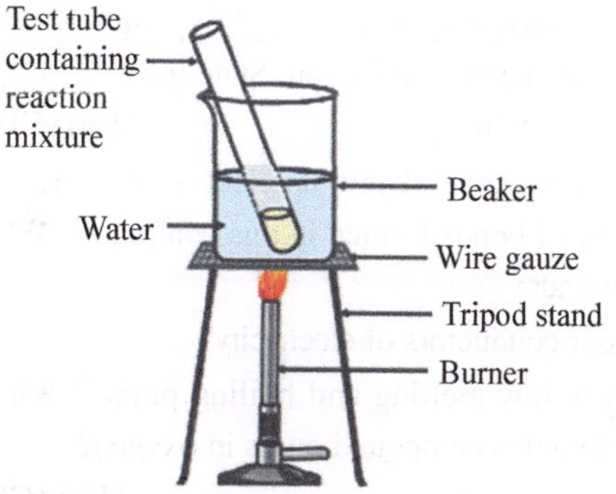

Later, when the product "P" reacts with a base, one of the reactants from the original mixture is recovered.

(*a*) Identify the product "P" formed in the reaction.

(*b*) What will be the reactant that is recovered when "P" reacts with a base? Explain the chemical reactions involved.

8. Answer the following questions:

(*a*) An organic compound burns with a blue flame. Is it a saturated or unsaturated compound?

(*b*) What is the effect of drinking methanol? (*Re*)

9. Answer the following questions:

(*a*) Name one hydrocarbon which undergoes substitution reaction.

(*b*) A compound has the molecular formula C_2H_6O. It is usable as a fuel. Identify the compound. (*Un*)

10. (*a*) Out of hydrophobic and hydrophilic end, which is water insoluble?

(*b*) What is scum? (*Re*)

Short Answer Type Questions (3 M)

1. Carbon, a member of group 14, forms a large number of carbon compounds estimated to be about three million. Why is this property not exhibited by other elements of this group? Explain. (*Re*) (CBSE 2020)

2. You are provided with an organic compound having the molecular formula, C_2H_6. Give the name and formula of the compound formed when. (*Ap*)

(*a*) One H atom of C_2H_6 is replaced by a OH group.

(*b*) One H atom of C_2H_6 is replaced by a CHO group.

(*c*) One H atom of C_2H_6 is replaced by a COOH group.

3. Shown below are the structural formulae of four carbon compounds.

$CH_3-C(=O)-CH_3$ P	$CH_3-CH(OH)-CH_3$ Q	$CH_3-CH_2-C(=O)-OH$ R	CH_3-OH S

(*a*) Two of these compounds are more likely to have similar chemical properties.

Identify these two compounds. Give a reason for your answer.

(*b*) Identify which of these compounds are likely to have the same boiling point. Justify your answer. (*An*) (CFPQ)

4. (*a*) Name the functional groups present in the following compounds

(*i*) $CH_3COCH_2CH_2CH_2CH_3$

(*ii*) $CH_3CH_2CH_2COOH$

(*iii*) $CH_3CH_2CH_2CH_2CHO$

(*iv*) CH_3CH_2OH (NCERT Exemplar)

(*b*) What change will you observe if you test soap with litmus paper (red and blue)? (*Un*) (NCERT)

5. (*a*) Define the term 'isomer'.

(*b*) Two compounds have same molecular formula C_3H_6O. Write the name of these compounds and their structural formula.

(*c*) How would you bring the following conversions:

(*i*) Ethanol to ethene

(*ii*) Propanol to propanoic acid **(*Un*) (CBSE, 2019)**

6. Alkanes are saturated compounds of carbon and hydrogen that can be represented by the general formula C_nH_{2n+2} where 'n' is the number of carbon atoms. An example of such a compound is ethane C_2H_6.

Maya has a compound of carbon and hydrogen whose formula is C_3H_4.

(*a*) What is true about the type of flame this compound will give on combustion?

(*b*) Draw all the possible straight chain structures of this compound. **(*An*) (CFPQ)**

7. You are a chemical engineer working in a food processing plant, where you are responsible for converting unsaturated fats into saturated fats through the process of hydrogenation. Hydrogenation involves adding hydrogen to unsaturated hydrocarbons in the presence of a catalyst such as palladium or nickel. This process is also used in the hydrogenation of vegetable oils to improve their stability and texture. **(*Un*)**

Consider the following hydrocarbons and their reactions:

(*a*) Identify which of the following hydrocarbons will undergo addition reactions: C_2H_6, C_3H_8, C_3H_6, C_2H_2, and CH_4.

(*b*) Explain the type of fatty acids that are predominantly found in animal fats.

8. 3 mL of ethanol is taken in a test tube and warmed gently in a water bath. A 5% solution of alkaline potassium permanganate is added first drop by drop to this solution, then in excess.

(*i*) How is 5% solution of $KMnO_4$ prepared?

(*ii*) State the role of alkaline potassium permanganate in this reaction. What happens on adding it in excess?

(*iii*) Write chemical equation of this reaction.

(*Un*) (CBSE 2020)

9. "Two different forms of carbon — diamond and graphite have different structures and very different physical properties even though their chemical properties are same." Explain why? **(*Un*) (CBSE, 2022 Term-II)**

10. What do you understand by esterification and saponification reactions of organic compounds. Explain this with the help of the chemical equation for each. **(*Re*)**

11. A compound X is formed by the reaction of a carboxylic acid $C_2H_4O_2$ and an alcohol in presence of a few drops of H_2SO_4. The alcohol on oxidation with alkaline $KMnO_4$ followed by acidification gives the same carboxylic acid as used in this reaction. Give the names and structures of (*a*) carboxylic acid, (*b*) alcohol and (*c*) the compound X. Also write the reaction. **(*Un*) (NCERT Exemplar)**

12. A student is performing an experiment to study the properties of acetic acid. Answer the following questions :

(*i*) Name the substance he must add to acetic acid to produce carbon dioxide.

(*ii*) Give the relevant chemical equation for the reaction.

(*iii*) How would he test CO_2 gas in the laboratory?

(*Un*) (CBSE 2019)

13. Complete the following reactions.

(*a*) $CH_3COOH + NaOH \longrightarrow$

(*b*) $R_2C=CR_2 + H_2 \xrightarrow{Ni}$

(*c*) $CH_4 + O_2 \longrightarrow$

(*d*) $CH_2=CH_2 + Br_2 \longrightarrow$

(*e*) $CH_3COOC_2H_5 + NaOH \longrightarrow$

(*f*) $CH_2=CH_2 + H_2O \xrightarrow{H_2SO_4}$ **(*Ap*)**

14. Why does micelle formation take place when soap is added to water? Will a micelle be formed in other solvents such as ethanol also? **(*An*) (NCERT)**

Long Answer Type Questions (5 M)

1. (*a*) (*i*) A compound 'A' with a molecular formula of $C_2H_4O_2$ reacts with a base to give salt and water. Identify 'A', state its nature and the name of the functional group it possesses. Write chemical equation for the reaction involved.

(*ii*) When the above stated compound 'A' reacts with another compound 'B' having molecular formula C_2H_6O in the presence of an acid, a sweet smelling compound 'C' is formed. **(*An*)**

(1) Identify 'B' and 'C'.

(2) State the role of acid in this reaction.

(3) Write chemical equation for the reaction involved.

OR

(*b*) (*i*) Name the compound formed when ethanol is heated at 443 K in the presence of conc. H_2SO_4 and draw its electron dot structure. State the role of conc. H_2SO_4 in this reaction.

(*ii*) What is hydrogenation? Explain it with the help of a chemical equation. State the role of this reaction in industry. **(*Un*) (CBSE, 2023)**

2. What is methane? Draw its electron dot structure. Name the type of bonds formed in this compound. Why are such compounds:

(*i*) poor conductors of electricity?

(*ii*) have low melting and boiling points? What happens when this compound burns in oxygen?

(*Un*) (CBSE 2019)

3. (*a*) What is covalent bonding?

(*b*) Define functional group.

(*c*) Give names of the following:

(*i*) An alcohol containing 5-carbon atoms.

(*ii*) An acid with 4-carbon atoms.

(*iii*) Simplest aldehyde. **(*Un*) (CBSE 2020)**

4. Identify the compounds 'P' to 'T' in the following sequence' **(*Ap*)**

(*a*) $CH_3CH_2OH \xrightarrow[\text{Heat}]{KMnO_4/KOH} P + H_2O$

(*b*) $CH_3CH_2OH + P \xrightarrow[\Delta]{Conc.H_2SO_4} Q + H_2O$

(*c*) $Q + NaOH \rightarrow R + CH_3CH_2OH$

(*d*) $P + NaHCO_3 \rightarrow R + S + H_2O$

(*e*) $CH_3CH_2OH + T \rightarrow CH_3CH_2ONa + H_2$

5. A salt 'X' is formed and a gas is evolved when ethanoic acid react with sodium hydrogen carbonate. Name the salt 'X' and the gas evolved. Describe an activity and draw the diagram of the apparatus to prove that the evolved gas is the one which you have named. Also write the chemical equation of the reaction involved. **(*Cr*)**

6. A carbon compound *P* has six carbon atoms and twelve hydrogen atoms.

(*a*) Is *P* a saturated or unsaturated carbon compound. Justify your answer by drawing the structural formula.

(*b*) Describe a test that can be used to determine if compound *P* is saturated or unsaturated.

(*c*) Name the products that are formed on burning compound *P* in an excess of air.

OR

A carbon compound *P* is found to be neutral when tested with red and blue litmus. A gas, that burns with a 'pop' sound, is produced when a metal reacts with carbon compound *P*.

(*a*) Write the chemical equation for the reaction.

(*b*) The carbon compound *P* is heated with concentrated sulphuric acid to produce carbon compound *Q*.

(*i*) Write the chemical equation for the reaction.

(*ii*) Describe the type of flame that *Q* produces on combustion.

(*c*) What is likely to be observed on heating compound *P* with ethanoic acid with an acid as catalyst?

Write the chemical equation for the reaction.

(*An*) (CBSE APQ, 2023)

7. (*a*) Compare soaps and detergents on the basis of their composition and cleansing action in hard water.

(*b*) What happens when ethanol is treated with sodium metal? State the behaviour of ethanol in this reaction.

(*c*) Draw the structure of cyclohexane.

(*d*) Name the following compound

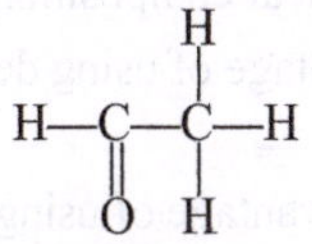

(*Un*) (CBSE 2020)

8. An organic compound 'P' is a constituent of wines. 'P' on reacting with acidified $K_2Cr_2O_7$ forms another compound 'Q'.

When a piece of sodium is added to 'Q', a gas 'R' evolves which burns with a pop sound when a burning matchstick is brought near it.

(*a*) Give the chemical name of compound P.

(*b*) Mention another use of the compound 'P' apart from the use mentioned in the question.

(*c*) Illustrate with the help of chemical equation the conversion of 'P' into 'Q'.

(*d*) Give a balanced equation to depict the reaction of Q with sodium.

(*e*) What happens when 'P' is heated with conc. H_2SO_4 at 443 K, write its chemical equation.

OR

An organic compound 'X' is a liquid at room temperature. It is also a very good solvent and has the molecular formula C_2H_6O. Upon oxidation 'X' gives 'Y'. 'Y' releases a gas 'W' with brisk effervescence on reacting with $NaHCO_3$. X reacts with Y in the presence of conc.H_2SO_4 to give another compound 'Z' which has a pleasant smell. Z.

(*a*) Give the chemical name and chemical formula of Y.

(*b*) How will you test for the gas 'W'?

(*c*) Depict the formation Y and Z using chemical equations.

(*d*) Name the reaction of formation of 'Z'.

(*e*) Give any one use of 'Z'? **(*Un*) (CBSE APQ, 2023)**

9. (*a*) Ethyl propanoate is a colourless compound with a pineapple-like smell. It is present naturally in some fruits such as kiwis and strawberries.

The structural formula of ethyl propanoate is given below.

$$CH_3-CH_2-\underset{\underset{O}{\|}}{C}-O-CH_2-CH_3$$

(*i*) Write the names of the carboxylic acid and the alcohol from which this compound is formed.

(*ii*) Apart from mixing the carboxylic acid and the alcohol, what should be done to form this compound?

(*b*) Bromine water is a reddish solution of bromine (Br_2) in water. When shaken with an unsaturated hydrocarbon, the red colour of the bromine water disappears because the bromine is used up in an addition reaction.

Kohli has three test tubes containing hexane, hexene and hexyne respectively. Which of the three compounds can he identify using the bromine water test? Give a reason for your answer. **(*Ap*) (CFPQ)**

Case Based Questions

Case Based-I: Carbon is a versatile element that forms the basis of all living organisms and many of the things we use. A large variety of compounds is formed because of its tetravalency. Compounds of carbon are formed with oxygen, hydrogen, nitrogen, sulphur, chlorine and many other elements.

Answer the following questions : **(*Un*) (CBSE 2024)**

(*i*) What are hydrocarbons? *(1 M)*

(*ii*) List two properties by virtue of which carbon can form a large number of compounds. *(1 M)*

(*iii*) Write the formula of the functional group present in (1) aldehydes, and (2) ketones. Write chemical equation for the reaction that occurs between ethanoic acid and ethanol in the presence of a catalyst. *(2 M)*

OR

What are structural isomers? Write the structures of two isomers of butane (C_4H_{10}). *(2 M)*

Case Based-II: Given below is a four carbon skeleton of a hydrocarbon compound. **(*Ap*) (CBSE APQ, 2023)**

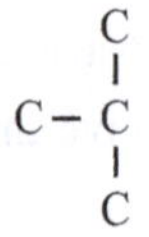

(*i*) Fill in the hydrogen atoms/bonds to form: *(2 M)*

(*a*) a saturated hydrocarbon

(*b*) an unsaturated hydrocarbon

(*ii*) If the four-carbon skeleton is of a straight chained alkene, draw the structures of all the possible compounds. *(2 M)*

OR

If the four-carbon skeleton is of a straight chained alkyne:

(*a*) How many carbon atoms may NOT be bonded to any hydrogen atoms? *(1 M)*

(*b*) How many hydrogen atoms will there be in the compound? *(1 M)*

Case Based-III: The table given below shows the hints given by the quiz master in a quiz. **(*An*) (CBSE SQP, 2023)**

S.No.	HINT
(*i*)	Substance 'C' is used as a preservative.
(*ii*)	'C' has two carbon atoms; 'C' is obtained by the reaction of 'A' in presence of alkaline Potassium permanganate followed by acidification.
(*iii*)	Misuse of 'A' in industries is prevented by adding Methanol, Benzene, and pyridine to 'A'.
(*iv*)	'F' is formed on heating 'A' in presence of conc Sulphuric acid.
(*v*)	'F' reacts with Hydrogen gas in presence of Nickel and Palladium catalyst.

Based on the above hints answer the following questions

(*i*) Give the IUPAC names of A and F *(2 M)*

(*ii*) Illustrate with the help of chemical equations the changes taking place. (A $\rightarrow$ C and A $\rightarrow$ F) *(2 M)*

OR

Name the chemical reactions which occur in steps 2 and 5. Identify the compounds formed in these steps if 'A' is replaced with its next homologue. *(2 M)*

Case Based-IV: Ethanoic acid is commonly called acetic acid and belongs to a group of acids called carboxylic acids. 5-8% solution of acetic acid in water is called vinegar and is used widely as a preservative in pickles. The melting point of pure ethanoic acid is 290 K and hence it often freezes during winter in cold climates. This gave rise to its name glacial acetic acid.

The group of organic compounds called carboxylic acids are obviously characterised by their acidic nature. However, unlike mineral acids like HCl which are completely ionised, carboxylic acids are weak acids. **(*Re*)**

On the basis of above paragraph, answer the following questions.

(*i*) (*a*) What is glacial acetic acid? Write the chemical formula? *(1 M)*

(*b*) Write the complete reaction when ethanoic acid reacts with sodium hydroxide. *(1 M)*

(*ii*) (*a*) What is the melting point of acetic acid and glacial acetic acid in degree celsius? *(1 M)*

(*b*) Write the reaction when ethanoic acid reacts with sodium hydrogen carbonate. *(1 M)*

OR

What is the difference between mineral acid and carboxylic acid? Write the involvement of both with the help of different chemical reactions. *(2 M)*

Case Based-V: Soaps and detergents are household products used for cleaning purposes. Soaps are made from natural ingredients and have a low environmental impact, but are not effective in hard water. Detergents are synthetic compounds, more effective than soaps in removing tough stains, but not biodegradable and can have a negative impact on the environment. Choose the product that best suits your needs while minimizing harm to the environment. **(*Re*)**

(*i*) What is the chemical composition of soap? *(1 M)*

(*ii*) What is the chemical composition of detergent? *(1 M)*

(*iii*) What is the advantage of using detergents over soaps? *(1 M)*

(*iv*) What is the disadvantage of using detergents? *(1 M)*

ANSWER KEYS

Multiple Choice Questions

1. (c)	**2.** (d)	**3.** (b)	**4.** (b)	**5.** (b)	**6.** (c)	**7.** (b)	**8.** (b)	**9.** (a)	**10.** (b)
11. (b)	**12.** (b)	**13.** (b)	**14.** (c)	**15.** (d)	**16.** (a)	**17.** (b)	**18.** (d)	**19.** (b)	**20.** (b)
21. (c)	**22.** (c)	**23.** (c)	**24.** (d)	**25.** (a)	**26.** (c)				

Assertion and Reason

1. (b)	**2.** (a)	**3.** (c)	**4.** (b)	**5.** (a)	**6.** (d)	**7.** (c)	**8.** (d)	**9.** (d)	**10.** (b)

HINTS & EXPLANATIONS

Multiple Choice Questions

1. (c) Option (c) is the correct representation of the electron dot structure of the water molecule.

2. (d) All the given factors are responsible for the huge *number of carbon compounds*

3. (b) CO_2 molecule can be represented as $O=C=O$. Hence, it contains double covalent bonds.

4. (b) $C_2H_4 + H_2 \rightarrow C_2H_6$

$C_2H_2 + 2H_2 \rightarrow C_2H_6$

Ethene (C_2H_4) will become ethane (C_2H_6) after the addition of 1 mole of hydrogen (H_2), while ethyne (C_2H_2) will require 2 moles of hydrogen to become ethane, undergoing two successive addition reactions.

Therefore, the correct answer is (b) only Q.

5. (b) Camphor and naphthalene are both likely to produce a yellow, sooty flame. Ethanol typically burns with a blue flame, indicating a cleaner combustion with less soot production.

6. (c) *Diamond does not conduct electricity. Hence it is a* poor conductor of electricity.

7. (b) In a diamond, each carbon atom is bonded to four other carbon atoms, forming a rigid three-dimensional tetrahedral structure.

8. (b) Benzene contains the presence of double bonds. Hence it is not a saturated compound.

9. (a) Mineral acids are completely ionized whereas carboxylic acids are partially ionized. Hence mineral acids are stronger than carboxylic acids.

10. (b) Dehydration: Ethanol is first dehydrated to form ethene (C_2H_4). This involves the removal of water (H_2O) from ethanol.

$$CH_3-CH_2OH \xrightarrow[H_2SO_4]{\text{Hot Conc.}} CH_2=CH_2+H_2O$$

Addition of H_2: Ethene is then reduced to ethane. This reduction is commonly carried out using hydrogen gas (H_2) in the presence of a catalyst such as nickel (Ni).

$$C_2H_4+H_2 \xrightarrow{Ni} C_2H_6$$

11. (b) They have the same general formula.

The given compounds contain only C – H and C – C single bonds and therefore, the given compounds belong to alkane series, whose general formula is C_nH_{2n+2}.

12. (b) The structure of ethane is:

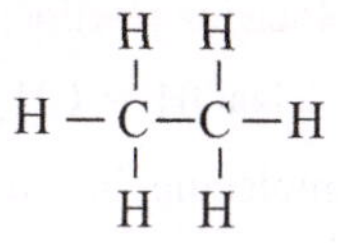

No. of covalent bonds between carbon and hydrogen atoms = 6

No. of covalent bond between carbon and carbon atom = 1

Total number of covalent bonds in ethane = 7

13. (b) In the given compound, ester(–COOR) and carboxylic acid (–COOH) groups are present.

14. (c) The given structure corresponds to propanoic acid.

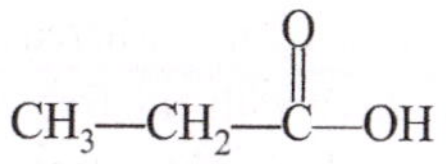

(Propanoic acid)

15. (d) Butane, 2-Methyl Butane, and 2,3-dimethyl Butane, all of them have the difference of $-CH_2$ unit and belong to the same general formula that of alkanes. Hence, they form a homologous series.

16. (a) $CH_2=CH_2+Br_2(aq) \rightarrow Br-CH_2-CH_2-Br$

(1,2-Dibromoethane)

17. (*b*)

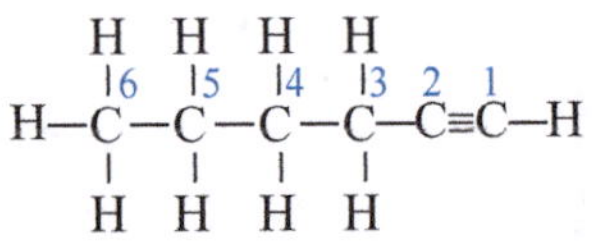

IUPAC Name: Hex-1-yne

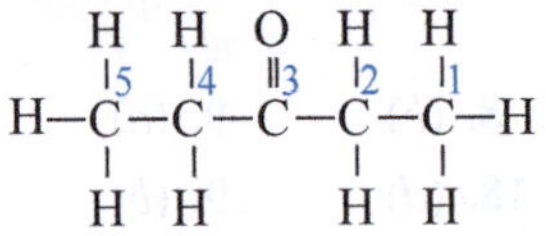

IUPAC Name: Pentan-3-one

18. (*d*) 2-methylpropane

19. (*b*) $HC \equiv CH \xrightarrow[+H_2]{Pd} CH_2 = CH_2$ (Ethene)

$$CH_3 - CH_2OH \xrightarrow[H_2SO_4]{\text{Hot Conc.}} CH_2 = CH_2 + H_2O$$

20. (*b*) While cooking, if the bottom of the vessel is getting blackened on the outside, it means that the fuel is not burning completely. Sometimes, due to lack of oxygen, the fuel does not burn completely. When the fuel does not burn completely, a sooty flame appears, which makes the bottom of the utensil black.

21. (*c*) This reaction is an example of addition reactions.

22. (*c*) $CH_4 + Cl_2 \xrightarrow{hv} CH_3Cl + HCl$

Those reactions in which one atom or group of atoms of a compound is replaced by some other atom or group of atoms, is known as substitution reaction.

23. (*c*) $C_2H_5OH + CH_3COOH \xrightarrow{H^+} CH_3COOC_2H_5 + H_2O$

24. (*d*) Esters when treated with alkalis such as NaOH, gives alcohol and sodium salt of carboxylic acid. This reaction is known as saponification reaction.

$$CH_3COOC_2H_5 + NaOH \rightarrow CH_3COONa + C_2H_5OH$$

25. (*a*) The soap molecule has a hydrophilic head and a hydrophobic tail.

26. (*c*) Detergent forms lather with hard and soft water both, while soap forms lather with soft water only.

Assertion and Reason

1. (*b*) Chemically, graphite is more reactive than diamond. This assertion is correct because carbon atoms in diamond are sp^3 hybridised with no free electrons, whereas carbon atoms in graphite are sp^2 hybridised with one free electron. Hence, Graphite is more reactive due to free electrons.

2. (*a*) For third member, n = 3

Putting 3 in general formula of alkanes, we get the chemical formula of propane as C_3H_{10}.

3. (*c*) Assertion is True but reason is False

For the compounds belonging to homologous series, the difference between the molecular masses of the two consecutive members is 14u and not 144u.

4. (*b*) Esterification is the reaction of carboxylic acid with alcohol to produce the sweet-smelling chemical ester.

When an ester interacts with sodium hydroxide, it produces an alcohol as well as the sodium salt of carboxylic acid. This is referred to as ester hydrolysis. This alkaline hydrolysis of ester is called saponification.

Hence, Both Assertion and Reason are true but reason is not the correct explanation of Assertion.

5. (*a*) According to the locant rule, the numbering of the parent chain occurs from that direction which gives the lowest sum of the carbon positioned with double, triple or any functional group.

Thus, pent-3-en-1-yne is the correct IUPAC name.

6. (*d*) Assertions is false because ethanol does not turn blue litmus red but it does react with Na to evolve H_2 gas.

7. (c) In esterification reaction, carboxylic acid and alcohol reacts in the presence of acid to give ester.

On treating esters with sodium hydroxide, which is an alkali, the ester is converted back to alcohol and sodium salt of carboxylic acid. This reaction is known as saponification. Hence, saponification is the reverse of esterification, not same .

8. (*d*) The combustion of hydrocarbons produces carbon dioxide and water. The hydrocarbons when burnt in the presence of oxygen, undergo a chemical reaction where the carbon in the hydrocarbons reacts with oxygen to form carbon dioxide (CO_2), and the hydrogen reacts with oxygen to form water (H_2O).

9. (*d*) Assertion is false but Reason is true as vegetable oils are healthier than animal fats.

10. (*b*) Soaps contain unbranched hydrocarbon chain which are easily degraded by bacteria.

Subjective Questions

Very Short Answer Type Questions

1. Covalent compounds are formed by the sharing of electrons between atoms. *(1 M)*

They are different from ionic compounds as they are formed by the complete transfer of electrons from metals to non-metals. *(1 M)*

2. (*a*) The valency of carbon is four. *(½ M)*

Carbon shares its four valence electrons with other atoms and forms four single covalent bonds to complete its octet thereby showing tetravalent nature. *(½ M)*

(*b*)

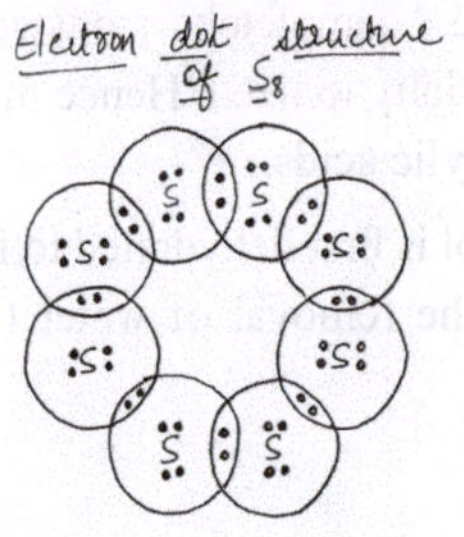

(1 M)

3. (a) (i) Bromopentane

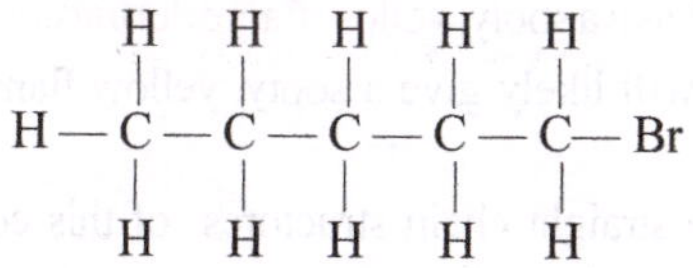

(½ M)

(ii) Butanone

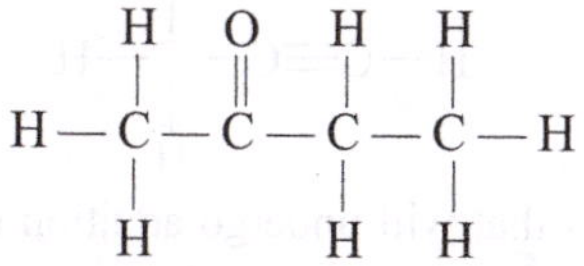

(½ M)

(b) (i) In HCHO, there is only 1 carbon atom, and there is also an aldehyde group (-CHO) present; hence, its name is methanal. (½ M)

(ii) In this compound, there are 6 carbon atoms and one triple bond; hence, its name is Hex-1-yne. (½ M)

4. (a) Saturated hydrocarbons are compounds in which the valency of carbon is satisfied by single bonds only. (½ M)

Some examples of saturated hydrocarbons are methane, ethane, propane etc. (½ M)

(b) $C_{11}H_{20}$ (1 M)

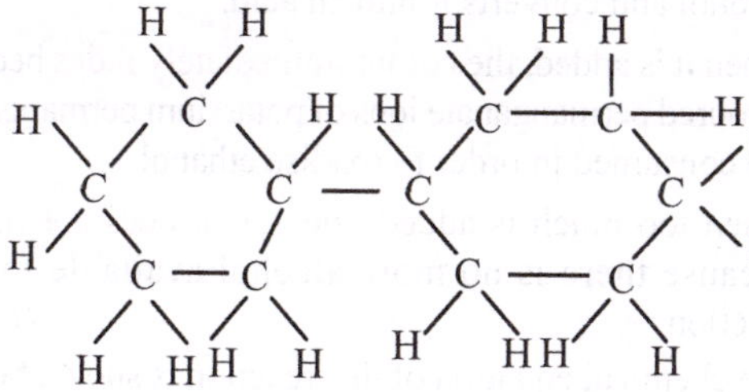

5. (a) The white curdy precipitate is likely to form in Test Tube (B) which contains hard water and soap solution. (1 M)

(b) When greasy dirt or oil is mixed with soapy water, the soap molecules arrange themselves into tiny clusters called micelles. (1 M)

6. **Conclusion:**

1. Low melting and boiling point shows that carbon compounds have weak intermolecular forces of attraction. (1 M)

2. Since they don't conduct electricity, this shows they do not have any free ions and they form covalent bonds. (1 M)

Topper Explanation

22 (1) The intermolecular forces of attraction between carbon compounds is weak. Due to this, they have low melting & boiling point.

(2) The carbon compounds do not contain ions and they form covalent bonds. As they don't conduct electricity.

7. (a) The product "P" formed in the reaction is an ester. (½ M)

(b) When the ester (product "P") reacts with a base, it undergoes a reaction called saponification, resulting in the formation of the original alcohol and the sodium salt of the carboxylic acid. (½ M)

For example:

$CH_3COOCH_2CH_3 + NaOH \rightarrow$

(P) $\quad CH_3CH_2OH + CH_3COONa$ (1 M)

8. (a) Saturated hydrocarbons burn with a clean blue flame and unsaturated hydrocarbons burn with a sooty flame. (½ M)

The given compound is saturated with a high percentage of hydrogen. (½ M)

(b) Methanol, even in trace amounts, can be fatal. In the liver, methanol is converted to methanal. Methanol can potentially damage the visual nerve, resulting in blindness. (1 M)

9. (a) Methane (CH_4) (1 M)

(b) Ethanol (C_2H_5OH) is the compound. Ethanol is utilised as a fuel in some regions because it is cleaner, producing just carbon dioxide and water when burned in sufficient air. (1 M)

10. (a) Hydrophobic end is insoluble in water. (1 M)

(b) When soap is applied in hard water, the Ca^{2+} and Mg^{2+} ions present in hard water react with soap to form white insoluble precipitate. This insoluble precipitate is known as scum. (1 M)

Short Answer Type Questions

1. Carbon(C) is the first element belonging to group 14. Carbon has the unique ability to form bonds with other atoms of carbon, giving rise to large molecules. This property is called catenation. This property can be explained on the basis that carbon has smaller nuclei which enable it to hold a shared pair of electrons tightly. (1 M)

Other members of this group do not form large number of compounds because of greater atomic size. As the size of the atom increases, the hold of the nucleus on the shared electrons decreases, therefore, the bond formed is not stable and strong. Hence, they are not able to form a large number of compounds as carbon does. (2 M)

2. (a) When one H atom of C_2H_6 is replaced with the -OH group, then,

The chemical formula of the compound formed : C_2H_5OH or C_2H_6O (½ M)

Name of the compound formed : Ethanol (½ M)

(b) When one H-atom of C_2H_6 is replaced with the -CHO group, then the chemical formula of the compound formed: C_2H_5CHO or C_3H_6O (½ M)

Name of the compound formed : Propanal (½ M)

(c) When one H-atom of C_2H_6 is replaced with the -COOH group, then

The chemical formula of the compound formed:

C_2H_5COOH or $C_3H_6O_2$ (½ M)

Name of the compound formed: Propanoic acid (½ M)

3. (*a*) Q and S, will have similar chemical properties (½ M)

They have the same functional group. (1 M)

(*b*) None of them are likely to have the same boiling point. (½ M)

Since they are all different chemical substances. (1 M)

4. (*a*) The functional group present in the compounds are–

(*i*) Ketone (½ M)

(*ii*) Carboxylic acid (½ M)

(*iii*) Aldehyde (½ M)

(*iv*) Alcohol (½ M)

(*b*) As soap is basic in nature it will turn red litmus blue. However, the colour of blue litmus will remain blue. (1 M)

Key Takeaways

This teaches students the following concept

Alcohol	Suffix - ol	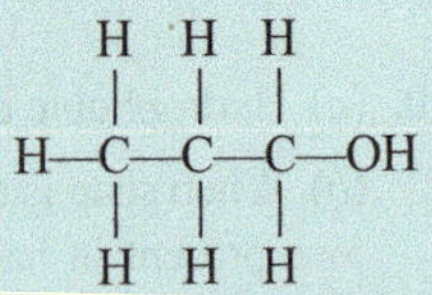
Aldehyde	Suffix - al	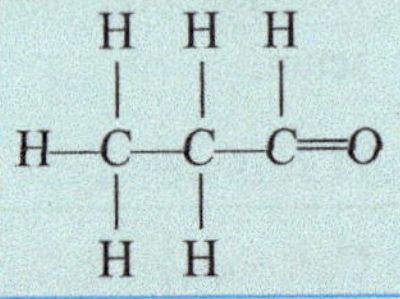
Ketone	Suffix - one	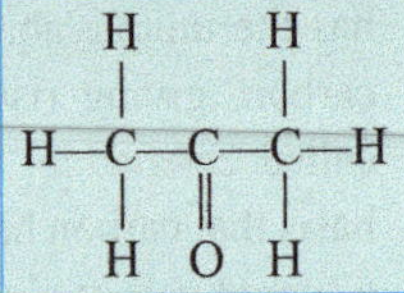
Carboxylic acid	Suffix - oic acid	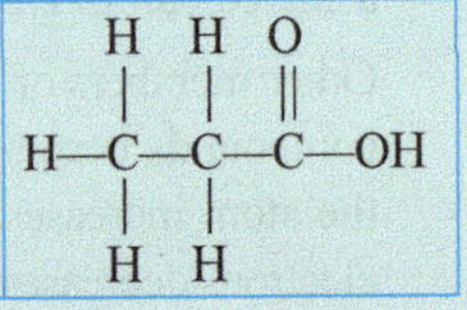

5. (*a*) When one or more compounds have the same molecular formula but different structures, then those compounds are known as isomers. (1 M)

(*b*) CH_3COCH_3 and CH_3CH_2CHO are functional isomers which have same molecular formula but different functional groups attached

CH_3COCH_3 - Propanone (½ M)

CH_3CH_2CHO - Propanal (½ M)

(*c*) (*i*) $\underset{\text{Ethanol}}{CH_3CH_2OH} \xrightarrow[160-170°C]{conc.H_2SO_4} \underset{\text{Ethene}}{CH_2=CH_2} + \underset{\text{Water}}{H_2O}$ (½ M)

(*ii*) $\underset{\text{Propanol}}{CH_3-CH_2-CH_2-OH} \xrightarrow[\text{Heat}]{\text{alkaline } KMnO_4}$

$\underset{\text{Propanoic acid}}{CH_3-CH_2-\overset{\overset{O}{\|}}{C}-OH}$ (½ M)

6. (*a*) In general, unsaturated hydrocarbons (like alkenes and alkynes) tend to have a sooty, yellow flame during combustion. The compound will likely give a sooty, yellow flame during combustion. (1 M)

(*b*) The possible straight chain structures of this compound are:

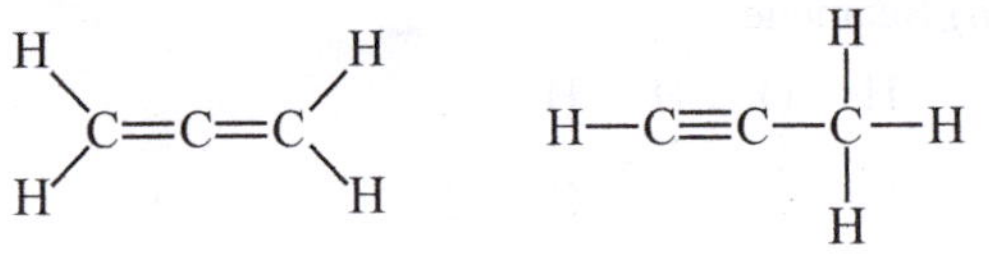

(2 M)

7. (*a*) The hydrocarbons that will undergo addition reactions from the given list are:

C_3H_6 (propene): Contains a double bond. (1 M)

C_2H_2 (acetylene): Contains a triple bond. (1 M)

(*b*) Animal fats predominantly contain saturated fatty acids. (1 M)

8. (*i*) Preparation of 5% Potassium permanganate : 5% solution of $KMnO_4$ is prepared by dissolving 5 grams of $KMnO_4$ in 100 mL of water. (½ M)

(*ii*) Role of alkaline potassium permanganate:

1. Alkaline potassium permanganate acts as a strong oxidising agent in this reaction since it adds oxygen to alcohol and converts it into an acid.
2. When it is added, the colour immediately fades because coloured permanganate ions of potassium permanganate are consumed in order to oxidise ethanol.
3. When too much is added, the colour does not change because there is no more alcohol available for the reaction. (1½ M)

(*iii*) The chemical equation of this reaction is shown below:

$\underset{\text{Ethanol}}{C_2H_5OH} \xrightarrow{\text{alk } KMnO_4 + \text{heat}} \underset{\text{Ethanoic acid}}{CH_3COOH}$ (1 M)

9.
- Two different forms of carbon -diamond and graphite have different structures. These are known as allotropes of carbon. The carbon-carbon bonding in both the cases varies. (½ M)
- In diamond, each carbon atom is bonded to four other carbon atoms in a tetrahedral fashion with strong covalent bonding forming a rigid three-dimensional structure. Hence, it is hard in nature. (½ M)
- In graphite, each carbon atom is bonded to three other carbon atoms in the same plane giving a hexagonal array being placed in layers one above the other. Due to the presence of weak forces between the atoms, the layer of graphite may slip past one another. Hence, graphite is smooth and slippery in nature. (1 M)

These structures are given as,

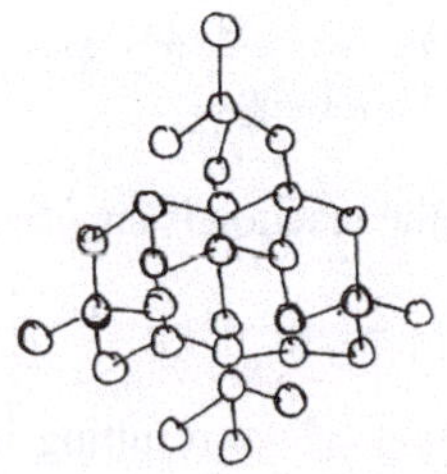

Structure of diamond

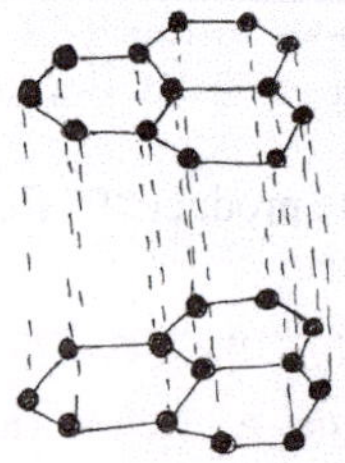

Structure of graphite

(½ M)

These two different structures result in diamond and graphite having very different physical properties even though their chemical properties are the same. *(½ M)*

10. Esterification is a process in which alcohol and carboxylic acid react together in the presence of an acid catalyst to give an ester. The reaction is shown below:

$$\underset{\text{Ethanoic Acid}}{CH_3COOH} + \underset{\text{Ethanol}}{CH_3CH_2OH} \xrightarrow{\text{Conc. } H_2SO_4} \underset{\text{Ethylethanoate}}{CH_3COOC_2H_5} + H_2O$$ *(1½ M)*

Saponification is the process, in which an ester reacts with sodium hydroxide to give sodium salt of acid and alcohol. The reaction is shown below:

$$\underset{\text{Ethyl ethanoate}}{CH_3COOC_2H_5} + \underset{\text{Sodium Hydroxide}}{NaOH} \xrightarrow{\text{Heat}} \underset{\text{Sodium ethanoate}}{CH_3COONa} + \underset{\text{Ethanol}}{C_2H_5OH}$$

(1½ M)

Mistakes 101 : What not to do!

- Students might forget to include the acid catalyst in the equation of esterification reaction.
- Students may mistakenly write incorrect names of the reactants involved and products formed in the reaction.

11. (*a*) Carboxylic acid is ethanoic acid *(½ M)*

(*b*) Alcohol is ethanol *(½ M)*

(*c*) X is ethyl ethanoate *(½ M)*

$$\underset{\text{Ethanoic acid}}{CH_3-COOH} + \underset{\text{Ethanol}}{C_2H_5OH} \xrightarrow{H_2SO_4} \underset{\text{Ethyl ethanoate}}{CH_3-COOC_2H_5} + H_2O$$

(1½ M)

12. (*i*) He must add sodium carbonate (Na_2CO_3) or sodium hydrogen carbonate ($NaHCO_3$) to produce carbon dioxide. *(1 M)*

(*ii*) $CH_3COOH + NaHCO_3 \rightarrow CH_3COONa + H_2O + CO_2\uparrow$ *(1 M)*

OR

$2CH_3COOH + Na_2CO_3 \rightarrow 2CH_3COONa + H_2O + CO_2\uparrow$

(*iii*) He would test CO_2 gas by passing the gas through "lime water," which is a diluted solution of calcium hydroxide.

The lime water turns milky when CO_2 gas is passed through it due to the formation of $CaCO_3$. *(½ M)*

$Ca(OH)_2(aq.) + CO_2(g) \rightarrow CaCO_3(s) + H_2O(aq.)$ *(½ M)*

13. (*a*) $CH_3COOH + NaOH \longrightarrow CH_3COO^{\ominus}Na^{\oplus} + H_2O$ *(½ M)*

(*b*) $R_2C=CR_2 + H_2 \xrightarrow{Ni} R_2CH-CHR_2$ *(½ M)*

(*c*) $CH_4 + O_2 \longrightarrow CO_2 + H_2O + \text{heat and light}$ *(½ M)*

(*d*) $CH_2=CH_2 + Br_2 \longrightarrow \underset{Br}{CH_2}-\underset{Br}{CH_2}$ *(½ M)*

(*e*) $CH_3COOC_2H_5 + NaOH \longrightarrow CH_3COONa + C_2H_5OH$ *(½ M)*

(*f*) $CH_2=CH_2 + H_2O \xrightarrow{H_2SO_4} CH_3CH_2OH$ *(½ M)*

14. Micelle formation takes place when soap is added to water, this is because the large number of molecular ions of soaps get accumulated and form a colloidal solution. Soap consists of the hydrophobic tail (hydrocarbon), which does not dissolve in water and hydrophilic part (ionic end) which dissolves in water. *(1½ M)*

Micelles are formed when the hydrocarbon chains come together and faces inwards and the polar ends are projected outwards. *(½ M)*

In less polar solvent like ethanol, micelle formation does not take place because the hydrocarbon chain of the soap will get dissolved in ethanol. *(1 M)*

Long Answer Type Questions

1. (*a*) (*i*) A is acetic acid (CH_3COOH). *(½ M)*

It is acidic in nature. *(½ M)*

Carboxylic group (-COOH) is present in it. *(½ M)*

$CH_3COOH + MOH \rightarrow CH_3COOM + H_2O$ *(1 M)*

Where M is any metal

(*ii*) (1) B is ethanol (C_2H_5OH) *(½ M)*

C is ester that is ethyl acetate ($C_4H_8O_2$) *(½ M)*

(2) Acid acts as a catalyst in this reaction to speed up the reaction. *(½ M)*

(3)
$$\underset{\text{(Ethanoic acid)}}{CH_3-COOH} + \underset{\text{(Ethanol)}}{CH_3-CH_2OH} \xrightarrow{\text{Conc.}H_2SO_4} CH_3-\underset{\underset{O}{\|}}{C}-O-CH_2-CH_3 + H_2O$$ *(1M)*

OR

(*b*) (*i*) The compound formed when ethanol is heated at 443K in the presence of conc. H_2SO_4 is ethene. *(½ M)*

$CH_3-CH_2OH \xrightarrow[H_2SO_4]{\text{Hot Conc.}} CH_2=CH_2 + H_2O$ *(½ M)*

Its electron dot structure -

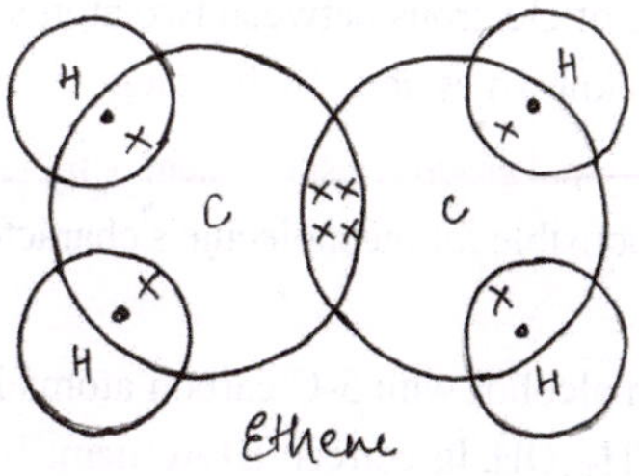

(1 M)

The role of concentrated sulphuric acid in this reaction is of dehydrating agent which removes water from ethanol. *(½ M)*

(*ii*) Hydrogenation is the process of addition of hydrogen to unsaturated hydrocarbons in the presence of catalysts such as palladium or nickel to give saturated hydrocarbons. *(1 M)*

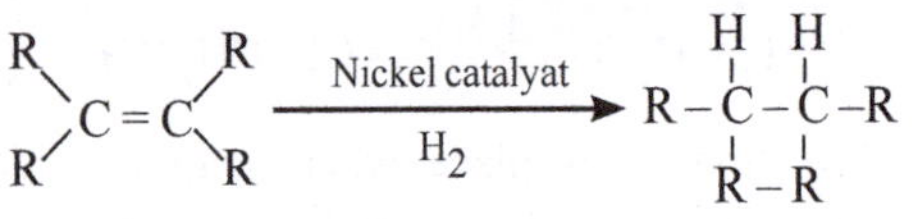

(½ M)

This reaction is commonly used in the hydrogenation of vegetable oils in the food industry.

It is used to convert unsaturated fatty acids in vegetable oils into saturated fats (ghee), which improves the texture, stability, and shelf life of food products. *(1 M)*

2. Methane (CH_4), the major component of natural gas, is a colourless, odourless, and extremely combustible gas. *(½ M)*

The electron dot structure of methane is-

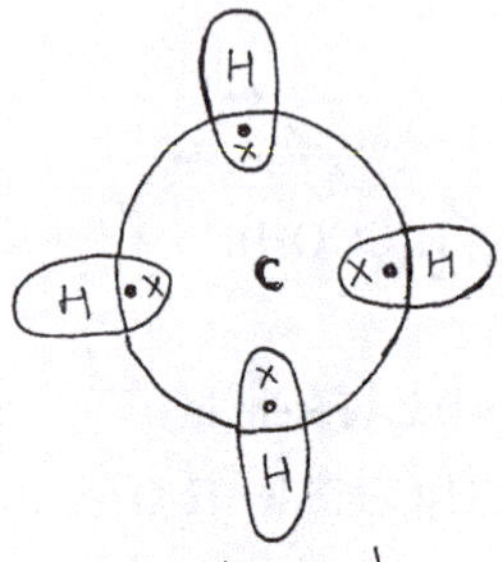

(Methane)

(1 M)

Covalent bonds exist between four hydrogen atoms and a single carbon atom in the molecule's core. *(½ M)*

(*i*) Methane is a poor conductor of electricity because all bonds in methane are covalent bonds, and thus no free electrons are present in the molecule to assist the conduction of electricity. *(1 M)*

(*ii*) Covalent compounds have low intermolecular forces of attraction, resulting in low melting and boiling points. Because methane is also a covalent molecule, it has an extremely low melting and boiling point. *(1 M)*

When methane is burned in the presence of oxygen, it produces CO_2 and water as a by product. The reaction takes place as

$CH_4 + 2O_2 \longrightarrow CO_2 + 2H_2O$ *(1 M)*

3. (*a*) A covalent bond consists of the mutual sharing of one or more pairs of electrons between two atoms. Such a type of bonding is known as covalent bonding. *(1 M)*

(*b*) A functional group is a substituent or moiety in a molecule that is responsible for the molecule's characteristic chemical reactions. *(1 M)*

(*c*) (*i*) An alcohol with 5-C carbon atoms is $CH_3CH_2CH_2CH_2CH_2$–OH. Its correct IUPAC name is pentanol. *(1 M)*

(*ii*) Butanoic acid ($CH_3CH_2CH_2COOH$). *(1 M)*

(*iii*) The simplest aldehyde is formaldehyde with the molecular formula of HCHO. *(1 M)*

4. (*a*) $CH_3CH_2OH \xrightarrow[\text{heat}]{KMnO_4/KOH} \underset{\text{'P'}}{CH_3COOH} + H_2O$ *(1 M)*

(*b*) $CH_3CH_2OH + \underset{\text{'P'}}{CH_3COOH} \xrightarrow[\Delta]{\text{Conc.}H_2SO_4} \underset{\text{'Q'}}{CH_3COOCH_2CH_3} + H_2O$ *(1 M)*

(*c*) $\underset{\text{'Q'}}{CH_3COOCH_2CH_3} + NaOH \longrightarrow \underset{\text{'R'}}{CH_3COONa} + CH_3CH_2OH$ *(1 M)*

(*d*) $\underset{\text{'P'}}{CH_3COOH} + NaHCO_3 \rightarrow \underset{\text{'R'}}{CH_3COONa} + \underset{\text{'S}}{CO_2\uparrow} + H_2O$ *(1 M)*

(*e*) $2CH_3CH_2OH + \underset{\text{'T'}}{2Na} \longrightarrow 2CH_3CH_2ONa + H_2\uparrow$ *(1 M)*

Hence, 'P' is CH_3COOH, 'Q' is $CH_3COOCH_2CH_3$, 'R' is CH_3COONa, 'S' is CO_2, and 'T' is Na (Sodium metal)

5. $CH_3COOH + NaHCO_3 \longrightarrow \underset{\text{'X'}}{CH_3COONa} + H_2O + CO_2\uparrow$

The salt 'X' is sodium ethanoate. The gas evolved is CO_2. *(1 M)*

Pass the gas through lime water. It will turn milky. It shows that gas evolved is CO_2.

$Ca(OH)_2 + CO_2 \longrightarrow CaCO_3 + H_2O$ *(½ M)*

Aim: To demonstrate the reaction of carboxylic acid with sodium hydrogencarbonate.

Materials Required: Ethanoic acid, sodium hydrogen-carbonate, lime water.

Procedure:

1. Set the apparatus as shown in diagram.
2. Take 1 g of $NaHCO_3$ and add 2 mL of ethanoic acid into it.
3. Pass the gas formed through lime water and note down the observations. *(1 M)*

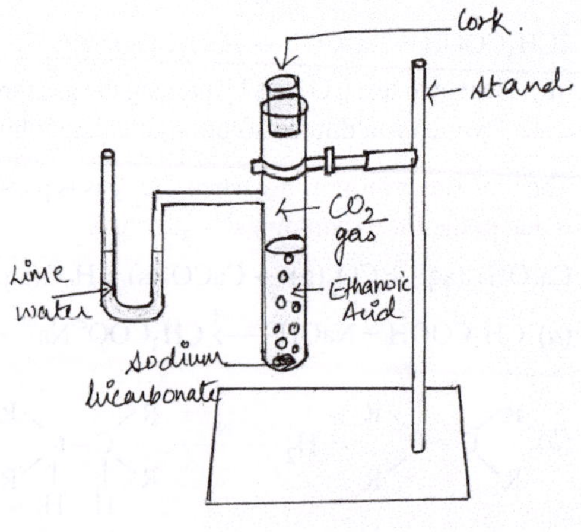

Observation: Brisk effervescence due to carbon dioxide formed which turns lime water milky.

Conclusion: Carboxylic acid reacts with sodium hydrogencarbonate to liberate CO_2 gas which turns lime water milky. *(½ M)*

Chemical Reaction:

$$CH_3COOH(l) + NaHCO_3 \longrightarrow CH_3COONa(aq) + H_2O(l) + CO_2\uparrow(g) \quad (1\ M)$$

$$\underset{\text{Lime water}}{Ca(OH)_2(aq)} + CO_2(g) \longrightarrow \underset{\text{(White ppt.)}}{CaCO_3(s)} + H_2O(l) \quad (1\ M)$$

Nailing the Right Answer

To ensure full credit student should include balanced chemical equations. Describe the procedure step by step: Outline the experimental steps in a clear and logical order, as you would perform them. Mention materials required for the experiment, observation and conclusion clearly. Include a well-labelled diagram: Draw the experimental setup accurately and label all parts clearly.

6. (*a*) Compound P may be either saturated or unsaturated. *(1 M)*

- Saturated compound: cyclohexane *(1 M)*

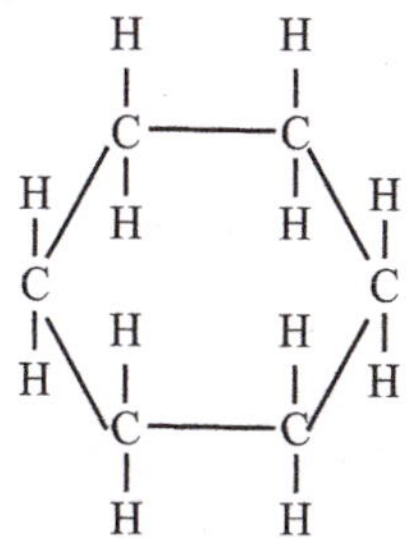

- Unsaturated compound: 2-hexene *(1 M)*

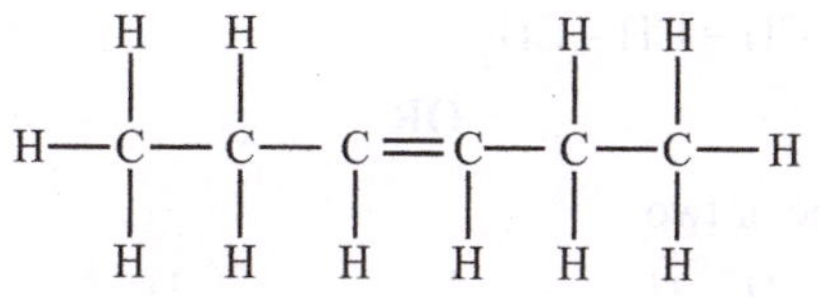

(*b*) Burning the compound in an excess of air will produce a sooty flame if it is unsaturated and a clean flame if it is saturated *(1 M)*

(*c*) The products formed are Carbon dioxide and Water. *(1 M)*

OR

(*a*) $2Na + 2CH_3 - CH_2OH \rightarrow 2CH_3 - CH_2O^- Na^+ + H_2\uparrow$ *(1 M)*

(*b*) (*i*) $CH_3 - CH_2OH \xrightarrow{\text{hot conc. } H_2SO_4} CH_2 = CH_2 + H_2O$ *(1 M)*

(*ii*) Compound ***Q*** (ethylene) burns with a yellow flame with black smoke. *(1 M)*

(*c*) A compound with a fruity smell i.e., ester will be produced. *(1 M)*

$$CH_3COOH + CH_3CH_2OH \xrightarrow{\text{Conc. } H_2SO_4} CH_3\,COOCH_2CH_3 + H_2O$$ *(1 M)*

7. (*a*)

Properties	Soaps	Detergents
Composition	Soaps are sodium or potassium salts of long chain fatty acid/carboxylic acids	Detergents are generally sodium salts of sulphonic acids or ammonium salts with chlorides or bromides ions
Cleansing action in hard water	Soaps are unable to work in hard water because the Ca^{2+} and Mg^{2+} ions present in hard water react with soap to form a white sticky substance called scum.	They work well in both hard and soft water.

(2 M)

(*b*) Ethanol reacts with sodium metal to produce sodium ethoxide and hydrogen gas. This salt is colourless and soluble in water. The reaction takes place as:

$$2Na + \underset{\text{Ethanol}}{2CH_3CH_2OH} \rightarrow \underset{\text{Sodium ethoxide}}{2CH_3CH_2ONa} + H_2 \quad (½\ M)$$

In this reaction, ethanol behaves like an acid. *(½ M)*

(*c*) 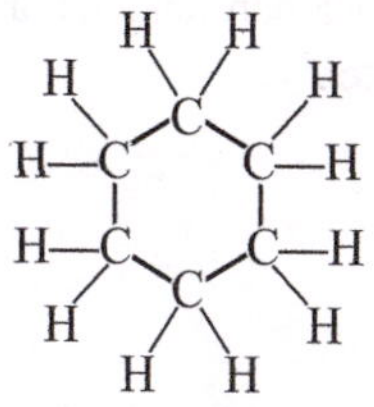 *(1 M)*

Cyclohexane

(*d*) The name of the given compound is Ethanal. *(1 M)*

8. (*a*) The chemical name of compound P is ethyl alcohol/ethanol. *(1 M)*

(*b*) Other uses of ethanol are

- Industrial solvent
- Ingredient of cough syrup
- Homeopathic medicine
- Lab reagent *(1 M)*

(*c*) $\underset{(P)}{C_2H_5OH} \xrightarrow{\text{Acidified } K_2Cr_2O_7} \underset{(Q)}{CH_3COOH}$ *(1 M)*

(*d*) $2Na + \underset{(Q)}{2CH_3COOH} \rightarrow \underset{(R)}{2CH_3COONa} + H_2\uparrow$ *(1 M)*

(*e*) Dehydration of ethanol occurs, when ethanol is heated with Conc. H_2SO_4

$$\underset{(P)}{C_2H_5OH} \xrightarrow{\text{conc.}H_2SO_4} C_2H_4 + H_2O$$ *(1 M)*

OR

(*a*) Ethanoic acid, Y = $CH_3—COOH$ *(½+½ M)*

(*b*) The gas evolved 'W' is CO_2 which will turn lime water milky. *(1 M)*

(*c*) $\underset{(X)}{C_2H_5OH} + \text{Acid}.K_2Cr_2O_7 \longrightarrow \underset{(Y)}{CH_3COOH}$ *(1 M)*

$$\underset{(X)}{C_2H_5OH} + \underset{(Y)}{CH_3COOH} \xrightarrow{\text{Acid}} \underset{(Z)}{CH_3COOC_2H_5} + H_2O$$ *(1 M)*

(*d*) Esterification reaction *(½ M)*

(*e*) Ester is used in making perfumes or cosmetics. *(½ M)*

9. (*a*) (*i*) Ethyl propanoate is an ester, and it is formed by the reaction of propanoic acid (a carboxylic acid) with ethanol (an alcohol).

- Carboxylic acid: Propanoic acid (CH_3CH_2COOH) *(1 M)*
- Alcohol: Ethanol (CH_3CH_2OH) *(1 M)*

(*ii*) To form ethyl propanoate (an ester) from propanoic acid and ethanol, an acid catalyst is needed, typically concentrated sulphuric acid (H_2SO_4). *(1 M)*

So, apart from mixing the carboxylic acid and alcohol, heat the mixture with a strong acid catalyst (such as sulphuric acid) to promote the esterification reaction. *(1 M)*

(*b*) Hexane. *(½ M)*

Hexane is a saturated hydrocarbon (alkane), and it will not decolourise bromine water. *(½ M)*

Case Based Questions

Case Based-I

(*i*) Hydrocarbons are the organic compounds that contains only carbon and hydrogen in it. *(1 M)*

(*ii*) Two properties are

(*a*) Tetravalency *(½ M)*

(*b*) Catenation *(½ M)*

(*iii*) Functional group present are:

(*a*) Aldehydes- 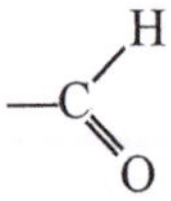 *(½ M)*

(*b*) Ketones - 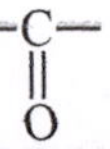 *(½ M)*

Reaction between ethanoic acid and ethanol:

$$\underset{\text{(Ethanoic acid)}}{CH_3—COOH} + \underset{\text{(Ethanol)}}{CH_3—CH_2OH}$$

$$\xrightleftharpoons{\text{Acid}} CH_3—\underset{\underset{O}{||}}{C}—O—CH_2—CH_3 + H_2O$$ *(1 M)*

OR

Structural isomers: Compounds with identical molecular formula but different structures are called structural isomers. *(1 M)*

Structures of two isomers of butane (C_4H_{10}):

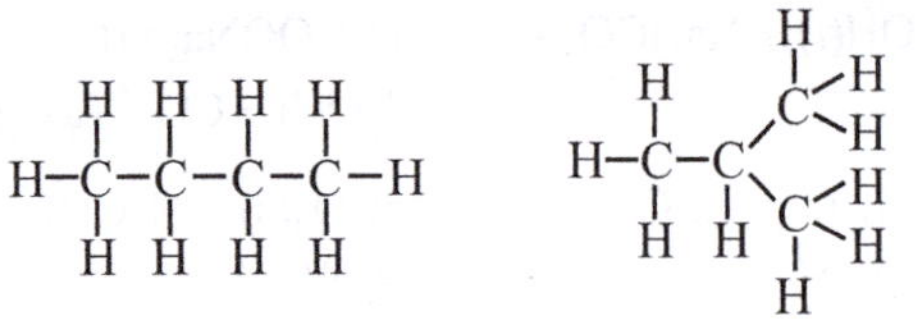

(*a*) (*b*) *(1 M)*

Topper's Explanation

(a) Hydrocarbons are the organic compounds which contain only hydrogen and carbon in it.

(b) (1) Catenation or self combination

(2) Tetravalency.

(c) (i) (1) Aldehyde → $-\overset{\overset{O}{||}}{C}-H$

(2) Ketone → $-\overset{\overset{O}{||}}{C}-$

$CH_3COOH + C_2H_5OH \xrightarrow{\text{conc. }H_2SO_4} CH_3COOC_2H_5 + H_2O$

Case Based-II

(*i*) (*a*) $CH_3-\overset{\overset{CH_3}{|}}{\underset{\underset{CH_3}{|}}{C}}-H$ *(1 M)*

(*b*) $CH_3-\overset{\overset{CH_2}{||}}{\underset{\underset{CH_3}{|}}{C}}$ *(1 M)*

(*ii*) $H_3C-CH_2-CH=CH_2$ *(1 M)*

$H_3C-CH=CH-CH_3$ *(1 M)*

OR

(*a*) One or two

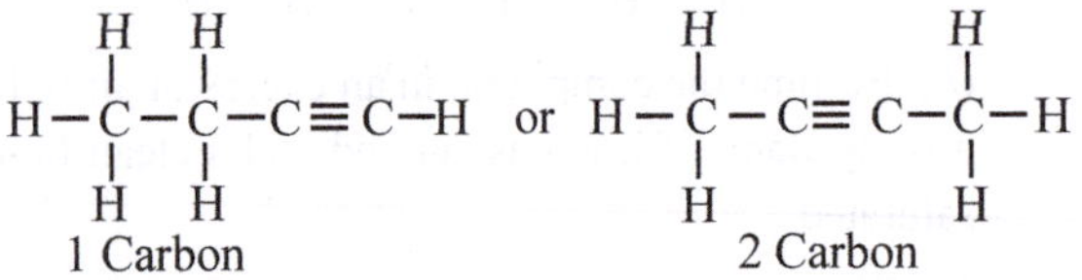

1 Carbon 2 Carbon

(1 M)

(*b*) Six hydrogen *(1 M)*

Case Based-III

(*i*) A - Ethanol; F - Ethene *(2 M)*

(*ii*) $$\underset{A}{CH_3–CH_2OH} \xrightarrow[\text{Or acidified }K_2Cr_2O_7 + \text{Heat}]{\text{Alkaline }KMnO_4 + \text{Heat}} CH_3COONa \xrightarrow{H^+} \underset{C}{CH_3COOH}$$

$$\underset{A}{CH_3-CH_2OH} \xrightarrow[H_2SO_4]{\text{Hot conc.}} \underset{F}{CH_2=CH_2} + H_2O$$ *(2 M)*

OR

Step 2: – Oxidation

Step 5: –Addition/ Hydrogenation

If A is replaced with propanol, then C is propanoic acid and F is propene

Case Based-IV

(*i*) (*a*) Glacial acetic acid is a concentrated form of acetic acid where it is almost 100% pure, known for solidifying at cooler temperatures and used in various chemical processes. It's chemical formula is CH_3COOH *(1 M)*

(*b*) The complete reaction when ethanoic acid reacts with sodium hydroxide is given as.

$NaOH + CH_3COOH \longrightarrow CH_3COONa + H_2O$ *(1 M)*

(*ii*) (*a*) The melting point of both acetic acid and glacial acetic acid is 16.6°C. *(1 M)*

(*b*) The reaction when ethanoic acid reacts with sodium hydrogen carbonate is given as.

$CH_3COOH + NaHCO_3 \longrightarrow CH_3COONa + H_2O + CO_2\uparrow$ *(1 M)*

OR

Mineral acids are strong acids, that means they ionize completely in aqueous solution, releasing H^+ ions.

Examples: Hydrochloric acid (HCl), sulphuric acid (H_2SO_4) *(½ M)*

$HCl_{(aq)} + NaOH_{(aq)} \rightarrow NaCl_{(aq)} + H_2O_{(l)}$ *(½ M)*

Carboxylic acids are weak acids, that means they only partially ionize in aqueous solution.

Examples: Acetic acid (CH_3 COOH), citric acid. *(½ M)*

$CH_3\ COOH_{(aq)} + NaOH_{(aq)} \rightarrow CH_3\ COONa_{(aq)} + H_2O_{(l)}$ *(½ M)*

Case Based-V

(*i*) Soaps are sodium or potassium salts of long-chain carboxylic acids. *(1 M)*

(*ii*) Detergents are made of sodium salts of sulphonic acids or ammonium salts with chlorides or bromides ions, etc. *(1 M)*

(*iii*) Detergents are more effective in hard water because they do not react with the minerals in the water, which means they can clean effectively without forming scum. *(1 M)*

(*iv*) The disadvantage of using detergents is that they are not biodegradable and can have a negative impact on the environment. *(½ M)*

Additionally, some of the chemicals in detergents can be harmful to human health and can cause skin irritation or other health problems. *(½ M)*

❑❑❑

5 LIFE PROCESSES

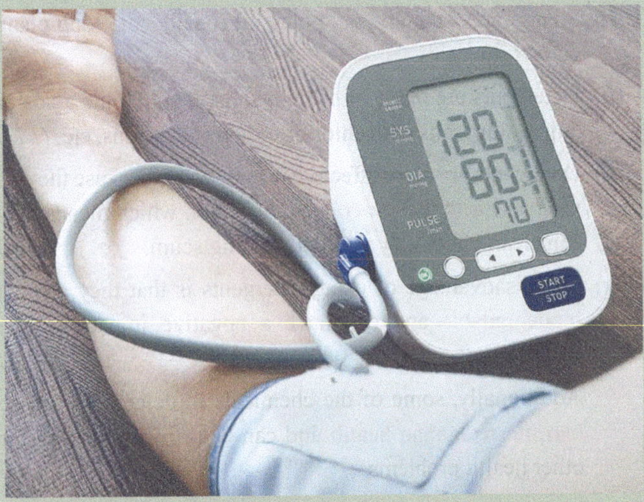

The measurement of blood pressure, a critical life process indicating cardiovascular function. The digital display of the monitor shows a systolic pressure of 120 mmHg and a diastolic pressure of 80 mmHg, which are considered normal values for a healthy adult. The display also indicates a pulse rate of 70 beats per minute. High or low blood pressure can be indicative of underlying health conditions.

SYLLABUS & WEIGHTAGE

LIST OF CONCEPT NAMES	YEARS				
	2020	2022 TERM-I	2023	2024	2025
Nutrition (Living Being: Basic concept of nutrition in plants and animals)	1 Q (3 M)	6 Q*	2 Q (1 M Each) 1 Q (3 M)	1 Q (1 M) 1 Q (2 M)	1 Q (1 M)
Respiration (Basic concept of respiration in plants and animals)	—	4 Q*	1 Q (1 M) 1 Q (3 M)	1 Q (1 M) 1 Q (3 M)	—
Transportation (Basic concepts of transport in plants and animals)	1 Q (5 M)	2 Q*	1 Q (2 M)	—	1 Q (2 M)
Excretion (Basic concepts of excretion in plants and animals)	—	5 Q*	1 Q (2 M)	—	1 Q (3 M)

For the year 2021, the exam was not conducted.

** All questions were of MCQ type and carried equal marks.*

CONCEPT MAP

To Access One Shot Revision Video Scan This QR Code

Life Processes

Nutrition
Process by which organisms take food and convert it into energy

Types of Nutrition

Autotrophic Nutrition
- Synthesis of food from inorganic substances
- Uses sunlight/ chemical energy (e.g., photosynthesis)

Key events in photosynthesis

Equation of photosynthesis

$$6CO_2 + 12H_2O \xrightarrow[\text{Sunlight}]{\text{Chlorophyll}} C_6H_{12}O_6 + 6O_2 + 6H_2O$$

(Glucose)

- Absorption of light energy by **chlorophyll**
- Conversion of **light energy** to **chemical energy** and splitting of **water molecules** into **hydrogen** and **oxygen**.
- Reduction of **carbon dioxide** to **carbohydrates**.

Adaptations in Desert Plants for Photosynthesis

Due to closed stomata in daytime desert plants absorb CO_2 at night and utilize it for photosynthesis during the day.

Heterotrophic Nutrition
Organisms obtained their food from other organisms

Saprophytic Nutrition (CBSE 2023)
- Obtain food from dead and decaying organisms
- Break down the food material outside the body and then absorb it. **E.g:** Bread mould (*Rhizopus*), yeast, and mushrooms.

Parasitic Nutrition

Derive nutrition from plant and animals without killing them.
E.g: *Cuscuta*, lice, leeches etc.

Holozoic Nutrition

Organisms ingest solid food and digest it internally.
E.g: *Amoeba*, *Paramoecium*, Humans, Dog etc.

In Unicellular Organisms (CBSE 2025)

Food may be taken in by the entire surface
E.g: *Amoeba* and *Paramoecium*

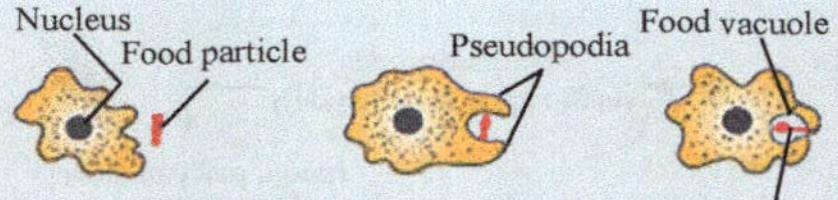

Nutrition in *Amoeba*

In Multicellular Organisms (Humans) (CBSE 2025, 2024)
- Accomplished by the use of alimentary canal.
- Consist of following steps: **Ingestion, Digestion, Absorption, Assimilation** and **Egestion**

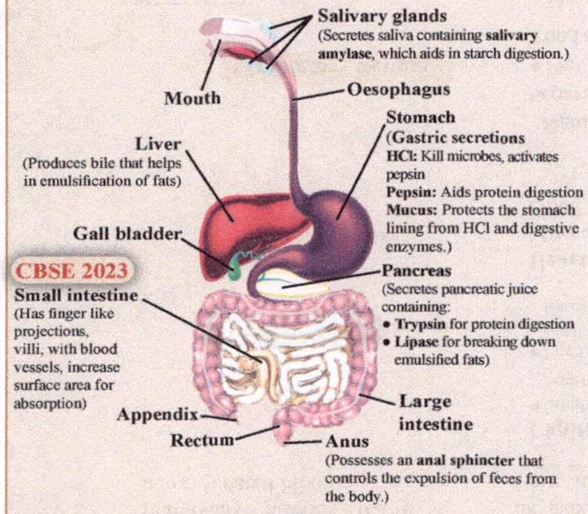

Human Alimentary Canal

Respiration
Involves utilisation of O_2 by cell and exchange of gases

In Animals

Human Respiratory System: Parts and its functions (CBSE 2020)

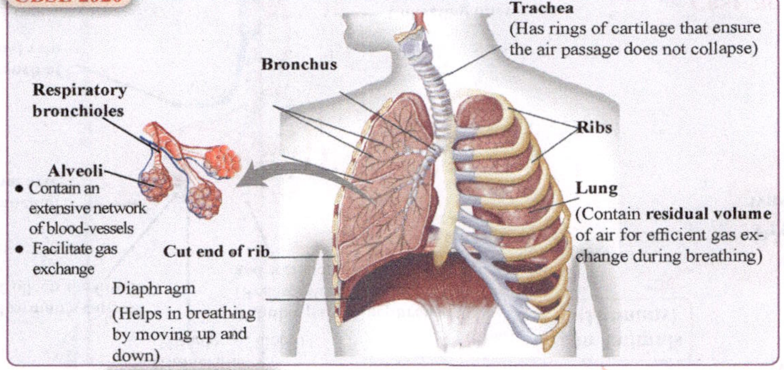

Inhalation vs Exhalation (CBSE 2022 Term-I)

Inhalation	Exhalation
Diaphragm flattens and move downwards	Diaphragm become dome shaped and raised upwards
Chest cavity enlarges and ribs move upwards	Chest cavity reduces and ribs move downwards

Aquatic vs Terrestrial (CBSE 2024, 2020)

Aquatic organisms breathe faster than terrestrial due to less dissolved oxygen in water vs air.

Hemoglobin (CBSE 2025)

(Why it is needed in organisms with large body size?)
- Large bodies require more oxygen than diffusion alone can supply.
- It has a higher affinity for oxygen

In Plants

Occurs through

Stomata (CBSE 2024, 2023, 2022 Term-I)

Tiny pores found on the surface of leaves

Opens when
- Needs CO_2 for photosynthesis
- Water flows into the guard cells

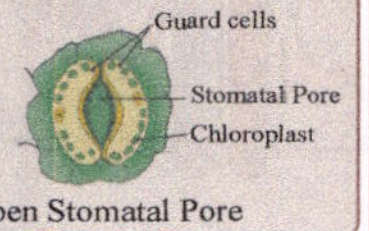

Open Stomatal Pore

Closes when
- Does not need CO_2 for photosynthesis,
- Water flows out of the guard cells

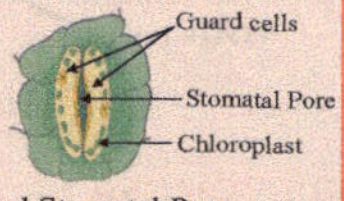

Closed Stomatal Pore

Glucose Metabolism (CBSE 2022 Term-I)

Glucose (6-carbon molecule) → In cytoplasm → Pyruvate (3-carbon molecule) + Energy
- Absence of oxygen (in yeast) → Ethanol + Carbon dioxide + Energy (2-carbon molecule)
- Lack of oxygen (in our muscle cells) → Lactic acid + Energy (3-carbon molecule)
- Presence of oxygen (in mitochondria) → Carbon dioxide + Water + Energy

Breakdown of glucose by various pathways

CBSE 2023, 2020

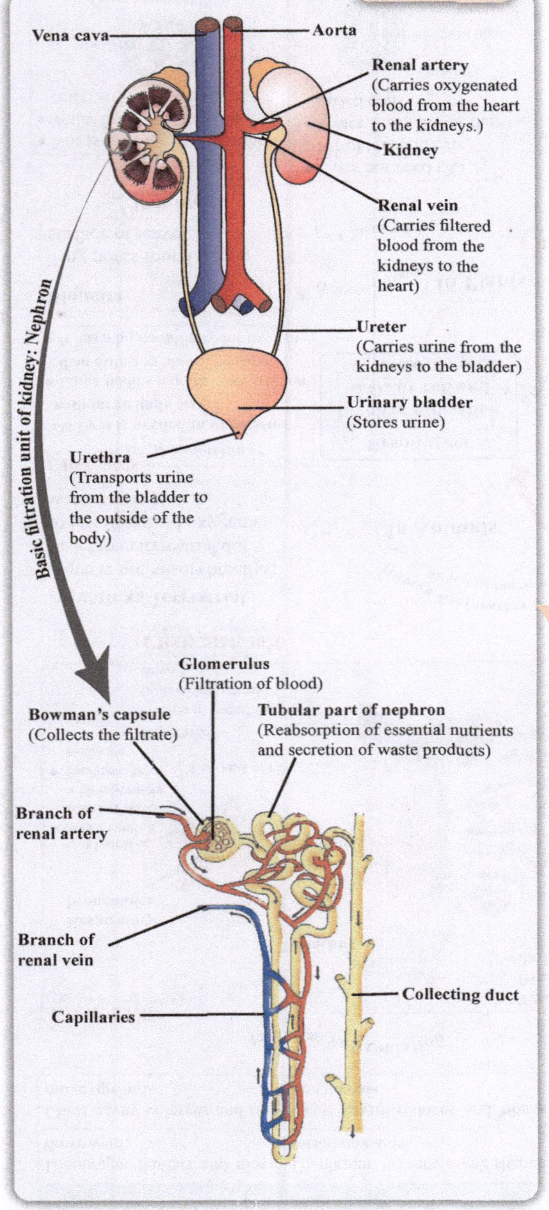

Life Processes

Transportation

Process of transferring substances (water, nutrients, waste products, etc.) from one place to another

In Animals (Humans)

Circulatory System

Blood vessels

Arteries (CBSE 2025)
Carry oxygenated blood away from the heart except pulmonary arteries (carry deoxygenated blood).

Veins
Carry deoxygenated blood to the heart except pulmonary veins (carry oxygenated blood).
Have valves to ensure one-way flow.

Capillaries
- Smallest blood vessels connecting arteries and veins; one cell thick.
- Facilitating nutrient and waste exchange between blood and tissues.

Heart
Muscular organ that pumps blood throughout the body.

CBSE 2023

Significance of Heart Chamber Separation in birds and mammals
- Prevents mixing of oxygenated and deoxygenated blood
- Ensures efficient oxygen supply to the body.
- Supports high energy requirements for body temperature regulation.

CBSE 2023

Double Circulation

The flow of blood through the heart twice in one cycle: once for oxygenation (pulmonary circulation) and once to deliver oxygen to the body (systemic circulation).

Veins (Deoxygenated blood) → Vena cava → Right atrium → Right ventricle → Pulmonary artery → Lungs → Pulmonary veins (Oxygenated blood) → Left atrium → Left ventricle → Aorta → Arteries → Capillaries in body organs apart from lungs → Veins

Lymphatic System

CBSE 2025

Lymph
- **Tissue fluid** similar to plasma.
- Formed by plasma, proteins, blood cells escape through capillary pores into intercellular spaces in the tissues.
- Colorless and contains less protein
- Drains into the lymphatic system and returns to veins

In Plants

Phloem
Bidirectional movement of organic compounds, primarily sugars produced during photosynthesis, throughout the plant.

Accomplished by →

CBSE 2022 Term-I

Sieve tubes, aided by companion cells

CBSE 2023

Xylem
Upward transport of water and minerals from the roots to the leaves and other parts of the plant.
- **Root pressure:** Ion absorption in roots creates pressure to push water upwards; active at night.
- **Transpiration pull:** Evaporation from leaves creates suction, pulling water upward during the day, aiding mineral transport and cooling.

Accomplished by →

Tracheids and vessels

Excretion

Process in which metabolic waste is eliminated from the body of an organism

In Animals (Humans)

(See kidney and nephron diagram.)

In Plants

CBSE 2025, 2022 Term-I

Different strategies for excretion of waste product in plants
- Oxygen as a byproduct of photosynthesis
- CO_2 and excess water through transpiration
- Leaves shed to dispose waste
- Dead cells and cellular vacuoles in plant store waste
- Resins and gums in old xylem store additional waste

1 NUTRITION

NCERT Definitions (Commonly asked in 1 mark)

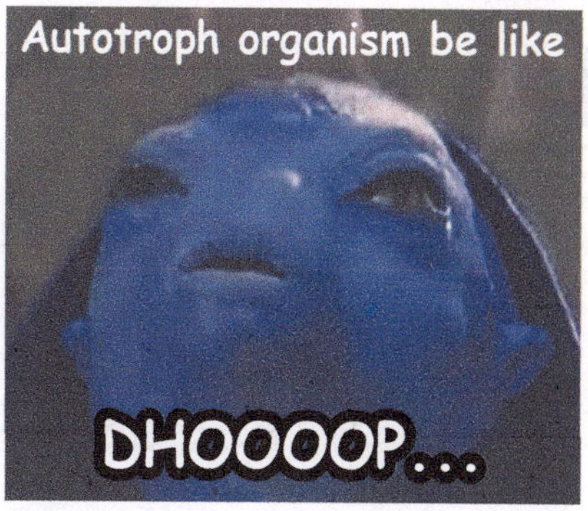

- **Life Processes:** The essential maintenance functions that living organisms must perform to sustain life, even when not actively engaged in any particular activity.
- **Nutrition:** The process of taking in food and using it for growth, metabolism, and repair. Essential for energy and life sustenance.
- **Autotrophic Nutrition:** The mode of nutrition in which organisms synthesize their own food through photosynthesis.
- **Heterotrophic Nutrition:** The mode of nutrition in which organisms depend directly or indirectly on autotrophs for their food.
- **Guard Cells:** Specialized cells that regulate the opening and closing of stomatal pores.
- **Pseudopodia:** A temporary finger-like extensions of the cell surface of *Amoeba* for movement and feeding.
- **Alimentary Canal:** A long tube extending from the mouth to the anus.
- **Saliva:** A digestive fluid secreted by the salivary glands, containing enzymes like salivary amylase.
- **Salivary Amylase**: An enzyme in saliva that starts the digestion of starch by breaking it down into simpler sugars.
- **Oesophagus:** The food pipe that connects the mouth to the stomach.
- **Peristaltic Movement:** Rhythmic contractions of muscles in the digestive canal that help to push food along the digestive tract.
- **Gastric Glands:** *Glands found in the wall of the stomach.*
- **Mucus:** A slimy substance that protects inner lining of the stomach from the action of the acid.
- **Bile Juice:** Secretion from the liver that neutralizes acidic food from the stomach and breaks down fat globules, enhancing enzyme efficiency.
- **Bile Salts:** Components of bile that emulsify fats, breaking them into smaller globules for easier enzyme action.
- **Intestinal Juice:** Secretions from the small intestine's glands containing enzymes for the final digestion steps, converting food into absorbable substances.
- **Villi:** Finger-like projections in the small intestine's lining that increase surface area for absorption and contain blood vessels for nutrient transport.
- **Anal Sphincter:** A muscle controlling the exit of waste material from the body.
- **Photosynthesis:** A process by which autotrophs take in substances from the outside (carbon dioxide and water) and convert them into stored forms of energy, using sunlight and chlorophyll.
- **Chlorophyll:** A green pigment found in the chloroplasts of plants, essential for photosynthesis.
- **Stomata:** Tiny pores on the surface of leaves through which exchange of gases takes place.
- **Enzymes:** Biological catalysts that speed up the breakdown of complex substances into simpler ones.

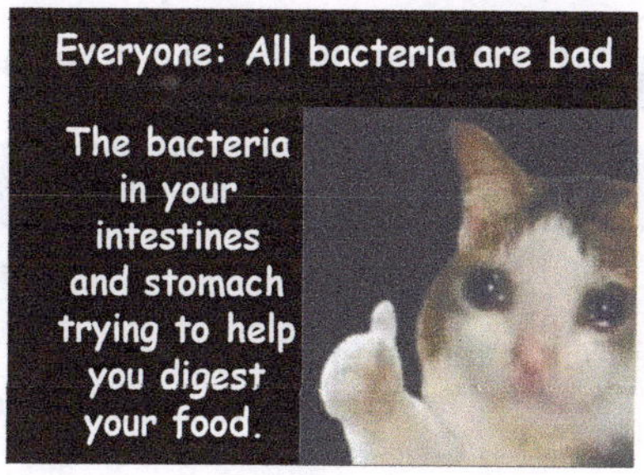

Important Facts

01 The storage form of carbohydrates in plants. *~Starch*

02 The storage form of carbohydrates in humans. *~Glycogen*

03 The length of an intestine varies by diet; herbivores have longer small intestines for cellulose digestion, while carnivores have shorter ones as meat digests easier.

04 Trypsin and pepsin are protein digestive enzymes; trypsin acts in the small intestine, while pepsin in the stomach.

05 The site of complete digestion of proteins, carbohydrates, and fats in the body. ***~Small intestine***

06 The secretions of gastric glands in the stomach that facilitate the action of enzymes involved in protein digestion. ***~Hydrochloric acid***

Classification

- **Nutrition**
  - **Autotrophic** (Green plants, Blue green algae)
  - **Heterotrophic** (Fungi, *Amoeba*, Man)
    - **Saprophytic** (Fungi, Yeast)
    - **Parasitic** (*Cuscuta*, *Plasmodium*)
    - **Holozoic** (Man, Dog, *Amoeba*)

Digestive Enzymes
(Enzymes vital for effectively breaking down food into absorbable nutrients, optimizing digestion and nutrient utilization)

Characteristic	Salivary Amylase	Pepsin	Gastric Lipase	Trypsin	Pancreatic Lipase
Source	Salivary glands	Stomach	Stomach	Pancreas	Pancreas
Substrate	Starches	Proteins	Fats	Proteins	Fats
Products	Maltose	Peptides	Fatty acids and glycerol	Peptides	Fatty acids and glycerol

Difference Between (Commonly asked in 2-3 mark)

Nutrition - Autotrophic v/s Heterotrophic

Feature	Autotrophic Nutrition	Heterotrophic Nutrition
Mode of nutrition	Synthesize their food from simple inorganic raw materials such as CO_2 and H_2O	Directly or indirectly depends on autotrophs for food
Energy source	Light energy (in photosynthesis) or chemical energy (in chemosynthesis)	Organic compounds ingested or absorbed from other sources
Carbon source	Carbon dioxide (CO_2)	Organic carbon compounds
Chlorophyll	Present	Absent

Amoeba* v/s *Paramoecium

Amoeba	*Paramoecium*
Unicellular organism with irregular body shape	Unicellular organism with definite body shape
Moves by forming pseudopodia	Moves by beating the cilia
Pseudopodia helps in engulfing food particles and removing waste	Have specific spots for engulfing food particles and removing waste

Real Life Application Based Questions

1. **Why might some people experience a burning sensation in their chest after eating spicy foods, especially close to bedtime?**

Ans. Eating spicy foods close to bedtime can lead to acid reflux, where stomach acid flows back into the esophagus, causing a burning sensation known as heartburn. This occurs more easily when lying down, as the position allows acid to travel up the esophagus more freely.

2. **Why might some individuals experience discomfort after consuming a glass of milk or milk products, whereas others do not?***

Ans. Some individuals lack sufficient lactase, the enzyme needed to digest lactose in milk, leading to lactose intolerance. This results in undigested lactose causing symptoms like bloating, diarrhea, and gas upon consuming milk or milk products, unlike those who produce enough lactase.

3. **Recall those times when, after a long play session outdoors, your mother would give you Glucon D? Why do you think she chose this for you?***

Ans. After outdoor play, your mother gave you Glucon D mainly because its simple sugars are easily digested, offering a quick energy boost. The glucose in Glucon D is rapidly absorbed, efficiently restoring your body's depleted energy reserves and aiding in quicker recovery and hydration.

4. **Why is induced vomiting considered an unhealthy and ineffective method for weight control, particularly among models and individuals seeking rapid weight loss?***

Ans. Induced vomiting for weight control is harmful because it can lead to serious health problems like nutrient deficiencies, electrolyte imbalances, and damage to the digestive system. It doesn't effectively manage weight and can cause long-term physical and mental health issues.

Myth Buster

- **Myth: More sunlight always results in more photosynthesis.***
  Fact: Beyond a certain point, increasing light intensity does not increase the rate of photosynthesis due to other limiting factors like CO_2 concentration and temperature.
- **Myth: Oxygen is the primary product of photosynthesis.**
  Fact: While oxygen is a by-product, the primary purpose of photosynthesis is to produce glucose for energy and growth.
- **Myth: Photosynthesis occurs only in leaves.**
  Fact: Photosynthesis primarily takes place in green leaves, but it also takes place in other green parts of the plant such as green stems and green branches.
- **Myth: Digestion starts in the stomach.**
  Fact: Digestion begins in the mouth with mechanical chewing and the chemical action of saliva.
- **Myth: Digestive disorders are always due to what we eat.**
  Fact: While diet plays a significant role, factors like genetics, stress, and infections can also cause digestive disorders.
- **Myth: The liver has no role in digestion.**
  Fact: The liver produces bile, crucial for fat digestion and absorption.

** Concepts beyond the board exam syllabus, offering deeper insight and critical thinking on NCERT topics.*

Mnemonics

❐ **MESSI : Path followed by food in alimentary canal**

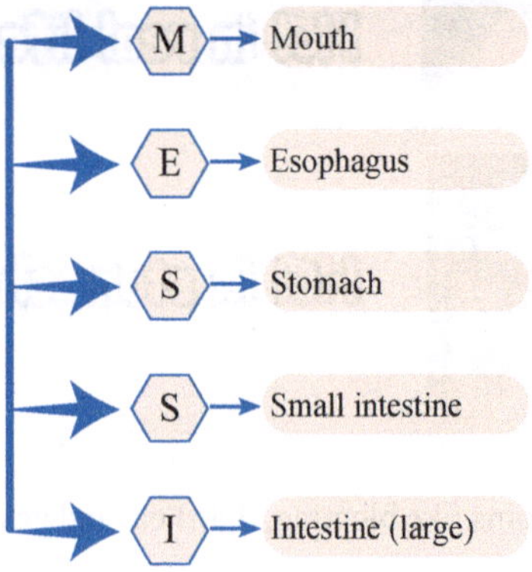

❐ **PIL: Organs that release their secretions into the small intestine**
VIL: Structure found in small intestine

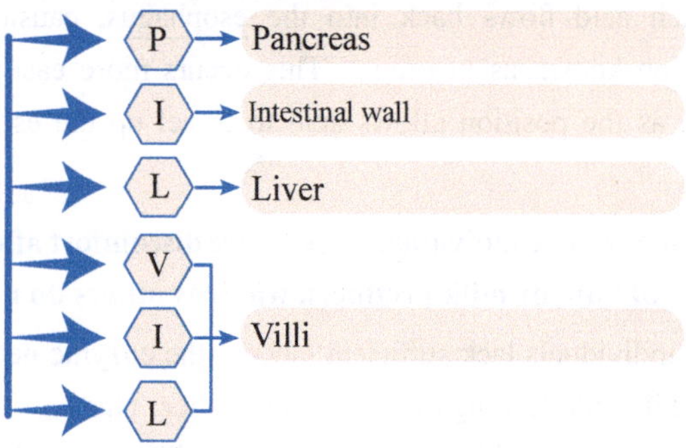

COMPETENCY BASED SOLVED EXAMPLES

Multiple Choice Questions (1 M)

1. Select the correct statement. **(*Re*) (NCERT Exemplar)**

(*a*) Heterotrophs do not synthesise their own food

(*b*) Heterotrophs utilise solar energy for photosynthesis

(*c*) Heterotrophs synthesise their own food

(*d*) Heterotrophs are capable of converting carbon dioxide and water into carbohydrates

2. Which one of the following conditions is true for the state of stomata of a green leaf shown in the given diagram? **(*An*) (CBSE, 2022 Term I)**

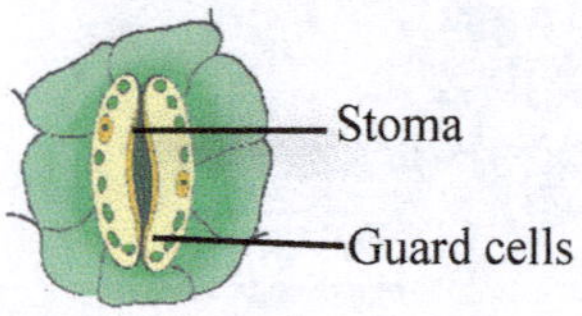

(*a*) Large amount of water flows into the guard cells.

(*b*) Gaseous exchange is occurring in large amount.

(*c*) Large amount of water flows out from the guard cells.

(*d*) Large amount of sugar collects in the guard cells.

3. Identify the two components of phloem tissue that help in transportation of food in plants. **(*Re*)(CBSE, 2022 Term I)**

(*a*) Phloem parenchyma & sieve tubes

(*b*) Sieve tubes & companion cells

(*c*) Phloem parenchyma & companion cells

(*d*) Phloem fibres and sieve tubes

4. An organism which breaks down the food material outside the body and then absorbs it is **(*Re*) (CBSE, 2023)**

(*a*) a plant parasite, *Cuscuta*

(*b*) an animal parasite, Tapeworm

(*c*) a bacteria, *Rhizobium*

(*d*) a fungi, *Rhizopus*

5. Which of the following equations is the summary of photosynthesis? **(*Re*)**

(*a*) $6CO_2 + 12H_2O \rightarrow C_6H_{12}O_6 + 6O_2 + 6H_2O$

(*b*) $6CO_2 + H_2O + \text{Sunlight} \rightarrow C_6H_{12}O_6 + O_2 + 6H_2O$

(*c*) $6CO_2 + 12H_2O + \text{Chlorophyll} + \text{Sunlight} \rightarrow C_6H_{12}O_6 + 6O_2 + 6H_2O$

(*d*) $6CO_2 + 12H_2O + \text{Chlorophyll} + \text{Sunlight} \rightarrow C_6H_{12}O_6 + 6CO_2 + 6H_2O$

6. A student was asked to write a stepwise procedure to demonstrate that carbon dioxide is necessary for photosynthesis. He wrote the following steps. The wrongly worded step is **(*An*) (CBSE, 2022 Term I)**

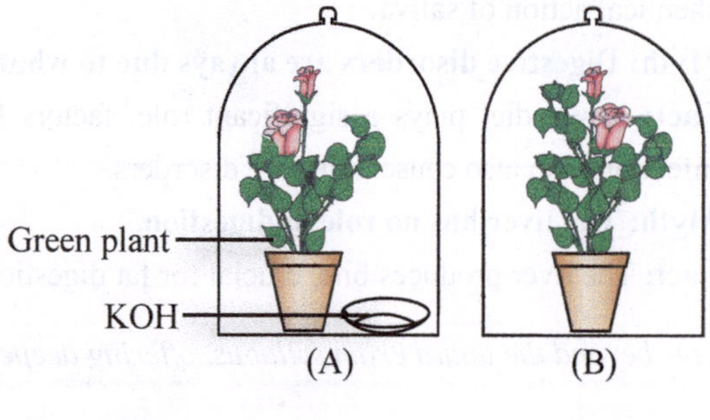

(a) Both potted plants are kept in dark room for at least three days.

(b) Bottom of the bell jars is sealed to make them air tight.

(c) Both potted plants are kept in sunlight after the starch test.

(d) A leaf from both the plants is taken to test the presence of starch.

7. Patient X was suffering from a pancreatic condition due to which the pancreas was not functioning adequately. Which of the following is a doctor likely to suggest to such an individual? (*Un*)

(a) including a large amount of protein in the diet

(b) eating a diet with low-fat content

(c) eating only carbohydrates

(d) including only liquid foods

8. Gastric juice is secreted by gastric glands and contains hydrochloric acid, mucus, and pepsin. Which activity will be affected in the absence of hydrochloric acid? (*Un*)

(a) Digestion of proteins

(b) Digestion of carbohydrates

(c) Digestion of lipids

(d) Digestion of starch

9. Gaurav in a pharmacy was searching for a remedy to relieve indigestion after a meal. He consulted with the pharmacist, who suggested a specific compound commonly used in the manufacturing of medicines for indigestion. What is the name of this compound? (*Un*)

(a) Anti-inflammatory (b) Antibiotic

(c) Antacid (d) Antiseptic

10. Which is the correct sequence of parts in human alimentary canal? (*Re*) (NCERT Exemplar)

(a) Mouth → stomach → small intestine → oesophagus → large intestine

(b) Mouth → oesophagus → stomach → large intestine → small intestine

(c) Mouth → stomach → oesophagus → small intestine → large intestine

(d) Mouth → oesophagus → stomach → small intestine → Large intestine

Assertion and Reason (1 M)

Direction: The following questions consist of two statements – Assertion (A) and Reason (R). Answer these questions by selecting the appropriate option given below:

(a) Both A and R are true, and R is the correct explanation of A.

(b) Both A and R are true, but R is not the correct explanation of A.

(c) A is true, but R is false.

(d) A is false, but R is true.

1. **Assertion (A):** A lot of difference in the concentrations of ions was observed by a scientist between the fluid in xylem cells of roots and that of the soil.

   Reason (R): Xylem cells in the roots of plants which come in contact with the soil actively take up ions. (*Un*)

2. **Assertion (A):** The food coming from the stomach into the small intestine is acidic.

   Reason (R): The acidic nature of the food is neutralized by bile juice from the pancreas to facilitate the action of pancreatic enzymes. **(*Re*)**

3. **Assertion (A):** The inner walls of the small intestine have finger like projections called villi which are rich in blood.

   Reason (R): These villi have a large surface area to help the small intestine in completing the digestion of food. **(*Re*) (CBSE, 2023)**

4. **Assertion (A):** Carbohydrate digestion mainly takes place in small intestine.

   Reason (R): Pancreatic juice contains the enzyme lactose. **(*Re*)**

5. **Assertion (A):** *Amoeba* takes in food using finger - like extensions of the cell surface.

   Reason (R): In all unicellular organisms, the food is taken in by the entire cell surface. **(*Un*) (CBSE SQP, 2023)**

Subjective Questions

Very Short Answer Type Questions (2 M)

1. State one role of each of the following in human digestive system: (*Re*) (CBSE, 2024)

(i) Hydrochloric acid (ii) Villi

(iii) Anal Sphincter (iv) Lipase

Ans. The role of the following in human digestive system are:

(i) Hydrochloric acid: Creates an acidic environment which facilitates the action of the enzyme pepsin. (½ M)

(ii) Villi: Finger-like projections on the inner lining of small intestine increase the surface area for absorption of nutrients from digested food. (½ M)

(iii) Anal sphincter: Controls the release of feces from the body. (½ M)

(iv) Lipase: Digestive enzyme that digests emulsified fats. (½ M)

2. (a) If you were a herbivore, what would you expect the length of your small intestine to be?

(b) Do you think the coiling of the small intestine has any significance in the digestion process? Explain your answer. (*Un*)

Ans. (a) If, I were a herbivore, I would expect the length of my small intestine to be longer than that of a carnivore, as herbivores require more time and space to digest cellulose. (1 M)

(b) Yes, the coiling of the small intestine has significance in the digestion process as it increases the surface area for absorption of nutrients. (1 M)

3. Amit placed plant X in a glass jar with mice and plant Y in a separate jar without mice, both under the same light conditions.

Which plant is more likely to photosynthesize more, and what is the reason behind it? (*Ap*)

Ans. By evaluating CO_2 consumption and respiration, we can infer which plant is more likely to photosynthesize more:

CO_2 consumption: Plant X, in the jar with mice, is more likely to photosynthesize more due to higher CO_2 levels from the mice's respiration. *(1 M)*

Respiration: The mice's respiration increases CO_2, which is a raw material for photosynthesis, potentially boosting Plant X photosynthesis rate under the same light conditions. *(1M)*

Nailing the Right Answer

When answering, students should clearly mention the impact of CO_2 consumption and respiration on photosynthesis. They should integrate the concept of how animal respiration influences CO_2 levels and, consequently, plant photosynthesis.

4. Two green plants are kept separately in oxygen free containers, one in the dark and other in sunlight. It was observed that plant kept in dark could not survive longer. Give reason for this observation. *(An)* (CBSE, 2023)

Ans. Plants rely on photosynthesis to generate energy using sunlight to convert CO_2 and water into glucose and oxygen.

Photosynthesis enables the plant in sunlight to produce glucose for energy and oxygen for respiration, ensuring its survival. *(1 M)*

Absence of light in the dark container prevents the plant from performing photosynthesis, thereby hindering glucose and oxygen production essential for its metabolic processes and survival. *(1 M)*

5. Where does digestion in *Amoeba* takes place? Explain it with the help of diagram. *(Re, Cr)*

Ans. Digestion in *Amoeba* takes place inside the food vacuole. It engulfs food through pseudopodia forming a food vacuole, where enzymes break down food. The soluble food is absorbed, and the undigested remains are expelled. *(1M)*

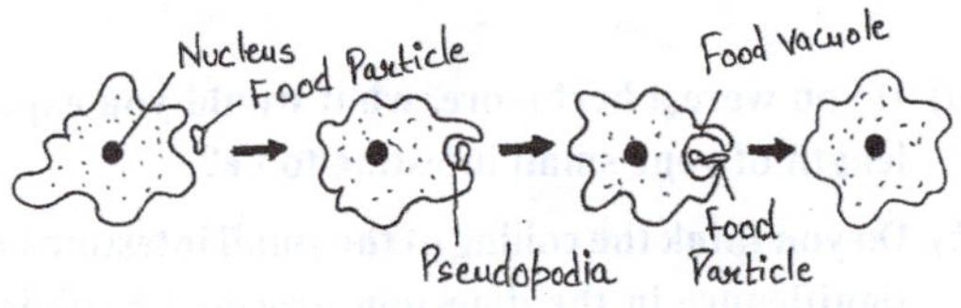

(1 M)

6. Can fats be properly digested without emulsification? *(Un)*

Ans. No, fats cannot be properly efficiently digested without emulsification. *(1M)*

Bile salts produced by the liver break down large fat molecules in food into smaller molecules. This crucial step increases the surface area of fats, enabling enzymes like lipase to efficiently act on and digest them. *(1M)*

7. Imagine you have eaten a meal high in starch but have a condition that inhibits salivary amylase production. Predict how this condition would affect your digestion process. *(Ap)*

Ans. Without salivary amylase, the chemical digestion of starch in the mouth would be inhibited, resulting in starch remaining in its complex form as it passes into the stomach and intestines. The digestive burden would shift to other enzymes in the small intestine, such as pancreatic amylase, to break down the starch into simple sugars. This might lead to slower digestion and reduced efficiency in starch absorption. *(2 M)*

Short Answer Type Questions (3 M)

1. *(i)* How does *Paramecium* obtain its food?

***(ii)* List the role of each of the following in our digestive system: *(Re)* (CBSE, 2023)**

***(a)* Hydrochloric acid**

***(b)* Trypsin**

***(c)* Muscular walls of stomach**

***(d)* Salivary amylase**

Ans. *(i)* *Paramecium* obtains its food by moving it to a specific spot using the cilia that cover its surface. *(1M)*

(ii) Role of given components in our digestive system:

	Component	Role
(a)	Hydrochloric acid	Creates an acidic medium that facilitates the action of the enzyme pepsin.
(b)	Trypsin	Digests proteins into smaller peptides and amino acids.
(c)	Muscular walls of stomach	Helps in churning and mixing the food thoroughly with digestive juices.
(d)	Salivary amylase	Breaks down complex molecules of starch into simpler sugars.

(½ × 4 = 2 M)

2. List in tabular form three distinguishing features between autotrophic nutrition and heterotrophic nutrition. *(Re)*

Ans.

Features	Autotrophic Nutrition	Heterotrophic Nutrition
Mode of nutrition	Synthesize their food from simple inorganic raw materials such as CO_2 and H_2O	Directly or indirectly depends on autotrophs for food
Energy Source	Light energy (in photosynthesis) or chemical energy (in chemosynthesis)	Organic compounds ingested or absorbed from other sources
Carbon Source	Carbon dioxide (CO_2)	Organic carbon compounds

(1 × 3 = 3 M)

3. **(a) Why does a piece of bread taste sweet when chewed some time?**

   (b) Cellulose acts as a roughage in man but serves as a source of nutrients in cow. Justify the statement. **(Ap)**

Ans. (a) The piece of bread tastes sweeter after being chewed for some time due to

Starch breakdown: Saliva contains an enzyme called salivary amylase. This enzyme breaks down starch, a complex carbohydrate present in bread, into simpler sugars. The conversion of starch into sugar gives the sweet taste. *(1½ M)*

(b) Humans cannot digest cellulose due to the absence of cellulase, thus it acts as roughage aiding digestion. Cows, with specialized stomach compartments and cellulase-producing bacteria, convert cellulose into absorbable nutrients. *(1½ M)*

4. **What would happen if green plants disappear from earth? Explain.** **(An) (NCERT Exemplar)**

Ans. If green plants disappeared from Earth, the consequences would be:

Oxygen depletion: Green plants produce oxygen through photosynthesis. Without them, oxygen levels would drop, affecting all aerobic life forms. *(1½ M)*

Disruption in carbon cycle: Plants absorb carbon dioxide for photosynthesis. Without them, carbon dioxide levels would increase, intensifying global warming and disrupting climate patterns. *(1½ M)*

5. **We often hear people complain about 'acidity' in the stomach.**

   (a) Overproduction of what substance is most likely the reason for the complaint?

   (b) Why is the production of this substance necessary?

   (c) How does the stomach prevent itself from the harmful effects of overproduction of the substance? **(Un) (CFPQ)**

Ans. (a) Hydrochloric acid *(1 M)*

(b) It creates an acidic medium for functioning of enzyme pepsin. *(1 M)*

(c) The stomach produces mucus that coats the inner wall lining to prevent damage by hydrochloric acid. *(1 M)*

6. **(i) What is the internal energy reserve in plants and animals?**

   (ii) How desert plants perform photosynthesis if their stomata remain closed during the day? **(Un) (CBSE, 2023)**

OR

Name the site where carbohydrates, proteins, and fats are completely digested in humans, and specify which part of the body secretes the enzymes necessary for this digestion. **(Re)**

Ans. (i) Carbohydrates which are not used immediately are stored in the form of

In plans – Starch *(½ M)*

In animals – Glycogen. *(½ M)*

(ii) Desert plants take up carbon dioxide at night because stomata are closed during day time to prevent water loss. They prepare an intermediate which is acted upon by the energy absorbed by the chlorophyll during the day time. *(2 M)*

OR

Nutrient	Site of Complete Digestion	Enzyme and their Source
Carbohydrates	Small Intestine	Pancreatic amylase (Pancreas), Enzymes in intestinal juice (Small Intestine)
Proteins	Small Intestine	Trypsin (Pancreas), Enzymes in intestinal juice (Small Intestine)
Fats	Small Intestine	Bile for emulsification (Liver), Lipase (Pancreas), Enzymes in intestinal juice (Small Intestine)

(1 × 3 = 3 M)

Long Answer Type Questions **(5 M)**

1. **(a) List three events that occur during the process of photosynthesis.**

   (b) Design an experiment to show that sunlight is essential for photosynthesis. **(Cr)**

Ans. (a) Events during Photosynthesis:

Absorption of light energy by chlorophyll: Chlorophyll in the chloroplasts absorbs sunlight, which is the initial step in the process of photosynthesis. *(½ M)*

Conversion of light energy to chemical energy: The absorbed light energy is converted into chemical energy, leading to the splitting of water molecules into hydrogen and oxygen. *(½ M)*

Reduction of carbon dioxide to carbohydrates: The chemical energy is used to reduce carbon dioxide into carbohydrates like glucose, which are used as food by the plant. *(½ M)*

(b) Experiment to show that sunlight is essential for photosynthesis:

1. Take the potted plant and keep it in a dark place for 2-3 days so that the leaves get destarched.
2. Attach light proof black paper strips on both sides of the leaf with the help of paper clips.
3. Place the plant in sunlight for 3-4 hours.
4. Pluck the selected covered leaf and remove the black paper covering it.
5. Perform starch test by boiling leaf first in boiling water followed by boiling in alcohol over a water bath and then rinsing with cold water and again placing it in iodine solution. *(2 M)*

Observation: In the experiment, the leaf displayed a distinct blue-black color in areas exposed to light, indicating starch presence. However, regions covered and thus deprived of light showed no such color change, signifying an absence of starch due to the lack of photosynthesis. *(1 M)*

Result: Light is essential for photosynthesis. *(½ M)*

2. Based on the figure labeled I, II and III, answer the questions that follow: ***(Re, Un)***

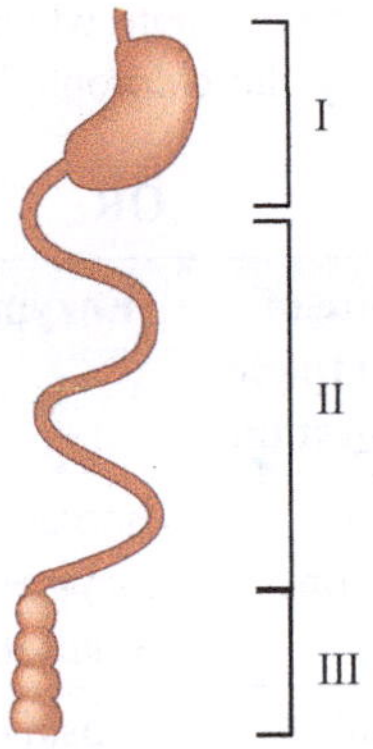

(a) What secretions are produced in part I, and what are their functions?

(b) Are the secretions produced in part I reason for acidity in adults? If yes, how do part I and II protect themselves from such acidic secretions?

(c) How is transport of food from part I to II regulated?

(d) How do the structural features of part II facilitate nutrient absorption in an individual?

(e) Compare the digestion and absorption processes in parts II and III.

Ans. (a) Secretions in part I (Stomach):

1. Hydrochloric acid (HCl) - Kill microbes and provide acidic medium for the action of pepsin.
2. Pepsin- Digestion of proteins.
3. Mucus - Protects stomach lining from action of acid under normal conditions. *(1 M)*

(b) Yes, HCl causes acidity. *(½ M)*

- Stomach (Part I) secretes mucus to protect its lining.
- In the small intestine, bile and pancreatic juice are released to neutralise acid. *(½ M)*

(c) Transport of food from the stomach (part I) to the small intestine (part II) is regulated by the sphincter muscle which releases food in small amounts. *(1 M)*

(d) Part II contains numerous finger-like projections called villi, which increase the surface area for nutrient absorption. Blood vessels in the villi transport absorbed nutrients to each and every part of the body. *(1 M)*

(e) In part II, digestion is completed, and nutrients are absorbed into the bloodstream. In part III, water and salts are absorbed, and solid waste is formed from indigestible food. *(1 M)*

3. (a) Compare the feeding mechanisms of *Amoeba* and *Paramoecium*, highlighting their differences and similarities.

(b) After digestion, how are the simpler substances obtained from the food distributed within the *Amoeba* cell?

(c) How does the specialized feeding process in *Paramoecium* contribute to its overall survival and functioning as a unicellular organism? ***(An)***

Ans. (a) Difference in feeding mechanisms of *Amoeba* and *Paramoecium*:

Method of Ingestion: *Amoeba* engulfs food through pseudopodia, forming a food vacuole, whereas *Paramoecium* utilizes a specific spot or oral groove for food intake.

Similarity in feeding mechanisms of *Amoeba* and *Paramoecium*:

Similarity in Digestion: In both organisms, digestion occurs within food vacuoles where complex substances are broken down into simpler ones, which then diffuse into the cytoplasm.

(b) In *Amoeba*, nutrient distribution after digestion is efficient and direct due to its unicellular structure.

- Direct Absorption: Simpler substances from the food vacuole diffuse into the cytoplasm by diffusion.
- No Blood System Needed: Being unicellular, *Amoeba* doesn't require a blood system for nutrient distribution.

(c) *Paramoecium's* specialized feeding process plays a crucial role in its survival and function.

- Targeted Feeding: Cilia guide food precisely to the specific spot that serves as a mouth, enhancing nutrient absorption.
- Improved Digestion: Intracellular digestion inside the food vacuole in the cell aids in growth and energy production.

Nailing the Right Answer

If comparing the feeding mechanisms of *Amoeba* and *Paramoecium*, make sure to highlight both the similarities and differences between the two organisms. This could include differences in feeding structures and methods of food capture.

4. (a) Priya was taking a stroll around a park and she noticed a fallen log covered in mushrooms. These mushrooms were thriving on the decaying wood, extracting nutrients from it. What kind of nutrition does this depict? How is it different from holozoic nutrition? Explain.

(b) State the functions of liver and pancreas.

(c) Name the organ which performs the following functions in humans.

(i) Absorption of digested food

(ii) Absorption of water. ***(Un)***

Ans. (a) *Saprotrophic nutrition* *(½ M)*

- The mushrooms exhibit saprotrophic nutrition, where organisms obtain nutrients by breaking down dead and decaying matter. *(½ M)*
  - Difference in saprotrophic and holozoic nutrition: Unlike holozoic nutrition, which involves ingestion, digestion, absorption, and assimilation of solid food, saprotrophic nutrition involves absorbing dissolved nutrients from decay. *(1 M)*

(b) Functions of Liver and Pancreas

Liver: Produces bile, which aids in the digestion and absorption of fats. It also plays a vital role in metabolizing proteins and carbohydrates, and detoxifying substances. *(1 M)*

Pancreas: Produces pancreatic juice containing digestive enzymes for carbohydrates, proteins, and fats. *(1 M)*

(c) Organs for Absorption

(i) Absorption of Digested Food: Small Intestine, where nutrients are absorbed into the bloodstream. *(½ M)*

(ii) Absorption of Water: Large Intestine, where water is absorbed from undigested food, forming solid waste. *(½ M)*

5. (a) Draw the diagram of alimentary canal and label the following parts: Mouth, Oesophagus, Stomach, Intestine

(b) Name the longest part of the alimentary canal.

(Re, Cr)

Ans. (a)

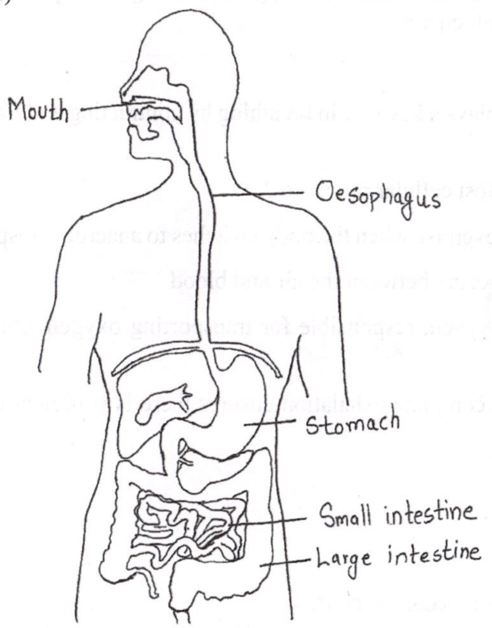

(4 M)

(b) The longest part of the alimentary canal is small intestine. *(1 M)*

Hints & Explanations

Multiple Choice Questions

1. (a) Heterotrophs are the organisms that depend on other organisms for obtaining their food and nutrition.

2. (c) The diagram illustrates the closure of stomatal pores. They open and close *via* specialized cells called guard cells. When these cells lose water, they shrink, causing the pores to close.

3. (b) The two components of phloem tissue that help in the transportation of food in plants are sieve tubes and companion cells. Sieve tubes transport sugars, while companion cells support and regulate their activity.

4. (d) Fungi like *Rhizopus* decompose organic matter by secreting enzymes outside their body, breaking it down into simpler molecules for absorption and use as energy and growth.

5. (c) $6CO_2 + 12H_2O + \text{Chlorophyll} + \text{Sunlight} \rightarrow C_6H_{12}O_6 + 6O_2 + 6H_2O$

This equation accurately represents the process of photosynthesis, where carbon dioxide (CO_2) and water (H_2O), in the presence of sunlight and chlorophyll, are converted into glucose ($C_6H_{12}O_6$) and oxygen (O_2).

Key Takeaways

Students learned that photosynthesis is a complex process involving multiple components, including chlorophyll and sunlight, essential for converting CO_2 and H_2O into glucose and oxygen.

6. (c) The correct procedure should involve exposing the plants to sunlight before performing the starch test, as the purpose is to demonstrate that photosynthesis has occurred in the presence of carbon dioxide, which would result in starch formation in the leaves.

7. (b) The pancreas produces enzyme pancreatic lipase that helps digest fats. If the pancreas is not working properly, digesting large amounts of fat can be difficult, leading to gastrointestinal discomfort and further strain on the pancreas. A low-fat diet helps to reduce this strain.

8. (a) Hydrochloric acid creates an acidic environment, which is necessary for the activation of pepsin from its inactive form, pepsinogen. Pepsin is crucial for the digestion of proteins.

9. (c) The compound used in the manufacturing of medicines used in indigestion is called an antacid.

10 (d) The correct sequence of parts in the human alimentary canal is:

Mouth → Oesophagus → Stomach → Small intestine → Large intestine

Assertion and Reason

1. (a) A significant difference in ion concentration often exists between the fluid in xylem cells of roots and the surrounding soil. Xylem cells actively take up ions from the soil through root cells, creating this concentration gradient necessary for nutrient absorption.

2. (c) Bile is not produced by the pancreas but the liver, and its help in digestion of fats.

3. (c) Villi are finger-like projections rich in blood vessels, their primary role is to increase the surface area for absorption of nutrients, not to complete the digestion of food.

4. (c) Carbohydrate digestion begins in the mouth and completes in the small intestine, with pancreatic amylase breaking down carbohydrates. Lactase, produced by the cells lining the small intestine, specifically digests lactose, a milk sugar.

5. (c) Different unicellular organisms have evolved diverse mechanisms to take in food based on the needs and environment.

RESPIRATION

2

NCERT Definitions (Commonly asked in 1 mark)

- **Respiration:** The process of acquiring oxygen from outside the body and using it to break down food sources for cellular needs.
- **Aerobic Respiration:** The process where glucose breaks down into carbon dioxide and water, using oxygen, to release energy.
- **Anaerobic Respiration:** The process by which glucose is broken down in the absence of oxygen, resulting in the production of ethanol and carbon dioxide (in yeast)or lactic acid (in muscles)along with energy.
- **Pyruvate:** Key intermediate in the breakdown of glucose.
- **Diaphragm:** A large, dome-shaped muscle at the base of the lungs that plays a key role in breathing by contracting and flattening to enlarge the chest cavity.
- **ATP (Adenosine Triphosphate):** The energy currency of the cell for most cellular processes.
- **Lactic Acid:** Three-carbon molecule produced in muscles during rapid exercise when the body switches to anaerobic respiration.
- **Alveoli:** Tiny balloon-like structures in the lungs where gas exchange occurs between the air and blood.
- **Haemoglobin:** A protein in red blood cells with a high affinity for oxygen, responsible for transporting oxygen and carbon dioxide in the blood.
- **Residual volume:** The amount of air that remains in the lungs after a complete exhalation ensures there is sufficient time for oxygen to be absorbed and for carbon dioxide to be released.

Important Facts

01 The site where the first step of both aerobic and anaerobic respiration occurs in cells.

~ Cytoplasm

02 The process of respiration where glucose is completely broken down.

~ Aerobic Respiration

03 Fishes intake water through their mouths and expel it past the gills to absorb dissolved oxygen directly from water.

04 Respiratory pigment crucial for O_2/CO_2 transport in large animals where diffusion alone is insufficient.

~ Haemoglobin

05 Aerobic respiration, generating up to 38 ATP from one glucose molecule, is more efficient than anaerobic respiration, which produces only 2 ATP.*

06 Aquatic organisms breathe faster than terrestrial organisms because water has less dissolved oxygen than air.

07 The structure that prevents the air passage from collapsing.

~Rings of Cartilage

** Concepts beyond the board exam syllabus, offering deeper insight and critical thinking on NCERT topics.*

Classification

Respiration (On the Basis of Presence or Absence of Oxygen)		
Aspect	**Aerobic Respiration**	**Anaerobic Respiration**
Location in Cell	Mitochondria	Cytoplasm
Oxygen Requirement	Requires oxygen	Does not require oxygen
End Products	Carbon dioxide, water, and energy (ATP)	Ethanol and Carbon dioxide (yeast), Lactic acid (Muscle cells) along with energy
Energy Yield	High	Low
Examples	Most plants, animals, and many microorganisms	Yeast during fermentation, muscle cells under strenuous activity, some bacteria

Difference Between (Commonly asked in 2-3 mark)

Breathing v/s Respiration	
Breathing	**Respiration**
Intake of O_2 from air and removal of CO_2	Oxidation of food to form carbon dioxide, water and energy
Physical process	Biochemical process
No energy is released*	Energy is released in the form of ATP*
Extracellular process*	Intracellular process*
No enzymes involved	Large number of enzymes are involved
Confined to certain organs	Occurs in all the cells of the body

Breath In v/s Breath Out	
Breath in	**Breath out**
Chest cavity increases	Chest cavity decreases
Diaphragm become flat in shape	Diaphragm becomes dome shaped
Ribs lift upwards	Ribs move downwards
Volume of lungs increases and air enters the lungs	Volume of lungs decreases and air exits from the lungs.

Real Life Application Based Questions

1. **Have you noticed hiccups tend to occur more frequently after consuming large meals quickly? Why do you think it happens?***

Ans. When you eat a big meal quickly, your stomach expands rapidly. This sudden expansion can press against your diaphragm, the muscle that helps you breathe, causing it to spasm and create hiccups as you inhale. It's like your body's quirky way of saying, "Slow down!"

** Concepts beyond the board exam syllabus, offering deeper insight and critical thinking on NCERT topics.*

2. **Have you ever wondered why bread rises and becomes fluffy when baked, and where does the alcohol produced during this process go?**

Ans. In bread making, yeast ferments sugar into carbon dioxide and alcohol. Baking evaporates the alcohol and traps carbon dioxide, expanding the dough for a fluffy, alcohol-free texture.

3. **Have you ever wondered how fish manage to breathe underwater while humans need air? Consider the process you observed in the aquarium.**

Ans. Fish breathe underwater by drawing water into their mouths and forcing it over their gills, where oxygen is extracted. This process allows them to extract dissolved oxygen directly from the water, unlike humans who breathe air.

Myth Buster

- **Myth: Plants do not perform respiration; they only photosynthesize.**

  Fact: Plants engage in both photosynthesis, converting light into chemical energy stored as glucose, and respiration, breaking down glucose for energy in cellular processes, regardless of light presence.

- **Myth: Respiration and breathing are the same process.**

  Fact: Breathing involves taking in oxygen and expelling carbon dioxide using the lungs, while respiration is a cellular process that uses oxygen to generate energy from food, producing carbon dioxide.

- **Myth: Cellular respiration only occurs in the presence of oxygen.**

  Fact: Cellular respiration occurs aerobically (with oxygen) for high energy yield, and anaerobically (without oxygen or low oxygen), yielding less energy and byproducts like lactic acid in muscle cells.

- **Myth: You use only your lungs to breathe.**

  Fact: Breathing also involves the diaphragm, intercostal muscles, rib cage, and abdominal muscles.

- **Myth: The rate of breathing in fish and terrestrial animals is the same.**

  Fact: Fish breathe through gills and need to extract oxygen from water, which contains less oxygen compared to air. Therefore, the rate of breathing in fish is much faster than in terrestrial animals, which breathe oxygen directly from the air.

Mnemonics

- **Passage of air in human respiratory system (Outside to inside)**

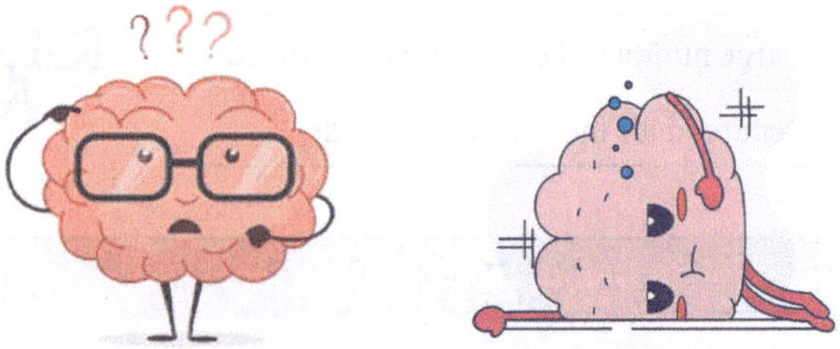

Not	Thinking?	Boring	Brain	Always!
↓	↓	↓	↓	↓
Nostril	Trachea	Bronchi	Bronchioles	Alveoli

COMPETENCY BASED SOLVED EXAMPLES

Multiple Choice Questions (1 M)

1. During exhalation, the exchange of gases takes place between ***(Re)***

(*a*) Alveoli of the lungs and blood.

(*b*) Alveoli of lungs and tissue fluid.

(*c*) Blood and body tissues

(*d*) Tissue fluid and blood capillaries

2. The correct sequence of anaerobic reactions in yeast is ***(Re)*** **(NCERT Exemplar)**

(*a*) Glucose $\xrightarrow{\text{Cytoplasm}}$ Pyruvate $\xrightarrow{\text{Mitochondria}}$ Ethanol + Carbon dioxide

(*b*) Glucose $\xrightarrow{\text{Cytoplasm}}$ Pyruvate $\xrightarrow{\text{Cytoplasm}}$ Lactic acid

(*c*) Glucose $\xrightarrow{\text{Cytoplasm}}$ Pyruvate $\xrightarrow{\text{Mitochondria}}$ Lactic acid

(*d*) Glucose $\xrightarrow{\text{Cytoplasm}}$ Pyruvate $\xrightarrow{\text{Cytoplasm}}$ Ethanol + Carbon dioxide

3. A student sets up an experiment to study human respiration using lime water, test tube and a straw. He fills a freshly prepared lime water in a test tube and blow air through straw into the lime water. It was observed that the solution turns cloudy as shown. What can be evaluate from this observation? ***(An)***

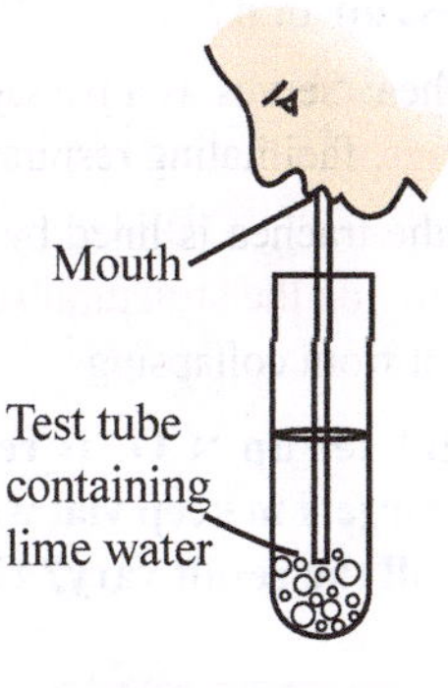

(*a*) Oxygen is exhaled during respiration

(*b*) Water vapours are produced during respiration

(*c*) Carbon dioxide is exhaled during respiration

(*d*) Glucose is produced during respiration

4. Which of the following statements are correct in reference to the role of A (shown in the given diagram) during a breathing cycle in human beings? ***(An)*** **CBSE, 2022 Term I)**

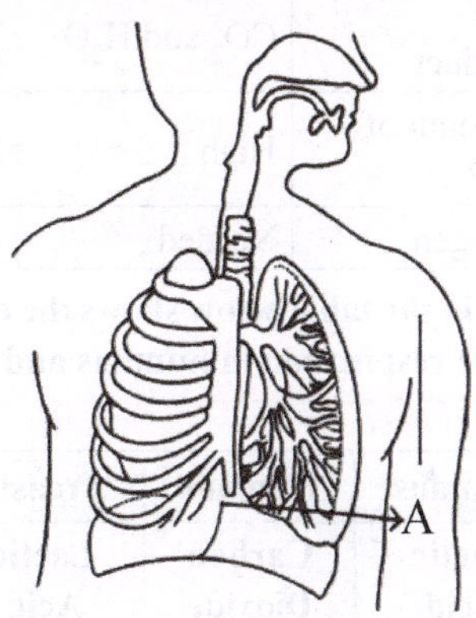

(*i*) It helps to decrease the residual volume of air in lungs.

(*ii*) It flattens as we inhale.

(*iii*) It gets raised as we inhale.

(*iv*) It helps the chest cavity to become larger.

(*a*) (*ii*) and (*iv*) (*b*) (*iii*) and (*iv*)

(*c*) (*i*) and (*ii*) (*d*) (*i*), (*ii*) and (*iv*)

5. As the cricket match progresses, some players begin to experience *muscle cramps*. The coach *gathers* the team to discuss the possible causes. What is the likely reason for these cramps? ***(Ap)***

(*a*) The conversion of pyruvate to ethanol

(*b*) The conversion of pyruvate to glucose

(*c*) The conversion of glucose to pyruvate

(*d*) The conversion of pyruvate to lactic acid

6. Oxygen saturation levels refer to the extent haemoglobin is bound to oxygen. As altitude increases, the atmospheric pressure decreases.

Which of the following graphs correctly represents the oxygen saturation levels as altitude increases? ***(An)***

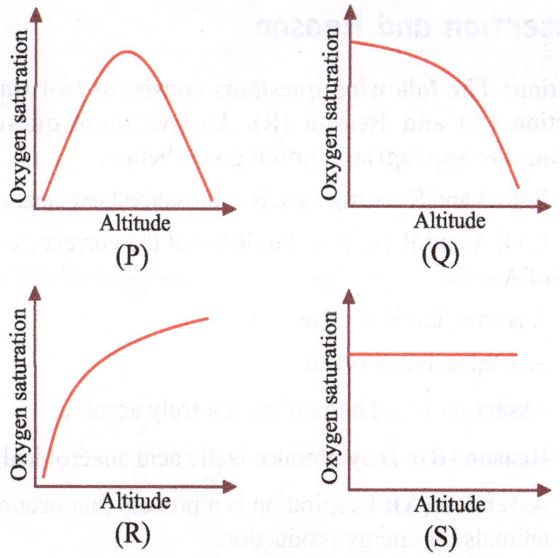

(*a*) P (*b*) Q

(*c*) R (*d*) S

7. **Study the table given below and select the option that has the incorrect information.** ***(Re)***

	Aspects	Aerobic	Anaerobic
(*a*)	Location	Cytoplasm	Mitochondria
(*b*)	End Product	CO_2 and H_2O	Ethanol and CO_2
(*c*)	Amount of ATP	High	Low
(*d*)	Oxygen	Needed	Not needed

8. **Which row in the table below shows the correct products of anaerobic respiration in humans and in yeast?** ***(Un)* (CFPQ)**

	Humans	Humans	Yeast	Yeast
	Lactic Acid	Carbon Dioxide	Lactic Acid	Carbon Dioxide
(*a*)	×	✓	×	×
(*b*)	✓	×	×	✓
(*c*)	×	✓	✓	×
(*d*)	✓	✓	✓	×

9. **Which is the correct sequence of air passage during inhalation?** ***(Re)* (NCERT Exemplar)**
   (*a*) Nostrils → Larynx → Pharynx → Trachea → Lungs
   (*b*) Nasal passage → Trachea → Pharynx → Larynx → Alveoli
   (*c*) Larynx → Nostrils → Pharynx → Lungs
   (*d*) Nostrils → Pharynx → Larynx → Trachea → Alveoli

10. **A study shows that smokers have a higher incidence of lung diseases compared to non-smokers. This can be attributed to:** ***(Un)***
   (*a*) Lower levels of carbon monoxide in the blood.
   (*b*) Increased ciliary movement.
   (*c*) Destruction of cilia in the respiratory tract.
   (*d*) Decreased air pollution exposure

Assertion and Reason (1 M)

Direction: **The following questions consist of two statements Assertion (A) and Reason (R). Answer these questions by selecting the appropriate option given below:**

(*a*) Both A and R are true, and R is the correct explanation of A.
(*b*) Both A and R are true, but R is not the correct explanation of A.
(*c*) A is true, but R is false.
(*d*) A is false, but R is true.

1. **Assertion (A):** Humans are not truly aerobic.
   Reason (R): They produce lactic acid anaerobically. ***(Re)***
2. **Assertion (A):** Respiration is a process that occurs only in animals for energy production.
   Reason (R): Respiration involves the breakdown of glucose into carbon dioxide and water, releasing energy. ***(Un)***
3. **Assertion (A):** Lungs always contain a residual volume of air.
   Reason (R): It provides sufficient time for oxygen to be absorbed and for carbon dioxide to be released. ***(Re)***
4. **Assertion (A):** The anaerobic respiration which takes place in yeast, has one of the end products as an acid.
   Reason (R): During anaerobic respiration, there is incomplete breakdown of glucose. ***(Un)* (CBSE, 2023)**
5. **Assertion (A):** Tobacco use can significantly affect the lungs.
   Reason (R): Tobacco smoke and chewable tobacco contain harmful substances that can cause diseases, including cancer and cardiovascular diseases. ***(Un)***

Subjective Questions

Very Short Answer Type Questions (2 M)

1. **All plants give out oxygen during the day and carbon dioxide during night". Do you agree with this statement? Give a reason.** ***(Ap)***

Ans. During day time, as the rate of photosynthesis is more than the rate of respiration, the net result is evolution of oxygen. At night there is no photosynthesis, so they give out carbon dioxide due to respiration. *(2 M)*

2. **What happens to the rate of breathing during vigorous exercise and why?** ***(Ap)***

Ans. The rate of breathing increases during vigorous exercise to
- Obtain more oxygen for ATP production, providing instant energy. *(1 M)*
- Remove the body of extra CO_2 produced during cellular respiration. *(1 M)*

3. **(*a*) State the function of trachea.**
   (*b*) Why do the walls of trachea do not collapse even when there is less air in it? ***(Un)***

Ans. (*a*) Function of trachea: Serves as a passageway for air to enter and exit the lungs, facilitating respiration. *(1 M)*

(*b*) The passage of the trachea is lined by C-shaped rings of cartilage which provide the structural support to the air passage and prevent it from collapsing. *(1 M)*

4. **In the experimental set up 'CO_2 is released during respiration', if one forgets to keep vial with KOH in the conical flask, how will the result vary? Give details.** ***(An)***

Ans. If KOH is not placed in the vial within the conical flask
- CO_2 produced by respiration will not be absorbed *(½ M)*
- No partial vacuum created in the conical flask *(½ M)*
- Air pressure inside the flask will not be reduced *(½ M)*
- Water level in the delivery tube will not rise *(½ M)*

5. **Write two different ways in which glucose is oxidized to provide energy in human body. Write the products formed in each case.** ***(Re)***

Ans. Glucose can be oxidized to provide energy in two ways in the human body: aerobic respiration and anaerobic respiration.

Aerobic respiration: It involves the oxidation of glucose in the presence of oxygen to produce carbon dioxide, water, and ATP.

$$\text{Glucose} \xrightarrow[\text{(in mitochondria)}]{\text{Presence of oxygen}} CO_2 + H_2O + \text{Energy (ATP)}$$

(1 M)

Anaerobic respiration: It occurs when body lacks oxygen and produces lactic acid and ATP.

$$\text{Glucose} \xrightarrow[\text{(in muscle cells)}]{\text{Lack of oxygen}} \text{Lactic acid} + \text{energy (ATP)}$$

(1 M)

Short Answer Type Questions (3 M)

1. Why diffusion is not sufficient to meet oxygen requirement of all the cells in multicellular organisms? (Ap)

Ans. In multicellular organisms, diffusion alone cannot meet the oxygen requirements of all cells due to:

Large body size: The body size of multicellular organisms is large, making diffusion an insufficient method for transporting oxygen to all parts. *(1 M)*

Complexity: The complexity of multicellular organisms necessitates a specialized system for oxygen delivery, as simple diffusion cannot adequately reach all tissues. *(1 M)*

Efficient transport: Respiratory pigments like hemoglobin in humans transport oxygen from the lungs to body tissues more effectively than simple diffusion can. *(1 M)*

2. (*i*) Why is respiratory pigment needed in multicellular organisms with large body size?

(*ii*) Give reasons for the following:

(*a*) Rings of cartilage are present in the throat.

(*b*) Lungs always contain a residual volume of air.

(*c*) The diaphragm flattens and ribs are lifted up when we breathe in.

(*d*) Walls of alveoli contain an extensive network of blood vessels. (*Un*) (CBSE, 2024)

Ans. (*i*) Respiratory pigment is needed in multicellular organisms with large body size to facilitate the transport of oxygen to all parts of the body, as diffusion alone is inadequate for this purpose. *(1 M)*

(*ii*) Reasons:

(*a*) Rings of Cartilage prevent the collapse of the air-passage (i.e., trachea) in the throat. *(½ M)*

(*b*) During breathing, the lungs retain residual air, ensuring efficient oxygen absorption and carbon dioxide release. *(½ M)*

(*c*) When we inhale, our ribs rise and our diaphragm flattens, causing the chest cavity to expand. This expansion draws air into the lungs, filling the expanded alveoli. *(½ M)*

(*d*) Walls of alveoli contain an extensive network of blood vessels to facilitate the gaseous exchange (O_2) and (CO_2) between the lungs and bloodstream. *(½ M)*

3. (*i*) State the role of ATP in cellular respiration.

(*ii*) What ensures sufficient exchange of gases in plants?

(*iii*) State the conditions on which the direction of diffusion of gases in plant depend upon.

(*Re*) (CBSE, 2023)

Ans. (*i*) The role of ATP in cellular respiration:

Energy storage: ATP stores energy released during respiration

Energy transfer: It captures energy released during respiration and makes it available for other cellular functions. *(1 M)*

(*ii*) The sufficient exchange of gases in plants is ensured by the presence of stomata on leaves and the large inter-cellular spaces that facilitate diffusion. *(1 M)*

(*iii*) The direction of diffusion of gases in plants depends upon the concentration gradients of gases (O_2 and CO_2) and environmental conditions, such as light and temperature. *(1 M)*

4. Study the following flow chart showing the breakdown of glucose by various pathways. In this flow chart, in four blocks some blanks are given as Ⓐ, Ⓑ, Ⓒ and Ⓓ. (*Re*)

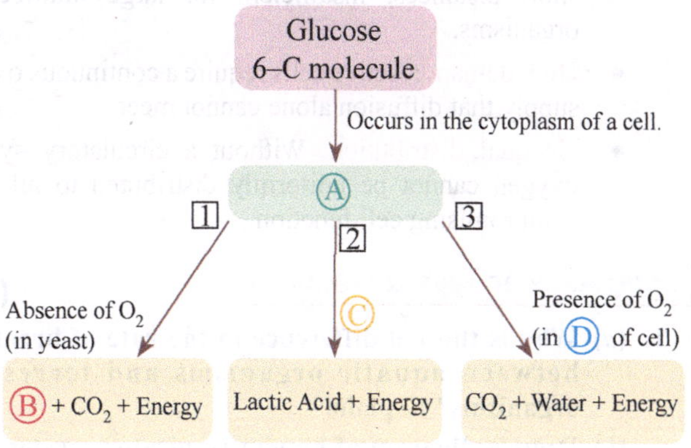

(*i*) Write the names of Ⓐ, Ⓑ, Ⓒ and Ⓓ.

(*ii*) Write the source of glucose molecule involved in cellular respiration in (a) plants, and (b) animals.

Ans. (i) In the given flowchart:

A: Pyruvate

B: Ethanol

C: Lack of oxygen (in muscle)

D: Mitochondria *(2 M)*

(ii) Source of glucose in cellular respiration:

(a) Plants: Glucose in plants is primarily produced through photosynthesis in the leaves using carbon dioxide, water, and sunlight. *(½ M)*

(b) Animals: Animals obtain glucose from the food they consume, which is broken down into glucose during digestion. *(½ M)*

5. Write the differences between inhalation and exhalation. (*Un*)

Ans.

Inhalation	Exhalation
1. Chest cavity enlarges	Chest cavity reduces
2. Ribs lift up	Ribs move downwards
3. Diaphragm flattens and move downwards	Diaphragm becomes dome-shaped and raised upwards

(1×3 = 3 M)

6. **How are the alveoli designed to maximise the exchange of gases?** **(*Un*) (NCERT)**

Ans. Alveoli are designed to maximise the exchange of gases as it has

- Extremely thin walls, enhancing the rate of diffusion of oxygen into and carbon dioxide out of the blood. *(1 M)*
- Rich network of blood vessels, ensuring that the blood comes into close contact with the alveolar air, maximizing the exchange of gases. *(1 M)*
- Balloon-like structures which provide the maximum surface area for the exchange of gases. *(1 M)*

7. **Imagine you're a tiny cell deep inside a large multicellular organism. Explain why depending solely on diffusion for oxygen may not be enough to keep you alive and functioning properly.** **(*Un*)**

Ans. In a large multicellular organism, simple diffusion is inadequate for oxygen delivery due to:

- Distance limitation: Diffusion is efficient only over short distances, insufficient for large multicellular organisms. *(1 M)*
- High demand: Active cells require a continuous oxygen supply that diffusion alone cannot meet. *(1 M)*
- Unequal distribution: Without a circulatory system, oxygen cannot be uniformly distributed to all cells, compromising cell function. *(1 M)*

Long Answer Type Questions (5 M)

1. **(*a*) Why is there a difference in the rate of breathing between aquatic organisms and terrestrial organisms? Explain.**

   (*b*) Draw a diagram of human respiratory system and label-pharynx, trachea, lungs, diaphragm and alveolar sac on it. **(*Un, Cr*) (CBSE, 2020)**

Ans. (*a*) The rate of respiration varies between aquatic and terrestrial organisms due to the following reasons:

Aquatic organisms, such as fishes, extract oxygen from water through their gills since it is present in a dissolved state. *(1 M)*

Since the amount of dissolved oxygen in water is lower compared to the oxygen in the gaseous form in air, aquatic organisms need higher breathing rates to fulfill their oxygen requirements. *(1 M)*

(*b*)

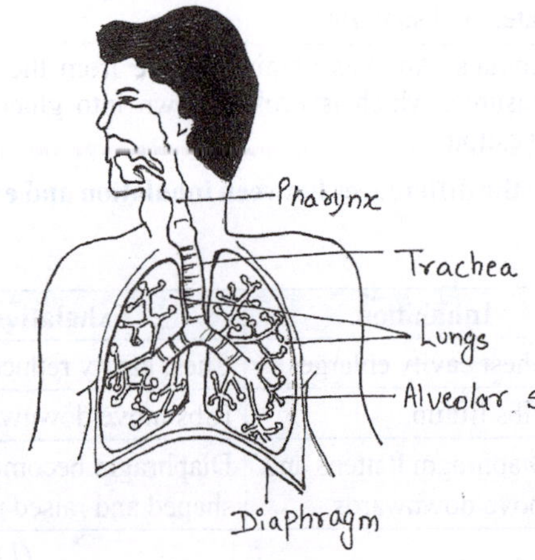

(3 M)

2. **What are the differences between aerobic and anaerobic respiration? Name some organisms that use the anaerobic mode of respiration.** **(*Un, Re*) (NCERT)**

Ans.

Aerobic respiration	Anaerobic Respiration
1. Takes place in the presence of oxygen	Takes place in the absence of oxygen
2. Complete breakdown of food occurs	Partial or incomplete breakdown of food occurs
3. The end products are CO_2 and H_2O	The end products may be ethyl alcohol, CO_2 or lactic acid
4. It produces a considerable amount of energy due to complete oxidation of food.	Much less energy is produced due to incomplete oxidation of food.

(1×4 = 4 M)

Organisms that use the anaerobic mode of respiration are yeast, bacteria and some parasitic worms. *(1 M)*

Hints & Explanations

Multiple Choice Questions

1. (*a*) During exhalation, the exchange of gases takes place between the alveoli of the lungs and the blood in the pulmonary capillaries. The deoxygenated blood releases carbon dioxide into the alveoli, which is then expelled during exhalation.

2. (*d*) Glucose $\xrightarrow{\text{Cytoplasm}}$ Pyruvate $\xrightarrow{\text{Cytoplasm}}$ Ethanol + Carbon dioxide

3. (*c*) When air is blown from the mouth into a test tube containing lime water, the lime water turns cloudy due to the presence of carbon dioxide.

4. (*a*) Figure A represents diaphragm. As we inhale, the diaphragm flattens and pulls downward, increasing the volume of the thoracic cavity. This action directly enlarges the chest cavity, allowing the lungs to expand and draw in air.

Mistakes 101 : What not to do!

A common error is to confuse the movements involved in inhalation with those of exhalation. Focus on the specific role of the diaphragm and thoracic cavity changes.

5. (*d*) The likely reason for muscle cramps during the cricket match is the conversion of pyruvate to lactic acid. This occurs when muscle cells utilize anaerobic respiration due to insufficient oxygen during intense activity, leading to the accumulation of lactic acid and muscle cramps.

6. (*b*) As altitude increases, atmospheric pressure decreases. As a result, less oxygen is available to bind with haemoglobin, reducing hemoglobin's oxygen saturation. Among the given graphs, Q correctly depicts this gradual decline in oxygen saturation with increasing altitude, aligning with physiological principles.

7. (*a*) Aerobic respiration takes place in the presence of oxygen in mitochondria whereas anaerobic respiration takes place in the absence of oxygen in cytoplasm.

8. (*b*) Humans produce lactic acid and yeast produce carbon dioxide and ethanol during anaerobic respiration.

9. (*d*) The correct sequence of air passage during inhalation is: Nostrils →Pharynx → Larynx →Trachea → Alveoli

Key Takeaways

Through this question, student learnt the sequence of air passage during inhalation.

10. (*c*) Smoking can harm the respiratory tract's cilia, which are vital for filtering out harmful substances, thus increasing the risk of lung diseases in smokers.

Assertion and Reason

1. (*a*) Lactic acid production in skeletal muscles during anaerobic activities in humans indicates they utilize both aerobic and anaerobic respiration.

2. (*d*) Respiration occurs in both animals and plants for energy production, involving the breakdown of glucose into carbon dioxide and water, releasing energy.

3. (*a*) During the breathing cycle, when air is taken in and let out, the lungs always contain a residual volume of air. It provides sufficient time for oxygen to be absorbed and for CO_2 to be released.

4. (*d*) Anaerobic respiration in yeast primarily produces ethanol and carbon dioxide, not an acid as the main product.

5. (*a*) Tobacco use can significantly affect the lungs because tobacco smoke and chewable tobacco contain harmful substances that can cause diseases, including cancer and cardiovascular diseases.

3 TRANSPORTATION

NCERT Definitions (Commonly asked in 1 mark)

- **Transportation:** The process by which nutrients, gases, and waste products are moved within the organism to support various functions like respiration, nutrition, and excretion.
- **Heart:** A fist sized muscular organ that pumps blood throughout the body.
- **Pulmonary artery:** Blood vessel that carry deoxygenated blood from the right side of your heart to your lungs.
- **Pulmonary vein:** Blood vessel that carry oxygenated blood from your lungs to your heart.
- **Capillaries:** Tiny blood vessels where the exchange of water, oxygen, carbon dioxide, and other nutrients and waste products occurs between blood and cells.
- **Plasma:** Fluid medium of blood in which various cells are suspended.
- **Double Circulation:** A mechanism in which blood circulates twice through the heart in one complete cycle.
- **Systemic circulation:** It is the movement of blood from the heart to the rest of the body and back.
- **Pulmonary circulation:** The exchange of gases between the blood and air in the lungs.
- **Blood pressure:** The force that blood exerts against the wall of a blood vessels.
- **Platelets:** Cells in the blood that help in clotting to prevent excessive bleeding from injuries.
- **Lymph:** A tissue fluid, transports substances in the body, formed from escaped plasma, proteins, and blood cells from capillary walls into intercellular spaces in the tissues.
- **Transpiration:** The process by which water vapor is lost from plants through stomata, aiding in upward movement of water and minerals and temperature regulation.
- **Translocation:** The movement of soluble products of photosynthesis and other substances within plants through the phloem.

Important Facts

01 A type of fluid is similar to blood plasma but is colorless and contains less protein.
~ Lymph

02 A device used to measure blood pressure.
~ Sphygmomanometer

03 The major driving force in the movement of water during night.
~ Root pressure

04 In fish, the heart pumps only deoxygenated blood in a single circulation; the gills facilitate blood oxygenation.

05 The reptile having 4 chambered heart.
~ Crocodile

Classification

❐ Components of Blood

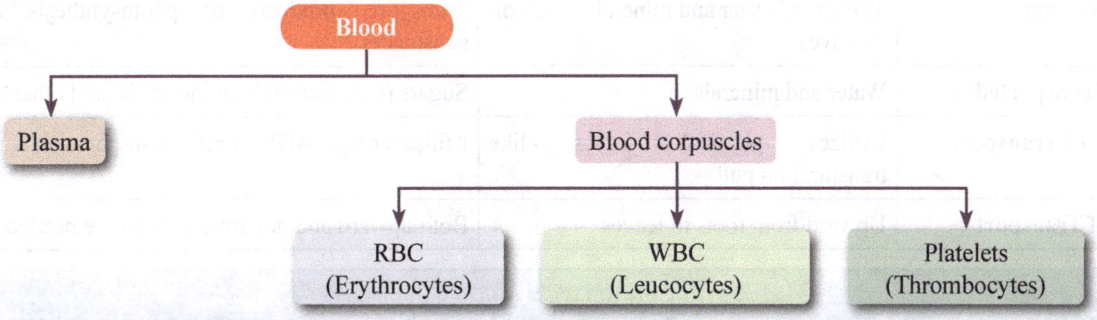

Blood Vessels			
Feature	**Arteries**	**Veins**	**Capillaries**
Function	Carry blood away from the heart to various organs	Bring blood back to the heart from different organs	Allow exchange of material between blood and cells
Wall Thickness	Thick, elastic walls	Thinner walls than arteries, not under high pressure	Walls are one-cell thick
Pressure	High pressure, since blood emerges from the heart	Lower pressure, as blood is not under significant pressure	Very low pressure, facilitating exchange
Valves	Absent	Present (Ensures one-directional blood flow)	Absent
Exchange of Material	Does not occur directly; arteries lead to capillaries for exchange	Does not occur directly; veins collect blood after exchange	Direct site of material exchange with cells

Difference Between (Commonly asked in 2-3 marks)

Systolic Pressure v/s Diastolic Pressure	
Systolic Pressure	**Diastolic Pressure**
Pressure in the artery during ventricular systole (contraction)	Pressure in the artery during ventricular diastole (relaxation)
Normal pressure is about 120 mmHg	Normal pressure is about 80 mmHg

Blood v/s Lymph	
Blood	**Lymph**
Fluid connective tissue with cells suspended in plasma	Fluid formed from escaped capillary contents in tissue spaces
Transports food, oxygen, salts and wastes,etc.	Carries digested and absorbed fats from intestine and, drains excess fluid back into the blood
Red in color due to hemoglobin in red blood cells	Colorless
High protein content in plasma	Lower protein content than blood plasma
Circulated by the heart through arteries, veins, and capillaries	Moves through lymphatic capillaries and vessels, eventually entering the venous circulation

Xylem v/s Phloem		
Feature	**Xylem**	**Phloem**
Primary Function	Transports water and minerals from soil to leaves	Transports products of photosynthesis and other substances
Materials Transported	Water and minerals	Sugars (e.g., sucrose), amino acids, and other substances
Mechanism of Transport	Utilizes physical forces like transpiration pull	Utilizes energy (ATP) for active transport
Direction of Transport	Upward from roots to leaves	Both upward and downward, to where needed

Transpiration v/s Translocation		
Feature	**Arteries**	**Veins**
Definition	The loss of water in the form of vapor from the aerial parts of the plant.	The transport of soluble products from the leaves to other parts of the plant.
Transported Substances	Water and minerals dissolved in it.	Products of photosynthesis (e.g., sucrose), amino acids, and other substances.
Transport Direction	Upward from roots to leaves.	Both upward and downward, according to the plant's needs.
Location	Occurs through stomata in the leaves.	Occurs in the phloem part of the vascular tissue.
Energy Utilization	Primarily passive, relying on physical forces like evaporation and root pressure.	Active, requires energy in the form of ATP to transport substances.

Real Life Application Based Questions

1. **Did you ever wonder how analyzing blood can determine if we are healthy, detect a multitude of infections, and detect or rule out various diseases and injuries?***

Ans. Blood analysis can reveal health status, infections, diseases, and injuries by measuring components like cells, proteins, and sugars, indicating normal function or abnormalities linked to specific health issues.

2. **You've likely noticed the small cuts or scratches stop bleeding after a few minutes? Why do you think that happens?**

Ans. When we get a small cut, platelets in our blood quickly gather at the injury site, forming a plug that stops the bleeding. This process is known as clotting.

3. **Have you ever wondered how water reaches the top of tall trees like the Banyan tree, defying gravity?**

Ans. Water reaches the top of tall trees, such as banyan tree, through a process called transpiration pull. This involves water evaporating from the leaves, creating a suction that pulls water upward from the roots through the xylem vessels, defying gravity.

4. **Have you ever puzzled why deserts are full of cacti, or why they have spines instead of leaves?***

Ans. Cacti thrive in deserts because they've evolved spines to minimize water loss through transpiration, a key adaptation to conserve water in arid environments.

5. **You've just finished a 30-minute jog and are using your digital watch to check your blood pressure. Why might your readings be higher immediately after exercise compared to before starting?**

Ans. Exercise increases heart rate and cardiac output to supply muscles with more oxygen, which temporarily raises blood pressure. A digital watch that measures blood pressure can reflect these changes, showcasing how systolic and diastolic pressures increase as the body's demand for oxygen goes up during physical activity.

** Concepts beyond the board exam syllabus, offering deeper insight and critical thinking on NCERT topics.*

6. When you are ill, the doctor measures your pulse by placing two fingers on your wrist. Why does he do this, and what does it represent?

Ans. The doctor puts his fingers on the wrist to check the pumping activity of the left ventricle and to measure the heart rate. The rate of throbbing felt in the arteries due to this pumping activity is called the pulse, which matches the heartbeat felt at the wrist. The pulse rate may change when we suffer from various diseases.

Myth Buster

- **Myth: Only the heart is involved in the transportation of substances within the human body.**

  Fact: While the heart plays a crucial role in pumping blood throughout the body, the transportation system in humans also involves blood vessels (arteries, veins, and capillaries) and the blood itself, which carries nutrients, oxygen, carbon dioxide, and waste products to and from cells.

- **Myth: Blood in the human body has only one function: to transport oxygen.**

  Fact: Blood in the human body has multiple functions, including the transportation of nutrients, oxygen, carbon dioxide, and waste products. It also plays a role in the immune response, temperature regulation, and hormone distribution.

- **Myth: Veins carry only deoxygenated blood.**

  Fact: While most veins carry deoxygenated blood back to the heart, the pulmonary veins are an exception as they carry oxygenated blood from the lungs to the heart.

- **Myth: Arteries carry only oxygenated blood.**

  Fact: Arteries carry oxygenated blood away from the heart to the rest of the body, with the exception of the pulmonary artery, which carries deoxygenated blood from the heart to the lungs.

- **Myth: Water transport in plants is driven solely by root pressure.**

  Fact: While root pressure plays a role, transpiration (the evaporation of water from leaves) creates a suction force that pulls water up through the plant from the roots to the leaves, known as the transpiration pull.

Mnemonics

- **How does blood travel through the heart?**

  Ray's R.V. went from L.A. to L.V.

VIP	Ray's	R.V.	went from	L.A.	to	L.V.	Amsterdam
↓	↓	↓		↓		↓	↓
Vena cava	Right Atrium	Right Ventricle		Left Atrium		Left Ventricle	Aorta

COMPETENCY BASED SOLVED EXAMPLES

Multiple Choice Questions (1 M)

1. Which of the following is not a mode of transportation? **(Re)**

(a) Ascent of sap (b) Translocation

(c) Circulation (d) Regulation

2. In which form the food is transported in plants? **(Re)**

(a) Starch (b) Sucrose

(c) Fructose (d) Glucose

3. Select the wrong statement from the following: **(Re)**

(a) Upper right chamber of the heart carries deoxygenated blood.

(b) Pulmonary vein carries deoxygenated blood.

(c) Blood pressure is measured using a sphygmomanometer.

(d) All the reptiles except crocodiles have three chambered hearts.

4. Observe the following diagram and identify the process and its significance from the following options: **(An) (CBSE, 2023)**

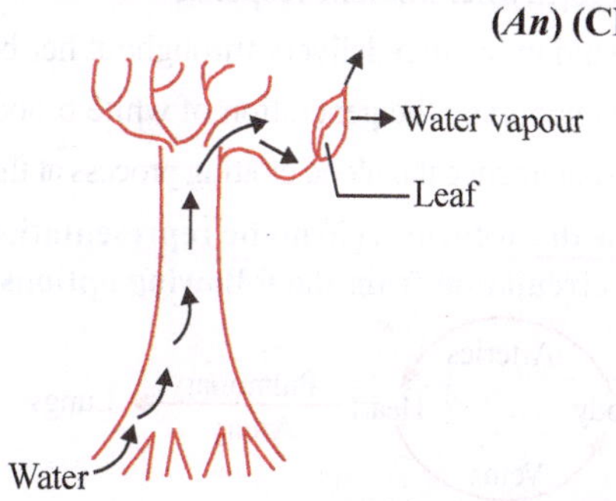

(*a*) Evaporation: Maintains water contents in leaf cells.

(*b*) Transpiration: Creates a suction force which pulls water inside the plant.

(*c*) Excretion: Helps in excreting out waste water from the plant.

(*d*) Translocation: Helps in transporting materials from one cell to another.

5. Consider the following statements in connection with the functions of the blood vessels marked A and B in the diagram of a human heart as shown.
(*An*) (CBSE, 2022 Term I)

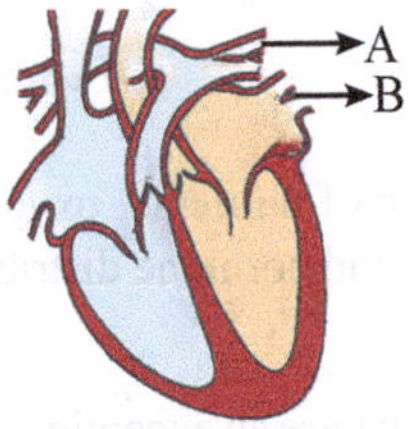

(*i*) Blood vessel A - It carries carbon dioxide rich blood to the lungs.

(*ii*) Blood vessel B - It carries oxygen rich blood from the lungs.

(*iii*) Blood vessel B - Left atrium relaxes as it receives blood from this blood vessel.

(*iv*) Blood vessel A - Right atrium has thick muscular wall as it has to pump blood to this vessel.

The correct statements are

(*a*) (*i*) and (*ii*) only (*b*) (*ii*) and (*iii*) only

(*c*) (*ii*), (*iii*) and (*iv*) (*d*) (*i*), (*ii*) and (*iii*)

6. Which of the following statements is TRUE about the uptake of water in plants? (*Un*)

(*a*) It occurs all the time due to diffusion.

(*b*) Water enters the roots due to osmosis.

(*c*) At night when transpiration is low, roots do not take up water.

(*d*) The movement of water from roots to leaves is bidirectional.

7. Blood from superior vena cava flows into (*Re*)

(*a*) right atrium (*b*) right ventricle

(*c*) left atrium (*d*) left ventricle

8. While gardening, Riya accidentally gets a deep cut on her hand. What is the primary function of platelets in that case? (*Re*)

(*a*) To fortify her immune response

(*b*) To aid in oxygen delivery throughout her body

(*c*) To encourage the generation of white blood cells

(*d*) To commence the blood clotting process at the wound site

9. Choose the accurate schematic representation of human blood circulation from the following options (*An*)

(*a*)
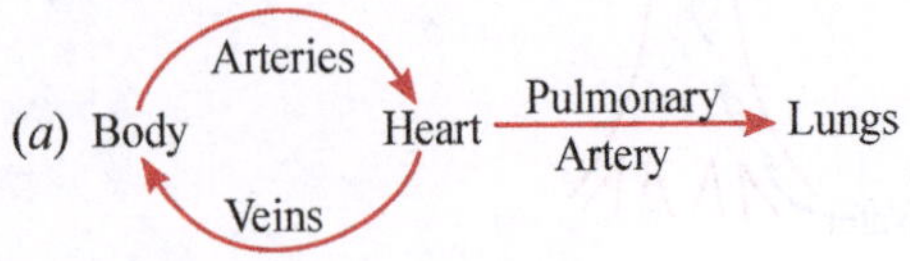

(*b*)
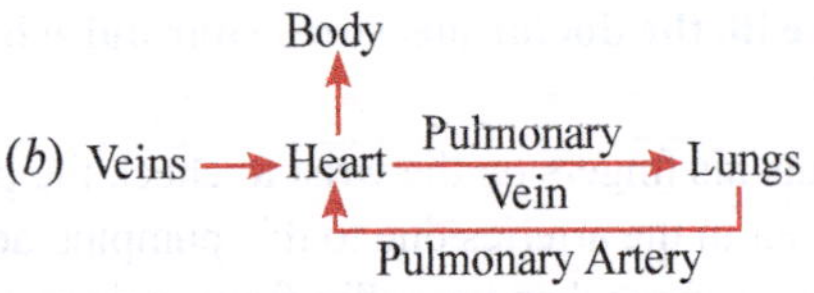

(*c*) Body —Veins→ Heart —Veins→ Lungs —Veins→ Heart

—Artery→ Heart

(*d*)
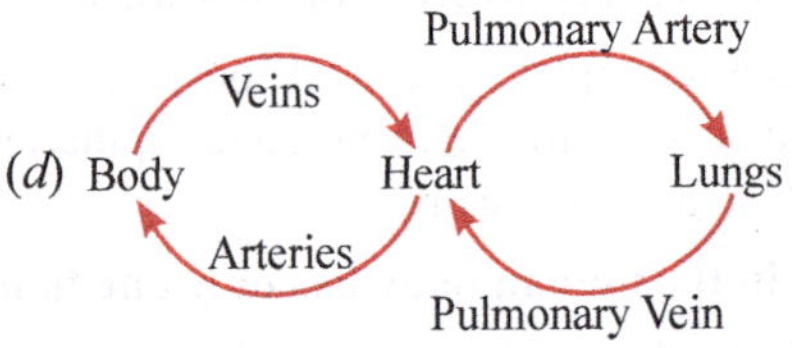

10. Which of the following statement (s) is (are) true about heart? (*Un*) (NCERT Exemplar)

(*i*) Left atrium receives oxygenated blood from different parts of body while right atrium receives deoxygenated blood from lungs

(*ii*) Left ventricle pumps oxygenated blood to different body parts while right ventricle pumps deoxygenated blood to lungs

(*iii*) Left atrium transfers oxygenated blood to right ventricle which sends it to different body parts

(*iv*) Right atrium receives deoxygenated blood from different parts of the body while left ventricle pumps oxygenated blood to different parts of the body

(*a*) (*i*) (*b*) (*ii*)

(*c*) (*ii*) and (*iv*) (*d*) (*i*) and (*iii*)

Assertion and Reason (1 M)

Direction: The following questions consist of two statements – Assertion (A) and Reason (R). Answer these questions by selecting the appropriate option given below:

(*a*) Both A and R are true, and R is the correct explanation of A.

(*b*) Both A and R are true, but R is not the correct explanation of A.

(*c*) A is true, but R is false

(*d*) A is false, but R is true.

1. **Assertion (A):** Valves are present in the arteries.

   Reason (R): Arteries carry oxygenated blood from the heart to different body parts except pulmonary artery. **(*Re*)**

2. **Assertion (A):** In the human heart, there is no mixing of oxygenated and deoxygenated blood.

   Reason (R): Valves are present in the heart which allows the movement of blood in one direction only. **(*Un*)**

3. **Assertion (A):** Double circulation in mammals involves two distinct pathways for blood flow, ensuring efficient oxygen and nutrient transport.

   Reason (R): The pulmonary circulation carries deoxygenated blood from the heart to the lungs, while the systemic circulation delivers oxygenated blood to body tissues. **(*Un*)**

4. **Assertion (A):** Lymph carries digested and absorbed fats from the intestine.

Reason (R): Lymph, which is similar to blood plasma but contains more protein. **(Re)**

5. **Assertion:** Transpiration is the upward movement of water and sugars from roots to leaves.

Reason: Movements of sugars in plants are bidirectional. **(Un)**

Subjective Questions

Very Short Answer Type Questions (2 M)

1. **Identify the figures given below and write the function of each.** **(Re)**

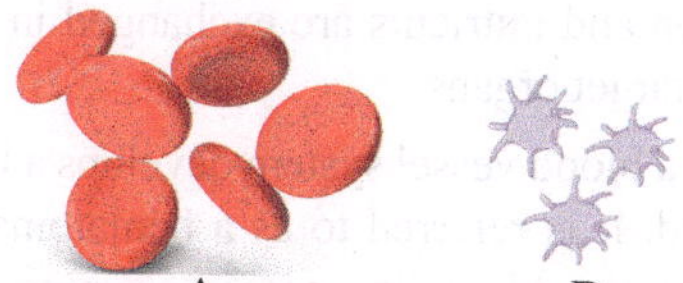

Ans. A: Red blood cells (½ M)

Function: Contain red pigment, hemoglobin that binds with oxygen and transports it to all the parts of the body. (½ M)

B: Platelets (½ M)

Function: Cell fragments that help in clotting of blood (½ M)

2. **Why do arteries have thick and elastic walls whereas veins have valves?** **(Ap) (CBSE SQP, 2023)**

Ans. The blood emerges from the heart under high pressure and flows through arteries. Hence, to bear this pressure the arteries have thick and elastic walls. (1 M)

Veins have valves to ensure that the blood flows in one direction only. (1 M)

3. **Identify the parts from the given diagram which carry oxygenated and deoxygenated blood.** **(Un)**

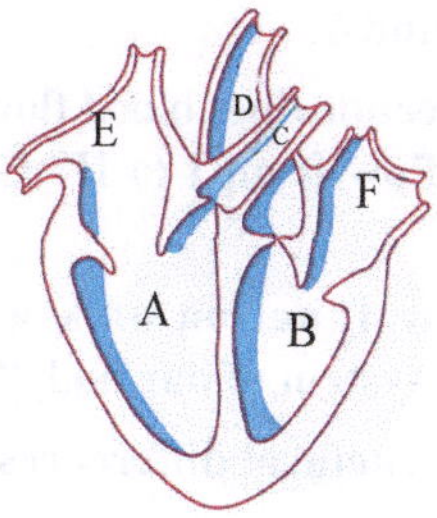

Ans. Oxygenated blood: B-left ventricle, D-aorta and F-left auricle (1 M)

Deoxygenated blood: A-right ventricle, C-pulmonary artery, E-right article. (1 M)

Short Answer Type Questions (3 M)

1. **(i) What is double circulation?**

(ii) Why is the separation of the right side and the left side of the heart useful? How does it help birds and mammals? **(Ap) (CBSE, 2023)**

Ans. (i) Double circulation involves the blood passing the heart twice in one complete cycle. It includes separate pulmonary and systemic circulation. (1 M)

(ii) The separation of the right side and the left side of the heart is useful to

- Prevent mixing of oxygenated and deoxygenated blood (½ M)
- Allows a highly efficient supply of oxygen to the body. (½ M)
- This separation is useful in birds and mammals as they
- Have high energy needs (½ M)
- Need to maintain their body temperature (½ M)

2. **What are the components of the transport system in highly organised plants?** **(Re)**

Ans. In highly organized plants, the transport system consists of specialized tissues designed to transport materials efficiently throughout the plant body.

Xylem: This tissue transports water and dissolved minerals from the roots to various parts of the plant. Driven by transpiration pull and root pressure. (1½ M)

Phloem: Responsible for transporting organic nutrients, particularly sucrose, from the photosynthetic parts of the plant to other parts. (1½ M)

3. **Given below is a table representing the characteristics of two fluids involved in the transportation of substances in the human body.** **(Un)**

Fluid A	Fluid B
Colourless	Coloured
Contains less protein	Contains more protein

(a) Identify fluid A and fluid B.

(b) With the help of a flow chart, describe the movement of fluid A from the intercellular spaces to the main circulatory system.

(c) What role does fluid A play in the digestion of food in humans?

Ans. (a) Fluid A - Lymph (½ M)

Fluid B – Blood (½ M)

(b) Intercellular spaces → lymphatic capillaries → lymph vessels → larger veins (1 M)

(c) Lymph carries digested and absorbed fat from the intestine and drains excess fluid from extracellular space back to the blood. (1 M)

4. **(a) What is translocation? Why is it essential for plants?**

(b) Where do the substances in plants reach as a result of translocation? **(Un)**

Ans. (a) Translocation is the process of moving soluble products of photosynthesis from the leaves to other parts of the plant, essential for distributing food. (1 M)

Function: It is crucial for growth and energy provision to non-photosynthetic parts such as roots and fruits. (1 M)

(b) Destination of Substances: As a result of translocation, substances reach all parts of the plant including roots, stems, flowers, and fruits, supporting their development and function. (1 M)

5. **Give reasons for the following:**

(*i*) **The two ventricles have thicker muscular walls than the two atria in human heart.**

(*ii*) **The capillaries have walls which are one-celled thick.** **(*Ap*)**

Ans. (*i*) The two ventricles have thicker muscular walls than the two atria due to

Higher Pressure Requirement: Ventricles pump blood to the entire body (left ventricle) and to the lungs (right ventricle), requiring more force than atria, which only pump to ventricles. *(1½ M)*

(*ii*) Capillaries have walls which are one-celled thick for

Efficient Exchange: The thin walls facilitate the quick and efficient exchange of nutrients, gases, and waste between blood and tissues. *(1½ M)*

Key Takeaways

Students understand the correlation between the thickness of heart chamber walls and their pumping force, and the capillaries' one-cell thickness aiding in material exchange.

6. **List four functions of the human heart. Why is double circulation necessary in the human body?** **(*Un*)**

Ans. Human heart has following functions

(*i*) Pump blood to the body

(*ii*) Pumping blood to lungs for oxygenation

(*iii*) Distributing substances via blood

(*iv*) Maintain blood pressure *(¼ × 4 = 1 M)*

Importance of Double Circulation in humans:

Efficient Oxygen Supply: Double circulation allows separation of oxygenated and deoxygenated blood, enhancing efficient oxygen supply to the body. *(1 M)*

Supports Higher Metabolism: Supports the high metabolic demands to maintain their body temperature *(1 M)*

7. (*i*) **How water enter continuously into the root xylem?**

(*ii*) **Name the process by which water loss occur in green plants.** **(*Un*)(NCERT Exemplar)**

Ans. (*i*) Water enters the root xylem continuously due to: Root pressure and transpiration pull.

Root pressure: Pressure that forces water upward in the xylem vessels

- Root cells actively absorb ions from the soil, creating a concentration gradient. *(½ M)*
- Increased ion concentration inside the root raises osmotic pressure, driving water movement from the soil into the root. *(½ M)*

Transpiration pull: Suction force aids in drawing the water upward from roots to leaves. *(1 M)*

(*ii*) The process by which water loss occurs in green plants is called transpiration. It involves the evaporation of water vapor through stomata, which are tiny openings on the surface of leaves. *(1 M)*

Long Answer Type Questions (5 M)

1. (*a*) **Write the correct sequence of steps followed during journey of oxygen rich blood from lungs to various organs of human body.**

(*b*) **What happens when the system of blood vessels develop a leak?** **(*Un*) (CBSE, 2020)**

Ans. (*a*) Sequence of steps followed by oxygenated blood during circulation are:

1. The pulmonary veins carry the oxygenated blood from both the lungs to the left atrium.
2. From here, the blood enters the left ventricle.
3. Left ventricle pumps blood to the aorta.
4. From the aorta, this oxygen-rich blood is distributed to various body organs through arteries.
5. Oxygen and nutrients are exchanged in the capillaries at the target organs. *(3 M)*

(*b*) When a blood vessel system develops a leak or a vessel is damaged, it is referred to as a hematoma. In response, platelets in the blood increase their numbers to reduce blood loss and form a clot over the site of the leak. *(2 M)*

2. **Given below are the two different types of blood vessels X and Y.** **(*An*)**

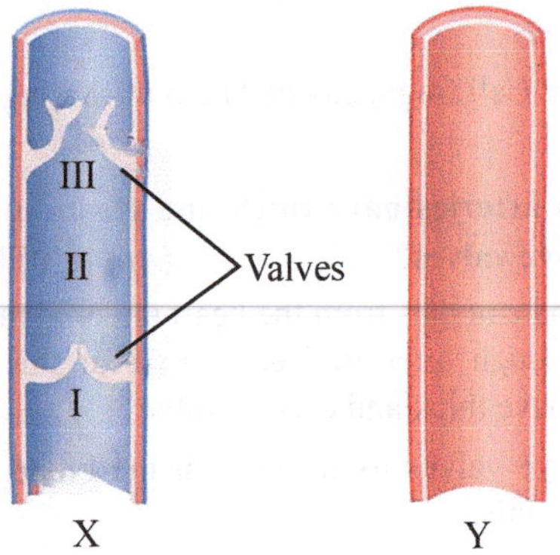

Based on your observation, answer the following questions:

(*a*) **Identify X and Y.**

(*b*) **In what direction does blood flow in X? Do you think blood will flow from I to II? Give reason for your answer.**

(*c*) **What is the function of X and Y found in the circulatory system of our body?**

(*d*) **Write the structural differences between X and Y.**

Ans. (*a*)

- X: Vein *(½ M)*
- Y: Artery *(½ M)*

(*b*) Blood in veins (X) flows from II to III since the valve is open. But blood will not flow from I to II point since the valve is closed. *(1 M)*

(*c*) Veins (X) carry deoxygenated blood from various tissues and organs and return it to the heart. *(½ M)*

Arteries (Y) carry oxygenated blood away from the heart to various tissues and organs. *(½ M)* (*d*) Veins (X): Veins have thinner walls and larger lumens compared to arteries. They contain valves that prevent backflow of blood, ensuring it flows only towards one direction. *(1 M)*

Arteries (Y): Arteries have thicker, more elastic walls to withstand the high pressure of blood being pumped from the heart. They do not have valves because the high pressure ensures unidirectional flow of blood away from the heart. *(1 M)*

3. Dr. Sharma uses an instrument X to measure blood pressure of a patient, Mr. Kumar, a 65 years old person, shows a reading of 145/90 mm Hg.

(*a*) Name the instrument used for measuring blood pressure.

(*b*) What does the reading indicate? Compare these values with standard blood pressure readings.

(*c*) Evaluate Mr. Kumar's risk of hypertension from his readings, and discuss potential health risks if untreated. ***(Re, Ev)***

Ans. (*a*) Sphygmomanometer *(½ M)*

(*b*) The blood pressure reading of 145/90 mm Hg shows that Mr. Kumar's systolic pressure (pressure of blood inside the artery during ventricular contraction) is 145 mm Hg and his diastolic pressure (pressure of blood inside the artery during ventricular relaxation) is 90 mm Hg. *(1 M)*

Normal values are typically 120/80 mm Hg for systolic and diastolic pressures, respectively. Mr. Kumar's higher readings suggest that he has elevated blood pressure. *(1 M)*

(*c*) Mr. Kumar's blood pressure readings (145/90 mm Hg) exceed the normal range (120/80 mm Hg), placing him at risk for hypertension. Untreated hypertension can lead to severe health issues, including increased resistance to blood flow and arteriole constriction, which may eventually cause the rupture of an artery and internal bleeding, among other cardiovascular problems. *(2½ M)*

Hints & Explanations

Multiple Choice Questions

1. (*d*) Regulation refers to the control mechanisms in biological systems, not the movement of substances.
2. (*b*) Food is transported in the form of sucrose in plants with the help of phloem.
3. (*b*) Pulmonary vein carries oxygenated blood from lungs to the heart.
4. (*b*) The process shown is transpiration: it's the evaporation of water from plant leaves, creating a suction force which pulls water up from the roots through the plant.
5. (*d*) Pulmonary Artery (A): Transports deoxygenated blood from right ventricle to lungs.

   Right ventricles have thick muscular walls for pumping blood to various organs, not the right atrium.

   Pulmonary Vein (B): Conveys oxygenated blood from lungs to the left atrium.

   Left atrium relaxes to allow more blood from the lungs to refill its chamber
6. (*b*)
   - Water uptake primarily occurs through osmosis, not diffusion.
   - Roots absorb water at night, although the rate may decrease without the transpiration pull.
   - Water movement is primarily unidirectional, from roots to leaves, driven by transpiration and capillary action.
7. (*a*) Superior and inferior vena cava empties deoxygenated blood into the right atrium. Blood from right atrium enters right ventricle and pulmonary arteries carry deoxygenated blood from right ventricle to lungs for oxygenation.
8. (*d*) The primary function of platelets in Riya's case is to commence the blood clotting process at the wound site. Platelets gather at the cut and form a plug to stop bleeding, initiating clot formation.
9. (*d*) Veins transport deoxygenated blood to the right atrium, which flows into the right ventricle and is pumped to the lungs *via* the pulmonary artery. Oxygenated blood returns *via* the pulmonary vein, enters the left atrium, and is pumped into the aorta for distribution to body tissues through arteries.
10. (*c*) Left atrium receives oxygenated blood from lungs, not body; right atrium receives deoxygenated blood from body, not lungs.

    Left atrium transfers oxygenated blood to the left ventricle, not right ventricle; right ventricle pumps to lungs, not body parts.

Assertion and Reason

1. (*d*) Valves are absent in arteries, whereas it is present in veins, which prevent backflow of blood.
2. (*a*) The human heart has 4 different chambers which prevent mixing of oxygenated and deoxygenated blood due to the partition between two sides called septum.

   Valves are present in the heart to prevent backflow of blood i.e., to allow the movement of blood in one direction only.
3. (*a*) Double Circulation in mammals consists of the pulmonary circulation (Carries deoxygenated blood from heart to lungs) and the systemic circulation (Carries oxygenated blood from heart to body tissues). These two distinct pathways ensures efficient oxygen and nutrient distribution.
4. (*c*) Lymph contains less protein compared to blood plasma.
5. (*d*) Transpiration is the process of water movement through a plant and its evaporation from parts, such as leaves, stems and flowers.

4 EXCRETION

NCERT Definitions (Commonly asked in 1 mark)

- **Excretion:** The biological process of removing harmful metabolic wastes from the body.
- **Nitrogenous Wastes:** Wastes that contain nitrogen, such as urea or uric acid, generated from metabolic activities and need to be excreted.
- **Kidneys:** Red-bean shaped organs located in the abdomen that filter blood to produce urine.
- **Ureters:** Tubes that connect the kidneys with the urinary bladder.
- **Urinary Bladder:** A muscular sac that stores urine until it is excreted through the urethra.
- **Urethra:** The tube through which urine is expelled from the urinary bladder to the outside of the body.
- **Nephrons:** The basic filtration units in the kidneys.
- **Bowman's Capsule:** A cup-shaped structure in the nephron containing a capillary cluster, where blood filtration begins.
- **Cellular Vacuoles:** Membrane-bound compartments within plant cells where waste products are often stored.
- **Resins and Gums:** Stored waste products especially in old xylem.
- **Artificial kidney:** A device to remove nitrogenous waste products from the blood through dialysis.
- **Organ Transplantation:** The surgical procedure of transferring an organ from one person (donor) to another (recipient) to replace a damaged or failing organ.

Glomerulus: Filters 180 litres of blood per day
Renal tubes: Reabsorbs 99% of that
Glomerulus:

Important Facts

01 The common process that facilitates nutrition, respiration, transportation and excretion in unicellular organisms.
~ Diffusion

02 The process can substitute for natural kidney function in cases of kidney failure.
~ Hemodialysis

03 A fluid used in hemodialysis that has the same osmotic pressure as blood but without nitrogenous wastes.
~ Dialysing Fluid

Classification

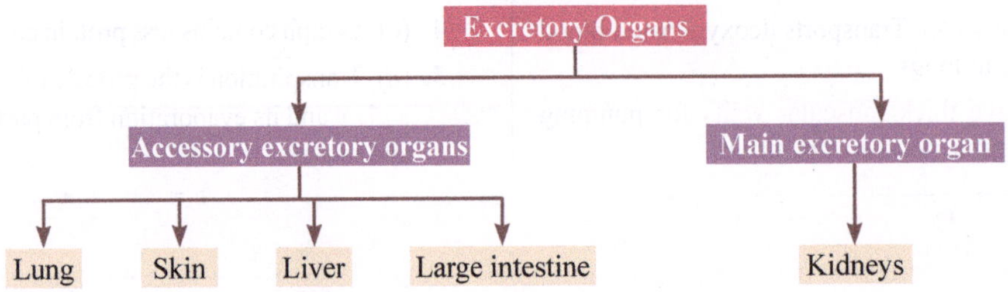

Difference Between (Commonly asked in 2-3 marks)

Excretion in Plants v/s Animals		
Feature	**Plants**	**Animals**
Method of Excretion	Transpiration, storage in dead tissues, loss of parts	Specialised organs for filtration and expulsion
Types of Wastes	O_2, CO_2, water, organic wastes	Nitrogenous wastes, CO_2, metabolic wastes
Excretion of Nitrogenous Wastes	Mostly stored in tissues or expelled into soil	Actively removed through kidneys

Excretion in Human Beings v/s Artificial Kidney (Hemodialysis)		
Aspect	**Human Beings**	**Artificial Kidney (Hemodialysis)**
Mechanism	Natural filtration and reabsorption	Dialysis through a semi-permeable membrane
Reabsorption	Present, for water and other substances	Absent, only filtration
Purpose	Remove nitrogenous waste and regulate fluid balance.	Remove nitrogenous waste in case of kidney failure
Components	Kidneys, ureters, urinary bladder, urethra	Dialysing fluid, semi-permeable tubes, dialysis machine
Dependency	Autonomous function of the body	Requires external machinery and supervision

Real Life Application Based Questions

1. **How do individuals with kidney failure continue to live, and what role does dialysis play in their survival? Is dialysis a permanent solution?**

Ans. Individuals with kidney failure survive through dialysis, which performs the kidneys' filtering functions to remove waste from the blood. While dialysis is life-saving, it's not a permanent cure; it's a treatment that requires ongoing sessions to maintain health.

2. **Why do health experts advise us to drink plenty of water, and what role does water play in the process of waste removal from our body through urine?***

Ans. Health experts recommend drinking plenty of water because it aids the kidneys in filtering and flushing out waste products from the body. Adequate hydration ensures efficient urine production, helping to maintain a healthy balance of bodily fluids and prevent kidney stones.

Myth Buster

- **Myth: Kidneys are the only organs involved in excretion.**

  Fact: Excretion involves multiple organs: kidneys remove urea, lungs expel CO_2, skin releases sweat, and the liver detoxifies substances for elimination.

- **Myth: Plants do not have specialized structures for excretion.**

  Fact: While plants do not have organs equivalent to the kidneys or lungs, they possess structures like stomata (for gas exchange and water vapor release) and lenticels (for gas exchange in woody plants), which play a role in the excretion process.

- **Myth: People with one kidney have a significantly reduced quality of life.**

  Fact: Individuals can live healthy, active life with just one kidney. The remaining kidney can adapt and compensate for the loss of the other, although it's crucial to avoid activities that could damage the remaining kidney and to maintain a healthy lifestyle.

* *Concepts beyond the board exam syllabus, offering deeper insight and critical thinking on NCERT topics.*

Mnemonics

❐ **Kidney functions – WET BREAD**

- W → Water balance
- E → Electrolyte balance
- T → Toxin removal
- B → Blood pressure control
- R → Renin formation
- E → Erythropoietin making
- A → Acid-base balance
- D → Vitamin D metabolism

COMPETENCY BASED SOLVED EXAMPLES

Multiple Choice Questions (1 M)

1. By analysing the urea levels in the blood of person A and B. It was found that person A's urea levels are higher than normal. ***(An)***

Individual	Urea in Blood
Person A	200 mg/dL
Person B	20 mg/dL

Considering the urea levels presented, which organ in Person A might be malfunctioning?

(*a*) Urinary Bladder (*b*) Liver
(*c*) Kidneys (*d*) Ureters

2. What is the primary purpose of the Bowman's capsule in the human kidney? ***(Un)***

(*a*) Production of urine
(*b*) Absorption of glucose
(*c*) Collection of blood filtrate
(*d*) Secretion of hormones

3. In an experiment to test kidney function, which substance would you expect not to be found in healthy urine? ***(Un)***

(*a*) Urea (*b*) Water
(*c*) Glucose (*d*) Salts

4. Considering the function of nephrons, what would likely happen if a person's blood flow to the kidneys decreases significantly? ***(An)***

(*a*) Urine volume increases
(*b*) Blood filtration rate decreases
(*c*) Reabsorption of salts increases
(*d*) Blood pressure decreases

5. If a patient's data shows the reabsorption rate in nephrons has decreased, which outcome is most likely? ***(Un)***

(*a*) Lower blood pressure
(*b*) Increased urine output
(*c*) Decreased urine output
(*d*) Higher blood sugar levels

6. Which statement best describes the role of the urinary bladder in the excretory system? ***(An)***

(*a*) Filters waste from the blood
(*b*) Stores urine until expulsion
(*c*) Reabsorbs essential nutrients
(*d*) Produces urine

7. How does the structure of nephrons facilitate their function in waste removal? ***(Un)***

(*a*) High permeability allows for efficient waste filtration.
(*b*) Large surface area enhances absorption.
(*c*) Presence of multiple nephrons speeds up the process.
(*d*) All of the above.

8. During a drought, how does the human body adjust urine production to conserve water? ***(Un)***

(*a*) Decreases reabsorption in the nephron
(*b*) Dilute urine is produced
(*c*) Increases reabsorption in the nephron
(*d*) Stops urine production entirely

9. **Which among the following procedures is used for cleaning the blood of a person by separating the waste substance from it?** **(*Re*)**

(*a*) Kidney transplant (*b*) Blood transfusion

(*c*) Dialysis (*d*) Hydrolysis

10. **Identify the correct path of urine in the human body.** **(*Re*)**

(*a*) Kidney → urinary bladder → urethra → ureter

(*b*) Urinary bladder → ureter → kidney → urethra

(*c*) Kidney → ureter → urethra → urinary bladder

(*d*) Kidney → ureter → urinary bladder → urethra

Assertion and Reason (1 M)

Direction: The following questions consist of two statements – Assertion (A) and Reason (R). Answer these questions by selecting the appropriate option given below:

(*a*) Both A and R are true, and R is the correct explanation of A.

(*b*) Both A and R are true, but R is not the correct explanation of A.

(*c*) A is true, but R is false

(*d*) A is false, but R is true.

1. **Assertion (A):** In humans a major amount of water is reabsorbed by the tubular part of nephron.

   Reason (R): Reabsorption of water depends on the dissolved waste to be excreted from the body. **(*Un*)**

2. **Assertion (A):** Haemodialysis can save the life of patients with kidney failure.

   Reason (R): Waste products like urea can be removed from the body by haemodialysis. **(*Re*)**

3. **Assertion (A):** Excretion is the biological process by which harmful wastes are removed from an organisms body.

   Reason (R): The mode of excretion is completely same in both unicellular and multicellular organism. **(*Re*)**

Subjective Questions

Very Short Answer Type Questions (2 M)

1. **Proteinuria is a condition in which significant amounts of protein can be detected in urine. Which process in the nephron is likely to be affected causing proteinuria? Justify.** **(*Un, An*)**

Ans. The process likely to be affected is filtration or selective reabsorption by the nephron. *(1 M)*

Justification:

- Improper filtration will lead to proteins getting filtered even though they are not waste.
- After filtration, useful substances such as proteins may not be getting reabsorbed, leading to their presence in urine. *(1 M)*

2. **What similarities and differences exist between the excretory processes in humans and plants?** **(*An*)**

Ans. Both plants and humans remove waste, but humans use a specialized organ like kidneys, whereas plants use simpler methods like transpiration and storing wastes in dead tissues or external structures like leaves. *(2 M)*

3. **What is the purpose of making urine in the human body? Name the organs that stores and releases the urine.** **(*Re*) (CBSE SQP, 2023)**

Ans. Purpose: To filter out nitrogenous waste products like urea and uric acid from the blood in humans. *(1 M)*

Organ for storage: Urinary Bladder *(½ M)*

Organ for release: Urethra *(½ M)*

4. **Reflect on the statement, "Kidneys processed 180 L of blood to make 1.8 L of urine."** **(*Ap*)**

Ans. The statement highlights the kidneys' efficiency and vital role in filtering blood and removing waste. Processing 180 liters of blood to produce just 1.8 liters of urine daily shows how kidneys concentrate waste into a much smaller volume, crucial for maintaining body fluid and electrolyte balance. *(2 M)*

Nailing the Right Answer

When answering, students should focus on the role of the kidneys in filtering blood and the selective reabsorption process.

5. **Write one specific function each of the following organs in relation with excretion in human beings:** **(*Re*)**

(*i*) Renal Artery

(*ii*) Urethra

(*iii*) Glomerulus

(*iv*) Tubular part of nephron

OR

(*a*) What role do Bowman's capsules play in urine formation?

(*b*) How do nephrons reabsorb necessary substances from the initial filtrate? **(*Un*)**

Ans. The functions of the given organs in relation to excretion are:

(*i*) Renal Artery: Supplies blood to the kidneys for filtration. *(½ M)*

(*ii*) Urethra: Excretes urine from the urinary bladder to the outside of the body. *(½ M)*

(*iii*) Glomerulus: Filters blood and removes waste products. *(½ M)*

(*iv*) Tubular part of nephron: Reabsorbs essential substances and nutrients from the filtrate into the bloodstream, and secretes additional wastes. *(½ M)*

OR

(*a*) Bowman's capsules collect the initial filtrate from the blood, starting the process of urine formation by filtering out waste products. *(1 M)*

(*b*) As urine flows along the nephron tube, essential substances like glucose, amino acids, salts, and water are selectively reabsorbed back into the bloodstream based on the body's needs. *(1 M)*

Short Answer Type Questions (3 M)

1. **List two major steps involved in the formation of urine and state in brief their functions.** *(Re)*

Ans. In the formation of urine, the two major steps include: Filtration and reabsorption. *(1 M)*

Filtration:

- Occurs in glomeruli and Bowman's capsule *(½ M)*
- Filter excess fluid and waste products out of the blood into the urine *(½ M)*

Reabsorption:

- Essential substances such as glucose, amino acids, salts, and significant amounts of water are reabsorbed in the nephron tubules. *(1 M)*

2. **Draw the well labelled diagram of functional unit of kidney.** *(Cr)*

Ans.

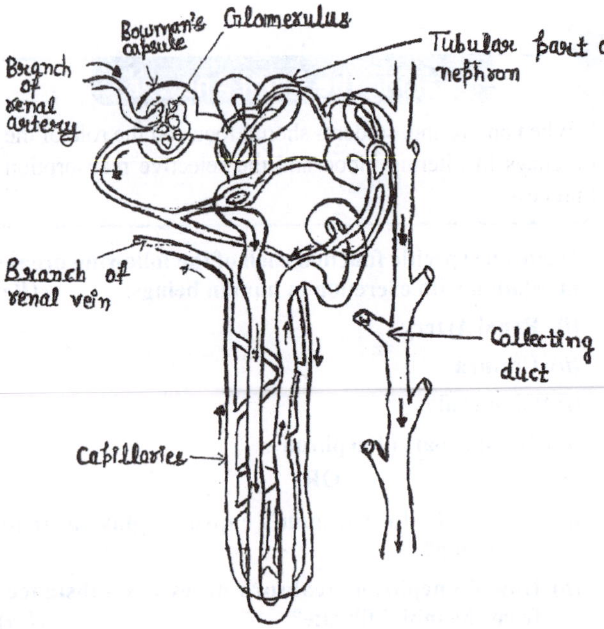

(3 M)

3. **How do leaves of plants help in excretion?** *(Un)* **(NCERT Exemplar)**

Ans. Leaves help in excretion in following ways:

- Removal of extra water by transpiration through stomata *(1 M)*
- Removal of CO_2 and O_2 from the stomatal aperture of leaves during respiration and photosynthesis *(1 M)*
- Plants shed leaves to expel accumulated excretory products. *(1 M)*

Long Answer Type Questions (5 M)

1. **Describe the process of urine formation in kidneys.** *(Un)*

Ans. Urine formation in kidneys involves three main processes: Filtration, Reabsorption, and Secretion.

- Filtration: Initially, blood is filtered in the nephron, specifically in the Bowman's capsule, where water and solutes are forced out of the blood. *(1½ M)*
- Reabsorption: The filtrate then travels through the renal tubules, where essential nutrients, water, and ions are reabsorbed back into the blood, based on the body's requirements. *(1½ M)*
- Secretion: Lastly, certain substances such as ions, toxins, and drugs are actively secreted into the tubule from the blood, completing the process of urine formation. *(1½ M)*
- The final urine, containing wastes and excess water, is transported by ureter to the bladder for storage until it is released by urethra. *(½ M)*

2. **(a) How does the artificial kidney help in treatment of patients with kidney failure?**

   (b) What is the role of the dialysing fluid in an artificial kidney?

   (c) Compare the efficiency of waste removal in an artificial kidney versus a natural kidney. *(Un)*

Ans. (a) The artificial kidney, or hemodialysis machine, removes waste products from the blood such as urea ,excess salts and water, using a semipermeable membrane, mimicking healthy kidney functions. *(1 M)*

(b) The dialysing fluid in an artificial kidney helps maintain a concentration gradient that facilitates the diffusion of waste products out of the blood. It has the same osmotic pressure as blood but lacks nitrogenous wastes, ensuring that only waste diffuses into the fluid, allowing the blood to be purified and returned to the patient. *(2 M)*

(c) The artificial kidney is less efficient than natural kidneys as

- It does not reabsorb filtered substances *(1 M)*
- Hemodialysis with an artificial kidney occurs several times weekly, causing periodic waste buildup between sessions. *(1 M)*

3. **The diagram provided shows the structure of a nephron and its various parts labeled P, Q, R, and S. Based on the diagram answer the following questions:** *(Re, Un)*

   (a) Identify the parts labeled P, Q, R, and S in the diagram.

   (b) Describe the process of filtration and reabsorption in the nephron, explaining the role of each labeled part (P, Q, R, and S).

   (c) Explain the importance of selective reabsorption in maintaining homeostasis in the body.

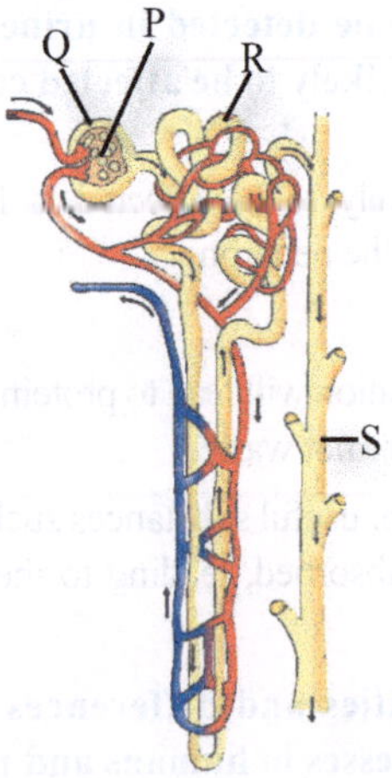

Ans. (*a*) P: Glomerulus

Q: Bowman's capsule

R: Tubular part of nephron

S: Collecting duct *(1 M)*

(*b*) Filtration: Blood enters the nephron through the glomerulus (P), where blood pressure forces water, ions, and small molecules out of the blood and into the Bowman's capsule (Q), forming the filtrate. Larger molecules such as proteins and blood cells remain in the bloodstream.

Reabsorption: As the filtrate passes through the tubular part of the nephron (R), essential nutrients, glucose, amino acids, and a significant amount of water are reabsorbed back into the bloodstream. This process is crucial for conserving valuable substances.

The remaining filtrate flows into the collecting duct (S), where further water reabsorption may occur based on the body's hydration needs. The urine then moves to the ureter and is stored in the bladder until excretion. *(3 M)*

(*c*) Selective reabsorption ensures that essential substances like glucose, amino acids, and water are not lost in the urine. It helps maintain the body's fluid balance, electrolyte levels, and overall homeostasis. This process allows the body to retain necessary nutrients and excrete only the waste products, such as urea and uric acid. *(1 M)*

Hints & Explanations

Multiple Choice Questions

1. (*c*) The kidney in Person A might be malfunctioning. Normally, the kidney regulates urea in the blood by filtering out excess from the bloodstream and excreting it in urine.
2. (*c*) The Bowman's capsule collects the blood filtrate that passes through the thin-walled capillaries, which is the first step in the formation of urine.
3. (*c*) Healthy kidneys reabsorb necessary substances like glucose back into the bloodstream; its presence in urine often indicates a dysfunction.
4. (*b*) Decreased blood flow to the kidneys would reduce the kidneys' ability to filter blood, leading to a decreased rate of blood filtration.
5. (*b*) A decreased reabsorption rate means that less water and salts are reabsorbed by the body, leading to an increase in urine output.
6. (*b*) The urinary bladder functions as a reservoir for storing urine until it can be expelled from the body.
7. (*d*) The structure of nephrons, including their permeability, surface area, and quantity, collectively enhances efficient filtration and waste removal.
8. (*c*) To conserve water during periods of low intake, the body increases the reabsorption of water in the nephrons, reducing urine output.
9. (*c*) Dialysis is the procedure used for detoxifying the blood by isolating the waste and unwanted constituents.
10. (*d*) Urine is formed in the kidney by filtering blood, then carried by the ureter to the urinary bladder for storage. Finally, it's expelled from the body through the urethra as waste.

Assertion and Reason

1. (*a*) A major amount of water is reabsorbed in the nephron, and this process indeed depends on the body's need to excrete dissolved wastes.
2. (*a*) Haemodialysis is a life-saving procedure for patients with kidney failure because it removes waste products such as urea from the body when the kidneys are unable to do so.
3. (*c*) The mode of excretion varies significantly between unicellular and multicellular organisms, with simpler organisms often relying on diffusion and complex ones using specialized organs.

MISCELLANEOUS EXERCISE

Multiple Choice Questions (1 M)

1. Patient X was suffering from a pancreatic condition due to which the pancreas was not functioning adequately.

   Which of the following is a doctor likely to suggest to such an individual? **(*An*)**

   (*a*) including a large amount of protein in the diet

   (*b*) eating a diet with low-fat content

   (*c*) eating only carbohydrates

   (*d*) including only liquid foods

2. The length of small intestine in a deer is more as compared to the length of small intestine of a tiger. The reason for this is **(*Un*) (CBSE, 2022 Term I)**

   (*a*) Mode of intake of food.

   (*b*) Type of food consumed.

   (*c*) Presence or absence of villi in intestines.

   (*d*) Presence or absence of digestive enzymes.

3. In the given diagram of a closed stomata: (1), (2), (3) and (4) respectively are **(*Re*) (CBSE, 2023)**

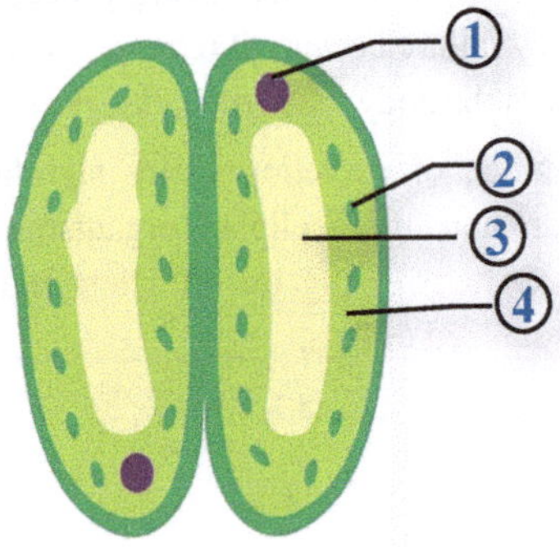

   (*a*) nucleus, chloroplast, guard cell, vacuole

   (*b*) nucleus, chloroplast, vacuole, guard cell

   (*c*) chloroplast, nucleus, vacuole, guard cell

   (*d*) vacuole, guard cell, nucleus, chloroplast

4. Opening and closing of stomata is due to: **(*Re*) (CBSE, 2023)**

   (*a*) High pressure of gases inside the cells

   (*b*) Movement of water in and out of the guard cells

   (*c*) Stimulus of light in the guard cells

   (*d*) Diffusion of CO_2 in and out of the guard cells

5.

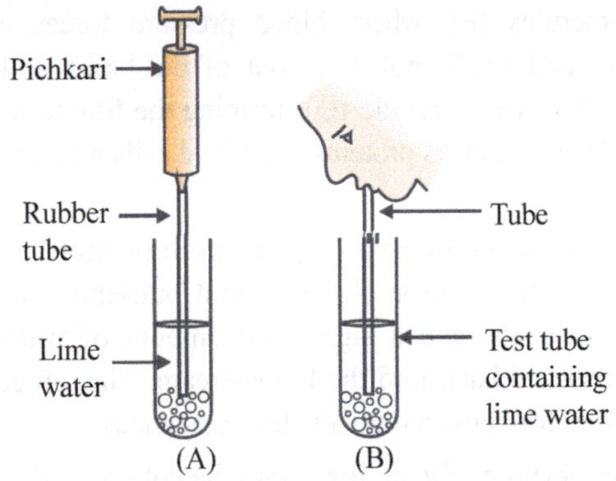

(*An*)

   Compare the reactions in setups (A) and (B). Which setup is likely to show a faster reaction, and why?

   (*a*) Setup (A), because atmospheric air has more oxygen.

   (*b*) Setup (B), because exhaled air has more carbon dioxide.

   (*c*) Setup (A), because atmospheric air has more nitrogen.

   (*d*) Setup (B), because exhaled air has more moisture.

6. Which of the following statement(s) is (are) true about human heart? **(*Un*) (CBSE, 2024)**

   (A) Right atrium receives oxygenated blood from lungs through pulmonary artery.

   (B) Left atrium transfers oxygenated blood to left ventricle which sends it to various parts of the body.

   (C) Right atrium receives deoxygenated blood through vena cava from upper and lower body.

   (D) Left atrium transfers oxygenated blood to aorta which sends it to different parts of the body.

   (*a*) (A) (*b*) (A) and (D)

   (*c*) (B) and (C) (*d*) (B) and (D)

7. In human respiratory system, when a person breathes in, the position of ribs and diaphragm will be: **(*Re*) (CBSE, 2024)**

   (*a*) lifted ribs and curve/dome shaped diaphragm.

   (*b*) lifted ribs and flattened diaphragm.

   (*c*) relaxed ribs and flattened diaphragm.

   (*d*) relaxed ribs and curve/dome shaped diaphragm.

8. Single circulation i.e., blood flows through the heart only once during one cycle of passage through the body, is exhibited by **(*Un*) (NCERT Exemplar)**

   (*a*) *Labeo, Chameleon, Salamander*

   (*b*) *Hippocampus, Exocoetus, Anabas*

   (*c*) *Hyla, Rana, Draco*

   (*d*) Whale, Dolphin, Turtle

9. One of the difference between blood and lymph is that **(*Re*)**
   (*a*) Blood has RBCs and WBCs while lymph has Lymphocytes.
   (*b*) blood has RBCs while lymph has no WBCs
   (*c*) blood has WBCs while lymph has RBCs
   (*d*) blood has dissolved organic salts while lymph has no such inorganic salt.

10. Given below is a diagram of a nephron. **(*An*)**

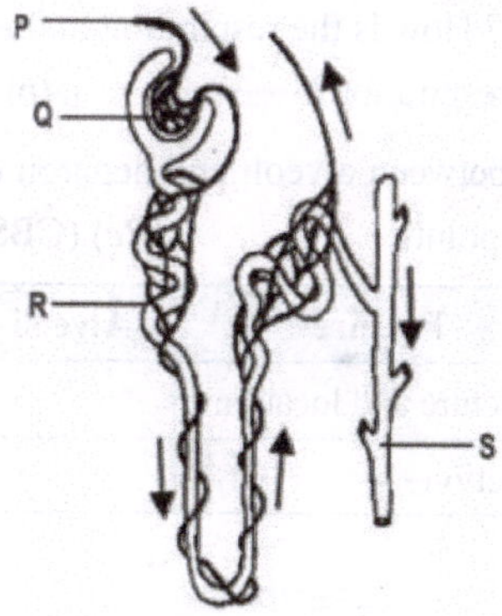

Which row of the following table correctly shows where filtration and selective reabsorption occur? **(*CFPQ*)**

	Filtration	Selective Reabsorption
(*a*)	P	Q
(*b*)	Q	S
(*c*)	Q	R
(*d*)	P	R

11. If the tubule segment of the nephron is completely non-functional in an individual, how will this impact the process of urine formation? **(*Un*)**
   (*a*) Urine formation will not occur.
   (*b*) The quality and quantity of urine remain unaffected.
   (*c*) Urine becomes more concentrated.
   (*d*) Urine becomes more diluted.

12. Respiratory structures of two different animals-a fish and a human being are as shown. Observe (*a*) and (*b*) and select one characteristic that holds true for both of them. **(*Un*) (CBSE, 2022 Term I)**

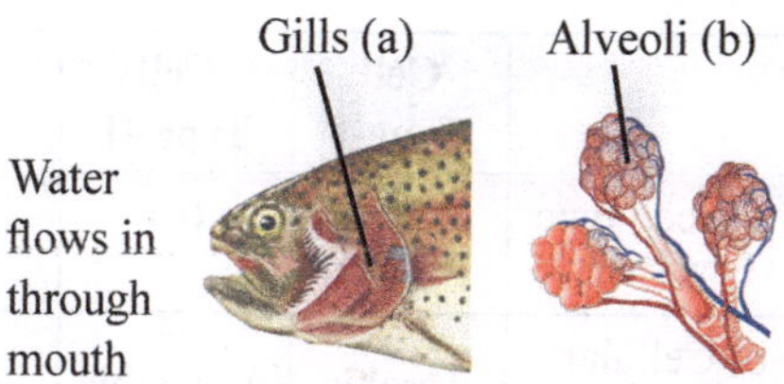

   (*a*) Both are placed internally in the body of animal.
   (*b*) Both have thin and moist surface for gaseous exchange.
   (*c*) Both are poorly supplied with blood vessels to conserve energy.
   (*d*) In both the blood returns to the heart after being oxygenated.

13. If the CO_2 concentration in the blood increases, the rate of breathing will **(*Un*)**
   (*a*) decrease (*b*) stop
   (*c*) increase (*d*) have no effect

14. Consider the following statements about small intestine and select the one which is NOT correct: **(*An*) (CBSE 2023)**
   (*a*) The length of the small intestine in animals differs as it depends on the type of food they eat.
   (*b*) The small intestine is the site of complete digestion of food.
   (*c*) The small intestine receives secretions from liver and pancreas.
   (*d*) The villi of the ·small intestine absorb water from the unabsorbed food before it gets removed -from the body via the anus.

15. Study the graph given below that represents the amount of energy supplied with respect to the time while an athlete is running at full speed. **(*An*)**

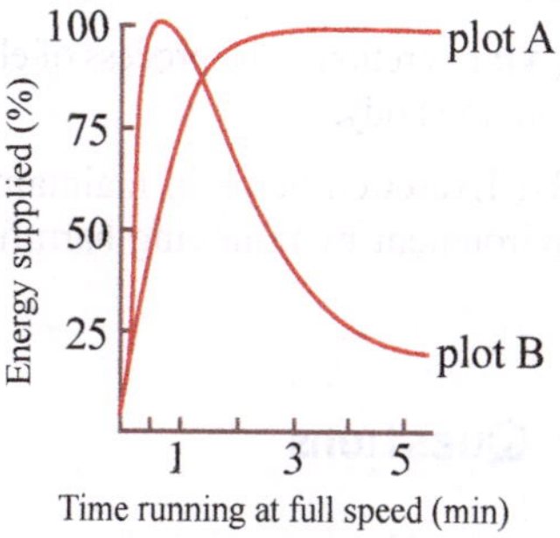

Choose the correct combination of plots and justification provided in the following table.

S. No.	Plot A	Plot B	Justification
(*a*)	Aerobic	Anaerobic	Amount of energy is low and inconsistent in aerobic and high in anaerobic
(*b*)	Aerobic	Anaerobic	Amount of energy is high and consistent in aerobic and low in anaerobic
(*c*)	Anaerobic	Aerobic	Amount of energy is high and consistent in aerobic and low in anaerobic
(*d*)	Anaerobic	Aerobic	Amount of energy is high and inconsistent in anaerobic and low in aerobic

Assertion and Reason **(1 M)**

Direction: The following questions consist of two statements – Assertion (A) and Reason (R). Answer these questions by selecting the appropriate option given below:

(*a*) Both A and R are true, and R is the correct explanation of A.
(*b*) Both A and R are true, but R is not the correct explanation of A.
(*c*) A is true, but R is false.
(*d*) A is false, but R is true.

1. **Assertion (A):** The translocation of food and other substances takes place by xylem.

   Reason (R): Translocation occurs with the help of adjacent companion cells. ***(Re)***

2. **Assertion (A):** Autotrophic nutrition occurs in green plants.

   Reason (R): Green plants self-manufacture their food from inorganic carbon source. ***(Re)***

3. **Assertion (A):** The rate of breathing in aquatic organisms is much faster than in terrestrial organisms.

   Reason (R): The amount of oxygen dissolved in water is very high as compared to the amount of oxygen in air. ***(Un)* (CBSE, 2024)**

4. **Assertion (A):** Birds have their left and right side of the heart separated for more efficient supply of oxygen to the body.

   Reason (R): Birds need high energy to maintain their body temperatures. ***(Un)***

5. **Assertion (A):** Excretion is the process of eliminating waste products from the body.

   Reason (R): Excretion helps in maintaining the body's internal environment by removing harmful metabolic by products. ***(Un)***

Subjective Questions

Very Short Answer Type Questions (2 M)

1. How do you think the digestive system would function if the sphincter muscle between the stomach and small intestine did not exist? ***(Un)***
2. Give the name of the enzyme present in the fluid in our mouth cavity. State the gland which produces it. What would happen to the digestion process if this gland stops secreting this enzyme? ***(Re)* (CBSE, 2023)**
3. Bile juice does not have any digestive enzyme but still plays a significant role in the process of digestion. Justify the statement. ***(Un)***
4. What will happen if mucus is not secreted by the gastric glands? ***(Un)* (NCERT Exemplar)**
5. Amount of urine produced generally decreases in summers as compared to other seasons if we don't keep ourselves sufficiently hydrated. Justify. ***(Ap)* (CBSE, APQ, 2023)**
6. In each of the following situations what happens to the rate of photosynthesis? ***(Un)* (NCERT Exemplar)**
   (*a*) Cloudy days
   (*b*) No rainfall in the area
   (*c*) Good manuring in the area
   (*d*) Stomata get blocked due to dust
7. X and Y pigments are found in humans and plants, respectively. X is found in RBCs whereas Y is responsible for light absorption in plants. Identify the pigments X and Y. Does the absence of these pigments affect their respective organisms? ***(An)***
8. Anita always gets confused between circulatory system and lymphatic system as both have a fluid flowing in them. Could you cite how lymph is different from blood? ***(Re)***

   OR

   List four precautions which a student should observe while preparing a temporary mount of a leaf peel to show stomata in his school laboratory. ***(Cr)***
9. Sometimes while running, the athletes suffer from muscle cramps. Why ? How is the respiration in this case different from aerobic respiration? ***(Ap)* (CBSE, 2024)**
10. Differentiate between alveoli and nephron on the basis of the following points: ***(Re)* (CBSE SQP, 2024)**

S. No.	Feature	Alveoli	Nephron
1.	Structure and location		
2.	Function		

Short Answer Type Questions (3 M)

1. In a study, Cell Type-I produces significantly more ATP per glucose molecule, compared to Cell Type-II and Cell Type-III, which yield minimal ATP. This highlights Cell Type-I's superior efficiency in cellular respiration. The data obtained from this study was presented in the graphical form as given below: ***(Un)***

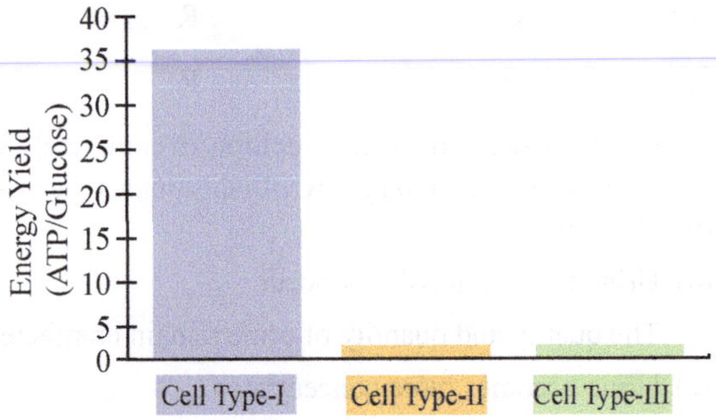

After observing the cells under various conditions, the student recorded the products obtained from each cell type. Some data (a to f) are missing from the table. Fill in the missing information based on the graph and experimental observations.

	Cell Type-I	Cell Type-II	Cell Type-III
Name the cell type	Human cell	(*a*)	(*b*)
Mode of Cellular Respiration	Aerobic	Anaerobic	(*c*)
Location of respiratory reaction in the cell	(*d*)	Cytoplasm	Cytoplasm
End Products of the reaction	(*e*)	(*f*)	Ethanol, CO_2, ATP

2. What is transpiration? List its two functions. ***(Re)***

3. (*a*) Give reasons for the following:

   (*i*) Alveoli in lungs are richly supplied with blood capillaries.

   (*ii*) Respiratory pigment in the blood takes up oxygen and not carbon dioxide.

   (*iii*) During anaerobic respiration, a 3-carbon molecule is formed as an end product instead of CO_2 in human beings. ***(Un)* (CBSE, 2024)**

OR

   (*b*) (i) Name the movements that occur all along the gut in human digestive system. How do they help in digestion?

   (*ii*) Where is bile juice stored in human body? List two roles of bile juice. ***(Re)* (CBSE, 2024)**

4. A student has set up an apparatus as given below to show that "CO_2 is released during respiration". After about 1 hour he observes no change in the water level in the delivery tube. Write three possible reasons for the failure of the experiment. ***(Ap)***

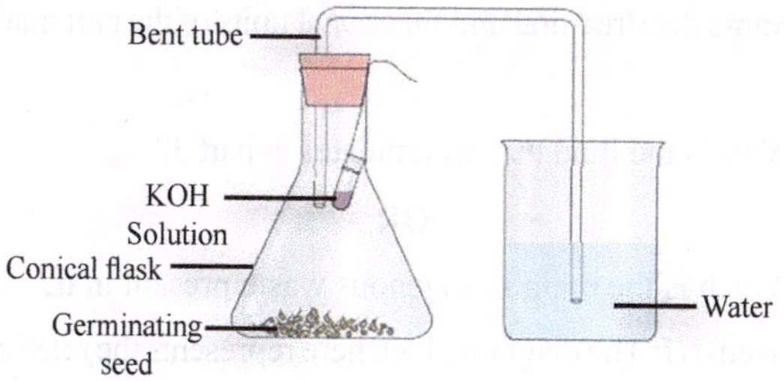

5. Imagine you are a tiny molecule of sucrose being transported through the phloem. Describe your journey from the leaves to the storage organs or growing organs of the plant? Can you explain it in a flow chart? ***(Cr)***

6. Explain the process of transport of oxygenated and deoxygenated blood in a human body. ***(Un)* (CBSE, 2023)**

7. Compare the functioning of alveoli in the lungs and nephrons in the kidneys with respect to their structure and functioning. ***(Un)* (NCERT)**

8. It is seen that in higher organisms like human beings there is a need for a proper circulatory system. However, in lower organisms there is no need for such systems ***(Un)***

   (*a*) Why is there such a difference?

   (*b*) How does human blood circulation differs from that of a fish?

Long Answer Type Questions (5 M)

1. A group of researchers conducted an experiment to study the effect of prolonged exercise on the concentration of lactic acid in the muscles. They monitored the lactic acid levels in athletes' muscles at different intervals during a 60-minute exercise. The graph below shows the relationship between the duration of the exercise and the concentration of lactic acid in the muscle. ***(Ap)***

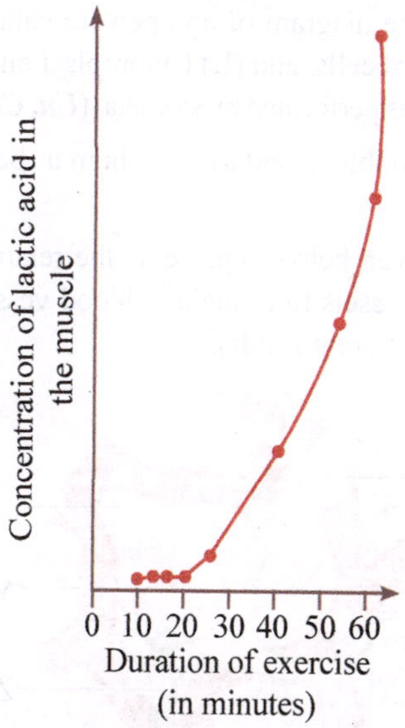

   (*a*) Based on the graph, at what point in time does the concentration of lactic acid in the muscle start to increase significantly?

   (*b*) What physiological change is indicated by the increase in lactic acid concentration in the athletes' muscle during the exercise?

   (*c*) Explain why the concentration of lactic acid in the muscle increases more rapidly after 40 minutes of exercise. What does this suggest about the athletes' oxygen levels?

   (*d*) What problem might be faced by the athlete as a result of prolonged exercise? Draw a flowchart showing breakdown of glucose in this case.

2. (*a*) Define excretion.

   (*b*) Name the basic filtration unit present in the kidney.

   (*c*) Draw excretory system in human beings and label the following organs of excretory system which perform following functions:

   (*i*) form urine.

   (*ii*) is a long tube which collects urine from kidney.

   (*iii*) store urine until it is passed out. ***(Cr)* (CBSE, 2020)**

3. (*i*)

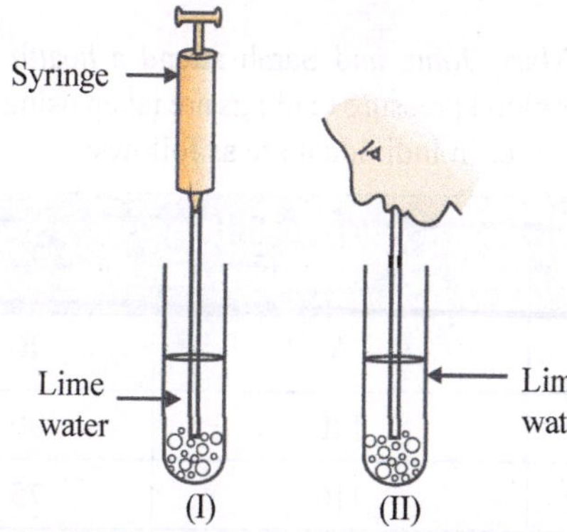

In the experimental set-up shown above in diagram (I) atmospheric air is being passed into lime water with a syringe while in diagram (II) air is being exhaled into lime water. The time taken for the lime water to turn milky in both the test tubes is different. Give a reason.

(*ii*) Draw the diagram of an open stomatal pore and label (I) Guard cells, and (II) Chloroplast on it. Mention two functions performed by stomata. **(*Un, Cr*) (CBSE, 2024)**

4. Describe double circulation in human beings. Why is it necessary? **(*Un*)**

5. A figure given below represents the relationship between lymphatic vessels to tissue and blood vessels. (Hint: X, Y and Z are different fluids). **(*Ap, An*)**

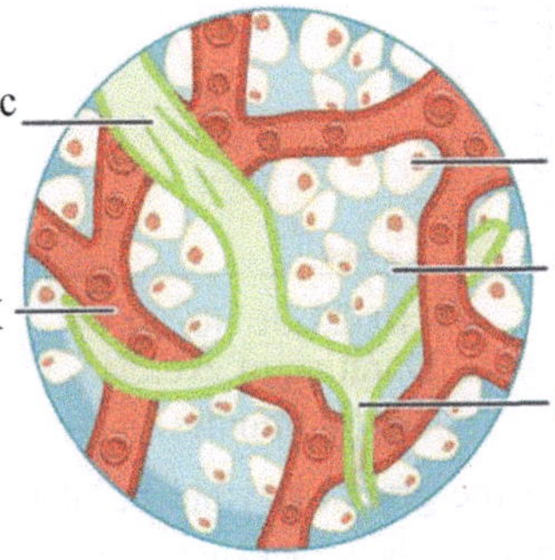

(*a*) Identify and describe the structure containing the fluid 'X' in the provided diagram and discuss its function in the circulatory system.

(*b*) Among X, Y, Z, which one of them carries digested and absorbed fat from intestine and drains excess fluid from extracellular space back into the blood?

(*c*) By observing the diagram, what structural similarity to veins can you find in lymphatic vessels?

(*d*) How is 'Y' compositionally different from X?

(*e*) Draw a flowchart suggesting the flow of lymph starting from intercellular spaces of tissue.

6. In few organisms well separated chambers are not present in the heart, however in humans, chambers are well separated. How does the heart prevent oxygen-rich blood from mixing with carbon dioxide-rich blood, and why is it essential to maintain this separation? Explain double circulation with a diagram. **(*Un, Cr*)**

Case Based Questions

Case Based-I: Mary, John, and Sarah attend a health checkup camp where their blood pressure readings are taken using a device X. The readings for each individual are as follows: **(*An*)**

Participants	Blood Pressure Readings (mmHg)	
	A	B
Mary	140	90
John	110	75
Sarah	160	95

(*i*) Based on the blood pressure readings of Mary, John, and Sarah, identify A and B. (*1 M*)

(*ii*) Identify the device X and what does X signify? (*1 M*)

(*iii*) Among Mary, John, and Sarah, which one of them shows a healthier body condition based on their blood pressure readings? Explain briefly. (*2 M*)

OR

By analyzing the Sarahs' blood pressure, what are the potential health implications she has been suffering from? (*2 M*)

Case Based-II: The diagram given below represents an organ system in the human body. Study the same and answer the questions that follow: **(*An*)**

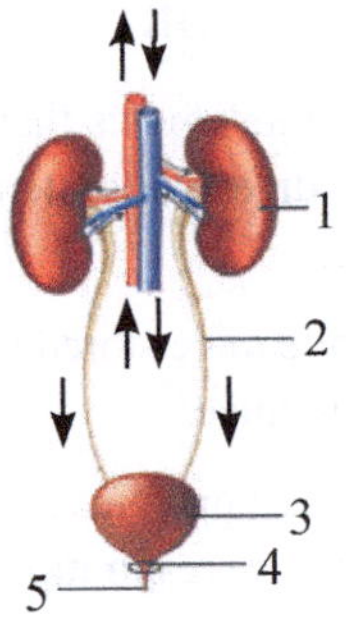

(*i*) Label the parts marked 2 and 4. Mention the function of part 5. (*2 M*)

(*ii*) Name the structural and functional units of the part marked 1. (*1 M*)

(*iii*) What is the fluid that accumulates in part 3? (*1 M*)

OR

Which is the main nitrogenous waste present in it? (*1 M*)

Case Based-III: The diagram given here represents the relationship between a mouse and a physiological process that occur in green plants. Study the diagram and answer the question that follows. **(*Un*)**

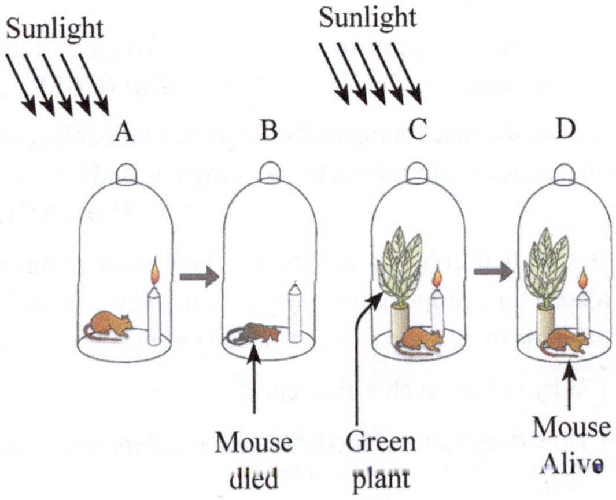

(*i*) Name the physiological process occurring in the green plants that have kept the mouse alive. (*1 M*)

(*ii*) Explain the physiological process mentioned above. (*1 M*)

(*iii*) Why did the mouse die in the bell jar B? (*2 M*)

OR

Reframe the above-mentioned physiological process in the form of a chemical equation. (*2 M*)

Case Based-IV: Look at the experiment setup A and B showing that heat is evolved during respiration when germinating seed are kept in the thermos flask. **(*An*) (CBSE APQ, 2023)**

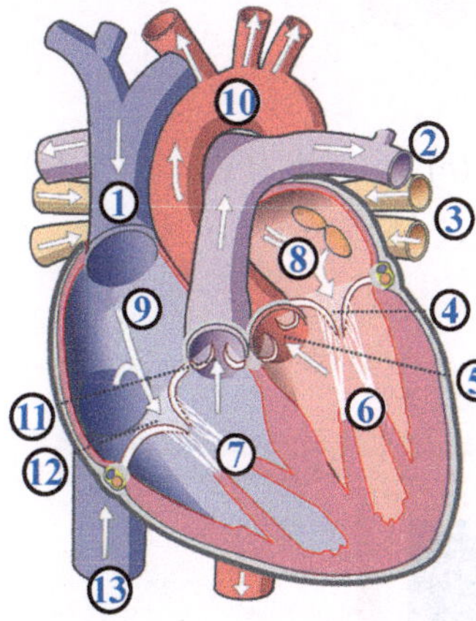

(*i*) Which chamber of the heart (6, 7, 8 or 9) pumps blood to the lungs for oxygenation, name it? Identify and name the blood vessels that carry blood to the lungs. *(1 M)*

(*ii*) Identify the structure at number 12 and state its function. *(1 M)*

(*iii*) Why do chambers 6 and 7 have thicker muscular walls than chambers 8 and 9? Name each of these chambers. *(2 M)*

OR

(*a*) Identify and name the chamber that receives oxygen rich blood and name the blood vessels which bring it. *(1 M)*

(*b*) State the significance of separation of right and left side of heart as seen in the above figure. *(1 M)*

Case Based-V: A, B and C represent the cross sections of the three blood vessels found in the human body. These are the channels or conduits through which blood is distributed to body tissues. Identify each of them and answer the following questions. **(*An*)**

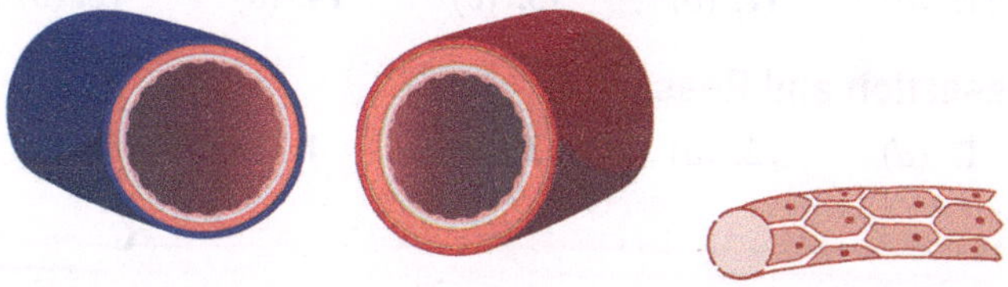

A B C

(*i*) Analyze the above figures and identify the blood vessel.

(*a*) responsible for supplying oxygenated blood to various tissues. *(½ M)*

(*b*) possess valves to prevent backflow of blood *(½ M)*

(*ii*) In which instances the functions of A and B exchange their role during the blood circulation? *(1 M)*

(*iii*) What is the significance of difference in thickness between the walls of the A and B? *(2 M)*

OR

What is the role of C in blood circulation? *(2 M)*

ANSWER KEYS

Multiple Choice Questions

1. (*b*)	**2.** (*b*)	**3.** (*b*)	**4.** (*b*)	**5.** (*b*)	**6.** (*c*)	**7.** (*b*)	**8.** (*b*)	**9.** (*a*)	**10.** (*c*)
11. (*d*)	**12.** (*b*)	**13.** (*c*)	**14.** (*d*)	**15.** (*b*)					

Assertion and Reason

1. (*d*)	**2.** (*a*)	**3.** (*c*)	**4.** (*a*)	**5.** (*a*)

HINTS & EXPLANATIONS

Multiple Choice Questions

1. (*b*) When the pancreas is not functioning adequately, it cannot produce enough enzymes to digest fats. Therefore, a doctor is likely to suggest a diet with low-fat content to reduce the burden on the pancreas.

2. (*b*) Deer have longer small intestines for digesting cellulose-rich plant materials, while tigers have shorter intestines suited for easily digestible meat.

3. (*b*) (1) nucleus, (2) chloroplast, (3) vacuole, (4) guard cell.

4. (*b*) The stomatal opening and closing are regulated by the osmotic flow of water in and out of the guard cells, influencing gas exchange and water balance.

5. (*b*) Exhaled air contains a higher concentration of carbon dioxide compared to atmospheric air. This increased carbon dioxide content will cause a faster reaction with the lime water, making it turn milky more quickly than setup (A).

6. (*c*) The incorrect statements are:

   (A) The right atrium receives deoxygenated blood through the vena cava, not oxygenated blood through pulmonary artery.

   (D) The left atrium transfers oxygenated blood to the left ventricle, which then sends it to the aorta, not directly from the left atrium to the aorta.

7. (*b*) When a person inhales, the diaphragm contracts and flattens, and the ribs are lifted, increasing the chest cavity volume and decreasing the pressure inside, which draws air into the lungs.

8. (*b*) Single circulation, where blood flows through the heart only once during one cycle of passage through the body, is exhibited by certain fish that have two-chambered hearts such as *Hippocampus* (seahorses), *Exocoetus* (flying fish), and *Anabas* (climbing perch), where the heart consists of one atrium and one ventricle.

9. (*a*) Blood is a complex tissue containing red blood cells (RBCs), white blood cells (WBCs), platelets, and plasma. Lymph, while similar to plasma, primarily contains lymphocytes, a type of WBC, and lacks RBCs and other components of blood.

10. (*c*) Filtration takes place at 'Q', which is the glomerulus, while selective reabsorption is carried out at 'R', the renal tubule.

11. (*d*) If the tubule segment of the nephron isn't functioning, reabsorption of vital substances (glucose, amino acids; Salts, water etc.) is impaired, causing an inability to concentrate urine, resulting in more diluted urine.

12. (*b*) The respiratory structures in both fish (gills) and humans (lungs) are adapted for efficient gaseous exchange. These structures are characterized by having thin surfaces that are moist, which helps in the diffusion of gases (oxygen and carbon dioxide).

13. (*c*) The increase in CO_2 concentration in the blood increases the rate of breathing as the body responds to remove excess CO_2.

14. (*d*) The absorption of water from undigested material occurs in the large intestine before it exits the body through the anus. Villi in the small intestine are not involved in water absorption from unabsorbed food.

15. (*b*)
    - Plot A seems to represent aerobic respiration as the amount of energy is high and more consistent.
    - Plot B seems to represent anaerobic respiration (lactic acid production) as the amount of energy is higher initially but decreases with time and less consistent.

Assertion and Reason

1. (*d*) Xylem is primarily responsible for the transport of water and minerals from roots to aerial parts of the plant. The translocation of food, particularly sugars, is carried out by the phloem, not the xylem.

2. (*a*) Autotrophs are those who have the capability of producing their own food by the process of photosynthesis. Photosynthesis is the chemical process of producing food which is glucose with the help of sunlight.

3. (*c*) The amount of oxygen dissolved in water is not very high compared to the amount of oxygen in air; it is actually much lower, which necessitates the faster rate of breathing in aquatic organisms to obtain the necessary oxygen.

4. (*a*) Birds have a heart divided into left and right sides, helping them get enough oxygen for their energy needs. This is important because birds need a lot of energy to keep their body temperature steady, needing a more efficient circulatory system.

5. (*a*) Excretion is indeed the biological process through which waste products and harmful metabolic by products are eliminated from the body. This process is crucial for maintaining the body's internal environment, as it helps remove substances that can be toxic or disrupt the body's normal functioning.

Subjective Questions

Very Short Answer Type Questions

1. If the sphincter muscle between the stomach and small intestine did not exist, the food would flow continuously into the small intestine, resulting in the digestive system being overwhelmed and unable to digest the food properly. *(1 M)*

   This sphincter allows only small quantity of food enter into the small intestine at a time for the proper digestion of food. *(1 M)*

2. Enzyme - Salivary amylase *(½ M)*

   Gland - Salivary glands *(½ M)*

   If the salivary glands stop secreting this enzyme, the digestion of starch into simpler sugars would not begin in the mouth, potentially leading to a less efficient overall digestion process and increased digestive workload further down the system. *(1 M)*

Topper's Explanation

The enzyme salivary amylase is present in the fluid in our mouth cavity, salivary gland produces the salivary amylase.
In the absence of this enzyme, digestion of complex starch to simple sugar (Maltose) would be difficult, thus affecting the digestive process.
Along with it, the ~~sig~~ swallowing of food would also be difficult as salivary amylase makes the food wet to easily flow down the oesophagus.

3. Bile is a digestive juice secreted by the liver. Although it does not contain any digestive enzymes, it plays an significant role in the process of digestion:

   (*i*) It neutralizes acidic stomach contents, preparing them for pancreatic enzyme action. *(1 M)*

   (*ii*) Bile salts emulsify large fat globules into smaller ones, enhancing enzyme efficiency. *(1 M)*

Mistakes 101 : What not to do!

Students often get confused between liver and gall bladder as bile juice is secreted from liver but stored in gall bladder.

4. Gastric glands in the stomach release hydrochloric acid, enzyme pepsin and mucus. Mucus protects the inner lining of the stomach from the action of hydrochloric acid and enzyme pepsin. If mucus is not released, it will lead to erosion of the inner lining of the stomach, leading to acidity and ulcers. *(2 M)*

5. The amount of urine produced is regulated by selective reabsorption in the renal tubule of the nephron. *(1 M)*

   During summers, the body loses more water through sweat to regulate temperature. Consequently, less water is available for urine production, leading to a decreased volume of urine if hydration is not maintained. *(1 M)*

6. (*a*) Decreases *(½ M)*

   (*b*) Decreases *(½ M)*

   (*c*) Increases *(½ M)*

   (*d*) Decreases *(½ M)*

7. Pigment X is haemoglobin in humans, crucial for gas transport. Pigment Y is chlorophyll in plants, essential for photosynthesis. *(1 M)*

   The absence of hemoglobin in humans impacts O_2/CO_2 transport. *(½ M)*

   Absence of chlorophyll in plants impacts their ability to produce sugars through photosynthesis, affecting overall organism function. *(½ M)*

8.

Blood	Lymph
Fluid connective tissue with cells suspended in plasma	Fluid formed from escaped capillary contents in tissue spaces
Transports food, oxygen, salts and wastes,etc.	Carries digested and absorbed fats from intestine and, drains excess fluid back into the blood

(1 × 2 = 2 M)

OR

Precautions that should be taken while preparing a temporary mount of a leaf peel to show stomata are:

- Use freshly plucked leaves for epidermal peels. *(½ M)*
- Select the lower leaf surface for epidermal peel as it bears more stomata. *(½ M)*
- Ensure a clean glass slide is used. *(½ M)*
- Place the cover slip carefully, avoiding any air bubble. *(½ M)*

9. While running, athletes suffer from muscle cramps due to the accumulation of lactic acid caused by anaerobic respiration in muscle cells when oxygen supply is insufficient. *(1 M)*

In anaerobic respiration, glucose is partially broken down into lactic acid, yielding less energy, whereas aerobic respiration completely oxidizes glucose to produce CO_2, H_2O, and yield more energy. *(1 M)*

(a) (1) Cramps are caused due to ~~formation~~ formation of lactic Acid in muscle cells.

(2) Due to lack of oxygen, another pathway for breakdown of glucose is chosen. This is an~~aerobic~~ anaerobic respiration as performed in absence of oxygen. The products are different from aerobic respiration i.e. Lactic Acid.

10.

S. No.	Feature	Alveoli	Nephron
1.	Structure and location	Balloon like structures present at the terminal ends of bronchioles in lungs	Tubular structure present in kidneys
2.	Function	Exchange of gases	Filtration of blood to form urine

(2 M)

Short Answer Type Questions

1. (*a*) – Muscle cell, (*b*) – Yeast cell,

(*c*) – Anaerobic, (*d*) – Cytoplasm and mitochondria

(*e*) – CO_2, H_2O, ATP (*f*) – Lactic acid, ATP *(3 M)*

2. Transpiration is the process of water movement through a plant and its evaporation from aerial parts, mainly from the leaves. *(1 M)*

It is an important process for plants as it serves two main functions:

(*i*) It provides the necessary pull for the absorption of water and minerals from the soil by roots. *(1 M)*

(*ii*) Cools the plant and prevents it from getting overheated by releasing excess water in the form of water vapour. *(1 M)*

3. (*a*) (*i*) Alveoli in the lungs are richly supplied with blood capillaries to provide a large surface area for the efficient exchange of gases between the air and the blood. *(1 M)*

(*ii*) The respiratory pigment haemoglobin in the blood has a high affinity for oxygen, which it carries from the lungs to tissues, rather than carbon dioxide which is more soluble in water and mostly transported in a dissolved form in our blood. *(1 M)*

(*iii*) During anaerobic respiration in human beings, pyruvate is converted into lactic acid, a three-carbon molecule, when oxygen is deficient, such as during intense physical activity, leading to muscle cramps. *(1 M)*

OR

(*b*) (*i*) The movements that occur along the gut in the human digestive system are called "peristaltic movements." *(½ M)*

They help in digestion by rhythmically contracting the muscles of the canal lining to push the food forward, ensuring it is processed properly in each part of the digestive system. *(½ M)*

(*ii*) Bile juice is stored in the gallbladder in the human body. *(1 M)*

Two roles of bile juice include:

- Making the acidic food coming from the stomach alkaline, so pancreatic enzymes can act on it. *(½ M)*
- Breaking down fat globules into smaller ones. *(½ M)*

4. The possible reasons for the failure of the experiment are given below:

(*i*) The setup was not air tight.

(*ii*) Germinating seeds were not moist.

(*iii*) One end of the U-shaped delivery tube is placed in the conical jar and another end was not immersed in the water of the beaker. *(3 M)*

5. Leaves (Photosynthesis)

↓

Sucrose is produced in the leaves during photosynthesis

↓

Sucrose is loaded into the sieve tubes of the phloem by companion cells

↓

Sucrose is transported downward towards the roots for storage or upward to the growing organs to support their development

↓

Sucrose reaches its destination in the roots or growing organs and is utilized for energy storage or growth support.

(3 M)

Nailing the Right Answer

Students should illustrate the journey of sucrose through the phloem, highlighting key steps from production in leaves to utilization in storage or growth organs. They must ensure clarity, sequence, and accurate depiction in the flow chart, addressing each stage comprehensively to earn full marks.

6. The human circulatory system is divided into systemic and pulmonary circulation.

Pulmonary Circulation: Deoxygenated blood is transported back to the heart through the vena cava into the right atrium, and then to the lungs via the right ventricle through the pulmonary artery for oxygenation *(1½ M)*

Systemic Circulation: Oxygenated blood is carried from the lungs to the heart via the pulmonary veins into the left atrium, and then pumped through the aorta to the rest of the body by the left ventricle, distributing oxygen to body tissues and collecting carbon dioxide for expulsion. *(1½ M)*

Topper's Explanation

27. The oxygenated blood from the lungs is transported to the heart for pumping through the pulmonary vein. The pulmonary vein transports blood to the left atrium which relaxes as it receives it then contracts to transport blood to the left ventricle which relaxes. When the left ventricle contracts, blood is pumped to all organs

through the thick walled Aorta.
The deoxygenated blood from the body is transported to the heart by vena cava from upper and lower body. The Right Atrium relaxes as it receives blood. when it contracts, the blood is transferred to Right ventricle which relaxes Finally the Right ventricle contracts to pump blood to Lungs, for oxygenation through pulmonary artery.

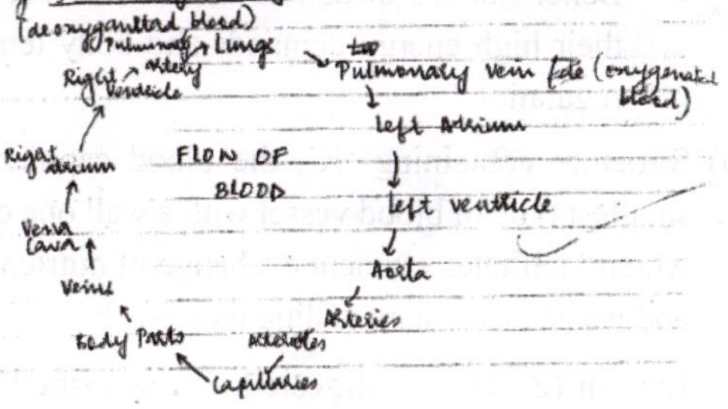

7. Alveoli

Structure: Tiny air sacs within the lungs where gas exchange occurs

Functioning: Surrounded by capillaries, allowing oxygen to enter the bloodstream and carbon dioxide to be expelled during respiration

Nephrons

Structure: Functional units of the kidneys

Functioning:

- Filters blood and reabsorb essential nutrients and water
- Excrete waste products as urine, maintaining homeostasis *(1½ + 1½ M)*

8. (*a*) Reasons for the difference in circulatory systems:

Complexity of organism: Higher organisms like humans are complex with multiple organs and tissues requiring efficient distribution of nutrients, oxygen, and removal of waste. Lower organisms, being simpler, can fulfill these needs through direct diffusion. *(1 M)*

Energy requirements: Higher organisms have greater energy needs due to their complex bodily functions, which requires a more sophisticated system to deliver oxygen and nutrients effectively across the body. Lower organisms have lesser energy requirements, making simpler systems sufficient. *(1 M)*

(*b*) Comparison of human and fish circulation:

Feature	Human Circulation	Fish Circulation
Type of Circulation	Double circulation i.e. blood flows through the heart twice.	Single circulation i.e. blood flows through the heart once.
Heart Chambers	Four chambers (two atria and two ventricles), preventing oxygenated and deoxygenated blood from mixing.	Two chambers (one atrium and one ventricle), leading to mixing of oxygenated and deoxygenated.

(½ × 2 = 1 M)

Long Answer Type Questions

1. (*a*) The concentration of lactic acid in the muscle starts to increase significantly after 20 minutes of exercise. *(½ M)*

(*b*) The increase in lactic acid concentration indicates that the athletes' muscles are switching to anaerobic respiration due to limited oxygen supply. *(½ M)*

(*c*) After 40 minutes, the rapid increase in lactic acid concentration suggests that the oxygen levels in the athletes' muscles are severely depleted. This forces their metabolism to rely more heavily on anaerobic respiration, which produces lactic acid as a byproduct. *(2 M)*

(*d*) Buildup of lactic acid in athletes' muscles due to prolonged exercise may cause muscle fatigue and cramps. *(1 M)*

Glucose (6-carbon molecule) —In cytoplasm→ Pyruvate (3-carbon molecule) + Energy —Lack of oxygen (in our muscle cells)→ Lactic acid (3-carbon molecule) + Energy *(1 M)*

2. (*a*) The process by which metabolic waste is eliminated from an organism is called excretion. This is primarily carried out by the lungs, kidneys and skin. *(1 M)*

(*b*) The basic filtration unit present in kidney is nephron. *(1 M)*

(*c*)

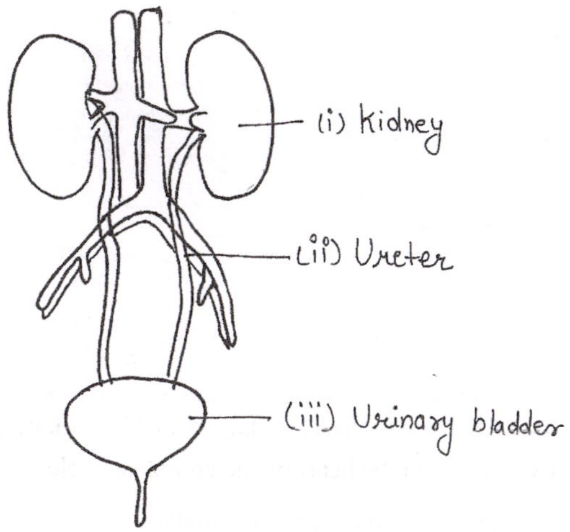

(3 M)

3. (*i*) Lime water turns milky due to the reaction of CO_2 with $Ca(OH)_2$, forming $CaCO_3$.

- In diagram (I), atmospheric air has a low concentration of CO_2 (0.04%), so it takes longer for the lime water to turn milky. *(1 M)*

- In diagram (II), exhaled air contains a higher concentration of CO_2 (4%), making the reaction faster, turning the lime water in a shorter time. *(1 M)*

(*ii*)

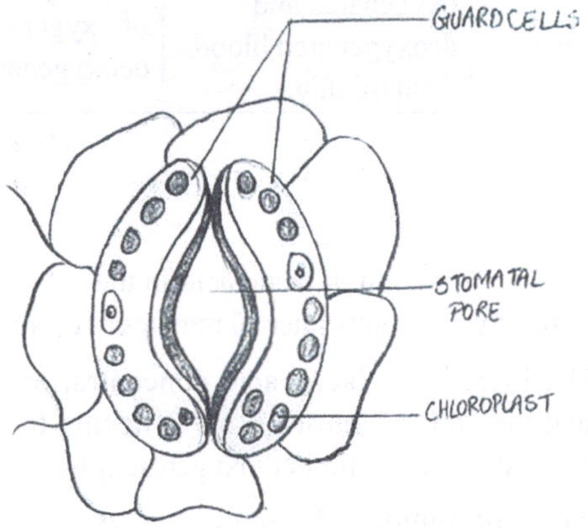

(2 M)

Functions of stomata:

1. Gaseous exchange – It allows the exchange of gases, such as oxygen (O_2) and carbon dioxide (CO_2), during photosynthesis and respiration. *(½ M)*
2. Transpiration – It helps in the loss of water vapor from the plant, which aids in cooling and maintaining water balance. *(½ M)*

Topper's Explanation

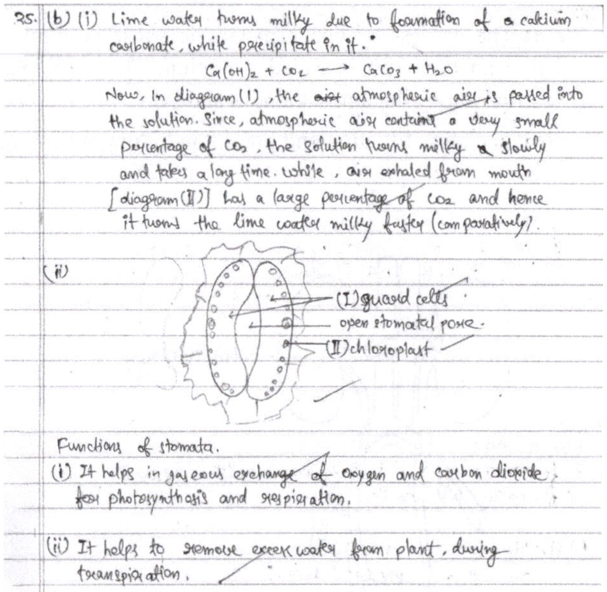
25. (b) (i) Lime water turns milky due to formation of a calcium carbonate, white precipitate in it.

$Ca(OH)_2 + CO_2 \longrightarrow CaCO_3 + H_2O$

Now, In diagram (I), the ~~air~~ atmospheric air is passed into the solution. Since, atmospheric air contains a very small percentage of CO_2, the solution turns milky ~~a~~ slowly and takes a long time. While, air exhaled from mouth [diagram (II)] has a large percentage of CO_2 and hence it turns the lime water milky faster (comparatively).

(ii)

Functions of stomata.

(i) It helps in gaseous exchange of oxygen and carbon dioxide for photosynthesis and respiration.

(ii) It helps to remove excess water from plant, during transpiration.

4. Double Circulation: A mechanism in which blood circulates twice through the heart in one complete cycle. *(1 M)*

It is present in birds and mammals.

It involves pulmonary and systemic circulation:

Pulmonary Circulation: Deoxygenated blood is transported back to the heart through the vena cava into the right atrium, and then to the lungs via the right ventricle through the pulmonary artery for oxygenation. *(1 M)*

Systemic Circulation: Oxygenated blood is carried from the lungs to the heart via the pulmonary veins into the left atrium, and then pumped through the aorta to the rest of the body by the left ventricle, distributing oxygen to body tissues and collecting carbon dioxide for expulsion. *(1 M)*

Double Circulation is necessary as it

- Prevents mixing of oxygenated and deoxygenated blood
- Allows a highly efficient supply of oxygen to the body
- Beneficial for birds and mammals as it supports their high energy demands and body temperature regulation. *(2 M)*

5. (*a*) Structure containing 'X', the blood capillary, is the smallest type of blood vessel with a wall one cell thick, which facilitates efficient exchange of nutrients, gases, and wastes with surrounding tissues. *(1 M)*

(*b*) Lymph (Z) carries digested and absorbed fat from intestine and drains excess fluid from extracellular space back into the blood. *(1 M)*

(*c*) By observing the figure, lymphatic vessels seem to have valves like those found in veins. *(1 M)*

(*d*) Tissue fluid (Y) is similar to blood plasma (X) but colourless and contains less protein. *(1 M)*

(e) Intercellular space (tissue fluid) → Lymphatic capillaries (Lymph) → Lymph vessels (Lymph) → Larger veins (Blood) *(1 M)*

6. The septum, located between the right and left sides of the heart, prevents the mixing of oxygen-rich blood from the carbon dioxide-rich blood. *(1 M)*

The separation of oxygenated and deoxygenated blood ensures efficient oxygen delivery to the animals like birds and mammals having high-energy needs, who require constant energy to regulate their body temperature. *(1 M)*

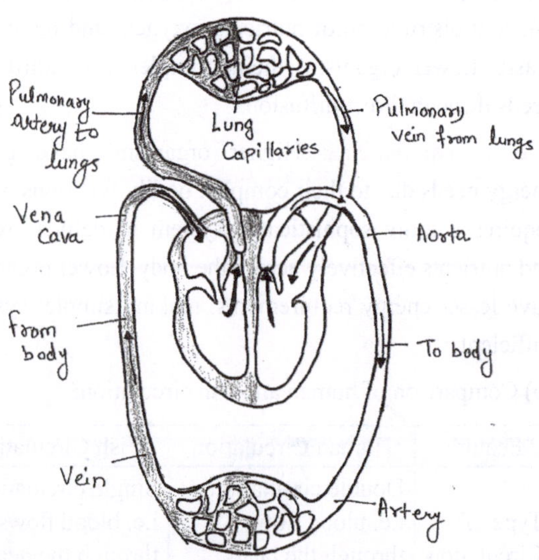

(3 M)

Case Based Questions

Case Based-I

(i) A and B represents systolic and diastolic blood pressure respectively. *(1 M)*

(ii) X is a sphygmomanometer. It is a medical device used to measure blood pressure. *(1 M)*

(iii) Among Mary, John, and Sarah, John shows a healthier body condition. Blood pressure slightly lower than 120/80 may be a sign of healthier body condition. *(2 M)*

OR

Sarah is suffering from hypertension. Hypertension signifies that the force of blood against the walls of the arteries is consistently higher than normal. High blood pressure often has no symptoms. Over time, if untreated, it can cause health conditions, such as heart disease and stroke. *(2 M)*

Mistakes 101 : What not to do!

Some students may get confused between systolic and diastolic pressures.

Nailing the Right Answer

Practicing different scenarios of high, low, and normal blood pressure readings can help you become more familiar with the range of values and their significance.

Case Based-II

(i) 2 is ureter and 4 is urethra *(1 M)*

Function of part 5 (Urethral opening): Convey urine from the urinary bladder to the outside of the body during urination. *(1 M)*

(ii) Nephron *(1 M)*

(iii) Urine *(1 M)*

OR

Urea *(1 M)*

Case Based-III

(i) Photosynthesis *(1 M)*

(ii) By Photosynthesis, plants make food and oxygen which keeps the mouse alive. *(1 M)*

(iii) The mouse died in bell jar B due to a lack of oxygen as photosynthesis could not occur in the absence of a green plant to produce oxygen. *(2 M)*

OR

Reaction of photosynthesis

$6CO_2 + 12H_2O \xrightarrow[\text{Sunlight}]{\text{Chlorophyll}} C_6H_{12}O_6 + 6O_2 + 6H_2O$ *(1 M)*

Reaction of respiration

$C_6H_{12}O_6 + 6O_2 \rightarrow 6CO_2 + 6H_2O$ *(1 M)*

Case Based-IV

(i) 7 - Right ventricle *(½ M)*

2 - Pulmonary arteries *(½ M)*

(ii) Valves (12) - It ensures that blood does not flow backwards when atria or ventricles contract. *(1 M)*

(iii) Left and right Ventricles (6 and 7) have thicker walls as compared to left and right atria (8 and 9). They have to pump blood out of the heart. They pump blood at a higher pressure to ensure it reaches all parts of the body. *(1+1 M)*

OR

(i) 8 - Left atrium *(½ M)*

3 - Pulmonary veins *(½ M)*

(ii) The separation of the right and left side of the heart is useful to prevent mixing of oxygenated blood and deoxygenated blood. *(1 M)*

Case Based-V

(i) (a) B- Artery *(½ M)*

(b) A-Vein *(½ M)*

(ii) The function of A(vein) and B(artery) exchange their role during the pulmonary circulation. The pulmonary artery carries deoxygenated blood from the heart to the lungs, while the pulmonary vein carries oxygenated blood from the lungs to the heart. *(1 M)*

(iii) Arteries (B) exhibit thicker walls, enabling them to handle the high pressure of blood pumped from the heart. Vein (A), designed for lower pressure, have thinner walls and incorporate valves for effective blood return to heart. *(2 M)*

OR

C represents capillaries that connect arteries and veins. They play a crucial role in delivering oxygen and nutrients to cells and removing waste products. *(2 M)*

6 CONTROL AND COORDINATION

"While hitting a cricket ball, the human brain seamlessly integrates visual input, motor coordination, and cognitive processing, showcasing its remarkable ability to manage multiple tasks simultaneously for accurate execution."

SYLLABUS & WEIGHTAGE

LIST OF CONCEPT NAMES	YEARS				
	2020	2022	2023	2024	2025
Nervous System (Nervous system; Voluntary, involuntary and reflex action)	—	—	—	—	2 Q (1 M)
Plant Movement (Tropic movements in plants; Introduction of plant hormones)	—	—	1 Q (1 M)	1 Q (5 M)	1 Q (1 M)
Human Endocrine System (Control and co-ordination in animals: Chemical co-ordination: animal hormones)	1 Q (4 M)	—	—	1 Q (1 M) 1 Q (5 M)	1 Q (4 M)

For the year 2021, the exam was not conducted.

CONCEPT MAP

To Access One Shot Revision Video Scan This QR Code

Control and Coordination

Nervous System in Humans

Peripheral Nervous System consist of

Cranial Nerves (CBSE 2025)
(Emerge from brain; 12 pairs)

Spinal Nerves (CBSE 2025)
(Emerge from spinal cord; 31 pairs)

Reflex Action (CBSE 2025, 2024, 2023)

Involuntary responses to stimuli

Reflex Arc:
Stimulus → Receptor → Sensory neuron → Spinal cord → Motor neuron → Effector (Muscle/gland) → Response

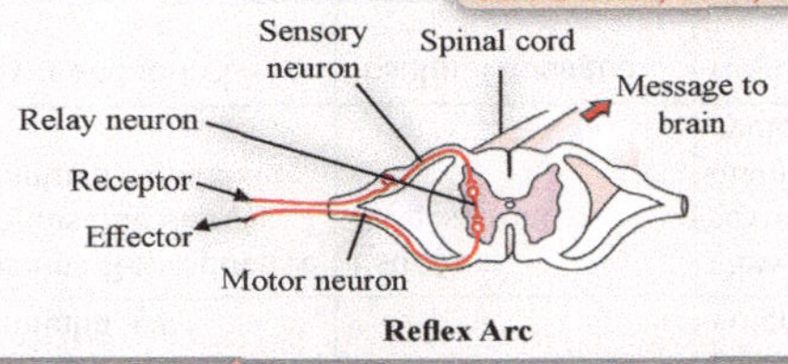

Reflex Arc

Are all involuntary actions reflex actions?

Involuntary Actions	Reflex Actions
Do not always require an external stimulus	Require external stimulus
Regulated by the brain	Regulated by the spinal cord
It may be quick or slow	Always quick
E.g., Heartbeat, digestion	E.g., Immediate withdrawal from a hot object, eye blinking

Central Nervous System

Parts and Functions of Human Brain (CBSE 2025, 2023)

Brain is protected by a bony skull and a fluid filled balloon (**cerebrospinal fluid**) that absorbs shocks.

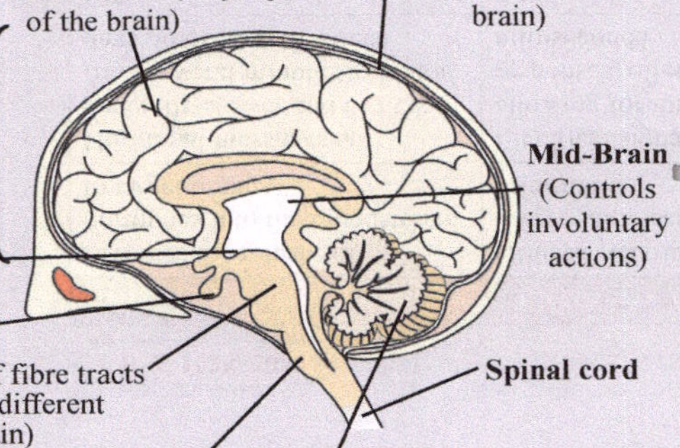

Spinal Cord (CBSE 2025)

- Connects brain to rest of the body.
- Reflex arc are formed here.
- Protected by vertebral column.

Nervous Tissue
(Made up of neurons, transmits signals)

Structure of Neuron

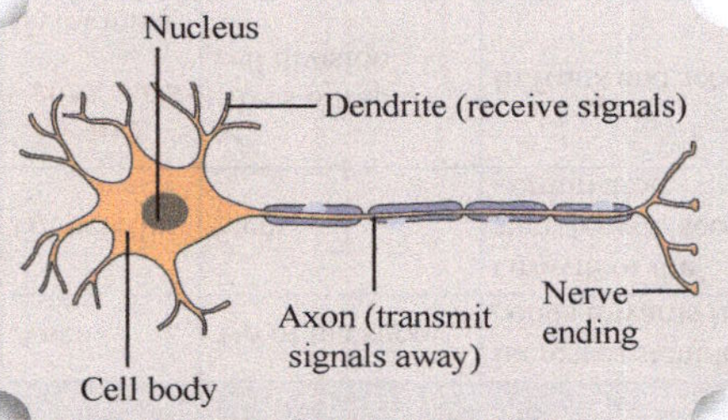

Direction of Nerve Impulse

Dendrites → Cell body → Axon → Nerve Ending → Dendrites

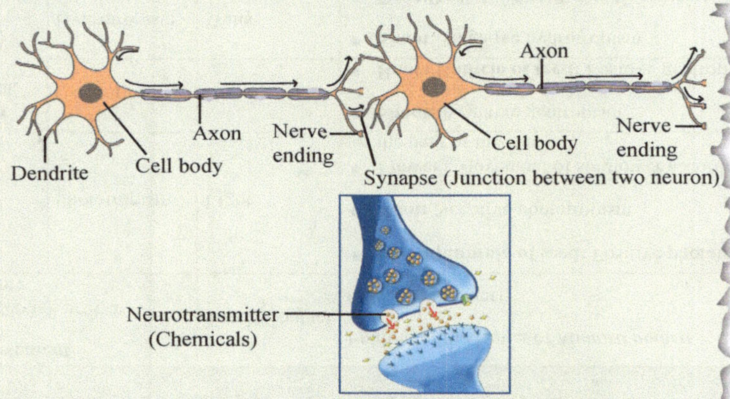

Control and Coordination

Coordination in Plants

Plant hormones: Functions and sites of action

Function	Hormone	Site of Action	Example
Increase Cell Growth	Auxin	Tip of the shoot	Increases stem length, bends towards light
	Gibberellin	Stem	Growth of the stem length, seed germination
	Cytokinins (CBSE 2025, 2023)	Areas of rapid cell division	In fruits and seeds
Inhibit Cell Growth	Abscisic Acid	Various parts of the plant	Wilting of leaves, closing of stomata

Plant Movements: Types and their stimuli

Type of Movement		Stimulus	Part of Plant Acting
Nastic Movement (Non-directional, growth independent)		Touch/Contact	Folding of the leaflet of *Mimosa pudica* (*Chhui-mui* plant)
CBSE 2023 **Tropic Movement** (Directional, growth dependent)	Phototropism	Light	• **Shoot/plumule of seed:** Positive phototropism • **Root:** Negative phototropism • **Flower:** Movement of sunflower according to the path of the sun
	Geotropism	Gravity	• **Shoot:** Negative geotropism • **Roots/Radicle of seed:** Positive geotropism
	Hydrotropism	Water	• **Shoot:** Negative hydrotropism • **Root/Radicle of seed:** Positive hydrotropism
	Chemotropism	Chemical	Growth of **pollen tubes** towards ovules
	Thigmotropism	Touch/Contact	Growth of **tendrils** (modified leaves or stem) of the climbing plant

Hormones in Animals

Endocrine Glands in Animals: Types, functions, and secretions

Endocrine Gland (Secrete Hormones in Blood)			
Gland	**Target Organ/Cells**	**Secreted Hormone**	**Function**
Pituitary Gland	Multiple organs	Growth hormone, TSH, etc.	Regulates growth, hormone production of different glands
Thyroid Gland CBSE 2024 (Malfunctioning can cause goiter)	Body cells	Thyroxin (Require iodine for production)	Regulates carbohydrate, protein, and fat metabolism
Adrenal Glands CBSE 2025	Kidneys, muscles	Adrenaline, Nor-Adrenaline	Manages stress responses during fight and flight reaction
Testes	Male Reproductive organs like external genitalia, etc	Testosterone	Development of secondary sexual characters in male like deep voice, beard, etc
Ovary	Female Reproductive organs like uterus, mammary gland, etc.	Estrogen, Progesterone	Development of secondary sexual characters in female like mammary glands, menstrual cycle, maintenance of pregnancy.
Pancreas (Malfunctioning can cause diabetes)	Liver and muscle cells	Insulin, Glucagon	Regulates blood sugar levels

Chemical communication Vs. Electrical communication

CBSE 2025, 2020

Chemical Communication	Electrical Communication
Involves the release of hormones into the bloodstream to target organs	Utilises electrical signals (nerve impulses) to transmit information
Hormonal messages are generally slower and can take from several minutes to hours/ days to exert their effect	Electrical signals are fast, allowing for immediate responses, often within milliseconds
Effects are usually longer-lasting and often widespread, affecting many cells throughout the body simultaneously	Effects are short-lived and highly localised, targeting specific cells or organs

1

NERVOUS SYSTEM

NCERT Definitions (Commonly asked in 1 mark)

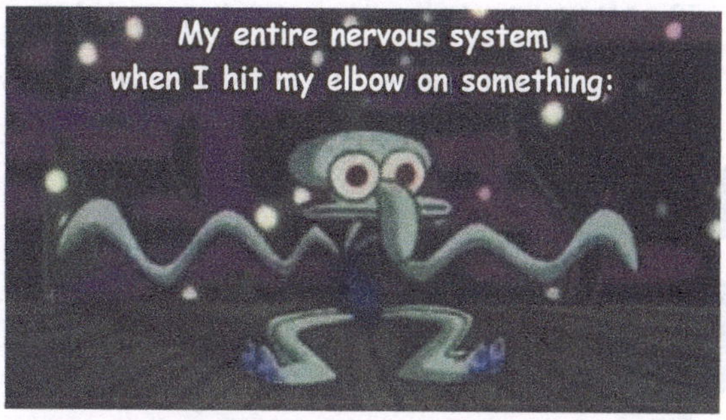

- **Stimuli:** The changes in the environment to which an organism responds and reacts.
- **Coordination:** The working together of various organs of the body of an organism in a proper order to produce appropriate reaction to a stimulus is called coordination.
- **Nervous System:** The network of nerve cells and fibers transmitting signals between different parts of the body.
- **Neuron:** The basic structural and functional unit of the nervous system, responsible for transmitting nerve impulses.
- **Dendrites:** Branch-like structures of neurons that receive messages and conduct impulses toward the cell body.
- **Cell Body:** The part of the neuron that contains the nucleus and connects to the dendrites and axon.
- **Axon:** The long, slender projection of a neuron that conducts electrical impulses away from the neuron's cell body.
- **Nerve Ending:** The terminal part of a neuron that communicates with other neurons or effectors (muscles/glands).
- **Synapse:** The junction between two nerve cells where chemicals (neurotransmitters) are released to transmit impulses.
- **Neuromuscular Junction:** A synapse between a motor neuron and a muscle fiber, facilitating muscle contraction.

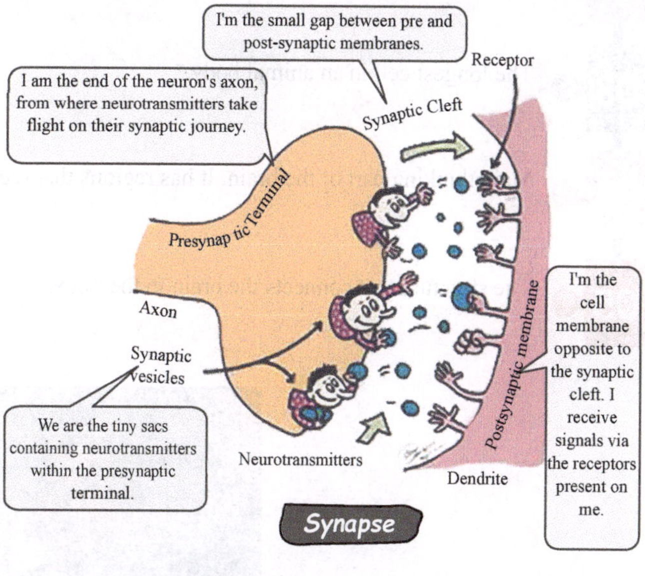

Synapse

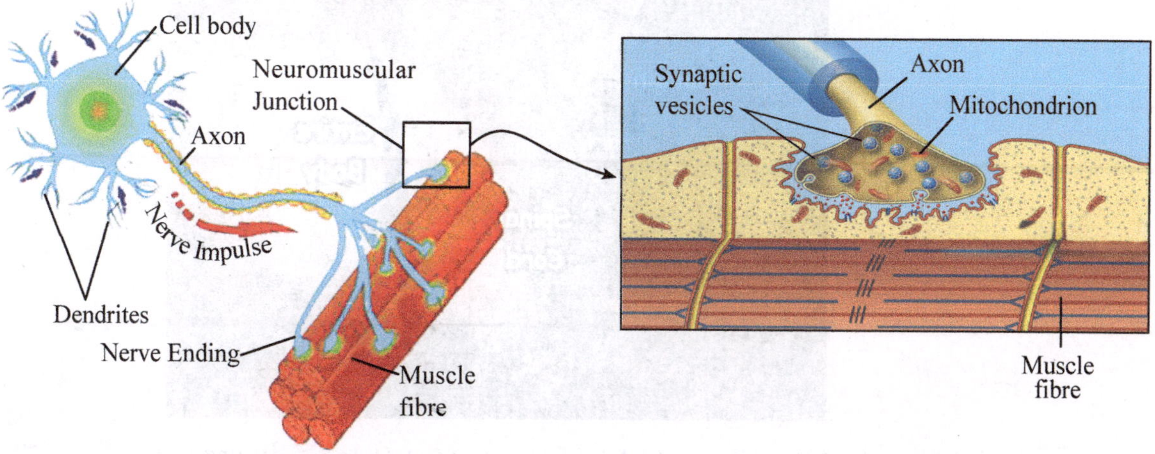

- **Impulse:** An electrical or chemical signal transmitted along the neurons.
- **Reflex Action:** An automatic and rapid response to a stimulus without involving conscious thought or decision-making.
- **Reflex Arc:** A neural pathway or circuit that facilitates a reflex action.
- **Spinal Cord:** A long, thin, tubular bundle of nervous tissue extending from the brainstem, involved in transmitting nerve impulses.
- **Human Brain:** The central organ of the human nervous system, responsible for processing information and controlling functions.
- **Cranium/Skull:** A protective bony structure enclosing the brain.
- **Fore-brain:** Main thinking part of the brain. Consist of cerebrum, thalamus and hypothalamus.
- **Hind-brain:** The posterior part of the brain, including the pons, cerebellum and medulla.
- **Mid-brain:** Located between the hypothalamus of the fore-brain and pons of the hind-brain.
- **Vertebral Column:** The spine or backbone, protecting the spinal cord.

Important Facts

01 The main processing unit of the body, which integrates and responds to bodily information.
~Central nervous system

02 Muscles respond to nerve impulses by changing their shape, facilitated by proteins within muscle cells.

03 The longest cell in an animal body.*
~Neuron

04 Main thinking part of the brain. It has regions that receive sensory impulses from various receptors.
~ Fore-brain

05 The structure that connects the brain to the body.
~Spinal cord

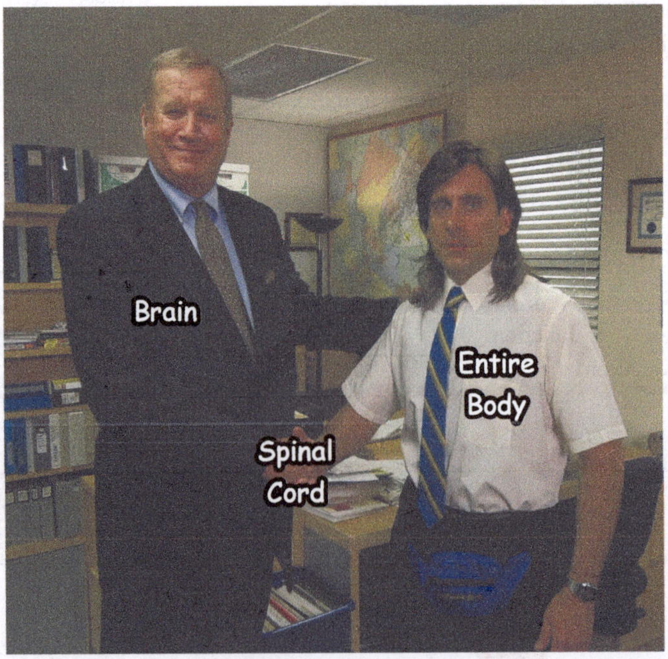

** Concepts beyond the board exam syllabus, offering deeper insight and critical thinking on NCERT topics.*

Classification

Neurons (According to their Function)			
Characteristic	**Sensory Neuron**	**Motor Neuron**	**Relay Neuron**
Function	Involved in sensing external stimuli like touch, sound	Executes actions like muscle movement	Integrates sensory information and extract motor response
Signal Direction	Carries signals from sensory receptors to the CNS i.e., toward CNS	Transmits signals from CNS to muscles and glands i.e., away from CNS	Connects sensory and motor neurons within the CNS i.e., Within CNS
Location	Mostly within sensory organs	Within effectors (muscles/glands)	Within the CNS

Receptors (Specialized Cells That Detect & Respond to External Stimuli)			
	Auditory Receptors	**Olfactory Receptors**	**Gustatory Receptors**
Function	Hearing (Hair cells)	Smell	Taste
Location	Inner ear	In the nose	Tongue (taste bud)
Stimuli	Sensitive to sound	Sensitive to volatile compound	Chemical interaction with food substance

Difference Between (Commonly asked in 2-3 marks)

Involuntary Action vs. Voluntary Action		
S. No.	**Involuntary Action**	**Voluntary Action**
1.	Automatic and rapid response to stimuli	Conscious and deliberate action
2.	Most controlled by **mid-brain** and **hind-brain**	Mostly controlled and coordinated by **fore-brain (cerebrum) and hind-brain (cerebellum)**
3.	Essential for immediate protection (e.g., withdrawal from pain)	Involves choice, planning (e.g., walking, talking)

Voluntary vs. Involuntary Muscles			
S. No.	**Characteristic**	**Voluntary Muscles**	**Involuntary Muscles**
1.	Control	Controlled consciously	Function automatically
2.	Location	Attached to bones	Found in internal organs and the heart
3.	Function	Enable intentional movement	Regulate body functions
4.	Fatigue Resistance	Fatigue more quickly with repetitive activities	More resistant to fatigue during sustained activity
5.	Examples	Bicep muscle, facial muscles	Muscles in the digestive system and the heart

Components of Nervous System (CNS vs. PNS)		
S. No.	**CNS (Central Nervous System)**	**PNS (Peripheral Nervous System)**
1.	Comprises the **brain** and **spinal cord**	Comprises **all neural elements** outside the CNS like cranial & spinal nerves
2.	Main control center for processing information	Connects the CNS to limbs and organs

Cranial Nerves Vs. Spinal Nerves		
S. No.	**Cranial Nerves**	**Spinal Nerves**
1.	Emerge directly from the brain	Emerge from the spinal cord
2.	Primarily serve the head and neck region	Connect the CNS to the rest of the body

Real Life Application Based Questions

1. **You've likely noticed how drunk individuals have trouble walking in a straight line. Why do you think that happens?**

Ans. Alcohol affects the cerebellum, a brain part responsible for coordinating muscle movements. When the cerebellum is impaired by alcohol, it leads to difficulties in maintaining balance, making it hard for drunk individuals to walk straight.

2. **Do you know which part of your brain is involved when you are reading this question?**

Ans. Parts of the midbrain coordinate the movement of the eyeball in response to visual stimuli received by a specialized area of the forebrain (cerebrum) for tracking moving images (such as a moving bike or a car) and scanning stationary images (as you are doing to read this sentence).

3. **It is believed that the higher number of folds in the human brain causes greater intelligence. Justify this statement*.**

Ans. It is believed that the more folds in the human brain, the more neuron cells are likely to be present. This increase in neuron numbers can lead to higher intelligence, as it allows for more complex brain functions and better problem-solving abilities.

4. **Have you ever observed that dogs tend to run away if you simply kneel down as if you are picking up a stone or how animals in the circus know many tricks and turns, whereas wild animals do not? Can you give a reason behind these behaviors?**

Ans. The conditioned reflexes observed in dogs, such as running away when someone kneels as if picking up a stone, and in circus animals performing tricks, are largely governed by repetitive training. In both of these conditions, the forebrain, which is the main thinking part of the brain, is majorly involved in recognizing and remembering these actions, indicating a cognitive aspect to their responses.

5. **Have you observed doctors examining patients experiencing numbness or tingling in the lower leg? They tap the patient's knee with a reflex hammer. What does this test indicate, and how does it aid in diagnosing the patient's condition?**

Ans. This test assesses the integrity of the reflex arc formed in response to the tapping, indicating spinal cord and nerve functionality. Abnormal reflexes may suggest nerve damage or neurological disorders like peripheral neuropathy, guiding diagnosis and treatment.

Myth Buster*

- ❑ ***Myth: Taste buds on specific regions of the tongue are specialized to detect only one taste as shown in the traditional taste map.***
  Fact: Certain regions of the tongue have higher concentrations of specific taste buds yet they can detect all five tastes. Thus, traditional taste maps inaccurately depict taste localization.
- ❑ **Myth: Hot and spicy are tastes, similar to sweet or sour.**
  Fact: Hot and spicy sensations, unlike tastes such as sweet or sour, are responses to **capsaicin**, a compound that activates pain receptors in the mouth, rather than stimulating taste buds.
- ❑ **Myth: Neural circuits in the CNS are always simple, with one presynaptic neuron stimulating a single postsynaptic neuron.**
  Fact: Neural circuits in the CNS can be much more complex. Presynaptic neurons can stimulate multiple postsynaptic neurons simultaneously, or multiple presynaptic neurons may synapse with a single postsynaptic neuron, integrating inputs from various sources.
- ❑ **Myth: All actions, including reflex actions, are formed and controlled by the brain.**
  Fact: Reflex actions are rapid and automatic responses managed by the spinal cord, not by the brain, to reduce response time. Although the information input also goes on to reach the brain.

Reflex actions are managed by brain

Reflex actions are managed by spinal cord

Mnemonics

- ❑ Reflex Arc: Order of propagation of nerve impulses.

"Snacks Ready, Sofa Cozy, Movies Every Night, Right"

Snacks → Stimulus
Ready → Receptor
Sofa → Sensory Neuron
Cozy → CNS

Stimulus → Receptor → Sensory Neuron → CNS

Movies → Motor Neuron
Every Night → Effector
Right → Response

Motor Neuron → Effector → Response

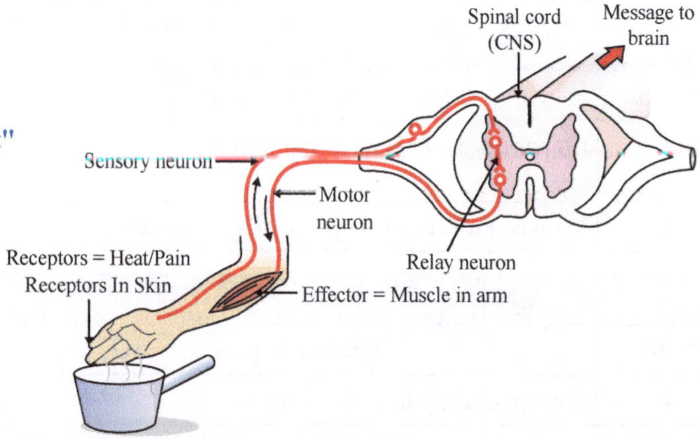

* *Concepts beyond the board exam syllabus, offering deeper insight and critical thinking on NCERT topics.*

- Impulse Transmission: Sequence of transmission of the impulse from one neuron to another:

"Daily Coffee Always Needs Sweet Doughnuts"

Daily	Coffee	Always	Needs	Sweet	Doughnuts
↓	↓	↓	↓	↓	↓
Dendrites →	Cell body →	Axon →	Nerve endings	→ Synapse →	Dendrites

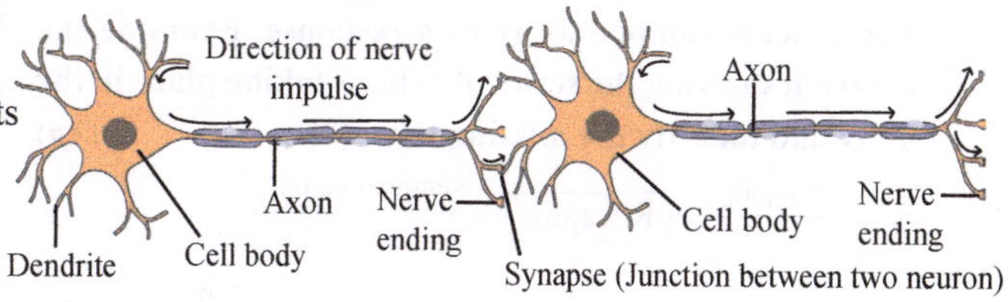

- Brain: Parts of brain
  - **Forebrain:** HTC Mobiles
  - **Midbrain**
  - **Hindbrain:** PCM subjects

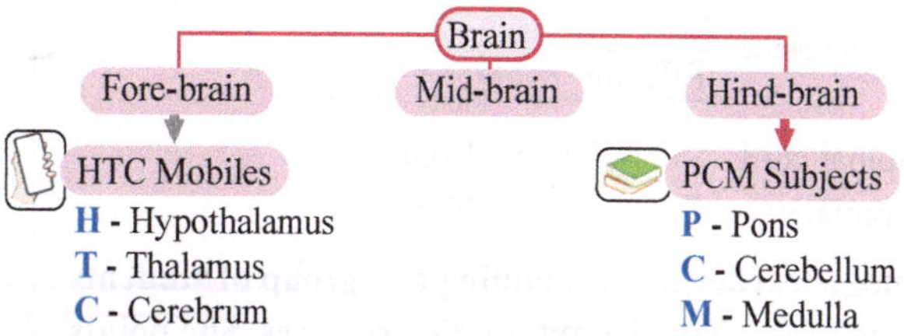

COMPETENCY BASED SOLVED EXAMPLES

Multiple Choice Questions (1 M)

1. Riya is enjoying her favorite meal at a restaurant. She smells the delicious aroma before taking a bite and savors the flavors as she eats. Which of the following correctly explains how her body detects the aroma and taste? *(Ap)*

(*a*) Olfactory receptors detect the aroma, and gustatory receptors detect the taste.

(*b*) Both olfactory and gustatory receptors detect only the aroma.

(*c*) Auditory receptors detect the aroma, and olfactory receptors detect the taste.

(*d*) Gustatory receptors detect the aroma, and olfactory receptors detect the taste.

2. Which of the following statements are true? *(Re)* **(NCERT Exemplar)**

(*i*) Sudden action in response to something in the environment is called reflex action.

(*ii*) Sensory neurons carry signals from the spinal cord to muscles.

(*iii*) Motor neurons carry signals from receptors to the spinal cord.

(*iv*) The path through which signals are transmitted from a receptor to a muscle or a gland is called a reflex arc.

(*a*) (*i*) and (*ii*) (*b*) (*i*) and (*iii*)

(*c*) (*i*) and (*iv*) (*d*) (*i*), (*ii*) and (*iii*)

3. A person suffering from a severe cold often experiences difficulty in perceiving certain sensations. Analyze the following scenarios and determine which sensory ability is most likely affected? *(An)*

(*a*) Identifying the taste difference between an apple and ice cream.

(*b*) Distinguishing the smell of a perfume from an *agarbatti*.

(*c*) Recognizing the difference between red light and green light.

(*d*) Feeling the temperature difference between a hot and a cold object.

4. In an experiment, neurons are exposed to a drug that blocks release of chemical "X" from the nerve endings. What will most likely to happen? *(An)*

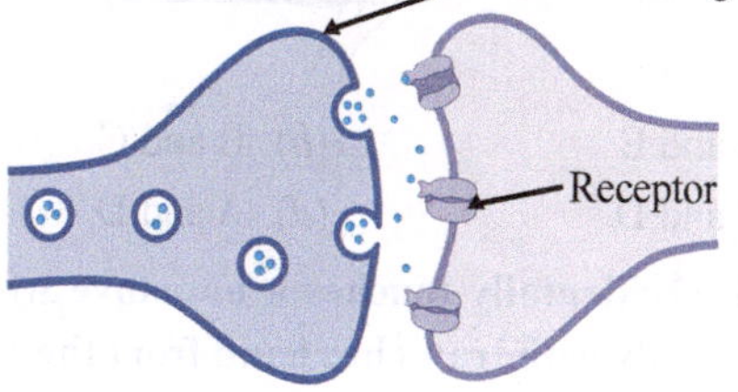

(*a*) Electrical impulses will stop traveling through the axon.

(*b*) Synapses will fail to transmit signals to the next neuron.

(*c*) Receptors will start detecting stimuli.

(*d*) The neuron will send the stimuli back to the axon.

5. What is the correct direction of flow of electrical impulses? *(An)* **(NCERT Exemplar)**

(*a*)

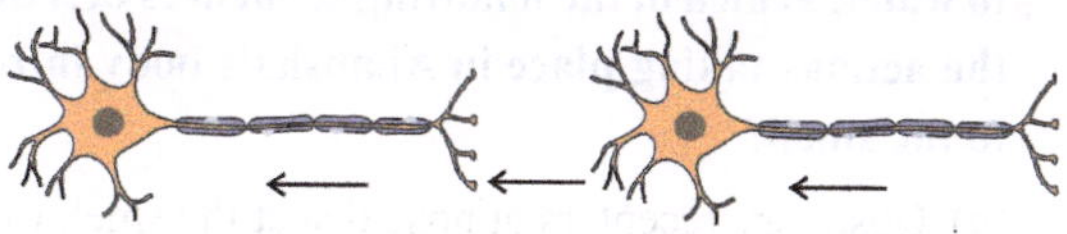

(*b*)

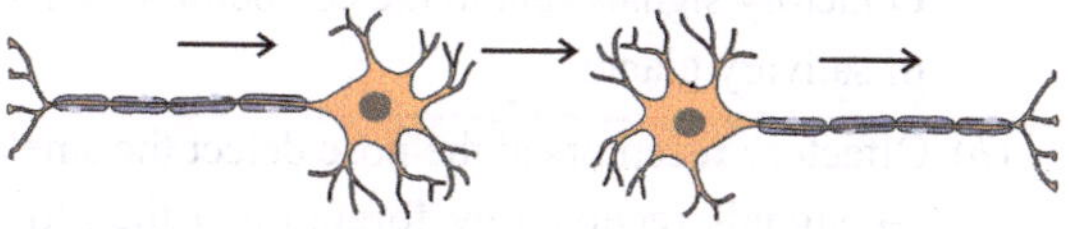

(*c*)

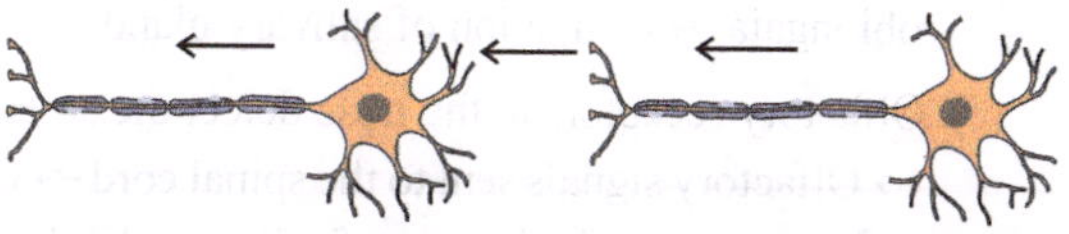

(*d*)

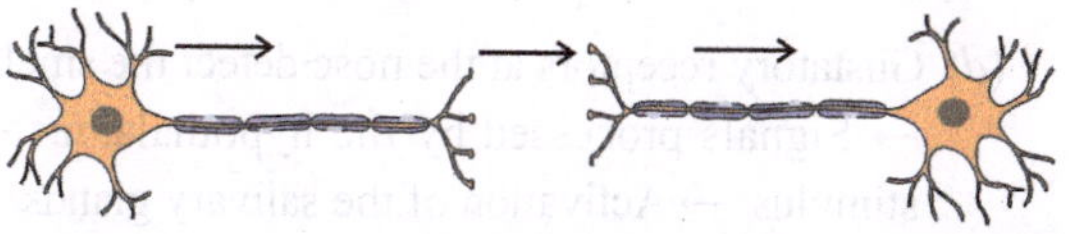

6. **While walking, you accidentally stepped on a sharp stone. You quickly jumped away as a response. Examine the diagram showing the series of actions taking place in the body and identify the missing term (?)** ***(An)***

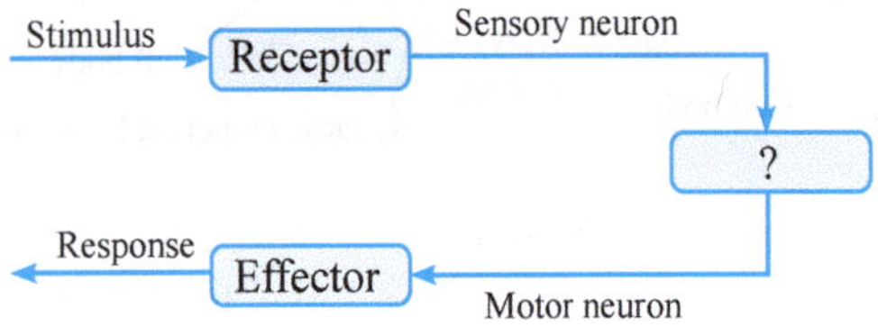

(*a*) Spinal cord (*b*) Brain
(*c*) Cranial nerve (*d*) PNS

7. **A biology teacher was explaining to a group of students how the brain manages automatic processes. She points out specific regions of the brain that are crucial for managing these involuntary actions. Referring to the diagram provided, identify which parts of the brain the teacher was discussing.** ***(An)***

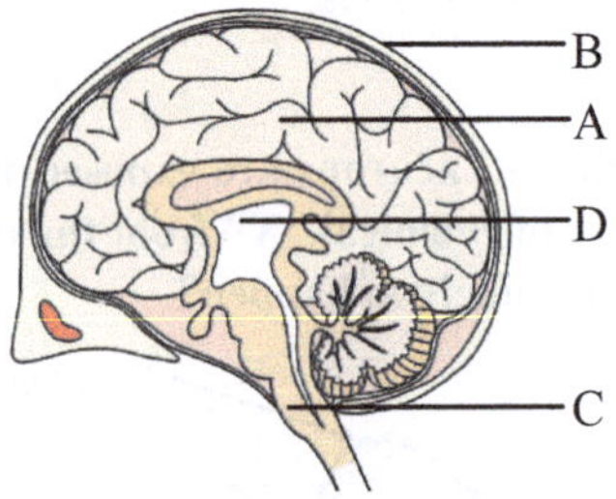

(*a*) A and B (*b*) B and C
(*c*) C and D (*d*) A and D

8. **Sarah accidentally touches a hot stove while cooking. She quickly withdraws her hand from the stove without consciously thinking about it. Explain the nature of this response and choose the correct option.** ***(An)***
(*a*) A conscious response to changes in the environment.
(*b*) An unconscious response to changes in the environment.
(*c*) A response that involves thinking about the situation.
(*d*) A response that involves feeling in control of our reactions.

9. **Akansha smelled imli at a food corner, her mouth started to water. Which of the following sequences best describes the actions taking place in Akansha's body in response to the smell?** ***(An)***
(*a*) Gustatory receptors at nose detect the smell of imli → Olfactory signals sent to the cerebellum → Activation of salivary glands
(*b*) Olfactory receptors at the nose detect the smell of imli → Signals received by forebrain→ then to medulla oblongata → Activation of salivary glands
(*c*) Olfactory receptors at the nose detect the smell of imli → Olfactory signals sent to the spinal cord → Generate reflex action → Activation of salivary glands
(*d*) Gustatory receptors at the nose detect the smell of imli → Signals processed by the hypothalamus → Send stimulus → Activation of the salivary glands

Assertion and Reason (1 M)

Direction: The following questions consist of two statements – Assertion (A) and Reason (R). Answer these questions by selecting the appropriate option given below:
(*a*) Both A and R are true, and R is the correct explanation of A.
(*b*) Both A and R are true, but R is not the correct explanation of A.
(*c*) A is true, but R is false.
(*d*) A is false, but R is true.

1. **Assertion (A):** The human tongue is responsible for the sense of taste.
Reason (R): Tongue consists of olfactory receptors. ***(Re)***
2. **Assertion (A):** We are able to detect the changes in the environment.
Reason (R): Different types of receptors are present all around the body that sense those environmental changes. ***(Un)***
3. **Assertion (A):** Reflex action has a very fast response that takes place without thinking.
Reason (R): Reflex action is controlled by the spinal cord. ***(Un)***
4. **Assertion (A):** Separate areas of the fore-brain are specialised for smell, hearing, etc.
Reason (R): Nerves from the nose are associated with the cerebellum. ***(Re)***
5. **Assertion (A):** Decisions involving voluntary actions are processed in the fore-brain.
Reason (R): The forebrain is the part of the brain responsible for complex thought processes and is associated with voluntary actions such as deciding when to eat, etc. ***(Re)***
6. **Assertion (A):** Riding a bicycle becomes a seamless activity over time, requiring minimal conscious thought.
Reason (R): The increased efficiency in riding a bicycle over time is due to the strengthening of muscle fibers in the legs, making the pedaling process more effortless. ***(Un)***
7. **Assertion (A):** An alcoholic person can not ride a bicycle in a straight line.
Reason (R): Alcohol affects the proper functioning of the cerebellum. ***(Un)***
8. **Assertion (A):** During intense physical exercise, the human brain reduces its cognitive functions to save energy for muscular activity.
Reason (R): Physical exercise increases the demand for oxygen and energy in the muscles, leading to and increased distribution of blood flow to the muscles. ***(Un)***

Subjective Questions

Very Short Answer Type Questions (2 M)

1. **Name the part of brain which is responsible for the following actions:** ***(Re)* (CBSE, 2023)**
   (*i*) **Maintaining posture and balance**
   (*ii*) **Beating of heart**
   (*iii*) **Thinking**
   (*iv*) **Blood pressure**

Ans. Each part of the brain is assigned specific functions/actions.

	Action	Part of the Brain
(*i*)	Maintaining posture and balance	Cerebellum
(*ii*)	Beating of heart	Medulla oblongata
(*iii*)	Thinking	Cerebrum (Cerebral cortex)
(*iv*)	Blood pressure	Medulla oblongata

(½ × 4 =2M)

2. How is an electric impulse created in the human nervous system? Identify the parts of a neuron which helps the nerve impulse to travel: ***(Re)***

(*a*) towards the cell body

(*b*) away from the cell body

Ans. A nerve impulse is generated when the stimulus triggers the receptors present in the sensory organs, causing electrical and chemical changes in the neuron. This impulse then travels through and across neurons as an electrical or chemical signal, effectively transmitting essential information and responses. *(1 M)*

The part of the neuron:

(*a*) Which helps the nerves impulse to travel towards the cell body is dendrite. *(½ M)*

(*b*) Which helps the nerve impulse to travel away from the cell body is axon. *(½ M)*

3. What is the function of receptors in our body? If receptors do not work properly in the body. What problems are likely to arise? ***(An)* (NCERT)**

Ans. The function of receptors in our body is to detect and respond to various signals or stimuli from the internal and external environment. Receptors are present in all parts of the body e.g., skin, eyes, tongue, etc. *(1 M)*

Consequences if receptors do not work properly:

- Sensation loss: Reduced ability to feel and respond to external stimuli. *(½ M)*
- Impaired coordination: Communication for coordinating actions and responses across the body would be disrupted. *(½ M)*

4. (*a*) State what would happen if your neurons were disc-shaped.

(*b*) Rohan stepped on a sharp stone while walking barefoot in his garden and immediately lifted his foot away. What type of action is this? Explain briefly. ***(Ap)***

Ans. (*a*) If neurons were disc-shaped, their ability to transmit signals efficiently would be impaired. The elongated shape of neurons is essential for quick signal transmission over long distances in the body. *(1 M)*

(*b*) Rohan's action is a reflex action. It is an involuntary and immediate response to a stimulus (pain). Sensory nerves detected the pain, and the spinal cord triggered a motor response to lift the foot, bypassing brain's conscious control. *(1 M)*

5. Based on the given diagram answer the following questions

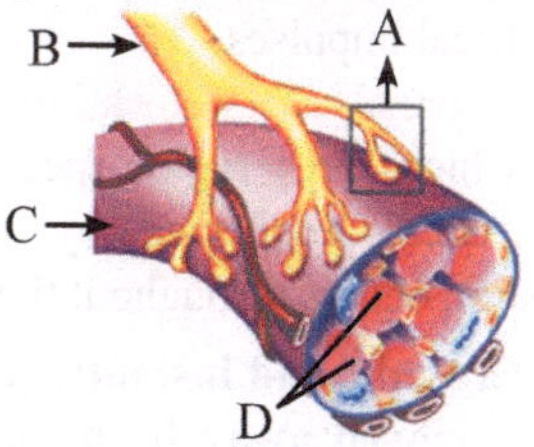

(*a*) Identify A, B, C and D.

(*b*) How does the structure labeled as B facilitate the function of A? ***(An)***

Ans. (*a*) A - Neuromuscular junction, B - Axon of motor neuron, C - Muscle fibre, D - Myofibrils. *(1 M)*

(*b*) The structure labeled as B (axon of the motor neuron) helps in functioning of A. As B carries electrical nerve impulses to the neuromuscular junction (A), where it triggers the release of neurotransmitters. These neurotransmitters then bind to receptors on the muscle fiber, initiating muscle contraction. *(1 M)*

Short Answer Type Questions (3 M)

1. State the functions of hind-brain. ***(Re)***

Ans. The hindbrain comprises pons, cerebellum and medulla. Their respective functions are as follows:

(*i*) Pons: Consists of fibre tracts that interconnect different regions of the brain. *(1 M)*

(*ii*) Medulla: Control involuntary functions like breathing, swallowing, regulation of heartbeat. *(1 M)*

(*iii*) Cerebellum: Control muscular coordination, maintaining equilibrium, balance and posture of the body. *(1 M)*

2. Draw a well-labeled diagram of a neuron, label any four parts, and briefly explain the function of any two parts. ***(Cr)***

Ans.

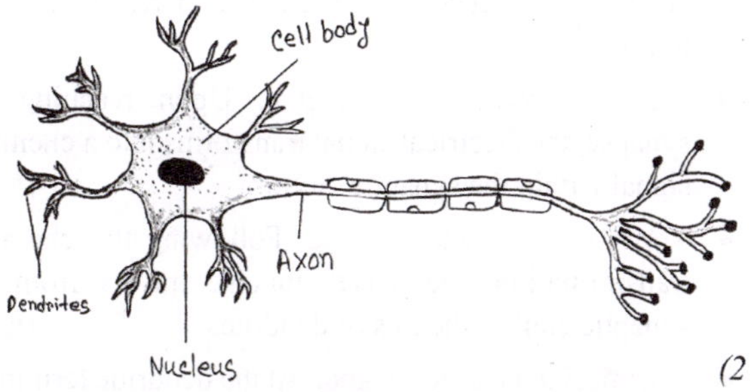

(2 M)

- Dendrites: Branch-like structures that receive signals from other neurons and transmit them towards the cell body. *(½ M)*
- Axon: Long, thin structure that carries electrical impulses away from the cell body to other neurons, muscles, or glands. *(½ M)*

3. Why is chemical communication better than electrical impulses as a means of communication between cells in a multicellular organism? ***(Un)* (CBSE, 2020)**

Ans. Chemical communication is a better means of communication than electrical impulses because:

1. It is mediated through hormones: Hormones can diffuse to different regions of the body, thereby allowing cells to communicate even without interacting with each other and can be maintained at a steady rate and easily regulated. *(1 M)*

2. It doesn't require specialized tissue like nervous tissue used in electrical impulses. *(1 M)*
3. Provide widespread communication: Unlike electrical impulses, which are region-specific and limited to specific areas connected by nerves, chemical communication occurs throughout the body. *(1 M)*

4. (*a*) Sheila saw a snake and instantly jumped back. She then slowly moved away from the snake. What is the difference between these two actions?

(*b*) 'Brain and spinal cord are two vital organs of our body.' How is our body designed to protect them?

(*An, Un*)

Ans. (*a*) Sheila's instant jump back is a reflex action, a quick, automatic response to a stimulus that does not involve conscious thought, primarily for protection and is mediated by the spinal cord. Whereas, slowly moving away involves voluntary action, which is a conscious, deliberate movement where she decides to avoid the snake, showing control and coordination of muscles after processing the situation. *(1½ M)*

(*b*) The brain is enclosed within a protective bony enclosure called the skull or cranium and is surrounded by a fluid-filled sac that shields it from shocks. The spinal cord is safeguarded by the vertebral column. *(1½ M)*

5. Why does the flow of signals in a synapse from the axonal end of one neuron to the dendritic end of another neuron take place but not in the reverse direction? Explain. **(*Un*) (CBSE, 2019)**

Ans.
- Nerve impulse as electrical signal: The nerve impulse originates as an electrical signal within the neuronal axon. *(½ M)*
- Transmission of impulse: Signals enter neurons through dendrites, travel along the axon, and reach the axon terminals. *(½ M)*
- Electrical to chemical signal: Upon reaching the synapse, the electrical signal transforms into a chemical signal within the synaptic cleft. *(½ M)*
- Movement to dendritic tips: Following the chemical transformation, the nerve impulse travels from the synaptic cleft to the tips of dendrites. *(½ M)*
- Chemical to electrical signal: At the dendritic terminals, the chemical signal is converted back into an electrical signal. *(½ M)*
- Direction of impulse: Neurotransmitters are synthesized exclusively in axon terminals, and receptors are located on dendritic terminals. This setup ensures that nerve impulses travel unidirectionally from one neuron's axonal end to another neuron's dendritic end. *(½ M)*

Nailing the Right Answer

For a high-scoring answer, students should emphasize the specialized roles of neuron parts, the conversion process impulse, and the specific arrangement of neurotransmitters and receptors that facilitate unidirectional signal flow. Frame the answer in points for better presentation.

Topper's Explanation

12.

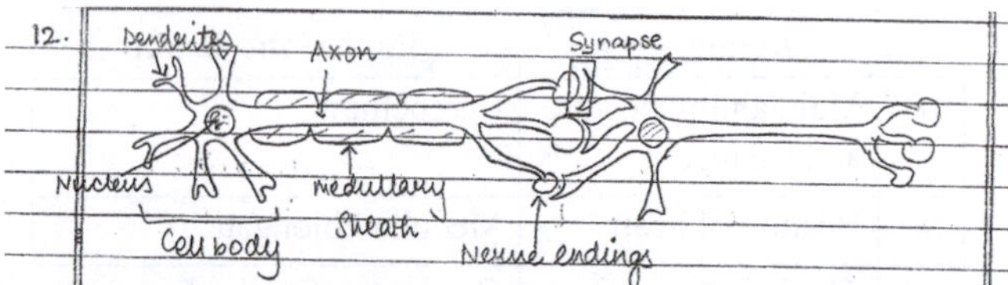

① The nerve impulses are transmitted from one neuron to the other in the form of electric impulses.

② They enter through the dendrites, move through axon and reach the nerve ending.

③ As soon as they reach there, they need to be converted into chemical signals and electric signals are unable to cross the gap i.e. synapse.

④ Thus, chemicals called 'neurotransmitters' are released from the vesicles that move from nerve ending of one neuron to the dendrite of the next one.

⑤ As soon as the chemicals reach the dendritic tip, they again get converted to electrical impulses and move on.

⑥ They chemicals are released and move only in one direction and do not reverse inorder to reach their destination that can be spinal cord or brain or effectors inorder to deliver the message.
(They are released in one direction.)

Long Answer Type Questions (5 M)

1. What is reflex arc? Draw a labelled diagram to show reflex arc on touching a very hot object.

(*Re, Cr*) (CBSE, 2017)

Ans. Reflex arc is the path taken by nerve impulses in a reflex action, an unconscious response to a sudden stimulus. *(1 M)*

In the figure below as hands touch the hot pan, afferent (sensory) neurons transmit the information to the spinal cord where a relay neuron passes it to the efferent (motor) neuron which causes the muscle to contract and pull our hand. *(2 M)*

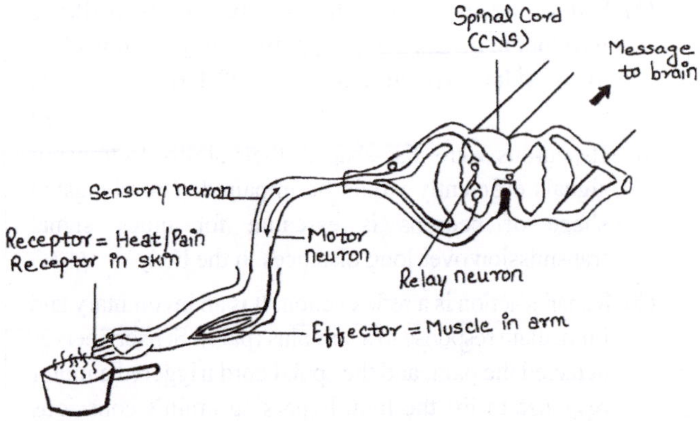

(2 M)

Nailing the Right Answer

Provide a precise reflex arc definition. Ensure all neural components are accurately labeled in the diagram. Use arrows to show impulse direction. Maintain a neat diagram and annotate each part's function. Link the diagram's labels to your written explanation to display a thorough grasp of the concept for full credit.

2. **(*a*) Draw a well-labelled diagram of Human brain.**
   (*b*) Which is the main thinking part of the brain? **(*Cr, Re*)**

Ans. (*a*)

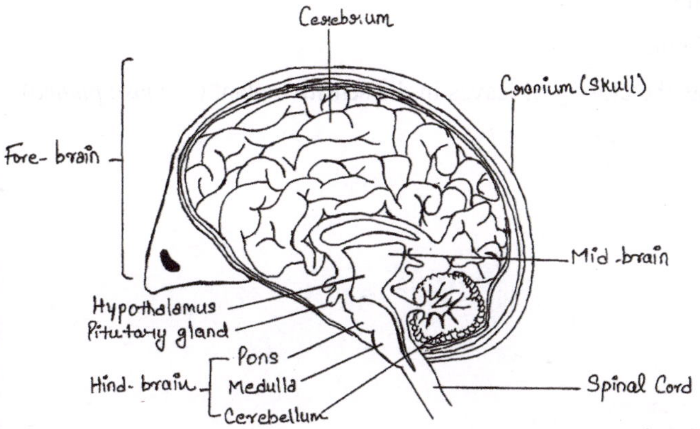

(4 M)

(*b*) Fore-brain is the thinking part of the brain. *(1 M)*

Hints & Explanations

Multiple Choice Questions

1. (*a*) Olfactory receptors in the nose detect smells like the aroma of food, while gustatory receptors on the tongue sense taste, helping Riya enjoy the combined flavors and fragrance of her meal.
2. (*c*) Sensory neurons transmit signals from receptors to the spinal cord or brain, while motor neurons carry instructions from the spinal cord or brain to the muscles, not the other way around.
3. (*b*) When a person is suffering from a severe cold, their nasal passages are congested, and their sense of smell is greatly impaired. This makes it difficult for them to differentiate between different smells, such as the smell of a perfume and that of an *agarbatti*.
4. (*b*) At the end of the axon, the electrical impulse triggers the release of some chemicals or neurotransmitters (X) that cross the synapse to generate a similar electrical impulse in the next neuron's dendrite. If the release of these chemicals is blocked (as in the experiment), the signal cannot be transmitted across the synapse, causing the communication between neurons to fail.
5. (*c*) The correct direction of flow of electrical impulses in a neuron is from the dendrites, which receive the signal, through the cell body, and along the axon toward the axon terminals.
6. (*a*) When you step on a sharp stone, skin receptors send a message *via* sensory neurons to the spinal cord, which then signals your muscles to react, making you jump away quickly.
7. (*c*) Most of the involuntary actions in the human brain are governed by the midbrain (D) and medulla (C) of the hind-brain.
8. (*b*) The nature of Sarah's response is an unconscious response to changes in the environment. When she touches the hot stove, her body automatically withdraws her hand as a reflex action without her consciously thinking about it. This rapid reaction is a protective mechanism to prevent injury.
9. (*b*) When Akansha smells imli, olfactory receptors in her nose send signals to the forebrain, which processes the sensory input. These signals are then transmitted to the medulla oblongata, triggering salivation and causing her mouth to water.

Key Takeaways

Through this question, students learnt the specific olfactory pathway leading to salivation, learning how scent detection takes place in everyday reflexes.

Assertion and Reason

1. (*c*) Tongue is responsible for the taste and it contains gustatory receptors. Olfactory receptors are responsible for the sense of smell and are present in the nose.
2. (*a*) Any change in the environment acts as a stimulus to us. These stimuli are received by a group of specialised cells called receptors. The receptor cells are spread all over and in the body and senses change.
3. (*a*) Reflex action is controlled by the spinal cord but the information also reaches the brain. Reflex arcs that produce a reflex action have evolved to reduce the response time.
4. (*c*) Separate areas of the forebrain are specialized for hearing, smell, sight, and so on, whereas the cerebellum is the part of the hind-brain responsible for the precision of voluntary actions and maintaining the posture and balance of the body.
5. (*a*) The forebrain, which includes the cerebral cortex, is involved in high-level thought processes and decision-making, which forms the basis of voluntary actions such as choosing when to eat, based on hunger and other factors.
6. (*b*) The primary reason riding a bicycle becomes seamless is the brain's ability to store procedural memory and automate motor activities, focusing on coordination and balance, particularly involving the cerebellum, rather than solely muscle strength.
7. (*a*) Cerebellum maintains the balance of the body during walking, standing, riding a bicycle, etc. Alcohol affects the proper functioning of the cerebellum. Hence, an alcoholic person finds it hard to ride a bicycle in a straight line.
8. (*d*) Physical exercise does increase the demand for oxygen and energy in muscles, leading to increased blood flow to these areas, but this does not result in any significant reduction of cognitive functions in the brain.

2 PLANT MOVEMENTS

NCERT Definitions (Commonly asked in 1 mark)

- **Tropism:** A directional growth response to stimuli in which the direction of the response is determined by the direction of the external stimulus.
- **Positive Topic Movement:** Plant movement in direction of stimuli.
- **Negative Tropic Movement:** Plant movement away from the stimuli.
- **Nastic Movements:** Non-directional response to stimuli, such as the closing of leaves in the sensitive plant (*Mimosa pudica*) upon being touched.

Important Facts

01 Plants lack the nervous system and muscle tissue.

02 Movements in plants that do not involve growth.

~ ***Nastic movements***

03 Growth-related movements within plants are slower.

04 Plant cells change their shape via alteration in cellular water content.

05 Plant hormones diffuse from their synthesis sites to action sites.

Classification

Plant Hormone			
Category	**Plant Hormone**	**Function**	**Example**
Growth Promotion	Auxin	Promotes cell growth & elongation	Directional growth towards light in plant stems
	Gibberellins	Promotes stem elongation, seed germination	Increase the length of grapes stalk and sugarcane stem, Breaking dormancy in seeds
	Cytokinins	Promote cell division, delay aging	Growth in fruits, shoots and seed
Growth Inhibition	Abscisic Acid	Stomatal closure, induce seed dormancy	Inducing wilting of leaves, seed dormancy, closing stomata during drought or under stress

Plant hormones which promotes cell division be like:

Difference Between (Commonly asked in 2-3 marks)

	Type of Tropism				
Aspect	**Phototropism**	**Geotropism**	**Thigmotropism**	**Chemotropism**	**Hydrotropism**
Definition	Growth or movement of an organism in response to light	Growth or movement of an organism in response to gravity	Growth or movement of an organism in response to touch or contact	Growth or movement of an organism in response to chemical stimuli	Growth or movement of an organism in response to water
Example	• Sunflowers tracking the sun throughout the day • Stem growing towards sunlight (positive phototropism) • Roots growing away from sunlight (negative phototropism)	• Roots growing downward (positive geotropism) • Shoots growing upward (negative geotropism)	• Tendrils of pea plant wrapping around a support structure	• Pollen tube growing towards the ovule	• Plant roots growing towards a water source
Advantage	Allows plants to optimize sunlight exposure for photosynthesis	Helps roots to anchor in the soil	Assists climbing plants in finding support and stability	Facilitates efficient fertilisation in plants	Assists in water uptake by guiding roots towards moisture-rich areas

Students who don't know phototropism, noticing plant bending towards sunlight

Students who know phototropism, noticing plant bending towards sunlight

Real Life Application Based Questions

1. Have you noticed that gardeners frequently trim plants in tea plantations and when forming hedges? Why do they do this?*

Ans. Trimming the shoot tips of plants removes the influence of auxin, a key plant hormone. This action encourages the previously dormant lateral buds to become active and start growing sideways, leading to a bushier appearance of the plant. This technique is extensively used in creating hedges and in the cultivation of tea to increase the density and yield of the plants.

2. Why are farmers often advised to apply gibberellin to their sugarcane crops?

Ans. Gibberellin promotes internodal elongation. By applying it to the crop, farmers can achieve longer sugarcane stems, directly leading to an increase in crop production by several tonnes per acre.

3. You must have read about carnivorous plants trapping insects to obtain food. Can you explain how this movement takes place in the plants?

Ans. This movement in carnivorous plants is a (growth-independent) nastic movement called thigmonasty, which involves a rapid response triggered by touch or mechanical stimulation. When an insect brushes against sensitive hairs present on the leaves, it initiates a rapid movement, such as the closing of specialized trapping leaves or structures.

4. You must have noticed leaves falling from trees when they are damaged or during autumn. Which plant hormone can be involved in these phenomena?

Ans. The plant hormone responsible for this phenomenon is ABA (abscisic acid). ABA functions by triggering stomatal closure to conserve water during stress or damage, leading to leaf wilting. During autumn, ABA levels rise, initiating leaf senescence and eventual shedding as part of the plant's seasonal changes.

Myth Buster

- **Myth: Plants do not use electrical signals for responses.**
  Fact: Plants use electrical-chemical means to convey information from cell to cell, but unlike in animals, there is no specialised tissue in plants for the conduction of information.
- **Myth: Plant hormones are only for growth and development.**
  Fact: Plant hormones extend beyond the function of growth and development. They also play critical roles in defense, stress response, and senescence.
- **Myth: Plants only respond to external stimuli.**
  Fact: Plants respond not just to external stimuli like light and touch, but also to internal cues, regulating processes such as flowering and fruiting.
- **Myth: Roots will not be able to grow without gravity.**
  Fact: Gravity influences the direction of root growth by directing the distribution of auxin towards the root cap. However, the absence of gravity can still lead to non-directional root growth, rather than completely stopping it altogether.

Mnemonics

- **To remember plant hormone and their functions:**

"A Great CD Album Always Give Classics"

A	Great	C	D	Album	Always	Give	Classics
↓	↓	↓	↓	↓	↓	↓	↓
Auxin	Growth (Cell growth)	Cytokinin	Division (Cell division)	Abscisic acid	Aging	Gibberellin	Cell elongation

** Concepts beyond the board exam syllabus, offering deeper insight and critical thinking on NCERT topics.*

- **To remember plant tropism and their stimuli:**

"Prachi lost her hat while carrying colorful gems so grandpa gave her a new one."

Prachi	lost	her hat	while	carrying	colorful	gems so	grandpa gave her a new one."
↓	↓	↓	↓	↓	↓	↓	↓
Phototropism	Light	Hydrotropism	Water	Chemotropism	Chemical	Geotropism	Gravity

COMPETENCY BASED SOLVED EXAMPLES

Multiple Choice Questions (1 M)

1. In plants the role of cytokinin is: ***(Re)*** **(CBSE, 2023)**

(*a*) Promote cell division.
(*b*) Wilting of leaves.
(*c*) Promote the opening of stomatal pore.
(*d*) Help in the growth of stem.

2. Which of the following are true about plant movements? ***(An)***

P. All plant movements are a result of growth.
Q. In plants electrical-chemical coordination takes place.
R. The sensitive plant moves its leaves in response to touch without growth.
S. Hormones can only act on the organ that secretes them.

(*a*) Only P and Q (*b*) Only Q and R
(*c*) Only R (*d*) P, Q and S

3. The growth of tendril in pea plants is due to ***(Re)*** **(NCERT Exemplar)**

(*a*) Effect of light.
(*b*) Effect of gravity.
(*c*) Rapid cell divisions in tendrillar cells that are away from the support.
(*d*) Rapid cell divisions in tendrillar cells in contact with the support.

4. Shown in the figure below is a plant in which auxin is synthesised at part X of the plant. Geeta took the potted plant and cut off part X. She then took the plant and kept it near a window with sunlight and observed it after 7 days.

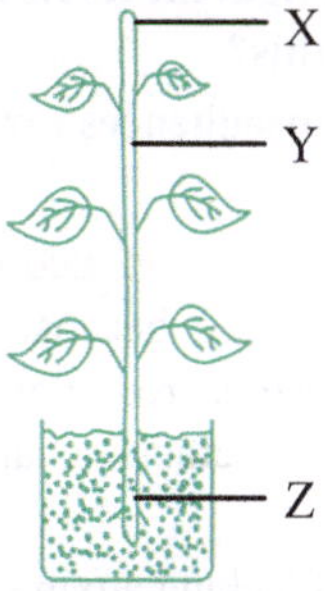

Which of the following is she likely to have observed? ***(An)***

(*a*) Part Y grew and bent towards the window.
(*b*) Part Z started growing upwards and out of the soil.
(*c*) Part Y did not grow at all.
(*d*) Part Y grew upwards.

5. Select from the following the correct statement about tropic movement in plants: ***(Re)*** **(CBSE, 2023)**

(*a*) It is due to stimulus of touch and temperature.
(*b*) It does not depend upon the direction of stimulus received.
(*c*) It is observed only in roots and not in stems.
(*d*) It is a growth related movement.

Assertion and Reason (1 M)

Direction: **The following questions consist of two statements – Assertion (A) and Reason (R). Answer these questions by selecting the appropriate option given below:**

(*a*) Both A and R are true, and R is the correct explanation of A.
(*b*) Both A and R are true, but R is not the correct explanation of A.
(*c*) A is true, but R is false.
(*d*) A is false, but R is true.

1. **Assertion (A):** Phototropism is the plant movement towards light.

   Reason (R): Root shows negative phototropism. ***(Re)***

2. **Assertion (A):** In a controlled laboratory setting under a high-resolution microscope, a botanist placed pollen grains on the stigma and observed the growth of a tube like structure inside the style showing pollen grains exhibit an attraction towards the stigma due to chemotropism.

   Reason (R): Pollen tube growth demonstrates positive chemotropism, guiding them towards the stigma for fertilization. ***(Un)***

3. **Assertion (A):** A farmer decided to treat one batch of seeds with a gibberellin solution before sowing while leaving another batch untreated. After sowing the seeds, he observed that the treated seeds germinated faster compared to the untreated ones.

   Reason (R): Gibberellins induce the production of auxin and cause cell division in the seed, facilitating the growth of both the plumule and radicle. ***(Ap)***

Subjective Questions

Very Short Answer Type Questions (2 M)

1. **(a) If a plant is subjected to a prolonged period of drought. How might the levels of abscisic acid change in response to this?**

   (b) Describe the consequences for a plant lacking auxin production. ***(Ap)***

Ans. (a) Plant subjected to a prolonged period of drought will promote ABA production because elevated ABA levels signal stomatal closure, reducing water loss through transpiration. This is a crucial change to conserve water during drought. *(1 M)*

(b) Consequences of lacking auxin

(i) Stunted development and reduced root formation. *(½ M)*

(ii) Impaired responses to environmental stimuli. *(½ M)*

Key Takeaways

Students learn the adaptive mechanisms plants use to survive under stress, such as drought, through increased ABA levels, and understand the fundamental role of auxin in plant development and environmental interaction.

2. **In Figure (a), (b) and (c), which appears more accurate and why?** ***(An)* (NCERT Exemplar)**

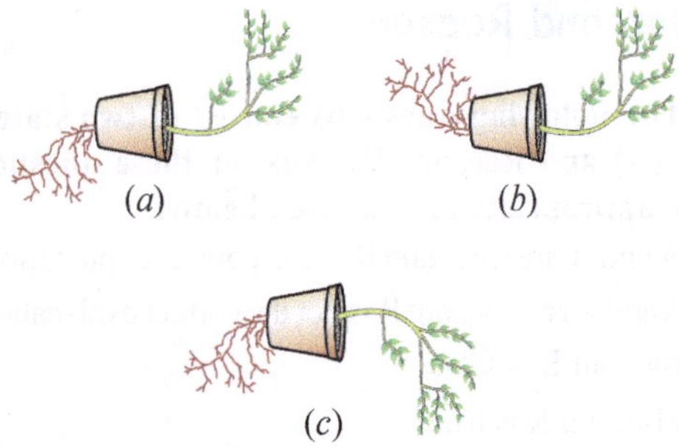

Ans. The directional growth response of plants to external stimuli is crucial in depicting plant behavior accurately. Figure (a) is more accurate as plant shoots exhibit negative geotropism and positive phototropism, growing upwards towards light and away from gravity. In contrast, roots display positive geotropism, growing downwards towards gravity. *(2 M)*

3. **Where are auxins synthesized in a plant? Which organ of the plant shows:**

   (i) Positive phototropism

   (ii) Negative geotropism

   (iii) Positive hydrotropism ***(Re)* (CBSE, 2023)**

Ans. Auxins are synthesized at the tip of the plant shoot. *(½ M)*

Phenomenon		Part of the Plant
(i)	Positive phototropism	Stem
(ii)	Negative geotropism	Stem
(iii)	Positive hydrotropism	Root

(1½ M)

4. **Dr. Smith, a botanist, sets up an experiment to study root behavior in plants. In his lab, he places a pot A with uniformly moist soil and another pot B with a clay pot filled with water.** ***(An)***

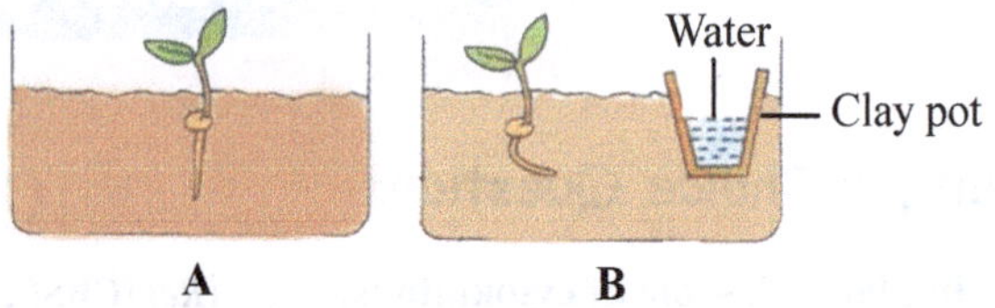

   (i) Why do roots in both pots grow downwards while shoots grow upwards?

   (ii) What type of tropism is observed in pot B, and how does it differ from the growth seen in pot A?

Ans. (i) Plants exhibit growth responses to gravity. In both pots, roots grow downward due to positive geotropism, while shoots grow upward and away from the earth due to negative geotropism. *(1 M)*

(ii) Pot B demonstrates hydrotropism, as roots grow toward the water source. In contrast, pot A shows uniform growth without such directional response, with roots growing straight in moist soil. *(1 M)*

Short Answer Type Questions (3 M)

1. ***A botanist calculated the change in hormones in plants as they grow old. Refer to the graph below showing the concentration of hormone X in young leaves attached to the plant and leaves about to wilt. Based on the graph and the provided scenario, answer the following questions:*** ***(An)***

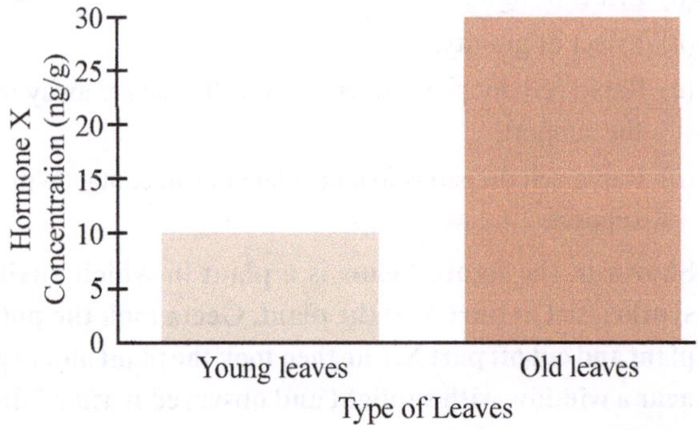

(*i*) **Identify the hormone X and propose a possible explanation for the observation.**

(*ii*) **Name two plant hormones that help in the growth of stem.**

Ans. (*i*) Hormone X is likely abscisic acid, which increases in concentration to inhibit growth and promote wilting in old leaves. This hormone helps the plant conserve resources by shedding older leaves during stress conditions, such as drought. *(2 M)*

(*ii*) Auxin and gibberellins *(1 M)*

2. Imagine you are a botanist assigned to design a classroom experiment to demonstrate phototropism. Frame an experiment and also write observations and results obtained. ***(Cr)***

Ans. To demonstrate phototropism in a classroom setting:

1. Fill a conical flask with water, cover with wire mesh, and place germinated bean seeds on it.
2. Place the flask inside a cardboard box open on one side, facing a light source.
3. Leave undisturbed for 2-3 days and observe shoot and root growth direction.
4. Rotate the flask, reversing shoot and root positions, and observe again after a few days. *(2 M)*

Observation: Initially, the shoot bends towards light and roots away from it. After turning the flask, the shoot moves away from light and roots towards it. However, after a few days, the shoot further bends towards light, and roots move away. *(½ M)*

Results: Shoot show positive phototropism, and roots exhibit negative phototropism. *(½ M)*

3. (*a*) **Plants do not have any nervous system but yet, if we touch a sensitive plant, some observable changes take place in its leaves.**

Explain how could this plant respond to the external stimuli and how it is communicated.

(*b*) **Name the hormone that needs to be administered to**

(*i*) **increase the height of a dwarf plant.**

(*ii*) **cause rapid cell division in fruits and seeds.**

(*Un, Ap*) (CBSE, 2019)

Ans. (*a*) When we touch the compound leaf of the sensitive plant, (*Mimosa pudica*) it collapses and its leaflets fold together. This response occurs due to:

- The change in amount of water in the cell at the region of contact. *(½ M)*
- The external stimulus of touch is communicated by the changes in concentration of ions. *(½ M)*

(*b*) (*i*) Gibberellin *(1 M)*

(*ii*) Cytokinin *(1 M)*

4. Emily, a passionate botany student, is conducting an experiment on plant movement. She notices that when she touches a specific part of a plant, movement occurs at a different location. Emily is intrigued by this phenomenon and begins investigating further? ***(Un)***

(*a*) **Explain how plants communicate information about touch from one cell to another without specialized tissue for information conduction?**

(*b*) **Discuss the role of water in plant cell shape changes and how it leads to swelling or shrinking?**

(*c*) **Provide examples of plant movements where cells changing shape play a significant role?**

Ans. (*a*) Plants communicate information about touch from one cell to another through electrical-chemical means. Unlike animals, plants do not possess specialized tissue for information conduction. Instead, they rely on intercellular communication pathways to transmit signals. *(1 M)*

(*b*) Changes in water content of plant cells are primarily regulated by osmosis. When water enters the cell, it exerts pressure on the cell wall, causing the cell to swell and expand. Conversely, when water exits the cell, it decreases the turgor pressure, causing the cell to shrink and lose its shape. *(1 M)*

(*c*) Examples of plant movements where cells changing shape play a significant role include the opening and closing of stomata, growth towards light (phototropism) for enhanced photosynthesis, curling of tendrils for anchor, and the response of leaves to touch (thigmonasty) for defense. *(1 M)*

Long Answer Type Questions **(5 M)**

1. Define geotropism. Draw a labelled diagram of a plant showing geotropic movements of its parts.

(*Cr*) (CBSE, 2020)

Ans. Geotropism is the growth of plant parts towards or away from gravity. Stem is negatively geotropic, it grows away from gravity whereas roots are positively geotropic. It grows towards gravity. *(2½ M)*

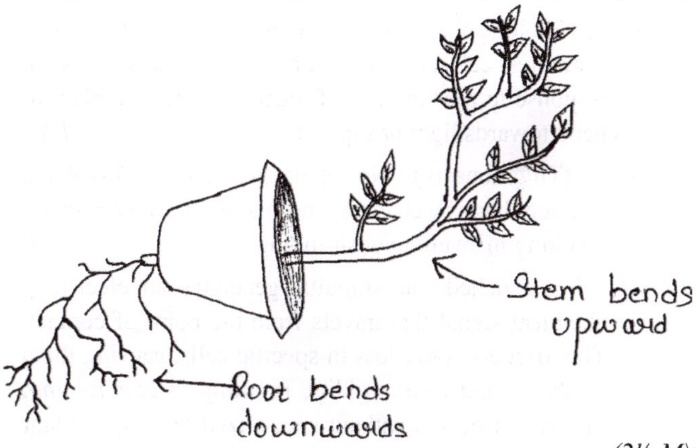

(2½ M)

2. Aradhya was studying plants and their movements. She observed different types of plant movements in response to stimuli and captured the following images: ***(An)***

(P)

(Q)

(R)

Analyze the images and answer the following questions:

(*a*) Name the type of movement shown in each of the images.

(*b*) State one difference between the types of movement observed in Q and R.

(*c*) Name the plant hormones involved in the movements shown in P, Q and R.

(*d*) Explain the mechanism of movement taking place in R.

Ans. (*a*) Types of movement:

P: Phototropism (½ *M*)

Q: Thigmotropism (½ *M*)

R: Nastic movement of *Mimosa pudica* (½ *M*)

(*b*)

Thigmotropism	Nastic movement of *Mimosa pudica*
Directional growth movement in response to touch (tendrils coiling around support).	Non-directional rapid movement in response to touch (folding of leaves in *Mimosa pudica*)

(1 *M*)

(*c*) Plant hormones involved:

- P (Phototropism) and Q (Thigmotropism): Auxin: Promotes cell elongation on the shaded side or in response to the stimulus of touch, causing the plant to bend towards light or support. (1 *M*)
- R (Thigmonasty): No plant hormone is involved. Change shape by changing the amount of water in them, resulting in swelling or shrinking. (½ *M*)

(*d*) When touched, the stimulus generates an electrical-chemical signal that travels from the point of contact. This triggers water loss in specific cells, causing them to shrink and lose turgidity, resulting in leaf folding. Movement occurs without specialized tissues, as plant cells regulate shape by altering water content. (1 *M*)

3. How do environmental stimuli affect the production of different plant hormones? ***(Un)***

Ans. Environmental stimuli significantly influence plant hormone production, affecting growth and adaptation.

(*a*) Light: In response to higher light intensity, auxin production increases, promoting cell elongation towards the light source, a phenomenon known as phototropism. (1 *M*)

(*b*) Water: During hydrotropism, roots sense moisture gradients, resulting in increased auxin concentration at the root tip, guiding roots towards water. (1 *M*)

(*c*) Touch: Thigmotropism involves auxin redistributing in response to touch, aiding in climbing or wrapping around objects. (1 *M*)

(*d*) Drought: Abscisic Acid (ABA) levels rise under drought conditions, causing leaves to wilt and inducing seed dormancy, conserving plant resources. (1 *M*)

(*e*) Germination: Favorable conditions trigger cytokinin production in seeds, breaking dormancy and initiating germination by promoting cell division and growth. (1 *M*)

Hints & Explanations

Multiple Choice Questions

1. (*a*) Cytokinins promote cell division in plants by stimulating the activity of meristems. Other activities like wilting of leaves (abscisic acid), stomatal pore opening (abscisic acid), and stem growth (auxins) are regulated by different hormones.

2. (*b*) Not all plant movements result from growth; for example, the movements of the sensitive plant's leaves in response to touch occur without growth. Additionally, hormones in plants do not act solely on the organ that produces them; instead, they are often synthesised in one part of the plant and affect various other parts, thus facilitating different growth and response mechanisms.

3. (*c*) Tendrils are sensitive to touch. When they come in contact with any support, the part of the tendril in contact with the object does not grow as rapidly as the part of the tendril away from the object. This causes the tendril to circle around the object and thus cling to it.

4. (*c*) Geeta likely observed that part Y did not grow at all, because auxin, which promotes growth, was no longer being produced after part X was cut off. Removal of shoot tips (decapitation) usually results in the growth of lateral buds.

5. (*d*) The movement of plants in response to the stimulus (light, chemical, gravity, water, etc.) resulting in growth of plants in a particular direction is called a tropical movement.

Assertion and Reason

1. (*b*) Phototropism is a directional growth movement of a plant, which is induced and determined by the direction of light stimulus. If a plant part such as the roots moves away from the light, then it is called negative phototropism.

2. (*d*) Pollen grains are not attracted rather they are carried towards stigma by the phenomenon of pollination. The pollen tube growth is an example of positive chemotropism as the growth of the pollen tube is triggered by chemical interaction between pollen and stigma.

3. (*c*) Gibberellins stimulate the germination of seeds and break down of stored food by stimulating the production of enzymes during germination, thereby ending seed dormancy.

HUMAN ENDOCRINE SYSTEM

3

NCERT Definitions (Commonly asked in 1 mark)

- **Hormone:** Chemical substances produced by glands, acting as messengers to regulate specific body functions.
- **Endocrine System:** A network of endocrine glands that produce and secrete hormones directly into the bloodstream to regulate various body functions.
- **Exocrine System:** A network of exocrine glands in the body that produce and secrete substances via ducts to specific external or internal surfaces.
- **Mixed Glands:** Glands that perform both exocrine and endocrine functions also known as mixed glands/ hetero glands.
- **Metabolism:** The set of life-sustaining chemical reactions in organisms, including anabolic (building of complex molecule from simple ones) and catabolic (breaking of complex molecule in simple ones) processes.
- **Feedback Mechanism:** The body's regulatory system, ensures hormone levels remain within the desired range. Any deviations in hormone levels prompt the activation of this mechanism. Within the body, two feedback mechanisms operate: positive and negative.
- **Goitre:** An abnormal enlargement of the thyroid gland, which can be caused by iodine deficiency, leading to disrupted production of thyroid hormones and potential metabolic issues.
- **Hyperthyroidism:** It is a condition characterised by the overproduction of thyroid hormones by the thyroid gland. This high level of thyroid hormones in the blood signals the pituitary gland to produce less TSH, leading to low TSH levels.
- **Hypothyroidism:** It is a condition where the thyroid gland underproduces thyroid hormones, leading to a slowdown in the body's metabolic processes. This can result in symptoms such as fatigue, weight gain, etc.
- **Dwarfism:** A condition resulting from a deficiency in growth hormone production by the pituitary gland during childhood, leading to shorter body structure.
- **Diabetes:** A metabolic disorder caused by malfunctioning of the pancreas gland or inability to use blood glucose by body cells, usually characterized by high blood sugar levels over a prolonged period.
- **Puberty:** A developmental stage in which the body undergoes physical changes to achieve reproductive maturity, driven by hormonal changes, including increased secretion of testosterone in males and oestrogen and progesterone in females.

Classification

Human Endocrine Glands

Category	Gland	Characteristics	Secreted Hormone	Function	Target Organ/Cell	Related Disorder
Endocrine System	Pituitary Gland	Pea-sized gland located at the base of the brain	Growth hormone	Regulates the growth and production of other hormones	Multiple organs	**In case if deficiency:** Dwarfism **In case of excess:** Gigantism
	Thyroid Gland	Butterfly-shaped gland located in the neck	Thyroxin	Regulates growth, metabolism of carbohydrate, fat, and protein	Body cells	**In case if deficiency:** Goiter
	Parathyroid Gland	Small glands located behind the thyroid gland	Parathyroid hormone (PTH)	Regulates calcium and phosphorus balance in the body	Bones, kidneys, intestine	**In case of deficiency:** Low blood calcium level **In case of excess:** Abnormally high level of calcium cause bone weakness
	Pineal Gland	Small gland located in the brain	Melatonin	Regulates sleep-wake cycles	Brain	Related to sleep disorders

Endocrine System	**Adrenal Glands**	Situated above the kidneys	Adrenaline	Manages stress responses, affects body metabolism	Kidneys, muscles	—
	Testes	Located in the male pelvis	Testosterone	• Drives male reproductive development • Maintenance of secondary sexual characteristics • Production of sperms	Reproductive organs like male genitalia	**In case of deficiency:** Inhibition of secondary sexual characteristics
	Ovary	Located in the female pelvis	Oestrogen, Progesterone	• Regulates female reproductive cycle • Development of secondary sexual characteristics • Production of egg	Reproductive organs like the uterus and mammary glands	Menstrual irregularities
	Hypothalamus	A region of the brain situated below the thalamus, connects the endocrine and nervous systems	Regulating pituitary gland secretions	Regulates the pituitary gland and various physiological processes	Pituitary gland	**In case of deficiency:** Various hormonal imbalances
	Thymus	A lymphoid organ situated in the chest, between lungs	Thymosin	Plays a role in the immune system	Immune cells	**In case of deficiency:** Impaired immunity
	Pancreas	Endocrine	Insulin	Decreases blood sugar levels.	Released into blood	**In case of deficiency:** Diabetes
		Exocrine	Pancreatic Juice (Not a hormone, but a digestive juice)	Helps in the digestion of protein and fat	Released in the small intestine	Digestive issues

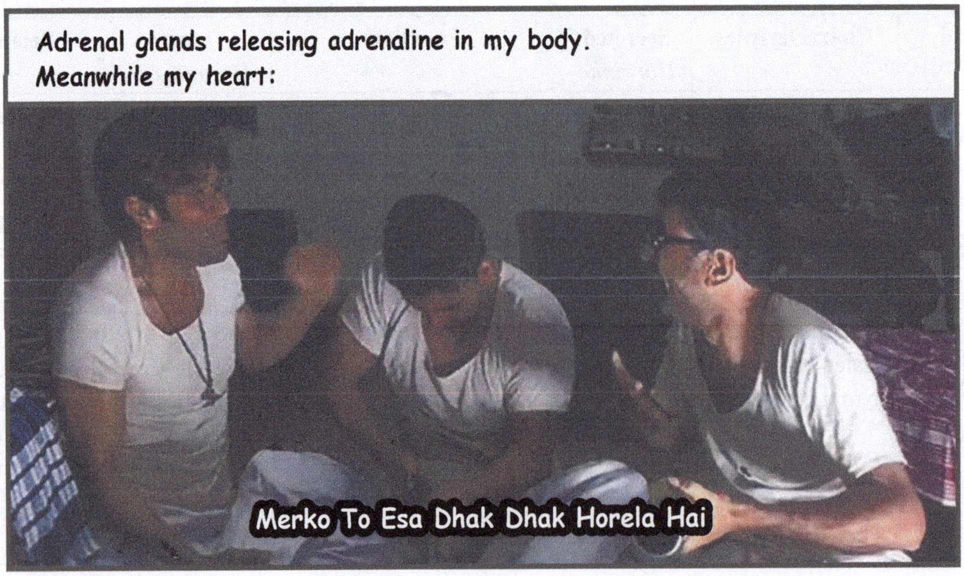

Important Facts

01 Chemical coordination is seen in both plants and animals.

02 Hormones produced in one part of an organism move to another part to achieve the desired effect.

03 A feedback mechanism regulates the action of the hormones.

04 The master gland of the body. ~ **Pituitary gland**

Real Life Application Based Questions

1. **Why do doctors recommend insulin injections for some diabetic patients, and which gland's function is directly influenced by this treatment?**

Ans. Insulin injections are prescribed to manage blood sugar levels in diabetic patients, compensating for the inadequate insulin production by the pancreas. This helps in the utilization and regulation of glucose within the body.

2. **Look around and you'll see everyone is a different height, with some not reaching the average height for their age group even after completing puberty. Why do some people remain shorter?**

Ans. Some individuals remain shorter than the average height for their age group due to their genetic or deficiencies in growth hormone secretion. This hormone, essential for the normal growth and development of bones and muscles, is produced by the pituitary gland.

3. **You've likely seen advertisements promoting iodine-enriched salt and its health benefits. Why is iodine considered essential for our health?**

Ans. Iodine is vital for our health because it enables the thyroid gland to produce thyroxin, a hormone that:

- Regulates our metabolism
- Impacting our energy levels, weight, and overall growth and development

Without adequate iodine, our bodies can't make enough thyroxin, leading to potential health issues like goiter characterized by an enlarged thyroid gland, and other metabolic disorders. Thus, using iodine-enriched salt helps prevent these deficiencies and supports overall bodily functions.

4. You must have noticed many dramatic changes in your appearance as well as that of your friends as you approached 10–12 years of age. What glands are involved in these changes?

Ans. The pituitary gland and the gonads are involved in these changes during the period of puberty.

Pituitary Gland:

- Releases growth hormones.
- Influences overall growth and development during adolescence.

Gonads:

- Testes in boys: Produce testosterone, which is responsible for muscle development, voice deepening, and other male secondary sexual characteristics.
- Ovaries in girls: Release oestrogen, promoting breast development, initiating menstrual cycles, and other female secondary sexual characteristics.

Myth Buster

- ❑ **Myth: Eating sugar causes diabetes.**

  Fact: Diabetes is more complex than just sugar intake. It involves insulin resistance or insufficient insulin production by the pancreas. While excessive sugar can contribute to obesity, a risk factor for diabetes but, it's not the direct cause.
- ❑ **Myth: Hormones are active throughout the entire body, affecting every cell they reach.**

  Fact: Hormones are specific in their action and only affect target cells with the appropriate receptors. For example, insulin primarily affects liver and muscle cells, even though it travels throughout the bloodstream.
- ❑ **Myth: Hormones only influence the physical aspects of the body, like growth and metabolism.**

  Fact: Hormones have a significant impact on both physical and psychological aspects, influencing mood, behavior, and cognitive functions alongside growth and metabolism.
- ❑ **Myth: Animals can consciously control their hormonal responses.**

  Fact: Hormonal responses are largely involuntary and regulated by complex feedback mechanisms within the body. For instance, humans cannot consciously control the release of insulin or adrenaline.
- ❑ **Myth: Only external stimuli can trigger hormonal changes in animals.**

  Fact: Both internal and external stimuli can trigger hormonal responses. For instance, internal changes in blood glucose levels can stimulate insulin release, while external stressors can trigger adrenaline release.

Mnemonics

- ❑ To remember human endocrine glands.

  Go along with peter parker to paris having the plate of noodles

Go	Along with	Peter	Parker	To	Paris	Having	The	Plate of noodles
↓	↓	↓	↓	↓	↓	↓	↓	↓
Gonads (Ovaries and testes)	Adrenal gland	Pancreas gland	Pituitary gland	Thyroid gland	Parathyroid gland	Hypothalamus	Thymus	Pineal gland

When you remember everything in your exams because you studied from PW books.

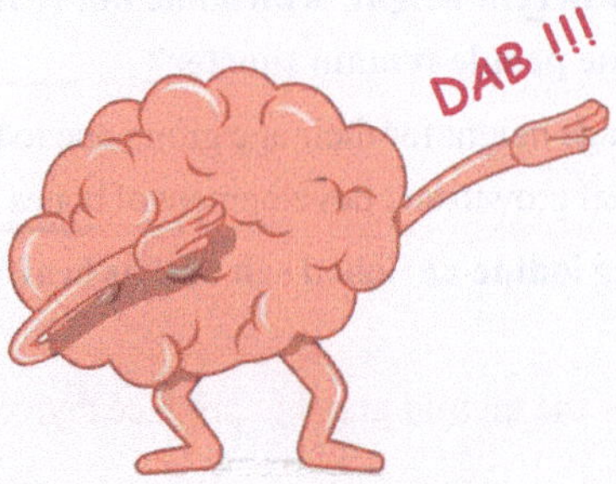

COMPETENCY BASED SOLVED EXAMPLES

Multiple Choice Questions (1 M)

1. **During an intense workout, an athlete notices an increase in muscle strength and endurance. Which hormone primarily mobilises energy stores to muscles during such physical activities?** ***(Un)***

   (*a*) Insulin (*b*) Thyroxin
   (*c*) Adrenaline (*d*) Glucagon

2. **Sapna suffers from a condition due to which her average blood sugar level is 174 mg/dL. The average blood sugar level in a healthy adult is <140 mg/dL.**

   Which of the following could be the cause of Sapna's condition? ***(An)***

   (*a*) Insufficient production of thyroxin in her body.
   (*b*) Insufficient production of insulin in her body.
   (*c*) Excess production of thyroxin in her body.
   (*d*) Excess production of insulin in her body.

3. **During a situation where a person is being chased by a wild animal, their body releases adrenaline to prepare for the "fight or flight" response. Considering this scenario, explain how the secretion of adrenaline affects:** ***(Ap)***

   (*i*) The concentration of glycogen in the liver.
   (*ii*) The concentration of glucose in the blood.

	Concentration of glycogen in the liver	Concentration of glucose in the blood
(*a*)	Decrease	Increase
(*b*)	Increase	Increase
(*c*)	No effect	Decrease
(*d*)	Increase	No effect

4. **In humans, the life processes are controlled and regulated by** ***(Re)*** **(NCERT Exemplar)**

   (*a*) Reproductive and endocrine systems.
   (*b*) Respiratory and nervous systems.
   (*c*) Endocrine and digestive systems.
   (*d*) Nervous and endocrine systems.

5. **A doctor is explaining to a teenage boy and girl about the changes they might experience during puberty. The doctor mentions that these changes are controlled by specific hormones secreted by their respective reproductive organs. Which of the following correctly identifies the hormones responsible for these changes?** ***(Ap)***

   (*a*) Oestrogen from testes and testosterone from ovary.
   (*b*) Oestrogen from adrenal gland and testosterone from pituitary gland.
   (*c*) Testosterone from testes and oestrogen from ovary.
   (*d*) Testosterone from thyroid gland and oestrogen from pituitary gland.

6. **A female patient visits a doctor with symptoms of irregular menstrual cycles and difficulty getting pregnant. The doctor suspects a hormonal imbalance. Which hormone is likely to be involved in this scenario?** ***(An)***

   (*a*) Insulin (*b*) Thyroxin
   (*c*) Progesterone (*d*) Cortisol

Assertion and Reason (1 M)

Direction: The following questions consist of two statements – Assertion (A) and Reason (R). Answer these questions by selecting the appropriate option given below:

(*a*) Both A and R are true, and R is the correct explanation of A.
(*b*) Both A and R are true, but R is not the correct explanation of A.
(*c*) A is true, but R is false.
(*d*) A is false, but R is true.

1. **Assertion (A):** Pituitary gland is also known as the master gland.
   Reason (R): It controls major endocrine glands by its secretion. ***(Re)***

2. **Assertion (A):** Endocrine glands sends their secretions directly into the bloodstream.
   Reason (R): Endocrine glands are ductless glands. ***(Re)***

3. **Assertion (A):** A person got his neck swollen.
   Reason (R): Iodine deficiency is responsible for goitre. ***(Re)***

4. **Assertion (A):** In controlled experiments where adrenal hormone levels are artificially increased, pancreatic cells respond by releasing more pancreatic juice to restore homeostasis in the body by metabolizing carbohydrates and fats in the small intestine for energy production.
   Reason (R): The feedback mechanism helps maintain metabolic homeostasis by adjusting the rate of metabolic reactions in response to changing internal or external conditions. ***(Ap)***

Subjective Questions

Very Short Answer Type Questions (2 M)

1. **A picture of the lady is given below. She might be having some problems. Can you depict the problem and what kind of diet is advised to treat the disease?** ***(An)***

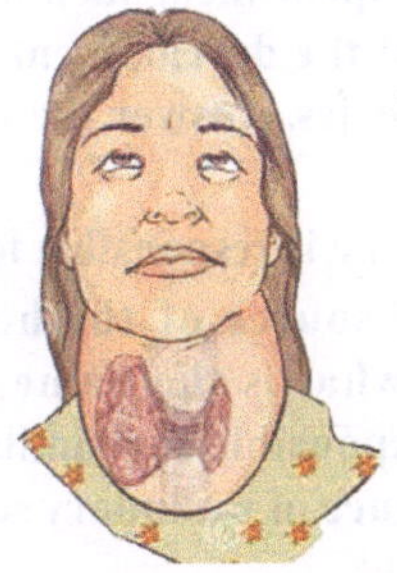

Ans. The given image suggests the woman may have hypothyroidism, indicated by the visible swelling in the neck region, which is a common sign of a goiter. *(1 M)*

A diet for hypothyroidism should be rich in iodine, and zinc, avoiding goitrogenic foods like soy and cruciferous vegetables in excess. *(1 M)*

2. Dr. Suman Lakhera is treating two patients:

Patient 1: Suffering from a digestive disorder, affecting enzyme secretion necessary for carbohydrate, fat, and sugar metabolism.

Patient 2: Suffering with anxiety issues.

Based on your understanding, answer the following question:

(*a*) Name the concerned gland in the case of Patient 1.

(*b*) Name the concerned gland in the case of Patient 2 and state one of its functions. ***(An)***

Ans. (*a*) The gland concerned in the case of patient 1 seems to be the pancreas. *(½ M)*

(*b*) The gland concerned in the case of patient 2 can be the adrenal gland. *(½ M)*

One of its functions includes secreting adrenaline, which prepares the body for a 'fight or flight' response by increasing heart rate and supplying more oxygen to muscles. *(1 M)*

3. What is the advantage of endocrine glands releasing their secretions into the blood? Give examples of endocrine glands associated with the brain. ***(Re)***

Ans. Advantages of endocrine gland secreting their secretion in blood:

- This ductless release mechanism facilitates rapid adaptation to varying conditions, crucial for maintaining homeostasis. *(½ M)*
- The lack of ducts allows hormones to reach and regulate multiple organs and systems, ensuring widespread physiological effects. *(½ M)*

Endocrine glands associated with the brain are:

- Pineal gland *(½ M)*
- Pituitary gland *(½ M)*

4. An old man is advised by his doctor to take less sugar in his diet. Name the disease from which the man is suffering. Mention the hormone due to imbalance of which he is suffering from this disease. Which endocrine gland secretes this hormone? ***(Un)***

Ans. The man is suffering with the disease diabetes. It is caused by an inability to produce or use insulin by the body. *(1 M)*

Insulin hormone is secreted by pancreas. *(1 M)*

5. A 14-year-old male student starts experiencing dramatic changes in his appearance, such as increased height, deeper voice, and the development of other secondary sexual characteristics. Answer the following questions: ***(Ap)***

(*a*) Which hormone is responsible for these changes?

(*b*) What is the source of the hormone described in (a), and what is the name and source of the hormone responsible for similar type of changes (i.e., appearance of secondary sexual characters) in females?

Ans. (*a*) Testosterone *(½ M)*

(*b*) Source: Testosterone is produced primarily in the testes in males. *(½ M)*

Hormone in females: Estrogen is the hormone responsible for secondary sexual characteristics in females. It is produced primarily in the ovaries. *(1 M)*

6. Aisha noticed that her height is shorter compared to children of her age. Meanwhile, her elder sister Sara has been experiencing irregular menstrual cycles. Can you identify the gland and the hormone responsible for these issues in both cases? ***(Ap)***

Ans. For Aisha (short height):

- Gland: Pituitary gland
- Hormone: Growth hormone *(1 M)*

For Sara (irregular menstrual cycles):

- Gland: Ovary
- Hormones: Estrogen and Progesterone *(1 M)*

Short Answer Type Questions (3 M)

1. (*a*) Infer the impact on an animal if its adrenal glands could not secrete adrenaline in response to stress.

(*b*) How the timing of secretion and amount of hormone secretion are regulated in human system? Explain with example. ***(Ap, Un)***

Ans. (*a*) Lack of adrenaline would impair the animal's ability to respond to stress, affecting heart rate, glucose metabolism, and muscle readiness, potentially compromising survival during critical situations. *(1 M)*

(*b*) The timing and amount of hormones released by various glands are controlled by the feedback mechanism which is in-built in the body.

For example, if the sugar level in the blood rises too much, they are detected by the cells of pancreas which respond by producing and secreting more insulin into blood. And as the blood sugar falls to a certain level, the secretion of insulin is reduced automatically. *(2 M)*

2. (*a*) Identify the endocrine glands B and C in the given diagram.

(*b*) Name the endocrine glands A and D and state its function. ***(Re)***

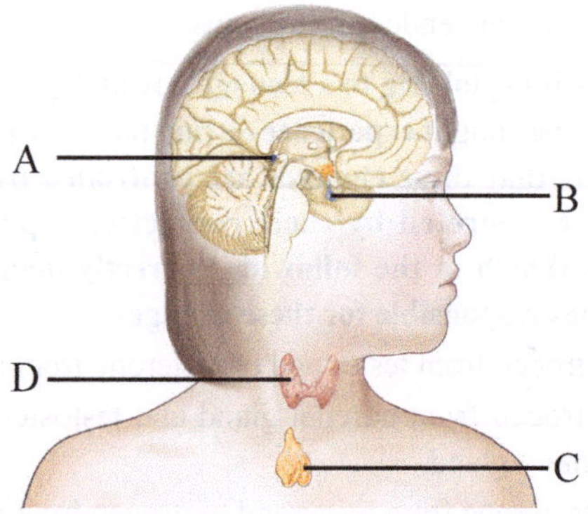

Ans. (*a*) B - Pituitary gland *(½ M)*

C - Thymus *(½ M)*

(*b*) A (Pineal Gland): The pineal gland regulates various biological rhythms, including sleep-wake cycles, by secreting the hormone melatonin. *(1 M)*

D (Thyroid Gland): It releases thyroxin, regulating growth, and metabolism of fats, carbohydrates, and proteins in the body. *(1 M)*

3. A squirrel is in a scary situation. Its body has to prepare for either fighting or running away. State the immediate changes that take place in its body so that the squirrel is able to either fight or run. ***(An)* (CBSE, 2020)**

Ans. Squirrels respond to threats with adrenal hormone-mediated fight or flight reactions. *(1 M)*

Changes that take place in the squirrel body involve:

- Increased Heart Rate: Ensures rapid blood flow, boosting alertness. *(½ M)*
- Enhanced Breathing: Increases oxygen intake for immediate activity. *(½ M)*
- Dilated Muscle Blood Vessels: Supplies extra oxygen, preparing muscles for intense action. *(½ M)*
- Liver Glucose Release: Cortisol prompts stored glucose release from liver, providing instant energy. *(½ M)*

4. Why is the use of iodised salt advisable? Name the disease caused due to deficiency of iodine in our diet and state its one symptom. ***(Re)* (CBSE, 2019, 2018)**

Ans. Iodised salt is recommended due to the role of iodine in production of thyroxine hormone which is crucial for the regulation of basal metabolism. *(1 M)*

Disease Caused by Iodine Deficiency:

Goitre: Abnormal growth of thyroid gland due to very high or little production of thyroid hormone. *(1 M)*

Symptom: Swollen neck due to the enlargement of the thyroid gland. *(1 M)*

5. Rahul, a 10 year old boy with a fear of public speaking, is asked to give an important speech in front of his entire class. As Rahul begins to speak, his anxiety escalates, and he starts to experience rapid heavy breathing and sweating. Given below is the graphical representation of the hormonal changes in Rahul's body during this challenging situation. Based on your analysis of the graph, respond to the following questions.

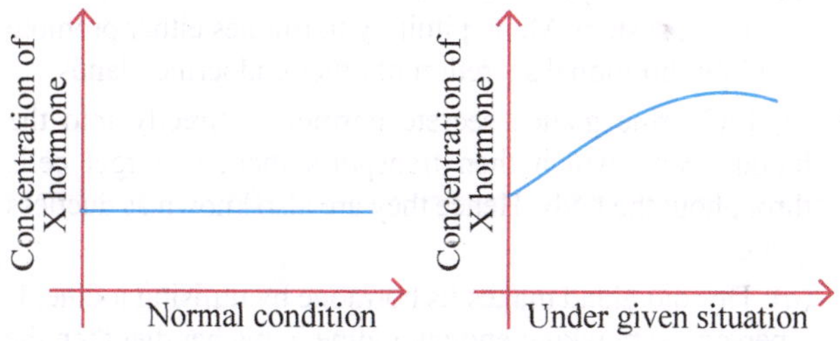

(*a*) Identify the hormone denoted as 'X'.

(*b*) Specify the organ responsible for producing the hormone 'X'.

(*c*) Explain the physiological role of hormone 'X'. *(An)*

Ans. (*a*) The hormone denoted as 'X' is adrenaline (also known as epinephrine). *(½ M)*

(*b*) The organ responsible for producing adrenaline is adrenal glands. *(½ M)*

(*c*) Physiological roles of adrenaline (Hormone-X) in triggering the "fight or flight" response during stress include:

- Increasing heart rate: Adrenaline accelerates heart rate and elevates blood pressure, ensuring rapid blood flow to essential organs and muscles. *(1 M)*
- Boosting energy availability: Adrenaline enhances the breakdown of glucose and increases blood sugar levels, providing immediate energy for the body's response. *(1 M)*

6. Write in tabular form, the location and function of the hormones secreted by each of the following glands present in the human body: ***(Re)* (CBSE, 2020)**

(*a*) Pituitary gland

(*b*) Thyroid gland

(*c*) Pancreas

Ans.

	Name of gland	Location	Function
(*a*)	Pituitary gland	Base of hypothalamus	• It controls functioning of several other glands by its hormones. • It secretes growth hormone.
(*b*)	Thyroid gland	In the neck region	Secretes thyroxin which controls basal metabolism of the body.
(*c*)	Pancreas	In the abdominal region below the stomach	Secretes insulin which reduces blood sugar and glucagon which increases blood sugar level

(3 M)

Long Answer Type Questions (5 M)

1. Explain with the help of an example, the feedback mechanism for the regulation of hormonal secretion in the human body. ***(Un)* (CBSE, 2020)**

Ans. The feedback mechanism of hormones is the mechanism through which the balance of hormone in the blood/body is maintained. The increase or decrease in the concentration of that hormone can either stimulate the secretion of that particular hormone or inhibit the hormone secretion. This is called feedback. *(1 M)*

There can be two types of feedback.

- Positive feedback: Stimulates the secretion or production of the hormone. *(½ M)*
- Negative feedback: Inhibits the secretion of the hormone. *(½ M)*

Example: Blood glucose regulation

- Positive Feedback: Consumption of carbohydrates leads to an increase in blood glucose levels. Which triggers the pancreas to release insulin. *(1 M)*

- Cellular uptake of glucose: Insulin signals boy cells to uptake glucose from the blood, reducing blood glucose levels. *(1 M)*
- Negative Feedback: As blood glucose levels drop, negative feedback mechanisms inhibit further insulin secretion, preventing hypoglycemia and maintaining blood glucose homeostasis. *(1 M)*

2. Give reasons: ***(Re)* (CBSE, 2014)**

(*a*) Pituitary is often termed as master endocrine gland.

(*b*) Pancreas helps in digestion and also regulates blood sugar level.

(*c*) Adrenaline are known as glands of emergency.

Ans. (*a*) The pituitary gland is sometimes called the "master" gland of the endocrine system because it controls the functioning of many of the other endocrine glands. *(1 M)*

(*b*) The pancreas helps in digestion and also regulates blood sugar levels due to its dual function as an exocrine and endocrine gland.

- Exocrine Function: The pancreas secretes digestive enzymes such as amylase, lipase, and proteases into the small intestine to aid in the breakdown of carbohydrates, fats, and proteins, respectively. These enzymes facilitate the digestion and absorption of nutrients from food. *(1 M)*
- Endocrine Function: The pancreas also produces hormones such as insulin and glucagon, which play critical roles in regulating blood sugar levels. Insulin helps to lower blood sugar levels by promoting the uptake of glucose into cells for energy production or storage, while glucagon acts to raise blood sugar levels by stimulating the liver to release stored glucose into the bloodstream. *(1 M)*

(*c*) Adrenaline is known as the emergency hormone because:

- It is secreted in large amounts by the adrenal glands during emergency conditions. *(1 M)*
- It prepares the body for flight or fight response by causing the heart to beat faster and increasing respiration rates to supply more oxygen to the muscles. *(1 M)*

3. Analyse the flow chart given below and answer the following questions. ***(An)***

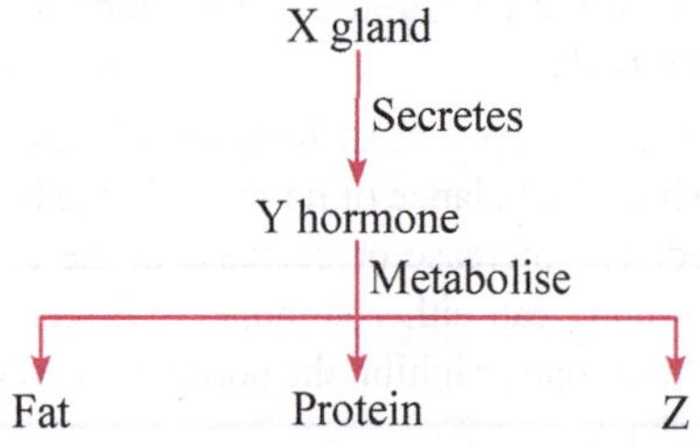

(*a*) Identify X, Y, and Z.

(*b*) Name the condition that develops from a deficiency in the dietary component necessary for synthesising the Y hormone with its symptoms.

(*c*) Suggest dietary recommendations to ensure the proper functioning of the X gland.

Ans. (*a*) X: Thyroid gland

Y: Thyroxine

Z: Carbohydrate *(½ × 3 = 1½ M)*

(*b*) The condition that develops from an iodine deficiency, which is necessary for synthesising the Y hormone thyroxine, is called goitre. The symptoms of goitre include a swollen neck, weight gain, and slow metabolism. *(1½ M)*

(*c*) To ensure the proper functioning of the thyroid (X) gland, it is important to include iodine-rich foods in the diet, such as iodised salt, seafood, dairy products, and eggs. *(2 M)*

Hints & Explanations

Multiple Choice Questions

1. (*c*) Adrenaline, released during physical exertion or stress, facilitates the mobilization of energy stores by increasing blood flow to muscles, enhancing oxygen delivery, and stimulating glucose release from energy reserves, thus improving muscle strength and endurance during workout.
2. (*b*) Insulin is a hormone produced by the pancreas that lower blood sugar levels by facilitating the uptake of glucose by cells. Insufficient insulin production can lead to elevated blood sugar levels which can be the cause of Sapna's condition.
3. (*a*) Adrenaline is secreted by body during fight or flight response. It increases the blood glucose level. This happens by increasing the rate of breakdown of glycogen to glucose in the liver and muscles.
4. (*d*) In humans, life processes are controlled and regulated by the nervous and endocrine systems. These systems coordinate bodily functions through electrical impulses and hormonal signals, maintaining homeostasis and responding to environmental changes.
5. (*c*) The dramatic body changes during puberty are primarily due to testosterone produced by the testes and oestrogen produced by the ovaries. These hormones are responsible for developing secondary sexual characteristics in males and females, respectively.
6. (*c*) Progesterone and oestrogen are critical in regulating the menstrual cycle and supporting pregnancy. It prepares the uterus for embryo implantation. An imbalance can lead to irregular menstrual cycles and fertility issues.

Assertion and Reason

1. (*a*) The pituitary gland is considered the master gland of the endocrine system because it controls the rest of the endocrine system. Many pituitary hormones either promote or inhibit hormonal secretion of other endocrine glands
2. (*a*) Endocrine glands secrete hormones directly into the bloodstream, which then transports them to target cells throughout the body. Hence they are also known as ductless glands.
3. (*a*) Thyroid gland makes its hormone by utilising iodine. If a person is not taking enough iodine in his/her diet then the thyroid gland swells up causing goitre.
4. (*d*) Elevated adrenal hormone levels don't directly stimulate pancreatic juice secretion for metabolising carbohydrates and fats for energy production. The adrenal hormones, like adrenaline, mainly regulate stress responses, such as increasing heart and breathing rates, preparing the body for action.

MISCELLANEOUS EXERCISE

Multiple Choice Questions (1 M)

1. A gardener wants the plants in the hedge that he is growing to become bushier with more branches. Which of the following should he do? ***(Ap)***
   (*a*) Spray water on the tips of the stems to increase growth.
   (*b*) Dig around the plant roots and apply more manure.
   (*c*) Trim the hedge by cutting off the tips of the stems.
   (*d*) Remove all the weeds that grow around the hedge.

2. A big tree falls in a forest, but its roots are still in contact with the soil. The branches of this fallen tree grow straight up (vertically). This happens in response to: ***(Un)***
   (*a*) Water (*b*) Minerals
   (*c*) Gravity (*d*) Light

3. In the context of the body's reaction to stress, a medical research team observes a rise in blood glucose levels in some individuals. Which of the following statements accurately explains the reason behind this physiological response? ***(An)***
   (*a*) During stress, the adrenal glands release adrenaline, which triggers an increase in blood glucose levels. This mechanism equips the body with the energy for the 'fight or flight' response.
   (*b*) The pineal gland secretes insulin in response to stress, aiming to enhance blood glucose levels.
   (*c*) While thyroxin, produced by the thymus gland, plays a crucial role in basal metabolism, it is a primary hormone responsible for the acute stress-induced rise in blood glucose levels.
   (*d*) Both (*a*) and (*c*)

4. If a person's spinal cord is injured at the lower back, what immediate effect would this injury have on the body's ability to perform reflex actions below the point of injury? ***(Un)***
   (*a*) Reflex actions in the upper body will be significantly enhanced.
   (*b*) Reflex actions in both the upper and lower body will remain unaffected.
   (*c*) Reflex actions in the lower body, below the point of injury will probably be impaired or paralyzed.
   (*d*) Only the involuntary actions in the lower body will be impaired or paralyzed.

5. If a person is unable to taste food unless it has very strong flavors, which part of their nervous system is likely not functioning properly? ***(An)***
   (*a*) Motor neurons
   (*b*) Sensory neurons in the tongue
   (*c*) Reflex arcs in the spinal cord
   (*d*) Muscles in the digestive tract

6. A female is suffering from an irregular menstrual cycle. The doctor prescribed her some hormonal tablets. Which of the following option is the hormone she lacks in her body? ***(Un)***
   (*a*) Oestrogen (*b*) Testosterone
   (*c*) Adrenalin (*d*) Thyroxin

7. A student studying late at night feels hungry and decides to eat. Which part of the brain is primarily involved in making him aware of the hunger sensation? ***(Ap)***
   (*a*) Cerebellum (*b*) Medulla oblongata
   (*c*) Forebrain (*d*) Mid-brain

8. In a nerve cell, the site where the electrical impulse is converted into a chemical signal is known as: ***(Re)* (CBSE, 2024)**
   (*a*) Axon (*b*) Dendrites
   (*c*) Neuromuscular junction (*d*) Cell body

9. Considering the hormone insulin, which of the following statement is correct? ***(Re)***
   (*a*) It decrease blood glucose level by breaking down glycogen in the liver.
   (*b*) It decreases blood glucose level by facilitating cellular uptake of glucose.
   (*c*) Insulin secretion decreases when blood glucose levels are high.
   (*d*) Insulin stimulates the conversion of excess glucose into proteins.

10. A student can still play a piano piece flawlessly even after not practicing for months. This ability to remember and execute the piano piece without recent practice involves which part of the brain? ***(An)***
   (*a*) Cerebrum (*b*) Cerebellum
   (*c*) Medulla (*d*) Hypothalamus

Assertion and Reason (1 M)

Direction: The following questions consist of two statements – Assertion (A) and Reason (R). Answer these questions by *selecting the appropriate option given below:*
(*a*) Both A and R are true, and R is the correct explanation of A.
(*b*) Both A and R are true, but R is not the correct explanation of A.
(*c*) A is true, but R is false.
(*d*) A is false, but R is true.

1. **Assertion (A):** Phototropism is a directional growth movement.
   Reason (R): It occurs in the direction of light. ***(Re)***

2. **Assertion (A):** In animals, adrenaline is released in response to stress, preparing the body for a 'fight or flight' reaction by increasing heart rate and blood flow to muscles.
   Reason (R): Adrenaline directly stimulates the digestive system to increase activity, ensuring immediate energy availability by rapidly breaking down stored nutrients. ***(Re)***

3. **Assertion (A):** The human brain uses electrical impulses to process information and coordinate responses to stimuli, while in plants, movement such as the closing of *Mimosa pudica* leaves involves only chemical signals without any involvement of the nervous system.

Reason (R): Although both organisms respond to stimuli, plants lack a nervous system and hence rely solely on chemical gradients to trigger movements, whereas the human brain processes information using rapid electrical impulses along neurons. ***(Un)***

4. **Assertion (A):** During a cooking class, Meera instinctively blinks when oil splatters from the pan as a reflex.

Reason (R): Blinking in response to sudden stimuli protects the eyes, a reflex action that involves the higher brain centers for decision-making and immediate processing to prevent injury. ***(Ap)***

Subjective Questions

Very Short Answer Type Questions (2 M)

1. (*a*) Name ONE plant hormone that controls directional growth.

(*b*) Plant hormones are also referred to as growth regulators and can be controlled by a number of stimuli. Mention ONE point of difference between the functioning of animal growth hormones and plant growth regulators with respect to such control. ***(Re)***

2. Hema bought some unripe tomatoes and left half of them in a brown paper bag and the other half in an open tray. After two days she noticed that the tomatoes in the paper bag had ripened, but the ones in the open tray had not.

(*a*) What hormone facilitated the ripening of tomatoes?

(*b*) Why did the tomatoes in the paper bag ripen faster? ***(An)***

3. A 40-year-old male has difficulty with writing, buttoning a shirt, and walking in a straight line, but does not experience any issues with breathing, swallowing, or other vital functions. Which part of the brain is most likely affected? Explain your answer briefly. ***(Ap)***

4. How do we detect the smell of an agarbatti (incense stick)? ***(Ap)* (NCERT Intext)**

5. A study was conducted to observe the concentration of plant hormones in different parts of a plant. The data collected is as follows: ***(Ap)***

Plant part	Hormone X (mg/g)	Hormone Y (mg/g)
Young leaves	1.2	0.5
Mature leaves	0.8	2.0

(*i*) Identify the hormones X and Y.

(*ii*) What would be the relevance of the highest concentration of Y in mature leaves?

6. If Aakash's cerebellum is damaged due to injury, what are the two things in his body that might not work well because of the damage? ***(Ap)***

7. Name the hormone responsible for the development of moustache and beard in men. State its two more function. ***(Re)***

8. (*a*) What would happen if reflex arcs were absent in humans? Provide an example to support your answer.

(*b*) Discuss one real-life situation where reflex arcs are beneficial. ***(Ap)***

9. How is the movement of leaves of a sensitive plant different from the downward movement of the roots? ***(Un)* (CBSE, 2024)**

OR

There is a hormone which regulates carbohydrate, protein and fat metabolism in our body. Name the hormone and the gland which secretes it. Why is it important for us to have iodised salt in our diet? ***(Un)* (CBSE, 2024)**

Short Answer Type Questions (3 M)

1. Taking the example of any two animal hormones along with their gland of secretion, explain how these hormones help (i) in growth and development and (ii) regulate metabolism, in the body. ***(Un)* (CBSE, 2024)**

2. A 10-year-old child was observed to be significantly shorter than other children of the same age. After a medical examination, it was found that the child had a deficiency of a particular hormone. Considering this scenario: ***(Ap)***

(*a*) Identify the hormone likely to be deficient and the gland responsible for its secretion.

(*b*) Identify the brain region involved in regulating the level of hormone in the given scenario and explain its role.

3. What is the difference between the manner in which movement takes place in a sensitive plant and the movement in our legs? ***(Un)* (NCERT)**

4. During an experiment, researchers expose a plant shoot to unilateral light and monitor its growth. They hypothesize that a hormone, "X," redistributes in response to light to regulate shoot bending. They tested three experimental setups: ***(An, Un)***

1. Hormone "X" is evenly distributed between the shaded and light-exposed sides of the shoot.
2. Hormone "X" accumulates on the shaded side of the shoot.
3. Hormone "X" accumulates on the light-exposed side of the shoot.

The researchers analyze the shoot's growth pattern for each setup to determine which distribution optimizes plant growth. Answer the following questions on the basis of your understanding.

(*a*) Predict the shoot's growth pattern for each experimental setup.

(*b*) Based on the results, which experimental setup ensures optimal shoot bending and growth? Justify your answer.

5. (*a*) Name the gland and the hormone secreted by it in scary situations in human beings. List any two responses shown by our body when this hormone is secreted into the blood. ***(Re, Un)* (CBSE, 2023)**

OR

(*b*) In the given diagram

(*i*) Name the parts labelled A, B, and C.

(*ii*) Write the functions of A and C.

(*iii*) Reflex arcs have evolved in animals ? Why ?

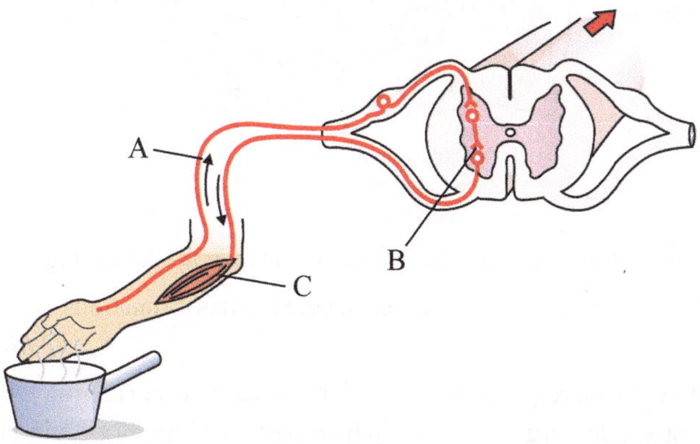

(*Re*) (CBSE, 2023)

6. Give reasons:

(*a*) Iodine plays a vital role in thyroid function and growth regulation.

(*b*) Pancreas helps in digestion and also regulates blood sugar level.

(*c*) Endocrine glands secrete hormones in precise quantities rather than in a continuous or unregulated manner. **(*Re*)**

Long Answer Type Questions (5 M)

1. (*a*) Sagar saw a beautiful rose and smelled it. As he was smelling it, he happened to touch a thorn and pull his hand away.
State TWO differences and similarities each in the way the nervous system performs these two actions.

(*b*) Are all involuntary actions reflex actions? Justify.

(Ap, *Un*) (CBSE APQ, 2023)

2. (*a*) A doctor has advised Sameer to reduce sugar intake in his diet and do regular exercise after checking his blood test reports. Which disease do you think Sameer is suffering from? Name the hormone responsible for this disease and the organ producing the hormone.

(*b*) Which hormone is present in the areas of rapid cell division in a plant and which hormone inhibits the growth? **(*An*) (CBSE APQ, 2023)**

3. Design an experiment to demonstrate hydrotropism. **(*Cr*) (NCERT Intext)**

4. (*a*) (*i*) Distinguish between hormonal co-ordination in plants and animals.

(*ii*) Which part of the brain is responsible for–

1. intelligence
2. riding a bicycle
3. vomiting
4. controlling hunger

(*iii*) How is brain and spinal-cord protected against mechanical injuries? **(*Un*, *Re*) (CBSE, 2024)**

OR

(*b*) (*i*) What are tropic movements? Give an example of a plant hormone which (1) inhibits growth and (2) promotes cell division.

(*ii*) Explain directional movement of a tendril in pea plant in response to touch. Name the hormone responsible for this movement. **(*Un*) (CBSE, 2024)**

Case Based Questions

Case Based-I: Questions numbers 1 to 4 are based on table given below. Study the table in which the levels of Thyroid Stimulating Hormone (TSH) in women are given and answer the questions that follow on the basis of understanding of the following paragraph and the related studied concepts.

Age Range	Normal (mU/L)	Low (mU/L)
18 – 29 years	0.4 – 2.34 mU/L	< 0.4 mU/L
30 – 49 years	0.4 – 4.0 mU/L	< 0.4 mU/L
50 – 79 years	0.46 – 4.68 mU/L	< 0.46 mU/L

Women are at greater risk for developing abnormal TSH levels during menstruation, while giving birth and after going through menopause. Around 5% of women in the United States have some kind of thyroid problem compared to 3% of men. Despite claims that high TSH increases your risk for heart disease, a 2013 study found no link between high TSH and heart diseases. But a 2017 study showed that older women are especially at risk for developing thyroid cancer if they have high TSH levels along with thyroid nodules. **(*An*) (CBSE, 2020)**

(*i*) A 35 year old woman has TSH level 6.03 mU/L. What change should she bring in her diet to control this level? *(1 M)*

(*ii*) When do women face a greater risk of abnormal TSH level? *(1 M)*

(*iii*) State the consequence of low TSH level. *(1 M)*

(*iv*) Name the mineral that is responsible for synthesis of hormone secreted by thyroid gland. *(1 M)*

Case Based-II: Given below is an experimental setup to demonstrate a particular tropic movement in germinating seeds. Study the diagram and answer the questions that follow: **(*An*) (CBSE, 2019)**

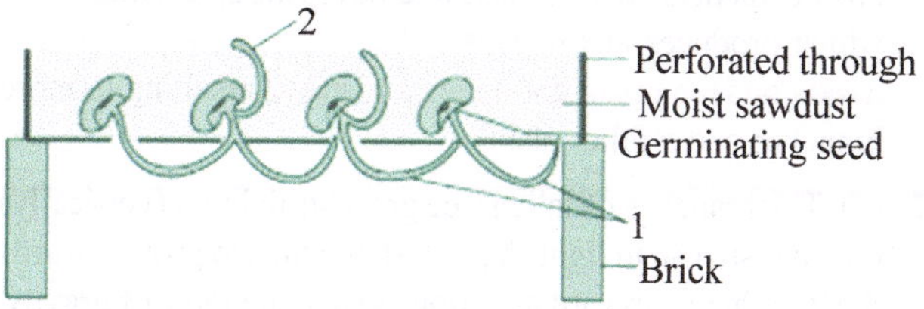

(*i*) Label the parts 1 and 2. *(1 M)*

(*ii*) Name the tropic movement shown by part 1. *(1 M)*

(*iii*) Part 1 is affected by two stimuli. Name them. Which one of the two is stronger? *(1 M)*

(*iv*) What do you understand by 'Positive' and 'Negative' tropic movements in plants? *(1 M)*

Case Based-III: The diagram given below represents a plant movement. Answer the following questions. ***(An)* (CBSE, 2020)**

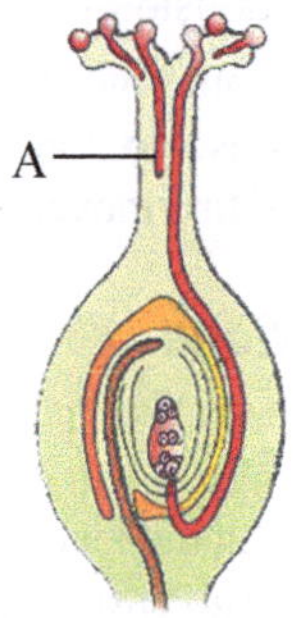

(*i*) Name the tropic movement shown in the diagram. *(1 M)*

(*ii*) Label the part marked 'A'. *(1 M)*

(*iii*) What is part A attracted to? *(1 M)*

(*iv*) Give an example of a plant which shows thigmotropism. *(1 M)*

Case Based-IV: Akanksha labeled various parts of the brain in the diagram below and noted their functions. However, some of her labels and descriptions are incorrect. ***(Re, Un)***

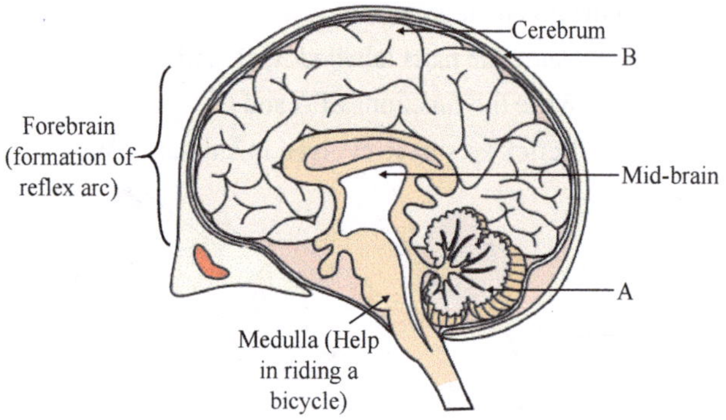

Carefully examine the image and answer the following:

(*i*) Identify and correct any mislabeled parts or functions. *(2 M)*

(*ii*) Akansha remembered that after a roller coaster ride she felt a sudden urge to vomit. Which part of Akansha's brain is responsible for this sensation? *(1 M)*

(*iii*) Explain the function of the A. *(1 M)*

OR

(*iii*) Explain the function of the B. *(1 M)*

ANSWER KEYS

Multiple Choice Questions

1. (*c*) **2.** (*d*) **3.** (*a*) **4.** (*c*) **5.** (*b*) **6.** (*a*) **7.** (*c*) **8.** (*c*) **9.** (*b*) **10.** (*a*)

Assertion and Reason

1. (*a*) **2.** (*c*) **3.** (*c*) **4.** (*c*)

HINTS & EXPLANATIONS

Multiple Choice Questions

1. (*c*) Trimming the hedge by cutting the tips stimulates bushier plant growth because it removes the apical meristem, which produces auxin. This reduction in auxin allows the lateral buds to break dormancy and grow, resulting in more branches and a fuller plant.

2. (*d*) The branches of fallen tree grow straight up (vertically) due to response to light. A plant stem tends to grow towards the light in the upward direction against the force of gravity.

3. (*a*) The rise in blood glucose levels during stress is primarily due to the release of adrenaline by the adrenal glands. Adrenaline triggers the liver to release stored glucose into the bloodstream, providing immediate energy for the body's response to stress, known as the 'fight or flight' reaction. The pineal and thyroid gland are not primarily responsible for stress response.

4. (*c*) A spinal cord injury at the lower back disrupts the nerve pathways that control involuntary, reflex and voluntary actions, leading to paralysis in that area.

5. (*b*) The gustatory receptors, which are types of sensory neurons in the tongue, are responsible for detecting taste. Dysfunction in these neurons can lead to diminished taste perception.

6. (*a*) The female may lack oestrogen, which is vital for female reproductive health and it significantly influences the regulation of the menstrual cycle.

7. (*c*) The forebrain contains regions responsible for processing sensory information, including hunger, making it primarily involved in making an individual aware of hunger sensations.

8. (*c*) The neuromuscular junction is the site where the electrical impulse from the nerve is converted into a chemical signal to stimulate muscle contraction.

9. (*b*) High blood glucose levels trigger the release of insulin, which lowers blood glucose by promoting glucose uptake into cells for energy or storing it as glycogen in the liver, not as protein. Glycogen breakdown occurs, particularly when blood glucose levels fall or cellular demand for glucose rises, to increase blood glucose levels, not due to insulin production.

10. (*a*) The cerebrum is the largest part of the brain associated with higher brain functions such as thought and action. It is responsible for remembering complex tasks and sequences of movements.

Assertion and Reason

1. (*a*) Phototropism is the growth driven movement of plant or its parts towards light. Hence, it is known as directional growth movement.
2. (*c*) Adrenaline prepares the body for 'fight or flight' but it decreases digestive activity, not increases it, to prioritize muscles and critical functions.
3. (*c*) The human brain does use electrical impulses to process information, and plants like Mimosa pudica do respond to stimuli with movements that do not involve a nervous system. However, the reason needs to be corrected because it suggests that plants use only chemical signals for their movement responses, ignoring that electrical-chemical changes can also be involved in plant responses, such as in the case of Mimosa leaves' movement.
4. (*c*) Meera's blinking is a protective reflex action. Still, it is primarily mediated by the spinal cord and brain stem for rapid response, not processed through higher brain centers for decision-making.

Subjective Questions

Very Short Answer Type Questions

1. (*a*) Auxin is a plant hormone that controls directional growth. *(1 M)*

   (*b*)

Plant Growth Regulators	Animal Growth Hormones
Respond to environmental stimuli like light and gravity (phototropism, gravitropism)	Can regulate growth and development without directional influence from external stimuli

(1 M)

2. (*a*) Ethylene *(1 M)*

   (*b*) In the paper bag, ethylene gas accumulates as it is emitted by the tomatoes. This concentrated ethylene environment speeds up the ripening process compared to the open tray where the gas disperses into the air. *(1 M)*

3.
   - The cerebellum is most likely affected. *(½ M)*
   - It plays a key role in coordinating voluntary movements, balance, and fine motor skills like writing and buttoning a shirt. *(1 M)*
   - Since vital functions such as breathing and swallowing are not impacted, the medulla, which controls these functions, is not affected. *(½ M)*

4. The smell of an agarbatti is detected by the nose. The olfactory receptors present in the nose sends electrical signal to the fore brain. The fore brain interprets this signal as the smell of the incense stick. *(2 M)*

5. (*i*) X: Cytokinins *(½ M)*

   Y: Abscisic acid *(½ M)*

   (*ii*) The highest concentration of abscisic acid in mature leaves inhibits growth, causes stomatal closure to reduce water loss, and signals the plant to stop growing, preparing it for adverse conditions. *(1 M)*

6. If Akash's cerebellum is damaged, he may experience difficulties with coordination and balance. Tasks like walking and maintaining posture could become challenging due to impaired motor control. *(2 M)*

7. Testosterone stimulates the growth of facial hair, such as mustaches and beards in men. *(1 M)*

   It also plays a crucial role in:
   - Muscle mass and bone density development *(½ M)*
   - Sperm production *(½ M)*

8. (*a*) Without reflex arcs, all responses would require conscious thought, delaying actions. For instance, withdrawing a hand from a flame would take longer, increasing the risk of injury. *(1 M)*

   (*b*) Reflex arcs are crucial in avoiding accidents, such as quickly pulling back from sharp objects to prevent cuts or injuries. *(1 M)*

9. The table outlining the differences in the movement mechanisms of the leaves of a sensitive plant compared to the downward movement of its roots:

Feature	Leaves of a Sensitive Plant	Downward Movement of Roots
Type of Movement	Nastic movement (rapid folding and drooping in response to touch)	Geotropism
Dependency	Independent of growth	Dependent on growth
Mechanism	Facilitated by changes in water content within cells	Influenced by environmental triggers
Trigger	Physical stimulus (touch)	Environmental stimulus (gravity)

(2 M)

OR

The hormone that regulates carbohydrate, protein, and fat metabolism in our body is thyroxine. *(½ M)*

It is secreted by the thyroid gland. *(½ M)*

Importance of Iodised Salt:

- Iodised salt is crucial because iodine is required for the thyroid gland to synthesize thyroxine. (½ M)
- Adequate thyroxine levels ensure proper metabolic balance for growth. *(½ M)*

Short Answer Type Questions

1. In animals, hormones play a crucial role in growth, development, and regulating metabolism. For example:
   - Growth hormone (Pituitary gland): It stimulates the growth of bones, muscles, and other tissues, aiding in overall development and growth. *(1½ M)*
   - Thyroxine (Thyroid gland): It regulates carbohydrate, protein, and fat metabolism in the body, ensuring the best balance for growth and maintaining overall metabolism. *(1½ M)*

Topper's Explanation

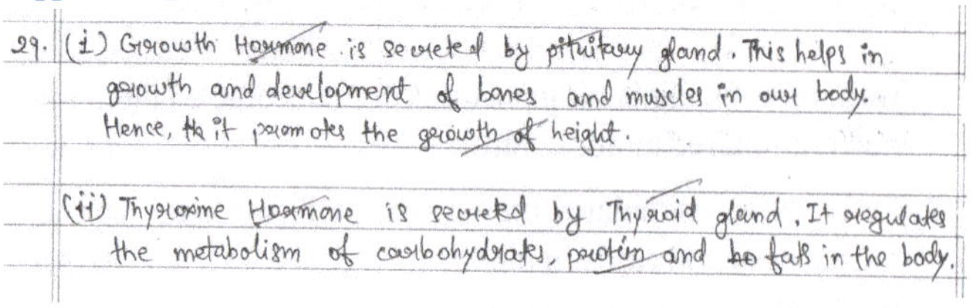
29. (i) Growth Hormone is secreted by pituitary gland. This helps in growth and development of bones and muscles in our body. Hence, it promotes the growth of height.

(ii) Thyroxine Hormone is secreted by Thyroid gland. It regulates the metabolism of carbohydrates, protein and fats in the body.

2. (*a*) The hormone likely to be deficient is the growth hormone, which is secreted by the pituitary gland. *(1 M)*

   (*b*) The hypothalamus is involved in regulating the level of growth hormone. It plays a crucial role by detecting low levels of growth hormone in the blood and releasing growth hormone- releasing hormone. This hormone stimulates the pituitary gland to secrete growth hormone, thereby maintaining proper growth and development in the body. *(2 M)*

3.

Sensitive Plant	Movement in our legs
The movement in a sensitive plant occurs in response to touch through rapid cell movement.	Movement in human legs is controlled by nervous system signals to muscles.
This movement serves as a defense mechanism against threats like predators or touch.	This movement facilitates locomotion and stability.
It is a passive reaction to stimuli.	This movement involves both voluntary and involuntary muscle control.
No special tissue is there for the transfer of information.	A complete system CNS and PNS is there for the information exchange.

(3 M)

4. (*a*) Predicted growth patterns for each setup:
   1. Even distribution: The shoot grows straight upward, showing no bending. *(½ M)*
   2. Accumulation on the shaded side: The shoot bends toward the light as cells elongate more on the shaded side. *(½ M)*
   3. Accumulation on the light-exposed side: The shoot bends away from the light, resulting in inefficient light capture. *(½ M)*

   (*b*) The second setup ensures optimal growth, as bending toward the light maximizes photosynthesis. Hormone "X," likely auxin, promotes cell elongation on the shaded side, causing phototropic bending. *(1 ½ M)*

5. (*a*) The gland responsible for secreting hormones during scary situations in human beings is the adrenal gland. The hormone secreted is adrenaline. *(1 M)*
   - Increased Heartbeat: Adrenaline prompts the heart to beat faster, enhancing blood flow to muscles and vital organs. *(1 M)*
   - Higher Breathing Rate: Adrenaline causes the diaphragm and rib muscles to contract and relax more rapidly, leading to an increase in breathing rate and providing extra energy for the body's needs. *(1 M)*

OR

   (*b*) (*i*) The parts labelled in the diagram are:
   - A: Sensory Neuron *(1 M)*
   - B: Relay Neuron
   - C: Effector/Muscle in Arm

   (*ii*) Functions:
   - A (Sensory Neuron): It detects the initial stimulus and carries the signal to the spinal cord/CNS. *(½ M)*
   - C (Effector/Muscle in Arm): It performs the required action in response to the signal, like moving the hand away from a painful stimulus. *(½ M)*

   (*iii*) Reflex arcs have evolved in animals to enable quick and involuntary responses to certain stimuli, ensuring immediate action without the delay of conscious thought, which can be crucial for survival. *(1 M)*

6. (*a*) Iodine is essential for thyroxin synthesis by the thyroid gland, which regulates fat and carbohydrate metabolism for optimal growth. Deficiency can leads to goitre and metabolic disorders. *(1 M)*

   (*b*) Pancreas acts as mixed gland:
   - Exocrine cells secrete digestive enzymes like lipase and trypsin that assist in the digestion of food. *(½ M)*
   - Endocrine cells secrete hormones such as insulin and glucagon, which are critical for regulating blood sugar levels. *(½ M)*

   (*c*) Endocrine glands control the body's functions by releasing just the right amount of hormones for:
   - Feedback Regulation: It accurately modulates hormone secretion in response to stimuli, for example, elevating insulin level when blood sugar rises and reducing it as blood sugar levels decline to a level. *(½ M)*
   - Health Impact: Maintaining hormonal balance is vital for health; imbalances can result in various conditions such as goitre, diabetes, dwarfism, and gigantism. *(½ M)*

Long Answer Type Questions

1. (*a*) Similarities:
   - Involvement of receptors: In both cases, the signal is initiated by receptors located at the specific sense organ. *(1 M)*
   - Involvement of neurotrans mitters: In both cases, neurotransmitters are released and accepted by neurons to carry the impulse. *(1 M)*

   Differences:
   - The action of smelling the rose is voluntary whereas pulling the hand away is a reflex action i.e. involuntary in nature. *(1 M)*

- While smelling the rose, the nerve impulse reaches the brain and back whereas on touching a thorn the nerve impulse travels only to the spinal cord and back. *(1 M)*

(*b*) No *(½ M)*

Involuntary actions occur with or without a stimulus like beathing of the heart whereas reflex actions always need a stimulus like removing hand when we touch a sharp/hot object. *(½ M)*

2. (*a*) Sameer's need to reduce sugar intake and exercise suggests:

- Sameer is suffering from diabetes. *(1 M)*
- The hormone responsible for this disease is insulin. *(1 M)*
- Insulin is produced by the pancreas. *(1 M)*

(*b*) Plant hormones and their effects on growth:

- The hormone present in areas of rapid cell division is cytokinins. *(1 M)*
- The hormone that inhibits growth is abscisic acid. *(1 M)*

Nailing the Right Answer

Carefully evaluate the doctor's dietary and exercise guidance in light of the blood test reports, particularly focusing on the mention of sugar intake. Use this information to logically deduce the health condition in question.

3. An experiment to demonstrate hydrotropism in plants.

Procedure:

(*i*) Plant a seedling in a vessel containing soil.

(*ii*) Adjacent to the seedling put a porous pot containing water.

(*iii*) Leave the set up for few days. *(2 M)*

Observation:

(*iv*) On examining the roots, it is observed that the roots bend towards the source of water and do not grow straight. *(1 M)*

Result: It confirms that plants show hydrotropism as the roots bend towards the porous pot of water. As hydrotropism is a plant-growth response in which the direction of growth is determined by a stimulus of gradient in water concentration. *(2 M)*

4. (*a*) (*i*)

Hormonal co-ordination in Plants	Hormonal co-ordination in Animals
Plant hormones regulate growth and responses to environmental stimuli.	Animal hormones regulate a variety of functions including metabolism, growth, and stress responses.
Hormones are synthesized in parts like roots and shoots, without specific glands.	Specific glands produce hormones, such as the thyroid gland and adrenal glands.
Hormones are transported via diffusion or vascular tissues.	Hormones are released directly into the bloodstream or ducts, reaching target organs.
Plant hormones do not typically have complex feedback mechanisms as seen in animals.	Hormone levels are tightly regulated by feedback mechanisms to maintain homeostasis.

(2 M)

(*ii*) The part of brain associated with their respective functions are:

(1) Intelligence - Cerebrum of the forebrain *(½ M)*

(2) Riding a bicycle - Cerebellum in the hindbrain *(½ M)*

(3) Vomiting - Medulla Oblongata in the hindbrain *(½ M)*

(4) Controlling hunger - Hypothalamus (Specific part of the forebrain) *(½ M)*

(*iii*) The brain is protected against mechanical injuries by the skull and surounded by fluid filled balloon that cushion it from shocks. Spinal cord is protected by the vertebral column (backbone) *(½ M)*

OR

(*b*) (*i*) Tropic movements are directional growth responses to environmental stimuli like light or gravity. *(1 M)*

- Abscisic acid is a hormone that inhibits growth, leading to effects like leaf wilting. *(1 M)*
- An example of a hormone that promotes cell division is cytokinins. *(1 M)*

(*ii*) The tendril in pea plants moves directionally in response to touch. When they contact a support, the side in contact grows slower than the opposite side, causing the tendril to coil around it for support.

This is part of the plant's tropic response to contact/touch. *(1 M)*

The hormone responsible for this movement is likely to be auxin. *(1 M)*

Case Based Questions

Case Based-I

(*i*) Women can monitor her diet and increase the intake of iodine-rich foods such as seaweed, seafood, and iodized salt. *(1 M)*

(*ii*) Women may face a greater risk of abnormal TSH levels during certain phases of life, such as pregnancy and menopause. *(1 M)*

(*iii*) Consequences of low TSH levels include

- Hyperthyroidism: Low TSH levels can indicate overactive thyroid gland function, also known as hyperthyroidism, speeds up the body's metabolism causing weight loss, anxiety, and other health issues. *(1 M)*

(*iv*) Iodine is responsible for thyroxin production. *(1 M)*

Case Based-II

(*i*) 1-Radicle, 2-Plumule (*1 M*)

(*ii*) Part 1 (radicle) exhibits gravitropism by growing downward in response to gravity, and hydrotropism by seeking moisture in the sawdust. (*1 M*)

(*iii*) Part 1 is affected by water and gravity, water is stronger stimuli as radicles are curving upwards towards moist sawdust. (*1 M*)

(*iv*) Positive tropic movement means movement towards the source of stimulus. (*½ M*)

Negative tropic movement means movement away from the source of stimulus. (*½ M*)

Mistakes 101 : What not to do!

Students can misinterpret the direction of the radicle's growth about the stimuli presented in the setup, leading to incorrect conclusions about which tropism is more influential. In labeling, students may confuse the parts of the seedling, mistaking the embryonic structures for one another.

Case Based-III

(*i*) Chemotropism (*1 M*)

(*ii*) A is pollen tube (*1 M*)

(*iii*) A is attracted towards chemical secreted by the embryo sac. (*1 M*)

(*iv*) Pea plant's tendrils show thigmotropism. (*1 M*)

Mistakes 101 : What not to do!

Students can misinterpret the cause of the growth direction of structure 'A' due to a lack of understanding of the topic tropism. Furthermore, can confuse 'A' with other plant structures.

Case Based-IV

(*i*) The functions of the fore-brain and medulla are incorrect. The correct functions will be:

- Forebrain: It is responsible for sensory processing, thinking, hearing, smell, sight and other voluntary actions. (*1 M*)
- Medulla: It controls involuntary actions like breathing, salivation, and blood pressure, etc. (*1 M*)

(*ii*) The medulla oblongata, part of the brainstem, is responsible for controlling the vomiting reflex. (*1 M*)

(*iii*) A (Cerebellum): It maintains body balance, posture, and coordinates voluntary muscle movements, ensuring smooth and precise actions. (*1 M*)

OR

(*iii*) B (Cranium): The cranium is the bony structure surrounding the brain, providing protection against mechanical injury. (*1 M*)

❑❑❑

7 HOW DO ORGANISMS REPRODUCE?

"Have you ever thought about why humans always have human babies and dogs always have puppies? Why doesn't it happen the other way around? This pattern happens because of a natural process called reproduction, which we're going to explore in this chapter. We'll learn how it ensures that every species produces its own kind, keeping the cycle of life going."

SYLLABUS & WEIGHTAGE

LIST OF CONCEPT NAMES	YEARS				
	2020	2022 TERM-II	2023	2024	2025
Asexual Reproduction	—	1 Q (2 M) 1 Q (3 M)	1 Q (5 M)	1 Q (1 M) 1 Q (4 M)	1 Q (5 M)
Sexual Reproduction in Plants and Animals, Reproductive health (Need and methods of family planning, Safe sex vs HIV/AIDS, Child bearing and women's health)	1 Q (3 M) 2 Q (5 M Each) 1 Q (4 M)	1 Q (2 M) 1 Q (4 M)	2 Q (5 M Each)	1 Q (3 M)	2 Q (1 M Each) 1 Q (5 M)

For the year 2021, the exam was not conducted.

CONCEPT MAP

To Access One Shot Revision Video Scan This QR Code

How do Organisms Reproduce? (Asexual Reproduction)

Do Organisms Create Exact Copies of Themselves?

- DNA copying during reproduction creates new cells with their own apparatus, storing inheritance and protein information, with small variations.
- Variations from minor DNA copying errors help species adapt to environmental changes, ensuring survival (e.g., heat-resistant bacteria in warming waters).
- Variations drive evolution and support species' survival in changing ecosystems.

Budding

CBSE 2025, 2024, 2023

In this a new organism develops from an outgrowth or bud due to cell division at one particular site on the parent body which then detaches to become a new, independent organism, e.g., *Hydra*.

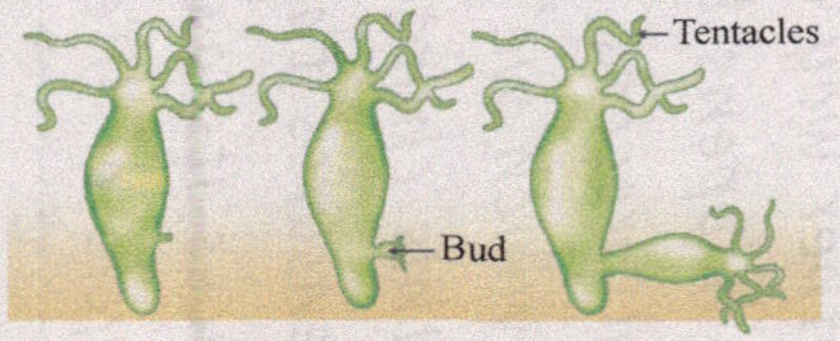

Budding in *Hydra*

Regeneration

CBSE 2025, 2023

Process of replacing lost parts or developing a full organism from its body, e.g., *Hydra* and *Planaria*.

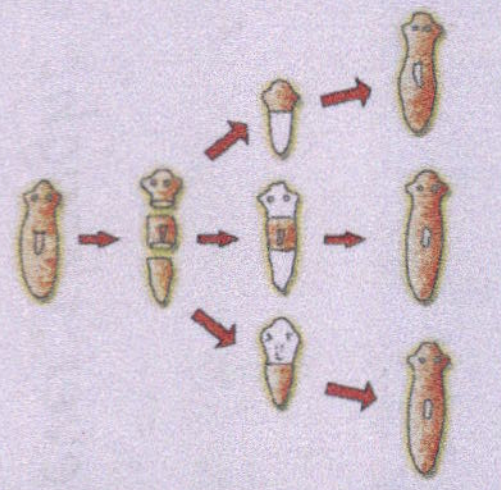

Regeneration in *Planaria*

Spore Formation

CBSE 2024, 2022 Term-II

New individuals grow from spores, e.g., *Rhizopus*.

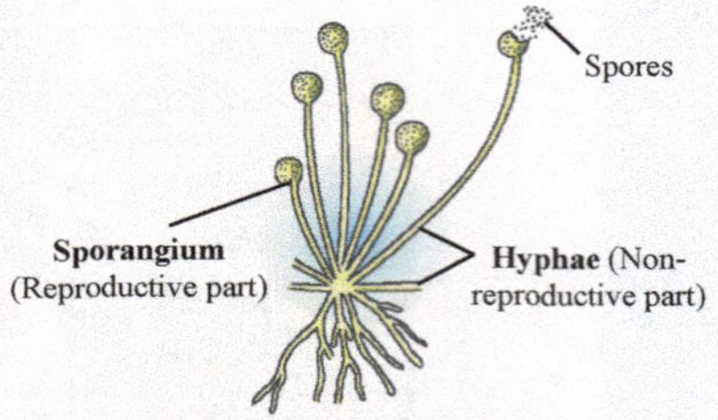

Spore Formation in *Rhizopus*

Fission

Splitting of unicellular organism or cell division where a single parent cell divides into two or more daughter cells.

Binary Fission (CBSE 2025, 2022 Term-II)

In this, single parent cell divides into two identical daughter cells

Binary Fission in *Amoeba*	Binary Fission in *Leishmania*
Binary fission can occur in any plane, as *Amoeba* lacks a fixed axis of division, allowing for random orientation during cell division.	Binary fission occurs in a definite orientation due to the presence of a flagellum at one end of the cell, determining the plane of division.
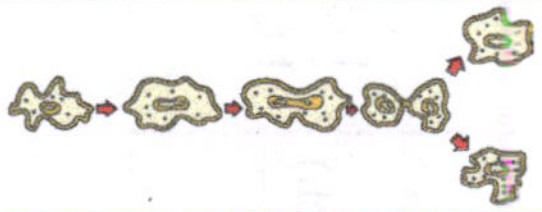	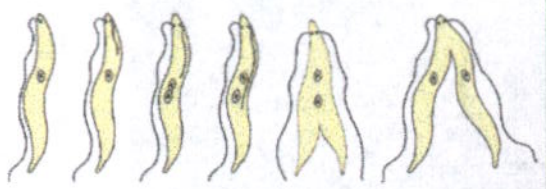

Multiple Fission (CBSE 2024, 2022 Term-II)

In this a single parent cell divides into multiple daughter cells simultaneously, after its nucleus undergoes multiple division.

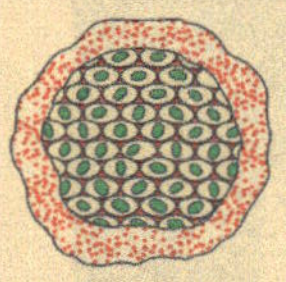

***Plasmodium* (Malaria parasite)**

Fragmentation

CBSE 2025

In simple multicellular organisms, main body get fragmented and fragments develop as new individuals, e.g., *Spirogyra*.

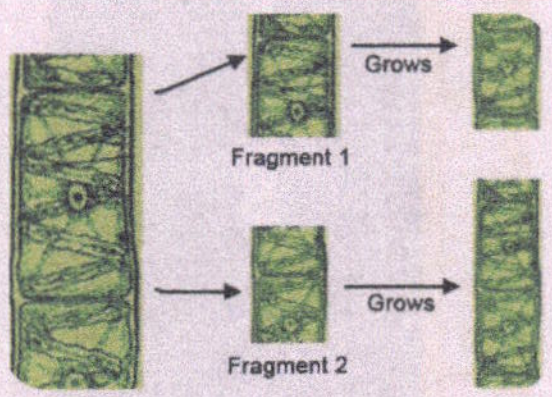

Fragmentation in *Spirogyra*

Vegetative Propagation

CBSE 2023

Many plants in which parts like root, stem and leaves develop into new plants under appropriate conditions, e.g., Sugarcane, Roses, *Bryophyllum*.

Leaf of *Bryophyllum* with Buds

Advantages of Vegetative Propagation (CBSE 2025, 2022 Term-II)

- Accelerates flowering & fruiting in plants compared to seed-grown plants.
- Restoration of seedless plants, such as banana, rose, etc.
- Vegetatively propagated plants are genetically identical to their parent plants.

How do Organisms Reproduce?

Sexual Reproduction in Plants

Flower (Reproductive Unit)

CBSE 2025, 2022 Term-II

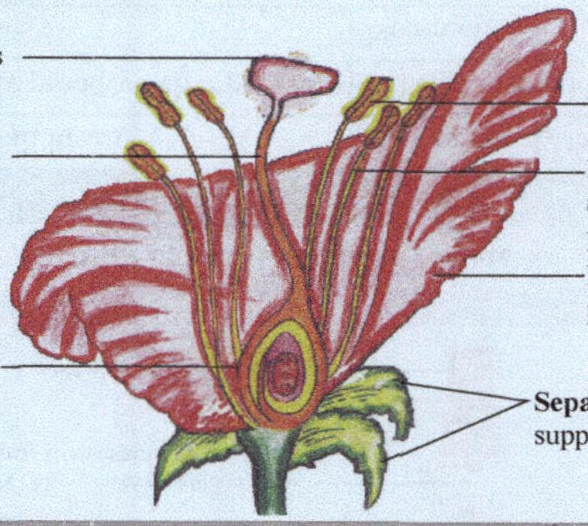

Type of Flowers

CBSE 2025

- **Unisexual:** Either stamen or pistil are present in the same flower, e.g., Papaya, watermelon.
- **Bisexual:** Both stamen and pistil are present in the same flower e.g., *Hibiscus*, mustard.

Pollination

CBSE 2025, 2020

Transfer of pollen grains to stigma.

Types of pollination

Self-pollination

Transfer of pollen grains from anther to stigma of same flower or different flower but on same plant.

Cross-pollination

Transfer of pollen grains from anther to stigma of the flower but on different plants.

Pollinating agents

Wind, water, insect, etc.

Significance of pollination:

- Facilitates fertilisation by bringing male gametes to female counterparts.
- It allows genetic exchange, enhancing plant diversity.

Fertilisation

CBSE 2022 Term-II, 2020

- Pollen tube grow towards ovary.
- **Double fertilisation** → Zygote and endosperm formation.

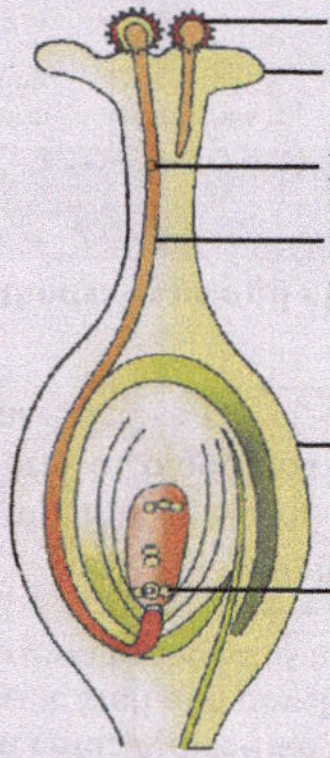

Germination of pollen on stigma

Post-Fertilisation Events

CBSE 2025

- **Zygote Development:** Zygote divides to form an embryo within the ovule.
- **Seed Formation:** Ovule develops a tough coat, converting into a seed containing the embryo.
- **Fruit Formation:** Ovary ripens to form fruit; petals, sepals, stamens, style, and stigma may fall off.
- **Germination:** Seed develops into a seedling under suitable conditions.

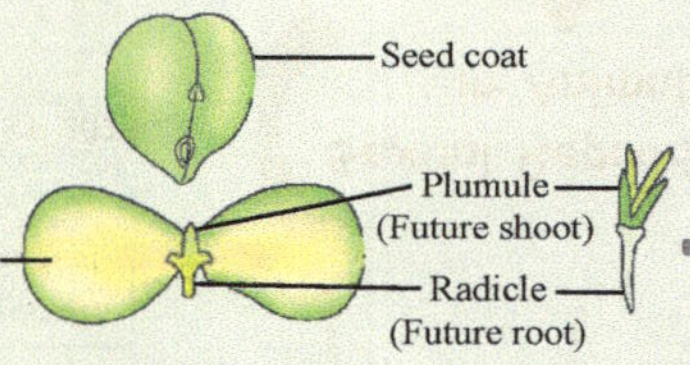

Germinated seed (Product of fertilisation)

Advantage of Seed Formation

Seeds ensure the survival of future plants by protecting the embryo and aiding dispersal for reproduction.

How do Organisms Reproduce?

Sexual Reproduction in Animals

Puberty

CBSE 2022 Term-II

It is the phase when adolescents undergo physical changes, reaching sexual maturity and reproductive capability.

Pubertal Changes in Males vs. Females

Males	Females
Enlargement of male genitalia (testicles, penis) and muscles.	Breast development, widening of hips, growth of pubic hair.
Deepening of voice.	Voice remains higher-pitched.
Production of sperm begins.	Menstrual cycles start, ovulation occurs.
Broadening of shoulders, more muscular physique.	Widening of hips, more rounded body shape.

Reproductive Systems

Male Reproductive System: Structures and Functions CBSE 2025

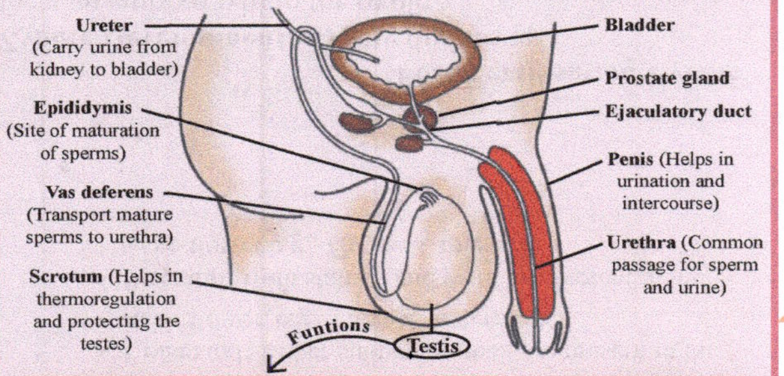

- Produce sperms and secretes testosterone
- Located outside the abdominal cavity in scrotum because sperm formation requires a lower temperature than the normal body temperature

Female Reproductive System: Structures and Functions

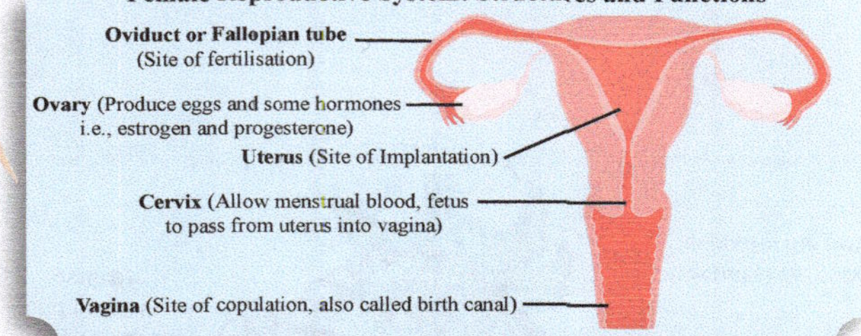

CBSE 2025

Male gamete vs. Female gamete CBSE 2025

Sperm	Ovum
They are small in size	Comparatively large in size
Continuously produced after puberty	All eggs formed before birth
Highly motile	Non-motile
Produced in testes	Produced in ovaries

Fertilisation: Union of sperm and egg.

Development
- Fertilisation→ Zygote $\xrightarrow{\text{Cleavage}}$ Blastocyst → Implantation → Embryo Development
- **Placenta:** A disc-like tissue present between uterine wall and developing embryo which provide nutrition to the fetus and help in waste removal.

What happens if egg is not fertilised?

Menstruation
The monthly cycle of shedding of uterus lining in the form of blood and mucus every month through vagina.

Reproductive Health

Definition: The well-being in all aspects of reproduction.

Contraceptive methods: Type and effects CBSE 2024, 2020

Type	Mechanism of Working	Example	Effects
Mechanical Barrier	Prevent sperm from reaching the egg	Condoms	Provides STD protection
Hormonal	Alters hormonal balance to prevent ovulation or fertilisation	Oral contraceptives (Pills)	May cause side effects
Intrauterine Device (IUD)	Creates an environment hostile to sperm and/or prevents implantation	Copper-T, loops	May cause uterine irritation and side effects
Surgical (Permanent) CBSE 2025	Involves blocking the ducts responsible for transporting sperm or eggs	• Vasectomy (male): Involves cutting or blocking the vas deferens. • Tubectomy (female): Involves blocking or sealing the fallopian tubes.	Risk of infections and complications if not performed properly.

Contraceptive Methods: Techniques or devices used to prevent pregnancy.

Sexually Transmitted Diseases (STDs): Infections transmitted through sexual contact.

STDs: Agents and Name

Causative agent	Name of the STD
Bacteria	Gonorrhoea
	Syphilis
Virus	Genital Warts
	HIV/AIDS

CBSE 2020

Sex Ratio Concerns
- Illegal sex-selective abortions of female fetuses harm the female-male sex ratio.
- Declining child sex ratio threatens societal health and balance.
- Prenatal sex determination is legally prohibited to prevent misuse.

Population size

The number of individuals present in a designated geographic range.

Factor that determine the size of a population are:
- **Birth rate:** Number of live births per thousand persons in a year.
- **Death rate:** Number of deaths per thousand persons in a year.

Concerns about an increasing population:
- Puts pressure on resources, making it difficult to raise everyone's standard of living.
- Leads to more environmental harm and uses up natural resources faster.

1 ASEXUAL REPRODUCTION

NCERT Definitions (Commonly asked in 1 mark)

- **Reproduction:** The biological process by which new offspring are produced from their parents.
- **Cell division:** It is the biological process where a cell duplicates its DNA, synthesises additional cellular machinery, and then divides into two fully functional, identical cells.
- **DNA copying mechanism:** A crucial process in reproduction where cells build copies of their DNA, ensuring that each new cell receives a complete set of genetic instructions. This process involves the creation of an additional cellular apparatus to ensure that each DNA copy has its cellular machinery, essential for the cell's survival and functioning.
- **Variation:** Slight differences in offspring's genetic makeup compared to their parents, arising from DNA replication errors.

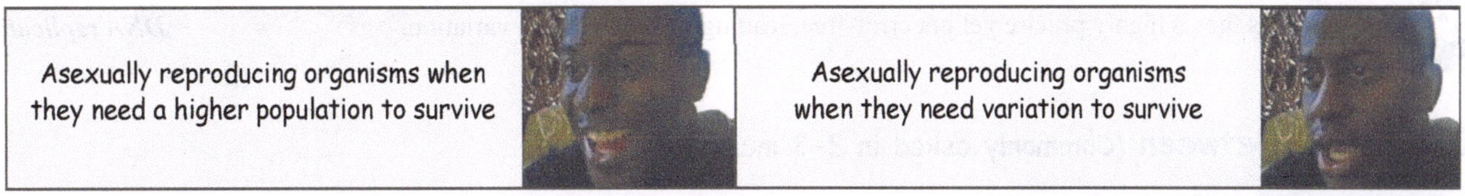

- **Asexual Reproduction:** A mode of reproduction where offspring are produced from a single organism without the involvement of gamete fusion.
- **Clone:** An organism or cell that is genetically identical to its parent.
- **Bud:** A bud is defined as an outgrowth from the parent body, which forms due to repeated cell division at a specific site.
- **Regenerative Cells:** Specialized cells capable of proliferating and differentiating into various cell types and tissues, enabling organisms to repair or reproduce like *Hydra* (budding) and *Planaria* (regeneration).
- **Tissue Culture:** A technique of growing new plants from a small tissue or a few cells in a suitable growth medium under controlled conditions.
- **Callus:** A mass of undifferentiated plant cells, often formed during tissue culture from which new plants can be grown.

- **Grafting:** A method of vegetative propagation where a plant segment (bud) is attached to another plant's stem, root, or branch (stock) to ensure they unite and grow together.
- **Layering:** A vegetative propagation method involves bending a plant branch to the ground, partially burying it in moist soil while keeping the end exposed. Over time, the submerged section sprouts new roots.
- **Sporangia:** The tiny blob-on-a-stick structures in certain plants, fungi, and algae that produce and store spores.
- **Spore:** A reproductive unit capable of developing into a new individual without fusion with another reproductive unit enclosed in thick walls.
- **Hyphae:** The long, branching, filamentous structure of a fungus.

Important Facts

01 A biological process which is not essential for individual survival but crucial for species continuity. *~Reproduction*

02 The DNA in the cell nucleus is the information source for making proteins.

03 Asexual reproduction gives rise to clones.

04 A unicellular organism causing kala-azar, featuring a whip-like structure and undergoing binary fission in a specific orientation. *~Leishmania*

05 In *Amoeba*, cell division can occur along any plane.

06 Regeneration is not the same as reproduction.

07 Mode of reproduction that enables plants to mature faster, allowing earlier flowering and fruiting compared to seed-grown plants. *~Vegetative propagation*

08 To initiate tissue culture and form callus, tissue or cells are extracted from a plant's growing tip.

09 A process that is highly precise yet not error-free, leading to slow genetic variation. *~ DNA replication*

Difference Between **(Commonly asked in 2-3 marks)**

Binary Fission vs. Multiple Fission	
Binary Fission	**Multiple Fission**
A form of asexual reproduction where a single organism divides into two parts, each forming a new organism.	A type of asexual reproduction where an organism undergoes multiple nuclear divisions before dividing into several new organisms.
Nucleus and cytoplasm divide simultaneously.	Only the nucleus divides initially, followed by the cytoplasmic division.
The plane of division can be transverse, longitudinal, or any axis, as in simple binary fission.	There is no exact axis for the fission; it may occur irregularly.
Typically occurs under favorable conditions.	Can occur under both favorable and unfavorable conditions.
Example: *Amoeba*	Example: *Plasmodium*

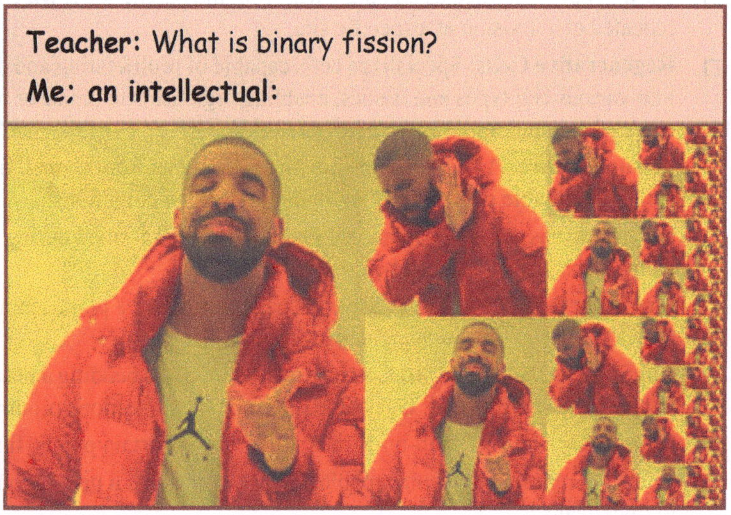

Fragmentation vs. Regeneration vs. Budding		
Fragmentation	**Regeneration**	**Budding**
Organism breaks into separate pieces, each becoming a new individual.	A process where lost or damaged parts are re-grown, can lead to the formation of new individuals.	In this, a new organism develops from a bud on the parent organism.
Organisms split due to internal or external factors.	Damaged or severed parts regrow into new individuals.	Outgrowth development doesn't require external triggers.
Occurs randomly or at specific breakage points.	Usually, it occurs in damaged parts, but not all parts can regenerate.	Specific site on the parent body where the bud forms.

Fragments develop independently after separation.	Regenerated parts usually don't detach to form new individuals.	Bud remains attached until it is mature enough to survive on its own.
Observed in *Spirogyra*	Seen in organisms like *Hydra* and *Planaria* (Have neoblasts)	Found in *Hydra*, yeast

Vegetative Propagation vs. Tissue Culture	
Vegetative Propagation	**Tissue Culture**
Involves the natural ability of plants to reproduce from organs like stems, leaves, and roots.	A laboratory technique that grows new plants from a small piece of plant tissue.
Seen in plants like potato, *Bryophyllum*, and strawberry.	It can be applied to a wide range of plants for rapid and large-scale propagation.
New plants are genetically identical to the parent plant, ensuring uniformity.	Allows for the production of disease-free and genetically uniform plants.
Does not require artificial growth media.	It involves the use of growth media and hormones to stimulate growth and development.

Real Life Application Based Questions

1. **You might have noticed that if there is any moldy fruit in your fruit basket, your mother advises you to remove it from the basket and wash both the basket and the remaining fruits. Explain the reasoning behind this advice.**

Ans. Mold/fungus reproduces by sporulation, i.e., by releasing tiny spores that float through the air. When these spores land on a suitable surface, like moist fruits, they grow and spread. Removing and washing the contaminated items will prevent these spores from contaminating other fruits, thereby hindering mold propagation.

2. **In your kitchen, you might have seen your parents or guardian planting a piece of garlic or onion in a pot or garden and later observing a plant growing from there. Can you explain how these pieces grow into new plants?**

Ans. Garlic and onion can grow into new plants through vegetative propagation, where a part of the plant, such as a bulb, is used to grow a new plant. These bulbs contain buds that develop into shoots. When planted, the bulb's stored nutrients support the initial growth of these shoots, eventually leading to the development of a new, genetically identical plant. This method allows garlic and onions to reproduce efficiently and consistently without the need for seed formation.

3. **You may have heard that a lizard can regrow its tail. Explain this phenomenon.**

Ans. Lizards can regrow their tails through a process known as regeneration, which is a form of asexual reproduction. When a lizard loses its tail, specialized cells at the injury site multiply and differentiate into various cell types, forming a new tail.

If you pull off a lizard's tail, it will grow back.
If you pull it off again, the lizard will be like:

4. **Have you noticed a green layer spreading over the surface of nearby ponds? Ever wondered what it is and how it manages to reproduce rapidly, covering the entire body of water?**

Ans. The green layer often seen on ponds is caused by algae, which reproduce rapidly through a process called binary fission, a form of asexual reproduction. In binary fission, a single algal cell divides into two, leading to quick population growth, especially under optimal conditions like abundant nutrients and sunlight, thus covering water bodies swiftly.

Myth Buster

- **Myth: Asexual reproduction only occurs in plants.**

  Fact: Asexual reproduction occurs in various organisms, including bacteria, protozoa, and some plants, enabling them to produce offspring without mating.

- **Myth: Asexual reproduction is exclusive to unicellular organisms.**

  Fact: Asexual reproduction is a common mode of reproduction among unicellular organisms yet it is not limited to unicellular organisms. Many multicellular organisms, like *spirogyra*, also reproduce asexually.

- **Myth: Regeneration means any part of an organism can grow into a new individual.**

  Fact: Regeneration depends on specialised cells that can proliferate and differentiate into various tissues through a process called development. Not all organisms or body parts have the capability for complete regeneration into new individuals.

- **Myth: All organisms use either sexual or asexual reproduction exclusively.**

  Fact: Some organisms can employ both sexual and asexual reproduction depending on environmental conditions or life cycle stages. This dual strategy allows them to adapt to varying environmental pressures and avail opportunities for both rapid population growth and genetic diversity.

- **Myth: Budding occurs at any random site in an organism.**

  Fact: Budding occurs at specific sites depending on the organism. For instance, in *Hydra*, budding happens at the junction of the stalk and gastric regions, indicating a regulated process.

- **Myth: Every part of a plant can propagate and produce new plants.**

  Fact: Not every part of a plant is capable of vegetative propagation. Specifically, flowers generally do not engage in vegetative propagation because their primary role is in sexual reproduction.

Mnemonics

- **Different Mode of Asexual Reproduction**

  "Fish and Frog R Buddies for Vegetable Soup"

  Fish → Fission

  and Frog → Fragmentation

  R → Regeneration

  Buddies → Budding

  for Vegetable → Vegetative propagation

  Soup → Spore formation

- **Example of Binary Fission**

  "ALBP shows Binary Fission"

  A → *Amoeba*

  L → *Leishmania* (Kala-azar)

  B → Bacteria

  P → Protozoa

- **Example of Multiple Fission**

  "PM show Multiple Fission"

  PM → *Plasmodium* (Malaria)

COMPETENCY BASED SOLVED EXAMPLES

Multiple Choice Questions (1 M)

1. **Offspring formed by asexual method of reproduction have greater similarity among themselves because** ***(Un)*** **(NCERT Exemplar)**
   (i) asexual reproduction involves only one parent
   (ii) asexual reproduction does not involves gametes
   (iii) asexual reproduction occurs before sexual reproduction
   (iv) asexual reproduction occurs after sexual reproduction
   (*a*) (*i*) and (*ii*) (*b*) (*i*) and (*iii*)
   (*c*) (*ii*) and (*iv*) (*d*) (*iii*) and (*iv*)

2. **Choose the correct order of the stages of binary fission in *Leishmania*.** ***(Re)*** **(CBSE, 2023)**

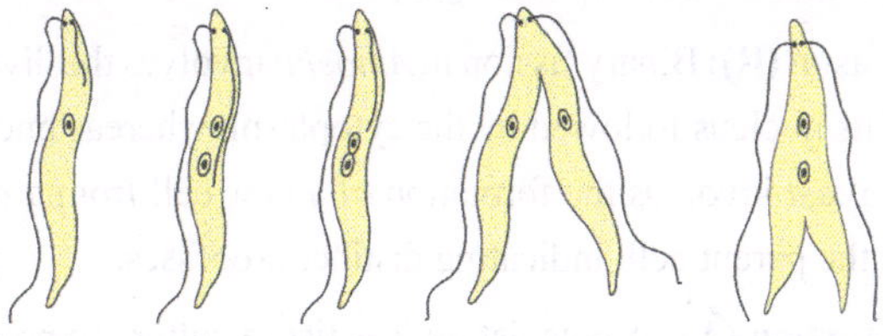

   (*a*) I, II, III, IV, V (*b*) I, III, II, V, IV
   (*c*) I, III, V, II, IV (*d*) I, II, III, V, IV

3. **In which of the following organisms, multiple fission is a means of asexual reproduction?** ***(Re)*** **(CBSE, 2024)**
   (*a*) Yeast (*b*) *Leishmania*
   (*c*) *Paramoecium* (*d*) *Plasmodium*

4. **Match the words in column-I with those which are most appropriate in column-II.** ***(Re)***

Column-I		Column-II	
A.	*Hydra*	1.	Binary fission
B.	*Amoeba*	2.	Spore formation
C.	*Rhizopus*	3.	Budding
D.	*Planaria*	4.	Regeneration

   (*a*) A-4, B-1, C-3, D-2
   (*b*) A-3, B-1, C-2, D-4
   (*c*) A-2, B-3, C-4, D-1
   (*d*) A-1, B-4, C-3, D-2

5. **In a biology lab, the teacher set up a slide showing binary fission in an *Amoeba*, but the stages were in the incorrect order as shown below. Carefully observe the image provided and choose the option showing the correct order.** ***(Re)***

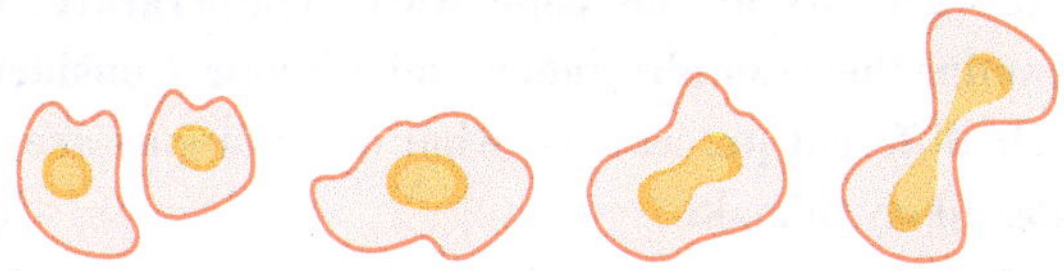

   (*a*) (*i*), (*iii*), (*iv*) and (*ii*) (*b*) (*ii*), (*iii*), (*iv*) and (*i*)
   (*c*) (*iv*), (*iii*), (*ii*) and (*i*) (*d*) (*iii*), (*iv*), (*ii*) and (*i*)

6. **Which one of the following organism is represented by this diagram?** ***(Re)*** **(CBSE, 2024)**

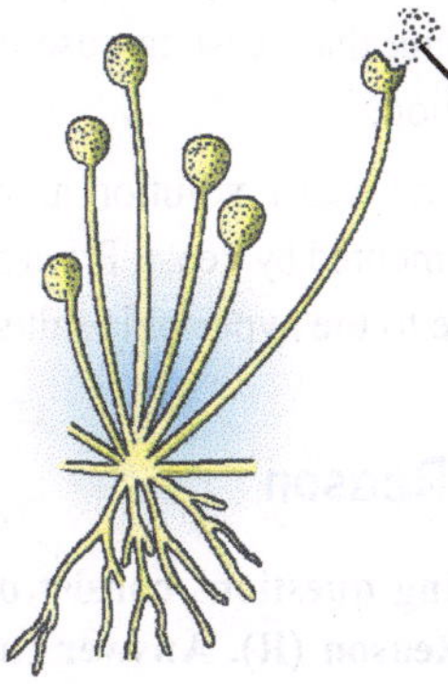

   (*a*) *Spirogyra* (*b*) *Planaria*
   (*c*) Yeast (*d*) *Rhizopus*

7. **In an experiment, two sets of plants are grown: one via vegetative propagation and one from seeds. Which of the following statements is the most accurate observation?** ***(An)***
   (*a*) Plants grown from seeds will mature, and bear flowers and fruits faster than those propagated vegetatively.
   (*b*) Plants grown by vegetative propagation will be the same as the plants grown from seeds.
   (*c*) Plants grown by vegetative propagation can bear flowers and fruits earlier than those produced from seeds.
   (*d*) Seed-grown plants will be genetically identical to their parent plant, while those from vegetative propagation will show slight genetic variation.

8. **Which experimental setup would best demonstrate the importance of genetic variation for survival in changing environmental conditions?** ***(An)***
   (*a*) Growing plants in constant temperature and light conditions
   (*b*) Exposing bacteria to antibiotics at varying concentrations
   (*c*) Observing fish behaviour in a large, stable aquarium environment
   (*d*) Measuring plant growth with different types of fertilisers

9. Rahul and Priya are both performing an activity. Rahul dissolves 10 gm of sugar in 100 mL of water and adds a pinch of yeast to 20 mL of this solution. Priya, however, dissolves 20 gm of salt in 100 mL of water and adds a pinch of yeast to 20 mL of this solution. After 2 hours at the same warm temperature, they examine their samples under a microscope. Considering their different procedures, what observations are they most likely to make? ***(An)***

(*a*) Rahul sees yeast reproducing by forming buds; Priya sees no budding because yeast cannot ferment salt.

(*b*) Rahul sees no yeast activity because the sugar concentration is not optimal; Priya sees intense budding because the salt stimulates yeast fermentation.

(*c*) Both Rahul and Priya see yeast reproducing by forming buds, indicating that yeast can use both sugar and salt for fermentation.

(*d*) Rahul sees the yeast solution unchanged as sugar cannot be fermented by yeast; Priya sees the yeast cells shrinking due to the hypertonic salt solution.

Assertion and Reason (1 M)

Direction: **The following questions consist of two statements – Assertion (A) and Reason (R). Answer these questions by selecting the appropriate option given below:**

(*a*) Both A and R are true, and R is the correct explanation of A.

(*b*) Both A and R are true, but R is not the correct explanation of A.

(*c*) A is true, but R is false.

(*d*) A is false, but R is true.

1. **Assertion (A):** Individual produced by asexual reproduction are known as clones.

   Reason (R): They are known as clones because they are genetically identical. ***(Re)***

2. **Assertion (A):** A genetically uniform population of asexually reproducing organisms in a conservation area becomes more susceptible to a new pathogenic outbreak.

   Reason (R): Lack of genetic variation compromises the population's ability to adapt to new threats. ***(Un)***

3. **Assertion (A):** If the body of *Planaria* gets cut into a number of pieces, then each body piece can be grown into a complete *Planaria*.

   Reason (R): *Planaria* possesses great power of regeneration. ***(Re)***

4. **Assertion (A):** DNA copying is necessary during reproduction.

   Reason (R): DNA copying leads to the transmission of characters from parents to offspring. ***(Re)***

5. **Assertion (A):** A tuber is thickened, swollen and underground stem or root.

   Reason (R): Potato tuber can be used for the vegetative reproduction of potato plants. ***(Re)***

6. **Assertion (A):** In an environment with no significant changes, organisms reproducing asexually will dominate.

   Reason (R): Asexual reproduction is more time and energy-efficient as it does not involve finding a mate or genetic recombination. ***(Un)***

7. **Assertion (A):** In an experiment, a horticulturist observes that certain pieces of a plant's stem with nodes are rooted faster when placed in a growth medium compared to other parts.

   Reason (R): The horticulturist concludes that the presence of nodes with pre-existing meristematic cells is the key factor for faster rooting and successful vegetative propagation. ***(Un)***

8. **Assertion (A):** In a classroom discussion, a student argued that binary fission in *Amoeba* and budding in Yeast are essentially the same because both result in the creation of new individuals from a single parent.

   Reason (R): Binary fission in *Amoeba* involves the division of its nucleus followed by the cytoplasm, whereas budding in Yeast involves the formation of a new cell from a bulge on the parent cell, indicating distinct processes. ***(Un)***

9. **Assertion (A):** A botanist utilises tissue culture to produce disease-free orchid plants from a single parent plant, aiming to replenish the orchid population in a conservation area quickly.

   Reason (R): Tissue culture allows for the multiplication of plants from a small amount of genetic material, ensuring all resulting plants are genetically better and can survive harsh conditions. ***(Ap)***

10. **Assertion (A):** The process of DNA replication during cell division ensures that the resulting cells are exact copies of the original cell, maintaining the organism's body design across generations.

    Reason (R): While DNA replication aims to accurately copy the organism's genetic material, minor errors during the process introduce variations, leading to cells that are similar but not identical to the original. ***(Un)***

Subjective Questions

Very Short Answer Type Questions (2 M)

1. Draw a labelled diagram in proper sequence to show budding in *Hydra*. ***(Cr)* (CBSE, 2019)**

Ans. The proper sequence of events of budding in *Hydra* is shown as follows:

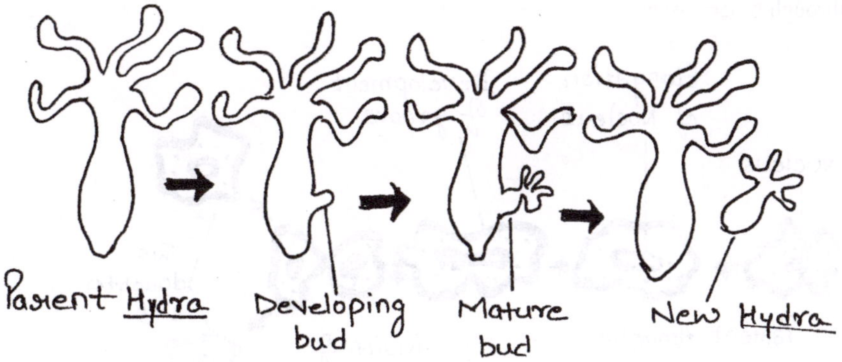

(2 M)

2. (a) Differentiate between binary fission in *Amoeba* and binary fission in *Leishmania*.

(b) How does reproduction take place in malarial parasite? **(*Re*) (CBSE, 2022)**

Ans. (*a*) The difference between binary fission in *Amoeba* and *Leishmania* is as follows:

Binary Fission in *Amoeba*	Binary Fission in *Leishmania*
In organisms such as *Amoeba*, the splitting of the two cells during division can take place in any plane.	In organisms such as *Leishmania*, which have a whip-like structure at one end of the cell, binary fission occurs in a definite orientation in relation to these structures.

(1M)

(*b*) The malarial parasite, *Plasmodium*, reproduces via

- Multiple fission, where the organism divides to produce multiple daughter cells. (½ M)
- During multiple fission, *Plasmodium* undergoes several rounds of nuclear division, creating numerous offspring from a single cell. (½ M)

3. Would a *Planaria* cut vertically into two halves regenerate into two individuals? Complete Figure D and E by indicating the regenerated regions. **(*Cr*) (NCERT Exemplar)**

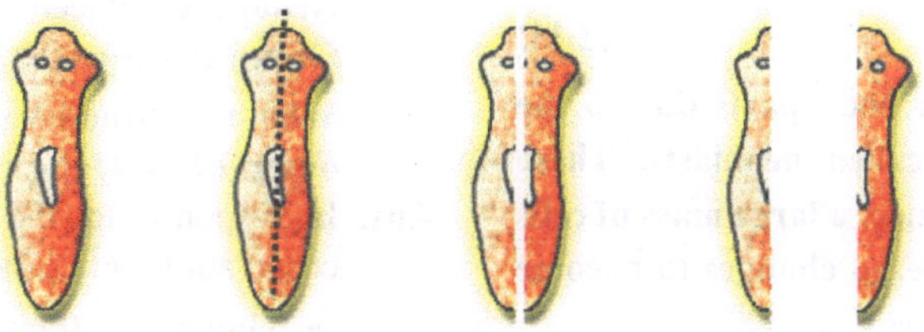

(A) (B) (C) (D) (E)

Ans. Yes, If a *Planaria* is cut vertically into two halves, both halves can regenerate the missing parts. Shaded part in Figures D and E represent the regenerated halves. (1 M)

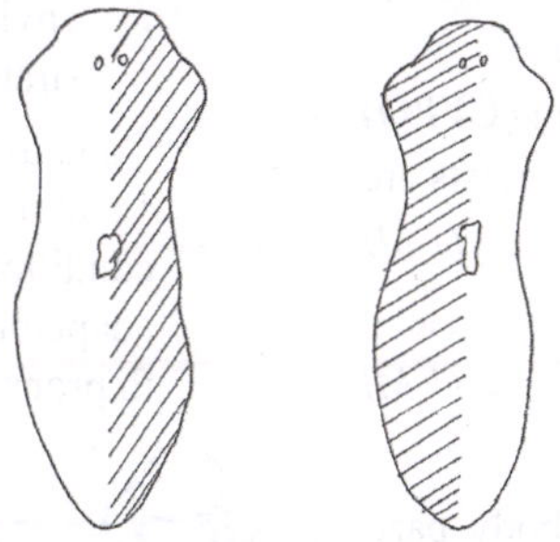

D E

(1 M)

4. Name the process by which an *Amoeba* reproduces. Draw the various stages of its reproduction in a proper sequence.

OR

A student is viewing under a microscope a permanent slide showing various stages of asexual reproduction by budding in yeast. Draw diagrams of what he observes. (in proper sequence). **(*Cr*) (CBSE, 2018)**

Ans. *Amoeba* reproduces through binary fission. (½ M)

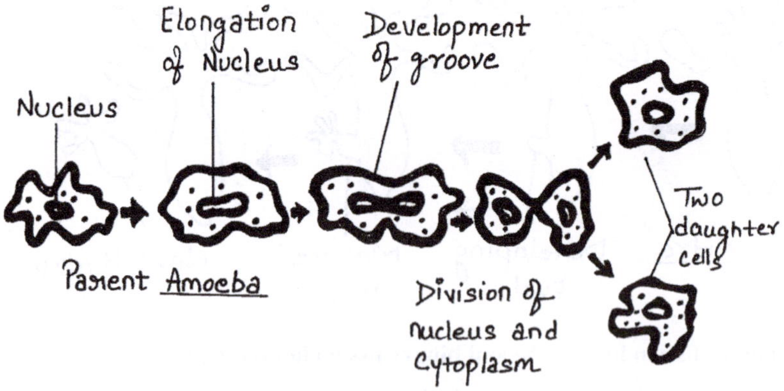

Binary fission in Amoeba

(1½ M)

OR

Budding in Yeast involves the formation of a new individual from an outgrowth on the parent's body, which detaches once it is fully developed. (½ M)

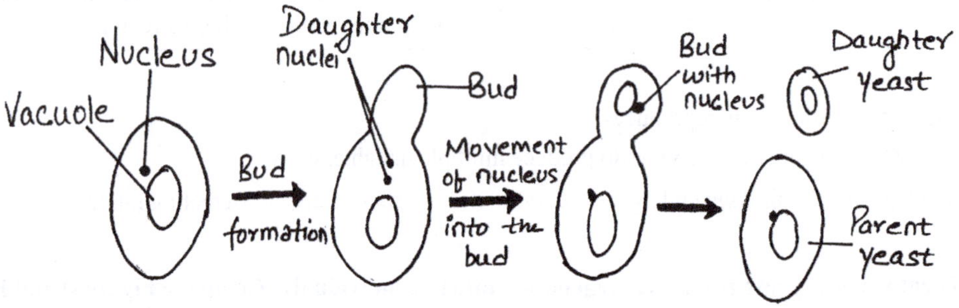

(1½ M)

Short Answer Type Questions (3 M)

1. Planarians can regenerate lost body parts due to the presence of specialised cells called neoblasts. These specialised cells multiply and make a large mass of cells from which different cells undergo changes to become different types of cells and tissues.

(a) In plants, in which type of tissue are cells that have a function similar to neoblasts found?

(b) How do the characteristics of a *Planaria* formed by regeneration compare with the characteristics of the original *Planaria*? Justify your answer.

(*Un, Ev*) (CFPQ)

Ans. (a) In plants, cells with a function similar to neoblasts are found in meristematic tissue. (1 M)

(b) A planarian formed by regeneration is very similar in characteristics to the original planarian. (1 M)

This is because:

- Neoblasts enable the regeneration of lost body parts with high precision, ensuring that the new tissues and cells closely match the original ones. (½ M)
- The DNA and genetic information remain largely unchanged, leading to remarkable similarity. (½ M)

2. In a controlled experiment, a student monitors two groups of *Amoeba*: Group A, placed in an optimal environment, and Group B, subjected to stressful conditions.

What reproductive strategy variations could the student observe? State the conclusion of the experiment. (*An*)

Ans. In response to the experiment following can be the observations and conclusion:

- Group A (Optimal Environment): May exhibits binary fission prominently, enabling rapid population expansion in favorable conditions. (1 M)
- Group B (Stressful Environment): Likely engages in multiple fission, delaying reproduction until environmental conditions improve, illustrating a strategic survival mechanism. (1 M)

Conclusion: The experiment highlights how Amoebas adapt their reproductive strategies based on environmental conditions, emphasizing their remarkable adaptability. This adaptability plays a crucial role in their survival and ability to propagate across varying environments. (1 M)

Key Takeaways

Students learns how environmental conditions *shape Amoebas'* reproductive strategies. They'll distinguish between growth methods in favorable and stressful environments, highlighting the crucial role of adaptability for survival and propagation in diverse habitats.

3. Aarav plotted a graph showing the variation frequency in generations of two populations: *(An)*

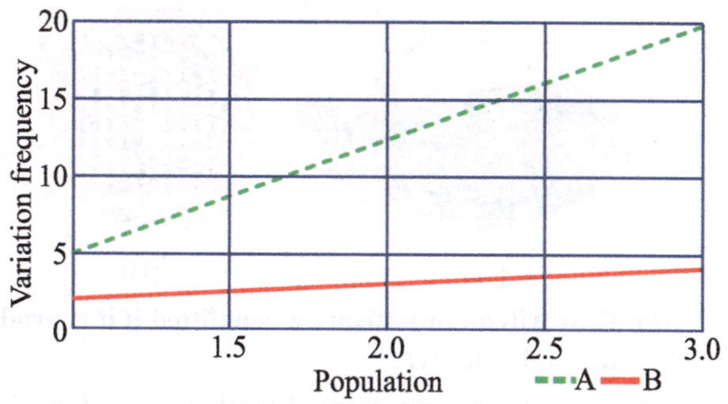

(a) State the reason for the difference in the variation frequency trends observed between populations A and B over time.

(b) Comment on the survival of organisms in both populations being affected by environmental changes?

Ans. (a) The reason for the difference in the variation frequency trends observed between populations A and B over time can be different mode of reproduction:

- Population A might be reproducing through sexual reproduction, resulting in higher genetic diversity and increased variation frequency. *(1 M)*
- Population B might be reproducing through asexual reproduction, leading to lower genetic variation and slower change in variation frequency. *(1 M)*

(b) Impact of environmental changes on survival:

- Population A: Higher variation, due to sexual reproduction, can help organisms adapt to environmental changes, increasing their chances of survival. *(½ M)*
- Population B: A slower increase in variation or negligible variation limits the ability to adjust of this population, making survival during environmental shifts more challenging. *(½ M)*

4. Three students, A, B and C, conducted an experiment to study potato propagation under different conditions. The table below summarizes their setup: *(An)*

Condition	Student A	Student B	Student C	Student D
Potato	With eyes	Without eyes	With eyes	With eyes
Soil	Yes	No	No	No
Moist cotton provided	No	Yes	No	Yes
Dry cotton provided	No	No	Yes	No

(a) Which student's setup is most likely to result in successful potato propagation or sprouting? Justify your answer.

(b) What changes would you make to the non-propagating setup(s) to ensure proper propagation?

Ans. (a) The setup which is most likely to result in successful potato propagation or sprouting are:

- Student A: Potato with eyes provides cells capable of sprouting, and soil offers essential nutrients and a stable environment for successful propagation. *(1 M)*
- Student D: Potatoes with eyes provide sprouting ability, and moist cotton offers an environment for growth. *(1 M)*

(b) Changes for

- Student B: Use potatoes with eyes along with either soil or moist cotton for sprouting or propagation. *(½ M)*
- Student C: Provide either soil or moist cotton to facilitate sprouting or soil to ensure propagation. *(½ M)*

5. A marine biologist is studying a population of bacteria found in temperate water bodies. Recent observations indicate that the water temperatures in these habitats are rising due to global warming. While a significant portion of the bacterial population seems to be perishing, a small subset appears to be thriving despite the changed conditions.

(a) Explain the cause behind the perishing of the bacterial population,

(b) Why a small subset of the bacterial population can survive and others did not. *(An)*

Ans. (a) Reasons for bacterial population decline:

- Environmental Sensitivity: Adapted to specific conditions, bacteria can't survive abrupt changes. *(½ M)*
- Genetic Homogeneity: Without diverse genes, bacteria lack adaptability to new stressors. *(½ M)*
- Temperature-induced Stress: Sudden warmth disrupts bacterial functions, causing fatalities. *(½ M)*

(b) Reason of persistence of certain bacteria:

- Genetic Diversity: Variations within the population lead to differences in survival capabilities. *(½ M)*
- Evolutionary Benefit: Some genetic traits offer survival benefits in warmer waters. *(½ M)*
- Reduced Competition: Fewer bacteria mean more resources, aiding survivors to flourish. *(½ M)*

Key Takeaways

After reading the answer, students will learn the importance of environmental adaptability and genetic diversity in the survival of bacterial populations.

Long Answer Type Questions (5 M)

1. A scientist conducts an experiment to study regeneration in three organisms:

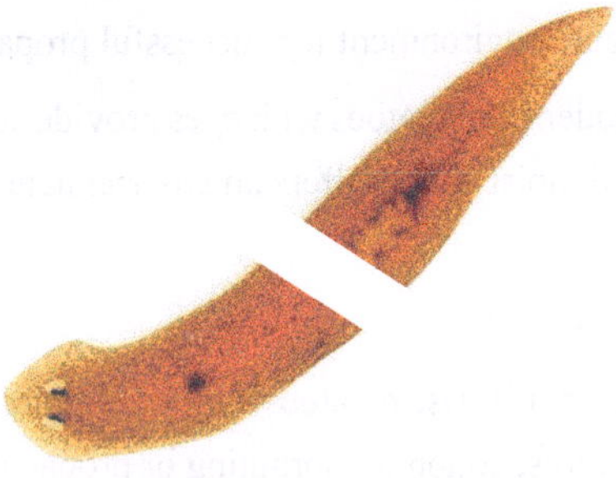

Organism X: Cut vertically into pieces.

Organism Y: Tail was severed.

Organism Z: Tail was severed. (*An*)

(*a*) Which of these organisms will or will not exhibit regeneration? Give reason.

(*b*) Based on the given experiment, which organism demonstrates a form of reproduction? Justify your answer.

Ans. (*a*) Organism X (*Planaria*) shows remarkable regenerative ability, where each fragment can develop into a complete organism. *(1 M)*

Organism Y can regenerate its tail but an entire new body cannot be regenerated from the severed tail. *(1 M)*

Organism Z cannot regenerate lost tails or other significant body parts. *(1 M)*

(*b*) X (*Planaria*) demonstrates a form of reproduction through regeneration, as each fragment can grow into a complete organism. Most organisms do not depend on being cut to reproduce. Organisms Y(Lizard) and Z(Rat) cannot reproduce in this manner. *(2 M)*

2. (*a*) Identify the organisms A, B and the mode of reproduction exhibited by them.

(A)

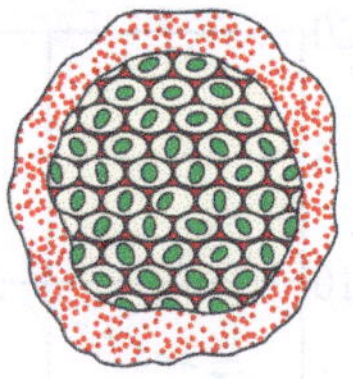

(B)

(*b*) How will an organism be benefitted if it reproduces through spores?

(*c*) Mention the two asexual methods by which *Hydra* can reproduce. Explain these methods. **(Re, *Un*)**

Ans. (*a*)
- Organism (A) is *Bryophyllum*, reproducing by vegetative propagation where new plants grow from the parent's leaves. *(½ M)*
- Organism (B) is *Plasmodium*, reproducing by multiple fission where one organism splits into many offspring. *(½ M)*

(*b*) Reproduction through spores offer various advantages like:
- Resistance to harsh conditions: Spores are encased in a thick protective layer, making them resilient during unfavorable conditions. *(1 M)*
- Enhanced dispersal: The lightweight nature of spores allows for easy transport by wind or water, facilitating the colonization of new areas suitable for growth. *(1 M)*

(*c*) *Hydra* reproduce asexually through budding and regeneration:
- Budding: A small outgrowth or bud forms on the body of the parent *Hydra* and eventually detaches to become a new individual. *(1 M)*
- Regeneration: *Hydra* can also regenerate lost body parts. Even if a *Hydra* is cut into pieces, each piece can develop into a complete new *Hydra* through cellular differentiation and growth, allowing for asexual reproduction. *(1 M)*

3. Answer the following questions:

(*a*) Certain specialised cells in animals called stem cells have the ability to divide and differentiate into different cell types. This helps in the replacement of a damaged organ.

Name and explain two methods of asexual reproduction that are similar to stem cells and occur mostly in multicellular organisms.

(*b*) Identify one reproductive organ in males and females that are functionally similar to each other in plants. Justify.

(*c*) Is it correct to say that asexual reproduction occurs only in unicellular organisms? Support your statement with reasons. **(*Un*)**

Ans. (*a*) In multicellular organisms, two methods of asexual reproduction similar to stem cells' functions are:

- Regeneration: Enables organisms like *Planaria* to rebuild complete organisms from parts. It utilizes specialized cells that can grow and differentiate into various cell types needed for the development of new organisms. *(1 M)*
- Fragmentation: *Spirogyra* involves the organism breaking into pieces, each capable of growing into a new individual. This method relies on the ability of each fragment to utilize cellular potential for growth, similar to stem cell function. *(1 M)*

(*b*) In plants, the male and female reproductive organs functionally similar to each other are like:

- Stamen is the male reproductive part, producing pollen grains containing male gametes. *(½ M)*
- Pistil is the female reproductive part, with the ovary containing ovules, which house the female gametes. *(½ M)*

(*c*) The statement that asexual reproduction is solely observed in unicellular organisms is not entirely accurate.

- Asexual reproduction in multicellular organisms: *Spirogyra*, which is a multicellular green alga, can reproduce asexually via fragmentation. *(1 M)*
- Sexual reproduction in unicellular organisms: While it is commonly thought that bacteria, which are unicellular, only reproduce asexually, many actually participate in sexual reproduction. *(1 M)*

4.

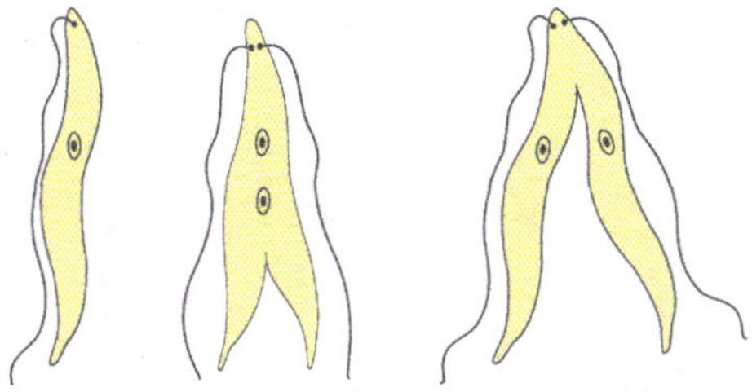

(*a*) Identify the organism given in the figure.
(*b*) What does the given figure represent?
(*c*) Name the disease caused by given organism?
(*d*) Give an example of organism that shows similar type of process like organism given here. Explain briefly. **(*Un*)**

Ans. (*a*) *Leishmania* *(1 M)*

(*b*) The given figure represents the binary fission in *Leishmania*. *(1 M)*

(*c*) The given organism (*Leishmania*) causes *Kala azar* disease in humans. *(1 M)*

(*d*) *Amoeba* is a unicellular organism, and just like *Leishmania*, it reproduces through binary fission. During binary fission, the genetic material in the nucleus replicates by mitotic division. Here the nucleus firstly divides into two daughter nuclei followed by division of cytoplasm and results into two daughter nuclei. *(2 M)*

Hints & Explanations

Multiple Choice Questions

1. (*a*) In asexual reproduction, there is no involvement of gametes, formation or fusion, leading to offspring that are genetically identical to the single parent. This results in a greater similarity among the offspring since no genetic mixing occurs.
2. (*b*) The correct order of binary fission stages in *Leishmania* is I, III, II, V, IV
3. (*d*) Yeast -Budding
   Leishmania - Binary fission
   Paramoecium - Binary fission
   Plasmodium - Multiple fission
4. (*b*) *Hydra* reproduce asexually by budding (through asexual buds). *Amoeba* reproduces asexually by binary fission. *Rhizopus* reproduces asexually by spore formation. *Planaria*, reproduce asexually by regeneration, it cuts its body into pieces and each piece of body grows into new individual.
5. (*b*) When *Amoeba* undergoes binary fission, the nucleus divides first and then the division of cytoplasm takes place. Thus, the correct sequence of binary fission is (*ii*), (*iii*), (*iv*) and (*i*).
6. (*d*) The diagram shows a sporangium with spores, characteristic of *Rhizopus*, a type of fungus, commonly known as bread mould.
7. (*c*) Plants grown by vegetative propogation allow plants to mature faster in terms of flowering and fruiting compared to those grown from seeds, and it ensures that all progeny are genetically similar to the parent plant, preserving its characteristics.
8. (*b*) Exposing bacteria to antibiotics at varying concentrations is an effective way to demonstrate the importance of genetic variation. Bacteria with genetic variations that show resistance to the antibiotic will survive and reproduce, illustrating how variation can ensure survival through environmental changes.
9. (*a*) Rahul will see yeast reproducing via budding as the provided sugar solution provides nutrients for yeast fermentation, whereas salt does not act the same hence Priya sees no budding in her slides.

Assertion and Reason

1. (*a*) The new individuals produced after cell division in asexual reproduction are always genetically identical or clone to each other and their parents because this process does not involve the fusion of gametes from two different organisms, resulting in offspring inheriting the exact genetic material of a single parent organism.
2. (*a*) In a genetically uniform population produced through asexual reproduction, all organisms share nearly identical genetic material. This genetic uniformity means that if a pathogen can infect one individual, it likely can infect all, making the entire population vulnerable to new diseases.

3. (*a*) The process of getting back a full organism from its body parts is called regeneration. *Planaria* possesses great power of regeneration. If the body of *Planaria* somehow gets cut into a number of pieces, then each body piece can regenerate into a complete *Planaria* by growing all the missing parts.

4. (*a*) DNA copying is necessary during reproduction because it leads to the transmission of characters from parents to offpsrings and brings about variation.

5. (*b*) A tuber is thickened, underground stem (or root) of a plant, which is swollen due to stored. It participates in vegetative reproduction, where vegetative parts of the plant contribute to reproduction, as seen in the potato.

6. (*a*) In stable environments, asexual reproduction's efficiency and rapidity enable organisms to quickly reproduce, outcompeting sexual reproducers due to the lesser energy and time required without mating or recombination processes.

7. (*a*) Nodes contain meristematic cells, which are essential for initiating new growth, explaining why stem pieces with nodes root faster and more efficiently in vegetative propagation than other parts.

8. (*d*) *Amoeba's* binary fission produces identical offspring through equal cell division, beginning with the nucleus and then cytoplasm. Yeast's budding is asymmetrical, generating a smaller bud on the parent cell that grows and separates into a new individual. Hence despite both processes creating new individuals, they remain distinct in terms of mechanism.

9. (*c*) Tissue culture is effective for cultivating disease-free orchids to support conservation projects. However, it does not enhance the plants' genetic resilience or adaptability. The technique yields genetically identical replicas of the parent plant, maintaining the original genetic traits without improving tolerance to adverse environments.

10. (*d*) DNA replication is highly accurate due to the precision of the enzymes involved, but it is not entirely error-free. Hence it does not create exact copies of the original cell. The minor errors that are not harmful and do not affect the organism's survival can indeed contribute to genetic variation within a population.

SEXUAL REPRODUCTION IN PLANTS AND ANIMALS, REPRODUCTIVE HEALTH

2

NCERT Definitions (Commonly asked in 1 mark)

- **Sexual Reproduction:** A biological process, involving two parents and a fusion of male and female gametes to create a new individual.
- **Gonads:** The organs that produce gametes.
- **Germ-cells:** Cells in the reproductive organs that develop into gametes.
- **Gametes:** Reproductive cells, consist of half the number of chromosomes (23) than normal body cells or somatic cells (46).

- **Sepal:** The outer parts of a flower, typically green, protecting the developing bud
- **Petal:** Colorful flower components attracting pollinators, surrounding reproductive structures.
- **Pistil:** The flower's female reproductive part, consisting of an ovary, style, and stigma.
- **Ovary (In plants):** Swollen bottom part of the pistil, which develops into fruit.
- **Stigma:** The sticky part of the pistil where pollen grains land and further germinate.
- **Style:** The pistil's part links the ovary and stigma, guiding pollen tubes to ovules for fertilisation.
- **Ovule:** Female gamete present within the ovary further develops into seed.
- **Stamen:** The male reproductive part of a flower, involved in producing pollen grains.
- **Filament:** The stalk-like part of the stamen that supports the anther.
- **Anther:** The bilobed part of the stamen where pollen grains are produced.
- **Pollen grains:** Yellowish grains produced by stamen containing male germ cells.
- **Pollination:** The transfer of pollen grains from the anther to the stigma of a flower.
- **Pollinator:** Organisms, often insects or birds, that transfer pollen from one flower to another, facilitating plant fertilisation.

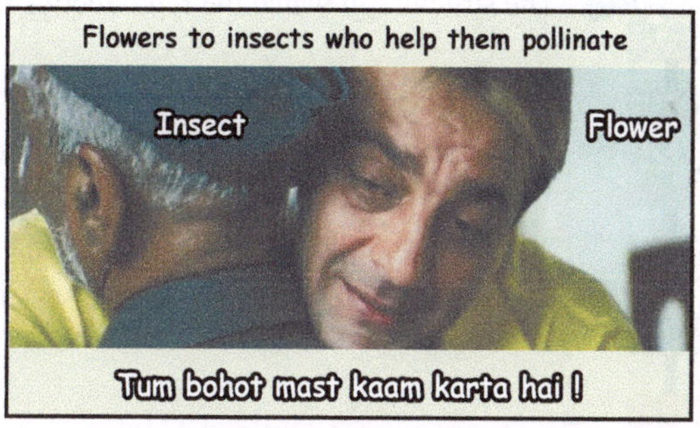

- **Germination:** The process where the embryo within a seed develops into a seedling under favorable environmental conditions, marking the initiation of a new plant's growth.
- **Male Reproductive System:** Comprises organs like testes, vas deferens, and penis, facilitating sperm production and delivery.
- **Female Reproductive System:** Includes ovaries, fallopian tubes, uterus, and vagina, responsible for egg production, site of fertilisation, and fetal development.
- **Sperm:** Male gametes produced in the testes. They are motile cells, primarily consisting of genetic material and a long tail that aids their movement towards the female gamete during fertilisation.
- **Ovum:** A female gamete produced in ovaries, containing nutrients vital for embryo development post-fertilisation.
- **Fertilisation:** The process of fusion of male and female germ cells to form a zygote.
- **Zygote:** The diploid cell (46 chromosomes) formed when a male gamete fertilises a female gamete.
- **Embryo:** An early development stage formed through division and differentiation of a zygote.
- **Blastocyst:** Early-stage embryo consisting of a hollow, fluid-filled structure.

- **Fetus:** The developing human from roughly eight weeks after conception until birth.
- **Puberty:** A period in human development when individuals acquire reproductive capabilities.
- **Menstruation:** The monthly shedding of the uterine lining in females when there is no implantation.
- **Reproductive Health:** A state of complete physical, mental, and social well-being in all matters relating to the reproductive system.
- **Pregnancy:** The period during which a fertilised egg develops into a fetus inside the uterus, typically lasting about nine months in humans.
- **Placenta:** A structure that connects the developing fetus to the uterine wall to allow nutrient uptake, waste elimination, and gas exchange via the mother's blood supply.
- **Family Planning:** The practice of controlling the number of children in a family and the intervals between their births.

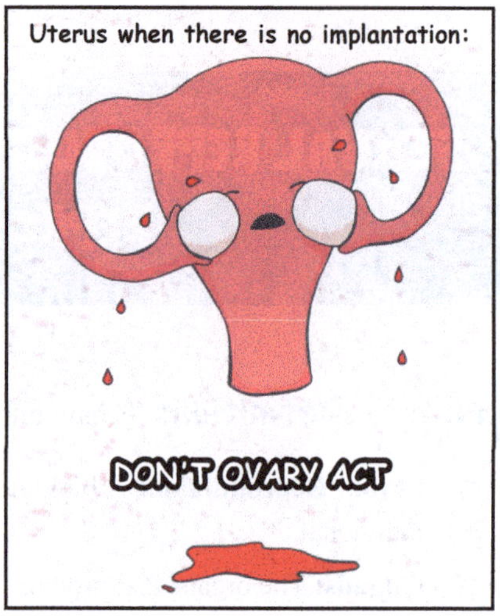

- **Contraceptive Methods:** Techniques or devices used to prevent pregnancy. These include barrier methods, hormonal methods, and surgical methods.
- **Sexually Transmitted Diseases (STDs):** Infections that are primarily spread through sexual contact, including bacterial (e.g., gonorrhoea, syphilis) and viral (e.g., HIV-AIDS, warts) infections.
- **Female Foeticide:** The practice of aborting a fetus because it is female, contributing to a disturbed sex ratio in many regions.
- **Sex Ratio:** Ratio of male to female population of an area.
- **Birth Rate:** The frequency of live births in a given population, usually expressed as the number of births per 1000 people per year.
- **Death Rate:** The frequency of deaths in a given population, typically measured as the number of deaths per 1000 individuals per year.

Important Facts

01 The structure in which the reproductive parts of angiosperms are located. *~ Flower*

02 The human gamete that can survive approximately one day if not fertilised. *~ Ovum*

03 The site in the female reproductive system where fertilisation occurs. *~ Fallopian tube*

04 Number of eggs the ovary releases every menstrual cycle. *~ One*

05 Placenta contains villi on the embryo's side of the tissue.

06 The mechanical barrier that greatly reduces the risk of transmitting many STIs. *~ Condom*

07 Population size and growth are determined by the rates of birth and death, affecting societal and environmental dynamics.

08 The component of the flower that sheds off after fertilisation as fruit development begins. *~ Petals, sepals, stamens, style, and stigma*

Difference Between (Commonly asked in 2-3 marks)

Pollination vs. Fertilisation	
Pollination	**Fertilisation**
Process of transferring pollen grains from the male anther to the female stigma.	The process where male and female gametes unite to form a zygote.
Occurs externally on the flower's reproductive organs.	Occurs internally within the plant's ovule in plants or the fallopian tube in humans.
Does not involve the fusion of genetic material.	Involves the fusion of genetic material from two gametes.
Can be facilitated by natural elements like wind, water, or animals.	Requires the direct contact of the gametes, usually following pollination in plants.
Pollination is specific to plants.	Fertilisation occurs in both plants and animals.

Self Pollination vs. Cross Pollination	
Self-Pollination	**Cross-Pollination**
Transfer of pollen from the anther to the stigma of the same flower or another flower on the same plant.	Transfer of pollen from the anther of one flower to the stigma of a flower on a different plant of the same species.
Genetic diversity is low, as the genetic material comes from the same plant.	Genetic diversity is high, due to the mixing of genetic material from different plants.
It can occur without the need for external pollinators such as insects or animals.	Often requires external pollinators
Examples: Peas, wheat, and orchid plants.	Examples: Apples, cherries, and most flowering plants.

Male vs. Female Reproductive Parts		
	Male Reproductive System	**Female Reproductive System**
Primary organ	• **Testes:** Paired glands where gamete production and synthesis of reproductive hormone takes place. • **Scrotum:** An external sac that consists of testes, crucial for regulating their temperature to support sperm production effectively.	• **Ovaries:** Two small, almond-shaped organs that produce gamete and reproductive hormones.
Accessory Ducts	• **Vas Deferens:** Duct for transporting mature sperm to ejaculatory ducts. • **Ejaculatory Ducts:** Tubes conveying semen to the urethra. • **Urethra:** Common passage for urine and semen expulsion.	• **Fallopian tube:** Tubular structures that transport eggs from the ovaries to the uterus and provide the site for fertilisation.
Accessory glands	Secretions of these glands constitute the seminal plasma which provides energy for sperm motility. • **Seminal Vesicles:** A pair of glands located at the back of the bladder base in men. • **Prostate Gland:** A small rubbery gland located below the bladder and in front of the rectum in men.	Secrete lubrication for the vagina.
Secondary organs	• **Penis:** The external genitalia used for sexual intercourse, capable of becoming erect for delivering semen into the female reproductive tract.	• **Uterus (Womb):** A muscular organ where a fertilised egg implants and develops into a fetus during pregnancy. • **Cervix:** The lower part of the uterus that connects it to the vagina. • **Vagina:** A muscular canal connecting the cervix to the external genitalia; serves as the birth canal during childbirth and also a passage for menstrual blood.
Gamete	Produces sperm, which are motile and numerous.	Produces eggs, which are larger and fewer in number.
Reproductive hormone	Consists of testosterone which regulates male reproductive functions and secondary sexual characteristics.	Consists of oestrogen and progesterone which regulate female reproductive functions and secondary sexual characteristics.
Reproductive cycle	Does not experience menstruation.	Undergo a regular reproductive cycle called menstruation.

Sperm vs. Egg	
Sperm	**Egg**
Smaller, mobile, and numerous.	Larger, non-motile, and typically released one per month.
It is produced continuously in large quantities.	*It is produced cyclically, with a finite number available from birth.*
It has a relatively longer lifespan, typically surviving for a few days within the female reproductive tract after ejaculation.	It has a shorter lifespan, capable of surviving for up to 24 hours after ovulation.
Sperms are formed in the testes.	Eggs are formed in the ovaries.

Bacterial STD vs. Viral STD	
Bacterial STDs	**Viral STDs**
Caused by various types of bacteria.	Caused by various types of viruses.
They are typically treatable with antibiotics.	Often managed with antiviral medications.
Many bacterial STDs can be cured.	Most viral STDs are chronic, with no cure, medications are available to treat symptoms only.
Examples: Chlamydia, Gonorrhoea, Syphilis.	Examples: HIV, HPV, Herpes, Hepatitis-B.

Real Life Application Based Questions

1. **While observing colorful flowers in gardens, have you ever wondered why plants display such a variety of colors?**

Ans. Flower colors act as attraction point for pollinators, optimizing pollination efficiency. This strategic variation enhances the chances of successful pollen transfer from one plant to another, playing a key role in plant reproduction and promoting genetic diversity among plant populations.

2. **While cutting a fruit like a guava, you observed small seeds. What structure have they developed from?**

Ans. The small seeds inside a guava have developed from the ovules within the ovary of the flower. After fertilisation, the ovule matures into a seed, while the ovary develops into a fruit.

3. **You must have heard about government campaigns emphasizing the importance of the girl child and prohibiting prenatal sex determination. Why are these initiatives crucial?**

Ans. Such campaigns are critical because determining a baby's gender before birth can sometimes lead to female foeticide due to a preference for male children. This practice unbalances the sex ratio, leading to fewer women in the population, which can seriously affect the health and stability of our society. These efforts aim to protect the girl child and ensure a fair and balanced community for everyone.

4. **You must have seen the news about the government extending the legal marriage age for boys and girls. Why is this age regulation important?**

Ans. The legal marriage age ensures individuals are mature enough for the responsibilities and challenges of marriage and parenthood. Just because a girl reaches biological maturity to bear children does not mean she's ready for the physical, emotional, and financial demands of childbearing and child-rearing. Setting a minimum age helps ensure better preparedness for these roles, promoting healthier families and societies.

5. **You might have encountered advertisements or discussions on contraception. Why is it crucial for family planning?"**

Ans. Contraception is crucial for family planning as:

- It allows couples to make informed decisions about their reproductive plans.
- It provides control over the timing and number of children, facilitating family size planning.
- Proper spacing between child through contraception enhances maternal and child health outcomes.

Myth Buster

❐ **Myth: Reproduction is essential for an individual life.**

Fact: Reproduction, unlike other life processes, is not essential to maintain the life of an individual organism. It is more about the survival and continuity of a species rather than individual necessity.

❐ **Myth: Menstruation is an illness that needs to be cured.**

Fact: Menstruation is a natural and healthy biological process signaling a female's reproductive system's functionality

❐ **Myth: Sexual education leads to increased sexual activity among teens.**

Fact: Comprehensive sexual education helps adolescents make informed decisions and practice safer sex.

❐ **Myth: Condoms guarantee absolute prevention of pregnancy and transmission of STDs.**

Fact: While condoms are highly effective in preventing pregnancy and STDs when used correctly, still they do not offer 100% protection. Proper usage significantly reduces but does not completely eliminate the risk of pregnancy or STD transmission.

Mnemonics

❐ **Example of Bisexual Flower**

"H & M has Biscuit"

H & **M** **B**iscuit
↓ ↓ ↓
Hibiscus Mustard are Bisexual

❐ **Example of Unisexual Flower**

"PW is Unique"

P **W** **U**nique
↓ ↓ ↓
Papaya Watermelon are Unisexual

- Reproductive parts of a Flower

  "A CAR belongs to Women but STeering belongs to MEN"

  Interpretation:

  CARpel: Female organ of the plant.

  STaMEN: Male part of the plant.

- Parts of Male Reproductive System (Human)

  "Eat Pizza, Save Spaghetti"

Eat	Pizza	Save	Spaghetti
↓	↓	↓	
External genitalia	Penis	Scrotum	

  "Amazing Singers Practice Everyday"

Amazing	Singers	Practice	Everyday
↓	↓	↓	
Accessory glands	Seminal vesicle	Prostate gland	

  "Astronauts Visit Universes Using Rockets"

Astronauts	Visit	Universes	Using	Rockets
↓	↓	↓	↓	
Accessory ducts	Vas deferens	Urethra	Ureter	

- Types of Contraceptive methods:

  "Make Cakes Have Pretty Icing, Chocolate, Sprinkles, Vanilla and Topping"

Make	Cakes	Have	Pretty	Icing	Chocolate	Sprinkles	Vanilla	Topping
↓	↓	↓	↓	↓	↓	↓	↓	↓
Mechanical barriers	Condom	Hormonal contraceptive	Pills	IUD	Copper-T	Surgical method	Vasectomy	Tubectomy

- Type of STIs

  Bacterial STIs – "CGS"

  - C → Chlamydia
  - G → Gonorrhoea
  - S → Syphilis

  Viral STIs – "HHH"

  - H → Herpes
  - H → Hepatitis B
  - H → HIV (Human Immunodeficiency Virus)

COMPETENCY BASED SOLVED EXAMPLES

Multiple Choice Questions (1 M)

1. A student planted seeds in two pots:

Pot 1: Moist soil with sunlight.

Pot 2: Dry soil without sunlight.

After 5 days, only Pot 1 showed germination. The student observed that between Z and Y, one structure emerged first, followed by the other. *(Ap)*

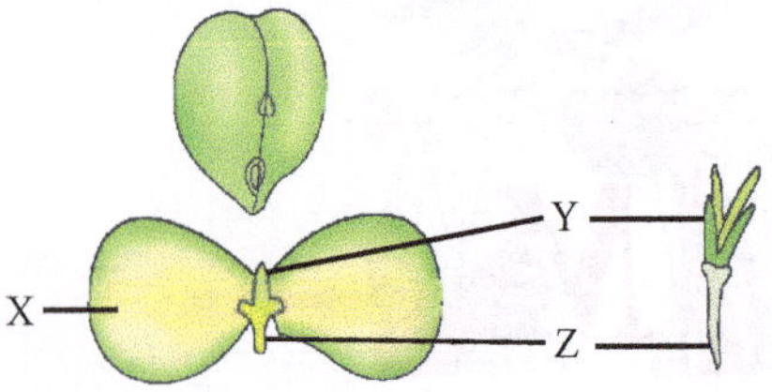

Which structure, Z or Y, emerges first, and what does this signify about its importance?

(*a*) The Z grows first to anchor the plant and absorb water and minerals, which are essential for the growth of the Y.

(*b*) The Y should emerge first to absorb sunlight and begin photosynthesis immediately.

(*c*) The Z emerges first only in case of lack of sunlight to grow to ensure anchoring the plant.

(*d*) The Y grows first to absorb sunlight for photosynthesis, providing energy for the growth of Z.

2. Carefully observe the image provided below and match the labeled structures A and B with their respective pre-fertilisation parts. *(An)*

(*a*) A-Petal, B-Ovary (*b*) A-Sepal, B-Ovules

(*c*) A-Carpal, B- Pistil (*d*) A-Stigma, B-Ovary

3. Which among the following statements are true for sexual reproduction in flowering plants?

(*Re*) (NCERT Exemplar)

(*i*) It requires two types of gametes

(*ii*) Fertilisation is a compulsory event

(*iii*) It always results in formation of zygote

(*iv*) Offspring formed are clones

(*a*) (*i*) and (*iv*) (*b*) (*i*), (*ii*) and (*iv*)

(*c*) (*i*), (*ii*) and (*iii*) (*d*) (*i*), (*ii*) and (*iv*)

4. A woman is undergoing pregnancy and she has noticed some changes in her body. Which of the following options is unrelated to her pregnancy? (*Re*)

(*a*) Development of the placenta

(*b*) Menstrual cycle

(*c*) Estrogen production

(*d*) Enlargement of mammary glands

5. Anita is studying the germination process in angiospermic flowers for her biology exam. Her teacher, Mr. Sharma, shows her several diagrams depicting different pathways of pollen tube growth and asks her to identify the correct one.
Which of the following shows the correct pathway of germination in the angiospermic flower? (*An*)

(*a*)  (*b*) 

(*c*)  (*d*) 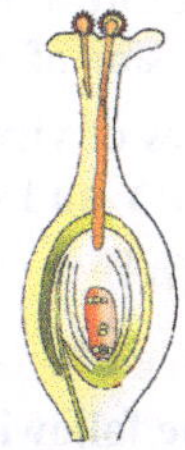

6. Consider the following three flowers namely X, Y and Z. Which flower(s) would develop into a fruit?

(*An*) (CBSE, 2023)

Flower X	Flower Y	Flower Z
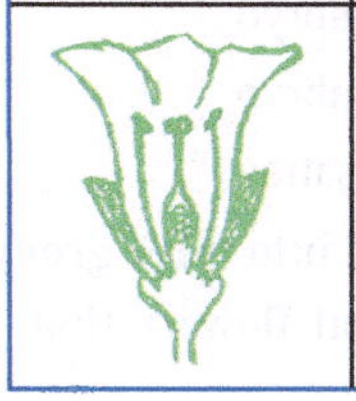		

(*a*) 'X' only (*b*) 'Z' only

(*c*) 'X' and 'Y' only (*d*) 'Y' and 'Z'

7. The graph below shows the number of eggs present in the ovaries of a girl at various stages of her life. Carefully analyze the graph and select the correct statement. (*An*)

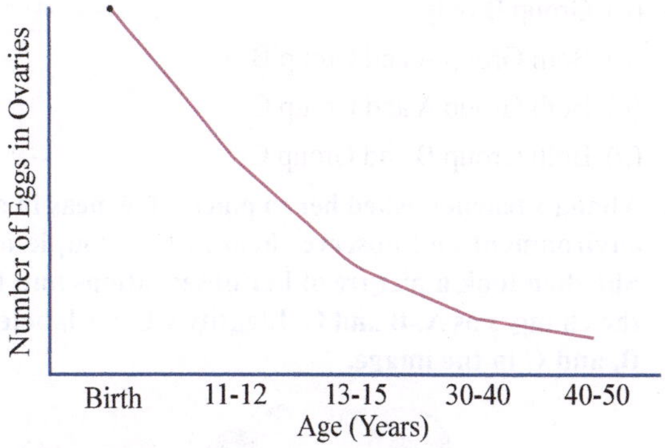

(*a*) A high number of immature eggs are present in the ovaries at the time of birth.

(*b*) A high number of mature eggs are present in the ovaries at the time of birth.

(*c*) Mature eggs are developed in the ovaries at the time of birth.

(*d*) A woman's ovaries continue to produce new eggs throughout her reproductive years, maintaining a constant number of eggs.

8. During a prenatal check-up, Seema undergoes an ultrasound to monitor her baby's health and growth. The focus of this procedure is a specific part of her reproductive system where the baby is developing. Identify the part of Seema's reproductive system being monitored to assess the baby's growth: (*An*)

(*a*) Cervix (*b*) Vagina

(*c*) Fallopian tube (*d*) Uterus

9. The female reproductive system includes almond-shaped glands. Which of the following hormones are secreted by these glands? (*Re*)

(*a*) Oestrogen and testosterone

(*b*) Testosterone and progesterone

(*c*) Oestrogen and progesterone

(*d*) Adrenaline and progesterone

10. In the flowering plants sexual reproduction involves several events beginning with the bud and ending in a fruit. These events are arranged in four different combinations. Select the combination that has the correct sequence of events. (*An*)

(*a*) Embryo, zygote, gametes, fertilisation

(*b*) Gametes, fertilisation, zygote, embryo

(*c*) Fertilisation, zygote, gametes, embryo

(*d*) Gametes, zygote, embryo, fertilisation

11. In a garden, plants were separated into three groups:

- **Group A plants have unisexual flowers that were wrapped in a bag.**
- **Group B plants have bisexual flowers that were wrapped in bags.**
- **Group C plants have unisexual flowers but were not bagged.**

Which group of plants will develop seeds? **(*Ap*)**

(*a*) Group B only

(*b*) Both Group A and Group B

(*c*) Both Group A and Group C

(*d*) Both Group B and Group C

12. Ahana's teacher asked her to place a few peas in a damp environment and observe them after a couple of days. She then took a picture of her observations and labeled the changes as A, B and C. Identify what is labeled as A, B, and C in the image. **(*An*)**

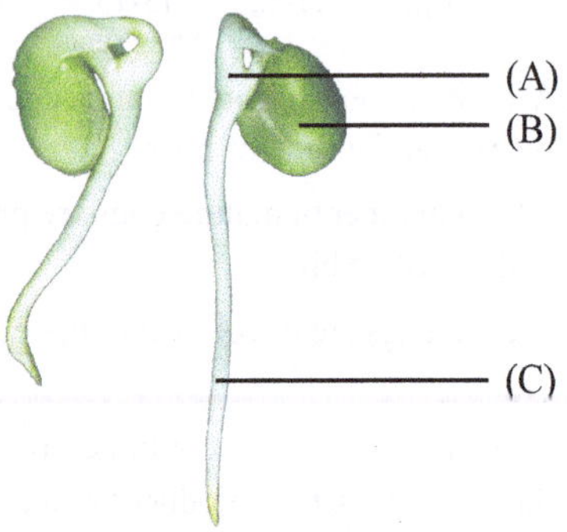

(*a*) A- Plumule; B- Radicle, C- Cotyledon

(*b*) A- Radicle; B- Cotyledon, C- Plumule

(*c*) A- Plumule; B- Cotyledon, C- Radicle

(*d*) A- Radicle; B- Plumule, C- Cotyledon

13. A and B are the two reproductive organs/tissues of females. A is responsible for nourishment of the developing embryo and B is where sperms encounter egg. A and B respectively are: **(*An*)**

(*a*) Vagina and uterus

(*b*) Ovary and fallopian tube

(*c*) Fallopian tube and uterus

(*d*) Placenta and fallopian tube

14. Which among the following statements are true for unisexual flowers? **(*Re*) (NCERT Exemplar)**

(*i*) They possess both stamens and carpel

(*ii*) They possess either stamen or carpel

(*iii*) They exhibit cross pollination

(*iv*) Unisexual flowers possessing only stamens cannot produce fruits

(*a*) (*i*) and (*iv*) (*b*) (*ii*), (*iii*) and (*iv*)

(*c*) (*i*) and (*ii*) (*d*) (*i*), (*iii*) and (*iv*)

15. Fertilisation is the process of **(*Re*) (CBSE, 2020)**

(*a*) Transfer of male gamete to female gamete.

(*b*) Fusion of nuclei of male and female gamete.

(*c*) Adhesion of male and female reproductive organs.

(*d*) The formation of gametes by a reproductive organ.

16. A scientist compares DNA content in two cells undergoing two types of cell division:

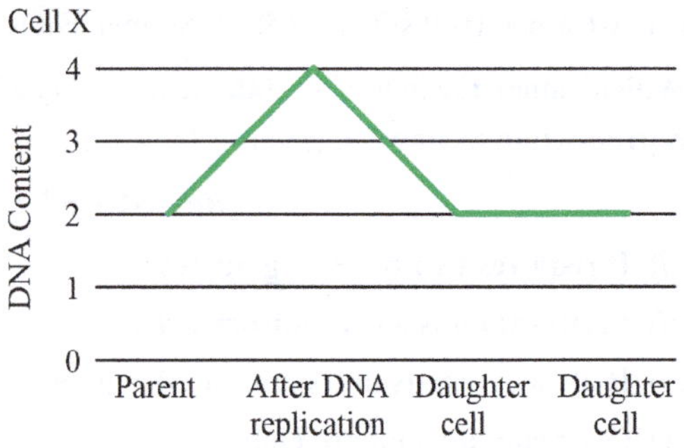

(A)

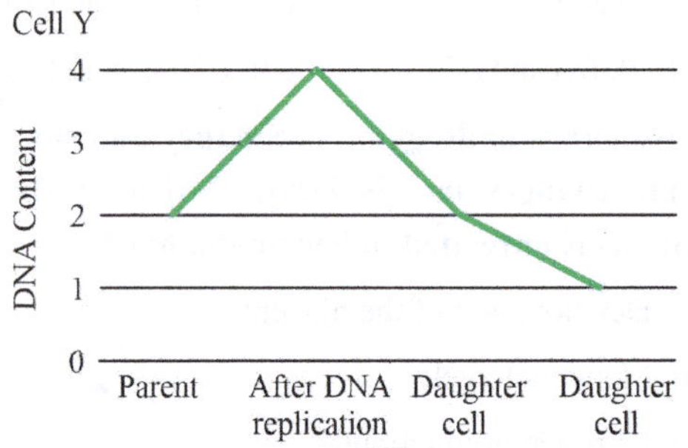

(B)

Which graph represents meiosis, and why is this process critical for sexual reproduction? **(*An*)**

(*a*) Graph A, because meiosis produces identical body cells.

(*b*) Graph B, as it reduces DNA to ensure stability in future generations.

(*c*) Both graphs represent meiosis as DNA is always divided equally.

(*d*) None, because meiosis halves DNA in germ cells.

17. Read the following statements about reproductive health and select the INCORRECT statements(s) from the given options. **(*Re*)**

(*i*) Diseases like gonorrhoea, syphilis and HIV/AIDS are sexually transmitted.

(*ii*) Gonorrhoea and syphilis are caused by fungus are transmitted sexually.

(*iii*) Using condoms during sex helps to prevent transmission of many of the infections to some extent.

(*iv*) Examples of viral and bacterial infection STDs are AIDS-HIV and syphilis respectively.

(*a*) (*ii*) and (*iv*) (*b*) (*ii*) and (*iii*)

(*c*) (*ii*) Only (*d*) (*i*) and (*iv*)

18. Consider the following statements: **(*Re*)**

(*i*) Copper-T is a contraceptive device used by women.

(*ii*) Sexually transmitted disease can be prevented by using condoms.

***(iii)* Increasing population size improves everybody's standard of living.**

***(iv)* Loop are placed in the cervix to prevent pregnancy.**

Which of these statement(s) is/are correct?

(*a*) (*i*) and (*ii*) (*b*) (*ii*) and (*iii*)

(*c*) (*i*) only (*d*) All of these

19. Match the entries of column-I with those of column-II.

Column-I		Column-II	
A.	Condom	(*i*)	A small portion of vas deferens is removed
B.	Copper-T	(*ii*)	Prevents ovulation
C.	Oral Pills	(*iii*)	Suppresses sperm motility
D.	Vasectomy	(*iv*)	Prevents entry of sperms into female genital tract

(*Re*)

(*a*) A-(*iv*), B-(*iii*), C-(*ii*), D-(*i*)

(*b*) A-(*iv*), B-(*iii*), C-(*i*), D-(*ii*)

(*c*) A-(*iii*), B-(*iv*), C-(*ii*), D-(*i*)

(*d*) A-(*i*), B-(*ii*), C-(*iii*), D-(*iv*)

20. If you were asked to plot a graph comparing the ability of asexual (Y) and sexual (X) organisms to survive in a changing environment, which of the given graphs would be the most accurate representation? (*An*)

(*a*)

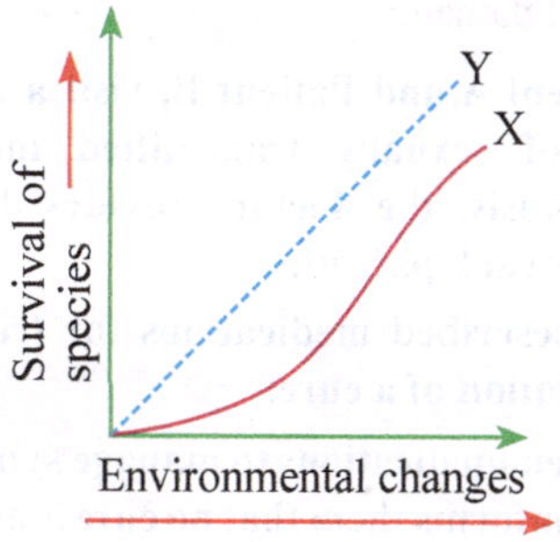

(*b*)

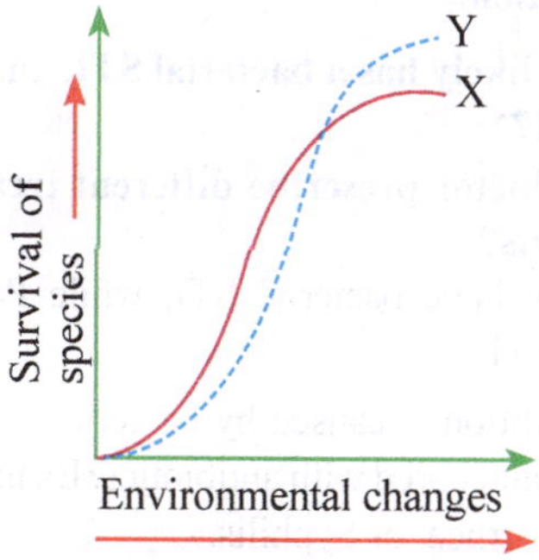

(*c*)

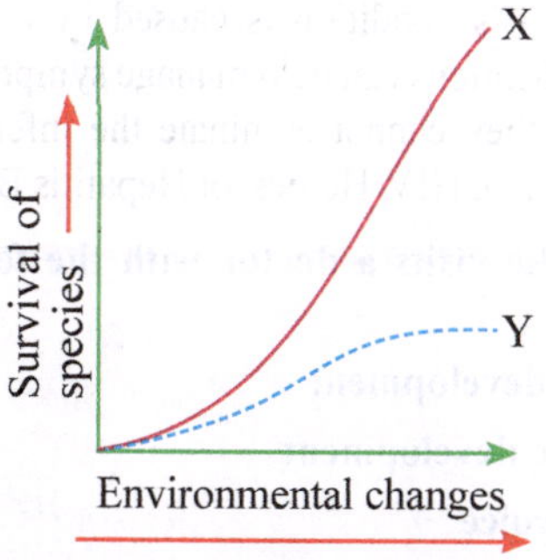

(*d*)

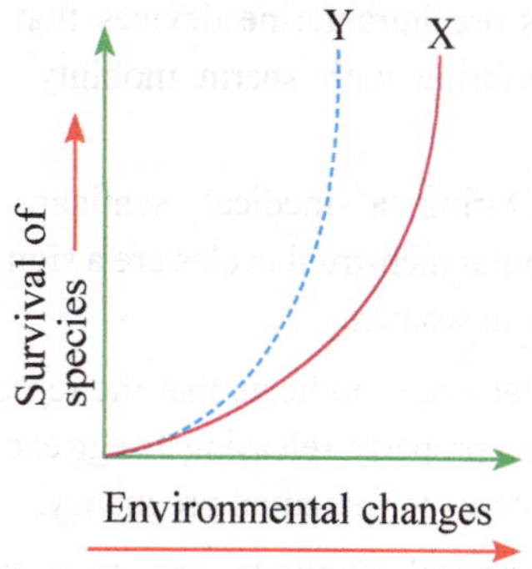

Assertion and Reason (1 M)

Direction: **The following questions consist of two statements – Assertion (A) and Reason (R). Answer these questions by selecting the appropriate option given below:**

(*a*) Both A and R are true, and R is the correct explanation of A.

(*b*) Both A and R are true, but R is not the correct explanation of A.

(*c*) A is true, but R is false.

(*d*) A is false, but R is true.

1. **Assertion (A):** Pollen grains fall from the pistil and stick to the stigma of the stamen.

   Reason (R): The fertilised egg cells grow inside the ovules and become seeds. **(*Re*)**

2. **Assertion (A):** Fertilisation occurs when the male gamete present in pollen grains fuse with the female gamete.

   Reason (R): The ovary of flower develops and becomes a fruit. **(*Re*)**

3. **Assertion (A):** Pollination is the act of transferring pollen grains from the male anther of a flower to the female stigma.

   Reason (R): In bisexual flowers, pollen grains are always transferred from the anther to the stigma of the same flower. **(*Un*)**

4. **Assertion (A):** Vagina is also called as birth canal.

   Reason (R): During birth, the baby passes through the vagina. **(*Re*)**

5. **Assertion (A):** Scrotum is present outside the abdominal cavity.

   Reason (R): It stores sperms which require a lower temperature than the normal body temperature. **(*Re*)**

6. **Assertion (A):** At puberty, in boys, voice begins to crack and thick hairs grows on face.

   Reason (R): At puberty, there is decreased secretion of testosterone in boys. **(*Re*)**

7. **Assertion (A):** A botanist observes that a papaya tree in the garden does not bear fruits despite having abundant flowers.

   Reason (R): The botanist concludes that all flowers on the tree only have stamens, which produces pollen but no ovules for fertilisation to occur. **(*An*)**

8. **Assertion (A):** A medical practitioner claims that undergoing an IUD is a reliable method for protecting against HIV/AIDS.

Reason (R): IUDs are intrauterine devices that prevent pregnancy by interfering with sperm mobility and egg fertilisation. ***(Re)***

9. **Assertion (A):** During a medical seminar, it was highlighted that regular menstrual cycles are a sign of good reproductive health in women.

   Reason (R): Regular cycles indicate that the reproductive system is functioning properly, releasing an egg each month and preparing the uterus for potential pregnancy. ***(Un)***

10. **Assertion (A):** Surgical methods are most effective methods of contraception done by removal of gamete producing organs.

    Reason (R): Surgical method blocks gametes transport and hence prevent fertilisation. ***(Re)***

11. **Assertion (A):** Vasectomy is a surgical method of birth control.

    Reason (R): In vasectomy, small portion of oviduct is cut or tied properly. ***(Re)***

12. **Assertion (A):** HIV-AIDS is a bacterial disease.

    Reason (R): AIDS does not spread through sharing of food and water. ***(Re)***

Subjective Questions

Very Short Answer Type Questions (2 M)

1. **Mention the functions of (*a*) Placenta (*b*) Fallopian tubes (*c*) Uterus and (*d*) Ovary in the human female reproductive system.** ***(Re)*** **(CBSE, 2022)**

Ans. The functions of the different parts of the female reproductive system are:

	Part	Functions
A.	Placenta	Provides oxygen and nutrients to the developing foetus.
B.	Fallopian tube	Transports the egg from the ovary to the uterus.
C.	Uterus	Provides a site for the fertilised egg to implant and develop into a foetus.
D.	Ovary	Produces and releases eggs (ovulation).

(2 M)

2. **A scientist conducted an experiment to study plant reproduction, dividing plants pollinated by birds and wind into three groups:** ***(Ev)***
   - **Group 1: Placed in an open field with birds.**
   - **Group 2: Placed in an open field without birds.**
   - **Group 3: Placed in a well-ventilated and sunlight-rich room.**

   Based on your knowledge answer the following questions:

   (*a*) Which group(s) of plants are most likely to produce fruits?

   (*b*) What conclusions can be drawn from this experiment?

Ans. (*a*) All groups can produce fruits. Group 1, with bird pollination, is most likely to produce fruit. Group 3 may produce fruit with wind pollination in a well-ventilated room, while Group 2 can still produce seeds because wind pollination can occur in the open field. *(1 M)*

(*b*) The experiment highlights the importance of pollinators in plant reproduction. Plants rely on biotic (birds, insects) or abiotic (wind, water) pollinators. Group 1 will most probably show higher fruit production due to pollinators availibility, while Groups 2 and 3 will most probably have reduced fruit production in their absence. *(1 M)*

3. **Give reasons:**

   (*i*) Placenta is extremely essential for foetal development.

   (*ii*) Uterine lining becomes thick and spongy after fertilisation. ***(Un)*** **(CBSE, 2022)**

Ans. (*i*) Reasons for placenta being essential for foetal development:
- Placenta helps in the exchange of oxygen and nutrients between the mother and the developing foetus. *(½ M)*
- Placenta removes waste products from the foetal bloodstream. *(½ M)*

(*ii*) Reason for the uterine lining becoming thick and spongy after fertilisation:
- The thickened uterine lining provides a suitable environment for the fertilised egg to implant and grow. *(½ M)*
- The thickened uterine lining helps to protect the embryo from mechanical damage. *(½ M)*

4. **Two patients, Patient A and Patient B, visit a hospital with complaints of sexually transmitted infections (STIs). After diagnosis, the doctor provides different treatment plans for each patient.** ***(An)***
   - **Patient A is prescribed medications for treatment with the expectation of a cure.**
   - **Patient B is given medications to manage symptoms, and the doctor informs them that no cure is available for their condition.**

   (*a*) Which patient likely has a bacterial STI, and which has a viral STI?

   (*b*) Why did the doctor prescribe different treatments for both patients?

Ans. (*a*) Patient A likely have bacterial STI, while Patient B likely have a viral STI. *(1 M)*

(*b*) Patient A's condition is caused by bacteria, which can typically be treated and cured with antibiotics. Example can be Chlamydia, Gonorrhea, or Syphilis. *(½ M)*

In contrast, Patient B's condition is caused by a virus in which antiviral medications can help manage symptoms and suppress the virus, they cannot eliminate the infection, as seen with viral STIs like HIV, Herpes, or Hepatitis B. *(½ M)*

5. **A 20-year-old make visits a doctor with the following signs:** ***(Ap)***
   - **No facial hair development**
   - **Lack of muscle development**
   - **High-pitched voice**

The doctor mentions that the patient has an underproduction of hormone X, also known as puberty hormones. Based on your understanding, answer the following questions:

(*a*) Identify hormone X and the organ responsible for its production.

(*b*) What other issues might the boy experience if the deficiency persists for years?

Ans. (*a*) The hormone X is testosterone, which is produced by the testes. *(1 M)*

(*b*) If the deficiency persists, the boy may experience underdeveloped sexual characteristics and low sperm production, impacting fertility. *(1 M)*

6. A couple is learning about different ways to prevent pregnancy and wants to know about a method that has the following characteristics:

1. **Prevents fertilisation.**
2. **Does not alter the body's mechanisms or cycles.**
3. **Does not require a medical procedure.**
4. **Should be a male-specific option.**

Identify this method and provide one example. ***(Ap)***

Ans. The method that matches the criteria is called the barrier method. *(1 M)*

A common male-specific option for this method is condoms. *(1 M)*

Short Answer Type Questions (3 M)

1. Draw a labelled diagram of the longitudinal section of a flower. ***(Cr)***

Ans. The labelled diagram of the longitudinal section of a flower is given below:

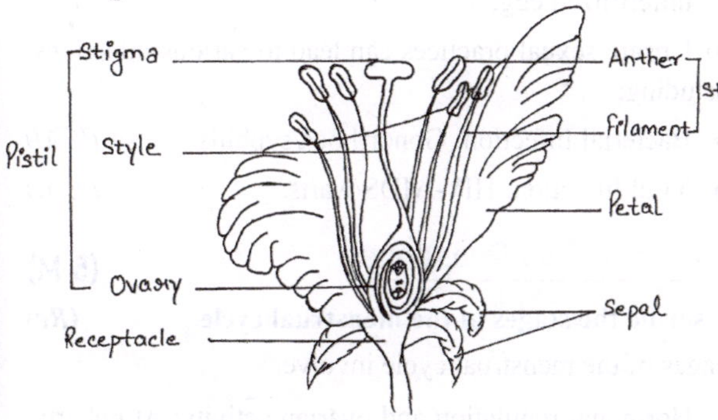

(3 M)

Nailing the Right Answer

When answering this question, ensure you focus on the correct positioning and clear labeling of each floral part.

2. (*a*) In angiosperms why fertilisation cannot take place in flowers if pollination does not take place? Where is zygote located in a flower after fertilisation? What does it develop into?

(*b*) Write the names of those parts of a flower which serve the same function as the following do in animals:
(*i*) testis (*ii*) ovary ***(Un)* (CBSE, 2024)**

Ans. (*a*) In angiosperms, fertilization cannot occur if pollination does not take place because pollination involves the transfer of pollen from the stamen (male part) to the stigma (female part). Without this transfer, the male germ cells cannot reach and fuse with the female gamete present in the ovule. *(1 M)*

The zygote is located in the ovule after fertilization. The zygote develops into embryo. *(1 M)*

(*b*) The parts of a flower serving the same function as:

(*i*) Testis in animals is the stamen in flower, which produces pollen grains, the male germ cells. *(½ M)*

(*ii*) Ovary in animals is the ovary in the flower, which contains the egg cells, the female germ cells. *(½ M)*

3. Draw the diagram of female reproductive system and mark the following parts:

1. **Where block is created surgically to prevent fertilisation.**
2. **Where Copper-T is inserted.**
3. **Entry point for sperm into the female reproductive system.** ***(Cr)***

Ans.

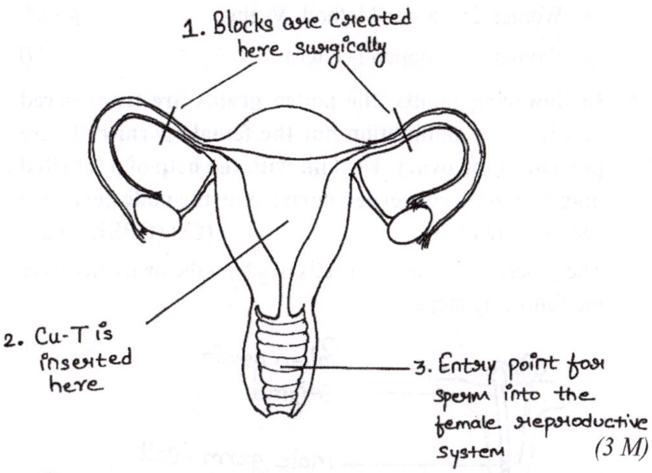

(3 M)

Mistakes 101 : What not to do!

Students might not accurately show where the cut is done to block the gamete transport to prevent fertilisation.

4. Seema conducted a survey with three women from a village to understand their family planning needs and health conditions. Analyze the given data and answer the following questions. ***(An, Ap)***

Woman	Age	Number of Children	Family Planning Need	Health Condition
Woman 1	28	3	Wants permanent prevention of pregnancy	Healthy

Woman 2	22	1	Wants temporary prevention of pregnancy	Sensitive to hormonal pills
Woman 3	30	2	Looking for long-term (5-10 years) prevention of pregnancy	Healthy

(a) Based on their family planning needs and health conditions, which contraceptive method is most suitable for each woman?

(b) Which part of the human reproductive system is involved by the contraceptive methods identified in (a)?

Ans. (a) Contraceptive Methods for Each Woman:

- Woman 1: Surgical method *(½ M)*
- Woman 2: Barrier method (No hormones, avoids side effects) *(½ M)*
- Woman 3: Copper-T (Long-term prevention but reversible) *(½ M)*

(b) Locations of the identified contraceptive methods:

- Women 1: Surgical Method- Fallopian Tubes *(½ M)*
- Women 2: Barrier Method- Vagina *(½ M)*
- Women 3: Copper-T- Uterus *(½ M)*

5. In flowering plants, the pollen grains are transferred to stigma by pollination but the female germ cells are present in the ovary. Explain with the help of a labelled diagram (only concerned parts), how the male germ cell reaches the ovary. (Cr) (CBSE, 2022)

Ans. The process of male germ cells reaching the ovary involves the following steps:

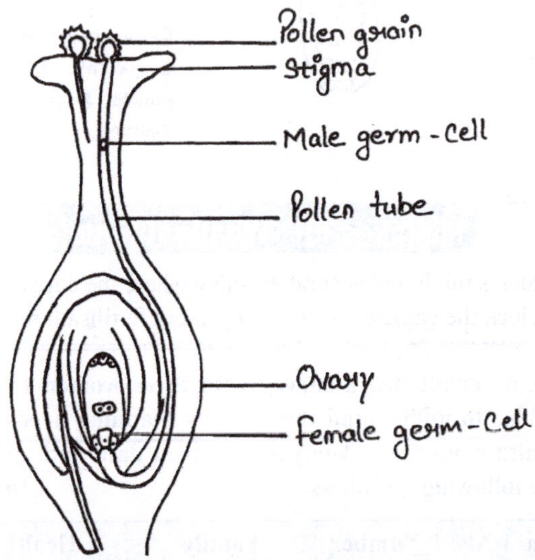

(3 M)

6. While dissecting a flower for a class project, a 10th-grade student observed yellow particles adhering to their fingers and noticed a distinct small bulging structure within the flower's central section.

(a) Identify the yellow particles and the bulging structure within the flower.

(b) State the key differences between these two structures, emphasizing their roles in plant reproduction. (An)

Ans. (a) The yellow particles on the student's fingers are pollen grains. *(½ M)*

The bulging structure inside the flower is an ovary. *(½ M)*

(b)

Feature	Pollen Grain	Ovary
Location	Produced in the anther of a flower.	Located at the base of the pistil in a flower.
Function	Contains the male gametes for plant reproduction.	Houses the ovules, which contain the female gametes and develop into seeds after fertilisation.

(2 M)

7. (a) What happens when in a human female the egg released by the ovary is not fertilised?

(b) Name one bacterial and one viral infection caused due to unsafe sex. (Un, Re) (CBSE, 2022)

Ans. (a) When an egg released by the ovary in a human female is not fertilised, the following outcome occur:

- Egg Lifespan: The unfertilized egg lives for about one day after being released from the ovary. *(1 M)*
- Menstruation: In the absence of fertilisation, the uterus, having prepared itself for a potential pregnancy by thickening its lining, shed and exits the body through the vagina as blood and mucous, along with the unfertilized egg. *(1 M)*

(b) Unsafe sexual practices can lead to various infections, including:

- Bacterial Infection: Gonorrhoea/syphilis. *(½ M)*
- Viral Infection: HIV-AIDS/warts. *(½ M)*

Long Answer Type Questions (5 M)

1. Describe the stages of the menstrual cycle. (Re)

Ans. Stages of the menstrual cycle involve:

1. Hormonal regulation and ovarian activity: At puberty, hormonal changes stimulate the ovaries, leading to the maturation and release of an egg (ovulation). *(1 M)*
2. Ovarian Cycle: Each month, an ovary releases an egg during ovulation, under the influence of these hormones. *(1 M)*
3. Uterine lining preparation: The uterus prepares itself every month for the potential implantation of a fertilized egg. This preparation includes the thickening of the uterine lining, creating a nutrient-rich environment for embryo development. *(1 M)*
4. Menstruation: The shedding of the uterine lining, mixed with blood and mucus, exits the body through the vagina, marking the menstrual phase of the cycle, typically lasting between two to seven days. *(1 M)*

5. Cycle Repeat: This cycle of preparation for potential fertilisation, and shedding (if fertilisation does not occur) repeats approximately every month, constituting the menstrual cycle. *(1 M)*

2. In a particular mammalian species, X cells fuse to form Y, which is then implanted in the female body for further development. Below is a graphical representation showing the number of chromosomes in the X and Y cells of different mammals. Based on your understanding, answer the following questions: *(An)*

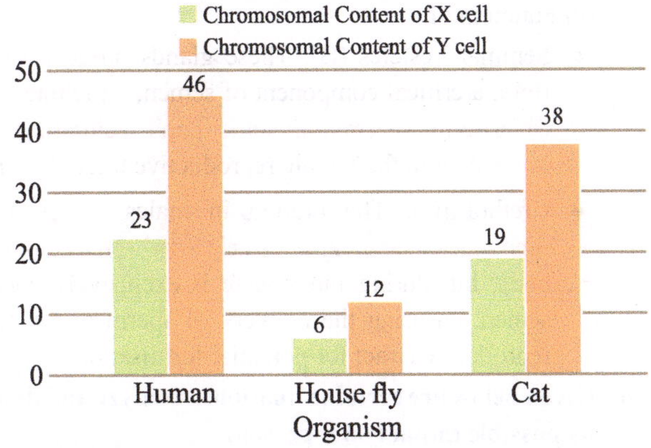

(a) Differentiate between cells X and Y.

(b) Explain the significance of the difference in the number of chromosomes between cells X and Y.

Ans. (a)

Aspect	Gamete (X)	Zygote (Y)
Definition	A gamete is a mature sex cell.	A zygote is the initial cell formed during sexual reproduction.
Chromosome Number	Gametes contain half the number of chromosomes of normal cells, being haploid (n).	Zygotes contain the full set of chromosomes, being diploid (2n).
Formation	Gametes are formed through a process called meiosis in the reproductive organs.	A zygote is formed when two gametes (sperm and egg) fuse during fertilization.

(3 M)

(b) Significance of the difference in the number of chromosomes between cells gamete and zygote:

- Maintenance of Chromosome Number Stability: Gametes are haploid (n), containing half the chromosome number to ensure the stable inheritance of genetic material. Upon fertilization, two gametes (sperm and egg) combine to form a diploid zygote (2n), restoring the species' normal chromosome number, preventing doubling with each generation. *(1 M)*
- Genetic Diversity and Proper Development: The fusion of genetic material from two different individuals introduces genetic variation. *(1 M)*

3. The diagram given below represents a system in the human body. Study the diagram and answer the following questions: *(Re)* (CBSE, 2019)

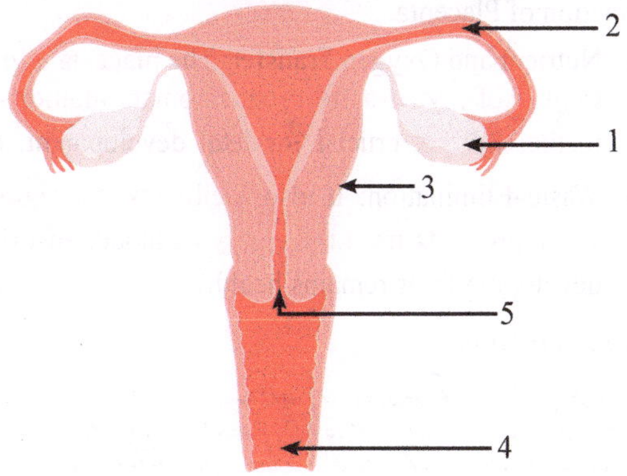

(i) Identify the system.

(ii) Label the parts marked 2 and 5.

(iii) Name the two hormones secreted by 1.

(iv) Mention the number and the name of the part involved in fertilisation and implantation from the above diagram.

(v) Mention the surgical methods of contraception in:

1. Human males

2. Human females

Ans. (i) Female Reproductive System *(1 M)*

(ii) 2-Oviduct, 5-cervix *(1 M)*

(iii) Estrogen and Progesterone *(1 M)*

(iv) 2, Oviduct is involved in fertilisation and *(½ M)*

3, Uterus is involved in implantation *(½ M)*

(v) 1. In Males - Blockage of vas deferens *(½ M)*

2. In females - Blockage of fallopian tube *(½ M)*

4. (a) Write the function of following parts in human female reproductive system:

(i) Ovary **(ii) Oviduct**

(iii) Uterus

(b) Describe in brief the structure and function of placenta. *(Re)* (CBSE, 2018, 2020)

Ans. (a) Functions:

(i) Ovary: Produces female gamete and secreted female sex and pregnancy maintenance hormones. *(1 M)*

(ii) Oviduct: Collects ovum and provides the path for sperm journey to fertilise the female gamete. *(1 M)*

(iii) Uterus: Site for implantation and growth of the embryo and path for sperm towards ovum. *(1 M)*

(b) Structure of Placenta:

- The placenta is a disc-shaped organ embedded in the uterine wall. *(½ M)*
- It contains villi on the embryo's side, which increases the surface area for absorption, facilitating nutrient and waste exchange. *(½ M)*

Function of Placenta:

- Nutrient and Oxygen Transfer: The placenta allows the transfer of oxygen and nutrients from the mother's blood to the embryo, crucial for fetal development. *(½ M)*
- Waste Elimination: It also facilitates the removal of waste products from the embryo's blood, ensuring the developing fetus remains healthy. *(½ M)*

Topper's Explanation

(a)(i) Ovary has following functions :-
• It releases matured egg (female germ cell) once every month & thus, is responsible for produce & release (oogenesis & ovulation) of ovum.
• It secretes oestrogen & progesterone. Oestrogen controls secondary sexual characteristics in females at time of puberty & also promotes release & maturation of egg.

(ii) • Oviduct / Fallopian tube carries the released egg to the uterus.
• Oviduct is also the site of fertilization.

(iii) Uterus in a bag like structure where embryo is developed & implanted.
It helps the embryo to grow into foetus & also, develops a thick lining of blood vessels every month in order to receive a fertilized egg.
• Its rythmic contraction helps the baby to come out from mother's body (womb).

(b) Placenta is a disc shaped tissue embedded in uterine wall once implantation of embryo takes place. It has villi on the embryo's side & blood spaces on mother's side.
→ It helps in nourishment of child inside mother's womb. It also helps in exchange of nutrients, oxygen & waste products (released by embryo) between mother's & embryo's blood & thus, is responsible for maturation of embryo.

5. Based on the given diagram answer the questions given below:

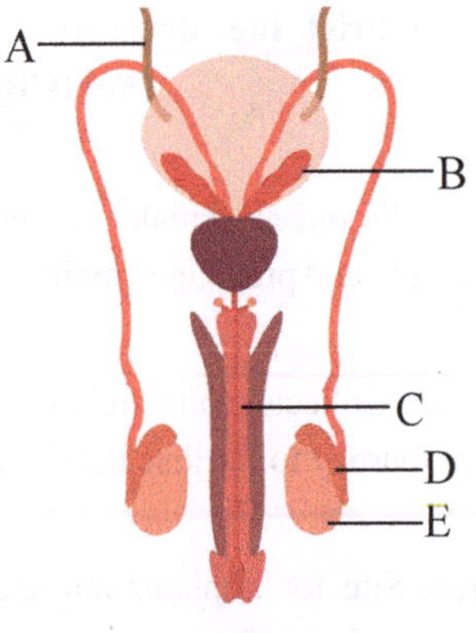

(*a*) Label the parts A, B, C and D.

(*b*) Name the hormone secreted by E and mention its role.

(*c*) State the functions of B and C in the process of reproduction. **(*Un*) (CBSE, 2020)**

Ans. (*a*) A- Ureter, B- Seminal vesicle, C- Urethra, D-Epididymis *(1 M)*

(*b*) The hormone secreted by the testes (E) is testosterone. *(1 M)*

Its roles include:

- Sperm production: Testosterone is crucial for the development and production of sperm in the testes. *(½ M)*
- Secondary sexual characteristics: It is responsible for the development of male secondary sexual characteristics during puberty, such as increased muscle and bone mass, and the growth of body hair. *(½ M)*

(*c*) Function of:

- Seminal Vesicles (B): These glands produce seminal fluid, a critical component of semen, enriching it with fructose for sperm nourishment and facilitating sperm movement in the female reproductive tract. *(1 M)*
- Urethra (C): The urethra in males serves a dual function, channeling both urine and semen out of the body, but during intercourse it exclusively conducts semen, ensuring the delivery of sperm to the female reproductive tract for potential fertilisation. *(1 M)*

6. Given below are certain situations. Analyze and describe its possible impact on a person:

(*a*) Testes of a male boy are not able to descend into scrotum during his embryonic development.

(*b*) Vas deferens of a man is plugged.

(*c*) Prostate and seminal vesicles are not functional.

(*d*) Egg is not fertilised in a human female.

(*e*) Placenta does not attach to the uterus optimally.

(*An*) (CBSE APQ, 2023)

Ans. (*a*) If a male boy's testes are not able to descend into the scrotum:

- Sperm formation will be adversely affected because it requires a lower temperature than the body temperature. *(½ M)*
- Could lead to fertility issues due to impaired sperm production. *(½ M)*

(*b*) If the vas deferens of a man are plugged sperm cannot travel to be mixed with semen, likely resulting in male infertility as there would be no sperm in the ejaculated fluid. *(1 M)*

(*c*) Consciences if prostate and seminal vesicles are not functional:

- Infertility: Non-functional prostate and seminal vesicles lead to infertility by impairing sperm viability and motility, due to the lack of seminal fluid which provides nourishment and energy for sperm movement. *(½ M)*
- Inference in sexual act: Reduced lubrication can cause discomfort and difficulties during intercourse. *(½ M)*

(*d*) When an egg is not fertilised in a human female, it lives for about one day. Then, the thickened lining of the uterus breaks leading to the discharge of blood and mucus along with the unfertilised egg. This is called menstruation. *(1 M)*

(e) If the placenta does not attach optimally to the uterus:

- It may not provide sufficient nutrients and oxygen to the foetus or effectively remove waste. *(½ M)*
- This condition can lead to complications such as fetal growth restriction, increased risk of preterm birth, and in severe cases, could result in fetal loss. *(½ M)*

7. **(i) Describe the role of prostate gland, seminal vesicle and testes in the human male reproductive system.**

(ii) How is the surgical removal of unwanted pregnancies misused?

(iii) Explain the role of oral contraceptive pills in preventing conception. **(Re, Un)**

OR

Describe sexually transmitted diseases and mention the ways to prevent them. **(Re)**

Ans. (i) Function of prostate gland and seminal vesicles:

- Production of seminal fluid: These glands secrete fluids that combine with sperm to form seminal fluid. *(½ M)*
- Aid in viability and mobility: This fluid provides essential nourishment and protection for sperm, aiding in their mobility and viability during ejaculation. *(½ M)*

Function of testes:

- Sperm production: The testes are the organs where sperm production occurs. *(½ M)*
- Reproductive hormone production: They also produce testosterone, the hormone responsible for developing secondary sexual characteristics and sperm formation in males during puberty. *(½ M)*

(ii) Surgical removal of unwanted pregnancies can be misused by aborting child on gender preference:

1. Female foeticide: It is often driven by societal and cultural preferences for male offspring, leading to the illegal selection and termination of female fetuses. *(½ M)*
2. Promoting gender imbalance: This practice creates significant gender imbalances within populations, affecting the natural demographic distribution and leading to long-term social issues. *(½ M)*
3. Violation of laws: Engaging in female foeticide through surgical removal of pregnancies directly violates legal prohibitions against gender-based abortion, challenging ethical and legal standards. *(½ M)*

(iii) Oral contraceptive pills in prevent conception by:

- Hormone regulation: Oral contraceptive pills contain hormones that prevent ovulation, ensuring no egg is released for fertilisation. *(½ M)*
- Thickening cervical mucus: They thicken the mucus around the cervix, making it difficult for sperm to enter the uterus. *(½ M)*
- Altering uterine lining: The pills change the lining of the uterus, making it inhospitable for implantation of a fertilised egg. *(½ M)*

OR

Sexually Transmitted Diseases (STDs), also known as Sexually Transmitted Infections (STIs), are infections spread primarily through sexual contact. They can be caused by bacteria, viruses, or parasites and can affect various parts of the body, including the genitals, mouth, throat, and rectum. Common STDs include chlamydia, gonorrhoea, syphilis, herpes, and AIDS. *(2 M)*

Ways to prevent STDs:

- Abstinence: The most effective way to prevent STDs is to abstain from any form of sexual activity. *(½ M)*
- Use of condoms: Consistent and correct use of latex condoms during sexual intercourse can significantly reduce the risk of many STDs. *(½ M)*
- Limiting partners: Reducing the number of sexual partners can decrease the risk of exposure to STDs. *(½ M)*
- Regular testing: Individuals who are sexually active should get regular STD screenings to detect infections early. *(½ M)*
- Avoiding high-risk behaviors: Avoiding practices such as sharing needles and blood transfusion with infected person. *(½ M)*
- Education and communication: Being informed about STDs, their symptoms, and risks can help individuals make responsible choices. Open communication with partners about sexual health is crucial. *(½ M)*

8. **During a medical test, a doctor observed a case where a pregnant woman, Mayra, was diagnosed with an underdeveloped disc-shaped tissue that forms after successful implantation of the embryo.** **(An, Ev)**

(a) Identify the tissue involved in this scenario.

(b) Describe the structure of this tissue in detail.

(c) Predict the consequences on fetal development if this tissue remains underdeveloped.

Ans. (a) The tissue involved in this scenario is the placenta. *(1 M)*

(b) The placenta is a disc-shaped structure that is embedded in the uterine wall after the embryo successfully implants. It has two main sides:

- Embryonic side: It contains finger-like projections called villi. These villi are rich in blood vessels and help facilitate the exchange of nutrients and gases between the mother and the embryo. *(1 M)*
- Maternal side: This side is characterized by blood spaces that surround the villi. These spaces allow the maternal blood to circulate, providing nutrients and removing waste from the embryo's blood. *(1 M)*

(c) If the placenta remains underdeveloped, several negative consequences could arise:

- Insufficient Nutrient Transfer: An underdeveloped placenta might not effectively transfer nutrients from the mother to the fetus, leading to malnutrition and delay in development. *(1 M)*
- Impaired Waste Removal: The waste products generated by the developing fetus might not be adequately removed, which can lead to the accumulation of harmful substances, potentially affecting fetal health. *(1 M)*

9. **Contraception has been significantly revolutionized the landscape of family planning in India, since it was introduced in a structured way. Elaborate on contraception means, and highlight three important advantages of utilizing contraceptive methods? (*Un*)**

Ans. Contraception or birth control, is the use of methods or devices to prevent pregnancy as a result of sexual intercourse. *(1 M)*

The advantages of adopting contraceptive measures are:

1. Planned parenthood: Contraceptive measures help individuals and couples to plan when they want to have children. This allows them to make informed decisions about their family size and spacing of children. *(1 M)*
2. Reduced risk of unintended pregnancies: Contraceptive measures reduce the risk of unintended pregnancies, which can have significant social, economic, and health consequences. *(1 M)*
3. Improved maternal and child health: Adequate spacing between pregnancies reduces the risk of maternal and infant morbidity and mortality. *(1 M)*
4. Prevents STDs: In addition to preventing pregnancies, certain contraceptive methods, especially barrier methods, play a crucial role in reducing the transmission of sexually transmitted infections (STIs), including HIV/AIDS. *(1 M)*

10. ***During the second trimester of a women's pregnancy, she was diagnosed with HIV. The medical team informs her of the high propability of the virus being transmitted to her unborn child. How is HIV transmitted from an HIV-positive mother to her fetus? Explain.*** **(*An*)**

Ans. HIV transmission from an HIV-positive mother to her fetus is a significant concern in prenatal care. The primary modes of transmission include:

- Transplacental Transmission: Generally the HIV virus do not but it can cross from the mother to the foetus via the placenta, especially when the mother's viral load is high or if the placenta is damaged, facilitating the passage of the virus into the fetal bloodstream. *(1½ M)*
- During Labor and Delivery: The risk of HIV transmission escalates during childbirth as the baby is exposed to HIV through contact with the mother's blood and vaginal fluids. The presence of HIV in these fluids can lead to infection at this critical stage. *(2 M)*
- Transmission through Breastfeeding: HIV virus can be present in breast milk, and breastfeeding can transmit the virus from the mother to the infant. This risk persists throughout the duration of breastfeeding. *(1½ M)*

11. **A research study was conducted on 50 men to evaluate the impact of surgical sterilization/ contraceptive on the male reproductive system. The study measured two key parameters and framed in two graphs:**

Graph A: Sperm count in semen – before and after the sterilization procedure.

Graph B: Hormone X levels – a hormone responsible for puberty changes and sperm production. (*An*)

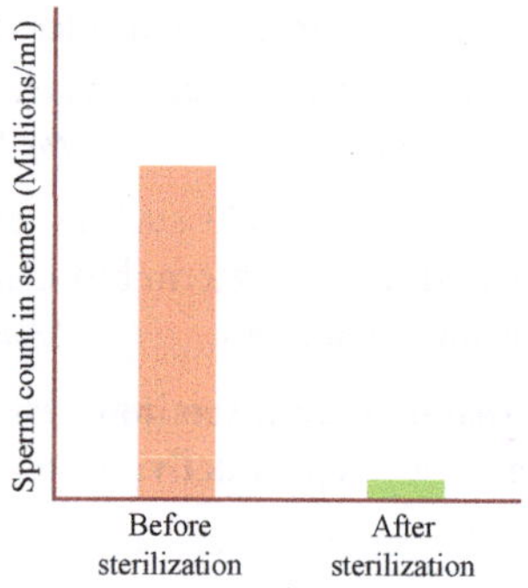

A

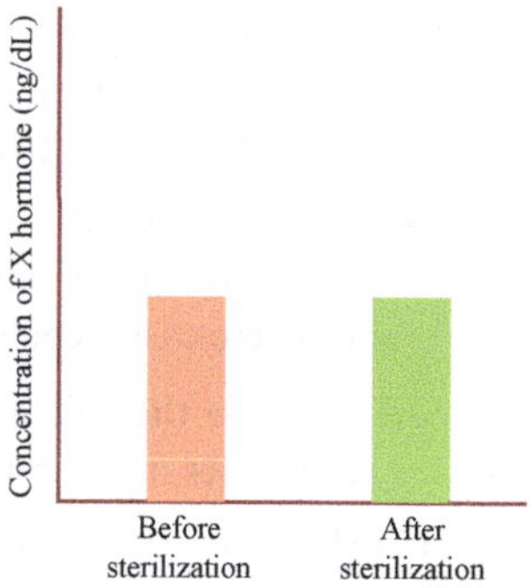

B

The findings were analyzed to understand the physiological and hormonal effects of the procedure. Based on the experiment and your knowledge, answer the following questions:

(*a*) After analysing the Graph A, comment on the effectiveness of surgical sterilization in preventing fertilization.

(*b*) Why is semen still released during intercourse after sterilization?

(*c*) Analyze Graph B and explain the effect of sterilization on hormone X levels.

(*d*) Identify the organ that produces hormone X and illustrate the sperm pathway from this organ to its release in a flow chart.

Ans. (*a*) After analyzing Graph A, which compares sperm count in semen before and after sterilization, the findings show a significant reduction in sperm count post-surgery. Since sperm are no longer present or present in negligible amounts in the semen after the procedure, this confirms that surgical sterilization effectively prevents sperm from being released during ejaculation, thus preventing fertilization. *(1 M)*

(*b*) Even after the surgery, semen is still released during intercourse because the procedure only blocks the sperm from reaching the semen. The seminal vesicles and prostate continue to produce seminal fluid, but without sperm, which means the ejaculate is still present but lacks the ability to fertilize an egg. *(1 M)*

(*c*) Graph B indicates no significant change in hormone X levels pre and post-sterilization, suggesting sterilization does not affect hormone production or the glands/ organs involved in its production. *(1 M)*

(*d*) Hormone X is produced in the testes. *(½ M)*

The sperm pathway is:

Testes → Vas deferens —(Seminal Vesicles + Prostate gland add their secretion)→

Urethra → Released out of the body *(1½ M)*

Hints & Explanations

Multiple Choice Questions

1. (*a*) The radicle (Z) i.e., future root grows first to anchor the plant and absorb water and minerals, which are essential for the growth of the plumule (Y) i.e., future shoot.

2. (*b*) In the given image, structure A is the remaining sepal, the outer protective part of a flower bud, and structure B is the ovules, found inside the ovary, which becomes a seed after fertilisation.
3. (*c*) Sexual reproduction in flowering plants requires two types of gametes (male and female), and fertilisation is a mandatory event leading to the formation of a zygote. However, sexual reproduction generates offspring with genetic diversity, not clones.
4. (*b*) Menstruation signifies the absence of fertilisation, leading to the shedding of the uterine lining. However, with fertilisation and the onset of pregnancy, this shedding is ceased to maintain the uterine lining, which is crucial for supporting and nourishing the foetus.
5. (*a*) Diagram (*a*) is correct as it shows the pollen tube growing through the style to the ovary for fertilization. Only one mature pollen tube is formed during fertilisation and carries male gamete to the egg in the ovary.
6. (*c*) Flower X and Y both contains pistils, the necessary organs for fertilisation and subsequent fruit development. Flower Z, however, has only stamens and no pistil, excluding it from developing fruit.
7. (*a*) At birth, a female's ovaries contain approximately 1 to 2 million immature eggs. These eggs are in an undeveloped state and remain dormant until puberty. After birth, the number of eggs decreases over time due to degeneration, and by puberty, only about 300,000 oocytes remain. Thus, the graph correctly represents the high number of immature eggs in the ovaries at birth.
8. (*d*) The uterus is the central focus of prenatal ultrasound because it is where the zygote implants itself and the embryo develops into the fetus.

Key Takeaways

The student will learn the specific part of the reproductive system where embryonic growth is monitored and understand its significance in prenatal care.

9. (*c*) The almond-shaped glands in the female reproductive system are the ovaries. They secrete several key hormones but primarily oestrogen and progesterone.
10. (*b*) In the reproductive cycle of flowering plants, it begins with the production of gametes. These gametes then participate in fertilisation, leading to the formation of a zygote. The zygote subsequently develops into an embryo.
11. (*d*) Group B contains bisexual flowers, meaning both male and female reproductive organs are present on the same flower. Self-pollination can occur even with the bag covering, as no cross-pollination is required. Group C has unisexual flowers but is not bagged, allowing cross-pollination to occur between male and female flowers, leading to seed development. However, in Group A, unisexual flowers are covered by a bag, preventing pollination, and thus, seeds will not develop.
12. (*c*) A is the Plumule (emerging upwards, developing into the shoot).

    B is the Cotyledon (store reserve food).

    C is the Radicle (emerging downwards, developing into the root).
13. (*d*) The placenta is the vital reproductive tissue providing nourishment and support for a developing embryo. The fallopian tube is the location where sperm and egg meet for fertilisation.
14. (*b*) Unisexual flowers do not possess both stamens and carpel. It is the characteristic of bisexual flower.
15. (*b*) Fertilisation is the process of fusion of nuclei of male and female gamete for the formation of zygote.
16. (*b*) Graph B represents meiosis as DNA content is reduced by half after two divisions. This ensures germ cells have half the DNA, preventing doubling in each generation and maintaining chromosome stability during sexual reproduction.
17. (*c*) Gonorrhoea and syphilis are sexually transmitted diseases caused by bacteria.
18. (*a*) Increasing population size puts more strain on resources and can lead to increased competition for those resources, potentially lowering the standard of living. The intrauterine device (IUD) like the loop, copper-T is inserted into the uterus where it can prevent pregnancy by various mechanisms including affecting the way sperm move and survive.
19. (*a*) A-(*iv*), B-(*iii*), C-(*ii*), D-(*i*)
20. (*c*) Species X, reproducing sexually, has a higher survival rate under environmental changes due to genetic variation, while species Y, reproducing asexually, has a lower survival rate due to lack of variation, reducing adaptability and survival.

Assertion and Reason

1. (*d*) Pollen grains are produced in anther of stamen. Through pollination pollen grains land on the stigma of pistil.
2. (*b*) Fertilisation is the process where the male gamete from the pollen fuses with the female gamete or egg in the ovule. Post-fertilisation, the fertilised ovule matures into a seed, and the ovary of the flower develops into a fruit.
3. (*c*) Bisexual flowers, containing both male and female parts, primarily undergo self-pollination, as both reproductive components are nearby, but not alway, as bisexual flower can also cross pollinate.
4. (*a*) Vagina is called birth canal, because the baby passes through the vagina during birth.
5. (*a*) Scrotum, a pouch containing testis is present outside the abdominal cavity because sperms require a lower temperature than the normal body temperature.
6. (*c*) Puberty in boys is regulated by male sex hormone called testosterone, which is secreted by testes. At puberty, secondary sexual characters like growth of hair on face,

chest, broadening of shoulders and deepening of voice occurs due to the increased production of testosterone.

7. (*c*) The lack of fruit production is directly related to the absence of female reproductive part (not male reproductive part), which would contain the ovules necessary for fertilisation and subsequent fruit development.

8. (*d*) IUDs effectively prevent pregnancy by creating an inhospitable environment for sperm and disrupting fertilisation, but do not prevent the transmission of sexually transmitted infections like HIV.

9. (*a*) Consistent menstrual cycles demonstrate a well-functioning endocrine system and reproductive organs, which is essential for potential fertility and overall reproductive health.

10. (*c*) Surgical method like vasectomy in males and tubectomy in females prevent pregnancy by blocking gamete transport and hence prevent fertilisation. It does not involve removal of gamete producing organs. They are very effective but reversibility is very poor.

11. (*c*) Vasectomy is a surgical method of birth control in which small portion of the sperm duct or vas deferens is cut or tied properly not oviduct.

12. (*d*) HIV/AIDS is caused by the Human Immunodeficiency Virus (HIV) and not by bacteria and it does not spread through casual contact such as sharing food and water. Transmission requires the exchange of certain bodily fluids, such as blood, semen, vaginal secretions, or breast milk.

MISCELLANEOUS EXERCISE

Multiple Choice Questions (1 M)

1. A farmer notices that one of his potato plants is resistant to a particular pest. He decides to use this plant for vegetative propagation. Which outcome is most likely due to this decision? ***(An)***

(*a*) The new plants will show resistance to various pest.

(*b*) The new plants will have resistance for the same pest.

(*c*) The propagated plants will have decreased resistance to the same pest.

(*d*) Each new plant will develop unique pest resistance.

2. Which of the following processes represents P and Q? ***(An)***

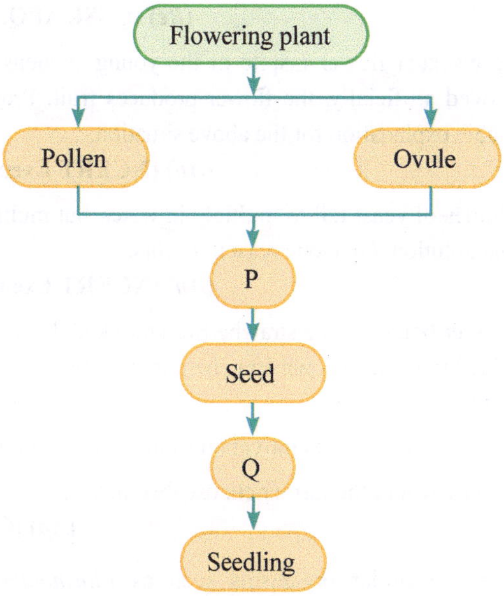

(*a*) Fertilisation, Pollination

(*b*) Pollination, Fertilisation

(*c*) Dispersal, Germination

(*d*) Fertilisation, Germination

3. The correct sequence of organs in the male reproductive system for transport of sperms is ***(Re)* (NCERT Exemplar)**

(*a*) testis → vas deferens → urethra

(*b*) testis → ureter → urethra

(*c*) testis → urethra → ureter

(*d*) testis → vas deferens → ureter

4. Which among the following is not the function of testes at puberty? ***(Re)* (NCERT Exemplar)**

(*i*) Formation of germ cells

(*ii*) Secretion of testosterone

(*iii*) Development of placenta

(*iv*) Secretion of estrogen

(*a*) (*i*) and (*ii*) (*b*) (*ii*) and (*iii*)

(*c*) (*iii*) and (*iv*) (*d*) (*i*) and (*iv*)

5. During adolescence, several changes occur in the human body. Mark one change associated with sexual maturation in boys ***(Re)* (NCERT Exemplar)**

(*a*) loss of milk teeth (*b*) increase in height

(*c*) cracking of voice (*d*) weight gain

6. The diagram below represents the male human reproductive system.

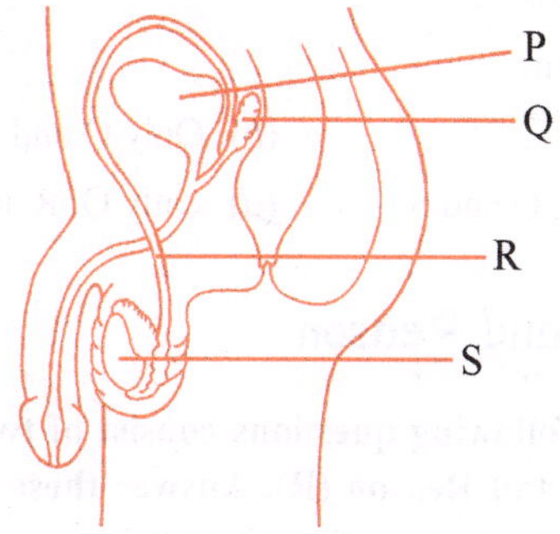

Identify the part that is responsible for the secretion of testosterone. ***(Re)* (CFPQ)**

(*a*) P (*b*) Q

(*c*) R (*d*) S

7. Characters that are transmitted from parents to offspring during reproduction show ***(Un)* (NCERT Exemplar)**

(*a*) only similarities with parents

(*b*) only variations with parents

(*c*) both similarities and variations with parents

(*d*) neither similarities nor variation

8. A feature of reproduction that is common to *Amoeba*, *Spirogyra* and Yeast is that ***(Re)* (NCERT Exemplar)**

(*a*) they reproduce asexually

(*b*) they are all unicellular

(*c*) they reproduce only sexually

(*d*) they are all multicellular

9. The number of chromosomes in parents and offsprings of a particular species remains constant due to ***(Re)* (NCERT Exemplar)**

(*a*) Doubling of chromosomes after zygote formation.

(*b*) Halving of chromosomes during gamete formation.

(*c*) Doubling of chromosomes after gamete formation.

(*d*) Halving of chromosomes after gamete formation.

10. Seema pointed out that the formation of a tough coat around the seed happens after the event of fertilisation in flowering plants. Which of the following statements accurately supports Seema's observation? ***(Un)***

(*a*) The tough coat stops the zygote from dividing, controlling the plant's growth rate.

(*b*) The tough coat provides necessary nutrients for the embryo's growth into a seed.

(*c*) The tough coat acts as a defence mechanism, protecting the seed from environmental stresses.

(*d*) The tough coat prevents the seed from being dispersed far from the parent plant.

11. Which of the following method/s are useful to prevent fertilisation even when ovulation occurs? **(*Re*) (CBSE APQ, 2023)**

(P) Surgical blocking of the fallopian tube

(Q) Copper-T

(R) Oral pills

(S) Condom

(*a*) Only P (*b*) Only Q and R

(*c*) Only P, Q and S (*d*) Only Q, R and S

Assertion and Reason (1 M)

Direction: The following questions consist of two statements – Assertion (A) and Reason (R). Answer these questions by selecting the appropriate option given below:

(*a*) Both A and R are true, and R is the correct explanation of A.

(*b*) Both A and R are true, but R is not the correct explanation of A.

(*c*) A is true, but R is false.

(*d*) A is false, but R is true.

1. Assertion (A): A particular plant species shows a high rate of vegetative propagation in a specific area, which indicates that the plant is an invasive species.

Reason (R): A high rate of vegetative propagation results in the production of a high number of genetically similar plants. **(*Un*)**

2. Assertion (A): Priya guessed that the ovule of an angiosperm flower develops into a fruit after fertilisation, so she decided to germinate it to produce seedlings.

Reason (R): Her mother explained that upon germination, the seed gives rise to the radicle and plumule. **(*Un*)**

3. Assertion (A): Zygote is the vital link between two generations of an organism.

Reason (R): The two gametes fuse to form a single zygote. **(*Re*)**

4. Assertion (A): Gonorrhoea and syphilis are viral diseases.

Reason (R): Gonorrhoea and syphilis can be sexually transmitted. **(*Re*)**

5. Assertion (A): Pregnancy can be prevented by adopting a method or procedure by which sperms released during copulation can be prevented from meeting the ovum and fertilising it.

Reason (R): Vasectomy and tubectomy are the two such methods of preventing pregnancy which do not allow sperms to meet ovum by acting as a barrier between them. **(*Re*)**

6. Assertion (A): A zygote is formed by the fusion of male and female gametes whereas an embryo is formed by the repeated cell division of a zygote.

Reason (R): The secretions of seminal vesicles and prostate gland provide nutrition to the sperms and also make their further transport easier. **(*Un*)**

Subjective Questions

Very Short Answer Type Questions (2 M)

1. (*i*) Name the reproductive and non-reproductive parts of ***Rhizopus*.**

(*ii*) How are the spores protected till they begin to grow? **(*Re*) (CBSE APQ, 2023)**

2. In a bisexual flower inspite of the young stamens being removed artificially, the flower produces fruit. Provide a suitable explanation for the above situation. **(*An*) (NCERT Exemplar)**

3. Colonies of yeast fail to multiply in water, but multiply in sugar solution. Give one reason for this. **(*An*) (NCERT Exemplar)**

4. A farmer bought some strawberries and liked the taste. He decided to grow his own strawberries that should have the same taste.

(*a*) Which method of cultivation should the farmer adopt?

(*b*) Why would the farmer choose this method? **(*Ap*) (CFPQ)**

5. Some unicellular organisms such as *Plasmodium* and *Leishmania* differ in the manner in which they reproduce. Name and explain the reproductive process taking place in them. **(*Un*) (CBSE, 2024)**

OR

What is puberty? Mention any two changes that are common to both boys and girls in early teenage years. **(*Re*) (CBSE, 2022)**

6. Name two types of germ cells present in human beings. List two structural differences between the two. **(*Re*) (CBSE, 2024)**

7. Ravi cultivated mustard, a plant with bisexual flowers, on his farm. His plants were diseased due to a gene defect and therefore had reduced yield. Ravi removed the stamens from the diseased plants and also planted fresh disease free mustard plants where he removed the pistils. How will Ravi's strategy help in improving the yield of mustard? **(*An*)(CBSE SQP, 2023)**

Short Answer Type Questions (3 M)

1. Write one main difference between asexual and sexual mode of reproduction. Which species is likely to have comparatively better chances of survival- the one reproducing asexually or the one reproducing sexually? Give reason to justify your answer. ***(Un)* (CBSE, 2018)**

2. (*a*) List three techniques that have been developed to prevent pregnancy.

   (*b*) Which technique of contraception used by females is not meant for males?

   (*c*) How does the use of these techniques have a direct impact on the health and prosperity of a family? ***(Re)* (CBSE, 2017)**

   OR

   A certain organism has the remarkable ability to break itself into multiple pieces, each capable of developing into a new individual. ***(Un)***

   (*a*) What is the specific term used to describe this method of reproduction?

   (*b*) Is this form of reproduction classified as sexual or asexual? Provide an explanation.

   (*c*) How does this process relate to the concept of regeneration, and what distinguishes it from the regeneration processes in other organisms?

3. Define the term pollination. Differentiate between self pollination and cross pollination. What is the significance of pollination? ***(Un)* (CBSE, 2020)**

4. A farmer enjoyed the sweet, low-acidity, and seedless Navel oranges he purchased. He wants to grow his own orange plants with the same traits. Answer the following questions. ***(Ap)***

   (*a*) Which cultivation method should the farmer use to grow oranges with identical traits and why?

   (*b*) If the orange plants were infected by a disease, would the chosen method in (*a*) needs to be changed? Why or why not?

5. A research team is studying a mutation in *Leishmania* that disrupts the whip-like structure during binary fission. ***(An)***

   (*a*) Predict the impact of this mutation on the process of binary fission and survival of the organism.

   (*b*) How could this mutation influence the spread of *kala-azar* in humans? Justify your answer.

   (*c*) How binary fission differ in *Amoeaba* and *Leishmania*?

Long Answer Type Questions (5 M)

1. (*a*) What happens when the egg is not fertilised?

   (*b*) How is sperm genetically different from a human egg/ova?

   (*c*) List any three contraceptive methods practiced for family planning. Mention how these methods work. ***(Un, Re)* (CBSE, 2023)**

2. The science lab teacher prepared two slides under the microscope, each showcasing a different unicellular organism. Students were tasked to observe and answer the following questions based on their identification of the organisms:

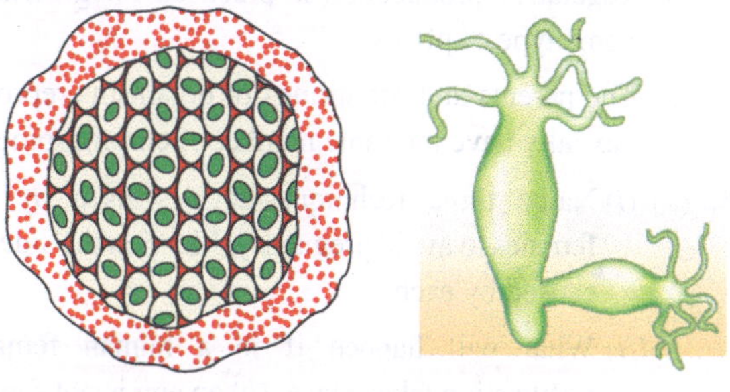

X Y

   (*a*) Identify Organism X and Y.

   (*b*) How does the mode of reproduction differ between Organism X and Organism Y?

   (*c*) If this division process taking place in Y stopped midway, what impact would it have on the organism's survival?

   OR

   (*a*) Identify the given diagram. Name the part 1 to 5.

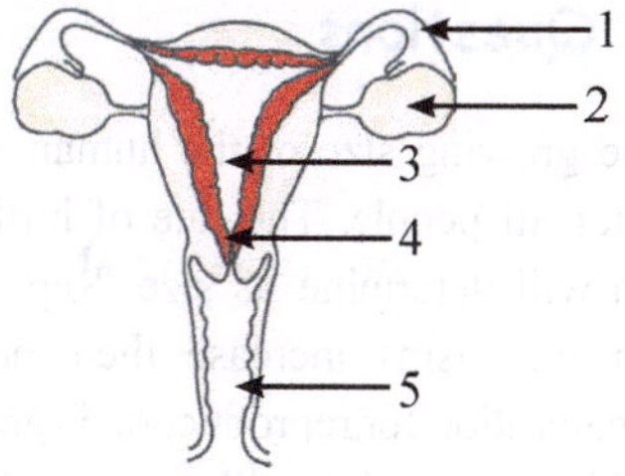

   (*b*) What is contraception? List three advantages of adopting contraceptive measures. ***(Re)* (CBSE, 2019)**

3. (*a*) Draw a diagram showing germination of pollen on stigma of a flower and mark on it the following organs/parts:

   (*i*) Pollen Grain (*ii*) Pollen tube

   (*iii*) Stigma (*iv*) Female germ cell

   (*b*) State the significance of pollen tube.

   (*c*) Name the parts of flower that develop after fertilisation into

   (*i*) Seed (*ii*) Fruit ***(Cr, Re)***

   OR

   (*a*) Use of a condom is beneficial for both the sexes involved in a sexual act." Justify this statement giving two reasons.

   (*b*) How do oral contraceptive help in avoiding pregnancies?

   (*c*) What is sex selective abortion? How does it affect a healthy society? (State any one consequence) ***(Un)* (CBSE, 2020)**

4. Give reason for the following : ***(Un, Ev)* (CBSE, 2023)**

   (*a*) During reproduction inheritance of different proteins will lead to altered body designs.

(*b*) Fertilisation cannot take place in flowers if pollination does not occur.

(*c*) All multicellular organisms cannot give rise to new individuals through fragmentation or regeneration.

(*d*) Vegetative propagation is practised for growing only some type of plants.

(*e*) The parents and off-springs of organisms reproducing sexually have the same number of chromosomes.

5. (*a*) (*i*) Name three techniques/devices used by human females to avoid pregnancy. Mention the side effects caused by each.

(*ii*) What will happen if in a human female (*a*) fertilisation takes place, (*b*) an egg is not fertilised? **(*Re*) (CBSE, 2024)**

OR

(*b*) (*i*) Draw a diagram showing spore formation in *Rhizopus* and label the (*a*) reproductive and (*b*) non-reproductive parts. Why does *Rhizopus* not multiply on a dry slice of bread?

(*ii*) Name and explain the process by which reproduction takes place in *Hydra*. **(*Cr, Un*) (CBSE, 2024)**

Case Based Questions

Case Based-I: The growing size of the human population is a cause of concern for all people. The rate of birth and death in a given population will determine its size. Reproduction is the process by which organisms increase their population. The process of sexual maturation for reproduction is gradual and takes place while general body growth is still going on. Some degree of sexual maturation does not necessarily mean that the mind or body is ready for sexual acts or for having and bringing up children. Various contraceptive devices are being used by human beings to control the size of population. **(*Re*) (CBSE, 2020)**

(*i*) List two common signs of sexual maturation in boys and girls. *(1 M)*

(*ii*) What is the result of reckless female foeticide? *(1 M)*

(*iii*) Which contraceptive method changes the hormonal balance of the body? *(1 M)*

(*iv*) Write two factors that determine the size of a population. *(1 M)*

Case Based-II: When an insect sits on the flower of a plant then some particles A present in the top of little stalks in the flower attached to its body hair. When this insect now sits on the flower of another similar plant, then particles A attached to the hair of insect are put on the top of a flask-shaped organ at the centre of the flower. The particle, A grows a long tube B from the top of a flask-shaped organ through which C moves down and reaches the bottom part of the flask-shaped organ. Here C fuses with the nucleus of D contained in structrue E. The fusion of C and D forms a new cell F which grows and develops into a seed of the plant. **(*An*)**

(*i*) What are particles A? What is the process of transferring A from one flower to another flower of the similar plant by an insect? *(1 M)*

(*ii*) What is the name of tube B? *(1 M)*

(*iii*) What will happen if C does not fuse with D? *(1 M)*

(*iv*) What does structure F develop into? *(1 M)*

OR

Where does the development of structure A take place? *(1 M)*

Case Based-III: Asexual reproduction involves a single parent to produce offsprings without the formation of gametes. It occurs by the following ways:

Fission, Budding, Fragmentation, Spore formation and Regeneration. In one of the methods like regeneration, *Planaria* A is cut horizontally into three pieces- L, M and N and *Planaria* B is cut vertically into two equal halves –O and P. **(*Un*) (CBSE, 2024)**

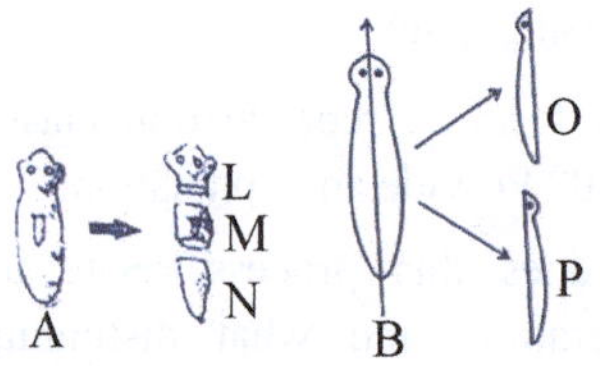

(*i*) Which of the cut pieces of the two *Planaria* could regenerate to form a complete organism? *(1 M)*

(*ii*) Give an example of another organism which follows the same mode of reproduction as *Planaria.* *(1 M)*

(*iii*) What is the meaning of 'development' in regeneration? *(2 M)*

OR

(*iii*) Differentiate between regeneration and fragmentation. *(2 M)*

Case Based-IV: X and Y are two human beings. The organ A in the reproductive system of X releases a mature gamete B once a month which goes into a tube-like structure C through a funnel-like opening. The organ D in the reproductive system of Y makes and releases gametes E which pass through a duct F and are introduced by an organ of Y, into the body of X. B and E fuse together in C to form a new cell G. The cell G divides repeatedly to form a ball of cells H which further develops and gets embedded in the lining of organ I of reproductive system of X where it grows and develops into a baby. **(*An*)**

(*i*) Describe the significance of organ I in the development of a baby. *(1 M)*

(*ii*) What will happen if E is not present to fuse with B? *(1 M)*

(*iii*) State one physical and genetical difference between B and E. *(2 M)*

OR

State the difference between organs A and D. *(2 M)*

Case Based-V: Radhika is an avid gardener who has a wide variety of flowering plants in her garden. One day, some mischievous children entered her garden and plucked a leaf X from some of the plants and scattering them around the garden. A few days later, Radhika noticed that new buds were sprouting from the leaves that had fallen on the ground. ***(Un)***

(*i*) Explain the process involved in the sprouting of new buds from leaf X. *(2 M)*

(*ii*) Discuss the significance of leaf X in the propagation of flowering plants. How can this natural process be advantageous for gardeners? *(1 M)*

(*iii*) In the case of the money plant, which plant part has the ability to reproduce through a process similar to that observed with leaf X? *(1 M)*

OR

Explain how the process adopted by leaf X contributes to genetic diversity. *(1 M)*

ANSWER KEYS

Multiple Choice Questions

1. (*b*) **2.** (*d*) **3.** (*a*) **4.** (*c*) **5.** (*c*) **6.** (*d*) **7.** (*c*) **8.** (*a*) **9.** (*b*) **10.** (*c*) **11.** (*c*)

Assertion and Reason

1. (*b*) **2.** (*d*) **3.** (*a*) **4.** (*d*) **5.** (*c*) **6.** (*b*)

HINTS & EXPLANATIONS

Multiple Choice Questions

1. (*b*) Vegetative propagation produces clones, ensuring that the new plants inherit the parent's pest resistance trait directly, maintaining genetic identity and consistency in resistance. It doesn't lead to decreased or development of any unique resistance traits in offspring, as there is no genetic variation or recombination involved.
2. (*d*) Pollen grains and ovule fertilise to produce seed. Seeds on germination produce seedling that emerges radicle (future root) and plumule (future shoot).
3. (*a*) The correct sequence of sperm transport is:

   testis ⟶ vas deferens ⟶ urethra
4. (*c*) Development of placenta and secretion of estrogen is not the function of testes. Placenta develops in females during pregnancy. Estrogen is a female hormone produces by ovaries.
5. (*c*) The cracking of voice during adolescence in boys is a direct result of sexual maturation, linked to hormonal changes that affect the larynx and vocal cords. This change is specific to sexual maturity, unlike general growth indicators such as height and weight gain, or loss of milk teeth.
6. (*d*) The testes (S) are the site of testosterone production, crucial for male sexual characteristics and reproduction. The bladder (P) stores urine, seminal vesicles (Q) contribute fluid to semen, enhancing sperm viability, and the vas deferens (R) channels sperm from the testes.
7. (*c*) Characters that are transmitted from parents to offspring during reproduction show both similarities (as half of chromosomes come from father and half from the mother) and variations (due to genetic combination, mutation etc.) with parents.
8. (*a*) *Amoeba*, *Spirogyra* and Yeast all of them show asexual mode of reproduction.
9. (*b*) Gametes are formed through reduction division that halves the number of chromosomes in each gamete. This ensures that gametes are haploid (n), containing half the chromosome number of the parent cells (2n). When two gametes, one from each parent, fuse during fertilisation, the diploid chromosome number is restored in the offspring.

10. (*c*) The tough coat around the ovule post-fertilisation is crucial for shielding the developing seed from environmental stress, ensuring its survival and germination. It does not prevent zygotic division or supply nutrients. Additionally, the coat doesn't inhibit but rather aids seed dispersion by providing durability during dispersal processes.

11. (*c*) (P) Surgical blocking of the fallopian tubes, i.e., tubectomy, blocks the egg's path; (Q) Copper-T creates a sperm-hostile environment; and (S) condoms prevent sperm from meeting the egg. In all these contraceptive methods, ovulation occurs, but fertilisation does not. However, (R) oral pills prevent fertilisation by inhibiting ovulation.

Assertion and Reason

1. (*b*) The invasive nature of a plant is determined by its ability to spread rapidly and outcompete native species, not just by its reproductive strategy or the genetic similarity of its offspring. Thus, while both statements are accurate, the reason (R) does not serve as an explanation for assertion (A).

2. (*d*) Priya's assumption is incorrect because it is the ovary that develops into a fruit after fertilisation, not the ovule. The ovule develops into a seed. Her mother's explanation is accurate: upon germination, the seed (which developed from the ovule) gives rise to the radicle and plumule, which are the embryonic root and shoot, respectively.

3. (*a*) The zygote carries genetic information from both parents to the offspring, forming through the fusion of parental gametes, thus ensuring species continuity. The creation of the zygote indeed links one generation to the next in sexual reproduction.

4. (*d*) Gonorrhoea and syphilis are bacterial diseases. Both of these diseases can be sexually transmitted.

5. (*c*) Vasectomy and tubectomy are surgical methods of contraception. Vasectomy prevent transfer of sperms from the testis to urethra and tubectomy prevents reaching of ova from the ovary to the uterus.

6. (*b*) The reason discusses sperm nutrition and transport, mechanisms involved before fertilisation which is unrelated to the assertion which explains the events occurring after fertilisation, namely zygote formation and embryonic development.

Subjective Questions

Very Short Answer Type Questions

1. (*i*) Non-reproductive parts of *Rhizopus* are hyphae and reproductive parts are the *sporangia* which contain the spores. *(1 M)*

   (*ii*) The spores are covered by thick walls that protect them until they come in contact with a moist surface and begin to grow. *(1 M)*

2. After the removal of stamens, a flower can still produce fruit due to cross-pollination, where, the flower can receive pollen from other flowers through agents like wind, insects, or animals, leading to successful fertilisation and fruit development. *(2 M)*

3. Yeast colonies thrive in sugar solutions due to the presence of glucose, which serves as a vital energy source for their growth and multiplication. Conversely, in plain water, the absence of essential nutrients, such as sugars, inhibits their ability to proliferate, as they lack the necessary resources for energy production and cellular processes. *(2 M)*

4. (*a*) The farmer should adopt vegetative propagation. *(1 M)*

   (*b*) The farmer would opt for vegetative propagation because it produces genetically identical offspring, ensuring the strawberries maintain the same desired taste as the original plant. *(1 M)*

5. *Plasmodium* reproduces asexually through multiple fission. In this process, the *Plasmodium* cell undergoes multiple nuclear divisions, forming several daughter nuclei within a single cell covered with a protective coat, which eventually burst and give rise to multiple offspring. *(1 M)*

   Leishmania reproduces asexually through binary fission, where one cell divides longitudinally into two identical cells in a definite orientation. *(1 M)*

Topper's Explanation

24. (1) Plasmodium reproduce by multiple fission. In this process a single cell of plasmodium forms a protective coating (cyst) during unfavourable condition. The cell divides multiple times at once producing several daughter cells.

(2) Leishmania reproduce by binary fission. In this process, the unicellular organism Leishmania divides into two daughter cells. This happens by division of nucleus and cytoplasm of the cell. longitudinally.

OR

Puberty is the process of physical maturation where an adolescent reaches sexual maturity and become capable of reproduction that typically occurs between the ages of 8 and 13 in girls, and 9 and 14 in boys. *(1 M)*

Two changes that are common to both boys and girls during early teenage years are:

- Both boys and girls experience a rapid growth during puberty. *(½ M)*
- Growth of hairs in some parts of the body such as armpits and genital areas. *(½ M)*

6. The two types of germ cells in human beings are the male gamete (sperm) and the female gamete (ovum). *(1 M)*

   The structural differences between male and female germ cells in human beings are:

Male Gamete (Sperm)	Female Gamete (Ovum)
Smaller in size, motile	Larger in size, non-motile
Contains little to no nutrient stores	Contains nutrient stores for the developing embryo

(½ + ½ M)

7. Ravi's strategy helps him in improving the yield of mustard by:

   - Enforcing cross-pollination: By manually creating unisexual flowers-removing stamens from diseased plants and pistils from healthy ones. Ravi ensures that cross-pollination is the only possible route for reproduction. This method prevents the diseased plants from self-pollinating and propagating the genetic defect. *(1 M)*

- Promoting genetic variation: The cross-pollination between healthy and diseased plants promotes genetic diversity, which can lead to a higher proportion of disease-resistant plants and improved yield. *(1M)*

Short Answer Type Questions

1.

Asexual Reproduction	Sexual Reproduction
Involves only one parent, and no fusion of gametes occurs leading to genetically identical offsprings.	Requires the fusion of male and female gametes from two different parents leads to offspring having genetic variation.

(1 M)

Species that reproduce sexually are likely to have a better chance of survival because it creates genetic variety, giving species the flexibility to adapt to changing environments and challenges, which greatly improves their ability to survive and evolve over time. *(2 M)*

2. (*a*) Three techniques that have been developed to prevent pregnancy are:

(*i*) Condoms: Barrier method of contraception that prevent the sperm from reaching the egg. *(½ M)*

(*ii*) Sterilisation: A surgical procedure that involves cutting and sealing the gamete carrying ducts or tubes in order to prevent fertilisation. Vasectomy in males and tubectomy in females. *(½ M)*

(*iii*) Intrauterine devices (IUDs): Small devices inserted into the uterus to prevent sperm from reaching the egg or for an egg to implant in the uterine lining. Eg. Loop, copper T, etc. *(½ M)*

(*b*) The technique that is not meant for males is intrauterine devices (IUDs). These are meant for females and are inserted into the uterus. *(½ M)*

(*c*) By preventing unintended pregnancies, these techniques help to reduce the burden of unwanted children on families. This can help to improve the economic and social well-being of families by allowing them to plan their families and invest in the education and health of their children. *(1 M)*

Topper's Explanation

13→ Pregnancy prevention techniques :

1) Mechanical barriers like cervical cap, condoms etc.
2) Surgical methods like Tubectomy, vasectomy.
3) Using IUCD's like loop, Copper-T.

Using IUCD's (like loop, copper-T) & also oral contraceptives are not meant for males.

Impact on health & prosperity of a family :

1) Better standard of living.
2) Better and improved resources.
3) More focus on children who are already born.
4) Prevention from STDs like HIV AIDS, syphilis etc.

OR

(*a*) The term for this method of reproduction is fragmentation. *(½ M)*

(*b*) This form of reproduction is classified as asexual. Fragmentation involves the splitting of an organism into pieces, and these pieces can develop into new individuals without the involvement of specialized reproductive cells (gametes) from different parents, which is characteristic of a sexual reproduction. *(1 M)*

(*c*) Fragmentation does align with the concept of regeneration, as it also involves the ability of an organism to regrow and develop from a broken or fragmented part. *(½ M)*

Feature	Fragmentation	Regeneration
Definition	A form of asexual reproduction where an organism splits into fragments, each capable of growing independently into a new organism.	A biological process where organisms regrow lost or damaged parts, sometimes potentially restoring a full organism.
Example	*Spirogyra*	*Planaria*

(1 M)

Mistakes 101 : What not to do!

- Not highlighting the intentional breaking of the organism into multiple pieces as a key aspect of fragmentation.
- Neglecting to mention that regeneration in other organisms typically involves the regrowth of specific lost or damaged body parts, whereas fragmentation involves the development of new individuals from the fragmented pieces.

3. The process by which transfer of pollen grains occurs from anther to stigma of the flower is known as pollination. *(1 M)*

Feature	Self-Pollination	Cross-Pollination
Definition	Pollination that occurs within the same flower or between flowers of the same plant.	Pollination that occurs between flowers of different plants.
Agents Involved	Does not typically involve external agents; relies on the flower's own mechanisms to transfer pollen.	Involves external agents such as wind, water, or animals to transfer pollen from one flower to another.

(1 M)

Significance of pollination:
Pollination play a crucial role in fertilisation by facilitating the transfer of male gametes to female eggs, leading to seed production and the subsequent generation of new offspring. Hence, pollination is important to develop new offsprings. *(1 M)*

4. (*a*) The farmer should use vegetative propagation. *(1 M)*

Vegetative propagation ensures that the new orange plants are genetically identical to the parent plant. This method preserves desirable traits of Navel oranges, as it bypasses sexual reproduction and directly uses plant parts like stems or buds. *(1 M)* (*b*) No, the method would not need to be changed unless the infection affects the plant at the genetic level. Diseases affecting the plant externally or at the tissue level can be avoided during propagation by using healthy, disease-free parent tissue. Since vegetative propagation does not alter DNA, the new plants will not inherit the disease if care is taken to select uninfected plant material. *(1 M)*

5. (*a*) The whip-like structure helps in maintaining orientation during binary fission. If disrupted, it may lead to unequal division, resulting in non-functional daughter cells or cell death, reducing survival chances. *(1 M)*

(*b*) Since *Leishmania* reproduction would be disrupted, its population would decline, potentially reducing infection rates and the spread of *kala-azar*. Without sufficient replication, the parasite's ability to infect and propagate in humans is significantly reduced. *(1 M)*

(*c*) In *Amoeba*, binary fission occurs in any plane because the organism has a simpler, irregular shape without specialized structures. *(½ M)*

In contrast, *Leishmania* undergoes binary fission in a specific orientation to ensure that both daughter cells inherit the whip-like structure, which is crucial for movement and survival. *(½ M)*

Long Answer Type Questions

1. (*a*) If the egg is not fertilised, it does not develop into a zygote or implant into the uterus without undergoing embryonic development. The body then expels the unfertilised egg along with the uterine lining during menstruation. *(1 M)*

(*b*) Genetic differences between sperm and egg:

Sperm	Egg/Ova
Contains 23 chromosomes, including either an X or a Y chromosome, determining the baby's sex.	Contains 23 chromosomes, always providing an X chromosome.

(1 M)

(*c*) Three contraceptive methods:

1. Condoms: Act as a physical barrier that intercepts sperm, preventing them from entering the female reproductive tract and reaching the egg. *(1 M)*
2. Oral contraceptive pills: These pills use a combination of hormones, inhibiting ovulation. Without the release of an egg, fertilisation cannot occur, effectively preventing pregnancy. *(1 M)*
3. Intrauterine Devices (IUDs): IUDs are small, T-shaped devices inserted into the uterus to create an inhospitable environment for sperm, thereby preventing fertilisation. *(1 M)*

2. (*a*) Organism X is *Plasmodium* and organism Y is *Hydra*. *(1+1 M)*

(*b*)

Aspect	*Plasmodium* (Organism X)	*Hydra* (Organism Y)
Mode of Reproduction	Asexual reproduction through multiple fission.	Asexual reproduction through budding.
Process of Division	The nucleus divides multiple times before the cytoplasm splits, forming many daughter cells.	A bud grows on the parent, develops into a new organism, and detaches.

(2 M)

(*c*) If the division process (e.g., budding) in Organism Y were interrupted midway, the organism would fail to reproduce. Over time, this would lead to a decline in the population, endangering its survival. Since asexual reproduction is the primary means of multiplication for such organisms, any disruption to this process could prove catastrophic. *(1 M)*

OR

(*a*) The given diagram shows the female reproductive system.

1- Oviduct/ fallopian tube *(½ M)*

2- Ovary *(½ M)*

3- Uterus *(½ M)*

4- Cervix *(½ M)*

5- Vagina *(½ M)*

(*b*) Contraception is the deliberate use of methods or devices to prevent pregnancy as a result of sexual intercourse. *(½ M)*

The advantages of adopting contraceptive measures are:

1. Planned parenthood: Contraceptive measures help individuals and couples to plan when they want to have children. This allows them to make informed decisions about their family size and spacing of children. *(1 M)*
2. Improved maternal and child health: Adequate spacing between pregnancies reduces the risk of maternal and infant mortality. Contraceptive measures also help prevent sexually transmitted infections (STIs), including HIV/AIDS. *(1 M)*

3. (*a*)

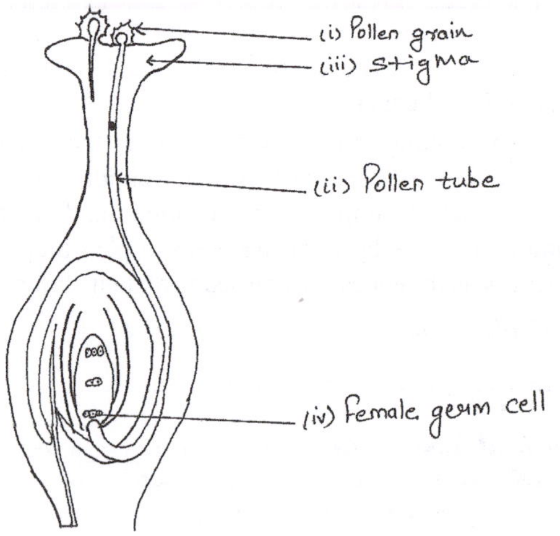

(2 M)

(*b*) The significance of the pollen tube is that it plays a crucial role in the process of sexual reproduction in plants by facilitating the process of fertilisation. Pollen tube carries the male germ cell to reach the ovary and fuse with the female germ cell. *(1 M)*

(*c*) (*i*) Seed: The ovules of the flower develop into seeds after fertilisation. *(1 M)*

(*ii*) Fruit: The ovary of the flower develops into the fruit after fertilisation. *(1 M)*

OR

(*a*) Use of a condom is beneficial for both the sexes involved in a sexual act as it:

- Protect, against sexually transmitted infections (STIs): Condoms provide a physical barrier that can help prevent the transmission of STIs such as HIV, chlamydia, and gonorrhoea. Both partners benefit from this protection. *(1 M)*
- Preventing unwanted pregnancies: Condoms are an effective method of contraception and can help prevent unwanted pregnancies. *(1 M)*

(*b*) Oral contraceptives help in avoiding pregnancies by:

- Releasing synthetic hormones that prevent ovulation (the release of an egg) from the ovaries. *(½ M)*
- Thickening the cervical mucus, making it difficult for sperm to enter the uterus and fertilize an egg. *(½ M)*

(*c*) Sex-selective abortion refers to the practice of aborting a fetus based on its sex. It is usually done in societies that value male children over female children. *(1 M)*

Sex-selective abortion can have several negative consequences for a healthy society, including:

Gender imbalance: A large number of male births and a smaller number of female births can lead to a gender imbalance in the population. *(1 M)*

4. (*a*) Proteins are the products of gene expression, determining the body design and genes are passed down from parents to offspring. Variation in the genetic material can lead to different proteins being synthesized, which can alter the physical characteristics of the resulting organisms. *(1 M)*

(*b*) Fertilisation cannot take place in flowers if pollination does not occur because pollination is the process by which pollen is transferred from the male part of a flower (the anther) to the female part of a flower (the stigma). Hence only after pollination can fertilisation happen. *(1 M)*

(*c*) Not all multicellular organisms can give rise to new individuals through fragmentation or regeneration. This limitation is due to the absence of cellular totipotency, particularly in complex species. *(1 M)*

(*d*) Vegetative propagation is ideal for plants that reproduce through parts like leaves, stems, or roots (consisting cells that are able to produce bud/new plant), especially when seeds are not viable or desirable. However, it is not suitable for all plant species, particularly those that do not naturally reproduce vegetatively. *(1 M)*

(*e*) In sexual reproduction, the consistent chromosome count between parents and offspring is ensured through the fusion of two haploid gametes by the process of fertilisation. This process combines their genetic material to form a diploid zygote, preserving the species-specific chromosome number across generations. *(1 M)*

Topper's Explanation

35. (a) Cellular DNA is the information source of making proteins in the cell. DNA provides the blueprint for all structure and functions of cell. Inheritence of ~~DNA~~ different proteins will thus lead to altered body designs. Proteins determine the function of hormones and enzymes in the body. Altered body design will lead to difference in efficiency of hormones, enzymes and body functions, and variation.

(b) Pollin~~ag~~ation is the transfer of pollen grains from anther of a flower to stigma ~~for flower~~ of a flower. If pollination does not occur, the pollen grains will not be able to reach the egg cell for fusion of male and female gametes (fertilization).

(c) It is unsuitable to depend on being cut accidentantly for mode of reproduction. The organisms cannot rely on being cut and divided at any point on body. Multicellular organisms have specialised cells for different functions. Their cells are divided and differentiated and specific. Thus, they have seperate gamete cells for reproduction. Gametes only can differentiate and divide to form tissues for different functions.

(d) Vegetative propagation is used for plants which have lost the ability to produce viable seeds for reproduction. Moreover, vegetative propagation provides ~~seed~~ little variations between parent and offspring. Variations are sometimes desirable.

(e) This is due to law of segregation, which states that during gamete formation, the alleles of genes separate and only one allele for each gene is taken up by the gamete. Thus, gametes are haploid and contain half the no. of chromosomes. When the male and female gamete fertilise, they restore the total no. of chromosomes in the offspring.

5. (*a*) (*i*) Three contraceptive techniques/devices are:

Surgical methods: Fallopian tubes in females are blocked *via* surgery. Side effects include infections if not performed properly. *(1 M)*

Hormonal contraceptives: Oral contraceptive pills alter hormonal balance to prevent egg release. Side effects can include nausea, weight gain, mood changes, hormonal imbalances. *(1 M)*

Intrauterine devices (IUDs): Devices like the copper-T are inserted into the uterus. They can cause side effects such as irritation of uterus. *(1 M)*

(*ii*) In human female if:

(*a*) Fertilisation takes place: The fertilised egg (zygote) begins to divide, forming an embryo that implants in the uterus lining, which thickens to nourish the growing embryo. *(1 M)*

(*b*) An egg is not fertilised: The unfertilised egg will live for about a day. The uterine lining slowly breaks and comes out through the vagina as blood and mucous, process called menstruation. *(1 M)*

OR

(*b*) (*i*)

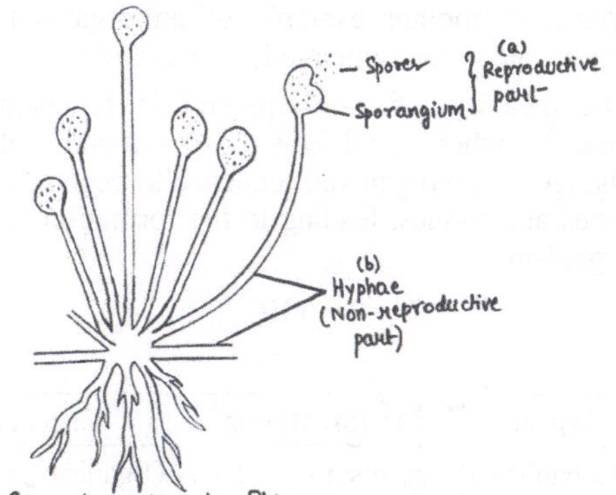

Spore formation in Rhizopus *(2 M)*

Rhizopus does not multiply on dry bread because the spores require a moist surface for growth, and a dry slice of bread does not provide the necessary moisture for spore germination. *(1 M)*

(*ii*) The reproduction in *Hydra* occurs through a process called budding. *(1 M)*

In this process, a small bud develops as an outgrowth due to repeated cell division at one specific site. *(½ M)*

This bud gradually grows and develops into a tiny individual and when fully mature, the bud detaches from the parent body to live independently. *(½ M)*

Case Based Questions

Case Based-I

(*i*) Two common signs of sexual maturation in boys and girls are:

(*a*) Growth of hairs in particular body regions like the pubic area and underarms. (½ M)

(*b*) Occurrence of acne. (½ M)

(*ii*) Reckless female foeticide refers to the illegal practice of aborting unborn female children, leading to an abnormal gender ratio between men and women. (1 M)

(*iii*) The oral contraceptive method works by changing the hormonal balance in the body, which in turn prevents ovulation in women who use these pills. (1 M)

(*iv*) Two key factors that determines the population size are: Birth rate and Death rate. (1 M)

Case Based-II

(*i*) A represents pollen grains (½ M)

The process of transferring A from one flower to another flower of a similar plant by an insect is called as cross-pollination. (½ M)

(*ii*) B represents the pollen tube. (1 M)

(*iii*) If C (the male gamete) does not fuse with D (the female gamete), fertilisation will fail, preventing the formation of a zygote and subsequent development of a seed. (1 M)

(*iv*) Structure F, formed from the fusion of the male and female gametes, develops into a seed, which can germinate to grow into a new plant. (1 M)

OR

Structure A, which are the pollen grains, develops in the anthers, the male reproductive part of the flower. (1 M)

Case Based-III

(*i*) Both cut pieces of *Planaria* A (L, M and N) and *Planaria* B (O and P) have the potential to regenerate into a complete organism. (1 M)

(*ii*) *Hydra* is another example of an organism which can regenerate in the same mode as *Planaria*. (1 M)

(*iii*) The meaning of 'development' in regeneration is the process where proliferated specialized cells undergo changes in an organized sequence to become different cell types and tissues, leading to the formation of a complete organism. (2 M)

OR

(*iii*)

Aspect	Fragmentation	Regeneration
Mechanism	Organism breaks into fragments and each fragment grows into an individual organism.	Organism regenerate new individuals from missing body parts.
Role	Always leads to reproduction; a primary mode of asexual reproduction for survival.	Doesn't always lead to reproduction; can regenerate lost body parts like a lizard's tail.

(2 M)

Case Based-IV

(*i*) Organ I, the uterus, is crucial as it provides a secure and nourishing environment where the embryo implants, grows and develops into a baby over nine months. (1 M)

(*ii*) If E (sperm) doesn't fuse with B (egg), no fertilisation occurs, preventing zygote formation. Consequently, the uterine lining sheds during menstruation, as the body disposes of the unfertilized egg. (1 M)

(*iii*)

Feature	Gamete B (Egg)	Gamete E (Sperm)
Physical	Larger and non-motile.	Smaller and motile, designed to reach the egg.
Genetical	Carries a single X chromosome contributing to female traits.	Can carry an X or Y chromosome, determining the sex of the offspring.

(2 M)

OR

Feature	Organ A (Ovary)	Organ D (Testes)
Function	Produces eggs and female hormones.	Produces sperms and male hormones.
Role in reproduction	Supports ovulation and maintains female reproductive health.	Crucial for sperm production and influencing male secondary sexual characteristics.

(2 M)

Case Based-V

(*i*) The sprouting of new buds from leaf X (*Bryophyllum* leaf) is due to vegetative propagation. Certain plant cells in the leaf retain the ability to divide and differentiate into new shoots and roots when conditions are suitable. This asexual method of reproduction allows for the generation of genetically identical offspring to the parent plant. (2 M)

(*ii*) The significance of leaf X (*Bryophyllum* leaf) lies in its role in vegetative propagation, which offers gardeners several advantages like:

- Trait conservation and predictability: It ensures the retention of desired characteristics in new plants and minimises seed-based variability, ensuring uniformity and predictability in gardening. (½ M)
- Enhanced growth rate: This method promotes faster plant development compared to seed germination, streamlining the cultivation process. (½ M)

(*iii*) In the case of the money plant, vegetative propagation similar to leaf X occurs primarily through stem cuttings. These cuttings can be rooted in water or soil to produce new money plant from the parent plant. (1 M)

OR

The process observed in Leaf X, vegetative propagation, generally contributes less to genetic variability because it creates genetically identical offspring, preserving the parent plant's traits and genetic makeup. (1 M)

8 HEREDITY

"'Her hair is just like her mother's'—many of us have heard similar statements at least once in our lives. Have you ever wondered how we can be so similar to, yet so different from, our parents? In this chapter, we will explore the mechanics behind this phenomenon of inheritance."

SYLLABUS & WEIGHTAGE

LIST OF CONCEPT NAMES	YEARS					
	2019	2020	2022 TERM-II	2023	2024	2025
Heredity & Mendel's Laws of Inheritance (Heredity; Mendel's contribution, Laws for inheritance of traits)	—	1 Q (3 M)	1 Q (2 M)	1 Q (4 M) 1 Q (1 M)	1 Q (1 M)	1 Q (2 M) 1 Q (3 M)
Sex Determination (Brief introduction)	1 Q (5 M)	1 Q (3 M)	1 Q (4 M)	—	1 Q (1 M)	—

For the year 2021, the exam was not conducted.

CONCEPT MAP

To Access One Shot Revision Video Scan This QR Code

CBSE 2025

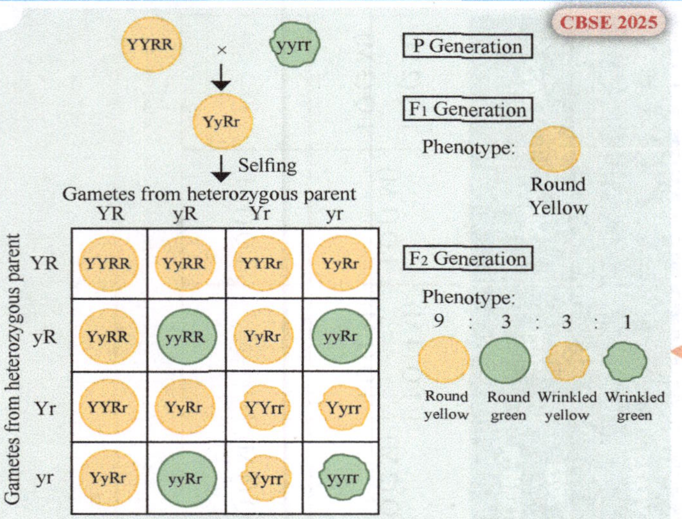

Dihybrid cross

(Mating between individuals differing in two observed traits)

CBSE 2025

Law of Independent Assortment: It states that alleles from different genes segregate independently during gamete formation, demonstrated by a dihybrid cross like seed shape and color, showing no linkage.

Contrasting Characters Used by Mendel

S. No.	Character	Trait	
		Dominant	Recessive
1.	Stem height	Tall	Dwarf
2.	Flower colour	Violet	White
3.	Flower position	Axial	Terminal
4.	Pod shape	Inflated	Constricted
5.	Pod colour	Green	Yellow
6.	Seed shape	Round	Wrinkled
7.	Seed colour	Yellow	Green

Mendel took pea plants with different characteristics (7 characters and 14 traits)

Mendel's Law of Inheritance

Law of Segregation: It states that alleles for a gene separate during gamete formation, ensuring each gamete carries one allele. Fertilization restores diploid alleles, inheriting one from each parent.

CBSE 2022 Term-II, 2020

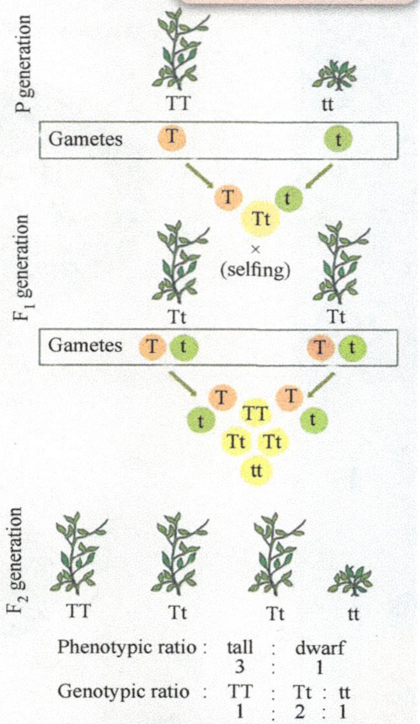

Monohybrid cross

(Mating between individuals differing in one genetic characteristic)

Heredity (Transmission of traits from parents to offspring)

Law of Dominance: It states that dominant alleles mask recessive alleles, as seen in a monohybrid cross, where the F_1 generation displays only the dominant trait, e.g., tall stem height.

Inherited Trait

A characteristic that is passed from parents to offspring through genetic material, contributing to the offspring's phenotype.

DNA: CBSE 2025

- Carries the information source for making proteins in cells.
- Minor inaccuracies during DNA copying produce variations.

Chromosome:

- Organized structures of DNA and proteins.
- Sex chromosomes (XX and XY) determine the sex of an individual.
- 22 pair of autosomes and 1 pair of sex chromosomes are present in humans.

Gene:

- A segment of DNA that controls characteristics or traits.
- Determine specific traits through its expression.

CBSE 2023

Dominant Trait Vs. Recessive Trait

Aspect	Dominant Trait	Recessive Trait
Expression in offspring	Appears when at least one parent contributes the allele	Only appears when both parents contribute the allele
Visibility in heterozygous condition	Visible even if paired with a recessive allele	Hidden when paired with a dominant allele
Expression of the trait	Will be expressed if inherited	May not be expressed even if inherited
Example	Tall plant height (T) is dominant and expressed in TT or Tt	Short plant height (t) is recessive and expressed only in tt

Heredity

CBSE 2025

DNA (Source of information)
↓
Gene (Encodes for protein)
↓
Protein/Enzyme (Catalyzes hormone production)

- Efficient → More hormone → Enhanced trait
- Less efficient → Less hormone → Diminished trait

How do Traits get Expressed?

Variation (Differences among individuals within a species or population)

Causes of Variation

- Inaccuracy in DNA copying mechanism: Small mistakes in DNA replication create new differences.
- Genetic recombination: Combining genes from two parents during sexual reproduction produces variety.

Importance of Variation

- Enhances species adaptability and survival in changing environments.
- Drives evolutionary processes through genetic diversity.
- Promotes the emergence of beneficial traits, aiding adaptation.

Sex Determination

Process by which sexual phenotype of an individual is determined in a species.

X Chromosome Vs. Y Chromosome

Feature	X Chromosome	Y Chromosome
Size	Larger	Smaller
Role in Sex Determination	Common chromosome in both genders	Determines male gender
Inheritance	Can be inherited from both parents	Only inherited from the male parent

Factors responsible for Sex Determination

Genetic Factor

In some animals like humans gender of an individual is determined by a pair of chromosomes called sex-chromosomes.

- XX - Female (Perfect pair of sex chromosome)
- XY - Male (Mismatched pair of sex chromosome)

Environmental Factor

CBSE 2025

In some animals, the temperature at which the fertilized eggs are kept, decides the gender. E.g., in few reptiles (turtle)

CBSE 2025, 2024, 2022 Term-II

Sex Determination in Humans

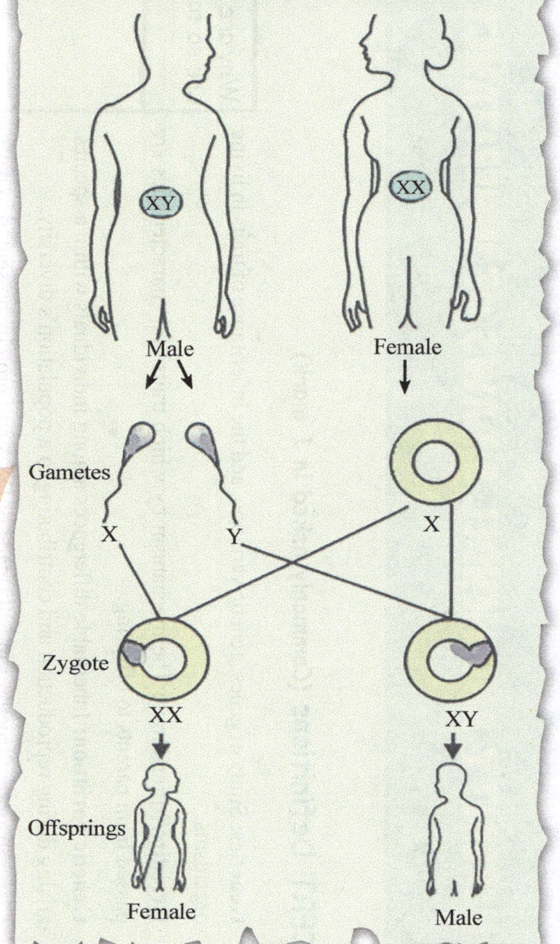

1 HEREDITY AND MENDEL'S LAWS OF INHERITANCE

NCERT Definitions (Commonly asked in 1 mark)

- **Genetics:** Study of genes, genetic variation, and the inheritance of traits in living organisms.
- **Heredity/Inheritance:** The mechanism by which traits and characteristics are passed from parents to offspring.
- **Genetic Variation:** Inheritable differences among individuals within a species, arising during reproduction and contributing to a population's diversity.
- **Chromosome:** Structures in cells made of DNA and protein, presented in pairs.
- **DNA (Deoxyribonucleic Acid):** The cellular material that carries genetic information for making proteins.
- **Gene:** A section of DNA responsible for a specific protein, influencing traits and characteristics in organisms.
- **Mendelian Inheritance:** The set of rules about the transmission of hereditary characteristics from parent organisms to their children, discovered by Gregor Mendel.
- **Factor:** A term used by Mendel, referring to what is now known as a gene, which controls the inheritance of traits.
- **Phenotype:** The observable physical traits of an organism.
- **Genotype:** The genetic makeup of an organism, dictate the complete set of genes of an organism.
- **Pure Line:** An organism that is homozygous for specific traits, consistently passing these traits to its offspring.
- **Inherited Trait:** A characteristic that is passed from parents to offspring through genetic material, contributing to the offspring's phenotype.
- **Hybrid:** Offspring resulting from the cross-breeding of genetically distinct parents, often showing heterozygosity for certain traits.

Important Facts

01 Segments of DNA that code for proteins. *~ Genes*

02 Variations arising during the process of reproduction can be inherited.

03 The plant on which Mendel's hereditary experiments were conducted. *~Pea plant (Pisum sativum)*

04 The genotypic ratio of the F_2 generation in the inheritance of a single character. *~1:2:1*

05 In the inheritance of two characters, the genotypic ratio of the F_2 generation. ***~9:3:3:1***

06 In individuals with the AB blood group, both of the alleles are dominant.

Classification

Generation used in genetic analysis

- **Parental Generation:** The initial set of parents in a genetic study, whose traits are analyzed in their offspring.
- **F_1 Generation:** The first generation of offspring from the parental generation, used to study inheritance patterns.
- **F_2 Generation:** The second generation of offspring, produced by intercrossing or self-pollinating F_1 individuals.

Difference Between

Character v/s Trait

Character	Trait
Each variant for a character like having blue or brown eye color	A heritable feature that varies among individuals such as the color of the eyes
Characters do not involve the concept of dominance and recessiveness	Traits can be dominant (visible) or recessive (hidden unless paired with another recessive)

Homozygous organism v/s Heterozygous organism

Feature	Homozygous Organism	Heterozygous Organism
Definition	An organism with two identical alleles for a character	An organism with two different alleles for a character
Expressed trait	The trait expressed is consistent	The trait expressed can vary depending on dominance
Genetic Variation	Lower genetic variation within the population	Higher genetic variation within the population
Predictability of Offspring Traits	Offspring traits are more predictable	Offspring traits can vary and include both dominant and recessive forms
Breeding	Self-breeding leads to similar offsprings	Self-breeding can produce varied offsprings
Example	Purebred organisms like tall (TT) or dwarf (tt) plants	Hybrid organisms like tall (Tt)

Dominant trait v/s Recessive trait		
Aspect	**Dominant Trait**	**Recessive Trait**
Expression	Expressed even when paired with a recessive allele	Only expressed in the absence of a dominant allele
Enzyme Production	Dominant allele produces a fully functional enzyme, leading to complete expression of the trait	Recessive allele results in an incomplete or non-functional enzyme, leading to non-expression of the trait in presence of dominant allele
Example of Phenotypic Effect	Height trait in pea plants where tall (T) is dominant (e.g., Tt or TT are tall)	Dwarf trait in pea plants only appears when both alleles are recessive (e.g., tt is dwarf)

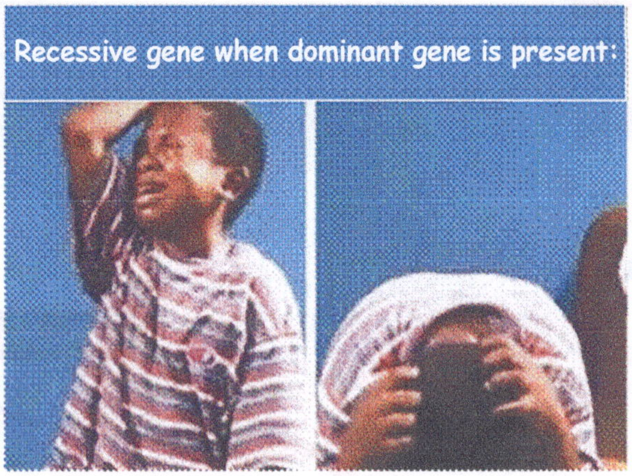

Monohybrid v/s Dihybrid Cross		
Aspect	**Monohybrid Cross**	**Dihybrid Cross**
Definition	A cross between two individuals concerning one character	A cross between two individuals concerning two characters
Phenotypic Ratio (F_2 Generation)	3: 1	9:3:3:1
Example of characters	Stem Height	Seed color (yellow or green) and seed shape (round and wrinkled)
Associated Mendel's Laws	Shows the principle of dominance and segregation.	Illustrates the principle of independent assortment along with dominance and segregation.

Real Life Application Based Questions

1. **When visiting a doctor for a routine check-up, why are patients often asked about their family's medical history?**

Ans. Doctors inquire about family medical history during check-ups because some diseases, such as heart disease and diabetes, can be inherited from parents. This information helps identify if a patient is more likely to develop certain illnesses, enabling early diagnosis and treatment.

2. **Have you ever wondered why the police collect blood or hair samples from a crime scene? How do these samples help in this scenario?**

Ans. Police collect blood or hair samples at crime scenes to utilize DNA for identifying individuals involved. These biological samples can be matched with DNA from suspects or databases, linking people to the crime scene.

3. **Have your friends ever approached you, showing off that they can roll their tongue or bend their thumb backward beyond 90 degrees? Why can some people do this while others cannot?**

Ans. Tongue rolling and thumb bending beyond 90 degrees involve genetic variations among individuals. However, research suggests these abilities are not determined by simple genetic inheritance alone but also by a combination of multiple genes and possibly environmental factors.

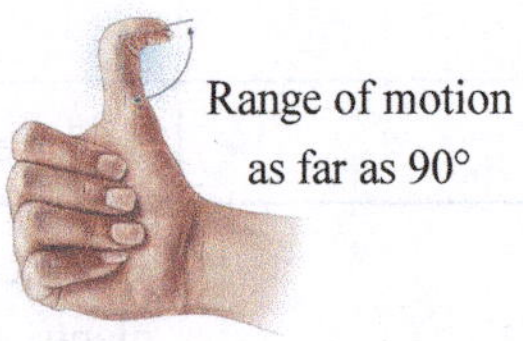

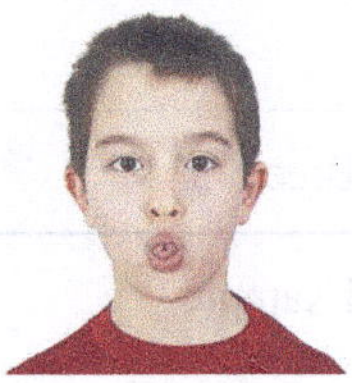

Myth Buster

- **Myth: Gene and DNA are the same.**

  Fact: DNA encompasses the entire set of genetic instructions for an organism, a gene represents only a fraction of that DNA, responsible for guiding the production of proteins that determine an organism's various characteristics.

- **Myth: One gene controls the expression of one trait always.**

  Fact: The idea that one gene controls the expression of one trait is overly simplistic for most traits. Many traits are influenced by multiple genes, and a single gene can also affect multiple traits. Moreover, environmental factors and interactions between different genes also play crucial roles in the expression of traits.

- **Myth: Traits inherited from parents are always visible in the offspring.**

  Fact: A trait influenced by a recessive allele must be inherited from both parents to be expressed in the offspring, meaning a trait can be inherited but not expressed if the dominant allele is also present.

- **Myth: All variations are beneficial and lead to evolution.**

  Fact: Not all variations are beneficial; some are neutral or even detrimental. Only beneficial variations are likely to contribute to an organism's fitness and have a chance of being passed on through generations.

- **Myth: Earlobes are either "free" or "attached," illustrating basic genetics.**

  Fact: Earlobe attachment varies continuously having intermediates phenotype for earlobes. Genetic studies have shown that the trait of earlobe attachment is likely influenced by multiple genes or by a single gene with more than two alleles.

- **Myth: If we take any random plant to duplicate Mendel's experiment, the results will be the same.**

  Fact: Mendel's success in predicting inheritance patterns was due to his selection of pea plants with highly specific traits like clearly visible contrasting traits, pure line breed of plant. Other plants might and might not follow the exact same results.

Mnemonics

- To remember 7 Pairs of contrasts traits in pea plants.

  "GRAVITY" (Dominant traits)

  - G → Green (Pod color)
  - R → Round (Seed shape)
  - A → Axial (Flower position)
  - V → Violet (Flower color)
  - I → Inflated (Pod shape)
  - T → Tall (Stem height)
  - Y → Yellow (Seed color)

Young Wizard train with charming Dragons Gladly (Recessive traits).

Young	Wizard	train	with	charming	Dragons	Gladly
↓	↓	↓	↓	↓	↓	↓
Yellow	Wrinkled	Terminal	White	Constricted	Dwarf	Green
(Pod color)	(Seed shape)	(Flower position)	(Flower color)	(Pod shape)	(Stem height)	(Seed color)

COMPETENCY BASED SOLVED EXAMPLES

Multiple Choice Questions (1 M)

1. **The statement that correctly describes the characteristic(s) of a gene is** ***(Un)***
   (a) In individuals of a given species, a specific gene is located on a particular chromosome.
   (b) A gene is not the information source for making proteins in the cell.
   (c) Each chromosome has only one-gene located all along its length.
   (d) All the inherited traits in human beings are not controlled by genes.

2. **In an experiment, two groups of same plants were grown under identical conditions. Group A had a gene that coded for an enzyme with high efficiency, while Group B had a mutation in the same gene, making the enzyme less efficient. The gene is responsible for the plant height. What result would you expect regarding the heights of the plants in both groups?** ***(Ev)***
   (a) Group A plants will be shorter, and Group B plants will be taller.
   (b) Group A plants will be taller, and Group B plants will be shorter.
   (c) Both groups will have plants of the same height.
   (d) Group B plants will produce more hormones than Group A plants.

3. **Attached earlobes in humans is an inherited condition. The allele for attached earlobes is recessive.**
   What are the chances of parents, both having attached earlobes, to have a child with attached earlobes? ***(Ap)***
   (a) 10% (b) 25%
   (c) 75% (d) 100%

4. **A monohybrid cross is conducted between one variety of pea plants having pods that are full (FF) and another having pods that are constricted (ff).**
   What is the percentage of heterozygous offsprings in F_1 generation? ***(Ap)***
   (a) 100% (b) 75%
   (c) 50% (d) 25%

5. **The plants obtained in the F_1 generation of a monohybrid cross involving height were** ***(Re)***
   (a) 25% tall and 75% dwarf
   (b) 50% tall and 50% dwarf
   (c) 100% tall
   (d) 75% tall and 25% dwarf

6. **Mendel's monohybrid cross ratio for height in F_2 generation was 1:2:1. It indicates.** ***(Re)***
   (a) One Tt, two TT and one tt
   (b) One TT, two Tt and one tt
   (c) One TT, two tt and one Tt
   (d) Two TT & two tt

7. **A cross between pea plant with white flowers (vv) and pea plant with violet flowers (VV) resulted in F_2 progeny in which ratio of violet (VV) and white (vv) flowers will be:** ***(Ap)*** **(CBSE, 2023)**
   (a) 1 : 1 (b) 2 : 1
   (c) 3 : 1 (d) 1 : 3

8. **Meena observed the following F_1 generation results after crossing two pea plants RrYy and RrYy. The observed results follow Mendel's law of independent assortment:**

Seed Shape	Seed Color	Number of Plants
Round	Yellow	180
Round	Green	60
Wrinkled	Yellow	60
Wrinkled	Green	20

   What might happen if the genes for seed shape and seed color are linked instead of assorting independently? ***(Ap)***
   (a) The phenotypic ratio would remain 9:3:3:1.
   (b) The phenotypic ratio would deviate from 9:3:3:1.
   (c) Only the dominant traits (Round Yellow) would appear.
   (d) The ratio would reverse, with more wrinkled green plants than round yellow plants.

9. **A doctor framed an inheritance chart of a family. She used symbols to denote the individuals of the family. In the family chart both parents do not show symptoms of the disorder, but one of their four children is affected.** ***(Ap)***

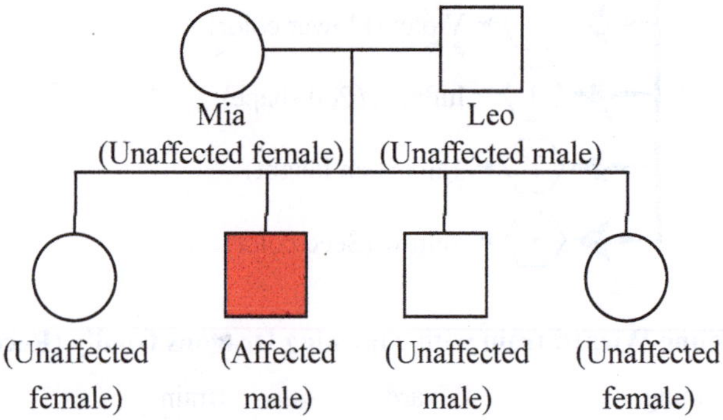

   Which of the following statements is correct about the inheritance of this disorder?
   (a) The disorder is caused by a dominant trait, and Mia and Leo are homozygous for the normal gene.
   (b) The disorder is caused by a recessive trait, and Mia and Leo are both heterozygous.
   (c) The disorder is caused by a dominant trait, and Mia and Leo are both heterozygous.
   (d) The disorder is caused by a recessive trait, and Mia is heterozygous and Leo is homozygous.

10. In a bacterial population where Trait X (heat resistance) and Trait Y (antibiotic resistance) exist, 80% of bacteria with Trait X survive a heat wave, while only 10% of those with Trait Y survive. If the heat wave lasts for 10 generations, which of the following is the most likely outcome for Trait X?

(*a*) The frequency of Trait X will decrease over time.

(*b*) The frequency of Trait X will remain constant.

(*c*) The frequency of Trait X will increase over time.

(*d*) The frequency of Trait X will initially increase and then decrease.

11. Two pea plants one with round green seeds (RRyy) and another with wrinkled yellow (rrYY) seeds produce F_1 progeny that have round, yellow (RrYy) seeds. When F_1 plants are selfed, the F_2 progeny will have new combination of characters. Choose the new combination from the following: *(Ap)*

(*i*) Round, yellow | **(*ii*) Round, green**

(*iii*) Wrinkled, yellow | **(*iv*) Wrinkled, green**

(*a*) (*i*) and (*ii*) | (*b*) (*i*) and (*iv*)

(*c*) (*ii*) and (*iii*) | (*d*) (*i*) and (*iii*)

12. Which among the combinations represents phenotypically similar, but genotypically different plants? *(Un)*

(*a*) RRYY and RrYy | (*b*) Rryy and rrYY

(*c*) rrYY and rryy | (*d*) RrYY and rrYy

13. Mendel selected garden pea plant for series of hybridization experiments as it had special features. Some statements are given below: *(Re)*

(*i*) This plant was easy to grow.

(*ii*) It has a short life cycle.

(*iii*) This plant had distinct, easily detectable contrasting variants of features.

(*iv*) In these plants artificial fertilisation could not be achieved.

Which statements are true?

(*a*) (*i*) and (*ii*) only | (*b*) (*i*) and (*iii*) only

(*c*) (*i*), (*ii*), (*iii*) and (*iv*) | (*d*) (*i*), (*ii*) and (*iii*) only

14. The following is the dihybrid cross done by Mendel and 556 progenies were produced. The plants with round and green coloured seeds will be *(Ev)*

(*a*) 315 | (*b*) 108

(*c*) 104 | (*d*) 32

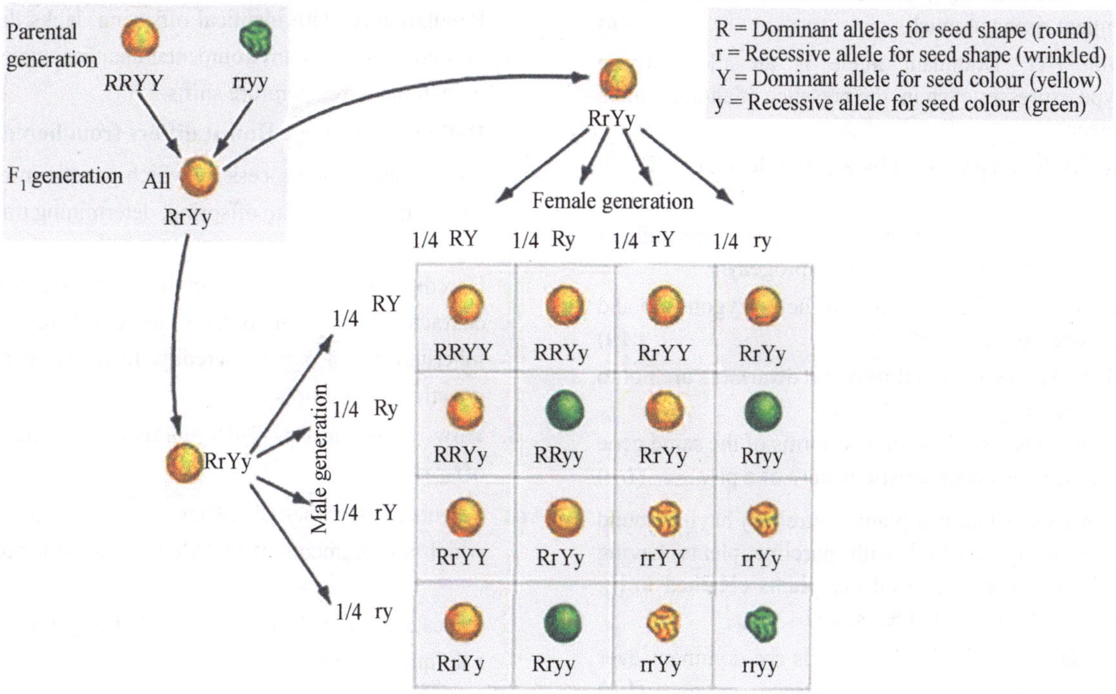

Assertion and Reason (1 M)

Direction: The following questions consist of two statements – Assertion (A) and Reason (R). Answer these questions by selecting the appropriate option given below:

(*a*) Both A and R are true, and R is the correct explanation of A.

(*b*) Both A and R are true, but R is not the correct explanation of A.

(*c*) A is true, but R is false.

(*d*) A is false, but R is true.

1. **Assertion (A):** Traits like eye colour or height are inherited traits.

   Reason (R): Inherited traits are not transferred from parents to young ones. ***(Un)***

2. **Assertion(A):** Variations are seen in offspring produced by sexual reproduction.

   Reason (R): Variations may be present between two individuals of same or different species. ***(Un)***

3. **Assertion(A):** In humans, height is a trait which shows variation.

   Reason (R): Some humans are very tall, some have medium height whereas others are short heighted. ***(Un)***

4. **Assertion (A):** Changes in non-reproductive cells can be passed on the DNA of the germ cells.

   Reason(R): The process of transferring characters from one generation to next is inheritance. ***(Un)***

5. **Assertion(A):** The genetic complement of an organism is called genotype.

   Reason(R): Genotype is the type of hereditary properties of an organism. ***(Un)***

6. **Assertion (A):** In humans, if gene (B) is responsible for black eyes and gene (b) is responsible for brown eyes, then the colour of eyes of the progeny having gene combination Bb, bb or BB will be black only.

   Reason (R): The black colour of the eyes is a dominant trait. ***(Un)***

7. **Assertion(A):** Accumulation of variation in a species increases the chances of its survival in a changing environment.

   Reason (R): Accumulation of heat resistance in some bacteria ensure their survival even when temperature in the environment rises too much. ***(An)***

8. **Assertion (A):** Dominant allele is an allele whose phenotype expresses even in the presence of another allele of that gene.

   Reason (R): It is represented by a capital letter, e.g. T. ***(Un)***

9. **Assertion(A):** A geneticist crossed two pea plants and got 50% tall and 50% dwarf plants in the progeny.

   Reason (R): Since the one plant was heterozygous tall and the other was dwarf. ***(An)***

10. **Assertion (A):** Genes for tallness and dwarfness are not to be considered as two different genes.

    Reason (R): They are just the two forms of the same gene which control one characteristic feature of a plant. ***(Un)***

11. **Assertion (A):** When pea plants (pureline) having round yellow seeds are crossed with pureline plants having wrinkled green seeds, then all pea plants obtained in F_1, generation bear wrinkled green seeds.

    Reason (R): Round and yellow seeds are dominant over wrinkled and green seeds. ***(Un)***

12. **Assertion (A):** Mendel's monohybrid cross based on law of independent assortment.

    Reason (R): Mendel's monohybrid ratio is 3:1. ***(Re)***

Subjective Questions

Very Short Answer Type Questions (2 M)

1. **Two populations are growing in a controlled environment with fluctuating temperatures.**

   In Population A, all offspring produced are nearly identical to their parents.

   In Population B, each generation shows small differences from the previous one.

   The graph below shows the number of individuals in each population across 7 generations subjected to temperature fluctuation starting from generation 3.

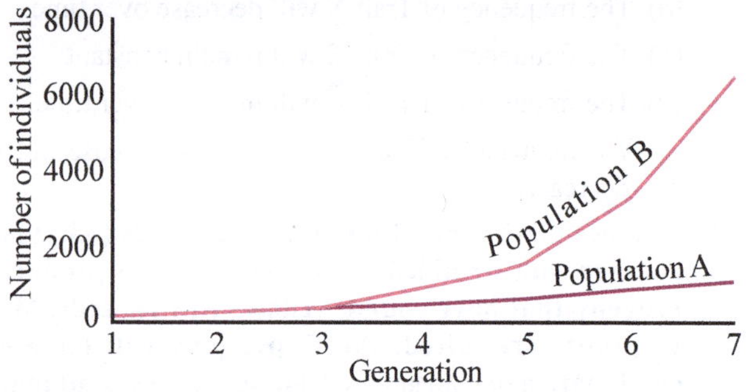

   Which population is more likely to survive over time in an environment with fluctuating temperatures, and why? ***(An)***

Ans. Population B is more likely to survive long-term in fluctuating temperatures. *(1 M)*

It is because genetic differences among individuals increase the likelihood of some surviving extreme conditions. Population A, with identical offspring, lacks the diversity needed to adapt to environmental changes, making it more vulnerable to temperature shifts. *(1 M)*

2. **Define inheritance. How it differs from heredity?** ***(Re)***

Ans. Inheritance is the process by which genetic information is passed from parents to offspring, determining traits like eye colour. *(1 M)*

Heredity refers to the overall transmission of genetic characteristics from parents to children. In essence, inheritance is a part of heredity, focusing specifically on genetic transmission. *(1 M)*

3. **How does the parent's characters transferred in offspring?** ***(Un)***

Ans. Parents transfer their characters to offspring through genes, which are segments of DNA inherited from both parents. *(1M)*

Genes determine the traits of the offspring, mixing to create a unique individual. *(1M)*

4. **How does the creation of variations in a species promote survival?** ***(Un)*** **(NCERT Intext)**

Ans. Variations in a species promote survival by enabling some individuals to adapt to changes in the environment, like climate or predators, increasing their chances of survival and reproduction. This genetic diversity helps the species withstand challenges. *(2 M)*

5. **Why Mendel results of his work remain hidden?** ***(Re)***

Ans. Mendel results remain hidden because communication was not easy (as it is now) in those days and his work could not be widely publicised. *(2 M)*

6. **Differentiate between a monohybrid and a dihybrid cross. Give example of both.** ***(Un)***

Ans.

Feature	Monohybrid Cross	Dihybrid Cross
Definition	Involves one trait	Involves two traits
Example	Crossing plants with purple flowers (PP) with plants having white flowers (pp)	Crossing plants with round yellow seeds (RRYY) with wrinkled green seeds (rryy)
Phenotypic Ratio	3 : 1 (Dominant : Recessive)	9 : 3 : 3 : 1 (Different combinations of traits)

(2M)

7. **Give two pair of contrasting traits of a characters in pea plant and mention which is dominant and recessive.** ***(Re)***

Ans.

Character	Dominant Trait	Recessive Trait
(*i*) Seed Color	Yellow	Green
(*ii*) Seed Shape	Round	Wrinkled

- For seed color in pea plants, the yellow color is dominant over green.
- For seed shape, round is dominant over wrinkled. *(2 M)*

8. **Using height (tallness/dwarfness) of a plant as an example, show that genes control the characteristics or traits in an organism.** ***(Ap)***

OR

In a cross between red coloured and white coloured flowers, when plants with red coloured flowers of F_1 generation were self pollinated, plants of F_2 generation were obtained in which 75% of plants were with red flowers and 25% plants were with white flowers.

Explain the inheritance of traits in the above cross with the help of a flow chart only along with the ratio of plants obtained. ***(An)***

Ans. Parents: TT × tt
(Tallness) Dominant (Dwarfness) Recessive
↓ ↓
Gametes: (T) (t)
F_1 generation: (Tt)
All tall plant

This result shows the genes controlling the traits, as all offspring are tall despite one parent being dwarf. *(2 M)*

OR

Parent : RR × rr
(Red flower) ↓ (White flower)
F_1 generation : All Rr (Red)
↓ Selfing
F_2 generation : RR : Rr : rr
25% : 50% : 25%
Genotypic ratio: 1 : 2 : 1
Phenotypic ratio : 3 : 1
(Red) (White)
75% : 25% *(2 M)*

Key Takeaways

From these examples, student will learns the fundamental principle of inheritance, where dominant alleles mask recessive ones in heterozygotes, and the significance of allele combinations in determining the traits of subsequent generations.

Short Answer Type Questions **(3 M)**

1. **Do all variation in a species have equal chances of surviving in the environment?** ***(Un)***

Ans. Not all variations in a species have equal chances of survival; their survival depends on the environment and how the variations affect an organism's fitness. Variations occur due to mutations, genetic recombination during sexual reproduction, and gene flow between populations. These processes introduce new genetic combinations, some of which may provide an advantage in specific environments, increasing the likelihood of survival and reproduction of those individuals. *(3 M)*

2. **At her school science fair, Riya studied the inheritance of earlobe types in families, as shown in the figure below. She observed two types of earlobes:** ***(Ap)***

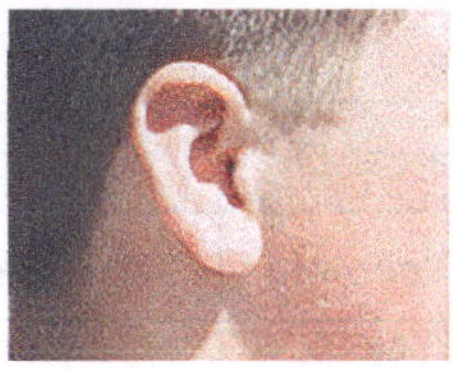

(*a*)
Free ear lobes
(dominant, represented by F)

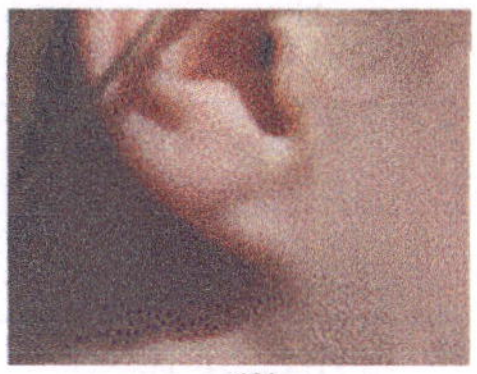

(*b*)
Attached ear lobes
(recessive, represented by f)

She observed two families with different parental earlobe traits:

- **Family 1: One parent has free earlobes (Ff), and the other has attached earlobes (ff).**
- **Family 2: Both parents have free earlobes (Ff and Ff).**

(*a*) In Family 1, draw a Punnett square to determine the possible earlobe types of their children. Why do attached earlobes appear only when a specific combination of alleles is inherited?

(*b*) In Family 2, explain why there is a chance of children having attached earlobes even though both parents have free earlobes. Use a Punnett square to justify your answer.

Ans. (*a*) In Family 1, the Punnett square for one parent (Ff) and the other (ff) gives:

	F	f
f	Ff	ff
f	Ff	ff

(1 M)

50% chance of free earlobes (Ff) and 50% chance of attached earlobes (ff).

Attached earlobes appear only when both alleles are recessive (ff) i.e. in the absence of the dominant F which allows the recessive alleles to express. *(½ M)*

(*b*) In Family 2, with both parents Ff, the Punnett square is:

	F	f
F	FF	Ff
f	Ff	ff

25% FF (free), 50% Ff (free), and 25% ff (attached) *(1 M)*

Attached earlobes (ff) appear when both parents contribute the f allele, even if hidden by the dominant F allele in heterozygous parents. *(½ M)*

3. "In a genetics experiment, the cross between two pea plants resulted in seeds where 50% were yellow(Dominant) and 50% were green(Recessive). **(*Ev*)**

(*a*) Identify the genotype of the parent plants that would result in this ratio. Use a Punnett square to justify your answer.

(*b*) Which Mendelian law is demonstrated in this experiment?

Ans. (*a*) The observed 1 : 1 ratio of yellow (dominant) and green (recessive) seeds suggests that one parent must be heterozygous (Yy) and the other parent must be homozygous recessive (yy). *(½ M)*

Punnett Square:

	Y (Parent 1)	y (Parent 1)
y (Parent 2)	Yy (Yellow)	yy (Green)
y (Parent 2)	Yy (Yellow)	yy (Green)

Result:

- 50% Yy → Yellow seeds
- 50% yy → Green seeds

This explains the 1:1 ratio observed in the progeny. *(1 M)*

(*b*) The Law of Segregation is demonstrated in this experiment. *(½ M)*

According to the Law of Segregation, during gamete formation, the two alleles (Y and y) segregate so that each gamete carries only one allele for a trait. *(1 M)*

4. In a 10th-grade biology class, a teacher discusses a family tree showing baldness in men across multiple generations but not in women. What inference can be drawn from this pattern? **(*An*)**

Ans.
- Baldness in the family tree appears to be a sex-linked trait, predominantly affecting men and not women, indicating it may be linked to genes on the X chromosome. *(1M)*
- Since men have only one X chromosome, a single copy of the baldness gene can express the trait, making it more common in men. *(1M)*
- Women, having two X chromosomes, would require two copies of the gene to express the trait, making baldness less likely in women. *(1M)*

5. If a trait A exists in 10% of a population of an asexually reproducing species and a trait B exists in 60% of the same population, which trait is likely to have arisen earlier? **(*Ap*) (NCERT Intext)**

Ans. Here, trait B is present in a higher percentage of the species. So, it has likely had more time to develop and spread to 60% of the population. Thus, it is likely to have appeared earlier. Trait A must be relatively new as it is present in only 10% of the population. *(3 M)*

6. Mendel crossed pure tall pea plants (TT) with pure short pea plants (tt) and obtained F_1 progeny. When the plants of F_1 progeny were self-pollinated, plants of F_2 progeny were obtained. **(*Ap, Ev*) (CBSE, 2024)**

(*a*) What did the plants of F_1 progeny look like? Give their gene combination.

(*b*) Why could the gene for shortness not be expressed in plants of F_1 progeny?

(*c*) Write the ratio of the plants obtained in F_2 progeny and state the conclusion that can be drawn from this experiment.

Ans. (*a*) Appearance and Gene Combination of F_1 Progeny:

- All F_1 progeny plants will exhibit the tall phenotype. *(½ M)*
- Gene combination: All the F_1 plants will have the genotype Tt. *(½ M)*

(*b*) The gene for shortness was not expressed in F_1 progeny because:

- The gene for shortness (t) is recessive, and since the F_1 plants are heterozygous (Tt), the dominant gene for tallness (T) masks the expression of the recessive shortness gene (t). *(½ M)*
- Therefore, despite the presence of the recessive t allele, the phenotype of the F_1 progeny is tall due to the dominance of the T allele. *(½ M)*

(*c*) Ratio in F_2 progeny: 3 tall plants: 1 short plants *(½ M)*

Conclusion: This experiment demonstrates Mendel's Law of Segregation, which states that each organism has two alleles for each trait (one from each parent), and these alleles segregate randomly during gamete formation. *(½ M)*

Topper's Explanation

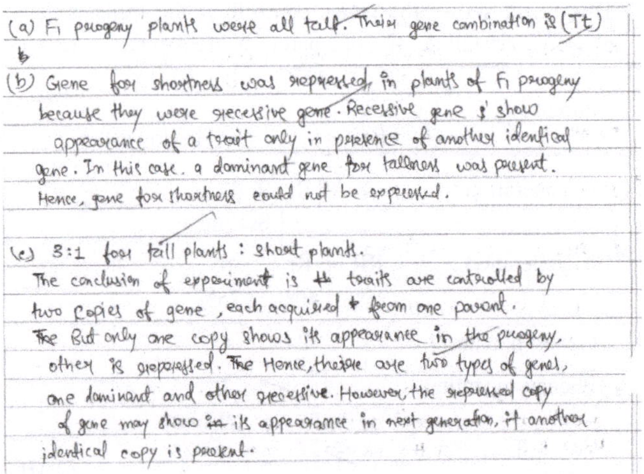
(a) F1 progeny plants were all tall. Their gene combination is (Tt)

(b) Gene for shortness was repressed in plants of F1 progeny because they were recessive gene. Recessive gene show appearance of a trait only in presence of another identical gene. In this case. a dominant gene for tallness was present. Hence, gene for shortness could not be expressed.

(c) 3:1 for tall plants : short plants.
The conclusion of experiment is the traits are controlled by two copies of gene, each acquired from one parent. But only one copy shows its appearance in the progeny, other is repressed. Hence, there are two types of genes, one dominant and other recessive. However, the repressed copy of gene may show its appearance in next generation, if another identical copy is present.

7. A man with blood group A marries a woman with blood group O and their daughter has blood group O. Is this information enough to tell you which of the traits – blood group A or O – is dominant? Why or why not?

(*An*) (NCERT Intext)

Ans. The given information suggests that blood group A is not enough to conclusively determine dominance over blood group O without additional context on how blood groups are inherited because:

(*i*) Blood group A can be genotypically AA (homozygous) or AO (heterozygous). Since the daughter has blood group O, the man must be heterozygous AO, passing the O allele to the daughter. *(1M)*

(*ii*) Blood group O is recessive, and for it to be expressed, an individual must inherit an O allele from both parents (OO). *(1M)*

(*iii*) The presence of blood group O in the daughter indicates she inherited the O allele from both parents, confirming O's recessive nature but not directly addressing the dominance of A over O without understanding the inheritance pattern of blood groups. *(1M)*

8. After self-pollination in pea plants with round, yellow seeds, following types of seeds were obtained by Mendel: **(*An*)**

Seeds	Number
Round, yellow	576
Round, green	192
Wrinkled, yellow	192
Wrinkled, green	64

Analyse the result and describe the mechanism of inheritance which explains these results.

Ans. The given results are explained by law of independent assortment.

The ratio obtained is 9:3:3:1 in which parental as well as new combinations are observed. This indicates that progeny plants have not inherited a single whole gene set from each parent. *(1½ M)*

Every germ cell takes one chromosome from the pair of maternal and paternal chromosomes. When two germ cells combine, segregation of one pair of characters occurs independent of the other pair. *(1½ M)*

Long Answer Type Questions **(5 M)**

1. In a classroom activity, students observed their classmates' earlobe types and noted whether they were free or attached. They also recorded the earlobe types of their parents. Consider that free earlobes (F) are dominant over attached earlobes (f). **(*Ap, Cr*)**

(*a*) If a student has free earlobes and one of their parents has attached earlobes, what are the possible genotypes of the student and their parents?

(*b*) If a person with genotype Ff marries a person with genotype ff, what are the possible genotypes and phenotypes of their children? Explain with the help of cross.

Ans. (*a*) If a student has free earlobes and one of their parents has attached earlobes, the student must have inherited one dominant allele (F) from the another parent. Therefore, the student's genotype could be Ff. The parent with free earlobes could have genotype either FF or Ff, while the parent with attached earlobes is ff. *(2 M)*

(*b*) When a person with genotype Ff marries a person with genotype ff, the possible genotypes and phenotypes of their children can be determined by performing the cross given below

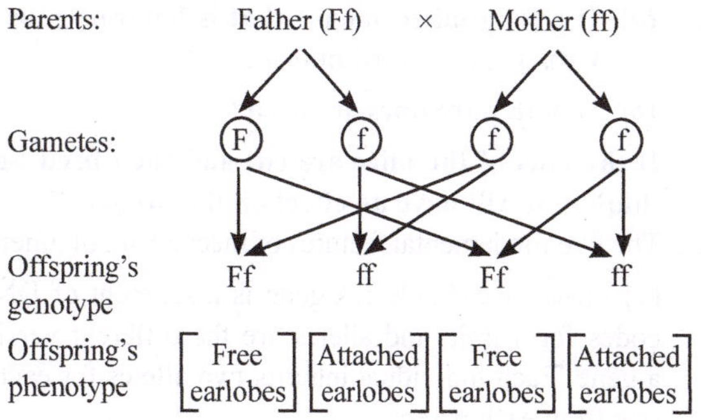

(3 M)

2. (*i*) Differentiate between dominant and recessive traits.

(*ii*) 'Gene control traits'? Explain this statement with an example. **(*Un*)**

Ans. (*i*) The differences between dominant vs recessive traits are as follows: *(3 M)*

Feature	Dominant Traits	Recessive Traits
Expression	Expressed in the phenotype even if only one allele is present (heterozygous).	Expressed in the phenotype only when both alleles are present (homozygous recessive).
Allele Symbol	Represented by a capital letter (e.g., 'A' for the dominant allele).	Represented by a lowercase letter (e.g., 'a' for the recessive allele).
Example	Brown eyes in humans where brown is dominant over blue.	Blue eyes in humans, expressed only when both alleles for eye color are blue.

(*ii*) The statement "genes control traits" refers to the fact that genes, which are segments of DNA, contain the instructions for the development of specific traits in an organism.

For instance, the gene for flower color in pea plants has different alleles, such as purple or white. The purple allele ('P') is dominant over the white allele ('p'). If a pea plant has at least one purple allele (PP or Pp), it will have purple flowers because the gene produces the pigment for purple color. If it has two white alleles (pp), it will have white flowers, as the dominant purple is not present to express that trait. This example illustrates how the presence or absence of certain alleles, and therefore genes, determines the trait expression in living organisms. *(2 M)*

3. Explain the key elements of the mechanism of inheritance, highlighting at least five fundamental features. **(*Re*)**

OR

A group of laboratory mice having long tails and short tails are bred together in various patterns and their progeny are studied. In mice, the gene for tail length has two alleles. A long tail(L) is dominant to a short tail(l).

What do you think would be the genotype of the new progeny and the percentage of short tailed offspring in the F_1 generation? (Draw the cross in each case to support your answer).

(*a*) If a long-tailed mouse that is heterozygous mates with a short-tailed mouse?

(*b*) If both pure lines are bred?

If the tails of the mice are cut and then bred , do you think that will have an effect on the progeny? (*An*)

Ans. The five fundamental features of mechanism of inheritance:

(*a*) Genes and Alleles: A gene is a segment of DNA that codes for a trait, and alleles are the different versions of a gene. Each individual inherits two alleles for each gene, one from each parent.

(*b*) Dominance and Recessiveness: Traits can be determined by dominant or recessive alleles. A dominant allele expresses its effect even if it's paired with a different allele, while a recessive allele only expresses its effect if it's paired with another recessive allele.

(*c*) Segregation of Alleles: During the formation of gametes (eggs and sperm), alleles for a gene segregate from each other so that each gamete carries only one allele for each trait. This is known as Mendel's First Law, the Law of Segregation.

(*d*) Independent Assortment: The alleles of different genes generally segregate independently of each other. This is Mendel's Second Law, the Law of Independent Assortment, which means the inheritance of one trait generally does not affect the inheritance of another.

(*e*) Probability and Genetics: The inheritance of genes follows the laws of probability. The likelihood of a particular trait appearing in an offspring can be calculated using Punnett squares that represent the possible genetic combinations from the parents' alleles. *(5 M)*

OR

(*a*) Heterozygous long-tailed mouse × short-tailed mouse

Parents: Ll (Heterozygous) × ll (Homozygous)

↓ ↓

Gametes: (L) (l) (l)

F_1 generation: Ll (Long-tailed heterozygous) : ll (Short-tailed homozygous recessive)

50% : 50%

(2 M)

(*b*) Breading pure lines (Homozygous long × Homozygous short):

Parents: LL (Homozygous long-tailed) × ll (Homozygous short tailed)

↓ ↓

Gametes: (L) (l)

F_1 generation: Ll

(Long-tailed, heterozygous)

100%

There will be 0% short-tailed of offspring because all offspring have at least one dominant allele (L) for long tails. *(2 M)*

Effect of Tail Cutting on Genetics:

Cutting the tails of the mice will not affect the genetic makeup of the progeny. This is because acquired traits such as cut tails do not alter the DNA sequence of the germ cells. The length of the tails in the offspring will still be determined by the alleles (L or l) they inherit, not by the physical appearance of the parents' tails. *(1 M)*

4. How do Mendel's experiments show that traits are inherited independently? (*Un*) (NCERT Intext)

Ans. Mendel's experiments with pea plants demonstrated that *traits are inherited independently through his dihybrid* crosses, which tracked the inheritance of two different traits at the same time. Hiswork supports the principle of independent assortment as follows:

- Selection of Traits: Mendel selected two traits with clear differences, such as seed shape (round vs wrinkled) and seed color (yellow vs green), each controlled by different genes.
- Parental Plants: He started with pure-breeding (homozygous) plants for the two traits. For example, one plant would be round and yellow (RRYY) and the other wrinkled and green (rryy).
- F_1 Generation: Crossing these plants resulted in an F_1 generation that were all heterozygous for both traits (RrYy), displaying only the dominant phenotypes (round and yellow).
- F_2 Generation: He then crossed the F_1 plants with each other (RrYy x RrYy). According to the principle of independent assortment, the allele a plant received for seed shape did not influence the allele it received for seed color.
- Observation of Ratios: The F_2 generation exhibited a phenotypic ratio of 9:3:3:1 for the traits (round yellow: round green: wrinkled yellow: wrinkled green). This ratio is what would be expected if the two traits were inherited independently.

Mendel concluded from these ratios that the genes for seed shape and seed color assort independently of one another when gametes are formed. This independent assortment is due to the genes for the traits being located on different chromosomes, a fact that Mendel inferred from his results. *(5 M)*

5. (a) Why is the F_1 progeny always tall when a tall plant is crossed with a short pea plant?

(b) How is F_2 progeny obtained by self-pollination of F_1 progeny different from F_1 progeny? Give reason for this observation.

(c) State a conclusion that can be drawn on the basis of this observation. **(*Un*) (CBSE, 2020)**

Ans. (*a*) F_1 progeny are all tall when a tall (TT) and a short (tt) pea plant are crossed because the tall allele (T) is dominant over the short allele (t), resulting in tall plants with genotype Tt. *(1 M)*

(*b*) F_2 progeny show a mix of tall and short plants upon self-pollination of F_1 individuals due to the segregation and recombination of T and t alleles during gamete formation, yielding genotypes TT, Tt, and tt with a 3:1 tall-to-short phenotypic ratio. *(2 M)*

(*c*) This pattern leads to the conclusion that alleles segregate ind0ependently during gamete formation, as per Mendel's Law of Segregation, and phenotype expression is determined by dominant and recessive allele interactions. *(2 M)*

6. A green stemmed rose plant denoted by GG and a brown stemmed rose plant denoted by gg are allowed to undergo a cross with each other. **(*Ap*) (CBSE, 2020)**

(a) List your observations regarding

(i) Colour of stem in their F_1 progeny

(ii) Percentage of brown stemmed plants in F_2 progeny if F_1 plants are self-pollinated.

(iii) Ratio of GG and Gg in the F_2 progeny.

(b) Based on the findings of this cross, what conclusion can be drawn?

Ans. Parents: GG (Green stemmed plant) × gg (Brown stemmed plant)

Gametes: G, g

$F_{1\ generation}$: Gg (Green stemmed plant)

F_1 selfing: Gg × Gg

G g G g

$F_{2\ generation}$: GG Gg Gg gg

The observations and conclusions based on the given cross:

(*a*) Observations:

(*i*) Colour of stem in their F_1 progeny: Green (as it is a dominant trait). *(1 M)*

(*ii*) Percentage of brown stemmed plants in F_2 progeny if F_1 plants are self-pollinated: The expected ratio of genotypes in the F_2 progeny will be 1 GG: 2 Gg: 1 gg. This ratio gives 25% brown-stemmed plants (gg) in the F_2 progeny. *(1 M)*

(*iii*) Ratio of GG and Gg in the F_2 progeny is 1:2. *(1 M)*

(*b*) Conclusion:

Based on the given cross, we can conclude that the stem colour trait is controlled by a single gene with two alleles, where the green stem (G) is dominant over the brown stem (g). The F_1 progeny will be heterozygous for the stem colour trait, and the F_2 progeny will show a 3:1 phenotypic ratio for stem colour. *(2 M)*

Topper's Explanation

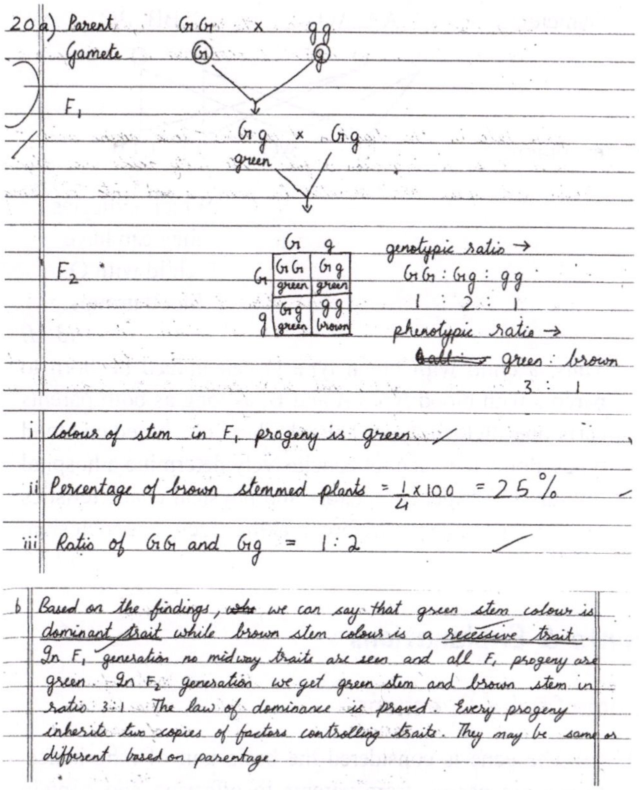
20 a) Parent GG × gg
Gamete G g
F_1
Gg × Gg
green
F_2
G g
G GG green Gg green
g Gg green gg brown
genotypic ratio →
GG : Gg : gg
1 : 2 : 1
phenotypic ratio →
green : brown
3 : 1
i Colour of stem in F_1 progeny is green.
ii Percentage of brown stemmed plants = $\frac{1}{4} \times 100$ = 25 %
iii Ratio of GG and Gg = 1 : 2
b Based on the findings, we can say that green stem colour is dominant trait while brown stem colour is a recessive trait. In F_1 generation no midway traits are seen and all F_1 progeny are green. In F_2 generation we get green stem and brown stem in ratio 3:1. The law of dominance is proved. Every progeny inherits two copies of factors controlling traits. They may be same or different based on parentage.

Mistakes 101 : What not to do!

Most students made errors while predicting the possible genotypes of gametes.

7. A couple with a newborn baby is troubled that the child does not resemble either of them. Suspecting that a mixup occurred at the hospital, they check the blood type of the infant. It is type O. Because the father is type A and the mother type B, they conclude that a mixup has definitely occurred. Are they correct ? Explain your answer with the help of cross. **(*An*)**

Ans. The couple's conclusion that a mix-up has occurred may not be correct solely based on the blood types because:

- If the father is type A, he can have either an AA or AO genotype. If he has the AO genotype, he carries one allele for type O blood.
- Similarly, if the mother is type B, she can also have either a BB or BO genotype. If she has the BO genotype, she carries one allele for type O blood.
- If both parents carry the O allele (father AO and mother BO), there is a possibility that the child can inherit an O allele from each parent, resulting in the OO genotype, which is blood type O.

Possible Blood Groups of Parents

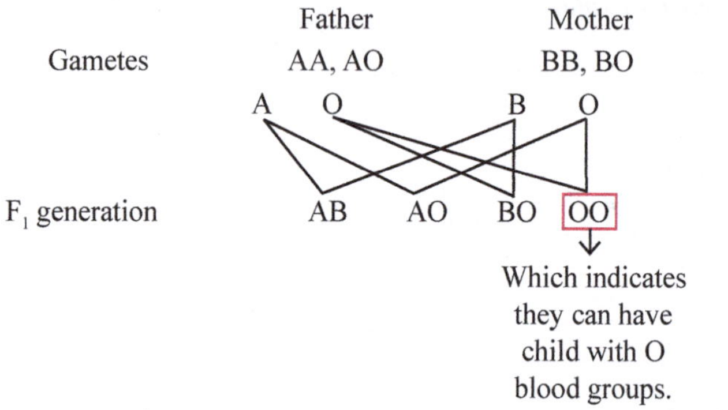

(3 M)

Thus, a child with blood type O can indeed be born to parents with blood types A and B, as long as both parents carry one allele for type O blood. Therefore, based on blood types alone, they cannot conclusively determine a hospital mix-up. Other genetic factors and physical characteristics must be considered before making such a conclusion. *(2 M)*

Hints & Explanations

Multiple Choice Questions

1. (*a*) The gene is considered the basic unit of inheritance. Genes are passed from parents to offspring and contain the information needed to specify biological and physical traits. Most genes code for specific proteins, or segments of proteins.
2. (*b*) The height of the plants depends on the amount of a specific hormone responsible for growth. Group A, with an efficient enzyme, produces more hormones, resulting in taller plants. In contrast, Group B has a less efficient enzyme due to the gene mutation, leading to reduced hormone production and shorter plants. This demonstrates how gene-controlled enzyme efficiency influences traits like height.
3. (*d*)
4. (*a*)
5. (*c*) A monohybrid cross is a genetic cross that involves a single trait of an organism. F_1 generation is the first progeny formed when two parents mate. Individuals of F_1 generation will show the dominant trait as they are heterozygous dominant. Tall height is a dominant trait over short height thus, all the plants in F_1 progeny will be tall.
6. (*b*) In Mendel's monohybrid cross in F_2 generation, 3 tall plants and 1 dwarf plant phenotypically or 1(TT) 2(Tt) 1(tt) genotypically are formed.
7. (*a*) The ratio of violet (VV) to white (vv) flowers in the F_2 progeny will be 1 : 1.

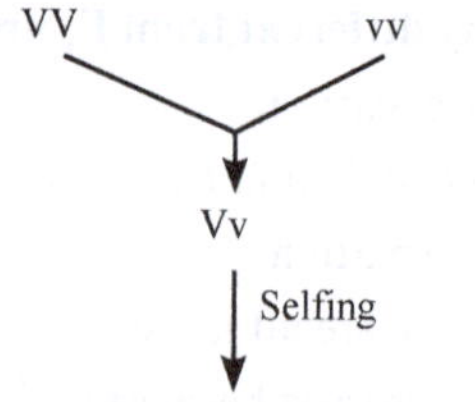

	V	v
V	VV (violet)	Vv (violet)
v	Vv (violet)	vv (white)

8. (*b*) If the genes for seed shape and seed color are linked, they would not assort independently during gamete formation. Instead, they would be inherited together more often, leading to a deviation from the 9 : 3 : 3 : 1 ratio observed in independent assortment. This is because the genes are physically close on the same chromosome and tend to co-segregate.
9. (*b*) The disorder is recessive, meaning it appears only when an individual inherits two recessive alleles. Mia and Leo are carriers (heterozygous), so they do not show symptoms but can pass the recessive gene to their children.
10. (*c*) As bacteria with Trait X (heat resistance) survive at higher rates during the heat wave, they will reproduce more, passing on this trait to offspring. Over time, the frequency of Trait X will increase.
11. (*b*) The new combination of characters in F_2 progeny when F_1 plants are selfed are round yellow and wrinkled green.
12. (*a*) RRYY and RrYy represents phenotypically similar but genotypically different plants as both produce round and yellow seeds.
13. (*d*) Mendel selected pea plants for his experiments due to their easily detectable, contrasting characters. These are bisexual plants and grow to maturity in a single season only. In these plants, cross-pollination can also be done artificially.
14. (*c*)

	Yellow	Green
Round	9/16 Round Yellow	3/16 Round Green
Wrinkled	3/16 Wrinkled Yellow	1/16 Wrinkled Green

In dihybrid cross, among the 16 progenies, 3 are round green.

So, in 556 seeds no. of round green seeds = 3/16 × 556 = 104

Assertion and Reason

1. (*c*) Inherited traits are present in a person since the time of birth and are passed on from one generation to another.
2. (*b*) Variations are differences present between individuals of same or different species. Changes in the structure of DNA leads to variations. It is because of sexual reproduction as DNA of two different individuals combine during fertilisation.
3. (*b*) In human, the features like height eye colour and hair colour come in lots of slightly different forms because they are regulated by many genes, each of which provides some amount to the overall phenotype.
4. (*d*) Assertion (A) is false because changes in non-reproductive cells generally do not affect the DNA in germ cells, which are responsible for passing genetic information to the next generation. Reason (R) is true as it correctly describes inheritance.
5. (*a*) Assertion (A) is true: the genetic complement of an organism, consisting of all the genes inherited from its parents, is called its genotype. Reason (R) is also true: the genotype refers to the specific hereditary makeup of an organism, including all of its genes.
6. (*d*)

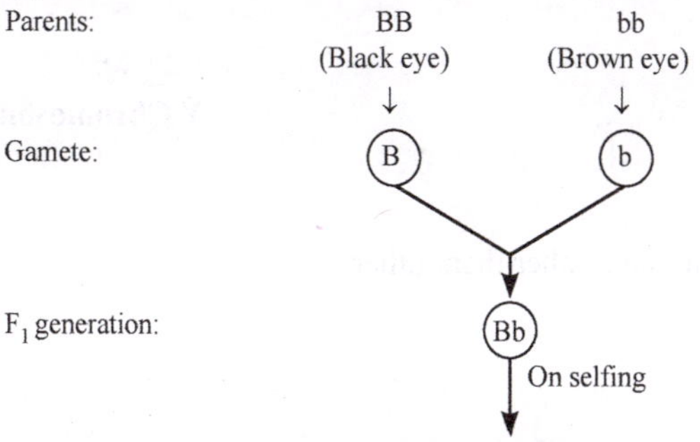

F_2 generation:

♀ \ ♂	B	b
B	BB	Bb
b	Bb	bb

Genotypic ratio: BB (Black eye) : Bb (Black eye) : bb (Brown eye)

Phenotypic ratio 1 : 2 : 1

7. (*b*) Variations promotes the survival of the species in the changing environment. The accumulation of 'heat resistant' variation (or trait) in some bacteria will ensure its survival even when the temperature in its environment rises too much due to a heat wave or some other reasons. On the other hand, the bacteria which did not have this variation to withstand heat would not survive under these circumstances and die.
8. (*b*) Statement (A) is correct: A dominant allele expresses its phenotype even when paired with a different allele for the same gene. This means its traits are visible in the organism even if only one copy is present. Statement (R) is also true and provides a method of representation, where dominant alleles are typically denoted by capital letters, such as "T", to distinguish them from recessive alleles.
9. (*a*) On crossing heterozygous tall and dwarf plant the result is as follows:

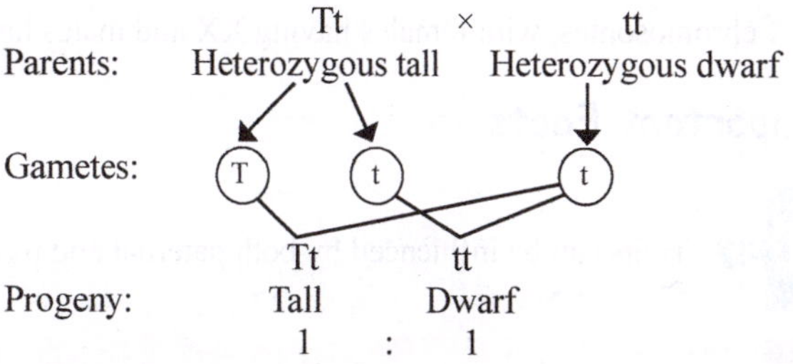

or 50% tall, 50% dwarf progeny.

10. (*a*) Assertion (A) is correct: Genes for tallness and dwarfness in plants should not be seen as separate entities but rather as different versions of the same gene. Reason (R) explains this by stating that these are two alleles, or forms, of the same gene that govern a single characteristic, such as height in plants. Each allele represents a variation of the gene that can influence the specific trait differently, in this case, resulting in either tall or dwarf plants.
11. (*d*) Round (R) and yellow (Y) traits are dominant over wrinkled (r) and green (y) traits, respectively. Therefore, when RRYY (round yellow seeds) plants are crossed with rryy (wrinkled green seeds) plants, the F_1 generation will inherit the RrYy genotype, expressing the dominant round and yellow seed traits, not the wrinkled green as initially stated.
12. (*d*) Mendel's monohybrid crosses, which yield a 3 : 1 phenotypic ratio in the F_2 generation, actually demonstrate the law of segregation, showing that alleles separate during gamete formation. This is distinct from the law of independent assortment, which applies to the inheritance of two or more traits and their distribution in gametes.

2 SEX DETERMINATION

NCERT Definitions (Commonly asked in 1 mark)

- **Sex Determination:** The biological process that decides the sex of an offspring, influenced by genetic, environmental, or a combination of factors.
- **Autosomes:** Chromosomes that are not sex chromosomes and are present in both males and females in pairs.
- **Sex Chromosomes:** The 23rd pair of chromosomes that determine the genetic sex of an organism. In humans, these are X and Y chromosomes, with females having XX and males having XY configurations.

Important Facts

01 Traits can be influenced by both paternal and maternal DNA.

02 In human beings, the sex of the individual is largely genetically determined.

03 In human, the sex chromosome present only in males. **~Y Chromosome**

04 In a male child (XY), the X chromosome always inherited from his mother, rather than father.

Classification

Methods of Sex Determination

- **Environmental Cues Changeable Sex**
  The temperature at which fertilized eggs are incubated can determine the sex of the offspring.
  Example: Certain Reptiles
- **Changeable Sex**
  Some species can change their sex, indicating sex is not fixed genetically.
  Example: Snails
- **Genetic Determination**
  Sex is determined by the genetic information inherited from parents.
  Example: Humans

Difference Between

Sex Determination in Humans vs Other Animals (General Perspective)

Humans	Other Animals
Genetically determined through the XX and XY chromosome system.	Can be genetically determined or environmentally influenced.
Sex is determined at fertilisation.	Sex can change after birth in some species.
Does not involve environmental factors in sex determination.	May involve environmental cues, like temperature.
XY leads to a male, XX leads to a female.	Mechanisms vary widely.

Myth Buster

- **Myth: The mother's genes determine the sex of the baby.**

  Fact: The sex of a baby is determined by the sex chromosome it inherits from the father. If the baby inherits an X chromosome from the father, it will be female (XX), and if it inherits a Y chromosome, it will be male (XY). The mother always contributes an X chromosome.

X and Y in Alphabet

X and Y in Maths

X and Y in Genetics

- **Myth: All human chromosomes are paired and identical.**

  Fact: While humans have 22 pairs of chromosomes that are the same in both males and females (autosomes), the 23rd pair, the sex chromosomes, differ between males and females. Females have two X chromosomes (XX), and males have one X and one Y chromosome (XY).

- **Myth: Sex determination mechanisms are the same across all organisms.**

  Fact: Different species use various strategies for sex determination. Some animals, like certain reptiles, rely on environmental cues like the temperature at which eggs are incubated, while in humans and many other species, sex is genetically determined through the combination of sex chromosomes inherited from the parents.

- **Myth: Changing environmental conditions can alter the genetic sex determination in humans.**

  Fact: In humans, the genetic determination of sex through the X and Y chromosomes is not influenced by environmental conditions. While environmental factors can affect the development and expression of secondary sexual characteristics to some extent, they do not change the genetically determined sex of an individual.

- **Myth: A single sperm contains both X and Y chromosomes.**

  Fact: During the process of gamete formation, the chromosome number is reduced by half, achieving a haploid state. This reduction ensures that each sperm cell contains only one set of chromosomes.

Real Life Application Based Questions

1. How do conservationists use sex determination studies to manage sex ratios in wild animal populations, particularly in endangered species recovery programs?

Ans. Studies on sex determination are vital for conserving species like turtles and snails, which exhibit temperature-dependent sex determination. By managing nesting temperatures, conservationists can influence sex ratios, ensuring balanced male and female populations. This approach is essential to maintain genetic diversity and prevent the decline of species affected by skewed sex distributions due to climate change.

2. How can knowledge of sex determination mechanisms be used to improve livestock breeding practices and other areas of agriculture?

Ans. Knowledge of sex determination mechanisms enhances livestock breeding by enabling the predetermination of offspring sex, thus optimizing productivity. Currently applied in cattle, this technology increases economic returns by producing preferred outputs, such as female dairy cows, and mitigates welfare concerns such as castration, supporting sustainable agricultural practices in response to growing global food demands.

3. How is sex determination utilized in medical genetics to improve health outcomes?

Ans. Sex determination is crucial in medical genetics for diagnosing X-linked genetic disorders. Diseases like hemophilia are primarily diagnosed in males who inherit the defective gene from their mothers. This understanding allows for targeted treatments and management strategies specific to the patient's genetic profile.

4. What role does sex determination play in paleontology and the study of fossils?

Ans. Sex determination in fossils helps paleontologists understand the evolutionary dynamics and behavior of ancient species. By identifying sexual dimorphism or characteristics specific to one sex, researchers can infer mating strategies, social structures, and ecological roles, shedding light on the past biodiversity of ecosystems.

COMPETENCY BASED SOLVED EXAMPLES

Multiple Choice Questions (1 M)

1. In an experiment on sex determination strategies in reptiles, a biologist observed the following:

- **At 28°C, 70% of the fertilized eggs developed into males and 30% into females.**
- **At 32°C, 40% of the fertilized eggs developed into males and 60% into females.**

Based on these observations, what can be concluded about sex determination in these reptiles? ***(Ap)***

(*a*) Higher temperatures increase the proportion of male offspring.

(*b*) Temperature has no effect on the sex of the offspring.

(*c*) The proportion of male to female offspring varies with temperature.

(*d*) Lower temperatures increase the proportion of female offspring.

2. Aarav and Pooja are a couple trying to conceive a child. They want to understand how the sex of their future child will be determined.Which of the following factors will determine the sex of Aarav and Pooja's future first boy child? ***(Ap)***

(*a*) The blood type of Aarav and Pooja

(*b*) The length of time between ovulation and copulation in Pooja

(*c*) The presence of the Y chromosome in Aarav 's sperm

(*d*) The presence of X chromosome in Pooja's ovum

Assertion and Reason (1 M)

Direction: **The following questions consist of two statements – Assertion (A) and Reason (R). Answer these questions by selecting the appropriate option given below:**

(*a*) Both A and R are true, and R is the correct explanation of A.

(*b*) Both A and R are true, but R is not the correct explanation of A.

(*c*) A is true, but R is false.

(*d*) A is false, but R is true.

1. **Assertion (A):** Genes inherited from the parents decide the sex of a child.
Reason (R): X chromosome in a male child is inherited from his father. ***(Re)***

2. **Assertion (A):** Sex determining chromosomes are X and Y in humans.
Reason (R): In some organisms environment can also determine sex. ***(Un)***

Subjective Questions

Very Short Answer Type Questions (2 M)

1. A woman has only daughters. Analyse the situation genetically and provide a suitable explanation.
(*An*) (NCERT Exemplar)

Ans. A woman having only daughters is due to the father's X chromosome fertilizing the egg each time, resulting in XX offspring, or females. Each pregnancy has a roughly 50% chance of being male or female, so having only daughters in multiple pregnancies can occur purely by chance, without underlying genetic factors.

2. Sex determination in humans happens through sex chromosomes. Along with other parameters, such processes often help in forensic studies in crime investigation and/or identification of accidents and natural calamities, In order to determine whether an accident victim is male or female, which cells can be used and why? ***(An)***

Ans.
- Any cell of the body
- Every cell has the sex chromosome as the 23rd pair

(2 M)

Short Answer Type Questions (3 M)

1. A scientist compared sex determination in three species, represented as X, Y, and Z: ***(An, Un)***

Species	Mechanism of Sex Determination
X	Genetic (XX for females and XY for males)
Y	Temperature-based sex determination during development
Z	Ability to change sex based on environmental cues

(*a*) Identify which organisms could be represented by X and Y. Justify your answer based on their mechanism of sex determination.

(*b*) Which mechanism of sex determination is more stable across generations? Justify your answer.

Ans. (*a*)

- X: Humans, as they follow genetic sex determination (XX for females, XY for males). *(1 M)*
- Y: Reptiles, because their sex is determined by temperature. *(1 M)*

(*b*) Genetic sex determination (as seen in X) is more stable across generations because it depends on the inheritance of chromosomes, ensuring consistency. In contrast, temperature or environmental factors (as seen in Y and Z) can fluctuate, leading to instability in sex ratios and population dynamics. *(1 M)*

2. (*i*) **Do genetic combination of mothers play a significant role in determining the sex of a new born?**

(*ii*) **Why do all the gametes formed in human females have an X chromosomes? (*Un*)**

Ans. (*i*) No, the genetic combination of mothers does not play a significant role in determining the sex of a newborn. Mothers provide an X chromosome to the offspring, while the sex of the newborn depends on whether the sperm cell from the father carries an X or a Y chromosome. *(1½ M)*

(*ii*) All gametes formed in human females have an X chromosome because females have two X chromosomes (XX) and during meiosis, each gamete receives one chromosome. Since females only have X chromosomes to give, all female gametes carry an X chromosome. *(1½ M)*

3. **In a family eagerly awaiting the birth of their third child, they already have two children—a son and a daughter. As they welcome their newborn, let's explore the role of sex chromosomes in determining the baby's sex.**

(*a*) **Mention the sex chromosomes present in the male and female children in the family.**

(*b*) **Describe the possible combination of sex chromosomes that lead to the birth of a male child for this family.**

(*c*) **Briefly explain how the inheritance of sex chromosomes from each parent contributes to the determination of the newborn's sex with the help of across. (*Re, Un*)**

Ans. (*a*) The sex chromosomes present in the male and female children in the family are as follows:

Male child: XY (The male has one x and one Y sex chromosome)

Female child: XX (The female has two X sex chromosomes)

(*b*) The possible combination of sex chromosomes that lead to the birth of a male child for this family is XY. When the X chromosome from the father during fertilization, it result in the XY combination, which determines a male child.

(*c*) The inheritance of sex chromosomes from each parent determines the child's sex. If can be understand with the help of cross as given below:

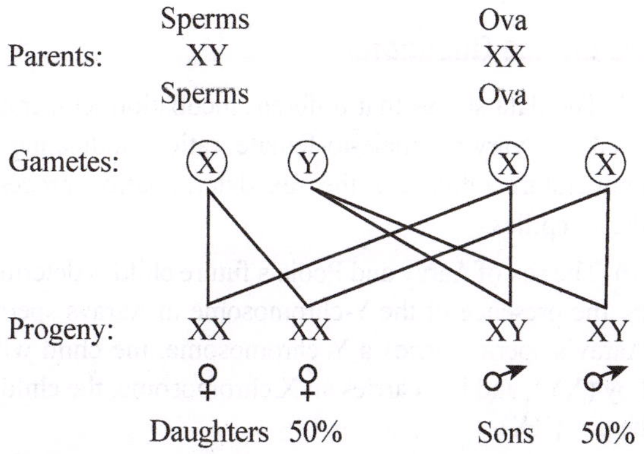

4. (*a*) **Name the two types of gametes produced by men.**

(*b*) **Does a male child inherit X chromosome from his father? Justify.**

(*c*) **How many types of gametes are produced by a human female? (*Re*) (CBSE, 2022 Term II)**

Ans. (*a*) The two types of gametes produced by men are X and Y. *(½ M)*

(*b*) No, a male child does not inherit an X chromosome from his father. The male child inherits the Y chromosome from his father, which pairs with the X chromosome inherited from his mother, resulting in an XY combination that determines male sex. *(2 M)*

(*c*) A human female produces one type of gamete, which is egg containing the X chromosome. *(½ M)*

Long Answer Type Questions (5 M)

1. **In a study of pea plants, a biologist finds that despite variations in sunlight and watering conditions, certain traits like seed color and shape remain consistent across generations.**

How does this observation support the idea of inherited traits and the stability of genetic information through sexual reproduction? (*Ap*)

Ans. (*a*) The observation that traits like seed color and shape remain consistent despite environmental variations indicates these traits are genetically determined and passed from parents to offspring through sexual reproduction. *(2 M)*

(*b*) The consistency across generations supports the idea that genetic information is stable and reliably transmitted through sexual reproduction, ensuring traits are inherited. *(2 M)*

(*c*) Sexual reproduction involves the fusion of gametes, mixing genetic material to produce offspring with a combination of traits from both parents, highlighting the principle of heredity. *(1M)*

2. **Rohan is a 5 year old boy. His parents inform Rohan that soon he will be an elder brother as Rohan's mother is pregnant. Rohan gets really excited and asks his mother whether it will be a boy or a girl. Rohan's mom explains that there is a 50 : 50 probability of either a boy or girl. Give a suitable explanation for this. (*Un*)**

Ans. The probability of getting either a boy or girl child in humans is 50:50 and can be attributed to the random nature of genetic inheritance during fertilization. Each time a couple conceives, the father's sperm carries either an X or a Y chromosome, while the mother's egg always contributes an X chromosome. The chance of fertilization by either an X or Y sperm is roughly equal. *(2 M)*

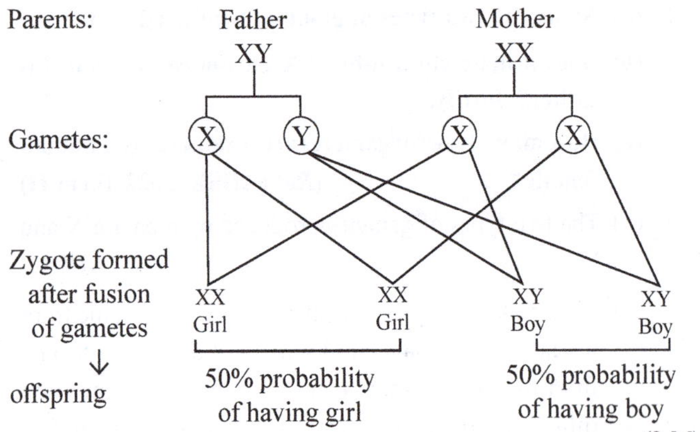

(2 M)

As a result, there is an equal chance of producing an XX combination (girl) or an XY combination (boy), leading to the 50:50 probability of having either a boy or girl child. *(1 M)*

> **Nailing the Right Answer**
>
> In case of sex determination, draw a simple punnett square to illustrate your answer. This can make your answer clearer & might fetch you extra marks for the efforts.

3. (a) How many pairs of chromosomes are present in human beings? Out of these how many are sex chromosomes?

(b) How many types of sex chromosomes are found in human beings?

(c) "The sex of a newborn child is a matter of chance and none of the parents may be considered responsible for it". Draw a flow chart showing determination of sex of a newborn to justify this statement. (*Un, Cr*) (CBSE, 2019)

Ans. (*a*) Human beings have 23 pairs of chromosomes, totaling 46. Out of these, one pair is the sex chromosomes, which determine the genetic sex of the individual. *(2 M)*

(*b*) There are two types of sex chromosomes found in human beings: X and Y chromosomes. Females have two X chromosomes (XX), and males have one X and one Y chromosome (XY). *(1 M)*

(*c*) The sex of a newborn child is determined by the combination of sex chromosomes received from the parents. Here's a flowchart to explain:

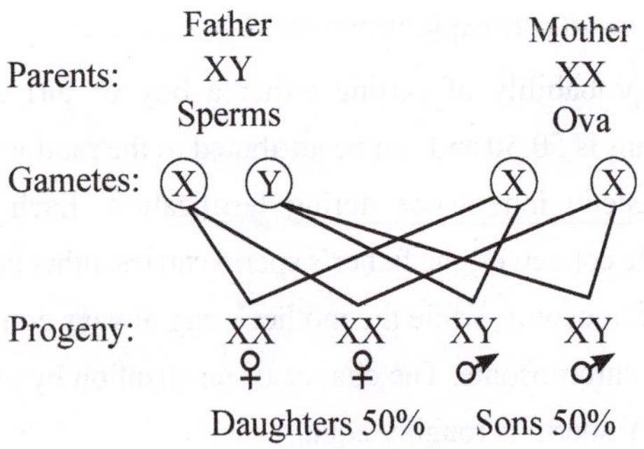

This flowchart shows that the sex of a newborn is determined by whether the sperm cell from the father carries an X or a Y chromosome, combined with the X chromosome from the mother, making it a matter of chance. *(1 M)*

4. The person A has only B chromosomes in all its gametes. On the other hand, another person C has chromosomes D in half of the gametes and chromosome E in the other half of gametes. When chromosomes B and D combine during fertilization, a female zygote results. On the other hand, the combination of B and E chromosomes produces a male zygote.

(*a*) What are chromosomes (*i*) B (*ii*) D, and (*iii*) E?

(*b*) Out of B, D and E, which two chromosomes are of the same type?

(*c*) Which chromosome is smaller in size?

(*d*) What is the general name of chromosomes such as B and E?

(*e*) Out of the two persons A and C, which one is (i) male, and (ii) female? (*An*)

Ans. (*a*) (*i*) The chromosome B represents X chromosomes because if person A is entirely made up of B chromosomes it means the person is a female and has all X chromosomes.

(*ii*) The chromosome D is X chromosome because when B and D combine a female offspring is produced. A female zygote can only be produced when both of the chromosomes in the gamete are 'X'.

(*iii*) The chromosome E is a Y chromosome because when B and E combine a male zygote is produced. *(1 M)*

(*b*) Chromosome B and D are of the same type, i.e. X chromosome. *(1 M)*

(*c*) Chromosome E is smaller in size since it is a Y chromosome. *(1 M)*

(*d*) Chromosome B (X) and chromosome E (Y) are known as Sex chromosomes. *(1 M)*

(*e*) (*i*) C is male since it has half of the gametes with D (X) and half of the gametes with E (Y) chromosomes. *(½ M)*

(*ii*) A is female since it has all B chromosomes in it i.e. X chromosome which is only present in females. *(½ M)*

Hints & Explanations

Multiple Choice Questions

1. (*c*) The data shows that different incubation temperatures result in varying male-to-female ratios, indicating that temperature influences the sex determination process in these reptiles.

2. (*c*) The sex of Aarav and Pooja's future child is determined by the presence of the Y-chromosome in Aaravs sperm. If Aarav's sperm carries a Y chromosome, the child will be boy (XY), and if it carries an X chromosome, the child will be girl (XX).

Assertion and Reason

1. (*c*) Assertion (A) is true, but reason (R) is false.

   Genes carry traits from one generation to another, they also determine the sex of the individual.

   In male (XY) and in females (XX) are sex chromosomes.

   Male child has X chromosome inherited from his mother and Y chromosome from his father.

   So, the reason (R) is false.

2. (*b*) In humans, the sex determination is XX-XY type. In some animals environmental factor such as temperature at which fertilised eggs are kept decide the gender. e.g., turtle.

MISCELLANEOUS EXERCISE

Multiple Choice Questions (1 M)

1. In a plant, red fruit (R) is dominant over yellow fruit (r) and tallness (T) is dominant over dwarf (t). If a plant with RRTt is crossed with a plant with rrtt, then **(*Ap*)**
   (*a*) 75% will be tall with red fruit
   (*b*) 100% will be tall with red fruit
   (*c*) 25% will be tall with red fruit
   (*d*) 50% will be tall with red fruit

2. The changes in non-reproductive tissues **(*Re*) (NCERT Exemplar)**
   (*a*) Cannot be passed on to the DNA of the germ cells
   (*b*) Cannot direct evolution
   (*c*) Are the acquired traits
   (*d*) All of these

3. In cattle, having horns is a recessive trait (*h*) to not having horns (*H*). When cattle with horns are crossed with cattle that do not have horns, the number of offspring having horns was equal to those not having horns. Which of the following is MOST LIKELY to be true? **(*Ap*)**
   (*a*) Both parents are homozygous dominant.
   (*b*) One parent is homozygous dominant.
   (*c*) Both parents are heterozygous.
   (*d*) One parent is heterozygous.

4. A mice with black colour (Bb) is mated with one with brown colour coat (bb). The chances of getting a brown colour is. (Assume black is dominant) **(*Ap*)**
   (*a*) 25% (*b*) 50%
   (*c*) 75% (*d*) 100%

5. A Mendelian experiment consisted of breeding tall pea plants bearing violet flowers with short pea plants bearing white flowers. The progeny will have all violet flowers, but almost half of them were short. This suggests that the genetic make-up of the tall parent can be depicted as **(*An*)**
   (*a*) TTWW (*b*) TTww
   (*c*) TtWW (*d*) TtWw

6. Study the data and answer the following question. **(*Ev*)**

Parental plants cross fertilised and seeds collected	F_1 First Generation offsprings	F_2 Offsprings of self pollination of F_1
Male parents always bear red flowers. Female parent always had white flowers.	330 seeds sown and observed. All 330 gave red flowers.	Out of 44 seeds 33 seeds gave plants with red flowers and 11 seeds gave plants with white flowers.

The genotype of F_2 progeny is
   (*a*) Homozygous recessive, Heterozygous dominant, Homozygous dominant
   (*b*) Homozygous recessive, Heterozygous Recessive, Homozygous dominant
   (*c*) Homozygous dominant and Heterozygous dominant
   (*d*) Homozygous recessive and Homozygous dominant

Assertion and Reason (1 M)

Direction: The following questions consist of two statements – Assertion (A) and Reason (R). Answer these questions by selecting the appropriate option given below:

(*a*) Both A and R are true, and R is the correct explanation of A.
(*b*) Both A and R are true, but R is not the correct explanation of A.
(*c*) A is true, but R is false
(*d*) A is false, but R is true.

1. **Assertion (A):** Sex determination in human beings is influenced by the presence or absence of specific sex chromosomes.
   Reason (R): The presence of an X chromosome from the father and an X chromosome from the mother results in a female offspring, while the presence of a Y chromosome from the father and an X chromosome from the mother results in a male offspring. **(*Re*)**

2. **Assertion (A):** A gamete contains a single allele for each trait.
   Reason (R): During gametogenesis, the two alleles of each trait segregate, one passing into each gamete at random. **(*Re*)**

3. **Assertion (A):** A geneticist crossed a pea plant having violet flowers with a pea plant with white flowers, he got all violet flowers in first generation.
Reason (R): White colour gene is not passed on to next generation. ***(Un)***
4. **Assertion (A):** The male is not responsible for the sex of the baby (boy or girl) which is born.
Reason (R): A male has one X chromosome and one Y chromosome whereas a female has two X chromosomes. XX combinations of sex chromosomes leads to a baby girl but the XY combinations of sex chromosomes leads to a baby boy. ***(Un)***
5. **Assertion (A):** In humans, if gene b gives blue eyes and gene B gives brown eyes, then the colour of the eyes of a person having Bb combination of genes will be blue.
Reason (R): The recessive gene cannot show its effect in the presence of dominant gene. ***(Un)***
6. **Assertion (A):** The characteristics (or traits) of an organism are determined by 'internal factors' (now called 'genes') which occur in pairs. Only one of a pair of such 'factors' can be present in a single gamete.
Reason (R): The genes which dominate other genes are called dominant genes and the genes which get dominated are called recessive genes. ***(Un)***

Subjective Questions

Very Short Answer Type Questions (2 M)

1. What should be the genotype of the parent plants to give green and yellow seeds in equal proportions? ***(Un)***
2. The farmer crosses two heterozygous green seeded plants and obtains 100 plants in the F_1 generation.
What would be the number of green and yellow seeds respectively in the F_1 generation? ***(Ap)***
3. (*a*) What process leads to the accumulation of variation during reproduction?
(*b*) What term describes an organism that has two identical alleles for a particular gene? ***(Un)***
4. Mendel crossed a pea plant having inflated green pod with a constricted yellow pod. ***(Un)***
(*a*) What type of a cross is it?
(*b*) What type of plants are obtained in F_1?

Short Answer Type Questions (3 M)

1. Name the plant Mendel used for his experiment. What type of progeny was obtained by Mendel in F_1 and F_2 generations when he crossed the tall and short plants? Write the ratio he obtained in F_2 generation plants. ***(Re)***
2. While conducting his research, Mr. Kumar crosses two pea plants:
• **Plant A:** Yellow seeds (Dominant)
• **Plant B:** Green seeds (Recessive)
Mr. Kumar expects all yellow seeds in the F_1 generation. However, his results were surprising:

Seed Color	Number of Seeds
Yellow	100
Green	100

Mr. Kumar is confused as to why green seeds appeared. ***(An)***
(*a*) How would the presence of green seeds in the F_1 generation affect your conclusion about the genotype of Plant A?
(*b*) If the dominant F_1 plants were self-crossed, what would be the phenotypic ratio of the F_2 generation?
3. A guinea pig having black colour is crossed with guinea pig having the same colour.
They produced 100 offsprings, out of which 75 were black and 25 were white.
(*i*) What is the possible genotype of parent guinea pigs?
(*ii*) Which trait is dominant and which is recessive? ***(Ev)***
4. If two pea plants having round and green seeds (*RRgg*) are crossed, identify the percentage of the following with respect to the F_1 generation: ***(Ap)***
(*a*) gametes having both the round and yellow seed traits
(*b*) offspring having the same genotype as the parents
(*c*) offspring having the same phenotype as the parents
5. A Mendelian experiment consisted of breeding pea plants bearing violet flowers with pea plants bearing white flowers. What will be the result in F_2 progeny? ***(An)*** **(CBSE, 2018)**
6. Explain the difference between the terms: gene, allele and chromosome. ***(Re)***
7. What is variation? List two main reasons that may lead to variation in a population. ***(Re)*** **(CBSE, 2022)**

Long Answer Type Questions (5 M)

1. Study the given data and answer the questions that follow:

1	2	3
Parental plant cross-fertilised and seeds collected.	F_1 generation offspring	F_2 generation offspring after self-pollination of F_1 hybrid.
Male parent: Round Green seeds Female parent: Wrinkled Yellow seeds	All seeds: Round Yellow	315: Round Yellow 108: Round Green 101: Wrinkled Yellow 32: Wrinkled Green

(*a*) What is the term given to this type of cross? ***(An)***
(*b*) What does the data in column 2 indicate?
State how you arrived at this conclusion.
2. Sex determination is an important developmental event in the life cycle of all Sexually reproducing plants. Recent studies of sex determination in many plant species, from ferns to maize, have been fruitful in identifying the diversity of genetic and epigenetic factors that are involved in determining the sex of the flower or individual."

The above is an excerpt from an article by two scientists Cristina Juarez and Jo Ann Banks.

(*a*) What is the most likely genetic factor for sex determination in unisexual plants?

(*b*) Epigenetic factors refer to factors external to the genetic component of an individual. Name evidence of ONE epigenetic condition that determines sexuality in animals.

(*c*) State Mendel's law of segregation and explain how sex determination violates the law.

(*d*) Which parent determines the sex of the offspring in human beings? Why? **(*An*)**

3. Imagine a student is curious about how certain traits are passed down from parents to their children and how genetic information remains stable. The student learns about structures within cells that play a crucial role in these processes. What are these structures, and how do they contribute to the inheritance of traits and the stability of genetic information? **(*Re, Ev*)**

4. (*i*) In a cross between violet flowered plants and white flowered plants, state the characteristics of the plants obtained in the F_2 progeny.

(*ii*) If the plants of F_1 progeny are self-pollinated, then what would be observed in the plants of F_2 progeny?

(*iii*) If 100 plants are produced in F_2 progeny, then how many plants will show the recessive trait?

(*Ap*) (CBSE, 2022)

5. The genotype of green-stemmed tomato plants is denoted as GG and that of purple-stemmed tomato plants as gg. When these two are crossed,

(*i*) What colour of stem would you expect in their F_1 progeny?

(*ii*) Give the percentage of purple-stemmed plants if F_1 plants are self-pollinated.

(*iii*) In what ratio would you find the genotypes GG and Gg in the F_2 progeny? **(*Ap*) (CBSE, 2022)**

6. (*a*) E is the gene for brown eye color and e is the gene for blue eye colour. Which gene is (*i*) recessive, and (*ii*) dominant?

(*b*) Both father and mother have the genes Ee in their cells. What color are their eyes?

(*c*) Which combination of genes in the zygote will produce children with blue eyes?

(*d*) Which combination of genes in the zygote will produce children with brown eyes? **(*An*)**

Case Based Questions

Case Based-I: In order to trace the inheritance of traits Mendel crossed pea plants having one contrasting character or a pair of contrasting characters. When he crossed pea plants having round and yellow seeds with pea plants having wrinkled and green seeds, he observed that no plants with wrinkled and green seeds were obtained in the F_1 generation. When the F_1 generation pea plants were cross-bred by self-pollination, the F_2 generation had seeds with different combinations of shape and colour also. **(*Un*)**

(*i*) Write any two pairs of contrasting characteristics of pea plant used by Mendel other than those mentioned above. *(1 M)*

(*ii*) Differentiate between dominant and recessive traits. *(1 M)*

(*iii*) State the ratio of the combinations observed in the seeds of F_2 generation (in the above case). What do you interpret from this result? *(2 M)*

OR

Given below is a cross between a pure violet flowered pea plant (V) and a pure white flowered pea plant (v). Diagrammatically explain what type of progeny is obtained in F_1 generation and F_2 generation:

Pure violet flowered plant × Pure white flowered plant.

(V V) (v v) *(2 M)*

Case Based-II: Four pea plants P, Q, R and S with different genotypes were cross-bred randomly for pod shape inheritance. The following pod shapes appeared in the progeny. Analyze the observations and answer the questions that follow.

Plant Cross	Generation 1 Observations
Plant P × Plant Q	All inflated pods
Plant R × Plant S	3 inflated pods : 1 constricted pod
Plant Q × Plant R	50% inflated pods : 50% constricted pods

(*An*)

(*i*) Predict the genotypes of the parents involved in each cross and explain the inheritance pattern for pod shape. *(2 M)*

(*ii*) How many genes control the inheritance of pod shape in the above crosses? *(1 M)*

(*iii*) Which Mendel's law is demonstrated in Plant R × Plant S cross? Justify with observations. *(1 M)*

OR

What will be the genotype and phenotype of the progeny if Plant P and Plant R are crossed together?. *(1 M)*

Case Based-III: A couple with normal hearing, have four children. Three of their children can hear normally, but one child is deaf. Deafness in their family is caused by a recessive allele. Despite no known history of deafness on either side, they seek to understand how this condition appeared in one of their children. **(*Ap*)**

(*i*) What are the likely genotypes of the parents based on the children's traits? *(1 M)*

(*ii*) What is the probability that the couple's next child will be deaf? *(1 M)*

(*iii*) Determine the possible genotypes of all the children given that one child is deaf. *(2 M)*

OR

Explain why deafness appeared in only one of the four children. *(2 M)*

Case Based-IV: Sex of an individual is determined by different factors in various species. Some animals rely entirely on the environmental cues, while in some other animals the individuals can change their sex during their life time indicating that sex of some species is not genetically determined. However, in human beings, the sex of an individual is largely determined genetically. ***(Un, Cr)***

(*i*) In what way are the sex chromosomes 'X' and 'Y' different in size? Name the mismatched pair of sex chromosomes in humans. *(1 M)*

(*ii*) Write the number of pair/pairs of sex chromosomes present in human beings. In which one of the parent (male / female) perfect pair/pairs of sex chromosomes are present? *(1 M)*

(*iii*) Citing two examples, justify the statement "Sex of an individual is not always determined genetically". *(2 M)*

OR

Draw a flow chart to show that sex is determined genetically in human beings. *(2 M)*

Case Based-V: All human chromosomes are not paired. Most human chromosomes have a maternal and a paternal copy, and we have 22 such pairs. But one pair called the sex chromosomes, is odd in not always being a perfect pair. Women have a perfect pair of sex chromosomes. But men have a mismatched pair in which one is normal sized while the other is a short one. ***(Un)***

(*i*) In humans, how many chromosomes are present in a Zygote and in each gamete? *(1 M)*

(*ii*) A few reptiles rely entirely on environmental cues for sex determination. Comment. *(1 M)*

(*iii*) "The sex of a child is a matter of chance and none of the parents are considered to be responsible for it." Justify it through flow chart only. *(2 M)*

OR

Why do all the gametes formed in human females have an X chromosome? *(2 M)*

ANSWER KEYS

Multiple Choice Questions

1. (*d*) **2.** (*d*) **3.** (*d*) **4.** (*b*) **5.** (*c*) **6.** (*a*)

Assertion and Reason

1. (*a*) **2.** (*a*) **3.** (*c*) **4.** (*d*) **5.** (*d*) **6.** (*b*)

HINTS & EXPLANATIONS

Multiple Choice Questions

1. (*d*) The cross between RRTt × rrtt will produce 50% red and tall and 50% red and short offsprings.

Parents: RRTt (red tall) × rrtt (yellow dwarf)

Gametes: (RT) (Rt) (rt) (rt)

F_1-generation:

♀ \ ♂	rt	rt
RT	RrTt Tall red	RrTt Tall red
Rt	Rrtt Short red	Rrtt Short red

2. (*d*) The changes in the non-reproductive body cells, i.e., *somatic cells of an organism cannot be inherited by its* offsprings, because only those traits can be transmitted to future generations in which changes have occurred in the DNA present in the reproductive cells of parent organism.

3. (*d*) The given problem states that the number of offspring with horns is equal to those without horns. This suggests a 1:1 phenotypic ratio, which typically occurs in a cross between a heterozygous dominant parent (Hh) and a homozygous recessive parent (hh).

Using a Punnett square: Hh × hh results in 50% offspring with horns (hh) and 50% without horns (Hh).

Hh X hh
(Cattle without horns) (Cattle with horns)

Male gamete ♂

Female gametes ♀	H	h
h	Hh (without horns)	Hh (without horns)
h	hh (with horns)	hh (with horns)

4. (*b*) On crossing black coat color (Bb) with brown coat color (bb).

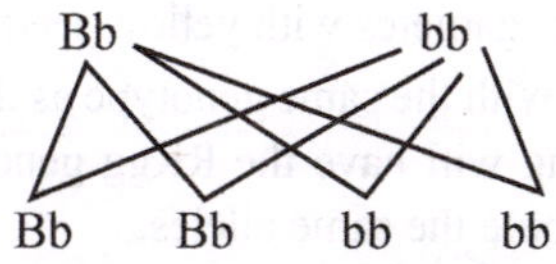

The chance of getting brown color is 50%.

5. (*c*) TtWW might be the genetic make-up of the tall parent. Since half the progenies have short pea plants, this means that the parent plant also will have a collection of dwarf genes; all progenies have violet flowers, further suggesting that violet color is dominant over white.

6. (*a*) The ratio of red to white flowers in the F_2 generation is approximately 3:1 (33 red: 11 white out of 44 total), which is a classic Mendelian ratio indicating a monohybrid cross involving heterozygous parents.

Thus, the gene types present in the F_2 progeny must include:

- Homozygous dominant (red flowers from two dominant alleles),
- Heterozygous dominant (red flowers from one dominant and one recessive allele),
- Homozygous recessive (white flowers from two recessive alleles)

Assertion and Reason

1. (*a*) The sex of an offspring in humans is indeed determined by the presence or absence of specific sex chromosomes. This is a fundamental concept in genetics. The sex of human offspring is determined by sex chromosomes: an X from the mother and either an X or Y from the father. An XX combination results in a female, while an XY combination leads to a male. This genetic mechanism ensures the determination of the offspring's sex at fertilization.

2. (*a*) "During the formation of gamete, each gene separates from each other so that each gamete carries only one allele for each gene."It was explained by Mendel's law of segregation.

3. (*c*) Assertion (A) is true: Crossing a pea plant with violet flowers (dominant trait) with one having white flowers (recessive trait) and obtaining all violet flowers in the first generation aligns with Mendelian genetics, indicating the dominance of the violet flower trait.

   Reason (R) is incorrect: The white color gene is passed on to the next generation, but it does not express itself in the presence of the dominant violet gene. In the F1 generation, the white flower gene is masked by the dominant violet flower gene, not absent.

4. (*d*) Sex of a child in humans is determined by the type of male gamete which fuses with the female egg. Male gamete contains either X or Y chromosome. The female egg always has an X chromosome. So if the male gamete with the X chromosome fuses with the female egg, the child will be female. Similarly, if the male gamete with the Y chromosome fuses with the female egg, the child will be male.

5. (*d*) If b gives blue eyes and B gives brown eyes in humans then the person having Bb gene combination has brown eyes. Since, the recessive gene cannot show its effect in the presence of dominant gene.

6. (*b*) During gamete formation, the alleles for each gene segregate from each other so that each gamete carries only one allele for each gene. This was proposed in the Law of segregation.

Subjective Questions

Very Short Answer Type Questions

1. For parent plants to produce green and yellow seeds in equal proportions, one parent must be homozygous for the yellow seed trait (YY or yy) and the other parent must be heterozygous (Yy). Assuming green is dominant (G) and yellow is recessive (g), the correct cross would be:

   One parent: gg (homozygous yellow)

   Other parent: Gg (heterozygous green)

   This cross would result in approximately 50% green (Gg) and 50% yellow (gg) seed offspring. *(2M)*

2. The cross between two heterozygous green seeded plants is as follows:

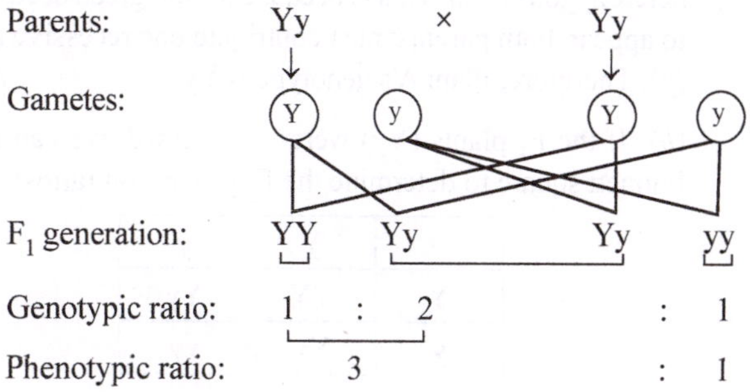

   So, for 100 plants,

   75% would have yellow seeds (3)

   25% would have green seeds (1) *(2M)*

3. (*a*) Variation accumulates during reproduction due to genetic recombination. When traits from both parents combine, resulting in unique genetic combination in offspring. *(1 M)*

   (*b*) An organism with two identical alleles for a particular gene is termed "homozygous", indicating that the alleles are the same, contributing to a consistent expression of that trait. *(1 M)*

4. (*a*) This is dihybrid cross. *(1 M)*

   (*b*) All plants are inflated, yellow pod plants. *(1 M)*

Short Answer Type Questions

1. The plant used by Mendel for his experiment is garden pea (*Pisum sativum*). *(1 M)*

When he crossed tall and short plants then he obtained all tall progenies in F_1 generation. To obtain F_2 generation he performed selfing of F_1 generation which produced both tall and short progenies in a ratio 3 : 1. *(1 M)*

Parents TT × tt

Gametes (T) (t)

F_1 generation (Tt) All tall plants (100%)

On selfing

F_2 generation

♀ \ ♂	T	t
T	TT	Tt
t	Tt	tt

Phenotypic ratio – 3 : 1

(Tall) (Short)

Genotypic ratio – 1 : 2 : 1

TT Tt tt

Tall Short

(75%) (25%) *(1 M)*

2. (*a*) The presence of green seeds (recessive trait) in the F_1 generation indicates that Plant A (Yellow seeds) is not homozygous dominant (YY). Instead, it must be heterozygous (Yy). This is because for the green seeds (yy) to appear, both parents must contribute one recessive allele (y). Therefore, Plant A's genotype is Yy. *(1 M)*

(*b*) If the F_1 plants (Yy) were self-crossed, we can use a Punnett square to determine the F_2 generation ratios:

	Y	y
Y	YY	Yy
y	Yy	yy

(1 M)

Phenotypic Ratio: 3 Yellow seeds : 1 Green seed

(Yellow includes YY and Yy; Green is yy)

Thus, in the F_2 generation, 75% of the seeds would be yellow, and 25% would be green. *(1 M)*

3. Given the offspring ratio of 75 black to 25 white guinea pigs from a cross that resulted in 100 offspring, we can deduce the following:

(*i*) Since the offspring exhibit a 3:1 ratio of black to white, this is indicative of a monohybrid cross involving two heterozygous parents for the trait. Therefore, the possible genotype of each parent guinea pig is Bb, where B represents the allele for black fur and b represents the allele for white fur. *(1½ M)*

(*ii*) The dominant trait is black fur, as indicated by the presence of this trait in the majority of the offspring (75 out of 100) when both parents carry alleles for both colors.

The recessive trait is white fur, which only appears in the absence of the dominant black fur allele (25 out of 100 offspring are white), meaning these offspring have the genotype bb. *(1½ M)*

4. Given that both parent pea plants have the genotype RRgg (round seeds, green seeds):

(*a*) Gametes with round and yellow seed traits: 0%, because both parents have green seed alleles (gg) and cannot produce gametes with yellow seed traits. *(1 M)*

(*b*) Offspring with the same genotype as the parents: 100% of the offspring will have the RRgg genotype, since both parents contribute the same alleles. *(1 M)*

(*c*) Offspring with the same phenotype as the parents: 100% of the offspring will have round and green seeds, matching the parents' phenotype. *(1 M)*

5. Mendelian parents were pure breed. Hence these plants must be PP (violet) and pp (white). The progeny will be Pp (purple) as shown in the cross. *(1 M)*

P gen PP (violet) pp (white)

Gametes P p

F_1 Pp (Purple)

Pp × Pp

F_2

	P	p
P	PP	Pp
p	Pp	pp

Phenotype Ratio: PP : Pp : pp

1 : 2 : 1

(2 M)

6. Gene are segments of DNA that code for characteristics. *(1 M)*

An allele is one of two or more versions of DNA sequence at a given genomic location. *(1 M)*

DNA gets condensed with proteins to form thread like structures called chromosome. *(1 M)*

7. Variation is the difference in characteristics of individuals in a population. It occur as a result of recombination and mutation. It enable organisms to adapt to environmental conditions. *(1 M)*

Two main causes of variation:

Mutation: It refers to a sudden change in the nucleotide sequence of the genetic material of an organism. Change in a particular gene causes variation which results in a change in the phenotype of the organism. *(1 M)*

Sexual reproduction: The fusion of gametes promotes the various combination of genes in a population leading to genetic variation. *(1 M)*

Long Answer Type Questions

1. (*a*) Dihybrid cross. (*1 M*)

   (*b*) Round shape and yellow colour in the pea plants are the dominant traits. On the other hand, wrinkled shape and green colour are recessive, and all the traits assort independently. (*1 M*)

   With the help of the punnet square we reach at this conclusion: (*2 M*)

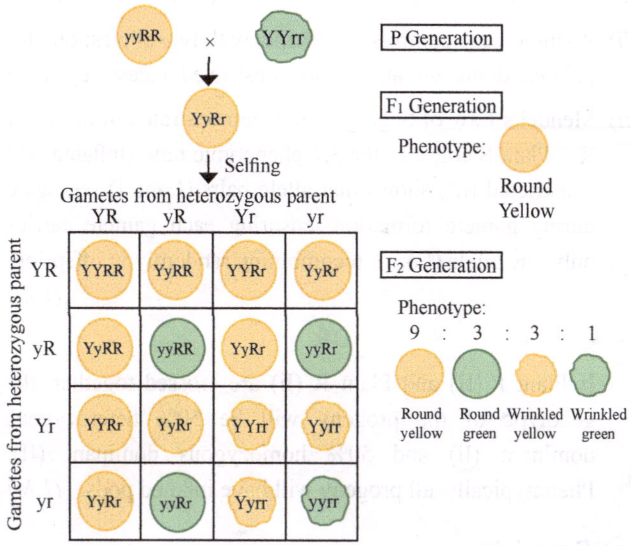

   Since in F_1, all are heterozygous for both traits, so yellow and round are dominant traits. These traits are not inherited together and hence there are two new recombinants. Thus, they are inherited independently. (*1 M*)

2. (*a*) Sex chromosomes (*1 M*)

   (*b*) Temperature of the fertilised egg determines sex of the embryo in some reptiles. (*2 M*)

   (*c*) The law of segregation states that a diploid organism passes a randomly selected allele for a trait to its offspring, such that the offspring receives one allele from each parent. (*1 M*)

   If sex determination in plants is governed by genetic factors, the offspring will get one copy of a gene from each parent. Sex determination violates the law of segregation as the human female does not have any copy of the Y-chromosomal genes.

   (*d*) 0.5 marks for each correct answer:

   The father because the father can pass either X or Y chromosome to the offspring. (*1 M*)

3. These structures are chromosomes, found in the nucleus of cells. Chromosomes carry genes, the units of heredity, which are made up of DNA. (*1 M*)

   During reproduction, parents pass on copies of their chromosomes to their offspring, thereby transmitting genetic information that determines traits. (*1 M*)

   Chromosomes ensure stability by pairing during sexual reproduction, with germ cells (sperm and egg) each receiving one chromosome from every pair. When these germ cells combine, they restore the normal chromosome number, maintaining DNA stability across generations. (*1 M*)

4. (*i*) In a cross between violet (dominant) and white (recessive) flowered plants, the F_2 progeny exhibits both violet and white flowers due to the segregation of alleles. (*1 M*)

   (*ii*) When F_1 progeny (all having violet flowers with a heterozygous genotype, Vv) are self-pollinated, the F_2 progeny will show a phenotypic ratio of 3 violet to 1 white flowered plants, following Mendel's principle of segregation. (*2 M*)

   (*iii*) If 100 plants are produced in the F_2 progeny, the expected distribution, according to Mendel's 3:1 ratio, would result in 75 plants displaying the dominant violet flower trait and 25 plants displaying the recessive white flower trait. Hence, 25 plants will show the recessive white flower trait. (*2 M*)

5. (*i*) The F_1 progeny would all have green stems. Since green stem (GG) is crossed with purple stem (gg), and assuming green stem is dominant over purple stem, all F_1 offspring would have the genotype Gg, expressing the dominant green stem trait. (*1 M*)

   (*ii*) When F_1 plants (Gg) are self-pollinated, the F_2 generation would follow a Mendelian 3:1 ratio of green to purple stemmed plants. Thus, 25% (or ¼) of the F_2 plants would have purple stems, displaying the recessive phenotype (gg). (*1 M*)

   (*iii*) In the F_2 progeny, the genotypic ratio of GG (homozygous dominant) to Gg (heterozygous) would be 1:2. This means for every homozygous dominant (GG) plant, there would be two heterozygous (Gg) plants expressing the green stem trait. (*1 M*)

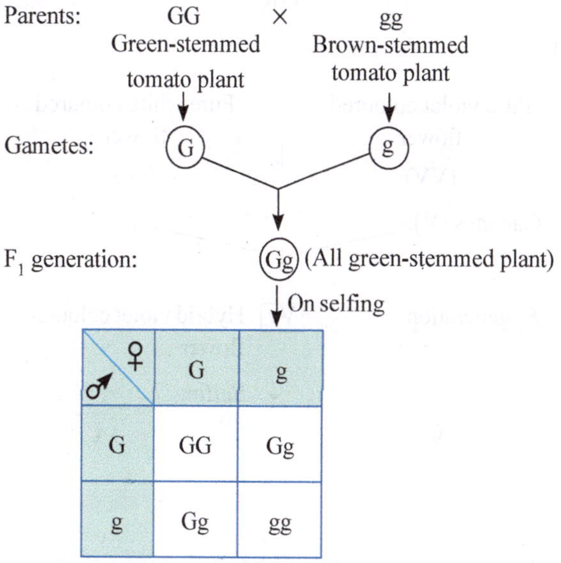

   Genotypic ratio: GG : Gg : gg

   Phenotypic ratio: 1 2 : 1

   3 : 1 (*2 M*)

6. (*a*) (*i*) e is recessive; (*ii*) E is dominant. (*1 M*)

   (*b*) The color of their eyes is brown. (*1 M*)

   (*c*) Combination ee will produce children with blue eyes. (*1½ M*)

   (*d*) Combination EE or Ee will produce children with brown eyes. (*1½ M*)

Case Based Questions

Case Based-I

(*i*) Contrasting trails like -

(*i*) Tall and Dwarf plant, (½ M)

(*ii*) Inflated and Constricted pod shape. (½ M)

(*ii*)

	Dominant Traits	Recessive Traits
(*i*)	Dominant traits are traits which gets expressed in F_1 hybrid plant or the plant having the heterozygous genotype.	Recessive traits are expressed only in plants having homozygous recessive genotype and doesn't get expressed in F_1 hybrid or heterozygous genotypic plant.
(*ii*)	Dominant traits are denoted by capital letter.	Recessive traits are denoted by small letter.

(*1 M*)

(*iii*) Plants produced in the F_2 generation yellow-round seeded plants, yellow-wrinkled seeded plants, green-round seeded plants and green-wrinkled seeded plants are produced with the ratio of 9 : 3 : 3 : 1. This result/ratio suggests the independent assortment of the genes of seed colour and seed shape. (*2 M*)

OR

(*iii*)

Pure violet coloured flower (VV) × Pure white coloured flower (vv)

Gametes (V) ↓ (v)

F_1 generation — Vv — Hybrid violet coloured flower

↓ Selfing

Vv × Vv

↓

F_2 generation

	V	v
V	VV Purple	Vv Purple
v	Vv Purple	vv White

Genotypic ratio — VV : Vv : vv — 1 : 2 : 1

Phenotypic ratio — 3 : 1

(*2 M*)

Case Based-II

(*i*)
- P = II (homozygous dominant). (¼ M)
- Q = ii (homozygous recessive). (¼ M)
- R= Ii (heterozygous dominant). (¼ M)
- S= Ii(heterozygous dominant). (¼ M)

Inheritance pattern: Pod shape follows Mendelian monohybrid inheritance, where inflated pod shape (I) is dominant over constricted pod shape (i). (*1 M*)

(*ii*) A single gene controls pod shape, with two alleles: one for inflated (dominant) and one for constricted (recessive). (*1 M*)

(*iii*) Mendel's Law of Segregation is demonstrated in the Plant R × Plant S cross, as the 3:1 phenotypic ratio (inflated (I) : constricted (ii)) shows that allele pairs (I and i) segregate during gamete formation, ensuring each gamete carries only one allele (I or i), recombining randomly in offspring. (*1 M*)

OR

If Plant P (II) and Plant R (Ii) are crossed together, the genotype of the progeny will be 50% heterozygous dominant (Ii) and 50% homozygous dominant (II). Phenotypically, all progeny will have inflated pods. (*1 M*)

Case Based-III

(*i*) The likely genotypes of the parents are both heterozygous (Hh), where 'H' represents the dominant normal hearing allele and 'h' represents the recessive deafness allele. This is because they have normal hearing but have produced a deaf child, indicating they must carry the recessive allele. (*1 M*)

(*ii*) The probability that the couple's next child will be deaf is 25%. This is because each child has a 1 in 4 chance of inheriting the 'hh' genotype from two heterozygous parents. (*1 M*)

(*iii*) The possible genotypes of the children are:
- Three children with normal hearing could be either 'HH' or 'Hh'.
- One child is deaf and must have the genotype 'hh'.

Parents: Father (Hh) (Heterozygous Normal) × Mother (Hh) (Heterozygous Normal)

↓

	H	h
H	HH	Hh
h	Hh	hh

HH: Child with normal hearing

Hh: Children with normal hearing but are carriers like parents

hh: Child with hearing loss (Deafness) *(2 M)*

OR

Deafness appeared only in one child due to the inheritance of two recessive alleles for deafness, one from each parent. The parents are carriers (heterozygous), with the genotype Hh, and only the child with genotype hh is deaf. *(2 M)*

Case Based-IV

(i) The sex chromosomes, X and Y, are different in size as the X chromosome is larger than the Y chromosome. *(½ M)*
In humans, the mismatched pair of sex chromosomes is XY in males. Males have one X and one Y chromosome, while females have two X chromosomes. *(½ M)*

(ii) Human beings have a total of 23 pairs of chromosomes, out of which one pair is the sex chromosomes. *(½ M)*
In males, the pair consists of one X chromosome and one Y chromosome (XY). In females, the perfect pair consists of two X chromosomes (XX). *(½ M)*

(iii) In some species of reptiles like turtles, the temperature at which the eggs are incubated determines the sex of the offspring.
Snails change their sex during their lifetime, which means that their sex is not genetically determined and depends on environmental factors. *(2 M)*

OR

A flowchart to show that sex is determined genetically in human beings:

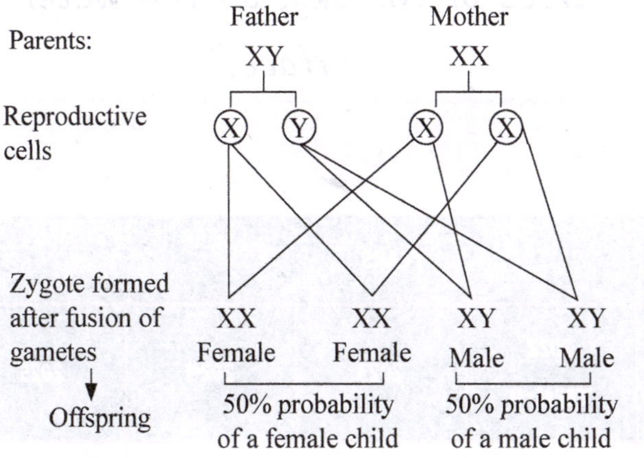

(2 M)

Case Based-V

(i) A human zygote, which is formed by the fusion of a sperm and an egg, contains 46 chromosomes, inheriting 23 chromosomes from each parent. Each gamete (sperm or egg) in humans contains 23 chromosomes, half the number in body cells, to ensure the offspring inherits the correct total number from both parents. *(1 M)*

(ii) Some reptiles use environmental cues, like temperature, to determine the sex of their offspring. This strategy does not rely on genetic differences but on external factors, showcasing nature's adaptability in reproductive strategies. *(1 M)*

(iii) *(2 M)*

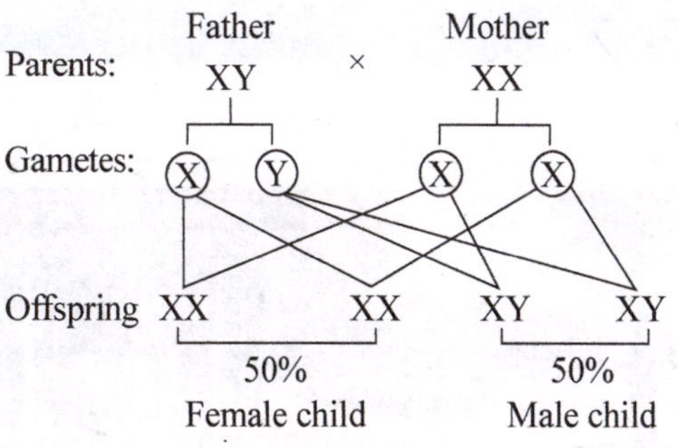

OR

All the gametes (eggs) formed in human females have an X chromosome because females have two X chromosomes (XX) in their genetic makeup. During the process of meiosis, each egg receives one set of chromosomes. Since females only have X chromosomes to pass on, each gamete formed by a female will invariably contain one X chromosome. This is in contrast to males, who have one X and one Y chromosome (XY), allowing them to produce gametes with either an X or a Y chromosome, which ultimately determines the sex of the offspring. *(2 M)*

Topper's Explanation

(a) chromosomes in zygote – 23 pairs – 46 chromosomes
chromosomes in each gamete – 23 chromosomes

(b) In few reptiles the temperature at which the fertilised egg is incubated determines the sex of the offspring. Thus few reptiles like lizards, depend on environmental cues.

~~(c) Women have perfect pair of sex chromosomes (XX)~~

(c)

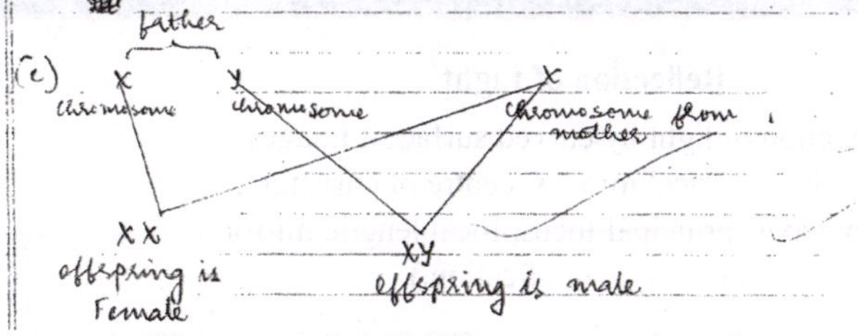

9 LIGHT-REFLECTION AND REFRACTION

"When you observe a fish in a pond, you notice that the fish appears to be in a different position from its actual one. Simultaneously, if the water's surface is calm and smooth, you can also see the reflections of the surroundings, such as trees or the sky, on the water's surface."

SYLLABUS & WEIGHTAGE

LIST OF CONCEPT NAMES	YEARS				
	2020	2022 TERM-II	2023	2024	2025
Reflection of Light (Reflection of light by curved surfaces: Images formed by spherical mirrors, centre of curvature, principal axis, principal focus, focal length, mirror formula, magnification.)	—	—	1Q(5M)	1Q (3M)	1Q (5M)
Refraction of Light (Laws of refraction, refractive index. Refraction of light by spherical lens: Image formed by spherical lenses: Lens formula, Magnification. Power of a lens.)	1Q (3M)	—	1Q (3M)	1 Q (2M) 1 Q (5M)	1 Q (1M) 1 Q (5M)

For the year 2021, the exam was not conducted.

CONCEPT MAP

To Access One Shot Reuision Video Scan This QR Code

Light-Reflection and Refraction

Concave Lens (CBSE 2024) / Convex Lens (CBSE 2023, 2022, 2020)

Concave Lens		Convex Lens	
Concave lenses are thinner at the center and thicker at the edges.	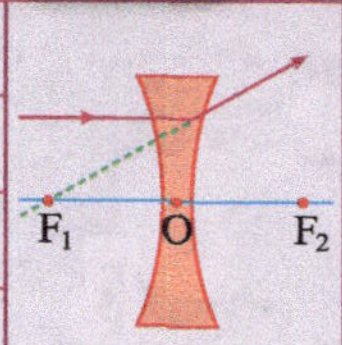	They have a thicker center and thinner edges.	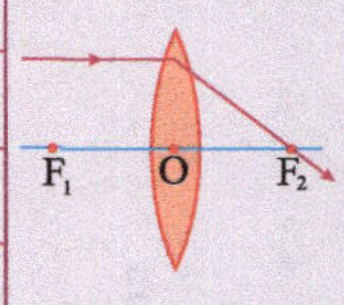
They diverge light rays, causing parallel rays to spread out.		Convex lenses converge light rays.	
Used in eyeglasses for nearsightedness (myopia)		Used in cameras, telescopes, and glasses to correct farsightedness (Hypermetropia)	
A concave lens always forms a virtual image.		Produce virtual, upright images for objects beyond the focus.	

Lens formula, Magnification and Power

Lens formula: $\frac{1}{f} = \frac{1}{v} - \frac{1}{u}$, where, (CBSE 2025)

u = object distance, v = image distance

Magnification: $m = \frac{v}{u} = \frac{h_i}{h_o}$, where,

h_i = height of image, h_o = height of object

Power of lens: The reciprocal of focal length in meter is defined as power of lens: i.e.

$P = \frac{1}{f(\text{in m})} = \frac{100}{f(\text{in cm})}$ (CBSE 2022)

S.I. Unit: Diopter (D), 1D = 1m^{-1}

What are the Laws of Reflection? (CBSE 2024)

1. Incident ray, reflected ray and the normal to the point of incident lie in the same plane
2. Angle of incident is equal to angle of reflection i.e. $\angle i = \angle r$

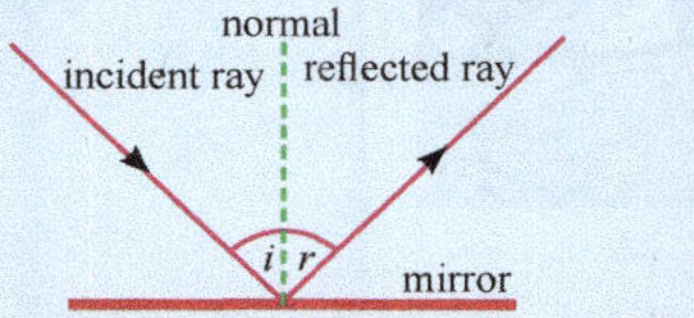

Refraction through a Rectangular glass slab (CBSE 2025, 2022)

Emergent ray is parallel to incident ray i.e., $\angle e = \angle i$

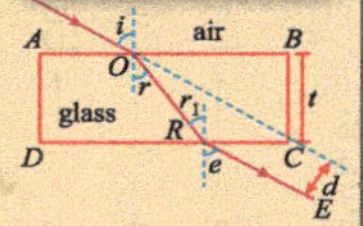

Types of Refractive Index

1. **Absolute refractive index:** $\mu = \frac{c}{v} = \frac{3 \times 10^8 \text{ m/s}}{v}$
2. **Relative refractive index:** $n_{21} = \frac{v_1}{v_2}$ or $n_{12} = \frac{v_2}{v_1}$

(CBSE 2024, 2022)

Refraction — Definition: The phenomenon of bending of light at the surface of second medium, when light goes from one medium to another.

What are the Laws of Refraction? (CBSE 2020)

1. Incident ray, refracted ray and normal to the surface lie in the same plane.
2. **Snell's law:** $\mu_1 \sin i = \mu_2 \sin r$

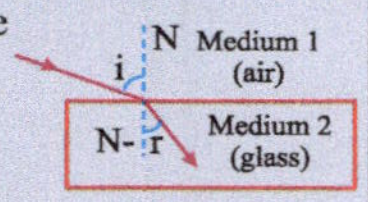

Reflection — Definition: The bouncing back of light from any surface in the same medium is called Reflection of light.

Sign Convention for Mirror (CBSE 2022)

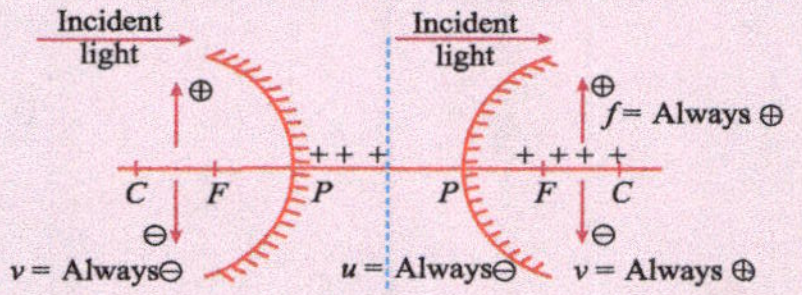

Mirror formula & Magnification (CBSE 2025, 2024, 2022)

Mirror formula: $\frac{1}{f} = \frac{1}{v} + \frac{1}{u}$,

Where, u = object distance, v = image distance

Magnification: $m = \frac{h_i}{h_o} = -\frac{v}{u}$

Where, h_i = height of image h_o = height of object

Types of Mirror (CBSE 2024, 2023, 2022)

Mirror		Shape of mirror	Nature of image	Magnification	Focal Length	Applications	Ray Diagram
Plane Mirror		Flat and smooth reflecting surface	It forms a virtual, erect and laterally inverted image of an object placed in front of it.	Magnification = +1	Infinity	solar cookers, periscopes, and scientific instruments for redirecting light, and enabling observation.	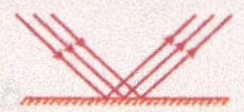
Spherical Mirror	Concave Mirror (Converging Mirror)	Reflecting surface that curves inward	It forms both real, inverted and virtual, erect image of an object	Magnification can be positive, negative, less than zero and more than zero.	Negative	Used in Torches, vehicles headlights, shaving mirrors. Large concave mirrors are used to concentrate sunlight to produce heat in solar furnaces.	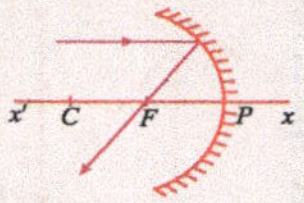
	Convex Mirror (Diverging Mirror)	Reflecting surface that curves outward	It forms only virtual, erect and diminished images of an object.	Magnification is always positive and less than 1	Positive	rear-view (wing) mirrors in vehicles offer safer driving by providing a wider field of view, always giving an erect image, and enabling drivers to see more traffic behind them.	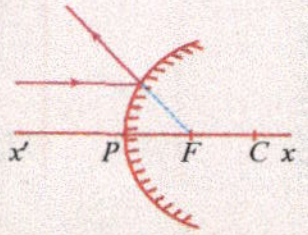

Image Formation by Spherical Mirror

Rules for Making Ray Diagram by Spherical Mirror

1. **A ray of light that is parallel to the principal axis, passes through the focus of the spherical mirror after reflection.**

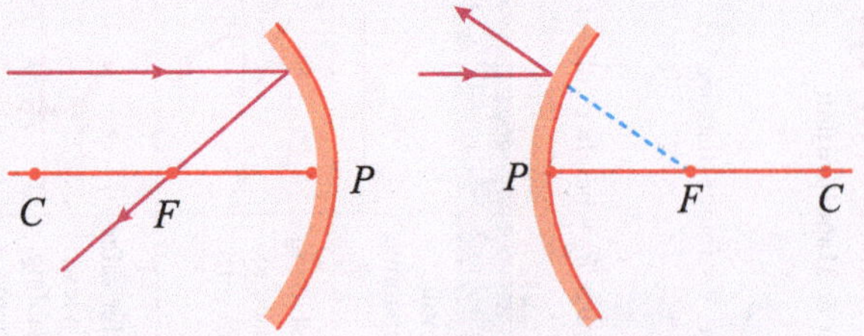

Concave mirror | Convex mirror

2. **A ray of light passing through or towards the center of curvature of a spherical mirror is reflected along the same path.**

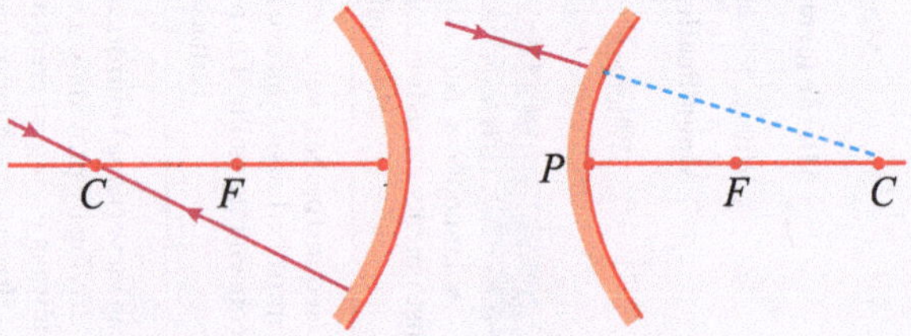

3. **A ray of light passing through or towards the focus of a spherical mirror becomes parallel to its principal axis after reflection.**

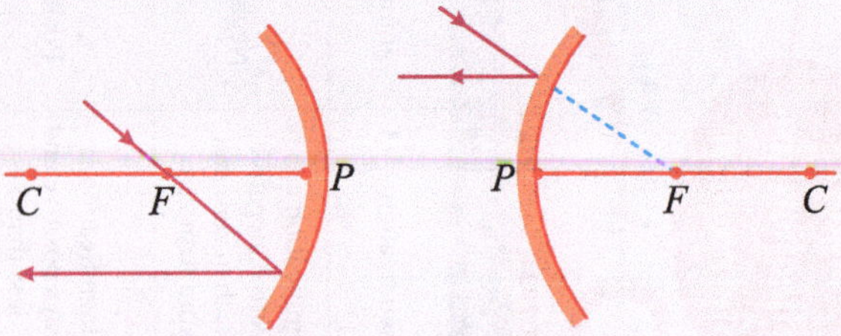

4. **A ray of light that is incident at the pole of a spherical mirror is reflected making the same angle with the principal axis.**

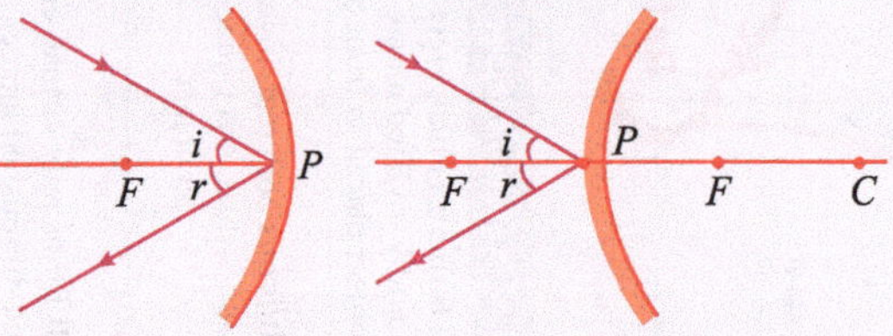

Nature of Object and Image

Real Object

Intersection of incident rays is actual

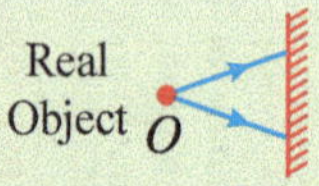

Real Image

- Intersection of Reflected rays is actual
- Inverted image

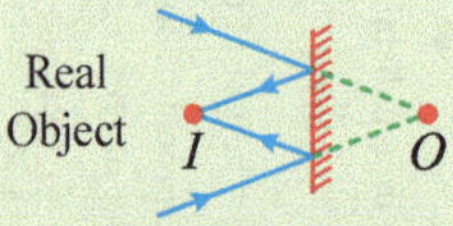

Virtual Object

Does not exist in real world

Virtual Image

- Reflected rays appear to meet
- Erect image

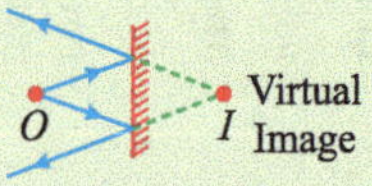

Magnification

Magnification: $m = \frac{h_i}{h_o} = -\frac{v}{u}$

- If m > 1 → Enlarged Image
- If m < 1 → Diminished image
- If m = 1 → Equal to the object
- If m > 0 → Virtual and erect Image
- If m < 0 → Real and Inverted Image

Image Formation by Spherical Mirrors for Different Positions of the Object

Image Formation by a Concave Mirror for Different Positions of the Object

CBSE 2023

Position of the Object	Concave Mirror	Position of the Image	Nature of the Image
At Infinity	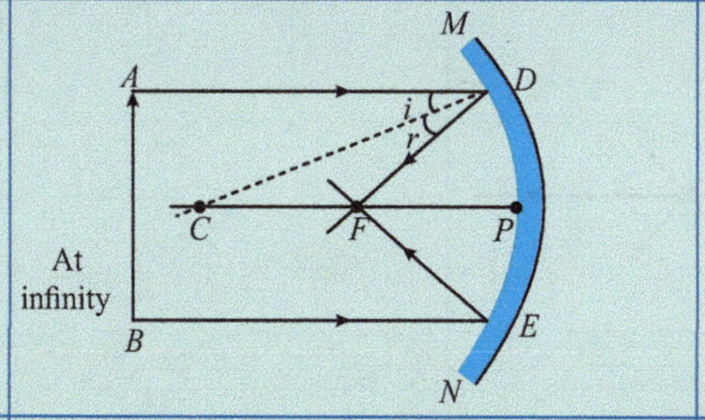	At Focus	Real, inverted, and highly diminished (point sized)
Between Centre of Curvature and Infinity	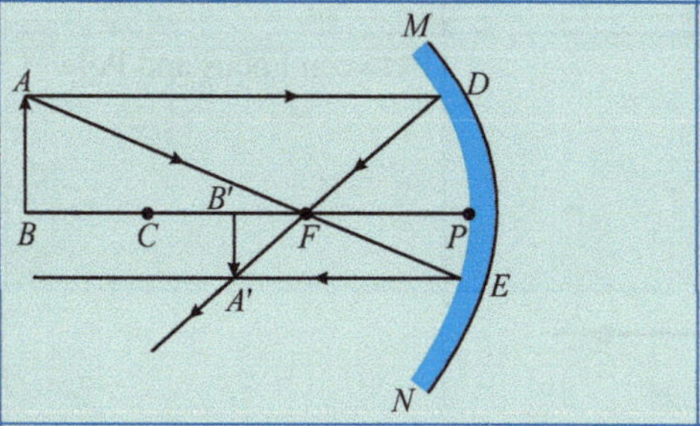	Between Focus and Centre of Curvature	Real, inverted, and diminished
At Centre of Curvature	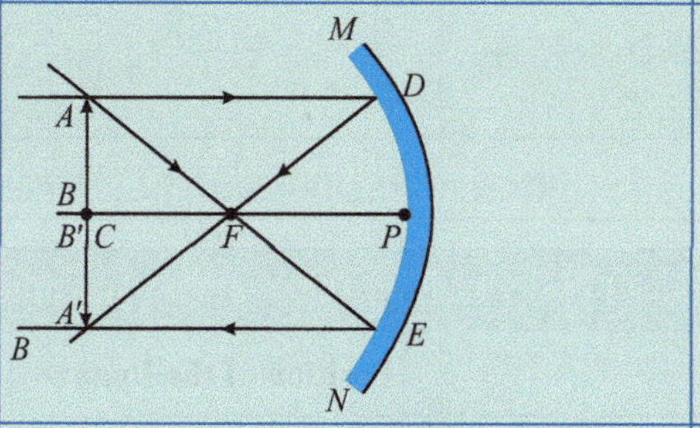	At Centre of Curvature	Real, inverted, and of the same size as the object
Between Centre of Curvature and Focus	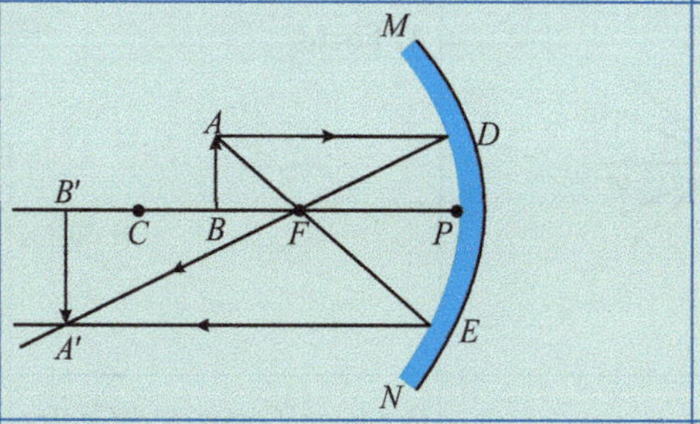	Beyond Centre of Curvature	Real, inverted, and highly magnified
At Focus	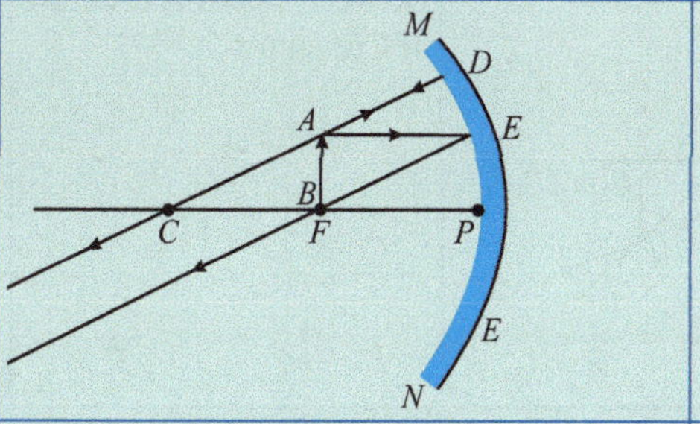	At Infinity	Real, inverted and highly magnified.
Between Focus and Pole	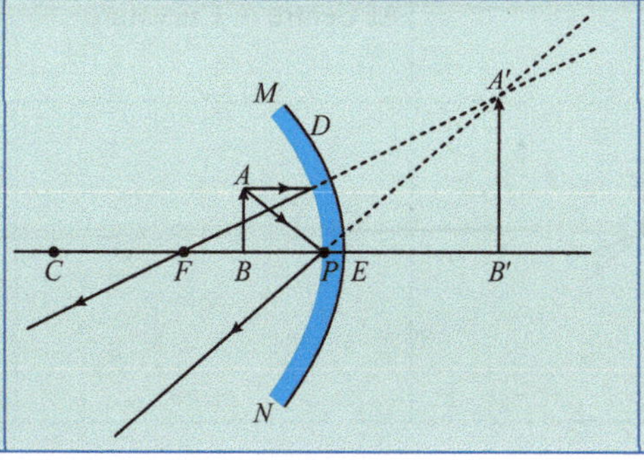	Behind the Mirror	Virtual, upright, and magnified

Image formation by a Convex Mirror for Different Positions of the Object

Position of the Object	Convex Mirror	Position of the Image	Nature of the Image
At Infinity	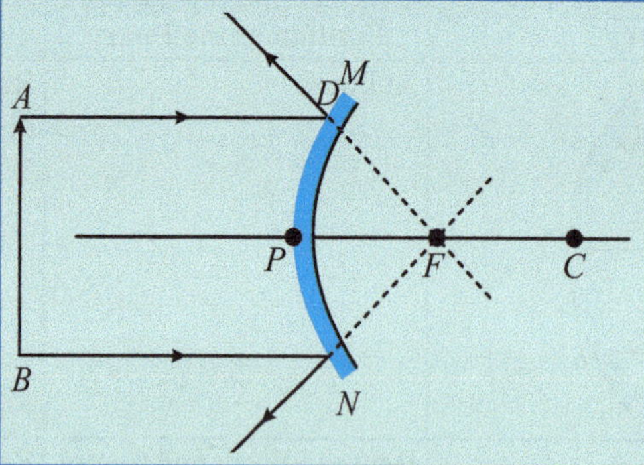	At Focus	Virtual, upright, and highly diminished (point sized)
Anywhere between Infinity and Pole	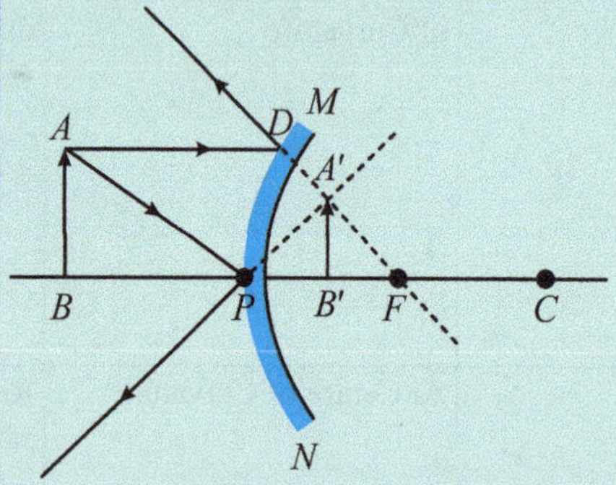	Between Focus and Pole	Virtual, upright, and diminished

Image Formation by Spherical Mirrors and Lenses for different Positions of the Object

CBSE 2023, 2020

Image Formation by a Concave Mirror and a Convex Lens for Different Positions of the Object

Position of the Object	Convex Lens	Position of the Image	Nature of the Image
At Infinity	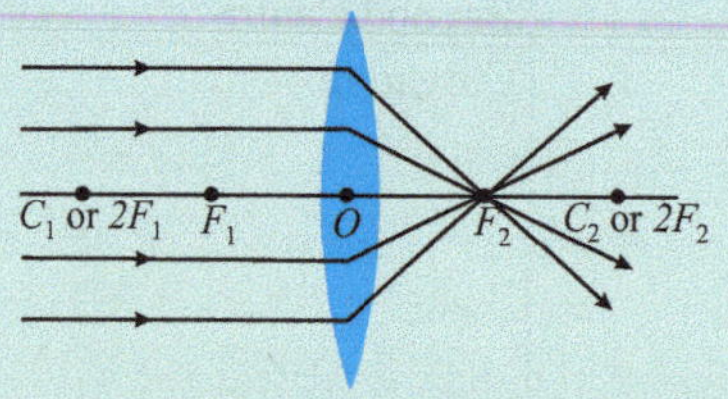	At Focus	Real, inverted, and highly diminished (point sized)
Between Centre of Curvature and Infinity	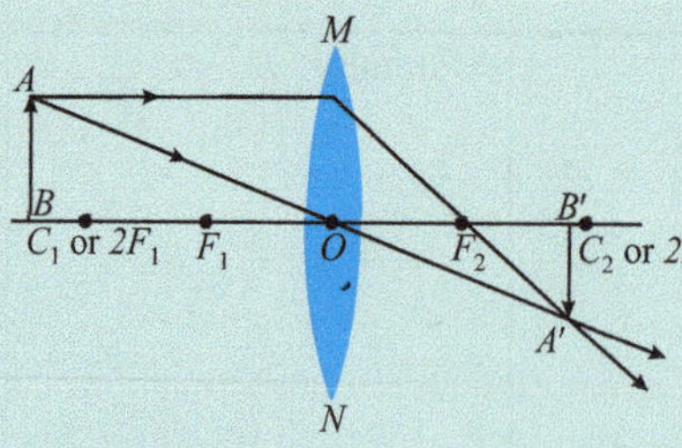	Between Focus and Centre of Curvature	Real, inverted, and diminished
At Centre of Curvature	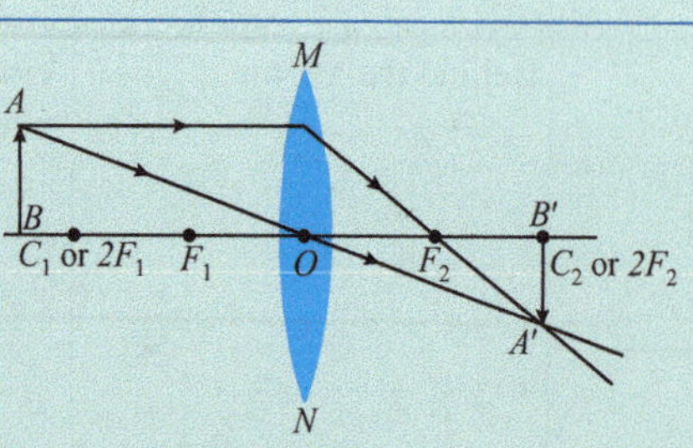	At Centre of Curvature	Real, inverted, and of the same size as the object

Between Centre of Curvature and Focus	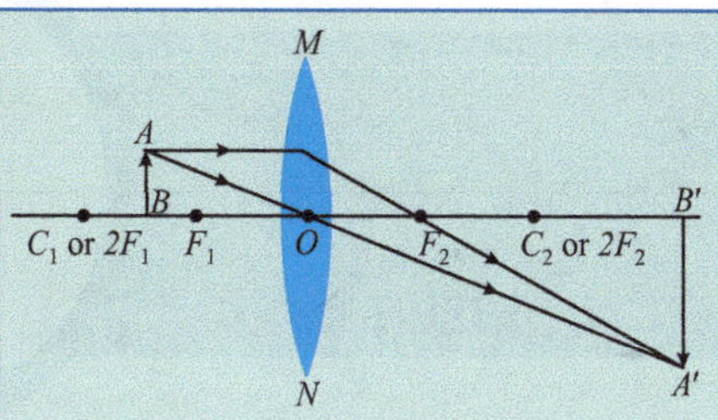	Beyond Centre of Curvature	Real, inverted, and magnified
At Focus	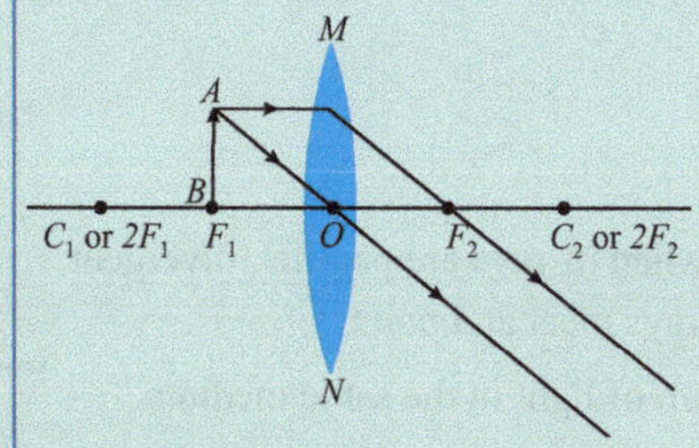	At Infinity	Real Inverted and highly magnified
Between Focus and Pole/ Optical Centre	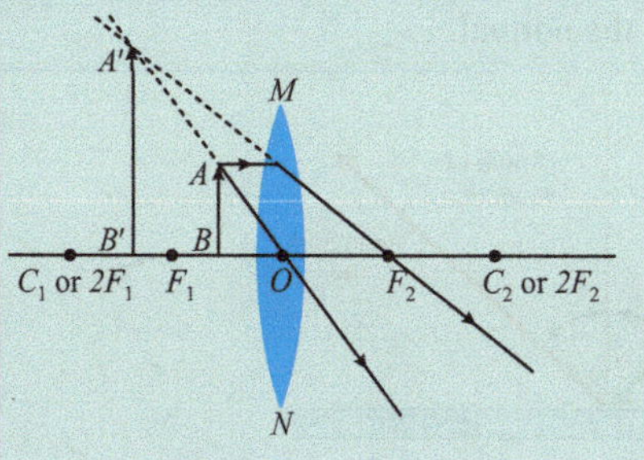	Behind the mirror in Concave mirror and On the same side of the object in the convex lens	Virtual, upright, and magnified

Image Formation by a Convex Mirror and a Concave Lens for Different Positions of the Object

Position of the Object	Convex Mirror	Concave Lens	Position of the Image	Nature of the Image
At infinity	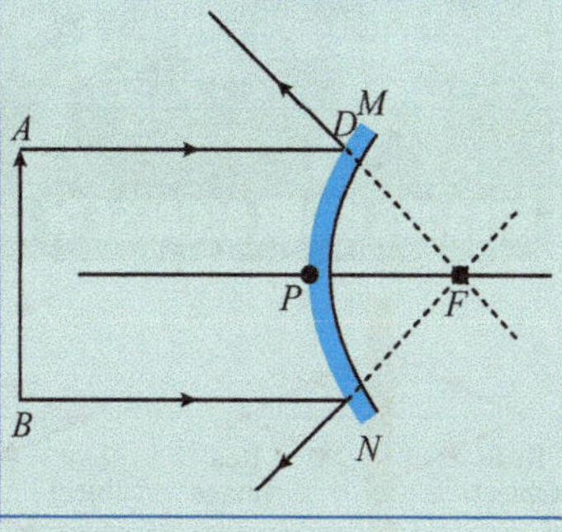	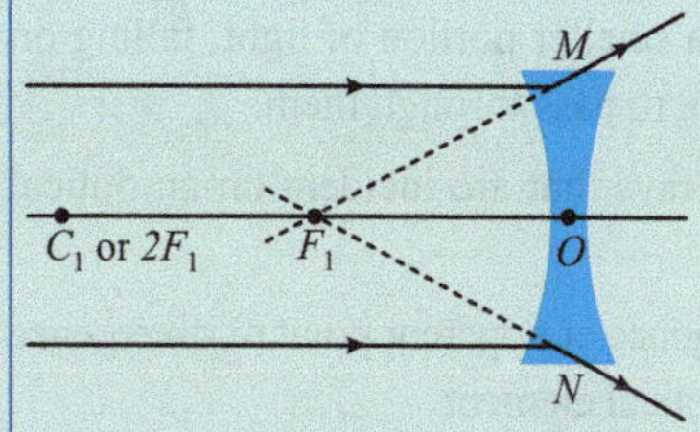	At Focus	Virtual, upright, and highly diminished (point sized)
Anywhere between Infinity and Pole/Optical Centre	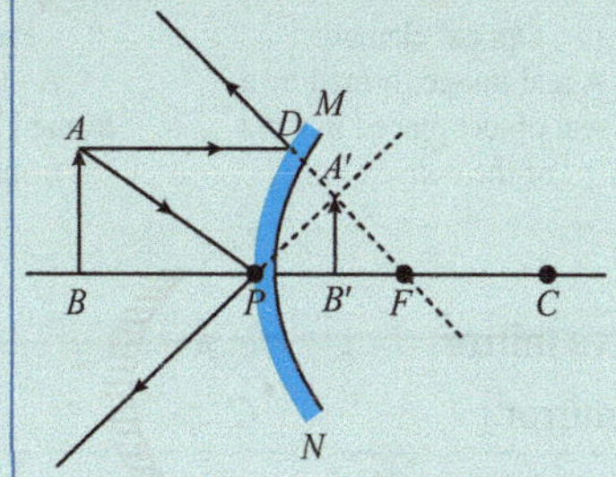	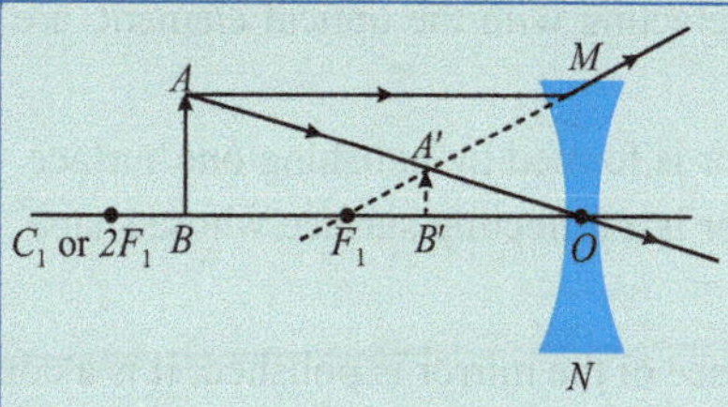	Between Focus and Pole/ Optical Centre	Virtual, upright, and diminished

REFLECTION

1

NCERT Definitions (Commonly asked in 1 mark)

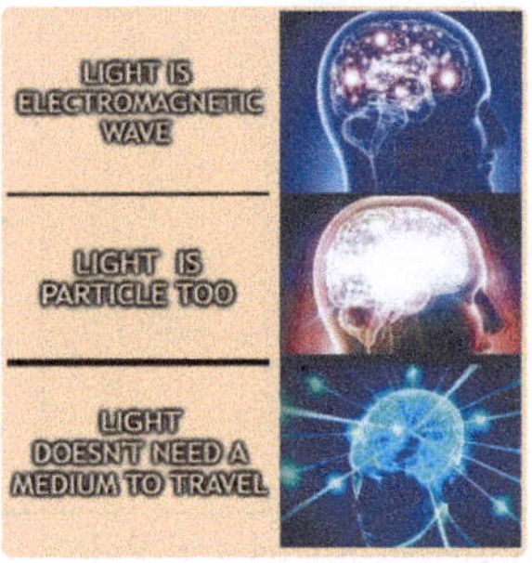

- **Light:** A form of energy that enables us to see.
- **A Ray:** The 'path' along which light travels is called a ray.
- **A Beam:** A bundle of rays is called a beam. A beam is parallel when its rays are parallel; divergent when its rays spread out from a point; and convergent when its rays meet at a point.
- **Reflection:** Reflection of light is the process of deflecting a beam of light in the same medium.
- **Angle of Incidence:** The angle between normal and the incident ray.
- **Angle of Reflection:** The angle between the reflected ray and the normal.

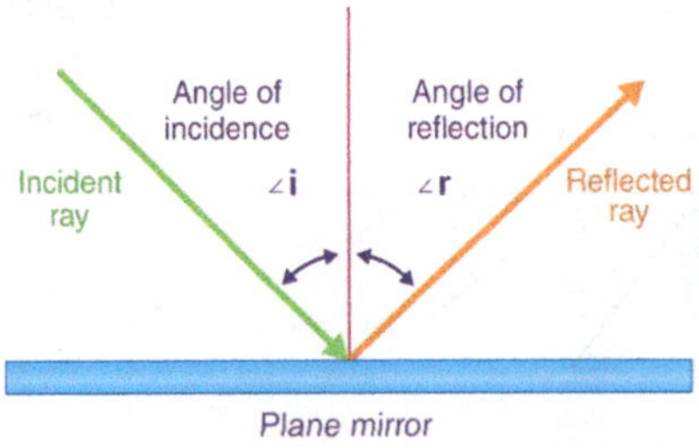

- **Mirror:** A mirror is a smooth and highly polished surface, usually made of glass with a reflective metal coating applied to one side, that reflects light.
- **Opaque:** Substances which allow no light to pass through them .e. g: -wood.
- **Transparent:** Substances which allow much light to pass through them.
- **Translucent:** Substances which allow a smaller portion of light, falling on them (or as we say, incident upon them), to pass through them.
- **Object:** An object is a source of light rays that are incident on an optical element (Mirror, lens).
- **Image:** An image is the point of convergence or apparent point of divergence of rays after they interact with a given optical element.
- **Real Image:** When rays after interacting with the optical element are of converging nature.
- **Virtual Image:** When rays after interacting with the optical element, are of diverging nature.

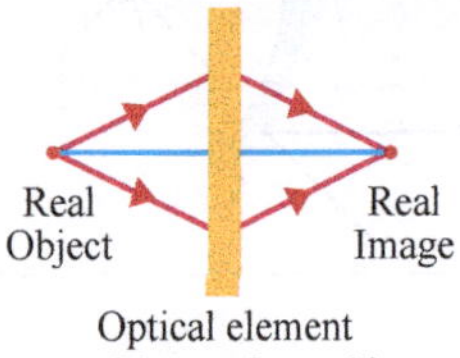

A real image formed by a real object placed in front of the convex lens

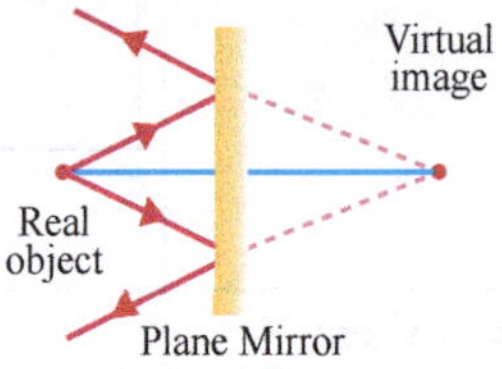

A virtual image formed by a real object in front of the mirror

- **Spherical mirror:** A spherical mirror is formed by polishing one surface of a part of sphere. A spherical mirror is a reflecting surface whose shape is a section of a spherical surface.
- **Concave Mirror:** If the outside surface of the mirror is polished, it is a concave mirror
- **Convex Mirror:** If the inside surface of the mirror is polished, it is a convex mirror.
- **Pole (P):** It is the geometrical center of the spherical reflecting surface.

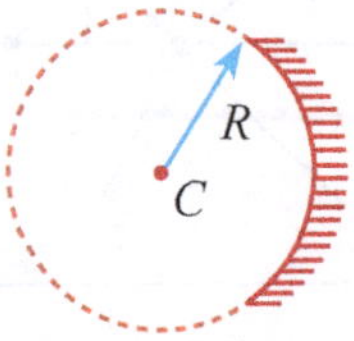

Concave Mirror

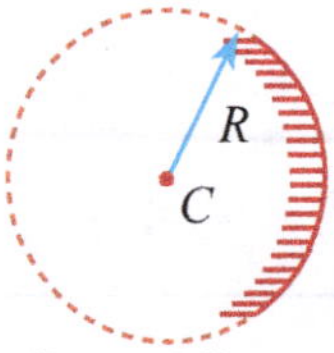

Convex Mirror

- **Center of Curvature:** The center of the sphere of which the mirror is a part, is called center of curvature (C).
- **Radius of Curvature (R):** The radius of the sphere of which the mirror is a part is called radius of curvature (R).
- **Principal Axis:** It is the straight line joining the center of curvature to the pole.

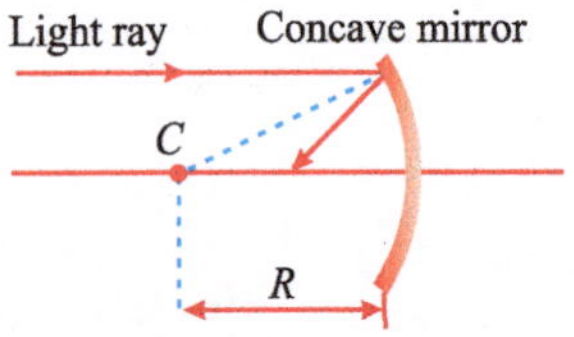

- **Principal Focus (F):** It is the point of intersection of all the reflected rays for which the incident rays strike the mirror (with small aperture) parallel to the principal axis.
- **Aperture (related to the size of mirror):** It is the diameter of the mirror.
- **Focal Length (f):** It is the distance between the pole and the principal focus. For spherical mirrors, $f = R/2$.
- **Focus (F):** When a narrow beam of rays of light, parallel to the principal axis and close to it, is incident on the surface of a mirror, the reflected beam is found to coverage to or appears to diverge from a point on the principal axis. This point is called the focus.
- **Magnification:** Magnification is a measure that describes how much larger or smaller an image is compared to the object itself.

$$m = \frac{\text{Height of the image } (h')}{\text{Height of the object } (h)}$$

Important Facts

01 Light travel in straight lines.

02 The nature, size, and orientation of images depend on the object's distance from the mirror.

03 The laws of reflection obey by all types of reflecting surfaces.

04 The speed of Light travels in vacuum. $\sim 3 \times 10^8\ ms^{-1}$

Classification

Mirror (According to their Function and Properties)			
Characteristic	**Plane Mirror**	**Convex Mirror**	**Concave Mirror**
Function	Reflects light to form a virtual image of the same size	Diverges light rays to form a virtual image that is smaller than the object	Converges light rays to form real or virtual images depending on the object's position
Image Type	Always virtual and erect	Virtual, diminished, and erect	Can be real and inverted or virtual and erect
Image Size	Same as the object	Smaller than the object	Larger or smaller than the object, depending on the object's position
Uses	Used in everyday life for personal grooming, decoration, and in vehicles for rear view mirrors	Used for safety in vehicles to see a wider field of view, in hallways for security, and in ATM machines	Used in various devices like telescopes, flashlights, head mirrors in medical examinations, and in solar cookers
Image Location	Behind the mirror, at the same distance as the object from the mirror	Behind the mirror, appears closer than the actual object	In front of the mirror for real images; appears behind the mirror for virtual images
Focal Length	Infinite (parallel rays of light reflected remain parallel)	Positive (focal point is behind the mirror)	Negative (focal point is in front of the mirror)

Difference Between (Commonly asked in 2-3 marks)

Feature	Real Image	Virtual Image
Formation	Formed by actual convergence of light rays.	Formed by the apparent divergence of light rays.
Projection	Can be projected onto a screen.	Cannot be projected onto a screen.
Image Orientation	Inverted compared to the object. Viewing	Upright compared to the object. viewer's position.
Location	In front of the mirror or beyond the lens.	Behind the mirror or into the optical device.
Examples	Image formed on a screen camera sensor or the retina.	Image seen in a plane mirror or behind a convex lens.

Important Formula

1. **Radius of Curvature:**

   $R = 2f$; Where, R = radius (in m), f = focal length (in m)

2. **Mirror Formula:**

   $\frac{1}{f} = \frac{1}{v} + \frac{1}{u}$; Where v = image distance from pole (in m), u = object distance from pole (in m)

3. **Magnification Formula:**

   $m = \frac{h_i}{h_0} = \frac{-v}{u}$; Where h_1 = height of image (in m), h_0 = height of object (in m)

Real Life Application Based Questions

1. **Why are rear-view mirrors in vehicles made convex?**

Ans. Convex rear-view mirrors are used because they reflect a wider field of vision compared to flat mirrors. The images formed are smaller than the objects they reflect, which allows drivers to see more from the rear of their vehicle, helping to monitor traffic and make safer driving decisions.

2. **How does a makeup mirror that magnifies your face work?**

Ans. A makeup mirror often has a concave surface that reflects light to magnify your image. When your face is within the focal point of the mirror, the reflected rays diverge in such a way that they appear to be coming from a larger, upright image behind the mirror, giving you a magnified view.

3. **What are optical mirrors, and in what applications are they commonly used?**

Ans. Optical mirrors are reflective surfaces that direct and focus light. They are commonly employed in scientific and industrial equipment, such as telescopes for astronomical observations, microscopes for magnifying small objects, and cameras for capturing images. Additionally, optical mirrors are integral to laser systems, where they are used in cutting and engraving materials with precision.

4. How do solar power systems utilize mirrors, and can you provide an example of such an application?

Ans. Solar power systems use mirrors to reflect and focus sunlight onto a specific point to generate electricity or heat. An example is the solar cooker at the Shirdi Sai Baba Temple in Maharashtra, India. This device, which is an alternative to traditional cooking methods, uses a large parabolic dish to concentrate sunlight onto a pot. The eco-friendly cooker tracks the sun's movement to maximize exposure, thus efficiently using solar energy for cooking meals for devotees.

5. What role do reflectors play in vehicle headlights, and what type of mirror is commonly used?

Ans. Reflectors in vehicle headlights, which are typically concave mirrors, direct light from the headlight bulb in a focused beam, enhancing road visibility ahead. Concave mirrors are used because they can converge light rays to a focal point, thereby creating a beam of light that illuminates the road more effectively.

6. How do mirrors function in binoculars and telescopes, and what is their purpose?

Ans. In binoculars and telescopes, mirrors are used to gather and focus light, which enables the magnification of distant objects for clearer observation. These mirrors collect light from far away and concentrate it into a smaller area, intensifying the image so that it appears closer and more detailed to the viewer.

7. What is the function of mirrors in microscopes?

Ans. Mirrors in microscopes reflect and direct light onto the sample being examined. This focused illumination is crucial for enhancing the visibility of small or transparent samples, allowing for detailed study and analysis under magnification.

8. How do kaleidoscopes use mirrors to create visual effects?

Ans. Kaleidoscopes use mirrors arranged in a triangular prism shape to reflect light and the fragments of coloured glass or other objects inside them. This arrangement causes multiple reflections, resulting in intricate and colourful symmetrical patterns that change as the kaleidoscope is turned. The mirrors refract and reflect light, enhancing the complexity of the visual patterns created.

Myth Buster

- **Myth: Reflection always results in an image.**
  Fact: While reflection can create an image of an object, it doesn't always do so. Reflection simply refers to the bouncing of light off a surface, and in some cases, the surface may not be smooth enough to produce a clear image.
- **Myth: Reflection occurs only with mirrors.**
  Fact: While mirrors are a common example of a reflecting surface, any object with a smooth surface can reflect light.
- **Myth: The reflection of light changes its wavelength.**
  Fact: Reflection does not change the wavelength of light. The reflected light has the same wavelength as the incident light.
- **Myth: The intensity of the reflected light is always the same as the incident light.**
  Fact: This is not always true, as some of the light can be absorbed or scattered by the surface, resulting in a decrease in intensity.

Mnemonics

- 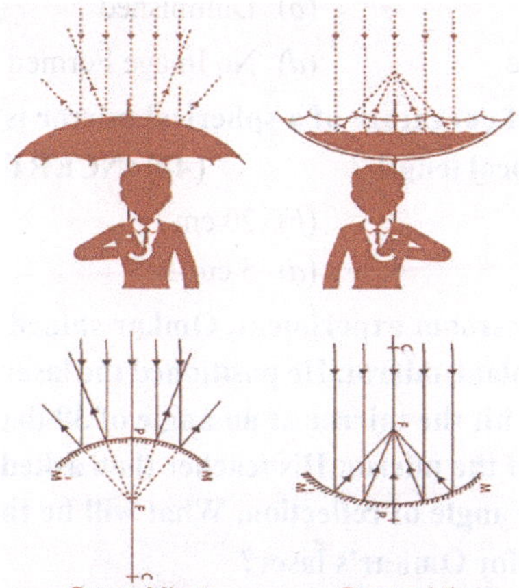

Convex Mirror (Diverging) | Concave Mirror (Converging)

❐ **Plane Mirror:** "VIRUS" - Virtual, inverted (laterally), Reversed, Upright, Same size. Characteristics of the image formed by a plane mirror.

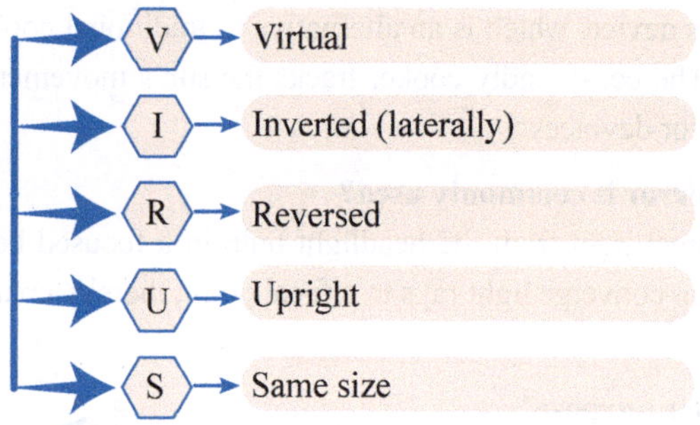

COMPETENCY BASED SOLVED EXAMPLES

Multiple Choice Questions (1 M)

1. When an object was kept at position X in front of a concave mirror, an enlarged and virtual image was formed. ***(Re)*** **(CBSE APQ, 2023)**

Which among the following identifies 'X' correctly?

(*a*) anywhere between the centre of curvature and principal focus

(*b*) anywhere between the pole and principal focus

(*c*) exactly at the centre of curvature

(*d*) exactly at the principal focus

2. An object is placed in front of a convex mirror. Its image is formed: ***(Re)*** **(CBSE SQP, 2023)**

(*a*) at a distance equal to the object distance in front of the mirror.

(*b*) at twice the distance of the object in front of the mirror.

(*c*) half the distance of the object in front of the mirror.

(*d*) behind the mirror and its position varies according to the object distance.

3. Riya was playing with her cat in her room when she noticed that the cat was fascinated by a spot of light moving on the wall. She realized that the spot of light was created by a small mirror directing sunlight into the room. What scientific concept is Riya observing? ***(An)***

(*a*) Refraction of light (*b*) Dispersion of light

(*c*) Reflection of light (*d*) Diffraction of light

4. Sonu observes a ray which seems to be traveling through the focus of a convex mirror passes ________ after reflection ***(An)***

(*a*) parallel to the axis

(*b*) along the same path in opposite direction

(*c*) through F

(*d*) through C

5. An object is placed at a distance of 10 cm in front of a plane mirror, then the distance of image from mirror will be ***(Un)***

(*a*) 5 cm (*b*) 10 cm

(*c*) 20 cm (*d*) 0

6. During an experiment in the laboratory, Meera and Rohan were investigating the properties of two spherical mirrors, AB and CD, which were cut from parts of a hollow spherical ball with its center at O, as shown in the diagram. Meera noticed that the arc length of AB is half the arc length of CD.

Given that the arc length of AB is $\frac{1}{2}$ the arc length of CD, determine the ratio of the focal lengths of the two mirrors. ***(Re)***

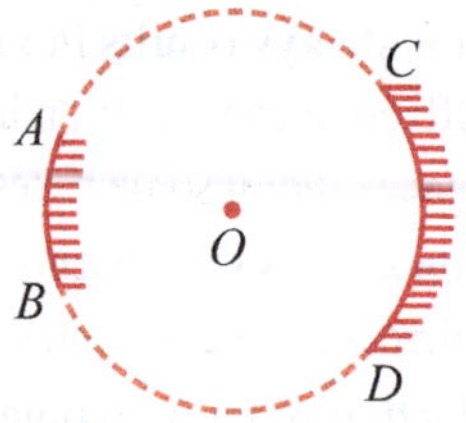

(*a*) 1 : 1 (*b*) 1 : 5

(*c*) 2 : 3 (*d*) 4 : 1

7. What happens to the size of the image formed by a concave mirror when the object is placed between the focus and the mirror? ***(Un)***

(*a*) Enlarged (*b*) Diminished

(*c*) Same Size (*d*) No Image Formed

8. The radius of curvature of a spherical mirror is 20 cm. What is its focal length? ***(Ap)*** **(NCERT Intext)**

(*a*) 10 cm (*b*) 20 cm

(*c*) 30 cm (*d*) 5 cm

9. During a classroom experiment, Omkar shined a laser pointer at a plane mirror. He positioned the laser so that the light ray hit the mirror at an angle of 30 degrees to the surface of the mirror. His teacher then asked him to calculate the angle of reflection. What will be the angle of reflection for Omkar's laser? ***(Un)***

(*a*) 30 degrees (*b*) 60 degrees

(*c*) 90 degrees (*d*) 120 degrees

10. **Under which of the following conditions a concave mirror can form a real image larger than the actual object?** **(*Un*) (NCERT Intext)**
   (*a*) When the object is kept at a distance equal to its radius of curvature
   (*b*) When object is kept at a distance less than its focal length
   (*c*) When object is placed between the focus and centre of curvature
   (*d*) When object is kept at a distance greater than its radius of curvature

11. **Ravi placed an object at a distance of 0.25 m in front of a plane mirror. The distance between the object and image will be** **(*Ap*)**
   (*a*) 1.5 m (*b*) 0.5 m
   (*c*) 1 m (*d*) 0.20 m

12. **The angle of incidence for a ray of light having zero reflection angle is** **(*Un*)**
   (*a*) 30° (*b*) 45°
   (*c*) 0 (*d*) 60°

13. **Which of the following optical devices can produce a real image for a real object?** **(*Re*)**
   (*a*) Concave lens (*b*) Concave mirror
   (*c*) Plane mirror (*d*) Convex mirror

14. **In the following cases, a ray is incident on a concave mirror. In which case is the angle of incidence equal to zero?** **(*Un*) (CBSE SQP, 2025)**
   (*a*) A ray parallel to the principal axis.
   (*b*) A ray passing through the centre of curvature and incident obliquely.
   (*c*) A ray passing through the principal focus and incident obliquely.
   (*d*) A ray incident obliquely to the principal axis, at the pole of the mirror.

15. **An object that is placed at a distance of 30 cm from a concave mirror gets its image at the same point. The focal length of the mirror is** **(*Ap*)**
   (*a*) –45 cm (*b*) 45 cm
   (*c*) –15 cm (*d*) +15 cm

16. **For an object that is at a distance of +15 cm and is moved slowly towards the pole of a convex mirror. The image will get** **(*Ap*)**
   (*a*) enlarged and real (*b*) shortened and real
   (*c*) enlarge and virtual (*d*) diminished and virtual

17. **For a concave mirror of radius 30 cm which is placed in water the focal length in air and water differ by** **(*Un*)**
   (*a*) 25 cm (*b*) 20 cm
   (*c*) 0 cm (*d*) 30 cm

18. **A concave mirror of focal length 20 cm forms an image twice the size of object. What will be the position of the object for the virtual image?** **(*Ap*)**
   (*a*) 20 cm (*b*) 30 cm
   (*c*) 10 cm (*d*) At infinity

Assertion and Reason (1 M)

Direction: The following questions consist of two statements. Assertion (A) and Reason (R). Answer these questions by selecting the appropriate option given below:

(*a*) Both A and R are true, and R is the correct explanation of A.
(*b*) Both A and R are true, but R is not the correct explanation of A.
(*c*) A is true, but R is false
(*d*) A is false, but R is true.

1. **Assertion (A):** A convex mirror always forms an image behind it and the image formed is virtual.
   Reason (R): According to the sign convention, the focal length of a convex mirror is positive. **(*Re*) (CBSE SQP, 2025)**

2. **Assertion (A):** A point object is placed at a distance of 26 cm form a convex mirror of focal length 26 cm. The image will not form at infinity.
   Reason (R): For above given system the equation $\frac{1}{u}+\frac{1}{v}=\frac{1}{f}$ gives $v=\infty$ **(*Ap*)**

3. **Assertion (A):** If both plane mirror and object are moved through a distance x, then the image moves through a distance $2x$.
   Reason (R): When the object is fixed and plane mirror moved through a distance x. Then the image is also moves through the distance $2x$. **(*Ap*)**

4. **Assertion (A):** The magnification of the real image is negative.
   Reason (R): Real image is inverted in nature. **(*Un*)**

5. **Assertion (A):** The image formed by a concave mirror is certainly real if the object is virtual.
   Reason (R): The image formed by a concave mirror is certainly virtual if the object is real. **(*Re*)**

Subjective Questions

Very Short Answer Type Questions (2 M)

1. **Search mirrors are mirrors that are used to look for hidden objects underneath the cars as shown. The hidden objects can be easily spotted as the mirror provides a wider field of view.** **(*Re*) (CBSE APQ, 2023)**

(*a*) **What type of mirrors are generally used to make search mirrors?**

(*b*) **With the help of a ray diagram describe the nature of image formed by the type of mirror identified in (*a*).**

Ans. (*a*) convex mirror *(1 M)*

(*b*) virtual, erect and diminished *(1 M)*

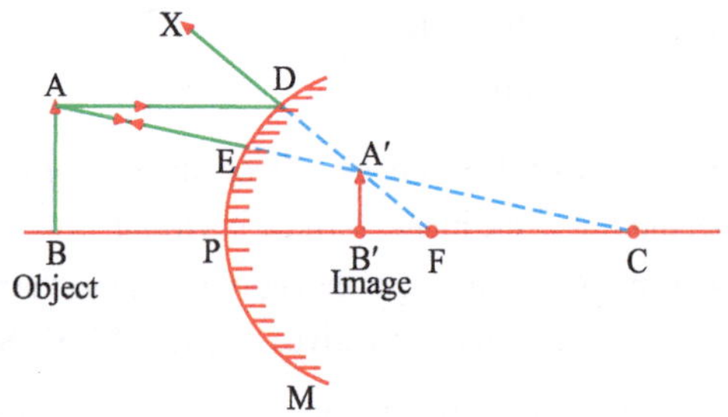

2. **Define the terms: a ray of light and a beam of light.** ***(Re)***

Ans. A Ray of light is a line drawn along the path of light. *(1 M)*

A bundle of rays originating from a single source of light in a particular direction is called a beam of light. *(1 M)*

3. **Write an observation which illustrates that light travels in a straight line.** ***(Un)***

Ans. A small source of light casts a sharp shadow of an opaque object that tells us that light travels in a straight line. In a slightly dusty atmosphere, the path of light appears to be straight. Light from sources such as a torch, train, or lamps always travels in a direct path. *(2 M)*

4. **While getting ready in the morning, Anu uses a large wall-mounted mirror in her bathroom to check her appearance. She notices that her reflection is exactly the same size as she is, upright, and appears to be the same distance behind the mirror as she is in front of it.**

What type of mirror is Anu using, and what are the properties of the image she sees? ***(An)***

Ans. Anu is using a plane mirror. The properties of the image she sees are that it is virtual, erect, the same size as the object, and as far behind the mirror as the object is in front of it. The image is also laterally inverted. *(2 M)*

5. **For what position of an object, a Real image equal to the size of the object is formed in front of the concave mirror. what would be the magnification in this case?** ***(Un)***

Ans. When an object is placed at the centre of curvature (C) of a concave mirror, a real image of size equal to that of the object is formed. *(1 M)*

Since, the size of image is equal to size of object and inverted to the object, therefore magnification(h_i/h_o) would be –1. *(1 M)*

6. **What should be the position of the object for which a concave mirror forms a real image that is highly enlarged?** ***(Un)***

Ans. To form a real, inverted, and highly enlarged image using a concave mirror, the object should be placed at the mirror's focus. *(2 M)*

7. **An object is placed at a distance of 10 cm from a convex mirror of focal length 15 cm. Find the position of the image formed by the mirror.** ***(Ev)* (CBSE, 2024)**

Ans.

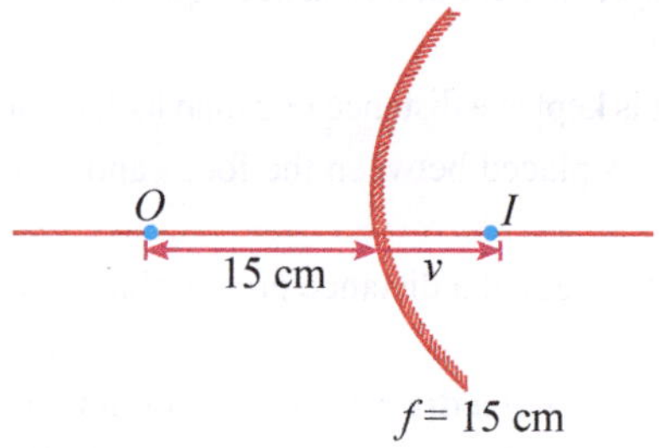

Given that,

$u = -10$ cm, $f = +15$ cm, $v = ?$

According to the mirror formula, $\frac{1}{f} = \frac{1}{v} + \frac{1}{u}$ where, u = the distance between the object and the pole of the mirror,

v = the distance between the image and the pole of the mirror,

f = focal length

$$\Rightarrow \frac{1}{v} = \frac{1}{f} - \frac{1}{u}$$ *(½ M)*

$$\Rightarrow \frac{1}{v} = \frac{1}{15} - \frac{1}{-10} \Rightarrow \frac{1}{v} = \frac{1}{15} + \frac{1}{10} \Rightarrow \frac{1}{v} = \frac{2+3}{30} = \frac{5}{30}$$

$$\Rightarrow v = \frac{30}{5} \Rightarrow v = 6 \text{ cm}$$ *(½ M)*

The image will be formed at a distance of 6 cm from the mirror behind it. The image will be formed erect and virtual. *(1 M)*

Nailing the Right Answer

- Focal length of concave mirror is always negative and for convex mirror it is positive.
- Familiarize yourself with the laws of reflection. Understand that the angle of incidence is equal to the angle of reflection.
- Understand the characteristics of images formed by mirrors. Learn about the different types of images (real, virtual, erect, inverted) and their properties (size, nature, and position).

8. **Specify the size of the image formed by a concave mirror when m > 1 and m < 1.** ***(Un)***

Ans. When the magnification m is greater than 1 (m > 1) for an image formed by a concave mirror, it indicates that the image is enlarged. This means that the size of the image is larger than the size of the object. *(1 M)*

When the magnification m is less than 1 ($m < 1$) for an image formed by a concave mirror, it indicates that the image is diminished. In this case, the size of the image is smaller than the size of the object. *(1 M)*

Short Answer Type Questions (3 M)

1. A concave mirror produces a three times magnified (enlarged) real image of the object placed at 10 cm in front of it. Where is the image located? (NCERT Intext)

Ans. Magnification produced by the spherical mirror:

$$m = \frac{\text{Height of the image}}{\text{Height of the object}} = -\frac{\text{Image Distance}}{\text{Object Distance}}$$

$$\Rightarrow m = \frac{h_i}{h_0} = -\frac{v}{u}$$ *(1 M)*

According to the question.

$h_i = 3h_0$

Then, height of the image $h_{(i)} = -3h$ (Image formed is real)

$$-\frac{3h_0}{h_0} = -\frac{v}{u}$$

$$\frac{v}{u} = 3$$

$\because \quad u = -10$ cm

$\Rightarrow v = 3 \times (-10) = -30$ cm *(1 M)*

Here, the negative sign indicates that an inverted image is formed in front of the concave mirror at a distance of 30 cm *(1 M)*

2. Under what condition in an arrangement of two plane mirrors, incident ray and reflected ray will always be parallel to each other, whatever may be angle of incidence. Show the same with the help of a diagram. (*Un*) (NCERT Exemplar)

Ans. When two plane mirrors are placed perpendicular to each other, the incident ray and reflected ray will always be parallel to each other, whatever may be the angle of incidence. *(1 M)*

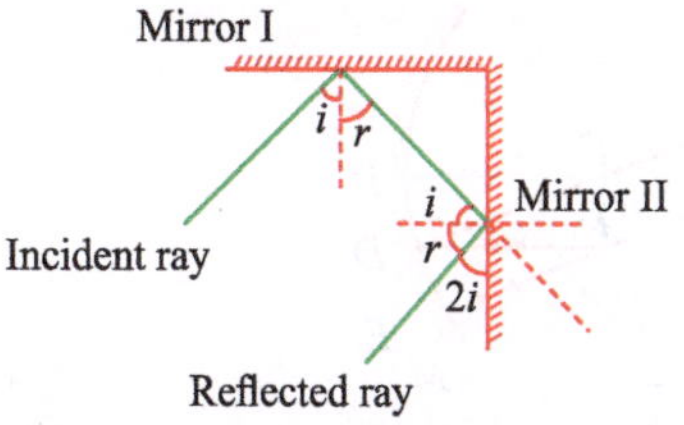

(2 M)

3. List two differences between the two images.

If the image formed by mirror for all positions of the object placed in front of it is always virtual and diminished, state the type of the mirror. Draw a ray diagram in support of your answer. (*An + Un*)

Where are such mirrors commonly used and why?

Ans. Convex Mirror

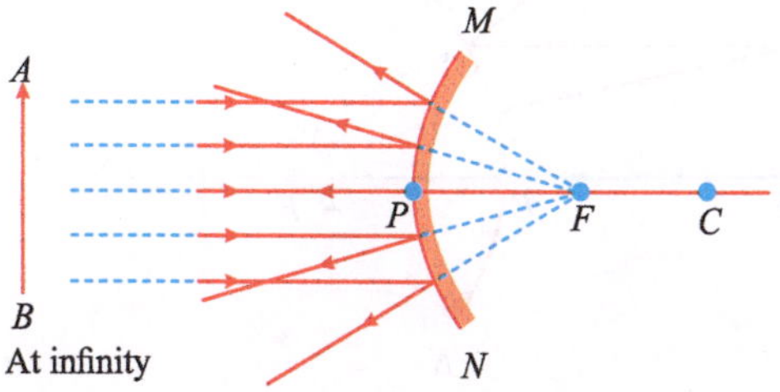

(1 M)

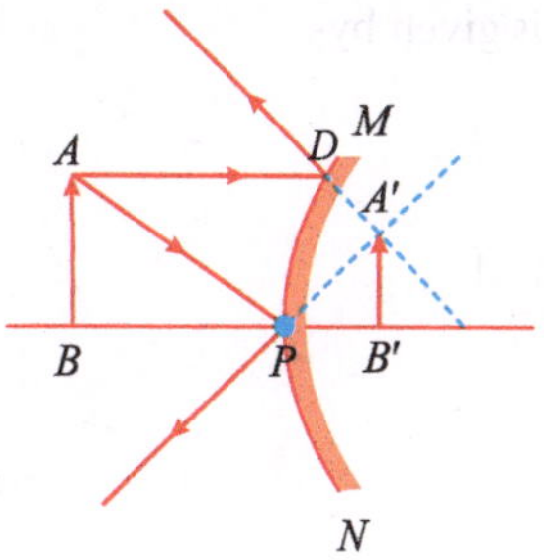

(1 M)

A convex mirror is commonly used as a rear-view mirror in vehicles because it always produces a virtual and erect image whose size is smaller than the object. Therefore, it enables the driver to see a wide field of view of the traffic behind the vehicle in a small mirror. *(1 M)*

4. An insect is at a distance of 1.5 m from a plane mirror. Calculate the distance:

(*i*) At which the image of the insect is formed.

(*ii*) Between the insect and its image. (*Ev*)

Ans. (*i*) It is given that the distance of insect from the plane mirror = 1.5 m

Therefore the image must be formed 1.5 m behind the mirror, since for a plane mirror image distance and the object distance are equal. *(1½ M)*

(*ii*) The distance between the insect and its image

= 1.5 + 1.5 = 3 m *(1½ M)*

5. An object 4.0 cm in size, is placed 25.0 cm in front of a concave mirror of focal length 15.0 cm.

(*i*) At what distance from the mirror should a screen be placed in order to obtain a sharp image?

(*ii*) Find the size of the image.

(*iii*) Draw a ray diagram to show the formation of the image in this case. (*Ev + Un*) (CBSE-2020)

Ans. (*i*) Given:

The size of object = 4.0 cm

Distance of the object = 25 cm (–*ve* as it is in front of mirrors) focal length of concave mirror = 15 cm (–*ve*) Distance of the image is given by-

$$\frac{1}{v} + \frac{1}{u} = \frac{1}{f}$$ *(½ M)*

$$\frac{1}{v} + \frac{1}{-25} = \frac{1}{-15}$$

$$\frac{1}{v} = \frac{1}{-15} + \frac{1}{25}$$ *(½ M)*

$$= \frac{-10+6}{150}$$

$$\frac{-4}{150} \Rightarrow v = -37.5 \text{ cm}$$

The screen should be at 37.5 cm in front of the lens.

(*ii*) The size of the image is given by-

$$\frac{h_i}{h_o} = \frac{-v}{u}$$ (½ M)

$$\Rightarrow h_i = \frac{-v \times h_o}{u} = \frac{-(-37.5)\times 4}{-25}$$

$$h_i = -\frac{150}{25} = -6\,\text{cm}$$ (½ M)

The images will be 6 cm high and it will be inverted.

(*iii*) The image will be formed at a distance of 37.5 cm form the mirror.

It will be an inverted image.

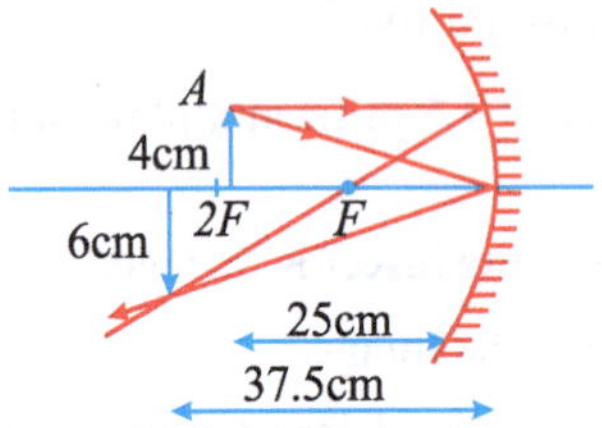

(1 M)

6. An object of height 3 cm is placed on the principal axis of a concave mirror. The distance of the object from the mirror is 15 cm, and the image formed is 30 cm away from the mirror on the same side of the mirror as the object. Calculate the height of the image formed. (*Ev*)

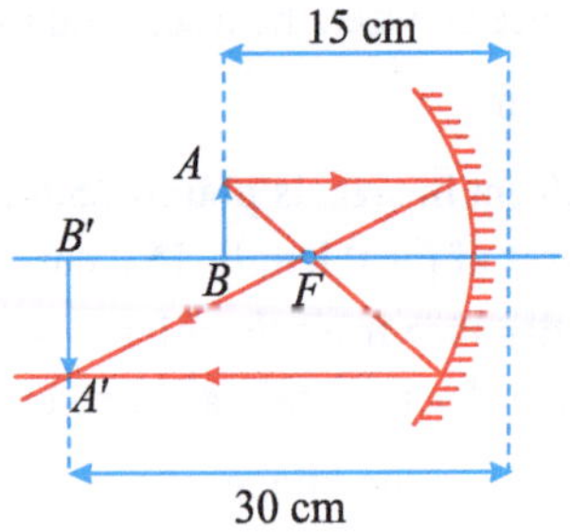

Ans. Given $u = -15$ cm and $v = -30$ cm

$h_o = 3\text{cm}, h_i = ?$ (1 M)

From the formula of magnification

$$m = \frac{h_i}{h_o} = -\frac{v}{u}$$

$$h_i = -\frac{v}{u} \times h_o$$

$$h_i = -\frac{-30}{-15} \times 3 = -6 \text{ cm}$$ (2 M)

7. An object is placed at a distance of 30 cm from a concave mirror of focal length 15 cm. List four characteristics (nature, position, etc.) of the image formed by the mirror. (*Ev + Un*) (CBSE 2017)

Ans. The object distance, $u = -30$

The focal length of the mirror, $f = -15$ cm

From Mirror formula

$$\frac{1}{u} + \frac{1}{v} = \frac{1}{f}$$ (½ M)

$$\frac{1}{-30} + \frac{1}{v} = \frac{1}{-15}$$

$$\Rightarrow \frac{1}{v} = \frac{1}{-15} + \frac{1}{30} = \frac{-1}{30}$$ (½ M)

Therefore, $v = -30$ cm

Magnification is given by, $\frac{v}{u} = -1$ (1 M)

Four characteristics of images

1. Real
2. Inverted
3. At centre of curvature
4. Same size of the object (1 M)

8. A student, holding a mirror in his hand, directed the reflecting surface of the mirror towards the sun. He then directed the reflected light on to a sheet of paper held close to the mirror.

(*i*) What should he do to burn the paper?

(*ii*) Which type of mirror does he use?

(*iii*) Will he be able to determine the approximate value of focal length of this mirror from this activity ?

Give reason and draw ray diagram to justify your answer in this case. (*Un*) (CBSE 2019)

Ans. (*i*) The student should adjust the distance between the mirror and the paper so that solar rays are sharply focussed on the paper. (1 M)

(*ii*) The mirror is a concave mirror. (1 M)

(*iii*) The student can find the approximate focal length by measuring the distance between the paper and the mirror.

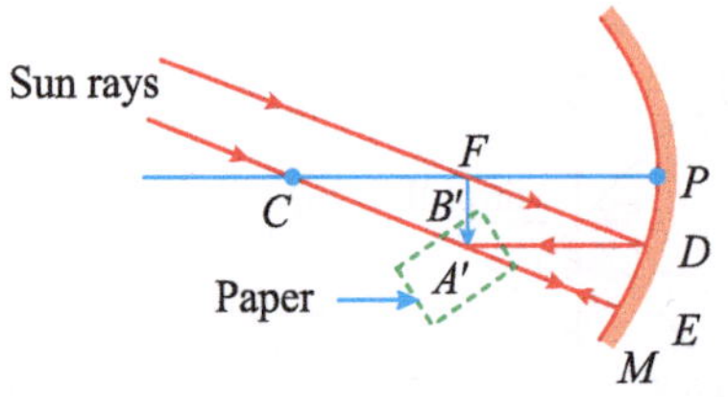

(1 M)

9. If the image formed by a spherical mirror for all positions of the object placed in front of it is always erect and diminished, what type of mirror is it? Draw a labelled ray diagram to support your answer. (*Un*) (CBSE 2018)

Ans. Convex Mirror (1 M)

Labelled Ray diagram for any position of object

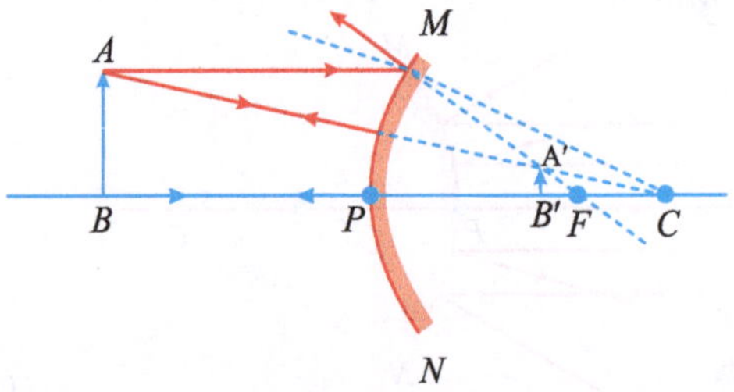

(1 M)

OR

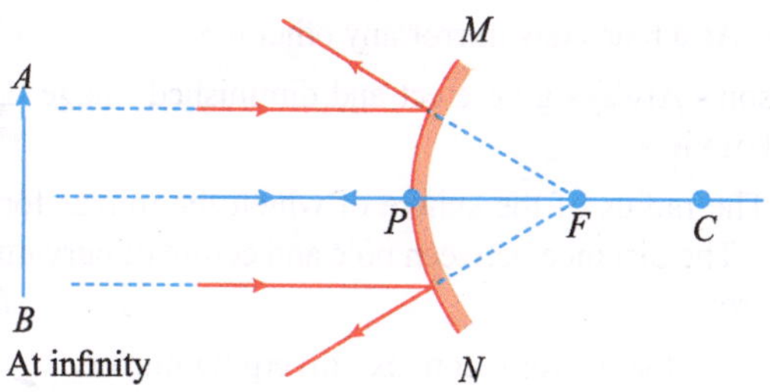

(1 M)

10. **(a) Define the following terms in the context of a diverging mirror**

(i) Principal focus **(ii) Focal length**

Draw a labeled ray diagram to illustrate your answer. **(Re)**

Ans. (a) (i) Principal focus: The principal focus of a diverging mirror is a point on the principal axis of the mirror where the rays of light parallel to the principal axis appear to diverge after reflection. It is denoted by the letter F. (1 M)

(ii) Focal length: The focal length of a diverging mirror is the distance between the pole (P) and the principal focus (F). It is denoted by the letter f. (1 M)

Here's a labelled ray diagram that illustrates the above explanation:

Convex or Diverging Mirror

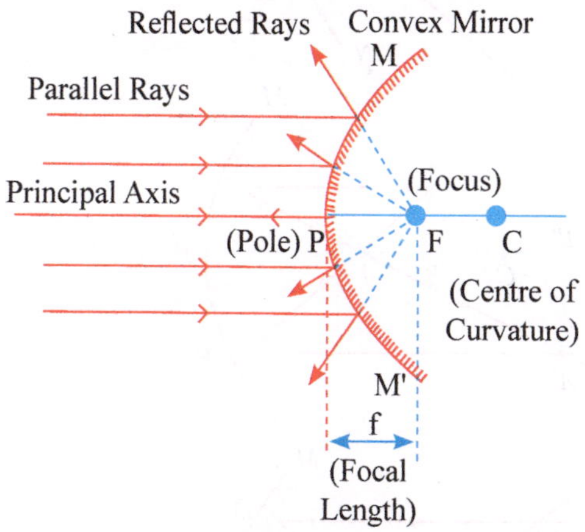

(1 M)

Long Answer Type Questions (5 M)

1. **(i) A concave mirror of focal length 10 cm can produce a magnified real as well as virtual image of an object placed in front of it. Draw ray diagrams to justify this statement.**

(ii) An object is placed perpendicular to the principal axis of a convex mirror of focal length 10 cm. The distance of the object from the pole of the mirror is 10 cm. Find the position of the image formed.

(Un + Ev) (CBSE, 2020)

Ans. (i) A concave mirror of focal length 10 cm can produce a magnified real image when the object is placed between the centre of curvature C and principal focus F. (½ M)

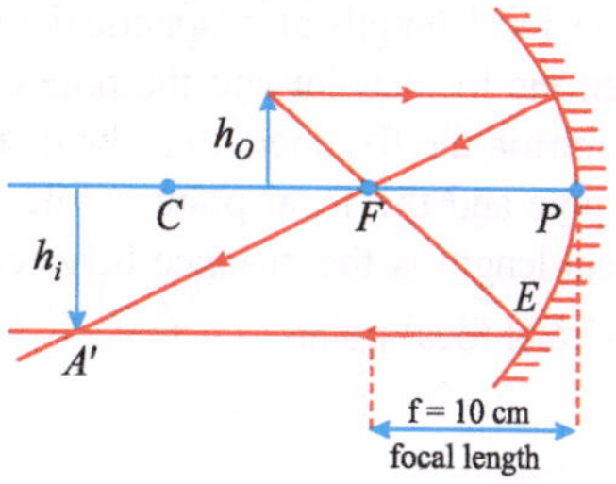

(1 M)

A concave mirror of focal length 10 cm can produce a magnified virtual image when the object is placed between the pole P and principal focus F (½ M)

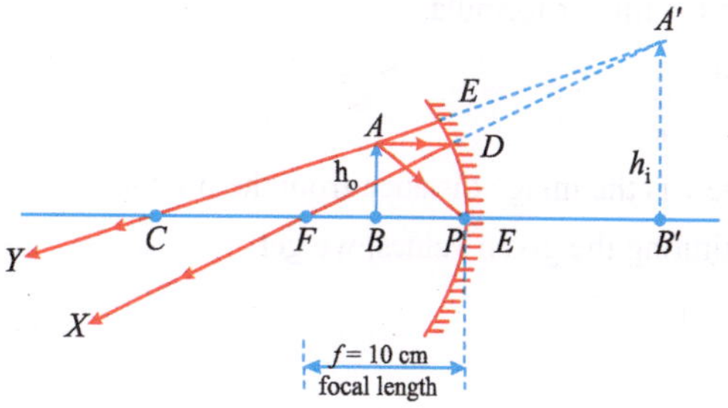

(1 M)

(ii) Focal length, $f = 10$ cm

Object distance, $u = -10$ cm (object distance is always taken negative as it is on the left side)

To find: Position of the image or image distance, v. (½ M)

From the mirror formula, we know that-

$$\frac{1}{v}+\frac{1}{u}=\frac{1}{f}$$ (½ M)

Substituting the given values in the formula, we get-

$$\frac{1}{v}+\frac{1}{(-10)}=\frac{1}{10}$$

$$\frac{1}{v}-\frac{1}{10}=\frac{1}{10} \Rightarrow \frac{1}{v}-\frac{1}{10}+\frac{1}{10} \Rightarrow \frac{1}{v}=\frac{1+1}{10} \Rightarrow \frac{1}{v}=\frac{2}{10}$$

$$\frac{1}{v}=\frac{1}{5}$$

$v = +5$ cm (1 M)

2. **(a) In the context of spherical mirrors, define the following terms:**

(i) Pole **(ii) Centre of curvature**

(iii) Principal axis **(iv) Focal length**

(b) An object of size 4 cm is placed at a distance of 15 cm in front of a concave mirror of focal length 10 cm. Find the distance of the image from the mirror and size of the image Formed. **(Re + Ev) (CBSE 2018)**

Ans. (a) (i) **Pole:** The pole is the point on the mirror's surface that lies on the principal axis and is equidistant from the mirror's surface. (½ M)

(ii) **Centre of curvature:** The centre of curvature is the centre of the sphere of which the mirror is a part of. It is located on the principal axis, and its distance from the mirror is called the radius of curvature. (½ M)

(iii) **Principal axis:** The principal axis is the imaginary straight line passing through the centre of curvature and the pole of the spherical mirror. (½ M) (*iv*) **Focal length:** The focal length of a spherical mirror is the distance between the focal point and the pole of the mirror. For a concave mirror, the focal length is the distance between the mirror's pole and the focal point, while for a convex mirror, the focal length is the distance between the mirror's pole and the virtual focal point. *(½ M)*

(*b*) Given:

Object distance, $u = -15$ cm

Object size, $h = 4$ cm *(½ M)*

Focal length, $f = -10$ cm (negative sign for concave mirror)

Using the mirror formula,

$$\frac{1}{f} = \frac{1}{v} + \frac{1}{u}$$ *(½ M)*

Where v is the image distance from the mirror.

Substituting the given values, we get

$$\frac{1}{-10} = \frac{1}{v} + \frac{1}{(-15)}$$

Simplifying the equation, we get

$v = -30$ cm *(½ M)*

Since the image distance is negative, the image is formed behind the mirror, which indicates that the image is real and inverted. *(½ M)*

Using the magnification formula,

$$m = \frac{-v}{u}$$ *(½ M)*

Substituting the given values, we get

$$m = \frac{-(-30)}{-(15)} = -2$$

$h' = m \times h$

Substituting the given values, we get

$h' = -2 \times 4 = -8$ cm

The negative sign indicates that the image is inverted and at a distance of 30 cm behind the mirror, and its size is 8 cm. *(½ M)*

3. (*a*) If the image formed by a mirror for all positions of the object placed in front of it is always diminished, erect and virtual, state the type of the mirror and also draw a ray diagram to justify your answer. Write one use such mirrors are put to and why.

(*b*) Define the radius of curvature of spherical mirrors. Find the nature and focal length of a spherical mirror whose radius of curvature is + 24 cm.

(*Un* + *Re*) (CBSE 2017)

Ans. (*a*) Convex/diverging mirror *(1 M)*

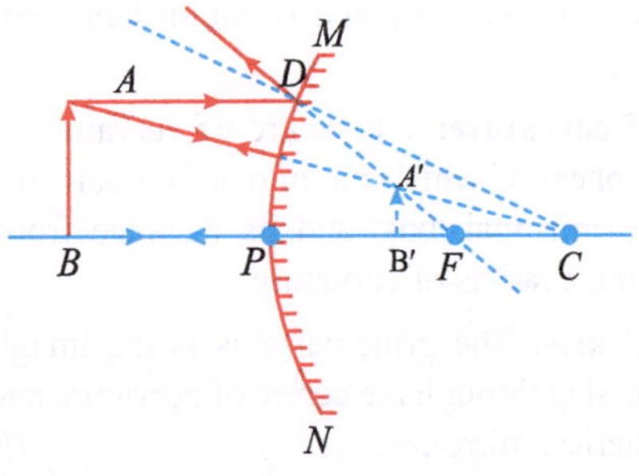

Direction of rays *(1 M)*

Use:- As a rear view mirror/any other use *(½ M)*

Reason:- Always give erect and diminished image/ Large field of view *(½ M)*

(*b*) The radius of the sphere of which the mirror forms a parts/ The distance between pole and centre of curvature of a mirror. *(1 M)*

Nature of the mirror – convex / diverging mirror

$R = 2f = 24$ cm

$\therefore \quad f = +12$ cm *(1 M)*

4. Draw ray diagrams showing the image formation by a concave mirror when an object is placed

(*a*) Between the pole and focus of the mirror.

(*b*) Between focus and center of curvature of the mirror.

(*c*) At the center of curvature of the mirror.

(*d*) A little beyond the center of curvature of the mirror.

(*e*) At infinity. (*Un*) (NCERT Exemplar)

Ans. (*a*) *(1 M)*

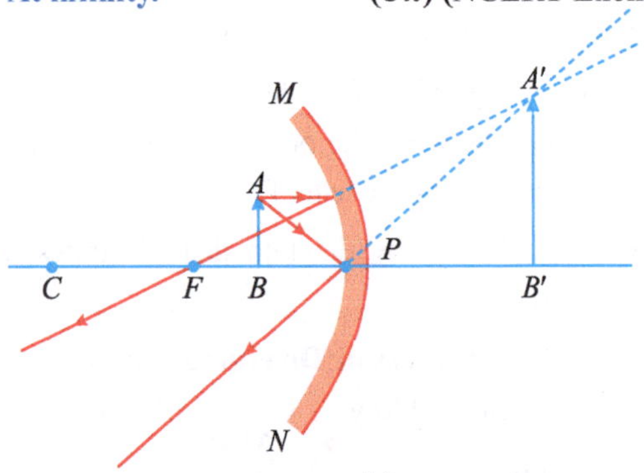

(*b*) *(1 M)*

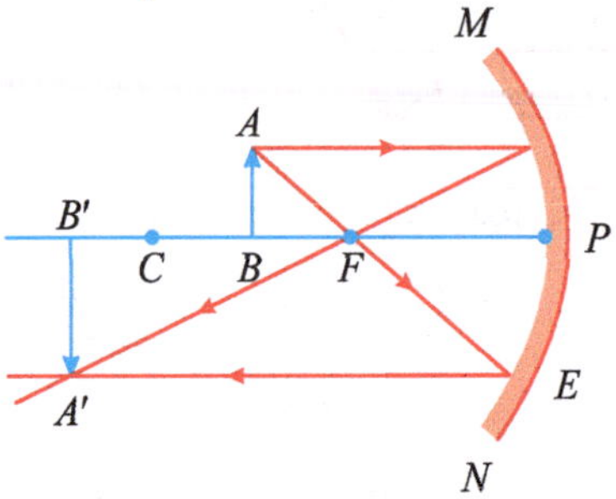

(*c*) *(1 M)*

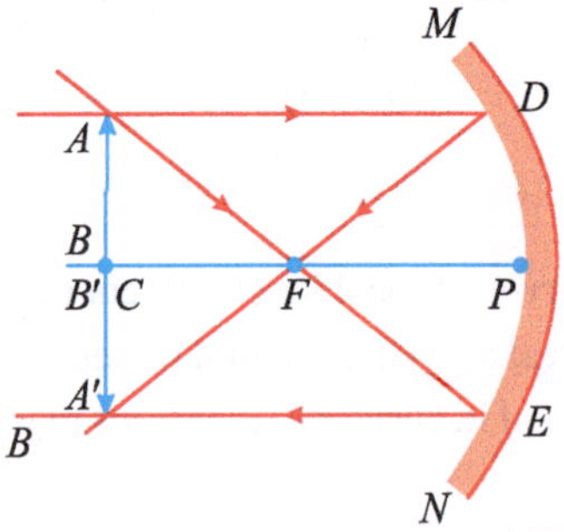

(*d*) *(1 M)*

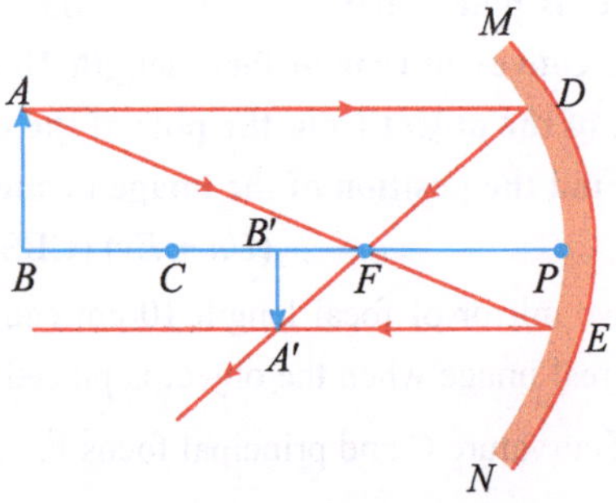

(e) 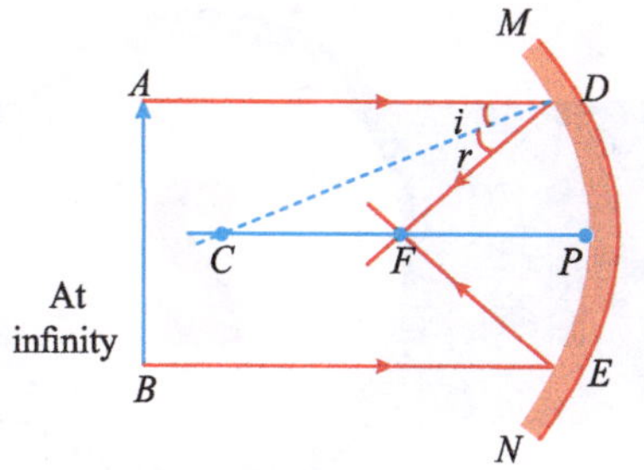

(1 M)

5. During a physics lab experiment, Rohan placed a 10 cm long pencil 5 cm in front of a concave mirror with a radius of curvature of 40 cm.

(a) Determine the position of the image formed by this mirror. **(Ev)**

(b) What is the size of the image? **(Ev)**

(c) Draw a ray diagram to show the formation of the image as mentioned in part (i). **(Cr)**

Ans. (a) $\frac{1}{f}=\frac{1}{v}+\frac{1}{u}$

where, $u=-5$ cm, $f=\frac{r}{2}=-20$ cm

$-\frac{1}{20}=\frac{1}{v}-\frac{1}{5}$

$\frac{1}{v}=-\frac{1}{20}+\frac{1}{5}=\frac{-1+4}{20}=\frac{3}{20}$

$v=\frac{20}{3}=6.67$ cm

The image is obtained at 6.67 m behind the mirror. *(2 M)*

(b) $m=\frac{h_2}{h_1}=-\frac{v}{u}=-\frac{\frac{20}{3}}{-5}=\frac{4}{3}$

Thus, the height of the image is = magnification × object size

$h_2=(4/3)\times 10=13.33$ cm *(2 M)*

(c)

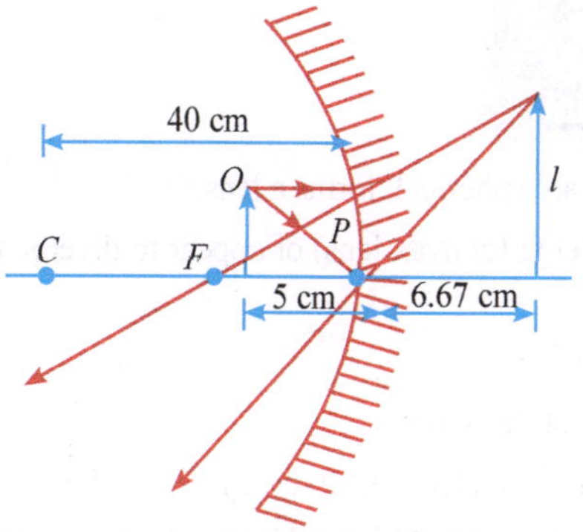

(1 M)

Hints & Explanations

Multiple Choice Questions

1. (b) anywhere between the pole and principal focus
2. (d) behind the mirror and its position varies according to the object distance.
3. (c) Riya is observing the reflection of light. Reflection occurs when light rays strike a surface and bounce back. In this case, sunlight hits the small mirror and reflects off its surface, creating a spot of light on the wall. The mirror redirects the sunlight because it acts as a reflective surface, causing the light rays to change direction and form a visible spot.
4. (a) parallel to the axis.
5. (b) The distance of image is equal to the distance of object from mirror. Therefore, the distance of image from mirror is 10 cm.
6. (a) Focal length of a mirror is given by

   Focal length = $\frac{\text{radius of curvature}}{2}$

   Since both the mirrors have same radius of curvature, therefore focal length of the two mirrors will be same, i.e.,

   $f_1/f_2=1:1$
7. (a) When the object is placed between the focus and the mirror, a magnified (enlarged) image is formed by the concave mirror.
8. (a) Focal length = Radius/2

   $f=20/2=10$ cm
9. (b)

   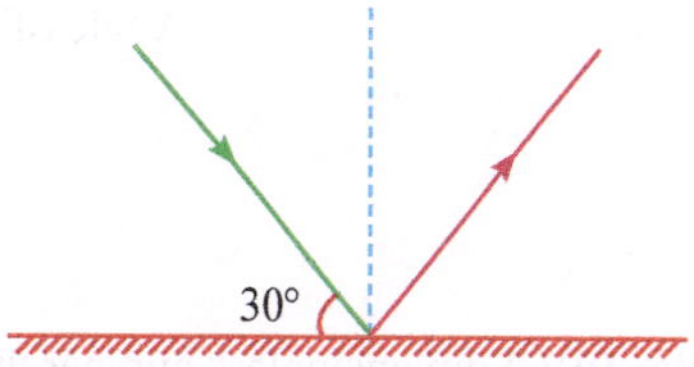

   The angle of incidence is the angle between the incident ray and the normal to the surface. If the laser hits the mirror at an angle of 30 degrees to the surface of the mirror, the angle of incidence is actually 60 degrees to the normal.
   According to the law of reflection, the angle of reflection is equal to the angle of incidence.
   Therefore, the angle of reflection is also 60 degrees.
10. (c)
11. (b) Distance between object and image = 2 × 0.25 = 0.5 m
12. (c) From laws of reflection. $\angle i=\angle r$
13. (b) Only a concave mirror produces a real image of an object.
14. (b) A ray passing through the centre of curvature and incident obliquely.
15. (c) When an object is placed at 2F, the image formed by a concave mirror is also at 2F. So 2F = –30 or F = –15 cm.
16. (d) Convex mirrors always form a virtual erect and diminished image when the object moves toward the pole, the image gets diminished.
17. (c) The focal length of the spherical mirror does not depend on the surrounding medium.
18. (c) For the image to be virtual.

Assertion and Reason

1. (b) Both (A) and (R) are true, but (R) is not the correct explanation of (A).
2. (c) Assertion (A) is true but reason (R) is false.
3. (c) Assertion (A) is true but reason (R) is false.
4. (a)
5. (c) Assertion (A) is true but reason (R) is false. The image of real object may be real in case of concave mirror.

REFRACTION

NCERT Definitions (Commonly asked in 1 mark)

- **Refraction:** Refraction is the bending of light as it passes from one medium to another with a different optical density.

Refraction of Light

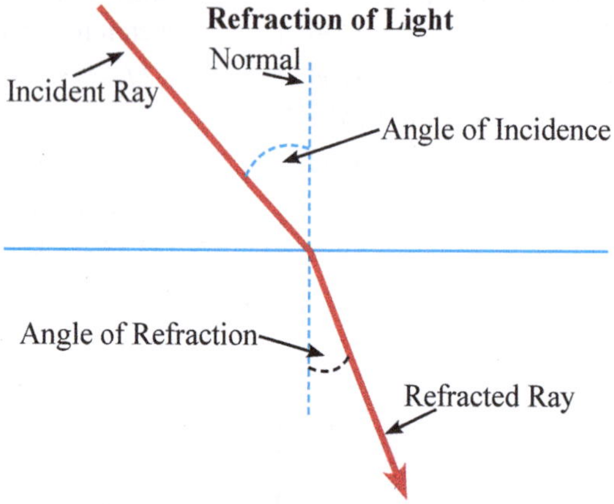

- **Refractive Index (n):** A dimensionless number that describes how light, or any other radiation, propagates through that medium. It is defined as the speed of light in vacuum divided by the speed of light in the medium.

- **Lens:** A transparent material bound by two surfaces, of which one or both surfaces are spherical, forms a lens.
- **Principal Focus (F):** The point where light rays parallel to the principal axis converge (convex lens) or appear to diverge (concave lens) after refraction.
- **Focal Length (f):** The distance between the optical center of a lens and its principal focus.
- **Optical Centre (O):** The central point of a lens through which light rays pass without deviation.
- **Lens Formula:** Relates the object distance (u), image distance (v), and focal length (f) of a lens, given by $1/f = 1/v - 1/u$.
- **Magnification (m):** The ratio of the height of the image to the height of the object, also related to the object and image distances.
- **Concave lens:** lens that is thinner at its center than at its edges and spreads out light rays, making them diverge away from a point.

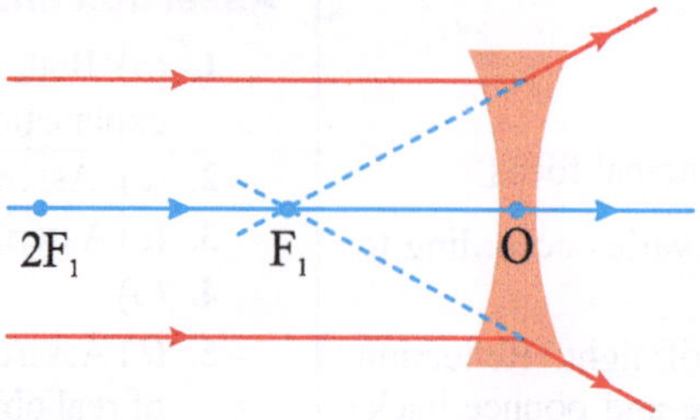

- **Convex lens:** Lens that is thicker at its center than at its edges and brings light rays together to a point.

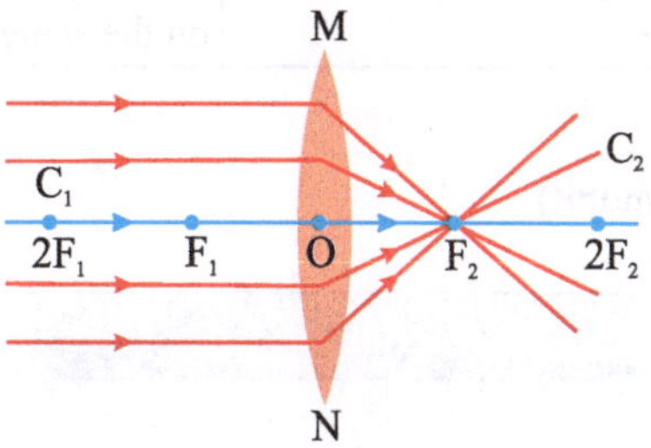

- **Power of a Lens (P):** The measure of the converging or diverging ability of a lens, defined as the reciprocal of the focal length (in meters). A positive power denotes a converging lens (convex), while a negative power indicates a diverging lens (concave).
- **Dioptre:** The unit of measure for the power of a lens, defined as the reciprocal of the focal length of the lens in meters. One dioptre equals the power of a lens with a focal length of one meter.

Important Facts

01 Convex lenses can produce real, inverted images or virtual, erect images depending on the object's position relative to the focal length.

02 Concave lenses always produce virtual, erect, and diminished images, regardless of the object's position.

03 The magnification value is positive for virtual images and negative for real images.

04 The power of a convex lens is positive, indicating it converges light rays, while that of a concave lens is negative, indicating it diverges light rays.

05 A lens' ability to bend light is significantly determined by its material's refractive index.

06 The optical center of a lens is a point through which light rays pass undeviated

07 Lenses use refraction, not reflection, to form images.

Classification

Lens (According to their Function and Properties)		
Feature	**Convex Lens**	**Concave Lens**
Shape	Thicker at the center than at the edges.	Thinner at the center than at the edges.
Surface Curvature	Outwardly curved surfaces.	Inwardly curved surfaces.
Light Convergence	Converges light rays to a point (focal point).	Diverges light rays, spreading them out.
Image Formation	Can form real and inverted or virtual and upright images, depending on the object's position relative to the focal length.	Always forms virtual, upright, and reduced images.
Uses	Used in magnifying glasses, cameras, and corrective lenses for farsightedness.	Used in peepholes, optical instruments, and corrective lenses for nearsightedness.

Focal Length	Positive focal length.	Negative focal length.
Ray Diagram	Parallel rays converge after passing through the lens.	Parallel rays diverge after passing through the lens, appearing to originate from a focal point on the same side as the incoming rays.

Difference Between (Commonly asked in 2-3 mark)

Reflection Vs. Refraction		
Feature	**Reflection**	**Refraction**
Definition	Bouncing back of light from a surface.	Bending of light as it passes between different media.
Laws	Angle of incidence equals angle of reflection.	Snell's law: the ratio of the sine of the angles of incidence to refraction is constant.
Image Formation	Can produce virtual or real images.	Typically results in a virtual image; can alter the apparent position of objects.
Medium Change	No change in medium.	Involves change from one medium to another.
Direction of Light	Remains in the same medium; angle may change.	Enters a new medium; direction and speed change.
Surface Requirement	Requires a reflective surface.	Occurs at the interface of two transparent media.
Applications	Mirrors, kaleidoscopes, optical instruments.	Lenses, magnifying glasses, corrective eye wear.

Lens Vs. Mirror		
Feature	**Lens**	**Mirror**
Medium	Transparent material (glass, plastic)	Reflective surface (silver, aluminum)
Light Behavior	Refracts (bends) light	Reflects light
Image Formation	By bending light through the lens body	By bouncing light off the surface
Types	Convex, Concave	Plane, Convex, Concave
Uses	Eyeglasses, cameras, microscopes	Reflecting telescopes,makeup mirrors

Important Formula

1. **Snell's Law:**

   $n_1 \sin(i) = n_2 \sin(r)$; Where n_1 = refractive index of medium 1, n_2 = refractive index of medium 2, i = angle of incidence, r = angle of refraction

2. **Refractive Index:**

   $n = \frac{c}{v}$; Where, c = speed of light in vacuum (in m/s), v = speed of light in medium (in m/s)

3. **Lens Power:**

   $p = \frac{1}{f}$; Where, f = focal length (in m)

4. **Lens Equation for Thin Lenses:**

   $\frac{1}{f} = \frac{1}{v} = \frac{1}{u}$; Where v = image distance from pole (in m), u = object distance from pole (in m)

5. **Lens Magnification:**

   $m = \frac{h_i}{h_0} = \frac{v}{u}$; Where h_1 = height of image (in m), h_0 = height of object (in m)

Real Life Application Based Questions

1. **How do magnifying glasses help us see small details more clearly?**

Ans. Magnifying glasses use convex lenses to enlarge the appearance of objects. When you hold a magnifying glass close to an object, the convex lens bends the light rays coming from the object, so they converge and then diverge. This creates a larger virtual image as seen by your eyes, making the small details easier to observe. The magnification allows for a closer inspection of fine details that would be difficult to see with the naked eye, such as small text or intricate patterns.

2. **Why are concave lenses used in peepholes of doors?**

Ans. Concave lenses are used in door peepholes to provide a wider field of view. When someone looks through a peephole with a concave lens, the lens diverges the light rays coming from the outside, allowing the viewer to see a larger area. This enables people inside to view a broad swath of the area outside their door, enhancing security by letting them see more than what's directly in front of the door.

3. **How do optical fibers transmit light signals over long distances?**

Ans. Optical fibers transmit light by guiding it through the fiber using the principle of total internal reflection. The core of the fiber, made of glass or plastic, is surrounded by a cladding with a lower refractive index. This causes light entering the fiber at a certain angle to reflect internally and propagate along the length of the fiber without significant loss, enabling long-distance transmission.

4. **How does refraction facilitate magnification in microscopy?**

Ans. In microscopy, refraction is used to magnify images of small objects by bending light rays with lenses. As light passes through these lenses, it's refracted in such a way that the image of the object is enlarged, allowing detailed observation that wouldn't be possible with the naked eye.

Myth Buster

❒ **Myth: Refraction always makes objects appear closer or larger than they really are.**

Fact: This is not true. Refraction can make objects appear closer or larger, but it can also make them appear farther away or smaller, depending on the specific conditions of the refraction. For example, when light passes from air into water, objects may appear closer and larger, but when light passes from water into the air, objects may appear farther away and smaller.

❒ **Myth: Refraction always results in a change of direction.**

Fact: This is also not true. Refraction only results in a change of direction if the light passes through the medium at an angle other than perpendicular. If the light passes through the medium at a perpendicular angle, it will continue in a straight line.

❒ **Myth: Refraction occurs only in transparent media.**

Fact: This is a common misconception. Refraction can occur in any medium, whether it is transparent or opaque. In fact, the phenomenon of mirages is caused by the refraction of light in the atmosphere, which is not transparent.

❒ **Myth: Refraction always causes dispersion.**

Fact: Dispersion is the separation of white light into its component colours as it passes through a prism or other medium. While refraction can cause dispersion, not all refraction results in dispersion. For example, if the light passes through a medium with a uniform refractive index, such as a piece of glass, it will not be dispersed.

Mnemonics

❒ **On other hand convex lenses are converging.**

Lions live in a Den that's a Cave.

↓ Lenses ↓ Diverging ↓ Concave

COMPETENCY BASED SOLVED EXAMPLES

Multiple Choice Questions (1 M)

1. The refractive index of transparent medium is greater than one because **(*Un*)**

(*a*) Speed of light in vacuum < speed of light in transparent medium

(*b*) Speed of flight in vacuum = speed of light in transparent medium

(*c*) Speed of light in vacuum > speed of light in transparent medium

(*d*) Speed of light wave changes when it moves from rarer to denser medium

2. The refractive index of water is 1.33. The speed of light in water will be **(*Ap*)**

(*a*) 1.33×10^8 m/s (*b*) 1.5×10^8 m/s

(*c*) $2.26\, x\, 10^8$ m/s (*d*) 2.66×10^8 m/s

3. Anil is given three media A, B and C of refractive index 1.33, 1.65 and 1.46. The medium in which the light will travel fastest is **(*Un*)**

(*a*) B (*b*) A

(*c*) C (*d*) equal in all three media

4. At what distance from a convex lens should an object be placed to get an image of the same size as that of the object on a screen? **(*Un*) (CBSE, 2024)**

(*a*) Beyond twice the focal length of the lens.

(*b*) At the principal focus of the lens.

(*c*) At twice the focal length of the lens.

(*d*) Between the optical centre of the lens and its principal focus.

5. The distance between the optical centre and point of convergence is called focal length in which of the following cases? **(*Un*)**

(*a*) 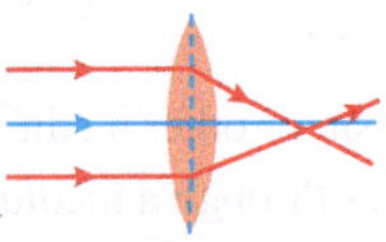

(*b*) 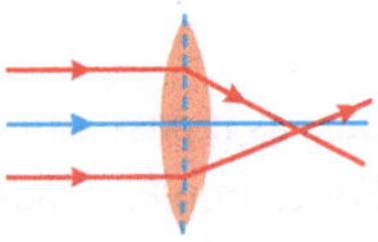

(*c*) 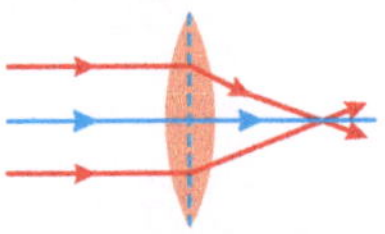

(*d*) 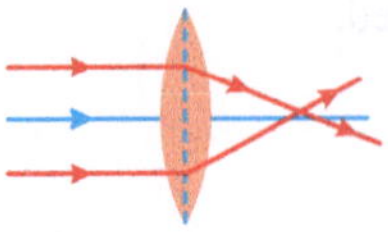

6. A ray of light travels from medium A to medium B as shown in the figure below. Refractive index of the medium B relative to medium A is **(*Ev*) (NCERT Exemplar)**

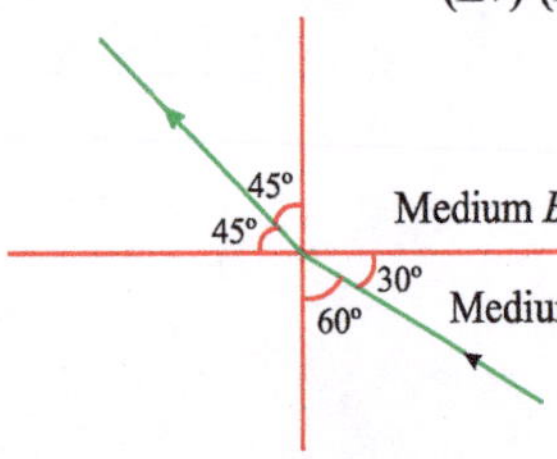

(*a*) $\frac{\sqrt{3}}{\sqrt{2}}$ (*b*) $\frac{\sqrt{2}}{\sqrt{3}}$

(*c*) $\frac{1}{\sqrt{2}}$ (*d*) $\sqrt{3}$

7. A light ray enters from medium B to medium A as shown in the figure. The refractive index of medium A relative to B will be **(*Un*) (NCERT Exemplar)**

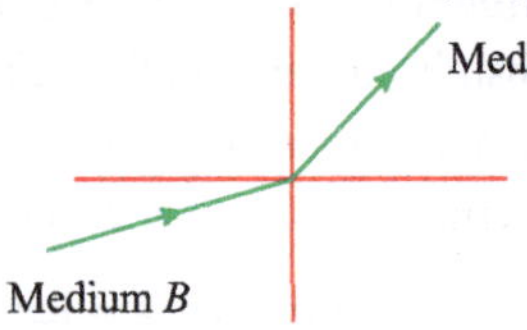

(*a*) > 1 (*b*) < 1

(*c*) =1 (*d*) None

8. A student obtains a blurred image of a distant object on a screen using a convex lens. To obtain a distinct image on the screen he should move the lens

(*a*) away from the screen

(*b*) towards the screen

(*c*) to a position very far away from the screen

(*d*) either towards or away from the screen depending upon the position of the object **(*Un*) (CBSE, 2017)**

9. Study the given ray diagrams and select the correct statement from the following: **(*Un*) (CBSE, 2017)**

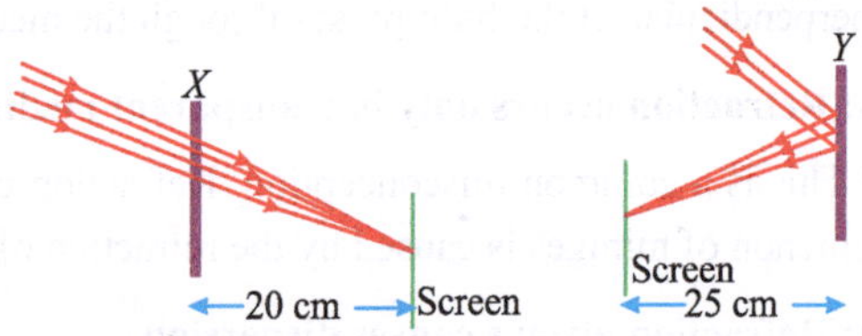

(*a*) Device *X* is a concave mirror and device *Y* is a convex lens, whose focal lengths are 20 cm and 25 cm respectively.

(*b*) Device *X* is a convex lens and device *Y* is a concave mirror, whose focal lengths are 10 cm and 25 cm respectively.

(*c*) Device *X* is a concave lens and device *Y* is a convex mirror, whose focal lengths are 20 cm and 25 cm respectively.

(*d*) Device *X* is a convex lens and device *Y* is a concave mirror, whose focal lengths are 20 cm and 25 cm respectively.

10. Beams of light are incident through the holes A and B and emerge out of box through the holes C and D respectively as shown in the Figure. Which of the following could be inside the box? **(*Un*) (NCERT Exemplar)**

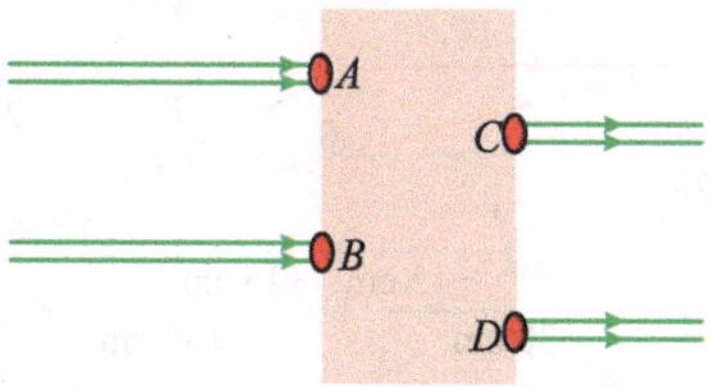

Box

(*a*) A rectangular glass slab (*b*) A convex lens

(*c*) A concave lens (*d*) A prism

11. A beam of light is incident through the holes on side A and emerges out of the holes on the other face of the box as shown in the Figure. Which of the following could be inside the box? (*Un*) (NCERT Exemplar)

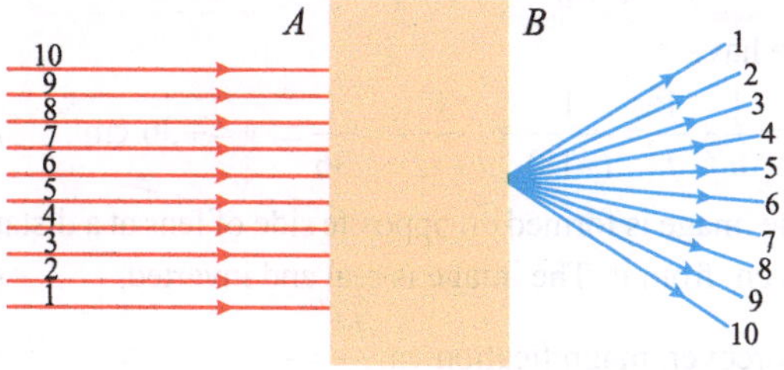

Box

(*a*) Concave lens (*b*) Rectangular glass slab

(*c*) Prism (*d*) Convex lens

Assertion and Reason (1 M)

Direction: **The following questions consist of two statements. Assertion (A) and Reason (R). Answer these questions by selecting the appropriate option given below:**

(*a*) Both A and R are true, and R is the correct explanation of A.

(*b*) Both A and R are true, but R is not the correct explanation of A.

(*c*) A is true, but R is false

(*d*) A is false, but R is true.

1. **Assertion (A):** During a physics experiment, Suman observed that when light passed from air into water, it bent at the interface. Her teacher explained that this phenomenon is called refraction.

   Reason (R): The teacher further explained that refraction occurs because the speed of light changes when it moves from one medium to another. **(*Un*)**

2. **Assertion (A):** Refractive index has no units.

   Reason (R): The refractive index is a ratio of two similar quantities. **(*Re*)**

3. **Assertion (A):** Higher is the refractive index of a medium or denser the medium, lesser is the velocity of light in that medium.

   Reason (R): Refractive index is inversely proportional to velocity. **(*Un*)**

4. **Assertion (A):** During a discussion in science class, Riya stated that glass is optically denser than air.

   Reason (R): Her friend Aryan explained that an optically denser medium is one in which the speed of light is comparatively high. **(*Un*)**

Subjective Questions

Very Short Answer Type Questions (2 M)

1. The refractive indices of three media are given below:

Medium	A	B	C
Refractive Index	1.6	1.8	1.5

A ray of light is travelling from A to B and another ray is travelling from B to C.

(*a*) In which of the two cases the refracted ray bends towards the normal?

(*b*) In which case does the speed of light increase in the second medium? Give reasons for your answer. (*Un*) (CBSE SQP, 2023)

Ans. (*a*) When light travels from an optically rarer medium to an optically denser medium it moves towards the normal. Since $n_B > n_A$ hence the light ray will bend towards the normal on passing from medium A to B. *(½ + ½ M)*

(*b*) The speed of the light will increase when the light travels from B to C, Since $n_C < n_B$ and $v = (c/n)$, the speed of light ray will increase in the second medium. *(½ + ½ M)*

2. The above figure shows the formation of an image by a lens shown by a thick line. (*An*) (CBSE SQP, 2025)

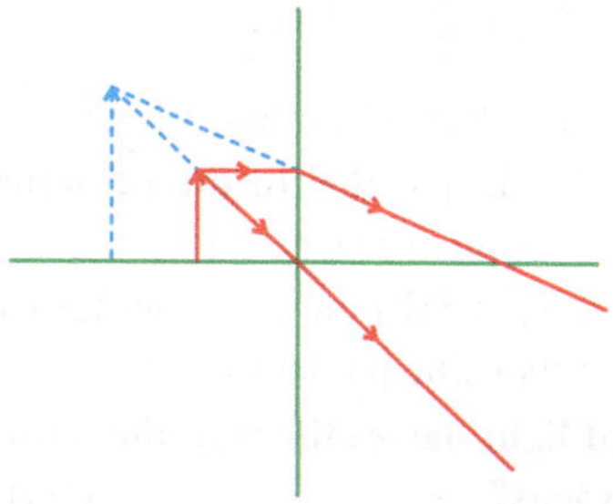

Analyse the figure and answer the following questions.

(*a*) What is the type of lens used?

(*b*) What is the nature of the image?

(*c*) If the image is formed at a distance of 30 cm from the lens and the image is twice the size of the object, then where is the object placed?

Ans. (*a*) The lens is a convex lens.

(*b*) The image is virtual.

(*c*) Magnification for lens $= \frac{v}{u} = \frac{h_i}{h_o} = 2.$

$$\frac{-30 \text{ cm}}{u} = 2$$

Hence $u = -15$ cm *(2 M)*

3. The image formed by which lens can be real as well as virtual, the power of a lens is measured in? (*Re*)

Ans. The image formed by the convex lens can be real as well as virtual. *(1 M)*

The power of a lens is measured in Dioptre. *(1 M)*

4. **When do light rays bend towards the normal during refraction, Define the aperture of a lens.** ***(Re)***

Ans. When light rays go from a rarer medium to a denser medium it bend towards the normal. *(1 M)*

The diameter of the lens is called the aperture of the lens. *(1 M)*

5. **Define the second principal focus.** ***(Re)***

Ans. The second principal focus of a lens is the point on the principal axis where parallel rays of light, after refraction through the lens, appear to converge or diverge from. In the case of a lens, there are two principal foci - the first principal focus where incident parallel rays converge after refraction, and the second principal focus where parallel rays appear to diverge after refraction. *(1 M)*

The second principal focus is located on the opposite side of the lens from the first principal focus. *(1 M)*

6. **A pencil when dipped in water in a glass tumbler appears to be bent at the interface of air and water. Will the pencil appear to be bent to the same extent, if instead of water we use liquids like, kerosene or turpentine. Support your answer with reason.** ***(Un)* (NCERT Exemplar)**

Ans. Refraction is dependent on refractive indices. Refractive indices of kerosene or turpentine would not be same as water. Hence degree of bend would be different in different mediums. *(2 M)*

Short Answer Type Questions **(3 M)**

1. **What happens after refraction, when:**
   (*i*) a ray of light parallel to the principal axis passes through a concave lens?
   (*ii*) a ray of light falls on a convex lens while passing through its principal focus.
   (*iii*) a ray of light passes through the optical center of a convex lens? ***(Un)* (CBSE 2020)**

Ans. (*i*) A ray of light parallel to the principal axis of the concave lens appears to be coming from focus after refraction through the lens. *(1 M)*

(*ii*) A ray of light crossing through a principal focus, after refraction from a convex lens, will be parallel to the principal axis. *(1 M)*

(*iii*) A ray of light passing through the optical centre suffers no refraction, that is, it passes un-deviated. *(1 M)*

2. **(*a*) The image of an object formed by a lens is of same size but inverted. If the object distance is 30 cm, calculate**
   (*i*) The distance between the object and its image.
   (*ii*) Focal length of the lens.
   (*b*) Draw a ray diagram to show the image formed in above case. ***(Un)* (CBSE 2023)**

Ans. (*a*) (*i*) As we know that the image of an object is of same size and inverted, this is only possible when object is placed at 2*F*. Now behind the lens it will 30 cm away. Hence the distance between object and its image is 60 cm. *(1 M)*

(*ii*) focal length $= 2f/2 = 15$ cm *(1 M)*

(*b*)

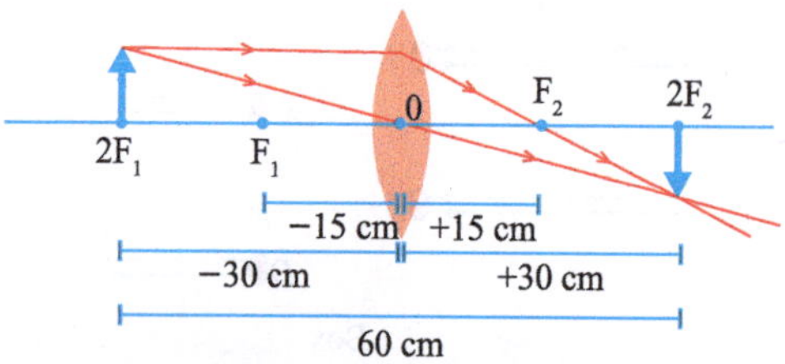

(1 M)

3. **A 10 cm tall object is placed perpendicular to the principal axis of a convex lens of focal length 12 cm. The distance of the object from the lens is 18 cm. Find the nature, position and size of the image.** ***(Ap)* (CBSE 2019)**

Ans. As per question $f = +12$ cm, $u = -18$ cm and $h = +10$ cm

As, $\Rightarrow \frac{1}{f} = \frac{1}{v} - \frac{1}{u}$ *(½ M)*

We have

$$\frac{1}{v} = \frac{1}{u} + \frac{1}{f} = \frac{1}{(-18)} + \frac{1}{(+12)} = \frac{1}{36} \Rightarrow v = +36 \text{ cm}$$ *(½ M)*

The image is formed on opposite side of lens at a distance of 36 cm from it. The image is real and inverted. *(½ M)*

Moreover, magnification m, $\frac{h'}{h} = \frac{v}{u}$ *(½ M)*

$\Rightarrow$ Size of image $h' = \frac{v}{u} \times h = \frac{(+36)}{(-18)} \times (+10) = -20$ cm *(½ M)*

So, the size of image is 20 cm tall and is formed below the principal axis. *(½ M)*

4. **A 5 cm tall object is placed perpendicular to the principal axis of a convex lens of focal length 20 cm. The distance of the object from the lens is 30 cm. Find the (*i*) position, (*ii*) nature, and (*iii*) size of the image formed.** ***(Ap)* (CBSE 2019)**

Ans. Here $h - +5$ cm, $f = +20$ cm, $u = -30$ cm

(*i*) Using lens formula $\frac{1}{v} - \frac{1}{u} = \frac{1}{f}$, *(½ M)*

we have

$$\frac{1}{v}, = \frac{1}{f} + \frac{1}{u} = \frac{1}{(20)} + \frac{1}{(-30)} = \frac{3-2}{60} = \frac{1}{60}$$ *(½ M)*

$v = +60$ cm

(*ii*) +ve sign of v means that image is being formed on the other side of lens i.e., the images is a real image. *(1 M)*

(*iii*) As $m = \frac{h'}{h} = \frac{v}{u}$ *(½ M)*

$\therefore\ h' = \frac{v}{u} \cdot h = \frac{(+60)}{-30} \times (+5) = -10$ cm. *(½ M)*

5. **An object is placed at a distance of 60 cm from a concave lens of focal length 30 cm.**
   (*i*) Use lens formula to find the distance of the image from the lens.
   (*ii*) List four characteristics of the image (nature, position, size, erect/inverted) formed by the lens in this case.
   (*iii*) Draw ray diagram to justify your answer of part (*ii*).
   ***(Ap)* (CBSE -2019/Set 3)**

Ans. We have,

(*i*) Object distance, $u = -60$ cm, Focal length of the concave lens, $f = -30$ cm

Using lens formula,

$$\frac{1}{v} - \frac{1}{u} = \frac{1}{f};$$

$$\frac{1}{v} - \frac{1}{(-60)} = \frac{1}{(-30)} \Rightarrow \frac{1}{v} = \frac{-1}{30} - \frac{1}{60}$$ (½ M)

$$\frac{1}{v} = \frac{-3}{60}$$

$v = -20$ cm

The images will be formed at a distance of 20 cm in front of the lens. (½ M)

(*ii*) Nature of the image is virtual. The position of the image is between F_1 and optical center O. (½ M)

Size of the image is diminish*ed*. The image is Erect. (½ M)

(*iii*) 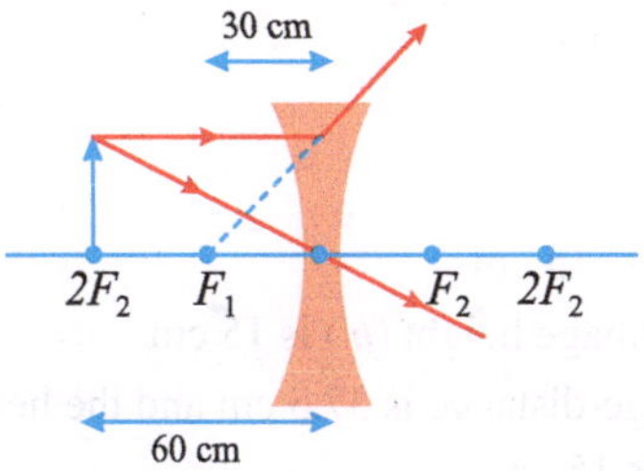

(1 M)

6. The power of a lens is +4D. Find the focal length of this lens. An object is placed at a distance of 50 cm from the optical centre of this lens. State the nature and magnification of the image formed by the lens and also draw a ray diagram to justify your answer.

***(Ap)* (CBSE 2023)**

Ans. Given, the power of the lens $P = +4$D.

We know that the relation between power (P) of a lens and its focal length (f) is given by:

$P = 1/f$ (½ M)

Substituting the value of P, we get:

$4 = 1/f$

Therefore, the focal length of the lens is $f = 1/4 = 0.25$ m or 25 cm. (½ M)

Now, the object is placed at a distance of 50 cm from the optical centre of the lens. Using the lens formula, $1/f = 1/v - 1/u$, we can find the image distance (v)

Substituting the values, we get,

$1/25 = 1/v - 1/-50$

$1/v = 1/25 - 1/50$

$1/v = (2 - 1)/50$

$v = 50$ cm

$v = 50$ cm

Therefore, the image distance is $v = 50$ cm. (½ M)

Now, to find the nature of the image, We can find the magnification (m) using the magnification formula:

$m = (v/u)$

Substituting the values, we get:

$m = 50/-50$ cm $= -1$

Therefore, the nature of the image is real and inverted and the magnification is $m = -1$. (½ M)

Here is the labelled ray diagram to justify the answer:

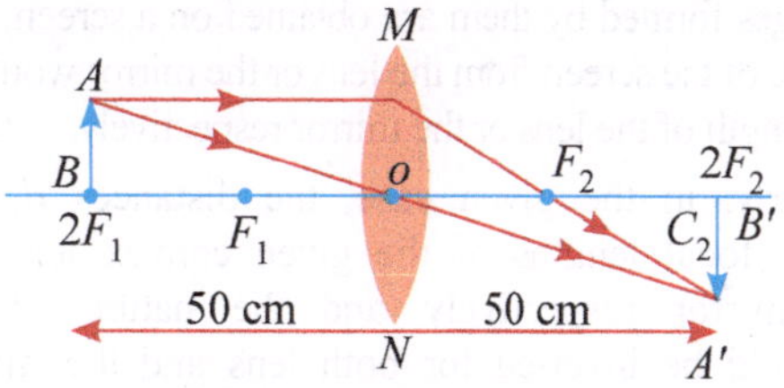

(1 M)

7. (*i*) Explain why the refractive index of any material with respect to air is always greater 1.

(*ii*) In the figure below a light ray travels from air into the semi-circular plastic block. Give a reason why the ray does not deviate at the semi-circular boundary of the plastic block.

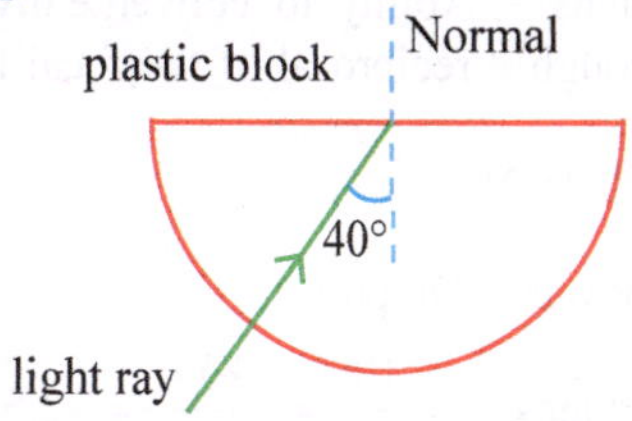

(*iii*) Complete the ray diagram of the above scenario when the light ray comes out of the plastic block from the top flat end. ***(Un)* (CBSE SQP, 2023)**

Ans. (*i*) The refractive index of a medium with respect to air is given by

$$\frac{\text{speed of light in air}}{\text{speed of light in the medium}}$$

Since speed of light in the medium is always less than the speed of light in air, hence the above ratio is always greater than 1. (½ + ½ M)

(*ii*) The ray of light is undergoing normal incidence at the air-plastic block interface. And for normal incidence there is no deviation. (1 M)

(*iii*) (½ + ½ M)

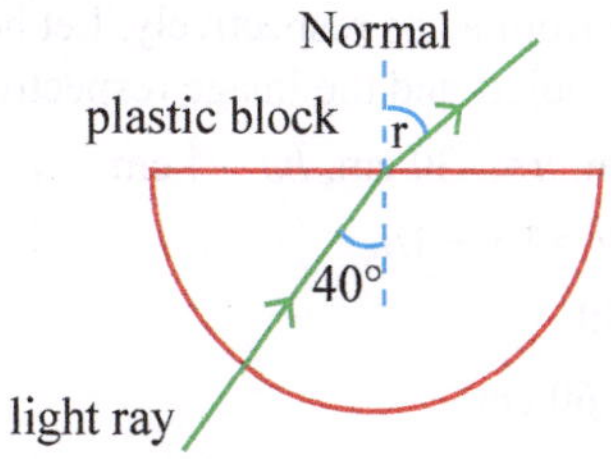

(Credit arrows, refracted ray moving away from normal)

8. A teacher gives a convex lens and a concave mirror of a focal length of 20 cm each to his student and asks him to find their focal lengths by obtaining the image of a distant object. The student uses a distant tree as the object and obtains its sharp image, one by one, on a screen. The distances d_1 and d_2 between the lens/mirror and the screen in the two cases and the nature of their respective sharp images are likely to be

(*a*) (20 cm, 40 cm) and (erect and erect)

(*b*) (20 cm, 40 cm) and (inverted and inverted)

(*c*) (20 cm, 20 cm) and (inverted and inverted)

(*d*) (20 cm, 40 cm) and (erect and inverted)

Give a reason for your answer. ***(Un)* (CBSE, 2019)**

Ans. ❒ A convex lens and a concave mirror both converge the rays coming from a distant object to their focal point to form an inverted image. *(1 M)*

❒ If images formed by them are obtained on a screen, then the distance of the screen from the lens or the mirror would be the focal length of the lens or the mirror respectively. *(1 M)*

❒ Similarly, in the given case, the distances d_1 and d_2 are the focal lengths of the given convex lens and concave mirror respectively and the nature of the image would be inverted for both lens and the mirror. Hence, the correct answer is an option (*c*) *(1 M)*

9. What is meant by the power of a lens? Write its SI unit. A student uses a lens of focal length 40 cm and another of –20 cm. Write the nature and power of each lens.

(*Re* + *Ap*) (CBSE, 2018)

Ans. Power of lens = Ability to converge/diverge light rays passing through it/reciprocal of the focal length in metres

$\therefore \frac{1}{f}$ (in meters) *(1 M)*

SI unit of power is Dioptre

Power of 1st lens $P_1 = \frac{100}{f_1} = \frac{100}{40\text{ cm}} = +2.5\ D$ *(1 M)*

Nature: Converging lens/Convex lens

Power of 2nd lens $P_2 = \frac{100}{f_2} = \frac{100}{-20\text{ cm}} = -5\ D$

Nature: Diverging lens/Concave lens *(1 M)*

10. An object of height 4.0 cm is placed at a distance of 30 cm from the optical centre '*O*' of a convex lens of focal length 20 cm. Draw a ray diagram to find the position and size of the image formed. Mark optical centre '*O*' and principal focus '*F*' on the diagram. Also find the approximate ratio of size of the image to the size of the object. (*Ap*) (CBSE 2018)

Ans. Let the focal length be *f*. Let *u* and *v* be the distance of the object and image from focus respectively. Let ho and hi be the heights of the object and the image respectively.

Given, $f = +20$ cm, $u = -30$ cm, $ho = 4$ cm

We know that, $1/f = 1/v - 1/u$

$1/20 = 1/v - 1/-30$

$1/v = 1/60 \Rightarrow v = 60$ cm

So, $h_i/h_o = v/u$

$h_i/4 = 60/-30 \Rightarrow h_i = -8$ cm

Thus, the height or size of the image is 8 cm. The minus sign shows that this height is in the downward direction, that is, the image is formed below the axis. *(1 M)*

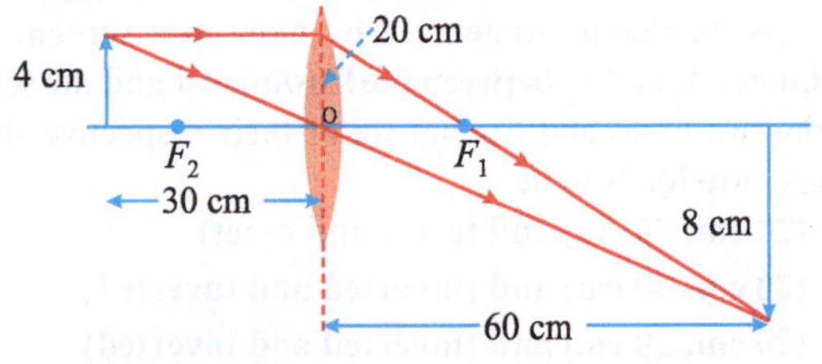

(1 M)

Position of *O* and *F*

Ratio = h_i/h_o approximately 2:1 *(1 M)*

11. An object of height 10 cm is placed 25 cm away from the optical centre of a converging lens of focal length 15 cm. Calculate the image-distance and height of the image formed. (*Ev*)

Ans. (*b*) Given,

Object height (*h*) = 10 cm

Object distance (*u*) = –25 cm (since the object is placed on the left side of the lens)

Focal length (*f*) = 15 cm

We can use the lens formula, $1/f = 1/v - 1/u$, *(1 M)*

Substituting the values, we get:

$1/15 = 1/v - 1/-25$

$1/v = 1/15 - 1/25 = 2/75 \Rightarrow v = 75/2 = 37.5$ cm

Therefore, the image distance (*v*) is 37.5 cm. *(1 M)*

Now, we can use the magnification formula, $m = v/u$, to find the magnification (*m*).

Substituting the values, we get:

$m = 37.5/-25 = -1.5$

Again, $m = h'/h$,

$-1.5 = h'/10$

$h' = -1.5 \times 10 = -15$ cm

Therefore, the image height (*h'*) is 15 cm.

Hence, the image-distance is 37.5 cm and the height of the image formed is 15 cm. *(1 M)*

Long Answer Type Questions (5 M)

1. State the laws of refraction of light. Explain the term 'absolute refractive index of a medium' and write an expression to relate it with the speed of light in vacuum. (*Re*)

Ans. Laws of Refraction of light:

(*i*) **First Law:** The incident ray, the normal to the transparent surface at the point of incidence and the refracted ray, all lie in one and the same plane. *(1 M)*

(*ii*) **Second Law:** The ratio of sine of the incidence angle ($\angle i$) to the sine of the refracted angle of the medium is called refractive index. It is denoted by *n*. *(1 M)*

i.e., $\frac{\sin i}{\sin r} = n$

Refractive index of second medium with respect to the first medium is denoted by $2n_1$,

Thus, eq.(*i*) can be written $^2n_1 = \frac{\sin i}{\sin r}$

This law is called Snell's law as it was stated by Prof. Willenbrord Snell (Dutch mathematical and astronomer). *(1 M)*

Absolute Refractive index:

Absolute refractive index of a medium is defined as the ratio of the speed of light in vacuum or air to the speed of light in the medium. It is denoted by *n*.

Then, $n = \frac{\text{speed of light in air}}{\text{speed of light in medium}} = \frac{c}{v}$

It has no unit. *(2 M)*

2. Draw a ray diagram in each of the following cases to show the formation of image, when the object is placed:

(*i*) between the optical centre and principal focus of a convex lens.

(*ii*) Anywhere infornt of a concave lens

(*iii*) At 2F of a convex lens.

State the signs and values of magnifications in the above-mentioned cases (*i*) and (*ii*). **(*Un*) (CBSE2020)**

Ans. (*i*) Let us suppose O be the object and I be the image then the image can be formed as:

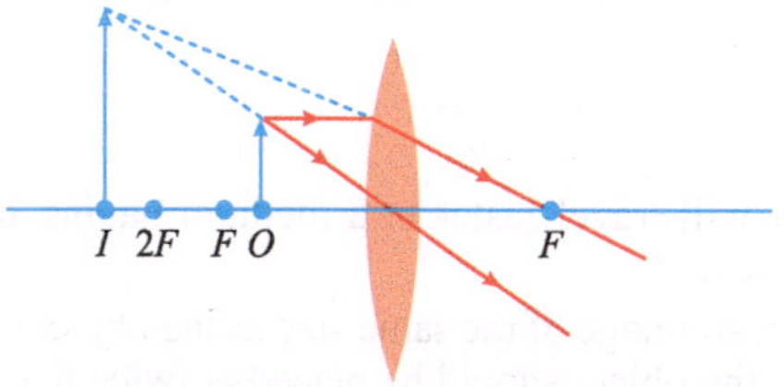

(1 M)

The image formed is enlarged and erect. Therefore its magnification will be positive and since it is enlarged therefore magnification will be greater than one. *(1 M)*

(*ii*) Anywhere in front of a concave lens.

Let us suppose O be the object and I be the image then the image can be formed as:

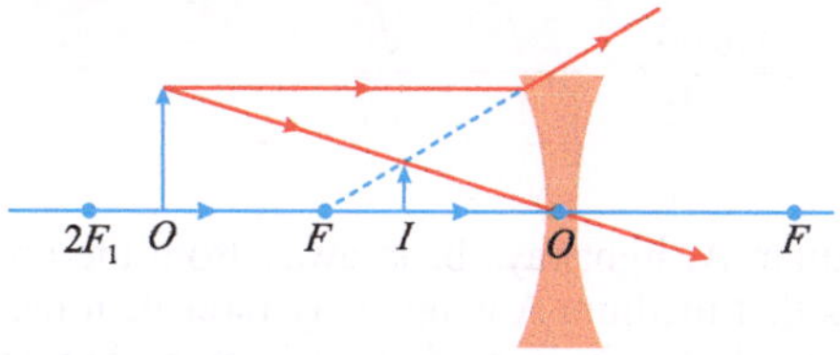

(1 M)

The image formed is diminished and erect. Therefore its magnification will be positive and since it is diminished therefore magnification will be less than one. *(1 M)*

(*iii*) at 2F of a convex lens.

Let us suppose O be the object and I be the image then the image can be formed as:

The image will be formed at 2F on the other side of the lens and its magnification will be the same as that of the object.

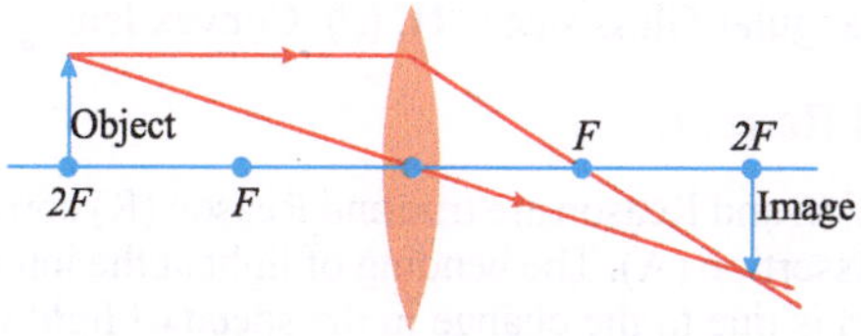

(1 M)

3. (*a*) Define the following terms: (*i*) Power of a lens (*ii*) Principal focus of a concave mirror (*b*) Write the relationship among the object distance (*u*), image distance (*v*) and the focal length (*f*) of a (*i*) Spherical lens (*ii*) Spherical mirror (*c*) An object is placed at a distance of 10 cm from optical centre of a convex lens of focal length 15 cm. Draw a labeled ray diagram to show the formation of the image in this case.

(*Re & Un*) (CBSE SQP, 2023)

Ans. (*a*) (*i*) Ability to converge/diverge light rays passing through it/reciprocal of the focal length in metres.

i.e., $P = \frac{1}{f}$ *(1 M)*

(*ii*) The point on which a parallel beam of light converges is known as principal focus. *(1 M)*

(*b*) (*i*) $\frac{1}{v} - \frac{1}{u} = \frac{1}{f}$ *(1 M)*

(*ii*) $\frac{1}{v} + \frac{1}{u} = \frac{1}{f}$ *(1 M)*

(*c*)

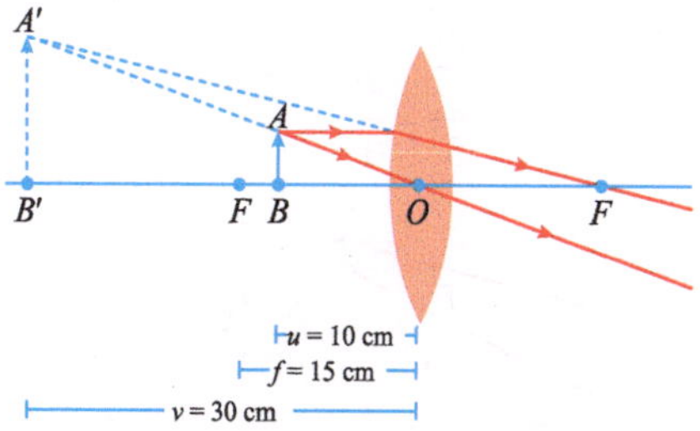

(1 M)

4.

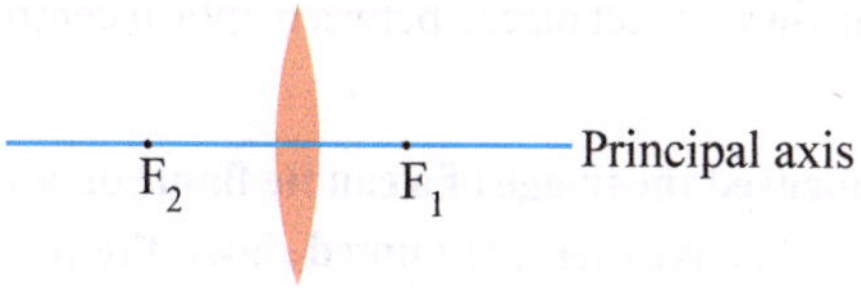

The above image shows a thin lens of focal length 5m.

(*i*) What is the kind of lens shown in the above figure?

(*ii*) If a real inverted image is to be formed by this lens at a distance of 7m from the optical centre, then show with calculation where should the object be placed?

(*iii*) Draw a neatly labeled diagram of the image formation mentioned in (*ii*)

OR

A 10 cm long pencil is placed 5 cm in front of a concave mirror having a radius of curvature of 40 cm.

(*i*) Determine the position of the image formed by this mirror.

(*ii*) What is the size of the image?

(*iii*) Draw a ray diagram to show the formation of the image as mentioned in the part (*i*).

(*Ap + Un*) (CBSE 2017)

Ans. (*i*) Convex lens *(1 M)*

(*ii*) $\frac{1}{f} = \frac{1}{v} - \frac{1}{u}$

In this case, v = 7m and f = 5m.

Putting the values in the equation we get-

$\frac{1}{5} = \frac{1}{7} - \frac{1}{u} \Rightarrow \frac{1}{u} = \frac{1}{7} - \frac{1}{5} = \frac{5-7}{35} = \frac{-2}{35}$ *(1 M)*

$u = -\frac{35}{2} = -17.5\,m$

The object will be placed 17.5 m on the left of the convex lens. *(1 M)*

(*iii*)

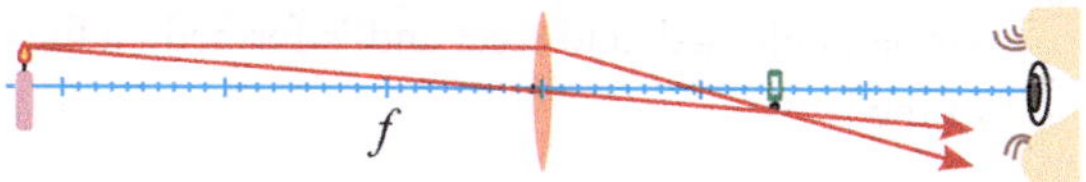

(two rays, arrows, object placed beyond 2f on the left) *(2 M)*

OR

(*i*) $\frac{1}{f} = \frac{1}{v} + \frac{1}{u}$ where u = −5 cm, $f = \frac{r}{2} = -20$ cm

$-\frac{1}{20} = \frac{1}{v} - \frac{1}{5}$

$$\frac{1}{v}=-\frac{1}{20}+\frac{1}{5}=\frac{-1+4}{20}=\frac{3}{20}$$

v = 20 ÷ 3 = 6.67 cm *(2 M)*

The image is obtained at 6.67m behind the mirror.

(*ii*) $m=\frac{h_2}{h_1}=-\frac{v}{u}=\frac{\frac{20}{3}}{5}=\frac{4}{3}$ *(1 M)*

(*iii*)

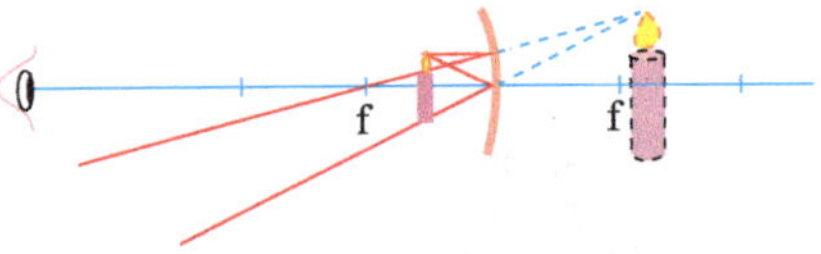

(two rays, arrows, object placed between optical centre and the focus) *(2 M)*

5. A student-focused the image of a candle flame on a white screen using a convex lens. He noted down the position of the candle screen and the lens as under

Position of candle = 12.0 cm

Position of convex lens = 50.0 cm

Position of the screen = 88.0 cm

(*a*) What is the focal length of the convex lens?

(*b*) Where will the image be formed if he shifts the candle towards the lens at a position of 31.0 cm?

(*c*) What will be the nature of the image formed if he further shifts the candle towards the lens?

(*d*) Draw a ray diagram to show the formation of the image in the case as said above.

***(Ap + Un)* (NCERT Exemplar)**

Ans. (*a*) $u = 50 - 12 = 38$ cm, $v = +38$ cm

Using the formula, $\frac{1}{v}-\frac{1}{u}=\frac{1}{f}$

$$\frac{1}{30}\left(-\frac{1}{38}\right)=\frac{1}{f}\Rightarrow\frac{2}{38}=\frac{1}{f}=19\text{ cm}$$ *(2 M)*

(*b*) Object distance $u = 50 - 31 = 19$ cm

Here, Object distance = focal length

Hence the image is formed at infinity. If the student moves the candle to a distance of 31.0 cm from the lens, the object distance is $u = (50 - 31) = 19$ cm. As a result, the candle lies at the focus. Hence an infinite image will be formed. *(1 M)*

(*c*) If he further shifts the candle towards the lens. The object comes between *F* and *O*. In this case. The image is virtual, enlarged, and erect and is formed on the same side of the lens. *(1 M)*

(*d*) *(1 M)*

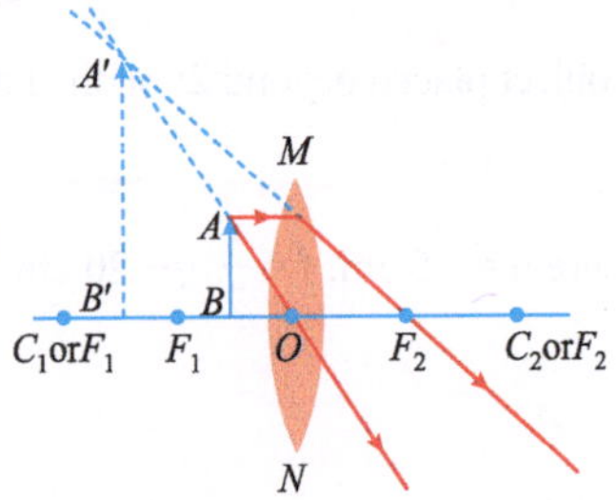

Hints & Explanations

Multiple Choice Questions

1. (*c*) Refractive index $\mu=\frac{\text{Speed of light in vacuum}}{\text{Speed of light in medium}}$

As $c > v$ so, $\mu > 1$.

2. (*c*) As refractive index $\mu=\frac{c}{\mu}$

So $v=\frac{c}{\mu}=\frac{3\times10^8}{1.33}=2.26\times10^8$ m/s

3. (*b*) As ${}_a\mu_m=\frac{v_a}{v_m}\Rightarrow v_m=\frac{v_a}{{}_a u_m}$

So, the light will travel faster in a medium having lower refractive index.

4. (*c*) To obtain an image of the same size as the object with a convex lens, the object should be placed at twice the focal length of the lens.

5. (*c*) Parallel rays after refraction meet at the focus of a convex lens.

6. (*a*) Given, $\angle i = 60°$, $\angle r = 45°$

From Snell's law of refraction, refractive index of medium B with respect to medium A.

$$n_{BA}=\frac{\sin i}{\sin r}=\frac{\sin 60°}{\sin 45°}=\frac{2\sqrt{3}}{\left(\frac{1}{\sqrt{2}}\right)}=\frac{\sqrt{3}}{\sqrt{2}}$$

7. (*b*) In medium A, light rays bend away from the normal. It indicates that medium A is optically rarer than medium *B*. Hence speed of light in medium A is more than that in medium *B*. Now, refractive index

$$n_{BA}=\frac{v_A}{v_B}$$

As $v_B > v_A \Rightarrow \frac{v_B}{v_A}$

$\therefore n_{BA} < 1$

8. (*d*) **9.** (*d*)

10. (*a*) A rectangular Glass slab **11.** (*d*) Convex lens

Assertion and Reason

1. (*a*) Assertion and Reason are true and Reason (R) correctly explains Assertion (A). The bending of light at the interface (refraction) is due to the change in the speed of light when it enters a different medium.

2. (*a*) Both assertion (A) and reason (R) are true and reason (R) is the correct explanation of assertion (A).

3. (*a*) Both assertion (A) and reason (R) are true and reason (R) is the correct explanation of assertion (A).

According to Snell's law,

$$\frac{\sin i}{\sin r}=\frac{n_2}{n_1}=\frac{c/v_2}{c/v_1}=\frac{v_1}{v_2}$$

$$n_1 v_1 = n_2 v_2$$

This shows that higher is the refractive index of a medium or denser the medium, lesser is the velocity of light in that medium.

4. (*c*) Assertion (A) is true but Reason (R) is false. The reason why glass is considered optically denser than air is that the speed of light is slower in glass compared to air.

MISCELLANEOUS EXERCISE

Multiple Choice Questions (1 M)

1. Which of the following can make a parallel beam of light when light from a point source is incident on it? **(*Un*) (NCERT Exemplar)**
   (*a*) Concave mirror as well as convex lens
   (*b*) Convex mirror as well as concave lens
   (*c*) Two plane mirrors placed at 90° to each other
   (*d*) Concave mirror as well as concave lens

2. A child is standing in front of a magic mirror. She finds the image of her head bigger, the middle portion of her body of the same size and that of the legs smaller. The following is the order of combinations for the magic mirror from the top. **(*Ap*) (NCERT Exemplar)**
   (*a*) Plane, convex and concave
   (*b*) Convex, concave and plane
   (*c*) Concave, plane and convex
   (*d*) Convex, plane and concave

3. In which of the following, the image of an object placed at infinity will be highly diminished and point sized? **(*Re*) (NCERT Exemplar)**
   (*a*) Concave mirror only
   (*b*) Convex mirror only
   (*c*) Convex lens only
   (*d*) Concave mirror, convex mirror, concave lens and convex lens

4. Find the angle of incidence and angle of reflection from the diagram. **(*Un*)**

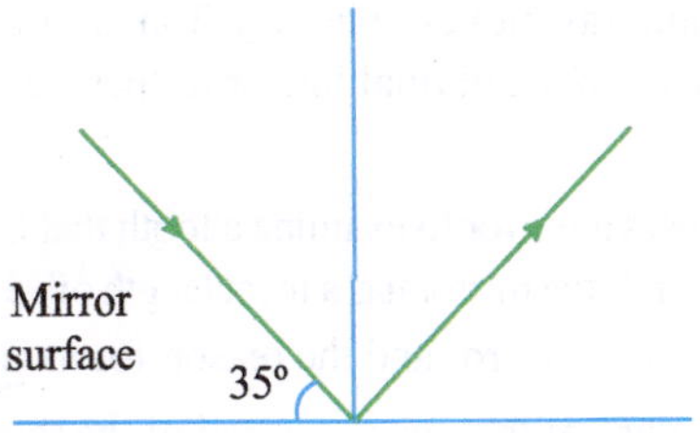

   (*a*) 45°, 40° (*b*) 55°, 55°
   (*c*) 60°, 60° (*d*) 30°, 30°

5. Velocity of light in air is 3×10^8 m/s. While its velocity in a medium is 1.5×10^8 m/s. Then, refractive index of this medium is **(*Ap*)**
   (*a*) 3 (*c*) 0.5
   (*b*) 5 (*d*) 2

6. An object is situated at a distance of f/2 from a convex lens of focal length f. Distance of image will be **(*Ap*)**
   (*a*) $+(f/2)$ (*c*) $+(f/4)$
   (*b*) $+(f/3)$ (*d*) $-f$

7. An object is placed 20 cm from the concave mirror of focal length 10 cm, then image is formed at **(*Ap*)**
   (*a*) behind the mirror
   (*b*) between the mirror and focus
   (*c*) at focus
   (*d*) centre of curvature of mirror

8. Light rays *A* and *B* fall on optical component *X* and come out as *C* and *D*. **(*Un*)**

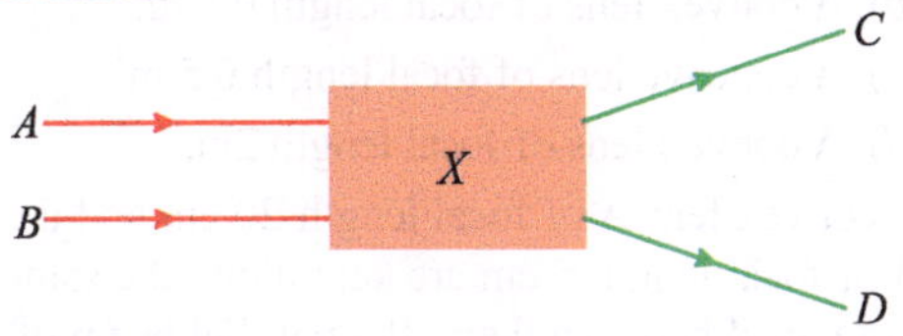

   The optical component is a
   (*a*) concave lens (*b*) convex lens
   (*c*) convex mirror (*d*) prism

9. If a spherical mirror has negative focal length then it is **(*Re*)**
   (*a*) Concave mirror
   (*b*) Convex mirror
   (*c*) Plane mirror
   (*d*) Both plane and convex mirror

10. Light of velocity 3×10^8 m/sec, falls on a glass prism. The frequency of light is 2×10^3 Hz. What will be its frequency after passing through glass prism: **(*Ap*)**
   (*a*) $\frac{2}{3} \times 10^{-5}$ Hz (*b*) $\frac{3}{2} \times 10^{-5}$ Hz
   (*c*) 2×10^3 Hz (*d*) None of these

11. A real and enlarged image can be formed by using a **(*Un*)**
   (*a*) concave mirror
   (*b*) place mirror
   (*c*) convex mirror
   (*d*) Both concave and a plane mirror

12. For an incident ray directed towards centre of curvature of a spherical mirror the reflected ray **(*Un*)**
   (*a*) retraces its path
   (*b*) passes through focus
   (*c*) passes through the pole
   (*d*) becomes parallel to the principal axis

13. Two mirrors M_1 and M_2 are placed at right angle to each other as shown in the figure. The total number of images of an object 'O' that can be seen are **(*Ap*)**

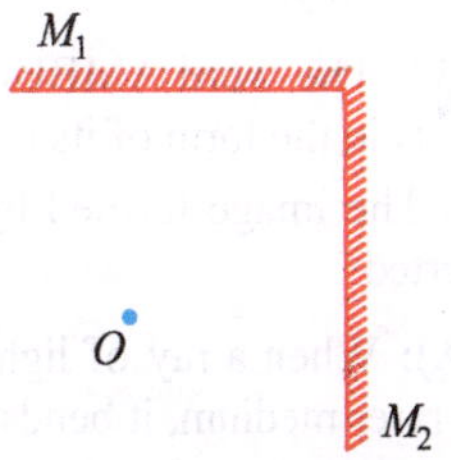

   (*a*) Two (*b*) Three
   (*c*) Four (*d*) Infinite

14. Consider the statements given below **(Un)**

(*a*) The speed of light is more in a rarer medium than in a denser medium.

(*b*) When a ray of light travels from air to water, its speed increases

Which of these statement(s) is/are correct?

(*a*) (*a*) only (*b*) (*b*) only

(*c*) Both (*a*) and (*b*) (*d*) Neither (*a*) nor (*b*)

15. A convex lens has a focal length of 0.5 m. It is combined with a second lens, so that the combination has a power of 1.5 diopter. Then the second lens is **(Ap)**

(*a*) A concave lens of focal length 2 m.

(*b*) A convex lens of focal length 0.5 m.

(*c*) A concave lens of focal length 0.5 m.

(*d*) A convex lens of focal length 2m.

16. A convex lens A of focal length 20 cm and a concave lens B of focal length 5 cm are kept along the same axis with a distance d between them. If a parallel beam of light falling on A leaves B as a parallel beam, then the distance d in cm will be **(Ap)**

(*a*) 25 (*b*) 15

(*c*) 30 (*d*) 50

Assertion and Reason (1 M)

Direction: The following questions consist of two statements. Assertion (A) and Reason (R). Answer these questions by selecting the appropriate option given below:

(*a*) Both A and R are true, and R is the correct explanation of A.

(*b*) Both A and R are true, but R is not the correct explanation of A.

(*c*) A is true, but R is false

(*d*) A is false, but R is true.

1. **Assertion (A):** A concave mirror can form a real and inverted image of an object.

   Reason (R): A concave mirror always converges the incident light rays towards a focal point **(Re + Un)**

2. **Assertion (A):** The refractive index of a medium is always greater than or equal to one.

   Reason (R): The refractive index of a medium is defined as the ratio of the speed of light in a vacuum to the speed of light in that medium. **(Re)**

3. **Assertion (A):** From a smooth surface incident light is reflected in only one direction.

   Reason (R): As the angle of incidence is always equal to the angle of reflection, therefore a parallel beam of rays falling on a smooth surface is reflected as a parallel beam of rays in one direction only. **(Re + Un)**

4. **Assertion (A):** The word AMBULANCE written on the hospital vans is in the form of its mirror image.

   Reason (R): The image formed by a plane mirror is not laterally inverted. **(Un)**

5. **Assertion (A):** When a ray of light passes from a denser medium to a rarer medium, it bends away from the normal.

   Reason (R): The speed of light decreases when it passes from a denser medium to a rarer medium. **(Re + Un)**

Subjective Questions

Very Short Answer Type Questions (2 M)

1. Sarah is presented with a challenge. She needs to explain how to identify the three types of mirrors (plane, convex, and concave) without physically touching them. **(Un)**

2. Sunlight enters the water at an angle of 30 degrees from the normal. If the water has a refractive index of 1.33, then find the angle of refraction of the sunlight inside water. **(Ev)**

3. A light ray is incident on a concave mirror with a radius of curvature of 20 cm. If the object distance is 15 cm, calculate the image distance. **(Ev)**

4. A converging lens has a focal length of 20 cm. An object is placed 30 cm away from the lens. Calculate the position of the image formed by the lens. Is the image larger or smaller than the object? Justify your response. **(Ev)**

5. What is the nature of image formed when object is placed at the centre of curvature of a concave mirror? Draw the ray diagram for the mentioned position. **(Re)**

6. A student is using a magnifying glass to examine a small object. They noticed that when they moved the magnifying glass closer to the object, the magnification increases. Explain why this happens and discuss the relationship between the distance of the magnifying glass from the object and the magnification. **(Ap)**

7. A diverging lens with a focal length of –15 cm is used to form an image of an object. If the object is placed at a distance of –20 cm from the lens, calculate the position and characteristics of the image formed. Is the image virtual or real? Provide a reason for your answer. **(Ev)**

8. Imagine that you are observing an object placed in front of a concave mirror. The object is at a distance greater than the focal length of the mirror. Describe the nature (real/virtual), position, and size of the image formed by the mirror. **(Un)**

9. When a light ray moves obliquely from air into water, does it shift closer to the normal line or farther from it? Explain. **(Un)**

10. A dentist uses a mirror to examine a tooth that is 1 cm in front of the mirror. If the mirror has a focal length of –5 cm, describe:

    (*i*) The type of mirror and the reason for its use.

    (*ii*) The nature of the image formed of the tooth. **(Ap)**

Short Answer Type Questions (3 M)

1. (*a*) Describe the relationship between the focal length and the power of a lens.

   (*b*) Imagine you are designing a magnifying glass, and you have two lenses to choose from: one with a focal length of 20 cm and another with a shorter focal length. How would you calculate the power of each lens?

   (*c*) Explain how a shorter focal length affects the magnification it provides. **(CBSE 2023)**

2. State laws of reflection of light. List four characteristics of the image formed by a plane mirror. **(Re)**

3. State the laws of refraction of light. Explain the term absolute refractive index and write an expression to relate it with the speed of light in vacuum. **(CBSE 2018)**

4. Draw a ray diagram to show the refraction through a rectangular glass slab. How is the emergent ray related to the incident ray? **(CBSE 2019)**

5. Write two different uses of a concave mirror. **(CBSE 2017)**

6. State two positions in which a concave mirror produces a magnified image. ***(Re)***

7. Absolute refractive indices of two media P and Q are 1.33 (n_P) and 2.52 (n_Q) respectively. The speed of light in medium P is 2×10^8 m/s.
   (*i*) What would be the speed of light in medium Q (V_Q)?
   (*ii*) If the angle of incidence for a ray of light travelling from medium P to Q is 0°, then what will be the path of light in the medium Q? ***(Un)* (CBSE APQ, 2023)**

8. Explain how the focal length of a mirror is related to its curvature. Find the focal length of a convex mirror whose radius of curvature is 32 cm. **(NCERT Intext)**

9. Identify the device used as a spherical mirror or lens in following cases, when the image formed is virtual and erect in each case.
   (*i*) Object is placed between the device and its focus, the image formed is enlarged and behind it.
   (*ii*) Object is placed between the focus and device, the image formed is enlarged and on the same side as that of the object.
   (*iii*) Object is placed between infinity and device, image formed is diminished and between focus and optical centre on the same side as that of the object.
   (*iv*) Object is placed between infinity and device, image formed is diminished and between pole and focus, behind it. ***(Un)* (NCERT Exemplar)**

10. A convex lens forms a real and inverted image of a needle at a distance of 50 cm from it. Where is the needle placed in front of the convex lens if the image is equal to the size of the object? Also, find the power of the lens. ***(Ap)***

Long Answer Type Questions (5 M)

1. An object, 4.0 cm in size, is placed at 25.0 cm in front of a concave mirror of focal length 15.0 cm. At what distance from the mirror should a screen be placed in order to obtain a sharp image? Find the nature and the size of the image. ***(Ap)***

2. A convex mirror used for rear-view on an automobile has a radius of curvature of 3.00 m. If a bus is located at 5.00 m from this mirror, find the position, nature and size of the image. ***(Ap)***

3. To construct a ray diagram we use two rays of light which are so chosen that it is easy to determine their directions after reflection from the mirror. Choose these two rays and state the path of these rays after reflection from a concave mirror. Use these two rays to find the nature and position of the image of an object placed at a distance of 15 cm from a concave mirror of focal length 10 cm. ***(Un)***

4. To construct a ray diagram we use two rays of light which are so chosen that it is easy to determine their directions after reflection from the mirror. Choose these two rays and state the path of these rays after reflection from a concave mirror. Use these two rays to find the nature and position of the image of an object placed at a distance of 15 cm from a concave mirror of focal length 10 cm. ***(Un + Ap)***
   (*a*) What is the minimum number of rays required for locating the image formed by a concave mirror for an object? Draw a ray diagram to show the formation of a virtual image by a concave mirror.
   (*b*) The linear magnification produced by a spherical mirror is+3. Analyse this value and state the (*i*) type of mirror and (*ii*) position of the object with respect to the pole of the mirror. Draw ray diagram to show the formation of image in this cased
   (*c*) An object is placed at a distance of 30 cm in front of a convex mirror of focal length 15 cm.
   Write four characteristics of the image formed by the mirror.

Case Based Questions

Case Based-I: Study the data given below showing the focal length of three concave mirrors A, B and C and the respective distances of objects placed in front of the mirrors: ***(An)* (CBSE, 2024)**

Case	Mirror	Focal Length (cm)	Object Distance (cm)
1	A	20	45
2	B	15	30
3	C	30	20

(*i*) In which one of the above cases the mirror will form a diminished image of the object? Justify your answer. *(1 M)*

(*ii*) List two properties of the image formed in case 2. *(1 M)*

(*iii*) What is the nature and size of the image formed by mirror C? Draw ray diagram to justify your answer. *(2 M)*

OR

An object is placed at a distance of 18 cm from the pole of a concave mirror of focal length 12 cm. Find the position of the image formed in this case. *(2 M)*

Case Based-II: The above image is that of a reflecting telescope. Reflecting telescopes revolutionised our ways of looking into the sky. They employ mirrors to gather and focus light, rather than relying solely on lenses as in their refracting counterparts. These telescopes utilise precisely shaped and polished mirrors to capture incoming light and reflect it to a focal point, where it forms an image for observation. ***(Un)* (CBSE SQP, 2025)**

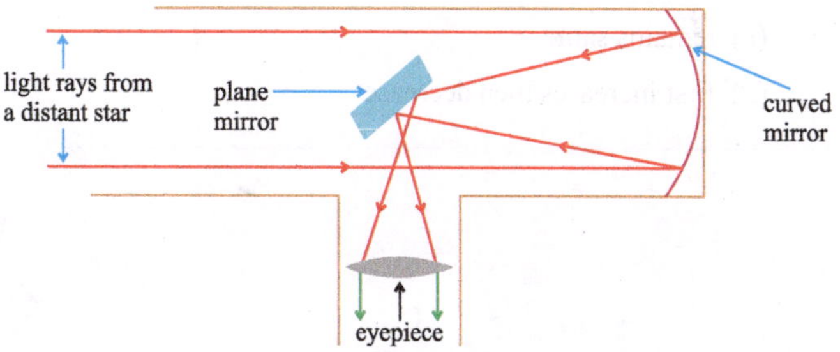

(*i*) What kind of image of the star is seen by the observer at the eyepiece?

(*ii*) What kind of mirror is used in this reflecting telescope?

(*iii*) Explain with reason what kind of optical device (type of lens or mirror) that is used at the eyepiece.

OR

What is the role of the plane mirror in the telescope?

Case Based-III: When the rays of light travel from one transparent medium to another, the path of light is deviate (*d*). This phenomenon is called the refraction of light. The bending of light depends on the optical density of the medium through which the light passes.

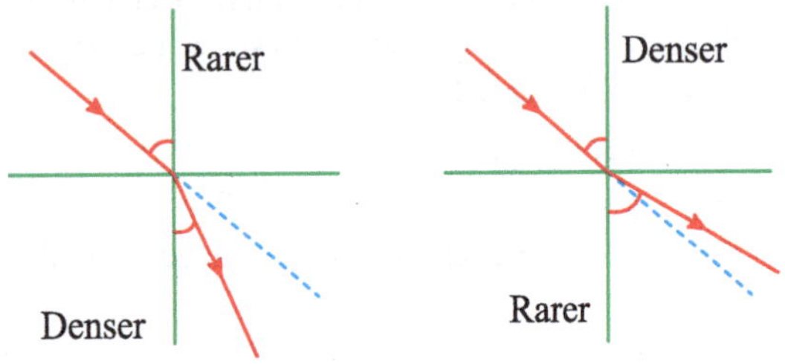

The speed of light varies from medium to medium. A medium in which the speed of light is more is an optically rarer medium whereas in which the speed of light is less is an optically denser medium. Whenever light goes from one medium to another, the frequency of light does not change; however, speed and wavelength change. It concluded that change in the speed of light is the basic cause of refraction. **(*Un*)**

(*i*) When light travels from air to glass, the ray of light bends (*1 M*)

(*a*) towards the normal (*b*) away from normal

(*c*) anywhere (*d*) none of these

(*ii*) A ray of light passes from medium A to another medium B. No bending of light occurs if the ray of light hits the boundary of medium B at an angle of (*1 M*)

(*a*) 0° (*b*) 45°

(*c*) 90° (*d*) 120°

(*iii*) When light passes from one medium to another, the frequency of light (*1 M*)

(*a*) increases (*b*) decreases

(*c*) remains same (*d*) none of these

(*iv*) When light passes from glass to water, the speed of light (*1 M*)

(*a*) increases

(*b*) decreases

(*c*) remains same

(*d*) first increases then decrease

(*v*) The bottom of a pool filled with water appears to be ______ due to the refraction of light (*1 M*)

(*a*) shallower (*b*) deeper

(*c*) at same depth (*d*) empty

Case Based-IV: The spherical mirror forms different types of images when the object is placed at different locations. When the image is formed on the screen, the image is real and when the image does not form on the screen, the image is virtual. When the two reflected rays meet actually, the image is real and when they appear to meet, the image is virtual.

A concave mirror always forms a real and inverted image for different positions of the object. But if the object is placed between the focus and pole. The image formed is virtual and erect. A convex mirror always forms a virtual, erect, and diminished image. A concave mirror is used as a doctor's head mirror to focus light on body parts like eyes, ears, nose, etc., to be examined because it can form an erect and magnified image of the object. The convex mirror is used as a rear view mirror in automobiles because it can form a small and erect image of an object. **(*Un*)**

(*i*) When an object is placed at the centre of curvature of a concave mirror, the image formed is (*1 M*)

(*a*) larger than the object

(*b*) smaller than the object

(*c*) same size as that of the object

(*d*) highly enlarged

(*ii*) No matter how far you stand from a mirror, your image appears erect. The mirror is likely to be (*1 M*)

(*a*) plane (*b*) concave

(*c*) convex (*d*) either plane or convex.

(*iii*) Which of the following characteristics is true for a concave mirror? (*1 M*)

(*a*) Always forms a virtual image

(*b*) Can form both real and virtual images

(*c*) Always forms a real image

(*d*) Only forms an inverted image

(*iv*) To get an image larger than the object, one can use (*1 M*)

(*a*) convex mirror but not a concave mirror

(*b*) a concave mirror but not a convex mirror

(*c*) either a convex mirror or a concave mirror

(*d*) a plane mirror.

(*v*) A convex mirror has wider field of view because (*1 M*)

(*a*) the image formed is much smaller than the object and a large number of images can be seen.

(*b*) the image formed is much closer to the mirror

(*c*) both (*a*) and (*b*)

(*d*) none of these

ANSWER KEYS

Multiple Choice Questions

1. (*a*) **2.** (*c*) **3.** (*d*) **4.** (*b*) **5.** (*d*) **6.** (*d*) **7.** (*d*) **8.** (*a*) **9.** (*a*) **10.** (*c*)
11. (*a*) **12.** (*a*) **13.** (*b*) **14.** (*a*) **15.** (*a*) **16.** (b)

Assertion and Reason

1. (*a*) **2.** (*a*) **3.** (*a*) **4.** (*c*) **5.** (*c*)

Case-Based Type Questions

Case Based-III

(*i*) (*a*) (*ii*) (*c*) (*iii*) (*c*) (*iv*) (*a*) (*v*) (*a*)

Case Based-IV

(*i*) (*c*) (*ii*) (*d*) (*iii*) (*c*) (*iv*) (*b*) (*v*) (*c*)

HINTS & EXPLANATIONS

Multiple Choice Questions

1. (*a*)

2. (*c*) 1. Head bigger and hence the mirror must be a concave mirror. A concave mirror here is producing an enlarged and erect mirror.

2. The middle portion unaltered and hence the middle part of the mirror must be a plane mirror.

3. The bottom part of the mirror produces a smaller image of the legs. The image is smaller since it is produced by a convex mirror. The convex mirror produced the erect and diminished image.

3. (*d*) When rays of light coming from infinity are incident on a concave mirror, convex mirror, concave lens or a convex lens, a highly diminished image is formed at the focus.

The same can be verified by using mirror equation and lens equation.

Mirror Equation:

$1/v + 1/u = 1/f$

Lens Equation:

$1/v - 1/u = 1/f$

Substituting

$u = -\infty, v = f$

Magnification

$m = v/u = f/\infty = 0$

Hence, image is point sized.

4. (*b*) 55°; 55°

5. (*d*) 2

Refractive index of medium with respect to air,

$${}_a n_g = \frac{\text{Speed of light in air}}{\text{Speed of light in medium}}$$

$${}_a n_g = \frac{3\times10^8}{1.5\times10^8} = 2$$

6. (*d*) $-f$

For a spherical lens $\frac{1}{v} - \frac{1}{u} = \frac{1}{f}$

For convex lens, $u = -f/2$ and f is Positive

$$\frac{1}{v} = \frac{1}{f} + \frac{1}{u} \Rightarrow \frac{1}{v} = +\frac{1}{f} - \frac{2}{f}$$

$$\Rightarrow \frac{1}{v} = \frac{-1}{f} \therefore v = -f$$

7. (*d*) centre of curvature of mirror

Given, focal length of concave mirror,

$f = -10$ cm

Distance of object from concave mirror,

$u = -20$ cm

From the mirror formula,

$$\frac{1}{u} + \frac{1}{v} = \frac{1}{f}$$

$$\frac{1}{-20} + \frac{1}{v} = \frac{1}{-10}$$

$$\frac{1}{v}=\frac{1}{20}-\frac{1}{10}=\frac{1-2}{20}=\frac{-1}{20}$$

$v = -20$ cm

Hence, the image is formed at the centre of curvature of mirror.

8. (*a*) concave lens

9. (*a*)

10. (*c*) Frequency remains unchanged while refraction.

11. (*a*)

12. (*a*)

13. (*b*)

14. (*a*)

15. (*a*)

16. (*b*) The situation is shown in figure. In the absence of concave lens, the parallel beam will be focussed at f_2 i.e. at a distance 20 cm from the lens. The focal length of concave lens is 5 cm. i.e. if this lens is placed at 5 cm from f_2, then the beam will become parallel.

So, d = 15 cm.

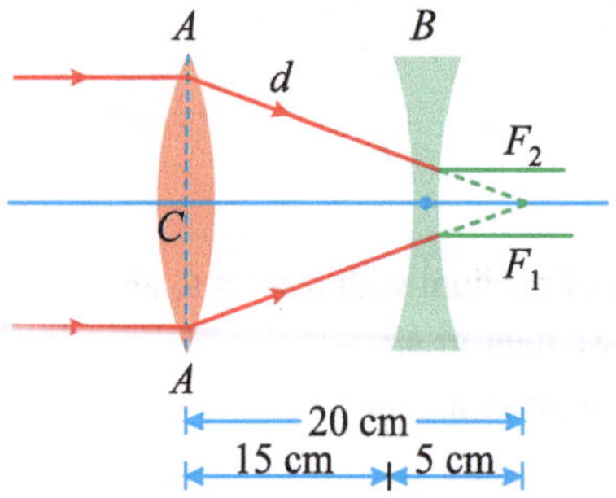

Assertion and Reason

1. (*a*) The assertion is correct. A concave mirror can form a real and inverted image of an object when the object is placed beyond the mirror's focal point. The reason is also correct. A concave mirror always converges the incident light rays towards a focal point. When the object is placed beyond the focal point, the reflected rays converge to form a real and inverted image.

2. (*a*) The assertion is correct. The refractive index of a medium is always greater than or equal to one. The reason is also correct. The refractive index of a medium is defined as the ratio of the speed of light in a vacuum to the speed of light in that medium. Since the speed of light in any medium is always less than or equal to the speed of light in a vacuum, the refractive index is always greater than or equal to one.

3. (*a*) Both the Assertion and the Reason are correct and the Reason is the correct explanation of the Assertion.

4. (*c*) Assertion is true, but Reason is false.

5. (*c*) The assertion is correct. When a ray of light passes from a denser medium to a rarer medium, it bends away from the normal.

This phenomenon is called refraction. The reason is incorrect. The speed of light increases when it passes from a denser medium to a rarer medium.

Subjective Questions

Very Short Answer Type Questions

1. (*a*) If the image formed is erect, of same size, and at equal distance behind the mirror as object is in front of the mirror, then mirror is plane.

(*b*) If the image is erect and magnified and becomes inverted if one moves away from the mirror, then it is a concave mirror.

(*c*) If the image is smaller and erect for all positions of the object from the mirror, then it is a convex mirror. *(2 M)*

2. In this scenario, the light enters the water at 30-degree angle from a line perpendicular to the water's surface. From snell's law,

$$\frac{\sin i}{\sin r}=\frac{\mu_2}{\mu_1}$$ *(1 M)*

$$\frac{\sin 30°}{\sin r}=1.33$$

$$\sin r=\frac{1}{2}\times\frac{1}{1.33}=\frac{1}{2.66}$$

$\sin r = 0.375$

$\therefore\ \angle r=\sin^{-1}(0.375)=\approx 22°$

Therefore, the angle of refraction is 22°. *(1 M)*

3. Given:

Radius of curvature (R) = –20 cm

Object distance (u) = –15 cm

Focal length $(f)=\frac{R}{2}=-\frac{20}{2}=-10\,\text{cm}$

Using the mirror formula: $\frac{1}{f}=\frac{1}{v}+\frac{1}{u}$ *(1 M)*

$$\frac{1}{-10}=\frac{1}{v}+\frac{1}{(-15)}$$

$$\frac{-1}{10}=\frac{1}{v}-\frac{1}{15}$$

$$\frac{-1}{10}=\frac{15-v}{15v}$$

$-15v = 150 - 10v$

$-5v = 150 \Rightarrow v = -30$ cm

Therefore, the image distance is 30 cm. *(1 M)*

4. Given:

Focal length (f) = 20 cm

Object distance (u) = –30 cm

To find: Position of the image and whether it is larger or smaller than the object.

Using the lens formula:

$$\frac{1}{f}=\frac{1}{v}-\frac{1}{u} \Rightarrow \frac{1}{20}=\frac{1}{v}-\frac{1}{(-30)} \Rightarrow \frac{1}{v}=\frac{1}{20}-\frac{1}{30}$$

$\Rightarrow v = +60$ cm *(1 M)*

To determine whether the image is larger or smaller than the object, we can use the magnification formula:

$$m=\frac{v}{u}=\frac{60}{-30}=-2$$

The negative sign indicates that the image is inverted. Since the magnification is greater than 1, the image is larger than the object. Therefore, the image is inverted and larger than the object. *(1 M)*

5. Image formed will be real, inverted and same size of the object if kept at centre of curvature.

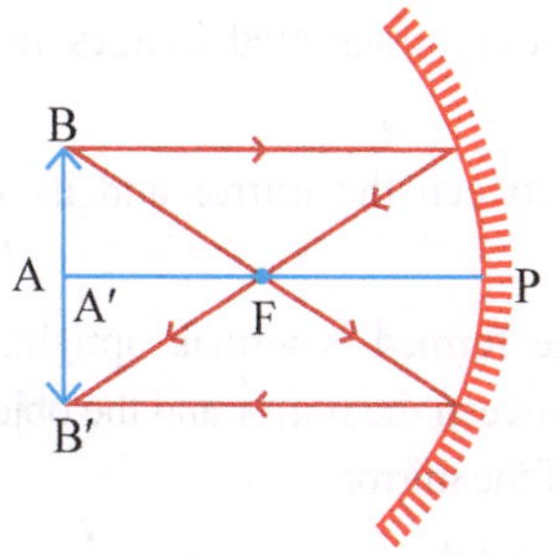

(2 M)

6. Moving the magnifying glass closer to an object increases magnification by changing the angle of view and the lens's focal length. The glass uses a thicker middle, thinner edges converging lens. Bringing it near the object reduces the lens-object distance, altering light entry angle. This wider angle refracts more rays, focusing more light and creating a larger magnified image. Adjusting distance changes effective focal length, impacting magnification. Magnification is inversely proportional to the glass-object distance: closer means higher magnification due to a wider angle and shorter focal length. *(2 M)*

7. Given:

Focal length (f) = –15 cm

Object distance (u) = –20 cm

Using the lens formula:

$$\frac{1}{f}=\frac{1}{v}-\frac{1}{u} \Rightarrow \frac{1}{-15}=\frac{1}{v}-\frac{1}{-20}$$

Solving for v, we get: $\frac{1}{v}=\frac{-7}{60}$ cm $\Rightarrow v = -8.57$ cm *(1 M)*

To determine the characteristics of the image formed, we can use the magnification formula:

$$m=\frac{v}{u}=\frac{-8.57}{-20}=+0.42$$

The positive sign indicates that the image is erected and virtual. Since the magnification is less than 1, the image is smaller than the object. *(1 M)*

8. When an object is placed in front of a concave mirror at a distance greater than the focal length, a real and inverted image is formed. *(½ M)*

The position of the image formed by the mirror is beyond the center of curvature of the mirror. The size of the image is bigger than the size of the object. *(½ M)*

The image formed by the concave mirror is real, which means it can be projected onto a screen. *(½ M)*

The image is inverted, which means that the top of the object is reflected at the bottom of the image, and the bottom of the object is reflected at the top of the image. *(½ M)*

9. The light ray shifts closer to the normal line. This bending towards the normal occurs because the ray is transitioning from a medium of lesser optical density (air) to one of greater optical density (water). Consequently, when light enters water from air, it bends towards the normal due to the increase in optical density. *(2 M)*

10. (*i*) The mirror is concave, chosen for its ability to produce magnified and erect images when the object is placed close to it, suitable for detailed examination. *(1 M)*

(*ii*) The image formed is virtual, erect, and magnified, facilitating a detailed view of the tooth. *(1 M)*

Short Answer Type Questions

1. (*a*) The relationship between the focal length (f) and the power (P) of a lens is given by

$P=\frac{1}{f}$, where f is in meter. *(1 M)*

(*b*) We can calculate the power of the lens from the focal length of the lens as power of lens is reciprocal of focal length.

Thus, for a lens with a focal length of 20 cm (0.2 m), its power is

$P=\frac{1}{0.2}=5D$ *(1 M)*

Hence, we will choose a lens of shorter focal length.

(*c*) A shorter focal length leads to a higher power. Thus, a magnifying glass with a shorter focal length can converge light more strongly, enabling larger magnification, making objects appear larger when viewed through it. *(1 M)*

2. The laws of reflection of light are:

1. The incident ray, the reflected ray, and the normal to the surface at the point of incidence all lie in the same plane. *(½ M)*
2. The angle of incidence is equal to the angle of reflection.

The four characteristics of the image formed by a plane characteristics mirror are: *(½ M)*

(*a*) The image is virtual, meaning it cannot be projected on a screen as it does not actually exist. *(½ M)* (*b*) The image is upright, meaning it is in the same orientation as the object. (½ M)

(*c*) The image is the same size as the object. (½ M)

(*d*) The image is located behind the mirror, at a distance equal to the distance of the object from the mirror, and appears to be located behind the mirror. (½ M)

3. The laws of refraction of light are:

1. The incident ray, the refracted ray, and the normal to the surface at the point of incidence all lie in the same plane. (1 M)
2. The ratio of the sine of the angle of incidence to the sine of the angle of refraction is a constant, which is known as the refractive index of the medium.

The term absolute refractive index is the ratio of the speed of light in a vacuum to the speed of light in a given medium. It is denoted by the symbol 'n' and is a dimensionless quantity.

The expression to relate absolute refractive index with the speed of light in a vacuum is: (1 M)

$n = c/v$

Where 'c' is the speed of light in a vacuum and 'v' is the speed of light in the given medium. This expression shows that the absolute refractive index of a medium is always greater than or equal to one, as the speed of light in any medium is always less than or equal to the speed of light in a vacuum. (1 M)

4. In the diagram, the incident ray (coming from the air) enters the rectangular glass slab and is bent towards the normal due to the increase in the refractive index of the glass. The refracted ray then emerges from the other side of the slab, bending away from the normal as it re-enters the air. (1 M)

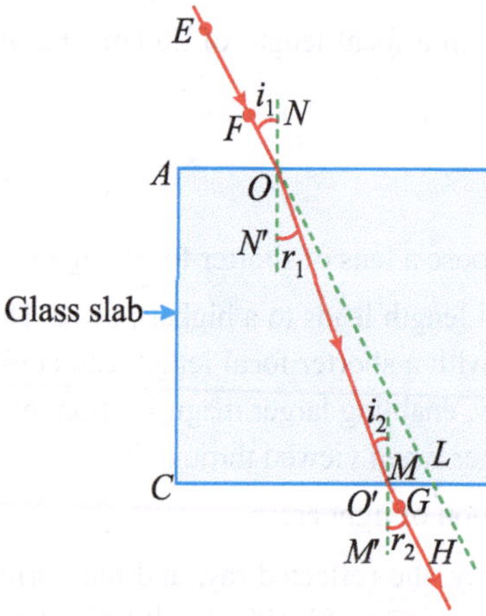

(1 M)

The emergent ray is related to the incident ray in that they are parallel and displaced laterally. The distance between the incident ray and the emergent ray is equal to the thickness of the glass slab. This displacement is known as lateral displacement and is caused by the deviation of the refracted ray from its original path due to the change in the medium. (1 M)

5. Concave mirrors have many practical applications, some of which are:

1. **Reflective Telescopes:** Concave mirrors are used in reflective telescopes to collect and focus light from distant objects. In a reflecting telescope, the concave mirror acts as the primary mirror and reflects light to a secondary mirror, which in turn reflects the light to the eyepiece. The concave mirror is used to produce a magnified image of the distant object being observed. (1½ M)
2. **Solar Furnace:** Concave mirrors are used in solar furnaces to focus sunlight to a point to generate high temperatures. The concave mirror reflects and concentrates the sunlight at its focal point, where a receiver is placed to absorb the concentrated solar energy. Solar furnaces are used in many industrial applications, including the production of electricity, materials processing, and chemical reactions. (1½ M)

6. Concave mirrors can produce magnified images in two different positions:

1. The Object placed between the mirror and its focal point (F): (½ M)

In this position, the image formed is virtual, upright, and magnified. The distance between the mirror and the object is less than the focal length of the mirror. (½ M)

2. The object placed beyond the focal point:

In this position, the image formed is real, inverted, and magnified. The distance between the mirror and the object is greater than the focal length of the mirror. (½ M)

Two differences between these two images are:

Orientation: The first position produces an upright image, while the second position produces an inverted image. (½ M)

Nature: The first position produces a virtual image, which cannot be projected on a screen, whereas the second position produces a real image, which can be projected on a screen. (1 M)

7. (*i*) n_P = (Speed of light in vacuum/speed of light in medium P) (½ M)

n_Q = (Speed of light in vacuum/speed of light in medium Q) (½ M)

Therefore,

$n_P/n_Q = V_Q/V_P$

$= 1.33/2.52 = V_Q/ 2 \times 10^8$ (½ M)

$V_Q = (1.33 \times 2 \times 10^8)/ 2.52$

$= 1.056 \times 10^8$ m/s (½ M)

(*ii*) The ray will travel un-deviated through the medium Q (1 M)

8. The focal length of a mirror is related to its curvature through the formula: $f = R/2$ (1 M)

For concave mirrors, where the focal length is negative, the radius of curvature is twice the focal length. (½ M)

For convex mirrors, where the focal length is positive, the radius of curvature is also twice the absolute value of the focal length. (½ M)

Given radius of curvature (R) = 32 cm

$R = 2 \times f$

$\Rightarrow f = \frac{R}{2} = \frac{32}{2} = 16$ cm

Hence, the focal length of the given convex mirror is 16 cm. (1 M)

9. (*i*) Concave mirror – In a concave mirror, if the object is placed between the mirror and the focus then the image formed is enlarged, erect and virtual. (¾ M)

(*ii*) Convex lens – In a convex lens, if the object is placed between the lens and its focus then the image formed is enlarged, erect, virtual and on the same side as that of the object. (¾ M)

(*iii*) Concave lens - In a concave lens, if the object is placed at infinity, the image formed is highly diminished, virtual, erect and between focus and optical centre on the same side as that of the object. (¾ M)

(*iv*) Convex mirror- In a convex mirror, if the object is placed at infinity, the image formed is highly diminished, virtual, erect and between pole and focus. (¾ M)

10. The position of the image should be at 2F, as the image is real and has the same size as that of the object. It is given that the image of the needle must be formed at a distance of 50 cm from the convex lens. Therefore, the needle is placed in front of the lens at a distance of 50 cm. (½ M)

Object

distance (u) = –50 cm

Image (½ M)

distance, (v) = 50 cm

Focal length = f

Using the lens formula,

$$\frac{1}{v} - \frac{1}{u} = \frac{1}{f} \quad (½ M)$$

$$\frac{1}{f} = \frac{1}{50} - \frac{1}{-50} = \frac{1}{50} + \frac{1}{50} = \frac{1}{25} \quad (½ M)$$

$$\text{Power of lens } P = \frac{1}{f(\text{in metres})} = \frac{1}{0.25} = +4D \quad (1 M)$$

Long Answer Type Questions

1. Object-size, $h = +4.0$ cm;

Object – distance, $u = -25.0$ cm;

Focal length, $f = -15.0$ cm; (½ M)

Image-distance, v = ?

Image-size, h' = ?

From mirror formula:

$$\frac{1}{v} + \frac{1}{u} = \frac{1}{f} \quad (1 M)$$

$$\text{or, } \frac{1}{v} = \frac{1}{f} - \frac{1}{u} = \frac{1}{-15.0} - \frac{1}{-25.0} = -\frac{1}{15.0} + \frac{1}{25.0}$$

$$\text{or, } \frac{1}{v} = \frac{-5.0+3.0}{75.0} = \frac{-2.0}{75.0} \text{ or, } v = -37.5 \text{ cm} \quad (½ M)$$

The screen should be placed at 37.5 cm from the mirror. The images is real. (½ M)

$$\text{Also, magnification, } m = \frac{h'}{h} = -\frac{v}{u} \quad (½ M)$$

$$\text{or, } h' = -\frac{vh}{u} = -\frac{(-37.5 \text{ cm}) \times (+4.0 \text{ cm})}{(-25.0 \text{ cm})} \quad (1 M)$$

Height of the image, h′ = – 6.0 cm

The images is inverted and enlarged (1 M)

2. Radius of curvature, R = + 3.00 m;

Object-distance, u = – 5.00 m;

Image-distance, v = ?

Height of the image, h' = ? (½ M)

$$\text{Focal length, } f = R/2 = \frac{3.00\text{m}}{2} = +1.50 \text{ m} \quad (½ M)$$

$$\text{Since } \frac{1}{v} + \frac{1}{u} = \frac{1}{f} \quad (½ M)$$

$$\text{or, } \frac{1}{v} + \frac{1}{f} - \frac{1}{u} = +\frac{1}{1.50} - \frac{1}{(-5.00)} = \frac{1}{1.50} + \frac{1}{5.00}$$

$$= \frac{5.00+1.50}{7.50}$$

$$\therefore v = \frac{+7.50}{6.50} = +1.15 \text{ m} \quad (1 M)$$

The image is 1.15m at the back of the mirror. (½ M)

$$\text{Magnification, } m = \frac{h'}{h} = \frac{-v}{u} = -\frac{1.15\text{m}}{-5.00\text{m}} = +0.23 \quad (1 M)$$

The image is virtual, erect and smaller in size by a factor of 0.23. (1 M)

3. The position of the image formed by a spherical mirror can be found by considering following two rays:

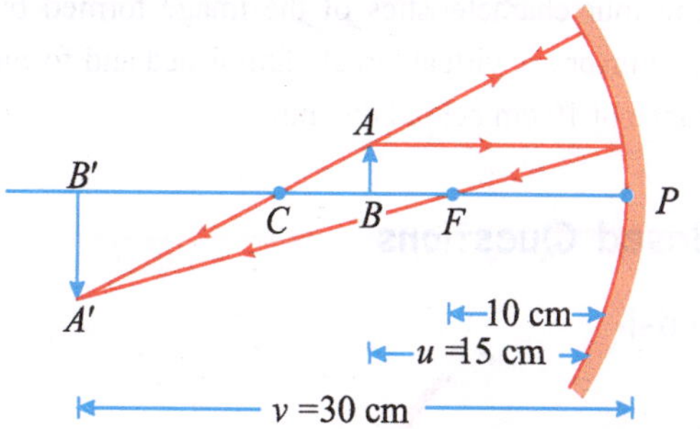

(1 M)

(*i*) The ray incident parallel to the principal axis, after reflection, passes through the principal focus of a concave mirror. (1 M)

(*ii*) A ray passing through the centre of curvature in a concave mirror after reflection, retraces its path. (1 M)

The image formation is shown in the adjacent figure. Here for every 5 cm distance we have 1 cm in the ray diagram. Here AB is the object and A′B′ is the real and inverted image formed on the basis of above mentioned two rays.

(1 M)

Actual measurement shows that the image is formed 30 cm in front of the concave mirror i.e., v = 30 cm. *(1 M)*

4. (*a*) Two rays are required

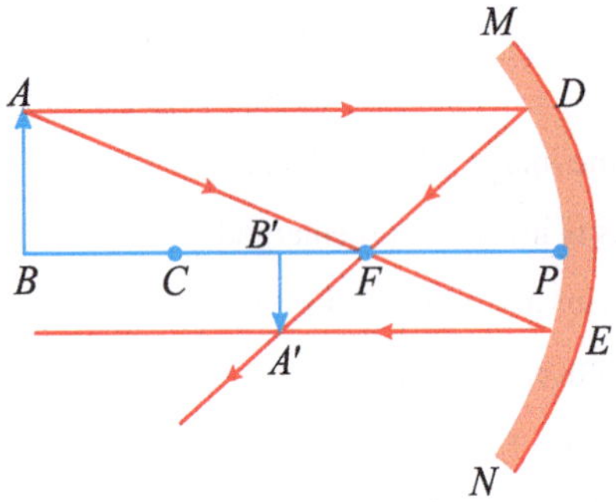

(1 M)

(*b*) The linear magnification produced by a spherical mirror is +3. It shows that the size of the image is three times the size of the object, the image is virtual and erect and formed behind the mirror. Hence *(1 M)*

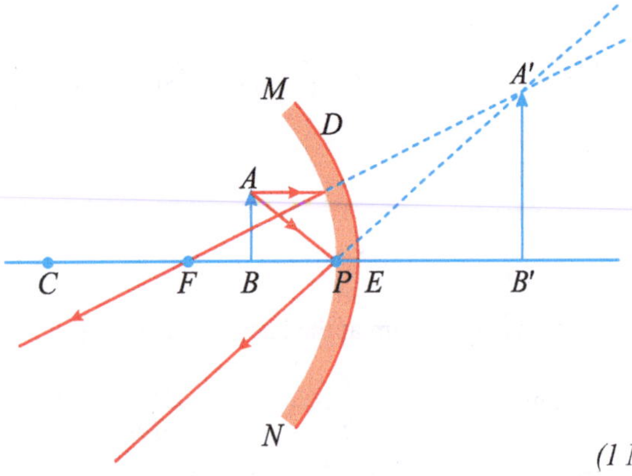

(1 M)

(*i*) The mirror is concave, and

(*ii*) The object is placed between the pole and the focus of a concave mirror. *(1 M)*

(*c*) The four characteristics of the image formed by the convex mirror are virtual, erect, diminished and formed at a distance of 10 cm behind the mirror. *(1 M)*

Case Based Questions

Case Based-I

(*i*)

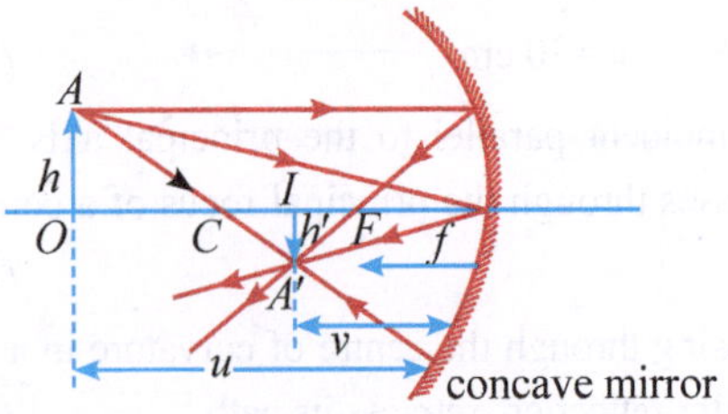

In Case (1), the object is positioned beyond the center of curvature (C). For concave mirrors, when the object is situated beyond C, the resulting image will form between C and the focal point (F), appearing inverted and diminished (smaller than the object). *(1 M)*

(*ii*)

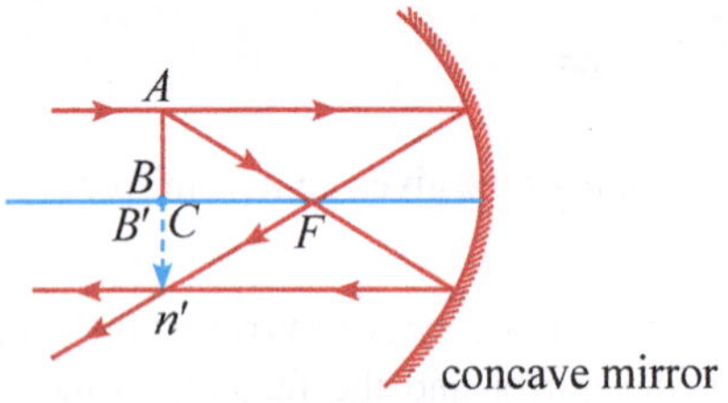

In Case (2), the object is located at the center of curvature (C), indicating that the image formed will be real and of equal size to the object. *(1 M)*

(*iii*) We are aware that a virtual and expanded picture is created when an object is positioned between P and F of a concave mirror. *(½ M)*

In case (3), the object distance (20 cm) is less than the focal length (30 cm). Therefore, the object is located between the mirror and the focal point. In such a case, the image formed will be virtual, erect, and larger than the object. *(1 M)*

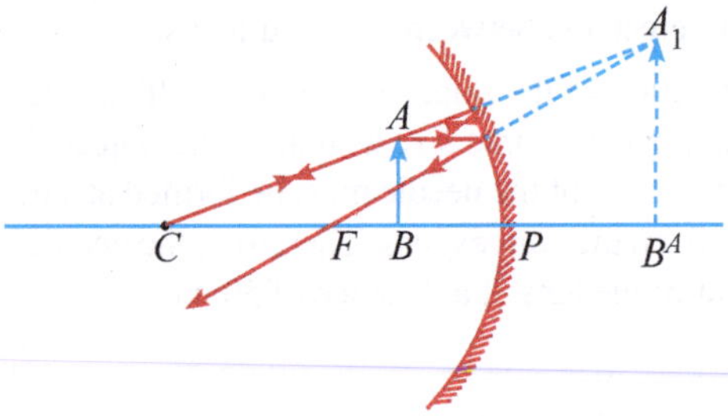

(½ M)

OR

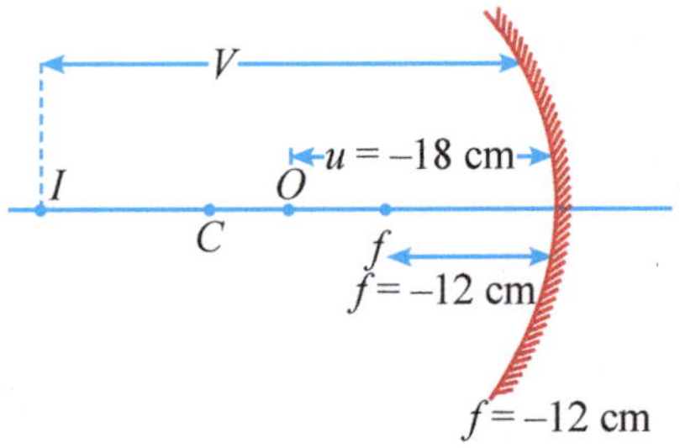

Given:

Focal length of concave mirror, $f = -12$ cm

Distance of object from the mirror, $u = -18$ cm

Now, put this value in mirror formula,

$$\frac{1}{f} = \frac{1}{v} + \frac{1}{u}$$ *(½ M)*

$$-\frac{1}{v} = \frac{1}{f} - \frac{1}{u}$$

$$-\frac{1}{v} = \frac{1}{-12} - \frac{1}{-18}$$ *(½ M)*

$$-\frac{1}{v} = -\frac{1}{12} + \frac{1}{18}$$

$$-\frac{1}{v}=\frac{1}{-36}$$

$-v = -36$ cm

Hence, image position is the 36 cm left side from the pole of the concave mirror *(1 M)*

Case Based-II

(*i*) Real Image (the final image is formed due to the lens at the eye-piece) *(1 M)*

(*ii*) Concave Mirror *(1 M)*

(*iii*) A converging lens is used at the eyepiece to collect the rays from the plane mirror and help the viewer to see a real erect image of the star. *(2 M)*

OR

The plane mirror laterally inverts the image formed by the curved mirror and its position helps to direct the rays towards the eye-piece. *(2 M)*

Case Based-III

(*i*) (*a*) When, a ray of light travels from air to glass, it bends towards the normal. *(1 M)*

(*ii*) (*c*) No bending of light occurs when light is incident normally or perpendicularly on a boundary of two media since angle of incidence and angle of refraction both are zero. *(1 M)*

(*iii*) (*c*) When light goes from one medium to other medium, its frequency does not change. *(1 M)*

(*iv*) (*a*) The speed of light increases when light passes from glass to water as water is optically rarer medium. *(1 M)*

(*v*) (*a*) The bottom of a pool of water appears to be less deep than it actually is due to refraction. *(1 M)*

Case Based-IV

(*i*) (*c*) *(1 M)*

(*ii*) (*d*) *(1 M)*

(*iii*) (*b*) *(1 M)*

(*iv*) (*b*) *(1 M)*

(*v*) (*c*) *(1 M)*

❑❑❑

10 THE HUMAN EYE AND THE COLOURFUL WORLD

"Imagine sitting by a window on a rainy afternoon, when suddenly a beautiful rainbow appears across the sky. This moment connects us to how light works, similar to what we've learned about how lenses bend light to create images. Just like those lenses, our eyes have a special lens that helps us see all the colors and shapes around us, making up the beautiful world we live in."

SYLLABUS & WEIGHTAGE

LIST OF CONCEPT NAMES	YEARS				
	2020	2022	2023	2024	2025
Human eye and its defects (Structure of an eye, Power of Accommodation, Myopia, Hypermetropia, Presbyopia, cataracts, and astigmatism)	1 Q (1 M)	—	1Q (2 M) 1Q (3 M)	3Q (1M each)	1Q (2 M) 1Q (3 M)
Prism and Atmospheric Refraction (Definition, Dispersion, TIR in prism, Tyndall Effects, Twinkling of stars, scattering of light, advanced sunrise and delayed sunset, Blue color of the sky)	2Q (3 M)	3Q (1 M)	1Q (2 M)	1Q (4M)	1Q (2 M)

CONCEPT MAP

The Human Eye and The Colorful World

Human Eye

Human eye and its structure — CBSE 2024

The human eye is a sensory organ that responds to visible light and is a component of the sensory nervous system.

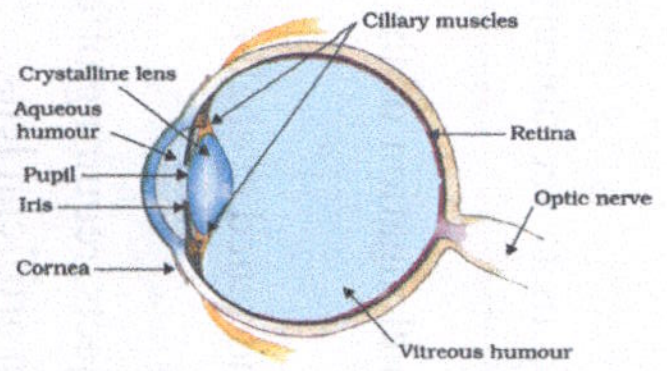

Accommodation of Eye

Ability of the eye lens to focus on nearby, and distant objects by changing their shape is called accommodation.

$$\text{Power of accommodation} = \frac{1}{\text{focal length } (m)}$$

(SI Unit: Diopter(D))

Defects & their Corrections

CBSE 2023

Presbyopia

Cause: (*a*) Hardening of the lens of your eye as you age

(*b*) Loss in flexibility of the eye lens

Correction: Glass of Bifocal Lens.

The upper component for distant vision and lower portion for reading.

Astigmatism

It is a common refractive error of the eye. It causes blurred of distorted vision due to an irregular shape in the cornea or lens.

- Symptoms include blurred vision at various distances, eye strain, and headaches.
- Correction options include glasses, contact lenses, or refractive surgery.

Cataract

Cataracts make the eye's lens cloudy, blurring vision, common in older age. Surgery is the usual fix: doctors remove the cloudy lens and replace it with a clear one. This surgery helps people see better.

CBSE 2025, 2024, 2023, 2020

Defects	Causes	Correction	Diagram
Myopia	(*a*) Elongated Eyeball (*b*) Increased power of Crystalline lens	Glass of Concave lens	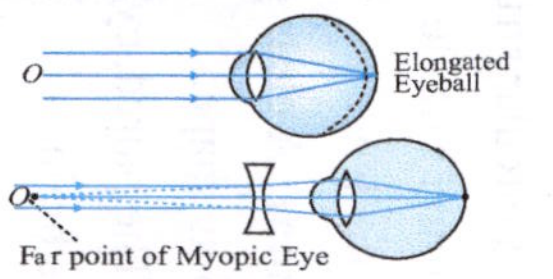
Hypermetropia	(*a*) Compressed Eyeball (*b*) Decreased power of Crystalline lens	Glass of Convex Lens	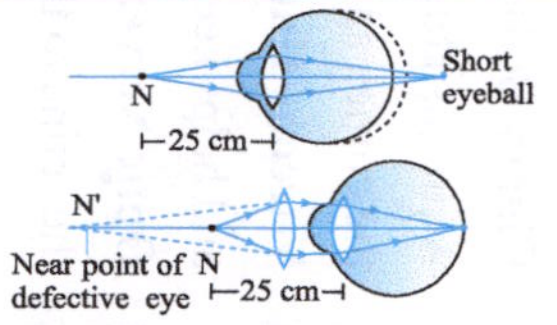

Colorful World

Scattering of Light — CBSE 2025, 2022, 2020

Light scattering is the dispersion of light in different directions when it interacts with particles or irregularities in a medium.

- Reddishness of the sun at sunrise and sunset
- Blue colour of the sky, are phenomena's of scattering of light.

What is Tyndall Effect?

The Tyndall effect, is the scattering of light by colloidal particles, distinguishing colloids from true solutions. When light passes through a colloid, it scatters due to particles, making the beam visible.

Dispersion of Light

The phenomenon of splitting white light into its component colors is called dispersion.

CBSE 2025, 2023, 2022

In Glass Prism

The colors of the spectrum include violet, indigo, blue, green, yellow, orange, and red

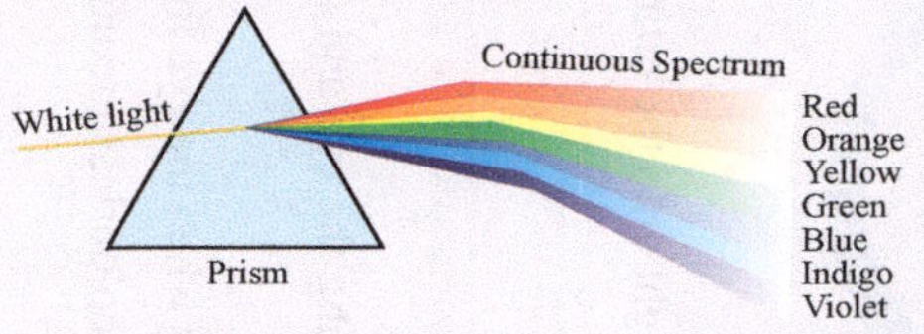

(VIBGYOR). Each color corresponds to a different wavelength of light.

CBSE 2025

How is rainbow formed in nature?

The phenomena involved in the formation of a rainbow are dispersion, internal reflection and refraction.

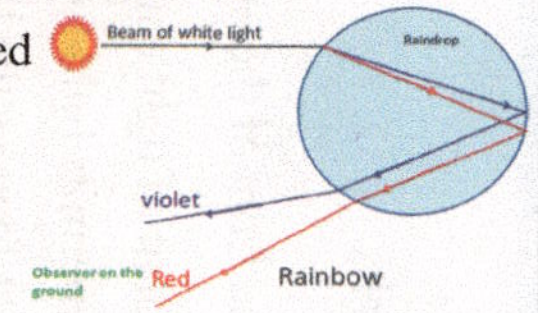

Atmospheric Refraction

It is the bending of light rays as they pass through the Earth's atmosphere.

Advanced sunrise and delayed sunset

Due to atmospheric refraction, the sun seems to rise early by 2 minutes and set late by 2 minutes.

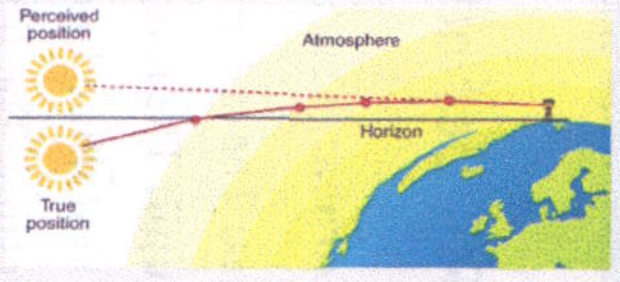

1 HUMAN EYE AND ITS DEFECTS

NCERT Definitions (Commonly asked in 1 mark)

- **Cornea:** A small, transparent, bulged-out portion at the front of the eyeball that functions to focus light onto the retina.
- **Iris:** The colored part of the eye that regulates the amount of light entering the eye.
- **Pupil:** The round opening in the center of the iris that permits light to pass towards the retina.
- **Crystalline Lens:** A transparent biconvex structure that focuses the light rays onto the retina.
- **Retina:** The light-sensitive layer of nerve tissue at the back of the eye that captures the light entering the eye and translates it into images we see.
- **Ciliary Body:** A circular structure connected to the iris that changes the shape of the crystalline lens when the eye focuses.
- **Aqueous Humour:** The clear liquid between the cornea and the lens that provides a transparent and colourless medium between the cornea and the lens.
- **Vitreous Humour:** A clear gel-like substance that occupies the space behind the crystalline lens provides nutrients to the eye and helps keep its shape.
- **Optic Nerve:** The paired, cylindrical structures extending from the back of the eyeball that transmits all visual information from the retina to the brain.

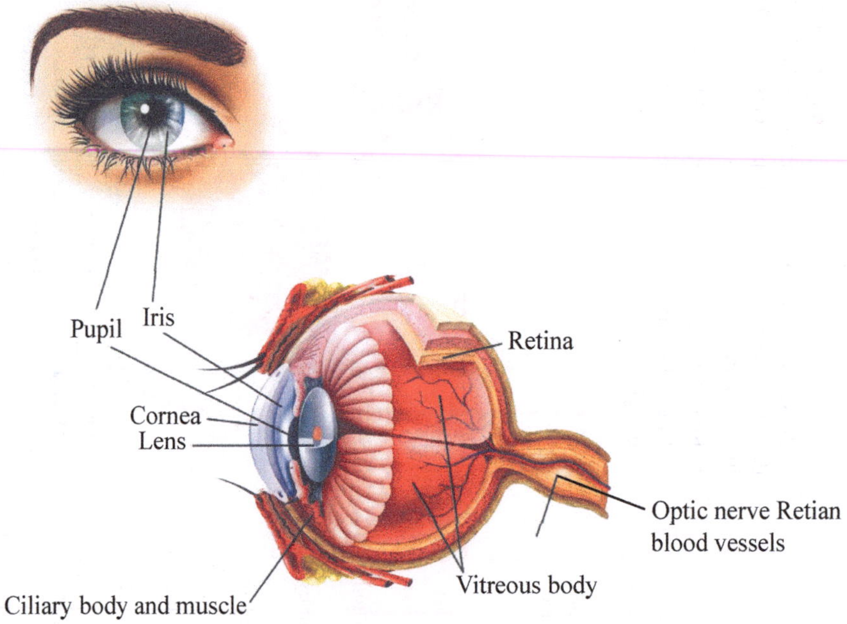

- **Power of Accommodation:** The power of accommodation is the ability of the eye to adjust its focus to see objects clearly at different distances.
- **Myopia:** A vision defect where close objects are seen clearly, but distant ones are blurred due to elongation of the eyeball or increased lens power.
- **Hypermetropia:** A condition causing difficulty in seeing close objects clearly, resulting from a shortened eyeball or decreased lens power.
- **Presbyopia:** Age-related vision defect marked by a decrease in the eye's ability to focus on close objects, requiring bifocal lenses.
- **Cataract:** Clouding of the lens causing vision loss, correctable by surgery and replacement with an artificial lens.
- **Astigmatism:** A defect caused by irregular curvature of the cornea or lens leading to blurred vision, corrected with cylindrical lenses.

Important Facts

01 Adjustments in the eye to control light include dilation and constriction of the pupil.

02 The near point of the eye, around 25 cm for a young adult with normal vision, is the closest distance at which objects can be seen clearly without strain.

03 The retina converts light into electrical signals sent to the brain, creating the images we see.

Classification

Functions of an Eye		
S. No.	**Function**	**Description**
1.	Adjustment to Light	Iris and pupil regulate light entry
2.	Refraction of Light	Lens bends light rays to form a sharp image
3.	Visual Processing	Retina converts light into electrical signals for the brain

Vision Defects and Corrections of an Eye			
S. No.	**Defect**	**Causes**	**Correction**
1.	Myopia (Nearsightedness)	Elongated eyeball or increased lens power	Concave lenses
2.	Hypermetropia(Farsightedness)	Compressed eyeball or decreased lens power	Convex lenses
3.	Presbyopia	Age-related hardening of the lens	Bifocal lenses
4.	Cataract	Lens clouding typically due to aging	Surgical removal and lens replacement
5.	Astigmatism	Irregular curvature of cornea or lens	Cylindrical lenses

Difference Between

Pupil v/s Iris	
Pupil	**Iris**
The opening that allows light into the eye	Muscular ring around the pupil that gives eye color
Size adjusts to light intensity	Controls the size of the pupil
Does not have color	Pigmented to provide eye color
Directly involved in light entry	Indirectly involved by adjusting pupil size
Remains black in appearance	Can have various colors

Myopia v/s Hypermetropia	
Myopia (Nearsightedness)	**Hypermetropia (Farsightedness)**
Caused by an elongated eyeball	Caused by a compressed eyeball
Distant objects are blurred	Close objects are blurred
Corrected with concave lenses	Corrected with convex lenses
Far point is closer than normal	Near point is farther than normal
Light focuses before the retina	Light focuses behind the retina

Important Formula

1. **Power of accommodation of an eye**

$$P = \frac{1}{\text{focal length } (m)}$$; S.I. unit of power is diopter (D)

Real Life Application Based Questions

1. **How do cameras use the concept of the human eye to capture images?**

Ans. Cameras utilize a lens to focus light onto a sensor, similar to how the cornea and lens of the human eye focus light onto the retina. The aperture of the camera, like the pupil, regulates the amount of light that reaches the sensor. Professional photographers can adjust these settings, just as the iris adjusts the pupil size, to control the exposure and clarity of the images captured.

2. **Why are eyes considered an important channel of communication?**

Ans. The eyes are crucial for understanding our surroundings as they collect visual information that the brain processes into images. This visual information, stored as memory tags, helps in communication and learning about our environment, making eyes a vital organ for interaction.

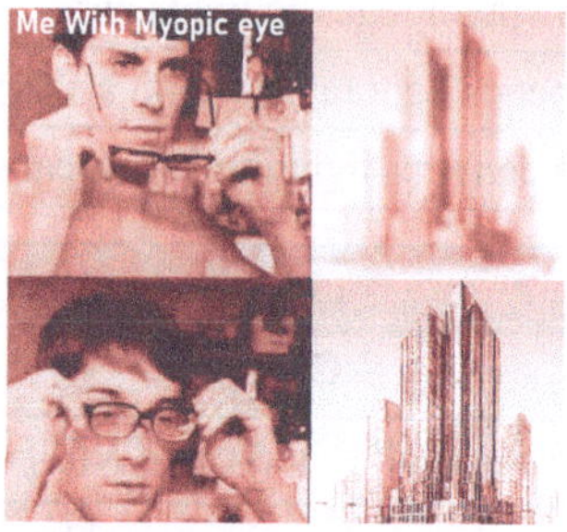

3. **How can the concept of the power of accommodation be applied in everyday life to promote healthy vision habits? Provide three practical examples.**

Ans. 1. Taking short breaks during study or screen time helps prevent eye strain and fatigue.

2. Adjusting font size and screen brightness on devices reduces the need for excessive eye accommodation.
3. Doing simple eye exercises, like focusing on distant objects, improves accommodation flexibility.

Myth Buster*

- **Myth: Reading in dim light weakens your eyes.**

  Fact: Reading in dim light can cause eye strain but doesn't permanently weaken eyesight. Proper lighting can reduce strain and discomfort.

- **Myth: Eating carrots can cure poor eyesight.**

  Fact: While carrots are nutritious, they can't cure vision problems. A balanced diet with various nutrients supports overall eye health but won't correct refractive errors.

- **Myth: The Power of Accommodation remains constant throughout life.**

  Fact: While the Power of Accommodation is highest during youth, it gradually decreases with age due to changes in the flexibility and elasticity of the lens. This decrease in accommodation ability is known as presbyopia and is a natural part of the aging process.

- **Myth: Presbyopia only affects older adults.**

  Fact: While presbyopia is commonly associated with aging, it can also occur in younger individuals due to certain medical conditions or medications. Presbyopia is characterized by the gradual loss of near vision due to the decreased flexibility of the lens.

- **Myth: Cataracts can only be treated with surgery.**

  Fact: While cataract surgery is the most effective treatment for advanced cataracts, early-stage cataracts can be managed with prescription glasses or contact lenses to improve vision. Regular eye exams are crucial for monitoring cataract progression and determining the appropriate treatment plan.

** Concepts beyond the board exam syllabus, offering deeper insight and critical thinking on NCERT topics.*

Mnemonics

- **MNC:** **M**yopia → **N**ear Sightedness → **C**oncave lens
  (Defect) (Defect) (Correction)
- The following trick will help you to remember the sign of power for myopia or hypermetropia.

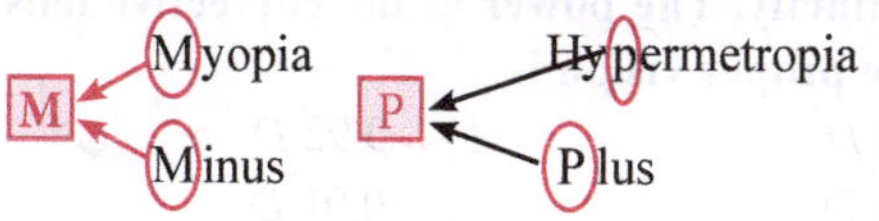

- **VISTA:** To remember functions performed by parts of human eye.

  - **V** → **Visual Sensitivity** (Retina)
  - **I** → **Iris Regulation** (Controls pupil size)
  - **S** → **Sclera Protection** (Outermost layer)
  - **T** → **Transparent Media** (Cornea, Lens, Vitreous humor)
  - **A** → **Aqueous Humor Production and Drainage** (Maintains pressure balance)

COMPETENCY BASED SOLVED EXAMPLES

Multiple Choice Questions (1 M)

1. Riya and Arjun are in a science class where they are learning about how the human eye works. Their teacher asks them to describe the journey of light as it travels through the different parts of the eye until it is detected by photoreceptor cells.
Explain to Riya and Arjun the correct sequence of structures that light passes through in the human eye, starting from where it first enters the eye to where it is finally detected by the photoreceptor cells? *(Re)*

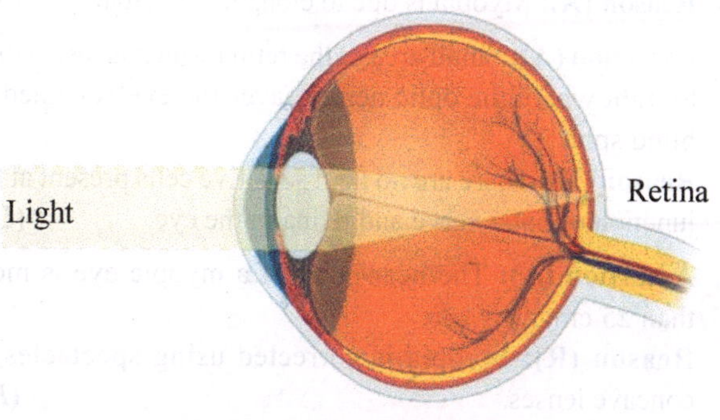

(*a*) Cornea → Lens → Pupil → Retina
(*b*) Cornea → Pupil → Lens → Retina
(*c*) Lens → Cornea → Pupil → Retina
(*d*) Pupil → Cornea → Lens → Retina

2. The size of the pupil is controlled by the muscular diaphragm called. *(Re)*
(*a*) Iris (*b*) Ciliary muscles
(*c*) Cornea (*d*) Rod and cones

3. The lens system of human eye forms an image on a light sensitive screen, which is called as: (CBSE, 2024)
(*a*) Cornea (*b*) Ciliary muscles
(*c*) Optic nerves (*d*) Retina

4. The nature of image formed on the retina of the human eye is *(Re)*
(*a*) Virtual and inverted (*b*) Real and inverted
(*c*) Real and erect (*d*) Virtual and erect

5. The ability of eye lens to adjust its focal length to form a sharp image of the object at varying distances on the retina is called *(Un)*
(*a*) Converging power of the eye
(*b*) Power of accommodation of the eye
(*c*) Power of adjustment of the eye
(*d*) Diverging power of the eye

6. **Far and near points of a young person's normal eye respectively are** ***(Un)***

(*a*) Infinity and 0 (*b*) Infinity and 25 cm

(*c*) 0 and 25 cm (*d*) 150 cm and 25 cm.

7. **Having two eyes facilitates in** ***(Re)***

A: Bringing three-dimensional view

B: Increasing the field of view

C: Observing the concept of height and distance

The correct option is/are

(*a*) A only (*b*) B only

(*c*) A and B only (*d*) A, B and C

8. **Consider a person with presbyopia, a condition where the eye loses its ability to focus on nearby objects due to the hardening of the lens. Which type of corrective lens would be most suitable for such a person and why?** ***(Un)***

(*a*) Convex lens, because it converges light rays onto the retina, compensating for the reduced flexibility of the lens.

(*b*) Concave lens, because it diverges light rays onto the retina, compensating for the reduced flexibility of the lens.

(*c*) Bifocal lens, because it has two parts with different focal lengths to correct both near and distant vision.

(*d*) Cylindrical lens, because it corrects the uneven curvature of the lens, addressing both near and distant vision problems.

9. **A person with a certain visual defect can see distant objects clearly but experiences difficulty focusing on nearby objects. Which corrective lens should be prescribed and why?** ***(Re)***

(*a*) Convex lens, because it converges light rays before they enter the eye, shortening the focal length.

(*b*) Concave lens, because it diverges light rays before they enter the eye, shortening the focal length.

(*c*) Convex lens, because it converges light rays before they enter the eye, increasing the focal length.

(*d*) Concave lens, because it diverges light rays before they enter the eye, increasing the focal length.

10. **What is the function of the retina in the human eye?** ***(Re)***

(*a*) To control the amount of light entering the eye

(*b*) To produce tears that keep the eye moist

(*c*) To focus light onto the back of the eye

(*d*) To detect light and transmit signals to the brain

11. **What is the name of the condition in which the lens of the eye becomes cloudy, causing vision to become blurry?** ***(Re)***

(*a*) Glaucoma (*b*) Cataract

(*c*) Myopia (*d*) Hyperopia

12. **Which of the following statements about color blindness is true?** ***(Un)***

(*a*) Color blindness affects only men

(*b*) Color blindness is caused by a lack of vitamin A

(*c*) Color blindness affects the ability to see certain colors

(*d*) Color blindness is a temporary condition

13. **Which of the following is a common vision problem that causes distant objects to appear blurry?** ***(Un)***

(*a*) Presbyopia (*b*) Astigmatism

(*c*) Myopia (*d*) Hyperopia

14. **A person with a myopic eye cannot see object beyond 1.2m distinctly. The power of the corrective lens used to restore proper vision is** ***(Ev)***

(*a*) –0.83 *D* (*b*) –0.92 *D*

(*c*) +0.21 *D* (*d*) +0.91 *D*

15. **Ravi, a student, experiences difficulty in reading books when they are held closer than 40 cm to his eyes. He visits an optometrist who diagnoses him with hypermetropia (farsightedness) and prescribes him corrective lenses. Calculate the power of the lens that should be prescribed to Ravi.** ***(Ev)***

(*a*) + 1.5 D (*b*) – 1.5 D

(*c*) + 2.5 D (*d*) + 0.5 D

16. **A person cannot see distinctly objects kept beyond 2m. This defect can be corrected by using a lens of power** ***(Ev)*** **(NCERT Exemplar)**

(*a*) + 0.5 *D* (*b*) – 0.5 *D*

(*c*) + 0.2 *D* (*d*) – 0.2 *D*

17. **A student sitting on the last bench can read the letters written on the blackboard but is not able to read the letters written in his text book. Which of the following statements is correct?** ***(Un)*** **(NCERT Exemplar)**

(*a*) The near point of his eyes has receded away

(*b*) The near point of his eyes has come closer to him

(*c*) The far point of his eyes has come closer to him

(*d*) The far point of his eyes has receded away

Assertion and Reason (1 M)

Direction: The following questions consist of two statements – Assertion (A) and Reason (R). Answer these questions by selecting the appropriate option given below:

(*a*) Both A and R are true, and R is the correct explanation of A.

(*b*) Both A and R are true, but R is not the correct explanation of A.

(*c*) A is true, but R is false

(*d*) A is false, but R is true.

1. **Assertion (A):** Myopia is the defect of vision in which a person cannot see the distant objects clearly.
Reason (R): Myopia is due to elongated eye-ball. ***(Re)***

2. **Assertion (A):** Small area of the retina which is insensitive to light where the optic nerve leaves the eye is named as blind spot.
Reason (R): There are no light sensitive cells present at the junction of optic nerve and retina in the eye. ***(Un)***

3. **Assertion (A):** The near-point of a myopic eye is more than 25 cm away.
Reason (R): Myopia is corrected using spectacles of concave lenses. ***(Re)***

4. **Assertion (A):** A normal human eye can clearly see all the objects beyond certain minimum distance.
Reason (R): The human eye has capacity of adjusting the focal length of eye lens. ***(Re)***

Subjective Questions

Very Short Answer Type Questions (2 M)

1. **Imagine you are helping a younger sibling understand how the human eye works for their school science project. To explain the basics of vision, you need to describe the process of how light enters the eye. Where does light enter the eye?** ***(Un)***

Ans. Light enters the eye through a thin membrane called the cornea, passes through the pupil, and is then focused by the lens onto the retina. This process allows us to perceive visual information from our surroundings. *(2 M)*

2. **You are explaining to a younger brother how the different parts of the human eye work together to help us see. They are particularly curious about the cornea and its role in vision. What is the role of the cornea in the human eye?** ***(Re)***

Ans. The cornea's role in the human eye includes allowing light to enter, focusing it onto the retina, protecting the eye from external harm, and maintaining transparency for clear vision. It is essential for both the clarity and protection of our vision. *(2 M)*

3. **Imagine you are explaining the basics of vision to your friend who is curious about how we see. He asks you to explain how the brain makes sense of the images we see with our eyes. How does the brain interpret signals from the eye?** ***(Re)***

Ans. The brain interprets signals from the eye by receiving electrical signals generated by light-sensitive cells in the retina. These signals are transmitted via the optic nerves to the brain, where they are processed to perceive and understand visual information. *(2 M)*

4. **Why is the blind spot called so?** ***(Un)***

Ans. Blind spot is called so because,

(1) A blind spot is a small fragment of the visual field in each eye.

(2) Photo-receptors are absent in this region so no image or light detection occurs in this specific area and a blind spot is created.

(3) Visual perception does not occur in this region as the visual fields of both eyes overlap.

(4) The optic nerve leaves the eye through this area and the blind spot is present in all vertebrates. *(2 M)*

5. **When you enter from bright sunshine into a dark room, you are not able to see clearly for some time, why?** ***(An)***

Ans. When we enter a dark room from bright sunshine, for sometime we cannot see anything clearly. After a short time our vision improves. This is because in bright sunshine the pupil of our eye is small and when we just enter the dark room, very little light enters our eye due to which we cannot see properly. After a while, when the pupil of our eye expands, more light enters our eye and we can see clearly. *(2 M)*

6. **A person with a myopic eye cannot see objects beyond 1.2 m distinctly. What should be the type of the corrective lens used to restore proper vision?** ***(Ev)*** **(NCERT Intext)**

Ans. The person should use a concave lens of focal length 1.2 m to restore proper vision.

Power, $P = \frac{1}{f} = \frac{1}{-1.2} = -0.83D$ *(1 M)*

Hence, the concave lens or diverging lens of $0.83D$ will bring the image back to the retina. *(1 M)*

7. **The far point of a myopic person is 80 cm in front of the eye. What is the nature and power of the lens required to correct the problem?** ***(Ev)*** **(NCERT)**

Ans. The lens should be such that an object at infinity must form its image at the far point of 80cm to make it visible to the myopic person.

It is given, $f = -80$ cm $= -0.8$ m

$$P = \frac{1}{-0.8\text{m}} = -1.25D$$

Therefore,

Power of the lens: The power of the lens is $-1.25D$. *(1 M)*

Nature of the lens: (*–ve*) sign implies that it is a concave lens. It is diverging in nature. *(1 M)*

8. **What happens to the image distance in the normal human eye when we decrease the distance of an object, say 10 m to 1 m? Justify your answer.**

Ans. There is no change in the image distance in the eye. The eye lens has the ability to adjust its focal length called accommodation. When object distance decreases, ciliary muscles contract and lens becomes thick and its focal length decreases. It facilitate the near vision. *(2 M)*

9. **What are the values of (*i*) near point and (*ii*) far point of vision of a normal adult person?**

Ans. (*i*) For a young person having normal vision, the near point is 25 cm. *(1 M)*

(*ii*) For a normal vision, far point is infinity. *(1 M)*

10. **An old person is unable to see clearly nearby objects as well as distant objects clearly. What defect of vision he is suffering from and how that can be corrected?**

Ans. The old person is suffering from presbyopia and that can be corrected by using bifocal lens. *(2 M)*

Short Answer Type Questions (3 M)

1. **Sohan is curious about how we are able to see objects clearly with our eyes. Describe the pathway of light through the human eye, starting from the point where light first enters the eye until it reaches the photoreceptor cells. Discuss the significance of each part of the eye in ensuring that we can see clear images.** ***(Re)***

Ans. Light enters the eye through the cornea, which refracts and focuses most of the light. It then passes through the aqueous humor, the pupil (controlled by the iris), and the lens, which fine-tunes the focus. The lens changes shape to adjust the focus for objects at different distances. Finally, the light reaches the retina, where photoreceptor cells convert it into electrical signals. These signals are transmitted to the brain via the optic nerve, allowing us to perceive clear images. *(3 M)*

2. **(a) Explain how a normal human eye is able to see distinctly the object placed at a large distance as well as those placed at a nearer distance.**
   (b) What is the far point and near point of a normal human eye? (Un)

Ans. (a) Ciliary muscles change the curvature of the eye lens as per the requirement of the eye. This changes the focal length of the eye lens. When muscles are relaxed, the lens becomes thin and distant objects are seen clearly. While seeing closer objects, muscles contract, which thickens the eye lens and focal length decreases. *(2 M)*

(b) Far point — Infinity. Near point — 25 cm from the eye. *(1 M)*

3. **State the function of the pupil and ciliary body. (Re)**

Ans. Pupil controls the amount of light entering the eye. *(1 M)*
The ciliary body is a circular structure that is an extension of the iris, the colored part of the eye. It produces the fluid in the eye called aqueous humour. It also contains the ciliary muscle, which changes the shape of the lens when eyes focus on a near object. *(2 M)*

4. **Study the diagram given below and answer the questions that follow: (Un & Re) (CBSE, 2024)**

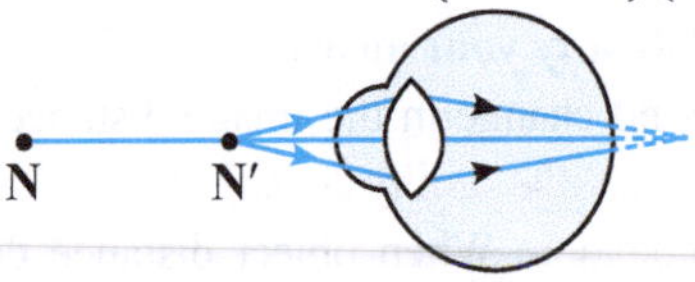

   (i) Name the defect of vision represented in the diagram. Give reason for your answer.
   (ii) List two causes of this defect
   (iii) With the help of a diagram show how this defect of vision is corrected.

Ans. (i) Hypermetropia as the image is formed beyond the retina. *(1 M)*

(ii) (a) Due to greater focal length of the, lens and
(b) As eyeball becomes smaller. *(1 M)*

(iii) It can be corrected by using a convex lens of suitable focal length as shown below.

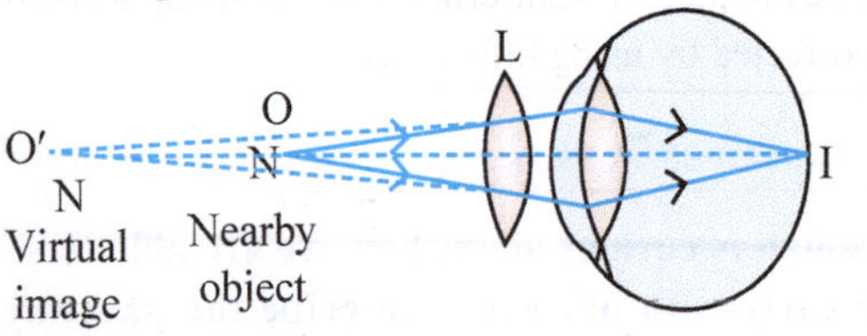

N
Virtual image formed at N

Nearby object

(1 M)

5. **Sushil went to an eye specialist for a check-up. He prescribed to use a spectacle lens of + 0.5D power.**
   (a) Name the defect of vision he is suffering from.
   (b) Find the focal length of the spectacle lens. (Un & Ev)

Ans. (a) Hypermetropia. *(1 M)*

(b) Power of spectacle $P = +0.5D$

$$f = \frac{1}{P} = +\frac{1}{0.5}m$$

or $f = +2m$ positive sign means it is a convex lens. *(2 M)*

6. **What is meant by the least distance of distinct vision? How does this vary between very young and old people? (Re)**

Ans. Least distance of distinct vision is the minimum distance between the eye and the object to see it. *(1 M)*
In young people, the least distance of distinct vision is about 25 cm and for old people, it is usually more than 25 cm. *(2 M)*

> **Mistakes 101 : What not to do!**
>
> **Guessing Randomly:** Guessing without any basis or strategy can read to incorrect answers, especially if there's a penalty for a wrong response.

7. **A person needs a lens of power –5.5 dioptres for correcting his distant vision. For correcting his near vision he needs a lens of power +1.5 dioptre. What is the focal length of the lens required for correcting (i) distant vision, and (ii) near vision? (Ev) (NCERT)**

Ans. Given: Power of the lens used for correcting distant vision $= -5.5D$.

(i) Thus, Focal length, $f = \frac{1}{P}, f = -\frac{1}{5.5} = -0.181m$

Power of the lens used for correcting near vision $= +1.5D$. *(2 M)*

(ii) Focal length, $f = \frac{1}{P}$

$$f = \frac{1}{1.5} = +0.667m$$ *(1 M)*

8. **Draw ray diagrams each showing (i) myopic eye and (ii) hypermetropic eye. (Un) (NCERT Exemplar)**

Ans. (i) *(1½ M)*

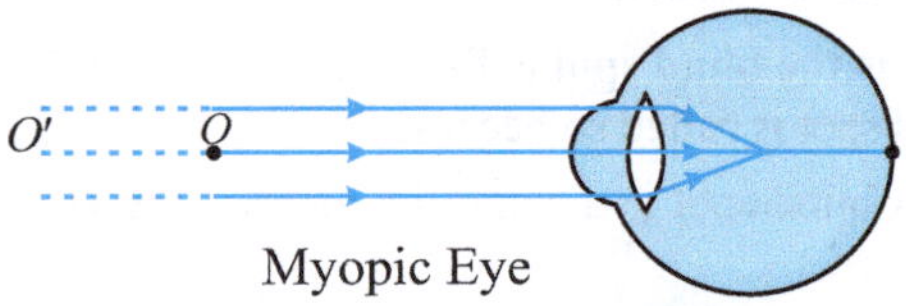

Myopic Eye

(ii) *(1½ M)*

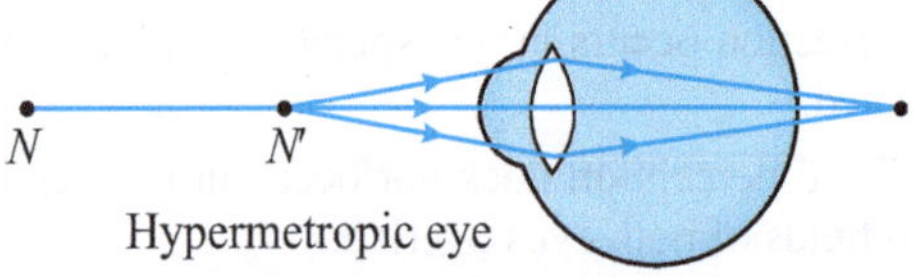

Hypermetropic eye

9. **A student sitting at the back of the classroom cannot read clearly the letters written on the blackboard. What advice will a doctor give to her? Draw ray diagram for the correction of this defect. (Un & Re) (NCERT Exemplar)**

Ans. The student is facing the problem of myopia, also known as nearsightedness. The doctor will advise the student to get her eyes checked and prescribe a suitable diverging lens that can be worn while looking at distant objects like the blackboard in the classroom. The power of the lens will depend on the degree of myopia and will be prescribed by the doctor. *(2 M)*

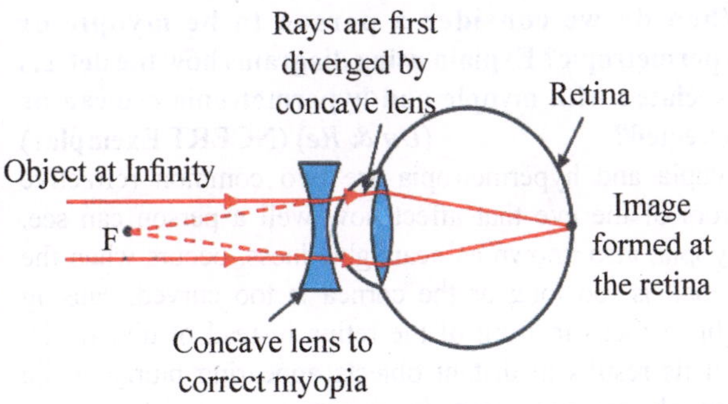

(1 M)

10. Trace the sequence of events which occur when a bright light is focused on your eyes. **(*Re*) (CBSE, 2019)**

Ans. When a bright light enters the eye then most of the refraction for the light rays entering the eye occurs at the outer surface of the cornea. Then, the crystalline lens merely provides the finer adjustment of the focal length required to focus objects at different distances on the retina. *(1 M)*

The pupil regulates and controls the amount of light entering the eye. At the retina, the light-sensitive cells get activated upon illumination and generate electric signals. These signals are sent to the brain via the optic nerves. The brain interprets these signals and finally, processes the information so that we perceive objects as they are. *(2 M)*

11. (*a*) List two causes of hypermetropia.

(*b*) Draw ray diagrams showing (*i*) a hypermetropic eye and (*ii*) its correction using suitable optical device. **(*Un*) (CBSE, 2020)**

Ans. (*a*) Hypermetropia is caused due to following reasons:

(*i*) Shortening of the eyeball *(½ M)*

(*ii*) Focal length of the crystalline lens is too long. *(½ M)*

(*b*)

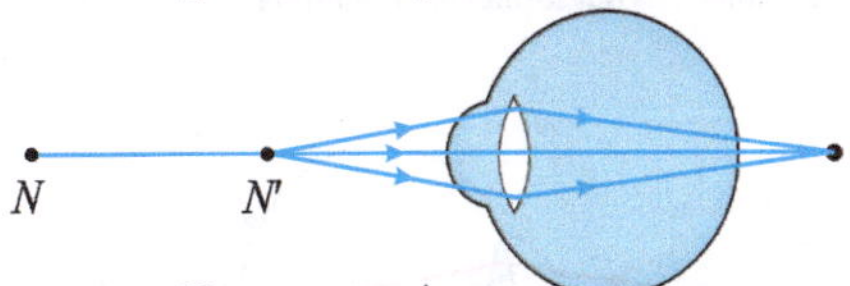

Hypermetropic eye

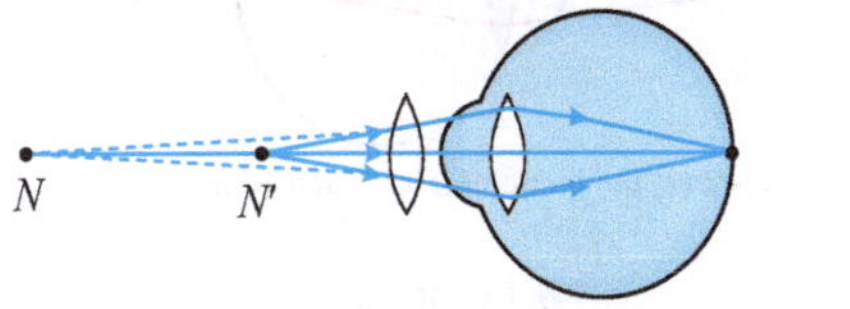

Correction for Hypermetropic eye *(2 M)*

12. A person may suffer from both myopia and hypermetropia defects.

(*a*) What is this condition called?

(*b*) When does it happen?

(*c*) Name the type of lens often required by the persons suffering from this defect. Draw labelled diagram of such lenses. **(*An*, *Un*) (CBSE, 2020)**

Ans. (*a*) This condition is called presbyopia. *(1 M)*

(*b*) It happens due to gradual weakening of ciliary muscles and diminishing flexibility of eye lens due to aging. *(1 M)*

(*c*) It can be corrected by using bifocal lenses.

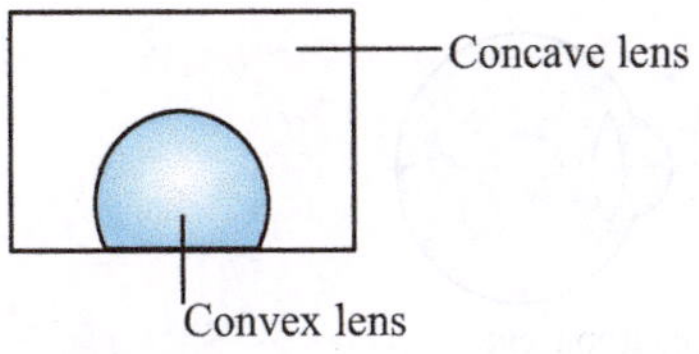

(1 M)

13. (*a*) What is the function of iris and pupil of the eye?

(*b*) How does the focal length of the eye lens change as per distance of the object in front of the eye?

Ans. (*a*) The iris controls the size of the pupil. It adjusts in size, and therefore, helps in regulating the amount of light entering the eye through a variable aperture 'pupil'. When the light is very bright, the pupil becomes very small. However, in dim light, it opens up completely through the relaxation of the iris. *(1 M)*

(*b*) The crystalline eye lens consists of a fibrous, jelly-like material. Its curvature can be modified to some extent by the ciliary muscles. The change in the curvature of eye lens can change its focal length. When the muscles are relaxed, the lens is thin and its focal length is more (about 2.5 cm). When the ciliary muscles contract and the eye lens becomes thicker. Consequently, the focal length of eye lens decreases. *(2 M)*

Long Answer Type Questions **(5 M)**

1. (*a*) A student is unable to see clearly the words written on the blackboard placed at a distance of approximately 3 m from him. Name the defect of vision the boy is suffering from State the possible causes of this defect and explain the method of correcting it. (*b*) If, in this case, the numerical value of the focal length of the corrective lens is 5 m, find the power of the lens as per the new Cartesian sign convention. **(*An*)**

Ans. (*a*) Defects of vision: Myopia or short-sightedness. Reasons: Excessive curvature of the eye lens and elongation of the eyeball. *(½ M)*

Correction: Using a concave lens *(½ M)*

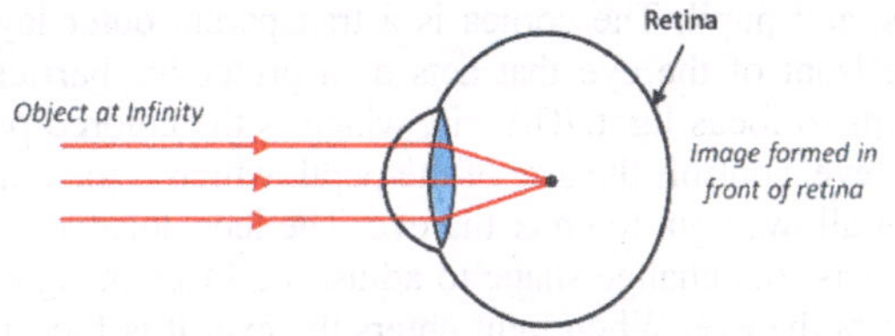

For a Myopic eye, image from infinity is formed in front of retina. It is **not formed on the retina**

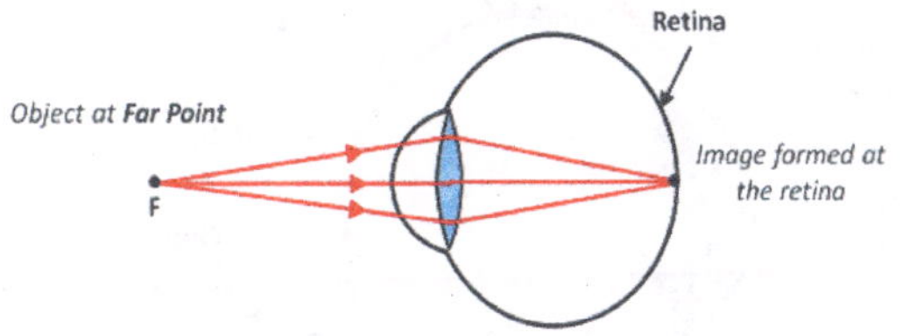

For a Myopic eye, the **far point is less than infinity**

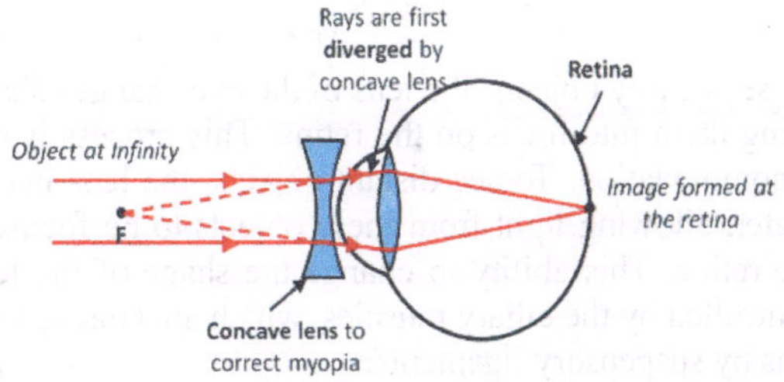

(2 M)

(*b*) Focal length, $f = -5$ m

$P = 1/f$ (in meters) or, $p = 1/-5 = -0.2D$

Hence, the power is –0.2 D. *(2 M)*

2. (*a*) Write the function of each of the following parts of the human eye:

(*i*) Cornea (*ii*) Iris

(*iii*) Crystalline lens (*iv*) Ciliary muscles

(*b*) Define the term power of accommodation. (*Re*)

Ans. (*a*) Function of the Human eye:

(*i*) Cornea focuses light rays to enter the eye. *(1 M)*

(*ii*) Iris control and regulate the amount of light entering the eye and control the size of the pupil. *(1 M)*

(*iii*) Crystalline lens is like a convex lens which converges light rays on the retina. *(1 M)*

(*iv*) Ciliary muscles adjust the focal length of the eye lens by contraction and relaxation so that a sharp image can be obtained on the retina. *(1 M)*

(*b*) The ability of the eye lens to adjust its focal length is called power of accommodation. *(1 M)*

Nailing the Right Answer

Manage Time Effectively: Keep Track of time during the test to ensure you can answer all the question. Try to answer section wise.

3. Explain the structure and functioning of Human eye. How are we able to see nearby as well as distant objects? (*Un* & *Re*) (NCERT Exemplar)

Ans. The human eye is a complex organ that allows us to see the world around us. The eye works by gathering light from the environment and focusing it onto the retina, a layer of light-sensitive cells at the back of the eye. This process is facilitated by several structures, including the cornea, lens, iris, and pupil. The cornea is a transparent outer layer at the front of the eye that acts as a protective barrier and helps to focus light. The iris, which is the colored part of the eye, controls the size of the pupil, which is the opening that allows light to enter the eye. The lens, located behind the iris, can change shape to adjust the focus of light as it enters the eye. When light enters the eye, it is focused by the cornea and lens onto the retina.

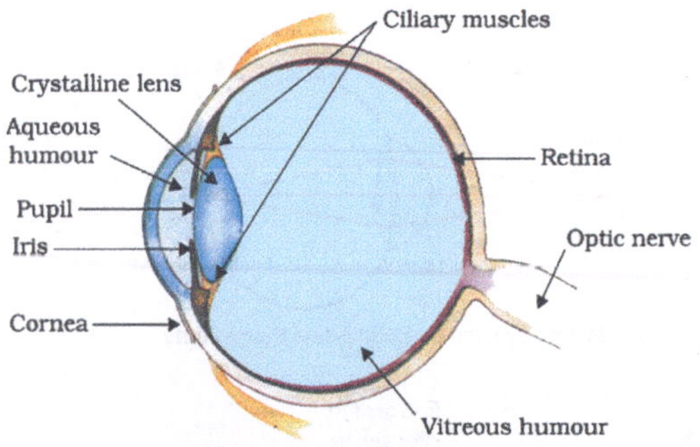

(3 M)

To see nearby objects, the lens of the eye changes shape to bring them into focus on the retina. This process is called accommodation. To see distant objects, the lens becomes flatter, allowing light from these objects to be focused on the retina. This ability to change the shape of the lens is controlled by the ciliary muscles, which are attached to the lens by suspensory ligaments. *(2 M)*

4. When do we consider a person to be myopic or hypermetropic? Explain using diagrams how the defects associated with myopic and hypermetropia eye can be corrected? (*Un* & *Re*) (NCERT Exemplar)

Ans. Myopia and hypermetropia are two common refractive errors of the eye that affect how well a person can see. Myopia, also known as nearsightedness, occurs when the eyeball is too long or the cornea is too curved, causing light to focus in front of the retina instead of directly on it. This results in distant objects appearing blurry, while near objects are clear. hypermetropia, also known as farsightedness, occurs when the eyeball is too short or the cornea is too flat, causing light to focus behind the retina instead of directly on it. This results in near objects appearing blurry, while distant objects may be clear. Both myopia and hypermetropia can be corrected with the use of corrective lenses or refractive surgery. *(1 M)*

To correct myopia, a concave lens (also called a diverging lens) is used. This lens is thinner in the center and thicker at the edges, causing light to diverge before it enters the eye. This helps to compensate for the excessive curvature of the cornea or elongation of the eyeball, allowing light to focus directly on the retina.

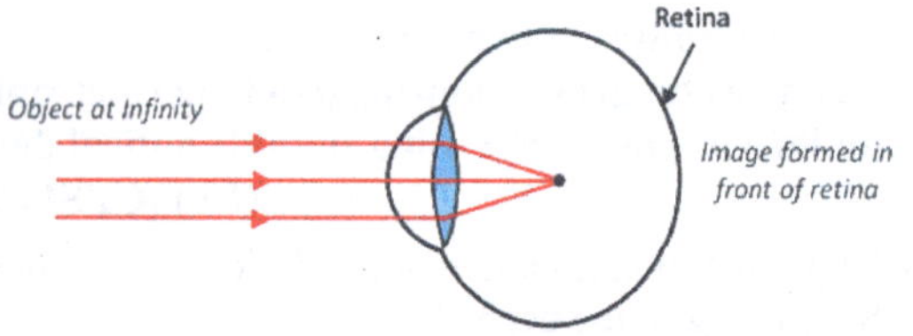

For a Myopic eye, image from infinity is formed in front of retina. It is **not formed on the retina**

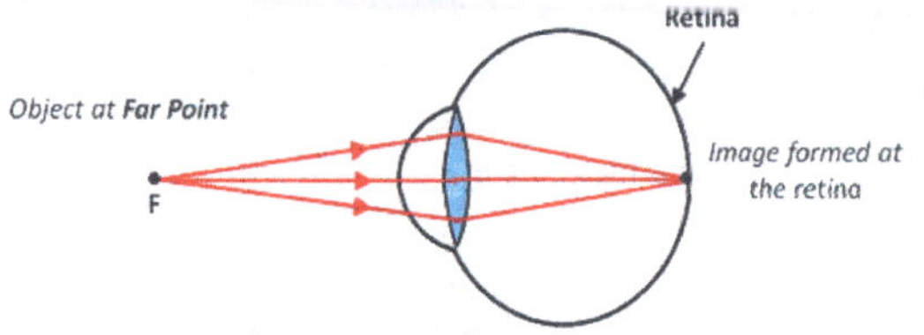

For a Myopic eye, the **far point is less than infinity**

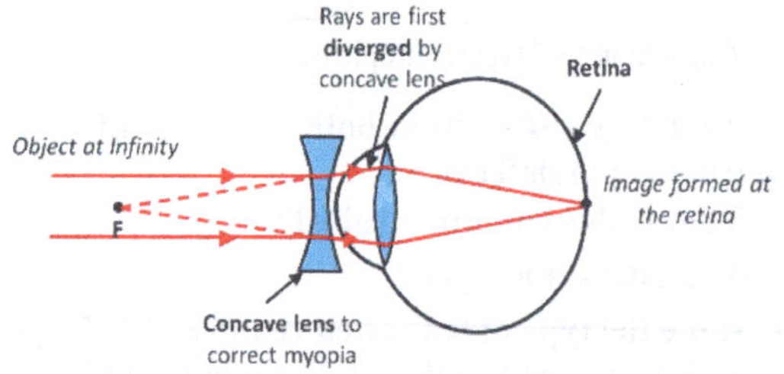

(2 M)

To correct hypermetropia, a convex lens (also called a converging lens) is used. This lens is thicker in the center and thinner at the edges, causing light to converge before it enters the eye. This helps to compensate for the insufficient curvature of the cornea or shortening of the eyeball, allowing light to focus directly on the retina.

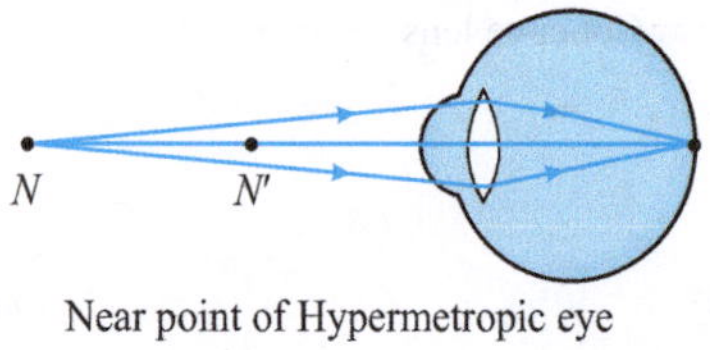

Near point of Hypermetropic eye

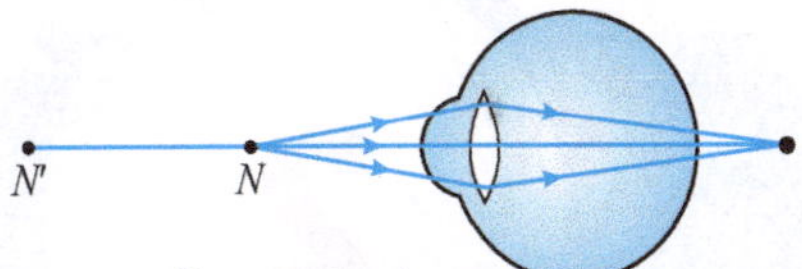

Hypermetropic eye

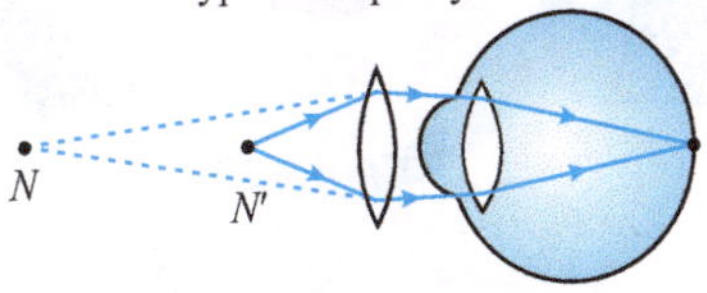

Correction for Hypermetropic eye *(2 M)*

5. A student sitting at the back bench in a class has difficulty in reading. What could be his defect of vision? Draw ray diagram to illustrate the image formation of the blackboard when he is seated at the (*i*) back seat (*ii*) front seat. State two possible causes of this defect. Explain the method of correcting this defect with the help of a ray diagram. (*Re & Un*)(CBSE 2018)

Ans. Student is suffering from myopia or shortsightedness or nearsightedness.

(*i*) When student is seated at the back seat.

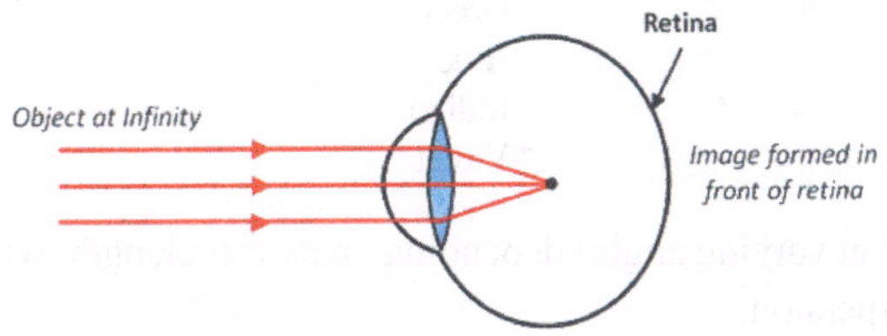

In this case student is suffering from myopia and have short focal length of eye lens. *(1 M)*

(*ii*) When student is seated at the front seat.

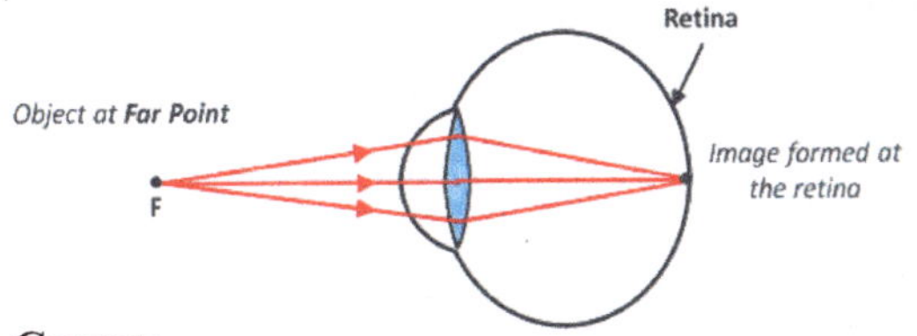

(1 M)

Causes:

(*i*) Excessive curvature of eye lens *(½ M)*
(*ii*) Elongation of eye ball. *(½ M)*

The defect is corrected by using a concave lens of suitable power placed in front of eye as shown below.

It diverge the rays and forms a virtual image of distant object at far point of the myopic eye. These diverged rays enter into the eye and form the image on the retina. Thus, the concave lens shifts the image back onto the retina instead of forming the image in front of it and the defect is corrected.

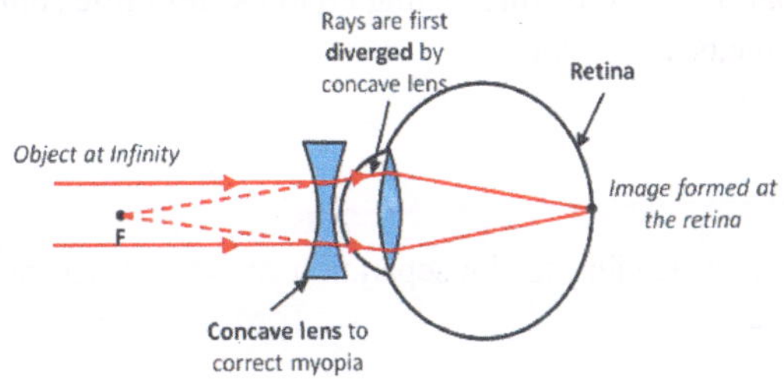

(1 M)

Hints & Explanations

Multiple Choice Questions

1. (*b*) Cornea → Pupil → Lens → Retina
2. (*a*) The size of the pupil is controlled by the muscular diaphragm called Iris.
3. (*d*) The lens system of the human eye forms an image on a light-sensitive screen called the retina.
4. (*b*) The nature of image formed on the retina of the human eye is real and inverted.
5. (*b*) The ability of eye lens to adjust its focal length to form a sharp image of the object at varying distances on the retina is called the power of accommodation of the eye.
6. (*b*) The far and the near point of a young person's normal eye respectively are infinite and 25 cm.
7. (*d*) Having two eyes facilitates in bringing three-dimensional view, increasing the field of view and observing the concept of height and distances.
8. (*c*) Bifocal lens, because it has two parts with different focal lengths to correct both near and distant vision.
9. (*a*) Convex lens, because it converges light rays before they enter the eye, shortening the focal length.
10. (*d*) The function of retina in the human eye is to detect light and transmit signals to the brain.
11. (*b*) Cataract is the name of the condition in which the lens of the eye becomes cloudy.
12. (*c*) Colour blindness affects the ability to see certain colours.
13. (*c*) Myopia is a common vision problem that causes distant objects to appear blurry.
14. (*a*) The corrective lens should form the image of far off object at the far point of the myopic person. So, by using lens formula,

$$\frac{1}{f}=\frac{1}{v}-\frac{1}{u}=\frac{1}{-1.2}-\frac{1}{\infty}=-\frac{1}{1.2}$$

$$f = -1.2m$$

Power of a lens, $P=-\frac{1}{1.2}=-0.83D$

15. (*a*) $\frac{1}{f}=\frac{1}{\upsilon}-\frac{1}{u}$

Here:

v is the image distance (which should be the near point of a normal eye, i.e., 25 cm or 0.25 m).

u is the object distance (which is the near point of Ravi's eye, i.e., 40 cm or 0.40 m).

$$\frac{1}{f}=\frac{1}{0.25}-\frac{1}{0.40}$$

$$\frac{1}{f}=4-2.5=1.5D$$

Therefore, P = + 1.5 D

16. (*b*) The defect can be corrected by using a lens of power –0.5 *D*.
17. (*a*) The near point of the student's eye has receded away.

Assertion and Reason

1. (*a*) Both A and R are true, and R is the correct explanation of A.
2. (*a*) Both A and R are true, and R is the correct explanation of A.
3. (*d*) A is false, but R is true.
4. (*a*) Both A and R are true and R is the correct explanation of assertion

2 PRISM AND ATMOSPHERIC REFRACTION

NCERT Definitions (Commonly asked in 1 mark)

- **Prism:** A solid optical element with flat, polished surfaces that can refract light, splitting it into a spectrum.
- **Dispersion:** The process by which white light is split into its constituent colors, such as violet, indigo, blue, green, yellow, orange, and red. Each colour corresponds to a distinct wavelength of light.

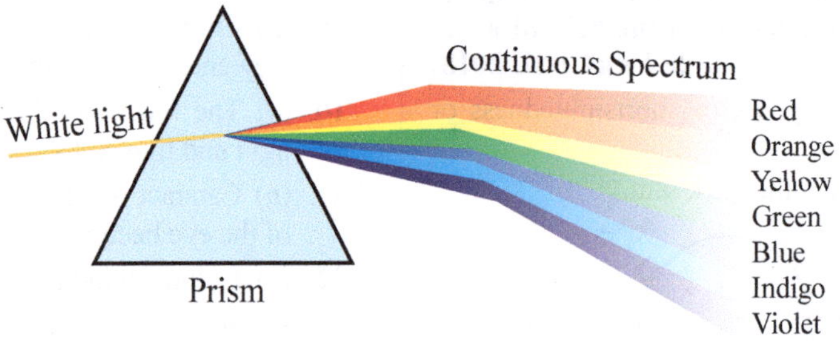

- **Shape of Prism:** The triangular shape of a prism causes light to bend at varying angles depending on its wavelength, with shorter wavelengths bending more than longer ones, resulting in angular dispersion.
- **Atmospheric refraction:** Atmospheric refraction refers to the bending of light rays as they travel through the Earth's atmosphere, which has varying densities. This bending causes phenomena such as the apparent.

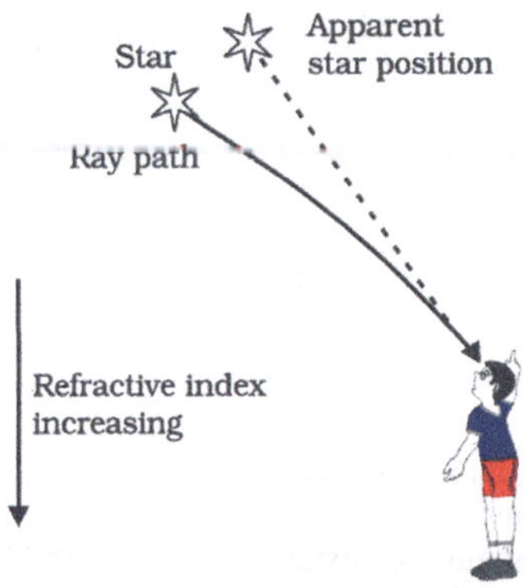

Apparent star position due to atmospheric refraction

- **Scattering of Light:** The scattering of light is the deflection of light rays from their direct path when they encounter particles in their path. This is why the sky appears blue, as the shorter (blue) wavelengths scatter more than the longer (red) wavelengths.
- **Tyndall Effect:** The Tyndall effect, is the scattering of light by colloidal particles, distinguishing colloids from true solutions. When light passes through a colloid, it scatters due to particles, making the beam visible.

Important Facts

01 Angular Dispersion is the variation in bending angle with wavelength, leading to the separation of white light into a spectrum.

02 Various instruments use reflective surfaces (mirrors) to focus and manipulate light for clearer visualization.

03 A natural spectacle resulting from refraction, dispersion and reflection of sunlight in water droplets. ***~Rainbow***

04 Sunrise and sunset exhibit a reddish hue as shorter light wavelengths scatter in the atmosphere, allowing longer wavelengths such as red and orange to prevail in the sky's color.

05 The angle of deviation produced by the prism depends on the angle of incidence, the refractive index of the prism material and the wavelength of light.

Difference Between

Atmospheric Refraction	Scattering of Light
Bends light as it travels through the atmosphere.	Makes light change direction by bouncing off particles in the air.
Due to differences in air density and temperature in the atmosphere.	Happens when light interacts with particles in the air.
Causes objects like the Sun and stars to appear higher in the sky than they actually are.	Makes the sky look blue and can cause the Sun to look red at sunrise and sunset.
Affects navigation and the timing of sunrise and sunset.	Affects visibility and the colors we see in the sky.

Atmospheric Refraction	Dispersion
Bending of light rays as they pass through the Earth's atmosphere.	Separation of white light into its constituent colors.
Differences in air density and temperature in the atmosphere.	Variation in the refractive index of a medium with respect to different wavelengths of light.
Causes celestial objects to appear higher in the sky than they actually are.	Creates a spectrum of colors, such as a rainbow, when light passes through a prism or a medium with varying refractive indices.
Affects the apparent positions of celestial objects and the timing of sunrise and sunset.	Used in optical instruments and spectroscopy to analyze the composition of substances.

Real Life Application Based Questions

1. **What is the reason behind the phenomenon of advanced sunrise and delayed sunset?**

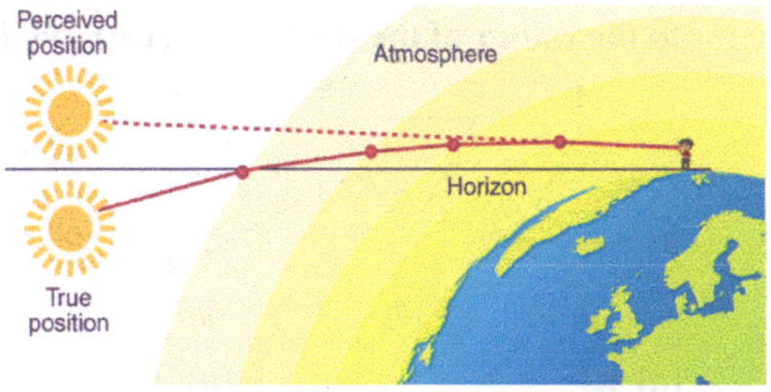

Ans. The phenomenon of advanced sunrise and delayed sunsets occurs due to atmospheric refraction. As light from the sun travels through the Earth's atmosphere, it bends from a rarer to a denser medium, causing the sun to appear in the sky when it is actually below the horizon. This makes the sun visible a few minutes before actual sunrise and a few minutes after the actual sunset.

2. **How are prisms utilized in optical instruments?**

Ans. Prisms are used in various optical instruments, like spectrometers and spectroscopes. In these devices, a prism disperses incoming light into its spectral components, allowing the measurement and analysis of different wavelengths. This helps in understanding the composition of light sources and is instrumental in various scientific and industrial applications.

3. **What is the mirage effect, and how does it occur in hot desert environments?**

Ans. The mirage effect is an optical illusion caused by the bending of light rays as they pass through layers of air with different temperatures. In hot desert environments, the ground absorbs heat, warming the air near the surface. This creates a temperature gradient, causing light to bend and creating the illusion of water or reflective surfaces on the ground.

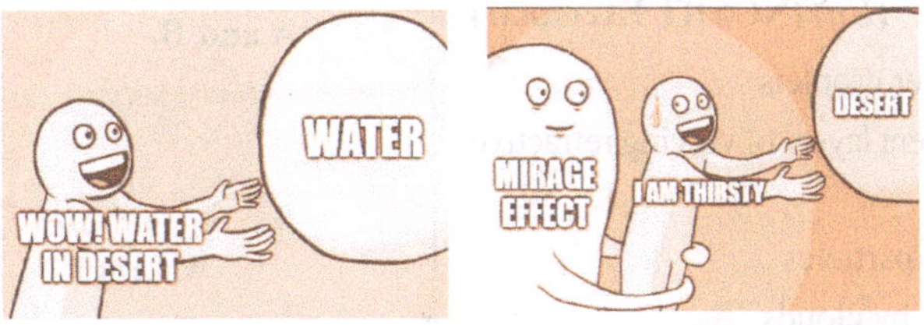

Myth Buster

- **Myth: The blue colour of the sky is caused by the reflection of the ocean.**
  Fact: The blue colour of the sky is primarily due to Rayleigh scattering, where shorter blue wavelengths are scattered more efficiently by air molecules in the atmosphere, making the sky appear blue.
- **Myth: Twinkling stars are caused by the stars themselves flickering or pulsating.**
  Fact: Twinkling stars are a result of the refraction of starlight as it passes through Earth's atmosphere, causing fluctuations in brightness due to atmospheric turbulence.
- **Myth: Total Internal Reflection (TIR) in a prism occurs due to the reflection of light off the prism's surface.**
  Fact: Total Internal Reflection (TIR) in a prism occurs when a light ray travelling from a denser to a less dense medium strikes the boundary at an angle greater than the critical angle, causing the light to be completely reflected back into the denser medium.

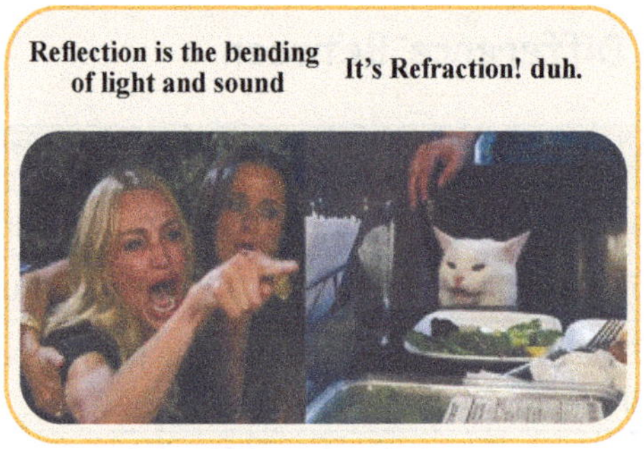

- **Myth: The Tyndall effect is caused by the reflection of light off particles suspended in a medium.**
  Fact: The Tyndall effect is a result of the scattering of light by particles suspended in a medium, such as dust or mist, making the light visible as it passes through the medium.

COMPETENCY BASED SOLVED EXAMPLES

Multiple Choice Questions (1 M)

1. A prism ABC (with BC as base) is placed in different orientations. A narrow beam of white light is incident on the prism as shown in Figure. In which of the following cases, after dispersion, the third colour from the top corresponds to the colour of the sky? (*Un*) (NCERT Exemplar)

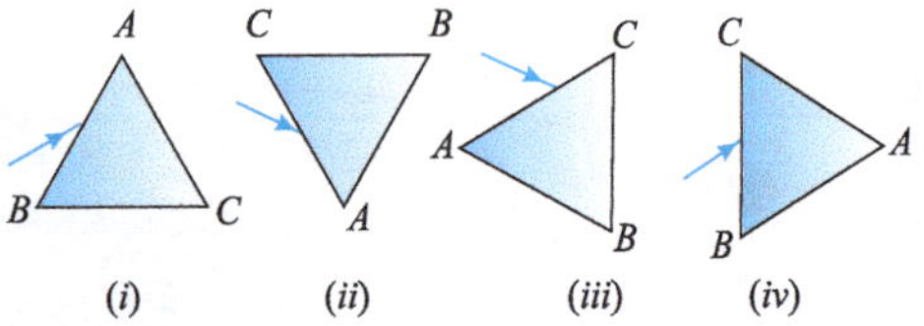

(*a*) (*i*) (*b*) (*ii*)
(*c*) (*iii*) (*d*) (*iv*)

2. At noon the sun appears white as (*Un*) (NCERT Exemplar)

(*a*) light is least scattered
(*b*) all the colours of the white light are scattered away
(*c*) blue colour is scattered the most
(*d*) red colour is scattered the most

3. Twinkling of stars is due to atmospheric (*Un*) (NCERT Exemplar)

(*a*) dispersion of light by water droplets
(*b*) refraction of light by different layers of varying refractive indices
(*c*) scattering of light by dust particles
(*d*) internal reflection of light by clouds

4. The clear sky appears blue because (*Un*) (NCERT Exemplar)

(*a*) blue light gets absorbed in the atmosphere
(*b*) ultraviolet radiations are absorbed in the atmosphere
(*c*) violet and blue lights get scattered more than lights of all other colours by the atmosphere
(*d*) light of all other colours is scattered more than the violet and blue colour lights by the atmosphere

5. Which of the following statements is correct regarding the propagation of light of different colours of white light in air? (*An*) (NCERT Exemplar)

(*a*) Red light moves fastest
(*b*) Blue light moves faster than green light
(*c*) All the colours of the white light move with the same speed
(*d*) Yellow light moves with the mean speed as that of the red and the violet light

6. Which of the following phenomena contributes significantly to the reddish appearance of the sun at sunrise or sunset? (*Un*) (NCERT Exemplar)

(*a*) Dispersion of light
(*b*) Scattering of light
(*c*) Total internal reflection of light
(*d*) Reflection of light from the earth

7. Choose the correct option for the colour of rays for A and B. (*Un*) (CBSE SQP, 2025)

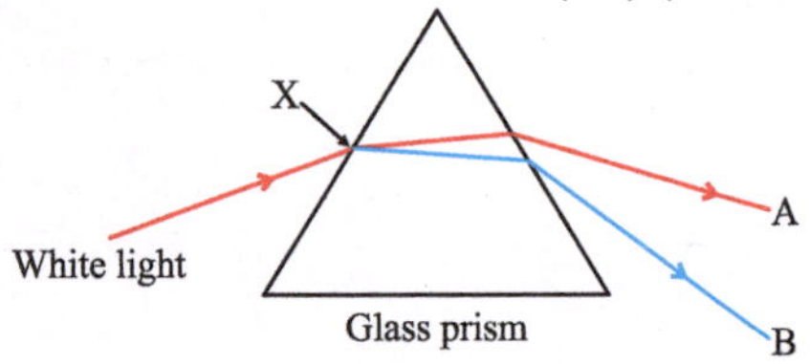

	Colour of Ray A	Colour of Ray B
(a)	Blue	Red
(b)	Green	Yellow
(c)	Red	Violet
(d)	Violet	Indigo

8. Which of the following statements is not true for scattering of light? ***(Un)*****(CBSE Term-II 2022)**

(a) Colour of the scattered light depends on the size of particles of the atmosphere.

(b) Red light is least scattered in the atmosphere.

(c) Scattering of light takes place as various colours of white light travel with different speed in air.

(d) The fine particles in the atmospheric air scatter the blue light more strongly than red. So the scattered blue light enters our eyes.

Assertion and Reason (1 M)

Direction: The following questions consist of two statements. Assertion (A) and Reason (R). Answer these questions by selecting the appropriate option given below:

(a) Both A and R are true, and R is the correct explanation of A.

(b) Both A and R are true, but R is not the correct explanation of A.

(c) A is true, but R is false

(d) A is false, but R is true.

1. **Assertion (A):** A prism disperses white light into its seven-colour components.
   Reason (R): Different colours of light bend through different angles with respect to the incident ray as they pass through a prism. ***(Un)***

2. **Assertion (A):** The stars twinkle while the planets do not.
   Reason (R): The stars are much bigger in size than the planets. ***(Un)***

3. **Assertion (A):** The twinkling of stars is due to the fact that refractive index of the earth's atmosphere fluctuates.
   Reason (R): In cold countries, the phenomenon of looming (i.e., ship appears in the sky) takes place, because of total internal reflection. ***(Un)***

4. **Assertion (A):** The sky looks dark and black instead of blue in outer space.
   Reason (R): No atmosphere containing air is in the outer space to scatter sunlight. ***(Un)***

5. **Assertion (A):** The light of violet colour deviates the most and the light of red colour the least, while passing through a prism.
   Reason (R): For a prism material, refractive index is highest for violet light and lowest for the red light. ***(Un)***

6. **Assertion (A):** The rainbow is a natural spectrum of sunlight in the sky.
   Reason (R): Rainbow is formed in the sky when the sun is overhead and water droplets are also present in air. ***(Re)*** **(CBSE, 2024)**

7. **Assertion (A):** Danger signals are made of red colour.
   Reason (R): Velocity of red light in air is maximum, so signals are visible even in dark. ***(Re)***

8. **Assertion (A):** The Sun appears flattened at sunrise and sunset.
   Reason (R): The apparent flattering of the Sun's disc at sunrise and sunset is due to atmospheric refraction. ***(Un)***

Subjective Questions

Very Short Answer Type Questions (2 M)

1. On what factor the colour of the scattered light depends? ***(Un)***

Ans. The colour of the scattered light depends on the size of the scattered particles. Fine particles scatter light mainly of shorter wavelength while large particles scatter light of longer wavelength. *(2 M)*

2. Define the dispersion of white light. Name the phenomena involved in the formation of a rainbow. ***(Re, Un)***

Ans. The splitting of white light into its constituents seven colours is called dispersion of light. *(1 M)*

The phenomena involved in the formation of a rainbow are dispersion, internal reflection and refraction. *(1 M)*

3. Why sky appears dark to passengers flying at high altitudes? ***(Un)***

Ans. The sky appears dark to passengers flying at very high altitudes mainly because:

(a) Scattering of light is not enough at such heights.

(b) There is no atmosphere at great heights.

(c) The size of molecules is smaller than the wavelength of visible light.

(d) The light gets scattered towards the earth. *(2 M)*

Key Takeaways

Remembering key facts can help answer straightforward questions correctly

4. Which colour of white light suffers (*i*) least deviation and (*ii*) maximum deviation when a beam of white light passes through a glass prism? ***(Un)***

Ans. Longer wavelength light (red) suffers the least deviation and shorter wavelength (violet) suffers maximum deviation when white light is passed through a prism. *(2 M)*

Short Answer Type Questions (3 M)

1. How will you use two identical prisms so that a narrow beam of white light incident on one prism emerges out of the second prism as white light? Draw the diagram. ***(An)*** **(NCERT Exemplar)**

Ans. By placing two identical prisms inverted with respect to the other, we get a narrow beam of white light incident on one prism and emerging out of the second prism again as white light. *(1 M)*

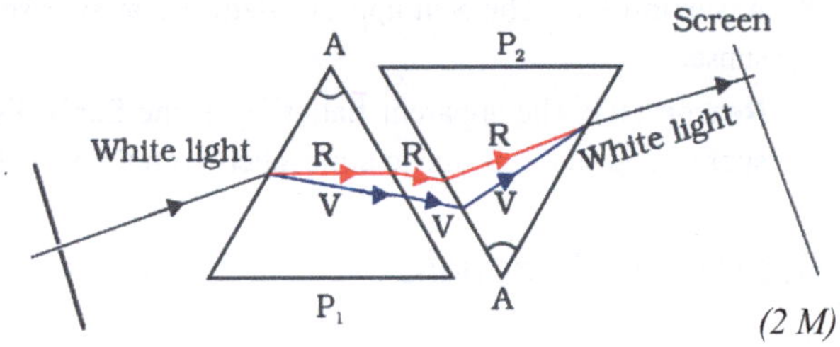

(2 M)

2. **Draw a ray diagram showing the dispersion through a prism when a narrow beam of white light is incident on one of its refracting surfaces. Also indicate the order of the colours of the spectrum obtained.**

(*An*) (NCERT Exemplar)

Ans. *(2 M)*

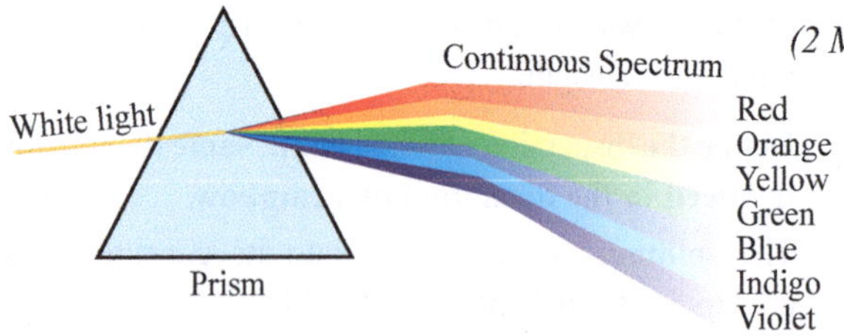

The order of colours from the bottom of the spectrum will be VIBGYOR.

V - Violet

I - Indigo

B - Blue

G - Green

Y - Yellow

O - Orange

R - Red *(1 M)*

3. **Is the position of a star as seen by us at its true position? Justify your answer.** **(*Re*) (NCERT Exemplar)**

Ans. The position of a star as seen by us is not its true position, but rather its apparent position. This is due to the fact that the light emitted by a star takes time to travel through space and reach us, and during this time, the star may have moved from its original position. Moreover, the apparent position of a star is also affected by various factors such as atmospheric refraction, which causes the apparent position of the star to be slightly shifted from its true position. To determine the true position of a star, astronomers use various techniques such as astrometry, which involves measuring the position and motion of stars relative to each other and to other celestial objects. These measurements can then be used to calculate the star's true position. *(3 M)*

4. **Why is the colour of the clear sky blue?**

(*Un*) (NCERT Exemplar)

Ans. The sky is blue due to a phenomenon called Rayleigh scattering. It refers to the scattering of white light by particles of a much smaller wavelength. The particles of the atmosphere scatter sunlight. Light with shorter wavelengths scatters more easily. These shorter wavelengths correspond to blue colours, which is why the sky appears blue to us. *(3 M)*

Nailing the Right Answer

Review your answer: If time permits, review your answer before submitting the test to catch any error or oversights.

5. **What is the difference in colours of the Sun observed during sunrise/sunset and noon? Give explanation for each.** **(*Un*) (NCERT Exemplar)**

Ans. The difference in colours of the Sun observed during sunrise/sunset and noon is due to the fact that sunlight travels through the Earth's atmosphere at different times of the day. During sunrise and sunset, the Sun appears to be red or reddish orange in colour. This is because the Earth's atmosphere scatters the shorter wavelengths of light (blue and green) more effectively than the longer wavelengths (red and orange). As the Sun's light travels through more of the atmosphere during sunrise and sunset, the blue and green wavelengths are scattered out, leaving the reddish and orangish colors to reach our eyes. *(2 M)*

At noon, when the Sun is highest in the sky, it appears to be bright white or yellowish in colour. This is because the sunlight is travelling through less of the Earth's atmosphere, so there is less scattering of the shorter wavelengths of light. The Sun appears smaller at noon because it is at its highest point in the sky, and the light has to travel a shorter distance through the atmosphere to reach our eyes. *(1 M)*

6. **Why is Tyndall effect shown by colloidal particles? State four instances of observing the Tyndall effect.**

(*Un & Re*) (CBSE 2020)

Ans. The Tyndall effect is shown by colloidal particles because the particles in a colloid are small enough to scatter light in different directions. When light passes through a colloid, the particles scatter the light in different directions, making the path of the light visible. This effect is not observed in a true solution, where the particles are much smaller and cannot scatter light effectively. *(1 M)*

Four instances where the Tyndall effect can be observed are:

1. **Fog:** When light passes through fog, the water droplets in the air scatter the light and make the fog visible. *(½ M)*

2. **Milk:** When a beam of light is passed through milk, the protein and fat particles in the milk scatter the light and make the path of the beam visible. *(½ M)*

3. **Smoke:** When light passes through smoke, the tiny particles in the smoke scatter the light and make the smoke visible. *(½ M)*

4. **Colored gemstones:** When light is passed through certain gemstones, such as a ruby or emerald, the particles in the gemstone scatter the light and create a beautiful display of colours. *(½ M)*

7. **Draw a labelled diagram to show (*i*) reddish appearance of the sun at the sunrise or the sunset and (*ii*) white appearance of the sun at noon when it is overhead.**

(*Un*) (CBSE 2020) (OS)

Ans.

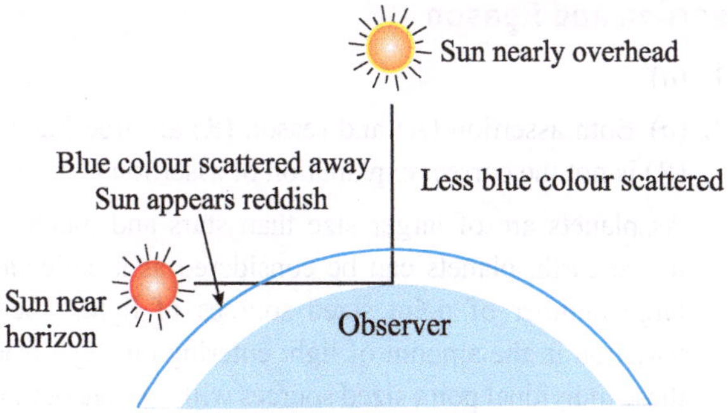

(3 M)

Long Answer Type Questions **(5 M)**

1. **State the cause of dispersion of white light by a glass prism. How did Newton, using two identical glass prisms, show that white light is made of seven colours? Draw a ray diagram to show the path of a narrow beam of white light, through a combination of two identical prisms arranged together in inverted position with respect to each other, when it is allowed to fall obliquely on one of the faces of the first prism of the combination.** ***(Re & Un)***

Ans. Cause of dispersion: From Snell's law of refraction, the angle of refraction of light in a prism depends on the refractive index of the prism material. Moreover, the refractive index of the material varies inversely with the speed of light and also varies inversely with the wavelength of light. Hence, different colours of white light bend through different angles with respect to the incident light, as they pass through the glass prism. *(2 M)*

Newton Experiment: Consider a prism A. When a beam of white light falls obliquely on one of the faces of this prism, it splits up into seven constituent colours. The violet colour deviates the most and the red colour deviates the least.

If another identical prism B is placed in an inverted position with respect to first prism A, the constituent coloured rays that emerge out of prism A will be made to merge together to come out as a beam of white light, as shown below.

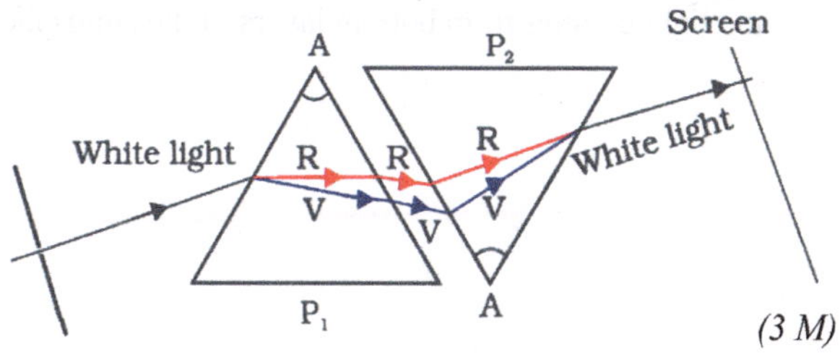

(3 M)

2. **(*a*) What is dispersion of white light? State its cause.**

   (*b*) "Rainbow is an example of dispersion of sunlight" Justify this statement by explaining, with the help of a labelled diagram, the formation of a rainbow in the sky. List two essential conditions for observing a rainbow. ***(Un & Re)***

Ans. (*a*) Dispersion of light refers to the process by which white light is separated into its component colours, which can be seen as a spectrum. This occurs when light passes through a medium, such as a prism, which bends the different colours of light at different angles, causing them to spread out and become visible as individual colours. *(1 M)*

The cause of dispersion of light is that different colours of light travel with different speeds in a denser medium. When light passes through a medium, the different colours of light are bent at different angles because the speed of light is different for each colour. This produces a spectrum.

In addition to prisms, other materials can also cause dispersion of light, such as water droplets in the atmosphere, which create rainbows when sunlight passes through them. *(1 M)*

(*b*) Rainbow: It is a natural spectrum, produced by the nature in the sky, in the form of a multicoloured arc. The rainbow is formed due to the dispersion of sunlight by water droplets suspended in the atmosphere after rainfall. These water droplets act like small prisms. The Sunlight enters the water droplets. At the point of incidence, it refracts and disperses then gets reflected internally and finally gets refracted again at the point of emergence as it comes out of the rain-drop.

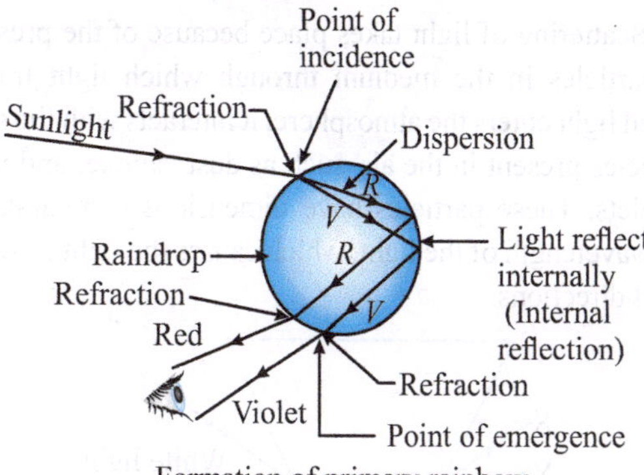

Formation of primary rainbow *(2 M)*

Therefore, due to refraction, dispersion and internal reflection of the sunlight, different colours reach the observer's eye along different paths and become distinct. It creates a rainbow in the sky.

Hence "Rainbow is an example of dispersion of sunlight."

Necessary conditions for the formation of a rainbow.

(*i*) The presence of water droplets in the atmosphere, and *(½ M)*

(*ii*) The sun must be at the back of the observer, i.e. the observer must stand with his back towards the sun. *(½ M)*

Mistakes 101 : What not to do!

Sometimes, students over analyze questions and choose incorrect answer due to second-guessing themselves.

Hints & Explanations

Multiple Choice Questions

1. (*b*) In the 2nd case (option (*b*)), after dispersion, the third colour from the top corresponds to the colour of the sky.
2. (*a*) At noon the sun appears white because of light is least scattered.

Nailing the Right Answer

Eliminate options: If uncertain, eliminate obviously correct option first. This increases the chance of selecting the correct answer from the remaining choice.

3. (*b*) Twinkling of stars is due to atmospheric refraction of light by different layers of varying refractive indices.
4. (*c*) The clear sky appears blue because violet and blue light get scattered more than lights of all other colours by the atmosphere.
5. (*c*) All the colours of the white light move with the same speed.
6. (*b*) Scattering of light contributes significantly to the reddish appearance of the sun at sunrise or sunset.
7. (*c*) Red Violet
8. (*c*) Scattering of light takes place because of the presence of particles in the medium through which light travels. When light enters the atmosphere, it interacts with the small particles present in the air, such as dust, smoke, and water droplets. These particles have dimensions comparable to the wavelength of the light, which causes the light to scatter in all directions.

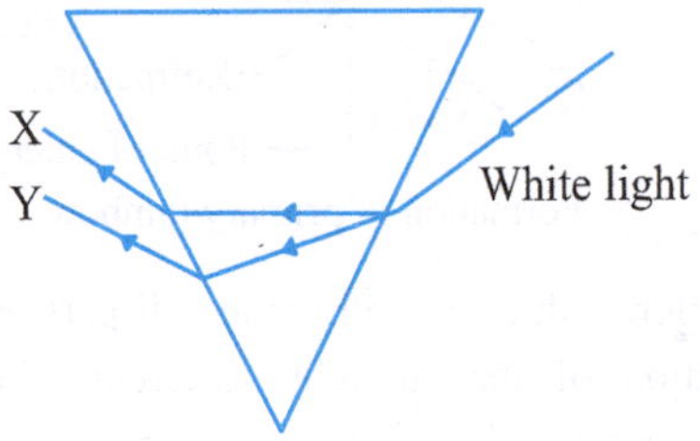

Assertion and Reason

1. (*a*)
2. (*b*) Both assertion (A) and reason (R) are true but reason (R) is not the correct explanation of assertion (A).

   As planets are of larger size than stars and much closer to the earth, planets can be considered as a collection of large number of point sized sources of light. The total variation in the amount of light entering our eye from all these individual point sized sources will average out to zero which nullify the twinkling effect of each other. Therefore, planets do not twinkle.
3. (*b*) Both assertion (A) and reason (R) are true but reason (R) is not the correct explanation of assertion (A).
4. (*a*) Both assertion (A) and reason (R) are true and reason (R) is the correct explanation of assertion (A).
5. (*b*) Both assertion (A) and reason (R) are true but reason (R) is not the correct explanation of assertion (A).

   The light of violet colour deviates most and the light of red colour the least, while passing through a prism.

   For a prism material refractive index is highest for violet light and lowest for the red light.
6. (*a*) The rainbow is indeed a natural spectrum of sunlight in the sky. When sunlight enters raindrops in the atmosphere, *it undergoes dispersion and internal reflection, resulting in* the separation of the white light into its component colors. This phenomenon occurs when the sun is low in the sky and raindrops are present, allowing for the formation of rainbows. Therefore, the presence of sunlight and water droplets in the air are necessary conditions for the formation of rainbows.
7. (*c*) Red colour scatters the least as it has the greatest wavelength. So red light is able to travel the longest distance through the fog, rain, and air particles. That is why the red colour is used in danger signals.
8. (*a*) The sun appears flat when near the horizon because of refraction of light. The atmosphere is made up of different layers of air each having a slightly different refractive index which causes uneven bending of sunlight. This bending causes the light coming from top layers to bend less than the light coming from bottom layers of the atmosphere.

MISCELLANEOUS EXERCISE

Multiple Choice Questions (1 M)

1. Which of the following phenomena of light are involved in the formation of a rainbow? **(*Re*) (NCERT Exemplar)**

(*a*) Reflection, refraction and dispersion

(*b*) Reflection, dispersion and internal reflection

(*c*) Refraction, dispersion and internal reflection

(*d*) Dispersion, scattering and internal reflection

2. The danger signals installed at the top of tall buildings are red in colour. These can be easily seen from a distance because among all other colours, the red light **(*Re*) (NCERT Exemplar)**

(*a*) is scattered the most by smoke or fog

(*b*) is scattered the least by smoke or fog

(*c*) is absorbed the most by smoke or fog

(*d*) moves fastest in air

3. The bluish colour of water in deep sea is due to **(*Un*)(NCERT Exemplar)**

(*a*) the presence of algae and other plants found in water

(*b*) reflection of sky in water

(*c*) scattering of light

(*d*) absorption of light by the sea

4. The sky appears dark to passengers flying at very high altitudes mainly because: **(*Un*)(CBSE-2020)**

(*a*) Scattering of light is not enough at such heights.

(*b*) There is no atmosphere at great heights.

(*c*) The size of molecules is smaller than the wavelength of visible light.

(*d*) The light gets scattered towards the earth.

5. In the diagram given below, X and Y are the end colours of the spectrum of white light. The colour of "Y represents the **(*An*)**

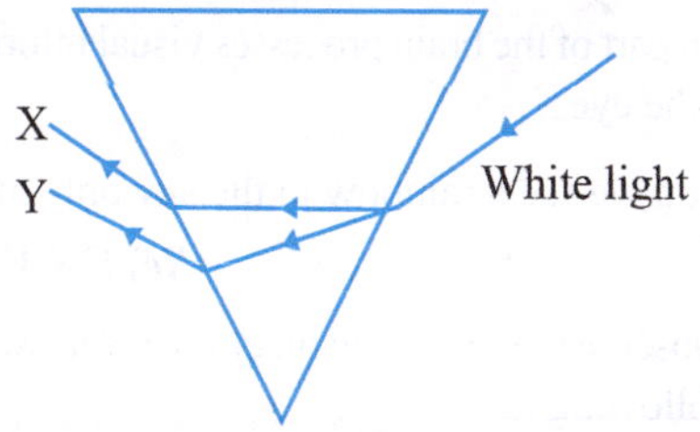

(*a*) Colour of sky as seen from earth during the day.

(*b*) Colour of the sky as seen from the moon.

(*c*) Colour used to paint the danger signals.

(*d*) Colour of sun at the time of noon

6. The near point and the far point are determined with regards to the function of which part of the eye? **(*An*)**

(*a*) pupil (*b*) retina

(*c*) eye-ball (*d*) ciliary muscles

7. Human eye is one of the most valuable and sensitive organ that **(*An*)**

(*a*) Enables us to see the wonderful world and colours around us

(*b*) Can identify the objects

(*c*) Is like a camera

(*d*) All of the above

8. Iris contracts the pupil **(*Re*)**

(*a*) In darkness (*b*) To allow less light to enter

(*c*) In bright light (*d*) Only (*b*) and (*c*)

9. Rohan is conducting an experiment to understand how the human eye adjusts to see objects at various distances. He is particularly interested in the process of accommodation. Rohan thinks that when the eye shifts focus from a distant object to a nearby object, the ciliary muscles play a crucial role.
Which of the following statements accurately explains the changes that occur during this shift in focus? **(*Re*)**

(*a*) The ciliary muscles relax, causing the lens to become thinner and decreasing its focal length.

(*b*) The ciliary muscles contract, causing the lens to become thicker and increasing its focal length.

(*c*) The ciliary muscles relax, causing the lens to become thicker and decreasing its focal length.

(*d*) The ciliary muscles contract, causing the lens to become thicker and decreasing its focal length.

10. If a person can see an object clearly when it is placed at 25 cm away from him but not distant objects he is suffering from: **(*Un*)**

(*a*) Myopia (*b*) Hypermetropia

(*c*) Astigmatism (*d*) None of these

11. Ravi is reading his favorite book under a dim light. He notices that the letters on the page appear blurry and strained after a while. **(*An*)**
What condition might Ravi be experiencing, and what is the solution?

(*a*) Myopia; use concave lenses

(*b*) Hypermetropia; use concave lenses

(*c*) Myopia; use convex lenses

(*d*) Hypermetropia; use convex lenses

12. The far point of a myopic person is 40 cm. To see the distant object clearly, the focal length and the power of the lens used should be: **(*Ev*)**

(*a*) –40 cm, –2.5 *D* (*b*) –25 cm, –4.0 *D*

(*c*) +40 cm, +2.5 *D* (*d*) –40 cm, +2.5 *D*

13. A normal eye is not able to see objects closer than 25 cm because **(*Un*)**

(*a*) The eye lens has the focal length of 25 cm

(*b*) The distance of the retina from the eye-lens is 25 cm

(*c*) The eye is not able to decrease the focal length beyond a limit

(*d*) The eye is not able to decrease the distance between the eye-lens and the retina beyond a limit

14. Nethra, who is a back-bencher, discovers one day in the class that she is unable to discern the details on the blackboard very well. When she visits an optician, he prescribes glasses for her. Which of the following statements is/are false? ***(Un)***

I. She suffers from myopia where the far point is nearer than the blackboard.

II. A concave lens with suitable power can help correct her vision.

III. Her eye is defective and is forming images in front of the retina.

IV. A concave lens or a convex lens may be used to correct her vision.

(*a*) Only I (*b*) I, II and III

(*c*) I, II and IV (*d*) Only IV

15. Match the following: ***(Un)***

Phenomenon		Reason	
A.	Rainbow	(*i*)	Scattering of light
B.	Twinkling of stars	(*ii*)	Dispersion of light
C.	Blue colour of sky	(*iii*)	Fluctuation in the refractive index of atmospheric layers
D.	Advancement of sunrise and delay of sunset	(*iv*)	Refraction of light

(*a*) A-(*ii*), B-(*iv*), C-(*i*), D-(*iii*)

(*b*) A-(*ii*), B-(*iii*), C-(*i*), D-(*iv*)

(*c*) A-(*ii*), B-(*i*), C-(*iii*), C-(*iv*)

(*d*) A-(*iv*) B-(*ii*), C-(*i*), D-(*iii*)

16. A person is suffering from both near sightedness and far sightedness. His spectacles would be made of ***(Un)***

(*a*) Two convex lenses with the upper lens having a larger focal length than the lower lens.

(*b*) Two concave lenses with the upper lens having a smaller focal length than the lower lens.

(*c*) A concave lens as the upper lens and a convex lens as the lower lens

(*d*) A convex lens as the upper lens and a concave lens as the lower lens

Assertion and Reason (1 M)

Direction: The following questions consist of two statements. Assertion (A) and Reason (R). Answer these questions by selecting the appropriate option given below:

(*a*) Both A and R are true, and R is the correct explanation of A.

(*b*) Both A and R are true, but R is not the correct explanation of A.

(*c*) A is true, but R is false

(*d*) A is false, but R is true.

1. **Assertion (A):** The phenomenon of scattering of light by the colloidal particles gives rise to the Tyndall effect.
Reason (R): The colour of the scattered light depends on the size of the scattering particles. ***(Un)***

2. **Assertion (A):** Sun appears reddish at the time of Sunrise and Sunset.
Reason (R): Distance travelled by sunlight in the atmosphere is lesser during sunrise and sunset as compared to noon. **(CBSE, 2022 Term-I) [OS]***

3. **Assertion (A):** Hypermetropia is corrected by using a concave lens.
Reason (R): Hypermetropia occurs when the image is formed behind the retina. ***(Un)***

4. **Assertion (A):** Presbyopia is commonly known as long-sightedness.
Reason r (R): Presbyopia is caused by the weakening of the ciliary muscles and loss of flexibility of the lens with age. ***(Re, Un)***

5. **Assertion (A):** A person with normal vision can see distant objects clearly as well as nearby objects.
Reason (R): The image formed by the lens of a normal eye falls precisely on the retina. ***(Un)***

6. **Assertion (A):** Cataract is the clouding of the lens inside the eye.
Reason (R): Cataract leads to a gradual loss of vision and can be corrected by using corrective lenses. ***(Re)***

7. **Assertion (A):** A person with color blindness cannot distinguish between certain colors, usually red and green.
Reason (R): Color blindness is a result of the absence or *malfunction of certain types of cones in the retina.* ***(Un)***

8. **Assertion (A):** The image formed by a myopic eye is in front of the retina.
Reason (R): Myopia is corrected by using a convex lens. ***(Un)***

Subjective Questions

Very Short Answer Type Questions (2 M)

1. Your friend is curious about how we see the world around us and asks you to explain the function of the human eye. To help them understand, you need to describe the main functions and processes involved in vision. What is the function of the human eye?

2. Which part of the brain processes visual information received from the eyes? ***(Re)***

3. Why do we see a rainbow in the sky only after rainfall? ***(Re)* (NCERT Exemplar)**

4. (A) Observe the following diagram and answer the questions following it: **(CBSE, 2023)**

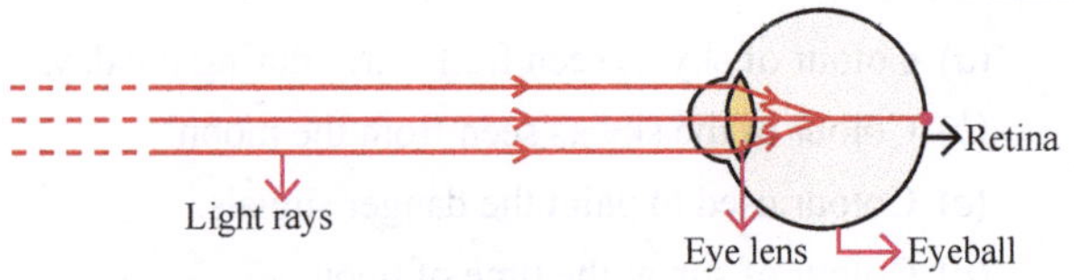

(*i*) Identify the defect of vision shown.

(*ii*) List its two causes.

(*iii*) Name the type of lens used for the correction of this defect.

OR

(B) The colour of clear sky from the earth appears blue but from the space it appears black. Why? ***(Re & Un)***

5. (*a*) A narrow beam *XY* of white light is passing through a glass prism *ABC* as shown in the diagram: ***(Un)* (CBSE, 2023)**

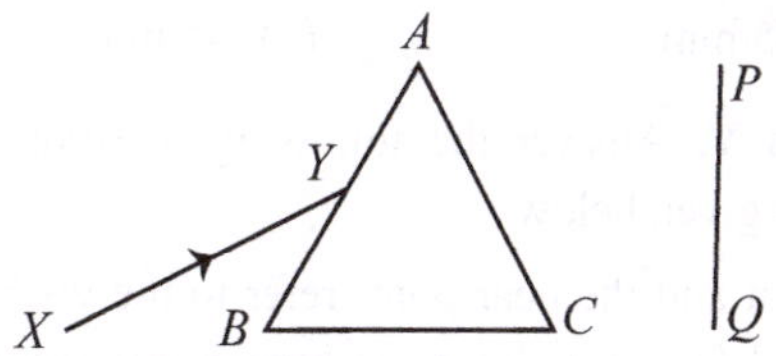

Trace it on your answer sheet and show the path of the emergent beam as observed on the screen *PQ*.

Name the phenomenon observed and state its cause.

OR

(*b*) It is observed that the power of an eye to see nearby objects as well as far off objects diminishes with age.

(*i*) Give reason for the above statement.

(*ii*) Name the defect that is likely to arise in the eyes in such a condition.

(*iii*) Draw a labelled ray diagram to show the type of corrective lens used for restoring the vision of such an eye.

6. Why is Tyndall effect shown by colloidal particles? State four instances of observing the Tyndall effect. ***(Un & Re)*(CBSE, 2020)**

7. Define the term power of accommodation. Write the modification in the curvature of the eye lens which enables us to see the nearby objects clearly? ***(Un & Re)*(CBSE, 2019)**

Short Answer Type Questions (3 M)

1. What is a rainbow? Draw a labelled diagram to show the formation of rainbow. ***(Cr & Re)* (CBSE, 2019)**

OR

Describe the formation of rainbow in the sky with the help of a diagram. **(CBSE, 2017)**

2. Due to gradual weakening of ciliary muscles and diminishing flexibility of the eye lens a certain defect of vision arises. Write the name of this defect. Name the type of lens required by such persons to improve their vision. Explain the structure and function of such a lens. ***(An, Un)***

3. Explain with the help of a diagram, how we are able to observe the sunrise about two minutes before the sun gets above the horizon. Hence, explain why does apparent duration of a day from sunrise to sunset is 4 minutes more than its actual duration. ***(An, Un)***

4. A person is suffering from an eye defect in which the far point of the eye is nearer than infinity. Identify the defect. List two main causes of this defect.
Draw a ray diagram to show how this defect is corrected by using a suitable lens. ***(Cr, Re & Un)*(CBSE 2019)**

5. (*a*) With the help of labelled ray diagram show the path followed by a narrow beam of monochromatic light when it passes through a glass prism. **(CBSE 2020)**

(*b*) What would happen if this beam is replaced by a narrow beam of white light?

OR

(*a*) A person is suffering from both myopia and hypermetropia. ***(Ev, Re & Un)***

(*i*) What kind of lenses can correct this defect?

(*ii*) How are these lenses prepared?

(*b*) A person needs a lens of power + 3D for correcting his near vision and –3D for correcting his distant vision. Calculate the focal lengths of the lenses required to correct these defects.

6. Draw a labelled diagram to show

(*i*) reddish appearance of the sun at the sunrise or the sunset and ***(Cr, Un & Re)***

(*ii*) white appearance of the sun at noon when it is overhead. **(CBSE, 2020)**

Long Answer Type Questions (5 M)

1. (*a*) What is presbyopia? State its cause. How is it corrected?

(*b*) Why does the sun appear reddish early in the morning? Explain with the help of a labelled diagram.

***(Cr, Re & Un)*(CBSE 2018)**

2. Explain the refraction of light through a triangular glass prism using a labelled ray diagram. Hence define the angle of deviation. ***(Cr & Un)* (NCERT Exemplar)**

OR

Explain the phenomenon of dispersion of white light through a glass prism, using suitable ray diagram.

(NCERT Exemplar)

3. How does refraction take place in the atmosphere? Why do stars twinkle but not the planets?

***(An, Re & Un)* (NCERT Exemplar)**

Case Based Questions

Case Based-I: Suppose a person is suffering from hypermetropia. The near point of the person is 1.5 m. The near point of the normal eye is 25 cm. ***(Ev)***

(i) Calculate the focal length of the lens. *(2 M)*

(ii) Which type of lens should be used in his spectacles? *(1 M)* ***(Re)***

(iii) Calculate the power of the lens. *(1 M)*

Case Based-II: Stars shine in the night sky due to their own light. When we look at a star in the sky on a clear night, we observe that the intensity of light coming from it changes continuously, however the planets do not appear to twinkle. ***(Un)***

(i) Explain why the planets do not twinkle? *(2 M)*

(ii) What happens to the intensity of starlight, when the atmosphere refracts less starlight towards us? *(2 M)*

Case Based-III: Atmospheric refraction is the phenomenon of bending of light on passing through the earth's atmosphere. As we move above the surface of the earth, the density of air goes on changing.

Local conditions like temperature etc. also affect the optical density of the earth's atmosphere. Following phenomena are due to atmospheric refraction of light: stars appear higher than they actually are; advanced sunrise; delayed sunset, the oval appearance of the sun at sunrise and sunset; twinkling of stars. **(Re)**

(*i*) Due to atmospheric refraction, the apparent length of the day (*1 M*)

(*a*) increases (*b*) decreases

(*c*) Remains the same (*d*) All of these

(*ii*) The apparent position of the star appears raised due to (*1 M*)

(*a*) Atmospheric refraction (*b*) Scattering of light

(*c*) Both (*a*) and (*b*) (*d*) None of these

(*iii*) The sun appears oval-shaped or flattened due to (*1 M*)

(*a*) Dispersion (*b*) Scattering

(*c*) Atmospheric refraction (*d*) Cannot say

(*iv*) In the absence of atmosphere, the colour of sky appears (*1 M*)

(*a*) Blue (*b*) Black

(*c*) Red (*d*) Yellow

Case-Based IV: Shushma is interested in photography and is learning about the role of lenses in capturing images. She is confused about how lenses work and what kind of lenses are used in cameras. She wants to learn the functioning of lenses in simple terms. Also, she is unaware of what kind of lenses are used in cameras and how they differ from the lenses in our eyes. **(Un)**

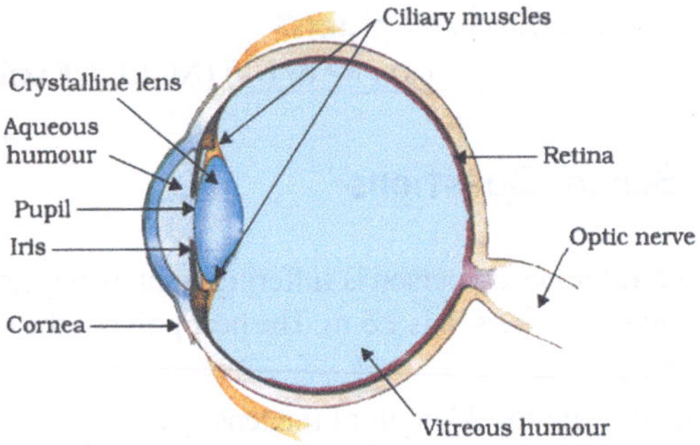

(*i*) How does the eye lens change shape to focus on objects at different distances? (*1 M*)

(*a*) It moves closer or farther away from the retina

(*b*) It changes color

(*c*) It changes shape by becoming more or less curved

(*d*) It expands or contracts

(*ii*) Far point of a normal eye is (*1 M*)

(*a*) 25 cm (*b*) infinity

(*c*) 50 cm (*d*) 75 cm

(*iii*) Round opening in the center of the iris is (*1 M*)

(*a*) Pupil (*b*) Cornea

(*c*) Retina (*d*) None of the above

(*iv*) What is the focal length of the human eye lens? (*1 M*)

(*a*) 15 mm (*b*) 25 mm

(*c*) 35 mm (*d*) 45 mm

Case-Based V: Answer the following questions based on the information given below:

The far point and the near point refer to the visibility of objects close by and far away from the human eye respectively. These are the maximum and minimum distances at which an object is clearly visible to a person.

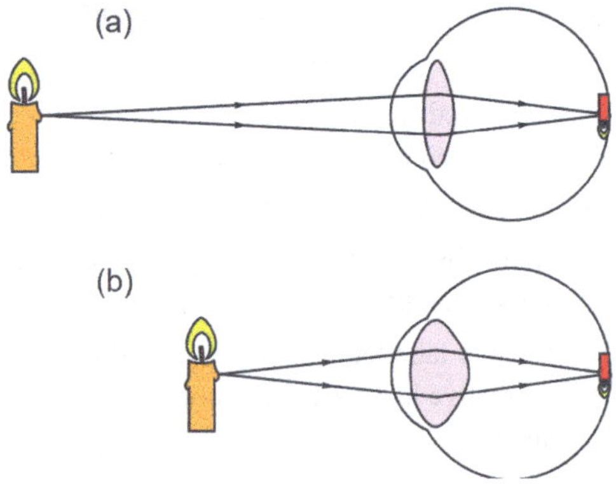

(*i*) The near point and the far point are determined with regards to the function of which part of the eye?

(*a*) pupil (*b*) retina

(*c*) eye-ball (*d*) ciliary muscles

(*ii*) Which of these is a reason why a far-sighted person needs a convex lens to correct his vision?

(*a*) The image forms in front of his retina.

(*b*) The image forms behind the retina.

(*c*) The image forms below the retina.

(*d*) The image forms on the retina.

(*iii*) Under which of these can myopia and hypermetropia be classified?

(*a*) breakdown of tissues

(*b*) incorrect bending of light in the eye

(*c*) incorrect reflection of light by surfaces around us

(*d*) incorrect coordination with brain for colour

(*iv*) What do the terms "far point" and "near point" refer to in the human eye?

(*a*) The maximum and minimum brightness levels visible to a person

(*b*) The maximum and minimum distances at which an object is clearly visible to a person.

(*c*) The points where the human eye focuses light most effectively.

(*d*) The ability of the eye to distinguish colors.

ANSWER KEYS

Multiple Choice Questions

1. (*c*)	2. (*b*)	3. (*c*)	4. (*a*)	5. (*c*)	6. (*d*)	7. (*d*)	8. (*d*)	9. (*d*)	10. (*a*)
11. (*d*)	12. (*a*)	13. (*c*)	14. (*d*)	15. (*b*)	16. (*c*)				

Assertion and Reason

1. (*a*)	2. (*c*)	3. (*c*)	4. (*a*)	5. (*a*)	6. (*a*)	7. (*a*)	8. (*c*)

Case Based Questions

Case Based-III

(*i*) (*a*) (*ii*) (*a*) (*iii*) (*c*) (*iv*) (*b*)

Case Based-IV

(*i*) (*c*) (*ii*) (*b*) (*iii*) (*a*) (*iv*) (*b*)

Case Based-V

(*i*) (*d*) (*ii*) (*b*) (*iii*) (*b*) (*iv*) (*b*)

HINTS & EXPLANATIONS

Multiple Choice Questions

1. (*c*) Refraction, dispersion and internal reflection of light are involved in the formation of a rainbow.
2. (*b*) The danger signals can be easily seen from a distance because among all other colours the red light is scattered the least by the smoke or fog.
3. (*c*) The bluish colour of water in deep sea is due to scattering of light.
4. (*a*) The amount of light scattering is much lower because of much less atmospheric substance at high altitudes. That's why sky appears dark to passengers.
5. (*c*) When white light falls on a prism, it splits into seven colours. The violet colour bends the most while the red colour least. Here in the given figure, y represents the red colour which is used to paint the danger signals.
6. (*d*) ciliary muscles.
7. (*d*) All of the above is correct.
8. (*d*) Iris contracts the pupil in bright light to allow less light to enter.
9. (*d*) The ciliary muscles contract, causing the lens to become thicker and decreasing its focal length.
10. (*a*) The person is suffering from myopia.
11. (*d*) Hypermetropia; use convex lenses.
12. (*a*) To see the distant object clearly, the focal length and the power of the lens used should be –40 cm and –2.5 D.
13. (*c*) A normal eye is not able to see objects closer than 25 cm because the eye is not able to decrease the focal length beyond a limit.
14. (*d*) Only option IV is false.
15. (*b*)
16. (*c*) His spectacles would be made of a concave lens as the upper lens and convex lens as the lower lens.

Assertion and Reason

1. (*a*) Both A and R are true, and R is the correct explanation of A.
2. (*c*) *Out of the Syllabus*
3. (*d*) Assertion is false, but the reason is true.

   The assertion is false because hypermetropia is corrected by using a convex lens. However, the reason is correct as hypermetropia occurs when the image is formed behind the retina.
4. (*a*) Both assertion and reason are true, and the reason is the correct explanation of the assertion.

   Both the assertion and reason are accurate. Presbyopia is indeed commonly known as long-sightedness, and it is caused by the weakening of the ciliary muscles and loss of flexibility of the lens with age, as explained in the reason.
5. (*a*) Both assertion and reason are true, and the reason is the correct explanation of the assertion.

   The assertion correctly describes the characteristics of normal vision, and the reason provides the explanation by stating that the image formed by the lens falls precisely on the retina, resulting in clear vision for both distant and nearby objects.

6. (*c*) Assertion is true, but reason is false.

Cataract is indeed the clouding of the lens inside the eye, and it can lead to a gradual loss of vision, which can not be corrected by using corrective lenses. It is possible to restore vision through a cataract surgery.

7. (*a*) Both assertion and reason are true, and the reason is the correct explanation of the assertion.

Both the assertion and reason are true. Colour blindness does result in the inability to distinguish between certain colours, typically red and green, and it is indeed caused by the absence or malfunction of certain types of cones in the retina, as explained in the reason.

8. (*c*) Assertion is true, but the reason is false.

The assertion is true, as a myopic eye forms the image in front of the retina. However, the reason is false because myopia is corrected by using a concave lens, not a convex lens.

Subjective Questions

Very Short Answer Type Questions

Nailing the Right Answer

- Explain the questions with the help of diagram.
- Mention the applicable concepts in each question.

1. The function of the human eye is to capture light from the environment, focus it onto the retina, convert it into electrical signals, and transmit these signals to the brain. The brain then processes these signals to produce the images we see, enabling us to understand and interact with our surroundings. *(2 M)*

2. The visual cortex is the part of the brain that processes visual information received from the eyes. It is located in the occipital lobe at the back of the brain and is responsible for interpreting and making sense of the electrical signals that are sent from the eyes through the optic nerve. *(2 M)*

3. We see a rainbow in the sky only after rainfall because raindrops act as tiny prisms that disperse, refract and reflect light. Sunlight is made up of different colours of light, each with a different wavelength and frequency. When sunlight passes through a raindrop, the light is refracted, or bent, and separates into its different colours due to the different speeds of the different wavelengths of each colour of light. *(2 M)*

4. **(A)** (*i*) The defect of vision is myopia. *(½ M)*

(*ii*) (*a*) The eye lens becomes too convex or curved.

(*b*) Depth of the eyeball is too much i.e. eyeball lengthened from front to back. When the length of the eyeball is too long as compared to the focusing power of the lens of the eye and cornea. *(1 M)*

(*iii*) Concave lens is used for the correction of this defect. *(½ M)*

OR

(B) The colour of the clear sky appears blue on the Earth because of the scattering of sunlight by the atmosphere. The blue light has a shorter wavelength and is scattered more than the other colours, making it more visible to our eyes. *(1 M)*

However, from space, the atmosphere is not visible, and the sky appears black. This is because there is no atmosphere to scatter the sunlight, and the scattered blue light does not reach space. Therefore, from space, the sky appears black. Hence, the colour of the sky appears blue from the Earth due to the scattering of sunlight by the atmosphere, while it appears black from space due to the absence of the atmosphere. *(1 M)*

5. (*a*)

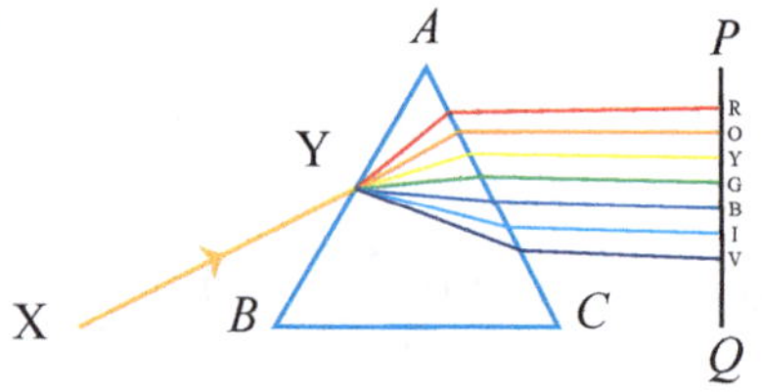

(1 M)

The phenomenon observed here is white light splits up into its constituent colours which is called dispersion of light. *(½ M)*

Different colours of white light have different wavelength, and as light passes through prism, the spread of each colour of light changes by different amount. The difference in speed causes the different colours of light to refract at slightly different angles, resulting in the separation of white light into its constituent colours, which is called dispersion of light. *(½ M)*

OR

(*b*) (*i*) It always happens in old ages because of loss of power of accommodation of the eye. *(½ M)*

(*ii*) The defect is called presbyopia. *(½ M)*

(*iii*) Presbyopia can be corrected by using both concave and convex lenses.

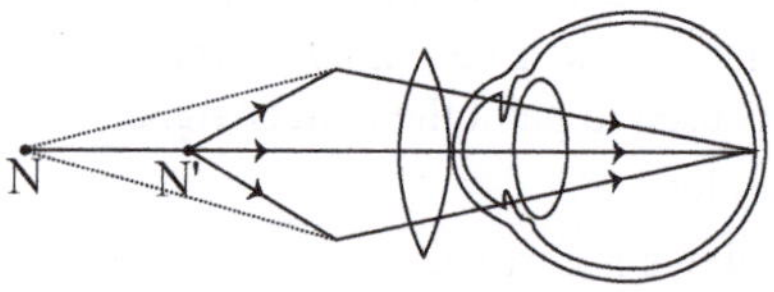

(1 M)

6. The Tyndall effect is shown by colloidal particles because of their small size and ability to scatter light. When light passes through a colloidal solution, the particles in the solution scatter the light, making it visible. This happens because the size of the particles is similar to the wavelength of visible light, causing the light to scatter in all directions. This scattering effect is known as the Tyndall effect. *(1 M)*

Four instances of observing the Tyndall effect are:

1. When sunlight passes through a cloudy sky, the scattered light makes the clouds visible.

2. When a beam of light is passed through a smoky room, the smoke particles scatter the light, making the beam visible.

3. When a flashlight is shone through a glass of milk, the scattered light makes the milk appear white or opaque.

4. When a laser beam is passed through a colloidal solution, the scattered light can be seen as a diffuse glow. *(1 M)*

7. Power of accommodation refers to the ability of the eye to adjust its focus to see objects at different distances. Accommodation is the modification in the curvature of the eye lens that enables us to see nearby objects clearly. *(1 M)*

When we look at a nearby object, the ciliary muscles surrounding the lens contract, causing the lens to become thicker and more curved. This increased curvature allows the lens to refract light more strongly and focus the image on the retina. The ability to accommodate decreases with age, resulting in presbyopia. *(1 M)*

Short Answer Type Questions

1. A rainbow is a natural spectrum appearing in the sky after a rain shower. Rainbow is caused by dispersion of sunlight by tiny water droplets hanging in the atmosphere after a rain shower. The water droplets act like small prisms. As shown in figure, the water droplets refract and disperse the incident sunlight. These rays are then reflected internally and finally refracted again and come out of rain drop. *(2 M)*

Due to the dispersion and internal reflection of light different colours reach the observer's eye and rainbow is seen.

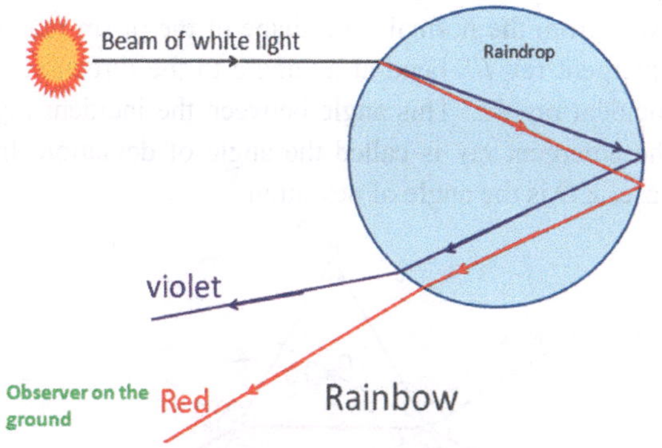

(1 M)

2. The defect of vision is Presbyopia. *(½ M)*

Bifocal lens is required by such persons to improve the vision. *(½ M)*

Structure and function of Bifocal lens

To view far off objects, the upper part of the bifocal lens is Concave or Diverging lens. *(1 M)*

To facilitate or view nearby objects, the Lower part of the bifocal lens is Convex or Converging lens. *(1 M)*

3. The air becomes rarer as its height above the earth increases. Its refractive index decreases. A ray of light from the Sun when it enters the atmosphere at the horizon gets refracted from a rarer to a denser medium. The rays, therefore gradually bend towards the normal and the Sun appears to be raised. *(2 M)*

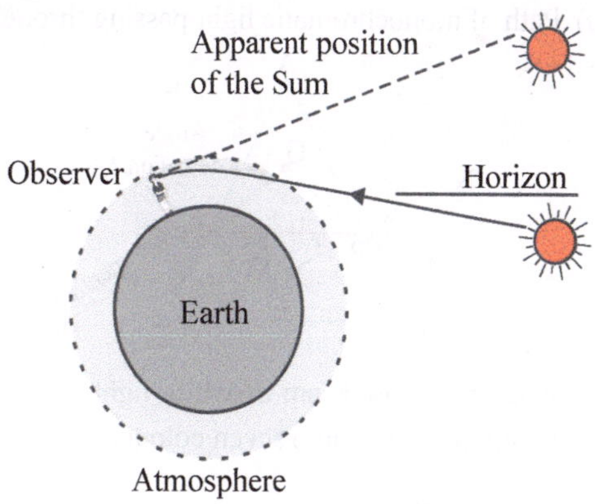

As a result, the Sun is visible to an observer nearly two minutes before actual sunrise at the horizon. Similarly, even after actual sunset, Sun is visible to us for about 2 minutes. Thus, in effect Sun is seen for 4 minutes more. It means that apparent duration of day (from sunrise to sunset) has increased by 4 minutes than its actual duration. *(1 M)*

4. Myopia is a defect in which person is able to see nearby objects but unable to see distinct object clearly. In it, an image of distinct object is formed in front of retina and myopic eye has its far point nearer than infinity.

Causes of Myopia:

(*i*) Eyeball becomes elongated

(*ii*) Eye lenses become more curved or increase in the curvature of the lens.

Correction of Myopia:

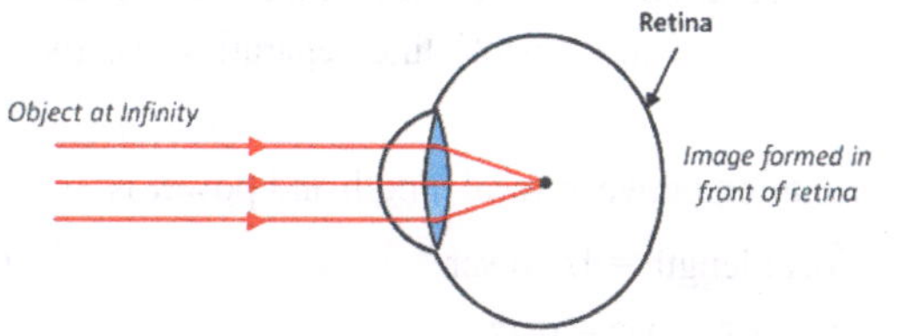

It is corrected by using concave lens as it helps to form image on the retina. *(1 M)*

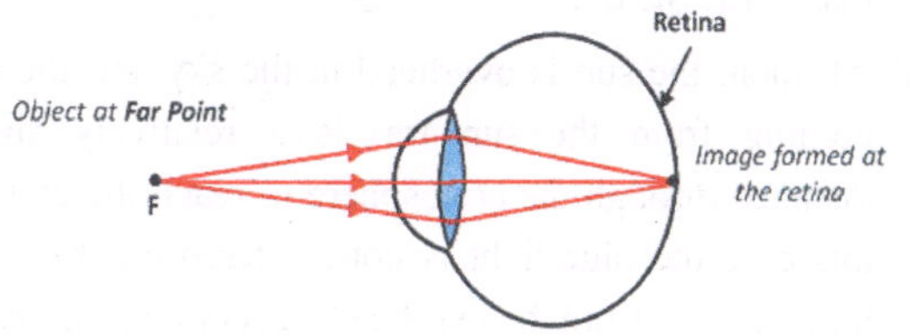

For a Myopic eye, image from infinity is formed in front of retina. It is not formed on the retina.

For a Myopic eye, the far point is less than infinity

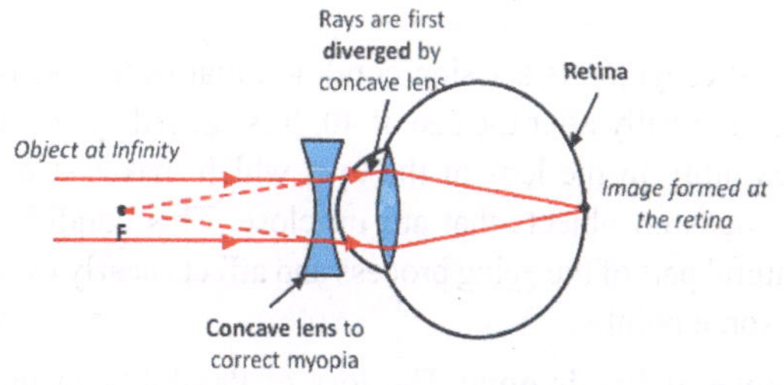

To correct myopia, we use a Concave lens *(2 M)*

5. (*a*) Path of monochromatic light passing through a prism

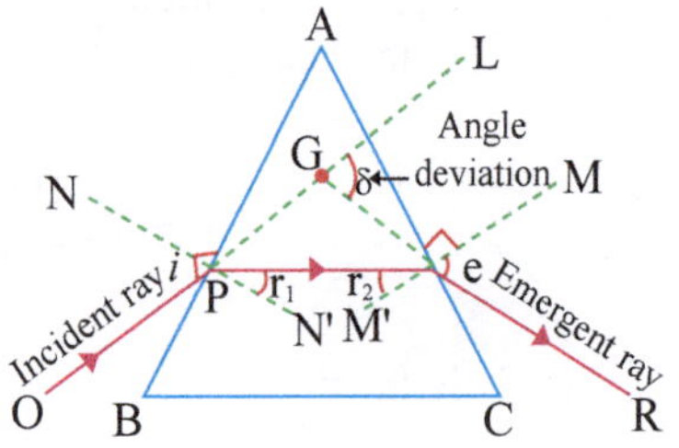

(*1½ M*)

(*b*) when a narrow beam of white light passes through a prism, it scatters into seven colours.

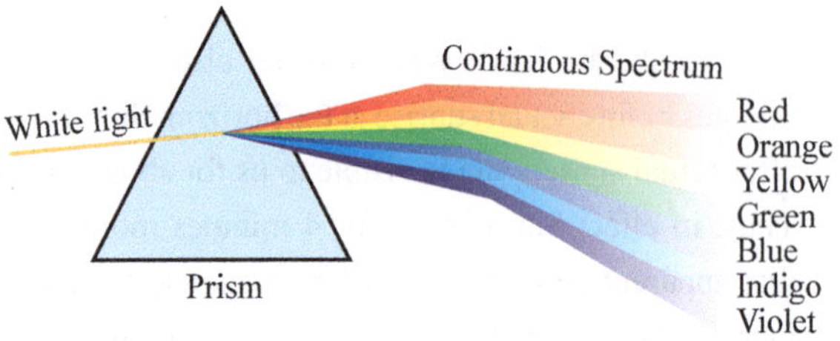

(*1½ M*)

OR

(*a*) A person suffering from both myopia and hypermetropia can correct their vision by using bifocal lenses. (*½ M*)

- Bifocal lenses have two different parts, one for nearsightedness (CONCAVE LENS) and the other for farsightedness (CONVEX LENS). (*½ M*)
- To prepare these lenses, the optician first determines the power of the lens needed for each condition and then combines them into a single lens with a visible line separating the two parts. (*½ M*)

(*b*) Relation between focal length and power is

Focal length = 1/ power (*½ M*)

Hence $f_1 = 1/3 = 0.33$ (*½ M*)

And $f_2 = 1/-3 = -0.33$ (*½ M*)

6. (*i*) *Out of the Syllabus*

(*ii*) At noon, the sun is overhead in the sky and the light coming from the sun travels a relatively shorter distance through the atmosphere to reach the earth. In this case the blue light is not scattered much. As the light coming from the overhead sun contains almost all its component colours in the right proportion, the sun appears white to us at noon. (*1½ M*)

Long Answer Type Questions

1. (*a*) Presbyopia is a vision condition that occurs as people age, typically after the age of 40. It is caused by the loss of flexibility in the lens of the eye, which makes it difficult to focus on objects that are up close. This condition is a natural part of the aging process and affects nearly everyone at some point. (*1 M*)

Cause of Presbyopia: The loss of flexibility in the lens occurs due to changes in the proteins in the lens, which makes it harder for the lens to change shape to focus on objects at different distances. As a result, people with presbyopia have difficulty reading or performing other tasks that require near vision.

Presbyopia can be corrected using glass of bifocal lens (*2 M*)

(*b*) Light coming from the sun near the horizon passes through thicker layers of air and travels considerable more distances in the earth's atmosphere before reaching our eyes. Therefore, most blue light and smaller wavelengths are scattered away by the particles near the horizon. As a result, the wavelengths of light that reach our eyes are longer. This gives rise to the reddish appearance of the sun. At noon, the sun appears white as only a little of the blue and violet colours are scattered. (*1 M*)

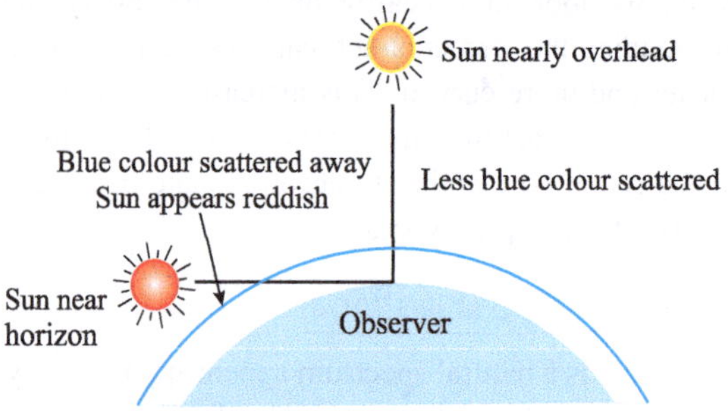

(*1 M*)

2. In the given diagram, *PE* is the prism's incident ray, *EF* is the refracted ray, and *FS* is the emergent ray from the prism. Incident ray of light *PQ* is entering from air to glass at the first surface *AB*. As the speed of light in glass is less than that in air, the refracted ray *EF* bends towards the normal. At the second surface *AC*, the light ray *EF* is incident from glass to air. As the speed of light in air is more than the speed of light in the glass, hence the emergent ray *FS* bends away from the normal. The shape of the prism makes the emergent ray *FS* bend at an angle to the direction of the incident ray *PE*. This angle between the incident ray and the emergent ray is called the angle of deviation. In this case, ∠*D* is the angle of deviation. (*3 M*)

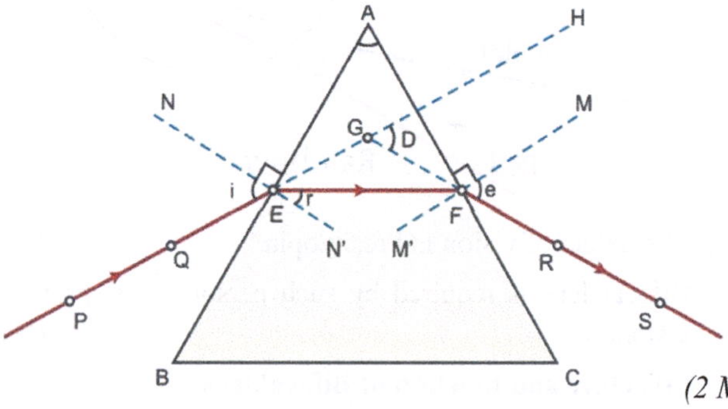

(*2 M*)

OR

The phenomenon of splitting white light into its seven components of colours when it passes through a glass prism is called dispersion of light. The different colours seen are Violet, Indigo, Blue, Green, Yellow, Orange and Red. The chronology of colours is known as VIBGYOR. The pattern of seven colours is called the spectrum of light. The different component colour of light bends at different angles for the incident angle. For example, red light bends the least while violet bends the most. (*3 M*)

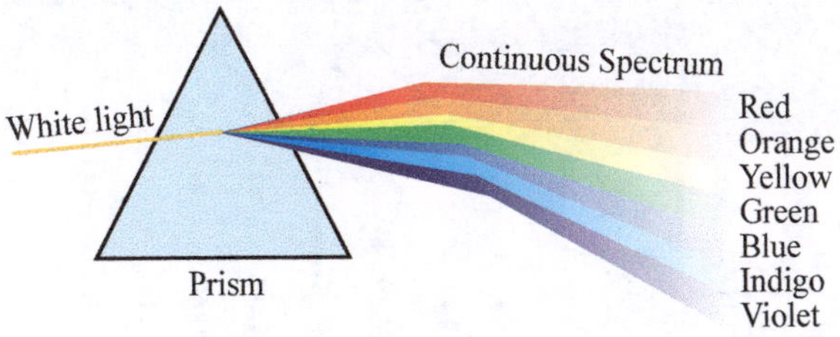

(2 M)

3. Refraction in the atmosphere occurs when light passes through the different layers of the Earth's atmosphere, each with a slightly different density. When light moves from one medium to another with a different refractive index, its direction changes. The atmosphere's varying density causes the light to bend, resulting in a phenomenon known as atmospheric refraction. *(2 M)*

Stars appear to twinkle because they are much further away from Earth than planets and are much smaller in size. When light passes through the Earth's atmosphere, the different layers of air with varying temperature and density cause the light to bend in different directions, leading to the twinkling effect. The effect is more pronounced for stars because their light has to travel a much longer distance through the Earth's atmosphere compared to planets, which are much closer to Earth. Planets do not twinkle because they are much closer and their light has to travel through less of the Earth's atmosphere, leading to less distortion and less of a twinkling effect. *(3 M)*

Case Based Questions

Case Based-I

(*i*) Given, near point (d) = 150 cm

D = 25 cm

v = – 150 cm

u = – 25 cm

From lens formula $\frac{1}{v} - \frac{1}{u} = \frac{1}{f}$

$$\Rightarrow \frac{1}{f} = \frac{1}{v} - \frac{1}{u} = \frac{1}{-150 \text{ cm}} - \frac{1}{-25 \text{ cm}}$$

$$= \frac{-1+6}{150 \text{ cm}} = \frac{5}{150 \text{ cm}} \Rightarrow f = 30 \text{ cm}$$ *(2 M)*

(*ii*) Convex lens is used to correct hypermetropia *(1 M)*

(*iii*) $P = \frac{1}{f(\text{in metre})} = \frac{1}{0.3} = 3.3D$ *(1 M)*

Case Based-II

(*i*) The planets are much closer to the earth and thus can be considered as the extended source of light. So, fluctuation in the light coming from various points of the planet gets averaged out due to atmospheric refraction and hence the plants do not twinkle. *(2 M)*

(*ii*) When the atmosphere refracts less starlight, then the star appears to be dim and when the atmosphere refracts more starlight towards us, the star appears to be bright. *(2 M)*

Case Based-III

(*i*) (*a*) Due to atmospheric refraction, the apparent length of the day increases by 4 minutes. *(1 M)*

(*ii*) (*a*) Apparent position of the stars appears raised due to atmospheric refraction. *(1 M)*

(*iii*) (*c*) atmospheric refraction *(1 M)*

(*iv*) (*b*) Due to no scattering of light. *(1 M)*

Case Based-IV

(*i*) (*c*) The eye lens changes shape by becoming more or less curved, which allows it to adjust its focal length and focus on objects at different distances. *(1 M)*

(*ii*) (*b*) Far point of a normal human eye is infinity. *(1 M)*

(*iii*) (*a*) Round opening in the center of iris is pupil. *(1 M)*

(*iv*) (*b*) The focal length of the human eye lens is approximately 25 mm. This means that the lens can converge light from an object at a distance of infinity to a sharp focus on the retina, which is located about 25 mm behind the lens. *(1 M)*

Case Based-V

(*i*) (*d*) Ciliary muscles *(1 M)*

(*ii*) (*b*) The image forms behind the retina *(1 M)*

(*iii*) (*b*) Incorrect bending of light in the eye *(1 M)*

(*iv*) (*b*) The maximum and minimum distances at which an object is clearly visible to a person. *(1 M)*

11 ELECTRICITY

"Electricity zips along at 300,000 km/s, just like light. It's crucial for powering everything from homes to gadgets, making our modern world possible in a flash."

SYLLABUS & WEIGHTAGE

LIST OF CONCEPT NAMES	YEARS				
	2020	2022	2023	2024	2025
Electric Current and Electric Potential (Electric current and circuit, Electric potential and potential difference)	—	—	—	—	—
Circuit Diagram and Ohm's Law (Circuit diagram, Ohm's law, Factors on which the resistance of a conductor depends)	1Q (3M)	—	—	1Q (1M) 1Q (2M)	1Q (4M)
Resistance of a System of Resistors (Resistors in series, Resistors in parallel)	—	1Q (3M)	1Q (1M)	1Q (1M)	1Q (1M)
Heating Effect and Electric Power (Heating effect of electric current, Practical applications of heating effect of electric current, Electric power)	1Q (1M) 1Q (3M)	1Q (3 M)	1Q (5M)	1Q (4M)	1Q (2M)

CONCEPT MAP

To Access One Shot Revision Video Scan This QR Code

ELECTRICITY

CBSE 2025, 2024, 2022, 2020

Electrical Energy(E):

E = P(in Kw) × T(in Hr)

1 KwH = 1000watts × 3600 sec

= 3.6×10^6 Joules

CBSE 2024

Electric Power(P):

Rate at which electrical energy is dissipated.

$$P = \frac{W}{t} = VI = I^2R = \frac{V^2}{R}$$

- Electric bulb to produce light
- Electric fuse that protects circuits and appliances.
- Electrical heating appliances.

Daily life applications

CBSE 2023, 2020

What is Joule's Law of Heating?

It states that the heat generated in a conductor by electric current is,

$H = I^2Rt = VIt$

1 Ampere:

When one coulomb of charge passes through a conductor in one second, the current flowing through it, is referred to as one ampere.

$$1 \text{ ampere} = \frac{1\text{coulomb}}{1 \text{ second}} = 1 \text{ C/s}$$

Electric Current

The flow of electric charge per unit of time.

$I = \frac{q}{t}$ or $q = It$

S.I. unit-Ampere(A)

What is an Electric Charge (Q)?

It is a basic property of particles that determines how they interact with electric and magnetic fields.

Types of charge:

1. Positive charge
2. Negative charge

S.I. unit – Coulomb (C)

Electric potential (V) is

The work done per unit charge to get a charge from infinity to a point in an electric field.

Potential Difference (V)

It is the potential created when transferring a charge from one point (A) in the field to another (B).

$$V = V_A - V_B = \frac{W}{Q}$$

1 Volt is defined as

The potential difference that exists when one coulomb of charge transfers between two points in an electric field with an energy change of one joule.

$$1 \text{ volt } (V) = \frac{1 \text{ joule } (J)}{1 \text{ coulomb} (C)} = 1JC^{-1}$$

Electric circuit

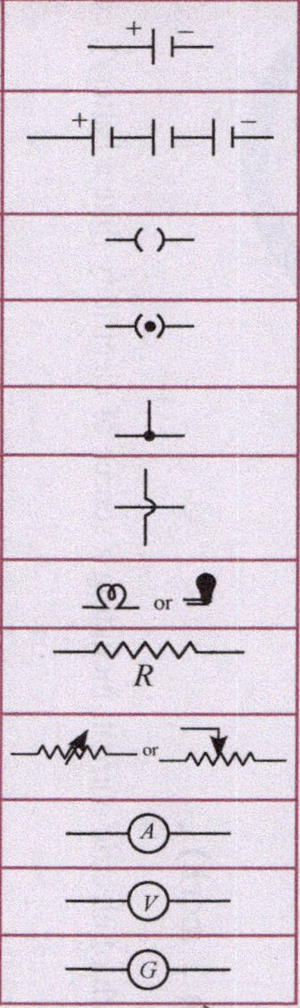

Components of Electric Circuit	Symbols
An electric cell	
A battery or a combination of cells	
Plug key or switch (open)	
Plug key or switch (closed)	
A wire Joint	
Wires crossing without joining	
Electric bulb	
A resistor of resistance R	
Variable resistance or rheostat	
Ammeter	
Voltmeter	
Galvanometer	

Ohm's Law states that

CBSE 2025, 2022

Voltage across a conductor directly relates to current when physical conditions and temperature remain consistent.

According to Ohm's law,

$V \propto I \Rightarrow V = IR$

The constant in the above relation is called resistance (R) of the conductor.

CBSE 2025, 2024, 2020

Factors Affecting the Resistance:

The resistance of a conductor depends upon (*i*) length (*ii*) cross-sectional area

$$\therefore R \propto \frac{\ell}{A} \Rightarrow R = \rho\frac{\ell}{A}$$

(ρ = constant of proportionality).

CBSE 2025, 2024, 2023, 2022, 2020

Resistors in parallel

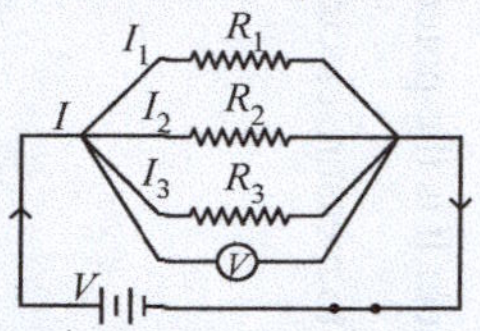

Equivalent Resistance of the Circuit:

$$\frac{1}{R_p} = \frac{1}{R_1} + \frac{1}{R_2} + \frac{1}{R_3} \quad \therefore \{R_p < R_1, R_2, R_3\}$$

Potential Difference: $V_p = V_1 = V_2 = V_3$.

Resistors in series

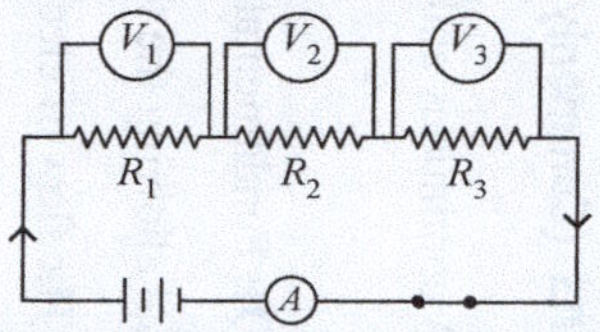

Equivalent Resistance of the Circuit:

$$R_s = R_1 + R_2 + R_3 \therefore \{R_s > R_1, R_2, R_3\}$$

Potential Difference: $V_s = V_1 + V_2 + V_3$.

ELECTRIC CURRENT AND ELECTRIC POTENTIAL

1

NCERT Definitions (Commonly asked in 1 mark)

- **Electric Circuit:** A continuous and closed path of electric current, including a source of electricity (like a battery), conductive path, and a load.
- **Electric Charge (Q):** Fundamental property of matter influencing it to experience a force within an electromagnetic field.
- **Conductor:** Material allowing the flow of electric charge due to the presence of free electrons, such as metals.
- **Electric Current:** The flow of electric charge through a conductor in a unit time, typically measured in amperes (A).
- **Ammeter:** An instrument for measuring electric current, connected in series with the circuit components.
- **Electric Potential:** The amount of work needed to move a unit positive charge from a reference point to a specific point inside the field without producing any acceleration, often called voltage and measured in volts (V).
- **Potential Difference:** It is the potential created when transferring a charge from one point in the field to another.
- **Voltmeter:** Device to measure electric potential difference, connected in parallel across the points of interest.

Important Facts

01 Electric charge is quantized (Q = ne), with the charge of one electron being approximately 1.6×10^{-19} coulombs.

02 Conventionally considered to flow from the positive to the negative terminal of a power source.
~Electric current

03 Voltage sources like batteries create potential differences to drive current flow in circuits, enabling the operation of electrical devices.

Classification

Charge	
Positive Charge	**Negative Charge**
Value- 1.6726×10^{-27} C	Value- 9.1094×10^{-31} C
Present inside the nucleus	Present in Electron Cloud
Moves towards negative	Moves towards positive
Repelled by other positive charges, attracted to negative charges	Repelled by other negative charges, attracted to positive charges
Creates outward electric field lines	Creates inward electric field lines
Conventional current flows in direction of positive charge	Electron flow (actual current) is opposite to direction of negative charge

Difference Between

Electric Potential vs. Potential Difference	
Electric Potential (V)	**Potential Difference (V)**
Refers to the work done per unit charge in bringing a charge from infinity to a point in space.	Refers to the work done to move a unit charge from one point to another.
Scalar quantity and has a value at a single point.	Always involves two points and indicates the difference in potential between them.
Indicates potential energy level at a point.	Measures energy difference that drives current.

Electric Current vs. Electric Charges	
Electric Charges (Q)	**Electric Current (I)**
It is a basic property of particles that determines how they interact with electric and magnetic fields.	It is the flow of electric charge through a conductor
Static (can be at rest) or dynamic (in motion as current)	Always dynamic, representing movement of charges
S.I unit is Coulombs (C)	S.I. unit is Amperes (A)

Important Formula

1. **Relation between Current and Charge**

$I = \frac{Q}{T}$; Where, I = Current(in A), Q = Charge(in C), T = Time(in sec)

2. **Relation between Potential Difference and Charge**

$V_{AB} = V_A - V_B = \frac{W}{Q}$; Where, V_A = Potential at point A(in V), V_B = Potential at point B(in V), W = Work done (in J)

Real Life Application Based Questions

1. **When we rub a balloon against our hair and bring it near the wall, it sticks. Can you give a reason behind this?**

Ans. Rubbing a balloon against hair transfers electrons from the hair to the balloon, giving it a negative charge. When brought near a wall, the balloon induces a positive charge on the wall's surface, causing attraction between opposite charges, making the balloon stick.

Static electricity

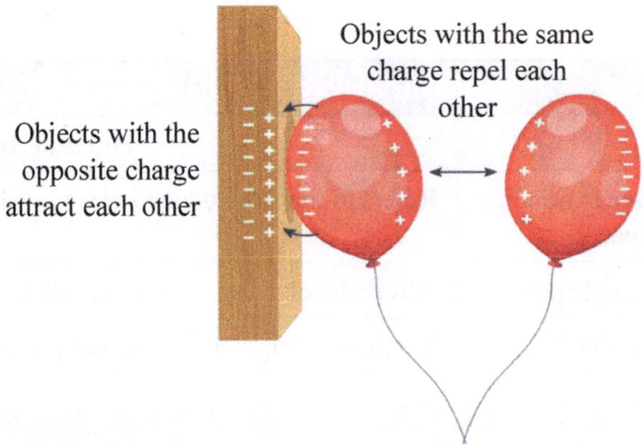

2. **How do the electrical circuits in your home work to turn lights on? Can you explain this process.**

Ans. In home lighting systems flipping a light switch either completes or breaks an electric circuit. Flipping the switch completes the circuit, enabling electricity to flow through the light bulb, producing light as the electrical energy is converted into light and heat energy by the filament inside the bulb.

3. **How do smartphones and electronic devices function smoothly, and what role do electric charges and currents play in this?**

Ans. When you power on or charge your smartphone or any other electronic devices, electrons flow through its circuits, creating an electric current. This current activates the device's components, allowing it to process data, illuminate the screen, and execute tasks.

4. **Why do electricians wear rubber gloves while working with electrical wires?**

Ans. Rubber is an excellent insulator and does not allow electric current to pass through it easily. By wearing rubber gloves, electricians protect themselves from electric shocks as the rubber prevents the current from passing through their body, ensuring their safety while handling live wires or components.

5. **Why do we often see birds sitting safely on high-voltage power lines without getting electrocuted, while touching a live wire on the ground can be fatal for humans?**

Ans. Birds can sit on high-voltage power lines without getting electrocuted because there is no significant voltage difference across their feet to create a current path. For current to flow, there needs to be a circuit, and a bird on a wire does not create one. In contrast, when humans touch a live wire on the ground, their body provides a path to the ground through which current can flow, potentially leading to electrocution.

6. **Do you know how electric vehicles get charged?**

Ans. During the charging process of an electric vehicle, the charger provides a higher electric potential compared to the EV's battery. This potential difference drives the flow of electric charges into the battery, storing energy. The charger must maintain a higher electric potential to ensure a continuous flow of charges until the battery reaches its full capacity, analogous to filling a tank with water from a higher-pressure source.

Myth Buster

- **Myth: The direction of conventional current flow is same as the direction of electron flow.**

  Fact: Conventionally, the direction of electric current is considered to be from the positive to the negative terminal of a power source, opposite to the direction of electron flow. This is known as conventional current direction.

❒ **Myth: Only metals can conduct electricity and overlooking the conductivity of other materials like electrolytes or semiconductors.**

Fact: While metals are excellent conductors, other materials such as ionic solutions (electrolytes) and semiconductors also conduct electricity under certain conditions. The mechanism of conductivity might differ, with ions carrying charge in electrolytes and electron holes in semiconductors.

Mnemonics

❒ $q = It$ can be memorise as ***quIt*** $(q = It)$

❒ **W = QV, Amount of work done by an electric current**

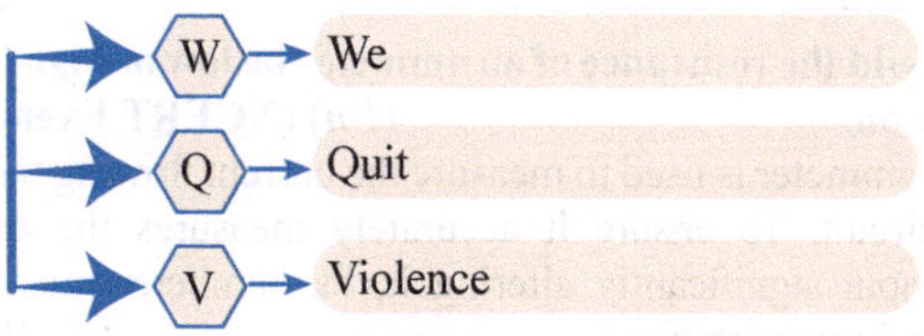

COMPETENCY BASED SOLVED EXAMPLES

Multiple Choice Questions (1 M)

1. A circuit contains cell, a resistor, a key, and an ammeter are arranged as shown in figure. ***(An)***

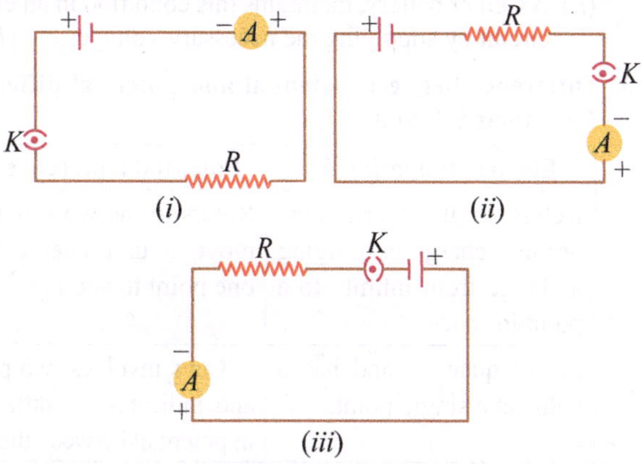

The current recorded in the ammeter will be

(*a*) maximum in (*ii*) (*b*) maximum in (*iii*)

(*c*) maximum in (*i*) (*d*) same in all the cases

2. Nisha is studying the concepts of electric circuits and electric potential in her physics class. Her teacher gives the class a problem to help them understand the relationship between electric charge, electric potential, and work done. The problem states that when one unit of electric charge moves from one point to another in an electric circuit, a certain amount of work is done.

When one unit of electric charge (1 Coulomb) moves from one point to another in an electric circuit, the amount of work done in joules, is known as: ***(Re)***

(*a*) Electric Current

(*b*) Electric Resistance

(*c*) Electric Potential difference

(*d*) Electric Power

3. Riya set up a simple circuit with a battery, a resistor, an ammeter, and a voltmeter. Riya varied the voltage applied to the circuit and recorded the current flowing through it.

Here is her observation

Voltage (V)	Current (A)
2	0.4

What is the resistance of the resistor used in Riya's experiment? ***(Ev)***

(*a*) 2 Ω (*b*) 4 Ω

(*c*) 5 Ω (*d*) 0 Ω

4. Which of these statement(s) is/are correct? ***(An)***

(A) Electric current is a vector quantity.

(B) The S.I. unit of electric charge is ampere.

(*a*) (A) only (*b*) (B) only

(*c*) Both (A) and (B) (*d*) Neither (A) nor (B)

5. Points *A* and *B* are at electric potentials 10V and 100V respectively. A charge *q* is taken from *A* to *B* and 18 Joule of work is done. The value of *q* is ***(Ev)***

(*a*) 2 Coulomb (*b*) 0.2 Coulomb

(*c*) 20 Coulomb (*d*) 0.02 Coulomb

6. In domestic electric circuits the wiring with 15A current rating is for the electric devices which have **(OS CBSE 2023)**

(*a*) higher power ratings such as geyser.

(*b*) lower power ratings such as fan.

(*c*) metallic bodies and low power ratings.

(*d*) non-metallic bodies and low power ratings.

Assertion and Reason (1 M)

Direction: The following questions consist of two statements. Assertion (A) and Reason (R). Answer these questions by selecting the appropriate option given below:

(*a*) Both A and R are true, and R is the correct explanation of A.

(*b*) Both A and R are true, but R is not the correct explanation of A.

(*c*) A is true, but R is false

(*d*) A is false, but R is true.

1. **Assertion (A):** Conductors allow the current to pass through themselves.
   Reason (R): Conductors have free charge carriers. ***(Re)***

2. **Assertion (A):** Electric current flows through a conductor when there is a potential difference across it.
   Reason (R): The potential difference creates an electric field that causes the free electrons in the conductor to move. ***(Un)***

3. **Assertion (A):** Doubling the time during which current flows through a circuit doubles the amount of charge that flows through it.
   Reason (R): The amount of charge (q) passed through a circuit is directly proportional to the time (t) and the current (I) as per the relationship q = It. ***(Un)***

Subjective Questions

Very Short Answer Type Questions (2 M)

1. **Name a device that helps to maintain a potential difference across a conductor.** ***(Re)*** **(NCERT Intext)**

Ans. Battery having one or more electric cells is one of the devices that help to maintain a potential difference across a conductor. *(2 M)*

2. **What is meant by saying that the potential difference between two points is 1 V?** ***(Un)*** **(NCERT Intext)**

Ans. When 1 J of work is done to move 1 C charge from one point to another, The potential difference between these two points is 1 V. *(2 M)*

3. **Aman is setting up a simple electric circuit to power a small light bulb for his school project. He uses metallic wires to connect the battery to the light bulb. To understand how the circuit works, he needs to know what causes the light bulb to light up. What constitutes the flow of charges in metallic wires in an electric circuit?** ***(Un)***

Ans. In a metallic wire, the flow of charges in an electric circuit is constituted by the movement of electrons. When the circuit is complete, the battery provides the necessary energy to push electrons through the wire, causing the light bulb to light up. *(2 M)*

4. **A circuit has a resistance of 20 ohms. If a current of 5 amperes flows through it for 10 seconds, calculate the charge passing through the circuit.** ***(Ev)***

Ans. Given: Resistance (R) = 20 ohms

Current (I) = 5 amperes

Time (T) = 10 seconds

Using the formula

Q = I × T, where Q represents the charge passing through the circuit, we can calculate: *(1 M)*

Q = 5 A × 10 s = 50 C *(1 M)*

Therefore, the charge passing through the circuit is 50 Coulombs.

5. **Define voltage and state its unit. Additionally, explain its role in electric circuits.** ***(Re)***

Ans. Voltage, also referred to as electric potential difference, is the measure of electric potential energy per unit charge in an electric circuit. It is quantified in volts (V) *(1M)*

Voltage serves as the driving force that prompts electric current to flow through a circuit. *(1M)*

Short Answer Type Questions (3 M)

1. **Should the resistance of an ammeter be low or high? Give reason.** ***(Un)*** **(NCERT Exemplar)**

Ans. An ammeter is used to measure the current flowing through a circuit. To ensure it accurately measures the current without significantly altering it, the ammeter must have very low resistance. *(1½ M)*

If it had high resistance, it would reduce the current flowing through the circuit, leading to incorrect measurements. Low resistance minimizes its impact on the circuit, allowing accurate current readings. *(1½ M)*

2. **(*i*) Mention the condition under which charges can move in a conductor.**
   (*ii*) Name the device which is used to maintain this condition in an electric circuit. ***(Re)***

Ans. (*i*) Setting up potential difference across the conductor, can result in the movement of charge through it. *(1½ M)*

(*ii*) A Cell or battery, maintains this condition in an electric circuit by supplying the necessary voltage. *(1½ M)*

3. **Difference between potential and potential difference. Give their S.I. unit.** ***(An)***

Ans.

Electric Potential (V)	Potential Difference (V)
Refers to the work done per unit charge in bringing a charge from infinity to a point in space.	Refers to the work done to move a unit charge from one point to another.
Scalar quantity and has a value at a single point.	Always involves two points and indicates the difference in potential between them.
Indicates potential energy level at a point.	Measures energy difference that drives current.

(3 M)

4. **A particle of charge 100μC is brought from infinity to a point in the electric field, 20 mJ work is done by the external forces. What is the potential at that point?** ***(Ev)***

Ans. Given $Q = 100\ \mu C = 100 \times 10^{-6}\ C = 10^{-4} J$

$W = 20\ mJ = 20 \times 10^{-3}\ J = 2\times10^{-2} J$ *(1 M)*

At infinity potential is zero

Using, $V_A - V_B = \dfrac{W}{Q}$ *(1 M)*

$\Rightarrow V - V_\infty = \dfrac{W}{Q}$ (let $V_A = V, V_B = V_\infty$)

$\Rightarrow V - 0 = \dfrac{2\times10^{-2}}{10^{-4}}$

$\Rightarrow V = 2\times10^{-2+4} = 2\times10^{2} = 200V$ *(1 M)*

Long Answer Type Questions (5 M)

1. **Explain the concept of electric charges, electric current, and voltage and their relationship in detail. Describe the factors that affect the flow of electric current through a conductor and how the resistance of a conductor can be determined. Also, provide some real-life examples of the use of these concepts and their importance in our daily lives.** ***(Re)***

Ans. **Electric charges:** Electric charges are a fundamental property of matter, and they can be either positive or negative. These charges are the source of electric fields, which cause electric forces between charged objects. The unit of electric charge is the coulomb (*C*). *(1 M)*

Electric current: Electric current is the flow of electric charges in a conductor. The unit of electric current is the ampere (*A*). The flow of electric current is influenced by various factors, such as the resistance of the conductor, the voltage applied, and the temperature. *(1 M)*

Voltage: Voltage is the potential difference between two points in a circuit, and it is measured in volts (*V*). Voltage is the force that drives electric current through a conductor. *(1 M)*

Relationship between electric charges, electric current, and voltage: Electric charges are the source of electric fields, which cause electric forces between charged objects. These electric forces can drive electric charges to move through a conductor, resulting in electric current. The amount of electric current that flows through a conductor is directly proportional to the voltage applied and inversely proportional to the resistance of the conductor. *(1 M)*

Factors that affect the flow of electric current: The flow of electric current is influenced by various factors, such as the resistance of the conductor, the voltage applied, and the temperature. The resistance of a conductor is determined by its length, cross-sectional area, and the material it is made of. The longer and thinner the conductor, the greater the resistance. The material of the conductor also affects its resistance, as some materials are better conductors than others. *(1 M)*

2. **(*i*) What is meant by electric current? Name and define its SI unit.**

(*ii*) In a conductor electrons are flowing from B to A. What is the direction of conventional current? Give justification for your answer.

(*iii*) A steady current of 1 ampere flows through a conductor. Calculate the number of electrons that flows through any section of the conductor in 1 second. (Charge on electron 1.6×10^{-19} coulomb). ***(Un + Ev)***

Ans. (*i*) **Electric current:** Electric current is defined as the flow of electric charge per unit of time.

When an electric charge (*q*) moves through a conductor during a certain period of time (*t*), the resulting flow of electric current (*I*) can be given as:

$$I = \frac{Q}{t} \qquad (2\ M)$$

Unit: Unit of electric current is Ampere(*A*)

(*ii*) **Definition of 1A:** When one coulomb of charge passes through a conductor in one second, the current flowing through it is referred to as one ampere.

$$1 \text{ ampere} = \frac{1\,\text{coulomb}}{1\text{ second}} \Rightarrow 1\,A = 1\text{ C/s} \qquad (1\ M)$$

Direction of current: The conventional direction of an electric current is the direction in which positive charges move in an orderly fashion. However, in metallic conductors, the current is actually carried by free electrons, which means that the direction of conventional current is opposite to that of electron flow.

In summary, conventional current and electron current flow in opposite directions in metallic conductors.

(*iii*) Charge, $q = It = ne$

$$n = \frac{It}{e} = \frac{1 \times 1}{1.6 \times 10^{-19}} = \frac{10^{19}}{1.6} = 6.25 \times 10^{18} \text{ electrons} \qquad (2\ M)$$

Hints & Explanations

Multiple Choice Questions

1. (*d*) The current would be the same in all cases as the values are not changing and the current does not change by changing the place of resistor, cell and ammeter or a key.
2. (*c*) The amount of work done to move one unit of electric charge (1 Coulomb) from one point to another in an electric circuit is known as the electric potential or voltage. It is measured in joules per coulomb (J/C), and the unit of electric potential is the volt (V).
3. (*c*) The resistance *R* of the resistor can be calculated using Ohm's law, $V = IR$.

   For the observations:

   When Voltage (V) = 2V, Current (I) = 0.4 A

   Using Ohm's law, $R = \frac{V}{I} = \frac{2}{0.4} = 5\Omega$
4. (*d*) Electric current is not a vector quantity. S.I. unit of electric charge is Coulomb.
5. (*b*) $W = \Delta V \times q = (V_B - V_A)q$

   $$\because q = \frac{W}{(V_2 - V_1)} = \frac{18}{100 - 10} = 0.2C$$
6. (*a*) Higher power rating such as geysers. This is because devices with higher power ratings require a higher current to operate and the wiring with 15*A* current rating can handle the load and prevent overheating and damage.

Assertion and Reason

1. (*a*) Conductors allow the current to pass through themselves by allowing the current to pass as easily as possible through their bodies. This is due to metals in conductors having free electrons that facilitate electricity flow, making both the explanation and the reasoning correct.
2. (*a*) Electric current flows through a conductor when there is a potential difference across it.

   An electric field in a wire, created by applying a potential difference, drives free electrons to move in the opposite direction at a drift speed.
3. (*a*) Assertion and Reason are True, and Reason correctly explains Assertion. According to the formula q = It, if you double the time, the charge flow also doubles.

CIRCUIT DIAGRAM AND OHM S LAW

2

NCERT Definitions (Commonly asked in 1 mark)

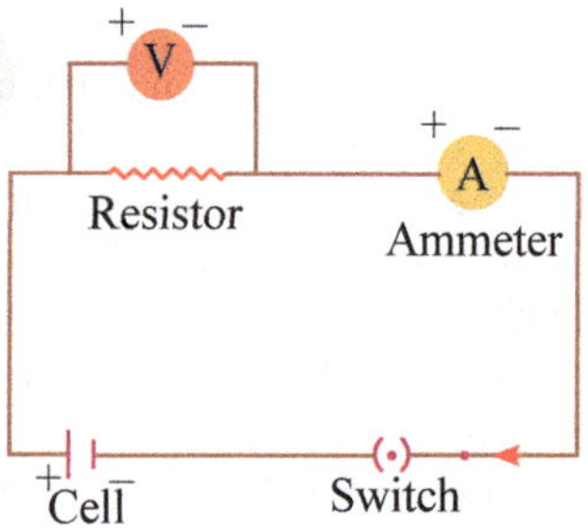

- **Circuit Diagram:** A visual representation of an electric circuit using symbols to depict components like cells, resistors, and switches.
- **Cell:** It is a device which generates a potential difference across its terminals, providing energy for current flow in a circuit.
- **Switch:** It is a component in a circuit used to open or close the path for current flow.
- **Ohm's Law:** A fundamental law stating that the current through a conductor between two points is directly proportional to the voltage across the two points.
- **Resistance:** A measure of the opposition to current flow in an electrical circuit, measured in ohms (Ω).
- **Resistivity:** A material property that indicates how much the material resists current flow, measured in ohm-meters (Ω-m).

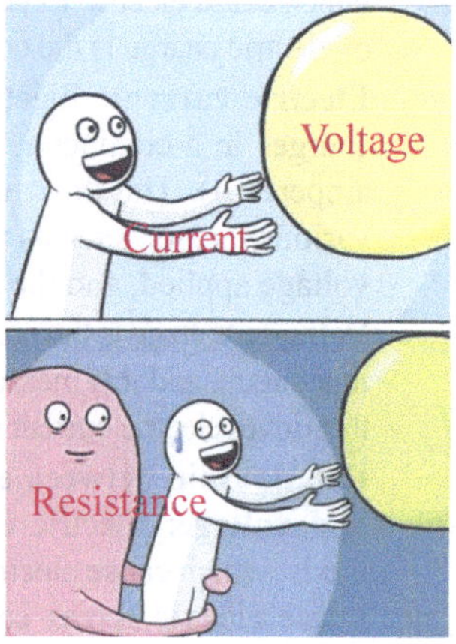

Important Facts

01 The resistance of a conductor is influenced by its material, length, and cross-sectional area.

02 The resistance of a conductor increases with length and decreases with an increase in cross-sectional area.

03 The resistivity of conductors increases with temperature.

04 Resistivity values of materials highlight the inherent property of materials to resist current flow, crucial for selecting appropriate materials for different electrical applications.

05 Insulators like rubber and glass have resistivity of the order of 10^{12} Ω m to 10^{17} Ω m.

Difference Between

Resistivity	Resistance
Intrinsic property of a material, indicating how strongly it opposes the flow of electric current.	Opposition to the flow of electric current through a conductor.
Does not depend on the dimensions of the material.	Depends on the dimensions: directly proportional to length and inversely proportional to cross-sectional area.
Measured in ohm-meters (Ω·m).	Measured in ohms (Ω).
Used to compare the inherent resistive qualities of different materials.	Used to understand how hard it is for current to flow through a specific conductor.
A constant for a given material at a given temperature.	Can be altered by changing the conductor's shape or material.

Important Formula

1. **Relation between Current and Voltage (Ohm's Law)**

   $I = \frac{V}{R}$; Where, I = Current(in A), V = Voltage(in V), R = Resistance(in Ω)

2. **Relation between Resistivity and Resistance**

   $R = \rho\frac{l}{A}$; Where, ρ = Resistivity (in Ω-m), l = Length(in m), A = Area(in m^2)

Real Life Application Based Questions

1. **Have you noticed that electrical wires are often made of copper or aluminum and not materials like iron or steel? What is the reason behind this preference?**

Ans. Copper and aluminium are preferred for electrical wiring because they have lower resistivity compared to materials like iron or steel, making them better conductors of electricity. Lower resistivity means less energy is lost as heat, improving the efficiency of power transmission. Additionally, copper and aluminium are more ductile, making them easier to bend and install.

2. **Ever wondered why the electrical wires used for transmission are thick? How does the concept of resistance affecting factors—length and cross-sectional area—justify the choice for thicker wires?**

Ans. Electrical resistance of a conductor is directly proportional to its length and inversely proportional to its cross-sectional area $\left(R \propto \frac{l}{A}\right)$. In power transmission, using thicker wires (greater cross-sectional area) significantly reduces their resistance, thereby decreasing the energy lost as heat and making the transmission more efficient. This principle ensures that more electrical power can be delivered over long distances without substantial losses.

Myth Buster

- **Myth: Ohm's Law is applicable under all circumstances in an electric circuit.**

  Fact: Ohm's Law holds true for ohmic materials where the resistance remains constant regardless of the voltage and current. However, it does not apply to non-ohmic materials where the resistance can change with voltage or current, like in semiconductor devices.

- **Myth: Resistance in a circuit decreases the amount of electricity.**

  Fact: Resistance does not reduce the quantity of electricity; it merely hinders the flow of electric charge. Resistance controls how quickly electrons can move through a circuit, impacting the current but not altering the actual amount of electrical energy supplied.

- **Myth: The thicker a wire, the higher its resistance.**

  Fact: The opposite is true. A thicker wire has a larger cross-sectional area, which allows more room for current to flow, reducing its resistance. Hence, a thicker wire has lower resistance compared to a thinner wire of the same material and length.

- **Myth: The resistance of a wire depends only on its material.**

  Fact: The resistance of a wire depends on its material, length, and cross-sectional area. A longer wire or one with a smaller cross-sectional area has higher resistance.

- **Myth: Resistance (R) and resistivity (ρ) are interchangeable and mean the same thing in electrical contexts.**

  Fact: Resistance is a opposition to the flow of electric current through a conductor and is measured in ohms (Ω). Resistivity is an intrinsic property of a material, measuring how strongly it resists current flow, and is expressed in ohm-meters (Ω·m).

Mnemonics

- **V = IR, Ohm's Law ("Veer")**

  V → Voltage (V)

  I → Current (A)

  R → Resistance (Ω)

COMPETENCY BASED SOLVED EXAMPLES

Multiple Choice Questions (1 M)

1. Which of the following is Ohm's Law? ***(Re)***

(*a*) $V = IR$ (*b*) $R = V/I$

(*c*) $I = VR$ (*d*) $V = I/R$

2. Raman wants to draw a graph to show how the resistivity (ρ) of a wire changes with the length (*l*) of the wire What should his graph look like? **(CBSE APQ, 2023)**

(*a*)
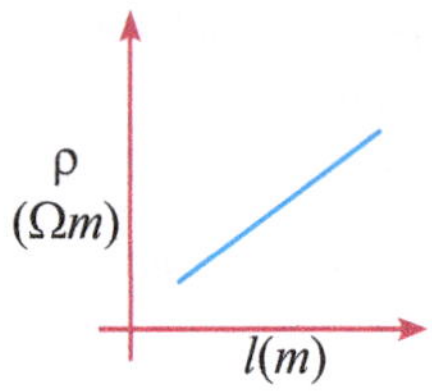

(*b*)
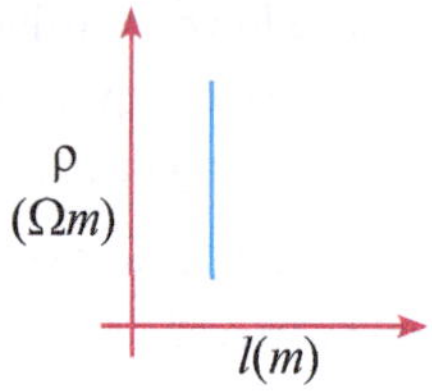

(*c*)
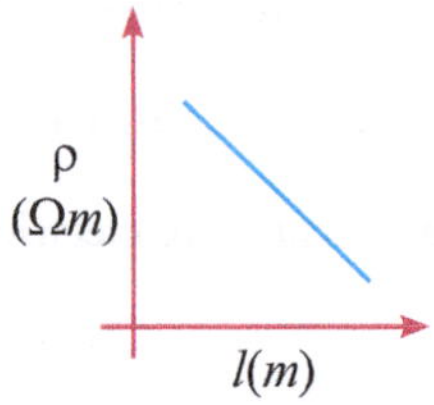

(*d*)
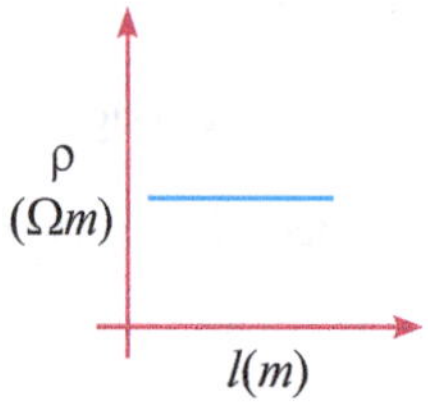

3. Which of the following materials has the highest resistivity? ***(Re)***

(*a*) Copper (*b*) Aluminum

(*c*) Tungsten (*d*) Silver

4. Which of the following statements is true about the resistance of a wire? ***(An)***

(*a*) Resistance is directly proportional to the length of the wire.

(*b*) Resistance is inversely proportional to the length of the wire.

(*c*) Resistance is directly proportional to the area of cross-section of the wire.

(*d*) Resistance is inversely proportional to the temperature of wire.

5. The resistance of a wire is 10 Ω. What will be its resistance if the length of the wire is doubled and the area of cross-section is halved? ***(Ev)***

(*a*) 10 Ω (*b*) 20 Ω

(*c*) 40 Ω (*d*) 80 Ω

6. The resistance of a wire is 2 Ω. If a current of 5 A is flowing through the wire, what is the voltage across the wire? ***(Ev)***

(*a*) 10 V (*b*) 2.5 V

(*c*) 7.5 V (*d*) 12.5 V

7. If you are conducting an experiment in your physics lab to verify Ohm's Law. As you set up your circuit with a resistor, voltmeter, and ammeter, you need to ensure accurate and reliable results. What are the crucial points you should keep in mind to verify Ohm's Law in this scenario? ***(Re)***

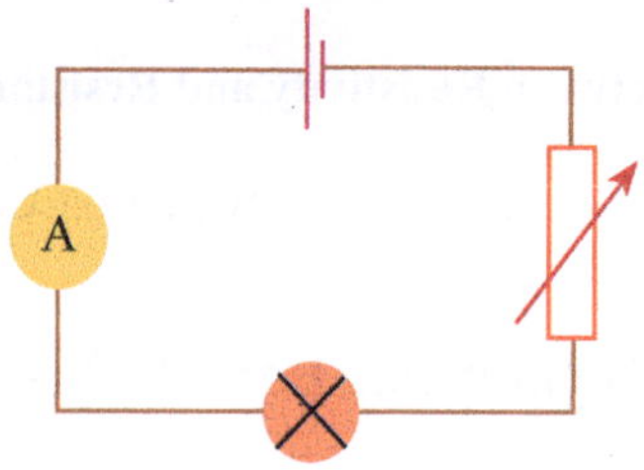

(*a*) Ammeter and voltmeter should be connected in series

(*b*) Ammeter should be connected in series and voltmeter in parallel

(*c*) Ammeter should be connected in parallel and voltmeter in series

(*d*) Ammeter and voltmeter should be connected in parallel

8. What will be the resistance of a wire if its length is 10 m and area of cross-section is 4×10^{-6} m^2, given that the resistivity of the material of the wire is 1.6×10^{-8} Ωm? ***(Ev)***

(*a*) 1.6 Ω (*b*) 4 Ω

(*c*) 10 Ω (*d*) 0.04 Ω

Assertion and Reason (1 M)

Direction: The following questions consist of two statements. Assertion (A) and Reason (R). Answer these questions by selecting the appropriate option given below:

(*a*) Both A and R are true, and R is the correct explanation of A.

(*b*) Both A and R are true, but R is not the correct explanation of A.

(*c*) A is true, but R is false

(*d*) A is false, but R is true.

1. Assertion (A): The current passing through a conductor is directly proportional to the potential difference across its ends.
Reason (R): This statement is in accordance with Ohm's law, which states that the current passing through a conductor is directly proportional to the potential difference across its ends. ***(An)***

2. Assertion (A): The resistance of a wire depends on its length, cross-sectional area, and resistivity.
Reason (R): Resistivity is a property of a material that determines the resistance of a conductor of unit length and unit cross-sectional area made of that material. ***(An)***

3. Assertion (A): The resistance of a conductor is directly proportional to its temperature.
Reason (R): When the temperature of a conductor increases, the atoms in the conductor vibrate with greater amplitude, which increases the resistance of the conductor. ***(Un)***

4. Assertion (A): The resistivity of a material depends on its temperature.
Reason (R): When the temperature of a material increases, the average velocity of the electrons in the material increases, which reduces its resistivity. ***(Un)***

Subjective Questions

Very Short Answer Type Questions (2 M)

1. State Ohm's Law and explain its significance in electrical circuits. ***(Re)***

Ans. Ohm's Law states that the current passing through a conductor is directly proportional to the potential difference applied across its ends, provided the physical conditions, such as temperature and pressure, remain constant. *(1 M)*

Ohm's Law is crucial in electrical circuits as it relates voltage, current, and resistance, enabling engineers to design efficient systems, ensure safety, and troubleshoot malfunctions effectively. *(1 M)*

2. Why do we use copper and aluminum wire for the transmission of electricity? Why not iron?(CBSE, 2017)

Ans. Copper and aluminium are good conductors of electricity because of it's low resistance and iron offers high resistance and it is not abundant in nature *(2 M)*

3. What is the resistivity of a conductor, write its S.I unit? ***(Re)***

Ans. The constant of proportionality 'ρ' is called specific resistance or resistivity of a material. *(1 M)*

$$\rho = \frac{RA}{l}$$

The S.I. unit of resistivity is ohm-m *(1 M)*

Short Answer Type Questions (3 M)

1. The values of current I flowing in a given resistor for the corresponding values of potential difference V across the resistor are given below: ***(Ap)*** **(NCERT Exercise)**

I (Ampere)	0.5	1.0	2.0	3.0	4.0
V (Volts)	1.6	3.4	6.7	10.2	13.2

Plot a graph between V and I and calculate the resistance of that resistor.

Ans. The graph between voltage and current is known as IV characteristic. The current is plotted in the y-axis while the voltage is plotted in the x-axis. The different values of current for different values of voltage are given in the table. The IV characteristics for the given resistor is shown below:

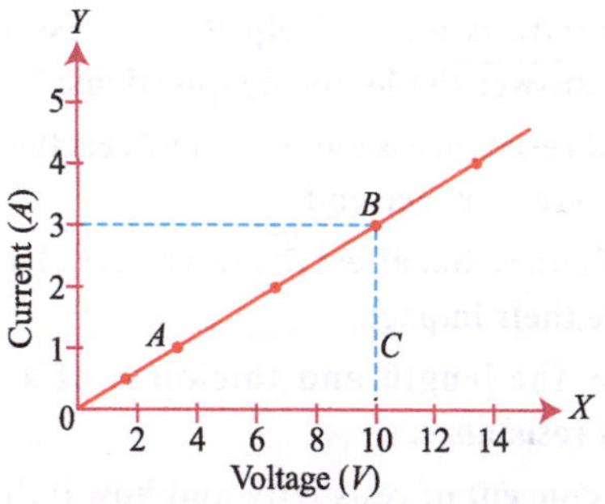

(2 M)

The slope of the line is equal to resistance.

The slope can be calculated as follows:

$$\text{Slope} = \frac{1}{R} = \frac{BC}{AC} = \frac{2}{6.8}$$

The resistance of the resistor, $R = \frac{6.8}{2} = 3.4\ \Omega$ *(1 M)*

2. Write the formula of resistance for a conductor, On what factors does the resistance of a conductor depend? ***(Un)*** **(NCERT Intext)**

Ans. The formula of resistance of the conductor $R = \rho(L/A)$, it depends on the following factors: *(1 M)*

(*i*) Length of the conductor *(½ M)*

(*ii*) Cross-sectional area of the conductor *(½ M)*

(*iii*) Nature of the material of the conductor *(½ M)*

(*iv*) Temperature of the conductor *(½ M)*

3. What is the resistance of a wire of length 2m and resistivity 10^{-8} Ωm and cross-sectional area 10^{-6} m²? ***(Ap)***

Ans. Resistance of a wire is given by $R = \rho(L/A)$, where ρ is the resistivity, L is the length of the wire and A is its cross-sectional area. *(1 M)*

Given, $L = 2\text{m}$, $A = 10^{-6}\ \text{m}^2$ and $\rho = 10^{-8}\ \Omega\text{m}$

$R = (10^{-8}\ \Omega\text{m} \times 2\text{m})/10^{-6}\ \text{m}^2 = 0.02\ \Omega$ *(2 M)*

4. Two wires of same material have their lengths in the ratio of 1:2 and diameters in the ratio of 2:1. What is the ratio of their resistances? ***(Ev)***

Ans. Resistance of a wire is directly proportional to its length and inversely proportional to its cross-sectional area.

Given, the lengths are in the ratio of 1:2, and diameters are in the ratio of 2 : 1. *(1 M)*

Hence, cross-sectional areas are in the ratio of $(2/1)^2 = 4$. *(1 M)*

Therefore, the resistance ratio is $(1/2) \times (1/4) = 1/8$ *(1 M)*

5. What is the effect of temperature on the resistance of a metallic conductor? ***(Un)***

Ans. The resistance of a metallic conductor increases with an increase in temperature due to the increase in the vibrations of the atoms of the conductor, which obstruct the flow of electrons. *(1½ M)*

Conversely, the resistance decreases with a decrease in temperature, as the vibrations of the atoms decrease, resulting in better flow of electrons. *(1½ M)*

6. What is the unit of resistivity, a current of 2A flows through a wire of resistance 10 Ω. Calculate the potential difference across the wire. ***(Ev)***

Ans. Unit of resistivity is ohm(Ω)-meter.

Using Ohm's Law, $V = IR$ *(1 M)*

Where V = potential difference, I = current, and R = resistance

Substituting the given values, we get:

$V = 2\ A \times 10\ \Omega = 20\ V$

Therefore, the potential difference across the wire is 20 V. *(2 M)*

7. **A wire has a resistance of 5 Ω and a length of 10 m. If the wire is stretched to double its length, calculate its new resistance.** **(*Ev*)**

Ans. Using the formula for resistance, R = ρ (L / A).

Volume of the wire = A × L

When the wire is stretched to double its length, L' = 2L, the cross-sectional area A' becomes A / 2 to conserve the volume. (A × L = A' × L') *(1 M)*

The new resistance R' = ρ (2L / (A/2)) = 4 × R.

Given R = 5 Ω,

R' = 4 × 5 Ω = 20 Ω.

So, the new resistance is 20 Ω. *(2 M)*

Nailing the Right Answer

- The mathematical equation for Ohm's Law is $I = V/R$, where I is the current, V is the voltage, and R is the resistance.
- The resistance of a conductor can be calculated using the formula $R = (\rho \times L)/A$, where R is the resistance, ρ is the resistivity, L is the length of the conductor, and A is its cross-sectional area.

8. **While studying the dependence of potential difference (*V*) across a resistor on the current (*I*) passing through it, in order to determine the resistance of the resistor, a student took 5 readings for different values of current and plotted a graph between *V* and *I*. He got a straight line graph passing through the origin. What does the straight line signify? Write the method of determining resistance of the resistor using this graph?** **(*An*) (CBSE 2019)**

Ans. When the student took 5 readings for different values of *R* and the student gets a straight line graph. *(1 M)*
This verifies Ohm's law.
Ohm's law states that the current through a conductor between two points is directly proportional to the voltage across the two points So, if you plot a graph of current against voltage you will get:

$I \propto V$

$I = \frac{V}{R}$

$R = \frac{V}{I}$ *(2 M)*

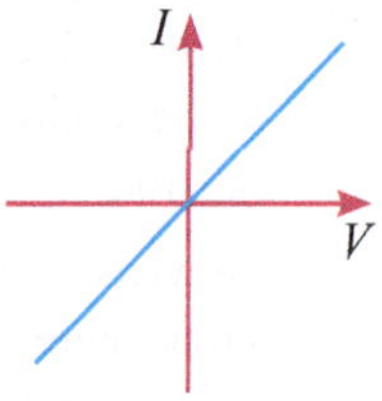

Long Answer Type Questions (5 M)

1. **Ravi is conducting an experiment to understand the relationship between the potential difference and the current through a conductor. He has a setup that includes a variable power supply, a conductor, and measuring instruments to record the potential difference across the conductor and the current flowing through it.**

   Explain Ohm's Law and how it describes the relationship between the potential difference across a conductor and the current flowing through it. **(*Un*)**

Ans. Ohm's Law states that the current (I) flowing through a conductor between two points is directly proportional to the potential difference (V) across the two points. This relationship is mathematically expressed as: *(1 M)*

V = I × R

Where:

V is the potential difference (voltage) across the conductor (in volts, V),

I is the current flowing through the conductor (in amperes, A),

R is the resistance of the conductor (in ohms, Ω). *(1 M)*

According to Ohm's Law, as the potential difference increases, the current increases proportionally, assuming the resistance remains constant. This relationship allows Ravi to determine the resistance of the conductor by rearranging the formula to R = V/I. *(1 M)*

2. **(*a*) List the factors on which the resistance of a conductor in the shape of a wire depends.**

   (*b*) Why are metals good conductors of electricity whereas glass is a bad conductor of electricity ? Give reason.

   (*c*) Why are alloys commonly used in electrical heating devices? Give reason. **(*Un*)**

Ans. (*a*) Resistance of a conductor depends upon the following factors:

(*i*) Length of the conductor : (Greater the length (*l*) of the conductor more will be the resistance (*R*).

$R \propto l$

(*ii*) Area of cross section of the conductor: (greater the cross-sectional area of the conductor, less will be the resistance.

$R \propto 1/A$

(*iii*) Nature of conductor. *(2 M)*

(*b*) Metal have very low resistivity and hence they are good conductors of electricity.

Whereas glass has very high resistivity so glass is a bad conductor of electricity. *(1½ M)*

(*c*) Alloys are commonly used in electrical heating devices due to the following reasons

(*i*) Alloys have higher resistivity than metals

(*ii*) Alloys do not get oxidised or burn readily. *(1½ M)*

3. **Rahul is conducting an experiment to investigate the relationship between resistance and various factors affecting it. He sets up a circuit consisting of a power supply, an ammeter, a voltmeter, and different resistors. He wants to understand how resistance is affected by the length and thickness of a wire, as well as the material from which the wire is made. Help Rahul design his experiment and answer the following questions:**

   (*a*) Explain what resistance is and how it affects the flow of electric current in a circuit. **(*Un*)**

   (*b*) Outline the factors that affect the resistance of a wire and describe their impact. **(*Un*)**

   (*c*) Discuss how the length and thickness of a wire influence its resistance. **(*An*)**

   (*d*) Explain the concept of resistivity and how it differs for different materials. **(*Un*)**

(*e*) **Suggest an experimental setup for Rahul to measure the resistance of wires of different lengths and thicknesses, and explain the procedure he should follow.** ***(An)***

Ans. (*a*) Resistance is the opposition offered by a material to the flow of electric current. It restricts the movement of electric charges through a conductor. A higher resistance means it is more difficult for the current to flow, while a lower resistance allows for easier current flow. Resistance is measured in ohms (Ω) and is denoted by the symbol '*R*'. According to Ohm's Law, resistance is directly proportional to the voltage across a conductor and inversely proportional to the current flowing through it. *(1 M)*

(*b*) Several factors affect the resistance of a wire, including its length, thickness (cross-sectional area), and the material from which it is made. Temperature also has an impact on resistance. An increase in length leads to higher resistance, as there is a longer path for the current to travel. On the other hand, an increase in thickness decreases resistance since a thicker wire provides more pathways for current flow. The material's electrical properties, such as resistivity, also affect resistance. *(1 M)*

(*c*) The length of a wire is directly proportional to its resistance. This means that as the length of the wire increases, the resistance also increases. The thickness of a wire is inversely proportional to its resistance. As the wire's thickness (cross-sectional area) increases, the resistance decreases. This is because a thicker wire allows for more current-carrying capacity and reduces the opposition to current flow. *(1 M)*

(*d*) Resistivity is a property of a material that determines its ability to resist the flow of electric current. It is denoted by the symbol 'ρ' (rho). Resistivity depends on the nature of the material and its temperature. Different materials have different resistivities, which is a measure of their inherent resistance to current flow. Materials with higher resistivities, such as rubber or glass, have higher resistance to current flow compared to materials with lower resistivities, such as copper or silver. *(1 M)*

(*e*) To measure the resistance of wires of different lengths and thicknesses, Rahul can set up the following experimental setup:

Connect the power supply, ammeter, voltmeter, and the wire whose resistance he wants to measure in series.

Choose wires of different lengths and thicknesses for the experiment.

Measure the length of each wire using a ruler and record the values.

Measure the diameter of each wire using a micrometer or vernier caliper and record the values.

Apply a constant voltage from the power supply and note the current reading from the ammeter.

Measure the voltage across the wire using the voltmeter. *(1 M)*

Hints & Explanations

Multiple Choice Questions

1. (*a*) The potential difference V across the metallic wire is directly proportional to the current flowing through it, provided its temperature is constant.

2. (*d*)

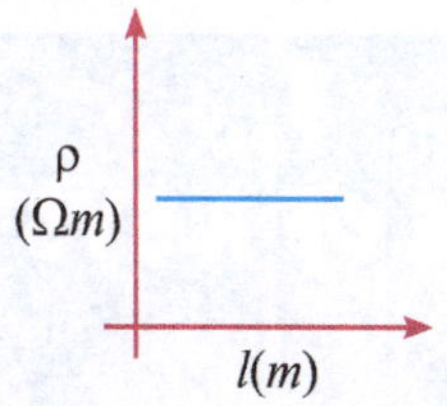

3. (*c*) Tungsten has the highest resistivity.

4. (*a*) Resistance is directly proportional to the length of a wire. It is inversely proportional to the area of cross-section the wire and directly proportional to the temperature of the wire as resistivity increases with temperature.

5. (*c*) Given R = 10Ω

$$R = \rho\frac{l}{A}$$

If l is doubled and A is having

$$R = 4\rho\frac{l}{A}$$

So $R = 40\Omega$

6. (*a*) Given $R = 2\Omega$

$I = 5A$

$V = IR$

$V = 5 \times 2 = 10V$

7. (*b*) Ammeter should be connected in series and voltmeter in parallel.

This setup ensures that the ammeter measures the current flowing through the resistor accurately, and the voltmeter measures the potential difference across the resistor correctly, allowing you to verify Ohm's Law.

8. (*d*) Given $l = 10$ m

$A = 4 \times 10^{-6}\ \text{m}^2$

$\rho = 1.6 \times 10^{-8}\ \Omega - \text{m}$

$$R = \rho\frac{l}{A}$$

$$R = 1.6 \times 10^{-8} \times \frac{10}{4\times10^{-6}} = .04\ \Omega$$

So, $R = .04\ \Omega$

Assertion and Reason

1. (*a*) Assertion and reason are both correct and are in agreement with Ohm's law.

2. (*a*) Both the assertion and reason are correct. The resistance of a wire is directly proportional to its length and inversely proportional to its cross-sectional area. The resistivity of a material is the constant of proportionality that relates the resistance of a wire made of that material to its length and cross-sectional area.

3. (*a*) Both the assertion and reason are correct. The resistance of a conductor increases with an increase in temperature due to an increase in the amplitude of atomic vibrations. This phenomenon is known as the temperature coefficient of resistance.

4. (*a*) Both the assertion and reason are correct. The resistivity of a material decreases with an increase in temperature due to an increase in the average velocity of the electrons in the material. This phenomenon is known as the temperature coefficient of resistivity.

RESISTANCE OF A SYSTEM OF RESISTORS

3

NCERT Definitions (Commonly asked in 1 mark)

- **Resistors in Series:** Configuration where resistors are connected end-to-end in a single path, resulting in the total resistance being the sum of individual resistances.

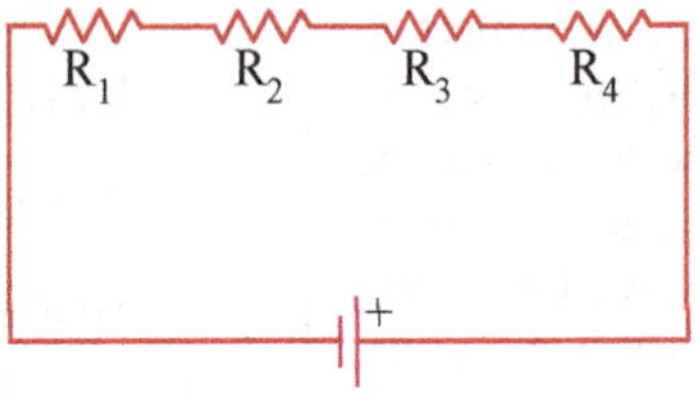

- **Resistors in Parallel:** Arrangement where resistors have both ends connected to the same two points, providing multiple paths for current flow and resulting in a decreased total resistance.

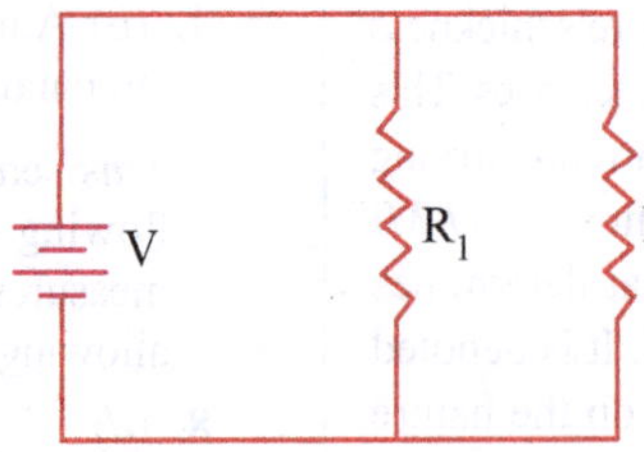

- **Equivalent Resistance:** Single resistance value that represents the total resistance of a circuit with multiple resistors, simplifying complex circuits for analysis.

- **Series Circuit:** An electric circuit in which components are arranged in a sequence such that the current has only one path to follow.

- **Parallel Circuit:** An electric circuit in which components are connected across common points, providing multiple pathways for the current.

Important Facts

01 In series connections, the current is the same through each resistor, while the voltage across the entire series is the sum of voltages across each resistor.

02 In parallel connections, the voltage across each resistor is the same, while the total current is the sum of currents through each resistor.

03 Adding a resistor in series increases the total resistance, while adding a resistor in parallel decreases the total resistance.

04 In series circuits, if one component fails, the entire circuit is interrupted. In parallel circuits, one component's failure does not affect the others.

Difference Between

Resistors in Series	Resistors in Parallel
Same current flows through all resistors.	Different currents flow through each resistor.
Voltage divides across resistors.	Voltage across each resistor is equal.
$R_{total} = R_1 + R_2 + R_3 + \cdots\cdots$	$\frac{1}{R_{total}} = \frac{1}{R_1} + \frac{1}{R_2} + \frac{1}{R_3} + \ldots\ldots$
A break in any part of a series circuit stops the current flow in the entire circuit.	A break in one parallel path does not stop the current flow in other paths.
Used when the goal is to increase the total resistance.	Used to decrease the total resistance below the smallest individual resistance.

Important Formula

1. **Equivalent Resistance in a series Circuit**

   $R_S = R_1 + R_2 + R_3$ $\{R_S > R_1, R_2, R_3\}$; Where, R_1, R_2, R_3 are resistance connected in series(in Ω)

2. **Potential Difference in a series Circuit**

   $V_S = V_1 + V_2 + V_3$; Where, V_1, V_2, V_3 are Voltages across resistance's connected in series(in V)

3. **Equivalent Resistance in a parallel Circuit**

   $\frac{1}{R_P} = \frac{1}{R_1} + \frac{1}{R_2} + \frac{1}{R_3}$ $\{R_P < R_1, R_2, R_3\}$; Where, R_1, R_2, R_3 are resistance connected in parallel(in Ω)

4. **Potential Difference in a parallel Circuit**

   $V_P = V_1 = V_2 = V_3$; Where, V_1, V_2, V_3 are Voltages across resistance's connected in parallel(in V)

Real Life Application Based Questions

1. **You've likely noticed that during a festival or celebration, decorative lights can easily be replaced without turning off the entire string. How does understanding circuit diagrams and parallel connections explain this?**

Ans. Decorative lights are often connected in a parallel circuit configuration. This means that if one bulb burns out or is removed, the circuit is not broken for the other bulbs; they continue to receive power and glow. Understanding circuit diagrams illustrates how each bulb receives an independent path for current flow, unlike in a series circuit where one broken connection would darken the entire string.

2. **Have you ever noticed that when multiple appliances are connected in a series at home, if one stops working, the others also stop functioning? Why does this happen?**

Ans. Yes, this happens because in a series circuit, the components share the same current. If one appliance stops working, it interrupts the flow of current, affecting the entire circuit. This is similar to how a broken link in a chain disrupts the entire chain's function.

3. **What are current limiters used for in circuits?**

Ans. Current limiters are combination of resistors used to restrict the amount of current flowing through a circuit, which is particularly beneficial in circuits where excessive current could potentially harm components.

Myth Buster

- **Myth: Believing that the current 'splits' in a series circuit or remains 'uniform' across different branches in a parallel circuit.**
  Fact: In series circuits, the same current flows through each component without splitting. In parallel circuits, the total current divides across the branches, with the sum of branch currents equating the total current entering the parallel configuration, reflecting Kirchhoff's current law.
- **Myth: Connecting electrical devices in series is always more efficient than connecting them in parallel.**
  Fact: While series connections have their advantages, such as sharing the same current, parallel connections are often more practical and efficient in real-life applications. Parallel connections allow devices to operate independently, ensuring optimal performance without affecting each other.

COMPETENCY BASED SOLVED EXAMPLES

Multiple Choice Questions (1 M)

1. If four identical resistors, of resistance 8 ohm, are first connected in series so as to give an effective resistance R_S, and then connected in parallel so as to give an effective resistance R_P, then the ratio R_S/R_P is **(*Ev*)**

(*a*) 32 (*b*) 2
(*c*) 0.5 (*d*) 16

2. Four resistors of resistance 2 ohms, 3 ohms, 4 ohms and 5 ohm are connected in series. The equivalent resistance of the combination is: **(*Ev*)**

(*a*) 14 ohm (*b*) 16 ohm
(*c*) 18 ohm (*d*) 20 ohm

3. Two resistors of resistance 4 ohms and 6 ohms are connected in parallel, and this combination is connected in series with a resistor of 8 ohm. The equivalent resistance of the combination is: **(*Ev*)**

(*a*) 3.2 ohm (*b*) 3.6 ohm
(*c*) 4 ohm (*d*) 10.4 ohm

4. Three resistors of resistance 2 ohm, 3 ohm and 4 ohm are connected in series, and this combination is connected in parallel with a resistor of 6 ohms. The equivalent resistance of the combination is: **(*Ev*)**

(*a*) 1.6 ohm (*b*) 2.4 ohm
(*c*) 3.6 ohm (*d*) 4.8 ohm

5. Two resistors of 2Ω and 4Ω are connected in parallel. This combination is then connected in series with a resistor of 6Ω. What is the equivalent resistance of the entire combination? **(*Ev*)**

(*a*) 2.0 Ω (*b*) 2.4 Ω
(*c*) 4.0 Ω (*d*) 7.3 Ω

6. Consider the following statements.

(A) In series connection, the same current flows through each element.

(B) In parallel connection, the same potential difference is applied across each element. **(*Re*)**

(*a*) both (A) and (B) are correct
(*b*) (A) is correct but (B) is wrong
(*c*) (A) is wrong but (B) is correct
(*d*) both (A) and (B) are wrong

7. When a 5Ω resistor is connected in parallel with a 10Ω resistor, the equivalent resistance is: **(*Ev*)**

(*a*) 2Ω (*b*) 3.33Ω
(*c*) 5Ω (*d*) 15Ω

Assertion and Reason (1 M)

Direction: **The following questions consist of two statements. Assertion (A) and Reason (R). Answer these questions by selecting the appropriate option given below:**

(*a*) Both A and R are true, and R is the correct explanation of A.
(*b*) Both A and R are true, but R is not the correct explanation of A.
(*c*) A is true, but R is false
(*d*) A is false, but R is true.

1. **Assertion (A):** Resistors connected in parallel have a lower equivalent resistance than resistors connected in series.

   Reason (R): In a parallel circuit, the current is split among the branches, leading to a decrease in total resistance. ***(Un)***

2. **Assertion (A):** When two resistors are connected in series, their equivalent resistance is equal to the sum of their individual resistances.

   Reason (R): In a series circuit, the same current flows through all the resistors, and the total resistance is the sum of individual resistances. ***(Un)***

3. **Assertion (A):** When resistors are connected in parallel, the equivalent resistance is always less than the smallest resistance in the circuit.

   Reason (R): In a parallel circuit, the current follows the path of least resistance, resulting in a lower total resistance. ***(Un)***

4. **Assertion (A):** The total resistance of a circuit containing only one resistor is equal to the resistance of the resistor.

   Reason (R): In a circuit with only one resistor, there is no other path for the current to flow, and the resistance of the resistor determines the total resistance of the circuit. ***(An)***

5. **Assertion (A):** The equivalent resistance of resistors connected in series is always greater than the resistance of any individual resistor.

   Reason (R): In a series circuit, the total resistance is the sum of individual resistances, which is always greater than any individual resistance. ***(Un)***

Subjective Questions

Very Short Answer Type Questions (2 M)

1. A piece of wire of resistance R is cut into three equal parts. These parts are then connected in parallel. If the equivalent resistance of this parallel combination is R_1, what is the value of the ratio $R_1 : R$? ***(Ev)***

Ans. Resistance of each part is $\frac{R}{3}\ \Omega$ (as resistance is proportional to the length of the wire.) *(½ M)*

$$\frac{1}{R_1} = \frac{3}{R} + \frac{3}{R} + \frac{3}{R} = \frac{9}{R} \quad (1\ M)$$

$$\therefore R_1 = \frac{R}{9} \because \frac{R_1}{R} = \frac{1}{9} \quad (½\ M)$$

2. What is the current passing through a 10 ohm resistor if it is connected in a series with a 5 ohm resistor and a 15V battery? ***(Ev)***

Ans. The current passing through the resistors is 1A $\left(\frac{15V}{10ohm+5ohm}\right)$. *(2 M)*

3. Priya is building a circuit with two resistors and a battery. She notices that when she adds a second resistor in a combination, the overall current from the battery increases.

In which combination Priya added the resistor and why the overall current increases when she adds another resistor? ***(An)***

Ans. Priya added the second resistor in parallel.

When resistors are connected in parallel, the overall resistance of the circuit decreases. According to Ohm's Law (I = V/R), when the total resistance decreases, the current from the battery increases, leading to an increase in the overall current in the circuit. *(2 M)*

4. Show how you would connect three resistors each of resistance 6 Ω, so that the combination has a resistance of 9Ω. Also justify your answer.

Ans. If resistor is connected in series $6\Omega + 6\Omega + 6\Omega = 18\Omega$ This is not correct

When they are connected in parallel

$\frac{1}{6} + \frac{1}{6} + \frac{1}{6} = 3$ This is also wrong *(½ M)*

Two 6Ω resistors are connected in parallel.

$$\text{Resistance} = \frac{1}{\frac{1}{6} + \frac{1}{6}} = \frac{6 \times 6}{6+6} = 3\Omega \quad (½\ M)$$

If 3rd resistor of 6Ω and 3Ω are connected in series, it becomes

$6\Omega + 3\Omega = 9\Omega$ *(1 M)*

5. How does the equivalent resistance of resistors change when they are connected in parallel? ***(An)***

Ans. When resistors are connected in parallel, the equivalent resistance decreases as compared to the individual resistances. This is because the current has multiple paths to flow through, which reduces the overall resistance. *(2 M)*

6. Ramya wants to measure the current flowing through the circuit shown below.

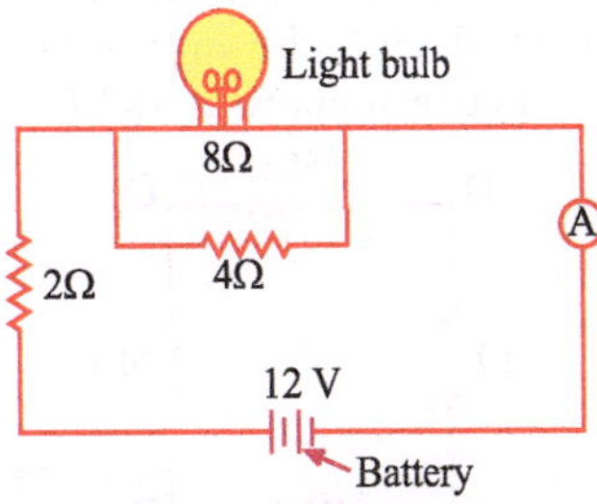

Which among the four ammeters can she use for the same? Show your calculations.

Ammeter	Minimum range	Maximum range
P	0 mA	1 mA
Q	0 mA	10 mA
R	0 A	1 A
S	0 A	10 A

Ans. From Ohm's law we have

$V = IR$

$I = V/R$

Given $V = 12$ V and $R_1 = 2$ ohm, $R_2 = 8$ ohm and $R_3 = 4$ ohm

Therefore,

net resistance $R = R_1 + (R_2 \times R_3)/(R_2 + R_3)$

$= 2 + (8 \times 4/8 + 4) = 2 + 32/12$

$= 2 + 2.66$

$R = 4.66$ ohm *(1 M)*

$I = 12/4.66 = 2.58$ A *(½ M)*

- She can use ammeter *S* to measure the current in the circuit. *(½ M)*

Nailing the Right Answer

- Familiarize yourself with the three basic types of combinations: series combination, parallel combination, and a combination of series and parallel resistors.
- Understand how resistors are connected in each type of combination.

Short Answer Type Questions (3 M)

1. Two resistors, one of 10 ohms and the other of 20 ohms, are connected in parallel. Calculate the current flowing through the 20 ohm resistor if a total current of 2 A flows through the combination. **(*Ev*)**

Ans. The total resistance of the combination is given by $(10 \times 20)/(10 + 20) = 20/3$ ohm. *(1 M)*

The current through the 20 ohm resistor can be calculated using Ohm's law as $I = V/R$, where V is the voltage across the resistor and R is its resistance. *(1 M)*

The voltage across the resistor is the same as the voltage across the combination, which can be calculated using Ohm's law as $V = IR = 2 \times 20/3$ V

Thus, the current through the 20 ohm resistor is $(2 \times 20/3)/20 = 2/3$ *A*. *(1 M)*

2. Four resistors, each of 5 ohms, are connected in a square as shown below. Calculate the equivalent resistance of the combination between points *A* and *B*. **(*Ev*)**

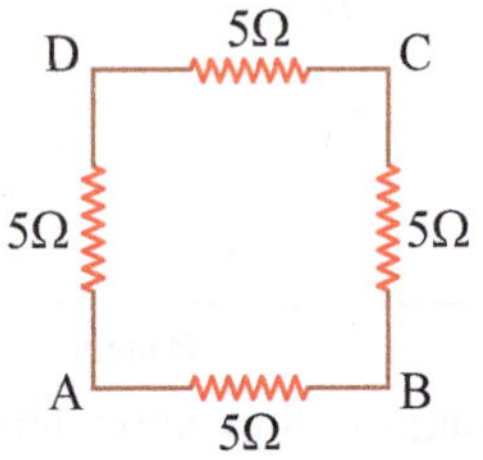

Ans. In the given figure, let's find the equivalent resistance between corners A and B.

Equivalent resistance of series combination of resistors AD, DC and CB

$= 5\Omega + 5\Omega + 5\Omega = 15\Omega$ *(1 M)*

Equivalent resistance between two adjacent corners A and B,

$$\frac{1}{R} = \frac{1}{15} + \frac{1}{5} = \frac{4}{15}$$

or, $R = \frac{15}{4} = 3.75\Omega$ *(2 M)*

3. (*a*) Vijaya connects three bulbs *P*, *Q* and *R* in series with a battery in two different ways using identical conducting wires as shown below. She notices that in case I all three bulbs glow but in case II only the bulbs *P* and *R* continue to glow. What could be the reason for the bulb *Q* to not glow in case II? Explain.

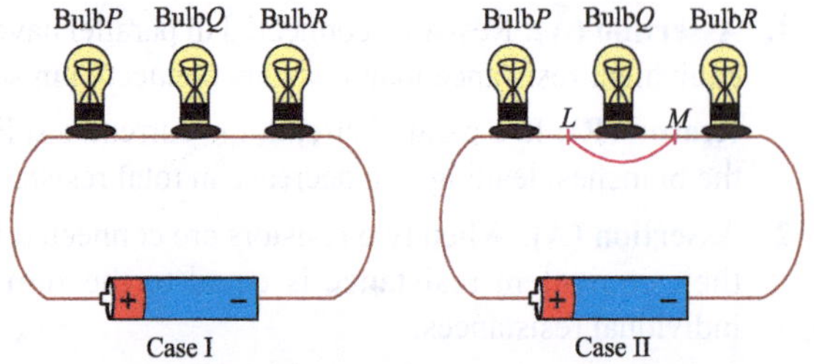

(*b*) Two resistances when connected in parallel give a combined resistance of 10/3 ohms. When the same two resistors are connected in series, the combined resistance becomes 15 ohms. Calculate the individual resistance of each resistor.

Ans. (*a*) The current will flow through the additional wire that connects the points L and M(avoiding the bulb) as it offers a path of least/lower resistance as compared with the bulb. *(1 M)*

(*b*) $3/10 = 1/R_1 + 1/R_2$ ...(*i*)

$R_1 + R_2 = 15, R_1 = 15 - R_2$

Substituting in (*i*)

$3/10 = (15 - R_2 + R_2)/ (15 - R_2)R_2$ *(1 M)*

$15R_2 - R_2^2 = 150/3 = 50$

$R_2^2 - 15R_2 + 50 = 0$

$R_2 = 10$ ohm, $R_1 = 5$ ohm

or

$R_1 = 10$ ohm, $R_2 = 5$ ohm *(1 M)*

4. How many 176 Ω resistors (in parallel) are required to carry 5 A on a 220V line? **(*Ev*) (NCERT Exercise)**

Ans. Let *n* resistors will be required for the purpose.

The equivalent resistance of the parallel combination of *n* resistors each of resistance *R* is given by

$$\frac{1}{R} = n \times \frac{1}{176} = R = \frac{176}{n}$$ *(1 M)*

Now, using Ohm's law,

$$R = \frac{V}{I}$$ *(1 M)*

Substituting the values, we get

$$\frac{176}{n} = \frac{V}{I}$$

$$n = \frac{176 \times 5}{220} = 4$$

The number of resistors required is 4. *(1 M)*

Long Answer Type Questions (5 M)

1. (*a*) How will you infer with the help of an experiment that the same current flows through every part of a circuit containing three resistors in series connected to a battery?

(*b*) Consider the given circuit and find the current flowing in the circuit and potential difference across the 15 Ω resistor when the circuit is closed.

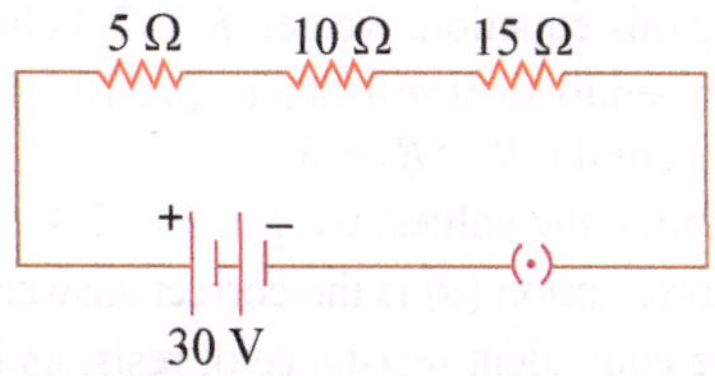

Ans. (*a*) To infer that the same current flows through every part of a circuit containing three resistors in series connected to a battery, you can perform the following experiment:

Set up the circuit with three resistors connected in series to a battery. Use a voltmeter to measure the voltage across each resistor. Use Ohm's law to calculate the current flowing through each resistor. Compare the current flowing through each resistor. If the circuit is in series, the current flowing through each resistor should be the same. *(2 M)*

(*b*) Total resistance R = 5 + 10 + 15 = 30 Ω *(1 M)*

As, $V = IR$

So, $I = 30/30 = 1A$ *(1 M)*

Hence, potential difference across 15 ohm resistor $= 1 \times 15 = 15\ V$ *(1 M)*

2. As shown in the figure above A and B are two lamps. Lamp A is rated at 12 V, 24W. Lamp *B* is rated at 6.0 V. When lamp B operates at its rated voltage, the current in it is 3.0 A. The values of R_1 and R_2 are chosen so that both lamps operate at their rated voltages.

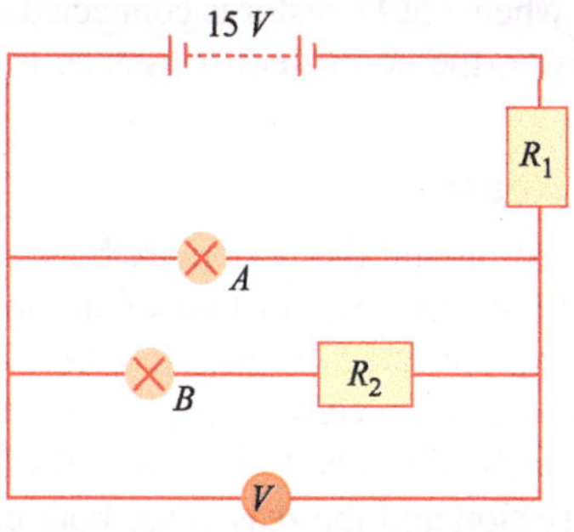

Based on the information given, answer the following.

(*i*) Calculate the current in Lamp A.

(*ii*) State and give reason for the reading of the Voltmeter.

(*iii*) Calculate the resistance of R_2.

(*iv*) Find the value of the resistance R_1.

Ans. (*i*) Use of P = IV *(½ M)*

I = P ÷ V = 24 W ÷ 12V

Current in lamp A – 2 A *(½ M)*

(*ii*) Voltmeter reading = 12 V *(½ M)*

Lamp A and Lamp B are in parallel.

Hence p.d. across the arm containing A = p.d. across arm containing B = 12 V (from a) *(½ M)*

(*iii*) p.d. across R_2 + p.d. across B = 12 V. *(½ M)*

p.d. across B = 6 V (given)

Hence p.d. across R_2 = 12 V – 6 V = 6 V *(½ M)*

Current through R_2 = Current through B = 3A (given) *(½ M)*

Use of $R = \frac{V}{I}$

$R_2 = \frac{6V}{3A} = 2\Omega$ *(½ M)*

(*iv*) Current through R_1 = Total Current = 3A + 2A = 5A *(½ M)*

p.d. across R_1 = 15 V – 12 V = 3 V

$R_1 = \frac{3V}{5A} = 0.6\ \Omega$ *(½ M)*

3. Show how would you join three resistors, each of resistance 9 Ohm so that the equivalent resistance of the combination is (*i*) 13.5 Ohm (*ii*) 6 Ohm? (CBSE 2017)

Ans. (*i*) Two resistors in parallel and then one is series

$1/R = 1/R_1 + 1/R_2 = 1/9 + 1/9 = 2/9$ *(1 M)*

$R = 9/2 = 4.5\Omega$ *(1 M)*

$R' = R + R_3$ *(½ M)*

$= 4.5 + 9 = 13.5\Omega$ *(1 M)*

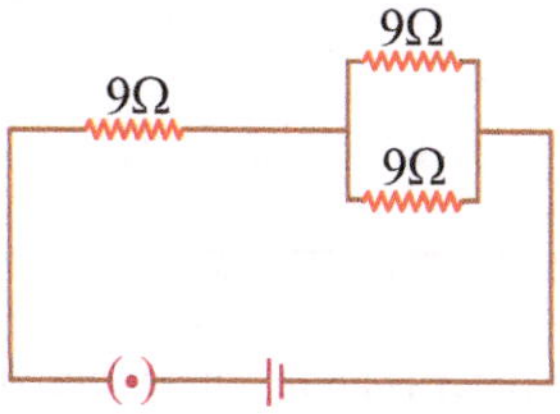

(*ii*) Two resistors in series and one in parallel $R = R_1 + R_2 = 9 + 9 = 18\Omega$

$1/R' = 1/R + 1/R_0 = 1/18 + 1/9 = 1 + 2/18 = 3/18$ *(½ M)*

$R' = 18/3 = 6\Omega$

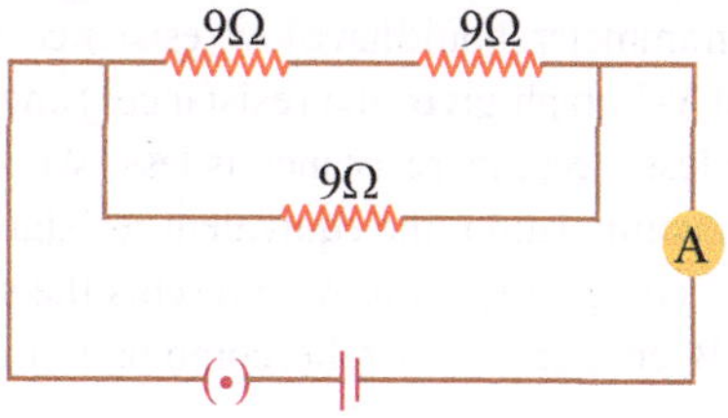

(1 M)

4. (*i*) How is electric current related to the potential difference across the terminals of a conductor? Draw a labeled circuit diagram to verify this relationship.

(*ii*) Why should an ammeter have low resistance?

(*iii*) Two V - I graphs A and B for series and parallel combinations of two resistors are as shown. Giving reason state which graph shows (*a*) series, (*b*) parallel combination of the resistors.

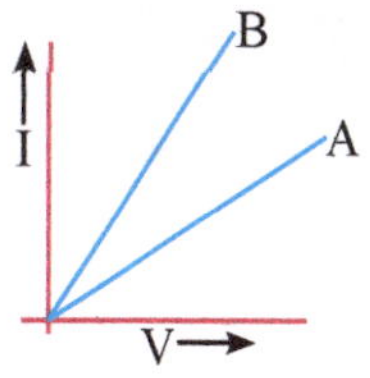

(CBSE 2023)

Ans. (*i*) Electric current is directly related to the potential difference across the terminals of a conductor. This relationship is described by Ohm's law, which states that the current flowing through a conductor is directly proportional to the potential difference across its ends, provided the physical conditions such as temperature remain constant. Mathematically, Ohm's law can be expressed as:

$I = V/R$

where I is the current flowing through the conductor, V is the potential difference across its ends, and R is the resistance of the conductor. *(1 M)*

To verify this relationship, here is a labelled circuit diagram:

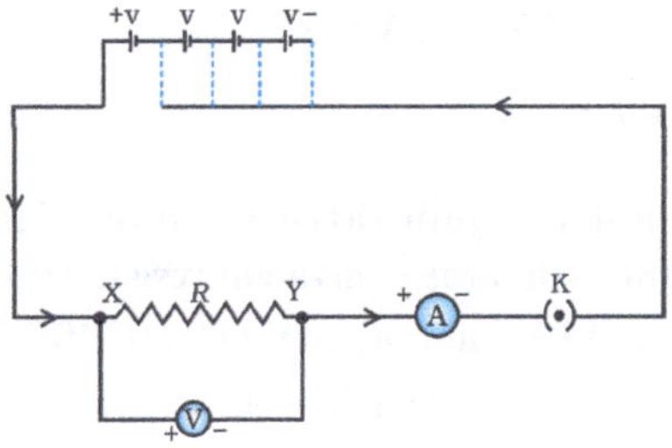

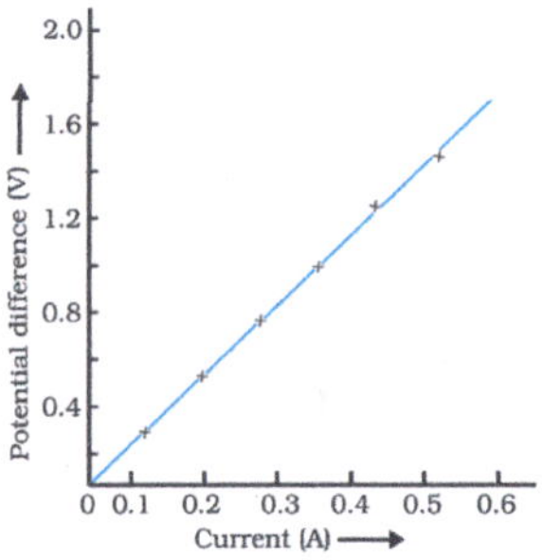

(2 M)

(*ii*) An ammeter is an instrument used to measure the flow of electric current in a circuit. It should have low resistance to prevent its own resistance from affecting the circuit being measured. If the ammeter has high resistance, it will draw a significant amount of current from the circuit, leading to inaccurate measurements. Therefore, to ensure accurate measurements, an ammeter should have low resistance. *(1 M)*

(*iii*) The slope of V-I graph gives the resistance. Since the straight line A is less steep, its resistance is less. We know that, in a parallel combination, the equivalent resistance is less than in series combination. So, A represents the series combination and B represents the parallel combination. *(1 M)*

Hints & Explanations

Multiple Choice Questions

1. (*d*) We know that,

$R_S = R_1 + R_2 + R_3 + R_4 + ...$

$R_p = \frac{1}{R_1} + \frac{1}{R_2} + \frac{1}{R_3} + ...$

If resistors are identical then

$R_s = nR$

$R_p = \frac{R}{n}$

Thus, $R_s = 4 \times 8\ \Omega = 32\ \Omega$

$R_p = 8\ \Omega/4 = 2\ \Omega$

$\therefore \frac{R_s}{R_p} = \frac{32\Omega}{2\Omega} = 16$

2. (*a*) The equivalent resistance of resistors in series is given by the formula: $R = R_1 + R_2 + R_3 + R_4$
Substituting the values, we get: $R = 2 + 3 + 4 + 5$
Solving this equation, we get: R = 14 ohm. Therefore, option (*a*) is the correct answer.

3. (*d*) The equivalent resistance of resistors in parallel is given by the formula: $1/R_p = 1/R_1 + 1/R_2$
Substituting the values, we get: $1/R_p = 1/4 + 1/6$
Solving this equation, we get: $R_p = 2.4$ ohm.
Now, the equivalent resistance of resistors in series is given by the formula: $R_s = R_1 + R_2$
Substituting the values, we get: $R_s = 2.4 + 8 = 10.4$ ohm.
Therefore, option (*d*) is the correct answer.

4. (*c*) The equivalent resistance of resistors in series is given by the formula: $R = R_1 + R_2 + R_3$
Substituting the values, we get: $R = 2 + 3 + 4 = 9$ ohms.
Now, the equivalent resistance of resistors in parallel is given by the formula: $1/R_p = 1/R + 1/R_4$
Substituting the values, we get: $1/R_p = 1/9 + 1/6$
Solving this equation, we get: $R_p = 3.6$ ohms.
Therefore, option (*c*) is the correct answer.

5. (*d*) First, we need to find the equivalent resistance of the two resistors in parallel, which we already know is 4/3 Ω. Then, we need to add this to the third resistor in series, which gives us a total of $4/3 + 6 = 22/3\ \Omega \approx 7.33\ \Omega$.

6. (*a*) Both (A) and (B) are correct

7. (*b*) Given resistors of 5Ω and 10Ω connected in parallel:

$\frac{1}{R} = \frac{1}{5\Omega} + \frac{1}{10\Omega}$

$\frac{1}{R} = \frac{2}{10} + \frac{1}{10} = \frac{3}{10}$

$R \approx 3.33\Omega$

Therefore, when a 5Ω resistor is connected in parallel with a 10Ω resistor, the equivalent resistance is approximately 3.33Ω.

Assertion and Reason

1. (*a*) The assertion and the reason are both correct, and the reason is the correct explanation of the assertion. When resistors are connected in parallel, the total resistance decreases because the current is split among the branches, and each branch offers less resistance to the flow of current.

2. (*a*) The assertion and the reason are both correct, and the reason is the correct explanation of the assertion. When resistors are connected in series, the total resistance is equal to the sum of individual resistances because the same current flows through all the resistors, and the voltage drop across each resistor is proportional to its resistance.

3. (*c*) The assertion is correct, but the reason is incorrect. When resistors are connected in parallel, the equivalent resistance is always less than any individual resistance, but it may not necessarily be less than the smallest resistance in the circuit. The reason given is not a correct explanation of the assertion.

4. (*a*) The assertion and the reason are both correct, and the reason is the correct explanation of the assertion. In a circuit with only one resistor, the total resistance is equal to the resistance of the resistor because there is no other path for the current to flow, and the voltage drop across the resistor is proportional to its resistance.

5. (*a*) The assertion and the reason are both correct, and the reason is the correct explanation of the assertion. When resistors are connected in series, the equivalent resistance is always greater than any individual resistance because the total resistance is the sum of individual resistances, and the current has to flow through all the resistors in series, resulting in an overall increase in resistance.

4 HEATING EFFECT AND ELECTRIC POWER

NCERT Definitions (Commonly asked in 1 mark)

- **Heating Effect of Electric Current:** The phenomenon where electrical energy is converted into heat when current flows through a conductor, leading to a rise in temperature.
- **Joule's Law:** This law states that the heat produced by a current flowing through a conductor is directly proportional to the square of the current, the resistance of the conductor, and the time for which the current flows.
- **Electric Power:** The rate at which electrical energy is transferred by an electric circuit, typically measured in watts (W).
- **1 Watt(W):** One watt of power is consumed when 1 A of current flows at a potential difference of 1 V
- **Electric Energy:** Electric energy is the power consumed or supplied by an electrical device over time, measured in kilowatt-hours (kWh). It is the energy generated or used when an electric current flows through an electrical circuit.
- **Kilowatt-hour (kWh):** A unit of energy commonly used to express electrical energy consumption, equivalent to the energy amount of energy used by a 1-kilowatt (1000-watt) device operating for one hour.
- **Fuse:** A safety device that prevents excessive current from damaging electrical circuits and appliances, illustrating the practical application of the heating effect.

Important Facts

01 The commercial unit of electrical energy is kilowatt hour (kWh). 1 kW h = 3,600,000 J = 3.6×10^6 J

02 Electric bulb filaments, like tungsten, withstand heat due to high melting points.

03 Electric power facilitates calculating energy costs, crucial for managing electricity usage economically.

04 Fuses melt to break circuits at excessive currents, preventing damage and fire hazards.

Difference Between

Joule's Law	Ohm's Law
The heat generated in a conductor is directly proportional to the square of the current (I), the resistance (R), and the time (t) the current flows through the conductor: $H = I^2RT$	The potential difference (V), across the ends is directly proportional to the current (I) flowing through it, provided its temperature remains the same. (R): $V = IR$.
Applies to thermal effects in electrical circuits, indicating how electrical energy converts into heat.	Describes the electrical relationship determining current flow and potential difference in a circuit.
Used to calculate the heat energy produced in electrical appliances, which can inform design and safety considerations.	Fundamental for designing and analyzing electrical circuits, determining how components should be connected to achieve desired performance.

Important Formula

1. **Relation for Electric Power**

   $P = \frac{W}{T} = VI$; Where, P = Power(in watts), W = Work done(in J), T = Time (in sec),

   V= Electric Potential(in V), I=Current(in A)

2. **Relation for Electrical Energy**

   $E = P \times T$; Where, E = Electrical Energy(in J),

3. **Joule's Law of Heating**

   $H = I^2 RT = VIT$; Where, H = Heat consumed(in J), R = Resistance (in Ω)

Real Life Application Based Questions

1. **Have you ever noticed that your mobile phone gets warm after being charged for a while or when you use it extensively? Can you explain why this happens based on your understanding of electricity and circuits?**

Ans. The warming up of your mobile phone is due to the heating effect of electric current. When the phone is being charged or heavily used, current flows through its internal components and circuits. Due to the resistance offered by these components, part of the electrical energy is converted into heat, causing the phone to warm up. This is similar to how electric heaters or irons work, utilizing the heating effect of electric current for a practical purpose.

2. **Have you ever noticed that electric kettles or toasters heat up quickly when plugged in, while other electronic devices like laptops or smartphones do not exhibit the same rapid heating effect? Can you explain the reason behind this observation?**

Ans. The rapid heating observed in electric kettles or toasters compared to devices like laptops or smartphones is due to the higher power consumption and resistance in the heating elements of the former. Electric kettles and toasters are designed to convert electrical energy into heat efficiently, utilizing the heating effect of electric current. The high resistance in the heating elements of these appliances causes them to heat up quickly, demonstrating the practical application of Joule's heating effect in generating heat for specific purposes.

3. **Have you ever wondered why incandescent light bulbs produce both light and heat when switched on, while LED bulbs remain cool to the touch even after prolonged use? Can you provide an explanation for this phenomenon?**

Ans. The dual production of light and heat in incandescent light bulbs is a result of the heating effect of electric current in the filament. When electricity flows through the filament, it heats up due to its resistance, emitting both light and heat. In contrast, LED bulbs operate on a different principle where electricity passes through a semiconductor material, producing light without significant heat generation.

Myth Buster

- **Myth: Increasing the resistance in a circuit always leads to a higher amount of heat generated by the electric current.**

  Fact: While resistance plays a significant role in the heating effect of electric current, the amount of heat produced also depends on the current flowing through the circuit. Higher current levels can generate more heat, even with lower resistance, as determined by Joule's Law.

- **Myth: All electrical devices primarily convert electrical energy into heat through the heating effect of electric current.**

  Fact: While many electrical devices do utilize the heating effect of electric current, not all devices convert electricity into heat. Some devices, like motors and LEDs, transform electrical energy into mechanical motion or light, showcasing diverse applications beyond heat generation.

- **Myth: A higher current means more power is always being consumed.**

  Fact: Power consumption depends on both current and voltage as per the relation P = VI. Two devices can draw different amounts of current but consume the same power if their operating voltages differ appropriately.

COMPETENCY BASED SOLVED EXAMPLES

Multiple Choice Questions (1 M)

1. Two bulbs of 100W and 40W are connected in series. The current through the 100W bulb is 1A. The current through the 40W bulb will be: (*Ev*) (CBSE 2020)

(*a*) 0.4*A* (*b*) 0.6*A*
(*c*) 0.8*A* (*d*) 1*A*

2. Which circuit shows the correct and safe positions for the fuse and the switch? (*Ap*) (CBSE APQ, 2023)

(*a*)
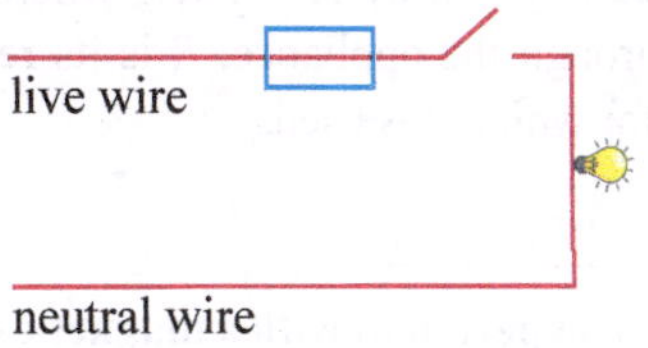

(*b*)
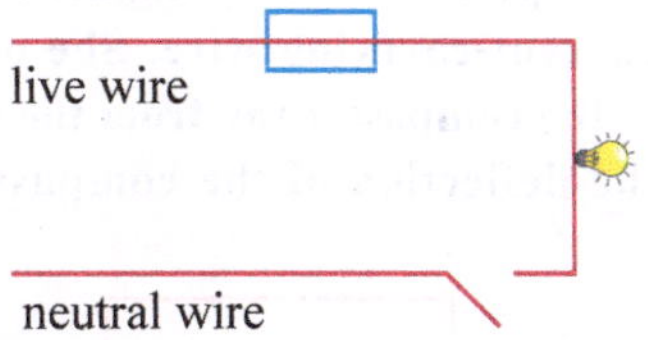

(*c*)
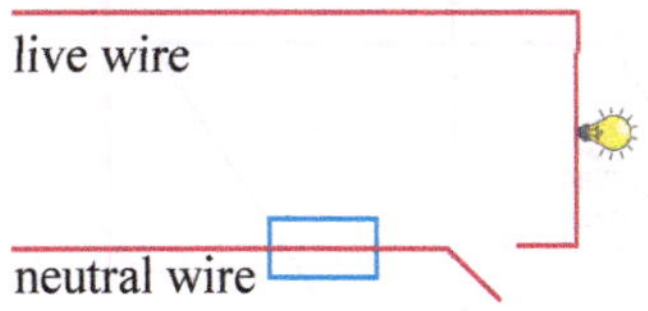

(*d*)
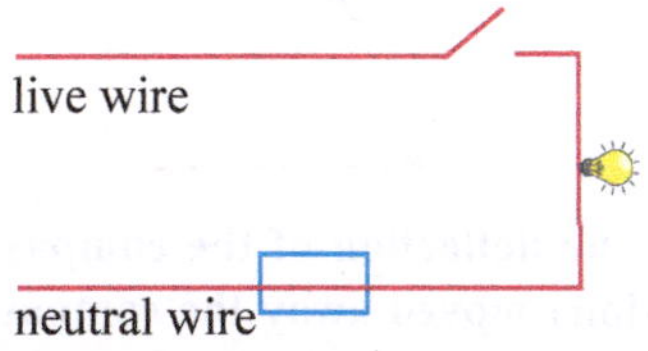

3. Which of the following factors affect the amount of heat produced in a conductor due to electric current? (*Un*)

(*a*) The current flowing through the conductor
(*b*) The resistance of the conductor
(*c*) The time for which current flows
(*d*) All of the above

4. Which of the following is the formula for calculating electric power? (*Re*)

(*a*) $P = V \times I$ (*b*) $P = V^2/R$
(*c*) $P = I^2 \times R$ (*d*) None of the above

5. A bulb of 60W is connected to a 220V source. What is the current flowing through the bulb? (*Ev*)

(*a*) 0.27 *A* (*b*) 0.36 *A*
(*c*) 0.45 *A* (*d*) 0.55 *A*

6. In an electric circuit three incandescent bulbs A, B and C of rating 40W, 60W and 100W respectively are connected in parallel to an electric source. Which of the following is likely to happen regarding their brightness? (*An*) (NCERT Exemplar)

(*a*) Brightness of all the bulbs will be the same
(*b*) Brightness of bulb A will be the maximum
(*c*) Brightness of bulb B will be more than that of A
(*d*) Brightness of bulb C will be less than that of B

7. An electric kettle consumes 1kW of electric power when operated at 220V. A fuse wire of what rating must be used for it? (*Un*) (NCERT Exemplar)

(*a*) 1*A* (*b*) 2*A*
(*c*) 4*A* (*d*) 5*A*

8. At the time of short circuit, the electric current in the circuit: (*Re*) (CBSE 2020)

(*a*) vary continuously (*b*) does not change
(*c*) reduces substantially (*d*) increases heavily

9. Which of the following is the unit of electrical energy? (*Re*)

(*a*) Watt (*b*) Joule
(*c*) Volt (*d*) Ampere

10. Two LED bulbs of 12W and 6W are connected in series. If the current through 12W bulb is 0.06A the current through 6W bulb will be: (*Ev*) (CBSE 2023)

(*a*) 0.04A (*b*) 0.06A
(*c*) 0.08A (*d*) 0.12A

11. The resistance of a resistor is reduced to half of its initial value. If voltage across resistor remains unaltered, the amount of heat produced in the resistor will become: (*Ev*) (CBSE 2023)

(*a*) Four times (*b*) Two times
(*c*) Half (*d*) One forth

12. An electric iron of 1500*W*, 200*V* and a flash light of 500*W*, 200*V* are used in homes. The rating of fuse to be used should be (*Ev*) (CBSE 2023)

(*a*) 5*A* (*b*) 10*A*
(*c*) 15*A* (*d*) 20*A*

Assertion and Reason (1 M)

Direction: The following questions consist of two statements. Assertion (A) and Reason (R). Answer these questions by selecting the appropriate option given below:

(*a*) Both A and R are true, and R is the correct explanation of A.
(*b*) Both A and R are true, but R is not the correct explanation of A.
(*c*) A is true, but R is false
(*d*) A is false, but R is true.

1. **Assertion (A):** The heating effect of electric current is utilized in electric heaters.

   Reason (R): When current flows through a conductor, some of the electrical energy is converted into heat energy due to the resistance of the conductor. (*Un*)

2. **Assertion (A):** When the current flowing through a resistor is doubled, the heat produced in the resistor doubled.

Reason (R): The heating effect of electric current is directly proportional to the square of the current flowing through the resistor. ***(Un)***

3. **Assertion (A):** It is observed that sometimes a bulb glows brighter and sometimes it glows dimly.

Reason (R): Glowing brighter and dimmer depends on the heating effect of the current. More current produces more heating effect making the bulb glow brighter and vice-versa. ***(Un)***

4. **Assertion (A):** The energy consumed by an appliance in a given time is equal to the product of its power rating and the time for which it is used.

Reason (R): The power rating of an appliance is defined as the amount of electrical energy it consumes per unit time. ***(Un)***

5. **Assertion (A):** A fuse wire of low melting point is used in an electric circuit to protect it from overloading.

Reason (R): When the current in a circuit exceeds the rated value, the fuse wire melts and breaks the circuit. ***(Un)***

Subjective Questions

Very Short Answer Type Questions (2 M)

1. **(*a*) Define the heating effect of electric current.**
(*b*) Describe how the heating effect occurs when electric current flows through a conductor. ***(Re)***

Ans. (*a*) The heating effect of electric current is the production of heat when electric current flows through a conductor. *(1 M)*

(*b*) This effect occurs due to the resistance encountered by the electrons as they move through the conductor. The collisions between the electrons and the atoms in the conductor result in the conversion of electrical energy into heat energy, causing the conductor to heat up. *(1 M)*

2. **In the given circuit calculate the power consumed in watts in the resistor of 2Ω:**

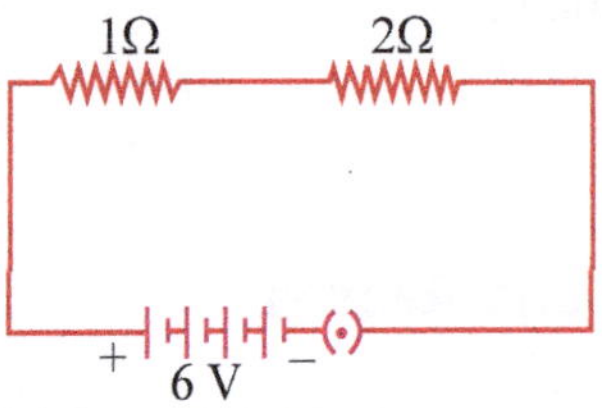

Ans. The circuit diagram is shown in fig,

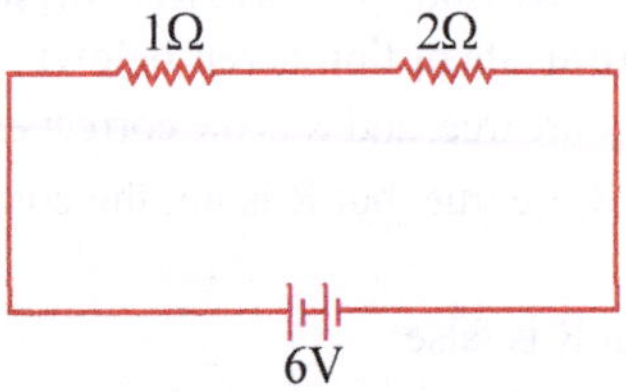

Total resistance, $R = 1 + 2 = 3\Omega$, *(½ M)*

Potential difference, $V = 6\ V$

Current, $I = \frac{V}{R} = \frac{6V}{3\Omega} = 2\ A$ *(½ M)*

Power used in 2Ω resistor $= (I)^2 R = (2)^2 \times 3 = 12W$. *(1 M)*

3. **How is the energy consumed by a device calculated, write the S.I unit of energy?** ***(Ap)***

Ans. The energy consumed by a device is calculated by multiplying the power of the device and the time for which it is used, i.e., $E = Pt$. *(1 M)*

The S.I unit of energy is Joule(J) *(1 M)*

4. **What is the relationship between power, voltage, and current in an electrical circuit?** ***(Re)***

Ans. The power of an electrical circuit is directly proportional to the product of voltage and current, i.e., $P \propto VI$. *(2 M)*

5. **What is the formula for calculating the heat produced by an electrical appliance?** ***(Re)***

Ans. The formula for calculating the heat produced by an electrical appliance is given by $H = I^2RT$, where I is the current flowing through the appliance, R is its resistance, and T is the time for which it is used. *(2 M)*

Short Answer Type Questions (3 M)

1. **Mona was doing an experiment with a magnetic compass and a straight current-carrying wire. She observed that as she moved the compass away from the current-carrying wire, the deflection of the compass needle reduced.**

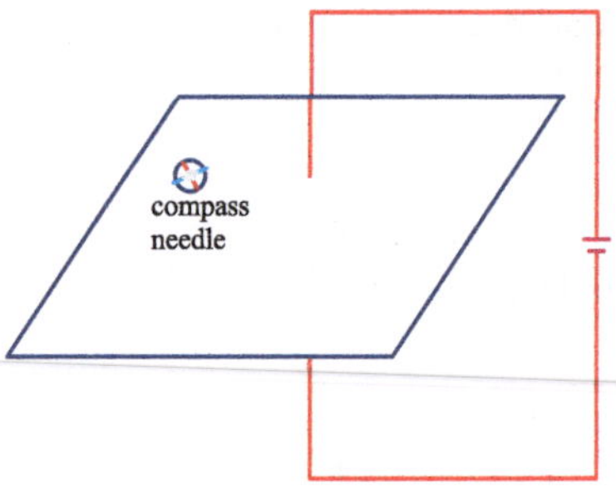

(*a*) Explain why the deflection of the compass needle reduced as Mona moved away the compass needle from the current carrying wire.

(*b*) Mention one thing that could have changed in the circuit of the wire that could increase the deflection of the needle.

(*c*) Explain with reason what will be the direction of the magnetic field associated with the wire for the case described by the above figure.

Ans. (*a*) Magnetic field strength is inversely proportional to the distance from the current carrying wire. Hence when Mona moved the compass away from the current carrying wire, the magnetic effect was less on it and hence the deflection was less. *(1 M)*

(*b*) Magnetic field strength is directly proportional to the current in the wire. So, Mona could increase the current in the circuit to observe a greater deflection in the compass needle. *(1 M)*

(*c*) The battery suggests that the current is going from top of the plane to the bottom of the plane. Using the right hand thumb rule we can say that the magnetic field will be clockwise. *(1 M)*

2. (*a*) **Write the mathematical expression for Joule's law of heating.**

(*b*) **Compute the heat generated while transferring 96000 coulomb of charge in two hours through a potential difference of 40 V.** **(*Ev*)**

Ans. (*a*) Joule's law of heating states that the amount of heat produced when a current flows through a conductor is directly proportional to the square of the current (I), the resistance (R) of the conductor, and the time (t) for which the current flows. The mathematical expression for Joule's law of heating is:

$H = I^2 R t$ *(1 M)*

(*b*) Time (t) = 2hr = 2 × 60 × 60 = 7200sec

Charge (Q) = 96000C

Potential difference (V) = 40V

Current (I) $= \frac{Q}{T}$

$I = \frac{96000}{7200} = 13.33A$ *(1 M)*

Now, heat generated

$H = V \times I \times t$

$H = 40 \times 13.33 \times 7200$

$H = 3.8 \times 10^6$ J *(1 M)*

Nailing the Right Answer

- Understand the relationship between resistance and heat production.
- Higher resistance in a conductor leads to more heat being produced when the same current passes through it, as per Joule's Law.
- Memorize the formula for calculating the heat produced in a conductor: Heat $(H) = I^2Rt$, where I is the current in amperes, R is the resistance in ohms, and t is the time in seconds.

3. **Kaveri conducted an experiment to study the energy efficiency of different bulbs. She connected a bulb A having a resistance of 100 ohms to a 240 V power supply in a laboratory.**

(*a*) **How much energy will be consumed by the bulb, if it is kept ON for 4 hours each day for a week? Express your answer in kJ.**

(*b*) **Kaveri connects another similar bulb B in series with bulb A and connects the combination to a 240 V supply. Will there be any change in the brightness with which bulb A glows now? Explain mathematically.**

Ans. (*a*) Given $V = 240$ V and $R = 100$ ohms

Therefore,

Power $(P) = V^2/R$

$= (240)^2/100 = 576$ W *(½ M)*

Energy consumed by bulb $A = P \times t$

$E = 576 \times 4 \times 7 \times 60 \times 60 = 58{,}060.8$ kJ *(½ M)*

(*b*) When bulbs A and B are connected in series:

$R_{net} = R_1 + R_2 = 100 + 100$

$R_{net} = 200$ ohms

Total power consumed by bulb A when connected in series with bulb B

$P_{tot} = V^2/R_{net} = (240)^2/200 = 288$ W *(½ M)*

$P_{A'} = P_{tot}/2 = 144$ W *(½ M)*

Power consumed by bulb A when connected without bulb B to 240 V

$P_A = V^2/R$

$= (240)^2/100 = 576$ W

As $P_{A'} < P_A$, the brightness of the bulb A decreases when connected in series with bulb B. *(1 M)*

Long Answer Type Questions (5 M)

1. (*a*) **Write Joule's law of heating.** **(*Ev*)**
(NCERT Exemplar) (CBSE, 2018)

(*b*) **Two lamps, one rated 100W; 220V, and the other 60W; 220V, are connected in parallel to electric mains supply. Find the current drawn by two bulbs from the line, if the supply voltage is 220V.**

Ans. (*a*) Joule's law of heating can be defined as: when current passes through a conductor, heat is generated. It is also known as Ohmic heating or resistive heating. *(1 M)*

$P = I^2R = V^2/R$ *(1 M)*

Where, P is in watt, I is in Ampere, R is in ohm and V is volt.

(*b*) Firstly we would find the resistance of the lamps.

$P_1 = 100W$

$V_1 = 220V$

$R_1 = V_1^{\,2}/P_1 = 484\Omega$

$P_2 = 60W$

$V_2 = 220V$

$R_2 = V_2^2/P_2 = 806.67\Omega$ *(1 M)*

The lamps are connected in parallel. Equivalent resistance $= R = (R_1 \times R_2)/(R_1 + R_2) = (484\Omega \times 806.67\Omega)$ $(484\Omega + 806.67\Omega) = 302.5\Omega$ *(1 M)*

From Ohm's law, current drawn is given by:

$I = V/R = 220V/302.5W = 0.727A$ *(1 M)*

2. **What is meant by electric circuit? Why does electric current start flowing in a circuit the moment circuit is complete? When do we say that the potential difference across a conductor in a circuit is 1 volt?**
Calculate the potential difference between the two terminals of a battery if 12 joules of work is done in transferring 2 coulombs of charge. **(CBSE, 2016 Term-I)**

Ans. (*i*) An electric circuit is defined as a continuous pathway for the flow of electric current, comprising of wires, resistances such as electric bulbs, and a switch. This circuit forms between the two terminals of a cell or battery, enabling the movement of electric current. *(1 M)*

(*ii*) Potential difference between the ends of the wire makes the current to flow in the wire. *(1 M)*

(*iii*) When the potential difference between two points measures 1 volt, it signifies that 1 joule of work is done in moving 1 coulomb of electric charge from one point to another point. *(1 M)*

1 volt = 1 joule/ 1 coulomb

$1V = 1J/1C$

(*iv*) We have been given: Work done (W) = 12 joules; Charge (Q) = 2 coulombs

Now, apply the formula for work done in moving a charge:

$$W = VQ \Rightarrow V = \frac{W}{Q}$$

$$V = \frac{12}{2} = 6\,\text{volts}$$ *(2 M)*

3. (*i*) Define electric power. Express it m terms of potential difference (V) and resistance (R).

(*ii*) An electric oven is designed to work on the mains voltage of 220 V. This oven consumes 11 units of electrical energy in 5 hours. Calculate:

(*a*) power rating of the oven

(*b*) current drawn by the oven

(*c*) resistance of the oven when it is red hot

Ans. (*i*) Electric power is defined as the rate at which electrical energy is transferred or converted in an electric circuit. *(½ M)*

It is expressed in terms of potential difference (V) and resistance (R) using the formula:

$$P = \frac{V^2}{R}$$ *(½ M)*

Where:

P is the electric power,

V is the potential difference (voltage), and

R is the resistance.

(*ii*) (*a*) To calculate the power rating of the oven, we can use the formula:

$$P = \frac{E}{t}$$

Where:

P is the power,

E is the electrical energy consumed (given as 11 units),

t is the time taken (given as 5 hours).

Substituting the given values:

$$P = \frac{11\,\text{units}}{5\,\text{hours}}$$

$P = 2.2$ units / hour *(1 M)*

(*b*) To find the current drawn by the oven, we can use the formula:

$P = VI$

Where:

P is the power (which we calculated in part (*a*)),

V is the voltage (given as 220 *V*),

I is the current.

Rearranging the formula to solve for *I*:

$$I = \frac{P}{V}$$

Substituting the given values:

$$I = \frac{2.2\,\text{units / hour}}{220V} \quad I = 0.01\text{ A}$$ *(1 M)*

(*c*) To find the resistance of the oven when it is red hot, we can rearrange the power formula:

$$P = \frac{V^2}{R}$$

to solve for *R*:

$$R = \frac{V^2}{P}$$ *(½ M)*

Substituting the given values:

$$R = \frac{(220V)^2}{2.2\,\text{units / hour}} \quad R = \frac{48400V^2}{2.2\,\text{units / hour}}$$

R = 22000 ohms *(½ M)*

So, the resistance of the oven when it is red hot is approximately 22000 ohms. *(1 M)*

4. Which uses more energy, a 250 W TV set in 1 hr, or a 1200W toaster in 10 minutes? (*Ev*) (NCERT Exercise)

Ans. The energy consumed by electrical device

$H = Pt$, where *P* is the power of the appliance and *t* is the time *(1 M)*

Using this formula, the energy consumed by a TV of power ration 250*W*, can be calculated as follows:

$H = 250W \times 3600$ seconds $= 9 \times 10^5$J *(2 M)*

Similarly, the energy consumed by a toaster of power rating 1200W is

$H = 1200W \times 600s = 7.2 \times 10^5$ J

From the calculations, we concluded that the energy consumed by the TV is greater than the toaster. *(2 M)*

5. Compare the power used in the 2Ω resistor in each of the following circuits: (*i*) a 6V battery in series with 1Ω and 2Ω resistors, and (*ii*) a 4V battery in parallel with 12Ω and 2Ω resistors. (*An*) (NCERT Exercise)

Ans. (*i*) The potential difference is 6*V* and the resistors 1Ω and 2Ω are connected in series, hence their equivalent resistance is 1Ω + 2Ω = 3Ω. The current in the circuit according to Ohm's law,

$$I = \frac{V}{R} = \frac{6}{3} = 2A \qquad (1\ M)$$

∴ 2A current will flow across all the components in the circuit because there is no division of current in a series circuit.

The power consumed by the 2Ω is

$$P = I^2R = (2)^2 \times 2 = 8W \qquad (2\ M)$$

(*ii*) When 12Ω and 2Ω resistors are connected in parallel, the voltage across the resistors remains the same. So, the power consumed by 2Ω the resistor is:

$$P = \frac{V^2}{R} = \frac{4^2}{2} = 8\text{W} \qquad (2\ M)$$

Hints & Explanations

Multiple Choice Questions

1. (*d*) In the series connection, the current remains the same, therefore current through the 40W bulb is also 1A.

2. (*a*)

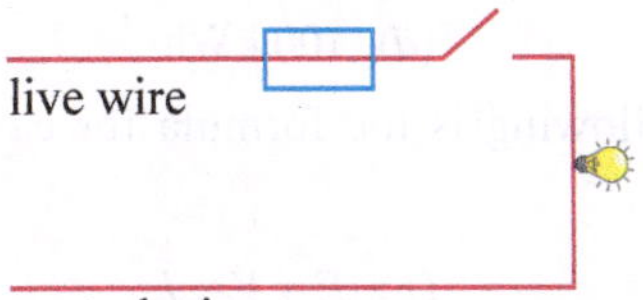

3. (*d*) The amount of heat H produced in the wire is directly proportional to the square of the current, resistance R of the wire, i.e., H ∝ R and the time t for which current is passed in the wire, i.e., H ∝ t.

4. (*a*) Electrical power can be calculated by

   P = VI

5. (*a*) Given P = 60W

   V = 220 V

   Then $I = \frac{P}{V} = \frac{60}{220} = 0.27\text{A}$

6. (*c*) We know that the bulb's brightness is proportional to the amount of power it consumes or the quantity of current it draws.

   Bulb C has the most power, and its brightness is the highest of the three. Bulb A has the lowest brightness. As a result, bulb B is sandwiched between these two.

7. (*d*) Power (*P*) = 1kW = 1000W

   Potential difference (*V*) = 220*V*

   We know,

   $P = VI$

   $I = \frac{P}{V} = \frac{1000}{220} = 4.54A$

   From all the given options, 5*A* fuse wire is correct.

   Hence, the correct answer is option (*d*).

8. (*d*) At the time of short circuit, the electric current in the circuit increases heavily.

9. (*b*) Unit of electrical energy is joule.

10. (*b*) The total power of the two bulbs connected in series is 18W (12W + 6W).

    Since they are connected in series, the current passing through both of the bulbs is the same.

    Therefore, the current passing through the 6W bulb is 0.06A.

11. (*b*) The resistance of a resistor is reduced to half of its initial value. If voltage across resistor remains unaltered, the amount of heat produced in the resistor will become two times.

12. (*b*) We know that, $P = VI$

    $\therefore I = \frac{P}{V}$

    Current in electric iron $= \frac{1500W}{200V} = 7.5A$

    Current in flash light $= \frac{500W}{200V} = 2.5A$

    Total current = 7.5*A* + 2.5*A* = 10*A*

Assertion and Reason

1. (*a*) The assertion is true, and the reason is also true and provides a valid explanation for the assertion. Hence, both the assertion and reason are true, and the reason is the correct explanation for the assertion.
2. (*d*) A is false, but R is true.

   When the current flowing through a resistor is doubled, the heat produced in the resistor quadruples.
3. (*a*) The assertion is true, and the reason is also true and provides a valid explanation for the assertion.
4. (*a*) The assertion is true, and the reason is also true and provides a valid explanation for the assertion.
5. (*a*) The assertion is true, and the reason is also true and provides a valid explanation for the assertion.

MISCELLANEOUS EXERCISE

Multiple Choice Questions (1 M)

1. Which of the following statements is true about electric current? **(Un)**

   (*a*) It flows from negative to positive terminals
   (*b*) It flows from positive to negative terminals
   (*c*) It flows randomly in a circuit
   (*d*) It flows from one end of a conductor to another

2. Which of the following materials is an insulator? **(Re)**

   (*a*) Copper (*b*) Aluminum
   (*c*) Rubber (*d*) Silver

3. Which of the following is the unit of electric current? **(Re)**

   (*a*) Ampere (*b*) Volt
   (*c*) Ohm (*d*) Watt

4. When a battery is connected to a circuit, which of the following statements is true? **(Re)**

   (*a*) Electrons flow from the positive terminal to the negative terminal of the battery
   (*b*) Electrons flow from the negative terminal to the positive terminal of the battery
   (*c*) Electrons do not flow in the circuit
   (*d*) Protons flow from the positive terminal to the negative terminal of the battery

5. Which of the following devices is used to measure electric current? **(Re)**

   (*a*) Voltmeter (*b*) Ammeter
   (*c*) Ohmmeter (*d*) Rheostat

6. Which of the following statements is true about electric circuits? **(Un)**

   (*a*) A closed circuit allows electric current to flow through it
   (*b*) An open circuit allows electric current to flow through it
   (*c*) A short circuit has no resistance
   (*d*) A parallel circuit has only one path for current flow

7. The resistance of a wire depends on which of the following factors? **(Re)**

   (*a*) Length of the wire (*b*) Thickness of the wire
   (*c*) Temperature of the wire (*d*) All of the above

8. The potential difference across a resistance of 5 ohm is 10 volt. What is the current flowing through the resistance? **(Ev)**

   (*a*) 0.5 A (*b*) 2 A
   (*c*) 5 A (*d*) 10 A

9. Which of the following statements is true about electric power? **(Un)**

   (*a*) It is the rate at which energy is consumed or produced
   (*b*) It is the amount of energy stored in a circuit
   (*c*) It is the resistance of a circuit
   (*d*) It is the potential difference between two points in a circuit

10. Which of the following is the correct formula to calculate electric power? **(Re)**

    (*a*) $P = V/R$ (*b*) $P = VI$
    (*c*) $P = IR$ (*d*) $P = V^2/R$

11. A heater consumes 1 kW of power for 10 hours. What is the energy consumed by the heater? **(Ev)**

    (*a*) 100 W (*b*) 1 kWh
    (*c*) 10 kWh (*d*) 100 kWh

12. Which of the following is the formula for calculating electrical energy? **(Re)**

    (*a*) $E = P \times t$ (*b*) $E = V \times I$
    (*c*) $E = V^2/R$ (*d*) $E = I^2 \times R$

13. Which of the following is the unit of electric power? **(Re)**

    (*a*) Watt (*b*) Joule
    (*c*) Volt (*d*) Ampere

Assertion and Reason (1 M)

Direction: **The following questions consist of two statements – Assertion (A) and Reason (R). Answer these questions by selecting the appropriate option given below:**

(*a*) Both A and R are true, and R is the correct explanation of A.
(*b*) Both A and R are true, but R is not the correct explanation of A.
(*c*) A is true, but R is false
(*d*) A is false, but R is true.

1. **Assertion (A):** The resistance of a conductor increases with an increase in its length.

   Reason (R): As the length of the conductor increases, the number of collisions between the electrons and the atoms of the conductor also increase, which results in an increase in the resistance of the conductor. **(An)**

2. **Assertion (A):** An increase in temperature increase the resistance of a metal wire.

   Reason (R): As the temperature of a metal wire increases, the number of collisions between the electrons and the atoms decreases, which results in a decrease in the resistance of the conductor. **(Un & An)**

3. **Assertion (A):** A circuit breaker is used to protect an electrical circuit from overload.

Reason (R): A circuit breaker works by opening the circuit when the current in the circuit exceeds a certain value, thereby protecting the circuit from damage. ***(Re)***

4. **Assertion (A):** In a series circuit, the total resistance is equal to the sum of the individual resistances.

Reason (R): In a series circuit, the current passing through each component is the same. ***(Un)***

Subjective Questions

Very Short Answer Type Questions (2 M)

1. What is the difference between: ***(Un)***
(*i*) a conductor and an insulator, (*ii*) a cell and a battery?
2. State the mathematical expression of Ohm's Law. ***(Re)***
3. What is the resistance, and what are the differences between series and parallel circuits? ***(Re)***
4. How does resistance affect the flow of current in a circuit? ***(Re)***
5. What is Ohm's law? ***(Re)***
6. How does the resistance of a conductor change with an increase in: (*i*) temperature (*ii*) length ***(Un)***
7. How does the resistance of a conductor change with a decrease in its cross-sectional area? ***(Re)***
8. How is the resistance of a conductor related to its conductivity? ***(Ev)***
9. Should the resistance of an ammeter be low or high? Give reason. **(NCERT Exemplar)**

Short Answer Type Questions (3 M)

1. How do you define electric potential difference? What is an electric circuit? ***(Un)***
2. Why is the resistance of a voltmeter very high? Why is it necessary to insulate the wires carrying electric current? ***(Re & Un)***
3. Explain Ohm's law. How does the resistance of a conductor affect the flow of electric current through it? ***(Re)***
4. How does the temperature affect the resistance of a conductor? ***(Re & Un)***
5. (*i*) State the law that explains the heating effect of current with respect to the measurable properties in an electrical circuit.
(*ii*) List the factors on which the resistance of a conductor depends. ***(Re & Un)***
6. What is the difference between series and parallel circuits? Two resistors of resistance 3Ω and 6Ω are connected in series. What is the total resistance of the combination? Two resistors of resistance 2Ω and 4Ω are connected in parallel. What is the total resistance of the combination? ***(Un & An)***
7. Resistances of three resistors are given as R_1 = 10 ohm, R_2 = 20 ohm and R_3 = 30 ohm. Calculate the effective resistance when they are connected in series. Also calculate the current flowing when combination is connected with the 6*V* battery. **(CBSE 2017)**
8. A student performs an experiment with 4 cells and a resistance wire and an ammeter in series and observes that when the number of cells in the circuit is decreased, the value of current through the wire also decreases. Name the law that is involved in the experiment and write its mathematical form. ***(Ap & Ev)***
9. A wire of resistivity 1.5×10^{-8} Ωm has a radius of its cross section is 0.8×10^{-3} m. Calculate the resistance of the wire if its length is 5 m. ***(Ev)***
10. What would you suggest to a student if while performing an experiment he finds that the pointer/needle of the ammeter and voltmeter do not coincide with the zero marks on the scales when circuit is open? No extra ammeter/voltmeter is available in the laboratory. **(CBSE 2020)**
11. A *V-I* graph for a nichrome wire is given below. What do you infer from this graph? Draw a labelled circuit diagram to obtain such a graph. **(CBSE 2020)**

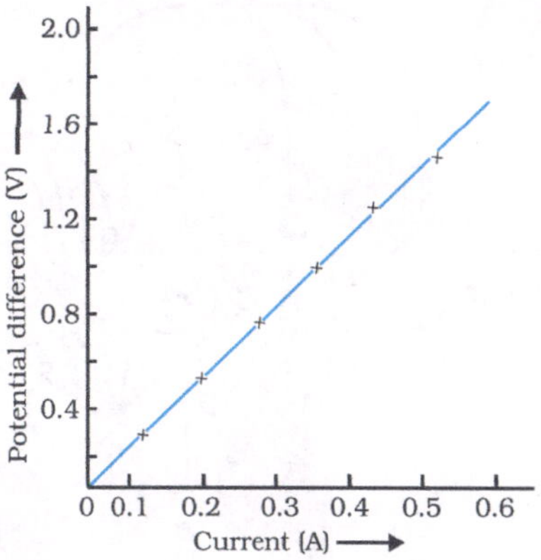

12. Draw a circuit diagram of an electric circuit containing a cell, a key, an ammeter, a resistor of 2W in series with a combination of two resistors of 4W each. Write net resistance of the circuit. **(NCERT Exemplar)**
13. What is meant by electrical power? ***(Re)***
14. A 100 W bulb is connected to a 220 *V* supply. Calculate the resistance of the filament. Why do the filaments of bulbs glow when electricity passes through them? ***(Ev)***
15. A circuit contains two resistors in parallel; one resistor has a resistance of 10 ohms and the other has a resistance of 20 ohms. If the total current in the circuit is 5*A*, what is the voltage across each resistor? ***(Ev)***
16. Two resistors with resistances of 20 ohm and 30 ohm are connected in series with a 6V battery. Find the current in the circuit and the voltage across each resistor. ***(Ev)***
17. A copper wire of length 10 m and diameter 1 mm is connected to a 6*V* battery. What is the current flowing through the wire if the resistivity of copper is 1.7×10^{-8} Ωm? ***(Ap & Ev)***

18. (*a*) Define the heating effect of electric current and explain its applications in daily life.

(*b*) Kaveri conducted an experiment to study the energy efficiency of different electric iron. She connected an iron of 1kW rating to a 220 V power supply in a laboratory. She has to calculate the current flowing through the electric iron.

(*c*) Draw a circuit diagram to represent a parallel combination of two resistors with resistance values 10 ohm and 20 ohm, respectively. **(*Ev*)**

19. (*i*) A 220*V* electric bulb is rated 100W. What is the current flowing through it?

(*ii*) An electric heater is rated at 220*V* and 500*W*. What is the resistance of the heater? **(*Ap* & *Ev*)**

Long Answer Type Questions (5 M)

1. The diagram above is a schematic diagram of a household circuit. The house shown in the above diagram has 5 usable space where electrical connections are made. For this house, the mains have a voltage of 220 V and the net current coming from the mains is 22A

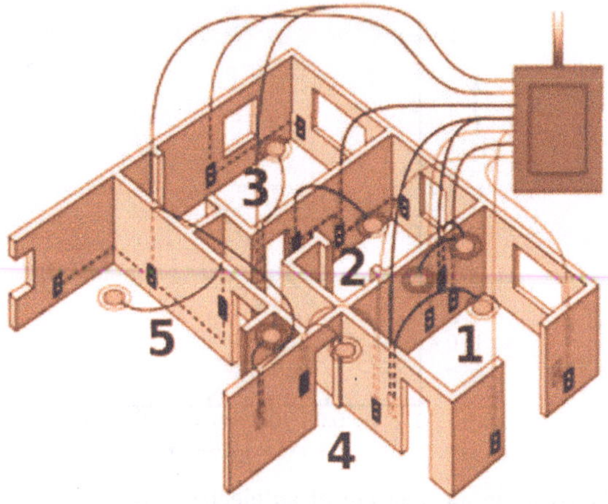

(*a*) What is the mode of connection to all the spaces in the house from the mains? **(*Ap*)**

(*b*) The spaces 5 and 4 have the same resistance and spaces 3 and 2 have respective resistances of 20Ω and 30Ω. Space 1 has a resistance double that of space 5. What is the net resistance for space 5. **(*An*)**

(*c*) What is the current in space 3? **(*An*)**

(*d*) What should be placed between the main connection and the rest of the house's electrical appliances to save them from accidental high electric current? **(*Un*)**

(CBSE SQP, 2022)

2. (*a*) With the help of a suitable circuit diagram prove that the reciprocal of the equivalent resistance of a group of resistances joined in parallel is equal to the sum of the reciprocals of the individuals resistance. **(*Cr* + *Un*)**

(*b*) In an electric circuit two resistors of 12Ω each are joined in parallel to a 6*V* battery. Find the current drawn from the battery. **(*Ev*) (CBSE 2019)**

3. (*a*) Write the relation between resistance R and electrical resistivity ρ of the material of a conductor in the shape of cylinder of length *l* and area of cross-section A. Hence derive the SI unit of electrical resistivity.

(*b*) The resistance of a metal wire of length 3 m is 60 Ω. If the area of cross-section of the wire is 4×10^{-7} m^2, calculate the electrical resistivity of the wire.

(*c*) State how would electrical resistivity be affected if the wire (of part '*ii*') is stretched so that its length is doubled. Justify your answer.

4. (*a*) Three resistors R_1, R_2 and R_3 are connected in parallel and the combination is connected to a battery, an ammeter, a voltmeter and a key. Draw suitable circuit diagram to show the arrangement of these circuit components along with the direction of current flowing. **(*Cr* + *Un*) (CBSE 2022)**

(*b*) Calculate the equivalent resistance of the following network: **(*Ev*)**

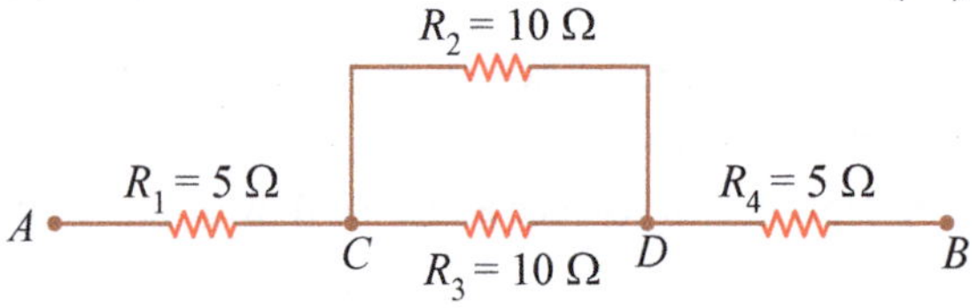

5. An electric lamp of resistance 20Ω and a conductor of resistance 4Ω are connected to a 6*V* battery as shown in the circuit. Calculate" **(*Ev*) (CBSE 2019)**

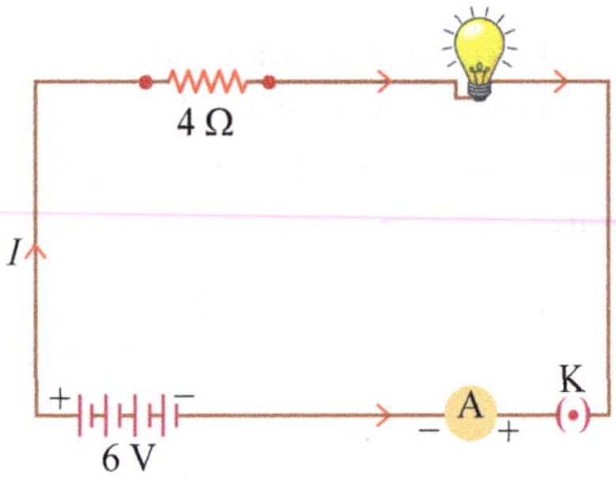

(*a*) the total resistance of the circuit,

(*b*) the current through the circuit,

(*c*) the potential difference across the (*i*) electric lamp and (*ii*) conductor, and

(*d*) power of the lamp

6. Show how you would connect three resistors, each of resistance 6Ω, so that the combination has a resistance of (*i*) 9Ω, (*ii*) 4Ω. **(*Un*) (NCERT Exercise)**

7. Explain the following. **(*Re*) (NCERT Exercise)**

(*a*) Why is tungsten used almost exclusively for filament of electric lamps?

(*b*) Why are the conductors of electric heating devices, such as bread-toasters and electric irons, made of an alloy rather than a pure metal?

(*c*) Why is the series arrangement not used for domestic circuits?

(*d*) How does the resistance of a wire vary with its area of cross-section?

(*e*) Why copper and aluminium wires are usually employed for electricity transmission?

Case Based Questions

Case Based-I:

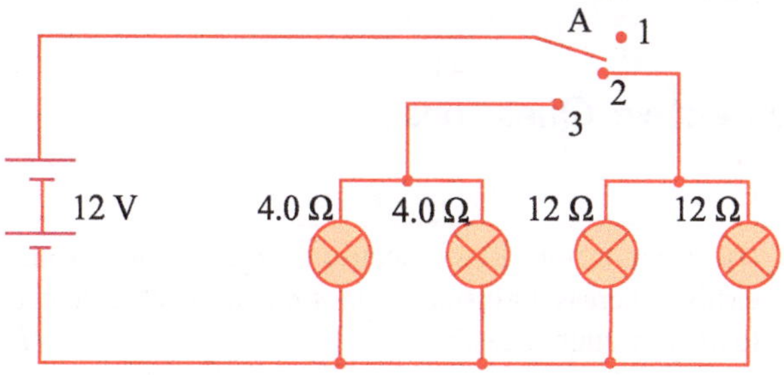

Vinita and Ahmed demonstrated a circuit that operates the two headlights and the two sidelights of a car, in their school exhibition. Based on their demonstrated circuit, answer the following questions.

(*i*) State what happens when switch A is connected to **(An)** *(1 M)*

(*a*) Position 2 (*b*) Position 3

(*ii*) Find the potential difference across each lamp when lit. **(An)** *(1 M)*

(*iii*) Calculate the current **(Ev)** *(2 M)*

(*a*) In each 12 Ω lamp when lit.

(*b*) In each 4 Ω lamp when lit.

OR

Show, with calculations, which type of lamp, 4.0 Ω or 12 Ω, has the higher power. **(Ev)** *(2 M)*

Case Based-II: Priya is a student who is learning about electric charge, current, and potential in her physics class. She is curious to understand these concepts and how they relate to each other. In order to grasp the concepts better, she relates them to a water flow analogy. **(Re)**

(*i*) Which of the following is a fundamental property of matter associated with the presence of electric fields? *(1 M)*

(*a*) Electric current (*b*) Electric potential
(*c*) Electric charge (*d*) Electric resistance

(*ii*) Ohm's Law relates which of the following quantities in a circuit? *(1 M)*

(*a*) Electric charge and electric current
(*b*) Electric resistance and electric potential
(*c*) Electric potential and electric current
(*d*) Electric charge and electric potential

(*iii*) What is the fundamental unit of electric charge? *(1 M)*

(*a*) Ampere (A) (*b*) Coulomb (C)
(*c*) Ohm (Ω) (*d*) Electron (e)

Case Based-III: Joule's Law of Heating Effects is a fundamental principle in electrical engineering and finds practical applications in various devices. It helps engineers and technicians design electrical circuits with appropriate resistance values to prevent overheating and ensure efficient energy transfer. It also plays a crucial role in the development of electrical appliances, heating elements, and other technologies that rely on controlled heat generation.

(*i*) The heating effect of electric current is commonly utilized in which of the following devices? **(Re)** *(1 M)*

(*a*) Electric motors (*b*) Solar panels
(*c*) Capacitors (*d*) Electric heaters

(*ii*) When a current of 2 amperes flows through a resistor with a resistance of 5 ohms for 10 seconds, the heat produced is: **(Ev)** *(1 M)*

(*a*) 10 J (*b*) 200 J
(*c*) 50 J (*d*) 100 J

(*iii*) The heating effect of electric current is primarily due to: **(Re)** *(1 M)*

(*a*) The flow of electrons
(*b*) The presence of magnetic fields
(*c*) The increase in resistance
(*d*) The conversion of electrical energy into heat energy

(*iv*) The electric energy consumed by an appliance with a power rating of 500 watts when operated for 2 hours is: **(Ev)** *(1 M)*

(*a*) 500 J (*b*) 1000 J
(*c*) 1000 Wh (*d*) 2000 Wh

ANSWER KEYS

Multiple Choice Questions

1. (*b*) **2.** (*c*) **3.** (*a*) **4.** (*b*) **5.** (*b*) **6.** (*a*) **7.** (*d*) **8.** (*b*) **9.** (*a*) **10.** (*b*)
11. (*c*) **12.** (*a*) **13.** (*a*)

Assertion and Reason

1. (*a*) **2.** (*c*) **3.** (*a*) **4.** (*a*)

Case Based Questions

Case Based-II

(*i*) (*c*) (*ii*) (*c*) (*iii*) (*d*)

Case Based-III

(*i*) (*d*) (*ii*) (*b*) (*iii*) (*d*) (*iv*) (*c*)

HINTS & EXPLANATIONS

Multiple Choice Questions

1. (*b*) It flows from positive to negative terminals.
2. (*c*) Rubber.
3. (*a*) Ampere.
4. (*b*) Electrons flow from the negative terminal to the positive terminal of the battery.
5. (*b*) Ammeter.
6. (*a*) A closed circuit allows electric current to flow through it.
7. (*d*) All of the above.
8. (*b*) 2 *A*.
9. (*a*) It is the rate at which energy is consumed or produced.
10. (*b*) $P = VI$.
11. (*c*) 10 kWh
12. (*a*) $E = P \times t$
13. (*a*) Watt

Assertion and Reason

1. (*a*) This assertion and reason pair are both true and related to Ohm's law, which states that resistance (*R*) is directly proportional to the length (*L*) of the conductor. Therefore, when the length of the conductor increases, the resistance also increases. The reason given for this assertion is correct as well. As the length of the conductor increases, the number of atoms in the path of the electrons increases, which results in an increase in collisions between the electrons and the atoms, which in turn increases the resistance of the conductor.
2. (*c*) Assertion is true and reason is false. The resistance of a metal wire increases with an increase in temperature. This phenomenon is known as the temperature coefficient of resistance. The reason given for this assertion is incorrect. As the temperature of the metal wire increases, the number of collisions between the electrons and the atoms increases, which results in an increase in the resistance of the conductor.
3. (*a*) This assertion and reason pair are both true. A circuit breaker is used to protect an electrical circuit from overload, which can cause damage to the circuit and lead to electrical fires. The reason given for this assertion is also true. A circuit breaker works by sensing the current in the circuit and opening the circuit when the current exceeds a certain value. This protects the circuit from damage and allows it to be safely reset and used again.
4. (*a*) This assertion and reason pair are both true. In a series circuit, the total resistance is equal to the sum of the individual resistances. This is because the current passing through each component is the same, and the voltage drop across each component is proportional to its resistance. The reason given for this assertion is also true. In a series circuit, the current passing through each component is the same because there is only one path for the current to flow.

Subjective Questions

Very Short Answer Type Questions

1. (*i*) A conductor allows electric charge to flow through it easily, whereas an insulator does not allow electric charge to flow through it easily. *(1 M)*

   (*ii*) A cell is a single unit that produces electrical energy, while a battery is a collection of cells. *(2 M)*
2. Ohm's Law can be mathematically expressed as $V = IR$, where V is the voltage applied across the conductor, I is the current passing through the conductor, and R is the resistance of the conductor. *(2 M)*
3. Resistance opposes the flow of current in a circuit, reducing the flow of current. *(1 M)*

   In a series circuit, the components are connected in a single path, while in a parallel circuit, the components are connected in multiple paths. *(1 M)*
4. Resistance affects the flow of current in a circuit by impeding the movement of electrons, causing a decrease in current as resistance increases. *(2 M)*
5. Ohm's law states that the current flowing through a conductor is directly proportional to the voltage applied across it and inversely proportional to its resistance. *(2 M)*
6. (*i*) The resistance of a conductor increases with an increase in its temperature. *(1 M)*

   (*ii*) The resistance of a conductor increases with an increase in its length. *(1 M)*
7. As the cross-sectional area of a conductor decreases, the resistance of the conductor increases. *(1 M)*

   This relationship is due to the fact that a smaller cross-sectional area provides less space for the flow of electrons, leading to more collisions and higher resistance in the conductor. *(1 M)*
8. The resistance of a conductor is inversely proportional to its conductivity. *(1 M)*

   Conductivity is a measure of how easily a material allows the flow of electric current, while resistance is a measure of how much a material opposes the flow of current. *(1 M)*
9. Resistance of an ammeter should ideally be zero so that it does not affect the flow of current in the circuit. Hence, resistance of an ammeter should be very low as zero resistance is not possible in real life. *(2 M)*

Short Answer Type Questions

1. Electric potential difference is defined as the difference in electric potential between two points in an electric circuit. It is measured in volts (*V*) and represents the amount of work needed to move a unit of electric charge from one point to another. *(1½ M)*

An electric circuit is a path or loop through which electric current can flow. It consists of a power source, conductors, and loads connected in a closed loop. The power source supplies energy to the circuit, and the conductors allow the current to flow, while the loads convert the energy into useful work. *(1½ M)*

2. The resistance of a voltmeter is very high so that it draws very little current from the circuit and does not affect the voltage being measured. *(1½ M)*
   It is necessary to insulate the wires carrying electric current to prevent electric shocks and short circuits. *(1½ M)*

3. Ohm's law states that the current through a conductor between two points is directly proportional to the voltage across the two points, provided that the temperature and other physical conditions remain constant. *(1 M)*
   In mathematical terms, it can be expressed as $I = V/R$, where I is the current, V is the voltage, and R is the resistance of the conductor. *(1 M)*
   The resistance of a conductor determines the amount of current that can flow through it. A higher resistance means that less current can flow, while a lower resistance means that more current can flow. The relationship between resistance and current is described by Ohm's law. *(1 M)*

4. The resistance of a conductor increases as its temperature increases. *(1 M)*
   This is due to the increase in the collisions between the atoms and electrons in the conductor, which increases the resistance to the flow of current. *(2 M)*

5. (*i*) Joules law of heating states that the heat dissipated across a resistor is directly proportional to *(½ M)*
   (*a*) the square of the current flowing through it
   (*b*) The resistance of the conductor
   (*c*) duration of flow of current. *(1½ M)*
   $H = i^2rt$ (alternative answer).
   (*ii*) Resistance of a conductor depends on
   (*a*) the length of the conductor
   (*b*) the area of the cross section
   (*c*) nature of material
   (*d*) temperature of the conductor.
   (Any two should fetch full marks). *(½ + ½ M)*

6. In a series circuit, the components are connected end to end, so that the current flows through each component in turn.
   In a parallel circuit, the components are connected across each other, so that the current can flow through each component independently. *(1 M)*
   Resistance of the series combination $= R_1 + R_2 = 3 + 6 = 9\Omega$ *(1 M)*
   Resistance of the parallel combination $= (R_1 \times R_2)/(R_1 + R_2)$ $= (2 \times 4)/(2 + 4) = 8/6 = 4/3\Omega$ *(1 M)*

7. Effective resistance = 10 + 20 + 30 = 60 Ohm *(1½ M)*
   Current, $I = V/R = 6/60 = 0.1A$ *(1½ M)*

8. The law involved in the experiment described is Ohm's Law. *(1 M)*
   Ohm's Law states that the current flowing through a conductor is directly proportional to the voltage across it, and inversely proportional to the resistance of the conductor. The mathematical form of Ohm's Law is given by:
   $V = I \times R$
   where:
   V is the voltage across the conductor,
   I is the current flowing through the conductor, and
   R is the resistance of the conductor. *(2 M)*

9. The resistance of a wire is given by the formula:
   $R = \rho \times (L/A)$ *(1 M)*
   where ρ is the resistivity of the wire, L is its length, and A is its cross-sectional area.
   Area of cross section of the wire, $A = \pi . r^2$
   $= 3.14 \times (0.8 \times 10^{-3})^2 = 2 \times 10^{-6}\ m^2$ *(1 M)*
   Substituting the given values, we get:
   $$R = \frac{(1.5\times10^{-1}\Omega m)\times 5m^2}{2\times10^{-6}m^2} = 0.0375\ \Omega$$
   Therefore, the resistance of the wire is 0.0375 Ω. *(1 M)*

10. If the circuit is open, the pointers/needles on the ammeter and voltmeter will not line up with the zero mark on the scale. If there is a zero error, it is recommended to subtract this error from the value when the circuit is closed (or subtract the value indicated by the ammeter from the value obtained after the current has flowed). Otherwise, an accurate current or potential difference will not be recorded. *(3 M)*

11. The *V-I* graph of the nichrome wire shows a straight line. It means that the resistance of the wire remains constant when the current supply is changed, it follows the ohm's low and therefore, it is considered as ohmic conductor.
    It follows the ohm's law $\rightarrow V = IR$ *(2 M)*
    $$R = \frac{V}{I}$$

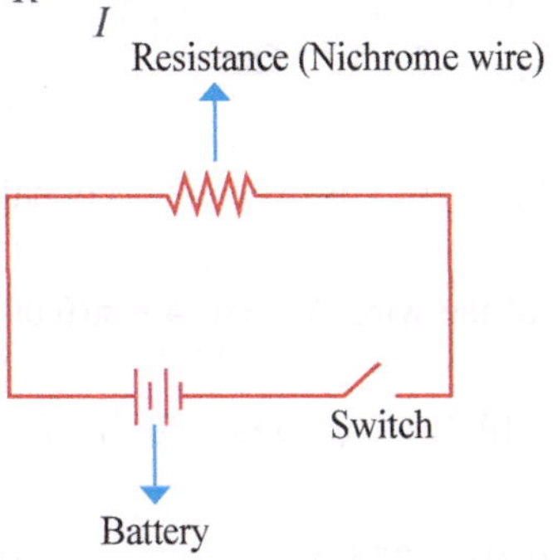

(1 M)

12.

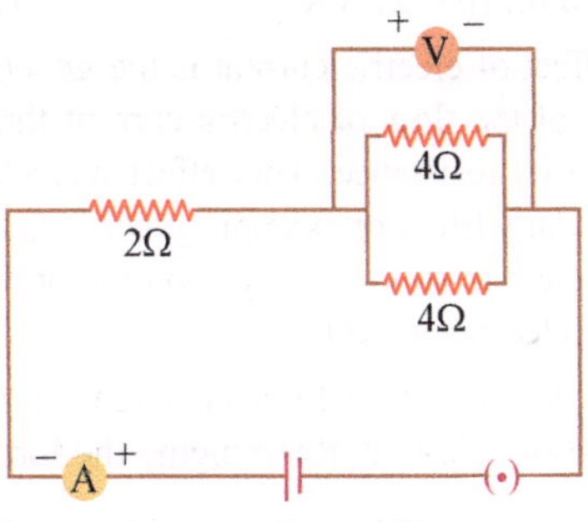

Net resistance of two 4Ω
Resistors connected in parallel is 2Ω
Since, we have two resistors of same resistance in series so the potential drop across each one of them will be same. *(3 M)*

13. Electrical power is the rate at which electric energy is transferred or consumed in an electric circuit. It is measured in watts (W) and is calculated by multiplying the voltage (V) and current (I) in the circuit. i.e.,

$P = VI$

Formula of electrical power can also be written as:

$P = V^2/R$ or $P = I^2R$ *(3 M)*

14. Given, Power (P) = 100W, Voltage (V) = 220V *(1 M)*

We know, $P = V^2/R$ *(1 M)*

Therefore, $R = V^2/P = 220^2/100 = 484\Omega$

The filaments of bulbs glow when electricity passes through them because of the heat generated by the resistance of the filament. *(1 M)*

15. Total resistance $R = (R_1 \times R_2)/(R_1 + R_2)$

= (10 ohm × 20 ohm)/(10 ohm + 20 ohm) = 6.67 ohm *(1 M)*

Current through $R_1 = I_1 = (R_2 / (R_1 + R_2)) \times I$

= (20 ohm/(10 ohm + 20 ohm)) × 5 A = 3.33 A *(½ M)*

Current through $R_2 = I_2 = (R_1/(R_1 + R_2)) \times I$

= (10 ohm / (10 ohm + 20 ohm)) × 5A = 1.67A *(½ M)*

Voltage across $R_1 = I_1 \times R_1 = 3.33A \times 10$ ohm = 33.3 V *(½ M)*

Voltage across $R_2 = I_2 \times R_2 = 1.67A \times 20$ ohm = 33.3 V *(½ M)*

16. Total resistance $R = R_1 + R_2$ = 20 ohm + 30 ohm = 50 ohm *(1 M)*

Current $I = V/R = 6V/50$ ohm = 0.12A *(1 M)*

Voltage across $R_1 = IR_1 = 0.12A \times 20$ ohm = 2.4V *(½ M)*

Voltage across $R_2 = IR_2 = 0.12A \times 30$ ohm = 3.6V *(½ M)*

17. Given, diameter of wire, d = 1 mm = 0.001 m

Length of wire, l = 10 m

Resistivity of copper, $\rho = 1.7 \times 10^{-8}$ Ωm

Voltage, $V = 6V$ *(½ M)*

Resistance, $R = \rho(l/A)$, where A is the cross-sectional area of the wire. *(½ M)*

Cross-sectional area of the wire, $A = \pi d^2/4 = \pi(0.001)^2/4 = 7.854 \times 10^{-7}$ m^2 *(1 M)*

Resistance, $R = (1.7 \times 10^{-8}) \times (10/7.854 \times 10^{-7}) = 0.216\ \Omega$ *(½ M)*

Current, $I = V/R = 6/0.216 = 27.8$ A *(½ M)*

18. (*i*) The heating effect of electric current is the generation of heat as a result of the flow of electric current through a conductor due to its resistance. This effect has several applications in our daily life. For example, electric heaters, electric irons, and electric stoves all work on the principle of heating effect of electric current. *(1 M)*

(*ii*) We can use the formula P = VI to calculate the current flowing through the electric iron. Rearranging the formula, we get

$$I = \frac{P}{V}$$

Substituting the given values, we get:

$$I = \frac{1000\text{ W}}{220\text{ V}}$$

Therefore, the current flowing through the electric iron is 4.54 A. *(1 M)*

(*iii*) Here's a circuit diagram to represent a parallel combination of two resistors with resistance values 10 ohm and 20 ohm, respectively:

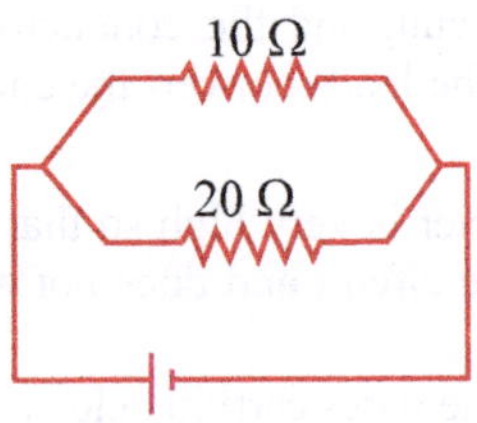

(1 M)

19. (*i*) Given, voltage, $V = 220V$

Power, P = 100W

Current, $I = P/V$ *(½ M)*

= 100/220 = 0.45A *(1 M)*

(*ii*) Given, voltage, $V = 220V$

Power, P = 500W

Resistance, $R = V^2/P$ *(½ M)*

= 220^2/500 = 96.8Ω *(1 M)*

Long Answer Type Questions

1. (*a*) All spaces are connected in parallel. *(1 M)*

(*b*) Let Resistance of Space 5 and 4 be R ohms respectively

Resistance of Space 1 = 2 R ohms

Resistance of Space 2 = 30 ohms

Resistance of Space 3 = 20 ohms

Current = 22 A

V = 220 V

Total Resistance = V/I

$$\frac{1}{R_1} + \frac{1}{R_2} + \frac{1}{R_3} + \frac{1}{R_4} + \frac{1}{R_5} = \frac{1}{R_{eq}}$$

$$\frac{1}{2R} + \frac{1}{30} + \frac{1}{20} + \frac{1}{R} + \frac{1}{R} = \frac{1}{R_{eq}}$$

$$\frac{30 + 2R + 3R + 60 + 60}{60R} = \frac{1}{R_{eq}}$$

$$\frac{150 + 5R}{60R} = \frac{1}{R_{eq}}$$

$$R_{eq} = \frac{60R}{150 + 5R} = \frac{220}{22}$$

$60R = 10(150 + 5R) = 1500 + 50R$

$10R = 1500 = 150\Omega$ *(2 M)*

(*c*) Current in space 3, 13 can be given by:

13 = V/R = 220/20 = 11 A *(1 M)*

(*d*) **Electric Fuses** can be used to protect circuits (and individual household appliances) from sudden surges in electric current. *(1 M)*

2. (*a*) *(1 M)*

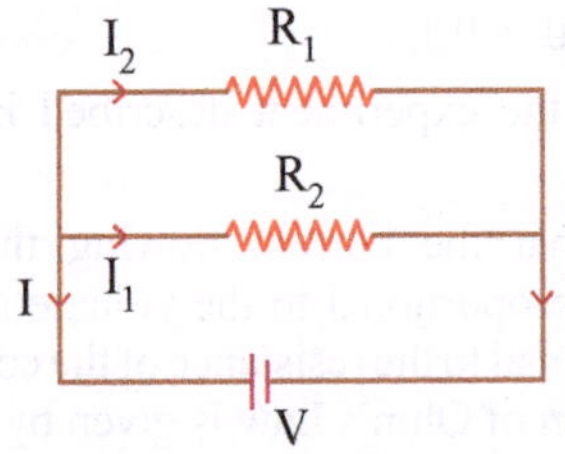

We know that V across, R_1 and R_2 will be same

$I = I_1 + I_2$

$$\frac{V}{R_{eq}} = \frac{V}{R_1} + \frac{V}{R_2} \Rightarrow \boxed{\frac{1}{R_{eq}} = \frac{1}{R_1} + \frac{1}{R_2}}$$ *(2 M)*

(*b*)

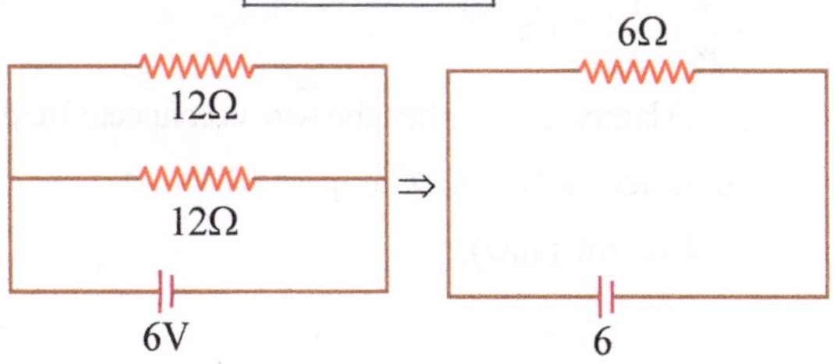

$V = iR$ $\qquad i = \frac{V}{R} = \frac{6}{6} = 1$ *(1 + 1 M)*

$$\boxed{\begin{array}{l} i = 1A \\ V = 6V \end{array}}$$

3. (*a*) The relation between resistance (R) and electrical resistivity (ρ) of the material of a conductor in the shape of a cylinder of length l and area of cross-section A is given by:

$$R = \frac{\rho l}{A}$$ *(½ M)*

To derive the SI unit of electrical resistivity, rearrange the equation:

$$\rho = \frac{RA}{l}$$ *(½ M)*

The SI unit of resistance (R) is ohms (Ω), the area (A) is in square meters (m^2), and the length (l) is in meters (m). *(½ M)*

Therefore, the SI unit of electrical resistivity (ρ) is ohm-meters ($\Omega \cdot m$). *(½ M)*

(*b*) Given:

Length of the wire (l) = 3 m

Resistance (R) = 60Ω

Area of cross-section (A) = $4 \times 10^{-7}\ m^{-2}$

Using the formula $R = \frac{\rho l}{A}$, we can rearrange it to solve for ρ:

$$\rho = \frac{RA}{l}$$ *(½ M)*

$$\rho = \frac{(60\Omega) \times (4 \times 10^{-7}\ m^2)}{3m}$$

$$\rho = \frac{240 \times 10^{-7}}{3}\ \Omega \cdot m$$ *(½ M)*

$\rho = 80 \times 10^{-7}\ \Omega \cdot$

$\rho = 8 \times 10^{-6}\ \Omega \cdot m$ *(½ M)*

(*c*) If the wire (from part '*ii*') is stretched so that its length is doubled, the new length l' would be $2 \times 3\ m = 6\ m$.

But we know that, the resistivity of a substance is unaffected by changes in its length or area of cross-section. It is solely determined by the material's inherent properties and temperature, leading to no alteration in its resistivity with changes in length or cross-sectional area.

Hence there is no change in resistivity of the wire. *(1 M)*

4. (*a*) *(2 M)*

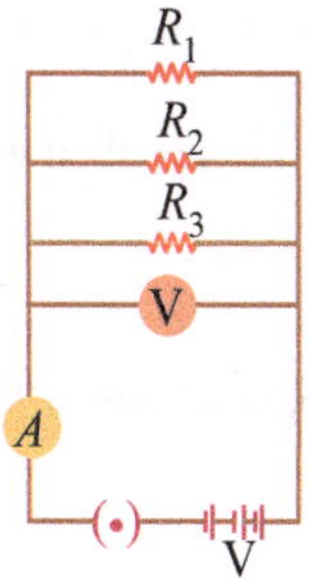

(*b*) Effective resistance = 5 + (10 × 10)/(10 + 10) + 5

= 15 ohm *(3 M)*

5. (*a*) The total resistance of the circuit = 20Ω + 4Ω = 24Ω *(1 M)*

(*b*) The current through the circuit = current through the bulb = current through the conductor.

The current through the circuit $= \dfrac{\text{voltage applied}}{\text{Total Resistance}}$.

The current through the circuit $= \dfrac{6}{24}$ A

The current through the circuit = 0.25A *(1 M)*

(*c*) The potential difference across the lamp and the conductor.

(*i*) The potential difference across the electric lamp = 0.25 × 20 = 5volt *(1 M)*

(*ii*) The potential difference conductor

= 0.25 × 4 = 1 volt *(1 M)*

(*d*) Power can be calculated as

P = VI

P = 5 × 0.25 = 1.15 W *(1 M)*

6. If all the three resistors are connected in series, their equivalent resistance would be [6Ω + 6Ω + 6Ω = 18Ω], which is not the desirable value, Similarly, if all the three resistors are in parallel, their equivalent resistor would be

$$\frac{1}{R} = \frac{1}{6} + \frac{1}{6} + \frac{1}{6} = \frac{3}{6} = \frac{1}{2} \quad \therefore R = 2\Omega$$ *(1 M)*

which is again not desirable value.

Case (*i*)

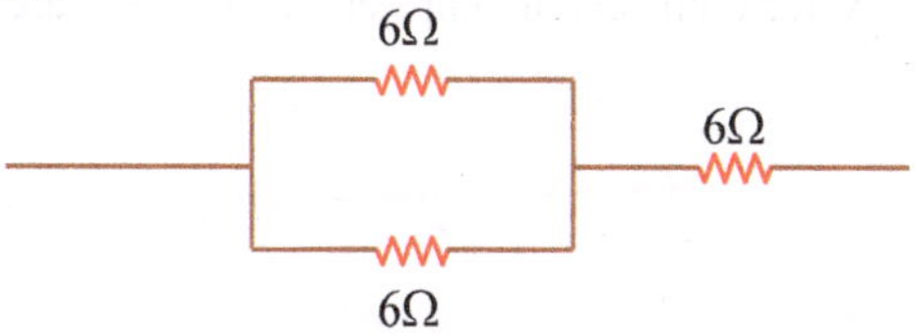

If two resistors are connected in parallel, then the net resistance is

$$\frac{1}{\frac{1}{6} + \frac{1}{6}} = \frac{6 \times 6}{6 + 6} = 3\Omega$$ *(1 M)*

The third resistor is in series, hence the equivalent resistance,

$R = 6\Omega + 3\Omega = 9\Omega$ *(1 M)*

Case (*ii*)

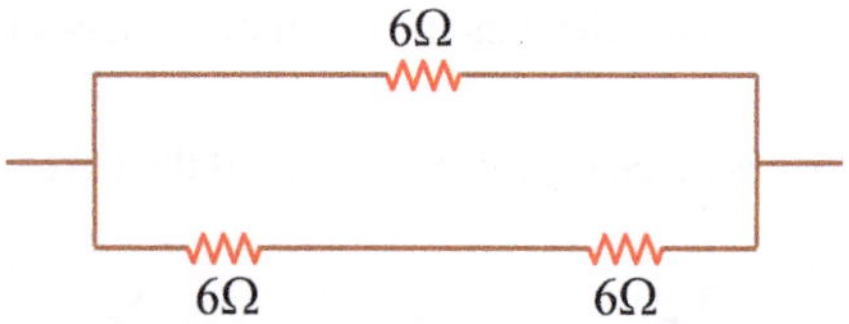

When two resistors are connected in series, their equivalent resistance,

$R = 6\Omega + 6\Omega = 12\Omega$

The third resistor is connected in parallel with 12Ω. *(1 M)*

Hence the equivalent resistance,

$R = \frac{1}{6} + \frac{1}{12} = \frac{12 \times 6}{12+6} = 4\Omega$ *(1 M)*

7. (*a*) Electric lamps operate at high temperature. The resistivity and melting point of tungsten is very high. So, it doesn't burn easily when heated. Hence, we use tungsten's filament for electric lamps. *(1 M)*

(*b*) Alloys have high resistivity than metals. So they produce more heat. *(1 M)*

(*c*) In a series circuit if one of the device is switched off then current through all the devices will be zero. Hence, all the devices will stop working. This is the reason why series combination is not used in domestic circuits. *(1 M)*

(*d*) We know, $R = \rho \frac{1}{A}$, thus

Resistance is inversely proportional to the area of cross section. When the area of cross section increases the resistance decreases and vice versa. *(1 M)*

(*e*) Copper and aluminium have low resistivity so they are good conductors of electricity they are usually employed for electricity transmission. *(1 M)*

Case Based Questions

Case Based-I

(*i*) (*a*) 12 Ω lamps (only) on.

(*b*) 4 Ω lamps (only) on *(½ + ½ M)*

(*ii*) 12 V for both sets of lamps and all of them are in parallel. *(1 M)*

(*iii*) (*a*) 12 Ω lamps are on when the wire is connected to position 2.

Voltage across both 12 Ω lamps = 12 V.

V = IR (Ohm's law).

$I = \frac{V}{R} = \frac{12}{12} = 1A$. *(1 M)*

(*b*) 4 Ω lamps are on when the wire is connected to position 3.

Voltage across both 4 Ω lamps = 12 V.

V = IR (Ohm's law).

$I = \frac{V}{R} = \frac{12}{4} = 3A$ *(1 M)*

OR

$P = V^2/R$

All lamps are in parallel and hence same V for all lamps.

For 4 Ω lamps → $P = \frac{12 \times 12}{4} = 36$ W

For 12 Ω lamps → $P = \frac{12 \times 12}{12} = 12$ W

Hence 4 Ω lamps will have higher power. *(½ × 4 M)*

Case Based-II

(*i*) (*c*) Electric charge *(1 M)*

(*ii*) (*c*) Electric potential and electric current *(1 M)*

(*iii*) (*d*) Electron *(1 M)*

Case Based-III

(*i*) (*d*) Electric heaters *(1 M)*

(*ii*) (*b*) To calculate the heat produced (H), we use the formula $H = I^2 \times R \times t$, where I is the current, R is the resistance, and t is the time.

$H = (2A)^2 \times 5\ \Omega \times 10s = 200$ J

Therefore, the heat produced is 200 J. *(1 M)*

(*iii*) (*d*) The conversion of electrical energy into heat energy *(1 M)*

(*iv*) (*c*) To calculate the electric energy consumed (E), we use the formula $E = P \times t$, where P is the power rating and t is the time.

$E = 500W \times 2$ hours $= 1000$ Wh *(1 M)*

❑❑❑

12 MAGNETIC EFFECTS OF ELECTRIC CURRENT

"Have you ever wondered at how a compass needle deflects near any current conducting wire? This happens because the electric current flowing through the wire generates a magnetic field around it, causing the compass needle, which aligns with magnetic fields, to deflect"

SYLLABUS & WEIGHTAGE

LIST OF CONCEPT NAMES	YEARS					
	2020	2021	2022	2023	2024	2025
Magnetic field and field lines (Electricity and magnetism interconnection, Properties of magnetic field lines, Magnetic field due to straight conductor, Magnetic field due to current in circular loop, Magnetic field due to current in solenoid, Right Hand thumb rule, Force on current carrying conductor in a magnetic field. Fleming's left - Hand Rule)	1Q (1 M) 1Q (5 M)	Exam not conducted	1Q (2 M) 1Q (4 M)	3Q (1M each)	1Q (1 M) 1Q (2 M) 1Q (3 M)	3Q (1 M) 1Q (3 M)
Domestic electric circuit (Wire - Live wire, neutral wire, earth wire, Meter Box: Electric meter, fuse)	—		—	1Q (3M)		—

CONCEPT MAP

To Access One Shot Revision Video Scan This QR Code

Magnetic Effect of Electric current

Force experienced in magnetic field

CBSE 2024, 2023, 2022

When a current-carrying conductor is placed in a magnetic field, a force is exerted on the conductor. Its direction is given by,

Fleming's Left – Hand Rule

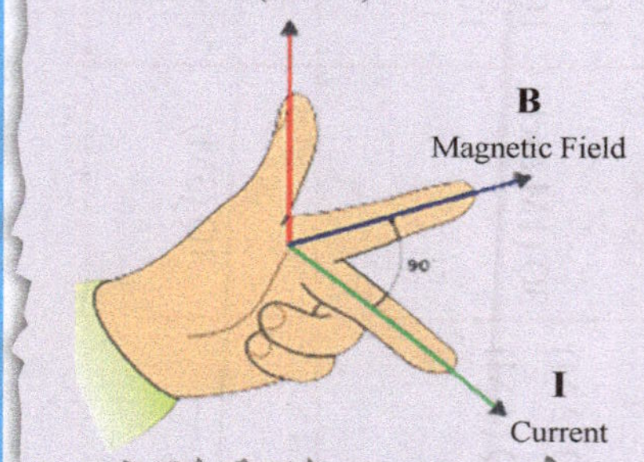

Direction of Magnetic field

CBSE 2025

Right-Hand Thumb Rule	
Straight current carrying conductor:	Circular Loop and Solenoid:
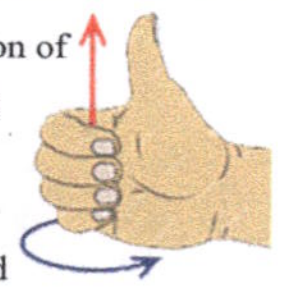	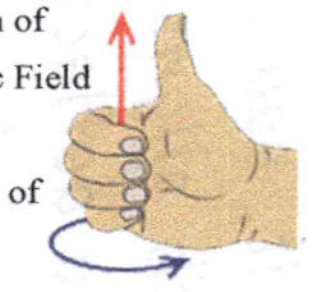

Magnetic field due to current carrying

Straight conductor

CBSE 2025, 2024

When a current is passed through a straight current - carrying conductor, a magnetic field is generated around it. The field lines are in the form of concentric circles at every point of the current carrying conductor.

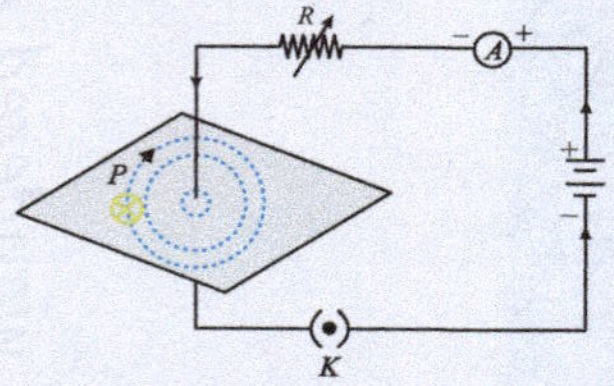

Circular loop

When a current passes through a circular loop, a magnetic field is generated around the loop. The direction of the magnetic field depends on the direction of the current.

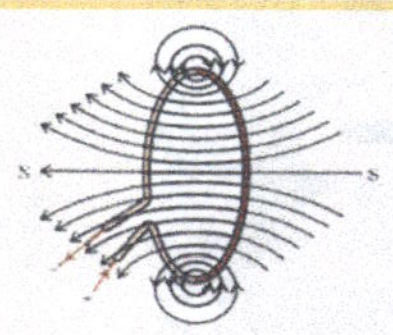

Solenoid

CBSE 2023

Solenoid is made up of coil of many circular turns of insulated copper wire wrapped closely in the shape of a cylinder.

The magnetic field inside a solenoid is uniform and parallel to its axis.

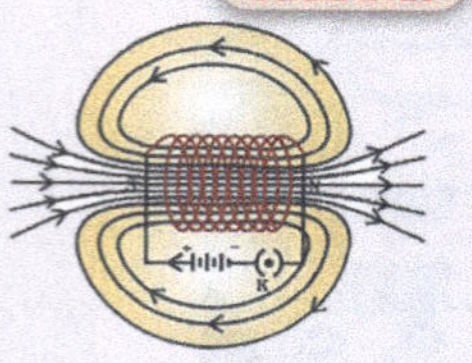

Electromagnetic Induction is a current produced because of voltage production due to a changing magnetic field.

An electromagnet is a type of magnet in which the magnetic field is produced by an electric current.

CBSE 2025, 2023, 2022

Properties of magnetic field lines for a bar magnet

1. Forms closed loops.
2. Never intersect with each other.
3. Crowded near the pole where the field is strong
4. Spread apart from each other where the field is weak.
5. Flow from the south pole to the north pole within a magnet and the north pole to the south pole outside.

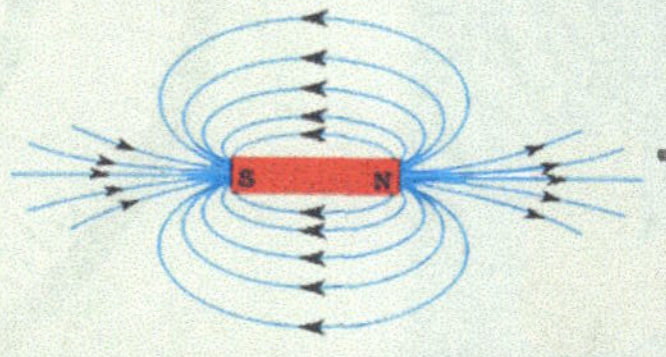

Who discovered the interconnection between electricity and magnetism?

Hans Christian Oersted in 1820 had accidentally discovered that a compass needle got deflected when an electric current passed through a metallic wire placed nearby.

What is a magnetic field?

The region around a magnetic material or a moving electric charge within which the force of magnetism acts.

Magnetism is the force exerted by magnets when they attract or repel each other.

Domestic electric circuit

CBSE 2023

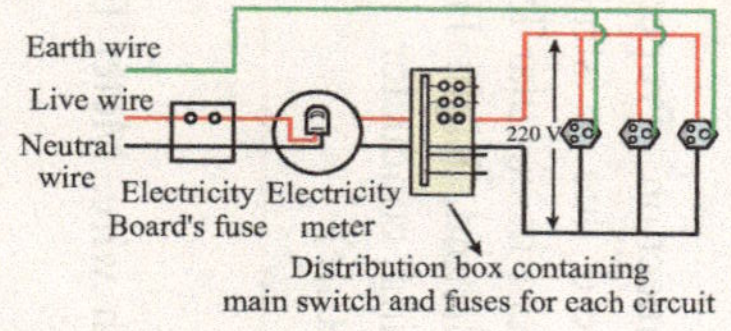

CBSE 2022, 2023

What is a fuse?

Fuse is used for protecting the circuits due to short-circuiting or overloading of the circuits.

In our households, AC electric power of 220 V with a frequency of 50 Hz is supplied.

Live wire (red)	carries current to appliances.
Neutral wire (black)	returns current to the source.
Earth wire (green)	connected underground, ensures safety against electric shocks.

MAGNETIC FIELD AND FIELD LINES

1

NCERT Definitions (Commonly asked in 1 mark)

- **Magnetism:** A property of matter by which it exerts an attractive or repulsive force on other materials.
- **Electromagnetism:** The interaction between electricity and magnetism where electric currents produce magnetic fields.
- **Magnetic Field:** The region surrounding a magnet, in which the force of the magnet can be detected.
- **Field Lines:** Imaginary lines used to represent the direction and strength of a magnetic field.
- **Right-Hand Thumb Rule:** A method to determine the direction of the magnetic field around a current-carrying conductor; the thumb indicates the current direction, and the curl of the fingers shows the direction of the field lines.

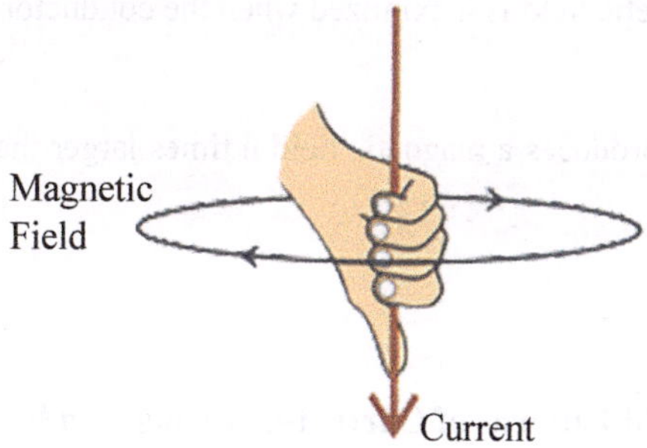

- **Magnetic Field due to a Current through a Circular Loop:** The magnetic field pattern created when current flows through a wire bent into a circular shape, characterized by concentric circles around the wire that become denser near the wire.

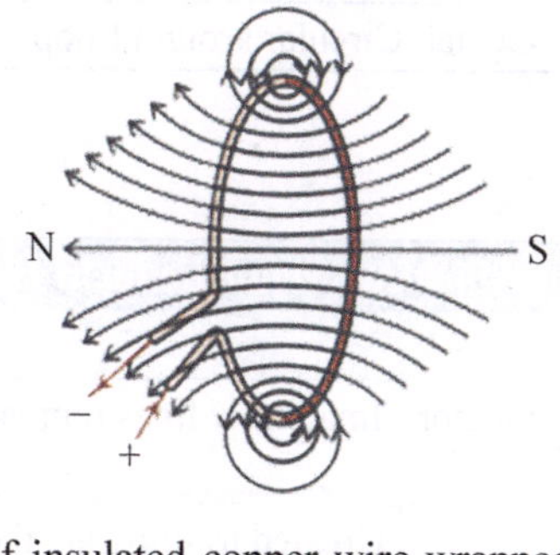

- **Solenoid:** A coil of many circular turns of insulated copper wire wrapped closely in the shape of a cylinder. It produces a magnetic field when current flows through it.

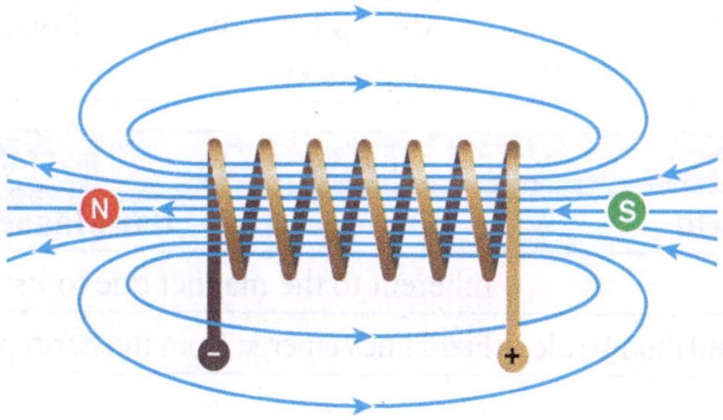

- **Magnetic Force:** The force experienced by a current-carrying conductor placed in a magnetic field. The direction of the force is perpendicular to both the direction of the current and the magnetic field, as determined by Fleming's Left-hand Rule.
- **Fleming's Left-hand Rule:** A rule used to determine the direction of the force experienced by a current-carrying conductor in a magnetic field. It states that if the thumb, forefinger, and middle finger of the left hand are held mutually perpendicular, the thumb points in the direction of motion, the forefinger in the direction of the magnetic field, then the middle finger points in the direction of the current.

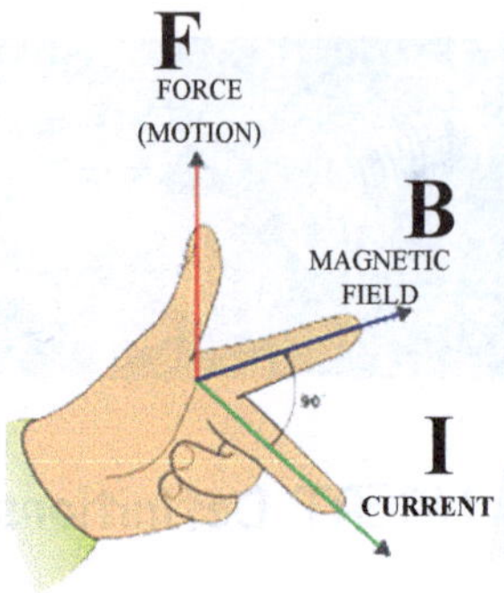

Important Facts

01 Magnetic fields are produced by electric currents, as demonstrated by Oersted.

02 Electromagnets can be turned on and off by controlling the electric current, making them versatile for various applications.

03 Magnetic field lines inside a solenoid are parallel and evenly spaced. *~ Uniform magnetic field.*

04 The force on a conductor in a magnetic field is maximized when the conductor is perpendicular to the field.

05 A circular coil with multiple turns produces a magnetic field n times larger than that of a single turn due to the additive effect of the fields.

Classification

Flow of Current and Resulting Magnetic Field Patterns of Current-Carrying Conductor

Current-Carrying Conductor			
	Straight Conductor	Circular Loop Conductor	Solenoid
Current Direction	Linear	Circular Path	Loops around Coil
Magnetic Field	Concentric Circles	Straight at Center, Circular around Loop	Uniform inside, Similar to Bar Magnet outside

Difference Between

Magnetic Field vs. Magnetic Field Lines

Magnetic Field	Magnetic Field Lines
A region around a magnet or a current-carrying conductor where magnetic forces are exerted.	Imaginary lines representing the direction and strength.
Can exist without being visually represented.	Created to illustrate the direction and strength of a magnetic field.
Its strength varies with distance from the magnet.	The closeness of lines indicates the strength of the field.
Does not have a directional property in itself.	Always have direction, from the north pole to the south pole outside the magnet.

Electric Current's Magnetic Field vs. Bar Magnet's Magnetic Field

Electric Current's Magnetic Field	Bar Magnet's Magnetic Field
Produced by moving electric charges.	Inherent to the magnet due to its magnetic domains.
Its direction can be determined by the right-hand thumb rule.	Field lines emerge from the north pole and enter the south outside the magnet.

Can be manipulated by changing the current's direction.	Fixed, based on the magnet's orientation.
Concentric circles around the conductor in a plane perpendicular to the current.	Field lines form closed loops from one pole to the other.
Strength depends on the current's magnitude and distance from the conductor.	Strength depends on the magnet's material and distance from the magnet.

Right-Hand Thumb Rule vs. Fleming's Left-Hand Rule	
Right-Hand Thumb Rule	**Fleming's Left-Hand Rule**
Used to determine the direction of the magnetic field around a current-carrying conductor.	Used to find the direction of force on a current-carrying conductor in a magnetic field.
Thumb points in the direction of current, fingers wrap in direction of magnetic field.	Thumb indicates force, first finger for magnetic field, and second finger for current.
Applicable for straight conductors.	Applicable for moving conductors in magnetic fields.
Simplifies understanding of magnetic field orientation.	Helps in understanding motor and generator principles.
Indicates the wrapping direction of field lines.	Indicates the movement direction of the conductor or charge.

Solenoid vs. Electromagnet	
Solenoid	**Electromagnet**
A coil of wire with a current running through it, producing a uniform magnetic field inside.	A solenoid with a ferromagnetic core inside, greatly amplifying the magnetic field.
Magnetic field similar to a bar magnet with a north and south pole.	Stronger magnetic field compared to a solenoid alone due to the core.
Used in devices like relays and valves.	Used in cranes for lifting heavy magnetic materials and in electric motors.
The strength of the field depends on the number of turns and current.	The strength can be adjusted by changing the current or modifying the core material.

Real Life Application Based Questions

1. **Have you ever wondered how electric fans, washing machines, and electric cars function smoothly and efficiently in our daily lives, making our chores and travel convenient without any manual effort?**

Ans. The seamless functioning of electric fans, washing machines, and electric cars is due to electromagnetism, where electric currents and magnetic fields interact. These devices employ electric motors that transform electrical energy into mechanical energy. The force on conductors within a magnetic field, a key aspect of magnetic effects of electric current, creates motion in these motors, powering these essential appliances and vehicles.

2. **Magnetic Resonance Imaging (MRI) can reveal intricate details of the body's internal structures, offering a peek inside the human body without the need for surgical procedures or invasive techniques. What's the secret behind this?**

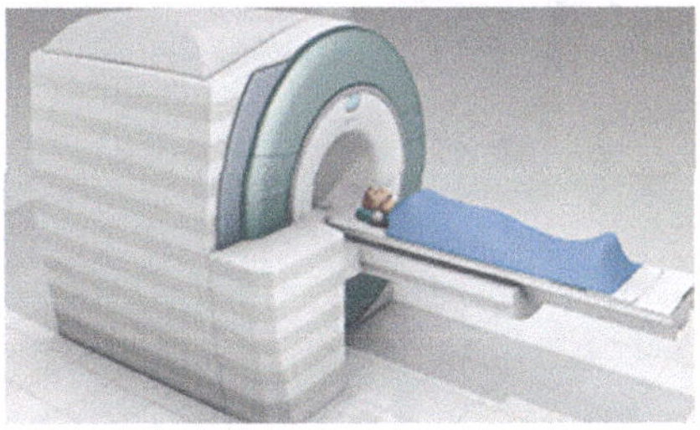

Ans. MRI uses magnetic fields and radio waves to create detailed images of the body's interiors. It aligns the body's atoms with a strong magnetic field, then disrupts this alignment with radio waves. The resulting signals form images, enabling non-invasive diagnostics and treatment planning without surgery, thanks to the principles of magnetic effects of electric currents.

3. **How do credit cards and security systems ensure secure transactions and controlled access using magnetism?**

Ans. Credit cards and security systems use magnetic strips to store data, read by magnetic sensors in card readers. This use of magnetism secures data transfer and access, leveraging magnetic effects from electric currents for reliable authentication and financial transactions, crucial in information security and financial services.

4. **How do solenoids function in various automotive systems to improve performance and functionality?**

Ans. Solenoids in automotive systems convert electrical energy to mechanical action, using a magnetic field from current in a coil. This enables precise control in starter motors, door locks, and transmission systems. Leveraging magnetic effects of electric current, solenoids efficiently translate electrical signals into movement, boosting automotive performance and functionality.

Myth Buster

- **Myth: Magnetic field lines are real physical entities.**

  Fact: Magnetic field lines are a imaginary lines used to represent magnetic fields. They show the direction and strength of the field but do not exist physically.

- **Myth: Two magnetic field lines can intersect each other.**

  Fact: Magnetic field lines never intersect. If they did, it would imply that a compass placed at the intersection could point in two different directions simultaneously, which is impossible.

- **Myth: The strength of a magnetic field produced by a current depends solely on the amount of current.**

  Fact: While the strength of the magnetic field does increase with the current, it also depends on the distance from the conductor and the medium in which the conductor is placed.

- **Myth: Magnetic fields can only be detected using heavily specialized equipment.**

  Fact: Magnetic fields produced by electric currents can be observed using simple tools like iron filings or a compass needle, as shown in experiments within the chapter.

Mnemonics

- **Direction of force on a current carrying conductor:**

  FBI-Fleming left hand rule

  - F → Force (Thumb)
  - B → Magnetic field (Index finger)
  - I → Current (Middle finger)

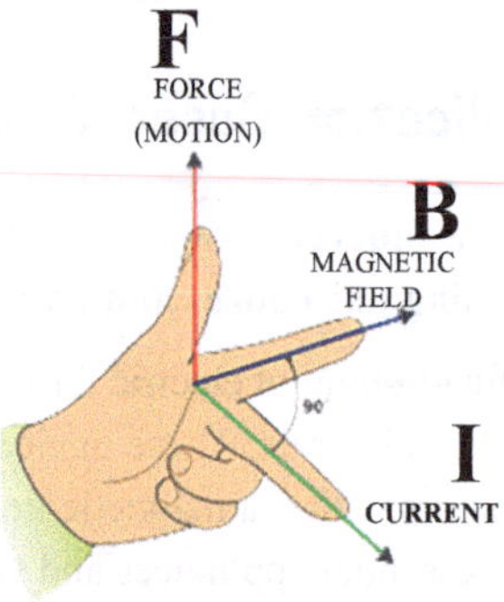

COMPETENCY BASED SOLVED EXAMPLES

Multiple Choice Questions (1 M)

1. Choose the incorrect statement from the following regarding magnetic lines of field

(*Un*) (NCERT Exemplar)

(*a*) The direction of magnetic field at a point is taken to be the direction in which the north pole of a magnetic compass needle points

(*b*) Magnetic field lines are closed curves

(*c*) If magnetic field lines are parallel and equidistant, they represent zero field strength

(*d*) Relative strength of magnetic field is shown by the degree of closeness of the field lines

2. If the key in the arrangement is taken out (the circuit is made open) and magnetic field lines are drawn over the horizontal plane *ABCD*, the lines are

(*Un*) (NCERT Exemplar)

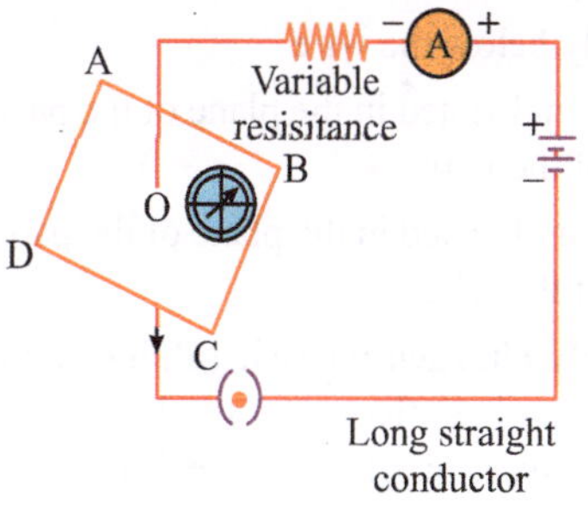

(*a*) concentric circles

(*b*) elliptical in shape

(*c*) straight lines parallel to each other

(*d*) concentric circles near the point *O* but of elliptical shapes as we go away from it

3. A circular loop placed in a plane perpendicular to the plane of paper carries a current when the key is ON. The current as seen from points *A* and *B* (in the plane of paper and on the axis of the coil) is anti clockwise and clockwise respectively. The magnetic field lines point from *B* to *A*. The N-pole of the resultant magnet is on the face close to

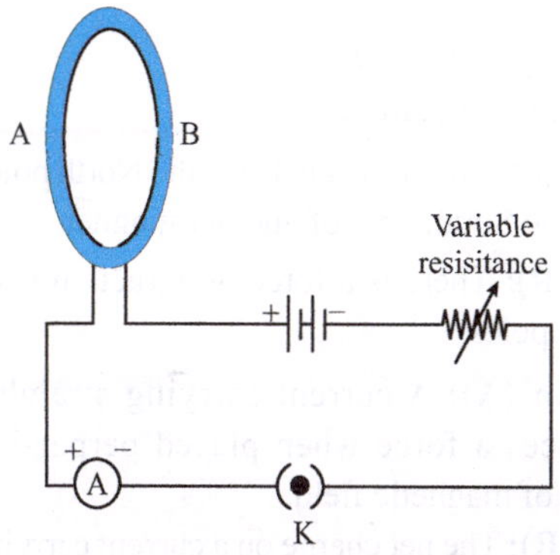

(*An*) (NCERT Exemplar)

(*a*) *A*

(*b*) *B*

(*c*) *A* if the current is small, and *B* if the current is large

(*d*) *B* if the current is small and *A* if the current is large

4. For a current in a long straight solenoid N- and S-poles are created at the two ends. Among the following statements, the incorrect statement is

(*Re*) (NCERT Exemplar)

(*a*) The field lines inside the solenoid are in the form of straight lines which indicates that the magnetic field is the same at all points inside the solenoid

(*b*) The strong magnetic field produced inside the solenoid can be used to magnetise a piece of magnetic material like soft iron, when placed inside the coil

(*c*) The pattern of the magnetic field associated with the solenoid is different from the pattern of the magnetic field around a bar magnet

(*d*) The *N*- and *S*-poles exchange position when the direction of current through the solenoid is reversed

5. A uniform magnetic field exists in the plane of paper pointing from left to right as shown in Figure. In the field an electron and a proton move as shown. The electron and the proton experience **(*Ap*) (NCERT Exemplar)**

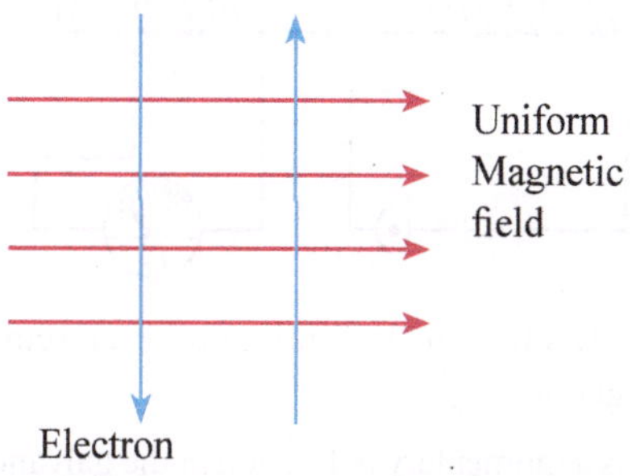

(*a*) forces both pointing into the plane of paper

(*b*) forces both pointing out of the plane of paper

(*c*) forces pointing into the plane of paper and out of the plane of paper, respectively

(*d*) force pointing opposite and along the direction of the uniform magnetic field respectively

6. The correct pattern of magnetic field lines of the field produced by a current carrying circular loop is:

(*An*) (CBSE, 2023)

(*a*)

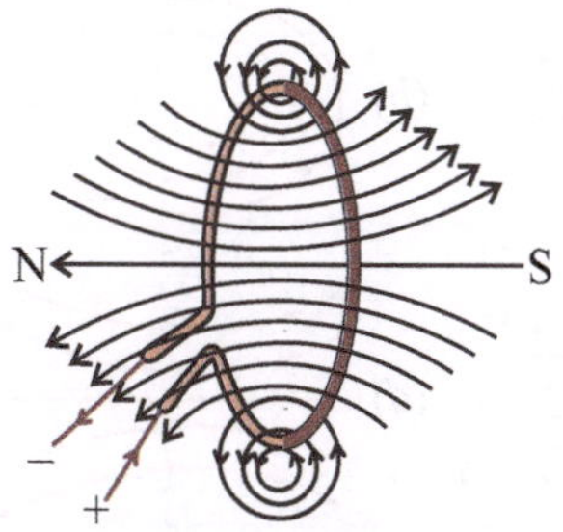

(*b*) 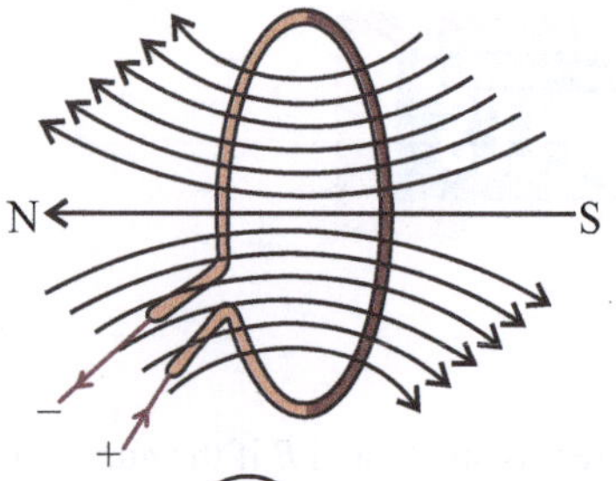

(*c*) 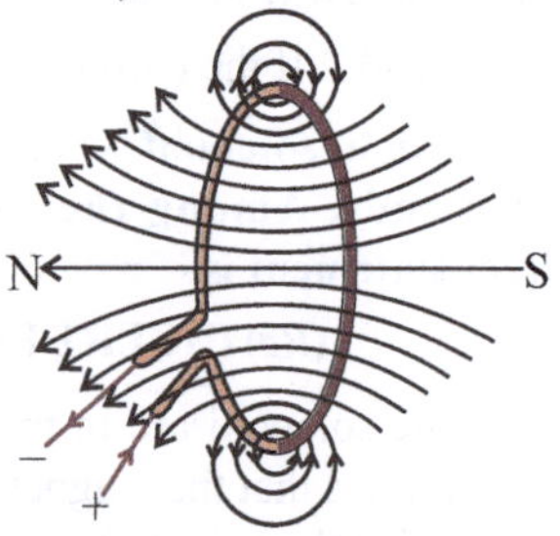

(*d*) 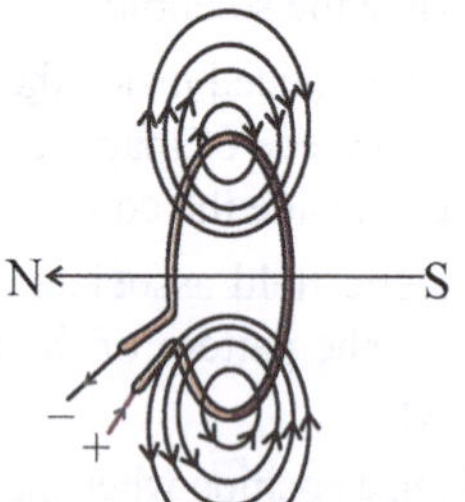

7. In the arrangement shown in Figure. There are two coils wound on a non-conducting cylindrical rod. Initially the key is not inserted. Then the key is inserted and later removed. Then **(*An*) (NCERT Exemplar)**

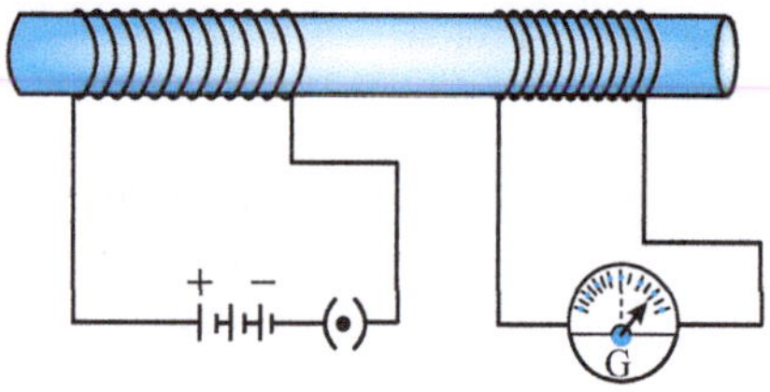

(*a*) the deflection in the galvanometer remains zero throughout

(*b*) there is a momentary deflection in the galvanometer but it dies out shortly and there is no effect when the key is removed

(*c*) there are momentary galvanometer deflections that die out shortly; the deflections are in the same direction

(*d*) there are momentary galvanometer deflections that die out shortly; the deflections are in opposite directions

8. The pattern of the magnetic field produced inside a current carrying solenoid is: **(*An*) (CBSE, 2024)**

(*a*) 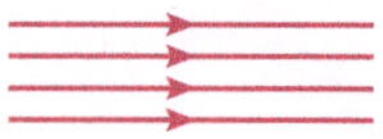 (*b*) 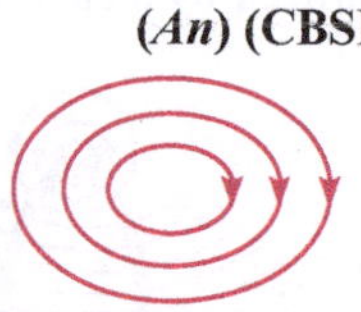

(*c*) 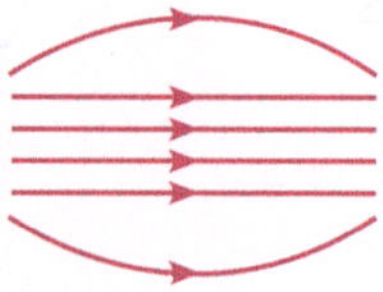 (*d*) 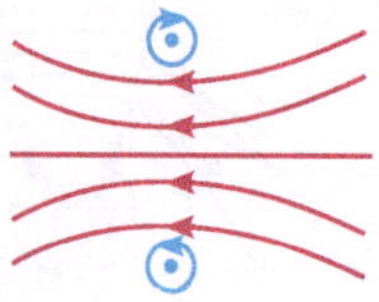

9. Choose the incorrect statement **(*Un*) (NCERT Exemplar)**

(*a*) Fleming's right-hand rule is a simple rule to know the direction of induced current

(*b*) The right-hand thumb rule is used to find the direction of magnetic fields due to current carrying conductors

(*c*) The difference between the direct and alternating currents is that the direct current always flows in one direction, whereas the alternating current reverses its direction periodically

(*d*) In India, the *AC* changes direction after every 1/50 second

10. A constant current flows in a horizontal wire in the plane of the paper from east to west as shown in the figure. The direction of magnetic field at a point will be North to South **(*Ap*) (NCERT Exemplar)**

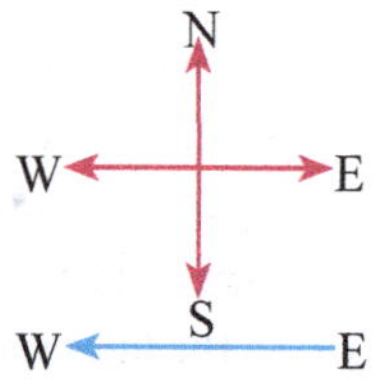

(*a*) directly above the wire

(*b*) directly below the wire

(*c*) at a point located in the plane of the paper, on the north side of the wire

(*d*) at a point located in the plane of the paper, on the south side of the wire

11. A positively-charged particle (alpha-particle) projected towards west is deflected towards north by a magnetic field. The direction of magnetic field is **(*Ap*) (NCERT Intext)**

(*a*) towards south (*b*) towards east

(*c*) downward (*d*) upward

Assertion and Reason (1 M)

Direction: The following questions consist of two statements – Assertion (A) and Reason (R). Answer these questions by *selecting the appropriate option given below:*

(*a*) Both A and R are true, and R is the correct explanation of A.

(*b*) Both A and R are true, but R is not the correct explanation of A.

(*c*) A is true, but R is false

(*d*) A is false, but R is true.

1. **Assertion (A):** It is easier to bring the North pole of a magnet towards the South pole of another magnet.

   Reason (R): There is a force of attraction between unlike magnetic poles. **(*Re*)**

2. **Assertion (A):** A current carrying straight conductor experiences a force when placed perpendicular to the direction of magnetic field.

   Reason (R): The net charge on a current carrying conductor is always zero. **(*Un*) (CBSE, 2023)**

3. **Assertion (A):** A compass needle is placed near a current carrying wire. The deflection of the compass needle decreases when the magnitude of the current in the wire is increased.
Reason (R): The strength of a magnetic field at a point near the conductor increases on increasing the current.
***(Un)* (CBSE SQP, 2023)**

4. **Assertion (A):** Iron filings scattered around a straight current carrying conductor in a plane perpendicular to the length of the conductor, arrange themselves in concentric circles.
Reason (R): Magnetic field has both magnitude and direction. ***(Un)* (CBSE APQ, 2023)**

Subjective Questions

Very Short Answer Type Questions (2 M)

1. **What are the properties of magnets?** ***(Re)***

Ans. Following are the properties of magnets :
(*i*) Magnets attract ferromagnetic materials.
(*ii*) The magnet's similar poles repel each other, whereas the opposite poles attract one other.
(*iii*) A hung magnet always comes to rest facing north-south.
(*iv*) The magnet's poles are arranged in pairs. i.e. magnetic monopole doesn't exist. *(2 M)*

2. **Two magnetic field lines do not intersect each other. Why?** ***(Re)* (CBSE, 2024)**

Ans. Two magnetic field lines do not intersect each other because if they were to intersect, it would imply that at the point of intersection, there would be two different directions for the magnetic field, which contradicts the fundamental property of magnetic field lines.
Magnetic field lines always represent the direction of the magnetic field at any given point, and at a single point, the direction of the magnetic field should be unique. *(2 M)*

3. **State the Flemings right-hand thumb rule.** ***(Re)***

Ans. The right-hand thumb rule is used to determine the direction of the magnetic field around a straight current-carrying conductor. When the thumb points in the direction of the current, the curled fingers indicate the direction of the magnetic field. *(2 M)*

4. **What is the purpose of using a solenoid in electromagnets, and how does the arrangement of coils in a solenoid contribute to its functionality?** ***(Un)***

Ans. A solenoid is used in electromagnets to increase the strength of the magnetic field by wrapping the wire into multiple turns, creating a concentrated magnetic field within the coil. This coil arrangement allows for a stronger and more uniform magnetic field, enhancing the electromagnet's overall effectiveness. *(2 M)*

5. **Refer to the image below and state how the magnetic field pattern indicates regions where the magnetic field is stronger outside the magnet? What happens to the magnetic field when the current in the circuit is reversed?** ***(An)* (CBSE SQP, 2023)**

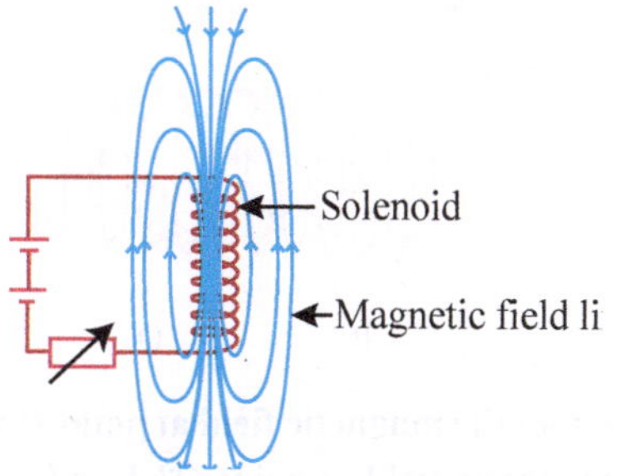

Ans. The magnetic field strength is more in the region where the field lines are crowded. This means the field strength is maximum near the poles and it reduces as we go away from the poles. *(½ + ½ M)*
The direction of the magnetic field is also reversed. *(1 M)*

6. **In the given circuit calculate the power consumed in watts in the resistor of 2Ω:** ***(Ap)* (CBSE, 2024)**

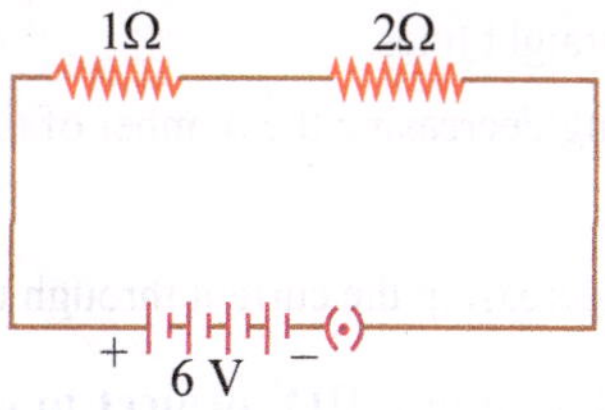

Ans. The circuit diagram is shown in fig,

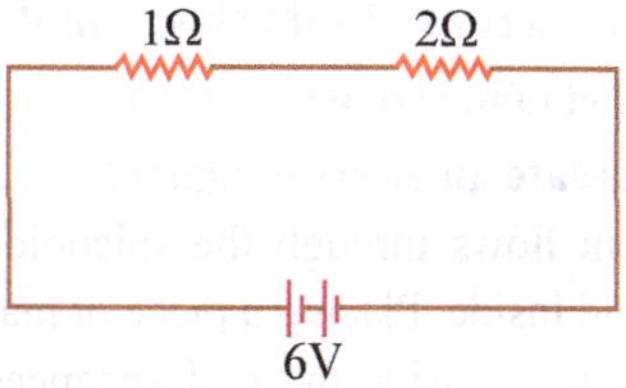

Total resistance, $R = 1 + 2 = 3\Omega$, *(½ M)*
Potential difference, $V = 6\ V$
Current, $I = \frac{V}{R} = \frac{6V}{3\Omega} = 2\ A$ *(½ M)*
Power used in 2Ω resistor $= (I)^2 R = (2)^2 \times 3 = 12$W. *(1 M)*

7. **What is the difference between a natural magnet and an artificial magnet?** ***(Un)***

Ans. Following are the difference between a natural magnet and an artificial magnet

Natural Magnet	Artificial Magnet
Natural magnet is found naturally on the earth.	Artificial magnets are man made.
It has regular or irregular shapes. Example- Lodestone.	It can be formed in different regular shapes. Example- Ring shape magnet.

(2 M)

8. **A helical coil whose length is greater than its diameter is connected to a battery as shown below.** **(CBSE APQ, 2023)**

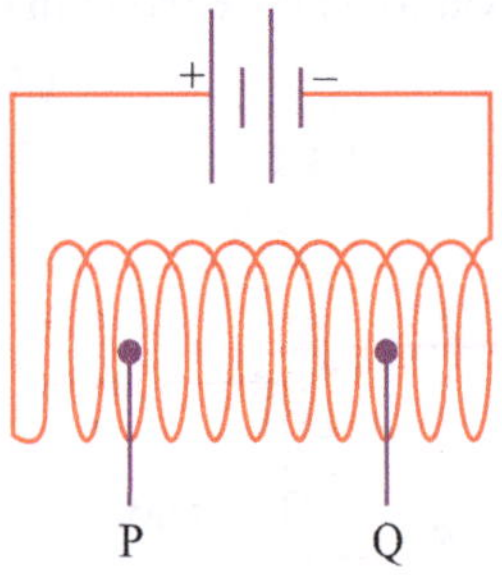

(*a*) **How does the magnetic field at point *P* compare with the magnetic field at point *Q*? Justify your answer.** **(*An*)**

(*b*) **State one way in which the strength of the magnetic field inside a current carrying helical coil can be changed?** **(*Un*)**

Ans. (*a*) The magnetic field at *P* and *Q* is the same. *(½ M)*

Because the magnetic field lines inside the helical coil of wire which behaves like a solenoid is uniform/in the form of parallel straight lines. *(½ M)*

(*b*) Increasing/decreasing the number of turn in the coil *(1 M)*

Increasing/decreasing the current through the coil

9. **If you are building a DIY project to create a simple lifting device that can pick up small metal objects like paperclips or screws. To do this, you decide to use an electromagnet made from a solenoid. How can a solenoid be used to create an electromagnet?** **(*Ap*)**

Ans. When current flows through the solenoid, it generates a magnetic field inside. Placing a piece of magnetic material, such as soft iron, inside the coil enhances this magnetic field, effectively creating an electromagnet. *(2 M)*

10. **Imagine you are on a hiking trip in the mountains, and you are using a compass to navigate your way. You notice that the compass needle, which usually points towards the north, suddenly deflects when you bring it close to a particular spot in your backpack where you have stored a small metal keychain.**

Why does the compass needle deflect when it is brought near the keychain in your backpack, which is actually a small bar magnet? **(*An*)**

Ans. A compass needle gets deflected when brought near a bar magnet because the compass needle itself acts like a small bar magnet. *(2 M)*

Short Answer Type Questions (3 M)

1. **Why does a compass needle get deflected when brought near a bar magnet?** **(*Un*) (NCERT Intext)**

Ans. When a compass needle is brought near a bar magnet, the North pole of the compass needle is attracted to the South pole of the bar magnet, and the South pole of the compass needle is attracted to the North pole of the bar magnet. This causes the compass needle to align itself with the magnetic field lines of the bar magnet, resulting in the deflection of the compass needle. *(3 M)*

2. **A current through a horizontal power line flows in east to west direction. What is the direction of magnetic field at a point directly below it and at a point directly above it?** **(*An*) (NCERT Intext)**

Ans. The current is in the east-west direction. Applying the right-hand thumb rule, we get that the direction of magnetic field at a point below the wire is from north to south. *(1½ M)*

The direction of magnetic field at a point directly above the wire is from south to north. *(1½ M)*

3. **Draw magnetic field lines around a bar magnet and list the properties of magnetic field lines.** **(*Cr*) (NCERT Intext)**

Ans. *(1 M)*

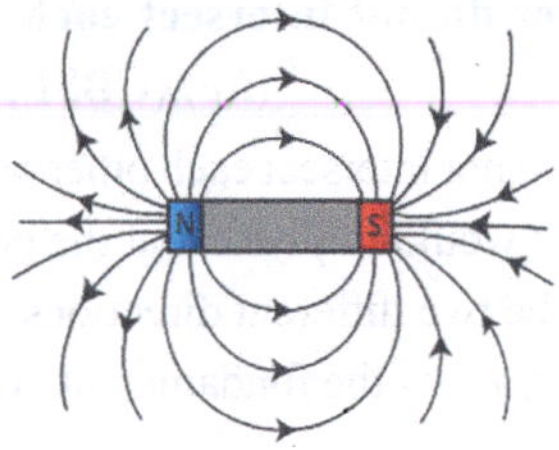

The properties of magnetic field lines:

- The tangent drawn to the magnetic field lines gives the direction of the magnetic field *(½ M)*
- Magnetic field lines appear to emerge or start from the north pole and merge or terminate at the south pole *(½ M)*
- Magnetic field lines never intersect with each other *(½ M)*
- Magnetic field lines form a closed-loop *(½ M)*

4. **Why don't two magnetic field lines intersect each other?** **(*Un*) (NCERT Intext)**

Ans. Two magnetic field lines do not intersect each other. If they intersect, that means the magnetic fields have two different directions at the same point, so it's impossible. The resultant force at the North Pole at any point can only act in one direction. If two magnetic field lines cross each other, it means that the net force of the north pole at the point of intersection acts in two directions, which is impossible. *(3 M)*

5. (*i*) State the rule used to find the force acting on a current carrying conductor placed in a magnetic field. (*Re*)

(*ii*) Given below are three diagrams showing entry on an electron in a magnetic field. Identify the case in which the force will be (1) maximum and (2) minimum respectively. Give reason for your answer.

(*An*) (CBSE 2023)

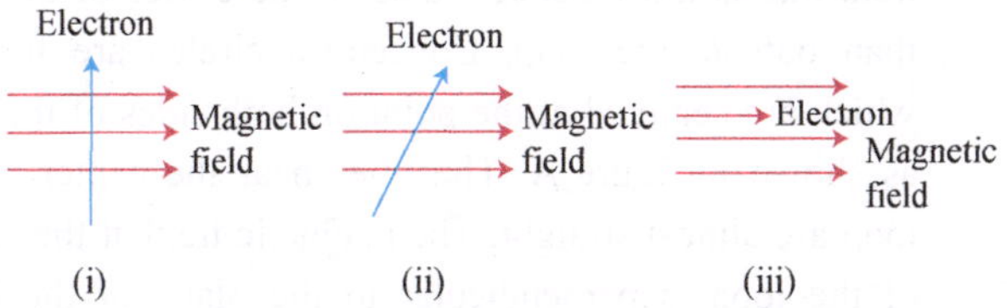

OR

(*i*) Draw the pattern of magnetic field lines of

(1) a current carrying solenoid

(2) a bar magnet (*Cr*)

(*ii*) List two distinguishing features between the two fields. (*Re*)

Ans. (*i*) We use Fleming's left hand rule to find the direction of force acting on a current carrying conductor, placed in a magnetic field. *(½ M)*

According to this rule, when we place the thumb, the index finger and the middle finger in such a way that they are mutually perpendicular to each other, then middle finger points to the direction of current flow, index finger points to the direction of magnetic field and thumb points to the direction of force acting on a current carrying conductor. *(1 M)*

(*ii*) Magnetic force acting on an electron, moving with velocity v in a magnetic field B is

$F = qvB\sin\theta$, Here θ is the angle between B and v.

In figure (*i*), electron is moving perpendicular to the direction of magnetic field.

i.e. $\sin 90° = 1$

Hence magnetic force will be maximum. *(1 M)*

And magnetic force will be minimum in figure (*iii*) as electron is moving parallel to the direction of magnetic field. *(½ M)*

OR

(*i*) (1)

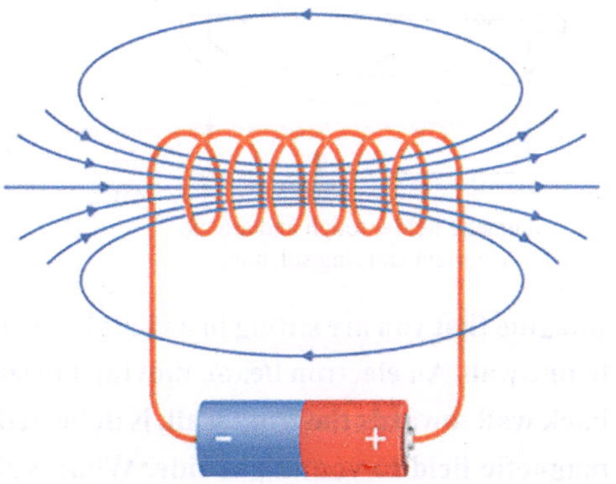

(1 M)

(2)

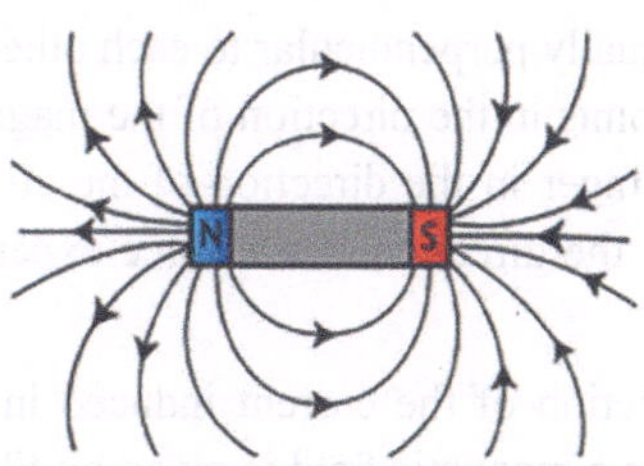

(1 M)

(*ii*) Two distinguishing features between the fields.

S.No.	Bar Magnet	Solenoid
1.	Magnetism always exists in a bar magnet.	Magnetism exists until an electric current flows through it.
2.	Poles can't be interchanged.	Poles can be interchanged.

(1 M)

6. Under what conditions permanent electromagnet is obtained if a current carrying solenoid is used? Support your answer with the help of a labelled circuit diagram.

(*Un*) (NCERT Intext)

Ans. The conditions to obtain a permanent electromagnet if a current-carrying solenoid is used are-

1. The current through the solenoid should be a direct current.

2. The magnetic material should be of high retentivity and should not lose it easily.

3. A iron core should be placed inside a solenoid.

(2 M)

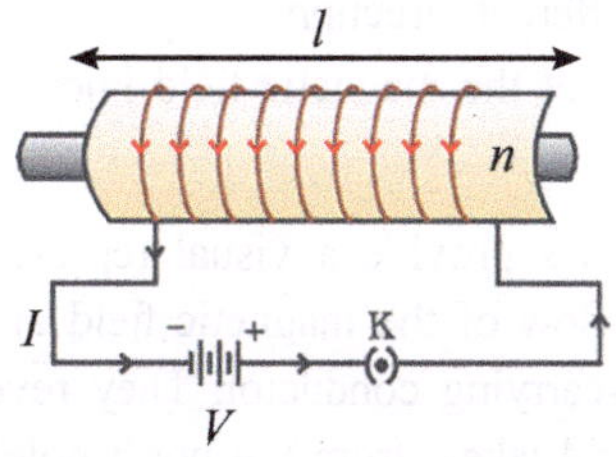

(1 M)

Long Answer Type Questions (5 M)

1. State the rule to determine the direction of a (*i*) magnetic field produced around a straight conductor-carrying current, (*ii*) force experienced by a current-carrying straight conductor placed in a magnetic field which is perpendicular to it, and (*iii*) current induced in a coil due to its rotation in a magnetic field.

(*Re*) (NCERT Exercise)

Ans. (*i*) The direction of the magnetic field produced around a straight conductor carrying current is given by the right-hand thumb rule. If the conductor is grasped in the right hand with the thumb pointing in the direction of the current, then the direction in which the fingers curl gives the direction of the magnetic field lines. *(2 M)*

(*ii*) The direction of the force experienced by a current-carrying straight conductor placed in a magnetic field that is perpendicular to it is given by Fleming's left-hand rule. If the thumb, forefinger, and middle finger of the left hand are held mutually perpendicular to each other such that the forefinger points in the direction of the magnetic field and the middle finger in the direction of the current, then the thumb gives the direction of the force experienced by the conductor. *(2 M)*

(iii) The direction of the current induced in a coil due to its rotation in a magnetic field is given by Fleming's right-hand rule. If the thumb, forefinger, and middle finger of the right hand are held mutually perpendicular to each other such that the forefinger points in the direction of the magnetic field and the thumb points in the direction of motion(Force) then the middle finger gives the direction of induced current. *(1 M)*

2. Why does a magnetic compass needle pointing North and South in the absence of a nearby magnet get deflected when a bar magnet or a current carrying loop is brought near it. Describe some salient features of magnetic lines of field concept. **(*Un*) (NCERT Exercise)**

Ans. A magnetic compass needle points towards the Earth's magnetic North pole because the Earth itself behaves like a giant magnet with its magnetic field lines running from the magnetic North pole to the magnetic South pole. However, when a bar magnet or a current-carrying loop is brought near the compass, it exerts a magnetic force on the needle, causing it to deflect from its original position. This is because magnets create their own magnetic fields, which can interact with the Earth's magnetic field and cause the needle to point in a different direction. *(2 M)*

Some salient features of the magnetic field lines concept include:

1. Magnetic field lines provide a visual representation of the direction and flow of the magnetic field around a magnet or a current-carrying conductor. They reveal the path the magnetic field takes, from the north pole to the south pole, allowing us to understand and analyze magnetic field behavior. *(1 M)*

2. Magnetic field lines never cross each other. If they did, it would imply that at the intersection point, there are two directions of magnetic force, which is not possible. *(1 M)*

3. The density of magnetic field lines indicates the strength of the magnetic field. The closer the lines are together, the stronger the magnetic field is. *(1 M)*

Nailing the Right Answer

- Apply Right Hand Thumb Rule to find the direction of magnetic field in case of straight current carrying conductor and circular loop.
- Apply Fleming's left hand rule to find the direction of force.
- Explain the question with the help of diagram.

3. Explain with the help of a labelled diagram the distribution of magnetic field due to a current through a circular loop. Why is it that if a current carrying coil has n turns the field produced at any point is n times as large as that produced by a single turn?

(*Un*) (NCERT Exercise)

Ans. The electric current in a circular loop creates a magnetic field that is more concentrated in the center of the loop than outside the loop. Concentric circles are formed, which are centered at the point on both sides of the loop as shown in figure A. The lines near the center of the loop are almost straight. The magnetic field at the center of the loop is perpendicular to the plane of the loop. The concentric circles become larger as we move away from the wire because as the distance increases from the current-carrying conductor the strength of the magnetic field fades away. *(2 M)*

In the same way, when we consider an electric current passing through a circular coil with n number of turns, say a solenoid, the strength of the magnetic field is directly proportional to the number of turns of the solenoid. That is, as the number of turns increases in the coil, the strength of the solenoid also increases. *(1 M)*

The diagrammatic representation is given above in Figure B.

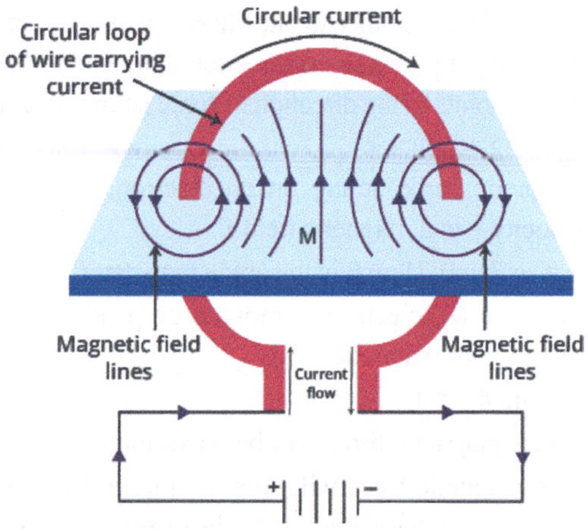

Magnetic lines of force

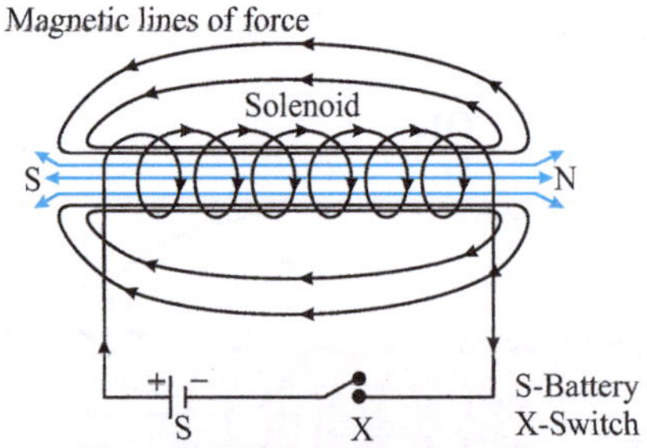

Magnetic field through and around a current carrying solenoid

(2 M)

4. Imagine that you are sitting in a chamber with your back to one wall. An electron beam, moving horizontally from back wall towards the front wall, is deflected by a strong magnetic field to your right side. What is the direction of magnetic field? **(*Un*) (NCERT Exercise)**

Ans. Since the particle deflects towards Right side, The force is in towards right side. Now, if negatively charged particle moves from back wall to front wall. Then, current is the opposite direction, i.e. Current is from front wall to back wall (Towards Inside our body) *(2 M)*

Applying Fleming's **left hand** rule,

Taking the forefinger, middle finger and thumb of the left hand in mutually perpendicular direction

- Pointing thumb towards right side (direction of force) *(1 M)*
- Middle-finger towards our body (direction of current) *(1 M)*
- We get that the direction of magnetic field is downwards (into the ground) *(1 M)*

5. Describe the activity that shows that a current-carrying conductor experiences a force perpendicular to its length and the external magnetic field. How does Fleming's left-hand rule help us to find the direction of the force acting on the current carrying conductor?

(*An*) (NCERT Exemplar)

Ans. In this experiment, you can take a wire or a conductor, such as a copper wire, and connect it to a power source to allow current to flow through it. Then, place the wire inside a magnetic field, which can be generated using a bar magnet or an electromagnet.

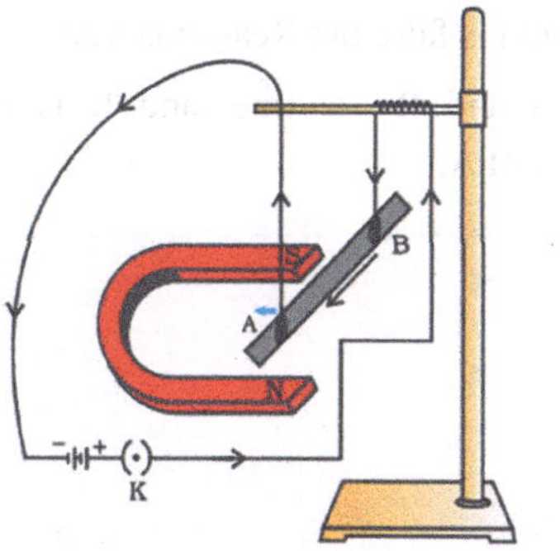

Now, if you position your left hand such that your thumb points in the direction of the current flow (from positive to negative), and your fingers represent the direction of the magnetic field, then your palm will indicate the direction of the force experienced by the conductor. *(1 M)*

According to Fleming's left-hand rule:

- The thumb represents the direction of the current.
- The index finger represents the direction of the magnetic field.
- The middle finger represents the direction of the force experienced by the conductor. *(2 M)*

By aligning your hand as described above, you can determine the direction of the force acting on the current-carrying conductor. This force is perpendicular to both the current direction and the magnetic field direction.

For example, if the current flows from south to north in the conductor and the magnetic field is directed from east to west, then the force experienced by the conductor will be directed upward or downward, depending on the orientation of your hand.

Fleming's left-hand rule provides a simple way to determine the direction of the force acting on a current-carrying conductor in a magnetic field, making it a useful tool in understanding and analyzing electromagnetic phenomena. *(2 M)*

Hints & Explanations

Multiple Choice Questions

1. (*c*) If the magnetic field lines are parallel and equidistant, they represent a uniform magnetic field and not a zero field strength.
2. (*c*) When the device's key is removed (circuit open), there is no current in the circuit, which means there is no magnetic field caused by the circuit. Therefore, only the Earth's magnetic field will exist in this region, and the resulting magnetic field will be straight lines parallel to each other in the horizontal plane *ABCD*.
3. (*a*) The right-hand thumb rule demonstrates that magnetic lines of force originate from the face close to A and enter the face close to B. In reality, magnetic fields exit from the north pole of a magnet and enter through the south pole.
4. (*c*) The magnetic field associated with the solenoid is different from the magnetic field around a bar magnet

   A current carrying solenoid behaves like a bar magnet with fixed polarities at its ends. The field lines of a solenoid are also very much like that of a bar magnet, where it originates from the north pole and moves towards the south pole outside the magnet and moves from south to north inside the magnet. These field lines form closed loops.
5. (*a*) Applying the Fleming's left hand rule, if we keep the index finger in the direction of the magnetic field, and the middle finger in the direction of current, which is same direction in which the proton is moving (since it is positively charged), and opposite to the direction in which the electron is moving (since it is negatively charged), the direction in which the force is experienced by them is given by the direction of thumb, which is pointing into the plane of the paper for both the cases
6. (*c*) The correct pattern of magnetic field lines of the field produced by a current carrying circular loop is concentric circles around the loop.
7. (*d*) When the key is inserted in the circuit of coil 1, there is a momentary increase of current. This change in current produces a change in the magnetic field.

   Since changing magnetic field induces a current, a momentary deflection is seen in the circuit of coil 2.

Similarly, on removing the key, the current becomes zero quickly, and there is a change in the current in coil (i) This current change induces a current in coil (ii) But this time the deflection happens in the opposite direction.

8. (*a*) The magnetic field pattern produced by a current carrying Solenoid is similar to the magnetic field produced by a bar magnet.

   The solenoid's one end acts as a magnetic north pole, while the other acts as a magnetic south pole.

   Within the solenoid, the field lines are in the form of parallel straight lines.

1. The magnetic field for the current-carrying solenoid

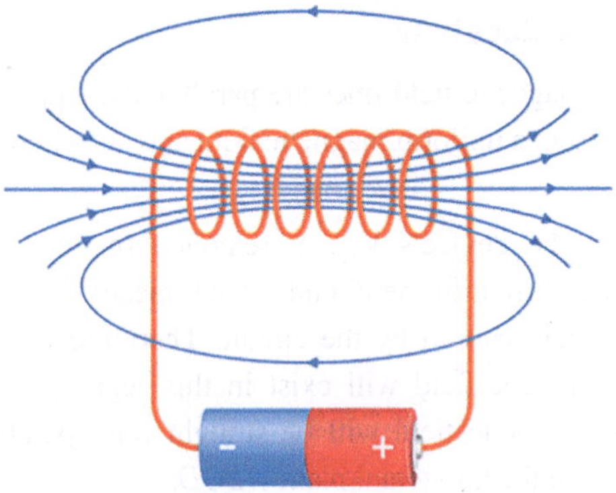

2. For bar magnet.

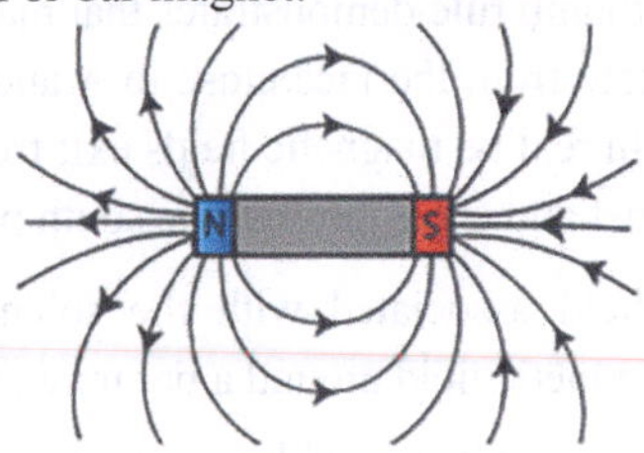

9. (*d*) The direction changes twice in each cycle so that change of direction takes place after every 1/100 second.

10. (*b*) The direction of the magnetic field can be determined by the right-hand rule: When the thumb points in the direction of the current, the direction of curling of fingers will give the direction of the magnetic field. Therefore, the magnetic field will be exactly from north to south only at a point directly below the wire.

11. (*d*) When an alpha particle, which carries a positive charge and is moving westward, is deflected northward by a magnetic field, the orientation of this magnetic field is upward, as determined by applying Fleming's left-hand rule.

Assertion and Reason

1. (*a*) Both the Assertion and the Reason are correct and the Reason is the correct explanation of the Assertion.

2. (*b*) Assertion (A) is correct because when a current-carrying straight conductor is placed perpendicular to the direction of magnetic field, it experiences a force known as magnetic force.

   Reason (R) is also correct because the net charge on a current-carrying conductor is zero. This is because the current is made up of equal and opposite charges moving in opposite directions, which cancel out each other's effect.

   Hence, both assertion (A) and reason (R) are correct, and reason (R) is not the correct explanation of assertion (A).

3. (*d*) Assertion is false but Reason is true

4. (*b*) Both A and R are true, and R is not the correct explanation of A.

DOMESTIC ELECTRIC CIRCUITS

2

NCERT Definitions (Commonly asked in 1 mark)

- **Live Wire:** A wire, typically with red insulation, that carries electric power from the supply to the household circuits.
- **Neutral Wire:** A wire with black insulation that completes the electrical circuit by returning power to the source.
- **Earth Wire:** Usually green insulated, this wire is connected to the earth and used as a safety measure to prevent electric shock by directing any leakage current into the ground.
- **AC Electric Power:** Alternating Current (AC) electric power supplied to households, typically at 220V and 50Hz frequency. It consists of live wire (red insulation), neutral wire (black insulation), and earth wire (green insulation) for safety.
- **Meter Box:** A housing unit containing the electric meter, which measures the amount of electricity consumed by a household or building.
- **Electric Meter:** A device installed in the meter box to measure the amount of electrical energy consumed in kilowatt-hours (kWh) by a household or building.
- **Fuse:** A safety device consisting of a strip of wire that melts and breaks an electric circuit if the current exceeds a safe level.
- **Main Fuse:** *Acts as the primary safety device in a household electric panel, preventing overcurrent from damaging the house wiring or causing fires.*
- **Main Switch:** A switch that controls the entire power supply to a house, allowing the power to be turned on or off as needed.
- **Circuit:** A complete and closed path through which electric current can flow.
- **Overloading:** A condition where more current flows through the wiring than it can safely handle, often caused by too many appliances being used simultaneously.
- **Short-Circuiting:** Occurs when the live wire and neutral wire come into direct contact, causing a sudden surge in current flow.

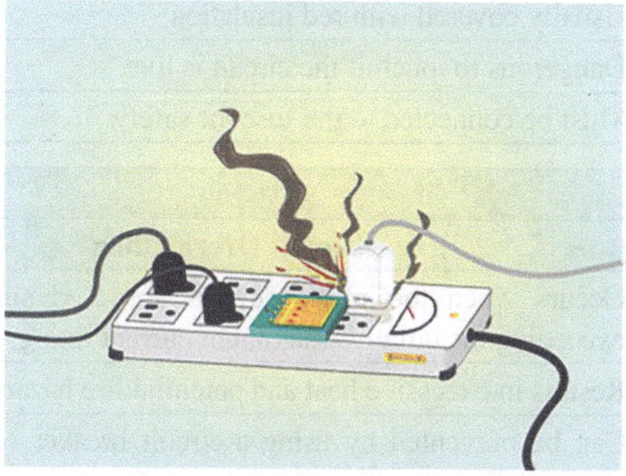

Important Facts

01 Fuse operates on the heating effect of electric current. A fuse contains a metal wire or filament that melts when too much current flows through it, thus interrupting the circuit.

02 Provides a low-resistance path to the ground, ensuring that any leakage current does not pose a hazard. *~The earth wire*

03 Safety measures in domestic circuits include the use of fuses and the proper installation of live, neutral, and earth wires.

04 The use of a main switch allows for controlling the overall power supply to a household, enabling power to be safely turned off for maintenance or in emergencies.

Classification

Types of Wires in Household Electrical Circuits		
Live Wire	**Neutral Wire**	**Earth Wire**
Red Insulation	Black Insulation	Green Insulation
Carries electricity from the supply to the house.	Completes the circuit by returning electricity to the supply.	Provides safety by grounding excess electricity.
Positively charged with respect to the neutral wire.	Consider zero or negative charge.	Connects metallic bodies of appliances to the earth for safety.

Electric Meter vs. Main Switch	
Electric Meter	**Main Switch**
Measures the amount of electric energy consumed by a residence or business.	Controls the entire power supply to a house.
Records consumption for billing purposes.	Can completely disconnect power for maintenance or emergencies.
Always on to measure continuous consumption.	Can be turned on or off as needed.
Located at the entry point of the electrical system of a building.	Positioned after the meter and before the distribution board.
Directly connected to the live and neutral wires.	Operates to connect or disconnect the live wire's flow.

Difference Between

Live Wire vs. Neutral Wire	
Live Wire	**Neutral Wire**
Carries electric power to the household circuits.	Completes the electrical circuit by returning power to the source.
Usually covered with red insulation.	Usually covered with black insulation.
Dangerous to touch if the circuit is live.	Normally safe to touch, but caution is advised as faults can occur.
Must be connected to the fuse for safety.	Directly connected to the earth pin at the socket for grounding.

Circuit Overloading vs. Short-Circuiting	
Circuit Overloading	**Short-Circuiting**
Occurs when too many devices are used simultaneously, exceeding the circuit's maximum current rating.	Occurs when there is a direct contact between the live and neutral wires, causing a sudden surge in current.
Results in excessive heat and potential fire hazard.	Leads to a rapid increase in current, posing a risk of damage and fire.
Can be prevented by using a circuit breaker or fuse of the correct rating.	Often results from damaged insulation or wiring faults.
Does not necessarily result in immediate circuit damage but poses long-term risks.	Causes immediate circuit damage and requires urgent repair.
Manifests as dimming lights, tripped breakers, or blown fuses.	Manifests as sparking, smoke, or an immediate loss of power.

Real Life Application Based Questions

1. **Have you ever wondered why we have different colored wires in our homes and what they signify, especially the ones with red and black insulation?**

Ans. Yes, in our homes, the electric power supply involves different wires where the one with red insulation is known as the live wire or positive, and the one with black insulation is called the neutral wire or negative. The color coding helps in identifying the wires for safe electrical installations and maintenance.

2. **How do domestic circuits ensure that appliances with higher power ratings don't interfere with or overload the system?**

Ans. Domestic circuits often use two separate circuits with different current ratings: one of 15 A for high-power appliances like geysers and air coolers, and another of 5 A for lower-power items like bulbs and fans. This segregation helps prevent overloading and ensures that each appliance operates within safe electrical parameters.

3. **Can you explain the role of the green-insulated earth wire in our household circuits?**

Ans. The earth wire, with its green insulation, is connected to a metal plate deep in the earth and to the metallic body of appliances. It provides a low-resistance path to the ground, ensuring that any leakage current does not pose a danger to users, thereby preventing electric shocks.

4. **How does a fuse function as an important safety component in domestic circuits to prevent damage due to overloading?**

Ans. A fuse in a domestic circuit plays a crucial role in preventing damage caused by overloading. When the current in the circuit exceeds a safe level, the fuse melts due to Joule heating, breaking the circuit and stopping the flow of unduly high electric current. This action safeguards both the appliances and the circuit from potential damage or hazards, ensuring the safety of the electrical system.

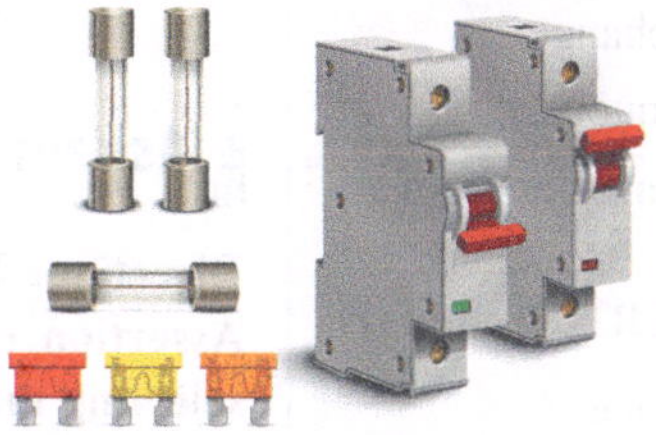

5. **How does the design of domestic circuits prevent potential damage when too many appliances are connected to a single socket?**

Ans. Overloading from connecting too many appliances to a single socket is prevented by the use of fuses and the segregation of circuits based on current ratings. Fuses ensure that the circuit breaks if the current flow abruptly increases beyond the safe limit, protecting the appliances and circuit from damage.

Myth Buster

- **Myth: Electricity in homes flows through a single type of wire.**
  Fact: Domestic electric circuits are made up of live, neutral, and earth wires, each serving a different purpose to ensure the safe use of electricity.
- **Myth: The earth wire in a household electrical system is used for grounding appliances to improve their performance.**
  Fact: The earth wire in a household electrical system is primarily a safety measure to prevent electric shocks. It provides a low-resistance path to the ground, ensuring that any leakage of current to the metallic body of appliances maintains the same potential as the earth, thus protecting users from severe electric shocks.
- **Myth: Live and neutral wires can be used interchangeably since they complete the circuit.**
  Fact: Live and neutral wires have specific roles; the live wire carries current to the appliance, while the neutral wire completes the circuit by returning the current to the source. Interchanging them can lead to serious safety hazards.
- **Myth: A higher number rating on a fuse indicates better protection for appliances.**
  Fact: Fuses are rated according to the maximum current they can handle before melting. Using a fuse with a rating too high for the circuit doesn't provide proper protection, as it may not melt soon enough to prevent damage during a surge.
- **Myth: Overloading and short-circuiting in an electric circuit are the same.**
  Fact: Overloading occurs due to too many devices drawing current from the same circuit, whereas short-circuiting happens when live and neutral wires come into direct contact, causing a sudden surge in current flow.
- **Myth: Using multiple extension cords in a household circuit is a safe way to increase the number of available outlets.**
  Fact: Relying excessively on extension cords can lead to overloading and overheating, posing a fire risk. It's safer to have additional outlets professionally installed where needed.

Mnemonics

- **Direction for DC and AC:**

DC-Direct Current

D → Don't
C → Change

AC-Alternate Current

A → Always
C → Changing

COMPETENCY BASED SOLVED EXAMPLES

Multiple Choice Questions (1 M)

1. At the time of short circuit, the current in the circuit **(*Un*) (NCERT Exercise)**

(*a*) reduces substantially. (*b*) does not change.
(*c*) increases heavily. (*d*) vary continuously

2. Why is the earth wire connected to a metallic body of an appliance in a household circuit? **(*Un*) (NCERT Exemplar)**

(*a*) To increase the resistance of the appliance
(*b*) To reduce the current flow in the circuit
(*c*) To provide a low-resistance path for current in case of leakage
(*d*) To regulate the voltage supply to the appliance

3. The most important safety method used for protecting home appliances from short circuiting or overloading is **(*Un*) (NCERT Exemplar)**

(*a*) earthing (*b*) use of fuse
(*c*) use of stabilizers (*d*) use of electric meter

4. In domestic electric circuits the wiring with 15A current rating is for the electric devices which have **(*Un*)**

(*a*) higher power ratings such as geyser.
(*b*) lower power ratings such as fan.
(*c*) metallic bodies and low power ratings.
(*d*) non-metallic bodies and low power ratings.

5. Which wire in a domestic electrical circuit is typically green colored? **(*Re*)**

(*a*) Neutral wire (*b*) Live wire
(*c*) Earth wire (*d*) Hot wire

6. What is the purpose of a fuse in a domestic electrical circuit? **(*Re*)**

(*a*) To control the flow of current through the circuit
(*b*) To prevent electrical shocks
(*c*) To protect electrical devices from overheating
(*d*) To prevent electrical fires

7. Which wire in a domestic electrical circuit is typically colored black? **(*Re*)**

(*a*) Neutral wire (*b*) Live wire
(*c*) Ground wire (*d*) Hot wire

8. What is the purpose of the neutral wire in a household electrical system? **(*Un*)**

(*a*) To carry current to the appliance
(*b*) To provide a return path for current
(*c*) To connect the appliance to the earth
(*d*) To regulate the voltage supply

9. What is the function of a circuit breaker in a domestic electrical circuit? **(*Un*)**

(*a*) To regulate the voltage of the circuit
(*b*) To prevent electrical shocks
(*c*) To protect electrical devices from overheating
(*d*) To automatically cut off power in the event of an overload or short circuit

Assertion and Reason (1 M)

Direction: The following questions consist of two statements. Assertion (A) and Reason (R). Answer these questions by selecting the appropriate option given below:

(*a*) Both A and R are true, and R is the correct explanation of A.
(*b*) Both A and R are true, but R is not the correct explanation of A.
(*c*) A is true, but R is false
(*d*) A is false, but R is true.

1. **Assertion (A):** Fuse is a safety device that is used to prevent electrical circuits from possible fires.

   Reason (R): A fuse consists of tin wire having low melting point, due to which it melts and breaks the circuit if the current exceeds a safe value. **(*Un*)**

2. **Assertion (A):** Heater wire must have high resistance and high melting point. **(*Un*)**

   Reason (R): If resistance is high, the electric conductivity will be less. **(*Un*)**

3. **Assertion (A):** The neutral wire in a household electrical system is essential for completing the circuit.

   Reason (R): The neutral wire carries current to the appliance. **(*Un*)**

4. **Assertion (A):** The earth wire in a domestic electrical circuit is connected to a metallic body of an appliance.

   Reason (R): The earth wire provides a low-resistance conducting path for current in case of leakage to prevent severe electric shocks. **(*Un*)**

Subjective Questions

Very Short Answer Type Questions (2 M)

1. What is the difference between the wires in an electric heater and in a fuse? **(*An*)**

Ans. The wire used in the element of electric heater has a high resistivity and have a high melting point, i.e. even at a high temperature element do not burn while fuse wire have a low melting point and high resistivity. *(2 M)*

2. Name any two parts of a human body where magnetic field is found significantly. **(*Un*)**

Ans. In the brain and heart of the human body, the magnetism produced is significant. The Magnetism present in the brain of a human is used to obtain the images of internal parts of the brain by using a technique known as MRI (Magnetic Resonance Imaging) *(2 M)*

3. **What is the colour of wire conventionally used for: (*Re*)**
   (*i*) **Live wire.**
   (*ii*) **Earth wire,**
   (*iii*) **Neutral wire, and explain the significance of these color codings?**

Ans. (*i*) Red. (*ii*) Green, (*iii*) Black.

These colour codings are crucial for safety and maintenance, ensuring clear identification of each wire's function. *(2 M)*

4. **What is the purpose of the ground wire in a domestic circuit? (*Re*)**

Ans. Earth wires are the important components of the electrical circuits. Following are their primary functions:

(*i*) Earth wire prevents live wire from overloading
(*ii*) Earth wire absorbs the excess electrons and channelize them to flow beneath the ground
(*iii*) It protects the electrical appliances from damages
(*iv*) It absorbs excess electricity from appliances *(2 M)*

5. **Explain the role of the live wire in a household electrical system. (*Un*)**

Ans. The live wire carries the current from the source to the appliance, providing the energy needed for the appliance to function. It is typically insulated with red colour for identification. *(2 M)*

6. **Describe the function of the neutral wire in a domestic circuit. (*Re*)**

Ans. The neutral wire completes the circuit by providing a return path for the current to flow back to the source. It ensures a balanced potential difference with the live wire and is usually insulated with black colour. *(2 M)*

7. **Explain the function of a circuit breaker in preventing electrical hazards in household circuits. What happens when it detects an overload? (*Un*)**

Ans. A circuit breaker's function in a domestic circuit is to safeguard against potential electrical hazards caused by overloading and short circuits. Upon detecting an overload, it interrupts the current flow by automatically tripping, thereby preventing damage to the circuit and connected appliances. *(2 M)*

8. **What is the purpose of a fuse in a domestic circuit, and how does its design ensure the protection of electrical systems from overloading? (*Un*)**

Ans. A fuse in a domestic circuit is designed to protect against overloading and short circuits by melting and breaking the circuit, thereby stopping the flow of excessive current. Its design incorporates a thin wire that melts easily when too much current passes through, ensuring immediate circuit disconnection. *(2 M)*

9. **What is the voltage of a standard household circuit and the standard frequency of AC used in the India? (*Re*)**

Ans. The voltage in India is 220 volts, alternating at 50 cycles (Hertz) per second. This is the same as, or similar to, most countries in the world including Australia, Europe and the UK. The frequency of Alternating Current in India is 50 Hz. *(2 M)*

10. **Discuss the role of the main fuse in a household electrical system. (*Un*)**

Ans. The main fuse acts as a protective device at the meter-board, preventing damage to the circuit and appliances by breaking the circuit in case of excessive current flow. It is crucial for ensuring the safety of the electrical system *(2 M)*

Short Answer Type Questions (3 M)

1. **Describe the working principle of a fuse in protecting domestic electrical circuits. (*Re*)**

Ans. A fuse contains a thin wire that melts when there is an overload or short circuit, breaking the circuit and preventing damage to appliances and the electrical system. The fuse operates based on the principle of Joule heating, where excessive current causes the wire to melt and interrupt the circuit. *(3 M)*

2. **Why is it important to have separate circuits with different current ratings in a household electrical system? (*Un*)**

Ans. Separate circuits with different current ratings are used to accommodate appliances with varying power requirements. Higher power appliances like geysers and air coolers need a higher current rating circuit (e.g., 15 A) compared to lower power devices like bulbs and fans (e.g., 5 A). *(3 M)*

3. **Explain the concept of overloading in domestic electric circuits and how it can be prevented. (*Un*)**

Ans. Overloading occurs when the current in the circuit abruptly increases, leading to potential damage to appliances and the circuit. It can be prevented by using safety measures like fuses, avoiding connecting too many appliances to a single socket, and ensuring proper insulation of wires to prevent short-circuiting. *(3 M)*

4. **What is the advantage of the third wire of earth connection in domestic appliances? (*Un*)**

Ans. In case of any electric fault in domestic appliances, current may come in appliance body. The third wire called earth wire transfer this current to the earth and user remains safe from any electric shock. *(3 M)*

5. **Why is series arrangement not used for domestic circuits? (*Un*)**

Ans. In domestic circuits, all appliances are connected in parallel not in series because

(*a*) In series combination same current is passed through each appliances whereas different devices may need different current. *(1 M)*

(*b*) In the case of series combination, if one appliance fails to work then circuit will be broken and all other appliances will stop to work. *(1 M)*

(*c*) In the case of series combination, if one appliance is switched off others also will stop working i.e. all appliance will work together *(1 M)*

6. **Explain what is short-circuiting and overloading in an electric supply.** ***(Re)***

Ans. When live wire and neutral wire come in contact with each other, short circuit takes place. This may be due to fault in electric circuit or when insulation of wire is damaged. During the short circuiting current increases abruptly due to decrease in resistance in the circuit. This short circuiting leads the spark and the house may catch fire. *(2 M)*

Over loading means to draw the current by all electric appliances in the circuit more than maximum permitted value of the current. *(1 M)*

7. **Anannya responded to the question: Why do electrical appliances with metallic bodies are connected to the mains through a three pin plug, whereas an electric bulb can be connected with a two pin plug?**

She wrote: Three pin connections reduce heating of connecting wires. **(CBSE SQP, 2023)**

(*i*) Is her answer correct or incorrect? Justify. ***(An)***

(*ii*) What is the function of a fuse in a domestic circuit? ***(Ap)***

Ans. (*i*) Anannya's answer is wrong. Electrical appliances with metallic bodies need an earth wire which provides a low resistance conducting path to the flow of current, in case there is an accidental leakage of current through the conducting body of the appliances. *(1 + 1 M)*

(*ii*) An electrical fuse is a safety device that operates to provide protection against the overflow of current in an electrical circuit. An important component of an electrical fuse is a metal wire or strip that melts when excess current flows through it. *(1 M)*

Long Answer Type Questions **(5 M)**

1. **(*a*) State the function of 'a fuse' in an electric circuit. How is it connected in the domestic circuit?**

(*b*) An electric fuse of rating 3A is connected in a circuit in which an electric iron of power 1.5 kilo watt is connected which operates at 220V. What would happen? Explain. ***(Ev)***

Ans. (*a*) Fuse is a safety device to prevent the damage of electrical devices from short circuit or overloading. A fuse is connected in series with the circuit. *(2 M)*

(*b*) Given Power $P = 1.5\ kW = 1500$ Watt and $V = 220$ Volt.

Power, $P = VI \Rightarrow I = \frac{P}{V} = \frac{1500}{220} = 6.8A$ *(2 M)*

The rating of fuse is $3A$ which is lesser the current drawn by electric iron which is equal to $6.8A$. So fuse wire will be blown. *(1 M)*

2. **(*a*) What is the function of an earth wire in electrical instruments? Why is it necessary to earth the metallic electric appliances?** ***(Un)***

(*b*) Explain what is short-circuiting and overloading in an electric supply. ***(Un)***

(*c*) What is the usual capacity of the fuse wire in the line to feed:

(*i*) lights and fans?

(*ii*) appliances of 2kW or more power instruments? ***(Ap)***

Ans. (*a*) We can get an electric shock on touching a faulty appliance, caused by the leakage of current from the appliance. Earthing provides a safety measure against the electric shock caused by the leakage of current. Earth wire brings this leakage current to the ground by a earth wire and we remains safe. *(2 M)*

(*b*) Short circuiting takes place when a live wire and neutral wire come in contact with each other due to damage of insulation of these wires. Due to short circuiting, resistance of the circuit becomes minimum and a very high current is passed through the circuit which produces spark and heat and may lead to fire in the house. Overloading take place when the amount of current flowing through the circuit exceeds the rating of the protective devices it is said that circuit is overloaded. *(2 M)*

(*c*) (*i*) Usual capacity of fuse wire for bulbs, fans etc. is $5A$, *(½ M)*

(*ii*) Usual capacity of fuse wire for heater - Micro-oven, Electric iron $15A$ *(½ M)*

3. **(*a*) Draw a schematic labelled diagram of a domestic wiring circuit which includes (*i*) a main fuse (*ii*) a power meter (*iii*) one light point and (*iv*) a power plug.** ***(Cr)***

(*b*) Why is it necessary to connect an earth wire to electric appliances having metallic covers? ***(Un)***

Ans. (*a*) *(3 M)*

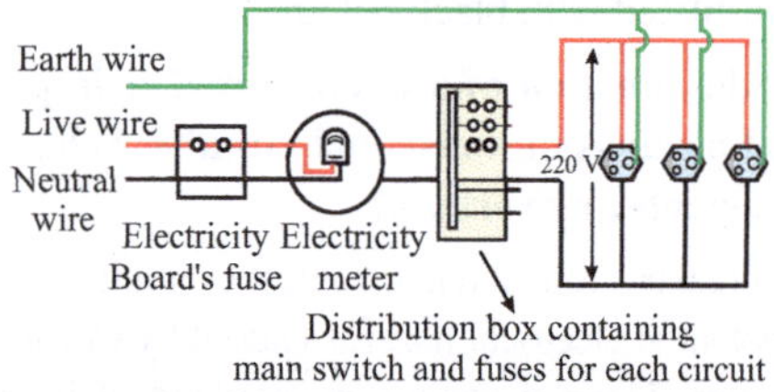

(*b*) The earth wire carry current due to any leakage or defective electric appliance to the earth keeping human beings safe preventing from any electric shock. *(2 M)*

4. ***(a) The given figure shows a domestic electric circuit. Study this circuit carefully. List any two errors in the circuit and justify your answer.***

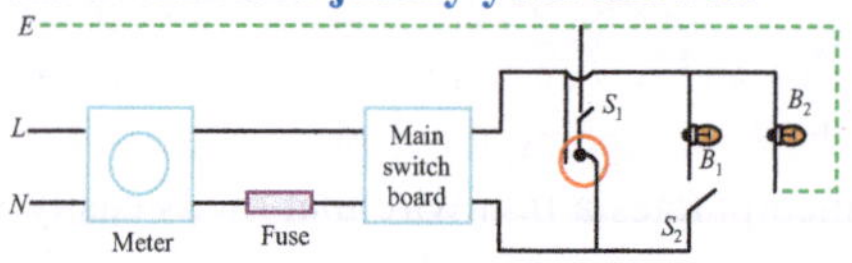

(An)

(*b*) Give one difference between the wires used in the element of an electric heater and in a fuse. ***(An)***

(*c*) List two advantages of parallel connection over series connection. ***(Un)***

Ans. (*a*) Errors in the circuit

(*i*) Fuse wire is connected to neutral wire (N) whereas it must be connected to live wire (L). *(1 M)*

(*ii*) Circuit of bulb B_2 is incomplete. *(1 M)*

(*b*) Element of electric heater has high resistance and high melting point whereas a fuse wire has high resistance and low melting point. *(1 M)*

(*c*) Advantages of parallel connection over series connection.

(*i*) In parallel combination if one appliance fails to work others keep working. *(1 M)*

(*ii*) Potential difference across each appliance remains same. *(1 M)*

Hints & Explanations

Multiple Choice Questions

1. (*c*) When a live wire and a neutral wire directly connect (short-circuit), the circuit's current spikes, flowing through the low-resistance path of wires instead of through the circuit's resistive elements.
2. (*c*) To provide a low-resistance path for current in case of leakage
3. (*b*) To protect the device from short-circuit or overloading, a fuse is commonly used. Fuse is a safety device which breaks the circuit and stops the excessive current flow when the current rating is more than the safe value.
4. (*a*) Higher power rating such as geysers. This is because devices with higher power ratings require a higher current to operate and the wiring with 15*A* current rating can handle the load and prevent overheating and damage.
5. (*c*) Earth wire in a domestic electrical circuit is typically green colored.
6. (*d*) Fuse is a protective device meant to protect electrical appliances from high voltage and short circuits. Which prevents electrical fires.
7. (*a*) Neutral wire in a domestic electrical circuit is typically colored black.
8. (*b*) To provide a return path for current
9. (*d*) The function of a circuit breaker in a domestic electrical circuit is to automatically cut off power in the event of an overload or short circuit.

Assertion and Reason

1. (*a*) Fuse is a safety device that is used to prevent electrical circuits from possible fires. A fuse wire is a wire with a low melting point.
2. (*b*) Both A and R are true, but R is not the correct explanation of A
3. (*c*) The neutral wire in a household electrical system provides a return path for current to flow back to the source, completing the circuit, rather than carrying current to the appliance.
4. (*a*) The earth wire is connected to the metallic body of appliances to ensure that any leakage of current to the body *keeps its potential to that of the earth, thus preventing* electric shocks to users.

MISCELLANEOUS EXERCISE

Multiple Choice Questions (1 M)

1. Which of the following is not attracted by a magnet? **(*Un*)**

   (*a*) Steel (*b*) Cobalt
   (*c*) Brass (*d*) Nickel

2. What is the SI unit of magnetic field strength? **(*Re*)**

   (*a*) Ohm (*b*) Ampere
   (*c*) Tesla (*d*) Joule

3. How does the strength of the magnetic field around a current-carrying wire change if the current is doubled? **(*Un*)**

   (*a*) It becomes half (*b*) It doubles
   (*c*) It remains the same (*d*) It cannot be determined

4. What happens to the direction of the magnetic field around a current-carrying wire if the direction of the current is reversed? **(*An*)**

   (*a*) The direction of the magnetic field remains the same.
   (*b*) The direction of the magnetic field reverses.
   (*c*) The magnetic field becomes weaker.
   (*d*) The magnetic field becomes stronger.

5. A straight wire carrying an electric current produces a magnetic field. If the wire is formed into a loop, what happens to the magnetic field inside the loop? **(*An*)**

   (*a*) The magnetic field becomes weaker.
   (*b*) The magnetic field becomes stronger.
   (*c*) The magnetic field is zero inside the loop.
   (*d*) The magnetic field remains the same.

6. Two parallel wires are carrying currents in the same direction. What is the effect of these currents on each other? **(*Un*)**

   (*a*) They attract each other.
   (*b*) They repel each other.
   (*c*) There is no interaction between the wires.
   (*d*) The interaction depends on the distance between the wires.

7. A current-carrying wire is placed in a magnetic field. In which direction will the wire experience a force? **(*Un*)**

   (*a*) In the same direction as the magnetic field.
   (*b*) In the opposite direction of the magnetic field.
   (*c*) Perpendicular to both the current and the magnetic field.
   (*d*) There will be no force acting on the wire.

8. Which type of current is used in most household appliances? **(*Re*)**

   (*a*) Alternating Current (*b*) Direct Current
   (*c*) Both *AC* and *DC* (*d*) None of the above

9. In a household circuit, what is the purpose of a fuse? **(*Un*)**

   (*a*) To regulate the voltage.
   (*b*) To regulate the current.
   (*c*) To prevent the circuit from overheating.
   (*d*) To prevent the circuit from overloading.

10. What happens if a household appliance is connected in reverse polarity? **(*Un*)**

    (*a*) The appliance will not work.
    (*b*) The appliance will work normally but with reduced efficiency.
    (*c*) The appliance will work normally.
    (*d*) The appliance may get damaged or cause a short circuit.

Assertion and Reason (1 M)

Direction: The following questions consist of two statements – Assertion (A) and Reason (R). Answer these questions by selecting the appropriate option given below:

(*a*) Both A and R are true, and R is the correct explanation of A.
(*b*) Both A and R are true, but R is not the correct explanation of A.
(*c*) A is true, but R is false
(*d*) A is false, but R is true.

1. **Assertion (A):** A current-carrying wire produces a magnetic field around it.

   Reason (R): This is due to the interaction between electric charges and magnetic fields. **(*Un*)**

2. **Assertion (A):** *The potential difference of 220 V in* household electrical systems is standardized for efficient appliance operation.

   Reason (R): Appliances require a specific voltage range for optimal performance and safety. **(*Un*)**

3. **Assertion (A):** Fuses are used in domestic circuits to protect against electrical overloading.

   Reason (R): Fuses regulate the voltage supplied to the appliances. **(*Un*)**

4. **Assertion (A):** When a straight wire carrying current is bent into a loop, the strength of the magnetic field inside the loop increases.

   Reason (R): The magnetic field lines become more concentrated outside the loop. **(*Un*)**

Subjective Questions

Very Short Answer Type Questions (2 M)

1. What is the SI unit of magnetic field strength? **(Re)**
2. What is the right-hand thumb rule used for? **(Re)**
3. What happens to the direction of the force experienced by a current-carrying wire in a magnetic field when the direction of the current is reversed? **(Re)**
4. What demonstrates the existence of a magnetic field around a current-carrying conductor? **(Un)**
5. How does the pattern of magnetic field lines change around a solenoid compared to a single straight wire? **(An)**

Short Answer Type Questions (3 M)

1. (*a*) State Fleming's left hand rule. **(Re)**

   (*b*) Write the principle of working of an electric motor. **(Un)**
2. Define magnetic field. Describe an activity to draw magnetic field lines around a bar magnet from one pole to another pole. **(Un)**
3. Name and state the rule to determine the direction of a:

   (*a*) magnetic field produced around a current carrying straight conductor.

   (*b*) force experienced by a current carrying straight conductor placed in a magnetic field which is perpendicular to it. **(Un) (CBSE, 2024)**
4. State the observation made by Oersted on the basis of his experiment with current carrying conductors **(Un)**
5. A compass needle is placed near a current carrying straight conductor. State your observation for the following cases and give reasons for the same in each case. **(Un)**

   (*a*) Magnitude of electric current is increased.

   (*b*) The compass needle is displaced away from the conductor.
6. Identify the type of magnetic fields represented by the magnetic field fines given below and name the type conductors which can produce them. **(An)**

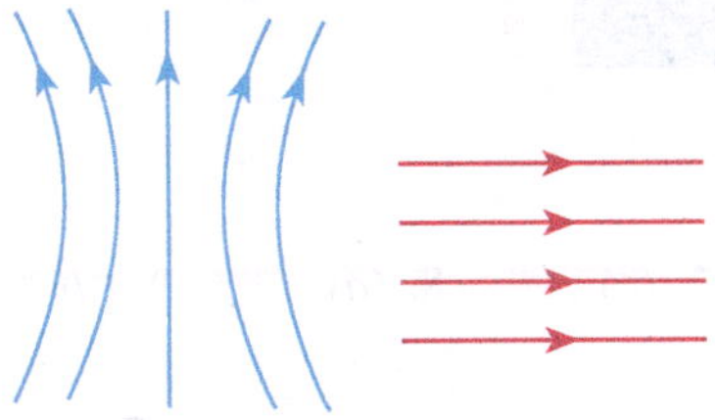

(*a*) (*b*)

7. On what factors does the force experienced by a current carrying conductor placed in a uniform magnetic field depend? **(Re)**
8. Why is series arrangement not used for domestic circuits? **(Un)**
9. Draw the pattern of lines of force due to a magnetic field through and around a current carrying loop of wire. How would the strength of the magnetic field produced at the centre of the circular loop be affected if the strength of the current passing through this loop is double? **(Cr)**
10. Differentiate overloading and short-circuiting. **(Re)**
11. For the circular coil carrying current shown alongside, draw magnetic field lines. Decide which of its face behaves as North Pole and which face as South Pole. Give reason to justify your answer. **(Un)**

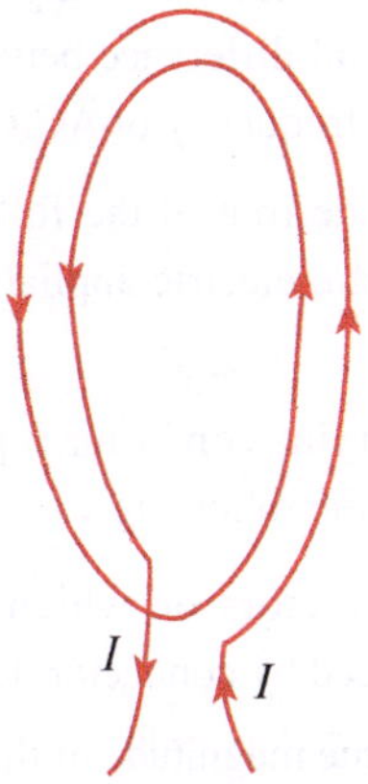

12. Find the direction of magnetic field due to a current carrying circular coil held: **(Ev)**

    (*i*) vertically in North - South plane and an observer looking it from east sees the current to flow in anti-clockwise direction,

    (*ii*) vertically in East - West plane and an observer looking it from south sees the current to flow in anti-clockwise direction,

    (*iii*) horizontally and an observer looking at it from below sees current to flow in clockwise direction.

Long Answer Type Questions (5 M)

1. (*a*) Describe an activity to determine the direction of magnetic field produced by a current carrying straight conductor. Also show that the direction of the magnetic field is reversed on reversing the direction of current. **(Un)**

   (*b*) An α-particle, (which is a positively charged particle) enters, a uniform magnetic field at right angles to it as shown below. Stating the relevant principle explain in which direction will this α-particle moves? **(Un)**

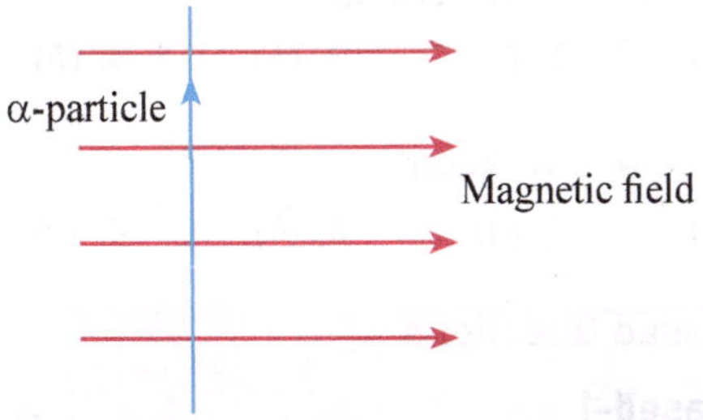

2. (*a*) Explain any three properties of magnetic field lines.

   (*b*) Give two uses of magnetic compass. **(Ap)**

3. (*a*) An electric current is passed in a horizontal copper wire from east to west. Explain your observations when a compass needle is placed (*i*) below this wire, (*ii*) above the wire. Draw inference from your observations. **(*An*)**

(*b*) List the factors on which the strength of the magnetic field due to a straight conductor carrying current depend. How should these be changed to decrease magnetic field at a point? **(*Re*)**

4. (*a*) Write the values of the following physical quantities in connection with domestic power supply in our country: (*i*) potential difference between live wire and neutral wire. (*ii*) frequency of AC. **(*Re*)**

(*b*) Explain the role of the following as safety measure in domestic electric appliance/circuits: (*i*) earth wire (*ii*) fuse. **(*Un*)**

5. A current carrying conductor is placed in a magnetic field. Now answer the following.

(*i*) List the factors on which the magnitude of force experienced by conductor depends.

(*ii*) When is the magnitude of this force maximum?

(*iii*) State the rule which helps, in finding the direction of motion of conductor.

(*iv*) If initially this force was acting from right to left, how will the direction of force change if:

(*a*) direction of magnetic field is reversed?

(*b*) direction of current is reversed?

Case Based Questions

Case Based-I: Field strength of the magnetic field produced by a current-carrying circular coil (or circular wire) depends on (*i*) Amount of current flowing through the coil. (*ii*) Radius of the circular coil, (*iii*) Number of turns in the circular coil. **(*Un*)**

(*i*) What type of curve we get between magnetic field and distance along the axis of a current carrying circular coil? *(2 M)*

(*ii*) A long horizontal power line is carrying a current of 100 A in the east-west direction. The direction of magnetic field at a point 1.0 m below it is *(1 M)*

(*a*) south to north (*b*) north to south

(*c*) east to west (*d*) west to east

(*iii*) If a current carrying straight conductor is placed in east-west direction, then the direction of the force experienced by the conductor due to earth's magnetic field is *(1 M)*

(*a*) downward (*b*) upward

(*c*) east-west (*d*) west-east

Case Based-II: An electric fuse is a safety device that prevents overloading of any electrical circuit. A fuse is always connected in the live wire and in series with the electrical circuit. Fuse wire is made from low-melting alloy of copper and tin. In urban areas, the conventional cut-out type fuses are being replaced by MCB. The maximum current which can be passed through a fuse without melting it is called its rating. **(*Un*)**

(*i*) What do you understand by the term fuse in an electric circuit? *(1 M)*

(*ii*) State two properties of a material, which make it suitable for making a fuse wire. *(1 M)*

(*iii*) Why is a fuse wire always placed in the live wire of an electric circuit? *(1 M)*

(*iv*) How does a fuse wire protect an electric circuit? *(1 M)*

(*v*) Two fuse wires A and B of the same length are rated 15 A and 5 A. Which amongst the A and B will be thicker and why? *(1 M)*

ANSWER KEYS

Multiple Choice Questions

1. (*c*) **2.** (*c*) **3.** (*b*) **4.** (*b*) **5.** (*b*) **6.** (*a*) **7.** (*c*) **8.** (*a*) **9.** (*d*) **10.** (*d*)

Assertion and Reason

1. (*a*) **2.** (*a*) **3.** (*b*) **4.** (*c*)

Case Based Questions

Case Based-I

(*ii*) (*b*) (*iii*) (*a*)

HINTS & EXPLANATIONS

Multiple Choice Questions

1. (*c*) Brass
2. (*c*) Tesla
3. (*b*) The strength of the magnetic field around a current-carrying wire is directly proportional to the current flowing through the wire. Therefore, if the current is doubled, the magnetic field strength also doubles.
4. (*b*) The direction of the magnetic field reverses.
   The direction of the magnetic field around a current-carrying wire follows the right-hand rule. Reversing the direction of the current results in reversing the direction of the magnetic field.
5. (*b*) The magnetic field becomes stronger.
   When a straight wire is formed into a loop, the magnetic field lines inside the loop become concentrated, resulting in a stronger magnetic field compared to the field produced by a straight wire.
6. (*a*) They attract each other.
   Parallel currents in the same direction generate magnetic fields that interact, resulting in a mutual attractive force between the wires.
7. (*c*) Perpendicular to both the current and the magnetic field.
   According to the right-hand rule, when a current-carrying wire is placed in a magnetic field, the force experienced by the wire is perpendicular to the current direction of current and the magnetic field.
8. (*a*) Alternating Current
   Alternating current (*AC*) is the type of current that is used in most household appliances.
9. (*d*) To prevent the circuit from overloading.
   A fuse is a safety device that is used to prevent a household circuit from overloading, which can result in fire or damage to the appliances.
10. (*d*) The appliance may get damaged or cause a short circuit.
    If a household appliance is connected in reverse polarity, it may get damaged or cause a short circuit, which can result in fire or damage to other appliances in the circuit.

Assertion and Reason

1. (*a*) Both the assertion and reason are true, and the reason is the correct explanation of the assertion.
   The assertion is true that a current-carrying wire produces a magnetic field around it. The reason is also true as the magnetic field is a result of the interaction between electric charges (moving electrons) in the wire and the magnetic fields they create.
2. (*a*) The assertion is true because the standard potential difference of 220 V ensures that appliances receive the required voltage for proper operation. This voltage level is suitable for most household devices, allowing them to function efficiently while maintaining safety standards.
3. (*b*) Both the assertion and reason are true, but the reason is not the correct explanation of the assertion.
   The assertion is true that fuses are used in domestic circuits to protect against electrical overloading. However, the reason is not correct as fuses do not regulate the voltage supplied to the appliances. Fuses primarily protect against excessive current flow.
4. (*c*) The assertion is true, but the reason is false.
   The assertion is true that when a straight wire carrying current is bent into a loop, the strength of the magnetic field inside the loop increases (not decreases). The reason is false as the magnetic field lines become more concentrated inside the loop, not outside.

Subjective Questions

Very Short Answer Type Questions

1. The unit of magnetic field is Tesla. It is the SI unit of magnetic field. Magnetic field is the measure of magnetic flux (Φ) per unit area. 1 Tesla=1 wb/m *(2 M)*
2. Right-hand thumb rule is used to determine the direction of the magnetic field around a current-carrying wire. It states that if you point your right thumb in the direction of the current flow, your curled fingers will show the direction of the magnetic field. *(2 M)*
3. The force experienced by a current-carrying wire in a magnetic field follows the right-hand rule. When the direction of the current is reversed, the force direction also reverses accordingly. *(2 M)*
4. The deflection of a compass needle placed near a current-carrying conductor demonstrates the existence of a magnetic field around it. The needle's orientation changes with the flow of current, illustrating the magnetic effect of electric current. *(2 M)*
5. Around a solenoid, the magnetic field lines form parallel straight lines inside the coil, indicating a uniform magnetic field. This contrasts with the concentric circles around a single straight wire, where the field strength decreases with distance from the wire. *(2 M)*

Short Answer Type Questions

1. (*a*) Fleming's left hand rule: If we stretch thumb, forefinger and middle finger of left hand perpendicular to each other in such a way that forefinger points in the direction of magnetic field, middle finger points in the direction of current then the thumb will point in the direction of motion/ force on the current carrying conductor. *(1½ M)*
   (*b*) Principle of working of electric motor: A current carrying coil placed in a magnetic field experience a torque. If the coil is free to move it will rotate in the magnetic field. *(1½ M)*
2. Magnetic field is the space around a magnet or a current carrying conductor in which its magnetic force can be experience.

Fix a plane white drawing sheet on a drawing board. Now take a bar magnet and a compass. Place the magnet at the middle of the paper and mark its boundary with the help of a pencil. Now place the compass near its N pole of the magnet and mark the positions of needle of the compass. Now move the compass on the drawing board. Coinciding south pole of the compass with the previous marked point of N pole of the needle and so on, move forward from one end

(N pole) to the another end (S pole) of the bar magnet.

Join all the marked points. You will get magnetic lines of force. *(2 M)*

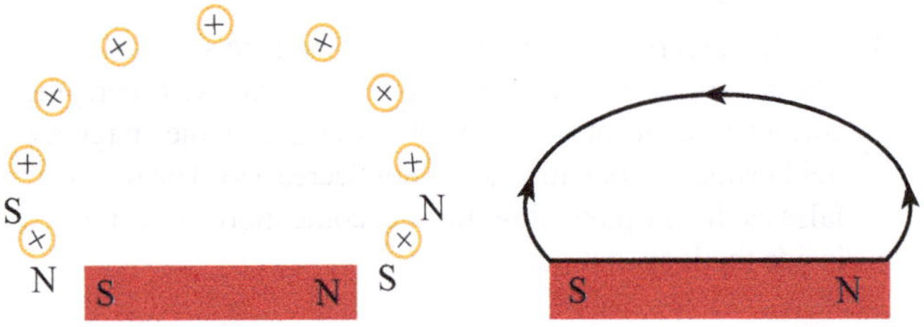

(1 M)

3. (*a*) The rule to determine the direction of the magnetic field produced around a current carrying straight conductor is known as the right-hand grip rule. *(½ M)*

   According to this rule, if you wrap your right hand around the conductor with your thumb pointing in the direction of the current flow, the direction in which your fingers curl around the conductor represents the direction of the magnetic field lines. *(1 M)*

   (*b*) The rule to determine the direction of the force experienced by a current-carrying straight conductor placed in a magnetic field perpendicular to it is known as the Fleming's left-hand rule. *(½ M)*

   According to this rule, if you extend your left hand such that your thumb points in the direction of the current flow and your index finger points in the direction of the magnetic field, then the direction in which your middle finger points represents the direction of the force experienced by the conductor. *(1 M)*

4. A magnetic field is produced near a current carrying conductor which last so long till there is current in the conductor on reversing the current the direction of magnetic field is also reversed. *(3 M)*

5. (*a*) As the amount of magnetic field strength is directly proportional to the amount of current, so the deflection of compass needle increases. *(1½ M)*

   (*b*) Since magnetic field strength at a point is inversely proportional to the distance from the wire. Hence deflection of compass decreases when it is displaced away from the conductor. *(1½ M)*

6. *(1 M)*

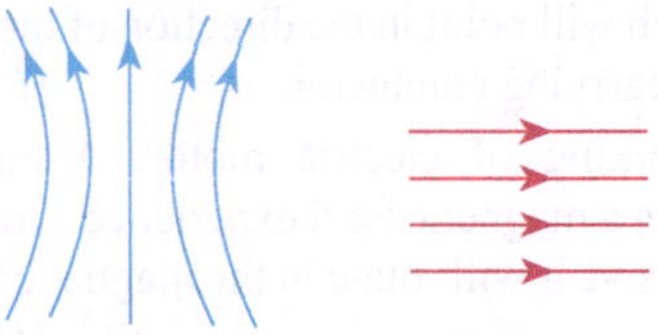

(*a*) (*b*)

(*a*) Magnetic filed lines of a current carrying circular. *(1 M)*

(*b*) Magnetic field lines in a solenoid. *(1 M)*

7. The force experienced by a current carrying conductor in a magnetic field depends upon

   (*a*) Length of the conductor *(1 M)*

   (*b*) Current in the conductor *(1 M)*

   (*c*) Magnetic field in which it is kept *(1 M)*

8. In domestic circuits, all appliances are connected in parallel not in series because

   (*a*) In series combination same current is passed through each appliances whereas they may need different current. If one appliance fails to work then circuit will be broken and all other appliances will stop to work. *(1 M)*

   (*b*) If one appliance is switched off others also will stop working i.e. all appliance will work together whether we require it or not. *(1 M)*

   (*c*) In series combination total potential difference is divided among all appliances in proportion to their resistance. So all appliance will not get required voltage to operate efficiently. *(1 M)*

9. The pattern of lines of force due to a magnetic field through and around a current carrying loop of wire is shown below

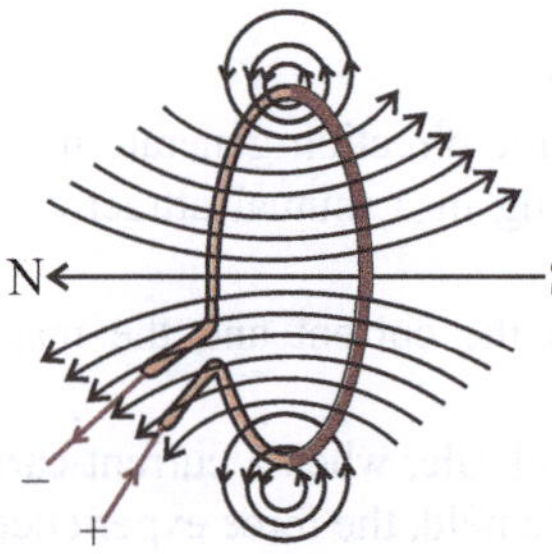

(2 M)

Strength of magnetic field is doubled when the current through the loop is doubled $B \propto I$. *(1 M)*

10. Overloading means to draw current more than the permitted maximum current in the circuit which may be due to connecting many appliances in one socket. *(1 M)*

    In short circuit, when live wire and neutral wire come in contact with each other then resistance of the circuit becomes minimum consequently the current in the circuit increases abruptly. It may be due to damage of insulation of wire. *(2 M)*

11. From the front face magnetic field emerges out of the coil and enters out from the back face so front face will behave as north pole and back face as south pole. *(1 M)*

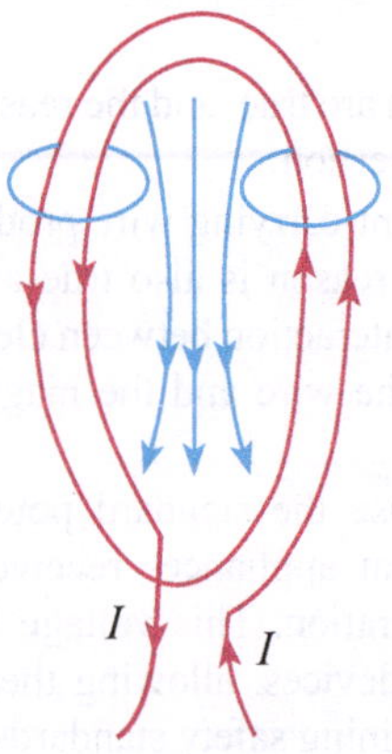

(2 M)

12. According to right hand rule, the direction of magnetic field is
(*i*) west to east (1 M)
(*ii*) north to south (1 M)
(*iii*) into the paper. (1 M)

Long Answer Type Questions

1. (*a*) Fix a cardboard and pass a straight wire through a hole in cardboard and connect the two ends of the wire with a cell through a rheostat and key with a cell. (1 M)
Sprinkle iron filings uniformly on the card board. Pass the current in the wire and gently tap the card board.
You would find that iron filings align themselves in concentric circles around the copper wire which represents the magnetic field around the current carrying conductor. The direction of magnetic field changes on reversing the direction of current. (1 M)
(*b*) According to Fleming's left hand rule the force on the α-particle will be inwards perpendicular to the plane of paper, so α-particle will move in the direction of force. (3 M)

2. (*a*) Properties of magnetic field lines:
   1. Magnetic field lines emerge from *N* pole and merge at *S* pole outside a bar magnet and travel from *S* pole to *N* pole inside the magnet. (1 M)
   2. These are continuous and closed curves. (1 M)
   3. Two field lines never intersect each other. (1 M)

   (*b*) Uses of magnetic compass:
   1. In navigation it is used to find direction. (1 M)
   2. It is used to detect the magnetic field. (1 M)

3. (*a*) The direction of deflection of a magnetic compass needle depends upon the direction of the magnetic field at that point. The direction of the magnetic field due to a current carrying wire is given by the right hand screw rule. The direction of magnetic field below and above the wire is opposite so deflection in compass needle changes as well i.e, the deflection is reverse direction. (2 M)
(*b*) The factors affecting strength of the magnetic field due to a straight wire carrying current depends on:
   1. Magnitude of current in the wire ($\propto I$) (1 M)
   2. Distance of the point from the wire ($\propto 1/d$) (1 M)

   By decreasing current or increasing the distance of the point from the wire, strength of magnetic field also decreases. (1 M)

4. (*a*) (*i*) 220V, (*ii*) 50 Hz (1 M)
(*b*) Safety measure in electric appliance/circuits:
(*i*) Earth wire is a safety device to protect us from electric shock due to leakage of current or faulty electric appliances. An earth wire is a thick copper wire connected to a metal plate buried deep in the earth. The metallic body of the electric appliance is connected to the earth wire, it provides a low resistance conducting path and leaked current goes to deep in the earth and human beings do not get a fatal electric shock. (2 M)
(*ii*) Fuse: It is also a safety device. It is a wire of an alloy with low melting point. If a current greater than a particular values flows in the circuit it will melt and circuit is broken and stops power supply in the circuit. (2 M)

5. (*i*) When a current carrying wire is placed in a magnetic field, it experiences a magnetic force that depends on
(*a*) current flowing in the conductor
(*b*) strength of magnetic field
(*c*) length of the conductor
(*d*) angle between the element of length and the magnetic field.
(*ii*) Force experienced by a current carrying conductor placed in a magnetic field is largest when the direction of current is perpendicular to the direction of magnetic field.
(*iii*) The rule used in finding the direction of motion of the conductor placed in a magnetic field is Flemings left hand rule.
Fleming's left hand rule is as follows:
Stretch out the thumb, the forefinger, and the second (middle) finger of the left hand so that these are at right angles to each other. If the forefinger gives the direction of the magnetic field (N to S), the second (middle) finger the direction of current then the thumb gives the direction of the force acting on the conductor.
(*iv*) (*a*) Direction of force will be reversed when direction of magnetic field is reversed, i.e., now force on conductor will act from left to right.
(*b*) Direction of force will be reversed, if the direction of current is reversed, i.e., the force on the conductor will act from left to right.

Case Based Questions

Case Based-I

(*i*) At smaller distances, the magnetic field will be described by concentric circles around the wire. As the distance increases, the circles become larger and larger. At the centre of the loop. The magnetic field will appear as straight line. (2 M)

(*ii*) (*b*) The current flows in the east-west direction. From right hand thumb rule, we get the direction of magnetic field as from north to south. The direction of magnetic field will be same at every point below the power line. (1 M)

(*iii*) (*a*) The force will act in downward direction perpendicular to both, the direction of current as well as to the field. (1 M)

Case Based-II

(*i*) Fuse is the weakest link in an electric circuit, which melts when the circuit gets overloaded or short circuited. (1 M)

(*ii*) (*a*) The material of the fuse wire should have high electric resistance. (1 M)
(*b*) The material of the fuse wire should have low melting point. (1 M)

(*iii*) When the fuse wire melts in the live wire circuit due to overloading, it completely disconnects the given appliance from the circuit. Thus, the appliance is safe to touch with bare hands and is also saved from any electrical damage. (1 M)

(*iv*) When the circuit gets overloaded, more current flows through the fuse wire, which in turn melts it. This cuts off the current in the given circuit and hence, it is protected from any damage, such as electric fire. (1 M)

(*v*) The wire A with 15 A rating is thicker. It is because, thicker the wire, less is its resistance and hence it can carry more current. (1 M)

13 OUR ENVIRONMENT

"One eats another to survive," just like a cheetah chases an impala, showing us the plain truth of nature's food chain. In the same way, everything in our environment, living and non-living, is interconnected. This chapter will take us through the basics of ecosystems and how they support these life and survival interactions.

SYLLABUS & WEIGHTAGE

LIST OF CONCEPT NAMES	YEARS				
	2020	2022 (TERM II)	2023	2024	2025
Ecosystem (Eco-system, Environmental problems)	1 Q (1 M) 1 Q (3 M)	1 Q (3 M)	1 Q (1 M) 1 Q (4 M)	1 Q (3 M)	1 Q (1 M) 1 Q (3 M)
Environmental Problems and its Management (Ozone depletion, Waste production and their solutions, Biodegradable and non-biodegradable substances)	—	1 Q (2 M)	1 Q (2 M)	1 Q (2 M)	1 Q (1 M)

For the year 2021, the exam was not conducted.

CONCEPT MAP

To Access One Shot Revision Video Scan This QR Code

Our Environment

Ecosystem

Types

Natural Ecosystem CBSE 2025
- Result of interactions between organisms and the environment.
- Does not need human assistance, E.g., Forest, Pond and Lakes.

Artificial Ecosystem
- Human-made structures where biotic and abiotic components are made to interact with each other for survival, E.g., Garden, crop fields, aquarium.

Components

Biotic	Abiotic
Producers (Organisms that produce their own food through photosynthesis)	Temperature, Soil, Water, Minerals, Wind
Consumers (Organisms that obtains energy by consuming other organisms)	
Decomposers (Organisms that break down dead or decaying materials) CBSE 2025	

Interaction among Biotic Components

Food Web: Network of interlinked food chains.

Food Chain Linear sequence of who eats whom. CBSE 2025

Trophic Levels CBSE 2022 Term-II

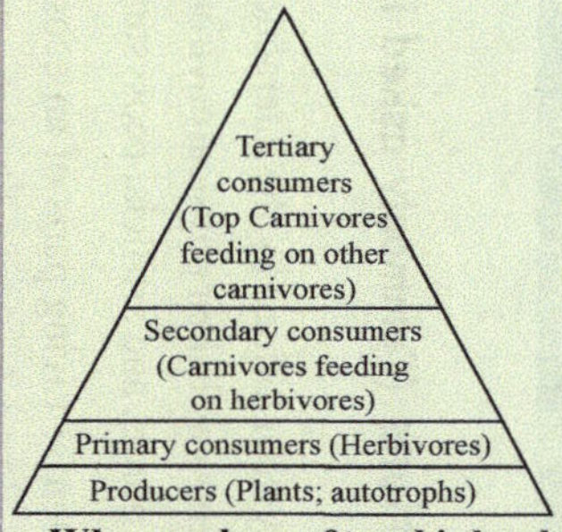

- **Why numbers of trophic levels limited?**
  - Loss of energy at each level
  - Only 10% of energy entering a trophic level is transferred to the next. CBSE 2025

Energy Transfer CBSE 2022 Term-II
- Unidirectional flow of energy:
  - Plants (Producers) → Herbivores (Primary consumers) → Carnivores (Secondary consumers) → Top Carnivores (Tertiary consumers). CBSE 2025
- **10% law:** Only 10% of energy entering a trophic level is transferred to the next.
- **Biomagnification:** CBSE 2025, 2023
  - Increase in toxic substance concentration up the food chain.
  - Greater risks to organisms at higher trophic levels.

Environmental Problems

Ozone layer CBSE 2024, 2022 Term-II

Role: Protects the Earth's surface from harmful UV radiations.

Effects of its depletion: Skin cancer, cataract, etc.

Cause of its depletion: Synthetic chemicals like chlorofluorocarbons (CFCs)

Measures: In 1987, UNEP froze CFC production at 1986 levels and mandated CFC-free refrigerators worldwide.

Waste CBSE 2025, 2023

Types

Biodegradable
Substances that are broken down by natural or biological processes, e.g., Paper, vegetables, food material, etc.

Non-Biodegradable
Substances that are not broken down by natural or biological processes, e.g., Plastic, Nylon, etc.

ECOSYSTEM

1

NCERT Definitions (Commonly asked in 1 mark)

- **Ecosystem:** A system formed by the interaction of a community of living organisms (biotic components) with their physical environment (abiotic components). Examples include forests, ponds, and artificial ecosystems like gardens.
- **Biotic Components:** Living parts of an ecosystem, including plants, animals, and microorganisms, which interact with each other and with the abiotic components.
- **Abiotic Components:** Non-living parts of an ecosystem that include physical factors like temperature, rainfall, wind, soil, and minerals, influencing the living organisms within.
- **Producers:** Organisms, like green plants and certain bacteria, that can make organic compounds from inorganic substances using sunlight energy through photosynthesis.
- **Consumers:** Organisms that rely on producers (either directly or indirectly) for their energy and sustenance, including herbivores, carnivores, omnivores, and parasites.
- **Omnivores:** Organisms that eat both plant and animal naturals as part of their diet. e.g., Humans.
- **Decomposers:** Microorganisms, such as bacteria and fungi, that break down dead organisms and waste products, converting them into simple inorganic substances useful for plants.
- **Food Chain:** A series of organisms each dependent on the next as a source of food, illustrating the flow of energy and nutrients from producers to various levels of consumers.
- **Trophic Levels:** The positions that organisms occupy in a food chain, which are indicative of their role in the flow of energy through the ecosystem.
- **Food Web:** A complex network of interconnected food chains within an ecosystem, showing the multiple paths through which energy and nutrients pass.
- **Biological Magnification:** The process whereby certain substances such as pesticides become more concentrated in the tissues of organisms at each successive trophic level of a food chain.

Important Facts

01 Components of an ecosystem. *~ Biotic and abiotic*

02 Percentage of sunlight energy capture by producers in an ecosystem. *~ 1%*

03 Percentage of energy transfer from one trophic level to the next in a food chain. *~ 10%*

04 Food chains rarely exceed four trophic levels because of significant energy loss at each step.

Classification

Levels of Food Chain				
Trophic levels	**First**	**Second**	**Third**	**Fourth**
Commonly known as	Producers	Primary consumers	Secondary consumers	Tertiary consumers
Examples	Plants, grass, phytoplankton	Rabbit, insect, zooplankton	Snake small fishes	Eagle, hawk, lions, tigers
Energy transfer (as per 10% low)	10,000	10,00	100	10
Nature of Organism	Autotrophs	Herbivores	Carnivores	Can be Carnivores or Omnivorous
Number in Ecosystem	Abundant	Less than producers	Less than primary consumer	Least, apex predators

Flow Chart for Ecosystem

ECOSYSTEM

Natural

- Occurs naturally without human intervention.
  Eg., Forest, oceans, lakes, deserts, etc.
- Higher biodiversity, more stable.

Artificial

- Created or modified by humans to achieve a specific purpose.
  Eg., Gardens, zoo, aquariums, urban parks, etc.
- Lower biodiversity, less stable.

Difference Between (Commonly asked in 2-3 marks)

Ecosystem vs. Environment	
Ecosystem	**Environment**
Community of living (biotic) and non-living (abiotic) components **interacting** as a system.	**All** living organisms and physical spaces, including biotic and abiotic components.
Can be **small** (aquarium) or **large** (desert).	Covers the **entire Earth,** including natural and built spaces.
Focuses on **interactions** within specific surroundings.	Broader concept affecting living beings, including **social** and **economic** factors.
Examples: forests, lakes.	More **generalized,** covers all surroundings.
Functional aspect, emphasizing **energy and matter flow.**	Covers all aspects affecting organisms, including **environmental conditions.**

Producers vs. Consumers	
Producers	**Consumers**
Synthesize **organic** compounds using light or chemical energy.	Rely on **consuming** other organisms for energy.
Autotrophs.	Heterotrophs.
Base of the food chain, converting **solar to chemical energy.**	Above producers, utilizing energy **stored by producers.**
Examples: green plants, algae.	Examples: deer (herbivores), lions (carnivores).
Do not consume others for energy.	Depend on other organisms for food.

Biotic vs. Abiotic Components	
Biotic Components	**Abiotic Components**
Living elements: microorganisms, plants, animals.	**Non-living elements:** sunlight, water, soil.
Interact through **predation, symbiosis.**	Determine **survival conditions** for biotic components.
Examples: bacteria, fungi.	Examples: temperature, humidity.
Evolve and adapt over time.	Change based on **natural or human actions** but don't evolve.
Influence **ecosystem structure and functions.**	Framework within which biotic components **live and interact.**

Food Chain vs. Food Web	
Food Chain	**Food Web**
Linear sequence of organisms, each eaten by the next..	Network of **interconnected** food chains.
Single path of energy flow.	**Multiple** paths of energy flow.
Simpler, showing **direct relationships.**	Complex, **realistic energy flow depiction.**
Involves **fewer** species.	Involves **more species** due to interconnectedness.
Vulnerable to **extinction if a link is removed.**	More **resilient** to changes.

Real Life Application Based Questions

1. **You're tasked with creating a self-sustaining aquarium for your science class.What features will you include to ensure it maintains a balanced ecosystem without frequent human intervention?**

Ans. Incorporate a mix of aquatic plants, fish, and a natural filtration system. Plants provide oxygen and food, while fish contribute to nutrient cycling, and the filtration system maintains water quality, creating a self-sustaining environment that mimics natural aquatic ecosystems.

2. **A local community is experiencing health issues due to pesticide use in farming. How could understanding biological magnification help address this problem?**

Ans. Educating farmers on biological magnification's impact can lead to reduced pesticide use, minimizing harmful accumulations in the food chain. Adopting integrated pest management (IPM) strategies can further mitigate health risks, ensuring safer food production and consumption.

Myth Buster

- **Myth: Only natural ecosystems contribute to conservation efforts.**

  Fact: Artificial ecosystems also contribute to conservation by providing habitats for endangered species, corridors for wildlife movement, and spaces for native flora and fauna in urban settings.

- **Myth: All food chains start with plants.**

  Fact: While many food chains start with plants, some begin with phytoplankton in aquatic environments or other autotrophic organisms capable of photosynthesis or chemosynthesis.

- **Myth: Apex predators have no natural enemies.**

  Fact: While apex predators are at the top of the food chain and have few or no predators, they can still be threatened by diseases, competition, and human activities.

- **Myth: All parts of an organism are consumed in a food chain.**

  Fact: Not all parts of an organism are consumed or assimilated in the food chain. Bones, shells, and other materials may not be directly used by the next trophic level.

- **Myth: Cooking or processing food eliminates the risk of biomagnification.**

  Fact: Cooking or processing food does not necessarily eliminate toxins that have biomagnified, as many of these substances are stable and resist breakdown under normal cooking temperatures.

Mnemonics

- **"Always Prefer Honey Over Dirty Green Salad"** - This stands for the following trophic levels:

Always	Prefer	Honey	Over	Dirty green salad
↓	↓	↓	↓	↓
Autotrophs	Primary Producers	Herbivores	Omnivores	Detritivores

- **"Time Rewards Smart Work Much"** - This stands for the following abiotic components of an ecosystem:

Time	Rewards	Smart	Work	Much
↓	↓	↓	↓	↓
Temperature	Rainfall	Soil	Wind	Minerals

- **"Sun Powers Healthy Chains"** - This stands for the flow of energy in an ecosystem

Sun	Powers	Healthy	Chains
↓	↓	↓	↓
Sunlight	Producers	Herbivores	Carnivores

COMPETENCY BASED SOLVED EXAMPLES

Multiple Choice Questions (1 M)

1. **Which of the following is not a biotic component in an ecosystem?** ***(Re)***

(*a*) Plants (*b*) Animals
(*c*) Sunlight (*d*) Microorganisms

2. **How does the number of organisms change as we move up the trophic levels in a food chain?** ***(Un)***

(*a*) Increases (*b*) Decreases
(*c*) Remains the same (*d*) Varies

3. **Which of the following is not a decomposer?** ***(Un)***

(*a*) Bacteria (*b*) Fungi
(*c*) Algae (*d*) Worms

4. **Identify the food chain in which the organisms of the second trophic level are missing:** ***(An)* (CBSE, 2024)**

(*a*) Grass, goat, lion
(*b*) Zooplankton, Phytoplankton, small fish, large fish
(*c*) Tiger, grass, snake, frog
(*d*) Grasshopper, grass, snake, frog, eagle

5. **Which of the following constitute a food-chain?** ***(Un)* (NCERT)**

(*a*) Grass, wheat and mango
(*b*) Grass, goat and human
(*c*) Goat, cow and elephant
(*d*) Grass, fish and goat

6. **Which one of the following is an artificial ecosystem?** ***(Re)* (NCERT Exemplar)**

(*a*) Pond (*b*) Crop field
(*c*) Lake (*d*) Forest

7. **In a food chain, the third trophic level is always occupied by** ***(Un)* (NCERT Exemplar)**

(*a*) carnivores (*b*) herbivores
(*c*) decomposers (*d*) producers

8. **An ecosystem includes** ***(Re)* (NCERT Exemplar)**

(*a*) All living organisms
(*b*) Non-living objects
(*c*) Both living organisms and non-living objects
(*d*) Sometimes living organisms and sometimes non-living objects

9. **In the given food chain, suppose the amount of energy at fourth trophic level is 5 kJ, what will be the energy available at the producer level?** ***(Ev)* (NCERT Exemplar)**

Grass → Grasshopper → Frog → Snake → Hawk

(*a*) 5 k J (*b*) 50 k J
(*c*) 500 k J (*d*) 5000 k J

10. **What is the ratio of average amount of energy absorbed by producers to the average amount of energy absorbed by the primary consumers?** ***(An)* (CFPQ)**

(*a*) 1 : 2 (*b*) 2 : 1
(*c*) 1 : 10 (*d*) 10 : 1

11. **Food web is constituted by** ***(Re)* (CBSE, 2020)**

(*a*) relationship between the organisms and the environment.
(*b*) relationship between plants and animals.
(*c*) various interlinked food chains in an ecosystem.
(*d*) relationship between animals and environment.

Assertion and Reason (1 M)

Direction: The following questions consist of two statements – Assertion (A) and Reason (R). Answer these questions by selecting the appropriate option given below:

(*a*) Both A and R are true, and R is the correct explanation of A.
(*b*) Both A and R are true, but R is not the correct explanation of A.
(*c*) A is true, but R is false.
(*d*) A is false, but R is true.

1. **Assertion (A):** Autotrophs can produce food on its own.
Reason (R): Green plants can absorb 1% energy of sunlight that fall on the leaves. ***(Un)***

2. **Assertion (A):** Food chains in an ecosystem rarely extend beyond four trophic levels.
Reason (R): The energy transferred from one trophic level to the next is insufficient to support viable populations at higher levels. ***(Un)***

3. **Assertion (A):** Energy flow in an ecosystem is unidirectional. ***(Un)***
Reason (R): Once energy is transferred from one trophic level to the next, it cannot return to the previous level.

Subjective Questions

Very Short Answer Type Questions (2 M)

1. **What is food chain? Write the common food chain of a pond ecosystem.** ***(Re)***

Ans. A food chain is a series of organisms in which transfer of energy takes place in the form of food from one organisms to another. *(1 M)*

The common food chain of a pond ecosystem is as follows:

Phytoplankton → Zooplankton → Small fish → Large fish *(1 M)*

2. **In the following food chain, 100 J of energy is available to the lion. How much energy was available to the producer?** ***(Ap)* (CBSE, 2017)**

Ans. As per 10 % law of energy transfer, if 100 J of energy is available at lion then deer should have 1000 J and grass will have 10,000 J of energy. *(2 M)*

Mistakes 101 : What not to do!

Students often miscalculate by overlooking the energy transfer rule, forgetting that energy diminishes at each level of the food chain.

3. How does an artificial ecosystem differ from a natural ecosystem? ***(Un)***

OR

Elaborate on how each component contributes to preserving the equilibrium within an ecosystem. ***(Un)***

Ans. Artificial ecosystems, like aquariums and agricultural fields, are human-made and often require external energy and monitoring to maintain, whereas natural ecosystems, such as forests and oceans, are self-sustaining and regulate themselves through internal processes *(2 M)*

OR

In an ecosystem, producers like plants convert solar energy into food, consumers ingest producers or other consumers, and decomposers break down organic matter, recycling nutrients and maintaining balance. *(1 M)*

Interactions among these components ensure energy flow and nutrient cycling, pivotal for ecosystem stability. *(1 M)*

4. List two main components of an ecosystem. **(*Re*) (CBSE 2019)**

Ans. Two main components of an ecosystem are:

(*i*) Biotic component: Plants, animals and microorganisms *(1 M)*

(*ii*) Abiotic component: Sunlight, water soil and air *(1 M)*

5. The following diagram shows a simple version of energy flow through the food web. ***(Ap)***

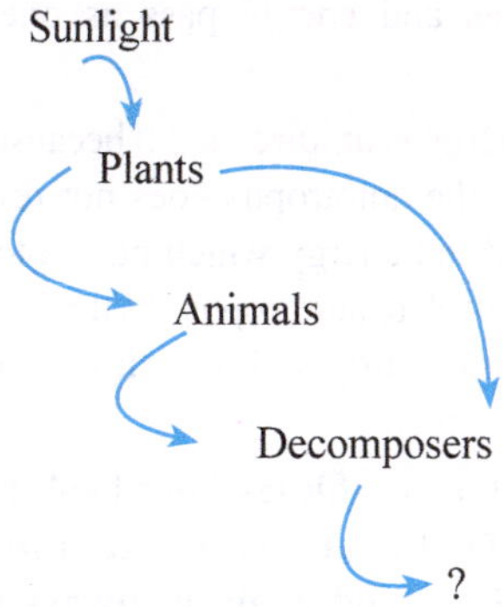

What happens to energy at the decomposers level?

Ans. After decomposers break down waste and dead matter, nutrients are cycled back to the soil, which are then absorbed by plants. *(1 M)*

However, most of the energy is converted to heat and released, not reused by living organisms. *(1 M)*

Nailing the Right Answer

When discussing the role of decomposers in energy flow, distinguish between the recycling of nutrients and the fate of energy.

6. Shown below are two food pyramids.

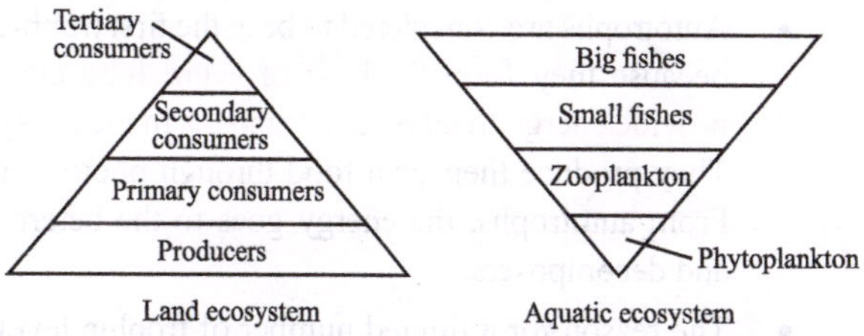

The pyramid representing the land ecosystem is traditional with producers being greater in mass than primary consumers and so on. Sometimes, in aquatic ecosystems, an inverted pyramid exists. Here, the total mass of producers (phytoplankton) is much smaller than the top consumers (big fishes). **(CBSE APQ, 2023)**

(*a*) Which level is likely to have the most amount of energy in such an aquatic ecosystem? Give a reason to support your answer.

(*b*) Such aquatic ecosystems are not considered to be sustainable. Justify this statement.

Ans. (*a*) Phytoplankton *(½ M)*

Producers will still have the highest amount of energy captured from sunlight which will continue to reduce as we move towards the top of the pyramid. *(½ M)*

(*b*) Since the total mass in the lower trophic level is lesser there will be lesser food available to higher trophic levels causing organisms to die sooner than usual. *(1 M)*

7. Will the impact of removing all the organisms in a trophic level be different for different trophic levels? Can the organisms of any trophic level be removed without causing any damage to the ecosystem? ***(An)***

Ans. Yes, the impact of removing all the organisms in a trophic level will be different for different trophic levels. For example, if plants are removed from food chain, herbivores and other primary consumers would not be able to survive. If herbivores are removed then carnivores will starve and die; producers will grow unchecked. Thus, it is not possible to remove any trophic level without causing any damage to the ecosystem. *(2 M)*

8. What is biological magnification? Will the levels of this magnification be different at different levels of the ecosystem? **(*An*) (NCERT)**

Ans. Biological magnification refers to the increasing concentration of a substance, such as a toxic chemical, in the tissues of organisms at successively higher levels in a food chain. *(1 M)*

The levels of magnification will indeed be different at various levels of the ecosystem, typically increasing as we move up the trophic levels because the substance accumulates progressively. *(1 M)*

Short Answer Type Questions (3 M)

1. What are trophic levels? Why are autotrophs considered to be at the first trophic level of all food chains? State the reason for limited number of trophic levels in nature. ***(Un)*** **(CBSE 2022, Term II)**

Ans.
- Trophic levels are the different levels in a food chain that show the transfer of energy from one organism to another. *(1 M)*
- Autotrophs are considered to be at the first trophic level because they form the base of every food chain and provide energy to all other organisms in the ecosystem. They produce their own food through photosynthesis. From autotrophs, the energy goes to the heterotrophs and decomposers. *(1 M)*
- The reason for a limited number of trophic levels in a food chain is due to the following reasons:
  - (*i*) Energy which is lost as heat and other physiological processes, is not transferred to the next trophic level. *(½ M)*
  - (*ii*) The amount of energy available decreases as it moves up to higher trophic levels. *(½ M)*

  As a result, there is not enough energy available to support more than a few trophic levels in a food chain.

2. Suggest one word for each of the following statements/ definitions. ***(Re)*** **(NCERT Exemplar)**

(*a*) The physical and biological world where we live in.

(*b*) Each level of food chain where transfer of energy takes place

(*c*) The physical factors like temperature, rainfall, wind and soil of an ecosystem

Ans. (*a*) The physical or biological world where we live in is called our environment. *(1 M)*

(*b*) The various steps in a food chain at which the transfer of food (or energy) takes place are called trophic levels. *(1 M)*

(*c*) Abiotic factor: The physical factors or climatic factors like light, temperature, pressure and humidity are considered as abiotic factor of ecosystem. *(1 M)*

3. Differentiate between food chain and food web. In a food chain consisting of deer, grass and tiger, if the population of deer decreases, what will happen to the population of organisms belonging to the first and third trophic levels? ***(An, Ap)*** **(CBSE, 2024)**

Ans.

Food Chain	Food web
A food chain is a linear sequence of organisms through which nutrients and energy flows from one organism to another.	A network of different food chains is called food web.
If one group of an organism is removed, the whole chain will become unstable.	The food web does not become unstable by the removal of one group of organisms.

(½ × 2 = 1 M)

Effect of Deer Population Decrease:

- First Trophic Level (Grass - Producers): With fewer deer grazing, grass population will increase due to reduced consumption. *(1 M)*
- Third Trophic Level (Tiger - Carnivores): The tiger population may decline due to a lack of sufficient prey (deer), leading to starvation and migration. *(1 M)*

Topper's Explanation

(1) Food chain is a ~~straight~~ series of organisms that feeds on one another. It is generally depicted by a 'straight line. However, one organism is fed by several other kinds of organisms which in turn ~~by~~ are fed by many more organisms'. So. ~~A branched chain of food chain~~ A food chain with several branches showing the flow of energy to different organisms from one is called food web.

(2) If population of deer decreases, then the population of organisms in 3rd trophic level ~~will~~ (Tigers) will decrease as they'll have less food to eat and hence, they'll die. In contrast, the population of organisms in first trophic level (~~deers~~ grass) will increase ~~dramatically~~. as ~~therefore~~ there will be less organisms to feed on them.

4. What are decomposers? State their role in our biotic environment. ***(Un)*** **(CBSE, 2018)**

Ans. Micro-organism which break down the complex organic compounds present in dead organisms like dead plants and animals and their products like feces, urine, etc., into simpler compounds are called decomposers. *(1 M)*

Following are the roles played by decomposers in the ecosystem are:

(*i*) They decompose biodegradable substances into useful substances.

(*ii*) They release nutrients into the soil by decomposing dead and decaying matter, (i.e.,maintaining, the nutrient pool) thus making the soil fertile. *(2 M)*

5. What is a food chain? Why is the flow of energy in an ecosystem unidirectional? Explain briefly. ***(Un)*** **(CBSE, 2019)**

Ans. A food chain is a linear sequence of organisms through which nutrients and energy pass as one organism eats another. *(1 M)*

The flow of energy is unidirectional because the energy that is captured by the autotrophs does not revert back to the solar input and the energy which passes to the herbivores does not come back to autotrophs. As it moves progressively through the various trophic levels, it is no longer available to the previous level. *(2 M)*

6. What is meant by trophic level in a food chain? Construct a terrestrial food chain with four trophic levels. The energy flow in a food chain is always unidirectional. Why? ***(Cr)*** **(CBSE, 2020)**

Ans. Each level in a food chain consists of living creatures that share the same function in the food chain, known as a trophic level. *(1 M)*

A terrestrial food chain with four trophic levels:

Grass → Insect → Frog → Eagle *(1 M)*

The energy flow in a food chain is always unidirectional because the energy transferred to the next trophic level cannot come back to the previous one, for example, the energy consumed by the plants from the sunlight cannot be revert back to the solar input and the energy consumed by the herbivores from the plants cannot be given back to plants. *(1 M)*

7. We do not clean ponds or lakes, but an aquarium needs to be cleaned. Why? **(*Ap*) (NCERT Exemplar)**

Ans. Aquariums, unlike ponds or lakes, lack natural self-cleaning processes. *(1 M)*

Ponds and lakes benefit from natural ecological cycles, including bacterial breakdown of waste, and have larger volumes of water that dilute pollutants. *(1 M)*

In contrast, aquariums are closed systems without these natural cleaning mechanisms, necessitating regular cleaning to remove waste and prevent toxin buildup, ensuring the health of aquatic life. *(1 M)*

8. (*a*) (*i*) Why does-a kitchen garden called an artificial ecosystem while a forest is considered to be a natural ecosystem?

(*ii*) While designing an artificial ecosystem at home, write any two things to be kept in mind to convert it into a self-sustaining system. Give reason to justify your answer.

(*An*) (CBSE, 2023)

OR

(*b*) (*i*) Construct a food chain of four trophic levels comprising the following: **(*Ev*) (CBSE, 2023)**

Hawk, snake, plants, rat.

(*ii*) 20,000 J of energy was transferred by the producers to the organism of second trophic level. Calculate the amount of energy that will be transferred by organisms of the third trophic level to the organisms of the fourth trophic level.

Ans. (*a*) (*i*) A kitchen garden is called an artificial ecosystem because it is created and maintained by humans, where plants are grown under controlled conditions, unlike a forest, which is a natural ecosystem that develops without human intervention. *(1 M)*

(*ii*) To create a self-sustaining artificial ecosystem:

1. Ensure a balanced mix of producers (plants) and consumers (insects, small animals) to maintain the food chain. Reason: This mimics natural ecosystem dynamics.
2. Include decomposers (fungi, bacteria) to recycle nutrients. Reason: Decomposers return nutrients to the soil, supporting plant growth. *(2 M)*

OR

(*b*) (*i*) Food Chain: Plants → Rat → Snake → Hawk. *(1M)*

(*ii*) If 20,000 J is transferred to the second trophic level, following the 10% rule, the third trophic level receives 2,000 J, and the fourth trophic level receives 200 J (10% of 2,000 J). *(2 M)*

9. Define an ecosystem. Draw a block diagram to show the flow of energy in an ecosystem. **(*Cr*)**

Ans. The ecosystem is defined as a biological community of interacting organisms and their physical environment, where energy flows from the sun to producers (like plants) and then through various trophic levels of consumers (herbivores, carnivores) and decomposers, with energy being lost as heat at each step. *(2M)*

The block diagram for the flow of energy in an ecosystem is as follows:

Producers	→	Primary Consumers	→	Secondary Consumers	→	Tertiary consumers
(10000J)		(1000J)		(100J)		(10J)

(1 M)

Long Answer Type Questions (5 M)

1. (*a*) Why is the maximum concentration of pesticides found in human beings?

(*b*) Give two methods which could be applied to reduce our intake of pesticides through food to some extent.

(*c*) What does various steps in a food chain represent?

(*d*) As per your understanding, humans occupy which trophic level in the food chain?

Ans. (*a*) The maximum concentration of pesticides is found in humans due to bio magnification, where these substances accumulate in higher concentrations in organisms at each trophic level. *(1 M)*

(*b*) Washing and peeling: Washing fruits and vegetables thoroughly under running water and peeling them can remove pesticide residues present on the surface. *(1 M)*

Organic eating: Consuming organically grown food, which is cultivated without the use of synthetic pesticides, can significantly reduce pesticide intake. *(1 M)*

(*c*) Various steps in a food chain represents a trophic level. *(1 M)*

(*d*) Humans occupy various trophic levels, primarily as primary consumers (herbivores) and secondary or tertiary consumers (carnivores or omnivores), depending on diet. *(1 M)*

2. (*a*) What do you understand by term 'environment'?

(*b*) What is meant by a primary consumer, secondary consumer and tertiary consumer? Give one example each.

(*c*) What will be the consequence of the absence of decomposers in the ecosystem? **(*Un, An*)**

Ans. (*a*) Physical and biological world where we live is called our environment. It includes our physical surroundings like air, (atmosphere) water (water bodies) (land) and all organisms such as animals, plants and micro-organisms. *(1 M)*

(*b*) Primary consumers are organisms that feed on producers (plants). Example: Rabbit. *(1 M)*

Secondary consumers feed on primary consumers. Example: Snake. *(1 M)*

Tertiary consumers feed on secondary consumers. Example: Eagle. *(1 M)*

(*c*) In the absence of decomposers, dead bodies of plant and animals would keep lying as such and the elements of which plant and animals bodies are made, would never be returned to their original pools of soil, air and to water. *(1 M)*

Hints & Explanations

Multiple Choice Questions

1. (*c*) Sunlight is an abiotic component whereas plants, animals and microorganisms are considered as biotic component.
2. (*b*) The number of organisms at any trophic level depends upon the amount of food and energy at the previous level. Therefore, the most food chains will have higher number of organisms at the producer level and the number decreases at each successive level.

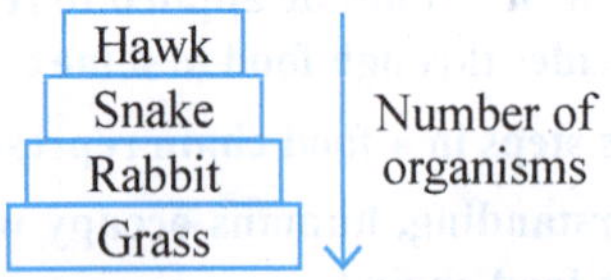

3. (*c*) Bacteria, fungi and worms are decomposers they decompose dead and decaying matter. Algae are not decomposers.
4. (*c*) Tiger, grass, snake, frog

Grass → [Herbivore is missing] → Frog → Snake → Tiger
(Producer) (Primary consumer) (Secondary consumer) (Tertiary consumer) (Top consumer)

5. (*b*) Grass serves as the producer, the goat as the primary consumer (eating the grass), and humans as the secondary consumer (eating the goat), forming a coherent food chain.
6. (*b*) Crop field is an artificial ecosystem whereas pond, lake and forest are natural ecosystem.
7. (*a*) In a food chain, the third trophic level is always occupied by carnivores. First trophic level is producers which are eaten by herbivores (second trophic level). These herbivores are eaten by carnivores (third trophic level).
8. (*c*) Ecosystem consists of both biotic component (living organisms like plants, animals and microorganisms) and abiotic component (non-living components of ecosystem like soil, water, air and sunlight).
9. (*d*) In an ecosystem, along with the food chain, there is a loss of energy and only 10 percent of the energy is transferred to each trophic level. 5000 kJ of energy is available at the producer level and at the next (or second) trophic level 500 KJ of energy will be available, at the next (or third) trophic level 50 KJ of energy will be available, at the next (or fourth) trophic level 5 KJ of energy will be available.
10. (*d*) The correct answer is 10:1. This is because, on an average, only about 10% of the energy from producers is transferred to primary consumers.
11. (*c*) Food web is consists of various interlinked food chains in an ecosystem.

Assertion and Reason

1. (*b*) The green plants in a terrestrial ecosystem capture about 1% of the energy of sunlight that falls on their leaves and convert it into food energy. The ability of autotrophs to produce food is due to their capacity to perform photosynthesis, not just their absorption of solar energy.
2. (*a*) Food chains typically do not extend beyond four trophic levels because the energy transfer from one trophic level to the next is only about 10%, making it insufficient to support viable populations at higher levels. This energy loss at each level limits the length of the food chain.
3. (*a*) Energy moves from producers to various levels of consumers and is not recycled back to the previous levels, making it unidirectional.

ENVIRONMENTAL PROBLEMS AND ITS MANAGEMENT

2

NCERT Definitions (Commonly asked in 1 mark)

- **Ozone Layer:** A layer in the Earth's stratosphere containing a high concentration of ozone, which protects living organisms from harmful ultraviolet radiation from the Sun.
- **Chlorofluorocarbons (CFCs):** Synthetic chemicals once commonly used as refrigerants and in aerosols, known to contribute to the depletion of the ozone layer.
- **Biodegradable:** Substances that can be broken down by biological processes, including the action of decomposers, into simpler, non-polluting compounds.
- **Non-Biodegradable:** Substances that cannot be broken down by natural processes and persist in the environment, potentially causing pollution and harm to ecosystems.

Important Facts

01 Chemical compound mainly responsible for the depletion of ozone layer. *~CFCs*

02 The process responsible for the accumulation of harmful chemicals in the bodies of organisms, particularly those at higher trophic levels. *~Biological magnification*

Difference Between (Commonly asked in 2-3 marks)

Biodegradable vs. Non-Biodegradable

Biodegradable	Non-Biodegradable
Broken down by **biological** processes into non-toxic substances.	**Persist in the environment,** cannot be easily broken down.
Decomposed by microorganisms.	Lead to **pollution** and harm to ecosystems.
Examples: food waste, paper.	Examples: plastics, metals.
Environmentally friendly but requires **proper management.**	Contribute to **long-term pollution,** and need **specialized disposal.**
Converted into **compost or organic matter.**	Cause **soil contamination, water pollution.**

A PLASTIC BAG NEEDS A 1000 YEARS TO FALL APART

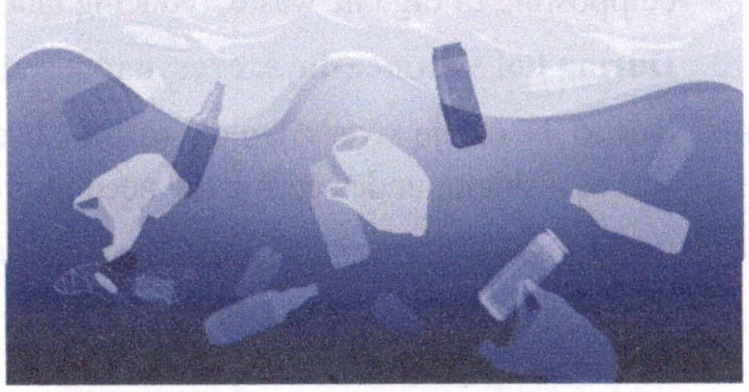

I ONLY NEED ONE AFTERNOOM

Disposable Paper-Cups vs. Disposable Plastic Cups		
Aspect	**Disposable Paper-Cups**	**Disposable Plastic Cups**
Biodegradability	More easily biodegradable.	Less biodegradable, persisting longer in the environment.
Environmental Impact	Lower impact, made from renewable resources.	Higher impact, made from fossil fuels.
Recycling	Easier to recycle in many areas.	Recycling can be more complex due to plastic types.
Manufacturing	Generally uses less energy.	Typically requires more energy to produce.
Decomposition	Decomposes faster, reducing landfill issues.	Slow to decompose, contributing to landfill mass.

Real Life Application Based Questions

1. **Have you ever encountered the blue or green colors dustbins at public places? How does using these bins correctly help the environment?**

Ans. Using blue bins for recyclables and green bins for organic waste significantly aids environmental conservation. It promotes effective recycling, reduces landfill waste, and conserves resources, helping to minimize pollution and support sustainable waste management practices.

2. **Your city council plans to improve waste management. What simple yet effective strategy can they employ to reduce landfill usage and promote recycling?**

Ans. Implement a city-wide segregated waste collection system, separating biodegradable, recyclable, and non-recyclable waste. This facilitates efficient recycling processes and composting of organic waste, reducing landfill strain and environmental pollution.

3. **During hot summer days, everyone insists on using sunscreen even during short outdoor trips. Why?**

Ans. Due to the ozone layer's depletion, more harmful UV rays can reach us, boosting the chance of skin damage. Daily sunscreen use acts as a shield, underscoring the need to protect the ozone layer for our safety.

4. ***Noticing the increased use of air conditioners (ACs) in your neighborhood during hot months, how does this trend impact the ozone layer?***

Ans. ACs often contain HFCs, which can deplete the ozone layer. Choosing ACs with eco-friendly refrigerants and minimizing use can reduce ozone depletion, protecting the environment and our health.

Myth Buster

- **Myth: Ozone is beneficial at ground level since it's good higher up in the atmosphere.**

  Fact: Ground-level ozone is a harmful air pollutant, contributing to smog and respiratory problems, unlike the protective layer of ozone in the stratosphere.

- **Myth: All biodegradable waste naturally decomposes quickly without harming the environment.**

  Fact: Some biodegradable waste can still release methane, a potent greenhouse gas, if not managed properly, such as in landfills without proper gas capture systems.

Mnemonics

- **"When the CFCs fly, the ozone says goodbye; let's keep it high, and not let the Earth cry."**
  This rhyme helps students recall the effect of CFCs on the ozone layer and the importance of preserving it.

- **"UVOO Trio"** - To remember the formation of Ozone.

  - **UV** → UV radiations splits oxygen molecule
  - **OO** → Splitting of O_2 to free O atoms & formation of O_3 (Ozone).
  - **Trio** → Highlights the three-part process (UV starts it, O_2 splits, and O_3 is the finale).

COMPETENCY BASED SOLVED EXAMPLES

Multiple Choice Questions (1 M)

1. Which of the following is the main cause of the depletion of the ozone layer? ***(Re)***

(*a*) Carbon dioxide emissions

(*b*) Deforestation

(*c*) Chlorofluorocarbon (CFC) emissions

(*d*) Overfishing

2. Increased exposure of UV rays to humans results in ***(Un)***

(A) Damage to immune system

(B) Damage to lungs

(C) Skin cancer

(D) Peptic ulcers

(*a*) (A) and (B) (*b*) (B) and (D)

(*c*) (A) and (C) (*d*) (C) and (D)

3. Which of the following features relates to biodegradable substances? ***(Re)* (CBSE SQP, 2023)**

(*a*) Broken down by biological processes

(*b*) Remain inert

(*c*) Persist in environment for long time

(*d*) May harm the ecosystem

4. The action of which among the following is crucial to the formation of ozone? ***(Re)* (CBSE APQ, 2023)**

(*a*) humans (*b*) sunlight

(*c*) carbon dioxide (*d*) chlorofluoro carbons

5. Samaira conducted an experiment where she buried three different types of solid wastes (P, Q, and R) under the soil in a pot to study their decomposition rates. The graph below shows the decomposition rates of these wastes over time. ***(An)***

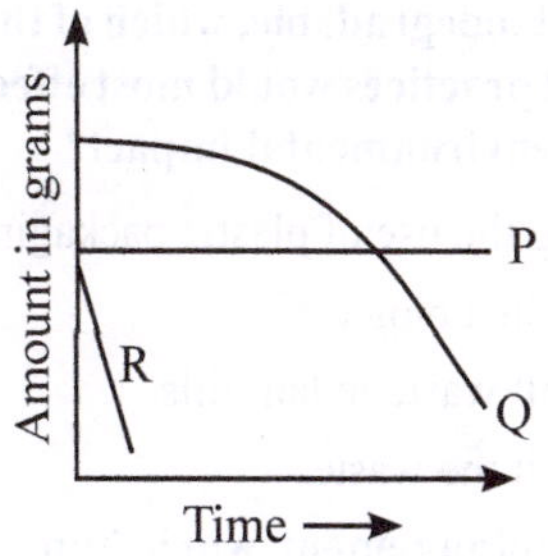

Select the option that correctly identifies P, Q, and R:

	P	Q	R
(*a*)	Banana peel	Plastic bottle	Paper cup
(*b*)	Polythene bag	Bone	Orange peel
(*c*)	Apple core	Metal can	Cardboard
(*d*)	Rubber tire	Vegetable scrap	Wooden stick

6. Which of the following steps is not related to formation of ozone? ***(Re)***

(*a*) Ozone is a toxic gas.

(*b*) UV radiations from sunlight split the oxygen molecule into atomic oxygen.

(*c*) Oxygen molecules combine with the atomic oxygen to form ozone.

(*d*) Ozone is formed at the higher levels of the atmosphere.

7. In an experiment to determine the biodegradability of different materials, which of the following observations would indicate that a substance is biodegradable? ***(An)***

(*a*) The substance changes colour after being buried for a week.

(*b*) The substance remains unchanged in size and appearance after several months.

(*c*) The substance shows signs of breaking down into smaller pieces after being exposed to microorganisms.

(*d*) The substance increases in size due to absorption of water.

8. Which of the following best describes the role of UV radiation in the formation of ozone? (*Re*)

(*a*) UV radiation provides the necessary heat for ozone formation.

(*b*) UV radiation splits O_2 molecules into free oxygen atoms.

(*c*) UV radiation combines two O_2 molecules to form ozone.

(*d*) UV radiation absorbs the excess oxygen released in the process.

9. What would be the consequence of a lack of specificity in enzyme action? (*Un*)

(*a*) Increased efficiency in digestion.

(*b*) No change in the digestion process.

(*c*) Breakdown of necessary molecules and potential harm.

(*d*) Faster synthesis of new molecules.

10. If a survey shows that 70% of waste produced by a household is biodegradable, which of the following waste management practices would most effectively reduce the household's environmental impact? (*Ap*)

(*a*) Increasing the use of plastic packaging.

(*b*) Investing in a biogas plant.

(*c*) Sending all waste to landfills.

(*d*) Burning all the waste.

11. In a waste management workshop, participants are given different groups of items to sort into categories. They need to identify which group contains an odd item that doesn't fit the category. An odd item in each group is italicized.

Which group has an incorrect odd one out? (*An*)

(*a*) Vegetable peels, *Plastic bottles*, Paper, Food scraps

(*b*) Newspaper, *Glass bottles*, Cardboard, Food waste

(*c*) Livestock wastes, *Polyethylene bags*, Leaves, Kitchen scraps

(*d*) Thermocol, Glass bottles, Metal cans, *Rubber*

12. An experiment comparing the decomposition of clay, plastic, and paper materials over time in a compost environment would likely show that: (*An*)

(*a*) Plastic decomposes fastest.

(*b*) Clay and paper decompose at similar rates.

(*c*) Clay decomposes, while plastic and paper do not.

(*d*) Paper decomposes faster than plastic but slower than clay.

13. If a certain area experiences a significant reduction in UV radiation due to atmospheric conditions, how would this affect local ozone production? (*Ap*)

(*a*) It would increase since less UV radiation means less ozone destruction.

(*b*) It would decrease since UV radiation is necessary to split O_2 molecules.

(*c*) It would remain unchanged since ozone production is constant.

(*d*) It would first decrease, then increase to maintain equilibrium.

Assertion and Reason (1 M)

Direction: The following questions consist of two statements – Assertion (A) and Reason (R). Answer these questions by selecting the appropriate option given below:

(*a*) Both A and R are true, and R is the correct explanation of A.

(*b*) Both A and R are true, but R is not the correct explanation of A.

(*c*) A is true, but R is false.

(*d*) A is false, but R is true.

1. **Assertion (A):** All kitchen waste cannot form compost.
   Reason (R): Material like milk packets may not be biodegradable. **(*Un*)**

2. **Assertion (A):** Biodegradable substances result in the formation of compost and natural replenishment.
   Reason (R): It is due to breakdown of complex inorganic substances into simple organic substances.
   (*Un*) (CBSE SQP, 2023)

3. **Assertion (A):** The reduction in atmospheric ozone levels was significantly noted around the 1980s.
   Reason (R): The increased use of chlorofluorocarbons (CFCs) leads to the destruction of ozone molecules. **(*Re*)**

Subjective Questions

Very Short Answer Type Questions (2 M)

1. Write the full name of the compound mainly responsible for the depletion of the ozone layer. Why is excessive use of this compound a cause of concern? (*Un*)

Ans. The compound mainly responsible for the depletion of the ozone layer is Chlorofluorocarbon (CFC). Excessive use of CFCs releases chlorine atoms in the stratosphere, which destroy ozone molecules, thinning the ozone layer and increasing harmful UV radiation exposure on Earth. *(2M)*

2. Use of several pesticides which results in excessive accumulation of pesticides in rivers or ponds, is a matter of deep concern. Justify this statement.
(*Un*) (CBSE, 2023)

Ans. Excessive pesticide use leads to accumulation in water bodies, posing risks through biological magnification. This process concentrates toxins at higher trophic levels, affecting aquatic life and humans who consume fish, potentially leading to health issues. *(2M)*

3. Name the harmful radiations that are absorbed by the ozone layer? Ozone layer is present in which layer of atmosphere? (*Re*)

Ans. UV radiations are absorbed by the ozone layer. *(1 M)*

Ozone layer is present in stratosphere layer of the atmosphere. *(1 M)*

4. **"The improvement in our lifestyle has led to the generation of large amount of waste material." List two reasons to justify this statement.**

OR

"The change in packaging has resulted in waste becoming non-biodegradable."

Giving two examples from daily life, justify this statement. **(*An*)**

Ans.
- Increased consumerism: More products purchased lead to more packaging and discarded items. *(1M)*
- Technological advancements: Frequent updates in technology result in higher electronic waste. *(1M)*

OR

- Plastic water bottles: Unlike paper-based alternatives, plastic bottles do not decompose naturally and persist in the environment. *(1M)*
- Plastic shopping bags: Commonly used for carrying groceries, these bags are non-biodegradable and contribute to plastic pollution. *(1M)*

5. **Marked decline in the thickness of ozone layer was noticed in the 1980s. Which human activity can be held accountable for this change? What is the possible effect of this on human health?** **(*Un*) (CBSE APQ, 2023)**

Ans. The production and use of chlorofluorocarbons (CFCs) in refrigeration and aerosols can be held accountable for the ozone layer depletion. *(1M)*

The thinning of the ozone layer increases UV radiation exposure, leading to higher risks of skin cancer and cataracts in humans. *(1M)*

6. **Why are some substances biodegradable and some non-biodegradable?** **(*Ap*) (NCERT Intext)**

Ans. Substances are biodegradable if naturally occurring microorganisms can break them down, like food waste and paper. Non-biodegradable substances, such as plastics and metals, resist microbial breakdown, persisting in the environment due to their synthetic or complex structures. That is why some waste materials are biodegradable, whereas some are non-biodegradable. *(2M)*

Short Answer Type Questions (3 M)

1. **Suggest any six activities in daily life which are eco-friendly.** **(*Un*)**

Ans. Some of the eco-friendly activities in our daily life:
- Segregation of waste: Separation of biodegradable and non-biodegradable substances. *(½ M)*
- Gardening: Planting potted plants at home and taking care of them. *(½ M)*
- Avoiding plastics: Use of gunny bags/paper bags in place of polythene/plastic bags. *(½ M)*
- Saving water: putting taps closed and also doing rain water harvesting. *(½ M)*
- Saving electricity: Switching off light/fans in unoccupied rooms. *(½ M)*
- Reusing: Reusing cereals bags, cans, plastic bottles.

2. **Name the wastes which are generated in your house daily. What measures would you take for their disposal?** **(*Un*) (NCERT Exemplar)**

Ans. Wastes generated at our homes:

(*i*) Vegetable and fruit peels and rind, stale food, food leftovers, used tea leaves.

(*ii*) Waste paper (newspaper, bags, envelopes), packing paper, empty bottles, cloth pieces, etc.

(*iii*) Milk pouches, polythene bags, empty cartons. *(1½ M)*

Different ways for Disposal waste:

(*i*) By Separating biodegradable and non-biodegradable waste, we can take out recyclable and non-recyclable wastes.

(*ii*) Recyclable wastes (waste paper, cloth, polythene or plastic bags, cartons, bottles, cans, etc.) can be given to rag pickers for recycling.

(*iii*) Kitchen wastes for home garden (kitchen garden) can be used for preparation of compost or vermicompost. *(1½ M)*

3. **A gas 'X' which is a deadly poison is found at the higher level of atmosphere and performs an essential function. Name the gas and write the function performed by this gas in the atmosphere. Which chemical is linked to the decrease in the level of this gas? What measures have been taken by an international organization to check the depletion of the layer containing this gas?** **(*Un*) (CBSE, 2024)**

Ans. Gas X: Ozone (O_3) *(½ M)*
- Essential Function: Shields Earth from harmful ultraviolet (UV) radiation from the sun. *(½ M)*
- Decrease in level of ozone is due to a chemical called chlorofluorocarbons (CFCs). *(1 M)*
- Measures taken by the United Nations Environment Programme (UNEP) in 1987:

  CFC Production Freeze: An agreement to halt CFC production at 1986 levels. *(½ M)*

  CFC-free Refrigerators: Now, it's compulsory for manufacturers worldwide to produce refrigerators without using CFCs, promoting eco-friendly practices. *(½ M)*

4. **Name the term used for the materials which cannot be broken down by biological processes. Give two ways by which they harm various components of an ecosystem.** **(*Un*) (CBSE, 2024)**

Ans. The term used for materials that cannot be broken down by biological processes is "non-biodegradable." *(1 M)*

The two ways by which they harm the components of an ecosystem are:
- They can persist in the environment for a long time, causing long-term pollution. *(½ M)*
- They may harm various members of the ecosystem by potentially entering the food chain and disrupting it. *(½ M)*

5. **Plastic cups were used to serve tea in trains in early days. These could be returned to the vendor, cleaned and reused. Later *Kulhads* were used instead of plastic cups. Now, paper cups are used for serving tea. What are the reasons for the shift from plastic to *Kulhads* and then finally to paper cups.** **(*An*)**

Ans. Plastic cups are non-biodegradable so it cannot be decomposed and its uses raised the concern towards hygiene thus they are replaced by *Kulhads*. *(1 M)*

Making of *Kulhads* required clay on large scale resulting in the loss of top fertile soil. *(1 M)*

So, now *Kulhads* are replaced by the paper cups as they are biodegradable and they can be easily disposed off and do not harm the environment. *(1 M)*

Mistakes 101 : What not to do!

When analyzing the transition from plastic to Kulhads and then to paper cups, a student might overlook environmental and sustainability reasons, focusing only on immediate utility and cost, instead of the broader ecological impacts.

6. How can we help in reducing the problem of waste disposal? Suggest any three methods.

(*Un*) (CBSE, 2019)

Ans. We can reduce the problem of waste disposal by the following methods–

(*i*) Recycling the non-biodegradable waste materials like plastic, glass and metals. *(1 M)*

(*ii*) Separating biodegradable and non-biodegradable waste before dumping them. *(1 M)*

(*iii*) By minimizing the use of disposable and promoting use of materials that can be recycled. *(1 M)*

Long Answer Type Questions (5 M)

1. (*a*) Define ozone depletion and explain its significance.

(*b*) Describe the main causes and sources of ozone depletion and their environmental consequences.

(*c*) How can we contribute to protecting the depletion of the ozone layer at an individual level? (*Un*)

Ans. (*a*) Ozone depletion refers to the gradual thinning of the ozone layer.

Significance of ozone layer:

The ozone layer plays a critical role in protecting life on Earth by absorbing and blocking the majority of harmful ultraviolet (UV) radiation from the sun which can lead to various adverse effects, including an increased risk of skin cancer, cataracts, and damage to terrestrial and aquatic ecosystems. *(1½ M)*

(*b*) It is primarily caused by the release of certain chemicals into the atmosphere, such as chlorofluorocarbons (CFCs), halons etc. These human-made chemicals contain chlorine atoms that can break down ozone molecules. Environmental consequences include increased harmful UV radiation, posing risks to human health, damaging ecosystems, and impacting marine life and crops. *(1½ M)*

(*c*) We can contribute to protecting the depletion of the ozone layer at individual level:

- Purchase air conditioning and refrigeration systems that utilize refrigerants other than CFCs.
- Choose aerosol products that do not rely on HCFCs or CFCs as propellants.
- Ensure routine inspection and maintenance of air conditioning and refrigeration equipment to prevent and reduce refrigerant leaks. *(2 M)*

2. In a small town, the streets were filled with trash because people kept throwing garbage everywhere. This made the town dirty and unhealthy. A teacher noticed this problem and decided to talk with her students. She asked the students to find out a solution to the problem of garbage. Finally they arrived at two main points – one is self-management of the garbage we produce and the second is to generate less garbage at individual level.

(*Ap*)

(*a*) Suggest two measures to manage the garbage we produce.

(*b*) As an individual, what can we do to generate the least garbage? Give two points.

(*c*) List two values the teacher instilled in his students in this episode.

Ans. (*a*) Segregation of Waste: Separate biodegradable waste from non-biodegradable waste. Biodegradable waste can be composted, turning waste into valuable compost for plants. *(1 M)*

Recycling and Reusing: Encourage the recycling of materials such as paper, plastic, metal, and glass. Reuse items whenever possible to reduce waste generation. *(1 M)*

(*b*) Avoid Single-Use Products: Use reusable bags, bottles, and containers instead of single-use plastics or disposable items to significantly reduce waste generation. *(1 M)*

Buy in Bulk: Purchase items in bulk to minimize packaging waste. Choosing products with minimal packaging also contributes to less garbage production. *(1 M)*

(*c*) Environmental Responsibility: The teacher encouraged students to understand their role in protecting the environment by managing waste effectively. *(½ M)*

Community Awareness: By discussing the issue and seeking solutions, the teacher fostered a sense of community responsibility among students, highlighting the importance of collective efforts in addressing environmental issues.

(½ M)

Hints & Explanations

Multiple Choice Questions

1. (*c*) Chlorofluorocarbon (CFC) emissions from refrigerator, air conditioners, etc., causes the depletion of the ozone layer.
2. (*c*) Exposure of humans to UV rays leads to health problems like skin cancer and damage to the immune system.
3. (*a*) Biodegradable substances can be broken down by biological processes.
4. (*b*) sunlight

5. (*b*)
   - P (Polythene bag): Non-biodegradable, slow decomposition
   - Q (Bone): Moderately biodegradable, moderate decomposition
   - R (Orange peel): Biodegradable, fast decomposition
6. (*a*) 'Ozone is a toxic gas' is a property and is not relevant to its formation.
7. (*c*) Biodegradable materials break down into smaller components due to the action of living organisms, such as bacteria and fungi. This is a direct observation of biodegradability in an experimental context.
8. (*b*) UV radiation provides the energy needed to split O_2 molecules into free oxygen atoms (O), which is the first step in the formation of ozone (O_3).
9. (*c*) If enzymes were not specific, they could act on unintended substrates, potentially breaking down molecules vital for health and causing harm.
10. (*b*) A biogas plant converts biodegradable waste into biogas, a renewable energy source, and digestate, a nutrient-rich fertiliser, making it an effective way to manage a large proportion of biodegradable waste sustainably.
11. (*d*) Rubber is incorrectly marked as the odd one out in this group. Rubber can decompose under certain conditions, while thermocol, glass bottles and metal cans are non-biodegradable.
12. (*d*) Paper decomposes faster than plastic due to its organic nature but slower than clay, which can merge with the soil naturally.
13. (*b*) UV radiation is necessary to split O_2 molecules into individual oxygen atoms, which are then available to form ozone. Less UV radiation would lead to a decrease in ozone production.

Assertion and Reason

1. (*a*) A is true because not all kitchen waste can be used for composting, especially if it includes non-biodegradable materials like certain plastics. R correctly explains A, as it highlights an example of kitchen waste (milk packets) that cannot be composted because it is non-biodegradable.
2. (*c*) The reason (R) inaccurately describes the breakdown process as it involves the conversion of complex organic substances into simpler organic or inorganic substances, not inorganic to organic.
3. (*a*) The reduction in atmospheric ozone levels was indeed significantly noted around the 1980s due to the increased use of chlorofluorocarbons (CFCs), which release chlorine atoms when broken down by ultraviolet light, leading to the destruction of ozone molecules.

MISCELLANEOUS EXERCISE

Multiple Choice Questions (1 M)

1. Which of the following statements is true about a food chain? **(*Un*)**
   (*a*) The arrows always point towards the prey.
   (*b*) The arrows always point towards the predator.
   (*c*) The arrows indicate the flow of energy.
   (*d*) The arrows indicate the flow of matter.
2. In a food chain consisting of grass → rabbit → fox, how does the energy content compare between the beginning and end of the chain? **(*An*)**
   (*a*) The energy content is highest in the fox.
   (*b*) The energy content is the same at all levels.
   (*c*) The energy content decreases from grass to fox.
   (*d*) The energy content increases from grass to fox.
3. Identify the incorrect statement
   'The energy available to the producers is maximum' because: **(*Re*) (CBSE SQP, 2024)**
   (*a*) It is the first trophic level which absorbs 1% of light energy directly from the source.
   (*b*) It utilizes the most of the chemical energy for its own respiration, growth, reproduction, movement etc.
   (*c*) It utilizes 10% of light energy and transfers the rest to the next trophic level.
   (*d*) It transfers only 10% of light energy to the next trophic level.
4. Rita's teacher was explaining the concept of a food chain using the image given below. **(*An*)**

If you were to draw a pyramid showing the number of organisms at each level, which option accurately represents the pyramid of numbers for this food chain?

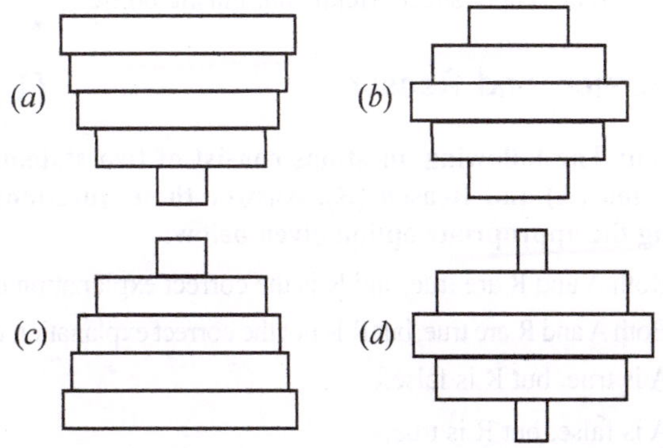

5. Imagine a farmer uses a new pesticide on his crops. What immediate action should be taken to minimise its entry into the food chain? **(*An*)**
   (*a*) Increase the use of the pesticide
   (*b*) Wash the crops with detergent after harvest
   (*c*) Ensure runoff is prevented from entering nearby water bodies
   (*d*) Replace all soil in the farm
6. An analysis of soil sample revealed 0.1 mg of a pesticide and 1 mg of the same pesticide was found in grains. However, in the adipose tissue of birds the concentration was 2 mg. The reason for this is the phenomenon known as **(*Un*)**
   (*a*) Bio-absorption (*b*) Bio-translocation
   (*c*) Biomagnification (*d*) Bio-multiplication
7. The chemicals that are non-degradable, get progressively accumulated at each trophic level, and their concentration is seen maximum in the bodies of top consumers. This phenomenon is known as: **(*Re*) (CBSE APQ, 2023)**
   (*a*) Eutrophication (*b*) Pollution
   (*c*) Accumulation (*d*) Biomagnification
8. In the following groups of materials, which group(s) contains only non-biodegradable items? **(*Re*) (NCERT Exemplar)**
   (*i*) Wood, paper, leather
   (*ii*) Polythene, detergent, PVC
   (*iii*) Plastic, detergent, grass
   (*iv*) Plastic, bakelite, DDT
   (*a*) (*iii*) (*b*) (*iv*)
   (*c*) (*i*) and (*iii*) (*d*) (*ii*) and (*iv*)
9. Choose the incorrect statement from the following: **(*Un*)**
   (*a*) Ozone is a molecule formed by three atoms of oxygen.
   (*b*) Ozone shields the surface of the Earth from ultraviolet radiations.
   (*c*) Ozone is deadly poisonous.
   (*d*) Ozone gets decomposed by UV radiations.
10. Arrange the four objects given below according to the time they take to get biodegraded, from the least time to the most time. **(*Ap*)**
   (*a*) Paper sheet, Bone, Metal can, Plastic bottle
   (*b*) Bone, Paper sheet, Plastic bottle, Metal can
   (*c*) Paper sheet, Bone, Plastic bottle, Metal can
   (*d*) Bone, Paper sheet, Metal can, Plastic bottle

Assertion and Reason **(1 M)**

Direction: The following questions consist of two statements – Assertion (A) and Reason (R). Answer these questions by selecting the appropriate option given below:

(*a*) Both A and R are true, and R is the correct explanation of A.
(*b*) Both A and R are true, but R is not the correct explanation of A.
(*c*) A is true, but R is false.
(*d*) A is false, but R is true.

1. **Assertion (A):** Aquarium needs regular cleaning. **(*Un*)**
   Reason (R): The absence of a naturally occurring balance of microbes in an aquarium necessitates manual cleaning and maintenance to remove harmful substances and ensure water quality.
2. **Assertion (A):** Accumulation of harmful chemicals is maximum in the organisms at the highest trophic level of a food chain.
   Reason (R): Harmful chemicals are sprayed on the crops to protect them from diseases and pests.
3. **Assertion (A):** Synthetic chemicals like chlorofluorocarbons (CFCs) have been found to deplete the ozone layer.
   Reason (R): CFCs release chlorine atoms in the stratosphere, which catalyse the breakdown of ozone molecules.
4. **Assertion (A):** All animals are consumers.
   Reason (R): Animal, from microscopic to macroscopic are dependent on producers or other animal for their food.
5. **Assertion (A):** Trophic levels are formed by only plants.
   Reason (R): Food chains and webs are formed due to linked organisms on the basis of their nutrition.

Subjective Questions

Very Short Answer Type Questions **(2 M)**

1. Study the food chain given below and answer the questions that follow: **(*An*) (CBSE SQP, 2023)**

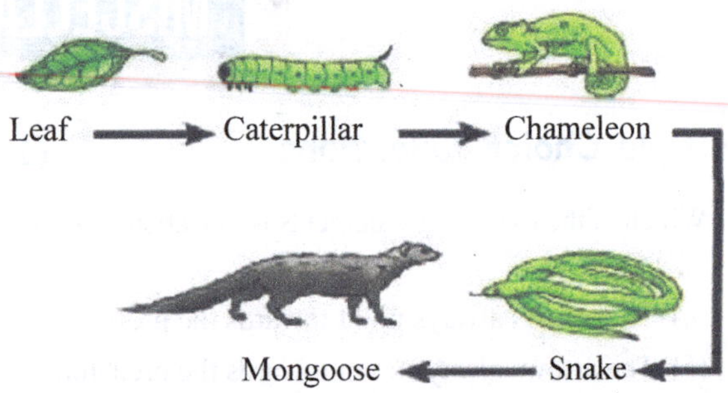

   (*a*) If the amount of energy available at the third trophic level is 100 joules, then how much energy will be available at the producer level? Justify your answer.
   (*b*) Is it possible to have 2 more trophic levels in this food chain just before the fourth trophic level? Justify your answer.
2. The cartoon below addresses a growing concern:

What impact will the process shown in the image have on Humans if they occupy the last trophic level? Explain. **(*An*) (CBSE SQP, 2024)**

3. State 10% law. Explain it with an example. **(*Re*)**
4. Mention TWO ways by which energy is lost from the trophic levels in the ecosystem. **(*Re*)**
5. If all the waste we generate is biodegradable, will this have no impact on the environment? **(*An*) (NCERT)**

Short Answer Type Questions (3 M)

1. Write one difference between biodegradable and non-biodegradable wastes. List two impacts of each type of the accumulated waste on environment if not disposed of properly. **(*Un*) (CBSE, 2023)**
2. (*a*) We do not clean ponds or lakes, but an aquarium needs to be cleaned regularly. Why?
   (*b*) Why is the ozone layer getting depleted at the higher levels of the atmosphere? Mention one harmful effect caused by its depletion. **(*Un*) (CBSE, 2022 Term-II)**
3. (*a*) Write the percentage of (*i*) solar energy captured by the autotrophs and (*ii*) energy transferred from autotrophs to the next level in a food chain.
   (*b*) What are trophic levels? Why do different food chains in an ecosystem not have more than four to five trophic levels? Give reason. **(*Un*) (CBSE, 2023)**
4. Observe the following food chain of grassland ecosystem and answer the questions that follow: **(*Ap*)**

   (*a*) Explain how grass captures energy and why it is essential in the grassland ecosystem.
   (*b*) Imagine a disease affects the frog population; how might this impact the grass population in the short term?
   (*c*) Applying your knowledge of food webs, how would this disease potentially affect the hawk's diet?
5. Use of pesticides to protect our crops affect organisms at various trophic levels especially human beings. Name the phenomenon involved and explain how does it happen. **(*Un*) (CBSE, 2024)**
6. What will happen? **(*An*)**
   (*a*) If all the lions (carnivores) are removed.
   (*b*) If all deer (herbivores) are removed.
7. What is ozone and how does it affect any ecosystem? **(*Un*) (NCERT Intext)**
8. In the following food chain, only 2J of energy was available at the level of peacocks. How much energy would have been present in Grass? Justify your answer. **(*Ev*)**
   Grass → Grasshopper → Frog → Snake → Peacock

   OR

   (*a*) What is meant by garbage? List two classes into which garbage is classified. **(*Un*) (CBSE, 2022 Term II)**
   (*b*) What do we actually mean when we say that the "enzymes are specific in their action"?

Long Answer Type Questions (5 M)

1. The given below diagram represents the food web that consists of many food chains. **(*An, Un, Ev*)**

   Based on your observation answer the following questions:
   (*a*) Which of the following animals in the given diagram can be categorised as top consumers?
   (*b*) Explain the significance of primary producers in this food web. What would happen if primary producers were drastically reduced?
   (*c*) Identify and discuss the impact of omnivores in this food web. How do they contribute to the stability of the ecosystem?
   (*d*) Evaluate the potential effects of an increase in the frog population on this food web. Which organisms would be most directly affected?
2. The stratosphere is very dry and rarely allows clouds to form. In the extreme cold of the polar winter, however, stratospheric clouds of different types may form. These clouds are called Polar Stratospheric Clouds (PSCs).

   Scientists recently discovered that polar stratospheric clouds, long known to play an important role in Antarctic ozone destruction, are occurring with increasing frequency in the Arctic. These high-altitude clouds form only at very low temperatures help destroy ozone in two ways: (1) They provide a surface which converts benign forms of chlorine into reactive, ozone-destroying forms, and (2) they remove nitrogen compounds that moderate the destructive impact of chlorine. In recent years, the atmosphere above the Arctic has been colder than usual, and polar stratospheric clouds have lasted into the spring. As a result, ozone levels have been decreasing.

(Information credit: NASA) ***(An)* (CFPQ)**

(*a*) How is ozone formed in the outer atmosphere?

(*b*) Ozone is being continuously destroyed due to extreme low temperatures. However, ozone formation is also a continuous process. Why is there a depletion in the ozone layer still?

(*c*) What can be a positive effect of global warming on the depletion of the ozone layer?

(*d*) How does ozone layer depletion impact human health?

3. (*a*) Name the group of organisms which form in the first trophic level of all food chains. Why are they called so? ***(Un)* (CBSE, 2022)**

(*b*) Why are the human beings most adversely affected by bio-magnification?

(*c*) State one ill-effect of the absence of decomposers from a natural ecosystem.

Case Based Questions

Case Based-I: As we know that sun is the ultimate source of energy for all organisms and all organisms are interconnected with each other by means of food chains. The food chain help in the survival of the species as by means of the food chain organisms obtain food.

The foundation of the food chain consists of primary producers. Primary producers, or autotrophs, can use either solar energy or chemical energy to create complex organic compounds, whereas species at higher trophic levels cannot and so must consume producers or other life that itself consumes producers. Because the sun's light is necessary for photosynthesis, most life could not exist if the sun disappeared.

Even so, it has recently been discovered that some forms of life, chemotrophs, appear to gain all their metabolic energy from chemosynthesis driven by hydrothermal vents, thus showing that some life may not require solar energy to thrive. ***(Ap)***

(*i*) Explain why decomposers are essential in an ecosystem.

(*ii*) Combine your knowledge of food chains and energy flow to explain why energy transfer between trophic levels is not 100% efficient.

(*iii*) (*a*) Imagine a world where chemotrophs are the primary producers instead of phototrophs. How would this change the structure of ecosystems around hydrothermal vents?

OR

(*b*) Given data on energy input and biomass output for a plant, derive a formula to calculate its energy conversion efficiency.

Energy input (from sunlight)	Biomass output
1000 J	10 J

Energy input (from sunlight) Biomass output
1000 J 10 J

Case Based-II: A food chain is a very important part of any ecosystem where one organism relies on another organism for its food source. In any food chain, there are different trophic levels starting from producers to top carnivores. ***(An)***

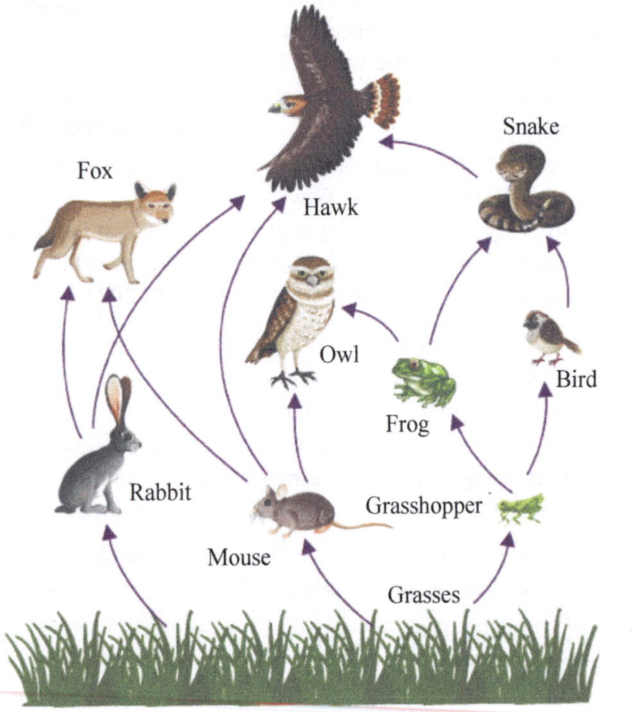

(*i*) What is the maximum number of trophic levels possible in any food chain in a given food web?

(*ii*) In the given food web, how many organisms are secondary consumers?

(*iii*) (*a*) Which organism is being eaten by the maximum number of organisms?

OR

(*b*) If DDT is sprayed on grass then which organism would have the maximum concentration of DDT?

Case Based-III: We are an integral part of the environment. Changes in the environment affect us and our activities change the environment around us.

Ozone (O_3) is a molecule formed by three atoms of oxygen. While O_2, which we normally refer to as oxygen, is essential for all aerobic forms of life. Ozone is a deadly poison. However, at the higher levels of the atmosphere, ozone performs an essential function. It shields the surface of the earth from ultraviolet (UV) radiation from the Sun. ***(Un)***

(*i*) How does ozone is formed? Write the chemical reaction for the formation of ozone?

(*ii*) In which layer of the atmosphere does ozone is present?

(*iii*) (*a*) What are the causes for ozone depletion?

(*b*) If the ozone layer was absent, how would the surface of the Earth be affected?

ANSWER KEYS

Multiple Choice Questions

1. (c) 2. (c) 3. (c) 4. (c) 5. (c) 6. (c) 7. (d) 8. (d) 9. (d) 10. (a)

Assertion and Reason

1. (a) 2. (b) 3. (a) 4. (a) 5. (d)

HINTS & EXPLANATIONS

Multiple Choice Questions

1. (c) In a food chain, arrows indicate the flow of energy.
2. (c) According to the 10% rule in ecological energy transfer, only about 10% of the energy at one trophic level is transferred to the next level. Therefore, the energy content decreases as you move from producers (grass) to tertiary consumers (fox).
3. (c) The producers (plants) capture only about 1% of the sunlight falling on them and convert it into chemical energy via photosynthesis. When this energy is transferred to the next trophic level, only 10% of it is passed on, while the rest (90%) is lost as heat or used for life processes like respiration and growth.
4. (c) Diagram (c) correctly represents the pyramid of numbers for the given food chain, with the widest base representing the large number of grass (producers) and the narrowing tiers representing fewer individuals at each successive trophic level.
5. (c) Preventing runoff having pesticides into nearby water bodies minimises their entry into the water ecosystem, thereby reducing their impact on the food chain.
6. (c) Biomagnification *is a process in which* poisonous chemicals like insecticides and pesticides gets accumulated as move from lower trophic level to higher trophic level. It has harmful effect on organisms.
7. (d) Biomagnification refers to the increase in concentration of non-degradable chemicals in organisms at each successive trophic level of a food chain.
8. (d) Polythene, detergent, PVC, plastic, bakelite and DDT are non-biodegradable items therefore (*ii*) and (*iv*) contain non-biodegradable items.
9. (d) UV radiations does not decompose the ozone layer in fact ozone acts as a shield to protect it from UV rays. Chloroflurocarbon deplete the ozone layer.
10. (a) Paper sheets degrade the quickest due to being organic. Bones take longer but still decompose faster than metal cans and plastic bottles, which are more resistant to degradation, with plastic bottles taking the longest due to their synthetic materials.

Assertion and Reason

1. (a) Aquarium needs regular cleaning as it is an artificial ecosystem and natural microbes (decomposers) *are not present to decompose the waste and make* water clean. Therefore, both assertion and reason are true and Reason is correct explanation of the assertion.
2. (b) The accumulation of harmful chemicals is indeed maximum in organisms at the highest trophic level due to biological magnification, where chemicals concentrate progressively up the food chain, not merely from crop spraying.
3. (a) CFCs release chlorine atoms when they are exposed to intense UV light in the stratosphere, leading to the breakdown of ozone molecules, directly linking chlorine release from CFCs to ozone depletion.
4. (a) Animals are called consumers as they do not make their own food. They are dependent on plants and other animals for their food. Therefore, assertion and reason are true and reason is the correct explanation of assertion.
5. (d) Trophic levels are formed by both plants and animals. Therefore, assertion is false but reason is true.

Subjective Questions

Very Short Answer Type Questions

1. (a) 10000J because only 10 % of energy is available for the next trophic level. *(1 M)*

   (b) No, since the loss of energy at each step is so great that very little usable energy will remain after 4 trophic levels. *(1 M)*
2. The image shows pesticide use in farming, leading to water contamination and affecting aquatic life. *(½ M)*

Pesticides are non-biodegradable and accumulate at each trophic level, a process called biomagnification. *(1 M)*

Since humans occupy the last trophic level, they will have the highest concentration of these harmful chemicals. *(½ M)*

3. According to 10% law, only 10% of the energy entering a particular trophic level of organisms is available for transfer to the next higher trophic level. *(1 M)*

   For example, in a food chain, if plants (producers) have 1000 J of energy, herbivores (primary consumers) will have about 100 J of energy, and carnivores (secondary consumers) will have about 10 J of energy. *(1 M)*

4. Energy is lost from trophic levels in the following ways:
   - Energy is lost through heat during metabolic processes. *(1 M)*
   - Energy is also utilised in maintaining life processes such as digestion and growth. *(1 M)*

5. Even if all waste were biodegradable, it would still impact the environment. Decomposition of organic waste requires oxygen, which can deplete oxygen in water bodies, affecting aquatic life. *(1 M)*

   Additionally, the process of decomposition can release greenhouse gases like methane, contributing to climate change. *(1 M)*

Short Answer Type Questions

1.

Waste Type	Difference	Impacts on Environment if Not Disposed off Properly
Biodegradable Waste	Can be broken down by living organisms.	1. Spread of diseases, 2. Attracts pests.
Non-Biodegradable Waste	Cannot be broken down naturally by living organisms.	1. Pollution, 2. Biological magnification.

(3 M)

2. (*a*) Natural ponds and lakes have ecosystems with decomposers and natural filtration processes that maintain balance. In contrast, aquariums lack these extensive ecosystems, requiring regular cleaning to prevent toxin buildup and ensure water quality. *(1½ M)*

   (*b*) The ozone layer is getting depleted due to human-made chemicals like chlorofluorocarbons (CFCs) releasing chlorine atoms in the atmosphere. One harmful effect is increased UV radiation reaching Earth, which can lead to higher rates of skin cancer in humans. *(1½ M)*

3. (*a*) (*i*) The percentage of solar energy captured by the autotrophs is about 1% of the energy of sunlight that falls on their leaves *(½ M)*

   (*ii*) The energy transferred from autotrophs to the next level in a food chain is roughly 10% of the energy that is present in the autotrophs *(½ M)*

   (*b*) Trophic levels are the different steps in a food chain at which the transfer of energy takes place. *(1 M)*

   Different food chains in an ecosystem typically have not more than four to five trophic levels because the energy transfer from one trophic level to the next involves a loss, usually about 90% per level, leaving insufficient energy to support viable populations at higher levels. *(1 M)*

Topper's Explanation

33. (a) (i) 1% of the total solar energy from the solar input is captured by the Autotrophs.

(ii) 10% of energy is available for and transferred to the next level trophic level.

(b) Each step or stage of a food chain is known as Trophic level.
Food chains consist of three or four trophic levels since the amount of energy lost (90%) at each trophic level is so great and massive that by the third or fourth trophic level there is really less energy usable energy left.

4. (*a*) Grass captures energy through photosynthesis, converting sunlight into chemical energy. It is essential as it forms the base of the food chain, supporting all higher trophic levels in the grassland ecosystem. *(1M)*

   (*b*) If a disease affects frogs, their population will decrease. This may lead to an increase in the population of insects, as frogs are their predators. Over time, this could result in overgrazing of grass due to the increased insect population and hence grass population will decrease. *(1M)*

   (*c*) If the frog population declines due to disease, hawks may face a food shortage as snakes will starve due to unavailability of frogs and their population declines. They may need to shift their diet to alternative prey in the food web, or their population could decline due to starvation. *(1M)*

5. The phenomenon involved is known as "biological magnification." *(½ M)*

   It happens because:
   - Pesticides used on crops can wash into soil or water bodies and are absorbed by plants. *(1 M)*
   - These non-degradable chemicals accumulate progressively at each trophic level. *(1 M)*
   - Human beings, at the top of the food chain, accumulate the highest concentrations of these chemicals in their bodies. *(½ M)*

6. (*a*) If all the lions are removed: Removing lions from an ecosystem could lead to an overpopulation of herbivores, such as deer, which lions typically prey upon. This could result in overgrazing and significant vegetation loss, disrupting the balance of the ecosystem and potentially leading to the degradation of the habitat. *(1½ M)*

   (*b*) If all deer are removed: Removing deer, a primary herbivore, would lead to an underutilization of plant biomass, causing an increase in vegetation density. This could reduce food availability for other herbivores and disrupt the food chain. Predators that rely on deer as a food source, like wolves and lions, might suffer from reduced food availability, potentially leading to a decline in their populations. *(1½ M)*

7. Ozone (O_3) is a molecule formed by three atoms of oxygen. At the higher levels of the atmosphere, ozone performs an essential function. It shields the surface of the earth from ultraviolet (UV) radiations from the sun. *(2 M)*
These radiations are highly damaging to organisms. Ultraviolet rays can also cause skin cancer, cataracts and skin diseases. *(1 M)*

8. According to the ten percent law of energy in a food chain, only ten percent of energy is transferred to the next trophic level. Thus, the energy keeps on decreasing by 10% at each level. *(1½ M)*

Grass →	Grasshopper →	Frog →	Snake →	Peacock
20,000 J	2,000 J	200 J	20 J	2 J

(1½ M)

OR

(*a*) Garbage refers to waste material discarded by human activities. It is commonly classified into two types: biodegradable (decomposes naturally, like food waste) and non-biodegradable (does not decompose easily, like plastic and metal). *(1½ M)*

(*b*) When we say "enzymes are specific in their action," it means that each enzyme only catalyzes a specific type of chemical reaction or acts on a specific substrate due to its unique active site, ensuring precise biological processes. *(1½ M)*

Long Answer Type Questions

1. (*a*) Animals such as tigers, eagles, owls, peacocks, and foxes can be categorized as top consumers in this food web, as they do not have any natural predators in it. *(1 M)*

(*b*) Primary producers, such as grasses and trees, are crucial as they convert solar energy into chemical energy through photosynthesis, supporting all other trophic levels. *(1 M)*

If primary producers were drastically reduced, the entire food web would collapse, leading to a decline in herbivores and subsequent trophic levels. *(1 M)*

(*c*) Omnivores, such as the bear and the fox consume both plants and animals, providing flexibility in their diet. They help stabilize the ecosystem by controlling populations of both producers and smaller consumers, preventing any single species from dominating and maintaining ecological balance. *(1 M)*

(*d*) An increase in the frog population would lead to a higher consumption of insects and small animals, potentially reducing their populations. *(½ M)*

Predators of frogs, like snakes and birds, would benefit from the increased food availability, potentially increasing their populations. *(½ M)*

2. (*a*) The higher energy UV radiations in the higher levels of atmosphere split apart some molecular oxygen (O_2) into free oxygen (O) atoms. *(1 M)*

These atoms then combine with the molecular oxygen to form ozone. *(1 M)*

(*b*) because the rate of destruction is higher than the rate of formation

(*c*) Rise in polar temperature might restrict the formation of PSCs and reduce the depletion of the ozone layer. *(1 M)*

(*d*) Removal of ozone layer allows harmful UV radiations to enter and cause diseases like skin cancer. *(1 M)*

Key Takeaways

Students will learn that UV radiation is essential in the ozone production process, as it provides the energy needed to split oxygen molecules, a critical step for ozone formation in the Earth's atmosphere.

3. (*a*) Producers form the first trophic level of all food chains. They are called so because they produce their own food through the process of photosynthesis, utilising sunlight, carbon dioxide, and water. *(1 M)*

(*b*) Human beings are most adversely affected by biomagnification because they often occupy the top position in the food chain. Bio-magnification leads to the accumulation of pollutants at each trophic level, and since humans consume a variety of organisms from different trophic levels, the concentration of pollutants is highest in them, leading to various health issues. *(2 M)*

(*c*) The absence of decomposers from a natural ecosystem would result in the accumulation of dead organisms and waste materials, leading to a lack of nutrients in the soil. This would disrupt the nutrient cycle, affecting plant growth and the overall balance of the ecosystem. *(2 M)*

Case Based Questions

Case Based-I

(*i*) Decomposers break down dead organisms, recycling nutrients back into the nutrient pool, ensuring the growth of producers and continuation of the food chains. *(1 M)*

(*ii*) Energy transfer isn't 100% efficient due to energy loss as heat in metabolic processes like respiration at each trophic level, limiting the length of the food chain. *(1 M)*

(*iii*) (*a*) Ecosystems would rely entirely on chemical energy from vents, potentially increasing the diversity of life forms adapted to extreme conditions, independent of solar energy. *(2 M)*

OR

(b) To calculate energy conversion efficiency: Efficiency (%) = (Energy stored in biomass / Energy input) × 100. If a plant receives 1000 Joules of sunlight energy and produces 10 Joules of biomass, its efficiency = (10/1000) × 100 = 1%. *(2 M)*

Case Based-II

(i) There is a maximum of 5 trophic levels possible when we consider a food chain comprising of grass eaten by grasshopper, grasshopper eaten by either frog or bird and then frog or bird eaten by a snake, and finally snake being eaten by a hawk. *(1 M)*

(ii) Secondary consumers are organisms that eat primary consumers. According to the given food web, there are 5 organisms that can be classified as secondary consumers.

- The fox, which eats the rabbit and the mouse.
- The hawk, which eats the mouse in one food chain of the food web.
- The owl, which eats the mouse.
- The frog, which eats the grasshopper.
- The bird, which may eat the grasshopper. *(2 M)*

(iii) (a) Mouse is being eaten by the most number of organisms (By Owl, Fox, Hawk). *(1 M)*

OR

(b) Hawk would have a maximum concentration of DDT. *(1 M)*

Case Based-III

(i) The UV radiations coming from the sun split the molecular oxygen into nascent oxygen. When this nascent oxygen is combined with molecular oxygen, it forms ozone (O_3).

$$O_2 \xrightarrow{UV} O + O$$

$$O + O_2 \rightarrow \underset{\text{Ozone}}{O_3}$$ *(1 M)*

(ii) The ozone is present in the stratosphere layer of the atmosphere just above the troposphere. *(1 M)*

(iii) (a) Synthetic chemicals like CFCs (Chlorofluorocarbons) which used as refrigerants and in the fire extinguisher.

(b) Without the ozone layer, Earth's surface would be exposed to high levels of UV radiation, leading to detrimental effects on life forms. *(1 M)*

MOCK TEST PAPERS

Scan Me
for Detailed
Mock Test
Explanations

MOCK TEST PAPER-1

Time allowed : 3 hours **Maximum Marks : 80**

NOTE:

(i) Q.P. Code given on the right hand side of the question paper should be written on the title page of the answer-book by the candidate.

*(ii) Please check that this question paper contains **39** questions.*

(iii) Please write down the Serial Number of the question in the answer-book at the given place before attempting it.

(iv) 15 minute time has been allotted to read this question paper. The students will read the question paper only and will not write any answer on the answer-book during this period.

GENERAL INSTRUCTIONS:

Read the following instructions carefully and follow them:

*(i) This question paper contain **39** questions. **All** questions are **compulsory**.*

*(ii) The question paper is divided into three sections - **A**, **B** and **C**.*

Section A : Biology (30 marks)

Section B : Chemistry (25 marks)

Section C : Physics (25 marks)

(iii) The question paper has MCQs, VSAs, SAs, LAs and CBQs. Marks are given against each question.

(iv) There are case based questions (CBQs) with three sub-questions and are of 4 marks each.

(v) Divide your answer sheet into three sections as per the question paper -

Section A (Biology), Section B (Chemistry) and Section C (Physics).

It is compulsory to answer each question in its respective section. Do not mix answers of one section into the other section.

(vi) Instructions are given with each section and question, wherever necessary.

(vii) Kindly note that a separate question paper has been provided for visually impaired candidates.

(viii) There is no overall choice in the question paper. However, an internal choice has been provided in few questions. Only one of the choices in such questions must be attempted.

SECTION - A

1. Identify *A* in the given flowchart representing the reflex arc. **1**

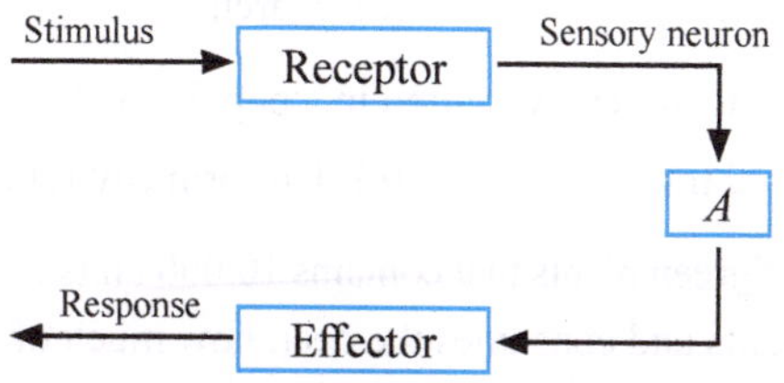

(*a*) Spinal cord (*b*) Brain (*c*) Spinal nerve (*d*) PNS

2. 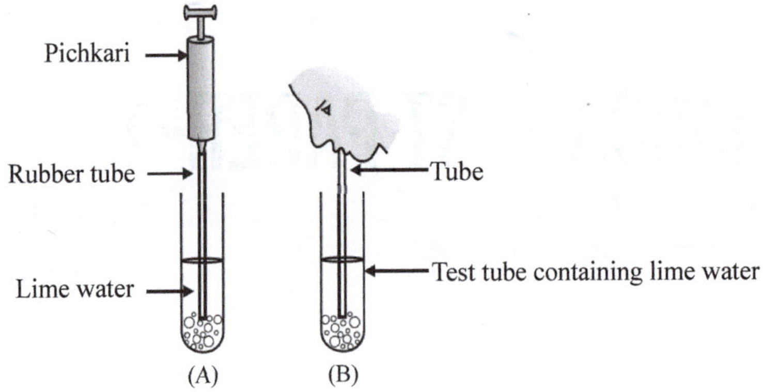

1

Compare the reactions in setups (A) and (B). Which setup is likely to show a faster reaction, and why?

(*a*) Setup (A), because atmospheric air has more oxygen.

(*b*) Setup (B), because exhaled air has more carbon dioxide.

(*c*) Setup (A), because atmospheric air has more nitrogen.

(*d*) Setup (B), because exhaled air has more moisture.

3. Raj was helping his younger sister prepare for her biology exam. He wanted to ensure she understood the reproductive process in angiosperms. He wrote down the steps in the wrong sequence and then asked his sister to choose the correct sequence from the following options: **1**

1. Fertilisation occurs, forming a zygote.
2. Pollen is transferred from the stamen to the stigma.
3. A tube grows out of the pollen grain and travels through the style to reach the ovary.
4. The ovary develops into a fruit containing seeds.
5. Zygote divides to form an embryo within the ovule.

(*a*) 2, 3, 1, 5, 4 (*b*) 2, 1, 3, 5, 4 (*c*) 3, 2, 1, 5, 4 (*d*) 3, 1, 2, 4, 5

4. Rita's teacher was explaining the concept of a food chain using the image given below. **1**

If you were to draw a pyramid showing the number of organisms at each level, which option accurately represents the pyramid of numbers for this food chain?

(*a*) 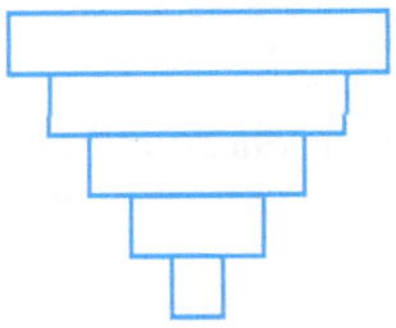

(*b*) 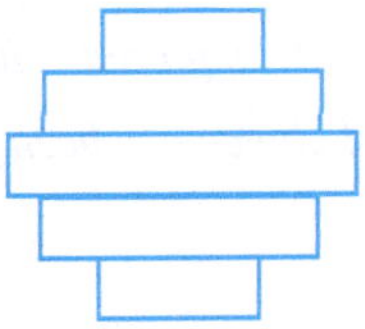

(*c*) 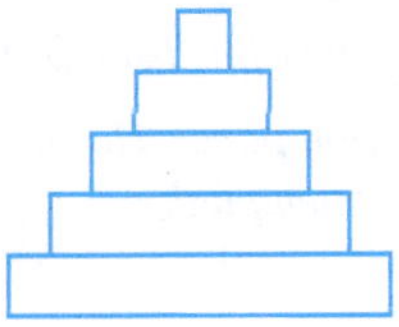

(*d*) 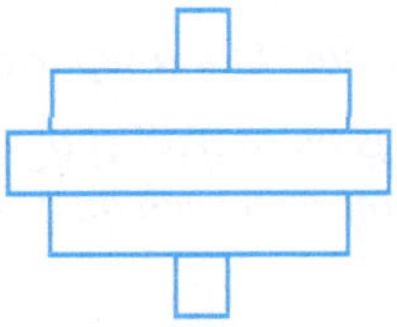

5. When a few drops of iodine solution are added to rice water, the solution turns blue-black in colour. This indicates that rice water contains: **1**

(*a*) Fats (*b*) Glycogen (*c*) Starch (*d*) Simple proteins

6. Which of the following majorly contributes to genetic variation in a population? **1**

(*a*) Asexual reproduction (*b*) Acquired traits (*c*) Uniform environment (*d*) Sexual reproduction

7. In a forest ecosystem, there's a lush layer of green plants that contains 10,000 units of energy. A group of deer feeds on these plants. When a predator, like a pack of wolves, hunts and consumes the deer, how much of the initial energy from the plants is typically found in the wolves? **1**

(*a*) 1000 units (*b*) 10 units (*c*) 100 units (*d*) 1 unit

The following two questions consist of two statements – **Assertion** (A) and **Reason** (R). Answer these questions by selecting the appropriate option given below:

(*a*) Both A and R are true, and R is the correct explanation of A.

(*b*) Both A and R are true, and R is not the correct explanation of A.

(*c*) A is true but R is false.

(*d*) A is false but R is true.

8. **Assertion (A):** Menstruation lasts for about 2-8 days in females.
Reason (R): Menstrual cycle repeats every 28 days and involves the shedding of the uterine lining if fertilization does not occur. **1**

9. **Assertion (A):** Sex determination in human beings is influenced by the presence or absence of specific sex chromosome.
Reason (R): The presence of an X chromosome from the father and an X chromosome from the mother results in a female offspring, while the presence of a Y chromosome from the father and an X chromosome from the mother results in a male offspring. **1**

10. In a controlled laboratory experiment, you place bean seedlings in two separate setups. Setup A has evenly distributed water and Setup B has water source only on the left side. After a week, you measure the root growth direction. Explain the observed results. **2**

11. (A) Consider two animals: a cow and a tiger. The cow primarily consumes grass, while the tiger primarily consumes meat. **2**

(*a*) Explain why the length of the small intestine differs between these two animals.

(*b*) Based on this information, predict the relative length of the small intestine in an omnivore like a bear, which eats both plants and meat. Justify your prediction.

OR

(B) Can fats be properly digested without emulsification? **2**

12. A guinea pig having black colour is crossed with guinea pig having the same colour. **2**
They produced 100 offsprings, out of which 75 were black and 25 were white.

(*a*) What is the possible genotype of parent guinea pigs?

(*b*) Which trait is dominant and which is recessive?

13. (*a*) Which hormone is essential for regulating metabolism for body growth in humans? **3**

(*b*) Give reasons for the following:

(*i*) The adrenal gland is important in stress responses.

(*ii*) Insulin is crucial for maintaining blood sugar levels.

(*iii*) The hypothalamus controls the release of many hormones.

(*iv*) Growth hormone is vital during childhood.

14. Nitin regularly consumes fruits and vegetables from the local market. He notices warnings about pesticide residues in these foods and starts to wonder about the process through which harmful chemicals enter the food chain and their impact on consumers like himself. **3**

(*a*) Describe the process through which harmful chemicals used in agriculture enter the food chain.

(*b*) Analyze the impact of these harmful chemicals on top-level consumers in a food chain, particularly humans.

(*c*) Discuss the challenges associated with removing pesticide residues from different types of food, and suggest potential methods to mitigate this issue.

15. Radhika is an avid gardener who has a wide variety of flowering plants in her garden. One day, some mischievous children entered her garden and plucked a leaf X from some of the plants and scattering them around the garden. A few days later, Radhika noticed that new buds were sprouting from the leaves that had fallen on the ground.

Buds

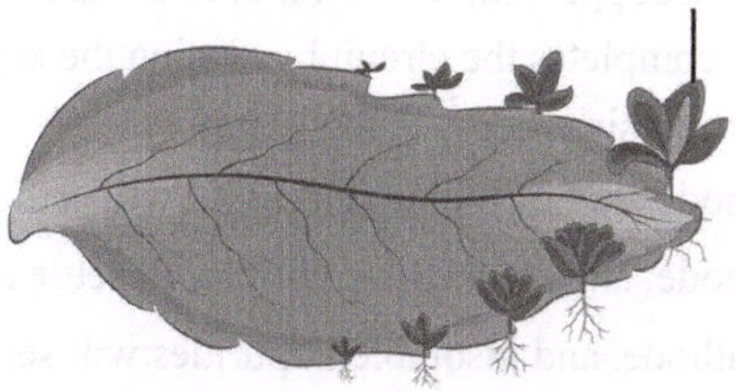

X

(*a*) Explain the process involved in the sprouting of new buds from leaf X. **2**

(*b*) Discuss the significance of leaf X in the propagation of flowering plants. How can this natural process be advantageous for gardeners? **1**

(*c*) Apart from plants having leaf X, mention some other plants that can be propagated through this method. **1**

OR

(*c*) Explain how the process adapted by leaf X contributes to genetic diversity. **1**

16. (A) (*a*) Write the correct sequence of steps followed during the journey of oxygen rich blood from lungs to various organs of the human body. **5**

(*b*) What happens when the system of blood vessels develops a leak?

OR

(B) Based on the figure labeled I, II, and III answers the questions that follow: **5**

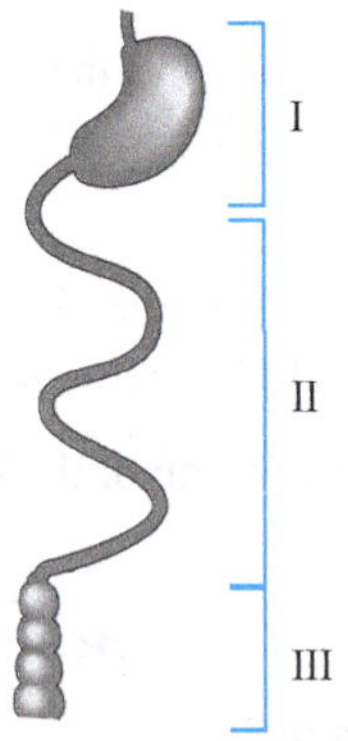

(*a*) What secretions are produced in part I, and what are their functions?

(*b*) Are the secretions produced in part I reason for acidity in adults? If yes, how do part I and II protect themselves from such acidic secretions?

(*c*) How is transport of food from part I to II regulated?

(*d*) How do the structural features of part II facilitate nutrient absorption in an individual?

(*e*) Compare the digestion and absorption processes in parts II and III.

SECTION - B

17. In a laboratory, Jack and Emily are conducting an experiment on the electrolysis of copper sulphate solution. They set up the apparatus as shown in the image.

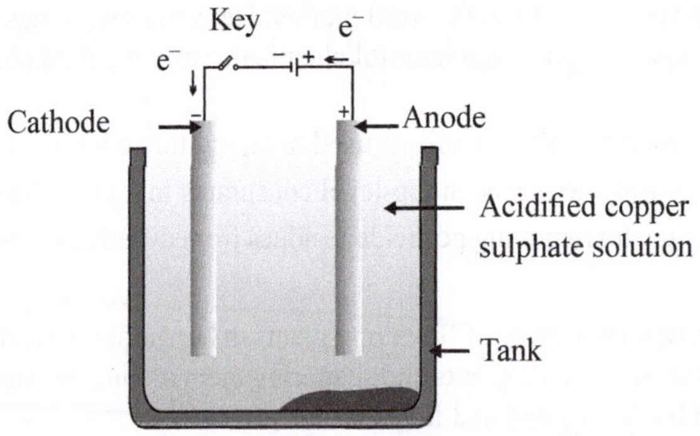

The setup includes a tank containing acidified copper sulphate solution. Jack uses the impure copper as the anode and a thin strip of pure copper as the cathode. When Emily completes the circuit by closing the key, electrolysis begins. **1**

What is the most likely outcome of the electrolysis process in this setup?

(*a*) Pure copper will be deposited at the anode, and insoluble impurities will settle at the cathode.

(*b*) Pure copper will be deposited at the anode, and soluble impurities will settle at the cathode.

(*c*) Pure copper will be deposited at the cathode, and insoluble impurities will settle down at the bottom of the anode.

(*d*) Pure copper will be deposited at the cathode, and soluble impurities will settle at the anode.

18. In a chemistry laboratory, students are conducting an experiment on the electrolysis of water. They have a setup with a plastic mug, graphite rods as electrodes, and a 6V battery. The experiment involves observing the gases produced at the anode and cathode during the electrolysis process.

Based on the experiment, which of the following observations would correctly identify the gases (X and Y) produced in the electrolysis of water? **1**

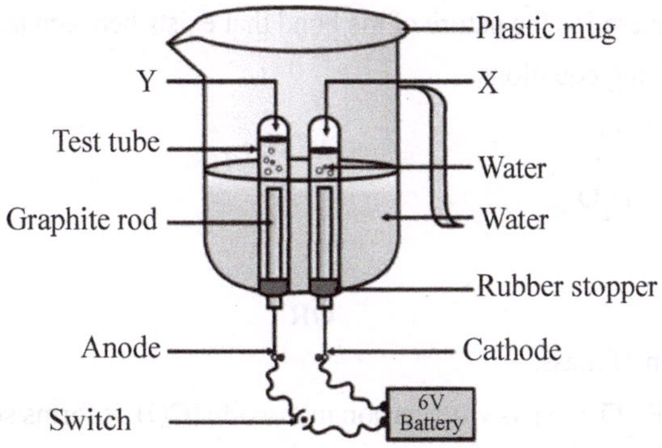

(A) The gas collected at the anode makes a glowing splint burn more brightly.
(B) The gas collected at the cathode turns lime water milky.
(C) The gas collected at the anode puts off a burning matchstick.
(D) The gas collected at the cathode produces a pop sound when exposed to a burning matchstick.

Select the correct option:

(*a*) Only (A) (*b*) Both (A) and (D) (*c*) Only (C) (*d*) Both (B) and (C)

19. 1 mole of ethene and 1 mole of ethyne are separately made to completely undergo addition reaction to form the respective saturated compound.

Which of the following will be DIFFERENT for the two reactions?
(P) the number of moles of the saturated compound formed
(Q) the number of moles of the hydrogen consumed **1**

(*a*) only P (*b*) only Q (*c*) both P and Q (*d*) neither P nor Q

20. Megha was at a family gathering, and her aunt starts complaining of severe stomach discomfort and burning sensations, which she believes are due to indigestion. She asks her for help in identifying the acid responsible for this discomfort:

"Do you know the name of the acid that causes this indigestion?" **1**

(*a*) Sulphuric acid (*b*) Hydrochloric acid (*c*) Methanoic acid (*d*) Nitric acid

21. Which of the following metals is found in its native or free state in nature? **1**

(*a*) Iron (*b*) Copper (*c*) Zinc (*d*) Aluminium

22. The reaction between iron(III) chloride ($FeCl_3$) and sodium hydroxide (NaOH) results in the formation of iron(III) hydroxide ($Fe(OH)_3$) and sodium chloride (NaCl). Identify the type of reaction, and what is the color of $Fe(OH)_3$ precipitate? **1**

(*a*) Double displacement reaction, reddish-brown (*b*) Combination reaction, white
(*c*) Displacement reaction, green (*d*) Decomposition reaction, brown

23. Imagine a milkman named Ravi, who delivers fresh milk to his customers every morning. One day, Ravi decides to add a small amount of baking soda to the fresh milk before delivering it. He is curious about how this addition will affect the milk's pH. **1**

What is the expected change in the pH of the milk after adding a small amount of baking soda?

(*a*) The pH will increase slightly, making the milk mildly alkaline.
(*b*) The pH will decrease slightly, making the milk more acidic.
(*c*) There will be no change in pH as baking soda is neutral.
(*d*) The pH will become neutral regardless of the initial pH of the milk.

The following two questions consist of two statements – **Assertion** (A) and **Reason** (R). Answer these questions by selecting the appropriate option given below:

(*a*) Both A and R are true, and R is the correct explanation of A.
(*b*) Both A and R are true, and R is not the correct explanation of A.
(*c*) A is true but R is false.
(*d*) A is false but R is true.

24. **Assertion (A):** Zinc sulphide can be directly reduced to zinc metal on heating with carbon.
Reason (R): Carbon is more reactive than zinc. **1**

25. Leena in a chemistry lab was conducting an experiment to investigate the properties of a newly discovered compound, XY. During her analysis, she discovered that atoms of X lost one electron each, while atoms of Y gained one electron each to form this compound.
Based on her observations, can you determine the nature of the bond that exists between atoms X and Y in compound XY? **2**

26. (A) Complete and balance the following equations:

(*a*) $NaOH + \_\_ \longrightarrow Na_2SO_4 + H_2O$

(*b*) $Ca(OH)_2 + \_\_ \longrightarrow CaCO_3 + H_2O$

(*c*) $FeSO_4 \xrightarrow{\text{heat}} Fe_2O_3 + \_\_\_\_ + \_\_\_\_$ **3**

OR

(B) (*a*) State the law of conservation of mass.

(*b*) When solid iron(III) oxide (Fe_2O_3) reacts with carbon monoxide (CO), it forms solid iron (Fe) and carbon dioxide (CO_2). Write the balanced chemical equation for this reaction.

(*c*) Identify the type of chemical reaction involved in part (*b*). **3**

27. During a chemistry lab session, students are tasked with analyzing the properties of three unknown solutions labelled A, B, and C. They are given a pH meter and a set of indicators, including methyl orange and litmus paper. After measuring the pH of each solution, they record the following values.

Answer the following questions based on their observations.

Solution	**pH**
A	2
B	7
C	12

(*a*) Which of these solutions will turn methyl orange red?
(*b*) Which of these solutions is most likely to react with a metal carbonate to produce carbon dioxide gas?
(*c*) Which of these solutions can be used to neutralise an acidic solution? **3**

28. Metal oxides are basic in nature. But some metal oxides, such as aluminium oxide, zinc oxide, etc., show both acidic as well as basic behaviour. Such metal oxides which react with both acids as well as bases to produce salts and water are known as amphoteric oxides. Most metal oxides are insoluble in water but some of these dissolve in water to form alkalis.

(*a*) Write the balanced chemical reaction of an amphoteric oxide with an acid. **1**
(*b*) (*i*) Why is potassium and sodium kept under the kerosene oil? **1**
(*ii*) What happens when copper is heated in the air? Give the equation for the reaction involved. **1**

OR

(*b*) (*i*) Name an oxide that is soluble in water and forms an alkali. Write the reaction also. **1**
(*ii*) Complete the following equation: $2Al(s) + 3H_2O(g) \rightarrow$ **1**
(*c*) Which of the following options correctly classifies the metal oxides? **1**
(1) Magnesium oxide (MgO) — Amphoteric oxide
(2) Copper(II) oxide (CuO) — Amphoteric oxide
(3) Potassium oxide (K_2O) — Basic oxide
(4) Zinc oxide (ZnO) — Basic oxide

29. (A) (*a*) Why are covalent compounds generally poor conductors of electricity?

(*b*) Name the following compound:

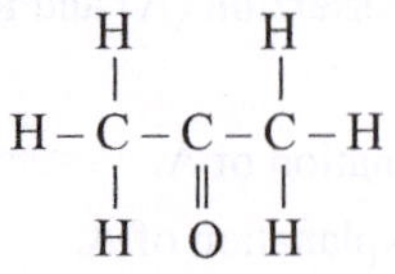

(*c*) Name the gas evolved when ethanoic acid is added to sodium carbonate. How would you prove the presence of this gas? **5**

OR

(B) The chemical properties of two elements X and Y are described below:

- Element X (2,4) is a non-metal with four valence electrons.
- Element Y (2,8,1) is a highly reactive metal with one valence electron.
- Both X and Y react with other substances to form different compounds.

Based on the information given above, answer the following questions: **5**

(*a*) When element X reacts with hydrogen, what type of bond is formed?

(*b*) Element Y reacts with water. Write the balanced chemical equation for this.

(*c*) The compound formed in (*a*) burns in air to form gas Z. What is the effect of gas (Z) dissolved in water on blue litmus paper?

(*d*) A compound YCl is formed from element Y. On electrolysis of its aqueous solution, which gases are released at the anode and cathode respectively?

(*e*) Element X forms many covalent compounds with hydrogen. What are these compounds called? How are they classified based on the type of bonds between carbon atoms?

SECTION - C

30. Rahul sir is assisting a student during a science experiment involving a convex lens with a focal length of 20 cm. They are setting up the apparatus and have some questions about the image formed by the lens. Which of the following statements is true about the image formed? **1**

(*a*) The image will always be real, inverted, and magnified.

(*b*) The nature of the image depends on the position of the object.

(*c*) The image will always be virtual, upright, and diminished.

(*d*) The nature of the image depends on the curvature of the lens.

31. During a classroom experiment, Omkar shined a laser pointer at a plane mirror. He positioned the laser so that the light ray hit the mirror at an angle of 30° to the surface of the mirror. His teacher then asked him to calculate the angle of reflection. What will be the angle of reflection for Omkar's laser? **1**

(*a*) 30° (*b*) 60° (*c*) 90° (*d*) 120°

The following two questions consist of two statements – **Assertion** (A) and **Reason** (R). Answer these questions by selecting the appropriate option given below:

(*a*) Both A and R are true, and R is the correct explanation of A.

(*b*) Both A and R are true, and R is not the correct explanation of A.

(*c*) A is true but R is false.

(*d*) A is false but R is true.

32. **Assertion (A):** The earth wire is used as a safety measure for appliances with a metallic body.

Reason (R): The earth wire provides a low-resistance conducting path, ensuring that any leakage of current to the metallic body keeps its potential to that of the earth, preventing severe electric shocks to the user. 1

33. Meera is designing a circuit that includes a light bulb and a battery. She notices that when she adds another light bulb in series, both bulbs become dimmer.

Meera wants to know why adding another bulb in series causes both bulbs to become dimmer. 2

34. (A) Sarah is presented with a challenge. She needs to explain how to identify the three types of mirrors (plane, convex, and concave) without physically touching them. 2

OR

(B) Explain how the focal length of a convex lens changes when it is submerged in water. Support your answer related to refraction of light. 2

35. (*a*) Define the power of a lens and state its unit. 3

(*b*) A concave lens has a power of –2.5 diopters. Calculate its focal length in centimeters.

(*c*) Explain how the power of a lens changes when two lenses of focal lengths 20 cm and –40 cm are combined.

36. (*a*) List the factors on which the resistance of a wire depends. 3

(*b*) Why are metals good conductors of electricity whereas glass is a bad conductor of electricity?

Give a reason.

(*c*) Why are alloys commonly used in electrical heating devices? Give a reason.

37. If you are working on a project that involves designing a small electronic device. You need to calculate the number of electrons that would constitute one coulomb of charge to better understand the flow of current in your device.

Calculate the number of electrons constituting one coulomb of charge. 3

38. Study the circuit shown in which three identical bulbs B_1, B_2, and B_3 are connected in parallel with a battery of 4.5V and answer the following questions.

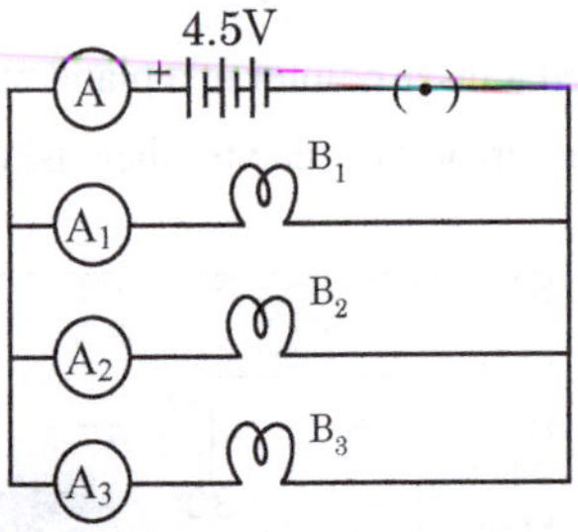

(*a*) What will happen to B_1 and B_2 bulbs if B_3 Bulb, gets fused? 1

(*b*) If the wattage of each bulb is 4.5W, what reading will the ammeter (A) show when all the bulbs glow simultaneously. 1

(*c*) Find the total resistance of the circuit. 2

OR

(*c*) How many resistors of 88 Ω are connected in parallel to carry 10 A current on a 220 V line? 2

39. (A) (*a*) Elaborate process of accommodation in the human eye. 1

(*b*) Explain how the ciliary muscles, lens, and retina work together to adjust the focus from distant to nearby objects. 2

(*c*) Discuss the role of the optic nerve in transmitting the final image to the brain and how the brain interprets this information to create visual perception. 2

OR

(B) (*a*) Define Atmospheric Refraction. 1

(*b*) Explain how it causes phenomenon such as the apparent shift in the position of stars and twinkling of star. 2

(*c*) Discuss the effect of atmospheric refraction on the duration of day and night. 2

MOCK TEST PAPER-2

Time allowed : 3 hours | **Maximum Marks : 80**

GENERAL INSTRUCTIONS:

*(i) This question paper consists of **39** questions in 3 sections. **Section A** is **Biology**, **Section B** is **Chemistry** and **Section C** is Physics.*

*(ii) All questions are **compulsory**. However, an internal choice is provided in some questions. A student is expected to attempt only one of these questions.*

SECTION - A

1. Akansha smelled imli at a food corner, her mouth started to water. Which of the following sequences best describes the actions taking place in Akansha's body in response to the smell? **1**

(*a*) Gustatory receptors at nose detect the smell of imli → Olfactory signals sent to the cerebellum → Activation of salivary glands

(*b*) Olfactory receptors at the nose detect the smell of imli → Signals received by forebrain→ then to medulla oblongata → Activation of salivary glands

(*c*) Gustatory receptors at the nose detect the smell of imli→ Olfactory signals sent to the spinal cord → Generate reflex action → Activation of salivary glands

(*d*) Olfactory receptors at the nose detect the smell of imli→ Signals processed by the pituitary → Send stimulus → Activation of the salivary glands

2. Which of the following statements about the inheritance of traits is correct? **1**

(*i*) Traits are influenced by both paternal and maternal DNA.

(*ii*) All traits are always expressed equally.

(*iii*) Traits can be dominant or recessive.

(*iv*) Traits are determined solely by the mother's genes.

The correct statements are:

(*a*) (*i*) and (*iii*) (*b*) (*ii*) and (*iv*) (*c*) (*i*), (*ii*), and (*iv*) (*d*) (*iii*) and (*iv*)

3. An analysis of soil sample revealed 0.1 mg of a pesticide and 1 mg of the same pesticide was found in grains. However, in the adipose tissue of birds the concentration was 2 mg. The reason for this is the phenomenon known as **1**

(*a*) Bio-absorption (*b*) Eutrophication (*c*) Biomagnification (*d*) Bio-remediation

4. Ravi cuts a ripened tomato to study its internal structure. He labels parts A and B in his notebook.
Carefully observe the image provided and match the labeled structures A and B with their respective pre-fertilisation parts. **1**

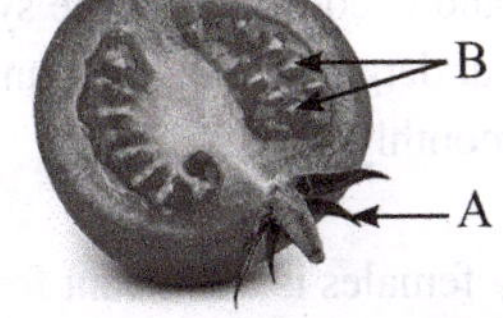

(*a*) A-Petal, B-Ovary (*b*) A-Sepal, B-Ovules (*c*) A-Carpel, B- Pistil (*d*) A-Stigma, B-Ovary

5. What is the purpose of dipping the variegated leaf in boiling water followed by boiling in alcohol when we check it for starch? **1**

   (*a*) To test the leaf's resistance to heat and alcohol. (*b*) To remove the green pigment from the leaf.

   (*c*) To enhance the coloration of the leaf. (*d*) To measure the leaf's growth rate.

6. Consider the following three flowers namely X, Y and Z. Which flower(s) would develop into a fruit? **1**

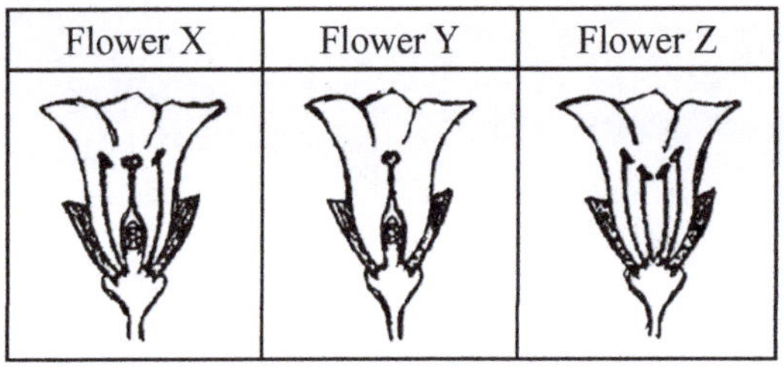

   (*a*) 'X' only (*b*) 'Z' only (*c*) 'X' and 'Y' only (*d*) 'Y' and 'Z' only

7. Samaira conducted an experiment where she buried three different types of solid wastes (P, Q, and R) under the soil in a pot to study their decomposition rates. The graph below shows the decomposition rates of these wastes over time. **1**

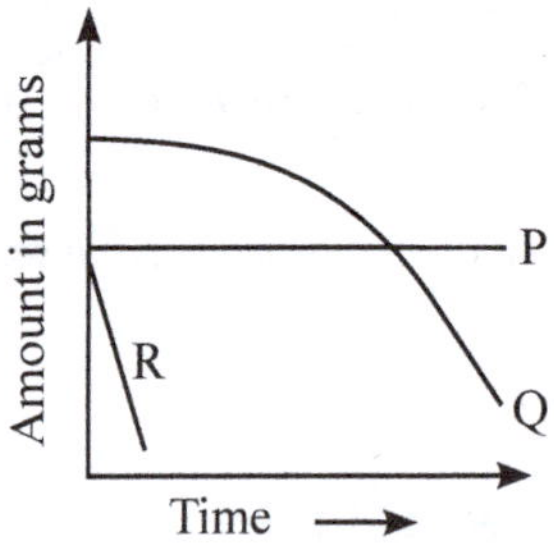

   Select the option that correctly identifies P, Q, and R:

	P	Q	R
(*a*)	Banana peel	Plastic bottle	Paper cup
(*b*)	Polythene bag	Bone	Orange peel
(*c*)	Apple core	Metal can	Cardboard
(*d*)	Rubber tire	Vegetable scrap	Wooden stick

The following two questions consist of two statements – **Assertion** (A) and **Reason** (R). Answer these questions by selecting the appropriate option given below:

(*a*) Both A and R are true, and R is the correct explanation of A.

(*b*) Both A and R are true, and R is not the correct explanation of A.

(*c*) A is true but R is false.

(*d*) A is false but R is true.

8. **Assertion (A):** Adrenaline, a hormone secreted from the pancreatic glands, plays a crucial role in preparing the body for fight or flight response in animals.

   Reason (R): *Adrenaline is secreted into the blood and acts on target organs, such as the heart, increasing heart rate, diverting* blood to skeletal muscles, and increasing breathing rate. **1**

9. **Assertion (A):** Dominant traits are always more common in a population than recessive traits.

   Reason (R): Dominant traits mask the expression of recessive traits in heterozygous individuals. **1**

10. In a population of an asexually reproducing species, trait X is found in 80% of the population while trait Y is found in 20% of the population. Given this information, which trait is more likely to have arisen more recently, and why? **2**

11. (A) (*a*) What is the term used for organisms that possess both male and female sex organs in the same individual?

    (*b*) Anwesha has just started her first period and is confused by the symptoms. Her elder sister, Aishwarya explains to her that it happens because the uterine lining undergoes thickening and sheds every month. Can you explain why does the uterine lining undergoes thickening on a monthly basis? **2**

OR

    (B) (*a*) Which technique of contraception used by females is not meant for males?

    (*b*) How does the use of contraception methods have a direct impact on the health and prosperity of a family?

12. Name the part/organ of the human female reproductive system: **2**

(*a*) where contraceptive devices such as loop or copper-T are placed to prevent pregnancy.

(*b*) which is blocked to prevent the transfer of eggs.

(*c*) where formation of ova takes place.

(*d*) from where the embryo gets nutrition from the mother's blood.

13. Consider the following food chain which occurs in a forest: **3**

Grass → Deer → Lion

If 10,000 J of energy is available at the grass, how much energy would be available at the lion?

14. Based on the figure provided below, answer the questions that follow: **3**

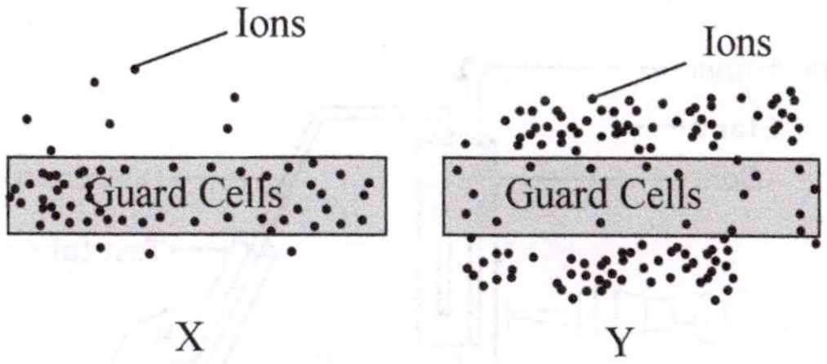

(*a*) Identify the direction of water movement in relation to the guard cells and describe the effect on the guard cells in conditions X and Y.

(*b*) Draw well-labelled diagrams of the stomatal complex for conditions X and Y, illustrating the changes in the stomatal pore size.

15. Emily, a passionate botany student, is conducting an experiment on plant movement. She notices that when she touches a specific part of a plant, movement occurs at a different location. Emily is intrigued by this phenomenon and begins investigating further.

(*a*) Explain how plants communicate information about touch from one cell to another without specialized tissue for information conduction. **1**

(*b*) Discuss the role of water in plant cell shape changes and how it leads to swelling or shrinking. **1**

(*c*) Provide examples of plant movements where cells changing shape play a significant role. **2**

OR

(*c*) How does the lack of specialized tissue for information conduction affect the efficiency of communication in plants? **2**

16. (A) **5**

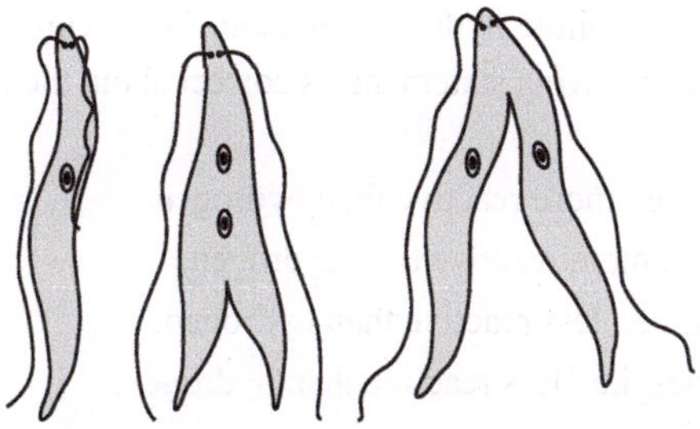

(*a*) Identify the organism given in the figure.

(*b*) What does the given figure represent?

(*c*) Name the disease caused by given organism.

(*d*) Give an example of an organism that shows a similar type of process like the organism given here. Explain briefly about the process.

OR

(B) (*a*) Define excretion. **5**

(*b*) Name the basic filtration unit present in the kidney.

(*c*) Draw excretory system in human beings and label the following organs of excretory system which perform following functions:

(*i*) form urine.

(*ii*) is a long tube which collects urine from the kidney.

(*iii*) store urine until it is passed out.

SECTION - B

17. Given below are the statements related to the allotropes of carbon: **1**

(*i*) Diamond is formed by carbon atoms bonded in a hexagonal array.

(*ii*) Graphite has carbon atoms bonded in layers forming a hexagonal array.

(*iii*) Graphite is a bad conductor of electricity.

(*iv*) Fullerene has carbon atoms arranged in the shape of a football.

The correct statements are:

(*a*) (*i*) and (*ii*) (*b*) (*ii*) and (*iii*) (*c*) (*ii*) and (*iv*) (*d*) (*i*) and (*iii*)

18. Sana, a science student, is conducting an experiment in her school's laboratory. She sets up an apparatus to observe the reaction between sodium carbonate and dilute hydrochloric acid. The setup is shown in the diagram. **1**

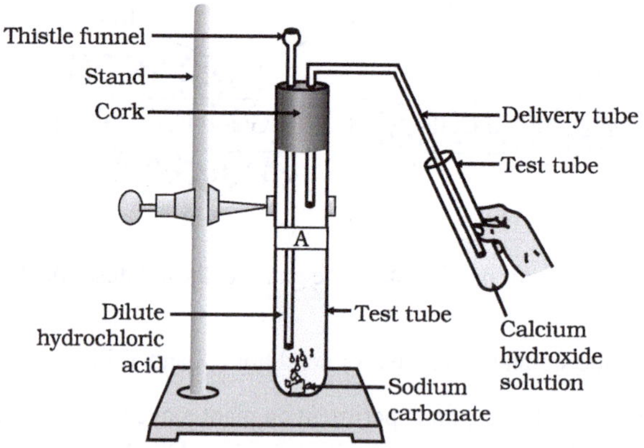

Based on the above experimental setup, determine which of the following statements is/are incorrect?

(A) Hydrogen gas is liberated on reacting sodium carbonate with hydrochloric acid.

(B) Sodium chloride is obtained as one of the products when sodium carbonate reacts with HCl.

(C) The lime water turns milky because of the formation of calcium chloride.

(D) The major product formed on reacting lime water and carbon dioxide turns blue litmus red.

(*a*) Both (A) and (B) (*b*) Only (C) (*c*) (B), (C) and (D) (*d*) (A), (C) and (D)

19. You have a shiny metal 'M' and decide to test its reactivity with hot water and dilute hydrochloric acid. The metal 'M' reacts, evolving hydrogen gas in both cases. Based on this experiment, which of the following statements is correct about the identity of the metal 'M'? **1**

(*a*) It can be copper because it lies above hydrogen in the reactivity series, i.e., more reactive than hydrogen.

(*b*) It can be gold because it lies below hydrogen in the reactivity series, i.e., more reactive than hydrogen.

(*c*) It cannot be gold because it lies above hydrogen in the reactivity series, i.e., less reactive than hydrogen.

(*d*) It cannot be copper because it lies below hydrogen in the reactivity series, i.e., less reactive than hydrogen.

20. Ravi has aqueous solutions of three salts, potassium nitrate, ammonium sulphate, and sodium acetate in three test tubes. The test tubes are not labelled. On checking, he finds the pH of the solutions to be 5.5, 7.0, and 8.9.

Which of the following correctly matches the salts with their respective pH? **1**

	pH 5.5	**pH 7.0**	**pH 8.9**
A.	potassium nitrate	ammonium sulphate	sodium acetate
B.	potassium nitrate	sodium acetate	ammonium sulphate
C.	ammonium sulphate	potassium nitrate	sodium acetate
D.	sodium acetate	ammonium sulphate	potassium nitrate

(*a*) A (*b*) B (*c*) C (*d*) D

21. A metal that exists as a liquid at room temperature is obtained by heating its sulphide in the presence of air. Identify the metal and its ore. **1**

(*a*) Hg, HgS (*b*) Ag, Ag_2S (*c*) Cu, Cu_2S (*d*) Na, Na_2S

22. Balance the given below reaction: **1**

$Fe + H_2SO_4 \rightarrow Fe_2(SO_4)_3 + H_2$

The correct equation is given in option:

(*a*) $Fe + 2H_2SO_4 \rightarrow Fe_2(SO_4)_3 + H_2$
(*b*) $3Fe + 4H_2SO_4 \rightarrow Fe_2(SO_4)_3 + 4H_2$
(*c*) $Fe + 3H_2SO_4 \rightarrow Fe_2(SO_4)_3 + 3H_2$
(*d*) $2Fe + 3H_2SO_4 \rightarrow Fe_2(SO_4)_3 + 3H_2$

23. A student mixed dilute hydrochloric acid (HCl) with solid sodium bicarbonate ($NaHCO_3$) in a test tube. As a result, a gas was evolved, which turned lime water milky when passed through it. Identify the gas. **1**

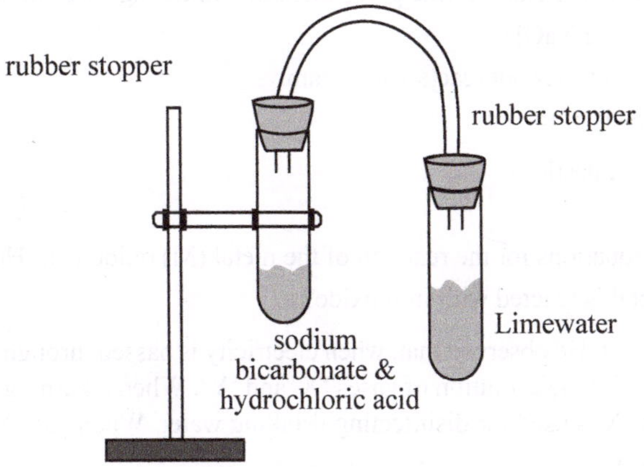

(*a*) H_2 (*b*) O_2 (*c*) SO_2 (*d*) CO_2

The following two questions consist of two statements – **Assertion** (A) and **Reason** (R). Answer these questions by selecting the appropriate option given below:

(*a*) Both A and R are true, and R is the correct explanation of A.
(*b*) Both A and R are true, and R is not the correct explanation of A.
(*c*) A is true but R is false.
(*d*) A is false but R is true.

24. **Assertion (A):** In a homologous series of alcohols, the formula for the second member is C_2H_5OH and the third member is C_3H_7OH.
Reason (R): The difference between the molecular masses of the two consecutive members of a homologous series is 144. **1**

25. During a laboratory experiment, you are given solutions of lead nitrate ($Pb(NO_3)_2$) and potassium iodide (KI). When these solutions are mixed, a yellow precipitate forms. **2**

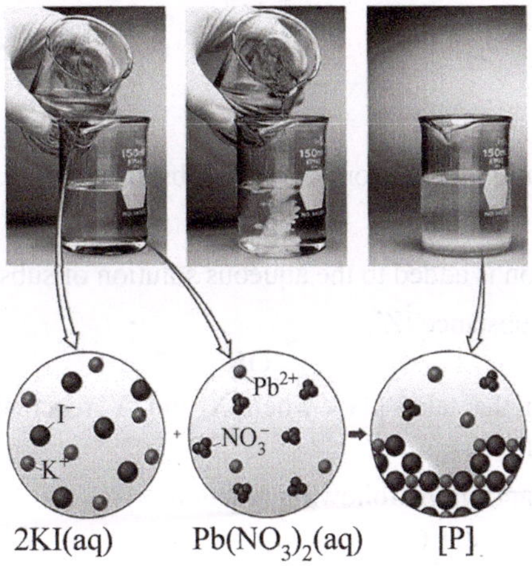

(*a*) Identify the compound that gives yellow precipitates.
(*b*) Briefly explain the reason.

26. (A) Shown below are the structural formulae of four carbon compounds.

$CH_3-\underset{\underset{O}{\|\|}}{C}-CH_3$	$CH_3-\underset{\underset{OH}{\|}}{CH}-CH_3$	$CH_3-CH_2-\underset{\underset{O}{\|\|}}{C}-OH$	CH_3-OH
P	Q	R	S

(*a*) Two of these compounds are more likely to have similar chemical properties.

Identify these two compounds. Give a reason for your answer.

(*b*) Identify which of these compounds are likely to have the same boiling point. Justify your answer. **3**

OR

(B) Write three different chemical reactions showing the conversion of ethanoic acid to sodium ethanoate. Write balanced chemical equation in each case. Write the name of the reactants and the products other than ethanoic acid and sodium ethanoate in each case. **3**

27. A teacher asks her students to identify a metal, M. She gives them the following clues to help them.

(P) Its oxide reacts with both HCl and NaOH.

(Q) It does not react with hot or cold water but reacts with steam.

(R) It can be extracted by electrolysis of its ore.

Based on this, answer the following questions:

(*a*) Identify the metal.

(*b*) Write the balanced chemical equations for the reaction of the metal (M) oxide with HCl and NaOH respectively.

(*c*) What would happen if the metal is reacted with iron oxide? **3**

28. Ashutosh is conducting an experiment. He observed that, when electricity is passed through an aqueous solution of a common salt, A substance 'Z' is produced along with the evolution of gases 'X' and 'Y'. When a burning matchstick is brought near the gas 'Y' it burns with a pop sound, whereas X is used for disinfecting drinking water. When gas 'X' is passed through a dry slaked lime, an insoluble substance 'A' is produced.

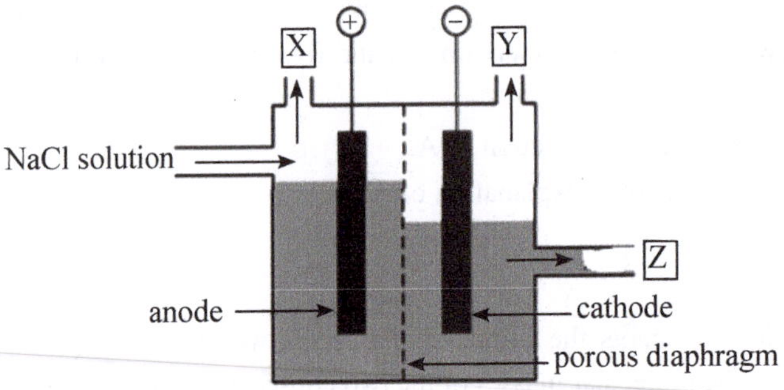

(*a*) Which of the following are the correct names of gases 'X' and 'Y' evolved during the electrolysis of aqueous solution of a common salt? **1**

(1) X – Hydrogen, Y – Chlorine

(2) X – Chlorine, Y – Hydrogen

(3) X – Oxygen, Y – Hydrogen

(4) X – Chlorine, Y – Oxygen

(*b*) Write the balanced chemical equation for the formation of substance 'A'. **1**

(*c*) Write your observations: **2**

(*i*) if a drop of blue litmus solution is added to the aqueous solution of substance 'Z'

(*ii*) if methyl orange is added to substance 'Z'.

OR

(*c*) Write a balanced chemical reaction that takes place when 'X' and 'Y' react with each other. The product so produced will turn blue litmus red only when wet, why? **2**

29. (A) Identify the oxidising agent (oxidant) in the following reaction: **5**

(*a*) $Pb_3O_4 + 8HCl \rightarrow 3PbCl_2 + Cl_2 + 4H_2O$

(*b*) $2Mg + O_2 \rightarrow 2MgO$

(*c*) $CuSO_4 + Zn \rightarrow Cu + ZnSO_4$

(*d*) $V_2O_5 + 5Ca \rightarrow 2V + 5CaO$

(*e*) $3Fe + 4H_2O \rightarrow Fe_3O_4 + 4H_2$

OR

(B) Imagine you are a chemical engineer working in a lab where you need to produce various compounds for different industrial applications. You have the following situations to handle: **5** (*a*) Situation 1: In one of the processes, you need to precipitate barium bromide from a solution. You have access to potassium bromide and barium iodide. Write the balanced chemical equation, and identify the type of reaction.

(*b*) Situation 2: You need to create a gas that turns lime water milky. You have zinc carbonate available. Write the balanced chemical equation, and name the type of reaction.

(*c*) Situation 3: In a laboratory project, you need to produce calcium nitrate. You have nitric acid (HNO_3) and calcium hydroxide [$Ca(OH)_2$] available. Provide the balanced chemical equation, and identify the reaction type.

(*d*) Situation 4: You are tasked with generating hydrogen gas to fill a small balloon. You have magnesium metal and hydrochloric acid. Write the balanced chemical equation, and classify the reaction type.

(*e*) Situation 5: You are tasked with producing aluminium chloride and copper using aluminium metal and copper chloride. Write the balanced chemical equation and classify the reaction type.

SECTION - C

30. A solenoid is used to create a strong magnetic field. If a piece of soft iron is placed inside the solenoid, what will happen to the iron piece? 1

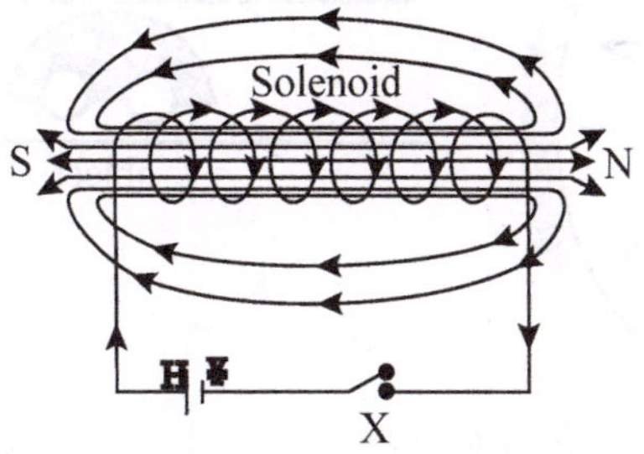

(*a*) It will become an electromagnet. (*b*) It will become a permanent magnet.

(*c*) It will lose its magnetic properties. (*d*) It will become a conductor.

31. A person in a room sees a rainbow formed by sunlight passing through a waterfall outside. Which optical phenomena are involved in the formation of this rainbow? 1

(*a*) Refraction, Reflection, Dispersion (*b*) Reflection, Scattering, Diffraction

(*c*) Dispersion, Interference, Reflection (*d*) Scattering, Refraction, Interference

The following two questions consist of two statements – **Assertion** (A) and **Reason** (R). Answer these questions by selecting the appropriate option given below:

(*a*) Both A and R are true, and R is the correct explanation of A.

(*b*) Both A and R are true, and R is not the correct explanation of A.

(*c*) A is true but R is false.

(*d*) A is false but R is true.

32. **Assertion (A):** Conductors allow the current to pass through themselves.

Reason (R): They have free charge carriers. 1

33. Rahul is setting up a home workshop and want to install proper lighting and electrical outlets. As he runs electrical wires through the walls, he becomes curious about how the electric current might affect the surroundings. What effect does an electric current flowing through a conductor have on its surroundings? 2

34. (A) Think about people you know who wear glasses. What are some common eyesight problems that these glasses can help fix? Write about any two. 2

OR

(B) Imagine you are explaining the basics of vision to your friend who is curious about how we see. He asks you to explain how the brain makes sense of the images we see with our eyes. How does the brain interpret signals from the eye? 2

35. While using multiple appliances in your kitchen, you notice that the circuit breaker trips frequently. 3

(*a*) Explain what might be causing the frequent tripping in terms of short-circuiting.

(*b*) Discuss how overloading could be a contributing factor and suggest ways to avoid overloading in household circuits.

36. Ravi is conducting an experiment to understand the relationship between the potential difference and the current through a conductor. He has a setup that includes a variable power supply, a conductor, and measuring instruments to record the potential difference across the conductor and the current flowing through it.

Explain Ohm's Law and how it describes the relationship between the potential difference across a conductor and the current flowing through it. 3

37. A wire of length 4 meter and uniform cross-sectional area of 0.5 square millimeter has a resistivity of 1.6×10^{-8} ohm-meter. If a potential difference of 10 volt is applied across the ends of the wire.

(*a*) Calculate the electric current flowing through it.

(*b*) State two factors that can affect the resistance of a conductor. **3**

38. Spherical mirrors display different image characteristics depending on the object's placement. A real image forms on a screen when reflected rays physically converge, while a virtual image does not. Concave mirrors consistently produce real and inverted images, except when the object is between the focus and pole, resulting in a virtual and erect image. In contrast, convex mirrors always produce virtual, erect, and smaller images. In medical practice, concave mirrors like doctor's head mirrors are used to focus light on body parts, for better illumination. Convex mirrors are employed as rear-view mirrors in vehicles, producing small and erect object images.

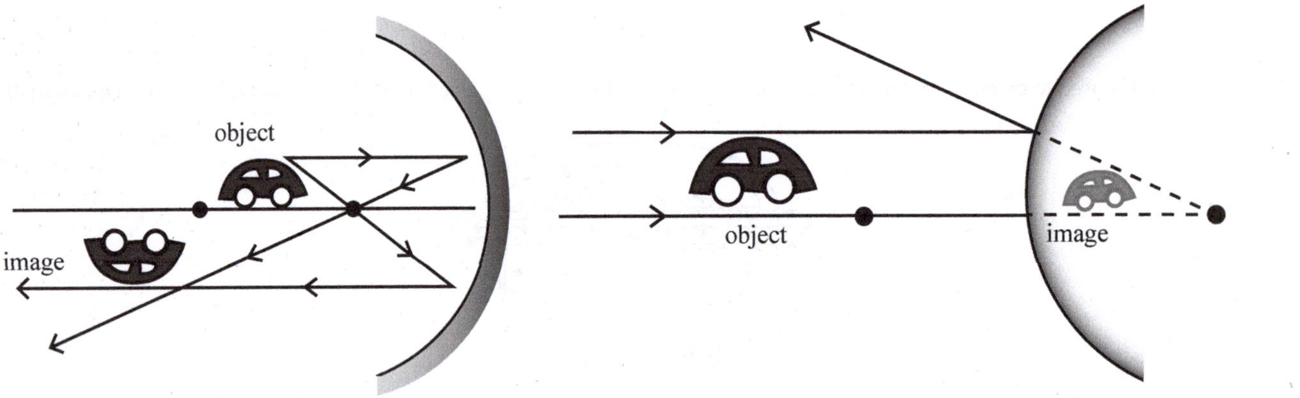

(*a*) What will be the combination of a magical mirror, if a boy is looking into it and he observes that his head is bigger, the middle portion of body is of same size and has smaller legs. **1**

(*b*) In what type of mirror, image always appear to be erect no matter how far you stand? **1**

(*c*) What is the nature of image formed when object is placed at the centre of curvature of a concave mirror? Draw the ray diagram for the mentioned position. **2**

OR

(*c*) Which type of mirror is employed to get larger image as compared to object? And how many types of images can be formed at that mirror? **2**

39. (A) A patient named Radha is at the eye doctor's office with Dr. Patel. She has some questions about the eye exam and asks Dr. Patel to explain the following doubts in detail

(*a*) What is power of a lens?

(*b*) A convex lens has a focal length of 20 cm. What is its power in dioptre?

(*c*) Draw a labelled diagram of a convex lens showing how parallel rays of light converge after passing through it. **5**

OR

(B) Ram situated a 12 cm tall object at a distance of 8 cm in front of a concave mirror with a radius of curvature of 30 cm. While observing his brother's activity, Rohan, his younger sibling, asked the following questions.

(*a*) What is the position of the image formed by this mirror?

(*b*) What is the size of the image?

(*c*) Draw a ray diagram to show the formation of the image as mentioned in part (*i*). **5**